The Journal and Letters of
FRANCIS ASBURY

FRANCIS ASBURY
Portrait by John Paradise at New York, 1812. From the steel engraving
by B. Tanner, 1814.

The Journal and Letters of
FRANCIS ASBURY

In Three Volumes

VOLUME I

The Journal
1771 to 1793

ELMER T. CLARK *Editor-in-Chief*

J. MANNING POTTS

JACOB S. PAYTON

Published Jointly By

EPWORTH PRESS
London

ABINGDON PRESS
Nashville

FIRST PUBLISHED IN 1958

PRINTED IN GREAT BRITAIN BY
HAZELL WATSON AND VINEY LTD
AYLESBURY AND SLOUGH

EDITORIAL STAFF

EDITORS

ELMER T. CLARK, A.B., M.A., B.D., S.T.D., Litt.D., LL.D.

Secretary of the World Methodist Council; Secretary of the International Methodist Historical Society; Executive Secretary of the American Association of Methodist Historical Societies; Author of *The Warm Heart of Wesley*, *An Album of Methodist History*, etc.; Editor of *What Happened at Aldersgate*, etc.

J. MANNING POTTS, A.B., M.A., Th.M., D.D.

Editor of *The Upper Room*; Member of the Executive Committee of the World Methodist Council and American Association of Methodist Historical Societies; Vice-President of the International Methodist Historical Society; President of the Southeastern Jurisdictional Methodist Historical Society; Collector of Asbury's Letters.

JACOB S. PAYTON, A.B., B.D., D.D.

Sometime Washington Correspondent for *The Christian Advocate*; President of the Northeastern Jurisdictional Methodist Historical Society; Member of the Executive Committee of the International Methodist Historical Society and American Association of Methodist Historical Societies; Author of *Our Fathers Have Told Us*, *The History of Methodism in Western Pennsylvania*.

REGIONAL RESEARCH EDITORS

FRANK BAKER, A.B., M.A., Ph.D.

Executive Secretary of the Wesley Historical Society of Great Britain; Secretary of the International Methodist Historical Society; Author of *A Charge to Keep*, *The Methodist Pilgrim in England*, *An Introduction to the People Called Methodists*, *Charles Wesley as Revealed by His Letters*, etc.

ALBERT DEEMS BETTS, A.B., M.A., B.D.

Author of *History of South Carolina Methodism*.

CULLEN T. CARTER

President and Member of Commission on Historic Places and Relics of the Tennessee Conference Methodist Historical Society; Secretary of the Southeastern Jurisdictional Methodist Historical Society; Author of *Methodist Doctrinal Beliefs*, *History of the Tennessee Conference of The Methodist Church*.

JOHN OWEN GROSS, D.D., L.H.D., Litt.D., LL.D., S.T.D., D.Sc.Ed.

Executive Secretary of the Department of Educational Institutions of the Board of Education of The Methodist Church.

VERNON BOYCE HAMPTON, Ph.D., Litt.D.

President, Newark Conference Methodist Historical Society; Author of *Francis Asbury on Staten Island*, etc.

WALLACE H. HARRIS, A.B., B.D., S.T.M.
Vice-President of the Northeastern Jurisdictional Methodist Historical Society; Biographical Secretary of the Philadelphia Conference Methodist Historical Society.

LEWIS O. HARTMAN, Ph.D., D.D., Litt.D., L.H.D.
Bishop of the Methodist Church; Librarian of the New England Methodist Historical Society. (Deceased.)

BROOKS B. LITTLE, A.B., M.A., B.D.
Editorial Associate and Librarian of *The Upper Room*; Associate Research Director and Collector of the *Letters of Francis Asbury*.

ISAAC P. MARTIN, D.D.
Librarian-Historian of the Holston Conference Methodist Historical Society; Author of *Elijah Embree Hoss, History of Methodism in Holston Conference, Church Street Methodists, A Minister in the Tennessee Valley.*

ARTHUR BRUCE MOSS, A.B., M.A., B.D.
Pastor of Old John Street Methodist Church, New York City; Secretary of the New York City Methodist Historical Society.

LOUIS D. PALMER, B.A.
Author of *Heroism and Romance: Early Methodism in Northeastern Pennsylvania.*

LAWRENCE SHERWOOD, B.A., B.D.
Research Historian, West Virginia Conference Methodist Historical Society.

WALLACE GUY SMELTZER, B.S., S.T.B., D.D.
Historian of the Pittsburgh Conference Methodist Historical Society; Vice-President of the Northeastern Jurisdictional Methodist Historical Society; Author of *Methodism on the Headwaters of the Ohio.*

WILLIAM WARREN SWEET, Ph.D., Litt.D., D.D.
Sometime Professor of American Church History at the University of Chicago and Southern Methodist University; Author of *The Methodist Episcopal Church in the Civil War, Circuit Rider Days in Indiana, The Rise of Methodism in the West, The Story of Religion in America, Religion on the American Frontier, Methodism in American History, Virginia Methodism, A History,* etc.

LESTER A. WELLIVER, A.B., M.A., B.D., D.D., LL.D.
Sometime President of Westminster Theological Seminary; President of the Northeastern Jurisdictional Methodist Historical Society.

ACKNOWLEDGMENTS

ATTENTION is called to the authorities cited in the footnotes and to the bibliography. The whole range of early Methodist literature, including periodicals, has been carefully searched. Contemporary maps have been studied to trace the routes of Asbury's travels. For local details scores of histories of states, counties, cities, and churches have been ransacked. The archives of most of the states through which Asbury passed have been investigated, and archivists and librarians have been uniformly helpful. County historians and genealogists have been contacted; and these have searched the old public records for deeds, wills, and other documents that might throw light on passages in the *Journal*. The Editors have traveled widely in all the states to trace the exact movements of the great Circuit Rider. It would be impossible to mention by name the hundreds of persons who provided local data and co-operated with unfailing kindness in the vast volume of research which has gone into the production of the work. Without their help thousands of local facts would not have been secured.

High credit is due to Mrs. Louise Stahl, my own secretary, who was responsible for a considerable part of the research and for drafting the whole *Journal* in its final form. She read numerous microfilms and photostats, accurately interpreted difficult hand-written documents, transcribed all the annotations, and with her helpers carried on the voluminous correspondence with the many persons who contributed much or little to the project.

Similar credit must be accorded to the Misses Annie and Clarice Winstead, secretaries to Dr. J. Manning Potts, for indefatigable work on the *Letters*. They co-operated in deciphering a large number of documents and transcribed all the *Letters* and the notes thereon.

In Washington the secretary to Dr. Jacob S. Payton, Miss Margery E. Rohman, rendered highly important service on large sections of the *Journal*. Proximity to the Library of Congress greatly enhanced her usefulness during the whole period of research.

Mr. Thoburn C. Lyon and Mr. Lewis Akin were responsible for making the maps used in this work. Each of Asbury's trips in each state was traced on an outline map of the state involved, and the hundreds of maps thus resulting were furnished to Mr. Lyon for guidance. Our indebtedness to Mr. Erle Prior of Washington, the illustrator, is evident throughout the book.

To express suitable gratitude to all the persons who have co-operated in the present work would involve listing the ministers in nearly all the areas through which Asbury moved for nearly half a century. Among the hundreds who deserve the thanks of the Editors the following must be mentioned:

GEORGIA: Mrs. Z. W. Copeland, Professor E. Merton Coulter, Dean S. Walter Martin, The Rev. Dr. A. M. Pearce, North Georgia Conference Historical Society, Professor Robert C. Wilson.

DELAWARE AND MARYLAND: Dr. William H. Best, Miss Annie P. Dalton, Mrs. S. J. L. DuLaney, Carlyle R. Earp, Dr. William M. Hoffman, Dr. Arthur J. Jackson, Ralph F. Martz, Dr. Walter M. Michael, Miss Hannah S. Parker, The Rev. Kenneth Ray Rose, The Rev. Edwin Schell, The Rev. Melvin Lee Steadman, The Rev. R. T. Thawley, Library of Congress, The Library of the Daughters of the American Revolution, Historical Society of the Peninsula Conference, Maryland Historical

Society, Methodist Historical Society of the Baltimore Conference, The Rev. William O. Hackett.

KENTUCKY: The Rev. O. B. Crockett, Russell Dyche, Sr., C. H. Greer, W. S. Hudson, E. C. Watts.

NEW ENGLAND: Mrs. William Kirk Kaynor, The Rev. Dwight H. McMahon, Mr. E. Farley Sharp, The Librarians of the Kent Memorial Library, The Public Library at Providence, R.I.

NEW JERSEY: Dr. Lynn H. Corson, Dr. B. Harrison Decker, The Rev. Frank D. Dennis, The Rev. John L. Ewing, Dr. William R. Guffick, The Rev. Albert E. Hartman, The Rev. George T. Hillman, Walter W. Hoover, Dr. Roland L. Luerich, Loring McMillen, The Rev. Raymond E. Neff, Dr. John B. Oman, The Rev. Frank Ostertag, Dr. Olin Y. Shute, Dr. Harold N. Smith, Dr. Frank B. Stanger, Miss Laura Yetman, William H. Zelley.

NEW YORK: The Rev. C. W. Christman, The Rev. Robert H. Dolliver, Dr. Robert C. Hunsicker, Mrs. Elizabeth D. Meier, The Trustees of John Street Methodist Church, Bishop Frederick B. Newell, Miss Dorothy Woodruff.

NORTH CAROLINA: Miss Alma Browning, Mrs. Mary L. Browning, The Rev. G. W. Bumgarner, W. Frank Burton, D. L. Corbitt, Department of Archives and History, Leon M. McDonald, Society of County Historians, Miss Amy Muse, S. T. Peace, William S. Powell, University of North Carolina Library, J. F. Pugh, Mrs. G. D. B. Reynolds, Stanley County Historical Society, Colonel Jeffrey F. Stanback, William S. Tarlton, Mrs. Stanley Whitaker, Mrs. Laura S. Worth, Randolph County Historical Society.

PENNSYLVANIA: Dr. Raymond Martin Bell, Ellsworth H. Bringinger, The Rev. Charles C. Chayer, The Rev. A. L. Cliffe, Mrs. Gladys DuPuis, William H. Irelan, Miss Ernestine M. Kashlin, S. S. Lesh, The Rev. Howard N. Reeves, Jr., Miss Catherine T. Shulenberger, The Rev. Edgar F. Singer, L. E. Wilt, Dr. T. Kenneth Wood, Libraries of the Philadelphia Conference Historical Society, Pennsylvania Historical Society, The Friends' Historical Society, The Germantown Historical Society, Delaware County Historical Society, The Historical Society of the Presbyterian Church, The Free Library of Philadelphia.

SOUTH CAROLINA: Dr. J. H. Easterby, South Carolina Historical Commission, Miss Cora Page Godfrey, Herbert Hucks, Jr., Wofford College Library, Dr. R. L. Meriwether, Library of the University of South Carolina.

TENNESSEE: The Rev. Dr. E. P. Anderson, Judge W. W. Faw, Dr. Robert L. Kincaid, Judge H. B. McGinis, Mrs. James K. Taylor.

VIRGINIA AND WEST VIRGINIA: Emory P. Barrow, Joseph Minton Batten (Deceased), Mr. and Mrs. H. Carstairs Bracey, Chaplain (Major-General) Charles I. Carpenter, Carroll C. Chowning, S. G. Cowan, Mrs. J. W. Dixon, Wallace R. Evans, R. H. Forrester, Bishop Paul Neff Garber, Miss Mabel F. Gardiner, The Library of Garrett Biblical Institute, Otis L. Gilliam, Garland E. Hopkins, J. Aubrey Hughes, H. H. Hughes, Frank A. Johnson, William A. Mabry, George Carrington Mason (Deceased), Mariner's Museum, Fred Newbraugh, Mrs. Theodore G. Owen, Major T. T. Perry, Jr., George S. Reamey, Roland P. Riddick, Henley S. Roane, Ellis W. Shuler, John C. Simpson, C. A. Steiding, Leland B. Tate, C. L. Wilkins, L. H. Youell.

INTRODUCTION

Elmer T. Clark

THE place of Francis Asbury in American history is secure. In Washington there stands a noble equestrian monument of the great Circuit Rider which was unveiled and presented to the nation by the President of the United States, who said on that occasion: "His outposts marched with the pioneers, his missionaries visited the hovels of the poor, that all might be brought to a knowledge of the truth. . . . Who shall say where his influence, written on the immortal souls of men, shall end? . . . It is more than probable that Nancy Hanks, the mother of Abraham Lincoln, had heard him in her youth. Adams and Jefferson must have known him, and Jackson must have seen in him a flaming spirit as unconquerable as his own. . . . He is entitled to rank as one of the builders of our nation." And Bishop Hamilton declared at the same ceremony: "He said, 'I must ride or die.' He printed the map of his ministry with the hoofs of his horse."

At Drew University there stands another memorial in bronze, depicting the man and his horse. Several American cities and towns, and numerous streets are called "Asbury." Many artists painted him in various moods and at different periods in his career. Across the land hundreds of churches and thousands of individuals bear his name, and notable institutions have been named for him. In stained-glass windows in many places the worshiping multitudes look into his blue eyes. In England his boyhood home has been designated as a notable site of history to be preserved by the Corporation which knew him as a lad.

Asbury was one of the greatest explorers of the American frontier. He was more widely traveled than any other man of his generation, and was known by more people. He was the welcome visitor in thousands of humble homes, and such notables as Washington, Meriwether Lewis, Ramsay, Rembert and Calhoun of South Carolina, Gough of Maryland, Bassett of Delaware, General Russell of Virginia, Governor Tiffin of Ohio, Lieutenant Governor Van Cortlandt of New York, and a multitude of others were numbered among his friends. For nearly fifty years he had no home save the road, and but a few months before his death he told a British correspondent that his mailing address was simply "America"; any postmaster would know that "the man who rambled America" would in due time pass that way. More than sixty times he crossed the eastern mountains; his annual circuit stretched from New England or New York to Charleston; his total mileage was more than a quarter of a million.

As the bearer of a moral culture and its civilizing consequences to the frontier settlements of America, Francis Asbury has no peer in history. He and his circuit riders went into every new community and nearly every log cabin in the wilderness; they were never more than a few weeks behind the earliest pioneers. In their saddlebags they carried the fundamentals of civilization—the Bible, the hymnbook, and religious literature of a varied nature. They brought news of the outside world. They fought intemperance and every form of wrongdoing; and they made godly, law-respecting citizens out of people who might otherwise have been ruffians. Asbury preached a gospel of personal salvation, as did all others in his day. Our modern social problems and the so-called "social gospel" did not exist. But on nearly every page of his *Journal* there is evidence of his keen social conscience, and his message bore fruit in social betterment.

Asbury was the educational pioneer of his day. He has long been credited with having established the first Sunday school in America. His preachers, most of whom had little formal education, were required to preach annually on education. Furthermore, they dotted their wide circuits with schools. As early as 1780, as will be noted in the *Journal*, a plan was drawn and money given for a school in North Carolina, although it was not opened for several years. In Virginia, Georgia, Kentucky, and both the Carolinas, Methodist schools were established; and the General Conference which organized the Church also founded a degree-conferring college in Maryland.

"How many institutions of learning, some of them rejoicing in the name of Wesleyan, all trace the inspiration of their existence to the service and sacrifice of this lone circuit rider!" exclaimed President Calvin Coolidge. Across the years Asbury's successors have established hundreds of schools and colleges in practically all the states. Many of these were suspended when the progress of public education, learning from the preachers, rendered them no longer necessary; but they blazed the way and laid down the challenge to the states. More than 150 of them are in operation today, and some of these are among the greatest in America.

In 1789 Asbury was instrumental in starting a publishing house which today is the world's largest religious publisher. In the same year he started a periodical which, under different names and with some lapses, has continued until this day. At once books and papers began to pour from the presses in a stream which has been constantly increasing in volume for more than a century and a half and is today far greater than it has ever been. He may almost be said to deserve the title of American Publisher Number One.

Such contributions give Francis Asbury a lasting and unique place in the history of the New World.

Asbury's Early Life

It has been pointed out that John Wesley's intemperate attack on the American cause in his *Calm Address to the American Colonies* cost the great founder of Methodism his influence in the New World.[1] Francis Asbury inherited that influence. He became the organizing genius and virtual father of American Methodism, and "the second man in Methodist history," as Dr. James Dixon called him, second only to John Wesley himself. Wesley's greatest biographer, Tyerman, regarded Asbury "with an almost equal veneration," and declared that "if the reader wishes to see his monument, we invite him to step within the living walls of the present Methodist Episcopal Church of America, and there, while surveying the grand edifice of spiritual order and beauty, we ask him, as the inquirer in St. Paul's Cathedral is asked, to 'look around.' "[2]

His *Journal* and *Letters* and the annotations thereto cover his entire career except sections of his early life in England and his last days following the end of his record; and while no interpretative biography is here intended, there seems to be need for information covering these sections[3] even though it covers ground already familiar to informed students.

Elizabeth and Joseph Asbury were poor but godly parents whose home was open to the preachers and whose hearts were turned seriously to religion by the death of a small daughter, their only other child. Francis was sent to school at Snails' Green, a mile away from the family home on Newton Road; and he was so apt in his studies that he could read the Bible at the age of six or seven years. The schoolmaster was a tyrant, however, and the boy's formal education ended when he was thirteen years old. For a few months he was in service in the home of a prosperous but irreligious family, and then he became an apprentice at the Old Forge nearby.

His immediate superior at the forge was a Methodist named Foxall. The work was of the manual sort, and all biographers have pointed out that the muscular strength developed by the hard labor admirably equipped Asbury for the tasks which were later to face him in the American wilderness. He also became an intimate of the superintendent's son, Henry Foxall, who in after years became a rich iron merchant in America and built and named the Foundry Church in Washington, reminiscent of the forge in England and the business in which the donor had prospered. Bishop Francis Asbury dedicated the noted premises in 1810.

The Asburys attended the parish church at Great Barr, which was a chapel-of-ease to Aldrich, and also All Saints' Church in West Bromwich.

[1] Lewis, *Francis Asbury*, 11.
[2] Tyerman, *Life and Times of John Wesley*, III, 250.
[3] A sketch of Asbury's life after he closed his *Journal* at Granby, South Carolina, on December 7, 1815, will be found at the end of the present work.

At the latter the young man heard the famous Edward Stillingfleet, who sympathized with and participated in the Wesleyan Revival. Among the parishioners was the rich and pious Earl of Dartmouth, who was a friend of Selina, Countess of Huntingdon, and whose seat at Sandwell Hall was open to the evangelical preachers like George Whitefield and Howell Harris, who were patronized by the Countess. Asbury himself has pointed out that he heard many notable preachers such as Ryland, Talbot, Mansfield, Hawes, and Venn.

Young Asbury naturally heard of the Methodists through Foxall and others, and with his mother's consent he attended one of their services at Wednesbury. This town was the scene of the bitterest persecutions which Wesley and his preachers had endured, and a large society developed there. It was embraced in the Staffordshire Circuit and under the ministry of Alexander Mather, who was to become the second president of the British Conference after the death of John Wesley. Asbury was most favorably impressed by the singing and the extemporaneous nature of the prayer and sermon.

Among Asbury's other intimates during the period were William Emery, Edward Hand, Thomas and Jabez Ault, James Bayley, Thomas Russell, and Richard Whatcoat, all of whom are mentioned in Methodist annals.[4] He was converted while he and young Emery were praying in the old barn at the Asbury home. In a matter of weeks he was reading the Scriptures and giving out the hymns in the women's meeting to which he accompanied his mother, and soon he was exhorting. At the age of eighteen he became a local preacher and delivered his first sermon while standing behind a chair in a cottage near Manwoods, a quarter of a mile south of Forge Mill Farm, a house erected in 1680 by a great-uncle of Dr. Samuel Johnson.

Events now moved rapidly. Asbury was still a blacksmith, but he says that he traveled widely through the region and preached several times each week. In 1766 he left his work and took the place of an ailing itinerant for nine months in Staffordshire and Gloucestershire. During this service he was rebuked gently by the "assistant" or preacher in charge of the Staffordshire Circuit, W. Orp, because of certain alleged neglect.[5]

The following year he was admitted on trial as a traveling preacher and appointed to the Bedfordshire Circuit. Other assignments followed regularly: 1768, in full connection and appointed to Colchester; 1769, Bedfordshire again; 1770, Wiltshire. Up to this time it appears that Asbury had never attended a conference.[6] But he had served well and made many friends.

[4] See Briggs, *Bishop Asbury*, ch. ii.
[5] See the letter from W. Orp, May 23, 1766, in the *Letters*; also *The Methodist Magazine*, 1831, 189–91.
[6] Briggs, *op. cit.*, 23. But see note on the first entry in Asbury's *Journal*.

Asbury seems to have had a sweetheart at Great Barr, named Nancy Brookes; and Dr. Tipple said that their romance was broken off by his mother.[7] The message that he sent to his "dear heart" in a letter to his mother seems to indicate that she took offense because he left abruptly without seeing her, although he tried to do so.[8] He apparently treasured his memories of her and declared that "what once befell me in England" was the first cause of his life-long celibacy,[9] although in later years he mentioned other reasons.

The fact that Asbury was held in affection by those among whom he ministered is attested by letters from his parishioners at Whitchurch and a preacher who in 1768 had served the Staffordshire Circuit on which Asbury's parents lived, but who at the time of writing was stationed in London.[10]

Such was the twenty-six-year-old man who attended the Bristol Conference in 1771 and answered, "Here am I, send me," when John Wesley declared, "Our brethren in America call aloud for help."

Francis Asbury was five feet and nine inches tall. He was a slender man, with bright and piercing blue eyes and a lofty forehead with flowing fair hair; his voice was clear and full, his presence dignified and commanding. It surprises many people to learn that he had a preference for light blue clothing.[11] He was a deeply serious man, though he had his moments of levity. His *Journal* is filled with references to his illnesses, and he suffered prolonged sickness on more than one occasion. Asbury was in general a robust and healthy man, and the fact that he traveled constantly and endured incredible hardships for nearly fifty years is proof enough of his strong constitution.[12]

Building the Church

Francis Asbury holds first place as the builder of American Methodism. Others were in the New World before him and more followed him, but to this day none rivals him as the supreme factor in establishing the church and enabling it to sweep the land in the face of manifold difficulties. He has never had a peer in American Methodist history, just as John Wesley has had none in Britain.

His greatest contribution was his successful insistence upon the principle of itinerancy, which he learned from Wesley. This was undoubtedly the

[7] Tipple, *Francis Asbury, the Prophet of the Long Road*, 316.

[8] See Asbury's letter to his parents, October 26, 1768.

[9] See the letter to his parents June 7, 1784.

[10] See the letter from his four parishioners on August 27, 1771, and the letter from the Rev. John Allen on January 20, 1772, in *The Methodist Magazine*, 1831, 194–96.

[11] See his letter to George Roberts on June 6, 1801.

[12] For descriptions of Asbury see Tipple, *op. cit.*, 302–7; Briggs, *op. cit.*, 3; Stevens, *Memorials of Methodism*, 145.

secret of Methodism's amazing success during the frontier period. As the *Journal* reveals, he had been in the country only three weeks when he discovered the preference of the preachers for the city, and with prophetic insight he discerned that this would mean failure for the evangelical movement. So the new arrival did not hesitate to rebuke his superiors and seniors. They did not want to leave the cities, but he would show them the way! He desired "a circulation of preachers, to avoid partiality and popularity!" "I am fixed," he wrote, "to the Methodist plan, and do what I do faithfully as to God. I expect trouble is at hand. This I expected when I left England, and I am willing to suffer, yes to die, sooner than to betray so good a cause by any means."

Thus stubbornly did he stand against those who presumably knew America better than he did. In the end he won, and the Conference adopted a time limit of six months for the preachers, with three months for those in New York. Under this rule they rode the eastern seaboard and continued everywhere, until the words "Methodist circuit rider" became and remained a part of the American vocabulary. Not otherwise could they have kept up with the advancing frontier. They were responsible for the amazing growth of Methodism in America. They moved with the pioneers everywhere, and their Church far outgrew the population and outstripped those which had been established a century or more before the Methodists came.

Asbury was called a dictator, and in a sense the charge was not wholly unfounded. When Dr. Thomas Coke came to ordain him and set up the Methodist Episcopal Church, Asbury insisted upon a democratic election, but he did not administer in democratic fashion. Had he done so, he might have averted some misunderstandings and schisms; but his church would not have spread to the Father of Waters and grown from 1,000 to 200,000 members in his lifetime. His control of the preachers and their appointments was the main element in this success, and he could not have exerted such control and escaped the charge of tyranny.

But if he was a dictator, he exercised a benevolent dictatorship. He loved his preachers next to God. He accepted the same small salary, endured the same hardships, lived the same life, and traveled more than any of them. He asked nothing of them that he did not impose on himself; and they knew that if he sent them on hard rounds, he had already made harder rounds and would make more. There were little rebellions, but they came to nothing. The schism led by O'Kelly was serious at first, leading even McKendree away for a brief period, and it gave the church a temporary setback; but when the Methodists numbered ten million souls, the O'Kellyites had grown not at all and had barely been able to survive.

If Francis Asbury was a dictator, he learned the art from John Wesley; and his dictatorship saved Methodism and built it into the largest Protestant body in all the land.

Asbury's Journal

For more than a hundred years the great church which Francis Asbury built neglected his writings; his letters were never collected and his famous *Journal*, the basic document of the church, became unknown to two generations of people. In 1951 the National Historical Publications Commission of the United States Government included Asbury among the sixty-six great Americans whose works the body recommended for proper editing and publication, along with Washington, Jefferson, Adams, Lincoln, and the other immortals of the land. That recommendation was accepted by two Presidents and both Houses of Congress.

Then world Methodism moved in the matter. In September, 1951, the World Methodist Council at Oxford, England, acting unanimously on a report of its affiliated International Methodist Historical Society, endorsed the preparation of a *Standard Annotated Edition of the Journal and Letters of Francis Asbury*, and the implementation of the resolution was turned over to the Association of Methodist Historical Societies in the United States.

Following the example of John Wesley, Asbury opened his *Journal* on the ship which carried him to the New World. He continued it until he could no longer move unaided; and the pen fell from his faltering fingers at Granby, South Carolina, on Tuesday, December 7, 1815, three months and seventeen days before his death. From his *Letters* it will be observed that he expected what he had written to constitute something like a history of the Methodist movement in America during the early period.

He was well aware of his literary shortcomings and took the most careful steps to ensure that his *Journal* would be in the best form when it was published. To this end he enlisted the aid of some of the outstanding Methodists of the day in selecting and editing the material to be preserved. Just what was eliminated we do not know, but much was undoubtedly discarded. A glance at one of the documents written by his own hand will show that extensive editing was necessary to cast his manuscripts in proper form.

The first publication of any part of Asbury's *Journal* consisted of extracts which were printed in the *Arminian Magazine*. This publication, fashioned after the periodical of the same name started by Wesley in England, was launched by Asbury and John Dickins in Halifax County, North Carolina, in 1788. The first volume appeared the following year, and there was a second in 1790; both were printed in Philadelphia under the editorship of Dickins, who thus became the first publishing agent of American Methodism. The periodical was then discontinued, to be revived in 1818 under the name of the *Methodist Magazine*.

In the first volume of the *Arminian Magazine* Asbury published an extract from his *Journal* covering the period of August 7, 1771, to February 27, 1772. In the second appeared the *Journal* from March 26, 1772, to April 14, 1773. These extracts are of considerable interest because (1) they contain the full names of most of the persons who are referred to by initials only in the *Journal* which was published in book form thirty years later, and (2) they contain numerous passages which were omitted from the three-volume *Journal* which first appeared in 1821. Reference is made to these hereunder in the explanation of the method of the present work.

The *Journal* passed through many later hands. On one occasion all or part of the manuscript was lost; in a letter to Ezekiel Cooper on October 4, 1798, Asbury declared that he had left his "long lost manuscript journal" with Mrs. Betsy Dickins, widow of the recently deceased John Dickins.

Probably Dickins and his wife were the first editors. Dickins was educated at Eton and London, drew the plan for the first Methodist school in America, edited the first *Discipline* in the present form, edited the *Arminian Magazine* and its successor, the *Methodist Magazine*, and was the first book editor and publishing agent of American Methodism. He was well qualified to serve as redactor of his chief's literary remains.

Asbury paid a hundred dollars to a second and unknown man who corrected his papers.[13]

Then Thomas Haskins worked on them. He was a notable Methodist of the period, a member of the Christmas Conference in 1784, whose diary now reposes in the Congressional Library at Washington. His wife was Martha Potts, the granddaughter of Mrs. Rebecca Grace of Pennsylvania, who entertained Washington and his officers when the army was encamped at Valley Forge; she refused the marriage proposal of Benjamin Franklin because of his religious beliefs, or lack of them, but at his request she sat by his bedside when he died and pointed him to "the Lamb of God that taketh away the sins of the world."[14]

Others who assisted Asbury with his documents were Joseph Lanston, Dr. Henry Wilkins, and Mrs. Ann Willis. Lanston was a preacher of prominence and the spiritual father of Henry Willis.

Dr. Wilkins was born in Annapolis, Maryland, in 1767, the son of Joseph Wilkins, who was a pioneer Methodist in Anne Arundel County before he moved from Annapolis to Baltimore. Dr. Wilkins was the editor of a book of family remedies entitled *The Family Adviser; or, A Plain and Modern Practice of Physic; Calculated for the Use of Families Who Have Not the Advantages of a Physician, And accommodated to the Diseases of America, To Which is Annexed Mr. Wesley's Primitive Physic*. This book passed through several editions and had a large circulation among Methodists and the general public. It contained a preface addressed "To

[13] See letter dated June 26, 1801.
[14] See *Journal* note under June 23, 1776.

the Members of the Methodist Episcopal Church" and signed by Coke and Asbury. Dr. Wilkins was the host of the sick Bishop McKendree at his home north of Baltimore when John Wesley Bond's messenger brought news of the death of Asbury.[15]

Ann Willis was the cultured widow of Henry Willis, the first preacher on whom Asbury laid ordaining hands, the daughter of Jesse Hollingsworth, a leading Baltimore merchant, and a sister of Francis Hollingsworth, the final transcriber of Asbury's *Journal*.[16]

Francis Hollingsworth was the last editor through whose hands the Asbury documents passed. He prepared the prefatory statement, "Notice of the Transcriber," and sent the material to the press. He lived near Baltimore and was a member of a prominent Methodist family. That he had the cultural ability to edit the *Journal* is brought out by a statement in the *Journal* of Bishop Beverly Waugh under the date of November 25, 1825:

I called in the afternoon to see Mr. Francis Hollingsworth, a man of eccentricities, but possessing a mind highly cultured. He was the particular friend of the late venerable Asbury. I found him sitting by his table upon which his Bible and spectacles were laid. After some conversation relative to his health, he remarked that he saw clearly that he was afflicted. He had not read the Bible as much as he should have done; that such had been his fondness for literature that he had been too much occupied in examining Greek, Latin, French, and Spanish works.[17]

Asbury and Hollingsworth met at York, Pennsylvania, on June 29, 1815; and the bishop made this entry in his *Journal*: "I sit seven hours a day, looking over and hearing my transcribed journal; we have examined and approved up to 1807. . . . I have buried in shades all that will be proper to forget, in which I am personally concerned." Asbury had previously printed the extracts from his *Journal* up to 1780, and copies of this edition are in the Library of Congress and at Westminster Theological Seminary. It has been said that an "extension" of that extract was printed later, but such has never come to light. In Hollingsworth's "Notice of the Transcriber," which is included in this work, it will be seen that he did not see the published extract of Asbury's *Journal* but confined his work wholly to the period following 1780. He points out that Asbury's manuscript

[15] Smith, *Recollections of an Old Itinerant*, 266–68; Paine, *Life and Times of Bishop McKendree*, 182.

[16] Warriner, *Old Sands Street Church of Brooklyn*, 76; Roberts, *Centenary Pictorial Album*.

[17] In his *Centenary Pictorial Album*, 56, Roberts says that the inscription at Hollingsworth's grave states that he "died on February 4, 1826, age 32 years and six months." He would thus have been only twenty-eight years old when he completed his work on the *Journal*, and only thirty-two when Waugh visited him. Miss Annie P. Dalton of Baltimore thinks that Roberts probably mistook the date of birth, 1773, for 1793, and that Hollingsworth finished the *Journal* at the age of fifty-two.

contained numerous errors of chronology and mistakes in the names of persons and places, and expressed the fear that his editorial work was not always correct.

Having undergone the scrutiny and revision of the numerous persons above-mentioned, the *Journal*, including the previously printed extract up to 1780, was published in 1821 by Nathan Bangs and Thomas Mason, the Methodist publishing agents at New York. It was reprinted in 1852 and again reprinted about two years later without date.

But before the first edition was published, there was another episode in the history of Asbury's documents.

At the Baltimore Conference in March, 1817, Bishop McKendree presented the matter of a biography of Bishop Asbury, to which the conference responded by naming a committee to carry the plan into execution. The committee, composed of N. Reed, S. G. Roszel, J. W. Wells, W. Ryland, and Dr. Henry Wilkins, employed Samuel K. Jennings, M.D., who had been president of Asbury College at Baltimore, to prepare the volume. The unpublished manuscript of the *Journal*, other papers secured by Bishop McKendree from Hollingsworth, "one small package sent from the west by Mr. Thomas L. Douglass," and twenty-five letters were turned over to Dr. Jennings as materials for the biography.

In 1818 Jennings outlined his plan orally to the conference, and it was "favorably received." The following year he reported further progress, and in June of that year he delivered a manuscript of 269 pages to a special committee which had been appointed to consider it. This committee read the document twice and unanimously decided that it was not worthy of publication. This episode led to an unfortunate controversy. Dr. Jennings contended that the material delivered by him to the committee was not a finished biography of Asbury but a collection of notes and data from which a biography was to be prepared, and he charged the committee with prejudice because of his *Reform* principles which later led him to become one of the founders of the Methodist Protestant Church. The arguments for the committee were published in the *Methodist Magazine* (1831, 82–94), to which Dr. Jennings' supporters replied in the appendix of his book *An Exposition of the Late Controversy in the Methodist Episcopal Church* (230–47).

Dr. Jennings reclaimed his materials and declined to deliver them again to the committee, and the final disposition of his manuscript or notes is not known. He returned the *Journal*, letters, and other materials to the committee. A number of the letters had been secured by John Emory, who later became a bishop; and his papers were deposited in the Emory Collection at Drew Theological Seminary. The manuscript *Journal* was burned in a fire which destroyed the publishing house in 1836. The *Journal* of Jesse Lee was lost in the same fire.

Editorial Method

The above history of Asbury's *Journal* largely determined the method employed by the Editors in producing the present work. They were not dealing with original manuscripts but with printed materials which had already been edited by several persons. Numerous alterations had admittedly been made, and there were numerous admitted inaccuracies. Asbury had little formal education, and his written documents had literary crudities and grammatical errors. His published letters were carefully edited. It was not possible to print his original work, and the Editors were not concerned about adhering exactly to the work of Hollingsworth.

The purpose has been to produce an accurate and readable edition of Asbury's *Journal*, never deviating from the bishop's words and meaning but without perpetuating the chronological, biographical, geographical, and grammatical errors which appeared throughout the earlier transcription. In this the Editors followed the advice of experts in the field, especially the officials of the National Historical Publications Commission.

It will be recalled that Hollingsworth mentioned the fact that he found certain chronological errors in Asbury's manuscripts. These were indeed numerous. All the dates in the first edition of the *Journal* were carefully checked with Fitch's *The Perfect Calendar for Every Year of the Christian Era* (Revised Edition, 1930), and it was discovered that more than three hundred mistakes were left by Hollingsworth in the first volume alone. Most of these were corrected in the second edition published in 1852, an indication that further editorial work was done after Hollingsworth. Many of these errors remained, however, and they were corrected without footnotes in the present work.

Scripture quotations were likewise checked, and numerous mistakes were found. These were also corrected without comment when possible.

The names of all persons and places which were referred to by their initials only were inserted in the text when they could be identified. An interrogation (?) was added when identification was highly probable but not actually established.

Mention has been made above of the differences among the extracts which Asbury published in his own lifetime in the *Arminian Magazine*. These concerned the names of persons and places as well as several sentences which were omitted from the text as published by Hollingsworth. Inasmuch as the magazine extracts antedated the first printed *Journal* by thirty-two years and were evidently inserted by Asbury himself, the Editors have in general followed the magazine in the matter of the names, and they have included the omitted sentences in brackets.

ADVERTISEMENT

THE FOLLOWING IS THE PREFACE WHICH MR. ASBURY PREFIXED TO THE
FIRST NUMBER OF THE SECOND VOLUME OF HIS JOURNAL, WHICH WAS
PRINTED DURING HIS LIFETIME.

IN the month of September, in the year of our Lord one thousand seven
hundred and seventy-one, I embarked in England for America; at which
time the memoirs I have written of my life commenced. As I considered
my station on the American continent, in the order of Divine Providence,
as a situation in which I should frequently be exposed to censure and
jealousy, I thought it highly expedient, for my own satisfaction and the
confirmation of my friends, to keep an impartial diary of my intentions,
resolutions, and actions, as a Christian and a minister, that I might have,
through this medium, a constant and reasonable answer for mine accusers.
From the nature and design of the work, it must have in it many things
both unpleasing and uninteresting to curious and critical readers; and
perhaps some things exceptionable even to those who enter into its spirit,
and read it with affection. In keeping a journal of my life, I have unavoidably laboured under many embarrassments and inconveniences; my
constant travelling, the want of places of retirement and conveniences to
write, my frequent calls to the pulpit, my extensive epistolary correspondence, and my debility, and sometimes inability of body, have all been in-
separable from my station in the Church, and so many impediments to
the perfection of the account of my labours and sufferings in this country.
The first volume of the extract of my journal was published, many years
after it was written, under the management of others, it being out of my
power to attend the press, or even to read over the copy before it was
printed:* several inconveniences attending that volume will be avoided in
this.

For many years I did not determine to publish a second volume of the
extract of my journal: but the advice of my friends, and the prospects of
my approaching dissolution, have determined me on its publication.†

As I have had no certain dwelling-place in America, my manuscripts
have frequently been exposed to be lost and destroyed; but, by the permission of Divine Providence, I have collected them together.

The Methodists of late years have become a more numerous body,

* This volume, now reprinted, was corrected by the author.

† This determination was not carried into effect, except one small number, which is
now republished with the corrections of the author.

consequently more obnoxious to their enemies. The Scripture is fulfilled even amongst us, "Also of your own selves shall men arise, speaking perverse things, to draw away disciples after them." Some, who were for a long time our confidential friends and fellow-labourers, are now become our most inveterate foes, and have written and published books against our characters, government, and discipline. And as I am considered the most ostensible character in the Methodist Church in America, I have frequently to bear the greatest weight of their invectives. But impartial readers will not, I am persuaded, give an implicit assent to the asseverations of those who may be under personal resentment against the body, or individuals, without duly considering the possibility of their being influenced by self-interest, jealousy, or prejudice. And as I have been (under God and my Brethren) the principal overseer of the work in America, and have constantly travelled from the centre to the circumference of the Connexion, I flatter myself that reasonable men will acknowledge that I have always had an opportunity of obtaining better information relative to the true state of the whole work than any other man could possibly have. Would it not then be highly injudicious to prefer a history of Methodism, written by men of small and contracted information, (and apostates from its principles,) to such a history of its progress as will be presented to the public in my journals? And, if I may be credited, I can declare, that in the critical and delicate circumstances that I have been necessitated to stand in relative to the characters of men, I have never knowingly deviated from the principles of that sacred charity which obligates us to treat each other with all possible tenderness.

If I have injured the character of man, woman, or child, in journal representation, I have done it inadvertently, and sincerely ask their pardon. In stationing the preachers I have known no man after the flesh; but have, to the utmost of my power, endeavoured to keep an eye to the glory of God, the usefulness of the ministry, and the benefit of the people. I have attempted to give a simple narration of facts in the integrity of my heart, and in the fear of God.

My intention is, as much as possible, to remove every hinderance out of the way, and to give no occasion for offence to any man. But if, after all, my attempts prove unsuccessful, I can, in the approbation of my own heart, and in the company of my old, faithful, and constant American friends and brethren, through the medium of my journal, look back upon what God has wrought, and say, "Hitherto the Lord hath helped." We can thus comfort and console ourselves with the past lovingkindness of the Lord; and the years in which his right hand hath been bare, will thus, to us, be rendered more delightful.

I had thoughts of leaving my manuscripts to the executors of my will, to be published by them after my death, but found, upon reconsideration, that their contents respecting persons and things were of such a nature that no person could do it so well as myself.* Should my life be spared, the volumes will be brought forward in course. As soon as one is disposed of, another will be put to press, until the whole is published.

FRANCIS ASBURY

* The greater part of the journal which follows was left in manuscript, but revised under the author's inspection as far down as the year 1807. See the Notice of the Transcriber.

NOTICE OF THE TRANSCRIBER

THE name of the venerable author of the following journal will create for the work so deep and enduring an interest, in the hearts and minds of those for whom it was more especially prepared, that it becomes proper the transcriber should give some account of the manner in which he conducted the work of transcribing, so that those who are concerned may have satisfactory assurances of its genuineness. The ill health by which Bishop Asbury was so much of his life a sufferer; the crowds in which he was too often compelled to live in the west and south; the succession of visitors he thought it his duty at all times of leisure to receive; his ministerial labours; and, above all, the constant occupation of mind which the important concerns of a Church, so great in membership, so widely extended and rapidly increasing, necessarily occasioned, left the first Superintendent of that Church few means of rendering his journal more perfect. The transcriber has not attempted to improve it by giving his own for the author's. Some things in the original work he has taken the liberty of leaving out of the transcript; but there are not many of these, and they are most of them in that part of it which the bishop himself examined during his life. The transcriber not unfrequently found a confusion of dates; and sometimes, as he thinks, a mistake in the names of persons and things, more especially in the author's geographical notices of the districts through which he made his annual tour; the emendations, in this last particular, are not, it is to be feared, always correct. In places where the author has left, by inadvertence, a sentence unfinished, a thing not uncommon, the transcriber has always tried to supply what was wanting; and where hurry has occasioned evident mistake, as is the case in a few instances, he has ventured upon correction; but he is not sure that in every attempt he has been successful. To those persons yet living, who had, by habits of intimacy with Bishop Asbury, become acquainted with the peculiarity of his conversational and epistolary manner of expressing himself, the style of the present work may not be so pleasing; because it is not so exactly the style they expected—not so decidedly the bishop's. But they must recollect that the author's intention in keeping his journal was, to make a faithful record for posterity; and the transcriber never forgot that its value, in this respect, would be better understood and more highly appreciated by those who can only know the author by his work. The abruptness of sentence in its beginning or its break—the sudden light flashed upon a subject by a suggestion conveyed in words few and strong; the names, descriptive as painting, he was wont to bestow upon persons

and things—all these live only in the memory of his surviving friends; and
with them must pass away; but that which is of more importance—the
identity of Bishop Asbury in the commencement, the continuance, and
wonderful increase of Methodism in this country, will give a perpetuity
of interest in the record here offered which nothing else can give. The
transcriber would not, however, have it supposed that he has entirely departed from Bishop Asbury's style; on the contrary, he presumes he has
been enough observant of this to satisfy most readers, inasmuch as the
bishop himself, when he examined what had been transcribed up to 1807,
altered but once, and then not much. The public may rest assured that the
work is the author's: but here the transcriber must be permitted to speak
in the first person. When I give this assurance, I must be understood to
mean from the year 1780 to the end of the journal; the original manuscript of all that preceded that date, I never saw: I only know that when
printed it did not please the author. The journal of Bishop Asbury might
have been better. I once ventured to express my unavailing wishes to him
that he had left out many of the uninteresting incidents and travelling
notices we find in it, and had put in more of the deep reflections and acute
remarks on men, books, and passing events continually afloat in his
powerful and observant mind; and that, for the sake of his brethren in
the ministry who should follow him, he had made the skeletons of his
sermons more perfect, and had added many more. His reply, uttered with
much feeling, would have satisfied every candid mind that it was by no
ordinary effort so much had been done.

F. HOLLINGSWORTH

March 28, 1821

August 7, 1771—December 29, 1772

1771

Asbury preaching in a gale on his way to America.

CHAPTER ONE

August 7, 1771 – December 29, 1772

On the 7th of *August*, 1771, the Conference began at Bristol, in England.[1] Before this, I had felt for half a year strong intimations in my mind that I should visit America; which I laid before the Lord, being unwilling to do my own will, or to run before I was sent. During this time my trials were very great, which the Lord, I believe, permitted to prove and try me, in order to prepare me for future usefulness. At the Conference it was proposed that some preachers should go over to the American continent. I spoke my mind, and made an offer of myself. It was accepted by Mr. Wesley and others, who judged I had a call. [It was my duty to go where the conference ordered; only one or two objected.]

From Bristol I went home to acquaint my parents with my great undertaking, which I opened in as gentle a manner as possible.[2] Though

---

[1] The *Minutes* contain the following: "Q.7: Our brethren in America call aloud for help. Who are willing to go over and help them? A. Five were willing. The two appointed were Francis Asbury and Richard Wright." Robert Strawbridge in Maryland and Philip Embury in New York had begun preaching several years previously. Robert Williams came to America in 1769, and John King followed in 1770, and in the latter year the British Conference sent Richard Boardman and Joseph Pilmoor. (The sentences in brackets in the early journal are those which were published in the *Arminian Magazine* but omitted in Hollingsworth's edition of Asbury's *Journal*. See the Introduction.)

[2] Asbury's boyhood home still stands in Newton Road, West Bromwich, about four miles from Birmingham, and is preserved by the Corporation as a historic site. His birthplace "near the foot of Hampstead Bridge in the Parish of Handsworth" has disappeared. It stood a little north of the Hampstead and Great Barr railway station. His parents were Joseph Asbury (1715?–98) and Elizabeth Rogers Asbury (1715?–1801). Their only other child was Sarah, who was baptized on May 3, 1743, and was buried on May 28, 1748, in the parish church at Handsworth. No support has been found for

it was grievous to flesh and blood, they consented to let me go. My mother is one of the tenderest parents in the world; but, I believe, she was blessed in the present instance with Divine assistance to part with me. I visited most of my friends in Staffordshire, Warwickshire, and Gloucestershire, and felt much life and power among them. Several of our meetings were indeed held in the spirit and life of God. Many of my friends were struck with wonder, when they heard of my going; but none opened their mouths against it, hoping it was of God. Some wished that their situation would allow them to go with me.

I returned to Bristol in the latter end of August, where Richard Wright[3] was waiting for me, to sail in a few days for Philadelphia. When I came to Bristol I had not one penny of money; but the Lord soon opened the hearts of friends, who supplied me with clothes, and ten pounds: thus I found, by experience, that the Lord will provide for those who trust in him.

On *Wednesday, September* 4, we set sail from a port near Bristol[4] and having a good wind, soon passed the channel. For three days I was very ill with the seasickness; and no sickness I ever knew was equal to it. The captain behaved well to us. On the *Lord's day, September* 8, brother Wright preached a sermon on deck, and all the crew gave attention.

Thursday, 12. I will set down a few things that lie on my mind. Whither am I going? To the New World. What to do? To gain honour? No, if I know my own heart. To get money? No: I am going to live to God, and to bring others so to do. In America there has been a work of God: some moving first amongst the Friends, but in time it declined; likewise by the Presbyterians, but amongst them also it declined. The people God owns in England, are the Methodists. The doctrines they preach, and the discipline they enforce, are, I believe, the purest of any people now in the world. The Lord has greatly blessed these doctrines and this discipline in the three kingdoms: they must therefore be pleasing to him. If God does

Herbert Asbury's statement in *A Methodist Saint,* 5–7, to the effect that Joseph Asbury had a son by a previous marriage to Susan Whipple and that Daniel Asbury was a descendant of that marriage. (*Journal* entries for July 24, 1774; July 16, 1792; February 22, 1795; April 5, 1802; Wakeley, "Mother of Bishop Asbury," *The Ladies' Repository,* August, 1867, 449 ff.; various biographies of Asbury.)

[3] Richard Wright had served one year as an itinerant before he came to America. He preached in Pennsylvania, New York, Delaware, and Maryland, and returned to England in 1774. He was appointed to West Cornwall for one year and then to East Cornwall for two years, after which his name disappears from the *Minutes.* He did not succeed in America because, according to Asbury, he "was spoiled by gifts" and "had no taste for spiritual subjects." (See *Journal* entry for May 29, 1774; this was also the judgment of Thomas Rankin, as stated in his *Journal,* now at Garrett Biblical Institute, p. 101. Wakeley: *Lost Chapters Recovered from the Early History of American Methodism,* 236 ff.; Atkinson: *The Beginnings of the Wesleyan Movement in America,* 322.)

[4] From the Port of Pill, John and Sebastian Cabot sailed to the New World in the fifteenth century. (Wood: *Elizabethan Sea Dogs,* 1 ff.) From there on Good Friday, 1773, Captain Thomas Webb, Mrs. Webb, Thomas Rankin, and George Shadford sailed for America. (Hurst: *History of Methodism,* II, 954.)

not acknowledge me in America, I will soon return to England. I know my views are upright now; may they never be otherwise.

On the *Lord's day, September* 15, I preached on Acts xvii, 30: "But God now commandeth all men everywhere to repent." The sailors behaved with decency. My heart's desire and prayer for them was, and is, that they may be saved: but O! the deep ignorance and insensibility of the human heart!

The wind blowing a gale, the ship turned up and down, and from side to side, in a manner very painful to one that was not accustomed to sailing; but when Jesus is in the ship all is well. O what would not one do, what would he not suffer, to be useful to souls, and to the will of his great Master! Lord, help me to give thee my heart now and forever.

Our friends had forgotten our beds, or else did not know we should want such things; so I had two blankets for mine. I found it hard to lodge on little more than boards. I want faith, courage, patience, meekness, love. When others suffer so much for their temporal interests, surely I may suffer a little for the glory of God, and the good of souls. May my Lord preserve me in an upright intention! I find I talk more than is profitable. Surely my soul is among lions. I feel my spirit bound to the New World, and my heart united to the people, though unknown; and have great cause to believe that I am not running before I am sent. The more troubles I meet with, the more convinced I am that I am doing the will of God.

In the course of my passage I read Sellon's Answer to Elisha Cole[5] on the Sovereignty of God; and I think, no one that reads it deliberately can afterward be a Calvinist.

On the *Lord's day, September* 22, I preached to the ship's company on John iii, 23; but alas! they were insensible creatures. My heart has been much pained on their account. I spent my time chiefly in retirement, in prayer, and in reading the Appeals, Mr. De Renty's life, part of Mr. Norris's Works, Mr. Edwards on the Work of God in New England, the Pilgrim's Progress, the Bible, and Mr. Wesley's Sermons.[6] I feel a strong

[5] Walter Sellon was once a Methodist itinerant and a master in Kingswood School. During the controversy over Calvinism, Sellon at Wesley's request defended the Church of England against the charge of predestination in *A Defense of God's Sovereignty Against the Impious and Horrible Aspersions Cast Upon It by Elisha Coles in His Practical Treatise on That Subject.* (See Wesley's *Journal,* V, 361.)

[6] John Wesley published *An Earnest Appeal to Men of Reason and Religion* in 1743 and *A Farther Appeal to Men of Reason and Religion* in 1745. These were frequently republished, separately and together; and Asbury probably used one of the collected volumes. M. de Renty was a French ascetic whose biography, *The Holy Life of Monr. De Renty, a late Nobleman of France, and some time Councellor to King Lewis the Thirteenth,* first published in 1651, was read by Wesley in Georgia (Wesley's *Journal,* I, 219, 414, 450). Wesley drastically abridged and published it in 1741, and it was this abridgment which Asbury read. John Norris (1657–1711) was a Platonist whose *Treatise Concerning Christian Prudence* was abridged and published by Wesley in 1734. Wesley also abridged and published two of Jonathan Edward's works, *A Narrative of*

desire to be given up to God—body, soul, time, and talents: far more than heretofore.

September 29, I preached to the ship's company again, on these words, "To you is the word of this salvation sent." I felt some drawings of soul towards them, but saw no fruit. Yet still I must go on. Whilst they will hear, I will preach, as I have opportunity. My judgment is with the Lord. I must keep in the path of duty.

On the 6th of *October*, though it was very rough, I preached on deck to all our ship's company, from Heb. ii, 3: "How shall we escape, if we neglect so great salvation?" The Lord enabled me to speak plainly, and I had some hopes that the interesting truths of the Gospel did enter into their minds. I remember the words of the wise man, "In the morning sow thy seed, and in the evening withhold not thy hand." As to my own mind, I long and pray, that I may be more spiritual. But in this I comfort myself that my intention is upright, and that I have the cause of God at heart. But I want to stand complete in all the will of God, "holy as he that hath called me is holy, in all manner of conversation." At times I can retire and pour out my soul to God, and feel some meltings of heart. My spirit mourns, and hungers, and thirsts, after entire devotion.

October 13. Though it was very windy, I fixed my back against the mizen-mast, and preached freely on those well-known words, 2 Cor. v., 20: "Now then we are ambassadors for Christ, as though God did beseech you by us: we pray you in Christ's stead, be ye reconciled to God." I felt the power of truth on my own soul, but still, alas! saw no visible fruit: but my witness is in heaven, that I have not shunned to declare to them all the counsel of God. Many have been my trials in the course of this voyage; from the want of a proper bed, and proper provisions, from sickness, and from being surrounded with men and women ignorant of God, and very wicked. But all this is nothing. If I cannot bear this, what have I learned? O, I have reason to be much ashamed of many things, which I speak and do before God and man. Lord, pardon my manifold defects and failures in duty.

Philadelphia

October 27. This day we landed in Philadelphia,[7] where we were directed to the house of one Mr. Francis Harris,[8] who kindly entertained us in the

the late *Work of God, at and near Northampton* and *Some Thoughts Concerning the Present Revival of Religion in New England,* and Bunyan's *Pilgrim's Progress.*

[7] Philadelphia at this time was the largest American city, having a population of 28,000. It was the Proprietary Capital of the Province until 1776. Carpenter's Hall, then nearing completion, was to house the Continental Congress three years later.

[8] Francis Harris was a prominent Philadelphia Methodist who frequently accompanied the preachers to their nearby appointments. (See Pilmoor's Manuscript *Journal* in the possession of the Philadelphia Conference Methodist Historical Society, Philadelphia.)

evening, and brought us to a large church,[9] where we met with a considerable congregation. Brother Pilmoor[10] preached. The people looked on us with pleasure, hardly knowing how to show their love sufficiently, bidding us welcome with fervent affection, and receiving us as angels of God. O that we may always walk worthy of the vocation wherewith we are called! When I came near the American shore, my very heart melted within me, to think from whence I came, where I was going, and what I was going about. But I felt my mind open to the people, and my tongue loosed to speak. I feel that God is here; and find plenty of all we need.

November 2. I find my mind drawn heavenward. The Lord hath helped me by his power, and my soul is in a paradise. May God Almighty keep me as the apple of his eye, till all the storms of life are past! Whatever I do, wherever I go, may I never sin against God, but always do those things that please him!

November 3. We held a watch-night. It began at eight o'clock. Brother Pilmoor preached, and the people attended with great seriousness. Very few left the solemn place till the conclusion. Towards the end, a plain man spoke, who came out of the country, and his words went with great power to the souls of the people; so that we may say, "Who hath despised the day of small things?" Not the Lord our God: then why should self-important man?

November 4. I was sent for to visit two persons who were under conviction for sin. I spoke a word of consolation to them, and have hopes that God will set their souls at liberty. My own mind is fixed on God: he hath helped me. Glory be to him that liveth and abideth forever!

November 5. I preached at Philadelphia my last sermon, before I set out for New York, on Romans viii, 32: "He that spared not his own Son, but delivered him up for us all, how shall he not with him freely give us all things?" This also was a night of power to my own and many other souls.

[9] This was St. George's Church, now the oldest Methodist place of worship in America and the first to be called a church. It was here that Asbury preached his first sermon in America on Monday, October 28, 1771. It was purchased from a German Reformed congregation on November 23, 1769. Its congregation was comprised mostly of members of the society organized by Captain Thomas Webb in 1767. Webb preached in a sail loft and later at 8 Loxley Place in a house which is still standing. Whitefield preached in Philadelphia in 1769; and one of his converts, Edward Evans, was preaching in the region before the arrival of Wesley's missionaries. (Pilmoor's *Journal*; Tees: *The Beginnings of Methodism in England and America*, 92, 93; Tees: *The Ancient Landmark of American Methodism*, 23–27; Atkinson, *op. cit.*, 145, 146.)

[10] Joseph Pilmoor (1739–1825) was one of the first two preachers sent by Wesley to America, arriving on October 24, 1769. He returned to England in 1774 and resumed his work in the British Conference. In 1784 he returned to America and was ordained by Bishop Samuel Seabury of Connecticut as a clergyman of the Anglican Church and served nearly seventeen years as the rector at St. Paul's Church in Philadelphia. (Wilson: *Life of Rev. William White*, 111; Atkinson, *op. cit.*, 447, 448; Seaman: *Annals of New York Methodism*, 67.)

New Jersey and Staten Island

November 6. I went to Burlington on my way to New York, and preached in the court house to a large, serious congregation.[11] Here also I felt my heart much opened. In the way from thence to New York I met with one Peter Van Pelt,[12] who had heard me preach at Philadelphia. After some conversation, he invited me to his house on Staten Island; and as I was not engaged to be at New York on any particular day, I went with him and preached in his house.[13] Still I believe God hath sent me to this country. All I seek is to be more spiritual, and given up entirely to God—to be all devoted to him whom I love.

On the *Lord's day*, in the morning, *November* 10, I preached again to a large company of people, with some enlargement of mind, at the house of my worthy friend Mr. P. Van Pelt; in the afternoon preached to a still larger congregation; and was invited to preach in the evening at the house of Justice Hezekiah Wright,[14] where I had a large company to hear me. Still, evidence grows upon me, and I trust I am in the order of God, and that there will be a willing people here. My soul has been much affected with them. My heart and mouth are open; only I am still sensible of my deep insufficiency, and that mostly with regard to holiness. It is true, God has given me some gifts; but what are they to holiness? It is for holiness my spirit mourns. I want to walk constantly before God without reproof.

New York

On *Monday* I set out for New York,[15] and found Richard Boardman[16] there in peace, but weak in body. Now I must apply myself to my old work—to watch, and fight, and pray. Lord, help!

[11] Asbury went by stage to Burlington en route to New York to assist Richard Boardman. (Pilmoor's *Journal.*) Captain Webb had formed a Methodist society in Burlington in December, 1770, with Joseph Toy as leader.

[12] Peter van Pelt lived on Staten Island, where his Dutch forebears settled in 1687. He was a prominent citizen, a soldier in the French and Indian War, and one of the leading early Methodists in the region. Pilmoor, Williams, and probably Boardman and Webb, preached on Staten Island; and van Pelt doubtless became a Methodist under the influence of one of these preachers. He is believed to have died in 1781.

[13] Van Pelt's house was a Dutch dwelling with low sloping roof, wide fireplaces and small windows, located on Woodrow Road about one-half mile from Woodrow Church. This church was built in 1787 and is still in use. Here Asbury preached his first sermon in New York State. (Leng and Davis: *Staten Island and Its People*, I, 466; Hampton: *Asbury on Staten Island*, 4.)

[14] Hezekiah Wright was a justice of the Court of Common Pleas of the province of New York, and a prominent citizen who operated a fleet of vessels engaged in coastal trade. His home was on Shore Road. (See *Journal* entry for May 22, 1802; Hampton, *op. cit.*, 5.)

[15] Asbury took a ferry from the foot of William Street at Stapleton to Whitehall at the lower end of Manhattan Island.

[16] Richard Boardman (1732–82) came to America with Pilmoor in 1769. He was designated by Wesley as "Assistant" with authority to station the preachers. He

Tuesday, 12.[17] I preached at New York to a large congregation[18] on 1 Cor. ii, 2: "I determined not to know anything among you, save Jesus Christ, and him crucified," with some degree of freedom in my own mind. I approved much of the spirit of the people: they were loving and serious; there appeared also, in some, a love of discipline. Though I was unwilling to go to New York so soon, I believe it is all well, and I still hope I am in the order of God. My friend Boardman is a kind, loving, worthy man, truly amiable and entertaining, and of a child-like temper. I purpose to be given up to God more and more, day by day. But O! I come short.

Wednesday, 13. I preached again at New York. My heart is truly enlarged, and I know the life and power of religion is here. O how I wish to spend all my time and talents for him who spilt his blood for me!

The *Lord's day*, 17, I found a day of rest to my soul. In the morning I was much led out with a sacred desire. Lord, help me against the mighty! I feel a regard for the people: and I think the Americans are more ready to receive the word than the English; and to see the poor Negroes so affected is pleasing,[19] to see their sable countenances in our solemn

brought twenty-five pounds in cash and some books which were sold for twenty-two pounds as a contribution from the British Conference to the New York Society. Boardman and Pilmoor returned to England together in 1774. The former resumed his itinerant status and preached in Ireland and London. He died from apoplexy in Cork and was buried in St. Barry's Churchyard there.

[17] In the early *Journal* there was an error of one day in each date between November 12 and December 2. Corrections have been made herein. Throughout the *Journal* erroneous dates have been corrected.

[18] This was Asbury's first sermon in Wesley Chapel, dedicated October 30, 1768. It was the house referred to by Wesley when he asked for volunteers for America in 1769. (Wesley's *Journal*, August 3, 1769.) It was the fourth Methodist preaching place in New York. The first was the home of Philip Embury in Augustus Street, where Embury preached the first sermon in New York in 1766. Then a house near the barracks was used, 1766–67. The society moved to the famous Rigging Loft, 120 Williams Street, in 1767, where Captain Thomas Webb joined Embury. On March 30, 1768, lots 44 and 46 on John Street, between Nassau and Williams, were purchased from Mrs. Mary Barclay, widow of a former rector of Trinity Church, the first property owned by Methodist trustees in America. The price, six hundred pounds, was loaned by Captain Webb and William Lupton, who with Thomas Taylor were trustees. Phraseology for the deed was secured from Wesley and was first used in the deed to St. George's Church in Philadelphia. This meetinghouse was 40 × 60 feet in size, built of stone, faced with plaster, and painted blue. Subscriptions for more than 418 pounds were received from 250 persons, including prominent vestrymen of Trinity Church. A Methodist church has stood on the site since that date. In 1817 a larger building was erected, and in 1841 the present John Street Church was built. It is still active and is one of the official shrines of American Methodism. Its society is the oldest in America, though the present building is not as old as St. George's in Philadelphia. (Seaman, *op. cit.*, 416–22, 448–53; *John Street Church Records*, I.)

[19] There were Negroes in the New York Society from the beginning. Barbara Heck's servant, Betty, was present at Embury's first sermon and a charter member. Others were subscribers to the building fund. Peter, slave of a tobacconist, James Aymar, was converted by Captain Webb in the Rigging Loft and was for many years the sexton of

assemblies, and to hear them sing with cheerful melody their dear Redeemer's praise, affected me much, and made me ready to say, "Of a truth I perceive God is no respecter of persons."

Tuesday, 19. I remain in New York, though unsatisfied with our being both in town together. I have not yet the thing which I seek—a circulation of preachers, to avoid partiality and popularity. However, I am fixed to the Methodist plan, and do what I do faithfully as to God. I expect trouble is at hand. This I expected when I left England, and I am willing to suffer, yea, to die, sooner than betray so good a cause by any means. It will be a hard matter to stand against all opposition, as an iron pillar strong, and steadfast as a wall of brass: but through Christ strengthening me I can do all things.

Thursday, 21. At present I am dissatisfied. I judge we are to be shut up in the cities this winter. My brethren seem unwilling to leave the cities, but I think I shall show them the way. I am in trouble, and more trouble is at hand, for I am determined to make a stand against all partiality.[20] I have nothing to seek but the glory of God; nothing to fear, but his displeasure. I am come over with an upright intention, and through the grace of God I will make it appear: and I am determined that no man shall bias me with soft words and fair speeches: nor will I ever fear (the Lord helping me) the face of man, or know any man after the flesh, if I beg my bread from door to door; but whomsoever I please or displease, I will be faithful to God, to the people, and to my own soul.

Saturday, 23. I went with Brother Sause[21] and brother White[22] to

Wesley Chapel. He was purchased by the trustees for forty pounds in 1783 when his owner returned to England and allowed to work out the sum for his emancipation. Peter was one of the founders of the African Methodist Episcopal Zion Church and laid the cornerstone of its first meetinghouse at Leonard and Church streets in 1800. (Wakeley, *op. cit.*, 439; Seaman, *op. cit.*, 485 ff.; Barclay: *Early American Methodism*, I, 291; *John Street Church Records*, I.)

[20] Asbury refers to his disagreement with Boardman and Pilmoor concerning the principle of itinerancy. Asbury insisted on frequent changes in appointments or a "circulation of preachers" while the other two believed in longer tenures. Pilmoor wrote in his *Journal*, page 197, "Frequent change . . . is never likely to promote the spirit of the Gospel nor increase true religion." This caused a conflict between the men which was reflected in numerous *Journal* entries and in correspondence with Wesley. The preferences of laymen for certain preachers and the acceptance of gifts became involved. (See *Journal* entries for October 9, 1772; July 1, 1773; May 29, 1774; and so on.) At the conference on May 25, 1774, after the departure of Pilmoor and Boardman, it was determined that the preachers should interchange each six months and that those in New York and Philadelphia should change quarterly. (See *Minutes*.) This action was "undeniably one of the chief means of the marvellous growth of Methodism in its first half century." (Tipple: *Prophet of the Long Road*, 119, 120.)

[21] Richard Sause came from Dublin with Charles White in 1766 and established a cutlery business. He was one of the original trustees of Wesley Chapel and a donor to the building fund. His home was open to the preachers, and he frequently escorted them on their travels. Asbury appointed Sause to succeed James Jarvis as the leader of the

Westchester,[23] which is about twenty miles from New York. My friends waited on the mayor[24] for the use of the court house,[25] which was readily granted. On the Lord's day morning, a considerable company being gathered together, I stood up in the Lord's power; yea, I felt the Holy One was nigh. I judged that my audience needed to be taught the first principles of religion: so I spoke from those words, "Now he commandeth all men everywhere to repent." Seriousness sat on the faces of my hearers, and the power of God came both on me and them, while I laboured to show them the nature and necessity of repentance, and the proper subjects and time for it. In the afternoon the congregation was increased, both in number and seriousness: some of the chief men of the town—the mayor and others, were present. I delivered my thoughts on those words, "This is his commandment, that we should believe on the name of his Son Jesus Christ, and love one another." I felt warmth in my soul while I set forth the nature and necessity of faith, and much enlargement towards my hearers. In the evening I preached at one Molloy's,[26] at a place called West Farms,[27] to many persons, on the love of God. The next day I preached at Westchester again to a large company, and felt a sense of God resting on my heart, and much love to the people. Being detained

class in 1774. (See *Journal* entries November 4, 7, 1774.) He was a Loyalist and returned to England soon after the Revolution, remaining an active Methodist there. The last word of him was in 1795 when Thomas Rankin in London wrote to John Staples in New York about the death of Staples' son, Thomas, named for Rankin. (*John Street Church Records*, 30–33, 69, 78, 416, 425–26, 446; Wakeley, *op. cit.*, 84–85; *Arminian Magazine*, XVIII, 413–15.)

[22] Charles White came from Dublin and was an original trustee of Wesley Chapel, a donor to the building fund, cotreasurer with Richard Sause, and treasurer when Sause returned to England. His house was open to the preachers, and he sometimes traveled with them. He was a Loyalist and went to Nova Scotia after the Revolution. Later he went westward, where Asbury found him "without property and without grace" in May, 1790. (Wakeley, *op. cit.*, 85–86; *Journal* entries for May 13, 1790, April 29, 1793; Seaman, *op. cit.*, 30–33, 416, 425–26.)

[23] Westchester was a village on the New York mainland, near Throg's Neck. The section visited by Asbury is now in the borough of the Bronx in New York City. Asbury traveled up Manhattan Island and crossed Harlem River by Kingsbridge about where the present IRT subway and bridge are located. (Scharf: *History of Westchester County*, I, 746; map of Kingsbridge, 1783.)

[24] The mayor was probably Nathaniel Underhill. (Scharf, *op. cit.*, I, 640.)

[25] The Westchester Courthouse stood near St. Peter's Church at the crossroads. It was built in 1720 and destroyed by fire in 1790.

[26] Molloy was perhaps related to M. Molloy, a barber who was active in Wesley Chapel and a close friend of Sause and White. (Pilmoor's *Journal*; *John Street Church Records*, I, 14.) The home became the center of West Farm's society. (See *Journal* entry for January 3, 1772.)

[27] West Farms, originally known as DeLancey's Mills, was a sprawling farming district along the Bronx River three miles or so west of the Westchester Courthouse. The area is still called West Farms and includes the southern part of Bronx Park and the thickly populated streets radiating from West Farms Road as it approaches Tremont Avenue.

another day by the roughness of the weather, I preached another sermon on this text, "Knowing therefore the terrors of the Lord, we persuade men." In the evening we went to the mayor's, where we lodged that night; and the next day at noon set out for New York.

The *Lord's day, December* 1, I found a day of rest to my soul, and much liberty, both in the morning and evening,[28] among the people. O that I may live to God and not to myself, and keep myself free from all worldly entanglements!

Saturday, December 7. As brother Boardman was still at New York, I thought it best to make another visit to Westchester. I spent the evening and lodged at the house of one Dr. White,[29] who appears to be an understanding man in the things of God. His wife is also of an amiable disposition, and is touched with a sense of her own state, and that of her neighbours. I spoke to her freely of the willingness of Christ to save now, but unbelief still prevailed. The next morning I went to the court house to preach, but the noise of the children, and the ill-behaviour of the unhappy, drunken keeper, caused much confusion. In the afternoon my friend Molloy informed me that the door of the court house was shut against me I felt myself at first a little troubled; but soon after a tavern-keeper gave me the offer of an upper room in his house,[30] where I spoke on those words, "If we confess our sins, he is faithful and just to forgive us our sins, and to cleanse us from all unrighteousness." The power of God was with us, and many of the vilest of those present will, I trust, remember it as long as they live. In the evening I made another visit to West Farms, and preached there; and my heart was there also touched with the power of God. I lodged that night at the house of Mr. Oakley.[31] After supper I asked the family if they would go to prayer. They looked at one another and said, there was need enough. The next morning, when I asked a blessing before breakfast, they seemed amazed. I told them, they wanted nothing but religion. The old father said it was not well to be too religious. The son said he thought we could not be too good. I soon afterwards took my leave of them, and preached in the evening at East-

[28] Asbury preached in Wesley Chapel on John Street in New York. Boardman may have been ill or on Staten Island. Pilmoor on this same date felt "great anxiety on account of hearing nothing from Mr. Boardman." (Pilmoor's *Journal*, December 2, 1771.)

[29] Ebeneezer White (1744–1825) was the son of the Rev. Ebeneezer White and attended Asbury in a later illness without charge. (See *Journal* entries for January 19–February 5, 1772.) He and his wife were deeply religious but do not appear to have been Methodists. (Scharf, *op. cit.*, I, 574.)

[30] Two weeks previously the use of the courthouse had been granted without question. On the present occasion no appeal seems to have been made to the mayor, perhaps because Sause and White were not now with Asbury. (See *Journal* entry and notes for November 24, 1771.) There were three inns in Westchester at the time.

[31] Lednum: *Rise of Methodism in America*, 76.

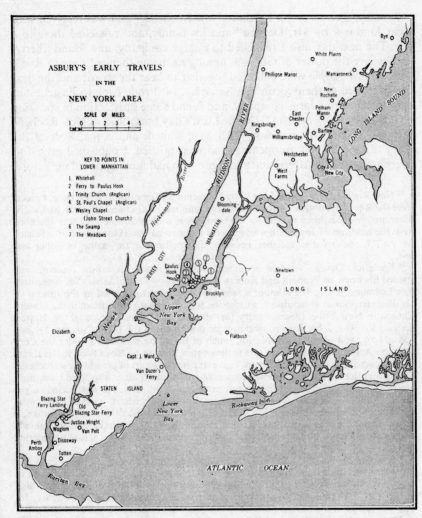

ASBURY'S EARLY TRAVELS

IN THE

NEW YORK AREA

SCALE OF MILES

KEY TO POINTS IN
LOWER MANHATTAN

1 Whitehall
2 Ferry to Paulus Hook
3 Trinity Church (Anglican)
4 St. Paul's Chapel (Anglican)
5 Wesley Chapel
   (John Street Church)
6 The Swamp
7 The Meadows

chester[32] to a few who seemed willing to hear, on those words, "As for
me and my house, we will serve the Lord." I found myself straitened and
shut up; but the Lord knoweth what he hath to do with me.

[32] The village of Eastchester was a mile or more inland from Eastchester Bay at the
lower part of Mount Vernon. Asbury perhaps preached in the home of Theodosius
Bartow, where Pilmoor also preached and where Asbury was to be cared for when ill
six weeks later. (See *Journal* entry for January 23–February 5, 1772; Scharf, *op. cit.*,
I, 727, and maps.)

Tuesday, December 10. I rode to New Rochelle,[33] and was received with great kindness by Mr. Deveau[34] and his family, and preached there to a few. The next day also I preached to a large company, and found liberty, and believe the power of God was among us. From thence I rode to Rye,[35] where a few people were collected together to hear the word: and the next day preached to them again. On *Saturday*, 14, I rode back to Eastchester, and preached to a large company, and found some satisfaction in speaking on "The one thing needful." On the Lord's day I preached at New Rochelle in the church.[36] My text was, "All have sinned, and come short of the glory of God." I felt an opening, and was satisfied. I published myself to preach again in the afternoon, and those who had most opposed me before,

[33] New Rochelle was settled in 1687 by Huguenot refugees from La Rochelle, France. Here the Rev. Theodotius Bartow, son of the man who befriended the first Methodist itinerants, was Anglican rector. As the town grew, a considerable area was absorbed from the holdings of John Pell, who gave his name to nearby Pelham Manor. (Scharf, *op. cit.*, I.) Scharf distinguishes between the spelling of the name of father and son.

[34] Frederick Deveau (variant spellings) was of French Protestant descent, who opened his home to Pilmoor and Robert Williams as well as to Asbury for preaching. (See Lednum, *op. cit.*, 70; Pilmoor's *Journal*.) Asbury later preached at the funeral of his daughter, Sarah Hutchinson, wife of the Rev. Sylvester Hutchinson, in the Bowery Church in New York. (*Journal* entry for May 30, 1802.) Another daughter, Hester, married the Rev. John Wilson, who became prominent in the Book Concern. Deveau was a Tory, and after the Revolution much of his estate was seized under the Confiscation Act of New York, and it is believed that he went to Nova Scotia. His three-hundred-acre farm called "Beechmont" gave its name to a part of present New Rochelle. This farm after its confiscation was presented to Thomas Paine, who lived there until hostile public opinion forced him to return to New York City. He was buried on the Deveau property, but his remains were later disinterred. (Scharf, *op. cit.*, I, 689, 690; *Dictionary of American Biography*, XIV, 163.) This man is identified as Mr. Drake in the extract of the *Journal* printed in the *Arminian Magazine*; however, nothing more is known about Drake, and it is presumed that the man in question was actually Frederick Deveau.

[35] Rye was established in the early 1660's and named for an English town. In 1676 a stone fort was built there. This was converted into a tavern by a Mr. Van Sicklin in 1728. Later it was acquired by John Doughty and operated under the name of "Sign of the Sun." When Asbury visited the place, it was operated by John Doughty, Jr., who was justice of the peace, and Asbury was doubtless entertained and preached there. (Scharf, *op. cit.*, II, 643 ff.) In 1868 the fort-tavern was purchased by the Methodist Episcopal Church and a parsonage erected on the property, which adjoined the church built years before. In 1950 the old well of the tavern was found between the church and the parsonage, and a bronze plaque was erected. (See article by the Rev. J. Lane Miller, "The Church Well at Rye Fort," *Christian Advocate*, October 29, 1953. Also see Baird: *History of Rye*.)

[36] The Anglican church at New Rochelle was a plain structure, 40 × 30 feet in size, built in 1710 on the Post Road near the center of the community. It had been continuously served by ministers of French descent ordained by the Bishop of London. The Rev. Michael Houdon was minister at this time. After his death in 1776 there was no resident minister during the Revolution. The Rev. Theodotius Bartow took the parish in 1790.

came to hear and behaved well.[37] In the evening I preached in the house of my friend Mr. Deveau [with liberty and power]. The next day I preached again at Mr. Deveau's, and on Tuesday went to Rye, where I had many to hear, and felt some freedom of spirit. The next day I preached at Mamaroneck,[38] to a company of people who at first took but little notice of the worship of God; but I trust some of them felt the power of truth in their hearts. On Thursday I returned to New York, and found my friends in peace.

Lord's day, December 22, I preached to a large company in the evening, and felt much power. I know that God was with us indeed, yea, was nigh to bless the people. On *Christmas day*, we had a very comfortable time. On *Friday the 27th*, I set off with two of my friends[39] for Staten Island. On *the 28th* we arrived at Justice Wright's, where we were entertained with the best his house afforded. From thence I went to my old friend Van Pelt's, who received me with his former kindness, and collected a congregation for the evening, to whom I preached, but had a violent pain in my head. After service I went to bed, and was very ill. However, the next day, being the Lord's day, I preached in the morning and also in the afternoon, with some freedom of mind. In the evening I returned and preached at Justice Wright's. Having received an invitation to preach at the house of one Mr. Ward[40] at the east end of the Island, I visited that place on my return to New York, where I had a comfortable time [and much power, and found the people kind].

On *Tuesday* we arrived in New York. We have been favoured here with a very solemn watch-night. Many felt the power of God.

[37] Pilmoor visited New Rochelle in 1771, and the Rev. Ichabod Lewis, Presbyterian minister at White Plains, objected to the Methodists preaching in the home of Frederick Deveau. Pilmoor preached, however, and Mrs. Deveau was converted. (Lednum, *op. cit.*, 70.)

[38] Mamaroneck had been founded on the Post Road halfway between Rye and New Rochelle in 1661 by John Richbell, an Englishman who secured the land from the Indians. Asbury had passed through the village three times but had not previously preached there. William Sutton was supervisor (1771–75), and Gilbert Budd was clerk (1771–1806). The descendants of the colonial Governor James de Lancy lived there. (Scharf, *op. cit.*, I, 846.)

[39] These friends were probably not Sause and White, who were involved with Pilmoor in the tense situation relative to the appointment of preachers at Wesley Chapel. One of them may have been Samuel Selby, who later cared for Asbury in illness and accompanied him to Staten Island in February. Perhaps Asbury absented himself from New York in order to leave Pilmoor free to adjust the situation there.

[40] Lednum, *op. cit.*, 76.

1772 *The society gathers at John Street Meetinghouse in New York*

January 1, 1772. I find that the preachers have their friends in the cities, and care not to leave them. There is a strange party-spirit. For my part I desire to be faithful to God and man. On Thursday evening, I preached my last sermon for a time, on 1 Thess. v. 6: "Let us not sleep as do others, but let us watch and be sober."

On *Friday*, brother Sause and myself set out for West Farms, and I preached in the evening. On the Lord's day I preached at brother Molloy's at half-past nine, in Westchester at three,[41] and at West Farms at six in the evening. A person showed me much kindness at West Farms, favouring me with a man and horse all the time I was there,[42] acknowledging the word came home to his heart, and that he was wicked. My friend Hunt,[43] who was a Quaker, said he never was so affected. The next day I went to Westchester, but had only a few to hear me. On *Wednesday* I preached at Hunt's, and felt much Divine power in my soul, and an opening among the people. I have found many trials in my own mind, but feel determined to resist. I see traps set for my feet.

Thursday, I preached at Deveau's, and had an attentive people to hear, and felt myself warm and zealous. On *Friday* I went to Mamaroneck had a large congregation, and felt the divine presence. Many of the people also felt the power of truth, and sunk under the word—it was laid home to the hearts of the people; but some contradicted and blasphemed. I believe God has a work to do among the people in this place. Lord, keep me faithful, watchful, humble, holy, and diligent to the end. Let me sooner choose to die than sin against thee, in thought, word, or deed.

[41] Asbury probably preached at the home of Ebenezer White or in the tavern at Westchester. (See note under December 7, 1771.)

[42] This man was probably Mr. Oakley. (See note under December 7, 1771.)

[43] The Quaker family named Hunt was prominent in the county. A promontory in East River is called Hunt's Point. (Scharf, *op. cit.*, numerous references.)

Saturday 11, I preached at one friend Burling's,[44] where many attended to the truth, and showed a willingness to hear. On the *Lord's day* I preached at Deveau's at ten in the morning, at three in the afternoon, and at six in the evening. Many attended, but I fear few felt such deep concern as will induce them to leave their sins, and flee from the wrath to come. At brother Hunt's on Monday evening, the house would not hold the congregation: there I felt liberty and power. I hope God will visit them. I have had many trials from Satan, but hitherto the Lord hath helped me against them all. I stand a miracle of mercy! O that I may always be found faithful in doing his will!

On *Tuesday* the 14th I went to Rye: but the people here are insensible. They cry, "The Church! the Church!" There are a few Presbyterians; but they have suffered their meeting house to go to ruin,[45] and have lost the power of religion, if they ever had it. I was not a welcome messenger to this people. On *Wednesday* the 15th I preached at two in the afternoon at Mamaroneck with some power, and in the evening returned, preached at Rye, to a large company, and felt my Master near.

Thursday 16, I was taken ill with a cold and chill. The next morning I rode to New City,[46] but the cold pinched me much. On New City island a congregation was assembled to receive me. I spoke to them with some liberty, and they wished me to come again. A wise old Calvinist said, he might experience all I mentioned, and go to hell. I said, Satan experienced more than I mentioned, and yet is gone to hell. After preaching I rode to Mr. Bartow's,[47] though in much pain. When I had preached there I went to bed. During the whole night I was very ill. My friends behaved very kindly, and endeavoured to prevail upon me to stay there till I was restored: but my appointment required me to set off from Eastchester, where I preached, and rode near eight miles in the evening to New Rochelle. On the 19th, the Lord's day, I preached three times, though very ill.[48] Many attended, and I could not think of disappointing them.

Monday the 20th, I rode to Pelham's Manor,[49] and preached there at

[44] Probably Thomas Burling of New Rochelle, whose house is reported to have been an early Methodist preaching place. (Lednum, *op. cit.*, 77; records of First Methodist Church, New Rochelle.)

[45] The Rye Presbyterian Church had been erected on the north side of the Post Road about 1730 and was served infrequently by the Rev. Ichabod Lewis of White Plains. The building was destroyed by fire during the Revolution.

[46] New City was a village on an island of the same name near the east shore of Eastchester Bay. It was connected with the mainland by a wooden toll bridge and was a part of Pelham Manor. It is now a part of the borough of the Bronx and called City Island.

[47] See note under December 10, 1771; Scharf, *op. cit.*

[48] Asbury was probably at the home of Frederick Deveau.

[49] In the early 1660's Thomas Pell purchased from the Indians a tract of about ten thousand acres east of the Hutchison River. This was called Pelham, and the Pell holding became a manor in the development of the county. About six thousand acres

noon, and at six in the evening at Peter Bonnette's[50] in New Rochelle. The next day I rode to Deveau's, but the day was extremely cold. In the night I had a sore throat, but through the help of God I go on, and cannot think of sparing myself:

> "No cross, no suff'ring I decline,
> Only let all my heart be thine!"[51]

Tuesday the 21st I preached at my friend Deveau's for the last time, on "Those things that ye have both learned, and received, and heard, and seen in me do." The people seemed deeply affected under the word. In the morning of the 22d, I set out for the New City, and preached there in much weakness and pain of body, and in the evening went to my friend Pell's.[52] That night I had no rest: and when I arose in the morning, the pain in my throat was worse. On the 23d I came in a covered sleigh to my friend Bartow's, where I took up my lodging, being unable to go any farther. I then applied to a physician,[53] who made applications to my ears, throat, and palate, which were all swelled and inflamed exceedingly. For six or seven days I could neither eat nor drink without great pain. The physician feared I should be strangled, before a discharge took place: but my God ordered all things well. I am raised up again; and cannot help remarking the kindness with which my friends treated me, as if I had been their own brother. The parents and children attended me day and night with the greatest attention. Thus, though a stranger in a strange land, God has taken care of me. May the Lord remember them that have remembered me, and grant to this family life forever more!

February 5. Still I feel myself weak. It is near a fortnight since I came to my friend Bartow's. Dr. White has attended me in all my illness, and did all he could for me gratis. Yesterday was the first day of my going out. I went to Westchester to hear a friend preach. My kind friends Sause and White brought up a sleigh from New York on Monday last, but my

were conveyed to Huguenot settlers and embraced in New Rochelle. The southern half of the remainder is now in the Bronx and called Pelham Bay Park, and the northern half is in Westchester County between Mount Vernon and New Rochelle and is known as Pelham Manor and North Pelham. Lednum and Tipple, as well as the *Journal* extract printed in the *Arminian Magazine*, identified this place as Phillipse Manor, but Phillipse was near the present Yonkers and beyond the territory which Asbury was now cultivating. (Scharf, *op. cit.*, I, 701 ff.)

[50] Peter Bonnette (1736–1823), of Huguenot descent, was a close friend of Frederick Deveau. After the Revolution he became a local preacher in the society at New Rochelle. (Lednum, *op. cit.*, 77, 102–3.)

[51] These are the closing lines of the hymn "Looking unto Jesus" from the Wesleys' *Hymns and Sacred Poems* published in 1740. It was probably composed by John Wesley and based on a German original in the Herrnhut collection. (*Poetical Works of John and Charles Wesley*, I, 222, 223.)

[52] Thomas Pell married Margaret Bartow and lived at the Pell homestead in Pelham. (Scharf, *op. cit.*, I.)

[53] Ebeneezer White of Westchester.

friends at this place would not suffer me to go with them. In the course of my recovery, I have read much in my Bible, and Hammond's *Notes on the New Testament*.[54] I have also met with a spirited piece against predestination. I did not expect to find such an advocate for general redemption in America. This day I ventured to preach at Mr. Anthony Bartow's to his family and a few other people. In the evening returned home, and found Mr. DeLancy,[55] the former governor's son, there; who lives in the woods near Salem, and invited me to his house. We spent the evening comfortably together.

On *Thursday, February 6*, I preached as I had appointed, the man of the house being in a consumption. Though I had not many people to hear me, yet I have reason to hope that my sermon did good to the poor invalid. I felt affected for my friends in this place, who had been in some measure moved by the word on my former visits, but are now returned to their old ways and company. I found myself weak and unfit to preach, but believe there were some who felt the word come close to their hearts. May God help them to profit by it! On *Friday*, the 7th I set out for New York in a sleigh,[56] and my friends seemed glad to see me. I want to be less concerned about anything except my own work—the salvation of souls. At present I seem determined to consecrate my all to God—body, soul, time, and talents.

On the *Lord's day* found myself weak, but brother Pilmoor being ill, I preached in the morning, and found life. Stayed at home on Monday, and read in Mr. Wesley's *Notes on the Old Testament*. On *Monday*, the 10th I went to the jail, and visited a condemned criminal, and preached to him[57] and others with some tender feelings of mind, on those words, "Joy shall be in heaven over one sinner that repenteth."

Tuesday, the 11th. This day I have visited many of my friends from house to house, and did not find much evil or much good stirring among them. Now I retire to hold communion with God, and to feel his power. In the evening my strength increased, and I preached with some freedom.

On *Wednesday* I walked out, but caught cold, and returned home chilled and very ill. In the evening when I went into the pulpit, my every

[54] Henry Hammond (1605–60) was a prolific writer and was known as the "father of English biblical criticism." His *The Paraphrase and Annotations on the New Testament*, published in 1653 and frequently republished, was his greatest work. (*Dictionary of National Biography*.)

[55] Stephen DeLancy (1736?–95), second son of the former Governor James DeLancy, inherited a tract of land in the town of Salem in the northern part of Westchester County, where he developed a community and erected a fine residence. He married Hannah, daughter of the Rev. Joseph Sackett. (Scharf, *op. cit.*, I, 865–66; II, 505.)

[56] Asbury's route from Bartow's in Eastchester was through West Farms, across the Bronx River at Williamsbridge to Kingsbridge, and through Manhattan Island to Wesley Chapel on John Street.

[57] Pilmoor had preached to this man ten days previously and on the twenty-first walked with him to the gallows and read the fifty-first psalm. (Atkinson, *op. cit.*, 304–6.)

limb shook; and afterward went to bed with violent pains in my bones. The sickness continued for three days, and kept me at home for above a week. On *Thursday*, the 20th, I gave an exhortation in public.

Staten Island

Having a desire to visit my friends on Staten Island, I set off in the afternoon of the 21st, contrary to the persuasion of my friends in New York. Samuel Selby[58] who was tender towards me in my illness, and took care of me as if I had been his father, accompanied me.

Justice Wright[59] received us and entertained us kindly; and though weak and weary, I preached at Peter Van Pelt's[60] to a few persons, with much satisfaction. Mr. Disosway[61] [a man of fortune] invited me to preach in his house, to which I consented; and Justice Wright sent us there on the Lord's day, with several of his family. I preached twice at that gentleman's house to a large company. Some, it appeared, had not heard a sermon for half a year; such a famine there is of the word in these parts, and a still greater one of the *pure* word. I returned in the evening to Justice Wright's, and preached to a numerous congregation with comfort. Surely God sent me to these people at the first, and I trust he will continue to bless them, and pour out his Spirit upon them, and receive them at last to himself!

February 24. I preached again at Justice Wright's to many people, and the Lord was with me. My labours increase, and my strength is renewed. Though I came here weak, yet after preaching three times I felt myself

---

[58] Samuel Selby was a prominent member and trustee of Wesley Chapel and conducted a saddlery business. He was a Patriot and was forced to leave New York when the city was occupied by British troops during the Revolution. (Seaman, *op. cit.*, 68, 431–32; *John Street Church Records*, Bk. I; *Journal* entry for April 23, 1780.)

[59] See note under November 11, 1771.

[60] See note under November 7, 1771.

[61] The prominent Disosway family lived near the present Tottenville, having removed from Brooklyn in 1684. Captain Cornelius Disosway operated Disosway's Mill on Staten Island opposite Perth Amboy, New Jersey, before the Revolution. His brother, Israel Disosway (1733?–1815), seems to have heard Asbury preach at Van Pelt's, and he became the leader of the first Methodist class on the island; the first quarterly meeting was held in his barn, and the first meetinghouse was built of lumber cut from his trees. Woodrow Methodist Church is the descendant of that chapel. He married Ann Doty, or Doughty (1766–1838); and they later moved to New York to educate their four sons in Columbia College. All were prominent in Wesley Chapel. One of the sons, Gabriel Poillon Disosway, was a manager of the Missionary Society and a founder of Randolph Macon College. He pledged the support of Melville Cox, the first missionary to Liberia in 1833, and was one of the supporters of the Oregon mission to the Indians. (Long and Davis, *op. cit.*, I, 166; Wakeley, *op. cit.*, 554, 555; Lednum, *op. cit.*, 421, 422; Hubbard: *History of Methodism on Staten Island*, 27–33; Clute: *Annals of Staten Island*, 290; Barclay, *op. cit.*, I, 291; North, "Reminiscences," *Christian Advocate, March* 2, 1933, 204; Hampton, *op. cit.*, 5–7.)

strong. Thanks be to God, who hath raised me up from so low a state! On the 25th I preached at Abraham Woglom's[62] at two in the afternoon, to a large company, and had an invitation to go to the south part of the Island:[63] in the evening also I preached at the same place. On the 26th, I preached at the ferry,[64] on my way to New York, to a few people, though some came two miles on foot. After preaching, I visited a young man who seemed to be at the point of death: he was full of unbelief, and I fear it was through his Calvinistic notions.

Thursday, the 27th, we arrived in New York. I found brother Pilmoor had set off for Philadelphia in the morning. In the evening I met the society, and felt myself assisted and enlarged. At night I slept with holy thoughts of God, and awoke with the same: thanks be to God!

Tuesday, March 3, 1772.[65] *Tuesday* próved to be a day of peace to my soul; part of which I spent in visiting the people. The next day I was employed in writing to England; and after preaching in the evening with power, I went to rest in sweet peace, and awoke in the morning in the same frame of spirit. May this day be spent to the glory of God! and may my soul yet praise him more and more!

[62] The house of Abraham Woglom was in the Rossville waterfront area about a mile from the Blazing Star Ferry to Perth Amboy, New Jersey. Several members of the Woglom family aided in establishing the Woodrow Church in 1787. (Lednum, *op. cit.,* 75, 77; Hampton: *Historical Address, 150th Anniversary of Asbury Church, Staten Island,* 1952; Hubbard, *op. cit.,* ch. ii.)

[63] The invitation probably came from Gilbert Totten, an extensive landowner whose family were active Methodists. Joseph Totten, his brother, became a prominent preacher; and John C. Totten was a printer whose name appeared on numerous early Methodist hymnbooks and tracts. The Tottens were among the founders of the Woodrow Church on Staten Island in 1787; and some of them are buried in its cemetery along with fifteen Methodist preachers, including Henry Boehm, one of Asbury's traveling companions and executors.

[64] Asbury's preaching place was in the vicinity of Quarantine Station in the Tompkins-ville-Stapleton area, where the Quarantine Station (Kingsley) Church later developed. Near here was the house of Cornelius Vandeventer, whose daughter, Gertrude, married Israel Disosway, Sr.; and here also was the home of Captain Ward, where Asbury also preached. (Morris: *Memorial History of Staten Island;* Hubbard: *History of Methodist Episcopal Churches of Staten Island;* Taylor and Skinner: *Revolutionary Map of Staten Island,* 1781; manuscript records of Vernon B. Hampton, 1928, 1955.)

[65] This section of the *Journal* through Tuesday, March 17, 1772, has been transposed to this position from a point immediately following April 14, 1773. In all previous editions and printings there has been a hiatus of approximately a month, February 27–March 26, 1772, with no statement as to Asbury's travels or activities during the period. Similarly there has been a brief entry dated at Philadelphia April 14, 1773, which was an interpolation caused by the insertion of a section of the *Journal* at the wrong point. This was doubtless due to an error on the part of the transcriber or printer, and the confusion has been noted by historians and biographers. Study of this material and cognate documents, especially the manuscript *Journal* of Joseph Pilmoor and the *Records of John Street Church,* shows that the interpolation of April 14–15, 1773, is in reality the record of the hiatus period, February 27–March 26, 1772. The section has therefore been placed in proper sequence.

On *Wednesday*, after spending a part of the day in visiting, I preached in the evening from these words: "So we see that they could not enter in because of unbelief:" and humbly hope it was not labour in vain, while unbelief, that destructive root of all other sin, was exposed to the people.

On *Thursday* there was an appointment for me to preach at Newtown.[66] Brother Sause and myself crossed the East River; but it was with difficulty that we obtained horses.[67] We then attempted to proceed on our way; but it was a severe morning, with much snow and wind. The snow came full in our faces, so that, after riding a few miles, we were lost in the storm, and imperceptibly turned our course back towards New York; which we never discovered till we overtook some people on the road. We then crossed the river back to the city, where I continued till Monday.

New York

Friday, I preached at New York on these words: "The Lord is good, a strong hold in the day of trouble;" and felt life and power in dispensing the word. On *Saturday* I visited the sick, and gave an exhortation to the people.

Sunday, March 8. After preaching in the morning on Heb. xii, 15, I went in the afternoon to church, and heard Mr. English preach a useful sermon:[68] in the evening I preached with much freedom on Eccles. xi, 9, "Rejoice, O young man, in thy youth," &c. The young people appeared deeply serious. May the blessing of the Lord attend it, and great fruit appear in time to come! The next day I rode to Bloomingdale,[69] and preached with satisfaction; and then returned home, and found it a

---

[66] Newtown was located about twelve miles east of colonial Brooklyn. A creek on Long Island opposite the present 23rd Street in New York is still known as Newtown Creek, and the village was two or three miles beyond the head of this stream. Captain Thomas Webb preached the first Methodist sermon there in 1767; and Williams, Pilmoor, and Boardman also preached there. The location is now a section of Queen's Borough, and the Middle Village Church is the descendant of the Newtown class.

[67] Liveries hesitated to let horses in unfavorable weather. On August 5, 1771, Pilmoor was denied a horse in the heat of midsummer. (Atkinson, *op. cit.*, 274.)

[68] The church attended by Asbury was Trinity Church, at present Broadway and Wall Street, or St. Paul's Chapel, at Broadway and Fulton Street; if the latter, as seems probable, the same building remains to this day. The Rev. Charles Inglis was assistant rector, whose name frequently appears as *English*. He was among the subscribers to the erection of Wesley Chapel in 1768. He was a Tory and after the Revolution went to Nova Scotia, where he was consecrated bishop in 1787. (Seaman, *op. cit.*, 438; *John Street Church Records*, Bk. I; Tipple, *op. cit.*, 43, identifies the preacher as "probably the Rev. William Eldred of the Protestant Episcopal Church" but gives no substantiating data; the records of the church show that no person named Eldred or whose name begins with *E* was ever there.)

[69] Bloomingdale was four miles north of Wesley Chapel.

blessing to labour in the vineyard of the Lord, both in season and out of season.

On *Tuesday* morning my mind was clear, my heart was fixed on God, and Christ was precious. Bless the Lord, O my soul! New York is a large city, and well situated for trade; but the streets and buildings are very irregular. The inhabitants are of various denominations, but nevertheless of a courteous and sociable disposition. There are several places of Divine worship: the Episcopalians have three; the High Dutch, one; the Low Dutch, three; the Lutherans, two; the French Protestants, one; the Presbyterians, two; the Seceders, one; the Baptists, one; the Moravians, one; the Methodists, one; and the Jews one.[70] The city abounds with inhabitants; but the exact number I could not ascertain.

Wednesday, 11. My soul enjoyed great peace, and the day was partly spent in religious visits. The next day my mind was in the same comfortable frame; and holy thoughts of God, with strong desires to do all things with a single eye to his glory, as well as to follow his Divine precepts, possessed my peaceful heart.

Friday, 13. This day was, as yesterday, a day of peace; and it was with great satisfaction I preached in the evening, though cold, to a considerable number of people, on the much-neglected duty of self-denial.

Lord's day, 15. I went through my morning exercises in church as usual, and in the afternoon heard Mr. C. preach a good sermon; but a more gay and undevout congregation I have seldom seen—they were talking,

[70] Asbury's list of churches is complete. The locations in present-day terms were as follows:

Episcopalians (Anglican or Church of England)
    1. Trinity—west side of Broadway at Wall Street
    2. St. Paul's—west side of Broadway at Fulton Street
    3. St. George's—Beekman Street, several streets east of Broadway, close to East River
Dutch (Reformed and Collegiate)
    1. Garden Street—south of Wall Street, east of Broadway
    2. Nassau and Cedar Streets
    3. Nassau Street, near John Street
    4. Fulton and Williams Streets
Lutheran (German)
    1. Broadway, just south of Wall Street
    2. North of Beekman Street, close to Swamp and Tan Yard
French Protestant—King Street east of Nassau, a short distance north of Wall Street
Presbyterian
    1. Wall and New Streets
    2. East of the Commons, north of Beekman Street
Seceders (Quakers)—east of Nassau Street on a lane just south of Maiden Lane
Baptist—Golden Hill (John Street) at Cliff Street, close to Wesley Chapel
Moravian—Fulton and Dutch Streets
Methodist—Wesley Chapel, John Street between Nassau and William Streets
Jews—synagogue on Mill Street east of Broad Street

laughing, bowing, and trifling both with God and their minister, as well as with their own unawakened souls.

New Jersey–Pennsylvania–Delaware

On *Tuesday* I took my leave of New York, after preaching from Philippians i, 9,[71] with an intention to spent some time on Staten Island, on my way to Philadelphia. During my stay on the island I preached several times, with power and satisfaction; but was sometimes greatly assaulted by Satan. Hitherto the Lord hath helped me. Glory to his name! He preserves and blesses my soul; he supplies me with all things necessary for the preservation and health of my body. May I be ever careful to please him, and devote all the powers of body and soul to his service.

March 26. After having preached in a large upper room, at Mr. Thompson's in Amboy,[72] where many came to hear, and I was much favoured in my soul, an innkeeper invited me to his house,[73] and kindly desired that I would call on him when I came again.

Friday, 27. I set off on a rough-gaited horse, for Burlington; and after being much shaken, breakfasted at Spotswood;[74] fed my horse again at Crosswick's,[75] and then thought to push on to Burlington; but the roads being bad, and myself and horse weary, I lodged with a Quaker, on whom I called to inquire the way. He not only invited me to tarry all night, but also treated me with great kindness. The next day I rode to town very weary; and on the Lord's day (*March* 29) preached in the court house to many hearers.[76]

[71] Asbury preached his farewell sermon on this visit at 5 A.M., an hour frequently observed on Tuesdays at Wesley Chapel.

[72] Amboy was the Indian name of Perth Amboy, New Jersey, which was founded about 1680 and incorporated in 1718; the word "Perth" was added in honor of the Earl of Perth. (*Columbia Encyclopedia*, 1376.) The owner of the upper room where Asbury preached has not been identified.

[73] This innkeeper may have been John Church, who kept "a good house of entertainment" at Amboy. (Watson: *Annals of Philadelphia*, I, 464.)

[74] Spotswood in Middlesex County was on the road to Bordentown and Trenton, about twenty-six miles from the latter place. Asbury had a choice of two routes from Inman's Ferry, now New Brunswick; and he took the "lower road," turning about five or six miles from the Raritan River and following a circuitous route toward Burlington. (Woodward and Hageman: *History of Burlington County*, 54; Gordon: *Gazeteer and History of New Jersey*, 241.)

[75] Crosswicks in Burlington County was a post town with a large Quaker meetinghouse. Methodist services were held in the schoolhouse, and a class was formed which grew into the Methodist church. (Gordon, *op. cit.*, 124, 125; Woodward and Hageman, *op. cit.*, 289.)

[76] Asbury, as well as Captain Webb, Richard Boardman, and John King, preached at the courthouse in Burlington until the county seat was moved to Mount Holly. Thereafter and until a church was built, the Methodists met in the home of George Smith. (Schermerham: *History of Burlington*, 195; Wakeley, *op. cit.*, 554, 555.)

Monday, 30. After riding to New Mills,[77] in company with some friends, in a wagon, I preached in a Baptist meeting house and was kindly received.

Tuesday, 31. Finding the people were divided among themselves, I preached from these words: "This is his commandment, that we should believe on the name of his Son Jesus Christ, and love one another;" and humbly hope my labour was not in vain. The same night we came to Burlington.

April 2. I came to Philadelphia, and finding brother Boardman[78] and brother Webb there, was much comforted. Brother Boardman's plan[79] was: that he should go to Boston; brother Pilmoor to Virginia; brother Wright to New York; and that I should stay three months in Philadelphia. With this I was well pleased; [and earnestly desire that my whole soul could be more devoted to God].

Friday 3. We dined with Mr. Roberdeau[80] who cannot keep Negroes for conscience' sake; and this was a topic of our conversation.

Saturday, 4. This morning my mind was composed and serene; [fixed, I humbly hope, on God alone. My desire is, to be more constantly devoted than ever: yea, to walk in holiness before the Lord].

April 7. In the evening I preached to a very large audience in the church, after preaching in the day to many poor mortals in the Bettering-house.[81]

---

[77] New Mills was the present Pemberton, New Jersey. Captain Webb preached there in 1770. In 1775 the Methodists built a meetinghouse on property deeded to the trustees by William Budd, Jr. (Woodward and Hageman, *op. cit.*, 407.)

[78] Richard Boardman (1738–82), whose unverified birthplace likely was Gillimoor, Ireland, came to America with Joseph Pilmoor in 1769. He acted as "assistant" until October 10, 1772, when Wesley assigned Asbury to the post. Boardman's ministry was confined mostly to New York and Philadelphia, but in 1772 he entered New England and organized in Boston a class of brief duration. After his return to England in 1774 he was appointed to circuits in Ireland, with the exception of 1780, when he was in London. He died during his pastorate at Cork and was buried in the churchyard attached to the St. Fin Barre Cathedral.

[79] This "plan" was a forerunner of American Methodism's system of making appointments at annual conferences.

[80] Asbury's host was doubtless General Daniel Roberdeau (1727–95), friend of Whitefield and a leader in Philadelphia. When a resident of Alexandria, Virginia, in 1785, he arranged the meeting of Asbury and Coke with General Washington at Mount Vernon to discuss slavery. (Lednum, *op. cit.*, 78; *National Cyclopedia of American Biography*, II, 18.)

[81] This was the Philadelphia Almshouse and Hospital maintained for the sick, insane, and dependent poor. It was the first nonsectarian hospital in the United States and was established in 1732 in the square now bounded by Third, Fourth, Spruce, and Pine streets. In 1767 the location was moved to Tenth and Spruce streets. Three modern institutions are the outgrowth of the Bettering House: The Philadelphia General Hospital; The Philadelphia State Hospital (Byberry); and Riverview, the home for the aged poor at Holmesburg, Philadelphia. (*History of Philadelphia General Hospital.*)

April 8. Set out for Bohemia[82] to find Mr. Wright, (who had been at his own discretion,) that he might wait on Mr. Boardman, in order to go to New York for five months. Stopping at Mrs. Withey's[83] in Chester,[84] to feed myself and my horse, I inquired about preaching in that town, and found this to be the house where Mr. Boardman and Mr. Pilmoor put up; and that the people were pleased with Methodist preaching. After leaving word that I would call to preach there on my return, I set off for Wilmington,[85] expecting to meet Mr. Wright there; but we accidentally met just as he was turning off to Mr. Tussey's[86] for lodging, about four miles from the town. He seemed glad to see me, and willing to be subject to order. The next morning Mr. Wright went on his way to Philadelphia. Having a desire to go, and see, and hear how things went, I desired him to call and preach at Chester; and I proceeded to the house of Mr. Stedham [in Delaware], a friend of the Methodists; and then rode on to Newcastle, and stopped at the house of brother Furness,[87] a tavern-keeper, but a good man. Preached there to a few people, but met with opposition, and found the Methodists had done no great good. The court house here is shut against us; but it is open for dances and balls; and brother Furness has lost his company by receiving us. However, we were comforted together.

Maryland

April 10. Set out for Bohemia, where I found that some mischievous opposers had thrown the people into confusion.

[82] The name given in honor of his homeland by Augustine Herman to some five thousand acres in Cecil County, Maryland, on the east side of the Elk River between the Bohemia River and Back Creek. The manorial grant, which was in payment to cartographer Herman by Governor Calvert for "an Exact Mapp of the country," fell into the hands of the Labadists after the grantee's death in 1686. This region was the scene of early Methodist activity and is associated with Methodist history through Governor Richard Bassett, who aided and entertained bishops and circuit riders at his estate there. (Wilstach: *Tidewater Maryland*, 108–10; Mathews: *The Maps and Map Makers of Maryland*, 368–86.)

[83] Mrs. Mary Withey was the widow of James Withey, an English officer. She kept the Columbia Hotel in Chester, Pennsylvania, called "the best Inn on the continent." Henry Boehm says that George Washington was often her guest. Asbury preached her funeral on May 5, 1810. (See entry for that date. Also July 16, 1773.)

[84] Chester, oldest town in Pennsylvania, was the Swedish settlement of Upland when William Penn arrived in 1682. Captain Webb is believed to have introduced Methodism there about 1769.

[85] Lednum lists those who preached there after Webb in this order: John King, whom Pilmoor licensed and sent to Delaware in 1770, Robert Williams, Boardman, Pilmoor, Wright, and Asbury. (*Op. cit.*, 58.) On his first visit to Delaware, Captain Webb preached in the home of J. Stedham in Wilmington. (Hallman: *The Garden of Methodism*, 9, 14.)

[86] This was Isaac Tussey, cousin of J. Stedham. He lived on Shell Pot Hill above Wilmington. (Hallman, *op. cit.*, 122; Scharf: *History of Delaware*, II, 911.)

[87] At New Castle, in Robert Furness's tavern, Asbury preached his first sermon in the state of Delaware. (Hallman, *op. cit.*, 117.)

I have had serious thoughts of going to Baltimore; but the distance, which is ninety miles, seems too much at present.

April 11. Found an inattention to study, and unsettled frame of mind, much insensibility of soul, and a backwardness to prayer. Lord, help me with an active warmth to move, and with a vigorous soul to rise!

Visited an old man who was sick, with whom I had some conversation, though not much; but came away without prayer; and was justly blamed both by my friends and myself. I would have prayed with him; but two men came in, whose countenances I did not like, and therefore neglected my duty through the fear of man. I have nothing to plead to palliate my omission. It is true, that to introduce prayer among prayerless people is not an easy matter; yet this is no excuse for me. Lord, forgive both my secret and open faults; my failings of omission and commission: help me to have respect to all thy commandments; and to be blameless before thee in all things!

Lord's day, 12. Preached to-day at my friend Hersey's,[88] as also the evening before. The house was filled both before and after dinner. The Lord gave me great liberty and power; and I humbly believe that some trembled under the word; [at least one, who was lord of the manor]. O, that it may not wear off! I preached from these words: "The wicked shall be turned into hell, and all the nations that forget God." After describing the wicked, and showing wherein they forget God, I attempted to prove the torments to be real and eternal, from the real joys and duration of heaven.

Monday, 13. Visited E. Thompson,[89] and saw his father, who is a hundred years old, or more. He had lately lost his wife, who was younger than he; and in her he lost his nurse and earthly comfort. [The old man was in great trouble; but had some sense of divine things, and joined me in prayer.]

Tuesday, 14. Was advised and invited to preach at Wilmington (Delaware) which I did, though there were but few to hear.

Pennsylvania

Wednesday, 15. Rode to Chester, and preached in the court house. The church minister and many Quakers were present; but the congregation

---

[88] Solomon Hersey lived at the head of Bohemia River. In his house the second society within the present Peninsula Conference was organized. It is perpetuated in Bethesda Chapel at Cayott's Corner near Chesapeake City, Cecil County, Maryland. (*Ibid.*, 105, 113, 292. For an account of the Hersey families see Marine: *Sketch of Rev. John Hersey*, 5, 6.)

[89] Ephraim Thompson and his brother Robert lived near Pivot Bridge, Cecil County, Maryland. At nearby Thompson's School House, Richard Wright is believed to have organized the Bethel Society. (See Hallman, *op. cit.*, 121, 290.)

appeared to be the wildest I had seen in America. [I felt much, myself; and believe that many others felt also.] But I humbly hope the labour was not all in vain. In the morning I visited, and spoke with great freedom to four men who were under sentence of death.

Thursday, 16. I rode through a heavy rain to Philadelphia, and preached the next morning with some freedom.

Tuesday, 21. My mind is quiet and serene. I am now free from company, which is very pleasing to me, having found that much company is both disagreeable and dangerous.

Wednesday, 22. Met the society, and found both life and liberty among the people. This night Brother Williams[90] came in from Virginia. He gives a flaming account of the work there. Many of the people seem to be ripe for the Gospel, and ready to receive us. I humbly hope, before long, about seven preachers of us will spread seven or eight hundred miles, and preach in as many places as we are able to attend. Lord, make us humble, watchful, and useful to the end of our lives!

April 23. Brother Williams set off for New York.

April 24. I preached at Philadelphia with freedom and power.

April 25. Preached to the people with some sharpness. In the evening I kept the door, met the society, and read Mr. Wesley's epistle to them.

Tuesday, 28. I intended to go out of town; but could not get a horse. So I stayed for Brother Wright, and heard that many were offended at my shutting them out of society meeting, as they had been greatly indulged before. But this does not trouble me. While I stay, the rules[91] must be attended to; and I cannot suffer myself to be guided by half-hearted Methodists. An elderly Friend told me very gravely, that "the opinion of the people was much changed, within a few days, about Methodism: and that the Quakers and other dissenters had laxed *their* discipline; that none but the Roman Catholics kept it up with strictness." But these things do not move me.

[90] Robert Williams, who became a member of the Irish Conference in 1766, preceded Boardman and Pilmoor to America in the summer of 1769 with the understanding with Wesley that he was to be subject to the regular preachers. Of his dramatic departure from Ireland see Lee: *A Short History of the Methodists*, 26 ff. Williams is said to have preached the first Methodist sermon in Virginia at Norfolk in 1769. The cash book of St. George's Church shows a disbursement on September 2, 1769, to Robert Williams for expenses from Norfolk to Philadelphia. After his marriage in 1774 he located. He died in Virginia on September 26, 1775; and his funeral sermon was preached by Asbury. (See *Journal* entries for September 26, 27, 1776.)

[91] Reference is to the General Rules drawn up in 1739 by John and Charles Wesley for governing the United Societies. Asbury, a strict disciplinarian, expressed constant concern over the laxity with which his colaborers applied these rules. He insisted that class leaders after each class meeting should report to the ministers and stewards on each member's attendance, conduct, contributions, and observance of the ordinances. Because of a restrictive rule the General Rules have undergone little revision since Asbury's day. (See *Doctrines and Discipline of the Methodist Church*.)

New Jersey—Pennsylvania

Wednesday, 29. Set out for Burlington,[92] where I met with brother Webb and brother John King,[93] and found the people there very lively. Two persons have obtained justification under brother Webb, and a certain Dr. T——t, a man of dissipation, was touched under brother Boardman's preaching last night. I admire the kindness of my friends to such a poor worm as I. O my God! remember them! remember me!

Thursday, 30. I humbly hope the word was blest to a large number of people who attended while I preached at the court house.

Set out for Philadelphia; but about a mile from the city found that the bridge could not be crossed on horseback; so I left my horse and walked to the ferry. Brother Wright took the horse and went to Burlington, on his way to New York. Was desired to attend the execution of the prisoners at Chester, and John King went with me. We found them penitent; and two of the four obtained peace with God, and seemed very thankful. I preached with liberty to a great number of people under the jail wall. The sheriff was friendly and very kind. John King preached at the gallows to a vast multitude; after which I prayed with them. The executioner pretended to tie them all up, but only tied one, and let the rest fall. One of them was a young man about fifteen. We saw them all afterward, and exhorted them to be careful. We returned to Philadelphia the same night, and I gave an exhortation.

Tuesday, May 5. Set out for Burlington again, and preached to a serious

[92] This journey initiated Asbury's labors on that part of the Philadelphia Circuit east of the Delaware River which included all of New Jersey. He therefore crossed the state line from time to time. Captain Webb had formed the first class in New Jersey at Burlington on December 14, 1770, and placed Joseph Toy, one of his converts, in charge as leader. (150th Anniversary Program of Broad Street Church, Burlington, 2; Atkinson: *Memorials of Methodism in New Jersey*, 36.)

[93] John King, M.D. (1746–95), was born in Leicestershire and educated at Oxford and a London medical college. It was to King that Wesley on July 28, 1775, wrote the well-known letter advising him to "scream no more at the peril of your soul." Disinherited by his father when converted under Wesley, he came to America in 1769 and was authorized by Pilmoor to preach. He began in the Potter's Field, now Washington Square, in Philadelphia; and in 1770 he preached the first Methodist sermon in Baltimore on a block in the front of a blacksmith's shop at Front and Center streets. He was present at the first conference in 1773 and assigned to New Jersey. The following year he was appointed to Norfolk, Virginia, and doubtless extended his circuit into North Carolina, to which state he was appointed in 1777. Having married Miss Sallie Seawell of a prominent Brunswick County, Virginia, family, he located in North Carolina and served as a local preacher. He was present at the first conference of the newly formed Methodist Episcopal Church at the home of his neighbor, Green Hill, near Louisburg, North Carolina, in 1785. (*Historical Sketches of Franklin County, N.C.*, 278–83, by Edward Hill Davis, a great-great-grandson of King; Moore: *Sketches of the Pioneers of Methodism in North Carolina and Virginia*, 51–56; Barclay: *History of Methodist Missions*, I, 33–34; see note under June 23, 1780.)

people. But how is my soul troubled that I am not more devoted! O my God! my soul groans and longs for this.

May 6. My heart was much humbled; but the Lord enabled me to preach with power in my soul.

Thursday, 7. Visited some prisoners; and one of them, who is to be tried for his life, seemed much affected. In the evening I preached, and felt my heart much united to this people. Next morning set off for Philadelphia, and got in time enough for intercession; after which, I visited a sick friend, who rested her soul on God, and then I preached in the evening.

Sunday, 10. Preached in the morning; attended two places of worship in the day; preached again at night; and had a comfortable time in meeting the society.

Monday, 11. Was much stirred up, and found an increase of life in visiting the society; and then preached in the evening.

Tuesday, 12. Set off for the Jerseys.[94] My mind enjoys sweet peace and the love of God. It is my desire to be entirely devoted to God, who opens the hearts of people to receive me, and my heart to deliver his counsel to them.

Wednesday, 13. Preached at three o'clock[95] on, "Behold I stand at the door and knock." O, what a time of satisfaction and power was this to my own soul! Went afterward to Mr. Thomas Taper's,[96] and many friends came at eight o'clock, when I was enabled to preach with life.

Thursday, 14. Went to the new church.[97] Surely the power of God is amongst this people. After preaching with great assistance, I lodged at Isaac Jenkins's,[98] and in the morning he conducted me to Gloucester; and thence we went by water to Philadelphia. Here I found a change. Brother Pilmoor was come, and the house was given up; which pleased me well, as it was a burden to the people. Brother Pilmoor went to Mr. Wallace's,[99] and I went to Mr. Wilmer's.[100] On Friday night I was heavily afflicted; and

---

[94] A name that persisted long after the division into East Jersey and West Jersey in 1676 had terminated when New Jersey became a royal province.

[95] This preaching place was probably within what was to constitute the Greenwich Circuit. (Atkinson, *op. cit.*, 144.)

[96] Lednum, *op. cit.*, 79, 80.

[97] This new church was probably in Greenwich and seems to have been the first Methodist meetinghouse built in New Jersey. (Atkinson, *op. cit.*, 144–45.)

[98] Atkinson, *op. cit.*, 144; Lednum, *op. cit.*, 79.

[99] Probably Burton Wallace, a bricklayer and member of St. George's Church. (Lednum, *op. cit.*, 80.)

[100] Lambert Wilmer and his wife were among the first fourteen persons to unite with St. George's Church. Charles M. von Wrangel, provost of Philadelphia Swedish Lutheran churches by appointment of the King of Sweden, visited John Wesley and from England advised Wilmer and his friend, John Hood, two of the provost's converts, to join the Methodists when they organized. This they did when Pilmoor and Boardman arrived. Wilmer became a class leader, as did his wife, the latter being the

dear sister Wilmer took great care of me. The next morning, through the mercy of God, I was something better, and preached in the evening.

Lord's day, 17. After preaching in the morning, I went to see George Hungary,[101] who was near to eternity. He had peace in his soul. Some slight me in this place on account of my attention to discipline; and some drop off. But my work is to please God.

Tuesday, 19. Went about sixteen miles into the country, and preached at eleven o'clock, with energy of soul.[102] A Presbyterian minister, who attended my preaching this morning, accompanied me part of the way back. We conversed by the way, on the evidences of religion, the work of God, and sending out preachers. This morning I arose with more spiritual strength, and felt a great desire to do the will of God with all purity of intention, desire, and thought; that in all things God may be glorified through Jesus Christ.

Wednesday, 20. Went to Trenton,[103] but as the court was sitting, I was obliged to preach in a school house to but few people; and as there were soldiers in the town, I could hardly procure lodging.

Thursday, 21. Preached on the other side of the river to[104] a few simple people; and in the evening at Burlington, where the congregation was also small on account of the fair.[105]

Friday, 22. In the morning I rode home in great pain; but after dinner went ten miles down the river.

second woman to hold that position in Philadelphia. Mrs. Wilmer, born in New Jersey, died in 1796; and her husband, a Marylander, died in 1824 or 1825. (Sweet: *Men of Zeal*, 86–88; Tees: *Ancient Landmark of American Methodism*, 26, 27.)

[101] Lednum, *op. cit.*, 80.

[102] This preaching place was probably Supplee's Chapel, oldest in Pennsylvania except St. George's. It was a stone chapel, afterward called Bethel, and now known as Bethel Hill. Pilmoor and Webb both preached there. It was named for Abraham Supplee, a local preacher who on several occasions entertained Washington and his officers. It was used as a hospital after the battle of Germantown, and a number of the soldiers were buried there. (Boehm: *Reminiscences, Historical and Biographical*, 99.)

[103] Whitefield had preached in Trent-Town on November 21, 1739, but did not establish a society. Captain Webb preached there in 1766; and Joseph Toy, who had moved from Burlington, organized a class in 1771. (*History of Mercer County*, 727; *History of First Methodist Church, Trenton*, 175th Anniversary, 1947.)

[104] Asbury's preaching place "on the other side of the river" was probably the present Morrisville, Pennsylvania. It was a part of the property of Robert Morris and had a small population, but was not so named until after the Revolution. There were three ferries across the Delaware at Trenton. (*Bucks County Historical Society Proceedings*, III, 237; Watson: *Annals of Philadelphia*, II, 68.)

[105] Fairs after the English type were held annually by legislative enactment at both Burlington and Greenwich, attracting numerous visitors from Philadelphia and elsewhere. The Greenwich Fair was discontinued in 1765. (Cunningham: "Calvalcade of Counties—Cumberland" in Newark *Sunday News*, November 9, 1952; Kull: *New Jersey—A History*, I, 310–11.)

Sunday, 24. We rode down to Greenwich, where I preached at ten o'clock to near three hundred people, collected from different parts; we then rode back to friend Price's[106] where we dined; and thence to Gloucester, which made near fifteen miles. I preached there at three o'clock to about two hundred people, and then went up the river in a boat to Philadelphia, where I preached at seven o'clock.

Monday, 25. Was unwell, but went to Burlington, and preached in the evening, though very sick.

Tuesday, 26. Found myself very unwell in the morning; but visited a prisoner under sentence of death, and strove much to fasten conviction on his heart. Through the mercy of God, I hope the poor man was humbled.

Wednesday, 27. Went to New Mills, where I preached at four o'clock; and again at ten o'clock the next morning. [In our lodgings we had much young company who had but little sense of religion. Mrs. Hulings went with me in a chair. I had many people, Baptists and others, though but little comfort in my own soul.]

Friday, 29. I preached under the jail wall; and for the benefit of the prisoner, attended him to the place of execution.[107] When he came forth, he roared like a bull in a net. He looked on every side, and shrieked for help; but all in vain. O how awful! Die he must,—I fear, unprepared. I prayed with him, and for him. How difficult it is (if I may use the term) to drench a hardened sinner with religion! I saw him tied up; and then, stepping on a wagon, I spoke a word in season, and warned the people to flee from the wrath to come, and improve the day of their gracious visitation, no more grieving the Spirit of God, lest a day should come in which they may cry, and God may refuse to hear them. We then rode home to Philadelphia, where I exhorted in the evening, and found myself much more drawn out than I expected.

Lord's day, 31. Preached morning and evening with some life; but found that offences increased. However, I cannot help it. My way is to go straight forward, and aim at what is right.

June 1. Preached this morning at five o'clock; and this day I wrote to Mr. Wesley, and experienced a great degree of purity in my soul.

Tuesday, 2. Rose this morning between four and five, and was much quickened in preaching; then went to Haddonfield[108] about noon. Satan assaulted me this day, but the Lord helped and delivered me, for his mercy and truth's sake, and granted me life in my soul.

[106] Lednum, *op. cit.*, 80.

[107] Asbury had returned to Burlington for the execution of the prisoner whom he had visited on the previous Tuesday.

[108] Asbury does not mention preaching at Haddonfield, and church records there do not indicate Methodist beginnings so early. (See note under September 23, 1784.)

Wednesday, 3. Preaching at five at Manta (Mantua) creek,[109] I was favoured with an opening and great power. After preaching there, about one hundred people went to Mr. Taper's,[110] one and a half mile off, and there also I preached with life.

Thursday, 4. At Greenwich I was weak in body, but had some liberty in preaching to about two hundred willing people; but at Gloucester, I preached only to a few dead souls, from this striking passage: "The word preached did not profit them, not being mixed with faith in them that heard it." I must observe, that in this journey I have been kept in peace, and had more freedom, life, and power, than I ever experienced in the city, [or perhaps ever shall].

Saturday, 6. Sailing four miles up the (Delaware) river, I came to Philadelphia in great comfort.

Lord's day, *June* 7. After preaching in the morning, I was at the table with Mr. Stringer,[111] and many felt the power of God, though I felt but little myself. We had a love feast to-day, and several could testify that God was with us: some of our Jersey friends spoke of the power of God with freedom.

Monday, 8. With much disagreeable company I set off for Trenton, where many felt the divine power accompanying the word preached.

Wednesday, 10. After preaching on the other side of the river,[112] I returned to Philadelphia, and preached in the evening.

Thursday, 11. Set off in the stage for Bristol, and crossed the water to see a man suspected of murder; but found him very ignorant of things relating to his soul: I then returned to Philadelphia very unwell.

Friday, 12. I was a little better, and rose to preach at five o'clock. The Lord was with me this day at intercession.

Saturday, 13. Hitherto the Lord hath helped. Praised be his dear name!

Lord's day, *June* 14. After preaching in the morning with some freedom of mind, I went to St. Paul's,[113] and afterward spent the afternoon in my room; then preached, and met the society in the evening; but felt great

[109] Mantua Creek flows through Gloucester County to the Delaware River above Maiden Island. (Gordon: *Gazeteer and History of New Jersey*, 173, 174; Heston: *South Jersey*, 397.)

[110] Lednum, *op. cit.*, 79, 80.

[111] Probably the Rev. Mr. Stringer, rector of St. Paul's Church, whose unusual sympathy for Methodism has been attributed to a belief that he was formerly a Wesleyan preacher. He came from England on August 20, 1768, with a letter of introduction from Whitefield. He was rector until October, 1777, and returned to England soon thereafter. He died at Barnet on June 12, 1799. (Barratt: *Outline of the History of Old St. Paul's Church*. See also *Journal* entries for December 2, 11, 18, 29, 1774; March 24, 1776. Atkinson: *The Wesleyan Movement in America*, 146; *The Methodist Magazine*, London, 1818, 641; Lednum, *op. cit.*, 80. See *Journal* entry for June 24, 1772.)

[112] Morrisville, Pennsylvania. (See note under May 21, 1772.)

[113] This church was organized in 1760 under the leadership of the Rev. Mr. Clenaghan, and the edifice was erected in 1762.

dryness, and was grieved to see so much conformity to the world, in the article of dress, among our people.

Tuesday, 16. Set off for Burlington;[114] and though weak and infirm, I preached at night with liberty.

Wednesday, 17. I bent my course for Newmills; but still groan for more life, and want to be more holy.

Thursday, 18. After preaching twice at Newmills with great liberty and life, I returned to Burlington; but was very ill that night; and though quite unwell the next morning, yet proceeded on my way to Philadelphia.

Lord's day, *June* 21. Finding myself much recovered, I preached with some animation.

Monday, 22. This day my heart was in deep exercise.

Tuesday, 23. Walked down to Gloucester-point, and then rode to brother Chew's;[115] and though very weak, weary, wet, and low, while it rained very hard, I preached with some power to many people from these words: "As the rain cometh down, and the snow from heaven, and returneth not thither, but watereth the earth, and maketh it bring forth and bud, that it may give seed to the sower, and bread to the eater; so shall my word be that goeth forth out of my mouth; it shall not return unto me void, but it shall accomplish that which I please, and it shall prosper in the thing whereto I send it."

Wednesday, 24. At Greenwich, I met with Mr. Stringer, who preached and baptized several people that seemed deeply affected. We then rode together, and had some conversation on the insult which Mr. Shirley[116] had given Mr. Wesley. As Mr. Stringer knew that Mr. Shirley had preached for Mr. Wesley, and was well acquainted with his doctrine, he was surprised at his conduct. He said Mr. Wesley was undoubtedly a good man, and had been useful to thousands.

Thursday, 25. Travelling back towards Gloucester, I called at 'Squire Price's;[117] and presented him with a petition for raising £150 to discharge the debt on our preaching house at Philadelphia. He promised both to give himself, and to propose it to others.

Friday, 26. Returned to Philadelphia, and preached at eight with some power. [But still I am not entirely holy in thought, word and deed. Will not the Lord get the victory? He surely will, and I shall be holy.] I find that Satan strives to sow discord among us; and this makes me desirous to leave the city.

Saturday, 27. Felt a great desire to live more to the glory of God; and preached at night with some life. Received a letter from Mr. Pilmoor

---

[114] There was no church in Burlington, and services were held in the courthouse or homes. In 1788 Ezekiel Cooper refused to use the courthouse and preached in the home of George Smith. Cooper noted that there was a "considerable work" there. (Phoebus: *Light on Early Methodism*, 83.)

[115] Jesse Chew. (Lednum, *op. cit.*, 80, 81.)   [116] Lednum, *op. cit.*, 80.   [117] *Ibid*,

replete with accounts of his preaching abroad,[118] in the church, to a large congregation, and the like. My heart is still distressed for want of more religion. I long to be wholly given up, to seek no favour but what cometh from God alone. I want to breathe after the Lord in every breath.

Lord's day, 28. This was a day of sweet rest to my soul; and the Lord gave me power to speak with some affection.

Monday, 29. Set out for Trenton with some loose and trifling company in the stage. After preaching in the evening with some life and energy, I went the next day to preach in the field, and then returned and preached with freedom to many people in the court house.

July 1. Went over the ferry and preached to many people; among whom were some fine women,[119] who behaved with airs of great indifferency. Returning to Trenton, I preached at night, and the next morning at five, after which I set off for Philadelphia with unprofitable company; among whom I sat still as a man dumb, and as one in whose mouth there was no reproof. They appeared so stupidly ignorant, sceptical, deistical, and atheistical, that I thought if there were *no other* hell, I should strive with all my might to shun that. Came home late and weary; but preached with some comfort. I have lately been blessed with much purity of intention, and fervour of spirit; but greatly thirst after living more in God.

Saturday, 4. Went to Burlington, in order to attend the execution of one Smart,[120] a murderer; and declared to a great number of people under the jail wall, "He healeth the broken in heart." The poor criminal appeared penitent, behaved with great solidity, and expressed a desire to leave the world.

Then returned to Philadelphia, gave an exhortation that night, and found the Lord's day a day of sweet peace.

Monday, 6. Set out for Burlington again, and spent three days labouring among them. Many seemed much stirred up to seek the kingdom of God.

Thursday, 9. Returned, and found some inward liberty in Philadelphia.

Saturday, 11. Was a day of peace and love to my soul.

Lord's day, 12. Went through the usual exercises of the day, and enjoyed some peace of mind. Our congregations here are small. They cannot bear the discipline and doctrine; but this does not move me.

Monday morning I preached with life, and long to be as an even-rising flame of fire.

Tuesday, 14. Went to the Jerseys and preached at friend Turner's to near one hundred people, though in the time of harvest; and while preaching from these words, "Ye were sometime darkness, but now are ye light

[118] Pilmoor left Philadelphia May 27, 1772, and had been preaching in Pennsylvania. (See Pilmoor's manuscript *Journal* for this period; also Atkinson, *op. cit.*, 318–20, 325, 339.)

[119] This was in Morrisville, Pennsylvania, where Summerset was a fashionable resort. (See note under May 21, 1772.)

[120] Lednum, *op. cit.*, 81.

in the Lord," many felt the power of truth, when the darkness and its properties were explained. After describing true religion to about one hundred souls, at Jessie Chew's,[121] I went on *Wednesday* to Greenwich, and felt much shut up while preaching to about the same number, on, "Fear not, little flock, &c." I then proceeded to Gloucester, which is one of the dullest places I have seen in this country. The same night went to Haddonfield; and the next day preached at Joseph Thorne's[122] to a few attentive hearers, who seemed somewhat affected by the truths of God; especially one S. K., who was greatly concerned on account of his past life, as he had been much devoted to company and liquor. I felt afraid that his concern would not be permanent. However, he accompanied me to the ferry.

Friday, 17. Returned to Philadelphia time enough for intercession, and found it a good time both then and at the evening preaching.

Lord's day, 19. After preaching in the morning, I set off in the afternoon for Trenton, came thither on Monday by noon, and found life in preaching at night.

Monday, July 20. Met with brother Sause from New York, who informed me that I was to go to New York; which was what I did not expect; but feel myself quite easy, not being fixed in any place.[123] He gave me an account of Mr. Wright's[124] good behaviour; though I fear, after all, he will settle at Bohemia.[125]

Wednesday, July 22. In meeting the small society of about nineteen persons,[126] I gave them tickets, and found it a comfortable time. They are a serious people; and there is some prospect of much good being done in this place. After preaching on Tuesday morning over the ferry, and in the evening at Trenton, I took leave of them on Wednesday morning, and set off for Philadelphia. Left Philadelphia[127] on the Lord's day evening, after

---

[121] Asbury was doubtless preaching near Carpenter's, sometimes called Smith's Landing, on Mantua Creek. (Lednum, *op. cit.*, 81; Atkinson, *op. cit.*, 44; Gordon: *New Jersey Gazeteer*, 173, 174.)

[122] Lednum, *op. cit.*, 81.

[123] Richard Boardman, returning from New England (*John Street Records*, I, May 14, 1772), found that affairs at Wesley Chapel had worsened under Wright's leadership and determined to transfer Asbury to New York sooner than had been planned. Finding that Richard Sause was going toward Philadelphia, Boardman requested him to explain the situation to Asbury and instruct him to proceed to New York.

[124] Richard Wright had accompanied Asbury to America in 1771, but the two men did not always agree, and Asbury became critical of Wright. (See *Journal* entries for April 2–4, 1772; and final remark of May 29, 1774.)

[125] In April, Boardman had made appointments for the preachers; and Asbury had carried the information to Wright at Bohemia Manor, instructing him to go to New York. Wright had been "at his own discretion" and apparently pleased with Bohemia Manor. (See *Journal* entries for April 2, 8, 1772.)

[126] This is the first mention of an organized society in Trenton.

[127] Asbury closed his work of nearly three months on the Philadelphia Circuit according to "Brother Boardman's plan." (See *Journal* entry for April 2, 1772.)

preaching on these words, "If I come again, I will not spare;" and on Monday met with brother Boardman. Went thence to New Mills, where I preached on Tuesday night and Wednesday morning, and found the people there very affectionate; then returned to Burlington, and found many friends from Philadelphia. We had power among us at night, and the next morning at three I set off for Amboy, and on the way had some conversation with one of Jacob Boehm's[128] disciples. We came to the stage-house through much rain and bad roads, about seven o'clock: thence we went to Amboy, and took lodging at a tavern. Have been kept in peace through this journey, felt great courage in the work of God, and go towards York in faith. The congregation at Amboy was small, and they appeared to be such as cared but little for the Gospel; so that my hope of that place is but slender. On Saturday evening, I preached with some power, to a large congregation of rich and poor, from these words, "Even from the days of your fathers, ye have gone away from mine ordinances, and have not kept them: return unto me, and I will return unto you."

New York

Sunday, August 2, 1772. After preaching with great liberty on the Lord's day, to many people at Peter Van Pelt's and justice Wright's on Staten Island, I set off on Monday in a boat for New York,[129] and arriving about five o'clock, found Mr. Richard Wright,[130] who that night had preached his farewell sermon, and told the people that he did not expect to see them any more. I have always dealt honestly with him, but he has been spoiled by gifts.[131] He has been pretty strict in the society, but ended all with a general love feast; which I think is undoing all he has done.[132] However, none of these things move me. My mind is calm, and my soul under a comfortable sense of God; and I am determined, by his grace, to keep on in the way of my duty, if it should be my lot to stand alone.

August 4. My soul felt life, and power, and renewed courage. Dis-

[128] Jacob Boehm was the grandfather of Henry Boehm. He was born in 1693 and came to this country in 1715. He was connected with the Mennonites.

[129] Asbury took the sailboat ferry from Stapleton on the northern end of Staten Island to Whitehall on lower Manhattan. (See note under November 12, 1771.)

[130] Wright had been in charge of Wesley Chapel since early in May. (*John Street Church Records*, I, 17. See *Journal* entries for April 2, 8, 1772.) Barclay's identification of "Mr. W." as Robert Williams is erroneous. (See Barclay: *Early American Methodism*, I, 30 ff.)

[131] Asbury discouraged the acceptance of personal gifts on the part of preachers and declined to accept them. Note his remark in the entry for August 4.

[132] Asbury was a strict interpreter of Wesley's rules. He maintained that society meetings and love feasts should be limited to the membership and not opened to the general congregation. (See III in *Journal* entry for September 5, 1772; also entries for October 3, 10, 1772, indicating Wesley's approval.)

covering the unfaithfulness of some who first spoil a man, and then condemn him, I intend to keep such at a proper distance. In the love feast this evening, I found that the living could not bear the dead.[133] Mr. Wright rose up and spake as well as he could, against speaking with severe reflections on his brother. But all this was mere talk. I know the man and his conversation.[134]

Wednesday, 5. Felt satisfaction and life in meeting the society last night, and spent this day in retirement.

Thursday, 6. Preached in New York, from Phil. i, 24, 25: "To abide in the flesh is more needful for you. And having this confidence, I know that I shall abide and continue with you all, for your furtherance and joy of faith." Found liberty in my mind while addressing the people, and am determined, in the strength of the Lord, to aim at promoting his glory, and to seek nothing but him.

Friday, 7. After preaching in the morning, I found the Lord near, and had great peace at intercession.[135] It pleases me much to see the people diligent in attending the word; and find myself favoured with liberty and the power of God in my labours among them; and humbly hope, that God will make known his power among this people, and drive Satan from them; and that we shall yet see good days in this place.

Saturday, 8. I found a degree of life in my soul; and on the Lord's day had power, and light, and life, and love, in speaking on these words: "Ye were sometime darkness, but now are ye light in the Lord: walk as children of light." The congregations are steady, and we look for the power of God both in our own souls and among the people. O, my God, make bare thine arm! After preaching in the evening of the Lord's day, with some opening of heart, and to a full house, I met the society; and then set out, on Monday morning, for New Rochelle,[136] and preached the same night at friend Deveau's,[137] about thirty miles from York.

Tuesday–Saturday, August 11–15. My soul does not forget God; but my desire is still towards him, and the remembrance of his name. On Wednesday I found my mind somewhat engaged; but on Thursday had some fears of coming short of eternal life. A cloud rested on my mind, which was occasioned by talking and jesting; I also feel at times tempted

---

[133] Asbury evidently means that one party in the society was spiritually "dead" and the other "living."

[134] Wright left New York immediately, going to Maryland to work with Robert Strawbridge and John King. Pilmoor was in Virginia, and Boardman remained in Philadelphia. (Lednum, *op. cit.*, 81.)

[135] Intercession was a service of prayer and praise widely observed in England. It was usually held on Friday. Pilmoor held the first such service at Philadelphia on November 23, 1771. This service later developed into the prayer meeting.

[136] New Rochelle was the focal-point of the circuit in Westchester County that had been organized in the preceding winter. (See notes, November, 1771, to February, 1772.)

[137] See note under December 10, 1771.

to impatience and pride of heart; but the Lord graciously blest me with life and power in preaching at night; and I afterward found my mind fixed on God, and an earnest longing to be always holy in heart and life. After preaching on Friday at New Rochelle,[138] from these words, "We ought to give the more earnest heed to the things which we have heard, lest at any time we should let them slip," I set out for New York on a bad horse, and met with indifferent fare, on the road;[139] but reached New York on Saturday, and there received a letter from my father and friend, Mr. Mather, who informed me of the preachers' returning to England. Preached also this evening with some satisfaction, but found broken classes, and a disordered society, so that my heart was sunk within me; but it is still my desire to commit myself to God.

Lord's day, August 16. Preached in the morning, and then went to preach at Newtown,[140] about twelve miles distant, in the evening. Friend Sause was in company with me, and we were obliged to lodge at a tavern; but we were more serious than usual, and spent our time in useful conversation. As it rained, we had but few people at preaching in the morning;[141] we then returned to New York about ten o'clock. In this journey I have found my soul comfortable and alive to God, a sacred nearness to God, and power to withstand temptations; though, in the afternoon of the next day, I had cause to blame myself for trifling conversation at noon.

Monday, August 17. This has been a day of distress to my soul. I was opposed for meeting the society, because one or two classes met at that time; which seemed to me a very weak objection, as those classes might meet at another time.

August, 21. Preached this morning with great life in my soul, and felt a strong desire to be devoted to God, and more and more engaged to promote his glory both in heart and life. O that my soul could be more intimately and sweetly united to the Lord! In the evening I preached with power; but have found my soul troubled within me, on account of a party-spirit which seems to prevail too much in this place. But they must answer for their own conduct. My business is, through the grace of God, to go straight forward, acting with honesty, prudence, and caution, and then leave the event to Him.

Lord's day, August 23. Preached morning and evening, and had peace

---

[138] Preaching at New Rochelle was doubtless in the home of Frederick Deveau (see note under December 10, 1771) or Peter Bonnette (see note under January 20, 1772).

[139] Asbury probably spent the night at one of the inns at or near Kingsbridge midway between New Rochelle and New York.

[140] On March 5, accompanied by Richard Sause, Asbury had attempted to go to Newtown on Long Island but was prevented by a heavy snowstorm. (See *Journal* entry for that date.)

[141] Asbury probably preached in the tavern where they lodged at Newtown.

in my own soul. In the evening I met the society, and read Mr. Wesley's letter.[142]

Monday, 24. Early in the morning we crossed the North river, in order to go to Staten Island.[143] Many people attended the word; but I know not what to make of them; for though they seem fond of hearing, yet they do not appear to be much affected. On Tuesday I went to Amboy (New Jersey), and dined with a mixed company of Assemblymen, Churchmen, Quakers, &c.[144] Many of them came to hear me in sport, but went away very still. On my return I preached at Mr. Ward's,[145] to many people; on Thursday returned to New York, and preached in the evening with some life. Friday my soul was kept in peace and love; and while preaching at night, both myself and others felt the power of God in our souls.

Saturday, 29. I preached with liberty, and can rejoice in God my salvation, finding an increasing desire to live to him alone. *Lord's day*, 30. Found life both morning and evening, and had many people; I also went to church, and heard Dr. Ogilvie[146] preach on the divinity of Christ.

Tuesday, September 1, 1772. My heart was fixed to seek the Lord; and found some nearness to him, and life in my soul: I preached also in the evening with some comfort.

Wednesday, 2. Preached at five, and found my soul this day fixed to do the will of God.

Thursday, 3. Preached in the morning, and found this a blessed day. My soul was lively, and my heart was filled with holy thoughts of God, and felt a strong and pure desire to pray, and mourn, and long for God. In the evening I preached from these words: "Whosoever shall confess me before men, him will I confess before my Father who is in heaven."

---

[142] On October 10, 1772, Asbury wrote that he received a letter from Wesley in which the founder required strict attention to discipline. The letter is otherwise unknown. An entry in *John Street Records*, I, 17, notes that immediately prior to this date ten shillings had been paid for postage on letters; and the letter that Asbury read may have been included in the packet.

[143] This was a roundabout way of reaching Staten Island. It involved crossing the North (Hudson) River to Paulus Hook, the present Jersey City, going overland through New Jersey, and crossing to Staten Island by another ferry, perhaps the "Blazing Star," over the Kills.

[144] Asbury probably preached in the tavern at Perth Amboy, New Jersey, where there was a long room for dining and assemblage. The New Jersey Assembly met in the town, which was headquarters of the still existent Corporation of East Jersey Proprieters.

[145] Lednum, *op. cit.*, 76.

[146] Asbury preached at 5 A.M. in Wesley Chapel and then went to Trinity Church at Broadway and Wall streets or St. Paul's Chapel at Broadway and Fulton streets, both of which were nearby. The Rev. John Ogilvie, D.D. (1723–74), was first assistant to Dr. Samuel Auchmuty, rector of Trinity. Ogilvie's sister-in-law was the wife of William Lupton, original trustee and first treasurer of Wesley Chapel; and he had given £1 12s. 6d. to the building fund of the chapel. He died after a stroke of apoplexy in the pulpit, and Asbury noted that fact in his *Journal* entry on November 24, 1774. (Seaman, *op. cit.* 428: *John Street Records*, I.)

Friday, 4. Found my soul grieved at the discovery of such parties among the people. Who can find a faithful man?

Saturday, 5. Found peace in my soul, and held a meeting for the better ordering of the spiritual and temporal affairs of the society. In this meeting I propounded the following queries:

I. How often shall there be public preaching? Agreed, that it should be on Tuesday, Thursday, and Friday nights, besides the Lord's day; and exhortation on Saturday night.

II. Shall we have morning preaching? This was agreed to.

III. Shall we have the Society meetings private? This was doubted by some; but I insisted on it, from our rules and Mr. Wesley's last letter.

IV. Shall we make a weekly and quarterly collection? Agreed.[147]

V. Can any other means be devised to lessen the debt? The debt was £1,100; but no other means could be found to relieve it.[148]

VI. Ought we not to be more strict with disorderly persons? Very little was said in answer to this.[149]

VII. Shall we have three stewards, for the satisfaction of the society? The majority voted against it.[150]

VIII. Are we as frugal as we can be? It was thought we were.

IX. Will the stewards meet me once a week? Agreed.

X. Do we endeavour to avoid all partiality in the things of God?

XI. Can we come at the balance of our accounts now or soon? It was thought we could.

XII. Who will stand at the door? Not determined.[151]

XIII. Shall we meet the society on Sunday nights? This was opposed by some. But I insisted upon its being the best time; and at last it was agreed to for a season.

[147] As a result of this action and Asbury's later appointment of a collector (see *Journal* entry for September 11, 1772), the financial situation in the society greatly improved. From April 1 to August 31 the income had been 73 pounds; between September 1 and January 31 it was 87 pounds; in the next five months it was 116 pounds. (*John Street Records*, I.)

[148] The society owed two hundred pounds to Captain Thomas Webb; three hundred pounds to William Lupton, trustee and steward; and six hundred pounds to Leonard Lispenard, a merchant and non-member who owned adjacent property and whose wife had contributed to the building fund. The Webb and Lupton items were for the purchase of the John Street lots in 1768, and the money had been borrowed from Lispenard for furnishings. These notes were reduced by a hundred pounds each on August 12, 1773; but otherwise the principal was not reduced though interest was paid. (*John Street Records*, I.)

[149] See *Journal* entry for October 6, 1772, for reference to one of the stewards whose conduct was not exemplary.

[150] The stewards were William Lupton and Henry Newton, and the treasurer was James Jarvis.

[151] The function of the guard was to enforce the rule barring unqualified persons from the society meeting.

XIV. Who shall be the collectors? This was not determined, though debated.[152]

XV. Can the preacher meet the children? Agreed.[153]

XVI. Can we spread the books? There was but little said on this head, and it was left undetermined.[154]

Monday, September 7. Richard Sause, Charles White and myself set off for New Rochelle. At night I felt myself unwell, and my mind under a cloud, but gave an exhortation at Mr. Deveau's in the evening.

Tuesday, 8. This was a day of heaviness, much trouble, sore temptation, and sorrow of heart; but in the evening I was happy in God, and spoke with power and feeling. On Wednesday my mind was warmly engaged, and I preached to many people, both at three o'clock and seven.

Thursday, 10. Mr. Deveau accompanied me as far as Kingsbridge,[155] on my way to New York, where Samuel Selby[156] met me, and rode with me the rest of the way.

I preached in the evening, and rose to preach next morning at five. It appears to me that trouble is at hand; but I fear nothing, being conscious of having acted uprightly before them all, and having no by-ends in view. Whoever has, must answer for it. Whatever comes, I am determined, while here, by the grace of God, to proceed according to the Methodist doctrine and discipline.

Friday, 11. I met the people in the morning to discourse with them about their temporal matters, and appointed Mr. Chave[157] to take an account of the weekly and quarterly collections. But the other two stewards[158] refused an exact entry of the money that is not settled. However, the people *must* have the same satisfaction concerning the other collections. *Saturday* morning I felt a strong desire to live to God, and act with a single eye to his glory in all that I do. On Saturday evening we had a comfortable meeting. After preaching to many people on the Lord's day

[152] A week later Asbury on his own initiative appointed John Chave as collector. (See *Journal* entry for September 11, 1772.)

[153] This is the first reference to the religious instruction of children in American Methodism. (See *Journal* entries for October 15, 18, 1772.)

[154] Several entries in the *John Street Records* record cash received from the sale of books.

[155] Kingsbridge was the community at the bridge connecting the northern tip of Manhattan Island with the mainland.

[156] See note under February 21, 1772.

[157] John Chave (1730?–1816) had come to America as an officer in the French and Indian War. He was associated with Captain Webb and William Lupton and had been a member of the group that met in the Rigging Loft. After the Revolution he lived in Greenwich Village, then a suburb of New York, and later moved to Walton, Delaware County, New York, where descendants of Lupton lived. He served as collector for over two years. (*John Street Records*, I; Wakeley, *op. cit.*, 509; Seaman, *op. cit.*, 444, 445.)

[158] The "other two stewards" were William Lupton and Henry Newton. (See note under October 9, 1772.)

at seven, I prepared to approach the table.[159] There was a great drawing among the people while these words were enforced: "This do in remembrance of me." Lord, prepare my heart. My bleeding Lord! let my soul feel thy melting love. Lord, make all thy people glad together in thee, that thou mayest be glorified in and by us both now and ever. At the table I was greatly affected with the sight of the poor Negroes, seeing their sable faces at the table of the Lord. In the evening I had a full house and much Divine assistance.

Monday, 14. I had liberty and love in preaching at five, and this day felt power to live to God.

Tuesday, 15. I spent great part of my time in company, and preached with some life to a small company at Bloomingdale.[160] Preaching at five the next morning, I had many people, and a comfortable sense of God; [and possess a humble hope that I shall live this day to God].

Wednesday, 16. I set off for Newtown, and found nearness to God, and more constancy of mind. Our journey was wet and troublesome;[161] however, there was a small company of people, and I preached with courage, disregarding my fatigue,[162] if any good can be done. We returned to New York in the night, which was very dark: but He to whom the darkness is known, conducted us in safety. Friday morning I found great peace; [but Satan was hard at my heels]. Lord, help me to be always guarded, and fly the very appearance of evil; so that in thy strength I may every moment conquer.

Saturday, 19. I felt comfortable in preaching this morning at five o'clock. O, my God! help me this day to eye thy glory! We had a melting power this evening also in public exhortation.

Lord's day, 20. In the morning we had a good time while I spoke from the latter part of the eighty-first psalm; and in the evening we had a very full house, and the Lord favoured me with warmth and power while I addressed the people from Rom. vi, 17, 18. After preaching on Monday morning, I went to Staten Island.[163] Justice Wright met me and informed

[159] The preachers and people of Wesley Chapel received the Sacrament at St. Paul's Chapel, Fulton Street and Broadway. (See *Journal* entry for June 13, 1773, when Asbury, Rankin, Wright, and Captain Webb received the Sacrament together there.)

[160] Asbury had preached at Bloomingdale on March 9, 1772. It was a community near the Post road about four miles north of Wesley Chapel.

[161] Practically every attempt to visit Newtown, as reported by both Pilmoor and Asbury, held some travel difficulties—heat, blizzard, obscure roads, rain, unwillingness of liveries to provide horses to the preachers.

[162] No one in Newtown is indicated as opening his house for the preaching in these early visits. Probably the tavern keeper offered his facilities. (See *Journal* entry for August 16, 1772.)

[163] Asbury went by the ferry from Whitehall, in New York, down the bay to Stapleton on Staten Island.

me that the people were very busy at that time in court;[164] so I went and preached to many attentive people at Bird's ferry. Hitherto the Lord hath helped me. I will endeavour to praise him with my whole heart, and glorify him more and more. Tuesday I crossed the bay, and preached in the evening at New York.

Wednesday, 23. In the morning I preached, and felt a measure of peace, and stronger confidence in my soul towards God.

I am now twenty-seven years of age, and have had a religious concern on my heart about fourteen years; though I felt something of God as early as the age of seven.

Thursday, 24. I preached in the morning from Psalm lxxxvi, 17; and found myself enlarged in the evening on the subject of the good Samaritan. This day my soul has felt much love towards God, and my mind has been bent on doing his will.

Friday, 25. Attending the lecture to-day, I heard the doctor[165] with much satisfaction, and in the evening preaching I laid open the plague of the human heart as I had felt it. It was a solemn time. This day we received tidings from Philadelphia of their doing well both in spiritual and temporal matters.[166] Some have been much dissatisfied with private society meetings, and collections in the classes. But, in the midst of every trial, the Lord keeps me in peace. On Saturday morning, though it was cold, we had many people, and a moving time at five o'clock; and a comfortable season in the evening exhortation.

Lord's day, 27. Preaching this morning on "building the tower," I had some assistance; but experienced some heavy exercises of mind this day. In the evening I was enabled to preach with power, on the awful subject of the judgment: attempting

I. To prove that the judgment will be universal.

II. To describe the person of the Judge.

III. To describe the awful events preceding and attending that period.

IV. To point out the business of the day.

V. To show the decision and consequences.

Monday, 28. Many people attended the preaching at five o'clock, and brother Sause and myself set off in the forenoon for New Rochelle. As we came unexpectedly on the people, I improved the occasion by preaching on these words: "In such an hour as ye think not, the Son of man cometh."

Tuesday, 29. At friend Deveau's I preached with fervency from Ezek.

[164] Justice Hezekiah Wright, close friend and frequent host to Asbury. Evidently Asbury was not aware of the court schedule, else he would have chosen a different time for the visit.

[165] The "doctor" was the Rev. Samuel Auchmuty, D.D., rector of Trinity Church, or his first assistant, the Rev. John Ogilvie, D.D. Both had contributed to the Wesley Chapel building fund and were friendly. (*John Street Records*, I.)

[166] Boardman was in Philadelphia, and the communication was doubtless from him.

xxxiii, 4. I have been much assaulted this day with temptations, but have been kept by the power of God. I find a degree of effeminancy cleaving to me, but abhor it from my very heart. The reading of Mr. Wesley's journal has been made a blessing to me, [and I hope for victory over all my foes].

Wednesday, 30. I was led to speak very closely at Peter Bonnette's, to a congregation in which were many old people; and then returned to Mr. Deveau's, where I preached again, and enforced the duty of meeting together among themselves.

October 1. I set off for New York; and preached to a small company at Kingsbridge[167] on my way. This day I received a letter from my mother, informing me she was weak in body, and had an earnest desire to see me once more before she dies.

October 3. Though I preached with liberty last night, yet my mind was troubled to-day: but I earnestly desire to renew my covenant with God. Mr. Wright received a letter from Mr. Wesley, enforcing our rules and discipline. My desire is to sit loose to every created object, [and through grace to be holy as my Lord is holy].

Lord's day, 4. I felt divine assistance in preaching both morning and evening; but was grieved at society meeting, to see the steward desirous to let strangers in.[168]

On *Monday*, I wrote to Mr. Wesley,[169] and communicated the true sentiments of my mind.

Tuesday, 6. This was a day of peace and rest to my soul. After preaching at night with some power, I spoke to our steward,[170] whose conduct did not altogether please me—frequently avoiding to speak to me—absenting himself from the meeting of the leaders—the appearance of dissimulation—opposing our rules—and consulting persons who were not members of our society. He appeared to be somewhat affected by the conversation.

Thursday, 8. In preaching both morning and evening, I had an opening of soul towards the people, [and found my mind in peace. My greatest concern is to be altogether holy in heart]. I met the society this evening, and told them plainly my mind relative to their state as a collective body.

Friday, 9. I met the leaders, and there were some sharp debates. After

[167] Asbury reversed his usual route. Kingsbridge was on the mainland opposite the northern tip of Manhattan Island near the famous bridge. Though Asbury had passed the community on each previous trip to and from Westchester, this is the first mention of preaching there.

[168] The steward who permitted the non-members to enter the society meeting was Henry Newton. (See note under October 9, 1772.)

[169] This letter to Wesley informing him of Asbury's sentiments regarding affairs in the New York society was written just before Asbury received Wesley's letter naming him as assistant in succession to Boardman and "requiring strict attention to discipline." (See *Journal* entry for October 10, 1772.)

[170] This steward was Henry Newton.

much had been said, I was charged with using Mr. Newton[171] ill, in saying he opposed my meeting the society. Mr. Lupton[172] told me I had already preached the people away;[173] and intimated that the whole work would be destroyed by me. Perhaps this was because I spoke so freely to Mr. Newton, and desired him to take care what company he kept.

Saturday, 10. I received a letter from Mr. Wesley, in which he required a strict attention to discipline; and appointed me to act as assistant.[174] He also enjoined that Mr. Williams might not print any more books without his consent.[175] I likewise received a letter from Mr. Williams,[176] informing me of the state of matters in Maryland; and that it was appointed for me to winter there.[177] For this I intend to prepare.

Lord's day, 11. Preached with power in the morning, and spoke freely to a large congregation in the evening. My soul is blest with peace and love to God.

Monday, 12. Read one of Mr. Wesley's sermons to the people, and believe some felt it reproving them for evil speaking. My mind is serene

[171] Henry Newton, a merchant, was an original trustee of the John Street property and one of the largest contributors to the building fund. He was steward, cotreasurer, and treasurer for many years. He later moved to the Second Mile Stone vicinity and was a prime mover in building the Methodist church on Forsyth Street, ordered by the conference in 1789. (See *Journal* entries for June of that year.) He was treasurer of the corporation that controlled both properties and one of New York's leading laymen well into the 1790's. He was buried at the Forsyth Street Church. His early difficulties with Asbury disappeared, and the two became warm friends. (*John Street Church Records*, I, numerous entries; Wakeley, *op. cit.*, 80–83; Seaman, *op. cit.*, 61, 429–30.) Forsyth Street Church on Forsyth (Second) Street near Division Street was dedicated November 8, 1789. Asbury frequently referred to it as the Bowery Church.

[172] William Lupton (1728–96), a merchant, came from England in 1753 as quartermaster in Thomas Webb's regiment and served with Webb in the French and Indian War. He joined the New York society under Webb in the Rigging Loft in 1767, and with Webb advanced funds for the John Street property in March, 1768. He later advanced other funds and was one of the original trustees and donor to the building fund and the first treasurer. He died on April 3, 1796, and was buried in his vault under Wesley Chapel. He and Asbury later became reconciled and were good friends. (*Journal* entries for July 10, 1774, and August 24, 1784; *John Street Church Records* (which Lupton started) I, numerous references; Wakeley, *op. cit.*, 75–79, 329–33, 533–38; Seaman, *op. cit.*, 61, 64, 69, 422–24.)

[173] Asbury's *Journal* references and the *John Street Church Records* for the period show that the congregations did not decrease and the society flourished.

[174] Asbury thus succeeded Boardman in authority and continued in the post until the arrival of Rankin on June 3, 1773. This letter greatly strengthened Asbury in his controversy with Newton, Lupton, Chave, and others in the New York society.

[175] Robert Williams had printed and sold Wesley's books until forbidden to do so by the conference in July, 1773. It does not appear that he was actuated by motives of personal gain, however. (*See Journal* entries for March 23 and July 14, 1773; *Minutes* of conference, 1773.)

[176] This was probably Robert Williams writing on behalf of Boardman with whom he had been in close contact.

[177] Asbury's appointment to Maryland had of course been made by Boardman before Asbury's appointment as assistant was received.

and comfortable. Part of Monday was spent in meeting classes; and on Tuesday morning, at five, I had many people. My intention is to deal faithfully with all; and it is my real opinion, that I am not so sensible of faults in any other person as in myself. Lord, help me to be faithful, and in all I do to glorify thee more than ever! Felt assistance this evening in preaching.

Wednesday, I went to Newtown, but was not expected. However, we collected many people to hear the word. I then returned to York, and, after preaching in the morning, was engaged in settling the classes, making up some bands, and meeting the children. I have reason to be thankful; though my trials have been great from many quarters, they have not moved me.

Friday, 16. Preached in the morning, and felt resigned to anything, having no choice; but am willing to go to the end of the world, if I can be holy and useful.

Lord's day, 18. Preached in the morning with some sensibility, and then went to hear Mr. Inglis,[178] who delivered a profitable discourse on the education of children. He proved the necessity, antiquity, and human authority of catechising; and made it evident, that, in the primitive Church, the best and ablest men were appointed for this work. He gave some account of the school in Alexandria; and told the audience, that in this duty there should be both precept and example, and sometimes severity. In the evening I was enabled to speak plainly to a large congregation, on Deut. xxx, 19: "I call heaven and earth to record against you this day, that I have set before you life and death, blessing and cursing: therefore choose life, that both thou and thy seed may live." This day we had a love feast. Many people spoke freely, but not long. This I have observed more here than in England, that the people speak short, and yet very full.

New Jersey—Pennsylvania

Monday, 19. Set off in the stage for Philadelphia.[179] The company was all pretty quiet, except one young man, who frequently profaned the name of the Lord. It was my intention to reprove him; but waiting for a proper time, I found an opportunity when there was only one person with him, and then told him how he had grieved me. He received the admonition very well; and excused himself by saying, he did not think of what he was doing. Afterward he seemed more careful. After dining at New Brunswick,[180] we came to Princeton, a place I had long wished to see for the sake

[178] The Rev. Charles Inglis, or English, was assistant to Dr. Samuel Auchmuty, rector of Trinity Church.

[179] Asbury ferried to Perth Amboy below the southern tip of Staten Island and proceeded by way of Brunswick and Princeton to Philadelphia.

[180] New Brunswick was on "the most ancient highway in New Jersey," an Indian trail centuries old leading from the site of the present Elizabeth. (Mellick: *Lesser Crossroads*, 76.)

of the pious Mr. Davies,[181] late president of the college there. Here I met Mr. Boardman, and we both agreed in judgment about the affairs of the society; and were comforted together. The next day I came to Trenton:[182] but a drunken sailor had locked up the court house, so I was obliged to preach in a school house, where we had a comfortable meeting; and also at five the next morning.

Thursday, October 22. In the morning I preached over the river,[183] and in the evening at Trenton, with some assistance. And many young people attended.

[*Friday*, 23. In the morning at five, preached over the ferry, and in the evening at Trenton. Glory to God! I have found peace, and power, and love.]

Saturday, 24. Leaving my horse at Bristol (Pennsylvania), I went to Burlington; and on the Lord's day my spirit was much dejected, though in preaching I felt greatly assisted, and Divine truth reached the hearts of the people.

Monday, 26. After preaching at five, I left them, and preached in the evening at Philadelphia. All things considered, the people here seemed to be quiet and in good order.

On *Tuesday*, preached both morning and evening. Richard Sause and myself set out on Wednesday for Bohemia Manor, and on our way we found a few friends at Newcastle (Delaware) that had not deserted the cause. In this journey I called at Chester jail, and saw the prisoners, who all seemed hardened to a man, and among them were the wretched three that I saw escape the gallows before;[184] two of these had behaved so badly they were now in chains. Lord, what is man! And what am I without thy grace! Keep me, keep me, holy Lord, and never let me go! Let me die rather than live to sin against thee! I spoke freely to one of them, who was a murderer.

Maryland

Thursday, 29. We reached Bohemia Manor where we found Solomon Hersey, a man hearty in the cause, and of a good understanding; but his spirit is too warm and easily moved.

On *Friday*, I visited Ephraim and Robert Thompson and saw their father in his hundredth year, eating, drinking, smoking, and talking. He

[181] Samuel Davies had been president of the Log College, later Princeton University. He went to Hanover County, Virginia, in 1747, on a preaching tour and moved there in 1748, remaining ten years. He was a friend and correspondent of John Wesley, and in 1754 he and Gilbert Tennent visited England and raised funds for the Log College. (Kull: *New Jersey—A History*, I, 348, 387; Sweet: *Virginia Methodism*, 21–25, 27–29, 31–36.)

[182] There was no meetinghouse in Trenton at this time.

[183] "Over the river" was evidently Morrisville, Pennsylvania.

[184] See *Journal* entry for May 30, 1772.

appeared as forgetful of eternity as if he had been at the most secure
distance from its brink. [It is well if his long life do not prove a curse in
the end.] I think he told me that his father lived to be a hundred and
nine, and never used spectacles.

Saturday, 31. Rose early this morning, and purpose, through grace, to
devote this day to God. I have traveled, since Monday week, one hundred
and fifty miles;[185] [and it has cost me about three pounds, which must
come out of my salary of twenty-four pounds per annum, as there is no
allowance for my expenses either by the society of Philadelphia or New
York].

Lord's day, November 1. After preaching at Hersey's in the morning, I
intended to preach in the school house in the afternoon; but it would not
contain half the people; so I stood at the door, and the people without.
Went to bed very unwell this evening; but rose at five, and feeling better,
set off for Susquehanna.[186] The next morning my soul longed for God. I
felt a comfortable sense of his love in my heart, and can rejoice in him as
my all-sufficient portion. In the afternoon we rode in company to the
bay side.[187] A few people, who came straggling after the time at friend
Nathaniel Giles's, felt themselves affected by the power of God. [Richard
Webster made one of the company; a man, who, I found by conversation,
was a mystic, and very fond of Mr. Law's works; but he spoke well of the
person of Christ.] At friend Giles's the family was called together in the
evening, and Richard Webster gave a moving exhortation. One person
seemed affected. The next morning I rose at five, my usual time, and
spent one hour in solemn, secret prayer. Friend Giles treated me with great
kindness, and pressed me to call again. I then went to Rocky Run,[188] and

[185] The 150 miles were over the main stage line from New York City to Philadelphia.
Leaving the latter place, Asbury and Sause probably crossed the Schuylkill River on a
raftlike ferry, at Gray's Ferry, the site of the present Gray's Ferry bridge, and proceeded through Darby, revisiting the points of his first trip to Bohemia Manor begun
the previous April.

[186] Asbury's course from Bohemia Manor was up the Elk River to Elkton (Head of
Elk), where at Hollingsworth's Tavern he took the main Western Shore Road which
led through Principio Furnace and Lower Susquehanna Ferry, the present Havre de
Grace.

[187] Crossing the Susquehanna River, Asbury entered into three centers of Methodist
influence created largely through the evangelistic labors of Robert Strawbridge. Richard
Webster, whom Asbury heard at the home of Nathaniel Giles, was among the earliest
Methodist local preachers of Harford County. After serving several circuits beginning
with 1774, he settled near Abingdon, Maryland, where for fifty years he was unsparing
in his service to Methodism. Among the monuments to his devotion is the Calvary
Chapel, erected in 1821.

[188] Rock, or Rocky, Run was named for George Rock, who built a mill on this
tributary of Deer Creek. Here previous to 1760 Nathaniel Giles, whose home was
Asbury's first Maryland preaching place, built a gristmill. Giles, who died in 1775,
owned the entire Susquehanna River water front between Heming Run and the mouth
of Deer Creek. (Mason: *Historical Sketches of Harford County, Md.*, 21, 22, 57.)

preached with freedom to a number of people, among whom were many Friends. For some days past my mind has been blest with much peace; so that I experience a present salvation, and hope to experience that which is eternal. Thanks be to God for what I feel! Glory, glory be given to my dear and gracious Saviour!

Wednesday, 4. This evening I had a very solemn family meeting; and spoke separately and pointedly to every one, both black and white.

On *Thursday morning*, rising at my usual time, I had a comfortable sense of God upon my heart. Glory be to thee, O Lord! After breakfast, Mrs. Giles, her brother, and myself set out for Deer Creek.[189] We called at a Friends' meeting, and heard two men and a woman speak. They all spoke to purpose. We then proceeded to Mr. Morgan's, and unexpectedly found the people, at two o'clock, waiting to hear the word. I preached with liberty, and the power of God was felt in the hearts of many, though some of them were principal men. The man of the house looked very earnestly at me while I was preaching. I then published preaching at Samuel Litten's where we had also a comfortable time. Samuel Litten himself was deeply affected. He had been a ranting Quaker, and a rebellious man; but God hath touched his heart, and wrought a good work on him and several others here. The next day we proceeded to Henry Watters',[190] whose brother is an exhorter, and now gone with Mr. Williams to Virginia. The Lord hath done great things for these people, notwithstanding the weakness of the instruments, and some little irregularities. Men who neither feared God, nor regarded man,—swearers, liars, cock-fighters, card-players, horse-racers, drunkards, &c., are now so changed as to become new men; and they are filled with the praises of God. This is the Lord's work, and it is marvellous in our eyes. Not unto us, O Lord, not unto us; but unto thy name be all the glory!

Saturday, 7. We had a powerful meeting at Henry Watters'; several

[189] Deer Creek, which empties into the Susquehanna River in northwest Harford County, was also a name which Asbury used for that community in which the families of Samuel Litten, Henry Watters, and other Methodists resided.

[190] One of the notable families in this region was that of Henry Watters, and Asbury seems to have made the Watters' home his headquarters in this community. At the time of Asbury's visit William Watters (1751–1827) was traveling through Virginia with Robert Williams on a preaching mission. Nicholas Watters (1739–1804), elder brother of William Watters, entered the traveling connection in 1776. William Watters was the first native American who became a regular itinerant Methodist preacher. He served in the itinerancy until 1783, when he purchased a farm near McLean, Virginia, and located. He again entered the active ranks in 1786, but became ill and was forced to discontinue traveling before the end of the year. His health improved, and he became active again in 1801. He finally located in 1805 and died in 1827. The graves of William Watters and his wife, Sarah Adams Watters, are in a neglected cemetery on El Nido Road, which leads off Old Dominion Drive about one mile east of McLean, Fairfax County, Virginia. In 1889 the Virginia Conference placed a monument and an iron enclosure on the spot. (Sweet: *Men of Zeal*, 133, 22 n.; Watters: *First American Itinerant of Methodism* and *The Watters Family*.)

from Mr. Morgan's followed me, and seemed to give good attention to the things of God. Here I met with Nicholas Watters, an exhorter, who appears to be a serious and sensible man. After appointing to meet the exhorters at my return, I went to Samuel Forwood's and preached to many people; then preached at a place about three miles on my way back, and came to Henry Watters' again, where we had a very comfortable time.

ROBERT STRAWBRIDGE

Lord's day, 8. We had a very melting time indeed, while I preached to about two hundred souls, from Rom. vi, 17, 18. We had also many people at Richard Webster's while I preached, with liberty in my soul, from 1 Cor. iv, 20: "The kingdom of God is not in word, but in power." This day I have been free from evil, happy, and joyful in my God. At the widow Bonds'[191] there were many people, both black and white, rich and poor,

[191] The Widow Bond was a member of a prominent Methodist family who lived one mile from Fallston, Maryland. Thomas Emerson Bond, a distinguished physician and local preacher (1782-1856), was long editor of *The Christian Advocate* (New York); and another son, John Wesley Bond (1784-1819), was present at the death of Asbury while serving as his last traveling companion.

who were all exhorted to seek the Lord while he may be found. Some of the young women of this family are serious and thoughtful.

Tuesday, 10. I enjoy peace and life in my soul; and am determined, through grace, to love and seek nothing but God. Preached to many people, both at Charles Baker's in the morning, and at James Moore's in the evening; and was favoured with much freedom.

Wednesday, 11. Many people attended preaching at Mr. Sinclair's, among whom were some Baptists, who went away displeased. The congregation was also large at friend Staniford's.[192] I have read Dr. Stonehouse on the non-eternity of hell torments.[193] But by his arguments, we may as well prove the non-eternity of heavenly joys; for he calls it an αἰώνιον, *aionion,* life. Now if the αἰώνιον, *aionion,* life of saints arises from a principle of spiritual life derived from Christ, then the ἰαώνιον, *iaonion,* death of the wicked arises from a principle of spiritual death in them; and the one will come to an end as soon as the other.

Thursday, 12. Preached at friend Galloway's. There are some Baptists in this neighbourhood, who oppose the work under us, and perplex and trouble our young beginners, though they let me alone. Then returning to friend Chamberlain's, the word flowed freely, while I preached to many people, at six o'clock, from 2 Cor. v, 20: "Now then we are ambassadors for Christ, as though God did beseech you by us: we pray you, in Christ's stead, be ye reconciled to God." Spoke on God's being reconciled to sinners, and showed on what terms they might be reconciled to God, and that none but Christ could bring about the reconciliation. My mind was greatly enlarged while describing the character of Gospel ministers. *Friday* morning my soul was happy in God. I rode about eight miles to meet John King. Many people attended the word at Mr. Gatch's; and after preaching John King came. We went together to town[194] and stayed all night. The next morning I returned to John Colgate's, where the congregation was large at twelve o'clock. This man's friends have rejected him on account of his religion. The family seem very serious; and I hope there will be a great and good work here. Then rode to Richard

---

[192] Asbury preached and was entertained in the home of Aquila Staniford. Henry Smith states in his *Recollections and Reflections of an Old Itinerant* that he found Staniford engaged as a local preacher in Kentucky (p. 57).

[193] The reference is probably to Sir James Stonehouse (1716–95), physician and divine, who in early life published a pamphlet against Christianity which had passed through two editions. A friendship with Philip Doddridge and James Hervey led to his conversion, and he took orders in 1749. At that time he burned the third edition of his pamphlet and later published numerous religious tracts. (*Dictionary of National Biography,* XVIII, 1304–5.)

[194] This was Asbury's first visit to Baltimore, where in 1770 his traveling companion John King had preached the first sermon. Among the members of the society organized in the home of Daniel Evans there were in addition to Philip Gatch, Sater Stephenson and Isaac Rollin.

Owings',[195] where some people came to see me, with whom we sung and prayed.

Tuesday, 17. This morning I found some peace and life in my soul; but want more retirement. My desire is, to be ever before the Lord. Many people attended the preaching, both in the forenoon and in the evening, when the congregation was much affected. The next morning I went to friend Strawbridge's,[196] and found his family well. Here we had Dr. Warfield and several polite people to dine with us. I spoke to the ladies about head-dresses; but the Doctor vindicated them, observing that religion did not consist in dress. I quoted the words of St. Peter; I stayed about an hour, and then departed. We then rode to Friend Durbin's,[197] and spent some time with his family.

Thursday, 19. Friend Durbin and I set off for Frederick.[198] We came to George Saxton's, where I expected to have preached, but there was a disappointment; so we pursued our way, though my little horse was unwell and very weary. A poor, unhappy man abused me much on the road: he cursed, swore, and threw stones at me. But I found it my duty to talk to him, and show him his danger. Frederick is a neat, little town, having one main street and three cross streets. It contains about a thousand houses, and the inhabitants are chiefly Germans. There are two German churches, one Calvinist, and one Lutheran. There is also one English church, and one Roman chapel. [About five and twenty Baptists are the greatest enemies the Methodists have in this place.] Many people came to hear me in this town.

Friday, 20. Found some peace of mind in the morning; but was sorely buffetted by Satan in the course of the day; I had but few people in the evening, and but little power.

Saturday, 21. My mind was greatly depressed. Not on account of any

[195] Richard Owings was one of the band of local preachers licensed under the ministry of Robert Strawbridge. Some claim that he was the first native American local preacher. His name appears on the first class book of the society in the home of Daniel Evans. He preached the funeral service of Strawbridge in 1781 and was admitted into the conference two years before his death in Leesburg, Virginia, in 1786. (*Minutes.* See Watters: *A Short Account of the Christian Experiences and Ministerial Labors of William Watters.*)

[196] Robert Strawbridge, a native of Ireland, formed a class in his home on Sam's Creek. The claim that this was the first society in American Methodism remains unconfirmed despite rather convincing evidence. He insisted on administering the sacraments. (See *Journal* entries for August 2, 1773; August 27, 1775.) Alexander Warfield and Mrs. Warfield, at whose home Asbury later dined, were members of the society formed in the Strawbridge house.

[197] William Durbin, also an original member of Strawbridge's class, was the father of John Durbin (1778–1805), who was received on trial in the Baltimore Conference in 1803. (Bibbins: *How Methodism Came*, 36.)

[198] Asbury, accompanied by William Durbin, proceeded to Frederick, Maryland, the county seat of the present Frederick County, where John King had preached the first Methodist sermon in 1770. The residents of this community were mostly members of the Dutch Reformed Church, a sect that shared the religious fervor of the Methodists.

outward, known sin; but partly from the state of my body, and partly from a deep sense of the very great work in which I am employed. I do not know when I sunk into deeper distress: though, thank God, there was no condemnation.

Lord's day. After preaching in the morning, brother John Hagerty[199] [his brother Paul,] friend Bonham[200] and myself set off to a place where I had to preach at two o'clock. Friend Bonham was awakened by the instrumentality of friend Strawbridge, and he told me that he had been much opposed [by the Baptists. He said they had used him very ill; but he was determined to have no more connexion with them. He appears to be a solid, sensible man]. I heard him give an exhortation greatly to the purpose; and gave him a note of recommendation, to do all the good he could. Happened in company with an old, stupid Quaker woman, who supposed me to be a half Quaker, and thought the Friends were the only people in the world, and that they were not fallen from their former lively and spiritual state. A man came twenty miles for me, to go and preach a funeral sermon. I accordingly complied, and had many people to hear me. Then went about two miles, to preach at Mr. Durbin's; and met with a German minister, Mr. Benedict Swope,[201] who heard me preach at both places. We had some conversation about the ordinances administered by Mr. Strawbridge. He advanced some reasons to urge the necessity of them, and said Mr. Wesley did not do well to hinder us from the administration of them. I told him they did not appear to me as essential to salvation; [and that it did not appear to be my duty to administer the ordinances at *that time*].

Tuesday, 24. Preached at Winchester,[202] in an unfinished house; and

[199] John Hagerty (1747–1818), a native of Prince George's County and a member of the society on Sam's Creek at the time of Asbury's visit in 1772, preached at Rodda's assignment at Linganore in the present Frederick County. In 1779 he entered the traveling connection and continued to preach until 1792, when because of illness of his wife he located. (*Methodist Magazine,* VII (1824), 209 ff.)

[200] Hezekiah Bonham, an early convert to Methodism on Sam's Creek, accompanied Asbury on his first journey to the Red Stone country in western Pennsylvania in 1784. A son, Robert, entered the traveling ministry in 1794 and died in 1800.

[201] Benedict Swope, or Schwope, was an elder in the Reformed congregation at Pipe Creek, Maryland, as early as 1754. Coming under the influence of Robert Strawbridge and William Otterbein, he became a leader in the Evangelical movement and stood high in the esteem of Bishop Asbury. Asbury records Swope's death in Kentucky at the age of eighty. (See Drury: *The Life of Rev. Philip William Otterbein,* 157, 191; *Methodist Review,* VI (1823), 249–54; Bibbins, *op. cit.,* 36.) Bishop John Christian Keener was a great-grandson of Benedict Swope. (Hough: *Christian Newcomer, His Life, Journal and Achievements,* 5 n.)

[202] The present seat of Carroll County, Maryland, was laid out by William Winchester (1710–64) in 1764, and bore the name of the founder until changed to Westminster by act of the General Assembly. The log meetinghouse stood on Marston Road, a mile south of New Windsor, Maryland. Those who give priority to this site as that on which the first Methodist preaching house in America stood have erected this marker:

while the rain beat in upon me, many people looked and wondered at the stranger. However, I delivered my message with some energy, and then road three miles to Richard Owing's, where the Lord enabled me to preach with much feeling to a great number of people.

Wednesday, 25. We rode about twenty miles to my old friend Joshua Owing's,[203] the forest home for the Methodists at that time, and found a very agreeable house and family. The old man is "an Israelite indeed." He was once a serious Churchman, who sought for the truth; and now God has revealed it to him. The Lord has also begun to bless his family. He has one son a preacher, and the rest of his children are very thoughtful. Though it was a rainy day, there were many people, and my heart was greatly enlarged towards them in preaching.

Thursday, 26. The congregation was also large at Mr. Samuel Merryman's,[204] and the Lord was with me. But on *Friday*, at Mr. Evans'[205] the congregation was small, and I was much straitened. The same evening I rode to Baltimore.

Saturday, 28. Preached at the Point[206] the first time.

Lord's day, 29. It was a rainy day, but I rode to the Point, and after preaching to a large congregation, returned to town and dined at William Moore's:[207] I preached in town both at three, and at six o'clock.

Monday, November 30. Rode in company with Mrs. Rachel Hulings, Mrs. Rogers, and the widow White,[208] to Nathaniel Perigau's,[209] and

"On this spot stood the log meeting house erected about 1764, the first Methodist meeting house in America." Its successor is Bethel Chapel located about a mile to the southwest of the original site and standing near the Alexander Warfield house. (Bibbins, *op. cit.*, 42–44; Roberts: *Centenary Pictorial Album*, 30, 32, 33, 34; Scharf: *History of Western Maryland*, II, 927.)

[203] Asbury now travels towards Baltimore. Joshua Owings was the father of Richard Owings of Sam's Creek. (For an account of the affiliation of the Owings family with the Garrison Church see Allen: *The Garrison Church, Sketches of the History of St. Thomas' Parish, Baltimore County, Maryland*, 1742–1852, 30, 175.)

[204] Samuel Merryman lived on the Hookstown Road about four miles from Baltimore. His devotion to Methodism dated from his early membership in the society on Sam's Creek. (Smith: *Recollections of an Old Itinerant*, 204, 205; Bibbins, *op. cit.*, 45, 46; *Maryland Historical Magazine*, X (1915), 176, 286; Lednum, *op. cit.*, 19.)

[205] In the home of Daniel Evans, in what is now Roland Park, Baltimore, the first society in the present Baltimore County was organized. (McLean: *Sketch of Rev. Philip Gatch*, 24; Stevens: *History of the Methodist Episcopal Church*, I, 74.)

[206] In 1772 an Irishman, Captain George Patton, or Paten, opened his house for preaching at Fell's Point. "The first meeting-house that was built by the Methodists in Baltimore was that at Fell's Point." (Lee: *A Short History of the Methodists*, 49; William Hamilton in the *Methodist Quarterly Review*, July, 1856. For a partial list of early members see Lednum, *op. cit.*, 89.)

[207] William Moore resided at the southeast corner of Water and South streets, Baltimore. (Lednum, *op. cit.*, 88.)

[208] Among Asbury's pioneer women helpers were Mrs. Rachel Hulings, who later engaged in evangelistic work with him; and Mrs. Rogers, mother of Philip Rogers, a Baltimore layman, long useful. (Lednum, *op. cit.*, 88, 89.)

preached to a large number of people. Then I rode to William Lynch's, to whom I was introduced by Mrs. Hulings, and had many to hear the word of truth.

[*Tuesday, December* 1. Lodged tonight in a damp bed, and though I expected some bad consequence, yet through mercy I received no injury.] The next day, at Joppa,[210] there were many people from the country, and some from the town.

Thursday, December 3. Preached at Joseph Presbury's, to many people who could feel the word, and with much power in my own soul. Then rode three miles into the Gunpowder Neck, and had a solemn, heart-affecting time, while preaching from Rev. ii, 11; a passage which, it seems, just suited their case: afterward returned to Joseph Presbury's.

Friday, 4. After preaching, Josias Dallam conducted me to his house, and treated me with great kindness. Preached at his house at three o'clock; and on Saturday, at Moses Brown's, about three miles off.

Lord's day, 6. Went about five miles to preach in our first preaching house.[211] The house had no windows or doors; the weather was very cold: so that my heart pitied the people when I saw them so exposed. Putting a handkerchief over my head, I preached, and after an hour's intermission (the people waiting all the time in the cold) I preached again.

Monday, 7. John King and I went about five miles to lodge; and the next morning set off for Bohemia Manor. We passed through Charlestown,[212] and dined at the head of the Elk.[213] We lodged at Robert Thompson's, where I spoke closely to the poor Negroes, who took some notice of

[209] Nathan Perigau, or Perrigo, spiritual father of Philip Gatch, resided about six miles northeast of the Baltimore of that day. About 1772 Perigau and Gatch organized a circuit in Pennsylvania along the Maryland border. (Gatch, *op. cit.,* 9–11, 22.) William Lynch, whose home was on Patapsco Neck, was a local preacher. He is believed to have attended the Christmas Conference. He died in 1806.

[210] The ancient town of Joppa when visited by Asbury was situated twenty miles northeast of Baltimore. It not only was at the head of navigation on Gunpowder River, but was at the crossroads of what was known as the Joppa Road running west to Towson and the main thoroughfare south from Lower Susquehanna. This once-historic place is now a cluster of houses on the Baltimore and Ohio Railroad and Highway 7. (Wilstach: *Tidewater Maryland,* 199, 205; *Journal* entry for Tuesday, January 19, 1773.)

[211] The first Bush Forest Chapel, six miles from Aberdeen, Maryland, was erected in 1769 by the society formed by Robert Strawbridge. Asbury described it as "the second house built for the Methodists in the State." (See *Journal* entry for Thursday, November 16, 1791.) On December 20, 1773, an acre of land was given by Benjamin Herbert to the society. The "Conveyance-Agreement" contains the names of such prominent Methodist families as Watters, Preston, Bull, Howard, Presbury, Armstrong, Baker, and Dallam. A photostat of the deed and text appeared in Bishop Charles W. Flint's *Report to the Jurisdictional Conference,* Harrisburg, Pennsylvania, June 11, 1952.

[212] Charlestown, Cecil County, Maryland, founded 1742, was halfway up the Northeast River, forty miles northeast of Baltimore. When Asbury visited it, and until 1784 when the county seat was moved to Elkton, it was a village that promised to rival Baltimore.

[213] This was the present Elkton.

what was said. Since I went from here last, my travels have been, perhaps, as much as three hundred miles in about six weeks. And, glory to God! I have been favoured with the presence of the Lord; and with zeal and power in my public exercises. Rode to Bird's tavern[214] for my trunk and box of books; and received a letter from Mr. Pilmoor which surpassed everything I ever had met with from a Methodist preacher. The Lord judge between him and me![215] Then I went to Solomon Hersey's, and after preaching to a few people, I spoke to them, one by one, concerning the state of their souls.

Tuesday, 8. I intended to have preached at Georgetown;[216] but in my way found a large house belonging to a certain Mr. Bayard,[217] in which Mr. Whitefield had preached some years ago, to some Hollanders, who were eminent for religion: but the old people are now dead. Then I proceeded on my way to Georgetown, and lodged at the house of a Quaker. He treated me with great kindness; and appeared to be an understanding man. His wife was somewhat tender in religious conversation. In the evening the Negroes were collected, and I spoke to them in exhortation. In the morning three or four white people also attended at prayer, to whom I spoke about their souls. The Friend went with me in the morning; and when I asked him what satisfaction he required, he told me, no more than what he had received.

Wednesday, 9. Preached to many people, rich and poor, at John Randall's,[218] and at another place in the evening.

Friday, 11. Went twelve miles into Kent county,[219] and had many great people to hear me. But before preaching, one Mr. Read, a church minister, came to me and desired to know who I was, and whether I was licensed.

[214] This may have been either Bird or Buck tavern. Each was a well-known hostelry in colonial times.

[215] This refers to Asbury's conflict with Pilmoor over the frequent change of the preachers. (See note under November 22, 1771.)

[216] Georgetown, now Galena, Kent County, was on the south bank of the Sassafras River, which divides Cecil and Kent counties, Maryland.

[217] Probably a descendant of Petrus Bayard, nephew of Peter Stuyvesant, who landed in New York City, 1647, and joined the Labidists at Bohemia Manor. In the Bayard mansion George Whitefield preached. James Asheton Bayard (1767–1815), American statesman, married a daughter of Governor Richard Bassett. The joint funeral services of Bayard and Bassett, who also died in 1815, were conducted by Ezekiel Cooper. (Mallery: *Ancient Families of Bohemia Manor, Their Homes and Their Graves*, 46 f.)

[218] In John Randall's house, near Worton, Kent County, Robert Strawbridge preached the first Methodist sermon on the eastern shore of Maryland. About 1780 the society erected a chapel. (Hallam, *op. cit.*, 119, 318; Jesse Lee, *op. cit.*, 39.)

[219] Asbury was probably in the neighbourhood in which the Old Kent Meeting House, the first Methodist place of worship on the Peninsula, was later erected. In the churchyard of the long-abandoned site between Chestertown and Rock Hall, William Gill and James Smith, two widely known itinerants, are buried. (Garrettson: *The Experiences and Travels of Mr. Freeborn Garrettson*, 76; Lee, *op. cit.*, 50; Wakeley: *Heroes of Methodism*, 199, 200.)

I told him who I was. He spoke great, swelling words, and told me he had authority over the people, and was charged with the care of their souls. He also told me that I could not, and should not preach; and if I did, he would proceed against me according to law. I let him know that I came to preach, and preach I would; and further asked him if he had authority to bind the consciences of the people, or if he was a justice of the peace; and told him I thought he had nothing to do with me. He charged me with making a schism. I told him that I did not draw the people from the Church; and asked him if his church was then open? He told me that I hindered people from their work; but I asked him if fairs and horse races did not hinder them? and, further, told him that I came to help him. He said, he had not hired me for an assistant, and did not want my help. I told him, if there were no swearers or other sinners, he was sufficient. But, said he, what did you come for? I replied, to turn sinners to God. He said, cannot I do that as well as you? I told him that I had authority from God. He then laughed at me, and said, You are a fine fellow, indeed! I told him I did not do this to invalidate his authority; and also gave him to understand that I did not wish to dispute with him: but he said he had business with me, and came into the house in a great rage. I began to preach, and urged the people to repent, and turn from all their transgressions, so iniquity should not prove their ruin. After preaching, the parson went out, and told the people they did wrong in coming to hear me; and said I spoke against learning. Whereas, I only spoke to this purpose—when a man turned from all sin, he would adorn every character in life, both in Church and state. I left him, and preached at John Randall's at seven o'clock.

Lord's day, 13. Preached twice with very little intermission, to many people collected at a school house near Robert Thompson's; and then rode to Solomon Hersey's, and found it a comfortable time while preaching at six o'clock.

Delaware

Monday, December 14, 1772. I rode to New Castle, and preached to a large company. My soul has lately been much bowed down.

Tuesday, 15. There were but few people attended preaching at Mr. Stedham's; and as the next day was wet, I stayed and had a family meeting. On *Thursday* I went to Mr. Tussey's.[220] My mind has been much affected lately. May the Lord support and teach me! After preaching at

[220] Asbury revisited the home of Isaac Tussey, a Methodist preaching place since Captain Thomas Webb held services there in 1769. The house built in 1765 still stands five miles below the Pennsylvania state line. (*Delaware, a Guide to the First State*, 325.)

Mr. Tussey's, I went to hear a New Light minister, and found but little satisfaction.

Lord's day, 20. Though it rained much, yet many people attended preaching at Isaac Hersey's. Then I preached at a place about five miles off; and rode thence to Newcastle, where many people attended at night. The Lord favoured me. My mind is now full of Divine peace.

Maryland

Monday, 21. I set out for Bohemia Manor; and though my body was much fatigued with my ride, and my head ached violently, yet in the evening I enforced these words: "Be diligent that ye may be found of him in peace, without spot, and blameless;" and endeavoured to show them, that in justification we have peace, in sanctification we are without spot, and in perfect love we are blameless; and then proceeded to show them wherein we must be diligent.

Tuesday, 22. On my way to Susquehanna, a person came for me to visit Mrs. Thomas in a dropsy. I then proceeded to Josias Dallam's; and the next day set off for Joseph Presbury's, to attend our quarterly meeting.[221] Many people attended, and several friends came many miles. I preached from Acts xx, 28: "Take heed, therefore, unto yourselves," &c. After showing to whom the charge was given, I proceeded to enforce the subject thus:—

I. Take heed to your spirits.
II. Take heed to your practice.
III. Take heed to your doctrine.
IV. Take heed to the flock.
  1. Those that are under deep conviction.
  2. Those that are true believers.
  3. Those that are sorely tempted.
  4. Those that are groaning for full redemption.
  5. Those that have backslidden.

I then urged the motives to this duty. We afterwards proceeded to our temporal business, and considered the following propositions:—

[221] Asbury now returned to the western shore to begin his second round of appointments in that part of Maryland. Josias Dallam lived near Aberdeen, Maryland, on the site of the present Aberdeen Proving Ground. Joseph Presbury conducted the meeting at which William Watters was spiritually awakened. Presbury served simultaneously as trustee of three Methodist chapels—Bush Forest Chapel built in 1768, and in 1773 those erected on Gunpowder Neck and at the mouth of Middle River. The quarterly conference held in his home is the first of which the minutes have been preserved. They indicate a growing cleavage between Asbury and Strawbridge over the administration of the sacraments by Mr. Wesley's unordained helpers. (Lee, *op. cit.*, 41; Stevens, *op. cit.*, I, 133, 134; *The Methodist Review*, N.Y., May, 1928.)

1. What are our collections? We found them sufficient to defray our expenses.

2. How are the preachers stationed? Brother Strawbridge and brother Owings in Frederick county. Brother King, brother Webster, and Isaac Rollins,[222] on the other side of the bay; and myself in Baltimore.

3. Shall we be strict in our society meetings, and not admit strangers? Agreed.

4. Shall we drop preaching in the day-time through the week? Not agreed to.

5 Will the people be contented without our administering the sacrament? John King was neuter; brother Strawbridge pleaded much for the ordinances; and so did the people, who appeared to be much biased by him. I told them I would not agree to it at that time, and insisted on our abiding by our rules. But Mr. Boardman had given them their way at the quarterly meeting held here before, and I was obliged to connive at some things for the sake of peace.

6. Shall we make collections weekly, to pay the preachers' board and expenses? This was not agreed to. We then inquired into the moral characters of the preachers and exhorters. Only one exhorter was found any way doubtful, and we have great hopes of him. Brother Strawbridge received £8 quarterage; brother King and myself £6 each. Great love subsisted among us in this meeting, and we parted in peace.

I then went to Josias Dallam's; and on Christmas day attended the Church,[223] and heard parson West preach a plain, useful sermon, which contained much truth; and afterward received the sacrament. Then rode five miles to Bush Chapel; but as Mr. Strawbridge did not give public notice, few people attended, and the preaching was late. [Perhaps Mr. Strawbridge omitted to give public notice, that it might prevent my going to church.] The next day I rode to Barnard Preston's,[224] where we had a

[222] Isaac Rollins (spelled "Rollings" by Lee), a member of Daniel Evans' class near Baltimore, was the third native American to become a traveling preacher. Of his unfortunate ministerial career and tragic death Asbury has left an extended account. (See *Journal* entry for Tuesday, August 5, 1783; also Lednum, *op. cit.*, 389, 390.)

[223] This was the historic Garrison Church of which from its erection in 1743 the Owings, Bond, Murray, Doughaday, Dallam, and several other later Methodist families had been members and vestrymen. Josias Dallam, on whose land at Abingdon, Cokesbury College later was erected, accompanied Asbury to hear "parson West." The Rev. William West (1734–91) and two others on December 31, 1784, invited Coke and Asbury to tea in Baltimore to discuss the prospect of a union of the Protestant Episcopal and the Methodist Episcopal Churches, only recently released from British ecclesiastical control. Thomas Worthington informed Asbury that the vestry of this church had decided to invite him to become its rector. (See *Journal* entry for Tuesday, August 26, 1777; also Allen: *The Garrison Church, Sketches of the History of St. Thomas Parish, Garrison Forest, Baltimore County, Md.*, 39, 46.)

[224] This was probably Barnard Preston, who among other Harford County Methodists signed the deed for the site of the Bush Forest Chapel, December 20, 1773. Or it may

large congregation, and a very comfortable meeting. On the same day, at the house of Henry Watters, Nicholas Watters[225] spoke with great care, but with little depth. He may improve, and make a useful preacher in time.

Lord's day, 27. Rode to the widow Bond's, and preached twice, with very little intermission, to a great number of people. Appointing a meeting in the evening, I had an opportunity of hearing Isaac Rollins exhort. His exhortation was coarse and loud enough, though with some depth. I gave him a little advice, which he seemed willing to take.

Monday, 28. Many people of various kinds attended at Aquilla Staniford's. Preached afterward at J. Moore's in the evening, and went thence to James Baker's, and met the class.

Tuesday, 29. At Mr. Sinclair's I found great peace of mind, and, thanks be to God, had power in preaching, though the people were dead and stupid. The next day at Mr. Chamberlain's I had many people, and preached with freedom; then went to Galloway's, where we had great consolation.

refer to Barnett Preston, who was a member of the first grand jury for Harford County, which met at "Harford Town" (Bel Air), August 23, 1774. (Preston, *op. cit.*, 65.)

[225] Nicholas Watters (1739–1804) was one of the seven sons of Henry Watters of Deer Creek, Maryland, and brother of William Watters, the first native American itinerant. Nicholas was received on trial at the conference in Baltimore with Freeborn Garrettson in 1776. He died of smallpox while stationed at Charleston, South Carolina. (*Minutes*, 1776; Hedges, *op. cit.*, 33–35; Betts: *History of South Carolina Methodism*, 33.)

large congregation, and a very comfortable meeting. On the same day, at the house of Henry Watters, Nicholas Watters[20] spoke with great care, but with little depth. He may improve, and make a useful preacher in time.

Lord's day, 27. Rode to the widow Bond's, and preached twice, with very little intermission, to a great number of people. Appointing a meeting in the evening, I had an opportunity of hearing Isaac Rollins there. His exhortation was coarse and loud enough, though with some depth. I gave him a little advice, which he seemed willing to take.

Monday, 28. Many people of various kinds attended at Austin Stanford's. Preached afterward at J. Moore's in the evening, and went thence to James Baker's, and met the class.

Tuesday, 29. At Mr. Sinclair's I found great peace of mind, and thanks be to God, had power in preaching, though the people were dead and stupid. The next day at Mr. Chamberlain's I had many people, and preached with freedom; then went to Galloway's, where we had great consolation.

refer to Daniel Ruston, who was a member of the first grand jury for Harford County, which met at "Harford Town," (Bel Air), August 23, 1774. (Preston, op. cit., 84).

[20] Nicholas Watters (1739-1804) was one of the seven sons of Henry Watters of Deer Creek, Maryland, and brothers of William Watters, the first native American itinerant. Nicholas was received on trial at the conference in Baltimore with each an Garrettson in 1776. He died of ... while stationed in Charleston, South Carolina. (Minutes 1776; Hudson op. cit., 3,858; Betts, History of South Carolina Methodism, 33).

1773

1773

The first American Conference, at St. George's Church in Philadelphia

CHAPTER TWO

Maryland

January 1, 1773. My body has been weak for some time; but my mind has enjoyed a good degree of peace, and I have a strong desire to be kept in the meekness of Jesus Christ. My heart has been affected by reading, lately, part of Sewel's History of the Quakers.[1] How great was the spirit of persecution in New England, when some were imprisoned, some had their ears cut off, and some were hanged! O that our God would arise, and bow the nations to himself!

January 2. After preaching to several people at John Murray's, a new place, I then rode back to Mr. Colgate's,[2] and preached in the evening.

January 3. Rode to Baltimore,[3] and had a large congregation at the

[1] William Sewel (1654–1720) wrote *The History of the Rise, Increase, and Progress of the Christian People called Quakers: Interspersed with several remarkable occurrences. Written in Low-Dutch and also translated into English.* London, 1725. (*Dictionary of National Biography*, XVII, 1221.)

[2] The text seems to indicate that Asbury rode back to Chamberlain's, who is mentioned on December 29, 1772; however, in the extract of the *Journal* printed in the *Arminian Magazine* this man is called Mr. Colgate. In Hollingsworth's edition he is referred to only as Mr. C.

[3] Asbury by appointment of the recent quarterly conference (see *Journal* entry for December 23, 1772) now made Baltimore his base of operations. Robert Williams and John King had preached in Baltimore before Joseph Pilmoor arrived on June 11, 1772, to spend eleven days. Pilmoor organized classes in Baltimore and at Fell's Point, a mile distant. The latter took its name from two Quaker brothers, Edward and William Fell, who settled north of Jones's Falls on land that projected into the northwest branch of the Patapsco River. At Fell's Point, or "the Point," lived Captain George Patton, "a friendly Irishman," who in 1766 chose a site for a wharf and later offered his home as a Methodist preaching place. (Scharf: *History of Baltimore City and County*, 45–55;

house of Captain Patton at the Point. Many of the principal people were there; and the Lord enabled me to speak with power. At night I preached in town. The house was well filled with people, and we have a comfortable hope the work of the Lord will revive in this place. Bless the Lord, O ye saints! Holiness is the element of my soul. My earnest prayer is, that nothing contrary to holiness may live in me.

Monday, 4. Rode to Sater Stephenson's,[4] and was much affected in preaching to the people. I then met and regulated the class.

Tuesday, 5. They were kind enough to offer me the court-house in town:[5] but judging it unfit, I preached in another house; then met the society, and settled a class of men.

Wednesday, 6. We had a pretty good gathering at Nathan Perigau's, about six miles from town; I then rode back to town, and after preaching with comfort in the evening, I formed a class of women.

Thursday, 7. Rose with a determination to live more to God. Preached twice in the country, met two classes, and settled them as well as I could. The class at Mr. Simm's[6] were lively, and had the power of God among them. They were the fruit of Nathan Perigau's labours, and many of them could give a good account of their experience.

Friday, 8. My mind is fixed on God. I both desire and purpose to exercise fasting, prayer, and faith. After some exercise of mind, the Lord enabled me to preach with warmth at Mr. Samuel Merryman's from these words: "Be not ye partakers with them." I showed: First, whom the words were spoken to. Secondly, with whom they were not to be partakers. Thirdly, how they were not to partake with them; namely, In spirit—in judgment— in practice.

Lord's day, January 10. Many people attended at Joseph Presbury's to whom I preached twice, with some life, and then went three miles into the Neck;[7] and felt much power while preaching on perfect love. The more I speak on this subject, the more my soul is filled and drawn out in love. This doctrine has a great tendency to prevent people from settling on their lees.

Pilmoor's manuscript *Journal*, June and July, 1772, and May, 1773; Atkinson, *op. cit.*, 333–42, 400, 401; Griffith: *Annals of Baltimore* (1824), 43.)

[4] Stephenson belonged to the society of Daniel Evans and, like his fellow members Isaac Rollins, Richard Owings, and Nathan Perigau, became a local preacher. (McLean: *Sketch of Rev. Philip Gatch*, 9; Lednum, *op. cit.*, 19, 117; Smith: *Recollections of an Old Itinerant*, 206, 210.)

[5] In 1768 a law was passed authorizing the erection of a courthouse and prison on the "uppermost part of Calvert Street near Jones' Falls," near the present Peace Monument. Because of rivalry between Oldtown and Fell's Point, Asbury may have judged the courthouse "unfit" as compared with "another house" more neutrally located. (Preston, *op. cit.*, 46; Scharf: *The History of Baltimore City and County*, 49–63.)

[6] In the Simm's home a class was organized, probably by Strawbridge, of which Philip Gatch was a member. (Lednum, *op. cit.*, 19.)

[7] Gunpowder Neck is a peninsula in Hartford County, Maryland, which projects into Chesapeake Bay between Gunpowder and Bush rivers.

Monday, 11. Preached with great plainness to many people at Daniel Ruff's,[8] and then rode to Mr. Dallam's.

Tuesday, 12. Rode to Moses Brown's; but as they had no previous notice, we collected but few. However, I preached, and afterward returned to Mr. Dallam's, and preached to his family.

Thursday, 14. It was late before I reached Samuel Litten's, and as there was much rain and snow, the company was small. Young Doctor Andrews took me home with him. The young man, with his sister and mother, seemed tender; but his father appeared to be a stiff old man, and I did by no means like his spirit.

Friday, 15. Many people attended preaching at Samuel Forwood's. I was shut up in speaking, and afterward rode home with friend Preston.

Saturday, 16. This morning I rose to glorify God, with a determination to do his will, and that only; to be wholly devoted to the Lord, in spirit, soul, and body. Many people came to hear the word of life to-day, though it was very cold.

Lord's day, 17. Preaching to-day at friend Preston's, on the barren fig-tree, I first showed that it was applicable to the Jews; and, secondly, to the Protestant Church; at the same time described the barren fig-tree as— one without leaves—or, one without blossoms—or, one without fruit—or, one that did not bear so much fruit as another might bear. I then rode to Josias Dallam's, and preached to his family with a few others. On *Monday* but few people attended at Bond's; and in the evening I preached at Mr. Duke's, but was shut up. The next day many country people came to hear the word at Joppa, though but few from the town. There are about forty houses in this town, and it stands on a neck of land near the water; but the people seem to be buried in trade, sensuality, and superstition.

Wednesday, 20. The weather being cold, there were but few at James Baker's; nevertheless I preached. If Israel be not gathered, yet I hope to be the Lord's.

Thursday, 21. After preaching with liberty at Mr. Chamberlain's, I went to Aquila Galloway's, and found life in preaching there. The next day at John Murray's, I preached to a stupid company, and then rode to John Colgate's. I was favoured with liberty in dispensing the blessed word in the evening at Joshua Owing's. How pleasant and profitable it is to feel Divine power in public exercises! *Saturday*, I rode to Baltimore, and had a large congregation.

[8] Daniel Ruff lived near Havre de Grace, Maryland. He was received on trial at the Philadelphia Conference, the second held in America, in 1774, and ceased to travel in 1781. He served extensively in New Jersey and experienced great trials in 1776 while stationed in New York City. Praise of Ruff by Asbury in his *Journal* in early March and May 18, 1774, and his membership on a committee of five at the Deer Creek Conference, May 20, 1777, "to act in the place of the general assistant (Thomas Rankin), in case they should all go before next conference" indicate his dependability. (Atkin-

Lord's day, 24. I preached twice at the Point, and once in town.[9] On *Monday* my heart felt great sorrow. This day I wrote to my mother;[10] and in the evening found great consolation.

Tuesday, 26. My mind was wholly given up to God, and I have a great hope that the Gospel will yet spread in this town. On *Wednesday* there was a moving among the people while I preached at Nathan Perigau's; and afterward returning to town, preached in the evening. On *Thursday* I felt power and life in my soul, while preaching to a large number of people at Mr. Gatch's. On *Friday* I preached in the Gunpowder Neck and at Joppa.

Saturday, 30. Perceiving the great wickedness of the people who were swearing and drinking in a tavern, great struggles arose in my mind about preaching there; however I broke through every difficulty, and felt both life and power in dispensing the word among them.

Lord's day, 31. This was a day of power and comfort. I rode to Joseph Presbury's, preached three times, and met the classes. Many of the people, through grace, were able to give a good account of their experience.

February 1. Was favoured in preaching to a number of people at Daniel Ruff's; and my mind has been kept by the grace of God.

Tuesday, 2. Was greatly assisted in preaching to-day, both at Swan Creek[11] and Mr. Dallam's. The next morning I breakfasted with Richard Dallam, and found that he was very fond of Mr. Law's works. He treated me with great kindness. After preaching and meeting the society at the ferry, I went to Jacob Giles's,[12] a man much talked of, but what he is, I know not. In principle he appeared to be a Quaker. He was much troubled with the gout, which, he told me, his father had before him. He said, his father cured himself of the gout by milk and moderate diet; but threw himself into a dropsy. On *Thursday*, after preaching at Deer Creek, I rode to Barnard Preston's. My present purpose is, to put all the people who are fit for it into bands.

Friday, 5. Many people attended at Forwood's, and my soul was enlarged in preaching to them. I then rode back to Barnard Preston's, and put the people into bands as I had designed.

---

son: *Memorials of Methodism in New Jersey*, 99-104; Wakeley: *Lost Chapters Recovered from the Early History of Methodism*, 255-58; Garrettson, *op. cit.*, 26; Watters, *op. cit.*, 57.)

[9] The "Point" was Fell's Point, one mile from Baltimore, which was the town referred to.

[10] See letter to his mother dated January 24, 1773.

[11] Swan Creek rises near the site of Bush Forest Chapel, flows north of Aberdeen, Maryland, into an estuary of Chesapeake Bay.

[12] Jacob Giles, one of the four owners of the Bush River Iron Works, acquired between 1735 and 1747 more than four thousand acres of land in Harford County. His kinsman Nathaniel Giles, who lived at Lapidum, Maryland, entertained Asbury on his first visit to the western shore. (Preston, *op. cit.*, 33, 34; Mason: *Historical Sketches of Harford County, Maryland*, 21, 44, 57.)

Saturday, 6. My mind was calm and serene this morning. I preached with some power, and we had a comfortable meeting. William Duke,[13] a lad about sixteen or seventeen years of age, exhorted the people. He appeared to be a promising youth, and I gave him a license to exhort.

Lord's day, 7. Some great critics attended at the preaching-house to-day; but I preached twice, and spoke freely.

Monday, 8. Though the weather was very cold, I went to William Bond's,[14] and enforced, on a dull congregation, these awful words of our Lord, "What shall it profit a man, if he shall gain the whole world, and lose his own soul?" I went afterward to the widow Bond's, and spoke closely to the girls, who appeared to be somewhat serious.

Tuesday, 9. After preaching to more people than usual, at Aquila Staniford's, I went to Baker's in the evening, and both met the class and formed some bands. I also gave them a copy of the proper deed for securing their preaching-house.[15]

Wednesday, 10. I went to Chamberlain's and preached. This perhaps will be the last time, for it is a disorderly house. I then went to Aquila Galloway's and preached with some comfort. There is room to hope that the Lord will do something for the people here.

Thursday, 11. The congregation was large at John Murray's, and I preached with plainness, so that the sleepy people seemed to awake. I then went back to Colgate's[16] and preached with some satisfaction; but Satan was close at my heels: however, the Lord gave me power to resist him.

Friday, 12. The Lord enables me to stand fast in the midst of tempta-

---

[13] William Duke (1757–1840), in whose father's house Asbury had preached on January 18, was admitted on trial in 1774 and withdrew in 1779. He was an intimate friend of Captain Thomas Webb, who presented him with his Greek New Testament. Duke entered the Protestant Episcopal Church, and in 1793 became the rector of the North Elk Parish on the eastern shore. Later in life he was professor of languages in St. John's College, Annapolis, Maryland, and later the rector of the parish. He was the author of *Observations on the Present State of Religion in Maryland*, 1795. (See letter to William Duke, March 4, 1774; Johnston: *History of Cecil County, Maryland*, 456; Atkinson: *Memorials of Methodism in New Jersey*, 104; McLean, *op. cit.*, 30; Duren: *Francis Asbury, Founder of American Methodism and Unofficial Minister of State*, 57, 68, which contains excerpt of a letter of Asbury to Duke dated March 4, 1774; Ethan Allen: *Historical Notices of St. Ann's Parish in Ann Arundel County, Maryland, Extending from 1649 to 1857*, 102, 104.)

[14] William Bond probably resided near Fallston, Maryland. In 1776 he was enrolled in the census of Brush River Lower Hundred, and in 1778 as a Maryland justice he made the returns to the Harford County Court of persons who took the oath of fidelity. (Brumbaugh: *Maryland Records*, II, 127, 636.)

[15] This third meetinghouse of Maryland Methodists was erected by the society organized in the home of James Baker, who was converted after listening to John King preach on a Baltimore street corner in early 1772. The Log Meeting House on Sam's Creek and the Bush Forest Chapel (1769) already were in use. (Lednum, *op. cit.*, 101; *The Methodist Quarterly Review*, July, 1856, 439; *The Methodist Review* (New York), May, 1928.)

[16] See note under January 2, 1772. The same situation applies here.

tions. My soul possesses inward and spiritual power. Many people attended preaching to-day at Joshua Owing's; I afterward met the class, and then gave an exhortation in the evening.

Lord's day, 14. Many country people came to hear the word of God at the Point; some came twelve miles before those of the town had left their houses; perhaps before some of them had left their beds. I found some life and power in preaching both at the Point and in Baltimore.

Monday, 15. Rose this morning with holy thoughts of God; and we had a good time in public worship.

Wednesday, 17. I preached and met the society, and employed Mr. Moreton to draw up a deed for the house in Gunpowder Neck.

Thursday, 18. Preached with power, both at Nathan Perigau's and Mr. Gatch's.[17]

Friday, 19. A few people attended at Mr. Merryman's: going afterward about four miles to Mr. Dallam's, I preached and met the society; most of them appeared to be under a good work of grace.

Lord's day, 21. The weather was excessively severe, yet many people came to hear the word at Joseph Presbury's. I rode about six or seven miles to preach in the Gunpowder Neck, but never felt colder weather. The water froze as it ran from the horse's nostrils; and a friend said, the water froze as it came from his eyes. However, after preaching to a few people, I returned.

Monday, 22. I had sixteen miles to ride to preach to a few people, and five more to Josias Dallam's to get my dinner. I have suffered a little by lodging in open houses this cold weather; but this is a very small thing when compared to what the dear Redeemer suffered for the salvation of precious souls.

Tuesday, 23. Glory to God! I had peace.

Wednesday, 24. After preaching with plainness to a considerable number of people, I then went to Josias Dallam's, where many people attended, and we had a comfortable time. My old opponent, Mr. Edmiston (?),[18]

[17] In Hollingsworth's edition of the *Journal* this man is called Mr. Galloway; however, in the extract printed in the *Arminian Magazine* he is called Mr. Gatch. Philip Gatch (1751–1835) was converted in 1772 under the preaching of Nathan Perigau. The Gatch home, about five miles from Baltimore, had become the center of pronounced religious interest aroused by Robert Strawbridge. Gatch became a traveling preacher in 1773. Near Bladenburg, Maryland, he sustained physical injuries from which he never fully recovered. (See McLean, *op. cit.*)

[18] The extract of the *Journal* printed in the *Arminian Magazine* identifies the old opponent as Mr. Evans; however, there is no evidence that either John or Daniel Evans opposed Asbury, although John may have held pro-Strawbridge sentiments. Some students have thought that the "old opponent" was William Edmiston, who was dismissed from St. Thomas' Parish, which included Garrison Church, for preaching against whigs and dissenters. Ethan Allen (*op. cit.*, 29, 33, 35) identifies the Josias Dallam where Asbury met Mr. Edmiston as John Doughaday, a vestryman who lived near the Beaver Dam east of the Garrison Church.

met me here, but he did not appear so forward as he had been. I rode thence to Rock Run, and preached there with satisfaction. Mr. Giles and his wife treated me with great kindness.

Thursday, 25. I had a good time and many people at Mr. Litten's. Two letters came to hand to-day, one from New York, and one from Philadelphia. They entreat me to return, and inform me that trouble is at hand. But I cannot fear while my heart is upright with God. I seek nothing but him; and fear nothing but his displeasure.

Lord's day, 28. After preaching yesterday at Samuel Forwood's, I returned to friend Preston's, and preached twice to-day. Then rode to Mr. Dallam's, and spent the evening comfortably.

Monday, March 1. Mr. Dallam and myself rode to Bond's, where I spoke with great plainness of speech. There appears to be some reason to doubt of the people in general here; though the young women seem to be deeply serious and thoughtful. I then went to Captain S——'s; but found very little satisfaction. The man and his wife are, I fear, too fond of their own opinions. After preaching here, I went to Bond's again, and spent some time in serious conversation; I afterward prayed and gave an exhortation. I then rode to Murray's and preached; and returned to Chamberlain's and preached there: but found the old man too much of a Quaker in principle. He objects against prayer in his family; and greatly discourages his daughter, who strives to live in the fear of God.

Friday, March 5. Went to Joshua Owings (?), where we had a melting time; and the people seemed much affected both in the day and in the evening. Satan has assaulted me very much of late: but hitherto the Lord hath helped and delivered me. I came next to Baltimore, and had many to hear the word.

Saturday, 6. Went to the Point but the people seemed very hard in their minds. In the evening at Baltimore, we had a moving, melting season. I humbly believe the labour was not in vain.

Monday, 8. Rose this morning with a determination to fight or die; and spent an hour in earnest prayer. Lord, keep me ever watchful. I was also much comforted by a letter which I lately received from Richard Owings, part of which was as follows: "I know not what it will come to. Almost every person seems to be under a religious concern. There are about twenty-two persons already joined in society at Seneca. At Georgetown four have been lately enabled to rejoice in God: and one at Rock Creek.[19] Blessed be God; who hath not forgotten to be gracious."

---

[19] Seneca, Georgetown, and Rock Creek were appointments on the circuit called "Frederich County," to which Strawbridge and Owings were assigned at the first quarterly conference in Maryland. Seneca is on the Potomac River near Seneca Creek, twenty-one miles northwest of Washington. Georgetown, where Methodism was introduced by Robert Williams and William Watters in October, 1772, is now a part of the District of Columbia; and Rock Creek is identified by Rock Creek Park in the same locality. (See *Journal* entry for December 22, 1772, and following; Watters: *The First American Itinerant of Methodism, William Watters*, 52.)

Tuesday, 9. This was a day of sweet peace to my soul. Went to dine with one Mr. Litten, and found him and his wife both serious. Preached in the evening with power.

Wednesday, 10. I went to Nathan Perigau's. It was a rainy morning; but a time of power to those who were present. In going thence to Mr. Gatch's, it was with great difficulty we crossed the water. The next morning I set off for Gunpowder Neck; but found the Great Falls very high; however, I got there about one o'clock, and found it a good time while preaching the word of God.

Friday, 12. Preached a funeral sermon at John Wilson's, from Isaiah lvii, 1, 2: "The righteous perisheth, and no man layeth it to heart: and merciful men are taken away, none considering that the righteous is taken away from the evil to come. He shall enter into peace: they shall rest in their beds, each one walking in his uprightness." This was a solemn time indeed. What melting and weeping appeared among the people! There was scarce a dry eye to be seen. O that it may not be as seed sown by the wayside! After preaching I rode to Mr. Dallam's,[20] and met with brother King and brother Webster,[21] and found myself abundantly comforted in their company.

Lord's day, 14. Preached at Bohemia Manor. There were but few people; though it was a melting time. Rode then to Solomon Hersey's, but was much shut up in preaching.

Monday, 15. Found my mind this morning free to do the will of God; and was more than ever strengthened in prayer. But set out for Worton[22] to-day, with my mind depressed in such a manner as I hardly ever felt it before. In my journey my heart sunk within me; and I knew not why. At a certain Mr. Dixon's, at the Cross Roads,[23] many people, who appeared to be strangers to the truth, were waiting to hear the word. I stood at the door and declared: "The time is fulfilled, the kingdom of God is at hand." I spoke with great feeling, and exerted myself much, but could not get my spirit free. They persuaded me to stay all night; but it was as if I had been bound in chains.

Tuesday, 16. Went to John Randall's, and found myself delivered from my shackles; but still my spirit is not altogether at home—it longs for God. I do humbly and confidently hope to live more to God than ever. Lord, keep me every moment!

---

[20] Although the *Journal* extract published in the *Arminian Magazine* identifies this man as Josias Dallam, some students have thought him to be a Mr. Dixon, who lived near Georgetown Crossroads, now Galena in Kent County, Maryland. (Hallman, *op. cit.*, 13, 109.)

[21] Richard Webster was one of the earliest preachers raised up in America. (Boehm, *op. cit.*, 24–25; Lednum, *op. cit.*, 169.)

[22] Worton was in Kent County, Maryland. (See note under December 9, 1772.)

[23] The Crossroads was at Georgetown, now Galena, Kent County, Maryland.

Wednesday, 17. Went down to the lower church,[24] but with some backwardness of mind. However, there were many people who were still and attentive; and I felt a melting sense of God in my own soul.

Delaware

Friday, 19. I spoke with power to many people at Newcastle. Went thence to Wilmington, and spoke to a few people with great feeling.

Lord's day, 21. But few attended at Isaac Hersey's,[25] because of the rain; but I felt myself greatly assisted. Went thence, through the rain, to Newport where many people attended in the evening. They appeared to have very little sense of religious things.

Monday, 22. Being a rainy day, we set out late for Marlborough. There was, notwithstanding, a large congregation waiting. Though unwell, I gave them an exhortation at night, and Isaac Rollins preached. He has been of some use to the people here.

Tuesday, 23. My mind was serene; and I felt a nearness to God—a determination to live to him alone.

Went to Thomas Ellis's, and felt much life while preaching to a large company there; but was afflicted with a violent pain in the head.

Wednesday, 24. Many great people attended the preaching at Woodward's; and we had a comfortable time. Rode thence to Samuel Hooper's;[26] many Quakers were present, and it was a moving season. I then went about twenty miles, through wet weather and bad roads, to Mr. Tussey's. The night was very dark, the road was through the woods, and it was late before we reached the place; but, by the help of a good guide, I got there safe at last.

> "In all my ways, Thy hand I own,—
> Thy ruling providence I see;
> Assist me still my course to run,
> And still direct my paths to Thee."

[24] Lednum mistakenly identifies this as "Hinson," or "Hynson," Chapel, originally called Old Kent Meetinghouse. The society did not erect a place of worship until the following year. The reference probably is to St. Paul's Anglican Church, known locally as "The Lower Church," which was located between Chestertown and Rock Hall, Maryland, about one mile from the original site of Old Kent Meeting House. (Lednum, *op. cit.*, 126; Hallman, *op. cit.*, 14, 116; Hurst: *American Methodism*, III, 111.)

[25] Isaac Hersey, a kinsman of Solomon Hersey, lived near Wilmington, Delaware. (Marine, *op. cit.*, 5, 6.)

[26] Asbury was preaching on both sides of Brandywine Creek, where Methodism had been introduced by Isaac Rollins. The following year the societies there seem to have been included in the newly formed Chester Circuit. The Rev. George W. Lybrand locates the Woodward home on the Brandywine of West Chester, and that of Samuel Hooper in Goshen Township, both in Chester County, Pennsylvania. (See Futhy and Cope: *History of Chester County*, "Methodism," 280; Hallman, *op. cit.*, 111, 114, 123.)

I was somewhat troubled to hear of Mr. Williams,[27] who had printed some of Mr. Wesley's books for the sake of gain. This will not do. It does by no means look well.

Friday, 26. Many young people attended among others, at Christeen-Bridge[28] while I preached from Eccles. xi, 9: "Rejoice, O young man, in thy youth; and let thy heart cheer thee in the days of thy youth, and walk in the ways of thy heart, and in the sight of thine eyes: but know thou, that for all these things God will bring thee into judgment." Deep seriousness sat on the faces of all; and the mouths of many gainsayers were in a great measure stopped.

Maryland—Delaware

Saturday, 27. Rode to Bohemia Manor and lodged with a Presbyterian elder. The next day I preached in the school house.[29] But these people, who profess religion, could scarce be serious during the time of preaching. Mr. B——, and some other great opposers of our doctrine, were present at Solomon Hersey's at three o'clock: I therefore changed my purpose, and preached from 1 John iii, 23: "And this is his commandment, that we should believe on the name of his Son Jesus Christ, and love one another; as he gave us commandment." And I had great hope that it was well received.

Monday, 29. Rode twenty miles to Susquehanna River; and just got in, almost spent, time enough to preach at three o'clock. Hitherto the Lord hath helped me. Praised forever be his dear and blessed name!

Tuesday, 30. Our quarterly meeting began.[30] After I had preached, we proceeded to business: and in our little conference, the following queries were propounded, namely:—

1. Are there no disorderly persons in our classes? It was thought not.

2. Does not dram-drinking too much prevail among our people?

3. Do none contract debts without due care to pay them? We found that this evil is much avoided among our people.

---

[27] Robert Williams, who had landed in Norfolk, Virginia, late in the summer of 1769, had been printing and selling the sermons of John Wesley. Members of the approaching Philadelphia Conference suspected him of doing so "for the sake of gain" and ordered him to cease publishing. Even during his lifetime his critics acknowledged that they had misjudged his motives. (See *Journal* entry for July 14, 1773; September 26, 1775; Lee, *op. cit.*, 42, 43; Bangs, *op. cit.*, I, 79; *Minutes*, 1773.)

[28] This was the present Christiana, Delaware.

[29] This was Thompson's schoolhouse. (See note under April 12, 1772.)

[30] This quarterly meeting somewhere in "Susquehanna" was the second convened by Asbury in Maryland. Noticeable is the expanding scope of these meetings in which preaching, organization, and sociability were emphasized. (Stevens, *op. cit.*, I, 138, 139; Lee, *op. cit.*, 41, 42.)

4. Are the band-meetings kept up?

5. Is there nothing immoral in any of our preachers?

6. What preachers travel now, and where are they stationed? It was then urged that none must break our rules, under the penalty of being excluded from our connexion. All was settled in the most amicable manner. Mr. Strawbridge preached a good and useful sermon from Joel ii, 17: "Let the priests, the ministers of the Lord, weep between the porch and the altar," &c. Many people were present at our love feast, among whom were some strangers: but all were deeply serious, and the power of God was present indeed. Brother Owings preached a very alarming sermon, and brother Stephenson gave a moving exhortation. The whole ended in great peace. And we all went, in the strength of the Lord, to our several appointments.

Saturday, April 3. Preached at Baltimore, where we had a comfortable meeting.

Lord's day, 4. I delivered a funeral discourse, but was much shut up in my mind. Went thence to the Forest (Garrison) and preached at seven o'clock, with great comfort. Several rich people attended preaching the last three days, and did not seem displeased with the plain truths of the Gospel. One or two persons here seem to be groaning for full redemption. My heart is grieved that I have not been entirely devoted to God; but have great reason to be thankful that I feel more and more desire after God.

Thursday, 8. I left Baltimore. John King and three exhorters being present, we held a watch-night at Preston's, and the Lord was powerfully with us.

Friday, 9. Preached at Litten's with power. But found it a heavy cross while preaching at Mr. Giles's.

Lord's day, 11. Preached at Bohemia Manor; but the people there seemed to be but little affected. Rode thence to Solomon Hersey's, where many people attended, and I was enabled to speak with solemnity from Deut. xxx, 19: "I have set before you life and death," &c. Went thence to Newcastle (Delaware) but found them out of order. Then rode to Red Clay Creek,[31] where I preached with power.

Tuesday, 13. Many people came to hear the word at Mount Pleasant (Delaware).

---

[31] Asbury, en route to Philadelphia along the main road, stopped to preach at an undisclosed place near Red Clay Creek, a tributary of Christina River, which flows into the Delaware two miles from Wilmington. Mount Pleasant on the Philadelphia Pike, north of Wilmington, later became the site of Matson's Chapel. Since late December when stationed with Baltimore as his base, Asbury had gone the rounds of his two-hundred-mile circuit, covering some six Maryland counties with appointments increasing to thirty. (Weslager: *Delaware's Forgotten River, the Story of the Christina*, 3; Hallman, *op. cit.*, 116, 117.)

Pennsylvania—New Jersey

Wednesday, 14. Came very weary to Philadelphia; but the sight of my friends greatly revived me; and all seem to be in peace.

Thursday, 15. I preached for the first time, on this visit in Philadelphia, on Ruth ii, 4. Many people attended, and the Lord filled my heart with holy gladness. All things are in peace here.

From *Saturday,* 17, till *Thursday* the 22, was spent in the Jerseys; where I preached at different places, and often to large congregations. The Lord was frequently with me in mercy and power; and my heart was greatly enlarged. How I long to be more holy—to live more with God, and for God! Troubles encompass me about; but the Lord is my helper. Before my return to Philadelphia I had the pleasure of seeing the foundation laid of a new preaching house, 35 feet by 30.[32] Then I returned and preached on *Thursday* evening, the Lord being with me.

Friday, 23. This morning my mind was in a calm and even frame—sweetly fixed on God as its prime object. But I greatly long for more grace—to receive esteem or disesteem with equal cheerfulness—to be something or nothing, as God would have me to be. My heart was at liberty, while employed in speaking for God this evening.

Tuesday, 27. The Lord has graciously assisted me in preaching every day; and my desires to be entirely devoted do still increase. But alas! what cause have I to mourn the want of life and zeal, both in public and private duties! Nevertheless, it is my determination to offer all I have to God. May he give me more to offer, and graciously accept the offering made! Had much conversation with Abraham Whitworth,[33] but found him unwilling to spend all his time in travelling. However, he agreed to take a part with John King. So my intention is to send them to the upper part of the Jerseys, where they may labour alternately, a fortnight at a time.

[32] This was the first Methodist meetinghouse in New Jersey. It was located at the corner of Greene, now Broad, and Academy streets, Trenton. The deed to the ground provided that the preachers were "to preach in the said house on every weekday evening, every week, and every morning at five o'clock, and every Sabbath-day at such time as shall be thought proper." The first society at Trenton had nineteen members, among whom was John Fitch, who built and operated a steamboat at Trenton twenty years before Robert Fulton launched his "Clermont" and in whose memory a memorial boulder has been erected near the site of the wharf where he landed. (Woodward and Hageman: *History of Burlington County,* 727; *One Hundred Seventy-Fifth Anniversary Program and Church History, First Methodist Church of Trenton,* 1772–1947.)

[33] Abraham Whitworth was a successful preacher whose efforts led to the conversion of the noted evangelist Benjamin Abbott. In 1774 or 1775 he became a victim of intemperance and was expelled from the ministry. He was believed to have been killed in battle while fighting with the British during the Revolution. He joined the conference in 1774. (McLean, *op. cit.,* 31; Lee, *op. cit.,* 319; Lednum, *op. cit.,* 102, 128; Atkinson: *Methodism in New Jersey,* 90, 91; Ffirth: *The Experience and Gospel Labors of the Rev. Benjamin Abbott,* 25. See *Journal* entry for July 23, 1774.)

Thursday, 29. Mr. Shadford[34] is just come from England, with strange accounts of their Calvinistic disputes. My mind is rather low, but serene and spiritual, and determined to follow Christ. How greatly do I long to die to every object which does not lead me to God! Blessed Master, hasten the time when I shall love thee according to the full extent of that desire which thou hast given me.

Saturday, 31. This was a day of delightful rest to my soul. After preaching in the morning, I spent part of the day in visiting some souls in distress. In the evening I preached again on these words, "Cut it down, why cumbereth it the ground?" My mind was much enlarged, perhaps to the offence of some, while showing the particular marks of such as do but cumber the ground in the Lord's vineyard.

Lord's day, May 2. My soul was favoured, both yesterday and this morning, with delightful and intimate accesses to God. In preaching this morning from these words, "Try the spirits whether they be of God," I took occasion to show, 1st, That this is the duty of all that profess religion; and 2dly, That they should bring their experience and practice to the word of God, to know if they be genuine. After preaching to a large congregation in the evening, I met the society, and thought it necessary to deal closely with the members.

Thursday, 6. After spending a few days in a country tour, preaching to many people at Goshen, Marlborough,[35] and other places, with some assistance, I returned and preached in Philadelphia this evening, on the subject of the stony-ground hearers. Some perhaps were displeased with me. But I must declare the whole counsel of God, and leave the event to him. This day a letter from Mr. Wesley came to hand, dated March 2, in which he informs me, that the time of his coming over to America is not yet, being detained by the building of the new chapel.

Lord's day, 9. My heart was much affected last evening, while many of

[34] George Shadford (1739–1816) was a native of Lincolnshire, and after serving in the British army he was converted in 1762. He preached occasionally for two years on the Epworth Circuit, which included Wesley's old home, and then became a regular itinerant. In 1773 he came to America with Captain Webb and the third contingent of Wesley's missionaries. It was to him that Wesley wrote the famous admonition: "I let you loose, George, upon the great continent of America. Publish your message in the open face of the sun." Shadford was the chief instrument of the great revival which broke out in the Brunswick Circuit in Virginia in 1775. This work reached fourteen Virginia counties and crossed the Roanoke River into North Carolina. In 1777 the *Minutes* show that 1,993 members were added in Virginia. Shadford probably stood first in Asbury's affection, but he was a loyalist and could not take the oaths, so he returned to England with Rankin in 1778. (Sanford, *op. cit.*, 244–84; *The Virginia Magazine*, I (1818), 11, 52, 90, 136, 169; Jackson: *Lives of Early Methodist Preachers*, VI, 137–81. See *Journal* entries for June 3, 1773; July 14, 1773.)

[35] Goshen is in the present Chester County, Pennsylvania. The preaching place was known later as the Valley Meetinghouse and still later as Grove, the present appointment in the Philadelphia Conference. Marlborough is also in Chester County. (See Nolan: *History of Southeastern Pennsylvania*, 259.)

the people felt the power of God. And this day my soul was filled with sweet peace. I had also the pleasure of hearing Mr. Toy (?)[36] preach with great sensibility.

Monday, 10. Visiting several families to-day afforded me great comfort of mind; and in preaching this evening, with close application to those who pursue earthly more than heavenly pleasures, my soul was filled with peace.

Travelling through the Jerseys I met with William Budd,[37] a man who has a great regard for us, but seems to be too much taken up with worldly cares. But speaking faithfully and closely to him, I showed him the deceitfulness of riches, in producing a spirit of independence towards God, hardness of heart, and pride in its various forms, while they promise us safety and happiness.

Pennsylvania

Thursday, 13. Through much rain I returned, wet and weary, to Philadelphia, after having preached at several places in the Jerseys, and sometimes with much freedom and power. Many people attended this evening, while I described an honest and good heart, under the similitude of the good ground which received the seed and brought forth fruit. This was free from the hardness of the way-side, from the shallowness of the stony ground, and from the obstructions of the thorny ground. The honesty of the heart appears in its conduct towards God, towards all mankind, and towards itself. As our Lord is pleased to denominate such a heart *good* as well as honest, is it not very wrong for a Christian to say he has a *bad* heart? Is not all that the Holy Ghost produces *good*? And so far as that blessed Spirit has changed the heart of a believer, is it not *good*? Through the unmerited grace of God, I have no desire to seek anything but Him, and that which may lead me to him.

Lord's day, 16. In preaching this morning from Gen. xviii, 19, I strongly enforced the great necessity of relative duties; and very pointedly pressed the same in meeting the society at night.

Monday, 17. All this day I was very unwell with a sore throat and violent pain in my head; but John King providentially came in and supplied my place. My indisposition continued also on *Tuesday*, so that I had but little power to read or think; but on *Wednesday*, I found myself, through mercy, much better. Although my body is weak, my soul is strong in the grace of God. May my heart, my lips, my hands, my life, my strength, my all, be constantly devoted to God!

---

[36] This may have been Joseph Toy. (See *Methodist Magazine*, 1836, 438.)

[37] William Budd lived at New Mills, the present Pemberton in Burlington County, New Jersey. (Lednum, *op. cit.*, 235; see note under May 4, 1776.)

Monday, 24. Sweet peace pervaded my soul; and my whole heart desired, prayed, longed, and panted to live a more spiritual life by faith in the blessed Son of God. In the evening I preached from Isa. lxii, 6: "I have set watchmen," &c.; and took occasion, First, to show that the Lord calls, authorizes, and qualifies all faithful ministers. Secondly, delineated their character as *watchmen*. Thirdly, observed that they were to keep watch on the *walls*. Fourthly, the duties enjoined, "they shall not hold their peace. Keep not silence." While opening this passage the Lord greatly comforted my soul. The next morning I expatiated on Canticles i, 7; and considered, First, the address, "Tell me, O thou whom my soul loveth." Secondly, the request, "where thou feedest," &c. This denotes the sincere desire of a true believer, in the time of division or persecution, or general declension of true piety. Thirdly, the humble query, "Why should I be as one that turneth aside by the flocks of thy companions?" This indicates a fear of being exposed to *false teachers*, who name the name of Christ, but deny him in experience, doctrine, and practice. How fearful is a pious soul of turning aside as a forlorn, neglected creature, exposed to the malice and designs of devils and ungodly men. Glory to God! Notwithstanding all the assaults of Satan, my soul is preserved in peace, and my heart is fixed, trusting in the Lord. My chief desire is to be found obedient and faithful at all times, and all occasions.

Thursday, 27. My text was Isaiah xxxiii, 16: "He shall dwell on high. His place of defence shall be the munition of rocks," &c. First, I inquired to whom this promise is made. Secondly, How "he shall dwell on high." High in faith, love, and church-privileges—above the power of Satan, the world, and all dangers; so that none of them shall injure his soul. Thirdly, "His defence shall be the munition of rocks,"—Christ shall be the rock of his defence—and the love, truth, faithfulness, mercy, and power of God shall enclose him on every side. Fourthly, "His bread shall be given him"— all things needful for life and godliness.

Friday, 28. It was a gracious season at intercession to-day. My soul was favoured with love and power.

Monday, 31. I went to Germantown,[38] and preached with freedom and comfort to a large congregation assembled in the Dutch Presbyterian Church.[39] I take God for my sufficient portion; and Christ is all in all to me.

[38] Germantown, a suburb of Philadelphia and now incorporated in the city, was noted as the starting place of several churches in the country. Henry Boehm said that "in 1802-3 the Methodists had scarcely a foot-hold in Germantown. There was a small class but the members were poor and of but little influence. They had preached in the school house but were now excluded from it." On February 9, 1803, Boehm started a subscription which resulted in the Haines Street Church and later First Church there. (See entries and notes under August 5, 1796; July 15, 1797; June 10, 1798; August 1, 1805; May 1, 1811; and so on.)

[39] This is the present Market Square Presbyterian Church in Germantown.

Tuesday, June 1. This day my soul was under gracious exercises; and went out in ardent desires after God. He has engrossed all my affections; and my heart is taken up with him.

Thursday, 3. To my great comfort arrived Mr. Rankin,[40] Mr. Shadford, Mr. Yearby,[41] and Capt. Webb. Mr. Rankin preached a good sermon on these words, "I have set before thee an open door, and no man can shut it." He will not be admired as a preacher. But as a disciplinarian, he will fill his place.

New Jersey

Lord's day, 6. After preaching both yesterday and this morning at Burlington, I went to Church in order to receive the sacrament. But the parson gave us a strange discourse, full of inconsistency and raillery. Leaving him to answer for his own conduct, I took no further notice of it, but preached at night from these words, "The natural man receiveth not the things of the Spirit of God," &c.; and showed, First, what the things of the Spirit of God are. Secondly, described the natural man. And, Thirdly, showed how they appear to be foolishness to him; and that he cannot know them, by the strength of his natural or acquired abilities. The little society in Burlington appears to be in a comfortable and prosperous state. On my way to Trenton, I met Abraham Whitworth on the road. We stopped at a house, and in the course of conversation I found he was much dejected in his mind; but before we parted he appeared to be somewhat comforted. Many people attended the preaching at Trenton, though the notice was but short.

Thursday, 10. My soul has been much assaulted lately by Satan; but by the grace of God it is filled with Divine peace. My heart thirsteth for God, even for the living God. I wrote to Mr. Wesley to-day, and in the evening addressed my discourse chiefly to the young people. May the Lord apply it to their hearts!

Friday, 11. Mr. Rankin came to Trenton. After dinner and prayer, we set off together for Princeton.

[40] Thomas Rankin (1736–1810) was born in Dunbar, Scotland. After eleven years as an itinerant he was appointed by Wesley in 1772 "to act as assistant" in America. The relationship between him and Asbury was one of strained compatibility. He returned to England in 1778, and resumed his association with Wesley, at whose death he was present. (Jackson: *The Lives of Early Methodist Preachers; Autobiography and Journal of Rankin*; Sanford: *Memoirs of Mr. Wesley's Missionaries in America,* 172–243.)

[41] Joseph Yearby, an English local preacher, also came with Captain Webb and his party. He was now stationed under Asbury on the Baltimore Circuit, and in 1774 he traveled the Chester Circuit. His name "unaccountably disappeared" from the *General Minutes* of 1775. (Lednum, *op. cit.,* 115, 116.)

New York

On Saturday we reached New York; and our friends there having previous notice of our coming, kindly met us on the dock where we landed. The sight of Mr. Richard Wright,[42] with some other concurring circumstances, affected Mr. Rankin so that he appeared to be rather cast down in his mind.

Lord's day, 13. I preached this morning to a considerable number of people. Mr. Rankin found his spirits raised, and was much comforted.[43] In the afternoon Mr. Rankin, Capt. Webb, Mr. Wright, and myself went to St. Paul's church, and received the sacrament.[44] At night, Mr. Rankin dispensed the word of truth with power. It reached the hearts of many, and they appeared to be much quickened.

Monday, 14. Many were present while I preached from 2 John 4: "I have no greater joy than to hear that my children walk in truth." The Lord favours me with great discoveries of my defects and unfaithfulness. But, blessed be God, my soul is humbled under these discoveries. My soul panteth for more of the Divine nature. When shall I be fully conformed to his blessed will? I received a letter this day from that venerable father in Christ, Mr. Wesley.[45]

Wednesday, 16. Captain Webb set out for Albany, and I for New Rochelle. On *Thursday*, Mr. Lewis[46] preached at Mr. Deveau's,[47] on these words, "To them that have obtained like precious faith with us." He spoke plainly and much to the purpose; though he did not show the necessity of assurance. We had some free and friendly conversation afterward; in which I gave him to understand how we hold this point: that assurance is suspended on an evangelical act of faith, by which we apply

---

[42] Richard Wright had succeeded Boardman in the leadership of the New York society. The reason for Rankin's disturbance on seeing him is not clear. Rankin sent Wright back to England after the conference in Philadelphia in 1774. (See *Journal* entry for May 25, 1774.)

[43] Rankin had been disturbed by a doubt of his widom in coming to America. (Stevens: *History of the Methodist Episcopal Church*, I, 158; Seaman, *op. cit.*, 64.)

[44] The ministers and members of the Methodist society were communicants of Trinity Parish, which included Trinity and St. Paul's churches. The original St. Paul's Church, built in 1766, still stands on Broadway at Fulton Street, and is the oldest church structure in New York. Washington attended services there.

[45] This letter from Wesley does not appear in Telford's standard edition of *The Letters of John Wesley*.

[46] Mr. Lewis was the Rev. Ichabod Lewis, a Presbyterian minister residing at White Plains, about ten miles northwest of New Rochelle.

[47] Ichabod Lewis occasionally preached at the home of Frederick Deveau. Williams and Pilmoor met him there in the spring of 1771 when Mrs. Deveau recognized Pilmoor as the man she had seen in the delirium of an illness and who rescued her from a swamp. She insisted that Pilmoor be allowed to preach, although Lewis objected because Pilmoor was not ordained. Mrs. Deveau was converted on that occasion. (Lednum, *op. cit.*, 70. See note under January 14, 1772.)

the merits of Jesus Christ for the removal of our guilt; and that we then receive the testimony of the Spirit. (Rom. viii, 16.)

Lord's day, 20. Satan, that malicious enemy of mankind, is frequently striving to break my peace. And the Lord graciously shows me all my involuntary defects; so that my soul is bowed down as in the dust; but Christ is precious, and the Spirit of all grace comforts my heart. This day I preached three times at Mr. Deveau's. The word reached the hearts of many, with Divine power. Our labours here have not been in vain. Many have a relish for religious exercises, and experience the spiritual benefit of frequently meeting together in the name of the Lord. My intention is to form a society here.[48]

Monday, 21. While preaching at Mr. Bonnette's, the Lord favoured me with sweet liberty; and there was no small moving amongst the people. Several seemed willing to meet in society here also.

Tuesday, 22. I received an account of the case of Sarah Deveau.[49] She is about sixteen years of age, and has been lately brought under serious and deep concern for the salvation of her soul. A few days after, she was taken ill, and was frequently troubled with fits; which, while they were on her, deprived her of her reason. About three days after she was taken ill, she was justified by faith, and had peace with God. She continued weakly in body about five weeks; but fasted, prayed, and sang, to the astonishment of all about her. After her recovery, she manifested a sound conversion—she had a settled peace, was conscientiously serious, meek, and patient in all her conduct; and the word of God was precious food to her soul.

Wednesday, 23. After preaching with some power on these words, "Blessed are they that hear the word of God, and keep it," I joined a few in society, and then set off for New York. I called on Mr. Bartow in my way, who renewed his former kindness, and treated me with great cordiality. On my return to New York, I found Mr. Rankin had been well employed in settling matters pertaining to the society.[50] This afforded me great satisfaction, and more especially the revival of religion, which has lately taken place in this city.

[48] Williams, Boardman, Pilmoor, and Wright had preached frequently in the New Rochelle area, and Asbury had established a circuit centering at the homes of Frederick Deveau and Peter Bonnette, but no organized society had been formed. Asbury completed the organization on the following Wednesday.

[49] Sarah Deveau (1757–1802) was the daughter of Mr. and Mrs. Frederick Deveau. She became the wife of the Rev. Sylvester Hutchinson, a Methodist itinerant. She died in May, 1802, at the home of her sister, Hester, wife of the Rev. John Wilson, pastor of the Forsyth Street Church in New York. Asbury conducted her funeral. (See *Journal* entry for May 30, 1802.)

[50] Rankin insisted on discipline within the societies, as did Asbury. This displeased Asbury's opponents in New York, who at one time threatened to exclude him from the chapel. (See *Journal* entry for July 16, 1773.)

Saturday, 26. Having preached a few times in New York, since my return, I set off for Staten Island; but the heat was so extremely powerful, that I stopped at my old friend Justice Wright's, and on the *Lord's day* heard Mr. Peabody,[51] a Presbyterian minister, preach twice; but thought he was too metaphysical and superficial. In the evening I preached in Mr. Wright's yard, from Heb. v, 12: "Ye have need that one teach you again which be the first principles of the oracles of God." My mind is filled with the peace of God, and is drawn out in love to Him and all mankind. Blessed be the Lord!

Monday, 28. While preaching to-day on Isaiah lxii, 6, Mr. Peabody, the minister, made one of the congregation. After service we had some conversation on religious subjects. He had imbibed that absurd scheme of Mr. B.'s; namely, that we are born again before we repent and believe. How strange, that any man should suppose the effect is produced before the instrumental causes exist! But, by the grace of God, none of these things shall move me from the gospel plan of salvation. Glory to God! He blesses me with the graces and comforts of his Holy Spirit in my own soul! The next day Mr. Peabody attended preaching again. I had lent him Mr. Fletcher's Second Check.[52] He approved of the latter part, though not of the first. May the truth of God spread here and in every place! Had some serious conversation with Mr. Israel Disoway and his wife. They both seem to have desires to be instructed in the ways of God. But the people in these parts appear in general to be ignorant of their own hearts; and are in danger of resting in the superficial knowledge of religion, without the power.

Wednesday, 30. Preached at the house of Abraham Woglom to more people than were expected, and my soul had near and sweet access to God, being filled with that peace which passeth all understanding.

Thursday, July 1. Set off for New York, and having a tedious passage over the North River,[53] I spent some time in serious conversation with two men in the boat, and hope it was not in vain. Then I came safe to New York, and preached from Habakkuk iii, 2: "O Lord, revive thy work in the midst of the years!" On *Friday* arrived the sorrowful news of the destruction of Mr. Whitefield's Orphan-house.[54] As there was no fire in the house, it was supposed to have been set on fire by lightning, which had been

---

[51] Asbury mentions Mr. Peabody again on August 14–15, 1774. (See *Journal* entry for that date.)

[52] The reference is to John Fletcher's famous *Checks to Antinomianism*, which was in several parts.

[53] Asbury perhaps followed a different route, crossing the river at the Blazing Star Ferry and proceeding northward by road to Paulus Hook, the present Jersey City. This involved a roundabout trip for which no reason is given.

[54] George Whitefield established his orphanage at Savannah, Georgia, in 1749. Asbury visited the ruins on January 29, 1793. It was later rebuilt, and its successor is still in operation.

in the morning, as some say, accompanied with a sulphureous smell. It broke out in a rapid flame about seven or eight o'clock at night, and consumed the whole building, except the two wings.

Lord's day, 4. Many people attended preaching both morning and night. In our love feast to-day, many were touched to the heart, and some were greatly comforted. Lord, let it not be as the morning dew! On *Monday*, my soul was in a delightful frame—my peace flowed as a river. I had power to resist every temptation of Satan before it could disturb my mind—and my heart was sweetly drawn out in love to all men.

Tuesday, 6. Having reason to fear that I had been rather too much elevated, my heart was humbled before the Lord; and was now fixed on him as its all-sufficient good. When shall I appear before Him!

Wednesday, 7. My soul is happy under a comfortable sense of God. May his grace always enable me to devote myself without reserve to him! The power of God was present while I preached to-day, behind the barracks[55] to a number of soldiers and others. Afterward I met a class, and preached again in the evening. But my spirit has been grieved by the false and deceitful doings of some particular persons.[56] Blessed be God! all are not so; some are faithful. But what is the chaff to the wheat? One undertook to reprove me, because I went in at a quarter after eight, and came out at twenty minutes after nine. What reason have I to be thankful, that this is the worst man can reprove me for! O that I had more zeal to preach the word in season and out of season!

Friday, 9. After intercession I went to see Mr. Lupton. Mr. Sause, Mr. White,[57] and myself, were charged with winking at the follies of some. We had a little debate on the subject; and Mr. Lupton was pleased to say, "He did not know but the church door would be shut against me;"[58] and that "some persons would not suffer matters to go on so." He moreover told me, "the preachers' gifts were taken away." How dangerous it is to be addicted to pride and passion, going from house to house, speaking perverse things!

Saturday, 10. After preaching this evening I enjoyed a comfortable time in meeting the leaders and band-society. My heart was blessed with a lively sense of God's gracious presence.

[55] The barracks were located on Barracks Street, between the present City Hall and Foley Square, in New York. The Methodists had contact with the soldiers from the beginning, and certain men of the Sixteenth Regiment attended the first service held by Philip Embury in 1766. (Seaman, *op. cit.*, 22.) *Journal* entries in July, 1774, indicate Asbury's contacts with men of the Twenty-third Regiment, then stationed in New York.

[56] These persons were perhaps William Lupton, Henry Newton, and others who opposed Asbury because of his insistence on discipline within the society.

[57] Richard Sause and Charles White. Lupton and Newton opposed Asbury, while Sause and White were friendly to him. After Boardman and Pilmoor returned to England in 1774, a reconciliation seems to have taken place. (See note under June 11, 1774.)

[58] A similar threat was made against Rankin. (See *Journal* entry for July 16, 1773.)

On the *Lord's day* I preached twice with great plainness to a large number of people; and then set off, in company with Mr. James Jarvis,[59] towards Philadelphia. Came safe to the city on Thursday, but did not find such perfect harmony as I could wish for.

Pennsylvania—Delaware

Wednesday, 14. Our general conference began:[60] in which the following propositions were agreed to:—

1. The old Methodist doctrine and discipline shall be enforced and maintained amongst all our societies in America.

2. Any preacher who acts otherwise, cannot be retained amongst us as a fellow-labourer in the vineyard.

3. No preacher in our connexion shall be permitted to administer the ordinances at this time; except Mr. Strawbridge, and he under the particular direction of the assistant.

4. No person shall be admitted, more than once or twice, to our love feasts or society meetings, without becoming a member.

5. No preacher shall be permitted to reprint our books, without the approbation of Mr. Wesley, and the consent of his brethren. And that Robert Williams shall be allowed to sell what he has, but reprint no more.

6. Every assistant is to send an account of the work of God in his circuit, to the general assistant.

There were some debates amongst the preachers in this conference, relative to the conduct of some who had manifested a desire to abide in the cities, and live like gentlemen. Three years out of four have been already spent in the cities. It was also found that money had been wasted, improper leaders appointed, and many of our rules broken.

[59] James Jarvis (1732–74), hatter and general merchant, was an early leader in the New York society and a contributor to the Wesley Chapel building fund. He frequently accompanied the preachers, and Pilmoor in his *Journal* mentions Jarvis several times as a traveling companion. Jarvis and John Southwell became trustees in 1770 when Philip Embury and Paul Heck left New York. He was the leader of an important class and succeeded Lupton as treasurer, continuing in that office until his death on November 4, 1774, when Sause and White became cotreasurers. (See *Journal* entries for November 3–7, 1774; *John Street Church Records*, numerous references; Wakeley, *op. cit.*, 79–80; Seaman, *op. cit.*, 69, 420, 425.)

[60] This was the first conference ever held in America. Asbury was one day late in arriving at St. George's Church, Philadelphia, the seat of the conference. Others present were Rankin, Shadford, Pilmoor, Webb, Boardman, Wright, King, Whitworth, and Yearby. Of these by 1778 death, apostasy, or the approaching Revolutionary War left only Asbury in the American itinerancy. The six proposals agreed to at the conference showed the disciplinary influence of Rankin, which pleased Asbury. Of the three members who recorded their impressions, Pilmoor and Asbury indicate lack of harmony; and concerning this Rankin is silent, adding, "We parted in love." (See their *Journals* for July 14–16 hitherto cited.)

Friday, 16. I set off for Chester,[61] and had a comfortable time in preaching. Mrs. Withey and two young women in her house, appeared to be under some religious concern. May the Lord make bare his holy arm, and revive his glorious work! I understand that some dissatisfied persons in New York, threaten to shut the church door against Mr. Rankin. If they should be bold enough to take this step, we shall see what the consequence will be; and no doubt but the Lord will bring all their evil deeds to light. O that it may be for the salvation of their precious souls!

Lord's day, 18. My soul has enjoyed great peace this week, in which I have rode near one hundred miles since my departure from Philadelphia, and have preached often, and sometimes great solemnity has rested on the congregations.

On *Monday*, brother Yearbry rode in company with me to Mr. Stedham's, where I preached with sweet freedom to a few attentive people. We took friendly counsel together, and our time was profitably and comfortably spent. On *Tuesday* morning my heart was still with the Lord, and my peace flowed as a river. Glory be given to God! On *Wednesday*, at Newcastle, the company was but small, though great power attended the word. Perhaps the Lord will yet visit this people, though at present too many of them appear to be devoted to pride, vanity, and folly. But, through abundant mercy, my heart is devoted to God and to his work. O that it may never depart from him!

I received a letter from my dear brother Wesley, written in Ireland, with his usual plainness and honesty of heart.

Maryland

Thursday, I came to Robert Thompson's, when the Lord enabled me to press home the word on the consciences of the people, many of whom had never heard us before. Set off the next day for Susquehanna and met with Isaac Rollins, who gave me an account of a considerable prospect of the work of God in Kent. In the evening we came, very wet and weary, to Josias Dallam's. We were kindly entertained, and soon forgot our fatigue and pains.

Lord's day, 25. I first preached in this neighbourhood, and then rode hard to reach Deer Creek in time. Was very unwell with a violent headache, but after preaching to many people, and meeting a large class, I felt myself much recovered. Thus the Lord graciously helpeth me! My soul is filled with peace, and drawn out in love to God and man.

[61] Asbury was appointed to the Baltimore Circuit with Robert Strawbridge, Abraham Whitworth, and Joseph Yearbry as colaborers. Appointed by Wesley October 10, 1772 to "act as assistant," Asbury had now been superseded by Rankin. Maryland had 500 members of the total 1,160 in the American societies. (See *Minutes*.)

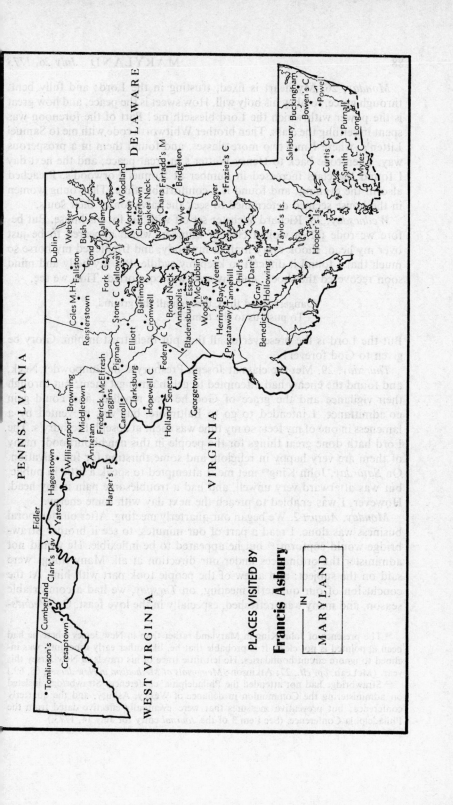

Monday, 26. My heart is fixed, trusting in the Lord; and fully bent, through grace, to obey his holy will. How sweet is the peace, and how great is the power with which the Lord blesseth me! Part of the forenoon was spent in settling the class. Then brother Whitworth rode with me to Samuel Litten's, where I met two more classes, and found them in a prosperous way. Then rode back to Henry Watter's in great peace; and the next day I found the class increased in number at Samuel Forwood's. Preached also in the evening; and found it a comfortable time. The young women in the house seemed determined to seek the salvation of their souls.

Wednesday, 28. Richard Webster set off with me for his house. But before we rode far, a violent clap of thunder, which appeared to be just over my head, shook every limb in my body, and frightened my horse so much that I found it difficult to keep my saddle. But my body and mind soon recovered the shock, and my soul was comforted. Thus we see,

> "Dangers stand thick through all the ground,
> To push us to the tomb."

But the Lord is the preserver of all that put their trust in him. Glory be given to God forever!

Thursday, 29. Met the class at Joseph Presbury's, in Gunpowder Neck, and found the enemy had attempted to get in amongst them; but through their vigilance and the grace of God he was repelled, and could gain no admittance. I intended to go to Baltimore, but was prevented by a lameness in one of my feet; so my time was spent at Joseph Presbury's. The Lord hath done great things for the people in this neighbourhood; many of them are very happy in religion, and some thirsting for full salvation. On *Saturday,* John King[62] met me. I attempted to speak a little in public, but was afterward very unwell, and had a troublesome pain in my head. However, I was enabled to preach the next day with some energy.

Monday, August 2. We began our quarterly meeting. After our temporal business was done, I read a part of our minutes, to see if brother Strawbridge would conform;[63] but he appeared to be inflexible. He would not administer the ordinances under our direction at all. Many things were said on the subject; and a few of the people took part with him. At the conclusion of our quarterly meeting, on *Tuesday,* we had a comfortable season, and many were refreshed, especially in the love feast. On *Wednes-*

[62] The presence of John King in Maryland rather than in New Jersey where he had been appointed is not clear. It is probable that he, like other early itinerants, was inclined to ignore circuit boundaries. He left little trace of his travels in New Jersey this year. (McLean, *op. cit.,* 27; Atkinson: *Memorials of Methodism in New Jersey,* 68, 69.)

[63] Strawbridge had not attended the Philadelphia conference. Strawbridge insisted on administering the Communion in defiance of Wesley, Asbury, and the quarterly conference; but preventive measures that were eventually effective dated from the Philadelphia Conference. (See item 3 of the *Journal* entry for July 14, 1773.)

day, I set out for Baltimore, but was taken very sick on the road; however, I pursued my way, though it was sometimes through hard rain and heavy thunder; and preached in Baltimore on *Thursday*, in Mrs. Triplett's new house,[64] which she freely lent for that purpose. There appeared to be a considerable moving under the word. After preaching the next morning at the Point, I went to see a woman, once happy in several respects, but now under distressing circumstances. Her husband was driven from her; and she was left with four children for three months.

Many people in general attend the preaching in Baltimore, especially after we have been long enough in town for the inhabitants to receive full knowledge of our being there. And I have a great hope that the Lord will do something for the souls in this place, though the little society has been rather neglected, for want of proper persons to lead them. I rode to Patapsco Neck, and after preaching, reduced the class to some order. Nathan Perigau told me, he had been grieved by some who had manifested too great a forwardness to speak in public. I then returned to Baltimore, and went thence to Backriver Neck, where I found contention in the class; but, through grace, was enabled to bring them to peace and order. Then I went to Charles Harriman's, and settled two classes in that neighbourhood. While preaching there, the Lord favoured us with a lively and profitable season. My mind has lately been much tortured with temptations; but the Lord has stood by and delivered me. O, my God! when will my trials end? At death. Lord, be ever with me and save me, or my soul must perish at last. But my trust is still in God, that he will ever help me to conquer all my foes.

Preached, and met the society, on *Wednesday*, at Joseph Presbury's, and on *Thursday*, set off for Kent county, but was troubled with a very uncommon pain in my head. In public worship, at Mr. Gibbs's, a serious Negro was powerfully struck; and though he made but little noise, yet he trembled so exceedingly that the very house shook. I then rode to Mr. Hinson's,[65] and was kindly entertained. Here we saw a little woman with

---

[64] Proper names were variously spelled. Mrs. Tribolett, Tribulet, and now changed by historians to Triplett, was a widow whose new three-story brick house stood on the corner of Baltimore Street and Triplett Alley. A daughter, Caroline Tribolett, married John Conrad Zollickoffer, who served as an American officer in the Revolutionary War and became a Baltimore merchant. Their son, Daniel Zollickoffer (1790–1862), and grandson of Mrs. Tribolett, was one of the founders of the Methodist Protestant Church. (Colhouer: *Sketches of the Founders of the Methodist Protestant Church*, 253–60; Smith: *Life and Labors of Francis Asbury*, 18, 29, 30.)

[65] Carvill Hinson (Hynson) lived near Rock Hall, Kent County, Maryland. The Hinson Chapel, also known as the Kent Meeting House, was between Rock Hall and Chestertown. In this area Robert Strawbridge preached the first Methodist sermon on the eastern shore of Maryland at John Randall's near Worton, in 1769. The first society was organized near Hinson's Chapel early in 1773, and the meeting house was completed the following year. It was the first Methodist chapel in the bounds of the present Peninsula Conference. (Hallman, *op. cit.*, 113, 115, 313, 316; Lee, *op. cit.*, 50.)

neither hands nor feet; yet she could walk, card, spin, sew, and knit. And her heart rejoiced in God her Saviour. But what is she at this time?

Friday, 13. The spirit of holy peace reigns in my heart. Glory be given to God! I received information to-day of W. F., who had threatened to stone one of our preachers, but was taken sick and died in a few days. Also of another person who had been under conviction for sin, but resisting and shaking it off, he left the house, and died in the dark, speaking evil of the ways of God. Likewise of Mrs. H., who was under conviction from the Spirit of God, but going from the house and indulging a trifling spirit, she soon after died. Thus it seems, when men slight the mercies of God, he visits them with his judgments! The congregation to-day at Mr. Gibbs's was very large, but they looked like fat bulls of Bashan, though they sat pretty still while I endeavoured to prove that the spirit, doctrine, sufferings, and practice of the holy apostles are exemplified in the people of God at this time. The Lord favoured me with freedom and power, as also in the evening at Mr. Hinson's.

On *Saturday*, a multitude of people attended the preaching of the word, and the Lord was with us of a truth.

Lord's day, 15. For some time past, the Lord has blessed me with abundant peace and love; but my soul longs for all the fulness of God, as far as it is attainable by man. O, when shall it once be? When shall my soul be absorbed in purity and love? The congregation assembled under a tree, at Mr. Gibbs's, and in the time of the first prayer, a woman fell down and lay there all the time of the sermon. The people here appear to be much affected with prejudice against Isaac Rollins; they will not bear with his rough address. But I know not what to do with them. If some other preacher could visit them in his stead, perhaps the work of God would prosper much better. But most of the society appears to be under a genuine work of grace; though a few of their cases are doubtful. The clerk of the church desired to be present in the class meeting; and was considerably affected.

Tuesday, 17. After preaching to a number of people at Mr. Hinson's, I was much delighted with the simple account of the work of God related and experienced by T. L., who I believe is saved from indwelling sin. He was born at Thornsbury, near Bristol in England; and came over to America about nineteen or twenty years ago. He was first brought to God in Gunpowder Neck; and was soon after in great distress for purity of heart. He said, he prayed and wept till his tears lay in small lakes on the floor; but was at last suddenly filled with spiritual glory. He was blessed with wonderful communications of peace and love. He appeared to be a holy, serious, happy man, and artless without colouring; so that there is no room to doubt but it is a genuine work of God.

Wednesday, 18. Several friends, both men and women, accompanied me to the bay (Chesapeake); and when we came to the water side, we kneeled down and prayed, recommending each other to the grace of God.

Thursday, 19. I felt myself unwell, but my heart longs to overflow with love to God. My resolution is, through grace, to make a total and perpetual surrender of myself to him, and his service. At Daniel Ruff's, on Friday, many people attended to hear the word, which was dispensed with some power; but my soul longs and pants for more of God. My heart rejoices in God, but I am troubled with too much freedom of temper, which may proceed from a great flow of animal spirits; but it has the appearance of levity. I long to be so guarded as to have a solemn, constant sense of the omnipresent God resting on my mind. *Saturday*, 21. Francis Hollingsworth[66] invited me home with him; and I called to see Richard Dallam, but found him too wise for me to do him much good. Rode to Henry Watter's, and preached with life and power from the first Psalm; and afterward met the class. Preached on the *Lord's day* at Henry Watter's in the morning at five, at Samuel Litten's at ten, and at Samuel Forwood's in the evening. My soul has been kept in tranquillity and peace.

Tuesday, 24. My heart swells with strong desire to live to God; and to trust constantly in him, that he may direct my paths. I. I., an honest old Friend, came to hear me. O that names and parties were done away! that Christians were all but one body! that pure love might reign alone in every heart! Lord, hasten the happy and desirable period.

Wednesday, 25. My body was very weak, but my soul was strengthened and blest with a delightful sense of God, while preaching to a large congregation at Mr. Bond's; and I afterward met the class. God is the portion of my soul; and to do his will is my constant desire and determination. I spoke with two exhorters at Mr. Cromwell's,[67] and gave them license to act in that character. *Friday*, 27. At Mr. Cromwell's we had a

---

[66] This was doubtless the transcriber of Asbury's *Journal* who wrote the "Notice of the Transcriber" signed "F. Hollingsworth, March 28, 1821." The Hollingsworth family came from near Elkton, Maryland, to Fell's Point about 1769. There Jesse Hollingsworth (1732–1810) built one of the docks and was a leader in erecting the Strawberry Alley Church. His daughter, Ann, became the wife of Henry Willis, whose services for thirty years were among the most extensive and distinguished in American Methodism. His youngest son, Francis Hollingsworth (1773–1826), mentioned above, married Mary Yellott, daughter of John Yellott. (Griffith, *op. cit.*, 55; Armstrong, *op. cit.*, 19, 20; *Journal* entry for June 29, 1815; Roberts: *The Centenary Pictorial Album*, 54–56; Hollingsworth: *The Hollingsworth Family*, 16.)

[67] The Cromwell family resided in Green Spring Valley, a locality also associated with the Owings, Merrymans, Moales, and other early Baltimore County Methodist families. Joseph and James O. Cromwell, brothers, became itinerant preachers; the latter accompanied Freeborn Garrettson to Novia Scotia and served as a presiding elder in New Jersey. Joseph located in 1793, and later while ill at the home of Josias Dallam he was persuaded to take brandy as medicine, against his own judgment. His former appetite for drink was revived, and he relapsed into intemperance and so died. John Jacob preached his funeral sermon. (Ridgly: *The Old Brick Churches of Maryland*, 101; Atkinson: *Memorials of Methodism in New Jersey*, 216–20; Payton: *Our Fathers Have Told Us*, 53, 54 n.; see *Journal* entry for August 25, 1804.)

comfortable time; and the work of God seems to be reviving there. Satan is still haunting my mind, but the Lord gives me power to resist him, and keeps me in constant peace. On *Saturday*, all my soul was love; no desire for anything but God had place in my heart. Keep me, O Lord, in this delightful, blessed frame. This day I met with Philip Ebert,[68] who has set out to preach, but I am doubtful of his call. Daniel Ruff, who lodged with me to-night, is under great exercises of mind from a conviction that it is his duty to preach. He ventured to open his mind to me on the subject, after he was in bed; and so exceedingly was he agitated, that the bed shook under him, while he was relating the exercises of his mind.

Lord's day. After preaching at Mr. Joshua Owing's in the morning, and at Mr. Daniel Evans's in the afternoon, I rode thence to town under heavy exercises of mind. Surely there will be good done here, or the place must be given up.

On *Monday*, I spent part of my time in reading Poole's account of the downfall of Antichrist.[69] Lord, hasten the time. While preaching this evening in town, there was a gracious moving amongst the people.

On *Tuesday* I rode to Mr. Dallam's, where a few attended, and I trust not in vain; then returned to town groaning in spirit. I was in company with Brother Whitworth, and Brother Strawbridge, on *Wednesday*, but was much distressed on account of so few preachers well qualified for the work, and so many who are forward to preach without due qualifications. My foolish mind felt rather disposed to murmuring, pride, and discontent. Lord, pardon me, and grant me more grace! The next day my conscience checked me for the appearance of levity. How seriously should we consider the presence of the Deity; and ever remember that we must render an account of all our conduct!

Friday, September 3. After enjoying a comfortable season with a few friends, at Mr. Hunt's,[70] about twelve miles from Baltimore, I preached at four o'clock at Mr. Joseph Armstrong's, in Middle River Neck, where there is a good prospect, and lodged with Matthew Alexander (?), whose heart the Lord hath touched; and on Saturday returned to town.

[68] Asbury's misgivings about Philip Ebert were confirmed. Having been admitted on trial in 1774, he was dismissed from his circuit after a year because he accepted the heretical doctrines of Abraham Whitworth. (Hurst, *op. cit.*, I, 130, 131; Atkinson, *op. cit.*, 90; Sweet: *Religion on the American Frontier*, IV, 128–30, contains a pathetic letter by Ebert.)

[69] *The Catalogue of the British Museum* lists twenty-seven published works by Matthew Poole (1624–79), an English Presbyterian. While none of the titles is identical with that suggested in the *Journal*, it is probable that Asbury was reading a work by this author. (See *Dictionary of National Biography*, XVI, 99, 100.)

[70] The home of Phineas Hunt and his wife, Susan, located twelve miles from Baltimore, was a preaching place until about 1780 when Hunt's Chapel was built. For sixty years prior to the death of Hunt in 1837 their home was a stopping place for Methodist preachers. (Lednum, *op. cit.*, 117; Armstrong, *op. cit.*, 155; Smith: *Recollections and Reflections of an Old Itinerant*, 208.)

Lord's day, 5. In the morning I preached at town, and then at the Point, where the people seem more attentive; and afterward returned to town, and preached at night to a large congregation. It is a matter of great grief to me, to see the inhabitants of this town so much devoted to pride, spiritual idolatry, and almost every species of sin. Lord, visit them yet in tender mercy, to reform and save their souls. On *Monday* I went to visit William Lynch, in Patapsco Neck. How is the scene changed there! He is no more ashamed of the truth as it is in Jesus. His wife has lately experienced great agonies of soul; and was, in a wonderful manner, delivered, being filled with the peace and love of God. This, by the mercy of God, has produced a gracious effect on his heart. The next day he accompanied me to George Prestbury's, and thence to Gunpowder Neck, where we had a comfortable time. Hitherto the Lord hath helped!

Wednesday, 8. I crossed Bush River, and then rode to Josias Dallam's: my heart was filled with peace and power; but what sore conflicts have attended me! I am weary of all that is wrong within me. Lord, purify my heart, make me wholly thine, and fill me with all the fulness of thy love! The next day I visited F—— H——, who treated me kindly. We entered into a close conversation on religious subjects; but I found he had been reading Mr. M——'s mystery of errors more than the Gospel. He has some good qualities. But how weighty is his charge; he has a family of not less than eighty souls under his care! They were collected in the evening to join in prayer, and receive a word of exhortation. I rode to Deer Creek on Friday, and had a refreshing season, as also at Henry Watters's in the evening at four o'clock. The Lord is still my friend, and fills me with peace and pure desire.

Monday, 13. Found it necessary on a particular occasion to go to Pipe Creek; and while preaching to a large number of people at Richard Owings's, the power of the Lord was present. My mind has been much stayed on God for some time past, and my body has felt but little weariness, though on some days I have preached four times. Came to William Lynch's, and found Mr. Lynch in spiritual trouble; but I hope the Lord will soon deliver him, and give him the "oil of joy for mourning." Glory to God! my mind is kept in sweet peace, and deeply engaged in every duty. Preached on *Thursday* at Mr. Lynch's, and there appeared to be some small awakenings amongst the people. Thence rode to Nathan Perigau's. He appears to be a man that fears God in some degree; but is very stiff, and in some things full of self-will. My mind was as it were in chains, while preaching at Mr. Harriman's;[71] but my soul was greatly blest while dispensing the word to a large congregation at Mr. Armstrong's, in Middle

---

[71] From this home Hezekiah Harriman (1770?-1818) was received into the Baltimore Conference in 1795. In 1800 he volunteered for pioneer work in Kentucky, and after five years returned to his home conference. (*General Minutes*; Redford, *op. cit.*, I, 288. 292-95.)

River Neck. There is a prospect of some good being done, by the grace of God, in this place. After preaching on *Saturday*, with freedom and satisfaction, to a number of people in Gunpowder Neck, I was taken very unwell; and after a very restless night, with much profuse sweating, I rose in the morning exceedingly indisposed, and in much weakness of body went through the public duties of the day; but the Lord was graciously and powerfully with me, both in preaching and society meeting.

Monday, 20. My soul was refreshed with the love of God. How do I long for a mind thoroughly refined, filled with perfect purity, and constantly devoted to God! The prospect and hope of this frequently transports my soul. Lord, hasten the blessed period! Let all my soul be swallowed up in love! I have lately been reading Mr. W. on the ruin and recovery of man: he is a judicious writer, in the main, and generally illustrates his subjects well; but some of his sentiments relative to infants, I think, are very exceptionable.

Tuesday, 21. I crossed the Chesapeake bay, in company with a few friends, to Kent County. After a good passage we reached the shore, sat down to rest and refresh ourselves, and then joined in prayer. We walked to John Randall's, where we were informed of the opposition which one of our preachers met with. But the work is the Lord's, and they that oppose his work oppose his omnipotence. On *Tuesday* my soul was kept in peace and rest. After preaching with some comfort, I was seized with a quartan ague, which was attended with much pain in my back and limbs. Mr. Kennard asked me home,[72] and treated me with much civility and kindness. I now read Smollett's description of the Methodists;[73] and cannot wonder that his readers, who have no personal knowledge of them, should treat the Methodists with contempt. But the day is coming when every one will appear in his true colours, and be constrained to render an account of all his conduct to God. A high fever and heavy sweats were my companions in the night; and the next morning I was too unwell to speak in prayer; but I ventured to ride in a carriage as far as Mr. Hinson's, in the afternoon.

Thursday, 23. At Mr. Carvill Hinson's the Lord was with me while preaching from Acts xiv, 10. Observing in John Randall the odious appearance of speaking too freely of absent persons, I felt a sense of my own imprudence; and saw both the propriety and necessity of retaining every such matter in my own breast, till an opportunity may offer of conversing with the person immediately concerned, face to face. Lord,

[72] Kennard resided near Worton, Kent County, Maryland. Asbury preached there July 27, 1778. (Hallman, *op. cit.*, 115.)

[73] Tobias George Smollett, M.D. (1721–71), popular English novelist who inveighed against evangelicals, generally made unusually splenetic attacks against the Methodists in his *History of England*. "Poor Doctor Smollett!" Wesley commented, "thus to transmit to all succeeding generations a whole heap of notorious falsehoods!" (Hurst: *The History of British Methodism*, III, 1165.)

pardon me in everything that is wrong in the least degree; and grant me more fortitude and evangelical wisdom for the time to come!

Friday, 24. My trials and exercises have been somewhat peculiar. May the God of mercy communicate more abundant power and love! Though this was the day in course for my ague to return, I preached to a small, serious congregation with inward power. My ague came on afterward with a severe pain in my back. I drove off the cold fit by walking and running, but went to bed in a high fever. The next morning my frame felt weak; but my heart was sweetly resigned.

Saturday, 25. While preaching to a large company at Mr. Gibbs's,[74] we had a moving, melting time. After preaching at nine o'clock the next morning at the same place, I went to church, and thought the minister intended to point at me, by speaking against idleness, and people who follow an unwarrantable employment, and doing what they have no business with. But, can any employment be more unwarrantable than the charge of souls without any real concern for their salvation? And, bad as idleness is, it is far preferable to leading immortal souls astray. The world can judge whether he is most like an idle man who reads a dry harangue every Lord's day, or he who toils and labours both day and night to save the souls of men. But these things I leave with the Lord. Many people attended my preaching in the evening, while I took occasion, from 2 Cor. v, 20, to show, amongst other things, the evangelical mission and life of a true ambassador of Christ.

Monday. We crossed the Chesapeake Bay, and rode to Jos. Presbury's. My ague coming on I went to bed in great torture; and thought my frame could not long endure it. My body is greatly weakened by this disorder; and perhaps I shall be dumb for a season, either for my own unfaithfulness, or the unfaithfulness of the people. May the Lord fortify my soul with patience!

Thursday, 30. Though very weak and low, the Lord favoured me with a good opportunity, life, and liberty, at Daniel Ruff's.

Friday, October 1. I was exceedingly ill at Mr. Dallam's; and now began to think my travelling would be interrupted. This is my greatest trouble and pain, to forsake the work of God, and to neglect the people, whose spiritual interest and salvation I seek with my whole soul. The next day, finding myself too weak to travel, I sent brother Ebert in my place; and must content myself to abide here awhile, where they treat me with the greatest care and kindness. My present purpose is, if the Lord spares and raises me up, to be more watchful and circumspect in all my ways. O Lord, remember me in mercy; and brace up my feeble soul!

Lord's day, 3. Every day I have endeavoured to use what little

---

[74] Asbury was again in that part of Kent County between Worton and Rock Hall where he had introduced Methodist preaching. In December, 1777, he returned to preach and meet a thriving society in Gibbs's home. (Hallman, *op. cit.*, 112.)

strength I had for God; and this day I felt something better in my body, and quite serene in my mind. Rode to Bush Forest Chapel, and preached to many people with considerable power. But had a violent fever at night, which held me nine hours. It is my desire to be resigned to the will of God in all things. Sent brother Whitworth in my place to supply the appointments.

Wednesday, 6. My disorder returned, and my body was in great pain for many hours. Felt some patience, but not enough. O that this affliction may answer the intended end! My will is quite resigned to the will of God, so that I cannot ask ease in pain; but desire to be truly thankful, and leave the disposal of all things entirely with him.

It is undoubtedly a gracious providence, that my lot should be cast in the family of Josias Dallam, during my indisposition to travel. I shall never forget the kindness, or discharge the obligations I am under, to Mrs. Sarah Dallam,[75] who watched and waited upon me day and night. God grant, that the same measure which she has meted to me, may return upon herself and her children! On *Thursday* and *Friday* my mind was kept in peace, though I could do very little but read. The language of my heart is, Lord, thy will be done!

My disorder has increased, and for several days my indisposition has been so great that I kept no journal. My friends wept around, and expected my dissolution was near. But the Lord thought on both them and me, to raise me up from the borders of death. O that my few remaining days may be spent to his glory!—that every valuable end may be answered by my future life!

Wednesday, 27. Mr. Dallam was so kind as to conduct me in a carriage to my friend Barnet Preston's, at Deer Creek. On *Friday* I found myself much better, and my soul was kept in peace and purity. May the Lord ever keep me near to himself!

Thursday, November 4. Our quarterly meeting came on,[76] and I attended the private business, though in much weakness of body. Some of my brethren did not altogether please me. My hand appears still to be against every man. Mr. Rankin conducted the meeting. At the close of the whole, I discovered the affectionate attachment which subsisted between many of my dear friends and me. It cut me to the heart when we came to part from each other. They wept and I wept; especially brother Lynch and his wife. May the gracious Lord remember them in mercy and love!

[75] The home of Josias William Dallam and his wife, Sarah Dallam, was among the very first opened to Wesley's missionaries when in the winter of 1769–70 Robert Williams preached there. It has been estimated that one-third of the time from midsummer 1773 to the end of the year, Asbury was confined to his bed. (Du Bose, *op. cit.*, 66; Atkinson: *The Beginnings of the Wesleyan Movement in America*, 198–200.)

[76] At this quarterly meeting held at Bush Chapel, Asbury was too indisposed to attend other than the business sessions. His rather gloomy report is in sharp contrast to that given by Rankin, who presided. (Sandford, *op. cit.*, 226.)

Saturday, 6. Was able to sit up and write to my dear friend Mr. S——y. It is but little I can do; but, thanks be to God for any help! Heard brother Williams preach, and thought it my duty to blame him for speaking against the knowledge of salvation. Was better on Thursday; but threw myself into a violent fever by my own imprudence.

Tuesday, 9. My disorder seems to be going off, though I mend but slowly. On *Wednesday* I went to Mr. Dallam's in a carriage, and met with Mr. Rankin, who preached there. The next day Mr. Rankin set off for Philadelphia, and left me still poorly.

Saturday, 13. Though I have not preached for a month, yet I ventured to attend the funeral of J. Gallin, a Presbyterian, but a man who had borne a Christian character. As they could get no preacher of their own profession, they made application to me. Many people attended on this solemn occasion; and it was a very moving time.

Monday, 15. Found myself much better in health, and concluded to set off on my Master's business as soon as I should be properly equipped. On *Thursday* my heart was fixed, trusting in the Lord; and as my body was gathering strength, I set out on *Monday* for Baltimore; and on *Friday* reached William Lynch's, who entertained me with the greatest kindness. Here I had the pleasure of seeing our new church begun on Back River Neck.[77] The next day he conducted me in his carriage to the Point, where I was enabled to preach with some power. Then returned to the Neck, and met with Mr. J. He heard the word of God with great freedom of mind; and I believe his false peace was broken. My spirit was greatly refreshed by meeting brother Yearby at Baltimore on Monday; and the next day I was much assisted in preaching to a large number of people in town, both rich and poor. May the Lord arise and show himself gracious to these people! Through abundant grace I feel nothing contrary to the purest intention; nor the least desire for anything but God. Bless the Lord, O my soul!

Thursday, 25. Had occasion to go to Annapolis,[78] and found some desire to preach there. But perceiving the spirit and practice of the people, I declined it. A tavern-keeper offered me the use of his house for preaching; but he was a Deist, and I did not feel free to open my mouth in his house.

[77] This was the Back River Meeting House about ten miles down Patapsco Neck and one mile east of Nathan Perigau's farm, near the present Eastern Avenue and North Point Road, Baltimore. The Society was organized and the edifice begun by Robert Strawbridge. (See article by Mrs. Arthur Barneveld Bibbins, *The Souvenir Book of the Methodist Sesqui-Centennial*, October 10-14, 1934, p. 26; Nelson Reed manuscript diary, November 19, 1773; Archives of Baltimore Conference Historical Society.)

[78] Asbury's visit followed by about five months that of Joseph Pilmoor, who on July 11, 1772, preached the first Methodist sermon in Annapolis under a "very large tree on a fine piece of ground," probably the old Treaty Tree on the campus of St. John's College. (Atkinson, *op. cit.*, 342–44; Bibbins: *How Methodism Came*, 76–78; Smith: *Recollections and Reflections,* 258, 259.)

After my return to Baltimore, Mr. J., the person mentioned a few days ago, came and invited me to his house. The next morning, at breakfast, he showed much freedom in conversation, and there was great appearance of a change.

Monday, 29. Have been able to officiate at the town (Baltimore) and Point every day; and the congregations rather increase. Lord, make me humble and more abundantly useful; and give me the hearts of the people that I may conduct them to thee! I feel great hopes that the God of mercy will interpose, and do these dear people good. This day we agreed with Mr. L. to undertake the brick work of our new building at the Point.[79] At night I was seized with a violent fever; and as many of my friends thought it improper for me to go immediately into the circuit, I concluded to abide for a season in town. Many are under some awakenings here; and they are very kind and affectionate to me. My heart is with the Lord. He is my all in all.

Wednesday, December 1. Preached at Nathan Perigau's and William Lynch's. At the latter place many more people attended than we could expect, considering the conduct of Abraham Rollins, who in his preaching had behaved more like a madman than anything else. Rode the next day to Richard Owings's, where a few attended the word who understood the things of God. My soul is in peace. But I wish to bear all things with perfect patience, and feel less affected by all that men may say of me, and every act of disagreeable conduct towards me.

Saturday, 4. I returned to Baltimore; and the house of Mr. William Moore[80] was crowded with people who attended to hear the word; and the next day I felt great satisfaction in preaching to a large number of people at the Point; most of them gave good attention, but some were unruly.

Tuesday, 7. Yesterday I was very ill all the day with a fever; but feel something better to-day. God is the portion of my soul. He favours me with sweet peace, and sanctifies all my afflictions. Lord, evermore keep me, and conduct me in safety to thy blessed presence above! I had a fever, and kept my bed on *Wednesday,* and should have thought the day had been lost, had it not been a season for the exercise of my patience.

Preached on *Friday* with some satisfaction, though in great weakness of body, having been very ill in the preceding night. On *Saturday* my mind

[79] This chapel located in Strawberry Alley on Fleet Street, Fell's Point, was the first to be begun in what is now Baltimore. (See article by the Rev. W. Hamilton, *The Methodist Quarterly Review,* July, 1856; Griffith, *op. cit.,* 55; Lee: *History of Methodism,* 49.)

[80] William Moore, an Irishman, arrived in Baltimore in 1762 and in 1770 built the stone house at the southeast corner of South and Water Streets to which Asbury refers. Two years later, on his first visit to Baltimore, Asbury with John King was a guest in this house, which soon became a center of Methodist activities. (Lednum, *op. cit.,* 88, 89; Griffith: *Annals of Baltimore,* 39, 48; Hamilton, *op. cit.,* July, 1856.)

was serene; though I greatly long to have a deeper sense of God continually resting on my heart. My soul pants earnestly for closer communion with the Lord; and to die, to be crucified, to every other object.

Lord's day, 12. While preaching at the Point, there was great solemnity very visible in the congregation. The power of God was eminently present, and one person fell under it. Such numbers of people attended to hear the word to-day in town, that we knew not how to accommodate them; and there appeared to be more seriousness than usual among them.

Tuesday, 14. We had a comfortable time at William Lynch's. The next day Mr. Chase, a Church minister,[81] was present at preaching. We had some conversation afterward, in which we did not disagree. But, poor man! one more ignorant of the deep things of God, I have scarcely met with, of his cloth. He knew brother King, and appearing to be angry with him, abused him for preaching in the church. Though very unwell, I rode twenty miles on Thursday, to preach at William Worthington's,[82] where a few of them felt the power of God. Mr. Worthington and his wife in particular were tenderly affected.

Saturday, 18. Though in a high fever, I rode twenty miles through the rain to Baltimore. But the Lord preserved me; and I was able to preach to a small company at night. Being unwell on the *Lord's day*, I did not attempt to preach till night. But then the people were serious, and the power of God was present.

Monday, 20. Mrs. Huling introduced me to the family of Mrs. Rogers,[83] where they treated me with great kindness and care. O that plenty may not hurt, nor ease destroy me! Lord, help me, in all things, to desire nothing but thee!

Thursday, 23. Richard Owings informed me that the work of God was gaining ground in Frederick county. I preached at John Deaver's, in the old town, and had a wild, staring congregation. On *Friday* the Lord graciously blessed me with sweet peace, and much love. My heart is greatly affected at times for the town of Baltimore; and I am almost ready to doubt whether it is my duty to tarry here. Yet the seriousness

[81] The Rev. Thomas Chase, a native of England, in 1741 arrived from near Princess Anne, Somerset County, Maryland, to become rector of St. Paul's Church. He was the father of Samuel Chase, an associate justice of the Supreme Court and a signer of the Declaration of Independence. (*National Cyclopaedia of American Biography*, I, 24.)

[82] Among early Methodist families in Elkridge, eight miles southwest of Baltimore, besides the Worthingtons were the Dorseys, the Howards, and the Hammonds. Asbury referred to the people at Elkridge as "wealthy and wicked." (Lednum, *op. cit.*, 116; Bibbins, *op. cit.*, 59.)

[83] Philip Rogers was among the leaders and contributors toward the erection of the Lovely Lane Meeting House, Baltimore. His wife was the daughter of Mrs. Woodward whose second husband was John Hesselius, an eminent portrait painter. Rogers was an original trustee of Cokesbury College, who often entertained Asbury at Greenwood, his Maryland estate. (Armstrong, *op. cit.*, 89; Bibbins, *op. cit.*, 79–80; Warfield: *Founders of Anne Arundel and Horner Counties*, 62.)

of the people appears to increase, and a few are concerned for their salvation.

Monday, 27. My soul was happy in God. Brother Whitworth brought good accounts from the country, where the congregations are large, and some coming to the Lord. I have great hopes that my acquaintance with the family of Mrs. Rogers will be rendered a blessing to them; and I expect to see the mother and son bow to the cross of Christ.

Tuesday, 28. Guyse's paraphrase[84] has lately afforded me great delight. It is a pity that such a man ever imbibed the Calvinistic principles. My soul was kept in peaceful composure to-day; and at night I made a religious visit, which I hope will not be labour lost. On my return home, I had great hopes that Philip Rogers will yet become a disciple of Jesus Christ. I still pray, and long, and wait, for an outpouring of the blessed Spirit on this town. O that the time were come! Lord, hasten it for thy mercy's sake!

[84] John Guyse (1680–1761) was an independent English minister who wrote *An Exposition of the New Testament in the Form of Paraphrase*, in three volumes.

13538

1774

1774

Strawbridge's log meetinghouse on Sam's Creek in Maryland

CHAPTER THREE

Maryland

Tuesday, January 4, 1774. My body has been indisposed for some days past; but the grace of God has rested on my soul, and I have been enabled to preach several times with freedom, power, and great boldness, the Lord being my helper. Feeling rather better to-day, I ventured to ride in a chaise ten miles to Mr. Lynch's, where we had some agreeable, Christian conversation. Returned the next day, and continued unwell—sometimes being confined to my bed for a day together; yet I preached at other times to large congregations. It frequently appears as if almost the whole town would come together to hear the word of the Lord. Surely it will not be altogether in vain. The Lord giveth me great patience, and all things richly to enjoy, with many very kind friends, who pay great attention to me in my affliction. Amongst others, Mr. Benedict Swope, a preacher in high Dutch, came to see me. He appeared to be a good man, and I opened to him the plan of Methodism.

Friday, 14. Though this was the day for the return of my disorder, yet I felt much better. A blister under my ear has removed the pain in my head. A great sense of God rested on my heart, while meeting the class to-day. There is an apparent alteration in this family; and I must conclude the Lord directed my steps among them.

Saturday, 15. My body is still weak, though on the recovery. Lord, if thou shouldst be pleased to raise me up, let it be to do more good! I desire to live only for this! Lord, I am thine, to serve thee forever, with soul and body, time and talents! O my God! now all I am and have is devoted to thee! Mercifully assist me, by thy grace, to persevere in all well-doing. Amen.

Lord's day, 16. While preaching in town this evening, two young men, in the midst of the sermon, came in, and broke the order of the meeting. On *Monday,* my heart felt an uncommon burden, on account of the inhabitants of this place. And sometimes I despair of ever doing them much good. But a constant sense of God resteth on my own soul.

Wednesday, 19. My mind is kept in peace, though my body is weak; so that I have not strength sufficient for travelling: nevertheless, I can read and think. O that it may be to the glory of Him, who, in his great wisdom, thinks proper to confine me! Lord, ever draw my heart after thee! May I see no beauty in any other object, nor desire anything but thee! My heart longs to be more extensively useful, but is, at the same time, filled with perfect resignation to God in all my affliction.

Therefore, I cannot choose for myself, but leave all to him. A young man, who disturbed the congregation on the evening of last *Lord's day,* has seen it expedient to excuse his conduct, as almost the whole town thought him culpable. Thus doth God bring good out of evil, and make the fierceness of man turn to his praise.

Lord's day, 23. Great numbers of people attended while I preached on the parable of the prodigal son.

Tuesday, 25. This was a day of sweet peace. I held a private conference with William Moore and Captain Stone, who both appeared to be convinced of sin.

Thursday, 27. Many people attended this evening, to hear an account of the rise, discipline, and practice of the Methodists; on which subject I enlarged with a warm exhortation, and had great liberty and satisfaction. If my labours should be in vain for the people, the Lord gives me a gracious reward in my own soul.

Friday, 28. My heart was fixed on God, and a great part of my time spent in reading. I also met a class, and received seven probationers into the society. May the Lord give them grace to stand!

Lord's day, 30. It appears that the people have a great desire to know the truth; for though it rained, and froze as it fell, yet a great many attended to hear. It was a very solemn time at night, while I discoursed on the awful day of judgment. Samuel Owings is tenderly affected for the salvation of his soul. And William Moore and Philip Rogers seem to be in earnest about this important matter. Glory to God for these things! Set out on *Monday* for our quarterly meeting, and met the preachers at brother Owings's. They all appeared to have their hearts fixed on promoting the work of God for the ensuing quarter; and we consulted together with great freedom and love. On the first day I inquired into the moral character of the local preachers, appointed them their work, and gave them written licenses to officiate. The preachers who spoke at this meeting, manifested great earnestness and zeal for the salvation of souls; and many of the people were much affected; all was harmony and love. For the next quarter we had our stations as follows: Philip Ebert, Edward Dromgoole,[1] and Richard Owings, in Frederick circuit; brother Yearbry and brother Rollins in Kent circuit; Henry Watters and brother Webster in Baltimore circuit; and myself in Baltimore town. We appointed our next quarterly meeting to be held in Baltimore on the first of May next. Much fatigued in my feeble frame by various exercises, I returned to town, and visited Mrs. Moore, who was afflicted in body and distressed in mind.

Thursday, Feb. 3. Last night, while we were all below stairs, my bed took fire by some unknown means, though it stood three yards from the fireplace. We happily came up in due time, and finding the room full of smoke, we discovered the fire, and extinguished it. Surely there was a kind providence in this! This day I wrote a letter to Mr. Otterbein,[2] a German minister, relative to his settling in Baltimore town. Though the weather was very disagreeable, yet many attended at night to hear the word. God is still my chief object; and my desire is to glorify and serve him. On *Saturday,* Mr. Swope came to consult me in respect to Mr. Otterbein's coming to this town. We agreed to promote his settling here; and laid a plan nearly similar to ours—to wit, that gifted persons amongst them, who may, at any time, be moved by the Holy Ghost to speak for God, should be encouraged; and if the Synod would not agree, they were still to persevere in this line of duty.

Lord's day, 6. We had a moving time at the Point; and after dining with

[1] Frederick Circuit included Frederick, Montgomery, Washington, Allegany, and Carroll counties in Maryland and Fairfax County in Virginia. Edward Dromgoole (1751–1835), whose name appears among the appointments for the first time, arrived from Ireland in 1770 with a letter of introduction to his fellow countryman Robert Strawbridge. In 1773 he began his ministry in Frederick County and preached from 1773 to 1780 and from 1783 to 1786. He then settled in Brunswick County, Virginia, where his home was a stopping place for preachers for nearly half a century, and the base from which he extended his ministerial labors to the regions thereabout. His home became known as "Dromgoole's Chapel." He was ordained an elder in his home by Asbury on February 12, 1815, having entered the ministry before Methodist ordination was instituted and located soon thereafter. Two of the five children born to him and Rebecca Walton, whom he married in 1775, became local preachers. Another son, George Coke Dromgoole, served three terms as a Congressman from Virginia; and a grandson, the Rev. Edward Dromgoole Sims, was a college professor. (*Arminian Magazine,* XIV, 219, 220; Sweet: *Religion on the American Frontier,* IV, 123, 124, for biographical sketch and reprints of some of the Dromgoole papers at the University of North Carolina.)

[2] The Rev. Philip William Otterbein (1726–1813) in 1774 organized and took charge of the congregation which he served for nearly forty years. He participated in the consecration of Bishop Asbury at the latter's request. In 1785 he led in the erection of what is now called the Old Otterbein Evangelical United Brethren Church, 112 West Conway Street, Baltimore, which is still in active use. (See Drury, *op. cit.,* 115; *Methodist Magazine,* VI, 210–14; Stevens: *History of the Methodist Episcopal Church,* I, 217–21.)

Mr. Swope, the German minister, many people attended at Mrs. Triplett's to hear me preach; but a company of men, who would wish to support the character of gentlemen, came drunk, and attempted an interruption: however Philip Rogers, once their intimate associate in sin, had courage enough to defend the cause of God: nevertheless, I thought it expedient to dismiss the congregation; and know not how this will end: but this I know, Satan and his emissaries are greatly displeased.

Monday, 7. According to appointment, I went to Elk Ridge, and was kindly received by Mr. John Worthington. I spent part of three days, labouring for the salvation of souls. In this place there are many wealthy and wicked people, destitute of all true religion. Numbers attended to hear the word, and some were affected. Lord, let it not be as the seed sown by the way-side! Returned to Baltimore on *Wednesday*, and the next day I advised the widow Triplett to seek redress of a magistrate, for the late riot made in her house. But they advised her to put up with it for this time. As Mr. William Moore offered the use of his house, I met the people there on *Friday* night, and found the disturbance had not diminished the congregation, but increased it. Thus Satan prepares a weapon to wound his own cause. After reading to the congregation part of the "Plain Account of the People called Methodists,"[3] I told them we were a united body, and as such would defend our own cause; that I had qualified myself according to the act of toleration[4] and had a legal right to preach the Gospel.

Friday, 11. Endeavoured to raise something by subscription, towards building a Methodist church; but as the whole lieth on my shoulders, I find the burden rather too heavy. However, God is my support, and my heart is with him.

Tuesday, 15. A lively sense of God rested on my soul, while preaching to a number of attentive people collected at William Lynch's; and in meeting the class at night, I found the members steady.

Wednesday, 16. Returning to the Point, I received a melancholy account of a poor, abandoned wretch, who staggered into a brothel at night, and was found dead the next morning. He was found at the door of Mr. L., and there were reasons to suspect he was murdered. Thus we see the vengeance of God frequently overtakes impenitent sinners, even in this life. How awful the thought! that a soul, in such a condition, should be unexpectedly hurried to the judgment-seat of a righteous God! Let every poor drunkard take the warning; lest the next time he brutifies his im-

---

[3] Wesley's tract under this title was published in 1749 and many times thereafter.

[4] The Act Concerning Religion, passed by the Maryland Assembly April 21, 1649, was known as the Act of Toleration. It provided that no person professing to believe in Jesus Christ should be molested. Asbury qualified himself legally under this statute. (Fiske: *Old Virginia and Her Neighbors*, I, 309–11, for copy of the statute; Smith: *Religion Under the Barons of Baltimore*, 318 ff.)

mortal spirit, by depriving it of the proper use of its rational powers, it should be suddenly driven out of the reach of divine mercy. On my return to town at night, William Moore gave me a pleasing account of the unspeakable peace with which God had blest him. But, let him that most assuredly standeth, take heed lest he fall. The next evening, I finished reading the "Plain Account of the People called Methodists;" and then exhorted the congregation with much warmth of heart.

Friday, 18. While preaching at the house of Mr. Moore, his father and mother were moved by the word of God. But after lying down at night to rest, my heart was oppressed with inexpressible feelings for the inhabitants of Baltimore. I am pressed under them as a cart full of sheaves; and would

LOVELY LANE MEETINGHOUSE

rather be employed in the most servile offices, than preach to them, if it were not from a sense of duty to God, and a desire to be instrumental in saving their souls. If honour and worldly gain were held out as motives to this painful work, they would to me appear lighter than vanity. But, Lord, thou knowest my motives and my ends! O prosper thou the work of my heart and my hands!

Saturday, 19. This day was chiefly spent in reading and prayer. Peace, purity, and a spirit of warm devotion filled my heart. Glory to God, the author of all my blessings! The next day the congregation at the Point were but little affected; but at night the attention of the people in town was much struck, while I preached from Matt. iii, 7.

Monday, 21. I rode eight miles and preached at Mr. Gatch's. Rode afterward to Middle River,[5] and had the satisfaction of seeing our new house raised and covered in. An opposer of the truth has been lately and suddenly summoned, by the smallpox, to answer for his conduct at the bar of Almighty God. Rode to Nathan Perigau's the next day, and found some whose hearts were tender. Stephen Watters gave me an account of the happy departure of his brother, John Watters, from this wicked and dangerous world. He had acted in the capacity of a steward among us; and was a serious, faithful man.

> "Happy soul, who, free from harms,
> Rests within his Saviour's arms."

Nathan Perigau rode in company with me to William Lynch's where we spent the evening comfortably. After preaching a few times, I returned on *Thursday* to town, and was much pleased to hear of the success which William Moore had met with in raising a subscription of more than a hundred pounds for our building.[6] Thus doth the Lord give us favour in the sight of the people. Mr. Rogers took up two lots of ground for the purpose of building; and Mr. Moore seemed determined to prosecute the work at all events. Surely the Lord hath stirred up their minds to this pious enterprise, and will bless them therein. As my body has now gained a little strength, I am determined to rise early, and make the most of my precious time.

Lord's day, 27. I rose with a solemn sense of God on my heart; and had many to hear, both in town and at the Point.

Tuesday, March 1. Several went with me to John Watters' where we found a large company of people collected, who appeared both ignorant and proud. While attempting to preach to them from these words, "May we know what this new doctrine, whereof thou speakest, is?" my mind was oppressed above measure; so that both my heart and my mouth were almost shut: and after I had done, my spirit was greatly troubled. O my soul! if confined to the society of the wicked, what couldst thou find but vexation and grief? But, "where the Spirit of the Lord is, there is liberty." Having frequently sixteen or twenty miles to ride, and then to preach before dinner, which is often as late as four o'clock, it shakes my constitution, and is painful to the flesh. But I cheerfully submit to these things for the sake of precious souls. What did the blessed Jesus suffer for

---

[5] Middle River Neck was eight miles from the home of Philip Gatch and lay between Gunpowder and Middle rivers.

[6] This building was the Lovely Lane Meeting House, the second Methodist place of worship in Baltimore. Its site is now occupied by the Merchants Club, 206 East Redwood Street, on which a bronze tablet reads: "Upon this site stood from 1774 to 1786, The Lovely Lane Meeting House in which was organized December, 1784, The Methodist Episcopal Church in the United States of America." Here Asbury and Coke were consecrated bishops. The successor to Lovely Lane was the first Light Street Church, at Light Street and Wine Alley, started in August, 1785, and dedicated by Asbury on May 21, 1786.

me! The next day, a champion in sin, a man who had been a famous ringleader in absurd and diabolical sports, was deeply wounded by the Spirit of God, while, in the course of my sermon, I was describing the horrible torments to which those would be exposed in hell, who had been instruments in the hands of Satan, to train up others in sin and disobedience. He afterward invited me home; and we had some serious conversation. I then returned to Baltimore.

Friday, 4. I was closely employed all this day, and enjoyed peace in my soul. But O! how does my spirit pant for more of God! The next morning my mind was somewhat dejected by the weight of my strong desires for more pure and undefiled religion. In reading the works of Mr. Brandon,[7] especially his meditations, my heart was greatly melted. Through grace, I feel a fixed determination to live more than ever to the glory of God. On the *Lord's day*, I laboured for my Master, both in the town and at the Point. Set off the next morning for Gunpowder Neck; and on *Tuesday*, preached at the funeral of W. P., who had waited for the consolation of Israel, and departed in peace, triumphantly declaring, "I have fought the good fight, I have finished my course, I have kept the faith." Here we have a lively and steady class. O that they may remain so! The next day, many people attended while I preached at the funeral of I. M., who also died in the Lord. My text was, "Blessed and holy is he that hath part in the first resurrection." The power of the Lord was present, and it was a melting time. The Spirit of God was present with us also at the upper ferry,[8] while I preached to a large congregation from Psalm cxxvi, 3: "The Lord hath done great things for us, whereof we are glad." Honest, simple Daniel Ruff has been made a great blessing to these people. Such is the wisdom and power of God, that he hath wrought marvellously by this plain man, that no flesh may glory in his presence.

Friday, 11. On my way to Joseph Presbury's my horse tired, and fell down with me on his back; but I was not in the least hurt. Calling at Dr. Henderson's, I met with I. R., a Quaker, who said it gave him pain to think that Joseph Pilmoor should go home for ordination, and expressed his disapprobation of our going to the Church for the ordinances, supposing we might have them amongst ourselves. But this was all a farce. He would rather that we should drop them altogether. And in the course of conversation, he laboured to overthrow them entirely. But when I told him it might appear to me as a duty to use them, though I should not suppose that all went to hell who did not use them; he asked, why we use them if they are not essential to salvation? What weak reasoning is this!

---

[7] John Brandon, an English divine, wrote *Happiness at Hand, or a Plain and Practical Discourse of Just Men's Souls in the State of Separation from the Body*, in 1687.

[8] The term "upper ferry" was applied to Bell's Ferry to distinguish it from the lower ferry at Havre de Grace. Bell's Ferry was established in 1727 and operated across the Susquehanna River from a point just south of Lapidum, Harford County, Maryland.

Do they think laying them aside is thus essential, or wearing their clothes in such a shape, or using (as they call it) the plain language? Why then do they follow these practices? But what makes them so contracted and bitter in their spirit as some of them are? There is One that knoweth.

After preaching the next day at Brother Presbury's, and having the pleasure to find that the society there had increased both in number and grace, I then returned to Baltimore, and, though much fatigued, spoke at Baltimore in the evening.

Blessed be God! Samuel Owings seems determined to give up all for Christ. And the little society in town are still pressing on. The Lord has been the keeper of my soul in this journey; my peace has been great, and my intention pure.

Monday, 14. Set out to-day with some agreeable company, for Mr. Worthington's; and though it rained, a small congregation attended; but they discovered very little sensibility in the things of God. My frame seems lately much affected by nervous disorders. But let the will of the Lord be done! After feeling much dejection of mind, and preaching on *Tuesday* at the house of Joshua Owings, on *Wednesday* I visited Joseph Cromwell, a very stiff, old Churchman. But as his parson, Mr. Edmiston, disagreed with him in the doctrine of predestination, he was much displeased with him, and willing to receive us. I preached at his house in the day with some freedom, and expounded at night. May the Lord apply the word to their conviction and conversion!

Returned on *Thursday* to Baltimore, and was favoured with liberty and power, while preaching to a considerable congregation at night.

Saturday, 19. The Lord blessed my soul with sweet peace in the day, and with the aid of his Holy Spirit in preaching at night. My heart is with God. The Lord Jehovah is my strength and my song: He also is become my salvation.

Satan assaulted me powerfully with his temptations on *Monday*; but by calling on the name of the Lord, I was delivered. How faithful and gracious is God! He will not suffer his people to be tempted above that they are able to bear; but will with the temptation make a way to escape. Precious truth! Sometimes we are tempted to the uttermost of our strength, but never beyond it. We always stand, at least, on equal ground with Satan: and by faith in Christ we may be more than conquerors.

Tuesday, 22. I rode a few miles into the (Garrison) Forest, and preached at Mr. E——'s. The people were much quickened; and there were great appearances of real good.

Wednesday, 23. At the house of William Lynch I preached a funeral sermon on the death of his brother Joshua. Many of his friends and neighbours were present. It was a very solemn, awful, warning season. May the people retain the impressions they then received, and be found prepared for their own departure! The next day I rode to meet Mr. Webb, but took cold, as the weather was severe, and found myself much indisposed. Mr. Webb preached an animating discourse from Rev. vi, 17. There is a great probability that his coming will be made a particular blessing to many.

Being much indisposed on *Friday*, Mr. Webb preached to a large congregation. There is something very singular in his manner; nevertheless the Lord owns and blesses his labours. Though I continued very unwell the next day, I went to church,[9] and heard Mr. Thomas Chase deliver a good discourse on retirement and private devotion; and afterward I attempted to preach at the Point, but found myself much worse at my return to town. My indisposition and weakness of body have so pressed me down for some time past, that I do not expect to abide long in this world of danger and trouble; neither do I desire it. But, come life or come death, let the will of the Lord be done! After the physicians have given over I—I—and thought they could do him no more service, we had recourse to that old-fashioned remedy, *prayer*; and had reason to believe the Lord in mercy heard us.

Thursday, 31. My illness has been so severe that I have preached but little for some days past; but felt myself rather better to-day. As Captain Webb had appointed to preach at Mr. W——'s, and was accidentally prevented, lest the people should be disappointed, I ventured to go in his stead. But after preaching was taken very ill, and obliged to go immediately to bed.

Lord's day, April 3. Though still very unwell, I attempted to preach. How difficult it is for a man who longs for the salvation of souls to be silent! Gratitude urges me to acknowledge the providence of God, and the kindness of my friends. The people who have had the chief trouble with me in my late afflictions, have shown remarkable care, tenderness, and concern. May the Lord reward their work and labour of love!

Wednesday, 6. My indisposition has been so great this week, that I have been incapable of all public exercises. Severe chills and burning fevers have been my portion both day and night. O that I may wisely and diligently improve these seasons of affliction! When shall I be all glorious within? My soul longs for the complete image and full enjoyment of God. Satan too often takes the advantage of my constitution, and betrays me into such a degree of cheerfulness as has, at least, the appearance of levity. But my prevailing and earnest desire is, to live and act as in the immediate presence of a holy and glorious God. Lord, make me more serious, watchful, and holy!

Ventured on *Thursday* to ride in a carriage twelve miles to town; but was very ill most of the night. On *Saturday* Captain Webb intended to have sailed in the packet; but when he saw the entertainment he was to have, he returned to abide with us for a short season. In great weakness of body, I

[9] Asbury attended St. Paul's Church in Baltimore.

met the congregation this evening, without any intention to preach; but seeing a great number of people collected, my spirit was moved within me, and I thought it my duty to exert what little strength I had, and preach to the people. But I was indisposed and confined all the next day. However, Captain Webb supplied my place.

Monday, 11. I was somewhat better. But I find myself assaulted by Satan as well in sickness as in health, in weakness as in strength. Lord, help me to urge my way through all, and fill me with humble, holy love, that I may be faithful until death, and lay hold on eternal life. On *Tuesday* I ventured to go as far as Mr. Lynch's, and my soul was kept in peace: though the next day my spiritual adversary assaulted me in a soft and artful way; but the Lord delivered me. May he ever grant me grace to confide in him, and devote my body and soul entirely to his service!

Thursday, 14. Rode back to town, and was enabled to preach with freedom and comfort, from the case of Naaman, the leper. My heart is much drawn out after God, with a determination to be more devoted to him, and more fervent in prayer.

Lord's day, 17. Both yesterday and to-day my soul enjoyed more peace and more love. May these graces never be interrupted! A great number attended at the Point, while I enforced these awakening words, "O earth, earth, earth, hear the word of the Lord!" After meeting the class of young men, I returned and spoke in town from Prov. xxiv, 30. Was much fatigued, but desire to be thankful to God that I am gathering some strength for duty. We have reason to think the spirits of hartshorn have been serviceable in my disorder.

Monday, 18. My soul was in peace, but my body weak. This day the foundation of our house in Baltimore was laid.[10] Who could have expected that two men, once amongst the chief of sinners, would ever have thus engaged in so great an undertaking for the cause of the blessed Jesus? This is the Lord's doing, and it is marvellous in our eyes. He hath touched and changed their hearts. He hath moved them to this acceptable undertaking; and he will surely complete it; and raise up a people to serve him in this place.

Tuesday, 19. My soul was in a comfortable frame; but I did not employ all my time in so useful a manner as I might have done. This was partly owing to my bodily weakness. But in class meeting this evening, we had a happy and blessed time indeed. Hitherto the Lord hath helped. So my labour hath not been in vain.

Wednesday, 20. Poor Mr. B. arrived here to-day from England. In great distress he applied to me for a little money. And is it come to this! Ah! what will be the end of those that forsake God, for wealth, a wife, or anything else? O my soul, keep these things always in remembrance as a perpetual caution. And may the Lord keep me ever humble, and dead to

[10] This was the Lovely Lane Chapel. (See note under February 21, 1774.)

all created good! I read the rules, and met the society in the evening; and it was a melting, happy time.

Thursday, 21. My heart was fixed on God, and kept in peace. I was able to walk some distance to-day, and believe the Lord is about to restore me to health. May it be to serve Him, and *Him only!*

Saturday, 23. Though weak in body, I have been able for a few days past to go through my public exercises; and was both instructed and delighted to-day in reading the Revelation with its comment. There we see the rise and spread of the Christian religion through the extensive and idolatrous empire of the Romans; the wars of the Saracens; the gradual rise and artful progress of Popery. What an amazing prophetic history is this, of all people and nations, in epitome! How expressive are the differently-coloured horses, and surprising representations seen by St. John! In this book, extraordinary events are foretold, as well as the proper rule of our faith and practice revealed. If this deep book were fully understood, need we go any farther after knowledge?

Monday, 25. The Lord favoured me yesterday with liberty in preaching to large companies both in town and Point. And this day my soul experienced a sweet mixture of peace, and joy, and grief. We had a very comfortable time at the class in the evening.

Wednesday, 27. We were all quickened by the grace of God in class meeting last night. Blessed be God! Calm serenity fills my mind; and my body recovers a little strength.

Friday, 29. What a miracle of grace am I! How unworthy, and yet how abundantly blest! In the midst of all temptations, both from without and from within, my heart trusteth in the Lord. I was greatly delighted to-day in reading Dr. John Guyse on the Reign of Christ, which on earth will be spiritual, and in glory personal and eternal. O the beauties and joys of which I have some prospect in that celestial world! It seems rather strange that, till lately, I could discover no beauties in the Revelation of St. John. But now I think it is the grand key of all mysteries, whether pure or impure; opening to view all the revolutions, persecutions, and errors of the Church from that time till the end of the world. And then it favours us with a glimpse of what shall remain forever. In preaching to-night from these words, "Bodily exercise profiteth little, but godliness is profitable unto all things;" I took occasion to show,

I. That bodily exercise, or what is called religious actions, cannot change a sinful heart, or purchase love.

II. Wherein godliness consisteth; namely, In repentance, faith, love to God and man, meekness, resignation, chastity, and the pure, spiritual worship of God.

III. Wherein this is profitable; namely, In all states, in all commerce, in the felicity of the possessor, in the general benefit of others, and finally in eternal glory. My mind has been grieved by some who have spoken evil of ministers. But I must be sure to take care of my own soul; that is more to me than all the world, and all the men in it. And blessed be God! he fills me with peace and purity. Lord, grant that this may be my portion, increasing forever!

Lord's day, May 1. Preached twice and met two classes. In the morning, at the Point, I had some feeling; but found myself rather shut up at night in town.

Monday, 2. My soul loveth the Lord God! What a great and blessed portion is he for worthless man! This evening was spent in company with two German ministers who are very friendly, and intend to be present at our quarterly meeting to-morrow.

Tuesday, 3. Our quarterly meeting began.[11] I preached in the morning; and in the afternoon we settled our temporal business, with great order and much love. When inquiry was made relative to the conduct of the preachers, there were some complaints of a few, who had been remiss in meeting the societies, and catechising the children. The next day several of us spoke in public, and then we parted in peace. Had a friendly intercourse with Mr. Otterbein and Mr. Swope, the German ministers, respecting the plan of Church discipline on which they intended to proceed. They agreed to imitate our methods as nearly as possible.

Friday, 6. I preached from Matt. xii, 50; but felt my mind dejected. Not meeting with success in this town as my soul ardently longs for, I rather feel a desire to depart, and to try some other people. But let the will of the Lord be done. My heart has been deeply affected by reading the Life of Col. Gardiner.[12] Blessed be God for so many who experience the same work of grace which we preach, and at the same time are not of us! This is a great confirmation of the work of God. And "whosoever doeth the will of my Father who is in heaven," of every denomination, "the same shall be my brother, and sister, and mother."

Saturday, 7. My soul longeth for God. My heart and my flesh cry out for him. O that I were wholly devoted to my God!

Lord's day, 8. Several appeared to feel something of the power which attended the word, both at the Point and in town. On *Monday* my soul was in peace, and God was the object of my love. Mr. Chase attended our class meeting, and expressed his approbation. The Lord was with us, and we were greatly blessed. Mr. W.[13] arrived to-day from Virginia. He gave us a circumstantial account of the work of God in those parts. One house of worship is built, and another in contemplation; two or three more preachers are gone out upon the itinerant plan; and in some parts the

---

[11] This was the first quarterly meeting held in Baltimore. (Lee: *A Short History of the Methodists,* 50.)

[12] This book was *Some Remarkable Passages in the Life of the Honourable Colonel James Gardiner* (1688–1745), by Philip Doddridge, 1747.

[13] Mr. W. was either John Wade or William Watters.

congregations consist of two or three thousand people. But some evil-minded persons have opposed the act of toleration, and threatened to imprison him. May the Lord turn their hearts, and make them partakers of his great salvation!

Wednesday, 11. I went to Mr. Lynch's, and preached to a large congregation; then called at Nathan Perigau's, and preached a funeral sermon on the death of his sister, who was once happy in religion. Returned to town on *Thursday*, and preached with freedom to an attentive audience.

Friday, 13. I packed up my clothes and books to be ready for my departure; and had an agreeable conversation with Mr. Otterbein. The next day some of my friends were so unguarded and imprudent as to commend me to my face. Satan, ready for every advantage, seized the opportunity and assaulted me with self-pleasing, self-exalting ideas. But the Lord enabled me to discover the danger, and the snare was broken. May he ever keep me humble, and little, and mean, in my own eyes!

Lord's day, 15. About to take my leave for a season, I went to the Point, and enlarged on these words, "I am afraid of you, lest I have bestowed upon you labour in vain;" and trust some felt at last the worth and weight of divine truths. My subject at night in town was this: "I take you to record this day, that I am pure from the blood of all men." In preaching from these words my mind was under some embarrassment. Perhaps my foolish heart desired to end with honour, and the Lord in mercy prevented it. May I ever be contented with that honour which cometh from God only!

Monday, 16. When the time of parting came, I felt some unwillingness to leave my kind and valuable friends: however, I took horse and rode sixteen miles to Mr. Giles's, where a large company attended to hear the word. Many were also present at Mr. Colgate's. In examining the leaders, I found them steady; but refused to give a license to an exhorter, who had been too unwatchful. After a long prejudice, Mr. Jacob Giles invited me to his house, and treated me kindly. In preaching at Mr. Bond's, my heart was troubled within me for the dullness and unbelief of the people.

Wednesday, 18. Rode to Susquehanna River and many of the leading men were present, with a large congregation. Simple Daniel Ruff has been an instrument of real and great good to the people in these parts.

Thursday, 19. I am happy in God after all my labours. But when amongst my friends, my mind inclines to a degree of cheerfulness bordering on levity. O for more watchfulness!—a more constant, striking sense of an omnipresent God! Preached to-day in the market house at Charlestown.[14] The congregation was somewhat large, and many of them very attentive. The company was large at Bohemia Manor on *Friday*, and my own heart was deeply affected, and much drawn out while speaking from Rev. iii, 3. At Newcastle (Delaware) on *Saturday*, Satan was there, diverting the

[14] Charlestown was in the present Cecil County, Maryland.

people by a play. However, several came to hear me enforce these words, "Be not ye partakers with them."

Pennsylvania

Monday, 23. After preaching yesterday at Newport and Red Clay Creek,[15] I rode to-day to Chester; and though weary, spoke from Gal. vi, 14. Here my old friends, Mr. Mann[16] and Mr. Sause, from New York, met me; and the next day we rode to Philadelphia. Hitherto the Lord hath helped.

Wednesday, 25. Our conference began. The overbearing spirit of a certain person had excited my fears. My judgment was stubbornly opposed for a while, and at last submitted to. But it is my duty to bear all things with a meek and patient spirit. Our conference was attended with great power; and, all things considered, with great harmony. We agreed to send Mr. Richard Wright to England; and all acquiesced in the future stations of the preachers. My lot was to go to New York. My body and mind have been much fatigued during the time of this conference. And if I were not deeply conscious of the truth and goodness of the cause in which I am engaged, I should by no means stay here. Lord, what a world is this! yea, what a religious world! O keep my heart pure, and my garments unspotted from the world! Our conference ended on Friday with a comfortable intercession.

Lord's day, 29. This was a day of peace, and the Lord favoured me with faith and energy while preaching to the people. I visited Mr. Wright, who is going to England; but found he had no taste for spiritual subjects. Lord, keep me from all superfluity of dress, and from preaching empty stuff to please the ear, instead of changing the heart! Thus has he fulfilled as a hireling his day. We had a very solemn love feast to day.

New York

Monday, May 30, 1774. My friends and I set off in the stage for New York,[17] where we arrived on Tuesday evening about eight o'clock. We had some trifling company on the way, who talked much but to little pur-

[15] Asbury went by Newcastle, Newport, and Red Clay Creek in Delaware, en route to Philadelphia.

[16] John Mann (1742–1816) was a local preacher in New York and was one of the preachers at Wesley Chapel during the Revolution. He was a Royalist and went to Canada after the war and continued to preach there. His brother, James, accompanied him to Nova Scotia and became a member of the conference there. (Seaman: *Annals of New York Methodism*, 54, 76, 120; Tipple, *op. cit.*, 65.)

[17] The party went by stage via Burlington to Perth Amboy and by ferry around Staten Island to Whitehall at the southern tip of Manhattan Island.

pose. My old friends in New York were glad to see me. But I still fear there is a root of prejudice remaining in the hearts of a few.[18] May the Lord prepare me for all events, that I may act and suffer, in all things, like a Christian! Captain Webb[19] preached a good sermon in the evening.

June 1. Considering my bodily weakness, and the great fatigue through which I have gone, it seems wonderful that my frame should support it, and be still so capable of duty. My mind is also kept in peace. My heart was much drawn out both towards God and the people, while preaching this evening from Sam. vii, 12. But too much of the old spirit is still discoverable in my few prejudiced friends. Mr. Chave,[20] not contented with his unkind and abusive letter, is still exerting all his unfriendly force. I feel myself aggrieved; but patiently commit my cause to God. Therefore their contention may subsist among themselves. I shall not contend with them.

Thursday, 2. In the public exercise of the evening, my heart was warmed with affection for the people. And except a very small number of dissatisfied, restless spirits, the hearts of the people are generously opened towards me. My heart is still fixed on God; and determined through grace, both to serve him, and promote the prosperity of his cause.

Friday, 3. Christ is precious to my believing heart. Blessed be God for this! it is infinitely more to me than the favour of all mankind, and the possession of all the earth. The next day my soul was also sweetly drawn out in love to God; and found great freedom and happiness in meeting the leaders and the bands.[21] I told them that the Spirit and providence of God would certainly assist in purging the society; that the time would come, when such as were insincere and half-hearted would have no place among us.

Lord's day, 5. Attended the old church,[22] as usual, but clearly saw

[18] The leader of the small group that was still opposed to Asbury was probably John Chave. (See *Journal* entry under June 1, below.) William Lupton was soon reconciled. (See *Journal* entry for July 10, 1774.)

[19] This was the last sermon preached by Webb in Wesley Chapel prior to his return to England because of the mounting political tension. (*John Street Church Records.*)

[20] Asbury had appointed John Chave collector in the New York society in 1772. (See *Journal* entry under September 11, 1772.) The contents of the letter and whether it was written to Asbury or others are unknown. Chave eventually became reconciled to Asbury and with Lupton met him at Newark on his return to New York after the Revolution. (See *Journal* entry for August 27, 1784.)

[21] Some changes had taken place in the leadership of the society. Boardman and Pilmoor returned to England in January, and Captain Webb and John Southwell no longer lived in New York, and their places as trustees of Wesley Chapel were taken by John Mann, John Staples, Samuel Selby, and David Johnson, while Stephen Sands and William Ellsworth were elected as "additional trustees." James Jarvis was still treasurer, and William Lupton and Henry Newton were the stewards. (*John Street Church Records*, I.)

[22] The "old church" was St. Paul's Chapel (Anglican) at Broadway and Fulton streets, where Asbury frequently worshiped.

where the Gospel ministry was. The Spirit of grace mercifully assisted me
in the public duties of this day. On *Monday*, I preached with great plainness and power in the Meadows;[23] but while preaching on *Tuesday* evening, my ideas left me, though I felt myself spirited in addressing the people
by way of exhortation.

Wednesday, 8. The fire of divine love glowed in my heart. My soul was
in peace. My affections were pure, and withdrawn from earthly objects.
But I fear, lest self-complacency should have any place in me. May the
Lord keep me in the spirit of humility, prayer, and loving zeal!

Thursday, 9. While reading a sermon of Mr. Brandon's on "Quench
not the Spirit," in company with a few friends, both they and I were much
quickened. Blessed be God! My soul is kept in peace, and power, and love.
Had great liberty this evening in pointing out the causes, why we have not
more of the spirit of devotion; of neglect or dullness in prayer; of too
much heart-attention to the world; of the want of more faith in the
realities of eternity, and the promises of God; of not looking more
earnestly to God in humble expectation of receiving his grace, &c.

Lord's day, 12. Both my body and mind are weak. As Mr. Ritzman[24]
was thought by many to be a great preacher, I went in the afternoon to
hear him. He was very stiff and studied in his composition, and dwelt
much on their favourite doctrine of imputed righteousness. He appeared
to have very little liberty, except in a short application. With great enlargement of heart, I spoke in the evening from these words, "If they hear
not Moses and the prophets, neither will they be persuaded though one
rose from the dead." In meeting the society at night, I spoke plainly of
some who neglected their bands and classes; and informed them that we
took people into our societies that we might help them to become entire
Christians, and if they wilfully neglected those meetings, they thereby
withdrew themselves from our care and assistance. The next day many
people attended the preaching at the Meadows.

Tuesday, 14. My heart seems wholly devoted to God, and he favours
me with power over all outward and inward sin. My affections appear to
be quite weaned from all terrestrial objects. Some people, if they felt as I

[23] Lispenard's Meadows was part of the estate of Leonard Lispenard. It was about a
mile and a half north of Wesley Chapel and a little south of present Canal Street.
Lispenard had loaned six hundred pounds to the trustees. (See notes under September
6, 1772.) They subsequently bought two lots adjacent to the chapel from him. Lispenard was coexecutor of the estate of Rector Barclay, from whose widow the first lots
were purchased; and as such he signed the original deed. (See note under November 13,
1771.)

[24] The Rev. John Ritzman was minister of the Reformed Dutch Church. Asbury
heard him at the Middle Dutch Church on Nassau and Cedar streets. In 1761 he married Miss Joanna Schuyler, related to General Schuyler, to William Lupton. Tipple's
identification (*op. cit.*, 66) of him as Thomas Rankin was erroneous, as Rankin was at
St. George's Church in Philadelphia at this time. (Seaman, *op. cit.*, 422, 440; see *Min-
ates.*)

feel at present, would perhaps conclude they were saved from all indwelling sin. O my God, save me and keep me every moment of my life! The next day my soul was under heavy exercises, and much troubled by manifold temptations; but still, all my care was cast on the Lord. I find it hurtful to pore too much on myself. True, I should be daily employed in the duty of self-examination, and strictly attend both to my internal and external conduct; but, at the same time, my soul should steadily fix the eye of faith on the blessed Jesus, my Mediator and Advocate at the right hand of the eternal Father. Lord, cause thy face to shine upon me; and make me always joyful in thy salvation.

Thursday, 16. My soul was more and more delighted in God. I felt myself uneasy to-day on account of riding out,[25] though I was conscious it was intended for my health. Yet to some it might have the appearance of pleasuring, and encourage them to seek their carnal pleasure in such things.

Saturday, 18. The Lord was my helper; and my mind was in peace.

Lord's day, 19. This was a blessed and delightful day to my soul. The grace of God was eminently with me in all my public duties. Heard Mr. E. Charles English at St. Paul's church preach from these words, "Put on the new man, which after God is created in righteousness and true holiness." He spoke well on man's fallen state, and the new creation; and brought good reasons to prove that we must be renewed in order to dwell with God. But he did not insist on the necessity of repentance and faith in order to obtain this change.

Monday, 20. Mr. Richard Sause, Mr. Charles White, and Mr. Thomas Tucker[26] bore me company as far as Kingsbridge, on my way to New Rochelle. Was much indisposed when I reached the house of my friend Mr. Frederick Deveau; nevertheless, thought it my duty to preach to the people. The Lord is doing something for several souls in this place. Though they have had but very few sermons for twelve months, yet the class is lively and engaged with God.[27]

Thursday, 23. After preaching as often as I could to many people who attended at New Rochelle,[28] I set off for New York, and was met at Kingsbridge by Mr. Sause and Mr. Jarvis. But on my arrival in the city I found myself very unwell, and had a painful, restless night.

Friday, 24. Found myself better; and was much refreshed by letters

---

[25] Certain friends, perhaps Sause, White, Jarvis, and Molloy, had probably arranged riding trips for Asbury. Sause narrowly escaped drowning on one such ride. (See *Journal* entry for June 27, 1774.)

[26] Thomas Tucker aided in the erection of Wesley Chapel and was later a vestryman of Trinity Church. (*John Street Church Records*; Seaman, *op. cit.*, 442.)

[27] See note under June 23, 1773.

[28] The preaching places from Monday evening to Thursday morning were probably the homes of Deveau and Bonnette, leaders of the class.

from Mr. Lindsay and Mr. Shadford,[29] in Maryland. But one of these letters informed me that Mr. Strawbridge[30] was very officious in administering the ordinances. What strange infatuation attends that man! Why will he run before Providence?

Saturday, 25. My fever was very high last evening, so I took an emetic this morning. I found liberty in my own soul, and great meltings amongst the people, while preaching on the *Lord's day*. Though my disorder has a tendency to oppress my spirits, yet, blessed be God! I am favoured with power to conquer every spiritual foe; and my heart is sometimes wonderfully raised, as on the wings of faith and love.

Monday, 27. Richard Sause, who accompanied me a few miles into the country to-day, was very near being drowned. He went into a stream of water to wash his horse and chaise, but accidentally got out of the horse's depth, and they must all have been unavoidably lost, had not two men swam in and dragged them to the shore. Thus the Lord preserveth both man and beast. I went to bed this evening in much pain, and had an uncomfortable night.

Tuesday, 28. Many of my good friends kindly visited me to-day; and in the afternoon I took another emetic. My heart is fixed on God, as the best of objects, but pants for more vigour, and a permanent, solemn sense of God. Rose the next morning at five, though very weak, and spent a great part of the day in reading and writing. Many people attended the public worship in the evening, though I was but just able to give them a few words of exhortation. Seeing the people so desirous to hear now I am unable to say much to them, Satan tempts me to murmuring and discontent. May the Lord fill me with perfect resignation!

Thursday, 30. My body was very weak and sweated exceedingly. If I am the Lord's, why am I thus? But in his word he hath told me, "If I be without chastisement, then am I a bastard and not a son." O that this affliction may work in me the peaceable fruits of internal and universal righteousness! An attempt to speak a little in exhortation this evening greatly augmented my disorder.

Friday, July 1. In prayer to-day with I. B.,[31] a soldier in the 23d regiment, the Lord greatly refreshed and strengthened my soul. My mind was strongly impressed with a persuasion, that God, through mercy, would restore me to health. If so, I am determined, by his assistance, to be more

---

[29] Robert Lindsay and George Shadford had been appointed to Baltimore. (See *Minutes*.)

[30] (See notes under November 12, 1772; December 22, 1772.) Strawbridge defied Asbury, Wesley, and the conference by insisting on administering the sacrament.

[31] The soldiers of the twenty-third regiment mentioned here and below (Monday, July 4) are otherwise unidentified. They were referred to as "my Christian brethren" by Asbury when they left New York on July 27, 1774. The daughter of I. B. was killed in the storm of July 28.

than ever intent on promoting his cause and his glory. Gave an exhortation at night, and met the leaders: but the next day I was much indisposed; nevertheless, I spent part of my time in reading the afflicted condition of the Waldenses, when so wickedly persecuted by the Dominicans, with the rise of those brutish men.

Lord's day, 3. Poor Mr. H. came to me in great distress. He is a native of Stowbridge, where, as he supposes, he has a wife now living; and he has been so unwatchful as to suffer his affections to stray. May the Lord deliver him out of this dangerous snare of Satan! If not, he may be undone. I spoke with freedom this morning from Job x, 2, and spent part of the day in reading of the holy war which was carried on against the Waldenses and Albigenses, by the devil, the pope, and their emissaries. Though my body is still weak, my soul is strong in the Lord, and joyful in his salvation. And at night I was able to preach with spirit, and found myself happy in addressing a large and attentive audience.

Monday, 4. I spent part of this day in visiting a few friends, and found my heart much united to I. S., a musician of the 23d regiment. Was much better to-night than I had been for some time, and enjoyed a good night's rest.

Tuesday, 5. In reading the Life of Calvin, it appeared that many, in his day, had opposed the doctrine of predestination; and all who opposed it were spoken of by him and his followers, as bad men. My fever returned this evening, and it was a painful, restless night. But the will of the Lord be done! Though he slay me, yet will I trust him! Found very great lassitude of body the next day also; but my soul hungered and thirsted for more of God. In reading Clark's Life of Origen, I felt a strong desire to imitate that great and good man, as far as he went right.

Thursday, 7. My disorder was much abated, and I had power to speak plainly and pointedly to both saints and sinners.

Lord's day, 10. My bodily weakness has been such, for a few days past, as to prevent my officiating much in public; however, I ventured to preach twice to-day, but in the evening was so weak that I could scarce stand in the pulpit: but while preaching on the parable of the prodigal son, the Lord greatly refreshed and strengthened me; though I went to bed very ill at night. Satan tempted me to-day to think much of my gifts. Alas! what poor creatures we are; and to what dangers we are exposed! What are all our gifts, unless they answer some good purpose? Unless properly improved, they neither make us holier nor happier. We have nothing but what we have received; and unless we are humble in the possession of them, they only make us more like devils, and more fit for hell. How wonderfully is the language and behaviour of Mr. Lupton changed towards me! Before, I was everything that was bad; but now, all is very good. This is a mistake: my doctrine and preaching are the same; and so is my manner. But such is the deceitfulness of the man. His favourite, Mr. ——,

is now gone.[32] Had I preached like an archangel it would have been to
no purpose, while I thought it my duty to oppose him.

Monday, 11. My soul is not so intensely devoted to God as I would
have it; though my desires for more spirituality are very strong. Lord,
when shall my poor heart be as a rising, active, holy flame? Blessed be God!
my illness is more moderate to-day than it has been for some days past.
On *Wednesday*, a letter from Samuel Owings[33] informed me that the house
in Baltimore was then ready to be enclosed.[34] He also expressed a great
desire to persevere. May the Lord give him grace so to do!

Thursday, 14. My mind is in peace. I have now been sick near ten
months, and many days closely confined; yet I have preached about
three hundred times, and rode near two thousand miles in that time;
though very frequently in a high fever. Here is no ease, worldly profit, or
honour. What, then, but the desire of pleasing God and serving souls,
could stimulate to such laborious and painful duties? O that my labour
may not be in vain! that the Lord may give me to see fruit of these weak,
but earnest endeavours, many days hence! After preaching this evening
with some warmth of heart, I was very close and pointed in meeting the
society.

Saturday, 16. My heart was much taken up with God. Letters from my
dear friends, Mr. James Foster[35] and Mr. Thomas Rankin, gave me
great satisfaction. In meeting the band society, I showed them the possibility of using all the means, and, without sincerity and spirituality, they
might still be destitute of true religion.

[32] Lupton's favorite was probably Joseph Pilmoor, who had returned to England on
January 2, 1774. Tipple (*op. cit.*, 69) thought the favorite was Richard Wright. However,
Wright had spent little time in New York and with indifferent success, most of his work
being in Philadelphia, Maryland, and Virginia. On March 27, 1771, Wesley wrote to
Pilmoor and addressed him at Lupton's house. In that letter Wesley said complaint had
been made that Boardman and Pilmoor had secured a deed to Wesley Chapel which
replaced the original deed. This second instrument included the doctrinal phrases of
Wesley's Model Deed and substituted the names of Boardman and Pilmoor for Embury
and Heck. It seems that some laymen had protested the naming of itinerating preachers
as improper. Sause and White had come from Dublin, from which place Wesley's
letter was written; and they may have written their objections to friends there. This was
probably a factor in the troubles of the New York Society in late 1771 and early 1772.
(See note under November 22, 1771, *et seq.* See *Letters of John Wesley*, V, 232.)

[33] Samuel Owings (1733–1803) was the nephew of Joshua Owings and cousin of
Richard Owings. (See *Journal* entry for November 25, 1772.) Samuel Owings was a
leader in the Baltimore Society and a trustee of Cokesbury College. (See notes under
November 12 and 25, 1772; Armstrong: *Old Baltimore Conference*, 18, 89.)

[34] This house was the Lovely Lane Chapel. (See *Journal* entry for October 19, 1774.)

[35] James Foster, whom Asbury had known in Baltimore, was admitted to the conference in 1776 and assigned to that city with Asbury. (Lednum, *op. cit.*, 168; *Minutes*,
1776.) Tipple identifies him as Mr. Fiddler, but gives no supporting data. (*Op. cit.*, 69.)
He probably had John Fiddler in mind. However, Fiddler did not enter the conference
until 1784, and it may be doubted that he was in familiar correspondence with Asbury
in 1774.

Monday, 18. The Lord assisted me in yesterday's duties; and he is the keeper and comforter of my soul to-day. A poor, unhappy young woman, who had abandoned herself to the devil and wicked men, being at the point of death, and expecting to go shortly and render an account of herself to God, sent for me to visit her. I felt some reluctance; but considering the danger her soul was in, thought it my duty to go. She was very attentive while I spoke plainly to her, and made prayer to God in her behalf. Strange infatuation! that men will not seriously think of preparing for death, till it comes upon them! If we were sure of dying in a few hours, most men would think it their duty to labour for a preparation: but when no man is sure of living a few hours, very few think seriously about it. So does the god of this world blind the minds of mankind!

Thursday, 21. My heart enjoys great freedom, with much peace and love both towards God and man. Lord, ever keep me from all sin, and increase the graces of thy Holy Spirit in my soul! A letter from Mr. Thomas Rankin brought melancholy tidings of Abraham Whitworth. Alas for that man! He has been useful, but was puffed up, and so fell into the snare of the devil. My heart pitied him: but I fear he died a backslider.[36]

Lord's day, 24. Ended the parable of the prodigal son. Does it not appear from this parable, that some, who, comparatively speaking, have all their lifetime endeavoured to please God, and are entitled to all his purchased, communicative blessings, are nevertheless not favoured with such rapturous sensations of divine joy as some others. I remember when I was a small boy and went to school, I had serious thoughts, and a particular sense of the being of a God; and greatly feared both an oath and a lie. At twelve years of age the Spirit of God strove frequently and powerfully with me: but being deprived of proper means and exposed to bad company, no effectual impressions were left on my mind. And, though fond of what some call innocent diversions, I abhorred fighting and quarrelling: when anything of this sort happened, I always went home displeased. But I have been much grieved to think that so many Sabbaths were idly spent, which might have been better improved. However, wicked as my companions were, and fond as I was of play, I never imbibed their vices. When between thirteen and fourteen years of age, the Lord graciously visited my soul again. I then found myself more inclined to obey; and carefully attended preaching in West Bromwich; so that I heard Stillingfleet,[37] Bagnel,[38] Ryland,[39] Anderson,[40] Mansfield,[41] and

[36] For the moral collapse of Abraham Whitworth see note under April 27, 1773. The phrase "I fear he died a backslider" was probably inserted at a later date, since Whitworth seems to have lived during the Revolution and died of wounds received while fighting with the British forces. (Lednum, *op. cit.*, 129.) In the following January, Asbury reported that he was still alive. (See *Journal* entry for January 7, 1775.)

[37] Edward Stillingfleet, descendant of Edward Stillingfleet, bishop of Worcester, was head minister of West Bromwich from 1757 to 1782. As chaplain to the Earl of Dart-

Talbott,[42] men who preached the truth. I then began to watch over my inward and outward conduct; and having a desire to hear the Methodists, I went to Wednesbury,[43] and heard Mr. Fletcher[44] and Mr. Ingham,[45] but did not understand them, though one of their subjects is fresh in my memory to this day. This was the first of my hearing the Methodists. After that, another person went with me to hear them again:[46] the text was, "The time will come, when they will not endure sound doctrine." My companion was cut to the heart, but I was unmoved. The next year Mr. Mather[47] came into those parts. I was then about fifteen; and, young as I

mouth he was one of the more important evangelical influences in the Midlands, and probably had greater influence on Asbury than anyone else.

[38] This was possibly Gibbons Bagnall (1719–1800), who was not otherwise known as an evangelical.

[39] John Ryland (1736–1822) was ordained in 1759 to serve as curate for his elder brother Richard, rector of Sutton Coldfield. In 1774 he was appointed the first vicar of St. Mary's, Birmingham, which became the home of the "Church Methodists" in the area. (*Proceedings* of the Wesley Historical Society, III, 193–96.)

[40] This was possibly Sir William Anderson, rector of Epworth, who was sympathetic to Wesley in 1780. (Wesley's *Journal*, VI, 287.)

[41] This was probably John Mansell, whom the Rev. John Fletcher lists as among the evangelical clergy in 1764.

[42] William Talbot (1719–74), vicar of Kineton, Warwicks, was the son of a wealthy family; and Samuel Walker of Truro, one of the earliest evangelicals, exerted considerable influence upon his ministry. (Elliott-Binns: *The Early Evangelicals*, 252, 291–92.)

[43] Wednesbury is about three miles from West Bromwich. It was the scene of the first Methodist preaching in Staffordshire, and here the Methodists encountered their worst persecution. Richard Whatcoat was also a member of the Wednesbury group, and it is believed that both Asbury and Whatcoat heard John Wesley preach there on March 4, 1760. (Baker: *A Methodist Pilgrim in England*, 74–77.)

[44] The Rev. John W. Fletcher (1729–85) was one of the greatest of John Wesley's evangelical collaborators among the Anglican clergy. Wesley designated Fletcher as his successor in charge of the Methodist societies after the death of himself and his brother Charles. (Tyerman: *Wesley's Designated Successor.*)

[45] The Rev. Benajmin Ingham (1712–72) was a member of the Holy Club at Oxford and a companion of the Wesleys on their mission to Georgia in 1735. On his return to England he became the pioneer evangelist in northern England and founded many religious societies which in later years he transferred to the care of the Moravians. In 1741 he married Lady Margaret Hastings, sister of the Earl of Huntingdon, but continued to itinerate widely from his headquarters at Aberford. Although the fresh societies he founded were known as Inghamites, he continued to preach to many Methodist congregations; however, negotiations for a fusion of the Inghamites and the Methodists fell through. (Tyerman: *Oxford Methodists*, 57–154.)

[46] Briggs (*op. cit.*, 17) suggests that Asbury's companion was named William Emery.

[47] Alexander Mather (1733–1800) was a Scots baker who was accepted by Wesley as an itinerant preacher in 1757. He became one of the leading preachers and in 1788 was ordained by Wesley as a "superintendent," apparently with the intention of serving as a bishop for England as Coke and Asbury had done for America. He was stationed in Staffordshire in the summer of 1760 and witnessed a widespread revival of religion there, one of the key points being the prayer meeting at Wednesbury. Mather was the second president of the British Conference after the death of Wesley. (Jackson: *Lives of Early Methodist Preachers*, II, 158–239.)

was, the word of God soon made deep impressions on my heart, which brought me to Jesus Christ, who graciously justified my guilty soul through faith in his precious blood; and soon showed me the excellency and necessity of holiness. About sixteen I experienced a marvellous display of the grace of God, which some might think was full sanctification, and was indeed very happy, though in an ungodly family. At about seventeen I began to hold some public meetings; and between seventeen and eighteen began to exhort and preach. When about twenty-one I went through Staffordshire and Gloucestershire, in the place of a travelling preacher; and the next year through Bedfordshire, Sussex, &c. In 1769 I was appointed assistant in Northamptonshire; and the next year travelled in Wiltshire. September 3, 1771, I embarked for America, and for my own private satisfaction, began to keep an imperfect journal.

To-day Dr. Ogilvie preached a pertinent discourse on the shortness of time. The Lord favoured me with great liberty in the evening, while preaching to a large congregation from Gen. xix, 17. And I was enabled to speak plainly and closely in meeting the society at night.

Tuesday, 26. My soul is in peace. But I long to be more spiritual—to be wholly devoted to God. Some circumstances make me fear that we have a few bad characters in the society here. These are the people that injure the cause of God. Like Judas, they betray the Lord with a kiss. It is not easy to conceive how such characters counteract the most faithful preaching. If their conduct is not fully known to the preachers, it is so known to many of their acquaintances, that Satan takes the offered advantage, and hardens the hearts of many against all the power of religion. Of all characters, that of a designing sinner under the fair appearance of religion, is the most odious. O that the Lord may strip all such unsound professors, in every place, of their covering, and show them to his servants in their own proper colours; that Israel may be able to put away the accursed thing from among them; and so increase both in strength and number!

Wednesday, 27. I rose early this morning to see my Christian brethren, the soldiers, go off; but was much affected at parting with those worthy men, I. S. and I. B.[48] May the Lord go with them!

Thursday, 28. The Lord shows me the snares of Satan, and enables me to avoid them. He favours me with the light of his countenance, and fills me with holy love. Surely we stand in jeopardy every hour! This day the thunder and lightning struck four people dead on the spot. Awful scene! And will man still venture to be careless and wicked? I made some improvement on the subject in the evening.

Friday, 29. I rose unwell this morning, and received a melancholy account, that the daughter of I. S. was beat overboard.[49] Poor man! He has lost both his children by going to sea. I was much blessed at intercession

---

[48] See *Journal* entry and note under July 1, 1774.   [49] *Ibid.*

to-day, but shut up in preaching at night. My soul is determined to live more to God.

Lord's day, 31. We had a feeling time this morning while I preached from Psalm i, 13.[50] After the various duties of the day, I met the society, and showed them the utility of our economy, the advantages of union and the fearful end of leaving our fellowship.

August 1. Some of my good friends accompanied me[51] as far as Kingsbridge, on my way to New Rochelle. I visited my little flock with some satisfaction. Here are some of the offspring of the French Protestants, who, on account of their religion, fled from Rochelle in France; and God has mercifully remembered them unto the third and fourth generation.[52]

I have great discoveries of my defects and weaknesses. My soul is not so steadily and warmly devoted to the Lord as it might be. Lord, help me, and supply me with grace always! In preaching from Ephesians ii, 12, 13,[53] I had great freedom. It seems strange, that sometimes, after much premeditation and devotion, I cannot express my thoughts with readiness and perspicuity; whereas at other times, proper sentences of Scripture and apt expressions occur without care or much thought. Surely this is of the Lord, to convince us that it is not by power or might, but by his Spirit the work must be done. Nevertheless, it is doubtless our duty to give ourselves to prayer and meditation, at the same time depending entirely on the grace of God, as if we had made no preparation. Rose early the next morning, but found myself weak both in body and mind. In this tabernacle I groan, earnestly desiring to be clothed upon with the house which is from heaven. My soul longs to fly to God, that it may be ever with him. O happy day, that shall call a poor exile home to his Father's house! But I must check the impetuous current of desire, for it is written, "He that believeth shall not make haste." After preaching to a large auditory in the evening at Peter Bonnette's, I rested in peace. Visited Mr. Burling (?) a partial friend, the next day, and had some serious, weighty conversation with him. I then went to Mr. Deveau's very unwell, and in trouble and pain spoke from Job xxi, 15. After a very restless night, I rose the next morning much indisposed, and was obliged to go to bed again. However, on *Friday*, 5, I set off for New York; and there met with William Watters.[54]

Saturday, 6. My mind is calm and comfortable, but grieved by the imprudence of some, and the loose conduct of a few others. Though much afflicted, I met the band leaders and body bands; and we had a singular blessing.

Lord's day, 7. We had a solemn, happy love feast. Though very weak,

[50] Psalm 1 has only six verses. The reference may be to Psalm 11:3.
[51] Sause or Selby, with White or Molloy, frequently accompanied Asbury.
[52] The homes of Deveau and Bonnette were focal to the group.
[53] The service was at the home of Frederick Deveau.
[54] William Watters had been appointed to Trenton, New Jersey.

made out to preach in the evening with some enlargement of heart. Brother Watters has much courage in preaching.

Tuesday, 9. My soul was assaulted by trials of a very severe kind: but the Lord was my keeper. I have been reading Newton on the Prophecies.[55] He is pretty clear in his views, and affords a good key for many passages; but confines himself too much to the literal meaning of the Revelation.

Wednesday, 10. My frame is much afflicted. But it is worse to be afflicted in mind by the misconduct of professors. It grieves me much to see the deceit of a few persons who have crept in amongst us. It is a thousand pities that such, whose hearts are not right with God, should ever thrust themselves in amongst the people of God. They are too apt to make all they are connected with as a rope of sand. I clearly see that professors who are rotten at heart, are a hinderance and curse to the rest. May the Lord thoroughly purge his floor! I was very low, but met my class, and preached in the evening. There appeared to be but little depth of religion in the class. It is a great folly to take people into society before they know what they are about. What some people take for religion and spiritual life is nothing but the power of the natural passions. It is true, real religion cannot exist without peace, and love, and joy. But then, *real religion is real holiness*. And all sensations without a strong disposition for holiness are but delusive.

Thursday, 11. My soul is in peace; and longs to be more devoted to God. My heart was enlarged and happy in exhorting the people this evening.

Friday, 12. This was a day of trouble and dejection of mind. But, committing my cause to God by faith and prayer, I have a hope that he will always stand by and deliver me. My soul was greatly straitened in public speaking. I received several letters to-day; some of which revived my spirits; but one from Mr. Rankin gave me pain. Satan makes use of all his cunning and tricks. But the Lord will rebuke him. My duty is clear—to bear all things patiently, and silently commit my cause to God. Even in this city there are some restless minds, who are not much disposed to spiritual union. Going into the pulpit this evening, I found an inflammatory letter without a name. My trials are multiplied and weighty: but glory to God! he strengthens and comforts me by an abundant manifestation of his love. Oh, how is my soul taken up with God! He is all in all to me! and if he is for me, I need not care who is against me.

Lord's day 14. Mr. Peabody[56] visited and dined with the rector to-day,[57] and what the event will be, I know not. Attending at church, as usual, I

---

[55] The Rev. Thomas Newton (1704–82), bishop of Bristol, wrote *Dissertations on the Prophecies, which have been remarkably fulfilled, and are at this time fulfilling in the world*, the first volume of which was published in 1754 and two other volumes in 1758. *Dictionary of National Biography*, XIV, 403–5.)

[56] Numerous references to this man appear until Monday, October 10, when Asbury with several others escorted him across the Hudson River to New Jersey. Evidently

heard Dr. ——[58] blow away on, "This is the day that the Lord hath made."
He makes a strange medley of his preaching; though he delivers many
good things, yet, for want of some arrangement of his ideas, all appears to
be incoherency and confusion. The Spirit of the Lord was with me, while
declaring his counsel to a large, listening audience. O that I could bring
them to the arms of Christ by thousands!

Monday, 15. I felt some conviction for sleeping too long; and my mind
was troubled on account of a conversation which had past between Mr.
Rankin, Mr. S.,[59] and myself. But the great Searcher of hearts knoweth
my intentions; and to him I submit all future events. Mr. Laidlie[60]
waited on Mr. Peabody, and told him he appeared to be more taken up
in reading Mr. Berridge's Christian World Unmasked,[61] than the Bible.
Mr. Berridge kept his room, in a very gloomy state of mind, about five
years ago; and now he is come forth with his facetious pen to dictate to
the Christian world. But Mr. Fletcher, in his Fifth Check,[62] has fully

---

Peabody carried on a preaching mission among nonconformist congregations. Asbury
heard him several times and had personal contacts with him. He preached at Wesley
Chapel on October 7, 1774.

[57] The Rev. Samuel Auchmuty, D.D., was the rector of Trinity Church. (See *Journal*
entry for August 28, 1774.)

[58] This was probably Dr. John Ogilvie at St. Paul's Chapel.

[59] This was probably George Shadford. There is a possibility that it was Robert
Strawbridge. Tipple (*op. cit.*, 72) identifies this man as Richard Sause, Asbury's close
friend in the New York Society; but the problem discussed appears to have been of
general administration and not local to New York. The conversation was evidently
of some time past, referred to in the painful letter recently received from Rankin
(*Journal*, August 12, 1774). Several references in the next six months attest a tense
situation with Rankin, to which either Shadford or Strawbridge, or both, may well have
been committed.

[60] The Rev. Archibald Laidlie, D.D. (1727–78) was minister of the North Dutch
Church at William and Fulton streets in New York and a religious and civic leader. He
had been brought from Scotland to conduct services in English for the Dutch congregation. He greatly influenced the girl who was to become Mrs. Livingston and the mother
of Mrs. Freeborn Garrettson. (See *Journal* entries for July 3, 1799, and August 1, 1800.)
Tipple (*op. cit.*, 73) identifies him as Lupton, but it seems improbable that the merchant
would have engaged in a theological argument with a trained preacher; Tipple identifies Laidlie on p. 474. (See Greenleaf: *History of the Churches in the City of New York*,
15, 16.)

[61] The Rev. John Berridge (1716–93), vicar of Everton, was one of the most learned
men and outstanding preachers of his day. He was a Calvinist, and in his early life he,
like Wesley, "sought to be justified by works," but in 1756 he experienced a change of
heart and became intimately related to the Methodist revival and an associate of Wesley.
In 1759 he was the leader of a revival at Everton, of which Wesley left accounts. He
wrote *Christian World Unmasked* and *Sion's Songs*. Asbury had heard him in England.
(Wesley: *Journal*, IV, 291, 317–22, 338–43 *et seq.*; Tyerman: *Life and Times of Wesley*,
II, 309–13, 331–33 *et seq.*; see Asbury's *Journal* entry for February 1, 1795.)

[62] John Fletcher of Madeley, the saintly man whom Wesley once designated as his
successor, was the author of the famous *Checks to Antinomianism*. (See *Journal* entry
for February 1, 1795.)

nswered all his witty arguments. Mr. Berridge was a good man, no oubt; but unfortunately drank deep into the principles of Antinomianism.

Wednesday, 17. My mind is free; and my soul delighteth in God. He aketh such possession of my heart, as to keep out all desire for created bjects. In due time, I humbly hope, through Jesus Christ, to enter into he full fruition. O blessed day, when my soul shall be swallowed up in iod!

> "In hope of that immortal crown,
>   I now the cross sustain;
> And gladly wander up and down,
>   And smile at toil and pain."

Friday, 19. I was very unwell; and in much pain of body spoke to the eople at night. Thus it seems, at present, weakness and pain are a part f my portion. O that my soul may be made perfect through sufferings!

Lord's day, 21. My body is afflicted, and my way is rough; nevertheless, cheerfully submit to the will of God. And though very unwell, I met a lass and preached at night.

Monday, 22. My heart panteth for God, even for the living God. A etter came to hand to-day from E.B., giving an account of the work of he Lord in Gibraltar, and inviting me to go. But my way is not open.

Tuesday, 23. A degree of the peace and happiness of heaven possessed ny soul to-day. And although it was a rainy evening, many people attended while I preached from 2 Kings v, 14, 15, 16.

Wednesday, 24. My mind is much exercised about going to Gibraltar. May the Lord direct my steps! On *Friday*, at intercession, my heart was greatly moved by the power of God.

Lord's day, 28. My soul was expanded and filled with love, while reaching from Isaiah lv, 1. Mr. Peabody attended at the church to-day, ut was not invited to preach.[63]

Monday, 29. I visited Second River,[64] where a number of Low Dutch eople attended the word, which was delivered with a blessing. J. K., one f our local preachers, has been made useful to the inhabitants of this eighbourhood.

Thursday, Sept. 1. My system gathers strength; and though variously nd sorely exercised, the Lord is graciously with me, blessing both my soul

---

[63] Peabody attended Trinity Church. He had dined with the rector, Auchmuty, on he 14th. (See *Journal* entry for that date.)

[64] Second River was a tributary of the Passaic River and the boundary between Belleille and Newark, in New Jersey. Arent Schuyler established a fund for the support of clergyman, and in 1725 a church was erected. There was a break in the pastorates in he 1770's, and during this period Methodist preaching began. After 1790 Asbury often raveled through Second River on his trips between New York and Philadelphia beause of improved roads and the Passaic and Hackensack bridges, and he preached here on occasions. (Disosway and Gregory: *Earliest Churches of New York and icinity*, 356 ff.)

and my labours. I clearly see that I must be cut off from every creature to do the will of God with an undivided heart. May the Lord sanctify m* wholly for himself, and every moment keep me from all appearance of evil

Saturday, 3. Calm serenity sat on my mind, and all my soul was fixe* on God, and sweetly inclined to do his will in all things. In the afternoo* I felt unwell, but met the leaders and bands. The next day, though my bod* was very feeble, I went through my public duties.

Monday, 5. I visited Mrs. D., who hardly escaped falling into ruin, bot* of body and soul. She opened the matter to me, and found deliverance A solemn report was brought to the city to-day, that the men-of-war ha* fired on Boston.[65] A fear rose in my mind of what might be the event o* this. But it was soon banished by considering—I must go on and mind m* own business,[66] which is enough for me; and leave all those things to th* providence of God.

Tuesday, 6. I rose very early this morning in great peace, and deter* mined not to let an hour of the day slip without earnest prayer to God Went the next day to hear Mr. Peabody preach at Flatbush.[67] He spok* pretty well, though very tenderly, on the fall and recovery of man. An* the report of his great abilities exceeds the reality. We returned just tim* enough for preaching: I spoke with great liberty from 2 Kings v, 17, 18 19; but afterward found myself very unwell.

Thursday, 8. Am both grieved and ashamed that my soul is not mor* steadily and fervently devoted to God

"And shall I ever live
At this poor, dying rate—
My love so faint, so cold to thee,
And thine to me so great?"

No: I will both labour and strive to be more swallowed up in the hol* will of God. My determination is strong; may Divine grace make i* stronger and stronger every day!

Friday, 9. My soul was happy in God: yet I felt some grief on account of the weakness and deceit of a few who profess religion.

Saturday, 10. God is still my principal object. Tidings came to-day, o* some dissatisfaction between Mr. Rankin[68] and the people in Philadelphia. But my duty is before me; I have my own business to mind.

[65] This was a false alarm, believed by many historians to have been circulated by patriot extremists to incite the people to action or to demonstrate to General Gates, the British commander, what would be the American reaction to attack. (Lossing: *Pictorial Field-book of the Revolution*, I, 511–12.)

[66] See *Journal* entry for September 10, 1774, for a similar expression of Asbury's determination to remain aloof from the political problems of the day.

[67] Flatbush was four or five miles southeast of Brooklyn. It is now a part of Brooklyn Borough of New York. It had a historic Dutch church built in the pre-British period.

[68] Thomas Rankin was then stationed at St. George's Church in Philadelphia. (See *Minutes*.)

Lord's day, 11. Dr. —— went on with his trumpery in his old strain; and the great Mr. Peabody had crowds to hear him in the French church. We also had a crowded audience and solemn time in the evening. A young woman of our society, who was seated in the congregation last Lord's day, is now a corpse. How short, how precarious is life! and yet what awful and weighty things depend upon it! On *Monday* evening I spoke on the occasion, from Job xix, 25, 26. We have lost a promising disciple of twenty-two years of age: but her flesh resteth in hope. When will the Saviour extend the arms of his mercy to make me perfectly and eternally free? I heard the celebrated Mr. Peabody again to-day. He insisted on eternal election; the gift of the Father to the Son; the renewal of the little flock by grace; and the Father's good pleasure; from Luke xii, 32. He detained us two hours; and had many devoted admirers. He spoke to the sinners with great words, but to little purpose.

Wednesday, 14. My mind is in great peace, and my body in better health. And though my heart cleaveth to the Lord, yet I long—O! I greatly long to be more swallowed up in the will of God.

Thursday, 15. All my desire is unto the Lord, and to the remembrance of his name. To please him is my chief delight; but there is more in view for which I pant:—

> "A heart in every thought renew'd,
>   And full of love divine;
> Perfect, and right, and pure, and good,
>   A copy, Lord, of thine."[69]

Friday, 16. I rose this morning dejected in mind. But my purposes to be wholly given up to God, are stronger than ever. And I hope to live to him in a more devoted manner than heretofore. Peace, and power, and love filled my soul, while speaking at night from Hosea xii. Glory be given to God!

Saturday, 17. My affections are raised from earth and all its objects. My treasure is above, and there also is my heart. In meeting the bands, I showed them the impropriety and danger of keeping their thoughts or fears of each other to themselves: this frustrates the design of bands; produces coolness and jealousies towards each other; and is undoubtedly the policy of Satan.

Lord's day, 18. Losing some of my ideas in preaching, I was ashamed of myself, and pained to see the people waiting to hear what the blunderer had to say. May these things humble me, and show me where my great strength lieth! In meeting the society I urged the necessity of more private devotion, and of properly digesting what they hear. Set off the next morning for New Rochelle, and found E. Deveau[70] in distress of soul.

[69] The quotation is from Charles Wesley's hymn "O for a heart to praise my God."
[70] The given name of Mrs. Frederick Deveau is not known. She was converted by the following Thursday. (See *Journal* entries and notes under September 22, 1774; December 10, 1771.)

This is an agreeable family, and the children are both affectionate and obedient to their parents. I hope she and the rest of them will become true Christians, and be finally bound up in the bundle of life. I preached from 2 Tim. iv, 2; and many strangers were present. Satan is frequently assaulting me with his temptations; but the Lord enables me to discover and resist his first attacks.

Tuesday, 20. Christ was precious. At Peter Bonnette's I spoke too plainly for some who were present. The next evening, at Frederick Deveau's we had a heart-affecting time; and I trust it will not be forgotten by all.

Thursday, 22. The Lord has graciously visited E. Deveau, and turned all her mourning into joy. Her soul is happy in the love of God. May the Lord carry on his work of grace through this family and neighbourhood turning all their hearts unto himself! The power of God was present in the congregation to-night, while I took my leave for a season from Isa. lxvi, 2.

Friday, 23. I set off for New York, and met some of my good friends at Kingsbridge. They brought me a letter from Thomas Rankin, who thought himself injured; but I am determined to drop all disputes as far as possible. Mr. Peabody is going on in New York with his Antinomianism unmasked. How prone is man to do what is wrong! And what watchfulness and diligence are necessary for a man to be right both in sentiment and practice!

Lord's day, 25. According to the particular request of sister G., preached her funeral sermon, from Isaiah xlix, 10. She had been brought up a Calvinist; but when she found peace with God, she renounced all her Calvinistic principles, which she said had been a check to her industry in seeking the Lord. In the time of her last illness, she manifested a great degree of patience, and expressed a strong desire for entire purity of heart. A little before her death, she was filled with perfect love; and seemed to want more strength and language to praise God. However, she did it to the uttermost of her power.

Monday, 26. My soul is sweetly drawn out after God, and satisfied with him as a sufficient portion. But O! how I long to be more spiritual!

> "Come, and possess me whole,
> Nor hence again remove;
> Settle and fix my wav'ring soul
> With ALL thy weight of love."

Thursday, 29. William Lynch[71] gave me an account of the manner of Mr. Rankin's treating him, because he would not go to Schenectady. But my mind is bent on loving God, and doing his will in all things. I have had

[71] Tipple (*op. cit.*, 74) identifies this man as William Lupton, but the merchant had little use for Rankin and would hardly have made such a request of him. (See *Journal* entries for November 20, 1772; September 5, 1773; January 8, 1775; Lednum, *op. cit.*, 84, 90, 116, 207.)

requent calls of late to visit the sick. May it prove a blessing both to them
and me! My heart was warm while addressing the congregation this evening, and I hope it was not labour lost. At two o'clock in the night, we were
all alarmed by a fire which burned down a house in Peck Slip.[72] What a
resemblance of the general judgment! But, if the cry of fire alarms us,
how much more shall we be alarmed by the archangel's trumpet! When
all the ungodly shall have ten thousand times more cause to fear, than the
loss of houses, and goods, and life, how will they endure the cutting anguish? But they are after the flesh; therefore they mind the things of the
flesh, and them only.

Lord's day, October 2. Though I have lately heard several preachers of
some fame, I am fully of the opinion that there is room enough for us to
preach repentance, faith, and all the work of God on the soul of man.
They almost leave this field entirely our own. We had a solemn love feast
to-day: though some imposed on us who will not meet in class.

Monday, 3. My soul was in peace, but assaulted by Satan. The next day
Mr. Peabody sent for me, and requested permission to preach in our house.
I told him, that as he had refused it at first, our people did not take it
well.[73]

Wednesday, 5. I rose early this morning, and found my soul devoted to
God. But it troubles my mind that I am not more so. Lord, come and save
me now with all thy great and glorious salvation! O, hasten the time!

> "Jesus, see my panting breast;
> See, I pant in thee to rest;
> Gladly would I NOW be clean;
> Cleanse me NOW from every sin."

Friday, 7. Mr. Peabody had appointed to preach in our house, and a
very large congregation attended on the occasion. He spoke on the chaff
and wheat, from Matt. iii, 12; and perhaps felt himself under some obliga-
tion to come as near to our doctrine as his principles would admit of;
and thereby gave tolerable satisfaction.

Saturday, 8. My heart was enlarged towards God. I saw a letter from
Mr. Pilmoor,[74] filled with his usual softness. Poor man! he seems blind to
his own conduct. We had a very happy time in meeting the bands this
evening.

[72] Peck Slip was a wharf embankment of an estuary a little less than a mile northeast
of Wesley Chapel. Nearby was Beekman's Swamp, where tanneries were located and
where Asbury preached on October 17, 1774. Present-day Peck Slip is between Fulton Street and Brooklyn Bridge near the Fulton Fish Market, but the estuary has been
filled in.

[73] Despite Asbury's critical reply the arrangement was made, and Peabody preached
at Wesley Chapel on Friday of that week. (See entry for that date.)

[74] Joseph Pilmoor had returned to England months before; and the letter was probably addressed to William Lupton, formerly one of Pilmoor's closest associates at
Wesley Chapel. (See *Journal* entry for July 10, 1774.)

Lord's day, 9. The Lord assisted me in my public exercises both morning and night: and going to church to-day, as usual, I heard a stranger preach; but he was a workman that needed to be ashamed. Attended Mr. Peabody on *Monday*, and found him very affectionate. The elders of the French church[75] wept over him with much tenderness. Several friends, with myself, conducted him across the river; then, after singing a parting hymn, he prayed very feelingly, and we took our leave of each other. I afterward went to preach in the Swamp,[76] where we had many people and a good time.

Tuesday, 11. Last night my soul was greatly troubled for want of a closer walk with God. Lord, how long shall I mourn and pray, and not experience all that my soul longeth for? And this day, my mind is in nearly the same frame.

Wednesday, 12. The Lord blessed me with great peace. I. Molloy[77] brought a letter from New Rochelle, containing an agreeable account of the work of God there. With much enlargement of heart, I preached to-night from 1 Kings xix, 11; and hope it was made a blessing to many present.

Thursday, 13. My soul is not so intensely stayed on God as it might be. O that he would bring me nearer to himself; and so transform me into his divine likeness, that there may be no diversity of will; but that it may be my meat and drink to promote his glory from moment to moment in all I do! I had much company in the course of this day.

Friday, 14. My heart was much devoted to God. But having been here now four months, preaching or exhorting every day, and twice on the Lord's day, besides society meetings; it seems to be too much for both the people and the preacher.[78] We have now more unity in the society here than we have had for some time past. But we want more of the life and power of religion amongst us.

Lord's day, 16. Yesterday Satan assaulted me powerfully; but the Lord was my keeper; so that I may with great propriety adopt the language of the poet,—

> "In all my temptations he keeps me, to prove
> His utmost salvation, his fulness of love."

This day the Spirit of grace assisted me in my public exercises. Mr. S. T.,

---

[75] The French Protestant Church was located on King Street east of Nassau.

[76] Beekman's Swamp lay north of Beekman Street and east of Gold Street in the direction of the East River. Adjacent to the swamp were the famous tan-yards with clusters of hovels and cottages of the workers. It was to the people of this location that Asbury preached, and he evidently went there quite often.

[77] I. Molloy was related to a family active in the society at New Rochelle. (See *Journal* entries for November 25, 1771; January 5, 1772.)

[78] Asbury's residence in New York at this time was to be almost six months because of prolonged illness.

nce a silversmith of this city, preached a good sermon at church;[79] hough his voice was so low that he could scarce be heard.

Monday, 17. Many people attended preaching in the Beekman's Swamp; nd my soul was greatly blessed in the discharge of my duty. But O, my eart is bowed down within me; and I feel strongly determined to be lore watchful and diligent in pleasing God.

Tuesday, 18. My heart was much taken up with God. I drank tea this fternoon with an old Moravian, who belonged to their fraternity in 'etter Lane, at the time when Mr. Wesley was so intimate with them.

Wednesday, 19. Captain Webb informed me by letter, the house in altimore was so far finished that he had preached in it. With great berty and satisfaction, I both met class and preached in the evening; nd feel more encouragement to hope for the people here.

Thursday, 20. Notwithstanding all my grievous temptations, God is still le object of my faith, my hope, my love, my joy. O that he may fill me lways with filial fear, and give me grace to die to all but him! My soul bounds with sweet peace; and an exhortation which I gave this evening, as made a blessing, I trust, to several that heard it.

Friday, 21. A solemn, comfortable sense of God rested on my mind, nd he has kept me from what I hate. And though Satan made some ttempts upon my soul, yet the Lord gave me power to withstand him. he next day we had a refreshing time in band meeting.

Lord's day, 23. Dr. Magaw,[80] from Dover, preached to-day at church, n fellowship with God. He spoke well on the subject, as far as it relates to le fruits and effects of the Spirit; but was deficient in respect to the witess, supposing that some may be in favour with God and not know it. ur carnal hearts are too prone to draw destructive conclusions from such doctrine as his. Dr. Ogilvie,[81] as usual, made a mighty clutter in the ulpit about Noah's ark. Our congregation was large, and we were not ft without a blessing.

Monday, 24. I still look to Jesus, the Author and Finisher of my faith, nd trust in him for supplies of strength and consolation. But O, when lall my attention be so fixed, that nothing may divert it a single moment om its beloved object! We are informed that three of our preachers are ming over from England, and that we may look for them every day.[82]

[79] This was either Trinity Church at Broadway and Wall Street or St. Paul's Chapel Broadway and Fulton Street.

[80] McGaw was rector of the Anglican Church in Dover, Delaware. (See *Journal* try for April 2, 1779.)

[81] This appears to be the last time Asbury heard Ogilvie preach. He was smitten with oplexy while preaching at St. Paul's on Sunday, November 20, 1774, when Asbury is in Westchester. (See note under August 30, 1772, and *Journal* entry for November , 1774.)

[82] These preachers were James Dempster, Martin Rodda, and possibly William lendenning.

Tuesday, 25. This morning my spirit wrestled with principalities an powers; but in the duty of prayer the Lord delivered me. After preachin at night from Matt. xxiv, 12, a man from Morristown[83] came to me t inquire into my principles; and told me the Lord was bringing souls t himself in his neighbourhood, and that more than one hundred wer converted there.

Wednesday, 26. My soul is in peace, but longs to be more spiritua After meeting a class and preaching in the evening, I found myself ir disposed with a cold and fever. The next day my disorder continue attended with a sore throat, so that it was with difficulty and pain I spok to the people.

Friday, 28. I do not sufficiently love God, nor live by faith in the suburb of heaven. This gives me more concern than the want of health.

> "'Tis worse than death my God to love,
> And not my God alone."

I was not able to preach, and was obliged to go to bed early; but coul not sleep. On *Saturday*, as my disorder continued, I felt a strong desir for more patience. Mr. Jarvis, his wife, and daughter, are all very ill brought on chiefly through fatigue.

Lord's day, 30. I kept close house till evening. And O! what happines did my soul enjoy with God! So open and delightful was the intercours between God and my soul, that it gave me grief if any person came int my room, to disturb my sweet communion with the blessed Father an the Son. When my work is done, may I enter into that fulness of joy whic shall never be interrupted, in the blissful realms above! In the evening ventured to preach from 1 Cor. i, 21; and spoke with great freedom an plainness; and felt better afterward than could have been expecte Found myself something better on *Monday*, and met two classes.

Tuesday, November 1. My soul was in a lively frame, and sweetly in clined to live to God, and to do all his holy will. Many people appeared feel the word, while I preached in the evening from Luke viii, 18.

Wednesday, 2. My friends in this city concluded to write to Mr. Rankin, requesting that I might continue some time longer in New York and th country adjacent, supposing it would endanger my life to go into the lo countries. But to stay or go, I submit to Providence. As my legs, hand and feet were swollen, it was thought proper to consult a physician, wh sent me a certain mixture of bitters.

Thursday, 3. My mind was much taken up with God; but I must lamel that I am not perfectly crucified with Christ. I visited Mr. Jarvis, wh

---

[83] Morristown was about twenty miles west from Newark or Elizabeth in Ne Jersey.

[84] For reasons of health Asbury had overstayed the normal period of residence New York. Evidently Rankin agreed that he might remain until relieved by one of tl new men expected from England.

appeared to be near death; and am ready to say, Art thou he? O, how changed! The next morning about eight o'clock he died, being about forty-two years of age, leaving a wife and six children behind him. At present a spirit of harmony subsisteth amongst our leaders; but I want to see them also deeply engaged to take the kingdom of heaven by violence.

Lord's day, 6. Both my body and mind were afflicted to-day. In the morning I showed the congregation the danger of settling on their lees; as all do who rest in dead formality, or trust in any past experience. In the evening, I addressed the people on the heartfelt inquiry of the trembling jailor, "What must I do to be saved?"

Monday, 7. My body was weak, and my mind was much tempted. Lord, support and comfort me under every trial! I met the class of Mr. Jarvis deceased: found much love amongst them; and by general consent, appointed Richard Sause[85] to act as their leader. I found much satisfaction in preaching the next evening; but had sore conflicts with Satan in the course of the day.

Wednesday, 9. My soul is strengthened with might, and filled with peace. But I see the propriety and great necessity of living every moment more and more to God. We are informed from Philadelphia, that it is eight weeks since the preachers sailed from England;[86] though they are not yet arrived.

Friday, 11. My heart is grieved, and groaneth for want of more holiness. A letter from E. Deveau, at New Rochelle, informs me of a gay young woman, and one or two more, who are turning to God through Christ Jesus. They call aloud for preachers to come amongst them.[87] On *Saturday* we had a blessed time in band meeting; though my mind had been somewhat depressed by finding one or two of my best friends drawn into a measure of party spirit.[88]

Lord's day, 13. Dr. Inglis, at St. Paul's, was on his old tedious subject of the Lord's supper. He cannot be at any great loss in saying the same thing over and over again so frequently. Many people attended at our church in the morning; and in the evening there were about a thousand who seriously listened, while I preached from Psalm i, 12.[89]

Monday, 14. I set off for New Rochelle; but by the disagreeable gait of

[85] In addition to being designated class leader in Jarvis' stead, Sause along with Charles White became treasurer of the society, succeeding Jarvis in that office. (*John Street Records.*)

[86] See entries for October 24, 1774, and November 19, 1774.

[87] Demands were being made in Westchester County for more frequent preacher visitation than could be provided from Wesley Chapel; and after the Revolution, New Rochelle became a separate appointment.

[88] Apparently this was a brief flare-up of the conflict between Lupton and Chave against Sause and White, caused by the emergence of Sause and White into posts of leadership following the death of Jarvis.

[89] There is no verse 12 in Psalm 1. This is probably a misprint for Psalm 1: 2. Note that Asbury used this text at New Rochelle the next day.

the horse, was exceedingly wearied on my arrival: nevertheless, I gave an exhortation to some serious people who were collected there. The next day my mind was troubled by turning on political subjects, which are out of my province. Alas! what a small matter may interrupt our communion with God; and even draw away our affections from him. Though we had a profitable time, while I preached from Psalm i, 2.

Wednesday, 16. I went to Peter Bonnette's,[90] where we had many people and some power. There is a very perceivable alteration in the people of these parts: they both hear and understand, in some measure, the things of God; and can feel his awful truths. I had some conversation with a certain Mr. Burling, a sensible man, though he is tainted with the indolent spirit of Quakerism.

Thursday, 17. All my desire was after God, and him alone: though my spirit was grieved by some involuntary thoughts which crowded in upon me. But in the midst of all, there was a calm and settled peace.

Friday, 18. Unguarded and trifling conversation has brought on a degree of spiritual deadness. But, by the grace of God, I will rouse myself, and endeavour to be more watchful and spiritual in all my ways; and in all things please him whom my soul loveth far above every other object.

Saturday, 19. I set off with an intention to go to New York, but at the bridge[91] was informed that Mr. Dempster[92] had come to the city. Therefore I returned to Mr. Bonnette's; and preached twice there the next day, as also once at Mr. Deveau's: and am persuaded that the power of God attended the word at both places. We have here a small class of about thirteen persons,[93] most of whom enjoy peace and consolation in Christ Jesus. I met them on Monday, and we were greatly comforted together.

Thursday, 24. My heart is weaned from visible objects; and, by grace, raised to its Best-beloved above. But, O! I greatly long for more solid,

[90] Peter Bonnette was co-leader with Frederick Deveau of the New Rochelle class.

[91] The reference is to Kingsbridge. Word of Dempster's arrival at New York had been sent forward by the officials at Wesley Chapel so that Asbury might complete his duties at New Rochelle, knowing that the preaching and work was now covered by the new arrival.

[92] James Dempster (?–1803) was born in Scotland and studied at Edinburgh University. He served the Wesleyan itinerancy about ten years before accepting Wesley's appointment to America. Arriving in America he was assigned to relieve Asbury at New York and was reappointed there at the 1775 conference. Later that year his health failed, causing his retirement; but after some months he was able to resume preaching. He later became pastor of the Presbyterian Church at Florida, Montgomery County, New York, where he remained until his death. His son, the Rev. John Dempster, D.D., became a distinguished Methodist minister and was "the father of theological education" in the Church. He assisted in the establishment of several biblical institutes, notably the present Garrett Biblical Institute. (Stevens, *op. cit.*, I, 264–65; Lednum, *op cit.*, 143; Wakeley, *op. cit.*, 250 ff.; Seaman, *op. cit.*, 69–70; Barclay, *op. cit.*, I, 44, 347 n.; *John Street Church Records*, I, several entries in 1775.)

[93] Asbury had inducted this group into the New York Society on June 23, 1773. (See note under that date.)

asting union—to be inwardly adorned with all the virtues and graces of evangelical religion. We were this day informed of the death of Mr. Ogilvie.[94] May the Lord help me to be faithful, lest I should not live out half my days! I set off the next day for New York, and met brother Sause at Kingsbridge. When we got within about ten miles of New York, we found that about fifteen minutes before a man had been robbed of his money and his coat from off his back. One of the rogues pursued us, but we were too far before him. We reached our church just as Mr. Dempster began to preach.

New Jersey

Monday, 28. After taking my leave of my good friends in New York the last evening,[95] from Phil. i, 27, Captain Webb and myself set off this morning for Perth Amboy. We met with a person who came a passenger with us from England in the character of a gentleman, by the name of Wilson, but now he calls himself Clarkson; and since then he has called himself Lavingston. He has been apprehended for passing a counterfeit bill, for which he was both imprisoned and whipped. When he saw me, he knew me and I knew him: but he was in such perplexity that he could eat no breakfast, and went off in the first wagon he could meet with. To what fears and anxiety are poor sinners exposed! And if the presence of a mortal man can strike such terror into the minds of guilty sinners, what must they feel when they stand without a covering before a heart-searching and righteous God? On *Tuesday*, we arrived at Burlington, very weary; and were saluted with the melancholy news, that two unhappy men were to be hung on the Monday following; one for bestiality, and the other for abusing several young girls in the most brutish and shocking manner. Alas for the dignity of human nature! The next day I visited them; and found one of them, who was a Papist, a little attentive; but he wanted to know if he might not trust for pardon after death. The other was a young man who appeared to be quite stupid. Both Captain Webb and I spoke freely and largely to them; though there was very little room to hope that we should do them any good. Here Mrs. H. gave an account of the triumphant death of her sister, whose heart the Lord touched about two years ago under my preaching. In preaching this evening, I showed the people the emptiness of mere externals in religion, and the absolute necessity of the inward power and graces thereof.

Friday, December 2. My soul enjoys great peace; but longs for more of

[94] The word received by Asbury on the 24th should have been of Ogilvie's impending death, as he did not succumb until two days later. (Dix: *A History of the Parish of Trinity Church in the City of New York*, I, 359–60; see *Journal* entry for November 30, 1772.)

[95] Asbury was not to see New York again until August 25, 1783.

God. We visited the prisoners again; and Captain Webb enforced some very alarming truths upon them, though very little fruit of his labour could be seen. Mr. Rankin came to Burlington to-day, and desired me to go to Philadelphia. So, after preaching in the evening from Prov. xxviii, 13, I set off the next morning for the city; and found the society in the spirit of love.

Pennsylvania

Lord's day, 4. I preached twice with some freedom; and went to hear Mr. Stringer,[96] but it was the same thing over again. The next day my mind was in a sweet, calm frame, and I felt a strong determination to devote myself wholly to God and his service. I spoke my mind to Mr. Rankin, but we did not agree in judgment. And it appeared to me, that to make any attempt to go to Baltimore would be all in vain.

Tuesday, 6. Visited some of my friends in the city; and wrote a letter to Mr. Wesley, which I read to Mr. Rankin, that he might see I intended no guile or secret dealings. It is somewhat grievous that he should prevent my going to Baltimore, after being acquainted with my engagements, and the importunities of my friends there. However, all things shall work together for good to them that love God. The next day Mr. Rankin appeared to be very kind; so I hope all things will give place to love.

Lord's day, 11. Mr. Rankin preached a close sermon, on the neglect of public worship. At church Mr. Stringer had the same thing over again; but the power of the Lord attended our preaching in the evening, from 2 Thes. i, 7, 8.

Tuesday, 13. Yesterday my heart was fervently engaged in acts of devotion; and with some enlargement of heart, I gave an exhortation at a private house near my lodging. But to-day, my cry is, O for more spirituality!—more purity of heart! Lord, form me by the power of divine grace according to all thy righteous will, that my soul may enjoy thee in glory forever! Though concurring circumstances required me to speak this evening, in a manner unprepared, yet we were blessed with a comfortable season.

Wednesday, 14. Mr. Rankin was sick, and Captain Webb was busy, so I spent my time in study and devotion; and enjoyed a blessed sense of the divine presence. But what need can there be for two preachers here to preach three times a week to about sixty people? On Thursday night about sixty persons attended to hear Captain Webb preach. This is indeed a very gloomy prospect. But my heart delighteth in God. He is the object of my hope; and I trust he will be my portion forever.

[96] The Rev. William Stringer was the rector of St. Paul's Church in Philadelphia (See note under June 7, 1772.)

Lord's day, 18. My soul was happy while preaching in the morning. Mr. Stringer gave us an old piece at church; and Mr. Rankin was very furious in the evening.

Monday, 19. My body was indisposed, but my soul enjoyed health. The Lord gives me patience, and fills me with his goodness. In meeting sister Mary Thorne's[97] class we had a mutual blessing.

"O that I could all invite,
   His saving truth to prove!
Show the length, and breadth, and height,
   And depth of Jesus' love."

Wednesday, 21. I began to read Neal's History of the Puritans.[98] The Lord keeps me from all impure desire, and makes me to abound with divine peace. In prayer meeting this evening all present were greatly blest.

Friday, 23. Mr. Neal, in his history, is tolerably impartial; though he seems rather inclined to favour the Non-conformists. But how strange! that the reformation should be carried on in such a reign as that of Henry VIII, and in the time of Edward VI, while he was but a child. The good bishops, no doubt, carried the matter as far as they could; but it was not in their power to disentangle themselves and the nation from all the superstition of Popery. But queen Elizabeth and her friends bore hard for the supremacy. It seems the dispute began at Frankfort; and Calvin was in the consultation. In the evening I preached from these words, "Neither give place to the devil:" and believe it was good for some that they were present. Took my lodging the next day at Mr. W.'s.

The next day, as the snow was near two feet deep, I did not go out, but had a comfortable time at home.

Thursday, 29. My soul is happy in the love of God. He gives me grace to die daily to the world, and all the desires of the flesh. Dr. Stringer delivered a good discourse from Isaiah xxvi, 20, 21, on the solemn occasion of a fast and preparation for the Lord's supper. I spoke at night from John i, 12, 13.

[97] Mrs. Mary Thorne was the first woman class leader at St. George's Church in Philadelphia. Of Welsh descent she was a native of Bristol in Buck County. Her parents, named Evans, settled at Newbern, North Carolina, where she joined the Baptists. After being widowed she went to Philadelphia, where she heard the preaching of Pilmoor and joined the Methodists. (Lednum, *op. cit.*, 42, 43.) In 1778 Mrs. Thorne married a Captain Parker and moved to England. (See *Letters*, 156.)

[98] Daniel Neal (1678–1743), Puritan historian and minister, published among other works the *History of the Puritans*, in four volumes.

1775

1775

Asbury nearing Norfolk in a wind-tossed bark

CHAPTER FOUR

Pennsylvania

Monday, January 2, 1775. I see the great necessity of always beginning to glorify God, with fresh vigour of soul. So prone is man to grow languid in devout exercises, that without fresh and powerful exertions he will soon sink into dead formality. At Mr. Bell's,[1] where we dined to-day, I was much grieved at the manner of Mr. Rankin's conversation: but let it be a caution to me to be prudent and watchful. The next day my soul was greatly alive to God. And the people here are so kind to me that it fills me with astonishment and gratitude.

Thursday, 5. For several days my throat has been much disordered, but it is now something better. Glory to God! he sweetly draws my heart into close and comfortable communion with himself. In reading the history of the Puritans, I am surprised at the conduct of Archbishop Laud. A monster of a man indeed!

Friday, 6. Find myself free, through grace, from all impure affections; but I am troubled on account of my disposition to trifle in conversation. Yet it is the will of God to save me from this also. May the happy hour speedily arrive when I shall be altogether such as my Lord would have me to be!

Saturday, 7. I had some conversation with that pious, good woman, the widow of Gilbert Tennent.[2] She greatly lamented the condition of her

[1] William Bell was a class leader at St. George's Church. He lived on New Street near Fourth in Philadelphia.

[2] This woman had been Tennent's third wife, formerly Mrs. Sarah Spafford of New Jersey. The Tennents had three children: Gilbert, here mentioned, who was lost at sea;

son, who was in the Jersey college;[3] a youth of about seventeen years of age, but under no deep impressions for the salvation of his soul. How grievous must this be to a pious parent! While carnal parents regard only the worldly prosperity of their children, truly religious parents are chiefly concerned about the eternal salvation of their souls. I was informed to-day that poor Abraham Whitworth is living with his wife, and appears to be industriously inclined.

Lord's day, 8. The Lord was pleased to bless my soul with that peace which passes understanding. A letter from my friend, William Lynch, informed me that three of my friends were coming to conduct me, if possible, to Baltimore. But it is a doubt with me if I shall, with consent, be permitted to go. May the Lord give me wisdom, patience, and faith, that in all cases I may know how to act or suffer, according to his will and my duty!

Thursday, 12. The conduct of Mr. Rankin is such as calls for patience. He has reported that I was the cause of Abraham Whitworth's becoming a preacher. Whereas when he was appointed it was by the conference. And the time when I wanted him to travel was a year before his appointment, when his heart was right with God. Moreover, at the last conference I was doubtful of him, and so expressed myself both by word and letter.

Friday, 13. As my throat was worse, I stayed at home and took physic. Part of my time was spent in reading the history of the Puritans: and I found my affections pure, and fixed on their proper object; though Satan did not fail to assault me with many temptations.

Lord's day, 15. I visited the Quaker meeting;[4] but wondered to see so many sensible men sit to hear two or three old women talk. In the latter part of the day I was much indisposed and kept at home. But the next morning I found myself something better; and earnestly longed for purity of heart, and perfect resignation to all the will of God.

Wednesday, 18. In the night my throat was bad, attended with a smart fever. My mind is variously exercised at different times. Sometimes thinking that my affliction is judicial; other times thinking that natural causes produce natural effects. But, blessed Jesus, I must be still and know that thou art God. From this time till *Lord's day*, 23d, I had a putrid sore throat, and two persons sat up with me every night; but I found relief from purges, and a mixture of nitre and fever powder. Mr. Rankin keeps driving away at the people, telling them how bad they are, with the wonders

---

a daughter who died early; and Cornelia, who married Dr. William Smith of Southampton on Long Island who became a physician in Philadelphia. Gilbert Tennent was pastor of the Second Presbyterian Church, Philadelphia.

[3] Jersey College later became Princeton University.

[4] The nearest Quaker meetinghouse was at present Fourth and Arch streets. It is now the Friend's Arch Street Center at 304 Arch Street.

which he has done and intends to do. It is surprising that the people are not out of patience with him. If they did not like his friends better than him, we should soon be welcome to take a final leave of them.

From the twenty-third of *January* till the first of *February*, my affliction was so severe that I was not able to write. There were several small ulcers on the inside of my throat; and the pain of the gatherings was so severe that for two weeks I could not rest of nights. My friends were very kind, and, expecting my death, they affectionately lamented over me. But on the 29th of *January* I was happily relieved by the discharge of near a pint of white matter. For a while my mind was in great heaviness; but after some severe conflicts with the powers of darkness, I was calmly resigned to the will of a wise and gracious God. O Lord, how wonderful are thy works! It is my desire to know the cause of this affliction, that, if it is in my power, I may remove it. Is it that I may know more of myself, and lie in the dust? Or, for my past unfaithfulness? But whatever may be the cause, I humbly hope that all those painful dispensations will work together for my good. In the course of this affliction I found that when my spirit was broken, and brought to submit with cheerfulness to the will of God, then the disorder abated, and I began to recover; though Satan was very busy, and, like Job's impious wife, suggested to my mind that I should curse God and die; nevertheless, through grace, I am more than conqueror, and can give glory to God. The gargle which I used first, to scatter, if possible, the inflammation, was sage tea, honey, vinegar, and mustard; then that which was used to accelerate the gathering, was mallows with a fig cut in pieces: and lastly, to strengthen the part, we used a gargle of sage tea, alum, rose leaves, and loaf sugar. On *Monday* the 30th, some letters came from Baltimore, earnestly pressing me to go. And Mr. Rankin was so kind as to visit me; when all was sweetness and love.

Wednesday, February 1. I am once more able to write, and feel a solemn, grateful sense of God's goodness resting on my soul. My all of body, soul, and time, are his due; and should be devoted, without the least reserve, to his service and glory. O that he may give me grace sufficient!

Thursday, 2. I am still getting better, but not able to speak in public; though the word of the Lord is like fire within me, and I am almost weary of forbearing. The next day my mind was much taken up with God, and several of my friends, who were so kind as to visit me, were melted in conversation and prayer.

Saturday, 4. My mind was filled with pure, evangelical peace. I had some conversation with Capt. Webb, an Israelite indeed, and we both concluded that it was my duty to go to Baltimore. And I feel willing to go, if it is even to die there; but, at present, am not permitted. I was confined to the house all the next day; but O! how painful are these dumb Sabbaths to me! However, it is my duty to submit to the providence of a wise God.

Monday, 6. My body is but weak, and my mind is somewhat distressed, lest I should be too much concerned about the ark of the Lord, and wish to take the cause out of his hand. How frail a creature is man! How little can he penetrate into the design and works of God!

Tuesday, 7. Mr. Taylor[5] took me in a chaise to dine with Mr. Rankin and Mr. Martin Rodda.[6] My mind is somewhat troubled with temptations but still I have peace. I am weak in body; and want more patience and resignation to submit to the will of God, till he is pleased to restore me. What is life? Lord, help me to be always ready to end it here!

Wednesday, 8. From the state of my body to-day, I feel great expectation of being restored to health. But O! how my soul longeth for more spiritual health! This day I wrote to Mr. Rogers,[7] at Baltimore, to come for me.

Thursday, 9. My body continues to recover. But I discover many weaknesses and failures in my inner man. When shall my soul be adorned as a bride for her bridegroom? When shall all within and all without be holiness to the Lord? Notwithstanding my illness, I have read Neal's History of the Puritans, consisting of four volumes, in about two months.

Friday, 10. How great a blessing is health! Though of late it is but seldom enjoyed by me. But, through mercy, my body now feels like being restored; and I am afraid of being thereby too much elated. The Lord shows me the excellency of affliction, and enables me to exercise resignation in all conditions of life. I am now reading Mosheim's Ecclesiastical History; but as a writer he is too dry and speculative.

Tuesday, 14. My heart pants to labour for God; to be once more employed in building up his spiritual house. O that he may strengthen me, set me to work, and greatly bless my poor endeavours! Preaching the glorious Gospel seems to be my proper employment; and when I am long detained from it, I appear to be out of my element. But hope, a blessed hope revives, that before long I shall be of some service in the Church of Christ.

Thursday, 16. My mind has been kept in great peace: but I am somewhat troubled on account of my defects in usefulness and spirituality. May the Lord make me more serious and more spiritual in all my internal and external actions! And though my mind was much taken up with God on *Friday*, yet I was too free in conversation. My earnest desire is, to have full power over every thought, word, and action. I now ventured to preach from Psalm cxxvi, 3: "The Lord hath done great things for us, whereof we are glad." Richard Sause wrote me a letter with his usual kindness, and informed me that Mr. James Dempster concurred in sentiment

---

[5] This was probably J. R. Taylor.

[6] Martin Rodda was one of Wesley's itinerants in 1763. Late in 1774 he came with Dempster to America by Wesley's appointment. In 1775 he was on the Baltimore Circuit with Richard Owings and John Wade. (Lednum, *op. cit.*, 151, 160.)

[7] Probably Philip Rogers.

elative to my going to Baltimore. And it is thought by many, that there will be an alteration in the affairs of our Church government.

Lord's day, 19. Mr. Rankin preached his farewell sermon, from Deut. xxx, 19. He has now been here ten months.

Monday, 20. Most of this day was spent in private devotion and reading. I am full of humble expectation that the Lord will restore me to better health and greater usefulness. May my eye be single, aiming at nothing but the glory of God, that my whole body may be full of light!

Wednesday, 22. I received a letter from Miss Gilbert at Antigua; in which she informed me, that Mr. Nathaniel Gilbert[8] was going away; and as there are about three hundred members in society, she entreats me to go and labour amongst them. And as Mr. Wesley has given his consent, I feel inclined to go, and take one of the young men with me. But there is one obstacle in my way—the administration of the ordinances. It is possible to get the ordination of a presbytery; but this would be incompatible with Methodism: which would be an effectual bar in my way. It appears very strange, that after so much affliction, my heart should be so languid and dull. This day Mr. Rankin set off for New York.

Thursday, 23. Mr. Ruff and Mr. Rodda came to town. I preached in the evening from Rom. i, 16: "I am not ashamed of the Gospel of Christ," &c. And showed, First, Of what he was not ashamed: the experience, precepts, and blessings, of the Gospel; to preach it in its purity; to suffer for it. Secondly, Why he was not ashamed of this: Because it is the power of God to salvation from the guilt, power, and remains of sin; the power of God is displayed in preaching the simple truths of the Gospel. Thirdly, To whom it became so: to them that believe, first, the threatenings, precepts, and invitations; and then in Jesus Christ for this present salvation.

Saturday, 25. I packed up my clothes in order to depart on *Monday* morning for Baltimore. And while giving a few words of exhortation in the evening, we found it a solemn, feeling time. We also had a very powerful season the next evening, while I preached to a full house on the awful subject of the rich man and Lazarus.

Monday, 27. My dear children in the Lord, Philip Rogers and Samuel Owings, with several other kind friends, accompanied me out of town. We stopped at Chester, where I preached from these piercing words of our Lord, "Thou knowest not the day of thy visitation." There are but little hopes of this place at present. Though, if they do not fill up the measure of their iniquity, the time to favour them may come. The Lord

---

[8] Nathaniel Gilbert was a descendant of Sir Humphrey Gilbert and a half brother of Sir Walter Raleigh. He and three of his servants were converted by John Wesley at Wandsworth in 1758. On his return to Antigua, Gilbert began preaching to the Negroes in 1760 and thus established Methodism in the West Indies. (See Wesley's *Journal,* IV, 247 n.; Findlay and Hollingsworth: *History of the Wesleyan Missionary Society,* II, ch. ii.) Gilbert died in 1774, but Asbury may not have heard of it or may have referred to his death as "going away."

hasten it, before the present generation drops into eternity! As it is some time since I have been accustomed to labour and fatigue, my body was exceedingly weak and weary at night.

Delaware

Tuesday, 28. Stopping at Wilmington to preach in the evening, a barber came to shave me, who once professed religion, and had been a soldier in the twenty-third regiment; but now he is a deserter both from God and man. On our way to Susquehanna the next day, we accidentally called on Mr. Isaac Hersey, whose heart was much affected while we prayed with him and his family. When we came to the ferry, we had an agreeable time, several joining us while we called on the Lord by prayer in our room.

Thursday, March 2. We called at the house of Mr. Josias Dallam and rested about an hour. Sister Dallam has treated me with all the tenderness of a mother towards a son: and may He that will not forget a cup of water given in his name, abundantly reward her!

Maryland

We then pursued our journey to Baltimore; and my heart was greatly refreshed at the sight of my spiritual children and kind friends there, for whose welfare my soul had travailed both present and absent. The next day I had the pleasure of seeing our new house,[9] and my old friends, with some new ones added to their number. Here are all my own with increase.

Lord's day, 5. Both in town and at the Point, large numbers attended to hear the word. The power of God was present; and I had an inward witness that it was the will of God I should, at that time, be amongst those people. Nicholas Jones is come home to God, and Richard Moale[10] is on his way.

Monday, 6. My mind was peaceful and calm. The next day I set out in

[9] Lovely Lane Meeting House had been completed, and the dedicatory sermon was preached by Captain Webb. The Strawberry Alley Chapel in Fell's Point was begun before Lovely Lane, but the latter was completed and opened for services first. (Roberts: *Centenary Pictorial Album*, 70; *Proceedings . . . of the Centennial Methodist Conference, Baltimore, Maryland, December 9–17, 1884*, article by Prof. H. B. Ridgaway, 119.)

[10] Nicholas Jones was a delegate to the meeting on May 25, 1774, to pledge assistance to Massachusetts upon receiving word from Samuel Adams that the British Parliament intended to tax the colonists. Jones was also one of the original trustees of Cokesbury College. Richard Moale and his brother John inherited considerable land from their father, John Moale, who died in 1740. In 1773 Richard Moale was one of the purchasers of the lot in Fell's Point on which the Strawberry Alley Chapel was erected. (Scharf: *History of Baltimore City and County*, 69, 70; Armstrong, *op. cit.*, 89.) The deed to the lot, found in the Maryland Historical Building, Baltimore, shows its location was not on the corner of Strawberry Alley and Fleet Street but fifty feet north of the latter.

a carriage for Mr. Taylor's, about nine miles from town, and found a large congregation, many of whom came from Elk Ridge. On *Wednesday*, I returned to town, and was powerfully assaulted by Satan. But, glory to God! He is my sun and my shield; he discovers to my mind the temptations, and keeps me from their power. May I ever feel my obligations, and delight in giving all my strength and time to his service!

Thursday, 9. My spirit was grieved within me to see the wickedness of mankind in this town—to see how they oppose the truth of God. The power of Satan is only checked in a small degree: but when shall he be quite cast out? Before he will suffer his kingdom to be entirely overthrown, he will, no doubt, do all he can in stimulating his trusty servants to defend his cause. Preaching on Friday at William Lynch's, the wealthy Mr. Charles Ridgely[11] was present. And who can tell but the Lord may reach his heart!

Saturday, 11. My body is somewhat unwell; but my soul is in health and peace. Though I have some cause of lamentation, for being too free in conversation with my friends.

Lord's day, 12. Much of the power of God was felt at the Point; and a divine energy went forth amongst the people that night in town, while I discoursed from that awakening scripture, Romans ii, 8, 9, 10: "But unto them that are contentious, and do not obey the truth, but obey unrighteousness, indignation and wrath, tribulation and anguish, upon every soul of man that doeth evil," &c. Christ was precious to my soul, which was filled with divine peace. I saw brother Strawbridge and entered into a free conversation with him. His sentiments relative to Mr. Rankin corresponded with mine. But all these matters I can silently commit to God, who overrules both in earth and heaven.

Monday, 13. After preaching at O. C.'s, about five miles from town, in a comfortable frame of mind, I returned. The next day I parted with brother Strawbridge and felt my mind depressed by temptations. But a holy flame glowed in my heart, while discoursing at night on the "cloud of witnesses." Believing that some souls were benefitted, I commended myself to the divine protection, and slept in peace. Though it rained on Thursday evening, yet many attended whilst I enforced the apostolic injunction: "Let us lay aside every weight, and the sin which doth so easily beset us." It is to be feared that many Christians do not "lay aside every weight" which impedes their spiritual progress. If they did, they

---

[11] Captain Charles Ridgely's sister Prudence was the wife of Henry Dorsey Gough. Ridgely acquired some ten thousand acres of land upon which he erected Hampton Hall, which required seven years to build. This historic house, which was completed in 1782 or 1790 is a few miles north of Towson, Maryland. Ridgely presented Robert Strawbridge with a farm at Long Green for a home during his life. Mrs. Ridgely was a devout Methodist. (*Methodist Quarterly Review*, July 1856, 439; Ridgely: *Old Brick Churches of Maryland*, 100; Wilstach: *Tidewater Maryland*, 200; *National Cyclopedia of American Biography*, IX, 299.)

would not halt, and go on as if they were weary; but be enabled to *run*
and that *with patience*, the race that is set before them.

Friday, 17. The glory of God and the salvation of men were my principa
objects. I went to preach at the Point, but they were training the militia
so that the town seemed all in confusion.[12]

Saturday, 18. Peace and pure desires filled my soul; and Christ was the
object of my love. Glory be to thee, O Lord! The next day the Spirit o
the Lord God was with me in preaching at the Point; and with grea
pathos I was enabled to deliver the truth at night in town. Many of the
audience felt the weight of God's word. May they yield to the sacred touch
and be saved! On *Monday* and *Tuesday*, I made a small excursion into the
country, and laboured to bring souls to Christ at Mr. Rodger's and Mr
Taylor's. It seems Caleb Dorsey has not lost all the concern he felt some
time ago. I afterward returned safe to town in the evening; and spent a
part of the next day in reading Taylor's Treatise on Holy Living.[13] This
book was made a blessing to me above seven years ago. I preached in
the evening from 1 Samuel x, 6: "The Spirit of the Lord will come upon
thee, and thou salt prophesy with them, and shalt be turned into another
man." Here I took occasion to show,

I. The operations of the Spirit on the heart of man—to convince, con-
vict, convert, and sanctify.

II. The effects of these operations.

1. A strong inclination to speak for God. This is the duty of every
Christian.

2. A great change—in judgment, desire, spirit, temper, and practice.

I found myself much indisposed when I returned to my lodgings, and
the disorder of my body depressed my spirits.

Friday, 24. I ventured to Patapsco Neck, and had a full house at Captain Ridgely's, whose wife is brought by grace to the knowledge of God in
Christ Jesus.

Lord's day, 26. My heart was delightfully taken up with God. In the
time of preaching at the Point this morning, my spirit was tender, and
many of the audience were much melted. I also found myself greatly
drawn out in preaching at night in town.

Tuesday, 28. Mr. Otterbein, the Dutch minister, accompanied me to

[12] Beginning with 1775 there were increasing signs of armed resistance to the Crown.
Military assistance to Massachusetts, which already had been promised by Maryland,
had resulted in the enrollment of all males from sixteen to sixty years of age and a levy
on all counties for arms and munitions. For a description of the patience, discretion,
and devotion to liberty with which Asbury met and endured the storm of war from 1775
to 1782 see Cooper's *The Substance of a Funeral Discourse . . . on the Death of the Rev.
Francis Asbury*, 83; Sweet's *Methodism in American History*, 78–99; *Maryland Historical
Magazine*, "Maryland During the Revolution," XXIV, 255.

[13] Jeremy Taylor (1613–67) was born at Cambridge, England, and published *The
Rules and Exercises of Holy Living* in 1650.

Joshua Owing's, where we had a blessed and refreshing season. The next day, at town, I met with brother Williams[14] from Virginia; who gave me a great account of the work of God in those parts—five or six hundred souls justified by faith, and five or six circuits formed: so that we have now fourteen circuits in America; and about twenty-two preachers are required to supply them. Thus we see how Divine Providence makes way for the word of truth, and the Holy Spirit attends it. May it spread in power, and cover these lands! Brother Williams is a very singular man, but honest in his intentions, and sincerely engaged for the prosperity of the work. I dined with Mr. Otterbein, the minister mentioned above, and spent the afternoon with him and Mr. Swope, another minister of the same profession. They both appear to be sincerely religious, and intend to make proposals to the German synod this year, to lay a plan for the reformation of the Dutch congregations.

Friday, 31. This was a day of joy and great consolation to my soul. I clearly saw the propriety and necessity of devoting every faculty and every hour to God.

Lord's day, April 2. Many people attended to hear the word, and there appeared to be much feeling amongst them. I had a desire to hear for myself, Mr. Patrick Allison,[15] the Presbyterian minister. His discourse was quite systematical and amusing, but if he had studied to pass by the conscience of his hearers, he could not have done it more effectually. *Monday* and *Tuesday* I spent comfortably, in labouring on a short tour in the country: and was graciously assisted on Tuesday night at town.

Wednesday, 5. I experienced the benefit of visiting the sick, and found much satisfaction in my own soul, while speaking plainly to a carnal young man. The next day Satan assaulted me with great violence, but he found my heart fixed on God.

Friday, 7. After visiting two sick persons, I went to brother Lynch's, and was enabled to speak freely and feelingly to a large number of rich and poor assembled there. On *Saturday* I returned, and found that a young man who had turned his back on the gospel, and devoted himself to sin, had been suddenly snatched away by death. How awful! Does not this appear like the judicial hand of God? Does it not seem as a powerful warning to surviving sinners, especially such as answer his character? And yet it is to be feared, many will not bear the rod, nor regard him that appointed it.

[14] For an account of the Great Awakening in Virginia and the part played by Robert Williams, see the letter from Devereux Jarratt. (*Journal* entry for December 19, 1776; Gewehr: *The Great Awakening in Virginia*.)

[15] The Rev. Patrick Allison arrived in Baltimore in 1763 and led the Presbyterian congregation in the erection of a log church on Fayette Street. When Congress fled from Philadelphia to Baltimore in December, 1776, it selected Allison as one of its chaplains. He died in 1802. (Scharf, *op. cit.*, 72; *Journal of the Congress for 1776*, proceedings for December 23.)

Lord's day, 9. Though my body was weak, and my mind grieved by the wickedness of the wicked, yet I was enabled to speak powerfully both at the Point and town. The blessing of the Lord attended us, both at Mr. Evans's on Monday, and at O. C.'s on *Tuesday*. Here I met with brother Strawbridge, and found we were of one heart and of one mind. Lord, grant that all the preachers may be thus united in sentiment and affection!

Thursday, 13. Had some conversation with Mrs. J., from Philadelphia. She appeared to be in distress about her soul, and said she was convinced of her lost estate the last Lord's day.

Saturday, 15. God is my portion, and my all-sufficient good. He fills me with pure, spiritual life. My heart is melted into holy love, and altogether devoted to my Lord. Many came to hear the word of life in the evening, and my soul was supplied with strength.

Lord's day, 16. The Spirit of God attended our endeavours both in town and Point. My heart was greatly enlarged in town especially. There is a very apparent alteration in this place. There is not so much drunkenness and neglect of the ordinances, as in former times; and the people are much more inclined to attend the places of public worship. So that, on the whole, I entertain a lively hope that the Lord will yet raise up for himself a large society in the town of Baltimore. On Monday my frame was weak and weary: nevertheless I had to preach once in town, and once in the country, about seven miles off.

Wednesday, 19. Having preached at several places in the country, I returned to town; and find that the Lord assisteth me from time to time. He frequently revives both body and soul, when I am almost ready to give over.

Thursday, 20. Just before preaching at the Point, six men were accidentally shot in the militia exercise. I will not venture to assert, the captain collected them for exercise because it was preaching night. However, I visited one of the wounded, and prayed with him.

Saturday, 22. I dined with Captain Ridgely, who appeared to be under some small awakenings. Afterward came to town, when brother Rankin and I met, like Jacob and Esau; and all was love and peace. In the evening Mr. Rankin preached a good sermon on John xii, 36: "While ye have the light believe in the light, that ye may be the children of light."

Lord's day, 23. Our congregations were large; amongst whom were Mr. G., Mr. C., and others. In the evening Mr. Rankin preached an alarming sermon. On Monday I visited a sick woman, who soon after went into eternity; and then I went to Mr. Evans's, where many found it beneficial to them that they were present to hear the word of the Lord. By particular invitation, I lodged on Tuesday night at Captain Ridgely's and in the course of a free conversation, he told me that he was brought under his first conviction at Mr. Taylor's, from Prov. xxviii, 13.

Saturday, 29. I have not been unassisted in the public exercises of this week, and now find my soul in a peaceful frame, though not without a serious concern for the cause of the country. Lord, turn aside thy displeasure, and mercifully interpose!

Lord's day, 30. I preached three times, and the cup of my blessing was full. What shall I render unto the Lord for all his benefits? But we have alarming military accounts from Boston, New York, and Philadelphia.[16] Surely the Lord will overrule, and make all these things subservient to the spiritual welfare of his Church. On *Monday* I visited the country, and, having preached at a few places, returned on *Tuesday* night to town; and found the people all inflamed with a martial spirit.

Thursday, May 4. My soul longs for a perfect conformity to the image and will of God in all things. I desire nothing but him, and he causeth my heart to overflow with peaceful joy. I preached at the Point this evening, but have more hope for the inhabitants of the town than for those of the Point. O that I could learn the holy art of doing more good for precious souls! It troubles me to think of being so unprofitable.

Friday, 5. At the appointed time for preaching we had an awful storm of thunder and lightning, which killed three horses. However, I began in the midst of it, and spoke with liberty of spirit, and confidence in God.

Saturday, 6. I was grieved to-day that I did not feel myself more steadily devoted to God. In the evening John King preached a good and profitable sermon, but long and loud enough.

Lord's day, 7. I preached twice and held a love feast; but heaviness is brought upon my mind by some that would once (comparatively speaking) have plucked out their eyes, and have given them to me; but now they slight me! "Cursed is the man that trusteth in man, and maketh flesh his arm; whose heart departeth from the Lord!" May my heart trust in the Lord!

Monday, 8. Several friends set out in company with me to the quarterly meeting. When we came to Jacob Giles's,[17] he did not appear to be so open and free as he was about a year ago. Prayer is almost neglected, and both his children and servants are almost like wild, untaught Indians. Ah! what is all the substance of this world, without the love and fear of God? I proceeded the next morning to meet the preachers and stewards. At ten o'clock we held our love feast; though my mind was under some exercises, so that I spoke but little. However, at four o'clock I preached from Isaiah xli, 13, with great enlargement, and to a large concourse of

[16] Three days before the news of the Battle of Lexington had reached Baltimore. For the most graphic account of the scenes in Baltimore, see Purviance's *Narrative of Events which occurred in Baltimore Town during the Revolutionary War.*

[17] En route to the quarterly meeting at the Forks Chapel, Asbury lodged with Jacob Giles, son of Jacob Giles, the old Quaker who in 1750 built "Mount Pleasant," the family home. (Silver: *History of Lapidum; Harford County Directory,* 320; *Journal* entry for February 2, 1773; Thomas Rankin's *Journal.*)

people. But was confined in the evening to the company of men who were destitute of religion, and full of sin and politics. My brethren and myself were glad to have prayer in the morning and leave them. If there were no other hell than the company of wicked men, I would say, From such a hell, good Lord, deliver me!

Thursday, 11, was appointed as a general fast:[18] I preached on the occasion, and the Lord made it a solemn, heart-affecting time, so that we did not conclude till about three o'clock. The next day I reached Bohemia Manor; but as it was late, some of the congregation had departed: I therefore exhorted those that were left; and then proceeded to Newcastle.[19]

Lord's day, 14. Both last night and this day, I hope my skirts were clear of the blood of the people in this little town, whether they reject or accept of an offered salvation.

Pennsylvania

Monday, May 15, 1775. After stopping to preach at Chester I then went on to Philadelphia.

Tuesday, 16. I had some friendly and close conversation with the preachers, in which we spoke plainly of our experience and doctrines. Mr. Rodda preached in the evening. From *Wednesday* till *Friday* we spent in conference, with great harmony and sweetness of temper. If the Lord spares me, I am now about bending my course towards Norfolk, to preach the glad tidings of salvation to perishing sinners there.

Monday, 22. Having preached the last evening with some sweet enlargement, I left Philadelphia this morning. and set off for Norfolk. Preached at night to a few people in Chester, and was conducted the next morning in a friend's chaise to Cecil court house,[20] where I embarked for Norfolk.

Virginia

Monday, 29. With a thankful heart I landed at Norfolk,[21] after having been much tossed about by contrary winds in the bay. My accommoda-

[18] This observance of a day of fasting and prayer was among the earliest called by civil and religious bodies, and was indicative of an aroused public. (Preston, *op. cit.*, 102.)

[19] Newcastle was in Delaware. Asbury's route was probably via Bohemia Manor and Elk River to Frenchtown, which is about four and a half miles below Elkton in Cecil County. Newcastle was about sixteen miles distant along the road over which stagecoach travel had been established as early as 1765.

[20] Cecil courthouse is the present Charlestown, Maryland.

[21] This was Asbury's first visit to Virginia. It has been claimed that he went to Winchester, Virginia, in 1772; but that early trip was to a town of the same name in Maryland. Because of the confusion the name of the Winchester in Maryland was later changed to Westminster. (Shellman: *The Pioneers of the Early Days of Westminster*.)

tions on board the vessel were also very indifferent, so that it was a disagreeable and fatiguing passage; but

> "In hope of that immortal crown
> I now the cross sustain;
> And gladly wander up and down,
> And smile at toil and pain."

Here I found about thirty persons in society after their manner;[22] but they had no regular class meetings. However, here are a few who are willing to observe all the rules of our society. Their present preaching house is an old, shattered building, which has formerly been a play-house. Surely the Lord will not always suffer his honour to be trampled in the dust. No; I entertain a hope that we shall have a house and a people in this town. My heart is filled with holy thoughts, and deeply engaged in the work of God. On *Tuesday* evening about one hundred and fifty souls attended to hear the word, and about fifty at five o'clock on *Wednesday* morning, which, by the presence of the Lord, was found to be a good time. I then went over to Portsmouth, and found my spirit at liberty in preaching to a number of souls there.

Friday, June 2. The Lord is pleased to show me the danger which a preacher is in of being lifted up by pride, and falling into the condemnation of the devil. How great is the danger of this! A considerable degree of ballast is highly necessary to bear frequent and sudden puffs of applause. Lord, fill me with genuine humility, that the strongest gusts from Satan or the world may never move me!

Saturday, 3. My body is weak, but my soul is in a sweet, pacific frame. I see the need of constant watchfulness and entire devotion to God. My heart was stayed on God while preaching in the evening from Psalm lxviii, 18.

Lord's day, 4. Many seemed willing to hear, both morning and evening, at Norfolk; but in the afternoon, at Portsmouth, the congregation, though large, seemed to have very little sensibility. On *Monday* I found myself better than could be expected, after preaching three times, and meeting the society the day before. May the Lord brace up my feeble frame, and by his grace I am determined to use it for his glory and the service of his Church. The congregation were attentive in the evening while I enlarged on the fruits of the Spirit.

Tuesday, 6. I went to the farthermost part of Portsmouth parish, through such a swamp[23] as I never saw before, and partook of a blessing with the people, some of whom are of a simple heart. After having preached

---

[22] These thirty persons represented the fruits of the labors of Robert Williams and Joseph Pilmoor. Pilmoor went to Norfolk on July 17, 1772, and stayed with Mr. Stephenson, whom he had known in New York. He preached in the "play-house" the same afternoon. (See note under April 22, 1772.)

[23] This was the Dismal Swamp near the border of North Carolina.

at Mr. Fulford's, in St. Bride's parish, then at Mr. Manning's[24] and Mr. Randle's, I returned to Portsmouth on *Thursday* evening, and found my soul in peace. I have lately read Mason on Self-Knowledge. This book, with Frank on the Fear of Man, and Thomas à Kempis, are most excellent books for a Christian.[25]

Wednesday, 14. I have continued labouring, with different degrees of encouragement, between Norfolk and Portsmouth; but have not met with that success which my soul longs for. Our friends set a subscription on foot to-day, for building a house of worship, and have raised only about £34. Had they the same spirit of liberality which they have in Baltimore, they might easily accomplish it.

Thursday, 15. I found thirteen serious souls in society about six miles from town, on the Suffolk road; but poor brother Owins[26] is subject to great heaviness through manifold temptations. The congregation here was small; however, some of them were much affected. I gave a close and pointed exhortation in the evening at Portsmouth; and there was a melting of heart amongst the people. I preached again the next day, and met both the classes, and felt my hopes for Portsmouth begin to revive.

Monday, 19. Yesterday's labour of preaching three times, &c., was not too much for me. And this day my soul enjoyed delightful communion with God. Satan assaults; but He that is for me is stronger than he that is against me.

> "Be thou my strength, be thou my way,
> Protect me through my life's short day;
> In all my acts may wisdom guide,
> And keep me, Saviour, near thy side."

Tuesday, 20. I preached at New Mill Creek, and joined two persons to the small society there. Went thence to Northwest Woods,[27] and preached at the house of Mr. A.; and after preaching at two or three more places, I returned on *Thursday* to Portsmouth.

Monday, 26. The God of hope fills me with joy and peace in believing. About seventy souls sat under the word this evening, and some of them were very deeply affected. But too often it is as the morning cloud, and as the early dew. How irrational it is, that rational beings should employ their thoughts with readiness on every trifling subject, when they can hardly be brought to think seriously on the things of eternity, although

[24] See Lednum, *op. cit.*, 185.

[25] John Mason (1706–63), an English noncomformist divine, published *Self-Knowledge, a Treatise*, in 1745. It ran through numerous editions as late as 1811 and was translated into Welsh. The Rev. Mark Frank, D.D. (1613–64), rector of Barley, is known for his *Course of Sermons for all the Sundays and Festivals throughout the year*, posthumously published in 1672. (*Dictionary of National Biography*, VII, 625; XII, 1317.)

[26] Mr. Owins lived five miles from Portsmouth. (See *Heads of Families*; Pilmoor's *Journal*.)

[27] Northwest Woods was near the North Carolina line. Pilmoor started a society at New Mill Creek and had preached at Northwest Woods. (See Pilmoor's *Journal*.)

he Holy Spirit awakens their sensibility, and alarms their fears! O, the strange perverseness, the deadly depravity of man!

Tuesday, 27. Preached at five in the morning, but am depressed in spirit, to see such an insensibility to the things of God amongst the people. Surely, I am now in a dry and barren land, but hope it will not be so long.

Thursday, 29. I preached at Mr. Bruce's,[28] a new place, and a large company was collected. The Lord stirred the hearts of the people under the preaching of the word at Harding's,[29] and on *Friday* I returned and preached at night in Portsmouth. After I had met the classes and put them into bands the next day, I then set off for Craney Island;[30] but found the weather excessively hot, such as I had never known in England. On my return some of the members appeared a little refractory in submitting to discipline. But without discipline we should soon be as a rope of sand; so that it must be enforced, let who will be displeased.

Lord's day, *July* 2. Our congregations consisted of many people from the country as well as the towns; and I knew by experience that "where the spirit of the Lord is, there is liberty."

Monday, 3, was spent in writing to the preachers, and reading; and I was much contracted in my ideas while preaching at night. But all my soul is taken up with God; so that my desire is unto the Lord, and the remembrance of his name.

> "Give me thyself; from every boast,
> From every wish set free;
> Let all I am in thee be lost,
> But give thyself to me."

Friday, 7. The last three days I have laboured at different places in the country, and preached this evening in Portsmouth. Though I feel some concern for the souls of my fellow men, yet not enough. If we could but see by faith the danger to which poor unpardoned sinners are continually exposed, if we could but have a realizing view of that unquenchable fire into which they must be plunged, dying in their present state, how could we rest day or night from using all possible endeavours to prevent their eternal damnation? O unbelief! thou most destructive sin! how dost thou destroy the vigour of Christians' endeavours, as well as the souls of the unregenerate!

[28] William Bruce lived on the road near Portsmouth and near the Mr. Owins mentioned on June 15, 1775. He is listed in *Heads of Families* as a man of property. Later he met Asbury at Berkeley (Bath) Springs, where he had gone for the curative value of the water. (*Heads of Families*, 93; see *Journal* entry for August 18, 1776.)

[29] Asbury refers later to a Mr. Harding whom he first knew around Portsmouth. He later moved to Petersburg. Some early writers call him Handing. (See May 11, 1780.)

[30] Craney Island, near the mouth of the Nansemond River in Hampton Roads, was one of the earliest Methodist preaching places. Asbury refers to it elsewhere and in one reference says there were fifty in the society. It is a very small island but appears larger in the old maps. (See *Journal* entry for April 2, 1800.)

Tuesday, 11. After preaching at five o'clock in Norfolk, I went to Portsmouth, met the classes, and read and explained the rules; telling them that every civil society has its proper rules, and persons appointed to see them kept, and that every member forfeited his right to membership if he wilfully transgressed them. If men see the necessity of being thus subject to order for the sake of temporary advantages, how much more cheerfully should we be subject for the eternal advantages which attend the salvation of our souls!

Friday, 14. I returned to town after a short tour, and preaching several times in the country. In this tour I lodged at the house of brother Owins, mentioned some time ago, a man of a gloomy spirit but solid piety. In his house there is a true spiritual Church—three souls all of one mind, and sincerely intent on seeking and serving the Lord. I met the classes in town and found my soul sweetly stayed on the Lord, though my animal spirits flagged by reason of the extreme heat. Friend Luke[31] is opposed to our rules; but no man can expect to abide with us, unless he is so satisfied with our rules as to manifest a proper respect and conformity. He may be, as I hope he is, a well-meaning man, but he is deficient in religious judgment.

Thursday, 20. I have now been a few days doing my Master's business in the country; but have taken cold, and am afflicted with a severe headache, so that I am almost ready to lie by. However, the next day I found myself something better, and came to Portsmouth, met the classes, and preached. My heart and my flesh cry out for God.

> "Fulfil, fulfil my large desires,
> Large as infinity!
> Give, give me all my soul requires—
> All, all that is in thee."

Lord's day, 23. There appeared to be many wild people in the congregation, though the grace of God is sufficient to make them tame. But the Almighty dealeth with man as with a rational creature: therefore we may go on in our folly, like the wild ass's colt, till we drop into endless perdition, unless we yield to the sacred touch of grace, and become workers together with God.

Wednesday, 26. I preached to a small company at brother Williams's;[32] and before the congregation was dismissed, an honest Christian who had been justified about twelve months before, rose up and spoke a few broken words, which affected the people more than all that had been said. What

---

[31] Isaac Luke of Portsmouth heard Robert Williams preach the first sermon at Norfolk and invited him to Portsmouth, where he preached the first Methodist sermon there under two persimmon trees. Luke was converted and fitted up a warehouse for preaching. (Bennett, *op. cit.*, 52, 53.)

[32] Robert Williams had married and located and was living on a farm on the Portsmouth–Suffolk road. The conference held the previous May had appointed him with four others to the Brunswick Circuit.

n excellent thing is simplicity of heart! How ready is God to own and
less it! It would be well for professors of some standing, to inquire im-
artially if they have not lost their first simplicity. Old professors are very
pt to become wise in their own esteem, and fools in God's esteem. I have
onstant inward fevers, and drag a cumbersome body with me; but my
ul is united to Jesus; though I ardently wish to feel more fervent love to
iy God and Saviour. Calling at brother Owins's in this little excursion, I
und his wife exceedingly happy in the love of God, and I know not but
ie is sanctified wholly.

Friday, 28. At my return to town, I found the people in some commotion;
ieir trading to the West Indies was prohibited. However, the little society
:emed determined to cleave to the Lord. The next day I went down the
ver to Mr. Ellis',[33] and preached, (perhaps to but little purpose,) to a
ompany of ignorant, careless people.

Lord's day, 30. I was greatly assisted in my public exercises both in
Norfolk and Portsmouth. If it were in my power, and consistent with the
ill of God, every soul of them should be brought to Christ. But alas!
iese are vain thoughts; for the Almighty has an infinitely greater desire
or their eternal welfare. But the whole of the matter is this: they "will
ot come to Christ," in the way he has appointed, "that they might have
fe;" and thus many will eternally perish in their sins.

Friday, August 4. I spent the preceding part of this week preaching in
ie country as usual, and with various prospects of success; but came back
)-day, met the classes, which appeared to be much more engaged for
eaven, and preached in the evening.

Saturday, 5. My spirit was a little dejected, but blessed with the peace
f God. I had some conversation with Mr. Stevenson,[34] who said the peo-
le should be kept in society, if they did not meet in class; and intimated,
iat, instead of preaching the Gospel, I had been exposing their faults.
o this is part of what I have gained by my labour. But I let him know
iat our rules were intended for use.

Monday, 7. I received a letter from Mr. Thomas Rankin, in which he
iformed me that himself, Mr. Rodda, and Mr. Dempster had consulted,
nd deliberately concluded it would be best to return to England. But I
an by no means agree to leave such a field for gathering souls to Christ,
s we have in America. It would be an eternal dishonour to the Methodists,
iat we should all leave three thousand souls, who desire to commit them-
:lves to our care; neither is it the part of a good shepherd to leave his
ock in time of danger: therefore, I am determined, by the grace of God,
ot to leave them, let the consequence be what it may. Our friends here

[33] Probably Samuel Ellis, who lived down the Western Branch from Portsmouth on
ie road to Mill Creek. (See *Heads of Families, Virginia*, 93.)
[34] Joseph Pilmoor in his *Journal* refers to a Mr. Stevenson, a Scotsman, as one of
e earliest Methodists in Norfolk.

appeared to be distressed above measure, at the thoughts of being forsake
by the preachers. So I wrote my sentiments both to Mr. Thomas Rank
and Mr. George Shadford.

Tuesday, 8. I set out on my little country tour, and after preaching
Mr. Bruce's, brother Williams's, and a few other places, returned c
Friday to Portsmouth and preached in the evening, though much in
disposed. This week we have had such thunder and lightning as I neve
knew before. Thus, by going from one climate to another, we may me
with things of which we had very little idea. Then how will it be when w
change worlds, instead of climates! And how surprised will impenite
sinners be, when they go from earth to hell! That God whose power pr
duces the thunder and lightning, of which the inhabitants of some par
of the earth have very little conception, is undoubtedly able to produce th
unquenchable fire, of which many impenitent sinners have very litt
belief.

Lord's day, 13. My own soul was enlarged in preaching, but the peop
were too little affected. On *Monday*, I spoke both morning and evening
but we were interrupted by the clamour of arms, and preparations of wa
My business is, to be more intensely devoted to God. Then,

> "The rougher the way,
> The shorter our stay;
> The tempests that rise
> Shall gloriously hurry our souls to the skies."

Wednesday, 16. Preaching at Mr. Harding's, about sixteen miles fro
town, I met with Mr. Pinner[?][35] from North Carolina, who invited me
go and form a circuit in Currituck county, where they have very litt
preaching but what they pay for at the rate of three pounds per sermo
I accepted the invitation, and appointed the 10th of September for th
time to visit them. A letter from brother George Shadford,[36] which can
to hand on Friday, gave an account of about two hundred souls broug
to Christ within the space of two months. Glory to God for the salvati
of sinners! Surely I am in a dry and barren place! And there is but litt
prospect of doing good; though the Spirit of holiness possesses my ow
heart. But O! how it pants for more faith and love! How it longs to
more useful in the Church of Christ!

Saturday, 19. My body is weak; but this does not concern me like th
want of more grace. My heart is too cool towards God: I want to feel
like a holy flame. I am also sometimes afraid that I shall never do an
more good.

Lord's day, 20. I preached three times as usual; and heard a sermon c

[35] The Mr. P. was probably Mr. Pinner. Asbury did not carry out his intention
visiting that state and did not do so until 1780.
[36] Shadford was one of the preachers on the Brunswick Circuit and a leader in t
great Virginia revival.

the dignity of human nature. Vain philosophy! "Every imagination of the thoughts of the heart (in an unrenewed man) is only evil continually." Then what is the dignity of depraved human nature? Received a letter from Mr. Thomas Rankin, expressing a change in his intention of returning to England. Rode to Mr. Bruce's, on *Tuesday*, where many of the people were much affected under preaching. Lord, water the seed sown, that sooner or later it may bring forth fruit to thy glory! The weather is now so hot, that my body is greatly enfeebled, and my mind almost unfit for every exercise. But I desire in patience to possess my soul. I went to Mr. Ellis's on Saturday, but there was so little prospect of doing them any good, I took my leave of them. My body was fatigued, my soul was tempted and cast down; but in meeting the people at night in town my spirit was refreshed.

Lord's day, 27. The Spirit of the Lord wrought powerfully in our congregations, and some were deeply affected. On *Monday,* I set off for Mill Creek,[37] to hold our quarterly meeting. We found it a peaceful, comfortable time. Mr. Strawbridge[38] discovered his independent principles, in objecting to our discipline. He appears to want no preachers: he can do as well or better than they. But it is likely self-sufficiency is the spring of all this. After preaching at a few other places on the way, I returned to Portsmouth on Friday; and on Saturday we had a most remarkable storm —the wind at north-east, and blew several vessels on shore; and among others the Mercury man-of-war. Houses were blown down; docks torn up; bridges carried away; abundance of trees broken and torn up by the roots; and several tracts of land overflowed with water. What a peculiar blessing is true religion!

> "Who in the Lord confide,
> And feel his sprinkled blood.
> In storms and hurricanes abide,
> Firm as the mount of God."

A more awful scene than this will be unfolded, when God shall judge the world by the man Christ Jesus. How then will poor sinners quake and tremble, when "the heavens shall pass away with a great noise, and the elements shall melt with fervent heat! O that they were wise, that they understood this, that they would consider their latter end!"

Monday, September 4. I was taken very ill with the fall fever, and being able to take but little nourishment, was much reduced. However, I put my trust in the Lord, and committed all my concerns to him; but was not able to keep any journal till the 26th instant, and then felt myself but very little better.

[37] Mill Creek is in Norfolk County. It is reached by going south along the Western Branch.

[38] Strawbridge insisted on administering the sacraments and refused to obey the rules to the contrary.

Tuesday, 26. Brother Williams[39] died. The Lord does all things well perhaps brother Williams was in danger of being entangled in worldl business, and might thereby have injured the cause of God. So he wa taken away from the evil to come.

Wednesday, 27. My body is still very weak, and there is too much weak ness in my soul, which passionately longs for more spirituality, and mor of God in Christ Jesus.

> "Come, O my God, thyself reveal;
> Fill all this mighty void:
> Thou only canst my spirit fill:
> Come, O my God, my God!"

Thursday, 28. I ventured to preach a funeral sermon at the burial o brother Williams. He has been a very useful, laborious man, and th Lord gave him many seals to his ministry. Perhaps no one in Americ has been an instrument of awakening so many souls, as God has awakene by him.

Friday, 29. My body recovers a little health and strength. Lord, hel me so to use my strength for thee, as never to provoke thee, in thy dis pleasure, to deprive me of either my life or my strength! Wrote to Mi Thomas Rankin, informing him of brother Williams's death.[40]

Lord's day, October 1. Preached in Portsmouth, for the first time sinc my illness, and the hearts of many were touched.

Tuesday, 3. My heart is fixed, trusting in the Lord. I sincerely desire t be entirely his—to spend the remnant of my days and strength altogethe for God. A company of marines have been ashore at Norfolk, ransacke the printing office, and taken the printers and press with them. The in habitants soon after embodied and got under arms. The people are als repairing the fort, which, if put in order, may sink all the ships that sha attempt to come into the harbour. But if it is thought expedient to watc and fight in defence of our bodies and property, how much more expedier is it to watch and fight against sin and Satan, in defence of our soul which are in danger of eternal damnation! But small dangers at hand hav a greater effect on fallen man, than the greatest dangers which are though to be at a distance. But, alas! the one may be as near as the other!

Saturday, 7. I ventured, though weak, on a small excursion into th country this week, and preached several times.

Lord's day, 8. Was greatly enlarged in preaching both at Norfolk an

[39] Robert Williams died on this day. It was said of him that he "preached the fir Methodist sermon on Virginia soil, he formed the first society, he printed the fir Methodist book, he aided in building the first church, he made out the plan of th first circuit, he was the first to marry, the first to locate, the first to die." (Bennett, *op cit.*, 71.)

[40] Thomas Rankin and Francis Asbury were made executors of Robert William will, and Rankin visited Mrs. Williams when he was in Virginia in 1776. (See Rankin' *Journal*.)

ortsmouth, and I venture to hope some good was done. But martial
lamours confuse the land. However, my soul shall rest in God during this
ark and cloudy day. He has his way in the whirlwind, and will not fail
ɔ defend his own ark.

Wednesday, 11. Satan assaults me, but cannot break my peace. My soul
, stayed on the Lord, and I find great sweetness in reading the Bible, and
omparing spiritual things with spiritual. Other books have too great a
ɛndency to draw us from this, the best of books; I therefore intend to
ɛad more in this, and less in all others.

Friday, 13. Preached at Mr. Fulford's, where I always find consolation
ɪ my soul: then I returned to Portsmouth, and found my spirit at liberty
ɩ preaching at night. Well may the kingdom of heaven be compared to a
ɛt, which is cast into the sea, and gathereth all, both good and bad; we
ɩad collected twenty-seven persons in our little society here, when I first
ame; but I have been obliged to reduce them to fourteen; and this day I
ut out a woman for excessive drinking. Here we see the necessity and
dvantage of discipline. No doubt but Satan will use all his endeavours to
ɪrust in some who are unsound and insincere, so that they, by their un-
ɔdly conduct, may help him to bring reproach on the spiritual Church
f Christ. And unless the discipline of the church is enforced, what
ɪncere person would ever join a society, amongst whom they saw un-
ɔdliness connived at?

Friday, 20. Having spent several days preaching in different parts of
ɩe country, I returned to Portsmouth, and was comforted. We have a few
s faithful and happy souls in this place, as perhaps in any part of Vir-
ɩnia; and unless Divine justice has determined destruction on these two
ɔwns, I hope the Lord will undertake for them, and increase their number.

Lord's day, 22. A painful swelling in my face prevented my preaching
ɩis morning; but it broke and gave me ease before night; so I exhorted
ɩ the evening.

Monday, 23. As I expect to go to Brunswick shortly, my heart rejoices
ɩ hopes of seeing good days, and many souls brought to God, in those
arts. True Gospel preachers may say with the poet,—

> "The love of Christ our hearts constrains,
> And strengthens our unwearied hands,
> We spend our sweat, and time, and pains,
> To cultivate Immanuel's lands."

Preaching at Mr. Bruce's to-day, some who had treated me with un-
ɩndness, were now affected and wept much at the thoughts of parting.
'he word went with power to the hearts of many at Mr. Harding's on
'*uesday*; as it did also the next day at the widow Ivey's;[41] where they
revailed on me to tarry all night and preach again for them on the

---

[41] Lednum, *op. cit.*, 185.

Thursday, which I did. Here is a prospect of doing good, and a preache
is acceptable; for they have no minister in the county, except one who i
occasionally hired at the extravagant rate before-mentioned. I explaine
something of our discipline and method of support to Mr. Pinner,[42] an
he seemed desirous that we should go amongst them. I then went to th
Northwest Woods, and preached at the funeral of a certain Mr. Manning,
who had desired that we should perform this last office for him. Man
people were present, who seemed serious, and some of them were muc
affected. On *Friday* I returned to Portsmouth.

Saturday, 28. I feel determined, by the grace of God, to use more privat
prayer. And may the Lord make me more serious, more watchful, an
more holy!

Lord's day, 29. There was great tenderness of heart amongst the peopl
at Norfolk, while I enlarged on these words of our Lord, "I will not leav
you comfortless; I will come unto you." It was also an affecting time a
Portsmouth while preaching from Deut. xxx, 19.

Monday, 30. I am now bound for Brunswick. Some that had bee
displeased with my strictness in discipline, were now unwilling to let m
go; but I fear they will not soon see me again, if they should even sa
"Blessed is he that cometh in the name of the Lord!" I am deficient i
many things; but my conscience beareth me witness that I have bee
faithful to these souls, both in preaching and discipline. After takin
leave of my friends, I set out for Brunswick; and having preached at M
Bruce's in the way, lodged at Mrs. Williams's.[44]

Wednesday, November 1. After we had passed Southampton cour
house,[45] we were stopped by one who had an order from the committee t
examine strangers. When we had given him an account of ourselves, h
treated us with great kindness, and invited us to dine with him, which w
did. My body is a little fatigued, but my soul is blessed with health an
vigour. Hitherto hath the Lord helped!

Thursday, 2. By the good providence of God I entered Brunswick circui
at the house of Mr. Mason,[46] and am now within a few miles of dea
brother George Shadford. God is at work in this part of the country; an
my soul catches the holy fire already.

[42] *Ibid.*
[43] *Ibid.* Manning had been a friend of Joseph Pilmoor.
[44] The widow of Robert Williams, in Nansemond County. (*Minutes*, 1775.)
[45] Southampton courthouse is now Suffolk, Virginia.
[46] Mason, one of the earliest Virginia Methodists, erected Mason's Chapel in Bruns
wick County. Conferences were held there in 1785 and 1801. (Clark: *An Album c
Methodist History*, 190.) It is said that Woolsey's Barn, Mason's, and Dromgoole
were ancestors of the present Olive Branch Church at Gasburg, Virginia. Howeve
Early's *Journal* shows that Woolsey's Barn was four miles away from Olive Branch
and preaching continued there for a while after Olive Branch was founded. Mason
was three miles from Olive Branch. Olive Branch was later moved to its present sit
(See Early's *Journal* in *Virginia Historical Magazine*, XXXV, 178.)

Friday, 3. God is my rest and my portion; my soul delighteth in him.
1y heart is elevated in flames of sacred fire, both in private and public
rayer.

> "Let others stretch their arms like seas,
> And grasp in all the shore:
> Grant me the visits of thy face,
> And I desire no more."

Lord's day, 5. Rode about ten miles to Samuel Yeargan's[47] chapel, and
1et brother George Shadford. My spirit was much united to him, and
ur meeting was like that of Jonathan and David. We had a large congre-
ation, and I was much comforted amongst them.

Monday, 6. I moved on towards our quarterly meeting; but in fording
1eherrin river, the water was so deep as almost to swim my horse and
arriage. On *Tuesday* our quarterly meeting began, at which there might
e seven hundred people. What great things hath the Lord wrought for
1e inhabitants of Virginia! Great numbers of them manifest a desire to
2ek salvation for their souls. At this meeting we admitted Francis
oythress, James Foster, and Joseph Hartley, as travelling preachers. I had
reat satisfaction in preaching both *Tuesday* and *Wednesday*, and was
1uch pleased with the manner and matter of the Christians' testimony in
1e love feast; having a correspondent witness of the same in my own
reast.

Thursday, 9. Spent this day profitably and comfortably with brother
ieorge Shadford. Happy are they who can open their minds freely to
1ch other, as we have done!

Friday, 10. I preached at Benjamin Johnson's,[48] and the power of the
ord was present, melting the hearts of the audience; and in class meeting
oth believers and penitents were all in tears. I have now a blooming
rospect of usefulness, and hope both to do good and get good. My heart
oes out in grateful thanksgiving and praises to God.

Lord's day, 12. Was much shackled in my ideas, and tempted against
1e place and people, while preaching at J. Mabry's.[49] But on *Monday* I
und an attentive, feeling people at I. Jay's. The preaching appeared to
e very seasonable, as the Baptists are creeping in amongst our societies
1 these parts. My soul possesses more and more of the Divine life and
ve, and is strongly bound to Jesus Christ my Lord. But still I hunger
nd thirst for more of the grace of God.

---

[47] Samuel Yeargan's chapel was on the Brunswick Circuit in Brunswick County. In
'75 the Brunswick Circuit embraced fourteen counties in Virginia and Halifax and
ute counties in North Carolina. Yeargan's was probably the first chapel in Virginia.
iewehr: *The Great Awakening in Virginia, 1740*, 156.)

[48] One of the earliest societies met at Benjamin Johnson's. (Lednum, *op. cit.*, 141.)

[49] Mabry lived in Greensville, formed from Brunswick County, and erected the fourth
ethodist Chapel in Virginia. (Bennett, *op. cit.*, 143; Sweet: *Virginia Methodism*, 121.)

Tuesday, 14. Preached at Mr. Cox's and Mr. Boisseau's,[50] and met with a few inquisitive people. It is a just observation, that those matters which are the least disputed in religion are the most essential, and those who are the most fond of controverted trifles have the least real religion. Satan will help us to the shell, if we will be satisfied without the kernel.

Wednesday, 15. The congregation at Mr. Haye's was but small; though I hope it was not labour in vain. The next day there was a good prospect at Mr. Featherstone's,[51] and a class of about fifty simple, faithful souls. The word was blessed on *Friday* at friend Smith's, and on *Saturday* I came to Samuel Yeargan's, a serious, sensible man.

Lord's day, 19. I began and ended the day with God. I had much liberty at the chapel in discoursing on the subject matter, manner, and end of the apostles' preaching.

Monday, 20. My soul is pure and peaceful; and blest with a more solid sense of God than heretofore. At V. Warren's we had a blessing both in preaching and class meeting.

Wednesday, 22. After preaching I met with brother Isaac Luke[52] and Mr. King,[53] who were on their way to Portsmouth, but could not pass the guards. Lord, help thy people to redeem their time, for the days are evil. I see the necessity of living to God, and improving our present privileges.

Thursday, 23. My soul was blessed with a delightful sense of the goodness of God this morning; and after I had preached at Warren's, brother Robert Lindsay[54] gave an exhortation. Then rode to F. Smith's, and went to bed with a fever on me; and in the morning felt so much pain that I thought of not going to the court house. However, I went and found a large congregation, and believe it was a profitable season. Thus we see the propriety of dragging a feeble body to duty, as far as it can bear; and if there be a willing and sincere mind, God will either give us strength for a profitable performance of duty, or accept of what we are able to do. At this time the Lord rewarded my weak endeavours with liberty, power, and consolation. So I kept on my way, and preached the next day at F. Smith's, and on the *Lord's day* at J. Mabry's, to about four hundred souls, where one person was struck with convulsive shakings. After preaching at Lane's,[55] on *Monday*, I met the class, but had not a satisfactory confidence in the testimony of some of the members. My own soul was in a comfortable frame, and felt a strong desire to glorify God more than ever. My mind was also strongly impressed with a desire to warn and stir up the

[50] Mr. Boisseau erected a chapel in Dinwiddie County, probably the third in Virginia. (Lednum, *op. cit.*, 140.)
[51] See note under September 17, 1780.
[52] Bennett, *op. cit.*, 52; *Journal* entry for July 14, 1775.
[53] Lednum, *op. cit.*, 141.
[54] Bennett, *op. cit.*, 74.
[55] Lednum, *op. cit.*, 140. Lane erected in Sussex the second Methodist chapel in Virginia.

eople to work out their salvation, in these dangerous and difficult times.

Tuesday, 28. The rain detained me in the house, to hold close and sweet ommunion with my God. But the next day I found many collected at Mr. loisseau's. Here Mrs. Jarratt[56] met me, and entreated me to go into their arish. Pursued my way on *Thursday* to Mr. Pegram's,[57] and found an nsettled society. And on *Friday* preached to a dry congregation at Mr. 'egram's, and the next day went on to Petersburg. Here I was unexectedly pleased with the sight of some of my friends from Norfolk. I reached twice in Petersburg, on the *Lord's day*, and though many of the eople seemed, like Gallio, to care for none of those things, yet I hope here will be some faithful souls found here.

Monday, December 4. I am frequently checking myself for the want of nore solemnity in my conversation; but still my heart is with the Lord.

> "In the heavenly Lamb
> Thrice happy I am,
> And my heart doth rejoice at the sound of his name."

Preached at Isaac Richardson's,[58] on *Tuesday*, and rode in company vith a few friends to George Booth's, and preached in the evening. We ad a melting time in preaching the next day, but especially in the class neeting. Satan still assaults me with his temptations, but the Lord is on ny right hand, that I may not be moved, if I trust in him. We must expect o be tempted, as our Lord was, while we are within the reach of the fallen pirits; but it is our duty to keep ourselves that the wicked one touch us ot. And if we yield in the least degree, even in desire or temper, we must xpect to suffer for it.

Thursday, 7. I saw brother John King,[59] whose heart seems to be yet a the work of God. We had a good time to-day at T. Andrews's, both in reaching and class meeting. My soul resteth in the love of God; and all ny powers are engaged to do his will. I also found my soul devoted to God n faith and prayer, the next day. And after preaching at F. Andrews's, net the society, which consisted chiefly of penitents.

Saturday, 9. Found a few simple souls at Mr. Ellis's,[60] and we were

[56] Devereux Jarratt (1732–1801) was born in Virginia and in 1763 went to England nd was ordained as an Anglican clergyman. On his return he became the rector of ath Parish in Dinwiddie County, where he served churches called Saponey, Hatcher's .un, and Butterwood. Saponey Chapel still exists, and Jarratt and his wife are buried nder its pulpit. He was an evangelical and co-operated heartily with the Methodists, inerating through twenty-nine counties in Virginia and North Carolina in addition o serving his own parish. He was one of the leaders in the great Virginia revival. (See is letter to Wesley in *Journal* entry for December 19, 1776.) He broke temporarily 'ith the Methodists after the organization of the Methodist Episcopal Church in 1784. Bennett, *op. cit.*, 60–64.)

[57] Lednum, *op. cit.*, 186.   [58] Lednum, *op. cit.*, 141.

[59] John King was on the Norfolk Circuit. (See note under April 29, 1772.)

[60] Mr. Ellis' chapel in Sussex County was probably the seventh meetinghouse in 'irginia. (Lednum, *op. cit.*, 141.)

comforted together. A man came to the house at night, asked for me
gave a curse, and went away.

Lord's day, 10. Rode to friend Lane's, and preached twice in their new
house, thirty feet by twenty-four. My own heart was enlarged, and many
of the people were moved and melted under the word. We have about
sixty persons in society here. Friend Lane, who had been ill for some
time, departed from this vale of woe, full of faith, and love, and joy, about
one o'clock on *Monday* morning. What a noble and delightful employment is ours, to be nursing immortal souls for the realms of eternal glory
And now and then we have the inexpressible comfort of seeing a soul
depart in peace, triumphing over the power of death! Is there joy among
the angels of God over one sinner that repenteth; and is there not joy
among them over one soul that has finally escaped the snare of the devil
Doubtless there is; and we will participate of their joy. Lord, help me, in
all humility and love, in all purity and faithful obedience, to devote all
my days to thee; that I may finally join all the glorious company of heaven
and praise thee eternally there!

Wednesday, 13. I left my circuit, and came back to preach at friend
Lane's funeral. There were many people, and a great melting among them
But I found myself very unwell at night, through much exercise, and went
to bed in a high fever. My mind was also dejected and tempted, so that
I have not had such a day these six weeks. Lord, give me patience, that in
the midst of all I may possess my soul!

Friday, 15. Was able to preach at N. Moss's, and met with brother
John King[61] and his wife, who were married yesterday. Found a happy
people at Mr. Tucker's, on *Monday*; and was greatly blessed with the
people, on *Tuesday*, at Mr. Boisseau's.

Wednesday, 20. I have now been twelve years a preacher, three years in
a local capacity, and nine years in the travelling connexion; about four
years and eight months in England, and about four years and four
months in America.

Thursday, 21. By a mistake of brother Glendenning's[62] I rode twelve
miles to Robert Jones's,[63] and then had to ride thirteen miles more to
Owens's, and met the people at night.

Monday, 25. Being Christmas day, I preached from 1 Tim. i, 15: "This
is a faithful saying, and worthy of all acceptation, that Christ Jesus came
into the world to save sinners." My spirit was at liberty, and we were

[61] John King married Miss Sallie Seawell of Brunswick County. (See note under Apr
29, 1772.)

[62] William Glendenning, a British immigrant, was admitted to the itinerancy in 1777
and appointed to the Brunswick Circuit. He was one of the preachers who attended the
Christmas Conference in 1784. (*Minutes*, 1775; Lednum, *op. cit.*, 413; Barclay, *op. cit.*
I, 57, 97 n.)

[63] Robert Jones erected in Sussex the fifth Methodist chapel in Virginia. (Lednum
op. cit., 140, 383.)

uch blessed both in preaching and class meeting. Hitherto the Lord hath
elped me both in soul and body, beyond my expectation. May I cheer-
illy do and suffer all his will, endure to the end, and be eternally saved!

Wednesday, 27. We have awful reports of slaughter at Norfolk and the
ireat Bridge; but I am at a happy distance from them, and my soul keeps
lose to Jesus Christ. And as we know not what a day may bring forth, I
an say with St. Paul, "For me to live is Christ, but to die is gain." Found
warm and lively society of about fifty souls at W. Featherstone's, on
'hursday; but the company was small at friend Smith's, on *Friday*.

Lord's day, 31. Being the last day of the year, we held a watch-night
t Samuel Yeargan's chapel, beginning at six and ending at twelve
'clock. It was a profitable time, and we had much of the power of God.

1776

1776
Baltimore alarmed at the approach of a British sloop

CHAPTER FIVE

Virginia

Monday, January 1, 1776. I am now entering on a new year, and am of late constantly happy, feeling my heart much taken up with God, and hope thus to live and thus to die. Or, if there should be any alteration, may it be for the better, and not for the worse! This is my earnest desire and prayer to God.

> "My residue of days or hours,
> Thine, wholly thine, shall be;
> And all my consecrated powers
> A sacrifice to thee;
> Till Jesus in the clouds appear
> To saints on earth forgiven,
> And bring the grand sabbatic year,
> The jubilee of heaven."

On *Wednesday* my soul was in a sweet and humble frame, and my heart was expanded both in preaching and meeting the class. I returned to Owen Myrick's[1] for lodging, and the next day after preaching spoke to about thirty lively souls at Warren's.

Wednesday, 10. Mr. and Mrs. Jarratt met me at friend Boisseau's and gave me a long narrative of a great work under Brother George Shadford. We held a watch-night, and Mr. Jarratt and I stood about two hours each. There appeared to be a great degree of Divine power amongst the people. Mr. Jarratt accompanied me to William Partridge's,[2] where I

[1] Lednum, op. cit., 185.   [2] Ibid., 303.

preached, and then pursued my way to Mr. Patrick's,[3] in Chesterfield, a
good old saint of God. The Lord was with us there; and I afterward wen
on to Petersburg; and was glad to see my friends, though they were in
some trouble about the times. To the great loss of many individuals, we
are informed that Norfolk was burnt by the governor.

Lord's day, 14. I found myself at liberty in preaching in the morning
and then went to hear parson H.,[4] who preached a good sermon. He came
in the evening and heard me preach on the Jubilee, Lev. xxv, 9, 10
Brother George Shadford then met the class with great animation.

Monday, 15. We had many people at friend Lee's:[5] I have been reading
Prideaux's Connexions, and my soul possesses peace and purity in Christ
my Redeemer.

Wednesday, 17. The Lord is graciously working on the hearts of the
people at F. Andrews's; but the Baptists endeavour to persuade the people
that they have never been baptized. Like ghosts they haunt us from place
to place. O, the policy of Satan! Some he urges to neglect the ordinances
altogether; others he urges to misunderstand them, or make additions to
them. Christ, speaking of children, says: "Of such is the kingdom of
heaven." But the practice of the Baptists says, They may be of the kingdom
of glory, but they cannot be of the kingdom of grace. But, knowing that
they who seduce souls must answer for them, I shall not break my peace
about it, but leave them to God. I look on them as objects of pity, rather
than objects of envy or contempt. The people also appeared to be much
alive, on *Thursday*, at the widow A's.[6] Had a blessing in class meeting,
and find my heart quite given up to God.

Friday, 19. Thanks be to God for his unspeakable love; my soul enjoys
it in a greater and greater degree. Many people attended to hear the word
to-day at the widow Lane's. The society consisted of about sixty souls,
who appeared to be very lively and spiritual.

Lord's day, 21. It was a powerful time while I preached from Isaiah
lxiii, 4: "The day of vengeance is in my heart, and the year of my Redeemed is come." Brother Jarratt, who was obliged to fly from Portsmouth, distressed by the late fire, met me here. On Monday we were all
deeply affected with a sense of our unworthiness, at friend Phillips's,
while I discoursed on the barren fig-tree.

Tuesday, 23. My soul was happy in God, and sweetly engaged in

---

[3] *Ibid.*, 186. He was known as "Father Patrick."

[4] Evidently a minister of the Established Church.

[5] Nathaniel and Elizabeth Lee lived in Prince George County, Virginia, about sixteen miles from Petersburg. They were the parents of Jesse Lee, one of the most famous
early Methodist preachers, the founder of Methodism in New England, and author of
the first history of American Methodism.

[6] On May 17, 1780, Asbury preached at Widow Heath's. (See *Journal* for that date.)
Inasmuch as A and H are sometimes confused, the widow A and the widow Heath
were probably the same person.

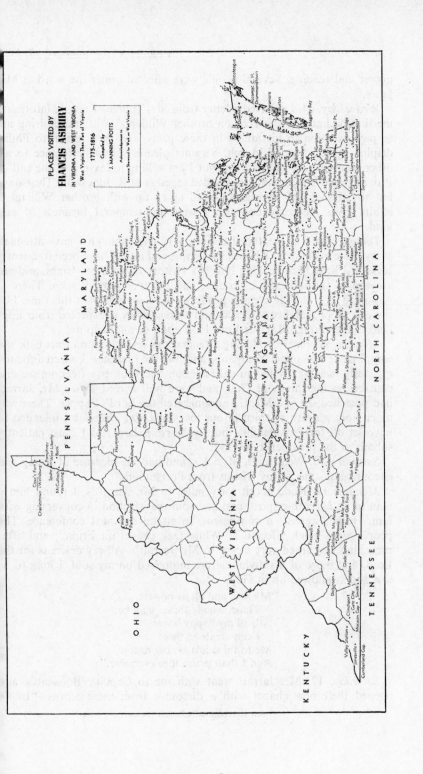

PLACES VISITED BY

FRANCIS ASBURY

IN VIRGINIA AND WEST VIRGINIA

West Virginia Then Part of Virginia

1775-1816

Compiled by

J. MANNING POTTS

Acknowledgment to
Lawrence Sherwood for Work on West Virginia

prayer and reading. Several people were affected under the word at Mr Lee's.

Wednesday, 24. I received a letter from Mr. Thomas Rankin, informing me that he had administered on brother Williams' will, and desiring me to pay attention to his affairs in these parts, and then return to Philadelphia by the first of March. Virginia pleases me in preference to all other places where I have been; but I am willing to leave it at the call of Providence. We were much comforted together at R. Jones's on Thursday but the thought of having my mind taken up with brother Williams's affairs gives me some concern. I want no temporal business of any kind.

Tuesday, 30. The weather has been very cold, though I have attended every place in course; and both the people and myself have been frequently blessed. I have been reading Burnet's History of his Own Times, and am amazed at the intrigues of courts, and the treachery of men. There is reason to fear, the same cause produces the same effects at this time. For there is no probability of peace, and a great army is expected from England in the spring. May the Lord look upon us and help us!

Monday, February 5. Having attended the several appointments in the way, I came to Samuel Yeargan's, and met the preachers collected for the quarterly meeting. With mutual affection and brotherly freedom we discoursed on the things of God, and were well agreed. After Mr. Jarratt had preached, he and Mr. C.[7] administered the Lord's Supper. There was much holy warmth of spirit in our love feast. On *Thursday* I intended to have set off for Philadelphia, but my horse is lame; so I must patiently submit to the providence of God.

Saturday, 10. Went to O. Myrick's, and had the pleasure of seeing and encouraging some of my friends from Portsmouth.

Monday, 12. Rode about forty miles to Mr. Jarratt's. I found him a man of an agreeable spirit, and had some satisfaction in conversing with him. He has agreed, if convenient, to attend our next conference. The people were much affected at White Oak chapel on Friday; and after preaching I returned very weary to Mr. Jarratt's. All my desire is for the Lord, and more of his divine nature impressed on my soul. I long to be lost and swallowed up in God.

> "My soul and all its powers,
> Thine, wholly thine, shall be;
> All, all my happy hours
> I consecrate to thee:
> Me to thine image now restore,
> And I shall praise thee evermore."

Saturday, 17. Mr. Jarratt went with me to Captain Boisseau's and opened their new chapel with a discourse from these words, "In all

[7] An Established Church rector.

laces where I record my name, I will come and bless thee." I spoke at ight, and we found the Lord with us.

Lord's day, 18. I preached twice at Petersburg. The last subject was the ich man and Lazarus, which struck the people with great solemnity; and nany seemed to feel the power of God. On *Monday* there were two Baptist reachers amongst the congregation. After the sermon was ended, they lesired to speak with me. So we conversed about three hours on experinental, practical, and controversial divinity; but ended where we began. thank the Lord, my mind was kept in peace and coolness. No doubt but atan is very active in promoting religious controversies. Many take a ontroversial spirit for the spirit of religion; while others dispute away vhat little religion they have. "Only by pride cometh contention. The visdom that cometh from above is pure and peaceable."

Wednesday, 21. Deep seriousness sat on the minds of the people under he preaching at friend Lynch's.[8] And my preaching, for five times together, has been attended with blessed effects. But let all the glory be given to God! I am only as a pen in the hand of a writer. My soul longs or more spirituality, and to be totally dedicated to God.

Friday, 23. I set off for Philadelphia; and after meeting with various ccurrences, heavy rains, and much fatigue, reached Leesburg on *Thursay*, 29. On *Friday, March* 1, my soul seemed to fix again on its centre, rom which it had been measurably removed by a variety of difficulties, nd found sweet peace with God. A company of lively people attended he word at Thomas Alliston's,[9] where I met with brother William Waters. The attention of the audience was also much engaged on the Lord's lay at the court house, while I discoursed with great affection and clearness of ideas. I afterward visited a poor unhappy man imprisoned for nurder, but found him very ignorant; though he was brought under some oncern before we parted.

Maryland

Left Leesburg on *Monday*, 4, and by the good providence of God, rrived safe at Baltimore on *Thursday*; but found the people greatly larmed by the report of a man-of-war being near. Many of the inhabitants were moving out of town.[10] Brother Watters preached in the evening.

Thursday, 7. My heart mounts heavenward on wings of strong desire or more of God; and the peace of God, which passeth all understanding,

[8] See Tipple, *op. cit.*, 94.

[9] *Heads of Families in Virginia*, 17.

[10] Hearing of the arrival of the British sloop "Otter," the inhabitants were thrown ato consternation, and many fled the city as hasty defense measures were begun. Scharf: *History of Baltimore City and County*, 72.)

keepeth my spirit in His knowledge and love. Here I met with brothe***
Rodda, and found him under some exercises of mind towards Mr***
Thomas Rankin. However, the temptation was removed before we parted***
On *Friday* the town was all in commotion. It was reported that the man***
of-war was in the river, which excited the serious attention of all th***
inhabitants; so that some were moving off, while others were gettin***
under arms. Alas, for fallen man! He fears his fellow creatures, whos***
breath is in their nostrils, but fears not Him who is able to destroy bod***
and soul in hell. If fire and sword at a small distance can so alarm us***
how will poor impenitent sinners be alarmed when they find, by woefu***
experience, that they must drink the wine of the wrath of God, poure***
out without mixture?

Lord's day, 10. The congregations were but small, so great has th***
consternation been. But I know the Lord governeth the world; therefor***
these things shall not trouble me. I will endeavour to be ready for life o***
death; so that, if death should come, my soul may joyfully quit this lan***
of sorrow, and go to rest in the embraces of the blessed Jesus. O delightfu***
felicity! There is no din of war; no unfriendly persecutors of piety; n***
enchanting world with concealed destruction; no malevolent spirit t***
disturb our peace: but all is purity, peace, and joy. Adapting my discours***
to the occasion, I preached this evening from Isaiah i, 19, 20: "If ye b***
willing and obedient, ye shall eat the good of the land: but if ye refuse an***
rebel, ye shall be devoured with the sword: for the mouth of the Lor***
hath spoken it."

Monday, 11. Pursued my way as far as Mr. Henry Gough's,[11] and wa***
treated with great kindness. May this family evince that all things ar***
possible with God; though their salvation should be attended with a***
much apparent difficulty as the passage of a camel through the eye of ***
needle! If they prove faithful stewards they will. I preached here the nex***
day to a large congregation, amongst whom were some of my old friend***
from the (Gunpowder) Forks; and the Lord gave us a blessing together

Wednesday, 13. Came to Josias Dallam's, and found his pious wif***
under hysterical complaints, and full of doubts about the state of her soul
Preached the next day, at a place by the way, with holy warmth of affec***
tion, to a considerable number of people.

---

[11] This was Perry Hall, home of Henry Dorsey Gough, located about twelve mile***
northeast of Baltimore. It was one of the most pretentious mansions opened to th***
early Methodist itinerants; and after 1775, when Gough and his wife were awakene***
under the influence of Asbury, it became a regular preaching place. Mrs. Gough wa***
among Methodism's most devout and influential women, and the Gough home i***
distinguished in Methodist history as the place in which Wesley's English emissarie***
met with Asbury and others for a week of preparatory planning before the Christma***
Conference. Only a remnant of the original manor-house remains. (Stevens, *op. cit.*, ***
235–40; Lednum, *op. cit.*, 153–57; *Maryland Historical Magazine*, XLV, 32–46***
Smith, *op. cit.*, 191–93, 201.)

Pennsylvania

Tuesday, 19. Under the divine protection I came safe to Philadelphia, having rode about 3,000 miles since I left it last. But heaven is my object, not earth. This springs my mind, and makes my burden light.

> "The things eternal I pursue,
> A happiness beyond the view
> Of those that basely pant
> For things by nature felt and seen:
> Their honours, wealth, and pleasure mean,
> I neither have nor want."

Here I met with Mr. Thomas Rankin in the spirit of love; and received a full account of what related to the unhappy Mr. (James) Dempster. I also received an affectionate letter from Mr. Wesley, and am truly sorry that the venerable man ever dipped into the politics of America.[12] My desire is to live in love and peace with all men; to do them no harm, but all the good I can. However, it discovers Mr. Wesley's conscientious attachment to the government under which he lived. Had he been a subject of America, no doubt but he would have been as zealous an advocate of the American cause. But some inconsiderate persons have taken occasion to censure the Methodists in America, on account of Mr. Wesley's political sentiments.

Wednesday, 20. By the power of God my soul is kept, in the midst of all company, sweetly reposed on Jesus Christ. My desire is, with the most fervent love, to devote myself to Him that died for me.

Thursday, 21. A perfect calm pervaded my soul; and I found myself at full liberty in preaching from 2 Cor. vi, 2.

Friday, 22. How changeable are all things here, and especially in these precarious times! but my determination is, to cast all my care on the Lord, and bear with patience whatsoever may occur. May the Lord make me more indifferent both towards persons and things, and only intent on doing his will! On *Saturday* I visited Mrs. M., above eighty years of age, and very infirm; she is a friend to all Gospel preachers, and opens her house to make them welcome. If she should at last receive the Lord into her heart, it will be well.

Lord's day, 24. Brother Webster[13] preached in the morning. Mr. Stringer at the Episcopal church was very severe upon the Quakers, but to little purpose. Two of their leading men, Gilbert Deacon and Alexander Bartram,[14] came very kindly to see Mr. Thomas Rankin.

[12] In 1775 John Wesley had severely attacked the position of the American colonies in his *A Calm Address to our American Colonies*. This was to be followed up in 1777 by a more moderate publication entitled *A Calm Address to the Inhabitants of England*.

[13] Richard Webster had been stationed on the Chester Circuit.

[14] Gilbert Deacon and Alexander Bartram were vestrymen at St. Paul's Church.

Monday, 25. I had an opportunity of speaking to John Wade relative to his leaving the work; and he manifested some inclination to return. My soul was greatly blessed in meeting sister Lambert Wilmer's class, and all present seemed to partake of the same blessing.

> "The opening heavens around me shine
> With beams of sacred bliss,
> If Jesus shows his mercy mine,
> And whispers I am his."

Tuesday, 26. My soul was blessed with divine serenity and consolation. May I ever be able to conduct myself with evangelical prudence, and so keep under my body, that I may always be the temple of God, by his Spirit that dwelleth in me! The next day also, my soul enjoyed the same delightful sense of the divine favour, and was fixed on God as on its centre, though in the midst of tumult. Glory to God! I can leave all the little affairs of this confused world to those men to whose province they pertain; and can comfortably go on in my proper business of instrumentally saving my own soul and those that hear me.

Friday, 29. Have been graciously assisted every time I have attempted to preach this week; and found a particular blessing to-day in speaking at the funeral of sister L., an old follower of Christ.

Saturday, 30. I persuaded John Wade to decline his thoughts of studying and settling, and return to his circuit. We had a powerful time in prayer meeting this evening.

Monday, *April* 1. My soul panted after God. We had a sudden and dreadful alarm of fire, which threatened a store-house, malt-house, and brew-house. It was not extinguished without great difficulty, and until much damage had been done. Man can neither defend his person nor his property in many cases, and yet how unwilling to commit himself and his property, in a proper manner, to God!

Tuesday, 2. My mind felt some dejection, but my peace was not interrupted. Amongst others in the congregation this evening, there was a woman of ninety years of age. The next day I was much employed in reading, and severely tempted by Satan, but was kept from all injury by the power of God.

Friday, 5. I heard a Moravian preach; but it was only a historical faith. And this being Good Friday, I preached from these pathetic words of Christ, "Father, if it be possible, let this cup pass from me; nevertheless, not as I will, but as thou wilt." What mortal can form any idea of the blessed Saviour's feelings at that time, when his agony was so great as to express from his sinless body great drops of blood and water! Was it ever heard before, that any man sweat blood? If Jesus found the punishment due to sin to be so severe, how will poor sinners themselves bear the eternal damnation of hell?

Lord's day, 7. The Lord graciously assisted me in my public exercises both morning and evening. And on *Monday* my soul was in a pure and spiritual state.

Tuesday, 9. We had a large congregation, and my heart was greatly expanded, while I discoursed on "the cloud of witnesses," from Heb. xii, 1. The power of God was eminently displayed on the minds of several; and one in particular was struck with deep conviction.

Thursday, 11. My soul was all on stretch for God both yesterday and to-day. Isaac Budd (?)[15] came to see me, and appeared to be in some distress. I prayed with him more than once, and he roared out for very anguish of spirit. Instead of being surprised that an awakened sinner should weep and cry aloud for mercy, we ought to be infinitely more surprised, that an unforgiven sinner should manifest but little or no concern. If a man expected to lose all his property, and be put to bodily torture, could he be unconcerned? But what is all this to the loss of God and heaven, and the torture of unquenchable fire? Truly, if it were not for unbelief, we should see sinners on every side weeping and roaring aloud both day and night.

Saturday, 13. Was desired to visit a prisoner under sentence of death. I found he was an Englishman, had been an old soldier, and had experienced the pardoning love of God in Ireland about twenty years ago, under Mr. Boardman. Thus we see that, although a soul has been blest with the favour of God, yet unfaithfulness may provoke the Almighty to give up such a person to work all kinds of sin with greediness. Then "let him that standeth, take heed lest he fall." On the *Lord's day*, my mind was shut up in preaching, and I felt the want of more faith for Philadelphia.

Monday, 15. I am not without a comfortable sense of the favour and presence of God, but labour under a lassitude of both body and mind. I went to the jail to visit the prisoners again, but could not obtain admittance. Mrs. Colesburgh (?), formerly the wife of Gilbert Tennent,[16] attended our class meeting today, and my soul was much blessed amongst them.

Tuesday, 16. My heart was sweetly enlarged towards God, both in my private exercises and my public preaching. A friend from New York informed us, that troops were raised and entrenchments made in that city. O Lord, we are oppressed; undertake for us. I received a letter from friend Ely[17] at Trenton, complaining that the societies in that circuit had been neglected by the preachers.

---

[15] This was probably Isaac Budd. Asbury had contact with the Budd family in Burlington County, New Jersey, and Philadelphia. (See *Journal* entries for April 25, 30, 31, 1776.)

[16] See note under January 7, 1775.

[17] George Ely was one of the trustees of the Trenton Society. (*History of First Methodist Church, Trenton, 175th Anniversary Program*, 1947.)

Wednesday, 17. My soul loves God and all mankind, but I canno
please all men. However, my conscience is void of offence both toward
God and towards man. On *Thursday* we heard of a skirmish between th
Philadelphia fleet and the Glasgow man-of-war. What will be the end o
these things? Lord, think upon us for good, and show us mercy! Preachin
this evening, the powers of my soul were at full liberty, and I trust it wa
made a blessing to many.

Friday, 19. Satan has been thrusting at me, but by grace I am still kept
and my soul is employed in holy and heavenly exercises, with constan
and delightful communion with God. O! how I long to find every powe
of soul and body one continual sacrifice to God!

> "If so poor a worm as I
>   May to thy great glory live,
>   All my actions sanctify,
>   All my words and thoughts receive:
>   Claim me for thy service; claim
>   All I have and all I am."

With great warmth of affection I went through the public exercises of
the evening. On the *Lord's day,* my soul was given up to God; and it
appeared to be a searching time in the public congregation.

Monday, 22. I found Christ in me the hope of glory: but felt a pleasing,
painful sensation of spiritual hunger and thirst for more of God.

New Jersey

On *Tuesday, April* 23 I rode to Burlington, and on the way my soul was
filled with holy peace, and employed in heavenly contemplations: but
found, to my grief, that many had so imbibed a martial spirit that they had
lost the spirit of pure and undefiled religion. I preached from Rom. xiii, 11,
but found it was a dry and barren time. And some who once ran well now
walk disorderly. On *Wednesday* I rode to Trenton; and found very little
there but spiritual coldness and deadness. Had very little liberty in preaching among them; thus has the Lord humbled me amongst my people. But
I hope, through grace, to save myself, and, at least, some that hear me.

Thursday, 25. I rode about eleven miles, and preached to a people who
were but very little moved: but at Isaac Budd's[18] the next day there was
more sensibility amongst the congregation; and, though very unwell, I
found my heart warm and expanded in preaching to them. It is my

---

[18] This was doubtless the person who visited Asbury on April 11. The Budd family
lived in Burlington County, New Jersey. The will of Thomas Budd, April 8, 1776,
mentioned his brothers, Isaac and Joseph, and left five pounds "to the Methodist
meeting house at New Mills when the house is finished." The will of Mary Budd, widow,
March 22, 1793, also left a similar amount to the New Mills church. (*New Jersey
Archives,* 1st Series, Vol. 34; *Abstracts of Wills,* V, 74–75; VIII, 57.)

resent determination to be more faithful in speaking to all that fall in my ay, about spiritual and eternal matters. The people were very tender at iend Fiddler's[19] on Saturday. And on the Lord's day I spoke feelingly nd pointedly to about three hundred souls at the meeting house. After- ard I returned, through the rain, to Trenton, and was well rewarded in ιy own soul, while preaching to the congregation at night. I felt every ord, which seemed to cut like a two-edged sword, and put me in mind f some of my former visits. May the Lord revive his work amongst ιem again; and make the time to come better than the former time!

Monday, 29. Satan beset me with powerful suggestions, striving to ersuade me that I should never conquer all my spiritual enemies, but be vercome at last. However, the Lord was near, and filled my soul with eace. Blessed Lord, be ever with me, and suffer me not to yield to the mpter; no, not for a moment!

Tuesday, 30. Went about nine miles to our quarterly meeting at Hope- ell;[20] and we had much of the power of God in our love feast, in which any declared their experience. I lectured in the evening at Isaac Budd's, ιough very weary: but my heart was with God; and I know we cannot re or wear out in a better cause. On *Wednesday* rode back to Trenton, here I preached to about a hundred souls, and then went about thirty iles more to William Budd's.[21]

Thursday, May 2. Some melted under the word at Mount Holly,[22] ιough at first they seemed inattentive and careless. The grace of God kept y spirit this day in sweet seriousness, without any mixture of sourness.

Saturday, 4. At New Mills I found brother Willmore [?] very busy ρout his chapel,[23] which is thirty-six feet by twenty-eight, with a gallery

[19] This was probably S. Fiddler, of "an old Methodist family" near Trenton. (Led- ιm, *op. cit.*, 236.)

[20] The Hopewell meetinghouse was "erected by the disciples of Mr. Whitefield, lled 'Newlights,' and stood about nine miles from Trenton." (*Ibid.*, 237.)

[21] The Budds were prominent in the area. John, Eli, Samuel, and Jonathan Budd ere trustees of the chapel.

[22] Mount Folly, formerly called Bridgeton, is the county seat of Burlington County, ew Jersey. The first Methodist to preach there was George Shadford, who preached the Presbyterian Church, as did Thomas Rankin in September, 1774. Nothing more heard of Methodist preaching there until 1781, when Caleb Pedicord and Joseph romwell were appointed to West Jersey. There was no society until 1805. In 1809 seph Totten held a quarterly meeting there and was obliged to preach in the door to ull house and large numbers in the yard. He urged the necessity of a meetinghouse, d in 1810 a brick chapel thirty-six feet square was built on Brainard Street. (Wood- ιrd and Hagaman: *History of Burlington County*, 189.)

[23] New Mills was the present Pemberton, New Jersey. Brother Willmore was probably ιmbert Willmore, one of the trustees of the first Methodist church there, although ιme historians have identified him with William Watters; however, Watters was in rginia at this time. The chapel was on an acre of land conveyed by William Budd, ., in 1774. It was a little south of the present Methodist church. In 1833 it was sold Solomon Middleton, moved to North Hanover Street, and remodeled into a resi- nce. (See Atkinson, *op. cit.*, ch. vi; DeCou: *The Historic Rancocas*, 76.)

fifteen feet deep. I preached in it from Matt. vii, 7, with fervour, but no
with freedom, and returned to William Budd's the same night.

Pennsylvania

Lord's day, 5. I preached at New Mills again, and it was a hear
affecting season: then returned to Philadelphia, but went under a heav
gloom of mind, and found my spirit much dejected and shut up.

Monday, 6. My mind was in a dissipated frame to-day: and we wer
alarmed with a report that ships-of-war were then in the (Delaware
river. However, I was blessed in meeting a class at night. My mind wa
more composed and comfortable the next day, but not so spiritual an
heavenly as I desire it should be.

> "Come, Lord, from above,
> The mountains remove,
> Overturn all that hinders the course of thy love:
> My bosom inspire,
> Enkindle the fire,
> And wrap my whole soul in the flames of desire."

Preached at night from a text which corresponded with my own feelings
"These are they which came out of great tribulation," &c.

Wednesday, 8. My spirit is much assaulted by Satan, but the Lord is m
keeper. About ten o'clock to-day tidings arrived that there had been
skirmish off Christiana,[24] between thirteen row-galleys and the Roebuc
man-of-war; that, after an encounter of three or four hours, the man-o
war withdrew, as it was thought, much shattered. At this news the i
habitants of the city were all in commotion; and the women especiall
were greatly shocked. Lord, what a world is this! Give me wisdom an
patience, that I may stand still and see the salvation of God.

Thursday, 9. My mind was free: and in meeting two classes we had muc
of the solemn power of God. At night I preached from these words, whic
are so applicable to the circumstances of the people: "We have no cor
tinuing city here." Many people seemed to feel the weight of this Divin
truth, so suitable to their present condition.

Friday, 10. My soul is in sweet peace; and I only want to feel my hea
continually flaming with pure love to God, carrying every desire an
every thought towards heaven. Brother William Bell arrived here to-day
and we are now informed that some men were killed in the galleys, and th
man-of-war was much damaged.

Lord's day, 12. Divine grace assisted and comforted me in all the exe
cises of the day. And although I spoke in strong and plain terms at night
yet the very soldiers bore it well. But the next day I was seized with

[24] Christiana was in Delaware.

:vere chill, and was carried to my lodging very sick. I was in a heavy
.weat till four o'clock the next morning, but nevertheless set out the next
ay, if possible to reach the conference: and came to Chester that night.

Wednesday, 15. I am still afflicted, but not forsaken; the Lord fills me
'ith peace and consolation. Attempted to reach a quarterly meeting, but
'hen I got to the place was obliged to go to bed. Though the next day,
'eak as I was, I went and held a love feast, and afterward preached; and
ie Lord gave me strength in my inward man.

Saturday, 18. My poor frame is much afflicted and shattered; but my
iind is full of Divine tranquillity, ardently desirous to submit to the
rovidence of God with inflexible patience. How amazing is the goodness
f God! He raiseth up the best of friends—such as love, for Christ's sake,
) show the kindest care for me in my affliction. Inasmuch as they have
one it unto me, one of the least of his servants, they have done it unto
hrist. And may he crown their kindness with an eternal reward! Was
:ry unwell all the *Lord's day*, but my great desire to be at conference in-
uced me to make an attempt, on *Monday*, to travel. But by the time I
ad rode three miles, I found, if I travelled, it would be at the hazard of my
fe: and was therefore obliged to decline it, though the disappointment
'as very great. Let it be, Lord, not as I will, but as thou wilt! Brother
/atters (?) went to a Quaker meeting, and began to speak; but some of
ie Friends desired him to sit down.

Tuesday, 21. My disorder seemed to be broken; but I was taken with a
leeding at the nose. The devil still bends his bow, and makes ready his
rrows on the string; but the Lord suffers him not to wound me.

Thursday, 23. Visited Mrs. Rebecca Grace,[25] an old disciple of Mr.
'hitefield's; but now she entertains the Methodists. And on the *Lord's
iy* I ventured to preach to a small company of people.

Monday, 27. Expecting the preachers were on their return from the
)nference, I appointed preaching at my lodgings, but had to preach my-
:lf, to a small, attentive, tender company, and felt much quickened in my
wn soul. At night brother Rankin arrived, and informed me that I was
ppointed for Baltimore: to which I cheerfully submit, though it seems to
: against my bodily health.

Wednesday, 29. My whole soul is devoted to God, and desires nothing
ut more of him. Brother Rankin and I both spoke to the congregation

---

[25] Mrs. Rebecca Grace (1718–1800), twice widowed, lived at Coventry and owned
onworks there by inheritance from her first husband, Samuel Nutt, Jr. She had been
. disciple of Whitefield but rejected his Calvinism after reading Wesley's sermon on
ee grace and was a devoted Methodist. George Washington and his officers were often
itertained by her while the army was at Valley Forge. Benjamin Franklin wanted to
arry her, but she rejected him because of his religious views; he sent for her when he
y dying, and she pointed him to religion. She died at the age of eighty-two. (McClin-
ck: *History of the Coventryville Methodist Church*; see *Journal* entries for March
', 1781; October 3, 1781; October 11, 1794.)

collected at night, and the power of God was eminently present. O
Thursday I wrote a letter to Mrs. W., who has departed from God, an
feel great hopes it may be the means of restoring her.

Maryland

Friday, 31. Though far from being in a good state of health, I set off fc
my appointment, and reached Josias Dallam's at night.

Lord's day, June 2. Went to the chapel, and preached after broth
Samuel Spraggs,[26] and the people appeared to be deeply affected; b
brother S. does not seem to enter into the Methodist plan of preachin;
He uses a few pompous, swelling words, which pass for something gre
with short-sighted people! but are not calculated to do them much spiritu
good. On *Monday* my soul enjoyed the peace of God; but I am frequentl
ashamed before the Lord, for indulging too great a flow of spirits in tl
company of my friends. Though I purpose, through grace, to begin anev
Lord, succour me by thy mighty power! We had a melting time among
the people on *Monday*, at Josias Dallam's.

Tuesday, 4. Went to the widow Presbury's; and after I had done preacl
ing, met a small class of about thirteen souls, who appeared to be sincer
My body is still very weak; but it is my determination to spend all th
little remains of my strength for God, and the salvation of precious soul

Wednesday, 5. Some felt the word of truth at the widow Phoebe Bond'
while I was showing what it is to walk after the flesh. But there appears t
be a general flatness amongst the members of the class: they are neith
so attentive nor so tender as they were two years ago. What a pity! th
the nearer souls approach to eternity, the more unfit they should be t
enter into that unchangeable place!

> "Help me to watch and pray,
> And on thyself rely;
> Assured if I my trust betray,
> I shall forever die."

Satan hunts my soul continually, and attacks me at times with the mo;
powerful temptations: but he does not get any advantage, nor break m
peace; but, on the contrary, drives me nearer to my Almighty Protecto.

[26] Samuel Spraggs became a traveling preacher in 1774. After serving in Virgini;
Philadelphia, and Maryland, Asbury conferred with him for the last time on Marc
10, 1778, before he, with George Shadford, disappeared behind the British lines. Durin
the seven years (1776–83) that New York disappeared from the *Minutes* because c
British occupancy, Spraggs joined John Mann in preserving the society in John Stree
Spraggs became the rector of the Old Protestant Episcopal Church in Elizabeth, Ne
Jersey, on the walls of which a marker acknowledges his services. (Lednum, *op. cit*
142; Stevens, *op. cit.*, I, 418–20; Wakeley, *op. cit.*, 279–90.)

nd I feel all my powers more abundantly given up to God, to serve him
ith all sincerity, fervency, and diligence.

Thursday, 6. Was greatly blessed in meditation and prayer, on my way
) Mr. Harry Gough's; and there met with my good friend, Mr. Philip
.ogers, and his wife. The next day my spirit was in heaviness through
1anifold temptations. I see the need of always standing sword in hand,
gainst my adversary the devil. Our Lord displayed both great wisdom
nd great mercy, when he commanded us to watch and pray ALWAYS.
'lay I show mercy on my own soul by always attending to this command!

Lord's day, 9. Yesterday I preached with some satisfaction at Mr.
iiles's; and rode to-day about twelve miles to the (Gunpowder) Forks,
'here I preached from Col. i, 28, and then met part of several classes.[27]
'ly feeble body was much fatigued with the exercises of the day, but my
)ul was delightfully taken up with God. On *Monday*, the congregation at
.quila Galloway's appeared as if they both understood and felt the two-
dged sword of the word. I see the need of having my thoughts constantly
mployed on the things of God, that no vacant moment may be left for
atan to fill up.

Tuesday, 11. Rose with a deep sense of God resting on my mind, and
t off for Mr. William Lynch's, which is about twenty miles from the house
'here I lodged; but by losing our way, we made it about thirty miles, and
id not reach the place till about two o'clock. The Lord then rewarded
1e for my toil, while I was preaching to a serious, tender people; and I
fterward endeavoured to unite the society, which Satan, by his diabolical
'iles, had divided. On *Wednesday* the congregation at Joshua Owing's
'ere so impenetrable that neither promises nor threats could move them.
Ior did the people at Mr. Alexander Warfield's (?) seem to have much
1ore sensibility, though I was greatly affected myself while preaching to
1em from 2 Corinthians vi, 2. The Lord has blessed me of late with much
ssistance in preaching, and with purity of heart.

Thursday, 13. Both the people and myself were moved by the word at
acob Cassell's. My feeble frame is much fatigued with preaching twice a
ay; but it must drag on as long as it can; for it is my meat and drink, yea,
: is the life of my soul, to be labouring for the salvation of mankind. I
esire nothing but God, and to spend the remainder of my strength in
uffering and labouring for him. Who that knows God, would be weary
f such a master! And who that knows the worth of souls would be weary
f striving to save them!

[27] The Fork Meetinghouse derives its name from its location near the forks of
iunpowder Falls near Fallston, Harford County, Maryland. It stands on land donated
y James Baker, who opened his home as a preaching place soon after hearing John
.ing preach at the corner of Front and French streets, Baltimore. Here Robert Straw-
ridge organized a Methodist society, and a chapel was erected in 1773. (*Maryland, a
iuide to the Old Line State*, 305; *Methodist Quarterly Review*, 1856, 439; Lednum, *op.
it.*, 154; Henry Smith, *op. cit.*, 212, 262.)

Saturday, 15. After preaching in the Dutch church,[28] and meeting th
class, I rode about five miles, through a heavy rain, and the wind was s
powerful that it blew down trees, barns, and houses; so that it was wit
difficulty I could urge my way through the woods; but at length came saf
to the widow Madeira's and enjoyed a comfortable hour in preaching fror
Luke xiv, 18, 19. On my coming to Baltimore, I met Mr. Thomas Rankir
and heard him preach. On *Monday* I rode to William Ridgely's, wher
we had a large company of people, and amongst the rest were two Baptis
preachers. All this day my soul was happy in God.

Tuesday, 18. Though temptations hung upon my spirit, yet I foun
myself greatly enlarged at Mr. Evans's, while enforcing these strikin
words: "The end of all things is at hand: be ye therefore sober, watchin
unto prayer." Returned on *Wednesday* to Baltimore, and spent some tim
with Mr. Otterbein. There are very few with whom I can find so muc
unity and freedom in conversation as with him. At night the words were
blessing to myself, and no doubt to others, while I expatiated on 2 Cor
iv, 5. I can rejoice in God, and cast all my care upon him.

Thursday, 20. Went to Nathan Perigau's and was fined five pounds fo
preaching the Gospel. But found my soul at liberty both in preaching an
class meeting. We then went to William Lynch's, and found N. L. unde
uncommon exercises of mind.

Saturday, 22. Returned to Baltimore; and although my peace is no
broken, neither is any wrong temper or desire indulged, yet I lament th
want of more spirituality. My soul, like the rising flame, would continuall
ascend to God.

Lord's day, 23. After preaching at the Point, I met the class, and the
met the black people, some of whose unhappy masters forbid thei
coming for religious instruction. How will the sons of oppression answe
for their conduct, when the great Proprietor of all shall call them to a
account! We had a serious audience in the evening at town.

Monday, 24. Spoke plainly on the nature of our society, and the neces
sity of discipline; which perhaps was not very pleasing to some who d
not choose to join. I told them we could not, would not, and durst no
allow any the privileges of members, who would not come under th
discipline of the society. I desire to know no man after the flesh. My sou
is in peace.

Tuesday, 25. James Foster, who has lately come from Virginia, gave m
an agreeable account of the glorious spreading of the work of God i
Virginia and North Carolina. The Lord is fulfilling his promises, an

---

[28] Reisterstown, eighteen miles from Baltimore, was settled by Germans, who wer
called "Dutch." Benedict Swope, who also served a congregation on Pipe Creek
labored among them. Freeborn Garrettson mentions preaching in two "Dutch"
churches in this general neighborhood in 1780. (Garrettson: *Experiences and Travels*
etc., 1791, 166, 170.)

)uring out his Holy Spirit on the people. Satan is still busy in his attempts
 disturb, if he cannot destroy me: but my soul stays, and waits, and
ings on God, who makes me more than conqueror over all the assaults
 the enemy. I preached to-day at the house of ——, a man who has
uch talk, and but little religion. The whole congregation appeared to be
ry stupid. Rode thence to John Kelso's,[29] and found a simple-hearted
ople. Here I met with poor M., who is keeping a school, which may per-
ips be his last and best shift.

Wednesday, 26. This was a general fast day; and my heart was fixed on
od. I preached at three o'clock at Mr. Darius Stansbury's and the
)wer of God was displayed among the poorer part of the congregation.
mes Foster then met the class, like another George Shadford.

Thursday, 27. This was a day of trials. Satan drew my thoughts into
train of reasoning on subjects which were out of my reach; for secret
ings belong to God, but things which are revealed belong to us and our
iildren. Thus, while I was soaring out of the region of my duty, I became
attentive to what immediately concerned me, and oversetting my chaise,
oke it very much. Though, blessed be God, my body was preserved. May
e Lord keep my soul united to himself, as its proper centre! However,
was greatly blessed in speaking to the people; and the power of God
sted on the congregation.

Friday, 28. Going to my appointment, it rained much, and I got wet,
hich brought on a sore throat, and laid me up till *July* 9. For the greatest
irt of the time I could neither eat, drink, nor sleep, till the tumour broke.
ut glory to God! I possessed my soul in patience under the whole of the
fliction; though my heart complains of its own ingratitude to my gracious
ord, who not only supported both soul and body under all my trouble,
it provided tender friends, who treated me with the greatest affection.
s a kind father dealeth with an afflicted son, so the Lord dealeth with me.
'hat shall I render unto the Lord for all his benefits? I will render thanks-
ving and praise, and devote both body and soul to the Most High.
uring this affliction my abode was at Mr. Gough's.

I have now come to a determination, God willing, to go to the warm
)rings,[30] and make a trial of them for the recovery of my health; perhaps
y strength may be thereby so restored for future services, that upon the

[29] John Kelso, a member of the Evans Meeting House, lived in the section of Balti-
ore now known as Mt. Washington. He was one of three brothers from Ireland.
'rook: *Ireland and the Centenary of American Methodism,* 168, 169.)
[30] This was Berkeley Springs, Morgan County, West Virginia. The official name is
ith, after the popular spa in England. George Washington was so impressed with the
edicinal value of the springs while surveying lands for Lord Fairfax in 1748 that during
ter seasons he visited it with his family. During Asbury's visit this health resort was
ronged with the gay and prosperous who sought safety from the armies of the Revolu-
)nary War. Their conduct met with the disapproval of Asbury.

whole there may be no loss of time. Richard Webster, William Lynch, ar
James Foster will supply the circuit in the mean time.

Thursday, July 11. My body is in some small measure restored, ar
God himself is the portion of my soul. May he ever keep me from eve
desire which does not directly or indirectly lead to himself!

Saturday, 13. My heart has been humbled and melted under a sense
the goodness of God. This day I set out for Baltimore on my way to th
springs; but by the time I reached the town I felt a great disposition
weariness in my shattered frame, and my soul, which seemed to sympathi
with the body, had not such a lively and steady sense of God as at son
other times, though there was no desire after anything else. I ventured
preach both this evening and the next day; and humbly hope the word wa
made a blessing to many.

Monday, 15. We set off for the springs. Mr. Dallam overtook us in th
evening; and that no opportunity might be lost, I lectured at night in th
tavern where we lodged. And both the tavern-keeper and his wife ap
peared to have some thoughts about their souls. On *Tuesday,* we reache
Frederick, and collecting as many people as we could by a short notice,
preached from 2 Corinthians vi, 2, and found my spirit at liberty. My bod
complains of so much travelling, for which it is almost incompetent; bt
the Spirit of the Lord is the support and comfort of my soul. I was throw
out of my chaise the next day, but was providentially kept from bein
much hurt. When we came to Hagerstown,[31] it seemed as if Satan was th
chief ruler there. The people were very busy in drinking, swearing, drun
ming, &c. My mind was disburdened and much comforted after I ha
delivered myself from Mark i, 16, though it seemed to answer but litt
purpose to the people. It is one thing for the preacher to do his duty, an
another thing for the audience to do theirs.

West Virginia

July 18, 1776 – August 27, 1776

Thursday, 18. After riding forty miles to-day, we reached the springs:
and at first we found it difficult to obtain lodgings. But after a while I pro

---

[31] Methodism probably had its beginning in and near Hagerstown, Maryland, i
association with resident preachers of the United Brethren in Christ, among who
were Christian Newcomer and George Adam Geeting. In 1793 a small Methodi
society had been organized in Hagerstown, and by 1812 Asbury preached in "the nea
new Methodist Chapel." (*The Methodist Magazine,* VI, 253–56; Boehm, *op. cit.,* 392

[32] This is the first time that it can be definitely shown that Asbury entered the prese
West Virginia. (Lednum, *op. cit.,* 169; *Journal* entries for July 23, 1776, and July 1.
1786.)

red a good lodging with Mr. Merryman.[33] Here was work enough for a
eacher, if he desired to be faithful. My soul was happy; and I felt
yself totally delivered from the fear of man—determined, by the grace
God, to discharge my duty.

Friday, 19. My soul was in peace; but the burden of the Lord rested
on me. I could not be satisfied till I declared to the people their danger
d duty: which I did from Isaiah lv, 6, 7. They all behaved with decency,
ough it is more than probable that some of them had enough of my
eaching.

Saturday, 20. We had a meeting in the evening (which we intend to
ve every evening at Mr. Gough's and Mr. Merryman's alternately) for
ayer and exhortation; at which about twenty people attended. My spirit
is grieved within me at the conduct of poor sinners; but in Jesus my
rd I had peace.

Lord's day, 21. A Church minister attended the public exhortation in
e morning; and in the afternoon a dissenting minister preached from
ese excellent words, "Believe in the Lord Jesus Christ, and thou shalt
saved." His discourse was very methodical—but dry, and full of
ademical stiffness. It was very unlikely to bring souls either to faith or
entance. I preached in the evening from Acts xiii, 26. But my spirit was
stirred up within me, by a desire that the people who were in their
uses might hear, that by speaking too loud I hurt myself. We afterward
d a good time in our prayer meeting.

Monday, 22. My soul enjoys sweet communion with God; but I am
liged to exercise patience in bearing with the manners of poor, blinded,
rdened sinners.

> "O might they at last with sorrow return,
> The pleasure to taste for which they were born;
> Our Jesus receiving, our happiness prove—
> The joy of believing, the heaven of love!"

Tuesday, 23. The peace of God abideth constantly with me. I preached
ain by the side of a hill, near the bath; and the word had a melting
luence on some of the congregation. The dissenting minister attended
r prayer meeting in the evening, and prayed with us. By the blessing
God, my body began to feel the benefit of the waters. May the Lord
ss these means for the entire restoration of my health; and in all my
ys may I acknowledge him, and ever study to serve him with all I have,
d all I am! Reading the lives of Halleburton, Walsh, and De Renty, has
d a great tendency to quicken my soul. Our not growing in grace is
dom for the want of knowledge concerning our duty; but generally for

---

Henry Dorsey Gough of Perry Hall, Maryland, and Samuel Merryman of Mary-
d (see December 26, 1772) had summer cottages at the springs. (See entry for July
below. Smith, *op. cit.,* 190, 204 ff.)

want of using proper means to bring the knowledge we have ir
spiritual use. Our dull spirits must have line upon line, and precept up
precept.

Wednesday, 24. The congregation was rather increased; many we
affected, and one man fell down. It clearly appears that I am in the line
my duty, in attending the springs: there is a manifest check to the ov
flowing tide of immorality, and the prejudices of many people are ir
great degree removed. So that I hope my visit to this place will be for t
benefit of the souls of some, as well as for the benefit of my own boc
though preaching in the open air, to a people who are almost strangers
a praying spirit, is more disagreeable to my feelings, and a much grea
cross than travelling and preaching in a circuit.

Friday, 26. My confidence was strong in the Lord, and accompani
with sweet consolation. My company and myself were quickened in o
own souls, by a diligent use of the means; and the hearts of several othe
were under some religious impressions. But the zealous conversation a
prayers of Mr. Gough seem to move and melt the hearts of the peoj
more than my preaching does. Lord, send by whom thou wilt: only se
to the conviction and salvation of immortal souls. I have found bc
reproof and instruction in reading the life of Mr. Walsh. At this tir
Christ is all in all to me. My heart is sweetly occupied by his gracic
Spirit. But alas! I am not watchful enough to keep up the spirit of pray

> "The praying spirit breathe,
> The watching power impart:
> From all entanglements beneath
> Call off my peaceful heart."

Saturday, 27. There were many to hear the word at three o'clock; a
the Lord was with us in the evening, when we were assembled for pray
and exhortation.

Lord's day, 28. My soul is kept in the love of God, but longs for
increase of the Divine gift. The workers of iniquity are not so bold as th
were: some of them have had convictions, but lost them. Others see
stiffly to oppose the influences of Divine grace. Mr. Hagerty,[34] who
commonly called the high-priest, on account of his height, preached t
day, and I stood clerk for him; but he seemed much dashed, and it w
with difficulty he proceeded in his discourse, which was very dry. Whil
was preaching, my heart was drawn out in compassion to the people, a
as the word was pointedly applied to their consciences, I believe son

---

[34] John Hagerty (1747–1823), a convert of John King, became an itinerant in 17
and was ordained deacon at the Christmas Conference in 1784. He could preach
German. He located in 1793. (See Joshua Soule's biography of Hagerty in *Methoa
Magazine*, VII, 209–12; and his letters in Sweet, *Religion on the American Frontier, t
Methodists*, "The Edward Dromgoole Letters." See *Journal* entries for August
1776; June 11, 1781; July 7, 1782; Lednum, *op. cit.*, 245.)

od was done. So much public speaking is almost more than my frame
n at present bear, but the Spirit within me constraineth me. I feel indeed
e want of retirement in this place, yet I make a substitute of family
ercises, and find communion with God. My soul has lately been much
awn out towards God in reading the life of Mr. Brainerd, and longs to
like him and every other faithful follower of Jesus Christ.

Monday, 29. My present mode of conduct is as follows—to read about
undred pages a day; usually to pray in public five times a day; to preach
the open air every other day; and to lecture in prayer meeting every
ening. And if it were in my power, I would do a thousand times as much
r such a gracious and blessed Master. But in the midst of all my little
ployments, I feel myself as nothing, and Christ to me is all in all.

Tuesday, 30. My spirit was grieved to see so little of the fear of God, and
ch a contempt of sacred things as appeared in many of the people in
is place. An enmity against God and his ways reigns in the hearts of all
e unawakened, from the highest to the lowest. The Rev. Mr. Webster
tended in the congregation to hear the word preached to-day.

Wednesday, 31. Spent some time in the woods alone with God, and
und it a peculiar time of love and joy. O delightful employment! All my
ul was centred in God! The next day I unexpectedly met with brother
ebster; and while preaching at three o'clock to an increased company,
e word produced great seriousness and attention. And we had a happy,
werful meeting in the evening at Mr. Gough's. But my mind is in some
gree disturbed by the reports of battles and slaughters. It seems the
erokee Indians have also begun to break out, and the English ships
ve been coasting to and fro, watching for some advantages: but what
n they expect to accomplish without an army of two or three hundred
ousand men? And even then, there would be but little prospect of their
ccess. O that this dispensation might answer its proper end! that the
ople would fear the Lord, and sincerely devote themselves to his service!
en, no doubt, wars and bloodshed would cease.

Friday, August 2. My soul was in a serious, solemn frame, but earnestly
sired to be more universally devoted to God. Brother Webster preached
day, and seemed a little abashed; but the Lord was with us in our
ening exercises. How difficult it is to be much amongst men of the world
d not imbibe their spirit in a greater or less degree! I am afraid my
ends begin to grow somewhat languid in their spirits. How watchful,
vout, and heavenly should we be, to keep up the power of inward
igion, in the midst of such a company of sinners of diverse principles
d manners! For my own part, I have had cause to lament the want of
re watchfulness. Lord, help us to be faithful in all things, to all persons,
d in all places!

Lord's day, 4. My heart was fixed, trusting in the Lord. Brother Webster
ached much to the purpose, though there were some little inaccuracies

in his language. I preached in the afternoon, and brother Webster aga
at night; and it appeared to be a time of power.

Monday, 5. Having withdrawn to the woods for the purpose of se
examination, and pouring out my heart in prayer to God, I found mys
much melted. Glory to God for a comfortable sense of the Divine favo
But alas! how serious, how solemn should I be, when so many immor
souls on every side are posting down to everlasting fire!

On *Tuesday* but few of the gentlemen attended to hear; but I was e
abled to deliver my message faithfully and freely; and the common peop
heard me gladly. The next day also many attended, and I hope my labo
will not be altogether in vain.

Thursday, 8. My heart was sweetly resigned to the will of my Lord
was willing to do or suffer whatsoever he might see proper to require
me. Met with a man to-day who came from a place about eighteen mi
from the springs. He never heard a Methodist before, nor saw one; yet
appeared to be a Methodist in principle, experience, and practice. He v
brought to the knowledge of himself and of God by the means of so
afflictions of body, prayer, and reading. Thus we see the Lord wor
where, and in what manner he pleases. My spirit has been much united
the faithful people of God of every denomination; and at this time I f
a spirit of unity with Mr. Hagerty,[35] a German minister,—though t
Germans in general, who dwell in these parts, seem very insensible to t
things of God. On Thursday night we had a mixed company of Germa
and English; Mr. Hagerty preached in German and I in English. O
exercises in the evening were as usual. Many have been much affect
lately, under the word which I have delivered from time to time for Go

Lord's day, 11. A fine, sensible, polite gentleman delivered a discou
on the new birth; he described it by its effects, but appeared to be at
total loss in respect to the manner in which it is wrought. I had spoken
the morning, and in the evening preached again, pressing religion on t
young people especially, and showing the superior advantages and sat
faction arising from it even in this life.

Monday, 12. I rode seventeen miles to see a saint indeed; a wom
confined to her bed for fifteen years, and quite happy in the love of Go
though she had never seen a Methodist, or any other truly religious peop
Where are the free-thinkers? Is this priestcraft? How can that be prie
craft, which no priest ever had a hand in? No! this is the effect of Divi
power and goodness: and so is all real, heart-felt religion. But if po
impenitent sinners will not give all diligence to know the comfort
enjoying religion, they will, they must, though much against their w
know, in due time, the misery of rejecting it. After I had preached, wi
some Divine assistance, to about one hundred people collected from t
country parts around, we returned and had a comfortable time in o

[35] Lednum, *op. cit.*, 259. See *Journal* entry for July 28, 1776.

ening meeting. The house in which we live, at the springs, is not the ost agreeable: the size of it is twenty feet by sixteen; and there are ven beds and sixteen persons therein, and some noisy children. So I vell amongst briars and thorns; but my soul is in peace.

Tuesday, 13. I found the parson had been encouraging the gentlemen oppose me, and intimating that it was very improper to permit me to each. My soul is amongst lions, but the God of Daniel is with me. I tempted to preach in the day, but my mind was shut up; though my irit was revived in the evening lecture. Is it strange to see a priest con- cting a persecution against the people of God? When did a persecution ke place in which men of that character had no hand? But although tan may be permitted to transform himself into an angel of light for a ason, yet he will not always have his own way in this matter.

Thursday, 15. My throat grew worse, and it was a rainy day, so I was liged to be dumb; but having faithfully declared to them, from time to ne, the whole counsel of God, both in his promises and threatenings, I t myself contented as having delivered my own soul.

Friday, 16. My throat growing worse, they put a blister behind my ear; t my conscience was pure, and I quietly submitted to the will of Heaven. ay the Lord keep me pure in heart, and humble at his feet, till he shall ake up his jewels, and bring them into his glorious presence, where rrow and sighing shall be done away! Glory to God, nothing has lately oken the peace of my tranquil breast!

Lord's day, 18. Found myself better, and felt a desire to preach, which lid; after having heard parson Webster (?), and found myself at liberty hile showing, 1. The natural state of the Gentile world: 2. Their spiritual ite: 3. The means and manner of their change: and lastly, I applied it to e Christian world, so called,—heathens in their hearts and practices; d showed how vain it is to substitute heathen morality, or religious rms and ceremonies, for true religion. My friend Mr. Bruce[36] and his fe, from Portsmouth, arrived here to-day.

Thursday, 22. My soul has been daily grieved by the practices of poor inded sinners; but the Lord has supported and comforted me. I have t spared, but preached plainly and pointedly every day this week; and -day Mr. Swope,[37] a German minister, went with me about nine miles a German settlement, where we both preached in our proper tongues.

Friday, 23. I had some serious conversation with a Quaker, on the bject of the Holy Scriptures as the grand criterion of all inward and utward religion. But to deny this, is to oppose the present dictates of the

[36] This was probably Mr. Bruce who lived just outside of Portsmouth. Asbury had ited and preached there.

[37] Benedict Schwope, or Swope, was an associate of Otterbein and one of the founders the United Brethren Church. (See Drury: *History of the United Brethren in Christ*, merous references; *Journal* entries for February 3 and 6, 1774; October 13, 1810.)

Holy Ghost to its former dictates; which would be a most dangerou
absurdity. How strange, how presumptuous, to exalt the dignity of moder
speakers beyond that of the prophets and apostles, who spake as the
were moved by the Holy Ghost, and have given us a sure word of pr
phecy, whereunto we do well that we take heed! (2 Pet. i, 19.) But v
must come to the law and to the testimony; if they speak not according
this word, it is because there is no light in them. (Isaiah viii, 20.) We a
sure that the Sacred Scriptures are of God; and we are as sure, if any ma
speak contrary to them, he is not of God.

   Lord's day, 25. I have had strong confidence towards God, but n
heart has not been so constantly and fervently employed in the spirit
prayer as it might have been. After preaching to-day, I fell in with one
the wildest Antinomians I had ever met with. He undertook to prove th
love is not love; and said, "they that are born of God do not sin; but th
they may sin in all manner of ways, and frequently do so." But what w
most surprising, he said, "he valued not my God and Christ; for the
could neither save nor damn him." Such language is enough to make
man shudder in repeating it.

   Tuesday, 27. Having taken my leave yesterday, in discoursing on th
parable of the sower, I this day turned my back on the springs, as th
best and the worst place that I ever was in; good for health, but mo
injurious to religion. We then rode about twenty-five miles, and called
see friend Rawlings,[38] but had to lodge on the boards. The next day
minister attended to hear the word at Dr. C.'s, and gave us a kind invit
tion to his lodging.

Maryland

   Saturday, 31. I met brother Lynch and brother Foster at Mr. Gough's
Thus hath the Lord preserved me through various trials, and his providen
hath conducted me back in safety. I enjoy more health, and perhaps posse
more grace than before I went to the springs. Now, O Lord, only make ar
keep me pure; and let me be wholly and only thine! My soul was enlarge
in preaching to-day, and many were melted under the word. I strove
prevail with brother Foster to go to Baltimore, but could not.

   Lord's day, September 1. I rode to Gunpowder Neck, and preach
twice. My soul was exceedingly happy in God, both in preaching ar
meeting the class; as it also was the next day at Josias Dallam's. B
alas! we hear of bloodshed and slaughter.[40] Many immortal souls a

[38] Stephen Rawlings lived on Back Creek in Berkeley County, West Virginia. (S
Journal entries for September 16 and 25, 1814.)

[39] Lednum, *op. cit.*, 167, 169.

[40] Apparently Asbury was referring to the Battle of Long Island a few days earlier
which the Americans suffered defeat with heavy loss. With the occupation of New Yo

iven to eternity by the bloody sword. This is a grief to my soul! Lord,
atter them that delight in war, and thirst for human blood! It is well
r the righteous that this is not their home. No: they are blessed with a
cific spirit, and are bound for a kingdom of peace, where

> "No horrid alarum of war
> Shall break our eternal repose;
> No sound of the trumpet is there
> Where Jesus's Spirit o'erflows:
> Appeased by the charms of thy grace,
> We all shall in amity join,
> And kindly each other embrace,
> And love with a passion like thine."

Friday, 6. Having been much fatigued by long rides, and preaching and
eeting classes every day, though for the most part both the people and
yself were much quickened, I came to-day to my old and faithful friend's,
enry Watters's, and the people felt the two-edged sword of the word.
lory to God! I find a constant sense of his divine love, though still
ame myself for being too free in conversation when amongst my friends.
Lord's day, 8. The congregation at Bush Forest[41] preaching house,
peared to be very insensible; and it seemed as if they had opposed the
ith so long, that they could feel it no more. But at Deer Creek,[42] my
art was warm, and the people were moved. On *Monday* I also preached
ice; but on *Tuesday* it seemed as if my labour was too much for my
ength. I have scarce had time to enter a few lines in my journal, but
ve been almost constantly employed in riding from place to place, and
eaking to the people.
Wednesday, 11. The people were serious at William Bond's (?). Here I
w the son of the famous Dr. Franklin (?); but how unlike his father
th in respect to grace and good sense! My soul now hangs on the Lord,
d dwells in the element of purity; desirous of nothing but to enjoy more
God, and to be entirely dedicated to his service. On *Thursday* I found

the British, the resentment created by Wesley's *Calm Address*, and the signing of the
claration of Independence, the persecution of Asbury and his associates was in-
asing. (Stevens, *op. cit.*, I, 417; Bangs, *op. cit.*, I, 117, 118.)
[41] This chapel, located about two and a half miles southwest of Aberdeen, on the
sh Chapel Road, is mentioned by all writers of early Maryland Methodism. In
ace Methodist Church, Aberdeen, is the cornerstone of one of the several meeting-
uses erected on the Bush Chapel site. It bears the original date, 1769. At present a
morial stone marks this historic spot. (See *Journal* entry for December 6, 1772.)
[42] Reference probably is to the residence of Henry Watters located on the Thomas
un road about three miles north of Shuck's Corner and near the present Thomas
·n church. The property, long in the possession of Judge James D. Watters, has
dergone such extensive remodeling that uncertainty exists as to whether the original
oms built in 1760 and used for worship now exist. (Forman: *Manors and Plantations*
Maryland, 121; Preston, *op. cit.*, 32; Miss Hannah S. Parker, Havre de Grace,
aryland.)

a loving, simple people at Thomas Bond's (?), and was comforted
meeting the class; though I had been undesignedly led to reach beyot
their capacity in my preaching. *Friday*, 13. I came to Mr. Gough's, ai
met with brother John Mann from New York, who brought painf
accounts of bloodshed and slaughter. On *Saturday*, I felt unwell, ai
was apprehensive that my return to Baltimore might bring on my old coi
plaints. We had a large company and a refreshing season at Mr. Gough
where brother Foster exhorted after I had preached.

Monday, 16. This was an abasing season. My soul was cast down ai
deeply humbled, under a consciousness of my spiritual wants. I did ni
enjoy such a cheerful sense of the divine goodness as at other times, bi
ardently panted for more of the Spirit of Christ.

Tuesday, 17. Both rich and poor came out to hear the word at E
Ridge, and some of the young and gay were made to weep. It will be wi
for them, if they prefer Jesus Christ and his cross to all the wealth ai
vanity of this world. I went home with Caleb Dorsey,[43] who was on
convinced of sin, but has now grown worse than ever. He had abo
forty souls in his family, untaught as the Indians in the forest. They see
to roll in plenty: but "there is no peace, saith my God, to the wicked
At Mr. R.'s on *Wednesday*, we had but few to hear. But many or few,
makes no difference with me. The Lord filled me with divine consolati
while I was dispensing the word of life to them.

Friday, 20. Returned to Baltimore, and found that a work which ha
cost some thousands of pounds, was burnt down. How easily can divii
Providence strip us of all our earthly objects! Are not such occurrenc
loud calls from a gracious God? "Lay up not for yourselves treasures upi
earth, but lay up for yourselves treasures in heaven." I have been mui
enlarged in preaching, and favoured with peculiar nearness to God
certain times, for this week past; but have been also sorely tempted by tl
enemy, and found it required great exertions of faith and prayer, to coi
quer every motion. Glory to God for his grace bestowed on me throug
Jesus Christ! We have now several exhorters raised up in different pai
of the country. This evening Mr. Rodda came to town.

Lord's day, 22. My labour was great. I preached twice, and met tl
white people and the black people separately at the Point; and aft
preaching in town, met a class. All this I could submit to with cheerf
ness; but my spirit was grieved for the want of more holiness, and more
God.

[43] Caleb Dorsey lived near Elk Ridge about eight miles southwest of downtov
Baltimore. His house, "Belmont," built for his bride, Priscilla Hill, is still standing.
plate on the main door is inscribed "C and P 1738." Dorsey, who operated nearby ir
mines, was among the first influential citizens to extend hospitality to the Method
itinerants. (Forman, *op. cit.*, 108; Bayard: *Travels of a Frenchman in Maryland a
Virginia with a Description of Philadelphia and Baltimore in 1791*; *Maryland, a Gui
to the Old Line State*, 309.)

"O grant that nothing in my soul
May dwell, but thy pure love alone:
O may thy love possess me whole,—
My joy, my treasure, and my crown:
Strange flames far from my heart remove;
My every act, word, thought, be love."

Monday, 23. My soul has been much harassed by Satan; though I found
eat freedom in preaching to a number of souls at the Point. On *Tuesday*
so my spiritual exercises were great and painful. Lord, I am oppressed;
dertake for me. Rode to Mr. Evans', and found the accuser of the
ethren had taken advantage of the society, by tempting them one
;ainst another. But most of them and the congregation seemed to feel
e power of the word preached.

Wednesday, 25. Though unwell, I returned to town, preached to a large
d serious congregation, and endeavoured to secure, in a proper manner,
r little building at the Point.[44] Having preached at Nathan Perigau's on
ursday, I found William Lynch very sick on *Friday*; but the small
mpany which was collected for worship, were deeply affected under the
ord. And, blessed be my all-sufficient Deliverer! my soul was in a great
easure disburdened of its temptations, and restored to delightful access
God, especially in the exercise of prayer. O my God! keep me always
ar to thee; always humble and watchful!

Saturday, 28. At Mr. Gough's, I met the preachers, John Mann and
1omas Foster, and we had a great melting in public worship: my own
ul also partook of the blessing.

Lord's day, 29. There were five or six hundred people at the Gunpowder
rks, to whom I discoursed on the judgments of God; and showed who
e the provoking cause—not religious people, as the ignorant say, but
ose who transgress the laws of God in defiance of his justice. Thus it
is with the antediluvians, with the Egyptians, with the apostate Israelites
the wilderness, with the inhabitants of Jerusalem after the coming of
1rist, and thus it is with us. After preaching we held a love feast, and
e power of God was present with us. Then went to Mr. Galloway's and
eached to a large company there. After which I went home with Mr.
olgate, but found that my labour was too much for my strength, and
d brought on a fever.

Monday, 30. Rode nine miles and preached at Mr. Merryman's (?), then
, miles farther, and preached and met the society at Mr. G——r's; and
e Lord was with us. I now find myself better both in body and mind,
d know the truth of our Lord's words, "My grace is sufficient for thee."

4 Strawberry Alley Chapel at Fell's Point was an unpretentious building 40 × 60
t in dimension. One who was familiar with it before it was demolished, about 1896,
scribes it as "a large, low brick building, with an old-fashioned tub pulpit, and a
nding board above it." (*Baltimore Methodism and the General Conference of 1908*,
.)

Friday, October 4. Having travelled through the Barrens,[45] and preache
at several places, I came to brother C.'s, and met with William Lync
And after preaching in a cold, open house, I rode to Mr. Rogers's ar
was happy in the company of my good friends. On *Saturday* I lodged
the house of Nicholas Jones, a happy, simple soul, the glory of this famil

Lord's day, 6. We had a great meeting at the widow M.'s. I preache
at eleven o'clock to six or seven hundred souls; and then we held a lo
feast, in which many spoke of the goodness of God. We had five or s
preachers and exhorters; so we also held a watch night from six o'cloc
till ten. And I felt as if it would have been no burden to have tarried
religious exercises all the night. The next evening likewise we had a ve
solemn watch night at William Ridgely's.

Wednesday, 9. Having received a letter from Mrs. M. of Middle Riv
Neck, requesting me to go and preach a funeral sermon at the burial
her sister, I set out this morning in compliance with her request. We four
it a serious, awful season: and after all was over, she offered me son
money; but being in a place where I could receive my six pounds p
quarter, which was sufficient for keeping me in clothes and a horse,
thankfully refused to take it. She was capable of making an excellen
useful Christian, and appeared to be under religious impressions.

Thursday, 10. At the head of the Middle River, I found a few poor, col
hearted, contentious people: but in the time of my preaching fro
Galatians v, 24, 25, most of them seemed much affected.

Saturday, 12. At Mr. Gatch's I met brother Rankin, who was ju
recovering from a late illness; and the next day we rode in company to t
Point, where he preached a very profitable sermon: and the Lord applie
the word to the hearts of the people, while I preached at night in tow

Monday, 14. My soul enjoyed the peace of God which passeth all unde
standing. Mr. Rankin went with me to Thomas Worthington's, and
he was unwell it fell on me to preach. I was greatly drawn out in my affe
tions and ideas; and it was a tender, melting time. On *Tuesday* I preache
with holy warmth at Mr. S.'s, though I had caught cold, and found myse
much indisposed.

Wednesday, 16. Met with brother Wade, and as I found myself unwe
I requested him to take my place for a day, but could not prevail; so
patiently submitted to go on, and think hard of nothing that may occu
If Jesus Christ suffered so much in purchasing salvation for men, we m
be willing to suffer a little in carrying the glad tidings amongst them.

Friday, 18. My body continued unwell, and my labour has been ti

---

[45] The Barrens was the early name of a region in upper Harford County, Marylan
and lower York County, Pennsylvania. The name was derived not from the lack
fertility but from having been denuded of trees by forest fires kindled by the Indians
improve their hunting-grounds. (Day: *Historical Collections of Pennsylvania,* 69
1953 Harford County Directory, 363.)

me to the flesh, but my soul has been much blessed with an uninter-
pted peace, and sweet communion with God. This is the time for suffer-
g and toil, but a *rest* remaineth for the people of God.

> "And what are all my suff'rings here,
>   If, Lord, thou count'st me meet,
> With thy enraptured host to appear,
>   And worship at thy feet?"

went to the Fell's Point, and delivered my message to the congregation
th much freedom. But the next day my spirit was grieved to find that the
ve of some was waxing cold. When Christ cometh, will he find faith on
e earth? What an ungrateful creature is man! to taste and see that the
ord is good, and then turn again to folly!

Lord's day, 20. My spirit was much refreshed in preaching and meeting
e little flock at the Point; and while I was preaching with peculiar sym-
thy in town, a poor sinner was so affected that he groaned as in an
;ony. If sinners could know as much of hell as the damned do, they
ould both groan and roar aloud: it is the blindness of their minds that
eps them so easy. On *Monday*, William Lynch, James Foster, brother
rawbridge and myself, held a watch night at the Point; and my soul was
uch quickened, though many of the people appeared to be dull.

Thursday, 24. At the funeral of Mr. T.'s son, I preached to about a
ousand souls, and gave him such a character as I thought he deserved.
me were affected; but the funeral parade engaged the attention of too
any. I spent about three hours in the different exercises suitable to the
casion, found myself pure from the blood of the people, and took
thing for my services.

Friday, 25. Being a day of rest from public exercises, I spent it in prayer,
editation, and reading; partly in Whitby's Notes,[46] and partly in the
fe of Solon, the Athenian philosopher.

Saturday, 26. Meeting with two of the preachers, we took sweet counsel
gether. And after I had preached the next day at Gunpowder Neck, we
ld a love feast. There was a great melting among the people, which I
pe will be the first-fruits of a gracious harvest.

Monday, 28. The people were too destitute of spiritual life at Mr.
allam's. But I found some faithful, lively souls, the next day, at Susque-
nna.[47]

[46] Daniel Whitby, D.D. (1638–1726), was prebendary of Salisbury in England and a
olific writer on theological subjects.

[47] Asbury may have had reference to Susquehanna Hundred in Harford County.
was a political division into which Maryland was divided for the purpose of levying
es, enumerating the population and recruiting troops. The two Jacob Giles, father
d son, the Litten and the Godfrey Watters families, and other supporters of Asbury's
rk lived within the bounds of Susquehannah. (*Maryland Genealogical Bulletin*, X,
. 4, 94; Brumbaugh: *Maryland Records*, II, 174–94; *Census of Susquehannah Hundred*,
76.)

Saturday, November 2. For a few days past I have been various
exercised in preaching at different places. Some congregations were war
and earnest in religion; others were dull, and seemed to have but litt
relish for Divine things. To-day I came home to Henry Watters's, an
except the time employed in public and private exercises, I was taken
in reading Whitby's Comments. He is steady to his purpose in confuti
Socinianism and Calvinism.

Lord's day, 3. "Truly my soul waiteth upon God: from him cometh n
salvation." I know they that wait upon him shall renew their strength. I
hath drawn me by the cords of his love, and blessed me with sweet co
munion. In preaching and meeting class at Deer Creek, I felt so much
the worth of immortal souls more than usual, that I seemed as o
awaking out of sleep.

Tuesday, 5. My spiritual trials have been heavy, but the Lord support
and gave me peace. Lord, sanctify me wholly, and keep me in the dus

Thursday, 7. Have read Whitby's first volume as far as the end of t
Acts. I preached and met class to-day at Thomas Bond's. And the ne
day at the Forks, I found a people that walk closely with God. Leavi
them for the present, I went to meet Mr. Rankin, who was then recover
from his illness. On the *Lord's day* we were employed in public exercis
at the widow Bond's. On *Monday* we had a heart-affecting time in pray
meeting at Deer Creek: and *Tuesday,* 12, we held our quarterly meeting
We had a very solemn time at the love feast, in which many spoke free
and feelingly of what God had done for their souls. After the preachi
was ended and the temporal business all settled, we then laid a plan f
regulating the public exercises of the local preachers; and concluded t
whole in much love and good order. But these public times interrupt n
private devotions and communion with God. It would be very disagre
able to live so always. One of the preachers brought an account of
apparition that appeared to a lad, and gave a particular account of bei
murdered by his fellow-soldier, requesting that the lad's father mig
lodge an information against the murderer: which was done. I was i
formed that the American and English armies were cannonading with
a mile of each other, near New Rochelle.[49] How much better would it
for mankind, to "seek peace and pursue it!"

---

[48] There is reason to believe that present at this quarterly meeting besides Fran
Asbury, James Foster, and John Wade, who were serving the Baltimore Circuit, a
Thomas Rankin, Wesley's American assistant, were Freeborn Garrettson and Willia
Watters. From the days of Robert Strawbridge many Maryland societies had produc
local preachers whose work had been indispensable. Under Strawbridge, who assum
spiritual offices beyond those granted Wesley's authorized helpers, a growing restle
ness occasioned the discussion to which Asbury refers. (Watters, *op. cit.,* 55, 56; T
Experiences and Travels of Freeborn Garrettson (1791), 55.)

[49] On October 27, 1776, occurred the Battle of White Plains, which was sufficien
near New Rochelle, New York, to cause Asbury to locate it there.

Wednesday, 13. Was spent comfortably in company with the preachers. ✓e had a public meeting, in which we all prayed and exhorted: and the ⸱ord gave us his blessing. Brother King and I spent *Thursday* at Mr. ⸱ough's; and on *Friday* I went to Baltimore.

Saturday, 16. The Spirit of the Lord applied the word to the hearts of ⸱e people, while I preached in town with much animation.

Lord's day, 17. It was difficult to reach the hearts of the congregation ⸱ the Point: but we had great satisfaction in the class meeting. Though my ⸱ody was weak, and there were symptoms of a fever, yet I was enabled to ⸱reach with spiritual life and power at night in town.

Monday, 18. My body was disordered, and my spirit sensibly felt the ⸱urden of the flesh; but under all my weakness and pains, my soul was ⸱xceedingly happy in God. On *Tuesday* I was still unwell, and took a ⸱omit. By *Thursday* I had got clear of my fevers, and on *Friday* met the ⸱reachers William Watters, William Lynch, and Caleb Pedicord. But my ⸱roat was now sore, and my mind a little uneasy on account of the dis-⸱ppointment in the circuit.

Lord's day, 24. I felt unwell, but went to the Point in the morning, where ⸱y mind was interrupted by the frequent coming of the people, almost to ⸱e very end of the sermon. After the preaching was over, I told them that ⸱ had rather they would stay at home, than come in such an irregular ⸱anner. The congregation were very serious in the evening at town. But I ⸱lt much exhausted.

Monday, 25. My soul was calm and comfortable. I have applied myself ⸱uch to reading Whitby: but he has so much to say about different men's ⸱pinions, that it makes the labour of reading him too dry and tedious. ⸱ow I began to read the Christian Library. On *Tuesday* intended to go to ⸱1r. Taylor's (?) but as there was a heavy rain, I thought it unsafe to ⸱enture so soon after my recovery. My soul has had complete victory ⸱ver all sin, and been blessed with peaceable and calm fellowship with the ⸱ather and the Son. Thanks be to God for his unspeakable gifts!

Wednesday, 27. I went to Mr. Rogers's, where we held a watch night. ⸱1y ideas were much contracted in preaching; but we had several exhorters ⸱resent, and they all spoke. A great part of what they said was very simple, ⸱hough well intended, no doubt. The society were greatly melted at Mr. ⸱resbury's on *Thursday*; and on *Friday* I went to a place of William Moore's ⸱ultivation, and I found a society of about thirty serious, steady people.

Saturday, 30. Returning to Baltimore, I preached from Rom. viii, 38, ⸱9. The congregation was small, but there was power in the word. It was ⸱ow reported that the British troops were on their march to Philadelphia. ⸱roubles may be at hand. But my design is, through grace, so to improve ⸱y time as to be always prepared for the worst. Poor sinners have cause ⸱ tremble at the approach of death; but even in that dreaded hour, the ⸱ighteous can rejoice in hope of the glory of God.

Lord's day, December 1. Preached as usual both at town and Point; bu some of the people seemed destitute of spiritual feelings. There is no sma danger of their being given up to hardness of heart. If the word preache does not prove the savour of life unto life, it will prove the savour of deat unto death. So that people may hear the word of God, and resist th operations of his Spirit, till they and their seats have an equal degree c spiritual sensibility when the word of God is preached.

Monday, 2. In reading Whitby on 1 Cor. iv, 4, I observed these words "Here also note in St. Paul another sense of justification; as it relates t our absolution from condemnation, and our approbation as righteous a the last day, which will be, saith he, according to our works, (2 Cor. v, 10 and our fidelity in execution of the trusts committed to us, verse 2." W are commanded to follow Jesus Christ. And he, for the joy that was se before him, endured the cross, despising the shame. So it is our duty t follow the example of Moses, who had respect unto the recompense c reward. Hence it appears, we are justified by the merits of Christ, throug faith, in the day of conversion; and by the evidence of works in the da of judgment. Happy is the Christian who abounds with them!

Tuesday, 3. I was informed that proposals were in agitation for settlin Mr. Swope, and allowing him a maintenance. But none of these thing shall give me much distress. My soul quietly resteth in the Lord. I hav some desire to know the issue of what relates to Philadelphia at thi critical juncture. But there is a God who overruleth all these matters.

Thursday, 5. My soul was much enlarged to-day in preaching at Natha Perigau's. I afterward went in company with Mr. Owings to brothe Lynch's [?]. And on *Friday,* Nathan Perigau, William Moore, and mysel held a watch night. *Saturday,* I returned to Baltimore, in a spiritual fram of mind, and preached from John viii, 12: "He that followeth me shal not walk in darkness."

Lord's day, 8. My present practice is, to set apart about three hours ou of every twenty-four for private prayer; but Satan labours much to inter rupt me; nevertheless, my soul enjoys a sweet and peaceful nearness t God, for the most part, in these duties. I found some at the Point mourn ing for an interest in Jesus Christ. May the Lord, whom they seek, com suddenly into the temple of their disconsolate hearts!

Monday, 9. My ideas were clear and my heart was warm, while I wa treating on the regal dignity of Christ, the nature of his government, an the privileges of his subjects.

Tuesday, 10. With the snow full in my face, I set out for Mr. Taylor's (? The flesh was reluctant for a while, but was brought to submit. When th mind is reconciled to duties and difficulties, then that which was har becomes easy.

Thursday, 12. I was greatly assisted and blessed in my own soul, whil preaching about two hours at a watch night at Mr. Presbury's. We hav

any alarming accounts of martial preparations. But I leave the troubles
to-morrow till to-morrow comes. My desire is to live more to God to-day
an yesterday, and to be more holy this hour than the last.

Lord's day, 15. The troubles of the times seemed so to engross the
tention of the people, that the congregation were very dull while I
reached at night in Baltimore, from Micah vi, 9: "The Lord's voice
ieth unto the city, and the man of wisdom shall see thy name; hear ye
e rod, and who hath appointed it." It seems Mr. Rankin is going to
ew York.

Thursday, 19. Received a narrative of the work of God in Virginia,
ritten by Mr. Jarratt, to be sent to Mr. Wesley. The Lord has been dis-
laying the power of his grace in a marvellous manner, through many
arts of Virginia. An extract of the narrative is here subjoined.

Brief Narrative

BRIEF NARRATIVE OF THE REVIVAL OF RELIGION IN
VIRGINIA. IN A LETTER TO A FRIEND.[50]

EAR SIR,—You were pleased, when in Virginia,[51] to desire a narrative of
e work of God in these parts. I shall give you matter of fact, in a plain,
rtless dress; relating only what I have myself seen and heard, and what
have received from men on whose judgment and veracity I can fully
epend.

That you may have a full view of the whole, I shall go back as far as my
rst settlement in this parish. August 29, 1763, I was chosen rector of
ath, in the county of Dinwiddie, in Virginia. Ignorance of the things of
od, profaneness, and irreligion, then prevailed among all ranks and
egrees. So that I doubt if even the form of godliness was to be found in
ny one family of this large and populous parish. I was a stranger to the
eople: my doctrines were quite new to them; and were neither preached
or believed by any other clergyman, so far as I could learn, throughout
e province.

My first work was, to explain the depravity of our nature; our fall in
dam, and all the evils consequent thereon; the impossibility of being
elivered from them by anything which we could do, and the necessity of

[50] The following insertion consists of (1) a letter from Devereux Jarratt to Thomas
ankin, who gave it to Asbury for transmission to Wesley (see *Journal* entry of Decem-
er 19, above), and (2) a letter from Rankin to Wesley. The Virginia revival was notable
the history of the area. This is a reproduction of a small book which was "printed
y R. Howes in London and sold at the Foundry in Moorfields and at the Rev. Mr.
esley's Preaching Houses in Town and Country, 1778. Price Three Pence." There
ere two known editions, one in 1778 and one in 1779.
[51] Rankin had been in Virginia in June and July, 1776.

a living faith, in order to our obtaining help from God. While I continue to insist upon these truths, and on the absolute necessity of being bor again, no small outcry was raised against this way, as well as against hi that taught it. But by the help of God, I continued to witness the sam both to small and great.

The common people, however, frequented the church more constantl and in larger numbers than usual. Some were affected at times, so as t drop a tear. But still, for a year or more, I perceived no lasting effect, onl a few were not altogether so profane as before. I could discover no hear felt convictions of sin, no deep or lasting impression of their lost estat Indeed I have reason to believe that some have been a good deal alarme at times. But they were shy of speaking to me (thinking it would be pr sumption) till their convictions wore off.

But in the year 1765, the power of God was more sensibly felt by a fev These were constrained to apply to me, and inquire, "What they must d to be saved?" And now I began to preach abroad, as well as in privat houses; and to meet little companies in the evenings, and converse freel on divine things. I believe some were this year converted to God, an thenceforth the work of God slowly went on.

The next year I became acquainted with Mr. M'Roberts,[52] rector of neighbouring parish; and we joined hand in hand in the great work. H laboured much therein; and not in vain. A remarkable power attended hi preaching, and many were truly converted to God, not only in his parisl but in other parts where he was called to labour.

In the years 1770 and 1771, we had a more considerable outpouring c the Spirit, at a place in my parish called White Oak.[53] It was here first formed the people into a society, that they might assist and strengthe each other. The good effects of this were soon apparent. Conviction were deep and lasting: and not only knowledge, but faith, and love, an holiness continually increased.

In the year 1772, the revival was more considerable, and extended itse in some places, for fifty or sixty miles round. It increased still more in th following year, and several sinners were truly converted to God. In sprin 1774, it was more remarkable than ever. The word preached was attende with such energy, that many were pierced to the heart. Tears fell plentifull from the eyes of the hearers, and some were constrained to cry out. goodly number were gathered in this year, both in my parish and in man of the neighbouring counties. I formed several societies out of those whic were convinced or converted; and I found it a happy means of buildin

[52] The Rev. Archibald McRoberts was an evangelical Anglican clergyman whos parish in Southside, Virginia, was adjacent to that of Devereux Jarratt. He welcome Robert Williams to the state and was a friend to the Methodists. He later became Presbyterian. (Atkinson, *op. cit.*, 377; Bennett, *op. cit.*, 56, 57.)

[53] This place was named for White Oak Creek.

ɔ those that had believed, and preventing the rest from losing their
ɪnvictions.

In the counties of Sussex and Brunswick, the work, from the year 1773,
ɪas chiefly carried on by the labours of the people called Methodists. The
ɪst of them who appeared in these parts was Mr. Robert Williams, who,
ɔu know, was a plain, artless, indefatigable preacher of the gospel: he
ɪas greatly blessed in detecting the hypocrite, razing false foundations,
ɪd stirring believers up to press after a present salvation from the remains
f sin. He came to my house in the month of March, in the year 1773. The
ɪxt year others of his brethren came, who gathered many societies both
ɪ this neighbourhood, and in other places, as far as North Carolina. They
ɔw began to ride the circuit, and to take care of the societies already
ɪrmed, which was rendered a happy means, both of deepening and spread-
ɪg the work of God.

I earnestly recommended it to my societies, to pray much for the pros-
ɪrity of Sion, and for a larger outpouring of the Spirit of God. They did
ɔ; and not in vain. We have had a time of refreshing indeed: a revival
f religion, as great as perhaps ever was known, in country places, in so
ɪort a time. It began in the latter end of the year 1775: but was more
ɔnsiderable in January, 1776, the beginning of the present year. It broke
ut nearly at the same time, at three places, not far from each other. Two
f these places are in my parish; the other in Amelia county—which had
ɪr many years been notorious for carelessness, profaneness, and im-
ɪoralities of all kinds. Gaming, swearing, drunkenness, and the like,
ɪere their delight, while things sacred were their scorn and contempt.
[owever, some time last year one of my parish (now a local preacher)
ɔpointed some meetings among them, and after a while induced a small
umber to join in society. And though few, if any of them were then
ɪlievers, yet this was a means of preparing the way of the Lord.

As there were few converts in my parish the last year, I was sensible a
ɪange of preachers was wanting. This has often revived the work of God:
ɪd so it did at the present time. Last December one of the Methodist
ɪeachers, Mr. Shadford, preached several times at the three places
ɔovementioned. He confirmed the doctrine I had long preached; and to
ɪany of them not in vain. And while their ears were opened by novelty,
ɪod set his word home upon their hearts. Many sinners were powerfully
ɔnvinced, and mercy! mercy! was their cry. In January, the news of
ɔnvictions and conversions was common; and the people of God were
ɪspired with new life and vigour by the happiness of others. But in a
ɪtle time they were made thoroughly sensible that they themselves stood
ɪ need of a deeper work in their hearts than they had yet experienced.
ɪd while those were panting and groaning for pardon, these were en-
ɪeating God, with strong cries and tears, to save them from the remains
f inbred sin, to "sanctify them throughout, in spirit, soul, and body;" so

to "circumcise their hearts," that they might "love God with all the
hearts," and serve him with all their strength.

During this whole winter, the Spirit of the Lord was poured out in
manner we had not seen before. In almost every assembly might be see
signal instances of divine power, more especially in the meetings of th
classes. Here many old stout-hearted sinners felt the force of truth, an
their eyes were open to discover their guilt and danger. The shakir
among the dry bones was increased from week to week: nay, sometim
ten or twelve have been deeply convinced of sin in one day. Some of thes
were in great distress, and when they were questioned concerning th
state of their souls, were scarce able to make any reply but by weeping an
falling on their knees, before all the class, and earnestly soliciting th
prayers of God's people. And from time to time he has answered thes
petitions, set the captives at liberty, and enabled them to praise a pardo
ing God in the midst of his people. Numbers of old and gray-headed, o
middle-aged persons, of youth, yea, of little children, were the subjects o
this work. Several of the latter we have seen painfully concerned for th
wickedness of their lives, and the corruption of their nature. We hav
instances of this sort from eight or nine years old. Some of these childre
are exceeding happy in the love of God—and they speak of the who
process of the work of God, of their convictions, the time when, and th
manner how, they obtained deliverance—with such clearness as migh
convince an atheist that this is nothing else but the great power of Go

Many in these parts who had long neglected the means of grace no
flocked to hear, not only me and the travelling preachers, but also th
exhorters and leaders. And the Lord showed he is not confined to mar
for whether there was preaching or not, his power was still sensible amon
the people. And at their meetings for prayer, some have been in suc
distress that they have continued therein for five or six hours. And it ha
been found that these prayer meetings were singularly useful in promotin
the work of God.

The outpouring of the Spirit which began here, soon extended itsel
more or less, through most of the circuit, which is regularly attended b
the travelling preachers, and which takes in a circumference of betwee
four and five hundred miles. And the work went on, with a pleasing pro
gress, till the beginning of May, when they held a quarterly meeting a
Boisseau's chapel, in my parish. This stands at the lower line of the paris
thirty miles from White's chapel,[54] at the upper line of it, where the wor
began. At this meeting, one might truly say, the windows of heaven wer
opened, and the rain of Divine influence poured down for more than fort
days. The work now became more deep than ever, extended wider, an

[54] This chapel was in Amelia County and was one of three where the revival bega
as Jarratt indicates in this letter. Nelson Reed makes frequent reference to this chapel i
his *Journal*.

as swifter in its operations. Many were savingly converted to God, and
a very short time, not only in my parish, but through several parts of
runswick, Sussex, Prince George, Lunenburg, Mecklenburg, and Amelia
unties.

The second day of the quarterly meeting a love feast was held. As soon
it began the power of the Lord came down on the assembly like a rush-
g mighty wind; and it seemed as if the whole house was filled with the
resence of God. A flame kindled and ran from heart to heart. Many
ere deeply convinced of sin; many mourners were filled with consolation;
d many believers were so overwhelmed with love, that they could not
oubt but God had enabled them to love him with *all* their heart.

When the love feast was ended, the doors were opened. Many who had
ayed without then came in; and beholding the anguish of some, and the
joicing of others, were filled with astonishment, and not long after with
embling apprehensions of their own danger. Several of them prostrating
emselves before God, cried aloud for mercy. And the convictions which
en began in many, have terminated in a happy and lasting change.

The multitudes that attended on this occasion, returning home all alive
God, spread the flame through their respective neighbourhoods, which
n from family to family: so that within four weeks, several hundreds
und the peace of God. And scarce any conversation was to be heard
roughout the circuit, but concerning the things of God: either the com-
aining of the prisoners, groaning under the spirit of bondage unto fear;
the rejoicing of those whom the Spirit of adoption taught to cry,
Abba, Father." The unhappy disputes between England and her colonies,
hich just before had engrossed all our conversation, seemed now in most
mpanies to be forgot, while things of far greater importance lay so near
e heart. I have gone into many, and not small companies, wherein there
d not appear to be one careless soul; and the far greater part seemed
rfectly happy in a clear sense of the love of God.

One of the doctrines, as you know, which we particularly insist upon,
that of a present salvation; a salvation not only from the guilt and power,
ut also from the root of sin; a cleansing from all filthiness of flesh and
irit, that we may perfect holiness in the fear of God; a going on to
rfection, which we sometimes define by loving God with all our hearts.
everal who had believed were deeply sensible of their want of this. I have
en both men and women, who had long been happy in a sense of God's
ardoning love, as much convicted on account of the remains of sin in
eir hearts, and as much distressed for a total deliverance from them, as
er I saw any for justification. Their whole cry was:—

> "O that I now the rest might know—
> Believe, and enter in;
> Now, Saviour, now the power bestow,
> And let me cease from sin!"

And I have been present when they believed that God answered th
prayer, and bestowed this blessing upon them. I have conversed with the
several times since, and have found them thoroughly devoted to God. Th
all testify, that they have received the gift instantaneously, and by simp
faith. We have sundry witnesses of this perfect love who are above a
suspicion. I have known the men and their communication for mai
years, and have ever found them zealous for the cause of God—me
of sense and integrity, patterns of piety and humility; whose testimoi
therefore may be depended on.

It has been frequently observed, that there never was any remarkab
revival of religion, but some degree of enthusiasm was mingled with it-
some wildfire mixed with the sacred flame. It may be doubted wheth
this is not unavoidable in the nature of things. And notwithstanding all t
care we have taken, this work has not been quite free from it; but it nev
rose to any considerable height, neither was of long continuance. In son
meetings there has not been that decency and order observed which
could have wished. Some of our assemblies resembled the congregati
of the Jews at laying the foundation of the second temple in the days
Ezra—some wept for grief; others shouted for joy; so that it was hard
distinguish one from the other. So it was here: the mourning and distre
were so blended with the voice of joy and gladness, that it was hard
distinguish the one from the other, till the voice of joy prevailed—t
people shouting with a great shout, so that it might be heard afar off.

To give you a fuller insight into this great work of God, I subjoin
extract from two or three of my letters.

TO THE REV. MR. M'ROBERTS

May 2, 1776

REV. AND DEAR BROTHER,—YESTERDAY I preached at Boisseau's chap
to a crowded and attentive audience. Afterwards the Methodists held the
love feast: during which, as many as pleased rose, one after another, ar
spoke, in few words, of the goodness of God to their souls. Before thr
had done speaking (although they spoke but few words) you might see
solemn sense of the presence of God visible on every countenance, whi
tears of sorrow or joy were flowing from many eyes. Several testified
the consolation they had received: some believed they were perfected
love. When the passions of the people were rising too high, and breakin
through all restraint, the preacher gently checked them by giving out
few verses of a hymn. When most of the congregation went away, son
were so distressed with a sense of their sins, that they could not be pe
suaded to leave the place. Some lively Christians stayed with them, ai
continued in prayer for the space of two hours, till fifteen mourners we
enabled to rejoice in God their Saviour; and some careless creatures of t

bliter sort, who would needs go in to see what this strange thing meant,
lt an unusual power, so that, like Saul among the prophets, they fell
bwn on their knees, and cried for mercy among the rest. O may they still
bntinue to pray till God has given them another heart!

May 3, 1776

Last night three or four score of my neighbours met together to keep a
atch night: at which it is the custom to spend three or four hours in
ligious exercises, and to break up at twelve. Such was the distress of
ose that were convinced of sin, that they continued in prayer all night,
ad till two hours after sunrise. Here also fourteen or fifteen received a
nse of pardon: so that in two days thirty of my own parish have been
stified, besides others of other parishes.

Indeed I do not take it for granted that all are justified who think they
e so. Some I fear are mistaken. But I shall judge better of this when I
e the fruits.

May 7, 1776

The work of God still increases among us: I believe, within these eight
ays, more than forty here have been filled with joy and peace in believing.
f these I have had an account; but there may be many more. And several,
ho have been justified some time, believe God has blessed them with
erfect love.

I have no doubt but the work now carrying on is genuine: yet there were
ome circumstances attending it which I disliked—such as loud outcries,
emblings, fallings, convulsions. But I am better reconciled, since I read
resident Edwards on that head, who observes, "That wherever these most
ppear there is always the greatest and the deepest work."

There is another thing which has given me much pain—the praying of
veral at one and the same time. Sometimes five or six, or more, have been
raying all at once, in several parts of the room, for distressed persons.
thers were speaking by way of exhortation: so that the assembly ap-
eared to be all in confusion, and must seem to one at a little distance,
ore like a drunken rabble than the worshippers of God. I was afraid,
is was not doing all things in decency and order. Indeed Dr. Edwards
efends this also. But yet I am not satisfied concerning it. I had heard of
, but never saw it till *Sunday* evening. But this is a delicate point. It re-
uires much wisdom to allay the wild, and not damp the sacred fire.

The first appearance of anything of the kind at my chapel, was last
aturday night. I was not there, but a young man who studies at my house
as. He is grave, prudent, and solidly religious, without the least tincture
f enthusiasm. He met the society there in the afternoon, and would have
eturned home, but that many who were in great distress begged him and

some others to stay and pray with them. They continued in prayer th
whole night, during which about twelve were set at liberty. But notwitl
standing all they could do, there were often two, three, or more, speakin
at one time.

I heard of this the next day, when I was at church, and hastened thenc
to the chapel. Some hundreds were assembled there, and were in muc
confusion when I went in. I went into the pulpit, and began to sing, addin
short exhortations and prayers. The confusion ceased: several spiri
were revived, and some mourners comforted.

Since that evening, this kind of confusion has never been known i
my neighbourhood. It continued longer in other places; but for som
time has been totally gone. But as this abated, the work of conviction an
conversion usually abated too. Yet, blessed be God, it still goes on, thoug
not with such rapidity. I have heard but of two or three that found peac
for three weeks; whereas sometime ago, seldom a week passed, but
could hear of eight or nine—sometimes between twenty and thirty, at on
meeting.

I have chiefly spoken of what was done in my parish. But that you ma
know a little of what was done elsewhere, I subjoin an extract from th
letters of two local Preachers, in the county of Sussex.[55]

July 29, 1776

REV. SIR,—WITH unspeakable pleasure I acquaint you of the gloriou
revival of religion in our parts. It broke out at our last quarterly meetin
and has since wonderfully spread throughout the circuit. The time seem
to be coming, when we shall not need to teach every man his neighbour t
know the Lord; for they daily know him, from the least to the greates
from little children to men of fourscore. Above seven years have I bee
exhorting my neighbours; but very few would hear. Now, blessed be Go
there are few that will not hear. It is no strange thing for two or three t
find the Lord at a class meeting: and at a Sunday meeting, although ther
was no preacher, ten, fifteen, yea, near twenty have been converted. At
place near me, thirty have found the Lord, within eight days. It is commo
with us for men and women to fall down as dead under an exhortation
but many more under prayer—perhaps twenty at a time. And some tha
have not fallen to the earth, have shown the same distress, wringing thei
hands, smiting their breasts, and begging all to pray for them. With thes
the work is generally quick; some getting through in less than a week
some in two or three days, some in one, two, or three hours. Nay, w
have an instance of one that was so indifferent, as to leave her brethre
at prayers, and go to bed. But all at once she screamed out, under a sens
of her lost estate, and in less than fifteen minutes rejoiced in God he

[55] This paragraph is a part of Jarratt's main letter.

aviour. And, blessed be God, many of these retain a sense of his favour.
Iany, who a few weeks ago were despisers and scoffers, are now happy
. the Lord. Many old Christians, who were always full of doubts and
ars, now walk in the light of his countenance. Some have a clear witness
. themselves, that they have given their whole hearts to God. O may God
.rry on his work among us, until we are all swallowed up in love!

Thomas Saunders[56]

Mr. Saunders lives twenty-two miles from me: the writer of the fol-
.wing letter, about thirty.[57]

July 29, 1776

EV. SIR,—ON *June* the 9th, we had a large congregation. I spoke on,
No man can serve two masters." Several appeared to be much distressed
-two women in particular. We spent above an hour in prayer for them,
nd they arose in peace. When we met the class, we suffered all that
esired it, to stay. The leader only put a question or two to each member.
his was scarce ended, when the fire of God's love was kindled. Praises
ung on the lips of many; and several cried out, "What must we do to be
ived?" Thus it swiftly went on; every now and then one rising with faith
. Jesus. Surely this was one of the days of heaven! Such a day I never
xpected to see in time. While we were met, one Isham Whitehead[58] was
bserved to be looking through the crack of the door; which being opened,
e came with it, and, being unable to stand, fell on the floor quite helpless.
ut in two or three hours he rose and praised a pardoning God: while
ne of the class who had been justified some time, received a blessing
reatly superior to anything he had known before. We have reason to
elieve, that on this day fifteen were enabled to believe in Jesus.
Saturday, June 15. I was speaking to the class, and one found peace to
er soul. *Sunday,* 16. I spoke from, "This is the victory that overcometh
.e world, even our faith," to four or five hundred people. This was also
day of Pentecost. Convictions seized on numbers, who wrestled with
iod till their souls were set at liberty. A young woman told me, "She
eard that many people fell down, and she would come to help them up."
'his she said in scorn. She came accordingly. The power of God soon
:ized her, and she wanted helping up herself. But it was not long before
.e Spirit of grace helped her, by giving her faith in Christ. We believe
.wenty souls found peace this day. O may we see many such days!
July 7. I spoke to a large congregation. Afterward I was going to give
ut a hymn, when one was so powerfully struck, that he could not hold a
.int still, and roared aloud for mercy. I immediately went to prayer; the
ries of the people all the time greatly increasing. After prayer, Benjamin

---

[56] *Heads of Families in Virginia,* 44.   [57] This sentence is of course Jarratt's.
[58] *Heads of Families in Virginia,* 44.

Tyus,[59] lately a great opposer, jumped up and began to praise God, wit
a countenance so altered, that those who beheld him were filled wit
astonishment. Our meeting continued from twelve at noon, till twelve a
night; during which God raised up about fifteen more witnesses.

The *Thursday* following, six of those who were convinced on *Sunda*
found peace in believing. We hear of many others converted in th
neighbourhood, several of whom were strong opposers; and some hoary
headed ones, who had been strict pharisees from their youth up.

Sunday, 21. We had a large and attentive auditory, and the power o
the Lord prevailed. The next day I was much tempted to doubt, whethe
I was sent of God to preach or not. I prayed earnestly to the Lord that h
would satisfy me, and that he would keep all false fire from among u
Afterward I preached. While I was speaking, a mother and her daughte
were so struck with conviction that they trembled every joint: but befor
I concluded, both found peace. Glory be to God! I am, &c.,

John Dickins

GOD has made examples of several opposers—examples not of justice, bu
of mercy. Some of them came to the assembly with hearts full of rancou
against the people of God, so that, had it been in their power, they woul
have dragged them away to prison, if not to death. But unexpectedl
their stubborn hearts were bowed down, being pierced with the arrows o
the Almighty. In a moment they were filled with distress and anguish
their laughter turned into mourning, and their cursing into prayer. An
frequently in less than a week their heaviness has been turned into joy
Of this sort are several of our most zealous and circumspect walkers a
this day. A goodly number of these are rich in this world; yet they ar
now brought so low, that they are willing to be taught by all, and to b
the servants of all.

A gentleman of this parish, in particular, had much opposed and con
tradicted; he was fully persuaded that all outward appearances, either o
distress or joy, were mere deceit. But as he was walking to his mill, abov
half a mile from his house, deep conviction fell upon him. The terrors o
the Lord beset him round about, and distress and anguish got hold upo
him. When he came to the mill and found no one there, he took tha
opportunity of prostrating himself before God, and of pouring out hi
soul in his presence. As his distress was great, his cries were loud, and hi
prayer importunate. The Lord heard him, and set his soul at liberty be
fore he left the place. And the power which came upon him was so grea
that it seemed as if his whole frame were dissolving.

Upon the whole, this has been a great, a deep, a swift, and an extensivel
glorious work. Both the nature and manner of it have been nearly th

[59] *Heads of Families in Virginia*, 44.

me, wherever its benign influence reached. Where the greatest work was
-where the greatest number of souls have been convinced and converted
God, there have been the most outcries, tremblings, convulsions, and
l sorts of external signs. I took all the pains I could that these might be
ept within bounds, that our good might not be evil spoken of. This I did,
ot by openly inveighing against them in the public assembly, but by
rivate advices to local preachers and others, as opportunity would per-
it. This method had its desired effect, without putting a sword into the
ands of the wicked. Wherever the contrary method has been taken—
here these things have been publicly opposed, when they have been
poken against in promiscuous congregations, the effect has always been
is: the men of the world have been highly gratified, and the children of
od deeply wounded. The former have plumed themselves, as though
ey were the men who kept within due bounds, and those that had
made so much ado about religion," were no better than hot-brained
nthusiasts. I cannot but think this has a great tendency to hinder the
ork of God. Indeed, if we thought that God wrought everything irre-
stibly, we should not fear this. But we know the contrary: we know,
at as some things promote, so others hinder his work. I grant, means
ould be used to prevent all indecency; but they should be used with
reat caution and tenderness, that the cure may be effected, if possible,
ithout damping the work of God.

With regard to the inward work, there has been a great variety as to the
ngth, and depth, and circumstances of the convictions in different per-
ons; but all in general have been at first alarmed with a sense of the
ultitude and heinousness of their sins—with an awful view of the wrath
f God, and certain destruction, if they persisted therein. Hence they be-
ook themselves to prayer, and as time permitted, to the use of all other
eans of grace; although deeply sensible of the vileness of their perform-
nces, and the total insufficiency of all they could do to merit the pardon
f one sin, or deserve the favour of God. They were next convinced of
eir unbelief, and that faith in Christ is the only condition of justification.
hey continued thus waiting upon the Lord, till he spoke peace to their
ouls. This he usually did in one moment, in a clear and satisfactory
anner, so that all their griefs and anxieties vanished away, and they
ere filled with joy and peace in believing. Some indeed have had their
urdens removed, so that they felt no condemnation; and yet they could
ot say they were forgiven. But they could not be satisfied with this.
hey continued instant in prayer, till they knew the Lamb of God had
ken away their sins.

Most of these had been suddenly convinced of sin: but with some it
as otherwise. Without any sense of their guilt, they were brought to use
e means of grace, by mere dint of persuasion: and afterward they were
rought by degrees to see themselves, and their want of a Saviour. But

before they found deliverance, they have had as deep a sense of their helpless misery as others. One in my parish was a remarkable instance of this. He was both careless and profane to a great degree; and remained quite unconcerned, while many of his companions were sorrowing after God, or rejoicing in his love. One of his acquaintance advised him to seek the Lord. He said: "I see no necessity for it as yet; when I do I will seek him as well as others." His friend persuaded him to try for one week, watching against sin, and going by himself every day. He did so: and though he was quite stupid when he began, yet before the end of the week he was thoroughly sensible of the load of sin, and is now happy in God.

If you ask, "How stands the case now with those that have been the subjects of the late work?" I have the pleasure to inform you, I have not heard of any one apostate yet. It is true, many, since their first joy abated, have given way to doubts and fears, have had their confidence in God much shaken, and have got into much heaviness. Several have passed through this, and are now confirmed in the ways of God. Others are in it still; and chiefly those over whom Satan had gained an advantage, by hurrying them into irregular warmth, or into expressions not well guarded. I have seen some of these in great distress, and just ready to cast away hope.

I have a great deal upon my hands at present, and have little time either to write or read. The difficulties and temptations of the lately converted are so many and various, that I am obliged to be in as many places as I can; for now is the critical hour. A man of zeal, though with little knowledge or experience, may be an instrument of converting souls. But after they are converted, he will have need of much knowledge, much prudence and experience, to provide proper food and physic for the several members, according to their state, habit, and constitution. This, at present, seems in a great measure to devolve upon me. And though I have been twenty years in the Lord's service, yet I find I am quite unequal to the task. However, I will do what I can; and may the Lord bless my endeavours.

The enemy is busy night and day, in sowing the tares of division among the wheat. And in some places he has prevailed so far as to plunge some of them in the water. In other places little feuds and animosities arise, to grieve the preachers and damp the spirits of the people. On these occasions they commonly apply to me; and all is well, at least for a season. When I consider what it is to watch over souls, and how much labour and pain it implies to discharge it in any degree, I cannot but cry out with the apostle, "Who is sufficient for these things?"

However, upon the whole, things are in as flourishing a condition as can reasonably be expected, considering what great numbers, of various capacities and stations, have been lately added to the societies.

But after all, a great part of Virginia is still in a very dark and deplorable condition. This province contains sixty-two counties; and the late work has reached only seven or eight of them. Nor has it been universal even

these, but chiefly in the circuit which is regularly visited by the preachers.
this alone very many hundreds have in a few months been added to the
ord. And some are adding still. May He continue to pour out his Spirit
pon us, and increase the number of the faithful every day!

Our highest gratitude is due to our gracious God; for he hath done
aarvellous things! In a short time he hath wrought a great work: and let
ho will speak against it, it is evident beyond all contradiction, that many
pen and profligate sinners, of all sorts, have been effectually and lastingly
hanged into pious, uniform Christians. So that every thinking man must
llow that God hath been with us of a truth, and that his "glory dwells in
ur land." I am your sincere friend, and brother in Christ,

September 10, 1776.

Devereaux Jarratt

To Mr. Thomas Rankin

*he following letter, which relates to the same work, was written some time
after.*

TO THE REV. MR. WESLEY

June 24, 1777[60]

EV. AND DEAR SIR,—YOU have the Narrative of the Rev. Mr. Jarratt.
send this as a supplement to it.

At our little conference, held in Philadelphia *May*, 1775, Mr. Shadford
as appointed assistant for Brunswick circuit, in Virginia. He found there
bout eight hundred joined together, but in a very confused manner.
Iany of them did not understand the nature of meeting in class; and
any of the classes had no leader. He resolved to begin in good earnest,
nd the preachers with him were like-minded. Their constant custom was,
s soon as preaching was over, to speak to all the members of the society,
ne by one. If the society was large, one preacher spoke to a part, and he
at came next, to the rest. By this means they learned more of our doc-
ine and discipline in a year, than in double the time before. The fruit
oon appeared: the congregations swiftly increased, and many were
ricked to the heart. Many that were a little affected, desired to see the

[60] There is some confusion as to the authorship and date of this letter. It must have
een written by Rankin since it was signed T. R. In the original printed *Journal* it was
ated June 24, 1778. However, Rankin was in England at that time and had apparently
een in touch with Wesley. (See Wesley's *Journal* for April 22, 1778; Asbury's *Journal*
r July 21 and October 22, 1777.) Either the authorship or the date is therefore erron-
us. The simplest and most likely solution is that there was an error of one year in the
ate as printed and that the letter was written on June 24, 1777, shortly before Rankin's
eparture for England.

nature of meeting in class; and while one was speaking either to those that were groaning for redemption, or those who had found peace with God these were frequently cut to the heart, and sometimes enabled on the spot to praise a pardoning God. Nay, sometimes four, five, or six found peace with God, before the meeting was over.

The work of God thus increasing on every side, more preachers were soon wanting. And God raised up several young men, who were exceeding useful as local preachers.

After Mr. Shadford had been about eight months in the circuit, Mr Jarratt desired his parish might be included in it; that all who chose it might have the privilege of meeting in class, and being members of the society. He soon saw the salutary effects. Many that had but small desire before, began to be much alarmed, and laboured earnestly after eternal life. In a little time numbers were deeply awakened, and many tasted of the pardoning love of God. In a few months Mr. Jarratt saw more fruit of his labours than he had done for many years. And he went on with the preachers hand in hand, both in doctrine and discipline.

When Mr. Shadford took an account of the societies, before he came to the conference in 1776, they contained two thousand six hundred and sixty-four persons: to whom eighteen hundred were added in one year Above a thousand of these had found peace with God; many of whom thirsted for all the mind that was in Christ. And divers believed God had "circumcised their heart, to love him with all their heart, and with all their soul."

This revival of religion spread through fourteen counties in Virginia and through Bute and Halifax counties in North Carolina. At the same time we had a blessed outpouring of the Spirit in several counties bordering upon Maryland.

Our conference was at Baltimore Town, on the 22d of *May*. Here received a letter from Mr. Jarratt, part of which I insert.

May 11, 1776

"I PRAISE God for his goodness, in so plentifully pouring out of his Spirit on men, women, and children. I believe threescore, in and near my parish have believed, through grace, since the quarterly meeting. Such a work never saw with my eyes. Sometimes twelve, sometimes fifteen find the Lord at one class meeting. I am just returned from meeting two classes Much of the power of God was in each. My dear partner is now happy in God her Saviour. I clap my hands exulting, and praise God. Blessed be the Lord, that ever he sent you and your brethren into this part of his vineyard! Many children, from eight to twelve years old, are now under strong convictions; and some of them are savingly converted to God. was much comforted this morning at the White Oak Chapel. The people there are of a truly teachable spirit—those particularly who profess to

ave obtained the pure love of God. They are as little children. When you
onsider how the work is spreading on every side, you will readily excuse
ie from being at your conference."

Monday, June 24. I left Leesburg, in company with W. B. (a truly
evout man, who now rests from his labours,) and came to Petersburg
n *Saturday* the 29th, where I preached, about three in the afternoon, and
nen rode on to Mr. Boisseau's, about ten miles farther. A little company
as waiting for me, and God was with us of a truth."

Sunday, 30. I was comforted by the sight of my dear brother Shadford.
ut I was weak in body, through riding so far in extreme heat, and much
xercised in mind; and did not know how I should be able to go through
ie labour of the day. We went to the chapel at ten,[61] where I had liberty
f mind, and strength of body beyond my expectation. After preaching I
iet the society, and was more relieved, both in body and mind. At four
i the afternoon I preached again, from "I set before thee an open door,
nd none can shut it." I had gone through about two-thirds of my dis-
ourse, and was bringing the words home to the present—Now, when
ich power descended, that hundreds fell to the ground, and the house
eemed to shake with the presence of God. The chapel was full of white
nd black, and many were without that could not get in. Look wherever
e would, we saw nothing but streaming eyes, and faces bathed in tears;
nd heard nothing but groans and strong cries after God and the Lord
esus Christ. My voice was drowned amidst the groans and prayers of the
ongregation. I then sat down in the pulpit; and both Mr. Shadford and
were so filled with the divine presence, that we could only say, This is
one other than the house of God! This is the gate of heaven! Husbands
ere inviting their wives to go to heaven, wives their husbands: parents
ieir children, and children their parents: brothers their sisters, and sisters
ieir brothers. In short, those who were happy in God themselves, were for
ringing all their friends to him in their arms. This mighty effusion of the
pirit continued for above an hour; in which time many were awakened,
ome found peace with God, and others, his pure love. We attempted to
peak or sing again and again: but no sooner we began than our voices
ere drowned. It was with much difficulty that we at last persuaded the
eople, as night drew on, to retire to their own homes.

Tuesday, July 2. I rode with Mr. Shadford to Mr. Jarratt's; who, with
Mrs. Jarratt, received us with open arms. I preached the next day, not
ir from his house, to a deeply attentive congregation. Many were much
ffected at the preaching; but far more at the meeting of the society. Mr.
arratt himself was constrained to praise God aloud, for his great love to
im and to his people.

Sunday, 7. I preached at White's chapel, about twenty miles from Mr.

[61] This was Boisseau's Chapel.

Jarratt's. I intended to preach near the house, under the shade of som
large trees. But the rain made it impracticable. The house was great
crowded, and four or five hundred stood at the doors and windows, ar
listened with unabated attention. I preached from Ezekiel's vision of t
dry bones: "And there was a great shaking." I was obliged to stop aga
and again, and beg of the people to compose themselves. But they cou
not: some on their knees, and some on their faces, were crying mighti
to God all the time I was preaching. Hundreds of Negroes were amor
them, with the tears streaming down their faces. The same power v
found in meeting the society, and many were enabled to rejoice with j(
unspeakable. In the cool of the evening I preached out of doors, and mar
found an uncommon blessing.

Every day the ensuing week I preached to large and attentive congreg
tions.[62] Indeed, the weather was violently hot, and the fatigue of ridir
and preaching so often was great. But God made up all this to me, by h
comfortable presence. *Thursday*, 11. I preached to a large congregation
the preaching house near Mr. Jarratt's.[63] After preaching at several plac
on *Friday* and *Saturday*,[64] on *Sunday*, 14, I came to Mr. Boisseau'
where I preached and met the society. The congregation was, as befor
abundantly larger than the chapel could contain. And we had almost su(
a day as fourteen days ago—only attended with a more deep and solen
work. What a work is God working in this corner of Mr. Jarratt's parisl
It seemed as if all the country, for nine or ten miles round, were ready
turn to God.

In the evening I rode to Mr. Smith's,[65] and found a whole fami
fearing and loving God. Mr. Smith, a sensible and judicious man, ha
been for many years a justice of the peace. By hearing the truth as it is
Jesus, he and his wife first, and then all his children, had attained th
peace that passeth all understanding. He observed, "How amazing tl
change was which had been lately wrought in the place where he livec
That before the Methodists came into these parts, when he was called b
his office to attend the court, there was nothing but drunkenness, cursin
swearing, and fighting, most of the time the court sat: whereas now nothir
is heard but prayer and praise, and conversing about God and the thin
of God."

Monday, 15. I rode towards North Carolina. In every place[66] tl

[62] Rankin says in his *Journal* that he preached at Booth's, Captain Colman's, ar
White Oak during the week.
[63] This was probably Sapponey Church. Jarratt also had Butterwood and Hatche
Run, all named after creeks. (Mason: *Colonial Churches of Tidewater, Virginia*, 92–97
[64] Rankin preached at Mr. Pigram's, an arbor, and at old Mrs. Pigram's. (See h
Journal.)
[65] See *Journal* entries for June 30, 1780 and January 12, 1782.
[66] During the week Rankin preached at Mabry's in Greensville County, Rose
Creek Chapel in Brunswick, John Seward's, and Mr. Harrison's. (See his *Journal*.)

ongregations were large, and received the word with all readiness of
ind. I know not that I have spent such a week since I came to America.
saw everywhere such a simplicity in the people, with such a vehement
irst after the word of God, that I frequently preached and continued in
rayer till I was hardly able to stand. Indeed there was no getting away
om them, while I was able to speak one sentence for God.

Sunday, 21. I preached at Roanoke chapel[67] to more than double of
hat the house would contain. In general, the white people were within
e chapel, and the black people without. The windows being all open,
very one could hear, and hundreds felt the word of God. Many were
athed in tears, and others rejoicing with joy unspeakable. When the
ociety met, many could not refrain from praising God aloud. I preached
a large company in the afternoon, and concluded the day with prayer
ad thanksgiving.

Tuesday, 23. I crossed the Roanoke river, and preached at a chapel in
orth Carolina.[68] And I preached every day to very large and deeply
tentive congregations: although not without much labour and pain,
rough the extreme heat of the weather.

On *Tuesday*, 30, was our quarterly meeting. I scarce ever remember such
season. No chapel or preaching house in Virginia would have contained
ne-third of the congregation. Our friends knowing this, had contrived to
ade with boughs of trees a space that would contain two or three thous-
nd persons. Under this, wholly screened from the rays of the sun, we
eld our general love feast. It began between eight and nine on Wednesday
orning, and continued till noon. Many testified that they had "redemp-
on in the blood of Jesus, even the forgiveness of sins." And many were
nabled to declare, that it had "cleansed them from all sin." So clear, so
ll, so strong was their testimony, that while some were speaking their
perience, hundreds were in tears, and others vehemently crying to God
r pardon or holiness.

About eight our watch night began. Mr. Jarratt preached an excellent

---

[67] Roanoke Chapel was an Anglican church on the Roanoke River near the Virginia-
orth Carolina border, in Mecklenburg or Brunswick counties in Virginia or the ad-
ining counties in North Carolina. Its exact location has not been determined because
conflicting evidence. Thomas Rankin and Bishop Coke, both of whom preached
ere, definitely state that it was in North Carolina. On the other hand, Asbury's
ferences to it and the distances from other spots seem clearly to locate it in Virginia,
d his letter of February 8, 1815, places it in Virginia. The same is true of later writers
ch as Early, Meade, Mason, and Bennett. The last named lists it among the Virginia
urches in 1789. None of them, however, gives the exact location. Meade says that he
d not know its site but stated that it was north of the river in St. Andrew's Parish in
unswick County. (See the *Journals* of Rankin and Coke; Meade: *Old Churches and
milies of Virginia*, I, 476, 477; Bennett, *op. cit.*, 276, 277; Vestry Book of St. Andrew's
rish, Brunswick County Court House.)

[68] Rankin indicates that this was an Established church, though he does not name it.
e stayed with a Mr. Haynes. (See Rankin's *Journal*.)

sermon; the rest of the preachers exhorted and prayed with divine energ
Surely, for the work wrought on these two days, many will praise God
all eternity.

Thomas Rankin

1777

Asbury's chaise shot through while on the way to Annapolis

CHAPTER SIX

Maryland

Thursday, January 2, 1777. My soul has had to wrestle with principalities d powers; but by the grace of God, in obstinately resisting the tempter, ave come off more than conqueror, and am now in peace. I was enabled speak plainly and closely at Mr. Gough's.

Lord's day, 5. After preaching and meeting the society, I think the ople were left more in earnest for the salvation of their souls than they re before. On Monday the Lord was the portion and comfort of my ul; and I enjoyed a very agreeable and happy season with the little flock William Watters'.

Tuesday, 7. The camp fever now rages much; of which several have d.

Thursday, 9. I have met with a few faithful, happy souls, both yesterday Susquehanna, and to-day at Edward White's (?). My own soul lives nstantly as in the presence of God, and enjoys much of his divine favour. s love is better than life!

> "My Jesus to know,
> And feel his blood flow,
> 'Tis life everlasting, 'tis heaven below."

Lord's day, 12. There was but little appearance of feeling while I eached in the day from John i, 14; but my soul was much blessed in the ening at William Evett's, and it was a solemn time amongst the people.

Monday, 13. We have constant rumours about the disagreeable war

which is now spreading through the country;[1] but all these things I s*
commit to God. Matters of greater perpetuity call for the exertion of *
mental powers. My soul is in a tranquil frame, but thirsting for more
God. After preaching at Samuel Litton's, I met the society, which seem*
but slow in their spiritual progress. Both the audience and myself w*
much more engaged the next day at Joseph Presbury's.

Thursday, 16. A certain person passed great encomiums, and sound*
my praise as a preacher to my face. But this is a dangerous practice; *
it is easier for a preacher to think too much of his gifts, than too little. *
Paul, describing the true Israelite, saith: "whose praise is not of men, b
of God."

Saturday, 18. I have heard much of many attending on the Lord's da*
to hear Thomas Chase, but for my part I see but little fruit. My heart w
warmly engaged to-day at Mr. Samuel Forwood's (?); and as sor
preachers met me in the evening, we held a watch night at Henry Watters*
There was a great number of people, and it was a solemn, profitable tim

Lord's day, 19. In preaching at Nathan Perigau's, from Zeph. i, 12
was particularly led, in the close of the sermon, to address the young
part of the congregation, in such a manner as greatly affected the parer
who were present.

Monday, 20. It is now a time of great and spreading sickness—but
this very time, the Lord keeps me in health and safety; for which my he*
is drawn out in grateful acknowledgments. There were more people th*
could have been expected, to hear the word at Mrs. Presbury's.

Tuesday, 21. A messenger from Mr. Gough's met me at the wid*
Bond's, informing me that Mr. Rodda and Mr. George Shadford we
there waiting to see me.[2] After preaching I set out, and met my brethr*
the same night, and found them inclined to leave America, and emba*
for England. But I had before resolved not to depart from the work *
any consideration. After some consultation it was thought best that M
Rodda should go to Mr. Rankin, and request his attendance here. *
Thursday brother Shadford preached a very argumentative and melti*
sermon. I intended to have gone forward on my circuit, but was prevent
by the rain.

Friday, 24. My heart has checked me for not being more watchful
company and conversation: but to-day my soul was greatly drawn o*
after God. How often do we grieve the Holy Spirit, and deprive ourselv

---

[1] Washington had attacked the Hessians at Trenton, New Jersey, and defeated
detachment of the British Army at Princeton a few days earlier. The war had alrea*
removed Norfolk, Virginia, from the list of appointments; and Philadelphia and N*
York were soon to fall behind the British lines.

[2] These men were soon to return to England. Rodda was a pronounced Tory, *
Shadford retained his popularity except among the extremists. (Lee, *op. cit.*, *
Lednum, *op. cit.*, 193; *Arminian Magazine*, London, XIII, 350–53; Cooper: *Discou*
on the Death of Asbury, 81.)

divine consolations, by not steadily attending to the duties of watching
d prayer. Lord, help me to be more attentive, and more faithful!

Lord's day, 26. After lecturing in Mr. Gough's family I rode to the
orks, and preached there; then through rain, and cold, and dirt, to meet
e congregation at Mr. Colgate's (?);[3] and afterward returned to Mr.
ough's, and lectured in the evening. And the Lord was with me, to sup-
ort and comfort me through all the exercises of the day.

Monday, 27. My spirit was assaulted by Satan, and felt itself in a heavy
ame; but in the Lord I have help. As brother George Shadford is willing
take this circuit for the present,[4] my intention is to move towards
nnapolis and its adjacent parts. May Divine Providence direct my
eps! I have had an agreeable conversation with my friend Mr. Otterbein.

Friday, 31. I was moved to speak in alarming terms at William Lynch's;
t am not yet so steadily and spiritually devoted to God as my soul
rnestly desires to be. Probably the Lord will be pleased to make me
erfect through sufferings. But, "our light affliction, which is but for a
oment, is not worthy to be compared with that glory which shall be
vealed in us," if faithful to the grace of God.

> "Who suffer with our Master here,
> We shall before his face appear,
> And by his side sit down;
> To patient faith the prize is sure;
> And all that to the end endure
> The cross, shall wear the crown."

Saturday, February 1. My soul is determined to labour more for the
irit of devotion. I found myself at liberty in preaching at Fell's Point,
"Casting all your care upon him, for he careth for you."

Lord's day, 2. The audience at Fell's Point were cold and unaffected
nd at town (Baltimore) on *Monday* evening, they were dispersed by the
arm of fire in the time of preaching.

Tuesday, 4. After a season of temptations and spiritual exercises, I found
y mind disburdened, and a holy, awful nearness to God. On *Thursday* I
t out for Reisterstown, in order to meet brother George Shadford, and
lling in at Mr. Warfield's (?), where brother King was then speaking, I
so spoke a few words, and found my soul refreshed. I met with brother
eorge Shadford the next day, and saw an affecting letter from Mrs.
ary Thorne of Philadelphia, in which, after she had given some account
the abounding wickedness of that city, she informed us of the declension
a few religious persons, of the fidelity of others, of the camp fever that

---

[3] This person was either Mr. Colgate or Mr. Cromwell.
[4] Neither Asbury nor Shadford was willing to take the Maryland oath which re-
ired bearing arms against England, and this explains why Shadford took the Balti-
ore Circuit temporarily. The increasing tension of the times is indicated by Asbury's
dency to be less explicit about names and places.

was then prevailing there, and that many died thereof—sometim
twenty, thirty, and even forty in a day. An awful account indeed! So
seems as if the Lord intends to bring us to our proper reflections and duti
by the sword, the pestilence, and famine. Alas! who can stand before t.
displeasure of the Almighty! How much better would it be, for men
please God, and live in love to him and one another, that they might pa
take of his blessing, instead of his curse! Lord, grant thy people wisdo
and protection in all times of danger!

Monday, 10. I went to the quarterly meeting[5] and met with broth
Rodda and brother Rankin. In our love feast several people were happ
but my mind was under a cloud and some severe exercises. However,
earnestly desire an increase of patience, and communion with God. O n
Lord, scatter every cloud, and cause they face to shine with beams
divine love upon my soul!

Thursday, 13. Mr. Rankin went to Baltimore; and on *Friday*, I felt
desire to be labouring for the salvation of souls. I cannot be idle, but mu
be occupied till my Lord shall come. O happy day, when the weary sha
be at rest! Lord, hasten thy work in me, and then hasten thy coming
judgment, or by death!

Saturday, 15. I have been reading some of both Greek and Hebrew
but my soul longeth to feel more deadness to everything but God, and a
increase of spiritual light, life, and love. I now parted with dear broth
George Shadford. On the *Lord's day* I found freedom and warmth
preaching to a larger congregation than could have been expected, at t
widow M.'s.

Monday, 17. Rode to Mrs. Rogers' [?]; and was grievously troubl
with inward temptations. O! when shall I rest with my Jesus in etern
glory? Lord, I am oppressed; undertake for me!

Tuesday, 18. It was a cold winter's day, but I rode twenty-three miles
Mr. Gough's, and found one had been brought to God since my departu
the last time. Several seemed to melt while I was discoursing on the visic
of the dry bones.

Thursday, 20. The weather was exceedingly severe, and I had twent
five miles to ride; which almost benumbed both body and soul. But n
mind was so exercised by the way, with various and heavy temptation

[5] The quarterly meeting was at Reisterstown, which was a new preaching place. Nume
ous Methodist families lived along the eighteen-mile route traveled by Asbury fro
Baltimore. Although three days elapsed, neither Asbury nor his contemporaries menti
any other names or places. (Armstrong, *op. cit.*, 39.) Rankin says the meeting was he
at John Worthington's, beginning on Tuesday, the eleventh. (See Rankin's *Journal*.)

[6] Asbury's Hebrew Bible, to which frequent reference is made, was bequeathed
Bishop William McKendree. It was left at Rembert Hall in South Carolina and pass
through several hands. In 1948 it was purchased by Dr. Vernon B. Hampton a
presented by him to Drew University. It was in two volumes. The second is now in t
collection in Lovely Lane Church, Baltimore.

d such a deep sense of my demerit and unprofitableness, that I thought
r suffering was much less than my desert. Satan frequently assaults me
every side, and with every species of temptations. Surely it is through
at tribulation we must enter into the kingdom of God. The righteous
ve great cause to rejoice that a rest remaineth for them.

Saturday, 22. The burden of my ardent desire was, to be more assimi-
ed to my spiritual Head, and to be more abundantly devoted, both day
d night, to the pure and uninterrupted service of my God.

> "I would be thine, thou know'st I would,
> And have thee all my own;
> Thee, O my all-sufficient good,
> I want, and thee alone."

Lord's day, 23. After riding twenty miles to John Worthington's, I
oke from these words, "How long halt ye between two opinions?"
any of the people displayed, by their looks, the carelessness of their
arts; but a few from among them have been brought to Christ, and some
ore are coming. On *Tuesday* we had severe weather, with a cold and
ty house; but my soul was much blessed in my little sufferings. On
ednesday, I was kindly entertained by old Mr. M. and his wife: though
roublesome little Irishman seemed much inclined to altercation. But as
lomon says, "A soft answer turneth away wrath;" so by coolness and
ekness, the ferocity of his temper was in a great degree subdued. I
ve had some doubts of late, whether I am in my proper route to bring
uls to God; however, the event must make it manifest.

Friday, 28. My heart was unfettered and quite happy in God, while
blishing glad tidings to poor sinners at Mr. Hammond's [?], from Acts
i, 38, 39. I had appointed the next day to enter Annapolis, but a great
ow prevented me. Meeting with brother Hartley,[7] who was about to
ter upon the circuit, we took some sweet counsel together relative to the
rk of God; and I gave him a plan which comprehended the greater part
the circuit, reserving for myself Annapolis and a few places adjacent.[8]
y soul is now kept in peace and love.

Lord's day, March 2. Though the weather was very cold, several mem-

Joseph Hartley of Sussex County, Virginia, was received on trial in 1776. He was
ested and fined in Queen Annes County, Maryland, and imprisoned in the Talbot
unty jail. Throngs came to hear him preach through the jail window, and Asbury
ted him there. Later Hartley married, located in 1781, died in 1785, and was buried
r his residence in Miles River Neck, Talbot County. (See *Journal* entries for Septem-
14 and December 28, 1779; October 11, 1783; Hallam, *op. cit.*, 113, 330, 336–37;
gs, *op. cit.*, I, 127, 142; Lednum, *op. cit.*, 232, 233.)
Asbury now disregards circuit boundaries. So swift are his movements and so
rded his disclosures of new preaching places that one follows him with difficulty.
rred on by the impending crisis and departure of the English preachers, he ranges
r parts of present Harford, Baltimore, Howard, Ann Arundel, Prince Georges,
Calvert counties.

bers of the convention attended to hear the word at the widow Dorsey
and I afterward preached in the play house,[9] now converted into a chur
In the beginning of the ensuing week, I was requested to preach in t
assembly room, but some of the members opposed it; so I returned to t
play house, and found my ideas contracted while preaching to a deisti
audience, from Rom. viii, 7, 8. Lord, if thou hast called me to preach
these souls, grant me divine assistance! But how difficult it is to decl
the plain truth to ungodly and sensual men in such a manner as not to
dismayed at their countenance! Our sufficiency is of God.

    Wednesday, 5. I had some hope for a poor, ignorant people at Bro
Neck, on the other side of the Severn.[10] My clothes were wet through,
riding twenty miles the next day to Mr. Perigau's; but I received
injury. Here I met with Mr. Otterbein and Wm. Moore, and my soul w
blessed with delightful communion with God.

    Lord's day, 9. Preached at Mr. Wilkins': and on *Monday* my heart w
inflamed with divine love, and the people were much melted, while I w
discoursing at Mr. Ridgely's (?)[11] from Amos v, 6, though my soul h
been bowed down by the weight of temptations; and, by the grace of G
I was ashamed before him, being base, unworthy, and contemptible in
own eyes. May the grace which thus abases me, in due time exalt me, a
bring me to glory!

    Tuesday, 11. I met with a dull congregation at Mr. G.'s,[12] and w
home with Mr. T., who appeared to be the only thoughtful man amon
them. I was much indisposed on *Wednesday*, and on my way to Annapo
stopped at Mr. Miller's, where a certain Mr. R. was taken sick; afte
had conversed with him about his soul and the things of eternity,
conduct proved that God hath a witness for himself in every breast, f
awaking in the night, he uttered expressive groans, and called upon t
name of the Lord. But alas! when men should attend to the voice of divi
grace, which speaketh in silence, though frequently with great power,
every conscience, they shake off the disagreeable sensation, and plun
into business and sensual pleasures: and when death comes they plun
into hell. Thus it was with the rich man mentioned by our Lord in t
parable: and thus it is with many every day. Unhappy creatures! How ri
how honourable, how easy, how happy once, avails them nothing the
There they must dwell in eternal poverty and nakedness, exposed to t
beating storms of the Divine displeasure. Then how much better is it,

---

    [9] On March 7, 1775, the playhouse at Annapolis was made into a preaching pla
(Allen: *Historical Notes of St. Ann's Parish in Anne Arundel County*, 86; Wilstac
Tidewater Maryland, 237; Ridgely: *Annals of Annapolis*.)
    [10] Broad Neck was on the peninsula between the Magothy and Severn rivers, abc
six miles northeast of Annapolis. It derives its name from that of an early Hundr
    [11] Absalom Ridgely was one of the first trustees of the Methodist Church in An
polis. (Phœbus, *op. cit.*, 104, 110, 112; Riley: *A History of Anne Arundel County*, 14
    [12] Mr. G. was probably either Mr. Gray or Mr. Griffith.

oose affliction with the people of God, than to enjoy the pleasure of sin
r a season!

Thursday, 13. At William McCubbin's (?)[13] many were much wrought
on by the Spirit of God, under the word: Alice Woodward especially
s so deeply affected, that she had scarce power to contain herself. I saw
resh proof that the life of man is quite uncertain: a tobacco house was
own down and killed a Negro man.

My heart was deeply engaged in prayer, especially for the inhabitants
Annapolis. My confidence in God was so great, that I could trust him
th my body and soul, and all my little concerns. He makes me a parker of his spiritual kingdom—righteousness, peace, and joy in the Holy
ost.

Friday, 14. My natural timidity depressed my mind at the thought of
eaching in Annapolis, where many people openly deny the Holy Scrip-
es, as well as the power of inward religion. But the Lord inspired me
th a degree of evangelical courage; and I felt a determination to adhere
the truth, and follow Jesus Christ, if it should be even to prison or to
ath.

Saturday, 15. Preaching in a private house in Annapolis, I found my
rit at liberty in a good degree. May the God of Daniel stand by me,
it I may never be ashamed to preach the pure gospel, or even afraid to
fer for it!

Lord's day, 16. After preaching at the widow Dorsey's, I rode back to
r. Hammond's, and was not very agreeably entertained by a company
gay, worldly people. And as they must either imbibe something of my
rit, or I something of theirs, if we were long together, I thought it most
oedient to depart in peace as soon as it was convenient; and was much
isted and comforted in preaching from Acts xvii, 30, 31; but felt myself
ary and unwell at the close of the day.

Monday, 17. Preaching when the house of assembly was adjourned,
iny of them came to hear for themselves. The Lord was with me, and I
ind my heart melted and expanded with love to the souls of the people.
t by imprudently venturing out when warmed by preaching, I have
ought on a sore throat. On *Tuesday* I went to get a sight of the poor
soners, but could not obtain admittance. At Broad Creek on *Wednes-*
y, there was a large company of wild and ignorant mortals, who, after
eaching, were communicating their thoughts to each other: some said
y did not like the doctrine; others said it was the truth—the very
th.[14]

ᵃ William McCubbin was a son of Moses McCubbin, who resided on the north side
South River in Anne Arundel County. (*D.C. Genealogical Records' Committee,*
. LXXIII, 68, 69; Warfield: *The Founders of Anne Arundel and Howard Counties.*)
ᵃ Asbury was apparently attempting to establish a new preaching place on Broad
ek, four miles west of Annapolis, Maryland.

Wednesday, 19. I rode to Major Thomas Rawling's, who treated r
with great kindness, and seemed desirous of knowing the truth: but tl
spirit of the times has engrossed too much of his attention. Our Lord h
told us that some, "when they have heard, go forth, and are choked wi
cares, and riches, and pleasures of this life." (Luke viii, 14.) No doubt b
this description comprehends a vast multitude of mankind: they (
not consider religion as the one thing needful.

Thursday, 20. By the providence of God, my throat was no worse, b
my mind was under some dejection. However, we had a powerful ar
profitable watch night at Mr. P.'s. And on *Friday* there were mar
attentive people at Mr. R.'s.

Saturday, 22. As sure as we draw nigh to God in sincerity, he will dra
nigh to us. I have given myself to private prayer seven times a day, ar
found my heart much drawn out in behalf of the preachers, the societie
especially the new places, and my aged parents. And while thus exercise
my soul has been both quickened and purified. Let the glory be given
God! But alas! after all, my heart is not so filled with generous gratitu
as it should be!

> "Eternal are thy mercies, Lord;
> Eternal truth attends thy word;
> Thy praise shall sound from shore to shore,
> Till suns shall rise and set no more."

Lord's day, 23. My mind was delightfully fixed on God. A few peop
who in dulness and religious stupidity exceeded all I had ever seen, car
to hear me to-day. But would they sincerely seek after God, they shou
find the way to heaven; for the prophet saith, "A fool shall not err therein

Thursday, 27. I have been variously exercised with the carelessness
the people, and the troubles of the times; though my soul has had intima
access to God. I received a letter from brother Shadford, intimating tha
according to rule, the time was drawing near for us to return. But S
Paul's rule is, that our spiritual children should be in our hearts, to li
and die with them. (2 Cor. vii, 3.) Then, doubtless, we should be willi
to suffer affliction with them. May the Lord give me wisdom sufficient
direct me in this and every intricate case!

Lord's day, 30. The congregation was large at Mr. Dorsey's (?),[15] ar
some of them felt the power of the word: though in the afternoon, at
school house near Annapolis, there was very little appearance of spiritu
feeling. On *Monday* I was under some exercise of mind in respect to tl
times: my brethren are inclined to leave the continent, and I do not knc
but something may be propounded to me which would touch my co
science; but my determination is to trust in God, and be satisfied if t
souls of my fellow-men are saved. A genteel woman met me to-day on t

[15] Asbury's preaching place was at either Caleb Dorsey's or Henry Duvall's.

road to John Hesselius's,[16] and asked me if I should not preach in town; but I had not the presence of mind to tell her I had no place there to preach in.

Wednesday, April 2. Having received information that some of my brethren had determined on their departure, I wrote to brother Shadford, that as long as I could stay and preach without injuring my conscience, it appeared as my duty to abide with the flock. But I must confess Satan has harassed me with violent and various temptations. However, my dependence is on the Lord, that he will always enable me to do what is right in the sight of God and man. I had about twenty-two miles to ride to-day, and to call by the way to preach: though both hungry and weary, yet my soul was much blessed in dispensing the word.

Thursday, 3. My soul had peace, and my body had rest: but Satan was still at hand. We had a comfortable watch night at Mr. P.'s. On *Friday* my heart was dissolved into tenderness while preaching at Mr. R.'s.

Saturday, 5. Mr. M. gave me an awful account of a man struck instantly dead at Deer Creek. The very relation of his crime is enough to make a man shudder—he had been cursing the Holy Spirit. This is a striking proof that God is not an inattentive spectator of the actions of men, though most men live as if they thought he were. No: "for God shall bring every work into judgment, with every secret thing, whether it be good, or whether it be evil." (Ecclesiastes xii, 14.) Much temptation has urged me to much prayer: so that I have lately retired as often as ten or twelve times a day to call upon my God. When the tempter finds that his violent assaults only drive us nearer to God, perhaps he will not be so maliciously officious.

Monday, 7. Satan seemed determined, if possible, to distract, if he could not destroy me—even blasphemous thoughts have been darted into my imagination. But I know where my help is to be found. Let our imaginations be ever so horrid, and haunt us ever so frequently, provided we hate them, and constantly resist them, they are not imputed to us; but we may still rejoice in God in the midst of them all. "It is enough for the servant to be as his Lord, who was in all points tempted like as we are, yet without sin." Glory to God, he hath promised that "we shall not be tempted above that we are able," (though sometimes it may be to the extent of our ability,) "but will with the temptation also make a way to

[16] J. H. may have been John Hesselius or John Hammond. The former was an artist who married the widow of Henry Woodward in 1763 and lived at "Bellefield" on the Severn River near Annapolis. One of the Woodward daughters married Philip Rogers, one of the trustees of the first meetinghouse in Annapolis. John Hammond lived at Annapolis. His daughter, Mrs. Anne Grice (1760–1839), lived in New York. She entertained Asbury and Henry Boehm during the General Conference of 1812, and there Paradise painted his well-known portrait of Asbury. (*Colonial and Revolutionary Lineages of America*, IX, 339–41; *Maryland Historical Magazine*, XXI, 277–79; Coles: *Heroines of Methodism*, 177, 178; Warfield, *op. cit.*, 178–84.)

escape, that we may be able to bear it." (1 Cor. x, 13.) I have now rea
Newton on the Prophecies three times over.[17]

Tuesday, 8. There was a large company of wild-looking people at M
Gray's, on the fork of Patuxent river.[18] And there was much such a co
gregation the next day at Mr. Childs'.[19]

Thursday, 10. My soul was much refreshed in speaking to the people
C. B.'s: and on *Friday* I met with Mr. Hanson,[20] and received a letter fro
Mr. Rankin; in which, after he had given me an account of the circui
and societies, he assigned his reasons for not travelling much for about tl
space of two months past.

Lord's day, 13. After preaching at Mr. D.'s, I found much freedom
preaching to a large company at Annapolis: and had an invitation to g
into Worcester county.[21]

Monday, 14. This was a day of rest to my fatigued frame, and of co.
solation to my immortal part. On *Tuesday* there was great decency in tl
congregation at Annapolis; though Satan, by his emissaries, had raise
an opposition. But Israel's God is above them all.

Wednesday, 16. God was with us, and the people were happy at M
M.'s. On my way I called and dined with Mr. R., who gave great attentic
to my explanatory and pointed conversation on the new birth. Ridir
after preaching to R. P.'s, my chaise was shot through; but the Lo
preserved my person. The war is now at such a height, that they a
pressing men for the sea service.

[17] Thomas Newton (1704–82), bishop of Bristol, published the first volume of l
*Dissertations on the Prophecies, which have been remarkably fulfilled, and are at this tir
fulfilling in the world*, in 1754; and two other volumes appeared in 1758. They we
printed in his *Works* in 1782 and many times separately. Dr. Johnson (Boswell, I
286) said it was "Tom's great work: but how far it was great, and how much of it w
Tom's, was another question." (*Dictionary of National Biography*, XIV, 403–5.)

[18] The Gray home was an early preaching place in Calvert County. (Watters, *op. ci
88; Sweet, *op. cit.*, 87.) The fork is near Priest Bridge on the Defence Highway betwe
Baltimore and Washington. Here the Big Patuxent and Little Patuxent join to form t
main stream that empties into Chesapeake Bay at Solomon's Island.

[19] Gabriel D. Childs, father of the Rev. John Childs and grandfather of the Re
John Wesley Childs, resided in the southern part of Anne Arundel County. (See *Jourr
entry for June 6, 1783; Whatcoat's *Journal* for December 17, 1789; Edward: *Life
John Wesley Childs*; Childs: *Reliques of the Rives*, 533–47.)

[20] Asbury probably met with Hollis Hanson to discuss plans for Hanson's beir
received on trial at the approaching annual conference, May 20, 1777. At that co
ference Hanson was appointed to serve with Philip Gatch on the Sussex Circuit
Virginia. Gatch says he did not serve. (McLean, *op. cit.*, 54.) Hanson was one of t
trustees of land deeded August 12, 1782, by Henry and Mary Watters for the site of t
Thomas Run Church, Harford County, Maryland. (See *Harford County Liber*, J.L.C
No. E Folio, 4, 5, 6, 7.)

[21] The invitation may have come from those who had heard Methodist itineran
Already they had preached in the home of Jephthah Bowen near Newark, Worces
County. Several years elapsed before Asbury reached that region. (Hallman, *op. ci
351.)

Thursday, 17. One of our Society died of a disorder in the throat and lungs, with only one day's illness. Such is the precarious tenure of life! But "blessed are they that die in the Lord!" May I always have my loins girded about, and my light burning, waiting for the will of my Lord! God has displayed great wisdom and goodness in hiding future events from man; that we may live without that painful anxiety which we should be apt to feel if we knew the hour of our death, and that we may be always ready to meet the unknown period.

Saturday, 19. My soul was much blessed at Richard Sewell's, in preaching from the Divine expostulation, "Why will ye die?" Mr. Josias Dallam invited me to lodge at his house, and treated me with great kindness.

Lord's day, 20. After preaching at Mr. Warfield's [?], I rode about twenty miles to lodge with a friend; but seeing a boy ploughing by the road-side, my conscience smote me for breaking the Sabbath, by riding when there was no real necessity for it.

Monday, 21. My heart was comforted in the company of an old friend:[22] but on *Tuesday* Satan raged against my soul as if he would immediately destroy it; but my divine Protector is too strong for him. The Lord visited and blessed my soul in the evening, while I was describing the faithful and wise servant.

Wednesday, 23. I found myself very unwell on my going to Thomas Webb's; but my spirit was at liberty in preaching. Though still unwell I rode twenty miles to John Worthington's on *Thursday*, and was blessed with a tranquil mind by the way. Satan cast several infernal darts at my soul; but I was enabled to repel them by the shield of faith, and the power of prayer.

Saturday, 26. A very genteel, polite company assembled at Annapolis; and though I spoke with great plainness, they bore it well.

Lord's day, 27. After meeting the congregation at the widow Elizabeth Town Dorsey's, I found a large company at Annapolis, who gave good attention to me, but I fear they were not disposed to give their hearts to God. My mind has been grieved at some who call themselves friends to religion and to the Methodists. But alas! how blind and ignorant is the unchanged mind of man! How little does he consider what will please or displease his Maker! I still desire to have every action, word, thought, and desire, entirely devoted to God. Lord, hasten the much wished for hour!

[22] This old friend was Captain Thomas Webb. In the following month he was reported as being suspected of spying. His attendant, John Carey, had fled but had been captured and imprisoned in Philadelphia, from where he wrote to explain his reason for being with Webb and asked for a hearing. (See Dawson: "The Early Methodists and the American Revolution" in *The Historical Magazine*, December, 1866.) Moravian records at Bethlehem, Pennsylvania, reveal that Webb, with his family of seven persons, arrived in or near Philadelphia on May 31, 1777, where he remained on parole as a prisoner of war until he was exchanged after fifteen months.

"Thou, my life, my treasure be,
My portion here below!
Nothing would I seek but thee,
Thee only would I know."

Monday, 28. About two hundred careless-looking people came to hea
the word at Pig Point:[23] they seemed entire strangers to such a doctrine
so some laughed and others wept. I rode fifty miles in going and coming t
preach that sermon; but hope it was not altogether labour lost.

Friday, May 2. At Mr. R.'s I spoke closely and pointedly for the la:
time during this visit; then rode through the rain and darkness to M.
Webb's (?), and felt my heart sweetly melted with gratitude and thank:
giving to God. On *Monday*, I went to Shadrach Turner's,[24] and met m
brethren at the Frederick quarterly meeting; where we were favoured wit
the Divine blessing.

Wednesday, 7. A letter came to hand from Mr. Jarratt, which gave u
hopes that there would be another revival in Virginia. He also advised u
to take no immature steps, which might have a tendency to alter our plar
After preaching the next day at Richard Sewell's, T. D. invited me to h
house. I found that he and his wife were seeking to be justified by th
deeds of the law, and I laboured with undissembled freedom to convinc
them of their error; but it appeared to be labour in vain.

Saturday, 10. At Annapolis the congregation was small, and so was m
power to preach. My soul has been kept in a calm and comfortable frame
but panting for more constant fervour towards God.

Lord's day, 11. Many attended at the widow Elizabeth Brown Dorsey':
to hear what I would say on my departure. I spoke from Acts xiii, 46; an
many seemed much affected. The congregation was also large at Anna
polis; where I spoke in plain terms to the rich and the gay, on our Lord'
awful account of the rich man and Lazarus. They behaved well; and som
were desirous to know if I intended to come again.

Monday, 12. Set out for our yearly conference, and having preached a
Mr. Perigau's (?), by the way, came safe to Mr. Gough's, and was glad t
see the preachers who were there.[25] We had some weighty conversation o

[23] Pig Point is situated on the eastern side of the Patuxent River in Anne Arund
County about twenty miles southwest of Annapolis. Several roads converged at th
ferry over the Patuxent River at Pig Point to make it familiar to early circuit rider
The first Methodist church near Pig Point was Wesley Chapel erected about 1839. (S
"Pig Point", by John L. Shepherd, in *300 Years with the Maryland Gazette* in suppl
ment, 1927.)

[24] The home of Shadrach and Sarah Turner was near Bladensburg, Prince George
County. (Lednum, *op. cit.*, 193; Brumbaugh: *Maryland Records*, I, 37.)

[25] It is not known how many of the twenty preachers who attended the Deer Cree
Conference participated in this seven-day "caucus" or preliminary session at Per
Hall. Asbury expressed an occasional minority viewpoint during "some weigh
conversation on different points."

fferent points: and among other things, it was asked whether we could
ve our consent that Mr. Rankin should baptize, as there appeared to be
present necessity. But it was objected that this would be a breach of our
scipline; and it was not probable that things would continue long
such a disordered state. The next day, with great harmony and joint
nsent, we drew a rough draught for stationing the preachers the en-
ring year. And on *Friday* we conversed on the propriety of signing
rtificates avouching good conduct for such of the preachers as chose to
to Europe. But I could not see the propriety of it at this time. We also
nversed on such rules as might be proper for the regulation of the
eachers who abide on the continent. And it was judged necessary that
committee should be appointed to superintend the whole. And on
onday we rode together to attend the conference at Deer Creek.[26]
So greatly has the Lord increased the number of travelling preachers
thin these few years, that we have now twenty-seven who attend the
rcuits, and twenty of them were present at this conference. Both our
blic and private business was conducted with great harmony, peace, and
ve. Our brethren who intend to return to Europe, have agreed to stay
l the way is quite open. I preached on the charge which our Lord gave
s apostles: "Behold, I send you forth as sheep in the midst of wolves:
ye therefore wise as serpents, and harmless as doves." Our conference
ded with a love feast and watch night. But when the time of parting
me, many wept as if they had lost their first-born sons. They appeared
be in the deepest distress, thinking, as I suppose, they should not see
e faces of the English preachers any more. This was such a parting as I
ver saw before. Our conference has been a great time—a season of un-
mmon affection. And we must acknowledge that God has directed,
vned, and blessed us in the work. A certificate, as mentioned above,
d been acceded to, and signed in the conference.
Lord's day, 25. My soul was quickened in preaching at the Bush chapel;[27]
lodged at Mr. Dallam's; and the next day collected my writings and
tters, in order to preserve them. On *Tuesday* went to Mr. Gough's; and
Wednesday began to read regularly Mr. Wesley's Notes.[28]
Thursday, 29. We had a profitable meeting at Gunpowder Neck. And

[26] There is uncertainty about the exact meeting place of the conference, though it
ms to have been at a meetinghouse near Deer Creek in Harford County, Maryland.
is fifth conference received fourteen preachers on trial, among them such notable
rsons as Edward Bailey, Caleb B. Pedicord, William Gill, John Tunnell, and John
ckins. (Lednum, *op. cit.*, 195–201; Preston: *History of Harford County*, 32.)
[27] Bush Forest Chapel, the second Methodist meetinghouse in America, was erected
1769. A second was built in 1842 and a third in 1878. The successor of these is the
erdeen Methodist Church, two miles distant.
[28] John Wesley completed his first edition of *The New Testament with Explanatory*
tes October 23, 1755. (See Wesley's *Journal* for that date; in Green's *Bibliography*
e work is number 172.)

on *Friday* I returned to preach at Mr. Gough's; where we had a sma
but warm congregation.

Saturday, 31. The Spirit of grace was with me: but I long for a mo
active life; to be constantly employed in bringing souls to God.

Lord's day, June 1. The Lord enlarged my heart, and opened a door
utterance, while preaching to a numerous congregation at the Forks; a
there were some among them who had for a long time been detained
prejudice from hearing us. But I could not find the same liberty at M
Gough's, in the latter part of the day.

Tuesday, 3. "As the hart panteth after the water-brooks, so panteth n
soul after God. My soul thirsteth for God, for the living God;" though
have been at times sorely beset by temptations. But shall I ever yield
the tempter, and sin against my Lord? No: in the strength of Jesus, n

Thursday, 5. Having been ten days off and on at Mr. Gough's, I set o
to-day for John Colgate's; and preached by the way at Phineas Hunt
On *Friday* I laid aside my wig, and began to use the cold bath for n
health: and rode as far as Mrs. Ridgely's, who was a mother in Israe
and both a friend and mother to me. After many heavy trials my soul w
comforted, but earnestly desirous of more purity and fellowship with Go

Saturday, 7. Some seemed to feel the weight of Divine truths at Reister
town; and on the *Lord's day*, my heart was melted and expanded towar
the people at Brother Colgate's.

Monday, 9. I met brother George Shadford at Mr. Colgate's, a
preached on Acts xvi, 30, 31; then called to see a sick person, and return
to brother Colgate's.

Wednesday, 11. I preached in town (Baltimore) on these affecting word
"How shall I give thee up, Ephraim?" And on *Thursday*, entering n
circuit at Mr. P.'s, we had a heart-affecting season, and a few joined t
society.

Friday, 13. We had great harmony and love in our increasing society
R.'s.

Lord's day, 15. There was a large, attentive audience in a school hou
on Elkridge; where I preached with usual energy and affection, on Am
iv, 11, and hope the time of favouring the souls of both rich and poor
now approaching. But after so great a blessing, Satan, as if moved wi
envy, attempted to wound me with his fiery darts. This was probably pe
mitted by my gracious Lord, lest I should be exalted above measur
Brother George Shadford came to accompany me into Virginia, to fet
our clothing and books.

Monday, 16. We set out and rode to Shadrach Turner's, where v
received this strange relation: "A person in the form of a man came to t
house of another in the night; the man of the house asked what he wante
He replied, 'This will be the bloodiest year that ever was known.' Th
other asked how he knew. His answer was, 'It is as true as your wife

ɔw dead in her bed.' He went back and found his wife dead. But the
ranger disappeared."

Virginia

On *Monday*, we went to brother Adam's;[29] and on *Wednesday* to Bryan
airfax's,[30] a kind man, but his ideas of religion were confused. *Thursday*,
e rode to Leesburg,[31] and found that brother Bealle had just departed
om this world of trouble and danger. My spirit was much drawn out
wards God and the souls of the people, while preaching on Matt. xxiv,
ɔ, &c.

Maryland

Tuesday we went on to Frederick, where I showed the people the danger
˙ postponing their duties to God, from Amos iv, 11. The next day we
ɔde forty-five miles to Reisterstown and came in about seven o'clock.
Wednesday, 25. By invitation, I visited Josias Dallam, who was very
, and hope it will be followed by the operations of the Holy Spirit, and
ɔve a permanent blessing to his soul. Then rode on to John Worthing-
ɔn's, and found myself unwell, but happy in God.
Friday, 27. I went to Mr. Hesselius's, and intended to preach in Anna-
ɔlis, but there was no house open for me. The next day two of the mem-
rs of the assembly promised to use their influence in procuring me a
ɔuse to preach in; but expected they could not succeed. Alas! What have
done? Whose ox or ass have I taken, or whom have I defrauded? But
e Lord permits it to be so; therefore I peaceably submit, and will not
ar the face of man, nor even a prison, while employed in the cause of
ɔd and of truth. However, contrary to my expectation, I preached in the
urch,[32] though the congregation was small, and the soldiers made a
eat noise before the door. I then concluded to preach the next time in

[29] William Adams lived in Virginia across the Potomac River from Georgetown,
aryland. Methodist preaching started near the Adams home in Fairfax County.
illiam Adams, Jr., was converted in 1775, entered the itinerancy in 1778, and became
and died December 3, 1779. (Lednum, *op. cit.*, 245–46.)
[30] Bryan Fairfax was converted in 1776 and attended the conference held at Balti-
ore that year. He was a relative of Lord Fairfax. (*Heads of Families in Virginia*, 86.)
[31] It has been thought that the first Methodist society in Virginia was at Leesburg,
ich was the nearest town to the Strawbridge meetinghouse on Sam's Creek in Mary-
nd. The date of the beginning of the society is not known; but the Old Stone Church
s begun in 1766, completed in 1770, and dedicated in 1790 by Joseph Pilmoor.
weet: *Virginia Methodism*, 46.)
[32] This was St. Anne's Church in Annapolis. The Rev. Thomas Read assumed his
ties Easter, 1777. (Allen's *Historical Notices of St. Ann's Parish* in Anne Arundel
ɔunty, Maryland.)

the commons. But the rain which fell the next day prevented me; an
there were but few people at Mrs. Dorsey's.

Tuesday, July 1. The Lord blessed me with joy and peace in believing
and I was enabled to cast all my care upon him. On *Tuesday* I went to M
P.'s, about twenty miles; and have been much delighted in reading D
Watts's Treatise on the Rest of Separate Spirits, and Mr. Baxter's Saint'
Rest.[33] In these books we find the marrow of Methodism; that is, pur
religion, and sound doctrine which cannot be condemned.

Wednesday, 2. Satan still manifesteth a desire to sift me as wheat; bu
the Lord supports me, and fills me with peace. A lowering cloud hang
threatening over our heads; but all my trust is in the Lord, who hat
stood by and preserved me for many years; and will stand by me still.

Thursday, 3. I rode about twelve miles, and preached a funeral sermo
on the death of Mr. W. It was a very affecting time, both to me and th
congregation. But after I had read the rules in the society, I told them m
doubts, and communicated my ideas of the approaching troubles, whic
produced a great melting amongst them.

Saturday, 5. I had some conversation with Mr. Montgomery [?]; bu
it was to no purpose, for he was still inflexible. Perhaps I have been to
forward in taking his part before, and now he requites me for it.

Lord's day, 6. There was a very serious congregation in the forenoo
where I enforced our Lord's affectionate declaration, Matt. xxiii, 37. B
in the latter part of the day, about eleven miles distant from the othe
place, the people seemed to be stupid and inattentive. As I have though
bacon was prejudicial to my health, I have lately abstained from it, an
have experienced the good effects of this economy. My soul has been kep
in great purity, and ardent pantings after more of God.

Monday, 7. In the evening Daniel Ruff and brother Hartley came an
brought me some account of the preachers, whom I love in the bowels c
Christ, with much affection. We spent the next day together in love, an
to edification; and on *Wednesday*, they set out for Virginia, and I fc
Annapolis. My spirit was somewhat dejected by the way, with a fear tha
the people would reject the Gospel of Jesus Christ, to their own destru
tion. But these matters must be left to the Lord, who "will judge the worl
in righteousness." I met a very insensible company at Mr. Childs's, an
laboured to fasten the truth on their hearts, from Malachi iii, 7; but
appeared to be labour in vain.

Thursday, 10. They received me at Mr. Hammond's [?] better than
expected; and some were touched by the power of grace. There was a
opportunity on Friday of speaking, at least to the judgment of some ric
and honourable men, on Psalm iv, 6, 7: "There be many that say, Wh

---

[33] Isaac Watts (1674–1748) was an English nonconformist hymn writer and theologian
Richard Baxter (1615–91) was the author of the devotional classic *Saints Everlastin
Rest*, published in 1650.

ill show us any good? Lord, lift thou up the light of thy countenance upon us. Thou hast put gladness in my heart, more than in the time that their corn and their wine increased." My heaviness of spirit was almost removed, and my soul was free and happy in God.

Lord's day, 13. Though I spoke closely and plainly at Mrs. Dorsey's, yet the audience did not seem properly to understand me. I had intended to preach in the commons this afternoon, but the rain prevented it, so I preached to a few desirous souls at Mr. Hesselius's. But my spirit is grieved within me, to see such multitudes of people in these parts so forgetful of God, and filled with the spirit and conversation of this world. Poor souls! If they were only convinced of their sinful and lost estate, their disposition and conversation would be immediately changed. My work at present is very heavy—it is chiefly among unawakened people. I have devised what I could to bring them to God; and know not what new method to take. May the Lord take the work into his own hand!

Monday, 14. There were forty or fifty, chiefly women, to hear the word at Annapolis: to whom I showed, "If our Gospel be hid it is hid to them that are lost; in whom the god of this world hath blinded the minds of them that believe not, lest the light of the glorious Gospel of Christ, who is the image of God, should shine unto them." Though I spoke freely yet but few of them seemed to feel it. On *Tuesday* my soul was under deep exercises. I am often purposing to pursue, with greater ardour, the summit of holiness, but still come short!

Wednesday, 16. At a place ten miles from Annapolis, there was some melting of heart under the word. I afterward met the class, and then returned with my mind fixed on God, and sweet nearness of soul to him.

Thursday, 17. The Spirit of the Lord was with me in preaching at Mr. —.'s; and there was a great moving among the society. Blessed be God for all things! My body has been in tolerable health, and my soul frequently refreshed with the dew of heavenly grace. My meditations in the Hebrew Bible have afforded me great pleasure. This is the book I study for improvement.

Lord's day, 20. Both at the school house, where I called on the people to consider their ways, from Haggai i, 5; and at Mr. Ridgely's [?], where I showed them, from Ezek. xxxiii, 31, how many of old time heard the word of the Lord, but did it not; there was very little appearance of anything more than attention, though I never laboured more earnestly to do good. It seems as if a judicial stupidity, in spiritual things, prevails among them.

Monday, 21. Heard Mr. Rankin preach his last sermon.[34] My mind was a little dejected; and I now felt some desire to return to England, but was

[34] Rankin wrote that he left Maryland in September and spent the winter in Philadelphia. He sailed for England from the "Capes of Delaware" on March 17, 1778. *Arminian Magazine*, London, II (1779), 198.)

willing to commit the matter to the Lord. There was a large congregatio
and some prospect of good things at Mr. Richard Sewell's, where I tol
the people, from the authority of Jesus Christ, "Except ye repent ye sha
all likewise perish." (Luke xiii, 3.)

Wednesday, 23. God was still my object and my hope. But I ha
lamented my backwardness in doing good by private conversation; whic
is in a great measure owing to the natural bashfulness of my dispositio
After visiting some poor people to pray and talk with them on the impo
tant subject of their salvation, I rode to C.'s, at the head of South River
but it is a miserable, stupid, careless neighbourhood; so I bid it farewel

Thursday, 24. There were many gay and giddy-looking folks to hear th
word of the Lord; and a few of them were serious and affected. Poo
souls! They are real objects of pity. Both their education and the circ
of their acquaintance, have a tendency to make them forget their latte
end, and to bend all the strength of their minds to present objects.

Friday, 25. We kept our general fast as appointed by conference; an
my soul was enabled to cast all its little cares, both spiritual and tempora
on Him that careth for me. May the Lord direct me how to act, so as t
keep myself always in the love of God! I have lately been reading a
account of Theodosius and his sons, with several of the ancient Father
which also communicates much information relative to the Eastern an
Western empires for about three hundred years,—so long were idolatr
and Arianism kept out of the Church of Christ. And while Chrysosto
was bishop, an Arian church was burnt at Constantinople. But since th
time, absolute, unconditional predestination has made its way into th
Church, which nullifies all laws, human and Divine—for if men cannot d
otherwise than they do, why should any law inflict punishment for the
crimes? Must quadrupeds be punished because they do not fly? Ho
easily might men, believing this doctrine, ascribe their envy, malice, an
most cruel inclinations, to the effect of Divine predestination; and co
clude that their most malignant dispositions were eternally decreed, an
therefore not to be conquered but complied with, though they shoul
produce the most pernicious and destructive consequences in huma
society.

Saturday, 26. My soul was composed, and in pursuit of more of Go
Having read the conquest of Rome by Alaric, and the rending of th
Western Empire by the Goths, I was led to observe how part of the Reve
lation of St. John was then fulfilled. But much more of this is yet to com

Lord's day, 27. After explaining the parable of the sower at Mr
Dorsey's, I preached at Annapolis to a large company—some serious, an
some gay and trifling—on these compassionate words of Christ, "Ho
often would I have gathered thy children together, and ye would not

---

[35] The head of South River is west of the village of Parole, Anne Arundel Count
between Annapolis and Washington.

Monday, 28. As the rain prevented my attending the appointment, I visited the jail, and found an unhappy mortal under sentence of death; who was very ignorant, but so susceptible of religious advice that he was melted into tears, and shook like a leaf.

Tuesday, 29. The Lord discovered to my view a greater depth of holiness, and my soul thirsted for it. I met with brother Hartley, who had been to Virginia, but having some scruples of conscience about taking the test oath, was obliged to return. May the Lord direct us all how to pursue the most wise and prudent measures! The next day I preached at Magothy,[36] where the work of God goes on successfully.

Thursday, 31. At Mr. P.'s there were about a hundred souls, who seemed much alive to God. Here I appointed a quarterly meeting and love feast, on my return from Baltimore and Frederick, next Saturday fortnight.

Friday, August 1. The Lord gave me spiritual peace, but my soul was on stretch for a greater degree of holiness, and deeper communion with God.

> "I pant to feel thy sway,
> And only thee to obey;
> Thee my spirit gasps to meet;
> This my one, my ceaseless prayer,
> Make, O make my heart thy seat!
> O set up thy kingdom there!"

have now finished reading sixteen volumes of the Universal History.[37]

Lord's day, 3. In the forenoon the poor rich sinners were very attentive in the school house on Elk Ridge,[38] and it is *possible* the Lord may raise people among them to fear and love him. But at Mr. R.'s in the afternoon, the congregation was very dull, though I spoke strong words from the Almighty's awful declaration concerning the ungodly: "These shall go away into everlasting punishment."

Monday, 4. Rode thirty-seven miles to the Frederick quarterly meeting[39] without breaking my fast, and was under the necessity of preaching when arrived. The next day our meeting began with a love feast; and we had a powerful, melting time.

Friday, 8. Having visited my friends in Baltimore, I rode to Mr. Gough's,

---

[36] Magothy was a political division of Anne Arundel County between the Severn and the Magothy rivers.

[37] *An Universal History from the Earliest Account of Time*, published in London from 1747–68. The original sixty-five-volume set was printed for T. Osborne.

[38] This small frame building stood one hundred yards south of Caleb Dorsey's Furnace on Furnace and Race roads, near where Deep Run flows into the Patapsco River. A quarter mile north of the Furnace site is the Melville Methodist Church (1834). (Information from a land plat in the Court House, Annapolis.)

[39] This quarterly meeting was probably held at Joseph Hobbs. (Rankin's *Journal*.)

met Mr. Rankin, and had some agreeable conversation on the work of
God in different parts of America. Went the next day to the Forks, when
I met with brother George Shadford in great harmony, and found Divine
assistance in dispensing the word.

Monday, 11. We settled all our little affairs in the spirit of love; and
brother Shadford partly agreed to go with me to the quarterly meeting
But alas! though my confidence in Christ was not shaken, yet I felt myself
less than the least in the company, and unworthy of the favour of both
God and man. How merciful is God in giving us such abasing views of
ourselves, which have a powerful tendency to drive us closer to him, and
keep us always in the dust!

Tuesday, 12. After I had publicly declared to the righteous, "The God
whom we serve is able to deliver us," we then had a solemn, comfortable
love feast; and having done our business, I returned to Mr. Gough's
where many people attended to receive the word of truth. And we have
reason to believe the work of God is now reviving.

Wednesday, 13, was spent at Mr. Gough's, and after some conversation
I found brother Shadford was not to go with me, because Mr. Rankin
did not choose to spend a quarter in Baltimore circuit. Indeed, he had
not taken a regular circuit since we have been in America; so I was
obliged to go into a new circuit[40] with a young exhorter who had deserted
me once before. But all contentions wound my spirit, so I passively
submitted.

Thursday, 14. My mouth was opened and my heart was enlarged at
William Lynch's (?); and I hope the word was made a blessing to many
souls.

Friday, 15. Rode to Curtis's Creek[41] to hold a quarterly meeting there
and the next morning we began with a love feast. It was a time of great
power, and exceeded all we had ever seen in these parts. There was some
thing very admirable in the Christian simplicity of the people, who spoke
the language of warm and artless love. Brother Shadford preached a
moving sermon on the barren fig-tree; and many sinners wept.

Lord's day, 17. The rain prevented my going to Elk Ridge, and brother
Shadford from going to Baltimore; so we had a very melting time in dis
coursing on the subject of the Canaanitish woman. And I believe, brother
Shadford was persuaded that he ought to be in this circuit with me.

Monday, 18. This was a day of much temptation, but my Deliverer was

[40] Asbury's name appears beneath Rankin's among the assistants, but not in the
appointments of the May conference. The "new circuit" which Asbury was obliged to
enter remains nameless, although it appears to have comprised many preaching places
on the older Maryland circuits as well as several hitherto unvisited regions.

[41] The source of Curtis Creek is south of Baltimore. At the Patapsco River it forms
Curtis Bay within the city limits. It is probable that the quarterly meeting was held at
the home of Samuel Dorsey, son of Caleb Dorsey, who managed the forge at Curtis
Creek.

hand. At Catherine Small's, I found a few from the Ridge, who in-
•rmed me that some attended yesterday in the rain. Hence I conclude,
any of them had a desire to be saved; and that it is best for a preacher
• attend his appointments, if the apparent risk is not too great. I preached
• the people with much affection; many felt the weight of the word, and
young woman was convinced of sin.

Tuesday, 19. The pacific spirit of grace had possession of my willing
:art. After preaching at Mr. G.'s to a few souls as dull as usual, I crossed
ιe Severn river in the rain; and though I expected to feel the consequence,
:t suffered no injury.

Wednesday, 20. How unlike real Christians are some that bear the name!
he Lord hath enabled me, of late, to be faithful to the families which
ιve come in my way. And we must overcome our natural bashfulness
ιd backwardness, to assist the precious souls of our fellow-men, who
·e on the brink of endless ruin, and see it not. On *Thursday*, both
ιe public congregation and the class were powerfully melted at Mr.
.'s.

Lord's day, 24. I was much fatigued by riding twenty-five miles and
·reaching twice. A report that a British fleet was sailing up the Chesa-
:ake Bay, has induced many people to quit Annapolis. Lord, give thy
:ople faith and patience sufficient for their day of trial!

Monday, 25. My soul confided in God, but was sweetly distressed with
ι ardent desire for more complete holiness. I have lately read Walker's
:rmons with much pleasure. We had an awful storm this evening at nine
·clock. The thunder, lightning, and sweeping winds, were all in commo-
 on. With reverence I turned my mind on the dread majesty and power of
·od, who, by the elements in which we live, contends with man. Such a
:ene as this was enough to strike the boldest sinner with terror, and make
ιm even shudder at a wicked thought. And how dare wicked men sin at
ιy time before a God so terrible? Is he less present at one time than
ιother? No, verily! But they desire not the knowledge of God. Their
ιrprise must be great beyond all expression, when disembodied they
ιddenly find themselves, by woeful experience, acquainted with nothing
:rtaining to their offended God, but his inexorable justice and vengeful
ɔwer, of which the awful scenes we now behold in the contending
:ments, are but a faint resemblance. Then how much better is it to
ιffer affliction with the people of God, than to enjoy the pleasures of
n for a season?

> "Happy the man whose hopes rely
> On Israel's God: he made the sky,
> And earth, and seas, with all their train;
> His truth forever stands secure;
> He saves the oppress'd, he feeds the poor,
> And none shall find his promise vain."

Tuesday, 26. Thomas Worthington informed me that they had ma choice of me to preach in the Garrison Church.[42] But I shall do nothir that will separate me from my brethren. I hope to live and die a Methodis

Wednesday, 27. Though it rained I rode twenty-five miles to Magoth but was tempted and shut up in my mind, while endeavouring to a nounce, "If God be for us, who can be against us?" But the next day m soul was happy at Mr. Perigau's,[43] and I admitted four persons int the society on trial. The militia were now collecting from all quarters. O the *Lord's day* my soul was much drawn out and blessed in preaching o 1 John ii, 16, 17. Perhaps it will not be in my power to preach much long with a clear conscience. But if it should be so, my greatest concern wou be for the people of God. For many of the poor sinners seem deaf to a entreaties; and I seem to be only a witness for God against them, that the damnation may be just, if they will not obey the Gospel.

Monday, *September* 1. The Lord refreshed my own spirit, while I e couraged the few faithful souls who were present, from the words of ou Lord, "Fear not, little flock, for it is your Father's good pleasure to gi you the kingdom." Brother Daniel Ruff, who had returned from Virgini met me to-day.

Wednesday, 3. My soul was watered with the peaceful influence c Divine grace. But what I enjoyed was a stimulus urging me to groan fo more. I spent much of my time in reading Law's Serious Call, and Baxter Call to the Unconverted;[44] and think the latter is one of the best pieces c human composition in the world, to awaken the lethargic souls of poc sinners.

My mind was under heavy exercises: so I fasted, and preached wit much freedom at Mr. Joseph Taylor's [?]; but it brought on a smar fever. Though I was much indisposed, necessity was laid upon me t preach twice on *Thursday*, which increased my fever; and with indifferen lodging and the noise of children, the night was very uncomfortable.

Lord's day, 7. After being blessed with a warm and comfortable seaso while preaching to a large company at Mr. Hunt's [?], I then rode to th widow P.'s, where the word went to the hearts of the people with Divin energy, while I exposed to their view the polluted state of the natural mar and pointed out the sovereign remedy.

Tuesday, 9. My mind was so intensely bent on seeking after more o God, that I devoted three hours to the exercise of private prayer and foun myself much drawn out by the Spirit of grace, in holy wrestling and com munion with God. Being informed that sister S. had slept in the Lord,

[42] This was a chapel of ease of the Established Church which derived its nam Garrison Forest, from the site of an outpost against the Indians. The present church i one and a half miles southeast of Owings Mills, Baltimore County.

[43] Tipple, *op. cit.*, 118.

[44] William Law (1686–1761), of England, published in 1729 his *Serious Call to Devout and Holy Life*. For Richard Baxter see note under July 1, 1777.

ongratulated her felicity. Happy soul! She is taken away from the evil
• come, and gone to Abraham's bosom, where the wicked cease from
oubling, and where the weary are at rest. I have endeavoured to banish
l anxiety from my mind, and devote much of my time to prayer; and have
aped the gracious benefit thereof in my soul. On *Wednesday* I went to
Iagothy, and had a large congregation; but found that some of our
embers had begun to backslide, and that the society stood in need of
urging.

Thursday, 11. By particular request I preached a funeral sermon at the
urial of Mr. William Ridgely. There were a great many people; and some
f them were cut to the heart while I enforced Eccles. ix, 10. But afterward
Mr. P.'s my mind was somewhat embarrassed.

Friday, 12. In performing the last office for L. S., who was a Christian
deed, I declared, for the comfort of true believers, "The last enemy that
all be destroyed is death." Some attended on this occasion who had
ever heard a Methodist before; and the Lord gave me utterance and
ower.

Monday, 15. We have great commotions on every side. But in the midst
war, the Lord keeps my soul in peace. My heart was warm in preaching
. Catherine Small's, though the congregation seemed dull. The two
ollowing days I had communion with God; but not in such a degree as I
ish to experience. I long "to comprehend the length, and breadth, and
epth, and height; and to know the love of Christ, which passeth know-
dge, that I may be filled with all the fulness of God"; to

"Live the life of heaven above,
All the glorious life of love."

Thursday, 18. At Mr. W.'s I met with brother Samuel Spraggs, who
formed me that the preachers in Virginia intended to abide there awhile
nger. Brother Spraggs preached twice, and there were some small
oving amongst the people.

Lord's day, 21. There was nothing remarkable under the word at Mr.
aylor's; but there was a large company and some melting of heart at
Ir. Perigau's.

Monday, 22. I met with brother George Shadford, who informed me
at my brethren, Mr. Rankin and Mr. Rodda, had left the continent. So
e are left alone. But I leave myself in the hand of God; relying on his
ood providence to direct and protect us; persuaded that nothing will
efall me, but what shall conduce to his glory and my benefit. There was
oth attention and concern in the congregation, which was pretty large,
Capt. Stansbury's.

Lord's day, 28. Brother George Shadford was unwell with an ague. At
eisterstown I urged the necessity of family duty, and showed them how
ey should train up their children in the ways of the Lord.

Monday, 29. My soul was stayed upon God, and resigned to his u¤ erring wisdom. I wish to be so subject to my Redeemer, as to move ¡ conformity to his divine will; and in all my ways to acknowledge him ¿ my God and my guide. I spent part of my time the next day in readir Mr. Baxter's Gildas Salvianus,[45] and esteem it as a most excellent book f¢ a Gospel preacher.

Saturday, October 4. I rode thirty miles to G. B.'s to meet broth¢ Pedicord.[46] My mind was spiritually employed in reading, meditation, an communion with God.

Lord's day, 5. The congregation at G. B.'s were dull; but at B. G. there was a melting.

Tuesday, 7. The word seemed to be made a peculiar blessing to th believers at John Hagerty's [?]; and the next day at Mr. John Evan the power of God was present, while I feelingly urged the people fro¤ Heb. iv, 16: "Let us therefore come boldly to the throne of grace, that v may obtain mercy, and find grace to help in time of need." My spirit w¿ also divinely animated in preaching afterwards at Richard Owings though I rode twenty miles between the two sermons. Several old pr¢ fessors felt the reviving influences of the grace of God; and I was in hop¢ they would press on their way with renewed vigour. Such is the langu¡ disposition of the human soul, that even pure minds require a consta¤ stimulation to keep them in the way of duty. This is one reason why Go permits our minds to be tempted by Satan, and our bodies to be afflicte with diseases.

Saturday, 11. I attended and spoke at the half-yearly meeting of th Germans. And on the *Lord's day,* after preaching at Mrs. D.'s, I returne to the meeting of the Germans, where brother George Shadford an myself both spoke.

Monday, 13. Commotions and troubles surrounded me without, b¤ the peace of God filled my soul within. We seemed to be in a strait; b¤ my heart trusted in the Lord. These distressing times have lately induce many people to pay a more diligent attention to the things of God. So have hopes that these temporal troubles will prepare the way for spiritu¿ blessings.

Wednesday, 15. A heavy gloominess hung on my mind. Brother Georg Shadford and I rode to Mr. H.'s; and after I had enforced these word "Therefore, my beloved brethren, be ye steadfast, unmovable, alway abounding in the work of the Lord, forasmuch as ye know that you

---

[45] *Gildas Salvianus,* or *The Reformed Pastor,* by Richard Baxter, was original published in 1656.

[46] Asbury had a special interest in Caleb B. Pedicord, then stationed on the Frederic Circuit and was soon to bring him to the Peninsula as colaborer. The first death noti¢ to appear in the *General Minutes* was the brief tribute to Pedicord by Asbury. (*Gener¿ Minutes,* I, 23; Ware, *op. cit.,* 54–60, 86, 174; Lednum, *op. cit.,* 387–88.)

our is not in vain in the Lord," then brother Shadford exhorted, and
hearts of the people melted under the power of the word. We likewise
w the merciful hand of God displayed the next day, at Mr. Willson's,[47]
the bank of the Potomac.

Lord's day, 19. As I was unwell, brother Shadford preached in the
orning on, "Thy kingdom come;" and there was a moving in the
ngregation. He also preached in the afternoon at Mr. B.'s, but it was
a large company of stupid souls.

Monday, 20. After I had preached brother Shadford met the class; and
was a very powerful season: he also met a class afterward at Mr. Sin-
ir's, and we were favoured with a similar blessing. This has been a day
spiritual and peaceful exercises to my soul. At Mr. Hunt's on *Tuesday*,
were blessed with an extraordinary visitation of grace.

Thursday, 30. We have been detained by heavy rains at W. S.'s, for
ee days. The times still wear a gloomy aspect; but our trust is in the
ovidence of a superintending God. We have been greatly blessed, and
n great displays of the divine goodness since we have been together.
d we have been made a blessing to each other. We now left Mr. S.'s
d rode to Rocky Creek.

Lord's day, *November* 2. I cried in the morning to a large congregation
Mr. Benjamin Johnson's, "We pray you in Christ's stead, be ye recon-
d to God;" and in the afternoon at the Sugar Loaf,[48] "Why will ye
?" And my soul was enlarged and blessed both times. I then rode to
G.'s, which made about twenty miles in the day.

Monday, 3. Our quarterly meeting began, and brother Shadford
ached on the subject of the barren fig-tree. On *Tuesday* we held our
e feast at nine, and I preached at twelve. Our brethren Owing, Samuel
aggs, and Shadford, all spoke. There were many friends from Virginia,
d the congregation was very large. It was a powerful, melting time, and
cluded in the spirit of love.

Wednesday, 5. After riding thirty-seven miles I came to Baltimore, but
s very weary; though my mind was calmly stayed on God.

Friday, 7. Went to Mr. Gough's; and on Saturday preached on 3 John 4:
have no greater joy than to hear that my children walk in truth."

Lord's day, 9. After preaching with freedom of spirit and speech at the
rks, I returned to Mr. Gough's and declared, "Ye are the salt of the
th." My soul has been kept by the grace of God; and

"Calm on tumult's wheels I sit."

7 This was probably John Willson, one of the sons of Jonathan Willson, who lived
r Comus, Maryland, in 1763. (Martz: *One Hundred Sixty-Fifth Anniversary of the
rksburg Methodist Church, Clarksburg, Maryland.*)
8 Sugar Loaf Society was established in the Bennetts Creek area on or near the
lson farm. It bore the name of Sugar Loaf Chapel, believed to be the first Methodist
tinghouse erected in that vicinity. It was replaced by a brick church known as the
untain Church, which no longer exists.

Monday, 10. We set out for the quarterly meeting at Deer Creek. (*Tuesday* our love feast began at ten, and at half-past two I began t public exercise, from Heb. xiii, 17, 18, "Obey them that have the rule ov you, and submit yourselves: for they watch for your souls as they th must give account, that they may do it with joy, and not with grief; f this is unprofitable for you. Pray for us: for we trust we have a go conscience, in all things willing to live honestly." The preachers we stationed without any trouble; and all was done in harmony and love.

Wednesday, 12. I rode back to Mr. Gough's, in order to attend quarterly meeting on Curtis's Creek.[49] The Lord has lately kept my sc in tranquil peace, not much disturbed by Satan. I now purposed, by t grace of God, as often as time will permit, to read six chapters every d in my Bible.

Saturday, 15. Great numbers of people attended at the quarterly mee ing. Preaching on Acts xiv, 22, I endeavoured to imitate the apostle "Confirming the souls of the disciples, and exhorting them to continue the faith, and that we must through much tribulation enter into the kin dom of God." The power of divine grace was greatly felt in the love fea and all our business was well conducted.

Lord's day, 16. Having first preached at the widow H.'s, I rode Baltimore and preached there. On *Tuesday* I was blessed in a visit to M G.'s.

Wednesday, 19. Rode to Reistertown, and found that God was n sufficient portion, and my exceeding great reward. I wanted nothi pertaining to this world more than I possessed; neither clothing, n money, nor food. Blessed be God, for his parental love and tender ca towards me!

> "Nothing on earth I call my own:
> A stranger, to the world unknown,
> I all their goods despise;
> I trample on their whole delight,
> And seek a country out of sight,
> A country in the skies."

Friday, 21. I have endeavoured to improve my time to the best advar age in reading; and have seen so much beauty in holiness, that I ha thirsted and longed for more. My desire is, like Abraham, the father of tl faithful, to maintain a constant walk with God.

Lord's day, 23. At Mr. S.'s I exposed the unjust plea which many mal against serving God, from Matt. xxv, 24, "Then he which had received tl one talent came, and said, Lord, I knew thee that thou art a hard ma reaping where thou hast not sown, and gathering where thou hast n

[49] It is probable that the quarterly meeting was held in the home of Samuel Dorse who managed the forge at Curtis Creek for his father, Caleb Dorsey, one of the iro masters of his day.

rewed." Thus do thousands charge God foolishly: "We cannot repent
[a]d bring forth fruits meet for repentance; we cannot cease from evil,
[a]d learn to do well; we cannot deny ourselves, and take up our cross;
[w]e cannot come to Christ that we may have life. At least, we cannot do
[th]ese things *now*; we must wait God's time." But God requireth these
[th]ings *now*; therefore, those who say they cannot do them, practically say
[h]e is a hard master. At Reisterstown in the afternoon, my heart was ex-
[te]nded, and my mouth was opened, while I declared, "He that, being
[of]ten reproved, hardeneth his neck, shall suddenly be destroyed, and that
[w]ithout remedy." On *Monday*, I parted with William Gill and Samuel
[D]raggs.

Wednesday, 26. I came to Mr. Gough's, on my way to the Eastern
[Sh]ore. On *Saturday* I intended to have crossed the bay, but was prevented
[by] the weather. My soul has lately felt much of the power of God, and I
[ha]ve been enabled to trust him with myself, and all my concerns.

Monday, December 1. I left Mr. Gough's, and after crossing the Chesa-
[pe]ake Bay, came in safety, at night, to Mr. Carvill Hinson's; having been
[ab]sent more than four years, though I was the first of our preachers who
[ca]rried the Gospel into this neighbourhood. My heart was thankful to
[G]od for his providential and gracious preservation of me. The next day
[I] went to Kent Island, and preached with some warmth, and then
[re]turned. The two following days, we had profitable times both in preach-
[in]g and class meetings.

Thursday, 4. Preaching and meeting the class at Mr. Edward Gibbs's,
[I] found the Lord had carried on a good work in the souls of many. Blessed
[be] God! my soul was in a comfortable frame, and my body was the
[be]tter for exercise.

Lord's day, 7. Though I spoke with feeling and warmth, yet the people
[w]ere dull both at F. T.'s and Mr. Hinson's. But my own soul was kept
[in] solemn nearness to God, and filled with peace and love. And I am
[pe]rsuaded that my appointment to this circuit is by Divine Providence.[50]

Thursday, 11. Early in the morning I felt a strong desire for more of
[G]od. At Mr. White's[51] my soul was much refreshed in preaching and class
[m]eeting. As the congregations are generally large, and most of the people
[at]tentive, we have a much greater prospect of doing good in this circuit
[th]an in some others.

Saturday, 13. I have been blessed with faith, and hope, and love. Lord,

[50] Neither the *General Minutes* of 1777 nor any other source records Asbury's ap-
[po]intment to Kent Circuit.
[51] Thomas White (1730–95), a magistrate who resided near Whitleysburg, Kent
[Co]unty, Delaware, and in whose home Asbury obtained sanctuary from November 9,
[17]78, to April 20, 1780. This influential family early espoused the cause of Methodism
[an]d gave it standing and its itinerants protection on the Peninsula. (Hallman, *op. cit.*,
[—]; Hurst, *op. cit.*, IV, 189, 190; Stevens, *op. cit.*, III, 61.) For Asbury's tribute to
[Ju]dge White, see *Journal*, Thursday, May 21, 1795.

if troubles are near, be thou nearer still to protect and comfort me; shall I not fear what man can do unto me!

Lord's day, 14. We had a good time in the forenoon, and I found t class in better condition than I expected. In the afternoon the Lord bless me with freedom and solid peace, while preaching at I. S.'s on Eze xxxiii, 11. There is a great prospect of saving souls in this neighbourhoo if preaching can be continued.

Monday, 15. There was a simple, loving people assembled at Mr. S. and many were powerfully wrought on while I enforced the divine co mand, "Seek ye first the kingdom of God, and his righteousness, and these things shall be added unto you." (Matt. vii, 33.) For some days pa my spirit has been rather hurried, and sometimes tempted by Satan; b wonderfully supported by the grace of God. An agreeable prospect ope to my imagination, if Providence should permit me to spend the win in this circuit.

Tuesday, 16. At Mr. White's I met with B. S., who once preached t gospel, and a blessing attended his labours. *Thursday* was a public fa day, and my soul was kept in a degree of peace, but struggled much fo more constant, fervent spirit of devotion.

Having preached at Mr. Gibb's, I rode to Thomas White's, and le tured in the evening, with satisfaction, from the first Psalm. On *Saturd* I was much embarrassed in preaching at Mr. Howard's; and under heavy cloud rode to Hinson's. But on the *Lord's day* my heart was e larged and inflamed with love, while preaching to a large audience on Thess. i, 6–8.

Monday, 22. I preached a funeral sermon near the Nine Bridges,[52] a met with a young minister who had been under Divine impressions: r heart at that time was much united to him; but he afterward became lawyer.

Tuesday, 23. Rode through Chestertown, about thirty miles, to M Hinson's, and enjoyed some rest from a part of my labour. In readi Josephus, I have been led to reflect on the disorder and confusion whi have always overspread the earth, in a greater or less degree, ever since t introduction of sin. Blessed be God! my mind is kept free from all to menting fear: and although my spiritual trials are various and great, l grace is always found sufficient for me. The next day I exhorted the peop who came together, and we spent some time in prayer.

Thursday, 25. Mr. W. read a good sermon, suitable to the day, church. Many people attended at the preaching house, where I declar from 1 Tim. i, 15, "This is a faithful saying, and worthy of all acceptatio that Christ Jesus came into the world to save sinners." The language my heart on this Christmas day was, "Whom have I in heaven but the

[52] This is the present Bridgeton, near the Mason Branch of the Tuckahoe Cree Caroline County, Maryland.

d there is none upon earth that I desire besides thee." The next morning
o I was in the spirit of devotion, and enjoyed the peace of God which
sseth all understanding. Having preached a funeral sermon in the
renoon, I addressed the congregation at Mr. Hinson's, from John i,
, 46.

1778

778

Judge White, Asbury's host, arrested at his home near Dover

CHAPTER SEVEN

Maryland

Thursday, January 1, 1778. Though the weather has been very cold for ~eral days, I have had to ride, sometimes a considerable distance, and ~ach every day. This day I preached a funeral sermon on the death of ~aughter of her who was buried last Friday. My text was, "This year ~u shalt die." Death, like a cruel conqueror, spareth none on whom he ~zeth; but sendeth them to the shades of eternity, without respect to age ~ condition!

~riday, 2. I experienced much of the love of Jesus Christ shed abroad ~ my heart; and through His meritorious mediation, found a delightful ~arness to God. Indeed I have found great happiness during this Christ-~.s season, and have endeavoured to redeem my time by diligent in-~stry. May the Lord keep me steadfast and faithful to the end, and bless ~ with abiding witness that I love him with all my heart! The people ~re lively to-day at Mr. John Chair's, and especially in the class meet-~.

~Lord's day, 4. The word of the Lord went to the hearts of the people ~th cutting power, both at Fredericktown (Cecil County) in the fore-~on, and at Mr. E. Hearn's in the afternoon. But my own mind has ~en under exercises from Satan. On *Monday* my spirit was grieved for ~nt of more spirituality, and more of God.

Delaware

The congregation at Mr. Scotten's was large, but dull. But the peo
seemed quickened both at Mr. Alfrey's on *Tuesday*, and at Mr. Howar
on *Wednesday*.

Thursday, 8. I enjoyed sweet communion with God this morning, a
was enabled to rest my soul on him as my never-failing support. God v
powerfully with us at Mr. Richard Shaw's (near Dover, Delaware)
Friday, and the people felt the weight of Divine truths.

Lord's day, 11. By reason of the snow the congregations were sm
but the Lord gave us his blessing. My soul has possessed a holy cal
and I have found the Lord constantly with me, in a greater or less degr
I have just finished the last volume of Whiston's Josephus,[1] and am s
prised that, at the age of seventy, Mr. Whiston should spend so much
his time in such a dry, chronological work. How much better was M
Baxter employed, when he thought himself near to eternity, meditati
and writing on the Saints' Everlasting Rest.

Tuesday, 13. A solemn, comfortable sense of God rested on my s
this morning; and at Mr. William Thomas's, there was a good congreg
tion of poor, but serious and desirous people. At the widow Jump's,
Wednesday, there was a general melting, and six were received into
society on trial. So there is some ground to hope that this place, which
appeared to be barren, will yet bring forth the fruits of righteousne
Many were also much affected at Mr. Virdenn's:[2] after the service v
ended, two men in arms came up; but they went away without maki
known their design.

Friday, 16. I found great liberty of spirit and speech at Mr. J. Gray
and there met with brother George Shadford.[3]

Lord's day, 18. After discoursing at Mr. A——n's on the parable of
sower, I thought it proper to remove the preaching to another house;
his religious sentiments did not agree with ours.

Tuesday, 20. My soul was kept humble and watchful: and I have be
enabled to put my whole trust in God, on all occasions. Brother Litt
john[4] sent me some account of the work of God; and I am stron
persuaded that he will defend his own cause, and his own people.

Wednesday, 21. The house was not sufficient to contain the congreg

---

[1] The English translation of the works of Flavius Josephus, Jewish historian a
military commander, by W. Whiston.

[2] William Virdenn lived in Kent County, Delaware. During this period Asbury v
in seclusion and spent most of his time in Delaware.

[3] Because the summer and winter spent in Maryland found him "brought t
straight," Shadford may have come to Sussex County, Delaware, to acquaint Asb
with plans for his early departure. (*Memoirs of Mr. Wesley's Missionaries*, compi
by P. P. Sandford, 275.)

[4] This was probably John Littlejohn.

n at the widow Woodland's, and the word went with power to the
rts of the people. *Thursday* was a very cold day, yet many, both rich
I poor, attended at I. K.'s. And the Lord enabled me to show them
inly, to what lengths a man may go in the externals of religion, and be
almost a Christian.

Friday, 23. My heart was fixed on God. I have lately found more sweet-
s and delight than ever before, in reading the Old Testament. And
ving met with Luther's Comment on the Galatians, I have begun to
d that. After riding eight miles to Mr. Z. Hazzard's, I found that I
I eight miles farther to ride, to preach a funeral sermon at Mr. Fowler's:
I the Spirit of the Lord rested upon my soul. Then rode five miles
re, in great peace and love, to lodge at Mr. Masten's.

Maryland

Lord's day, 25. Many attended at Mr. John Randall's in the forenoon,
I God gave me power to speak to their hearts. I then rode ten miles
ther to the meeting house,[5] and preached to about three hundred
emn and attentive people.

Tuesday, 27. Both my body and mind were under a heavy gloom. At-
npting to preach in Quaker Neck,[6] my mind was shut up, and I had no
wer to speak to the people. This is very painful and disagreeable; but
ught to be borne with patience. Physic is necessary sometimes, as well
food.

Wednesday, 28. My soul had peace, and enjoyed sweet rest in God,
er all my trials. May I ever glorify him, even in the fires! Dark pros-
cts, in temporal matter, present themselves to my view. But "the eyes
the Lord are over the righteous"; and he hath promised to be "a wall
fire round about" his Church, "and the glory in the midst of her." I
ached a funeral sermon at the meeting house on 1 Cor. xv, 20: "But
w is Christ risen from the dead, and become the first-fruits of them that
pt." There were many people on this solemn occasion, and my heart
s enlarged towards them.

Lord's day, February 1. We had a good time at Fredericktown in the
enoon, and I found myself at liberty in the afternoon at Mr. Hearn's.
y heart feels nothing contrary to love and purity; and the effect thereof
bundant peace. Troubles stare me in the face; but I have confidence
ards God, and without perplexing myself with anxious care, will leave
events to him.

After listening to a Christmas sermon in St. Paul's Church, Asbury rode to Kent
eting House, later called Hinson's.
Quaker Neck, Kent County, Maryland, is southeast of Pomona and is bordered
Chester River, Langford Creek, and the east fork of Langford Creek.

Delaware

Monday, 2. There was some appearance of a revival at Mr. Scotter and the Lord blessed my soul with liberty, peace, and love. On *Tues* we had a love feast at Lewis Alfrey's,[7] and many delivered their affecti ate testimony of God's goodness and love in Christ Jesus.

Wednesday, 4. I received a strange account, which had been attes on oath by the people who lived in the house but am at a loss to know w judgment to pass upon it. The fact was this: a wicked young fellow, wh friends countenanced the truths of the gospel, was disposed, it seems. curse the preacher; but being deterred from doing it openly, he went the place of worship, with a design to curse him in his heart. It seems was struck with terror, and soon after died. His own brother said, devil pulled his heart out.

Lord's day, 8. After preaching at Mr. Freeny's in the forenooon, I the congregation at Mr. Richard Shaw's, who is a striking instance of power and goodness of God: some time ago he was, like Saul, an poser of the truth, but grace hath changed his heart.

Thursday, 12. The Lord hath supported me in preaching at every pla and this day I came to Thomas White's, and met brother George Sh ford. The martial, threatening aspect of the times has had a great tende to keep me close to God: and my soul has experienced the benefit.

Saturday, 14. I had much peace, but too much company: my time v not spent to the greatest advantage. But the next day I felt the power Divine truths in my own heart, while preaching at Edward White's,[8] fr 1 Pet. i, 13–15.

Monday, 16. Our quarterly meeting began in Mr. White's barn, a numbers attended from different parts. On *Tuesday* morning we held love feast; and the Lord was with us. My heart was powerfully drawn o in preaching on the last three verses of the forty-eighth Psalm.

Wednesday, 18. I set my face unto the Lord God, to seek by prayer a supplications, with fasting. And although brother Shadford had ma fested a desire to leave the continent, he now agreed to abide in country with me awhile longer.

Lord's day, 22. Though the weather was disagreeable, yet many peo attended at Edward White's; and there appeared to be a promising pr pect, amongst the young people especially. I have great hopes that

[7] Lewis Alfrey resided in Fieldboro, Newcastle County, Delaware. In 1779 Alfr name appears as one of Asbury's four colleagues on the Delaware Circuit, bu disappears after that year.

[8] Edward White, M.D., in whose barn the quarterly meeting was held, was a nep of Judge Thomas White. After he moved to Cambridge, Dorchester County, Maryl in 1799, he continued his active interest in Methodism. He was instrumental in en ing Joseph Everett in the itinerancy and provided a house for him in his old age.

rd will show mercy, and make his power known in the family of the
ite's.

Monday, 23. Satan has made several violent pushes at my soul, but he
; not been able even to break my peace. The word was powerfully
)lied to the hearts of the people at Mr. J. Gray's to-day.

Wednesday, 25. After preaching with holy warmth at Mr. Robert
yton's, I met the class, in which were some faithful souls, but others
.t could hardly bear plain dealing. But we must deal plainly and honestly,
)ugh affectionately and tenderly, with all that come in our way, and
)ecially with such as put themselves under our pastoral care. If we seek
please men, unless it is for their good to edification, we are not the
vants of Christ.

Thursday, 26. I spoke closely and pointedly to many poor, ignorant
)ple at the widow Jump's. And on *Friday*, met a dull congregation at
. C.'s.[9]

Monday, March 2. Rode to I. K.'s, on Cedar Creek, an old Presbyterian,
)o keeps his coffin ready made. But both the congregation and the class
med very blind and ignorant in spiritual things.

Thursday, 5. Returned to Thomas White's, with a cold in my head and
inflammation in my throat, which detained me till the *Lord's day*.
t my time was chiefly spent in prayer and reading Flavell's and Hartley's
rks;[10] though no book is equal to the Bible. I have also received much
truction and great blessings of late in reading Mr. Wesley's Works.
ere is a certain spirituality in his works, which I can find in no other
man compositions. And a man who has any taste for true piety, can
rce read a few pages in the writings of that great divine, without imbib-
a greater relish for the pure and simple religion of Jesus Christ, which
herein so Scripturally and rationally explained and defended.

Monday, 9. Samuel Spraggs came in from the upper circuit;[11] but on
)sday both he and George Shadford left me. However, I was easy, for
Lord was with me. And if he will be with me, and bring me to my
ther's house in peace, he shall be my God forever. Yea; let him do with
as seemeth good in his sight—only let him not take his Holy Spirit
m me—and he shall be mine, and I will be his, in time and through
rnity.

Friday, 13. I was under some heaviness of mind. But it was no wonder:
ee thousand miles from home—my friends have left me—I am con-

This was either Cannon or Calloway.

John Flavell (1630–91), English Presbyterian, who wrote *Husbandry Spiritualized*
59). David Hartley (1705–57), English materialistic philosopher.

Asbury refers either to the upper part of Kent Circuit or to Chester Circuit. This
his last recorded interview with Spraggs. That Spraggs passed through the British
s almost immediately is apparent from the records of Old John Street Church, New
k City, which shows that his salary as its pastor began in May, 1778. (Wakeley,
cit., 382; Lednum, *op. cit.*, 206.)

sidered by some as an enemy of the country—every day liable to be seiz
by violence, and abused. However, all this is but a trifle to suffer f
Christ, and the salvation of souls. Lord, stand by me!

Lord's day, 15. My temptations were very heavy, and my ideas we
greatly contracted in preaching, neither was my soul happy as at ma
other times. It requires great resignation for a man to be willing to be la
aside as a broken instrument. But

> "In all my temptations
> He keeps me, to prove
> His utmost salvation—
> His fulness of love."

Monday, 16. I applied myself to the Greek and Latin Testament; b
this is not to me like preaching the Gospel. However, when a man cann
do what he would, he must do what he can.

Wednesday, 18. To make the best of my time in this partial confir
ment, I have attended closely to my studies, spent some time in instructi
the children, and intend to lecture frequently in the family. This day
received information that brother Wrenn[12] was cast into prison at Anr
polis.

Saturday, 21. My spiritual exercises have been various. I have fr
quently been under powerful temptations: but at other times my so
has been serene and comfortable. Much of my time is spent in study. Ar
my desire is, to glorify God in all I do, and spend all I gain in his servi

Lord's day, 22. A large congregation attended at Edward White's wh
I enforced the important inquiry, "What shall it profit a man if he ga
the whole world, and lose his own soul?" A warm, affectionate ze
glowed in my heart, and some of the people were affected. On *Monday*
met with brother Cox,[13] and sent him into the upper circuit, intendi
myself to abide here for a season till the storm is abated.

Wednesday, 25. Blessed be God! his providence hath cast my lot in
quiet, agreeable family; where I can make the best improvement of n
time in study and devotion. Brother Cooper[14] came from below, and v
had a meeting at Edward White's, where some were deeply cut to t
heart by the two-edged sword of the word.

---

[12] Both Robert Wooster and William Wrenn underwent persecution in Annapolis.
Wooster had gone to the "Redstone Country" as early as 1777, which is a dubic
assertion made by some, then Asbury's reference is to Wrenn. (Lednum, *op. cit.*, 2C
Smeltzer, *op. cit.*, 40, 41.)

[13] Philip Cox (*d.* 1793), from England, served as a supply before entering the rar
of the regular itinerants. For accounts of his evangelistic successes and his career
one of the Book Stewards, see *The Arminian Magazine,* London, XI, 1781, 486; *T
Arminian Magazine,* Philadelphia, II, 1790, 91; Phœbus, *op. cit.,* 258.

[14] This was probably John Cooper, a native of Caroline County, Maryland, who h
arrived from Sussex Circuit. (Lednum, *op. cit.,* 86; Wright: *Life and Labors of Jar
Quinn,* 34, 41, 42; *General Minutes,* I, 33.)

·iday, 27. The grace of God is a sufficient support, while I bear the
oach of men, and am rewarded with evil for all the good which I have
e, and desired to do for mankind. I want for no temporal convenience,
endeavour to improve my time by devotion and study; but all this
ıot give full satisfaction, while it is not in my power to labour more for
l in seeking the salvation of souls. But I am strongly persuaded that
ine Providence will bring about a change before long.

hursday, April 2. This night we had a scene of trouble in the family.
friend Mr. Thomas White was taken away,[15] and his wife and family
in great distress of mind. The next day I sought the interposition of
l by fasting and prayer.

aturday, 4. This was a day of much Divine power and love to my soul.
ıs left alone, and spent part of every hour in prayer; and Christ was
: and very precious. The next day I preached with great solemnity at
vard White's, on 2 Cor. vi, 20; and on *Monday* found freedom to
·e. After riding about fifteen miles, I accidentally stopped at a house
re a corpse was going to be buried, and had an opportunity of ad-
·sing a number of immortal souls. I then rode on through a lonesome,
.ous-road, like Abraham, not knowing whither I went: but weary and
·ell, I found a shelter late at night; and there I intended to rest till
vidence should direct my way. This was something like the faithful
·ts of old times, mentioned in Heb. xi: "They wandered about in sheep-
.s and goat-skins, being destitute, afflicted, tormented: (of whom the
ld was not worthy:) they wandered in deserts, and in mountains, and
·ens and caves of the earth." Though it must be acknowledged their
·s far exceeded.

Maryland

uesday, 7. My soul was kept in peace; and I spent much of my time
·ading the Bible and the Greek Testament. Surely God will stand by
deliver me! I have none other on whom I can depend. And he knows
· what intention and for what purposes I came into this distant and
·nge land, and what little I have suffered for his cause. At night a report
· spread which inclined me to think it would be most prudent for me to
·e the next day. Accordingly I set out after dinner, and lay in a swamp

A succession of pro-Tory manifestations, such as Wesley's *Calm Address*, the
.iiting of a so-called Tory company by Chauncey Clowe, a former Methodist, the
partisan sermons by Rodda and Rankin, and now the reception of the remaining
·ish missionary into White's home, stimulated the fury that led to the arrest and
· isonment of the judge. Among members of the White family who witnessed the
·essing scene was Samuel White, age eight, who was to attend Cokesbury College
· serve as a senator from Delaware, 1801–9. (Bangs: *Life of the Rev. Freeborn
·ettson,* 64, 65; *Biographical Directory of the American Congress,* 1774–1927, 1692;
·man, *op. cit.,* 123.)

till about sunset; but was then kindly taken in by a friend. My soul
been greatly humbled and blessed under these difficulties, and I thou
myself like some of the old prophets, who were concealed in time
public distress.

Thursday, 9. I promised God, that if he would lift me up, I would
wholly his, and spend as much time in returning thanks as I have sp
in seeking his protection,—which has been some part of every hour.
soul has been much comforted in reading J. Alleine's Letters,[16] which
wrote in prison. I felt strong confidence in God, that he would deliver
being conscious that I sought neither riches nor honour, and that wh
suffered was for the sake of his spiritual Church, and the salvation of
fellow-men. I was informed that brother Joseph Hartley was apprehen
last *Lord's day* in Queen Annes (County). May the Lord strengthen
support him, while he suffers for righteousness' sake! He shall be faithf
remembered by me in my addresses to the throne of grace. This ever
I was called upon to visit a person in distress of mind; and the Lord g
him rest for his soul. Perhaps Providence cast my lot in this place for
assistance of this man.

Friday, 10. My heart was kept pure, and panting after God, thoug
was in some sense a prisoner, and under the necessity of being concea
rather than sacrifice the peace of my conscience, and offend my God
my Lord, guide thy poor pilgrim through the rugged ways of this ungo
and dangerous world! And if I suffer with Christ here, may I finally re
with him in glory!

> "Who suffer with our Master here,
> We shall before his face appear,
>   And by his side sit down;
> To patient faith the prize is sure;
> And all that to the end endure
>   The cross, shall wear the crown."

My practice is, to keep close to God in prayer, and spend a part of ev
hour, when awake, in that exercise. I have lately begun to read
Wesley's Notes again; and have always found both them and his Serm
to be made an especial blessing to my soul. My exercises are very deep
various. The Lord makes great discoveries of my defects and sh
comings in many points. He melts my heart into humility and tendern
he graciously draws me nearer and nearer to himself; and fills me with
spirit of holy love.

Saturday, 11. God was my portion, and my soul rested in him. B
was at a loss to know what to do: my time was useless in respect to oth
though I carefully improved it for my own spiritual advantage, which
some years past, had been in a degree neglected, on account of my g

---

[16] This was Joseph Alleine, author of *Directions for a Thorough Conversation*
God, and *An Alarm to Unawakened Sinners* (1672).

ntion to the souls of others. And I know not what to determine—
:ther to deliver myself into the hands of men, to embrace the first
ortunity to depart, or to wait till Providence shall further direct.
: reason of this retirement was as follows.[17] From *March* 10, 1778, on
scientious principles I was a non-juror, and could not preach in the
:e of Maryland; and therefore withdrew to the Delaware State, where
clergy were not required to take the State oath: though, with a clear
science, I could have taken the oath of the Delaware State, had it been
:uired; and would have done it, had I not been prevented by a tender
 of hurting the scrupulous consciences of others. Saint Paul saith,
hen ye sin so against the brethren, and wound their weak conscience,
in against Christ." (1 Cor. viii, 12.)

ord's day, 12. This was one of my dumb and silent Sabbaths, and was
it in fasting and prayer, that the Lord may turn again my captivity.
 soul was greatly humbled, and not a little comforted in waiting before
1. I lament that part of the Lord's flock is carried away captive; but
e that those who remain in Zion will be holiness to the Lord, and found
ong the living in Jerusalem.

Ionday, 13. I formerly thought it would be death to me to keep silence
n declaring the word of God; but now I am in a measure contented,
 hope to see a day of liberty once again. It appears to be the will of
1 that I should be silent for a season, to prepare me for further useful-
s hereafter. Therefore my time shall be employed to the best advantage.

uesday, 14. I am not yet forsaken of all, but am happy in the family
re I stay, and my soul is fixed on God. I have a private chamber for
asylum, where I comfort myself in God, and spend my time in prayer,
litation, and reading. The next day brother John Fogwell[18] held a
lic meeting: he appeared to be a well-meaning, good man; and who
h despised the day of small things?

hursday, 16. My soul was blessed with peace; but I earnestly desire to
nore spiritual in all my thoughts, words, and actions.

riday, 17. Being Good Friday, I devoted myself to fasting and prayer.
w many such days have I spent in addressing large congregations on
 mournful subject of our blessed Lord's crucifixion; but am now deed of the privilege of making a public improvement of the day. I must
lown and weep, when I remember Zion, and the years of God's right
d. O! how I long to see his goings in the sanctuary, as in times past!

Asbury's retirement was not as complete as early historians believed. (For his own
unt of the latitude of his confinement, see Asbury's letter to Zachariah Myles,
ust 16, 1804.)

John Fogwell, who was transformed from a drunkard to an ardent Christian under
influence of a blind evangelist, a Mrs. Rogers, invited William Watters to preach
is home in 1773. It was in Fogwell's home near Sudlersville, Queen Annes County,
 Asbury took refuge from April 6–29, 1778. (Watters, *op. cit.*, 36, 37; Lednum,
it., 115, 162; Hallman, *op. cit.*, 12, 282, 322.)

Return, O Lord, to the many thousands of Israel, and cause us to reje
according to the days in which we have seen trouble! I now enjo
favourable opportunity of taking a circumstantial review of my past l
But alas! how am I shamed, and covered with blushing before God.
soul is bowed in awful reverence and melting humility before the me
seat. My intention has been pure, as far as I can judge; but on accoun
my imperfections, if there were no Mediator, there could be no hop
mercy. But, blessed be God, I can come with humble boldness to
throne of grace, knowing "that we have a High Priest that can be touc
with the feeling of our infirmities; who was in all points tempted like
we are, yet without sin." I hope to learn obedience by the things I suf
and walk more watchfully and piously before God for the time
come.

Saturday, 18. I labour to make the best use of my precious time; a
hope to be better prepared for future service on earth, or for eternal
vice in heaven. I bear our dear, suffering friends, on my heart.

Lord's day, 19. Another solitary Sabbath. Ezekiel's portion is mine—
be dumb for a season. But the Lord gives me patience, and supports
under it. The family amongst whom my lot is cast use me with g
kindness; and may the Lord show kindness to them according to all t
they have done unto me!

Monday, 20. Reading the Revelation, with Mr. Wesley's Notes,
made a particular blessing to my soul; but my conscience checked
severely for not reading more frequently that part of the sacred can
seeing such a blessing is pronounced on them that read and understand
But I intend for the future, if time and health will permit, to read
chapter in it every day.

Tuesday, 21. I purposed in my own mind, to spend ten minutes out
every hour, when awake, in the duty of prayer. May the Lord help me
pay all the vows which my heart hath uttered, and my mouth hath spo
in the time of trouble!

Wednesday, 22. I finished Mr. Wesley's Notes on the New Testame
and began to read Doddridge's Rise and Progress;[19] but am not so dec
ated with holy love as the temple of God should be. I am reconciled to
condition, and in faith and prayer commit all events to my Divine P
tector. This is an excellent season for dressing my own vineyard.

Thursday, 23. God was near, and my heart was exceedingly humb
before him. I finished Doddridge, and was pleased, instructed, and affec
thereby. I think an abridgment of this book would be of great service
our societies.

Friday, 24. I began reading honest John Bunyan's Holy War,[20] and

---

[19] Philip Doddridge (1702–51), English dissenting minister, was the author of
Rise and Progress of Religion in the Soul (1745).

[20] *The Holy War* (1682), by John Bunyan (*d.* 1688).

was kept in peace, but earnestly desirous of every branch and degree
erfect love. Holiness is far preferable to the greatest wisdom.
ord's day, 26. I was still confined and obliged to keep silence; but
nt much of the day in reading the Revelation, with Mr. Wesley's Notes
n it. As this Revelation was given on the Lord's day, what can be a
re proper subject for meditation on that day? Devoting much of my
e to the exercise of prayer, I pray frequently for my dear parents and
nds, as well as for myself.

Delaware

Vednesday, 29. Ventured to leave my asylum; and under the special
vidence of God, came safe to my old abode;[21] where I purpose spend-
these perilous days in retirement, devotion, and study. I want for
hing but more holiness, and wonder at the love and care of Almighty
d, towards such a dead dog as I am. My spirit was greatly comforted
Psalm cvi, 10: "He saved them from the hand of him that hated them:
redeemed them from the hand of the enemy."

riday, May 1. The minds of the people are so confused, and filled with
spirit and troubles of the times, that it does not appear to me as if God
uired me to treat with them on spiritual and eternal subjects, till they
, with some considerate calmness, pay attention to those momentous
tters. I have lately been grievously haunted by the temptations of
an; but my desire is to die rather than live to sin against God. Lord,
nd by me in the day of trial, and every moment support my feeble soul!
Saturday also my mind was much harassed by my spiritual adversary;
my study and devotion were interrupted, so that I could do but little
er for God or myself.

ord's day, 3. My mind was strangely twisted and tortured, not know-
what to do. It seems I know not how to fight, nor how to fly: but I
persuaded there will be a speedy change in the wheel of Providence,
er prosperous or adverse. Others are now free, but I am bound. Read-
at present no other books on the Lord's days, I have lately read the
velation, with Mr. Wesley's Notes, three times through.

Monday, 4. Satan hath a desire to destroy, or at least, to disturb my
l. But I pray mightily to God against him. O that he may rebuke the
pter, and make a way for my escape!

On Wednesday my temptations were so violent, that it seemed as if all
infernal powers were combined to attack my soul. Like Elijah, when

This abode was the home of Judge Thomas White. Just when the legal phases of
te's persecution ended is not known; but Freeborn Garrettson, who visited Asbury
White's home, says, "None but the Lord and himself (White) knew what he suffered
twelve months." (Bangs, *op. cit.*, 65.)

persecuted by Jezebel, I was ready to request for myself that I might
However, about noon the storm abated, and my soul was calm. I had
as though I could neither pray nor read; but the Lord blessed my trou
soul while endeavouring to pray with brother Edward White. My temp
tions have been such as I never experienced before in the course of my
But God will help me, and I shall yet praise him! Both *Friday* and *Sa*
day my spiritual enemies were upon me, but my soul had more strer
from the Lord. My practice is, to spend some part of every hour in pra
Lord, "what is man, that thou art mindful of him? and the son of m
that thou visitest him?" On *Saturday* brother White came home, a:
answer to prayer. On the *Lord's day* I read the Revelation three times o
and experienced great sweetness in my soul, both in reading and far
exercises.

Monday, 11. My mind was deeply exercised, not knowing what to
If the Lord delivers me, I shall be bound to praise him: if I had a thous
hearts and tongues, and a million of years to live, all would be insuffic
for paying the mighty debt of praise. Time, and language, and number:
fail in point of praise and adoration for the unmerited mercies of a graci
God.

> "Praise ye the Lord, ye immortal choirs,
>   That fill the realms above;
> Praise Him who form'd you of his fires,
>   And feeds you with his love."

Tuesday, 12. My exercises were still grievous; but I am persuaded t
all these trials will contribute to the spiritual advantage of my s
Temptations and prayer, as one observes, qualify a Gospel minister
his work. But I am ready to ask, as one of old, "Lord, are there few t
be saved?" May God vouchsafe to help and deliver his few afflicted peop

Wednesday, 13. I met a small congregation, and my soul was blessec
speaking to the people, as it usually is on such occasions. O my G
when wilt thou turn again my captivity? Surely Jacob shall rejoice, a
Israel shall be glad.

Thursday, 14. I still attend to prayer, study, and teaching the childr
but cannot be fully satisfied without preaching the Gospel, which appe
to be my peculiar province. Though I find more relish for the word of G
and greater sweetness in reading it, than ever before.

Friday, 15. My soul was, for the most part, in peace; though at ti
my own trials and the trials of others produced strong agonies of mi
But strengthened with Divine might, I am able to oppose the tempte
his most violent assaults, and am brought off more than conqueror.
study of the Holy Scriptures affords me great pleasure. Lord, help me
dig into the Gospel field as for hidden treasure!

Saturday, 16. It may be observed that two of our preachers have b
apprehended, rather than do violence to conscience; and the men

PLACES VISITED BY

Francis Asbury

— IN —

DELAWARE

PENNSYLVANIA

MARYLAND

DELAWARE BAY

MARYLAND

Cloud's C
Mount Pleasant
Wilmington
New Castle
Salem C
Forrest C
Green's C
Fartadd's M
Barratt's C
Todd's C
Hazzard
Quakertown
Johnstown
Lewis
Lewes
Brown's C
Lacey
Williams
Line C
Sound C

whom they were both taken, were dangerously wounded within a
weeks after they had laid hands upon them. I am now resigned to
confinement, and am persuaded that God, by his providence, will sl
me when and which way to go.

Lord's day, 17. As a congregation was collected to hear the wor
ventured to preach, and found my soul much drawn out both in speal
to God and the people. Perhaps this was a token of future enlargen
and usefulness.

Monday, 18. My spirit was oppressed by heavy temptations.
preachers and people began to convene for the quarterly meeting, wl
was to begin the next day.

Tuesday, 19. Brother Cox began our quarterly meeting, and the
preached with tender sensibility and warm affection a humiliation sern
on Joel ii, 16–18: "Gather the people, sanctify the congregation, assen
the elders, gather the children, and those that suck the breasts; let
bridegroom go forth to his chamber, and the bride out of her closet.
the priests, the ministers of the Lord, weep between the porch and
altar, and let them say, Spare thy people, O Lord, and give not thy heri
to reproach, that the heathen should rule over them: wherefore she
they say among the people, Where is their God? Then will the Lor
jealous for his land, and pity his people." The hearts of the people v
greatly melted under the word: and the power of the Lord was with u
the afternoon also. We were quiet and undisturbed; and I hope the w
will take root in the hearts of some who were present. On *Wednesday* tl
was so much company about me, that I could not keep in my usual
desirable track of walking with God.

Thursday, 21. My mind was somewhat dissipated. A young won
who had been awakened by the instrumentality of Captain Webb,
deprived of the means of grace for about four years, and had thought
could never be happy unless among the Methodists, was now brough
God by faith in Jesus Christ, and found peace in her soul. Another pe
was also brought into deep distress for an interest in Christ about
same time. Our family meetings are now attended with great power.

Friday, 22. Satan worried my mind with his temptations; but at n
we joined the two families together for worship, and the Spirit of
Lord was with us in power.

Saturday, 23. I set this day apart for fasting and prayer, especiall
behalf of brother Thomas White. My soul was comforted to hear
Mrs. P., near seventy years of age, knew by experience that she coul
born again, though she was old. This week the Lord has given me twc
the children of my bonds.

Monday, 25. Thomas White went back to have his case determined.
left his family in much distress of mind. I endeavoured to minister s
comfort to them: but in respect to myself, everything appeared tc

ler a cloud; so that I knew not, as yet, what the Lord would be pleased
lo with me. I now began to read Barclay's Apology,[22] and to make some
ctures.

riday, 29. I spent much of the forenoon in prayer, and read through the
ok of Job: but was sorely tempted by the devil. My spiritual trials have
n heavier and more grievous of late, than I have ever experienced before
ll the course of my pilgrimage. They seem to indicate to me, that I shall
e my soul, or lose my life, or live for some peculiar usefulness in the
urch of Christ. On *Saturday* Mr. Hartley came to see me; and I ven-
ed to set out for Mr. Williams';[23] but having been so long unaccustomed
riding, my body was exceedingly fatigued. However, my soul was much
reshed in meeting the people there.

Lord's day, 31. My body was indisposed: but many people came to-
her to hear the word of God: and as there had been some little disorders
ong them, I discoursed on 2 Tim. ii, 19, "Nevertheless, the foundation
God standeth sure, having this seal, the Lord knoweth them that are
. And, let every one that nameth the name of Christ depart from ini-
ty." We had a profitable time; and in the afternoon I went to hear Mr.
who appeared to be a well-meaning, though a weak man.

Monday, June 1. I rode about twenty miles and came home very unwell,
l continued for several days afflicted with a fever and boils; but my
l was peaceably stayed on the Lord, in the midst of various and heavy
ls both of body and mind.

Lord's day, 7. Being Whitsunday, I went to the barn,[24] weak as I was,
l preached on Rom. viii, 7–9. My heart was enlarged, and the people
re greatly melted and alarmed; and many of them felt the gracious
wings of the Father. But alas! I am as gold in the furnace! though I
st not think it strange concerning the fiery trial, which is to try me,
though some strange thing had happened unto me. In my patience may
ossess my soul: and the Lord, in his own time, will deliver me. Surely,
en this mortal shall put on immortality, then shall there be an eternal
y without a cloud, ease without pain, and joy without any mixture of
row! I preached again in the afternoon, and found great liberty in my
rit. Peradventure, the Lord will, in this barren place, raise up a seed to
ve him.

Wednesday, 10. I had both great peace and heavy trials; but have cause
complain of the want of more seriousness and devotion to God. I find
: more pious part of the people called Quakers, are exerting themselves

---

[2] Robert Barclay (1648–90), a Scot who was a member of the Society of Friends and
h William Penn was one of the proprietors of East New Jersey, wrote *Apology for
True Christian Divinity*.

[3] This was probably Reynear Williams, who lived south of Milford, Sussex County,
laware.

[4] This was Edward White's barn.

for the liberation of the slaves. This is a very laudable design; and what
Methodists must come to, or, I fear, the Lord will depart from them. I
there is cause to presume, that some are more intent on promoting
freedom of their bodies, than the freedom of their souls; without wh
they must be the vassals of Satan in eternal fire.

Saturday, 13. For a few days past my mind has been variously agitat
at certain times, by that restless, fallen spirit, who so often attempts
break my peace; but my soul has been kept by the same omnipote
gracious arm which has been so frequently displayed in my behalf. I w
to Reynear Williams', where all our souls were under the softening
fluence of Divine grace in the class meeting. With animation of spiri
preached twice on the *Lord's day*, to large congregations. As the Gos
of Jesus Christ meets with indulgence in this free State, I entertain a hc
that it will prove a general blessing to the inhabitants thereof; and th
Delaware will become as the garden of the Lord, filled with plants of
own planting.

Monday, 15. The congregation was large at Mr. K.'s, but showed
much appearance of spiritual insensibility. I have lately been surpris
and self reproved, for not feeling the same earnest desire that the wo
might profit the hearers, after it was delivered, as I have felt before
preaching began. My soul was deeply engaged with the Lord, at this tir
that the word might prove a permanent blessing. On *Tuesday* I heard N
Thorne preach a funeral sermon, which was well put together, but
calculated to reach the hearts of the people.

Thursday, 18. My trials, as usual, have been great, but the Lord has
left me comfortless. About this time it was currently reported, that
treaty of peace was like to take place.[25] I thought this would have bee
singular blessing, especially as it would have given the Gospel a f
course through the land. But my hope is, through grace, that I shall
found prepared for all changes and circumstances.

Lord's day, 21. I was enabled to press upon the consciences of
people, with great pungency, the awful declaration of God in Amos iv,
"I have overthrown some of you, as God overthrew Sodom and Gom
rah, and ye were as a firebrand plucked out of the burning: yet have
not returned unto me, saith the Lord." Some felt the word preached; a
at the class meeting the hearts of the society were melted.

Saturday, 27. We have had some refreshing times, both in our pub
and society meetings, through the course of this week; and my own so
has sometimes been greatly drawn out in affectionate devotion; but
other times sorely tempted by the enemy. We have had a very alarmi

[25] Reference is probably to the hopes aroused when on June 13, 1778, a copy dra
up by Lord North's commissioners proposing cessation of hostilities was received
Congress and the subsequent arrival of the commissioners in Philadelphia. (Howla
Annals of North America, 374.)

ught in this part of the country. Last *Friday,* we fasted, and prayed
t the Lord might water the earth: but though we had a fine shower, it
not seem to cover much more than the two adjacent farms.

Lord's day, 28. In the forenoon, I preached under an oak, on "Him
t cometh unto me, I will in no wise cast out;" but the people seemed
moved: though in the afternoon they were a little roused by that awful
eatening, Psalm ix, 17: "The wicked shall be turned into hell, and all
nations that forget God." Yet there seems to be a judicial hardness of
rt amongst many of the people. There was a large congregation at Mr.
w's on *Monday,* but they also were under the influence of a spiritual
por. My mind has been much agitated; and at present my prospect of
cess is but gloomy. Sometimes I have been afraid that I have done
ng in retiring from the work; though, as far as I can judge, the glory
God and the prosperity of his Church, were my chief objects.

Tuesday, 30. Brother Freeborn Garrettson[26] came to see me; and on
day the Lord sent us a plentiful rain after the threatening drought.

Saturday, July 4. I lamented my want of more spiritual life and Divine
mation; neither did I find myself so quietly and perfectly resigned to the
sent dispensations of Providence, as is necessary to keep my soul in
disturbed peace, and promote my advancement in all the beauty of
iness.

Lord's day, 5. The Lord favoured me with great assistance in preaching
ee times to-day; and at Mr. Calloway's, in the forenoon, we had a
y solemn season.

Tuesday, 7. It has been matter of grief to me, that I have not been more
ly and heavenly in all the powers of my soul. And it will be very wonder-
if my soul should be saved, after so many external trials, and such
ernal assaults from the banded powers of darkness. Death and destruc-
n seem to threaten me on every side; but,

> "Thou know'st the pains thy servants feel;
> Thou hear'st thy children's cry;
> And their best wishes to fulfil,
> Thy grace is ever nigh."

Wednesday, 8. My exercises were heavy, but I had some liberty in
aching, and there were some happy souls who possessed the spirit of
yer.

Friday, 10. Satan so beset me by different means, that it seemed as if I
ld do little else but endeavour to pray.

Saturday, 11. I rode to W. and found that Mr. C. had taken away
out half the society, and was gone to set up a church for himself. But
et those who were willing to abide with us, and preached twice on the
rd's day, perhaps to some purpose.

At the conference of May 20, 1778, Freeborn Garrettson had been appointed to
Kent Circuit, which then included the eastern shore of Maryland and Delaware.

Monday, 13. Preaching in Slaughter's Neck,[27] there appeared to be so impediment in the family: I therefore removed the preaching, and fou the children were openly wicked. We shall now meet the people at N Shockleys', whose family appears serious; and I hope the work of G will go on in this neighbourhood. The people were all attention at Richards' on *Wednesday*, but not much affected. On *Thursday* I preach at Boyer's,[28] and then returned to brother Thomas White's.

Saturday, 18. I laid a plan for myself to travel and preach nine days two weeks. This was one step towards my former regularity in what a pears to me as my duty, my element, and my delight. On the *Lord's* (I met a class in the morning, and then preached twice, with earnestness a affection, to large, attentive, and serious congregations. My spirit v afterward refreshed in the company of some of my old friends.

Monday, 20. My company being gone, my soul returned to its us exercises; and I was led to reflect on the fluctuating state of human life continual circle in which the soul can find no permanent centre to upon! We shall never have perfect rest till we come to the holy mount of the Lord.

Tuesday, 21. My soul keeps close to God in prayer, meditation, a reading. My internal exercises are very great, and I see no other way conquer and escape, but by resisting my malignant foe. On *Thursda* went about twenty miles to preach at one Twyford's,[29] in Sussex: th were about two hundred people who appeared to be kind, and willing receive instruction; and I was enabled to fix their attention, though th were ignorant and wild.

Maryland

I then rode ten miles on my way back to visit Joshua Barwick's,[30] who v in deep distress of soul. On *Saturday* my mind was sweetly stayed on G after riding about fifty miles since *Thursday*, seeking to bring poor w dering souls to the fold of Christ. I hope to travel and preach as long I live.

Lord's day, 26. My own soul was much enlarged while enforcing Ro x, 15, 16; though the hearts of the audience appeared to be proof agai

[27] Slaughter's Neck is located between Milford and Lewes, Sussex County, Delawa Among the pioneer Methodists were the Stradley, Richards, and Shockley famil The Zion Meeting House, which is located near the site of the former Hickman Me ing House, was rebuilt in 1945. (Hallman, *op. cit.*, 278.)

[28] See Hallam, *op. cit.*, 106.

[29] This was Charles Twyford, whose home was near Bridgeville, Sussex Cour Delaware.

[30] Joshua Barwick lived ten miles west, near Burrsville, Caroline County, Maryla Asbury spelled his name "Barack" when he preached his funeral sermon Octo 16, 1787.

: power of the word. Thus it is that the preaching of the gospel is too
en as seed sown in stony ground: the hearers do not prepare their
arts by prayer and meditation, and the Almighty does not destroy their
oral agency, to save them by irresistible grace; and therefore the word
nich was intended to be a "savour of life unto life," proves, by their
use of preventing grace, "a savour of death unto death."

Monday, 27. I am still in possession of the inestimable pearl; Christ
des in me, the hope of glory.

> "In the heavenly Lamb,
> Thrice happy I am,
> And my heart doth rejoice at the sound of his name."

e congregation to-day at Kennard's were dull and insensible, but in
: class meeting at Gilbert Simmon's we had a melting time.

Delaware

It was currently reported about this time that some of the British troops
ere so blocked up, that there was very little probability of their escape.
ad thus it is with the fallen spirits of mankind; having forfeited the favour
d protection of their offended Creator, they are environed by the in-
sible, malignant angels, who kept not their first estate, desirous to
volve the human race in their own condemnation and misery. But God,
oved with compassion towards our helpless race, has made it *possible*
at we may escape through the redemption that is in Jesus Christ. But
 melancholy thought! men are more inclined to listen to the voice of
eir enemies, than to the voice of their Divine Friend. Instead of putting
. the whole armour of God, and resisting the devil that he may flee from
em, they arm themselves against all the warnings of their gracious
eator, and resist the motions of his Holy Spirit, till they have filled up
e measure of their iniquity, and have their portion appointed with devils
d damned spirits. On *Wednesday* my soul was deeply exercised in seek-
g after more of the Divine nature. I long to be made perfect in love, to
ve all my heart wrapped up in Christ Jesus, to have my conversation in
aven, and to be completely prepared for every duty, and every suffering
at may lie before me! We had a lecture in the evening at Thomas
hite's, and the hearts of some were moved and melted by the power of
od. I begin to think it is my duty to abide for a season in this state; and
ve great hopes that the Lord will pour out his Spirit, and favour us with
revival of pure and vital piety.

Saturday, August 1. I went into the Fork: and on the *Lord's day*
eached at Mr. W. Ross's, and at Mr. Robert Layton's. The congrega-
ons were attentive and affected; so that, although they are rude and
polished, yet God is able, even of these unseemly stones, to raise up

children unto Abraham. Being informed that Mrs. James Peterkin v
dangerously ill, I rode about twenty miles to see her, arrived at the ho
about nine o'clock and found her confident and happy in the love of G
—a miracle of saving grace. But the power and the glory of this and
every other good work, belongs unto the Lord.

Tuesday, 4. We had a large congregation, and the presence and pov
of God were with us, while I enforced, on a funeral occasion: "Rememl
now thy Creator in the days of thy youth, while the evil days come n
nor the years draw nigh when thou shalt say, I have no pleasure
them."

Thursday, 6. After proclaiming the great salvation at Jessup's,[31] I ro
back to visit Mrs. Peterkin again; and found her still happy in God, a
patient under her affliction.

Lord's day, 9. Having been informed that some of the people were
danger of being led aside by impressions and dreams, and a weak-head
man having already drawn off a few simple souls, I thought it expedi
to urge upon them Isaiah viii, 20: "To the law and to the testimony: if th
speak not according to this word, it is because there is no light in then
While in theory, experience, and practice, we keep close to the writ
word of God, we are safe. And if an angel from heaven preach any ot
gospel, saith St. Paul, "Let him be accursed." (Gal. i, 8.)

Dreams may arise from various causes; and even diabolical impressic
may sometimes resemble those made by the Spirit of God. And it
evident that all such impressions as have a tendency to effect divisions,
interrupt the peace of the Church, to draw us off from any revealed du
or to make us contented in a lukewarm and careless state, cannot co
from God, because they are contrary to the revealed dictates of the H
Spirit—and the Spirit of truth cannot contradict itself. Therefore
impressions, dreams, visions, &c., should be brought to the standard
the Holy Scriptures, and if they do not perfectly correspond therewi
they should be rejected.

Monday, 10. At Mr. S.'s[32] there was an ignorant, hardened compa
who had heard much preaching, but, I fear, to bad purpose. May t
hammer of the word, in the hand of Omnipotent Mercy, break the
rocks into pieces! In the evening I returned to Reynear Williams'; a
was under painful exercises of soul the next day. Such views of my wa
of more of the Divine nature, and such a clear discovery of the wickedne
and obstinacy of the people, were opened to my mind, that my spi
was brought down to the dust before the Lord, and my heart poured c
streams of humble, earnest prayer. The words of the apostle are cc
tinually verified: "We must through much tribulation enter into the kir
dom of God." (Acts xiv, 22.) Such gracious discoveries as break up t

---

[31] At Jessup's, Asbury was in Caroline County, Maryland, for a single service.
[32] This was either Shaw or Shockley.

:at deep of the human heart, are painful, but profitable. Blessed be God,
r illuminating, quickening, sanctifying, and strengthening grace!

Thursday, 13. A sense of the Divine presence penetrated my soul, and
vas deeply humbled before the Lord; but was at the same time in the
rnace of temptations, and by all my prayers and efforts could not obtain
liverance from them. No doubt but it was then needful that I should be
heaviness through such manifold temptations. But the Lord knoweth
w and when to deliver. On *Friday* my soul was in peace, and I felt willing
die, rather than ever yield to temptation and sin against my God.

Lord's day, 16. After preaching at Mr. Brown's[33] in the Fork, I enforced
:ts xiii, 40, 41, at Robert Layton's, where many people were affected,
d about twelve were taken as probationers into the society. On *Monday*,
Mr. Flower's, I spoke with spiritual enlargement to a poor, ignorant
ngregation; and there were many persons much affected on *Tuesday* at
aarles Twyford's. It seemed as if the Lord was working on their willing
arts, to prepare them for his Church militant below, and for his Church
umphant above.

Though my body is feeble, and the weather is very warm, yet the Lord
pports me, and makes my labours successful.

> "How do thy mercies close me round!
> Forever be thy Name adored;
> I blush in all things to abound;
> The servant is above his Lord."

Thursday, 27. After preaching at the widow Jump's, I returned to Mr.
hite's; and was visited by my old friends, William Lynch and William
oore.

Lord's day, 30. For several days past I was extremely ill with a vomiting,
:., and was frequently delirious. It was a very heavy season of affliction;
t the Lord looked upon me in my trouble, and this day he granted me
me relief. Glory be given to God! my fever was greatly abated.

Lord's day, September 6. I am still unable to preach the glad tidings of
vation to my fellow-men. And my mind has been variously exercised
ough the past week: sometimes grieved at spending my time to so little
rpose; at other times deeply engaged for more inward religion, and for
ore of God.

Lord's day, 13. Another week has passed without public labour, except
e prayer meeting. But my soul has enjoyed a great degree of Divine
ace and consolation. Especially on last *Thursday*, my soul was favoured
th deep communion with God. How earnestly do I long for a more

---

³ White Brown, a nephew of Thomas White of Delaware, where Asbury stayed
·ing the Revolutionary War, lived "in the Forks" in Sussex County, Delaware.
bury preached in his home a number of times. Early in the nineteenth century Mr.
·wn emigrated to Ohio, where Asbury again visited him. (See *Journal* entry for
·tember 23, 1803, and note under September 8, 1805.)

holy and a closer walk with God—to have every thought devoted to
blessed Jesus! I ventured to preach to-day on Heb. xiii, 13, when my sp
was at liberty, and the people were affected.

Tuesday, 15. This was a day of peculiar temptations. My trials were s
as I do not remember to have experienced before; and for some tim
seemed as if I scarcely knew whether to fight or fly. My usefulness
peared to be cut off; I saw myself pent up in a corner; my body in a m
ner worn out; my English brethren gone, so that I had no one to cons
and every surrounding object and circumstance wore a gloomy asp
Lord, must I thus pine away, and quench the light of Israel? No: thou
he slay me, yet will I trust him.

> "Though in the paths of death I tread,
> With gloomy horrors overspread,
> My steadfast heart shall fear no ill,
> For thou, O Lord, art with me still:
> Thy friendly crook shall give me aid,
> And guide me through the dreadful shade."

Wednesday, 16. My body felt better, and my mind had rest. I could
pose myself in Christ Jesus; and felt a lively hope that through all
difficulties the Lord will finally conduct me to eternal rest.

Thursday, 17. While riding on the road, my soul was deeply affec
with a powerful, solemn sense of a present and gracious God. W
ecstatic sensations must be enjoyed in heaven, where a much deeper se
of the Divine presence is eternally enjoyed, without interruption
cessation! Well might St. Paul say, "To die is gain." Here our co
munion with the Deity is but partial and very imperfect: we dwell in sh
of infirmity—exposed to the assaults of wicked spirits, and surround
with countless numbers of amusing, empty objects; by which means
are in continual danger of forgetting God, or of being too well satisf
without the fruition of him.

I called to see Mr. S., and his wife,[34] who was sick, and I introduce
conversation on the benefit of affliction, as a proper means to excite
consideration, and humble us for our past sins. But she began to s
Whom the Lord loveth he chasteneth; and seemed inclined to presume t
she was in a state of acceptance. This I did not believe, and theref
broke off the conversation abruptly, and went to prayer. They were b
extremely affected; and especially Mrs. S. The Lord had touched a
broken her heart; so that her thoughts of herself and of the nature
religion were greatly changed; and I left her roaring and crying for mei

Lord's day, 20. There was a great melting in the congregation, an
pleasing prospect of a gracious work of God, while I attempted to descr
the solemn grandeur of the judgment day, and the woeful end of the
regenerate, from 2 Thess. i, 7–10.

[34] This was either Shaw or Shockley.

Thursday, 24. My frame has been indisposed all this week, so that I am almost a stranger to the enjoyment of health for any length of time. I have been reading the life of Mr. ——: but think it quite too pompous. The praise bestowed on him is too much to bestow on mortal dust. What is man, that such flowers should be strewed on his grave! May I ever be contented with the honour which cometh from God only! My soul at present is filled with his Holy Spirit; I have a glorious prospect of a boundless ocean of love, and immense degrees of holiness opening to my view; and now renew my covenant with the Lord, that I may glorify him with my body and spirit, which are his. Seven times a day do I bow my knees, to utter my complaints before him, and to implore an increase of his grace. But after all, and in the midst of all, I can feelingly say, I am an unprofitable servant. But though unworthy, utterly unworthy, I am blessed with the sweet gales of God's love. Blessed breezes!—how they cheer and refresh my drooping soul! What the Lord has for me to do, I know not; but wait to know, and gladly to obey every dictate of his unerring pleasure.

Friday, 25. My soul was still happy in my God, and I am powerfully persuaded that I shall yet live to be more useful than ever in the Church of Christ.

Saturday, 26. On my way to the Fork, I was in spiritual travail for the souls of the people; and there was some melting at Mr. W. Ross's; but a much more powerful moving at Layton's, while I discoursed on 2 Cor. v, 11: "Knowing therefore the terror of the Lord, we persuade men; but we are made manifest to God, and I trust also, we are made manifest in your consciences." I returned to my lodging, blessing and praising God that he had enabled me to deliver my own soul, and given me some cause to hope that my labour was not in vain.

Wednesday, 30. The malicious enemy of mankind still haunts, and powerfully tempts me; but my never-failing Friend makes me victorious. My soul is in constant search after more of God, and sweetly sinks deeper and deeper into the abyss of his fulness. I am much employed in the spirit and duty of prayer; but earnestly desire to be more so. My desire is that prayer should mix with every thought, with every wish, with every word, and with every action; that all might ascend as a holy, acceptable sacrifice to God.

Thursday, October 1. My heart was much devoted to Him who devoted himself to death for me. Peace and purity were my agreeable companions; and I saw the indispensable need of perpetual watching, and looking unto "Jesus, the author and finisher of my faith, who for the joy which was set before him, endured the cross, despised the shame, and is set down at the right hand of God." Endured the cross!—despised the shame! And shall the disciple desire to be above his master? Shall I ever shun the cross?—or dread the shame? God forbid! For it is only on condition that we suffer with him, that we shall also reign with him. At Twyford's to-day there was

a gracious melting in the congregation; and the prospect of a good wor
on the hearts of many. I then rode to Mr. Freeny's; and the untaught au
dience felt the weight of Divine truth. Mr. F. has been under religious in
pressions amongst the Nicholites, but suffers spiritual loss by the war
of more fortitude.

Friday, 2. I preached a funeral sermon on Nanticoke river; and we ha
a very solemn season.

Lord's day, 4. I was greatly assisted in my public exercises, though m
body was afflicted with a fever. After preaching twice, I rode to M
Thomas White's, and enjoyed consolation in my soul; though at preser
there is but a small prospect of my being permitted to preach long in thi
land, with a clear conscience. But to defile the conscience, would be doin
evil that good may come; which I look upon as a dangerous, yea,
diabolical sentiment—and therefore can never think of indulging it. M
conscience must be kept void of offence towards God, as well as toward
man. I am desirous to do what I can for the salvation of the immorta
souls which inhabit America; but if Providence should permit men t
prevent me, then I am clear, and must labour where the door is open.

Thursday, 8. I found some religious feelings in the congregation a
J. Gray's; but dead, dead times at Robert Layton's. And I was so unwel
as to be under the necessity of sitting down to teach the people. I re
turned very ill, and was unable to preach on the *Lord's day*.

Lord's day, 18. My body has laboured under affliction all the week; an
Satan has buffeted me with heavy temptations. I have been much tempte
to impatience, and to say, Show wherefore thou contendest with me? Bu
shall the clay complain in the hand of the potter? Lord, support me, an
enable me to resist the devil, that he may flee from me! This was a ver
solemn day in the great congregation, and I felt unusual power in preach
ing on Acts xx, 27. I left the people under the effects of what they ha
heard and felt; and then returned to Mr. White's. Bless the Lord, O m
soul; and all that is within me, praise his holy name!

Friday, 23. My indisposition still cleaveth to my shattered frame. Bu
my spirit is for the most part pacific and calm, though much tempted
Lord, grant me patience and resignation, on all occasions; that while
am a living man, I may never complain!

Tuesday, 27. My soul was impressed with a deeper sense of the presenc
and purity of God. And I felt determined to be more circumspect an
watchful in every part of my conduct. But what are all the resolutions o
man without the grace of God! And will God withhold his grace, withou
any fault in us? By no means: He hath encouraged us to ask, by promisin
that we shall receive, if we do not ask amiss. Lord, help me to fulfil al
my covenant engagements, that I may have respect to every precept of th
righteous law, and in all things do according to thy holy will. I spent par
of this day in reading, but a fever and pains produced a restless night.

Thursday, 29. I spoke with some animation at J. Gray's, and most of the ongregation felt the weight of Divine truths.

Friday, 30. I put the society in some order at Layton's, turning out the isorderly members—which always are a weight and a curse to any religious community. St. Paul said to the Corinthians, (though alluding) only one disorderly person among them,) "Know ye not that a little aven leaveneth the whole lump?" (1 Cor. v, 6.) And the anger of the Lord as kindled against Israel, for the covetousness of Achan, who then welt among them. (Josh. vii, 1.) And who can tell how often the Lord is ispleased with his Church for the wickedness of some of its members? o doubt but this frequently checks the spiritual progress of the righteous; specially if ungodly members are known and not dealt with according to e Gospel. I spoke plainly and closely to the people, and there was some oving of the Holy Spirit amongst them. But alas! I am not yet so devout, piritual, and heavenly, as I ought to be. Neither do I feel that burning ove to God which I want to feel. What small returns do I make, after my ate visitations of judgment and mercy! I may well say of myself, Ah! ngrateful wretch! May the Lord help me to be always mending!

Lord's day, *Nov.* 1. After I had preached a funeral sermon, at which the earts of many were powerfully wrought upon, I returned to Thomas White's, making twenty miles in the whole, and lectured in the evening; nd then lay me down and slept in peace.

Wednesday, 4. There was some melting among the people at Twyford's, nd a prospect of a work of grace. On *Thursday* I felt deep workings of eart, but was much taken up with God in prayer. I rode to Quantico,[35] nd found no want of anything there, but religion. I then returned to ussex, and found my spirit at liberty in preaching to those untaught eople, who behaved with seriousness and attention.

Monday, 9. I rode to Thomas White's; and cannot help esteeming his ouse as my temporary home; though I meet with more spiritual trials an in constant travelling. Lord, point out my way, and show what thou rouldst have me to do!

Saturday, 14. I have spent this week in reading and private exercises; nd have been much indisposed in my body. But, glory to God! I have een favoured with some access to his gracious presence, and felt strong esires to be abased as in the dust before him.

Lord's day, 15. This morning I felt very unwell, but ventured to set out or my appointment twenty miles off; and found both my body and mind trengthened far beyond my expectation.

Monday, 16. I preached to a few poor people at W. Richards's, and then

[35] Quantico, Maryland, was the village in which Freeborn Garrettson first preached a a home where Mr. and Mrs. Ryder were guests. Shortly thereafter a society was oranized, and a church was standing there in 1782. (Bangs: *Life of Freeborn Garrett-*on, 82, 83; Coke: *Extracts of the Journals of the late Rev. Thomas Coke*, 46.)

returned to my temporary home, in a much better state of health tha
when I went out. Thus is my life at present chequered: I come home, an
grow sick, then go out and grow better; and return to meet affliction agaii
So the Lord is pleased to deal with me, to keep my spirit down. Father (
mercies, let thy will be done! I am thine, and submit to be dealt wit
according to thy pleasure.

Wednesday, 18. My soul was much devoted to God. I spent part of th
day in visiting the sick; and then returning, I preached in the evening, wit
much liberty, at Edward White's.

Thursday, 19. Having had much time on my hands, I have endeavoure
to improve it by enriching my understanding with religious knowledg
and by frequent, earnest prayer to Almighty God, that he may enrich m
heart with all the graces of his Holy Spirit. I have lately read through th
first volume of Doddridge's paraphrase,[36] and am now waiting for sufficie
health, and a proper opportunity, to turn out and labour in the field, whic
is white for harvest. But alas! I cannot think that I grow in grace as
increase in knowledge. Come, dear Lord, come quickly into my pantin
soul, and by thy gracious beams transform my whole soul into thy Divin
likeness, that I may shine in all the image of Christ Jesus!

Dr. Doddridge's critical notes and improvements are excellent, ir
structive, and beautiful—well calculated for forming the minds of youn
preachers; to prevent wild and unwarrantable expositions, such a
some are apt to give. He must have been a man of extensive reading an
learning.

Lord's day, 22. Some souls were affected while I was preaching on
Cor. vi, 19, 20; and in class meeting the members of society were greatl
quickened. But it is matter of lamentation to me, that I do not glorif
God more perfectly. On *Monday*, I read Doddridge's paraphrase, an
admire his spirit, sense, and ingenuity; though I disagree with him, i
respect to the unconditional perseverance of saints. That this doctrine ha
a pernicious influence on the conduct of many is beyond all doubt. An
a man must live much above his principles, to be diligent and faithfu
under the persuasion of such a stupifying and dangerous sentiment.

Thursday, 26. My mind has lately been much taken up with God, an
I have frequently struggled, and wrestled, and pleaded for more of th
Divine nature.

> "Bid me in thy image rise,
>   A saint, a creature new;
> True, and merciful, and wise,
>   And pure, and happy too.
> This thy primitive design,
>   That I should in thee be blest;
> Should within the arms Divine,
>   Forever, ever rest."

[36] Philip Doddridge (1702–51) edited *The Family Expositor* in six volumes, 1739–56.

Friday, 27. I am much delighted in reading the second volume of Doddridge's paraphrase, and am occupied with various exercises; and my soul enjoys sweet peace. But all this is not travelling and preaching at large, for the salvation of souls. Lord, when shall I return to my beloved employment; and be every day casting the Gospel net to bring souls to the expanded arms of the willing Saviour?

Lord's day, 29. We had a large audience, and a very solemn time, at Jessup's. I then returned and lectured at Edward White's.

Thursday, December 3. Under some groundless apprehensions, I set out for Somerset. My soul poured out abundant prayer by the way; and the Lord, by his providence, conducted me in safety.

Tuesday, 8. After my little excursion to Broad Creek,[37] and its adjacent parts, I returned; and notwithstanding all the foreboding apprehensions of my mind, no person offered me the smallest insult.

Wednesday, 9. My mind was kept in a calm serenity; but as I did not enjoy such deep communion with God as my soul was favoured with in the course of the last week, I was much abased in my own eyes. Though, upon the whole, my obligations to praise and magnify the Lord are very great; and may his grace preserve me from every degree of ingratitude!

Friday, 11. As brother Joseph Hartley is incapable of travelling, there seems to be a necessity for my going to Maxfield's.[38] I have endeavoured, and do still endeavour to improve my time by prayer, meditation, and reading; but I cannot omit any opportunity of preaching, not knowing how soon my liberty or life may come to a final period. On *Saturday* I met the children and the black people, and found some gracious movings among them.

Lord's day, 13. With much freedom of spirit, I preached at Edward White's, on these words, so applicable to thousands: "But they made light of it, and went their ways,—one to his farm, and another to his merchandize; and the remnant took his servants, and entreated them spitefully, and slew them." The word, attended by the grace of God, wrought on the understandings of some, and on the affections of others.

Tuesday, 15. The Lord blessed me with sweet peace; though too much company interrupted my private meditations and study. It seems as if I must commit myself to Divine Providence, and go forth to declare the glad tidings of salvation to the children of men; lest others should follow my example of a partial silence without sufficient cause.

Thursday, 17. I have ended the fourth volume of Mr. Doddridge's paraphrase. He sets the apostle off to the greatest advantage, on the two Epistles to the Corinthians. My soul has been grievously exercised by temptations to impatience and discontent. With the greatest propriety St. Paul exhorted Timothy, to "war a good warfare." A "warfare" indeed!

---

[37] This was probably Broad Creek near Laurel, Sussex County, Delaware.
[38] Maxfield lived near Canterbury, Kent County, Delaware.

How powerful and subtle our enemies! And it is very remarkable, tha all the addresses to the seven churches of Asia, conclude with a promis to them that overcome. Lord, help me to stand in the evil day, fortifie with faith, meekness, patience and love; that, conquering every foe, b thy Almighty aid, I may at last eat of the tree of life which is in the mid of the Paradise of God!

Friday, 18. I am not altogether what I wish to be, and am much tempte by Satan; nevertheless the Lord is my portion and my support. My labour are still in some measure circumscribed, so that I generally preach c exhort but about three times a week. Lord, let not my weakness, timidity or unfaithfulness, provoke thee to lay me aside as a broken instrument, a fit for little or no service! But for twenty months before these troublesom times fully came, I foresaw the probability of them, and was much stirre up to rely upon God, and prepare for the worst. There is now an appoin ment for me to go to Kent, in Delaware, and my hope is, that the Lor will fortify and bless me in my labours.

Lord's day, 20. After preaching at Layton's, I returned and lectured a Thomas White's: and on *Monday* saw brother Wrenn,[39] who informed m of the prosperity of the work, which far exceeds my expectation. Althoug the labourers are driven from place to place, yet it seems the Lord wi help us in his own way and time.

Wednesday, 23. My temptations yesterday were very heavy and trouble some; but to-day my soul overflowed with gratitude to God. I hav lately observed the strong propensity in children to lie, and seen how th Lord kept me from that and many other abominations, from my earl days.

> "In all my ways thy hand I own,
>   Thy ruling Providence I see;
> Assist me still my course to run,
>   And still direct my paths to thee."

My soul has been much quickened by reading the Memoirs of Mr Doddridge, who was a man of great piety, and strict devotion to God There is something peculiarly animating in the lives of holy men—for i their experience we see the veracity of God in fulfilling his graciou promises; and in their holy tempers and godly conduct, we see the possi bility of complying with the precepts of the Gospel: therefore, in th perusal of such tracts, we feel an increasing appetite for more pure an undefiled religion.

Friday, 25. This being the day for commemorating the Saviour's birth I preached at Edward White's with much inward freedom; though th audience were not greatly moved.

I have lately begun to read, for the first time, Mr. (James) Hervey'

[39] William Wrenn's name first appears in 1776 under appointment to Kent Circui After 1777 his name disappears from the *General Minutes*.

:lebrated Dialogues; and cannot but observe his laboured endeavours to
:tablish the doctrine of "the imputed righteousness of Christ." He seems
» make it equal at least to the two grand commands of our Lord. And
hy not supersede them? But providence has brought forth that eminent
.an, Mr. John Fletcher, to manage this subject—whose language appears
» be more natural, and less studied than Mr. Hervey's, and yet in no
:spect inferior; and his arguments are incontestable, carrying their own
>nviction with them. But of this let the public judge.

Saturday, 26. I intended to set out for my appointment in Kent, but a
·eat snow prevented me.

Tuesday, 29. I have generally read of late about a hundred pages a day,
 Hervey's Dialogues, the Lives of Gilbert, Harper, Langston, Brainerd,
·c.[40] But alas! how is my soul abased. It is my deliberate opinion, that I
⊃ the least good in the Church of Christ, of any that I know, and believe
» be divinely moved to preach the Gospel. How am I displeased with
.yself! Lord, in mercy help, or I am undone indeed!

[40] James Hervey (1714–58) published *Theron and Aspasio, or a Series of Dialogues
·d Letters Upon the Most Important and Interesting Subjects.* Harper was probably
·r William Harper (1496?–1573), Lord Mayor of London. John Langston (1641–
'04) published what became popularly known as a *Vindication*. David Brainerd (1718–
') was an American missionary among the Indians. Jonathan Edwards in 1749 pub-
hed *An Account of the Life of the Rev. Mr. David Brainerd.*

1779

1779

In retirement during the Revolution, Asbury studies ancient languages

CHAPTER EIGHT

Delaware

January 1, 1779. A living miracle of Divine mercy, I am brought to the beginning of another year. How many of my friends are gone to eternity the past year, while I am spared amidst temptations and afflictions of various kinds! I humbly hope, upon the whole, I am more spiritual; but O! how unfruitful and unprofitable. This year seems to open with forebodings of uncommon distress. Lord, prepare me for every event of thy providence! My own soul was much affected, and there appeared to be a concern among the people, while preaching to-day at Lewis'. Blessed be God! my soul has intimate access to Jesus, and is much quickened.

> "My residue of days or hours,
> Thine, wholly thine shall be;
> And all my consecrated powers,
> A sacrifice to thee."

Saturday, 2. I reached my circuit in Kent,[1] and preached on my favourite subject: "This is a faithful saying, and worthy of all acceptation, that Christ Jesus came into the world to save sinners;" and there appeared to be some meltings of heart among the people.

Upon mature reflection, I do not repent my late voluntary retirement in the State of Delaware. Notwithstanding all my afflictions and fears, I

[1] Having left his retreat at Judge White's, Asbury began riding a fragment of the old Kent Circuit, confined largely to Delaware, although the *General Minutes* contain no record of this appointment. The conference of April 28, however, appointed Asbury with four others to the Delaware Circuit. He had considerably enlarged the old circuit since his arrival in December, 1777. (Lednum, *op. cit.*, 205, 226.)

entertain a hope, that after the people have been tried and humbled b their present calamities, the Lord will yet visit and bless them with spiritua light, purity, and consolation. Already I am informed that there is gracious work going on in Sussex, in Delaware, and in Accomack an Northampton counties, in Virginia.

Monday, 4. Being prevented from travelling, by a heavy fall of snow, finished the reading of the 2d vol. of Mr. Wesley's Sermons, which I bega on *Saturday*; and they were, as usual, made a peculiar blessing to my sou I trust the Lord favours me with an increase of love and gratitude.

Wednesday, 6. I ended the first volume of Prideaux's Connexions,[2] an had a clear view of the state of the nations at the different periods of th Church of God—a just view of which is highly necessary for the unde standing of the prophecies. The revolutions of kingdoms have bee wonderful in all ages; and it ought not to be thought strange, if they shoul be so now. But in all the various turns of Divine providence God had, an still has, spiritual ends, and the welfare of his Church, in view.

Thursday, 7. In reading the second volume of Prideaux, I was struc with the exact fulfilment of Daniel's prophecy "The seventy weeks bein divided into three periods,—that is, into seven, sixty-two, and one week,- the first reacheth from the time of the going forth of the commandme to Ezra, for the restoring of the Church and the state of the Jews, in th seventh year of Artaxerxes Longimanus, to the finishing of that work b Nehemiah, forty-nine years after; the second, from the end of that perio to four hundred and thirty-four years after, at which time the Messia appeared in the ministry of John; and the last, from that of his thu appearing, to his being cut off by his death on the cross—which was on week, or seven years; and all these put together, fully make up seven weeks, or four hundred and ninety years of this prophecy: and, accordin to this computation, every particular of it hath been fully verified in completion exactly agreeable thereto, and the whole number of yea pointed out thereby exactly answered to a month; for as the going out the commandment to Ezra, from whence they began, was in the month Nisan, so the crucifixion of Christ was also in the same month, just fo hundred and ninety years after." This day my heart was kept in peac My soul shall make her boast in the Lord.

Friday, 8. I rode to Mr. Boyer's, and conversed freely with him on th things of God. He appeared very kind, and inclined to hear instructio

Lord's day, 10. Though it rained, many attended to hear the word bot at Boyer's[3] and at Dover; and on *Monday* my heart was greatly enlarge

[2] Humphrey Prideaux (1648–1724) wrote *Connections of the Old and New Testamen in the History of the Jews*, etc. (1716).

[3] This was the Boyer home located near Magnolia, Delaware. From it went Cal Boyer, a convert under the ministry of Freeborn Garrettson, who was an itinerant fro 1780 to 1788, and who was one of the most eloquent and effective leaders that th Peninsula conference has produced. (Lednum, *op. cit.*, 304–5.)

1 preaching to a large congregation at Hilliard's, on Rom. i, 16. There ere present many persons of respectability; but every mouth was stopt, nd gainsayers had nothing to say or do.

Tuesday, 12. I preached at S.'s,[4] on the education of children, and elative duties: I then rode to Richard Shaw's, where I found a tender ongregation; and left one soul in deep distress. It seems that God, in ompassion to the souls of the people, has kept the way open for the reachers to travel, notwithstanding the imprudence of some, and the ickedness of others. If the Lord is pleased to work, who or what can inder?

Wednesday, 13. My soul has enjoyed a deep sense of God. The conregation was large at Stradley's, and I trust their coming together was rofitable, at least to some of them. In many circuits the preachers have ardly an opportunity of reading their Bibles, much less anything else. A reat part of the day is taken up in riding, preaching, and meeting the asses; and very often at night, there is a large family, but one room for ll, and sometimes no candle: so that I think it would be well, under such rcumstances, if the preachers could have one spare day in every week or the purpose of improving themselves.

Thursday, 14. I had many people at (William) Thomas's, to whom I reached with great freedom; and took occasion to explain and enforce amily duties. It affords me no small joy to find that my labours are not ltogether in vain.

Saturday, 16. I am grievously tempted by the enemy; but the Lord is ill my defender and friend. I am now reading the third volume of rideaux, and find it both entertaining and instructive. I still go on to nforce the education of children, and family duties.

Lord's day, 24. At the widow Jackson's I enforced Genesis xviii, 19: I know him, that he will command his children, and his household after im, and they shall keep the way of the Lord, to do justice and judgment; at the Lord may bring upon Abraham that which he hath spoken of im." In the evening I opened and applied Ezek. xxxvi, 25, &c., with light nd liberty, and the congregation felt the weight of the word.

Tuesday, 26. I spent much of my time in reading the third volume of Ir. Hervey's Dialogues. I like his philosophy better than his divinity. owever, if he is in error by leaning too much to imputed righteousness, nd in danger of superseding our evangelical works of righteousness, some re also in danger of setting up self-righteousness, and, at least, of a artial neglect of an entire dependence on Jesus Christ. Our duty and lvation lie between these extremes. We should so work as if we were to : saved by the proper merit of our works; and so rely on Jesus Christ, • be saved by his merits and the Divine assistance of his Holy Spirit, as we did no works, nor attempted anything which God hath commanded.

[4] Asbury preached at either Sturgis's or Scotten's.

This is evidently the Gospel plan of man's salvation:—St. Paul says i
one place, "By grace are ye saved, through faith; and that not of you
selves, it is the gift of God." In another place the same apostle saitl
"Work out your own salvation with fear and trembling." But some, wh
see the danger of seeking to be justified by the deeds of the law, turn a
their attention to those passages of Scripture which ascribe our salvatio
to the grace of God; and to avoid the rock which they discover on th
right hand, they strike against that which is equally dangerous on th
left, by exclaiming against all conditions and doings, on the part of man
and so make void the law through faith—as if a beggar could not cros
the street, and open his hand (at the request of his benefactor) to receiv
his bounty, without a meritorious claim to what he is about to receiv
What God hath joined together, let no man put asunder. And he havin
joined salvation by grace, with repentance, prayer, faith, self-denial, lov
and obedience, whoever putteth them asunder will do it at his peril. Bu
it is likewise true that others who see the danger of this, in order, as the
imagine, to steer clear of it, go about to establish their own righteousness
and although they profess to ascribe the merit of their salvation to Jesu
Christ, yet think they cannot fail of eternal life, because they have wrougl
many good deeds of piety towards God, and of justice and mercy toward
man; and they would think it incompatible with Divine justice, to sentenc
them to eternal punishment, for what they call the foibles of huma
nature, after having lived so moral and upright a life. Happy the man wh
so studies the Holy Scriptures, his own heart, and the plan of salvatioi
and daily prays with such earnest sincerity to Almighty God, as to se
that neither faith without works, nor works without that faith whic
justifies the ungodly, will suffice in the awful day of universal retr
bution!

Wednesday, 27. My soul is sensible that there is a declension amon
professors. This cannot but grieve the hearts of those who labour, and ar
engaged to promote the spiritual and eternal happiness of their fello
creatures. Lord, revive thy work of grace, in all our societies throughou
this extensive continent, and in every nation on the earth—and especiall
in my poor heart.

Thursday, 28. We had tidings of great troubles in the south as well a
the north.[5] The gathering cloud seemed to lower and threaten with grea
severity. O my God! I am thine: and all the faithful are thine. Mercifull
interpose for the deliverance of our land, and for the eternal salvation c
all that put their trust in thee. At present my way is measurably hedge
in by Providence; but the time may come when I shall be useful in th
Church of Christ. This would afford me more satisfaction than all th

[5] Asbury probably refers to the defeat of the Americans and the capture of Savanna
and occupancy of Georgia by the British. In the North anxiety prevailed over th
conduct of Benedict Arnold.

hes of the east, with all the pomp and grandeur of empires, and all the
easures that can gratify both the imagination and the flesh.

Monday, February 1. My conscience smote me severely for speaking
a idle word in company. O! how frail is man. It is very difficult for
e to check my rapid flow of spirits when in company with my friends.
he tongue is an unruly member: and St. James spoke a sacred truth when
e said, "If any man offend not in word, the same is a perfect man, and able
bridle the whole body." He that can on all occasions govern his tongue,
ill have power sufficient to keep his whole body in religious subjection.
This day our quarterly meeting began,[6] and my heart was expanded in
eaching to about seven hundred people, on Heb. ii, 2. I entertain great
opes that we shall see a gracious revival of religion. The Lord knoweth
at, next to my own salvation, this is my chief concern, and all my
terest in America, or in the whole world: I desire to live only for this.

Tuesday, 2. Our love feast began at nine, and public worship at twelve
clock. The operations of the Holy Spirit were very powerful in the
ongregation; so that there was a general melting; and amongst the young
ople, there were outcries and deep distress. Here was a blessed prospect,
od is gracious beyond the power of language to describe. Both preachers
d people were exceedingly quickened. The public labours of the day
ere too much for my feeble frame.

Friday, 5. I am still far short of what I wish to be in point of universal
oliness and fervent devotion; but my soul is kept in peace, and I am
etermined, by grace, to be more resolute, faithful, and diligent.

Lord's day, 7. There was a large company, and some melting of heart,
Boyer's, while I preached on Luke xix, 10. In the afternoon I was inted to preach in Dover court house; but my ideas were not very clear,
either was my spirit at liberty.

Tuesday, 9. My affections were warm, and my words flowed with ease
st night in town; and the attention of the people appeared to be fixed.
he people also were very lively today at Richard Shaw's. My body is in
feeble state; but glory to God, when I am weak, then am I strong.
hough this mortal frame is shaken by repeated afflictions, my soul is
pported by that peace which passeth all understanding. Lord, keep me
ways in the dust at thy feet, leaning continually on Jesus my beloved,
at as my body approacheth the grave, my soul may advance towards
e realms of light and glory, and there securely rest in Abraham's bosom
l the general resurrection.

> "There I shall see his face,
> And never, never sin;
> There, from the rivers of his grace,
> Drink endless pleasures in.

[6] This quarterly meeting was probably held in the home of Richard Shaw, two miles
st of Dover, Delaware. (Lednum, *op. cit.*, 226; Hallman, *op. cit.*, 120.)

"Yea, and before I rise
To that immortal state,
The thoughts of such amazing bliss
Should constant joys create.

"There I shall bathe my weary soul
In seas of heavenly rest,
And not a wave of trouble roll
Across my peaceful breast."

Saturday, 13. Having seen some good appearances at two or thre
places, I returned to my lodging,[7] but found, as usual, that heavy crosse
are to be borne here. Upon the whole, it appears sufficiently clear tha
God has other work for me to do, and that I must not abide here. If h
graciously intends me for more extensive service in his Church, may he b
pleased to open my way, and make it plain before me!

Monday, 15. Various trials beset me—from Satan, the world, and fro
friends; but hitherto the Lord hath helped. I am convinced there must b
no resting here, in any person, place, or other object; for it would b
bitter and painful in the end.

Thursday, 18. My soul was in sweet peace; and I humbly hope the Lo
will sooner take me out of the world, than let me live to sin against him
'Tis grace, almighty grace, must keep me; otherwise all my readin
praying, and labours of every kind, would be ineffectual. The means mu
be diligently used; but unless God's blessing accompany them, they wi
be used in vain.

Friday, 19. My soul was so terribly beset by Satan, that I was ready t
say, I had rather die than live thus. But grace, by reflection, brought m
to submit, and say, the Lord's will be done; though my sufferings we
even worse than death, yet let me go to heaven, to enjoy thy presence,
it be through fire and water. In reading Clarke's Martyrology,[8] I hav
observed, that notwithstanding the errors and superstitions of Poper
there has been a Church of faithful witnesses preserved, who have borr
witness to the truth—not in word only, but by a holy life, and triumpha
death.

Monday, March 1, 1779. I have of late, for the most part, had libert
in preaching, and the Spirit of the Lord has been with me: and from m
various and peculiar exercises, I am strongly impressed with a persuasio
that the Lord is preparing me for future services. But alas! what caus
for shame, on account of my great unfaithfulness! This present life ma
be well compared to a tempestuous ocean: sometimes the fair wind
prosperity blows a fresh gale; at other times the cross wind of adversi

[7] Asbury was lodging with Judge Thomas White.
[8] This was probably a work by Samuel Clarke (1675–1729), an English clergyma
who was a prolific writer on religious subjects.

es and threatens a hurricane. How difficult it is, in the midst of such posing diversity, to pay proper attention to the Divine compass, and l pursue the right course!

Wednesday, 3. Nothing grieves me so much as the want of holiness. But affords me some satisfaction to find that the people in these parts pear to advance in religion.

Friday, 5. Satan shot his fiery darts at me; but my soul was shielded, and darts repelled. My heart is humbled within me and I must be more thful to God, or I fear I shall not endure to the end.

Monday, 8. I had a large congregation yesterday at Jackson's, and my rit was at liberty. To-day my hopes were revived at Dover, while patiating on the experience of Hezekiah.

Lord's day, 14. For some days past my soul has been dejected: but upon mination, I am conscious that I have, in some good measure, walked sely with God, and in the time of my greatest heaviness, I have found ce: therefore conclude, that it must be owing to some natural cause, ugh intended to humble me. The most genteel people in Dover treat with great kindness and courtesy. I hope it will turn to their own ritual advantage. I have a witness within, that I seek not theirs (neither ney nor esteem) but them—as the purchase of my Lord's death, that y may be his willing servants forever. I have lately been reading Watson's dy of Divinity.[9] The general drift of it does not comport with my timents, yet it contains many good things. I had a mind to abridge his sermons on, "Lead us not into temptation, but deliver us from l."

On *Friday* I was inclined to believe, that the night before the Lord had sanctified my soul. It afforded me much comfort; and I was ready to nclude it had been so for many years past, if I had maintained and ieved it. But I fear I have been too slack in urging both myself and ers diligently to seek the experience of this great and blessed gift. y the Lord help me from this time, to live free from outward and in-rd sin, always maintaining the spirit of the Gospel in meekness, purity, l love!

At this time my body labours under much affliction, and I seem fit for le or no service. This, with the heavy temptations which frequently ack my soul, makes me feel as in the furnace; but grace surrounds me a wall of fire, and I trust my soul suffers no damage.

Tuesday, 23. My eyes being sore, the children[10] read for me the Life of

Thomas Watson (d. 1686), ejected English divine, was a man of considerable ning; and his works preserved his fame long after his death. His most famous rk was the *Body of Practical Divinity*, which appeared after his death. It consisted 176 sermons on the catechism of the Westminster assembly of divines. (*Dictionary National Biography*, XX, 948–49.)

These were the children of Judge and Mrs. Thomas White. For sketches of Mrs. ite and members of the family, see Lednum, *op. cit.*, 256, 270.

John Bruen.[11] He was an eminent man, truly pious, and much morti
in his affections, by deep meditation on the word of God, and ot
religious exercises. I see myself the least of all God's servants, whet
ancient or modern; and although he has done more for me than for ma
yet I have done less for him. From an observation of Mr. Bruen's, t
great blessings more frequently attended the labours of plain, sim
preachers than of the more sublime and eloquent, I was led to fear tha
had not been simple enough.

Thursday, 25. It appears to me very difficult to keep professors fr
placing too much confidence in past experience; and to keep them press
after grace with as much assiduity as at first. How prone is man to st
from God, and to embrace every excuse for the neglect of that best of
duties—living in close communion with the Father of spirits! Thoug
now pray not less than ten times a day, yet I find I have need to p
without ceasing.

Saturday, 27. A remarkable instance occurred of the watchful care
God over his people. Mr. Peddicord went to bed, but could not sle
though he tried again and again. At last he was obliged to rise; a
going down stairs with the man of the house, he found the house
fire.

Lord's day, 28. My mind was much drawn out in prayer, and I beli
I have not spent more time in this exercise for many years past, if ev
than I do now. But my mind has been much perplexed about wander
thoughts in prayer, though Mr. Wesley's deep and judicious discourse
that subject has afforded me no small satisfaction. He hath both sho
the causes of those thoughts, which are not sinful, and incontesta
proves that they contract no guilt. Yet a devout and tender mind must
grieved, to find any kind of temptation in that sublime exercise wher
the whole soul desires to be employed. This portion of Scripture—"Sh
not God avenge his own elect who cry unto him day and night?"—ha
followed me for some time, almost continually, and hath brought
much comfort. This day I preached at Edward White's. I am stron
persuaded in my own mind, that I have stayed in these parts too long.
black man, who had been liberated by Mr. Blades, gave such an ext
ordinary account of the work of God in his soul, and withal displa
such gifts in public exercises, that it appears as if the Lord was prepar
him for peculiar usefulness to the people of his own colour. Let the L
choose his own instruments, and send by whom he will.

Tuesday, 30. Several of my friends came to take their leave, and see t
last of me for the present. They manifested great affection: and well th
might, if they knew how much I had suffered among them. The next d

[11] William Hinde (1509?–1625) wrote *The Very Singular Life of J. Bruen, Esq.* (15
*1625), of Bruen-Stapleford, Cheshire, exhibiting a variety of Memorable and Exempl
Circumstances.* It was first published in 1641.

off,[12] and on my journey I gradually recovered my spirits. Meeting a man on the road, I began to speak to him about the things of God, saw how Providence had brought it about, for the Lord had reached 1eart the night before. I advised him to be diligent and faithful, and eft him. I then rode on to brother Shaw's, where I heard agreeable s.[13] Peradventure there is something in the womb of Providence, for h the Lord hath been preparing me, by bringing me through the fire water.

ursday, April 1, 1779. My soul was much blessed, and there was a t melting among the people, while I spoke strong words on the sub- of sanctification. The believers were greatly quickened, and in class ting we had much of the power of God. I live in great hopes of doing 1 in this journey. Bless the Lord, O my soul!

iday, 2. I had an interview with the Rev. Mr. Magaw,[14] a kind, sensible, idly minister of the Episcopal Church. I then returned to the house of Shaw, my quiet retreat for the present; and here I hope to spend my leisure in peaceable converse with God and Divine subjects. My soul s to be quite complete in the image of God.

ird's day, 4. I breakfasted with a Presbyterian minister, and en- oured to answer some objections which he started; but could not npt a vindication of those amongst us who had dipped deep in politics. n *Wednesday,* 7, there was a great moving among the people—some ing justification, and others perfect love.

ednesday, 14. My soul was in peace; but I have not sufficiently en- ed the doctrine of Christian perfection. This will press believers for- 1, when everything else is found insufficient; and the people in these s appear ripe for it—for there is little or no opposition. But I have ided too much to my own small and low experience. Brother Joshua ley and brother Richard Garrettson, two young preachers, both spoke ay, and I gave each of them a written license. On *Thursday* my mind deeply exercised on the subject of sanctification; and the result was, termination to preach it more frequently, and pursue it more diligently.

Asbury was leaving Judge White's home, which had offered him sanctuary since :mber 9, 1778.

This may be a reference to the fact that Asbury's letter to Thomas Rankin in 1777, ig been intercepted by American authorities, had caused a lessening of suspicion rd Asbury. This was reflected in the attitude of Governor Cæsar Rodney of ware. (Lednum, *op. cit.,* 226.)

Dr. Samuel Magaw (1735–1812) became rector of Christ Church, Dover, Delaware, '67. He befriended the Methodists by presenting to them their first frame meeting- e in Delaware. Its early name, Forest Chapel, was later changed to Thomas Chapel •nor of the Thomas family who first opened their homes for Methodist preaching, for a kinsman, the Rev. William Thomas, who became an itinerant preacher. num, *op. cit.,* 233, 254; *National Cyclopaedia of Biography,* I, 347; Barratt: *Outline e History of St. Paul's Church, Philadelphia,* 36, 97; Rightmeyer: *Anglican Church elaware,* 61–63.)

Friday, 16. My greatest trouble is, that I am not more holy. My
is constantly humble within me on this account. I visited the Rev.
Magaw, and presented him Mr. Fletcher's Checks; at the same time o
ing to his view the whole plan of Methodism. He treated me with exc
ing great kindness; and I spent some time very agreeably in his comp
The people of these parts (the most wealthy not excepted) are, for
most part, very courteous and friendly. Surely the Lord will raise up
himself a body of faithful witnesses among them. Sundry person
respectability attend my feeble exercises in public, and express satisfact
But shall this satisfy, or lift me up? God forbid! If this should be the c
God would punish me for my folly. And what is the esteem of man, wl
breath is in his nostrils, when compared with the approbation of the N
High?

Tuesday, 20. We have judgment weather—a hard frost, which
killed a great part of the fruit. I am now reading Newton on the Pro
cies.[15]

Tuesday, 27. Yesterday and today we held a quarterly meeting
Dover. A great concourse of people attended the ministry of the w
and many serious persons were present at our love feast.

Wednesday, 28. Our conference for the northern stations[16] bega
Thomas White's. All our preachers on these stations were present,
united. We had much prayer, love, and harmony; and we all agree
walk by the same rule, and to mind the same thing. As we had great rea
to fear that our brethren to the southward were in danger of separa
from us, we wrote them a soft, healing epistle. On these northern stat
we have now about seventeen travelling preachers. We appointed
next conference to be held in Baltimore town, the last Tuesday in A
next.

Monday, May 3, 1779. Yesterday we had some melting under the w
at the house of Edward White, and today I wrote to John Dickins
Philip Gatch, Edward Dromgoole, and William Glendenning, ur
them, if possible, to prevent a separation among the preachers in
south—that is, Virginia and North Carolina. And I entertain great h
that the breach will be healed; if not, the consequences may be bad. I
now reading Edwards on the Affections.[17] Excepting the small vein
Calvinism which runs through this book, it is a very good treatise,

---

[15] Thomas Newton (1704–82) was the author of a *Dissertation on the Proph
Which Have Been Remarkably Fulfilled and are at this time fulfilling in the World* (1

[16] This Delaware conference of northern preachers was held because of the impen
crisis of a division over the question of ordinances. Within a month the sou
preachers, led by Philip Gatch, were to break away from the North over this ques
The schism was healed in May, 1780. (See *Journal* entries for May 8–10, 1780;
Life and Times of Jesse Lee, 78–86; Sweet: *Virginia Methodism*, 80–85.)

[17] Jonathan Edwards (1703–58) wrote *A Treatise Concerning the Religious Affec
(1742–43).*

thy the serious attention of young professors. I have now been about
teen years employed in the work of God as a travelling minister; and
n a review, I have cause to be ashamed, but, at the same time, great
on to be thankful that I have not yet grown weary, and humbly hope
ver shall, while able to travel at all.

uesday, 4. I still find it pleasant and profitable to be employed in my
ster's service both in public and private. My conscience smote me
rely for lying in bed till six o'clock this morning, no indisposition of
y being the cause. O! why should we lose one hour, when time is so
rt and precious, and so many things to be learned and taught.

aturday, 8. Yesterday being a public fast day, we had a large congre-
ion, and a solemn time, while I preached on the fast of the Ninevites.
und about forty in society at the Draw-Bridge.[18] Thus it pleaseth the
d to work, and who shall hinder him? In the most troublesome times
can build up the walls of Jerusalem. I thought for some time that it
uld have been much better for the work of God in America, if brother
dford had stayed; but the Lord ruleth over all, and he ruleth for the
t. Many faithful, zealous men are raised up for the work in the States,
o only want a little instruction, and they are ready to spend and be spent
souls.

Vednesday, 12. Every day I have had more or less liberty in preaching
blessed Gospel. The people daily show great marks of affection and
em for me. May the Lord keep me humble! Yea, he is pleased to
nble me by afflictions, temptations, and frequent discoveries of my
ects and imperfections.

riday, 14. John Hagerty preached on: "May we know what this new
trine, whereof thou speakest, is?" He spake long, and much to the
pose. I feel some fears lest the people should be offended against the
th, by any improprieties, or undue rashness of expression. But how can
please such as delight in their sins? It is our duty, whether they will
r, or whether they will forbear, to declare, that if they die in their sins
y can expect nothing but hell and damnation.

aturday, 15. I received a letter informing me of the death of John
ws,[19] a young man whom I visited about a week ago. He had been in
eclining state about fifteen months, and the Lord was pleased to use me
an instrument to open his eyes, and show him the necessity and nature
religion. On my last visit I found him ripening fast for heaven, and have
doubt but that his spirit now rests in the bosom of Jesus.

The Drawbridge over the St. Jones River behind Barratt's Chapel, Kent County,
aware.
John Laws lived near St. Johnstown, Sussex County, Delaware; and his memory
erpetuated in the St. Johnstown Methodist Church about one mile east of Green-
d, Sussex County. The society was organized in May, 1779; and the first church
erected in 1780. (Lednum, *op. cit.*, 229; Hallman, *op. cit.*, 277.)

Lord's day, 16. I preached twice, and in the interim went to hear
Magaw, who preached so excellent a sermon on the sufferings of Ch
that I was amazed to think how such a contrariety of preaching and p
tice could be found in the same man. But what have I to do to ju
another man's servant? To his own Master he standeth or falleth.
whole of the public service—preaching and the Lord's Supper—la
about six hours. The *Friday* following was a day of fasting among
people, that God might revive his work, avert calamities, and send us r
that our hearts may be filled with food and gladness. My own soul
not been so steadily devoted to God as I wish it to be. How I long t
made as a pure seraphic flame! In the afternoon of our fast-day we ha
great rain with heavy thunder and lightning—mercy and judgment uni
a strong indication of our deserts, and God's goodness. On the *Lo*
day, at Johnstown, about a thousand people attended to hear the fun
sermon of John Laws, the young man before mentioned. His experie
and death have wrought powerfully on the hearts of many, both in
family and neighbourhood, so that even in this unpromising place th
is a prospect of religion. Thus we see the Lord can work, when, and wh
and how he pleaseth. I am ashamed of the littleness of my faith. Par
me, Lord, in this my weakness. I long to be altogether the Lord's—
preach and pray, believe and love, as when I first entered on the worl
the ministry.

Tuesday, June 1, 1779. Both yesterday and today my soul was enlar
in unfolding the truths of the Gospel. In several parts of this penins
the work of the Lord increases, and people are flocking in apace. The w
is his, and worthy of him. May the instruments he is pleased to work
be always humble, and give the glory to whom it is due! We have a so
of war from the southward;[20] Lord, think upon us, that we perish n
What reason have I to be thankful, that in the midst of war and confus
I am kept in peace and safety.

Thursday, 10. I feel an increasing desire to be the Lord's, every mome
in every thought and desire, and in all I speak and do.

Lord's day, 13. Many attended the word, and the Lord was with me
speaking on Acts xvi, 30. In the evening I treated on the great salvati

Monday, 14. Notwithstanding I was very unwell, I rode to Solom
Levinson's, and preached; had a very unfeeling company to hear me,
felt assisted and blessed in speaking to them. I have lately read Sherloc
Sermons:[21] he was doubtless a man of great abilities, and it is a pity

---

[20] This probably refers to the burning of Suffolk and the plundering of Portsmou
Virginia, by the expeditions commanded by Matthews and Collier. The total dam
including the burning of merchant ships in the James and Elizabeth rivers was estima
at two million dollars.

[21] Thomas Sherlock (1678–1760), English prelate, who published a collection
sermons in 1775. His father, William, was once dean of St. Paul's, London.

had been a more evangelical writer. I find some good things in his
tings, and others, in general, harmless, but not very interesting.

Wednesday, 16. Preached at Boyer's; found myself shut up, but the
ople appeared tender and attentive: next day I had more hearers than
xpected, at brother Shaw's. I have not spent so much time in private
ayer of late as I could wish, for want of time. My mind enjoys great
ace and sweetness in God, and I find myself much given up to him; 'tis
y seldom I feel a thought, much less a desire, contrary to his holiness.
st Monday night it appeared to me that I had as deep a sense of God,
though I could see, touch, handle, and feel him. This day I received a
nderful Arian and Socinian letter from H. C., a weak, wild mortal,
elled with pride and self-will. I rode seven miles to see a sick man, who
s more than seventy years of age deeply convinced of sin. I laboured
d prayed with him; he expressed some comfort, but had not a confidence
his acceptance with God.

Saturday, 19. My heart is kept in peace.

Sunday, 20. I preached at Shaw's, at eight o'clock, to about two hundred
arers, with great enlargement; a melting tenderness went through the
ngregation. I then rode to church at Dover, and heard a most excellent
mon on hypocrisy, by Mr. Magaw. In the evening I preached on the
aspel supper. The great (so called) attended; but, I fear, to little
rpose.

Wednesday, 23. Preached at a new place, in a meadow, to about one
ndred people, who were wild enough; after preaching, had to ride
elve miles for my dinner. In this our labour, we have to encounter hun-
r, heat, and many restless nights with mosquitoes, unwholesome pro-
ions, and bad water: but all this is for souls; were it for silver, I should
quire a great sum; but the Lord is not unrighteous to forget our labour
love, and our reward is with him.

Thursday, 24. I find the heat of the weather too great for close study;
flags the spirits, and strangely debilitates all the powers of body and
nd in a manner that is seldom felt in Europe, unless for one month in
: year.

Friday, 25. I am not as I long to be: I want to be more spiritual in all
thoughts, words, and works; to live wholly to God from moment to
oment.

Saturday, 26. I preached in Newcastle, and twice the next day: I find
ese people pay no great attention to, and do not manifest much affection
r, our Gospel and ministry; I had but little liberty to preach to them,
d not much satisfaction while there.

Tuesday, 29. Employed in reading. I see what I ought to be, as a
aristian and a minister, and mourn because I am not more holy. O! how
eat a thing to be a man of God!—to be in everything exemplarily good;
everything to do one thing—the will of God.

Wednesday, 30. I received the minutes of the Virginia Conference,[22] which I learn the preachers there have been effecting a lame separat from the Episcopal Church, that will last about one year. I pity the Satan has a desire to have us, that he may sift us like wheat.

Friday, July 2, 1779. Heard Mr. Magaw at the Forest chapel,[23] "Thy kingdom come."

Sunday, 4. At half past eight o'clock, I preached at the chapel, a then went to church, and heard Mr. Magaw preach an excellent serm on wavering in religion. The inflammatory disorder that had seized throat is growing worse.

Tuesday, 6. I applied to Dr. Abraham Ridgely,[24] who prescribed t blisters, of great strength: the two following days I was very ill.

Friday, 9. I began to mend, and am persuaded that the doctor's mea have been very successful, and feel myself under great obligations him.

Sunday, 11. Felt myself so much better in health, that I ventured speak to a small serious congregation; I hope not in vain.

Wednesday, 14. Set out for the sea-side, in a double carriage, brotl Alfrey with me. We rode thirty miles, and came to Shockley's[25] a li after twelve o'clock. Preached to about one hundred people, all serious great alteration since I was here, twelve months back. So does God wo I am in growing health, my voice much restored; feel a springing hope tl this journey will be attended with a blessing to myself and others. I a overcome with a sense of the goodness of God, in so suddenly raising up. O! What I laboured under this day week! How great the change find all my afflictions divinely sanctified to me; I am kept in great pea and a Divine serenity all day. A sweet peace sits upon my soul. I re some psalms, and a little of Haliburton's Life,[26] as I rode in the chair. how good it is to strive to do a little for God! My friends were frighter at my going out so soon, but the Lord will help me on my way. I spoke Shockley's on Eph. ii, 8–10.

Thursday, 15. We rode to the sea-side, about forty miles from Shockle I read part of the life of Mr. De Renty. We came in about two o'clock, a

---

[22] This was the conference at Broken-back Church on May 18. The *Minutes* omit the name of Asbury, and all but two of the circuits north of Virginia. (Lee: *Life* Times of Jesse Lee, 76–84; Tigert: *Constitutional History of American Episcopal Met dism,* 97–109.)

[23] See note under April 2, 1779.

[24] Dr. Abraham Ridgely (1756–1811) was a friend of Asbury and a member of Methodist Society at Dover, Delaware. He was educated as a physician with James Anderson of Chestertown as his preceptor, and he later married Dr. Anderso daughter. (*A Calendar of Ridgely Family Letters, 1742–1899,* in the state archives Delaware; Lednum, *op. cit.,* 220.)

[25] Shockley lived at Slaughter Neck.

[26] This was probably George Haliburton (1616–65), eminent Scottish Covenanter

and a kind reception. We prayed after dinner in the family and private;
ernoon went down to the sea to bathe, for my health; at night read a
apter, and gave an exhortation. Brother Alfrey and myself prayed; we
ted well.

Friday, 16. Am kept in peace of soul, yesterday and this day; feel myself
in the presence of God, growing in health of body and soul.

Saturday, 17. I preached on 1 John i, 8, 9, to about fifty people, simple,
t teachable. Some poor men in a boat came on shore, who had been
en prisoners: were English and Scotch, going to New York. I called
their tent, read the third of Romans, lectured to them; they seemed
ad and humble: I pitied an old man, near seventy, from Devonshire.
vent to bathe, called on the distressed people, prayed with them. This
orning I finished reading the book of Psalms, which has been my
gular reading this week past; likewise the eleventh volume of Wesley's
orks, and part of the lives of those men of God, Haliburton,
Renty, and Walsh[27]—one of the Church of Scotland, another from
Church of Rome, the latter a Methodist preacher; but the work of
od is one in all. To set aside a few particulars, how harmonious does
work of God appear, in men of different nations and Churches! I
ve been in peace, but not so much given up to God. I was humbled and
rred up to be more heartily employed: when shall every thought,
rd, and action in me be holiness to the Lord?

Sunday, 18. Rode to Wood's,[28] near Peleg Water's tavern; had about
ree hundred people, and apparently very ignorant in religion, yet
lling to be taught. I spoke on 1 John i, 3; I found I could not speak plain
ough to them: afternoon on Isa. lv, 6, 7; they understood me better.
vent to Law's[29] to lodge. I found the Baptists were fishing in troubled
ater, (they always are preaching water to people,) and are striving to
t into all the houses where we preach; they had taken one simple man
o was joined to us, into the water. They plead they did not want to
n, being Church people; but the ministers were good men, and they
uld not deny them their houses.

Monday, 19. I preached at J. Gray's to many feeling people: a good
ork is begun; and I fear that division is begun also. But what is to be
ne? Must we instrumentally get people convinced, and let Baptists
ke them from us? No; we will, we must oppose: if the people lose their
uls, how shall we answer it before God? I met with a woman who
rmly contended for dipping, as though it had been for life. Another
gan with me about going to their houses; and said, we must all live in

[27] Thomas Walsh (1730–59) was a native of Limerick, Ireland, and in the judgment
John Wesley one of the most learned preachers of early British Methodism.
[28] Members of the Woods family were among the early Methodist converts in Sussex
unty, Delaware. (Lednum, *op. cit.*, 258.)
[29] The Law family resided at the present Greenwood.

heaven. I said, there will be no rebaptizing there. She said, we m
imitate our Lord. I said, our Lord rebuked the wind, and walked upon t
sea. The point is this: the Baptists and Methodists came and preach
together; our simple young men not knowing how they would act; t
people being unacquainted with them, are for receiving both.

Tuesday, 20. I went to the water, and believe bathing has been
singular use to me. Preached at S. Evans', on Acts xxvi, 18. Had gr
freedom. About a hundred people were present, and I hope there will
a work here, if controversy does not prevent it. Afternoon, I called to s
a person in the dropsy, for whom I sent to Dr. White. At three o'clo
preached at West's, on Matt. vii, 7: "Seek, and ye shall find." I had mu
liberty, but the people in general were insensible. After preaching, so
poor people came with tears in their eyes, fearing from what I had sa
I was about leaving the houses where the Baptists would preach, a
thought we were going to leave them altogether, as the others had set
forth. I answered them, while we could get a house to ourselves, a
society, we would consider them as objects of our attention. Some ra
and my preaching twice, brought on a small inflammation in my thro
We rode to J. Gibbons's, fifteen miles, heavy road, very hot.

Wednesday, 21. I preached at twelve o'clock to about fifty peop
unfeeling enough. I spoke on Gal. iii, 22. I spoke all the truth. Aft
preaching, we rode to Joseph Moore's,[30] twenty miles, great part hea
travelling. An ulcer broke in my mouth while I was preaching, but
continued speaking.

Thursday, 22. I arose with a gracious sense of God upon my hea
cool weather after the rain. I hear good news from the people, of the wo
of God; though they are not competent judges, yet I hope the prospect
favourable. Many brought home to God, and hope more will be. I hav
in the course of my reading, attained to the end of Solomon's So
Preached at Joseph Moore's; a hundred serious people attended: a gre
change since I preached here nine or ten months ago. Then many
blindness,—now forty in society; some seeking, others have found t
Lord. One of the friends told me he thought he could number fifty prayi
families. Some who have not joined us yet, are stirred up by preaching
pray; before, the people were swearers, drunkards, fighters, horse-race
and such like; but the Lord hath done great things for them. I spoke
Eph. v, 8; had great liberty.

Friday, 23. Arose, as I commonly do, before five o'clock in the mornir
to study the Bible. I find none like it; and find it of more consequence
a preacher to know his Bible well, than all the languages or books in t
world—for he is not to preach these, but the word of God. I preached

---

[30] Joseph Moore, with whom Asbury lodged, was one of several prominent Methodi
of that name in the Mt. Pleasant neighborhood.

ting Bradley's,[31] in the woods, to about two hundred people, on Acts 26. Had considerable freedom. In the evening, at George Moore's,[32] Rev. xxi, 6–8. Great liberty; the serious people much affected.

aturday, 24. I rode to Joseph Turpin's, about thirteen miles; many ple, I judge about two hundred, attended. The Lord hath done great gs since I was here about nine months ago—numbers are inquiring r God; the Lord hath done great things for us. Not unto us, but unto be all the glory given.

unday, 25. I spoke on Matt. xxiii, 37, with uncommon freedom, to ut three hundred people, at Joseph Turpin's: we had a melting time . The Lord is striving mightily to save them. Rode through the rain wyford's, had a hundred people or more to hear; spoke on John xv, 20. Strove to comfort and encourage the seeking souls. Rode to ther Thomas White's that night.

onday, 26. Spent in writing to our dissenting brethren in Virginia, ing to reclaim them.[33] I am kept in peace, though not without inward outward war.

uesday, 27. I have peace: arose before three: I am much employed, it is good to make the best of every moment, and carefully to fill up space of time that may be lost. O! how precious is time! our moments, ugh little, are golden sands. I preached a funeral sermon for our late nd and brother Hardisty, to about one hundred people. I spoke on ah lvii, 1, 2. Had liberty in speaking to a solemn people: some were cted, and at the close brother Pedicord gave an exhortation. The prevails, and hath carried some off. Returning, I called at Mr. Micajah ruler's; afterward called at Mrs. Peterkin's, who is sick.

Vednesday, 28. Prepared my letters; am most severely tried at times, if for good, the Lord's will be done. Had a conversation with Mr. Neal[34] this week—a man of learning and understanding, who knows trines and men; is a minister of the Episcopal Church, in Maryland, on-juror. I ended the reading of Isaiah, in course, going through the le; have trials very heavy, but my soul is humbled before the Lord. I ached at Edward White's, on Zeph. i, 12; had a great time in preaching.

Gitting Bradley was a charter member of the old Moore Meeting House between rel, Delaware, and Sharptown, Maryland. For the erection of this church, now Mt. sant, Asbury circulated a subscription list.

George Moore became an itinerant minister of exceptional ability from 1780 to . (Lednum, *op. cit.*, 257.)

The conference at White's declared that it would be imprudent for Asbury to mpany William Watters to the Fluvanna Conference because he was needed in the nsula revival, and also because he had declined to sign the oath of allegiance. Thus ould exert his influence through correspondence only. (Watters, *op. cit.*, 73.)

Asbury doubtless refers to the Rev. Hugh Neill, a former rector at Dover but in ge of St. Paul's Church, Queen Annes County, 1767–82. During his latter years, ng to his Toryism, he retained his incumbency under much opposition. (Emory: ory of Queen Anne's County, 169, 174, 175.)

Thursday, 29. Set out for Kent; visited Mrs. Peterkin, going swiftly
her home; and also William Riche—about two months ago he was
opposer, proud and self-righteous, but now brought low, penitent, a
submits to prayer, and Methodist conversation; thus does God bring do
He held, yea, pressed my hand, unwilling to part. I came to brot
Shaw's, before B. D. had done preaching. I spoke a few words, and a
dinner went to see my very dear friend, Mr. Magaw again.

Friday, 30. Went to the widow Howard's; spoke freely to about t
hundred people, on John iii, 16. 1. The condition that all men must h
been in if God had not given his Son. 2. His great love. 3. The nature
faith. 4. The consequences of not believing. The people were seriou
went to Lewis Alfrey's. A man followed me that night, ten mi
distressed in soul; I talked to and prayed with him. He went away, w
clearer views and some hope, pleading for the blessing.

Saturday, 31. Rode to Shaw's; the weather was hot. Called on N
Wood, sick and distressed in his soul. There is an inquiry excited in ma
people, and an awakening power is going forth. I saw today a polit
libel; the Methodists are struck at, but every charge is false.

Sunday, August 1, 1779. Rainy. I rode to church, and heard an
cellent sermon on Luke xiv, 22. At three o'clock I preached in the squ
at Dover; many came to hear. I spoke on Ezek. xxxiii, 30, very plain a
pointed: how it was taken I know not. I am easy and clear in my o
mind.

Monday, 2. Our quarterly meeting began: I was detained by rain,
came in about one o'clock. Brother Philip Cox preached on Psa. xlv
12–14.

Tuesday, 3. In the morning the rain continues; all things look gloo
We appointed to meet at nine, if clear; if not, at twelve o'clock. Ab
twelve it cleared away, without such visible tokens as sometimes appe
We went to the arbour; it covers three or four hundred people. I
possible we had six or seven hundred people each day; from Sus
Somerset, Queen Annes, Caroline, Kent, Newcastle counties, and Ph
delphia. I preached on Psa. cxxvi, 3–6, and was greatly led out; God v
with us. Mr. ——, a clergyman, was with us, very friendly. The r
prevented Mr. Magaw's attendance.

Wednesday, 4. We held our love feast. Many spectators, and a melt
time; some power and life appeared to be amongst the people. Upon
whole we had a blessed time. About twelve o'clock I preached on Col
27, 28, with some freedom, and hope the people were profited. Brot
Garrettson[35] exhorted long: his speaking is mostly proposing cases

---

[35] It is quite certain that Asbury was describing the style of exhorting of one of
Garrettson brothers. Freeborn had left the Peninsula in mid-July, but he did not s
for Philadelphia until after "attending several quarterly meetings." Asbury's comm
might also be applied to Richard Garrettson, who was appointed to New Jersey

science, and answering them, and speaking about Christ, heaven, and
; yet this carries all before it. It is incredible the good he has been
trumental in doing; the people are generally moved under his preaching.
s, however, thought expedient to send him to the north. I go to Chop-
k.[36] We have had much of God in this meeting. Though I have had
little sleep, and unwholesome weather, yet I feel no injury; thank the
rd! We rode to Thomas White's after four o'clock.

Thursday, 5. Employed in writing.

Friday, 6. Part of the day taken up in writing; am not collected as I
ght to be, nor as I long to be. The same day heard a sermon from
other Cox at Edward White's.

Saturday, 7. Rode to Reynear Williams's; I was dejected in my own
l, on account of some things I felt in body and mind: met a few in
ss; all seemed tender.

Sunday, 8. Preached on Rev. xx, 11–15, to about three hundred people.
ad uncommon light; I never spoke there with such liberty in my life.
de to the Draw-Bridge, preached to about three hundred there, but not
h so much enlargement as in the morning. The Lord is at work here
a truth.

Monday, 9. This morning went to the Bay; afterward went to Caleb
rby's, spoke on 1 Pet. iv, 18. Met the class, and found them much en-
ged, and many joined. I am weak and feeble, the weather is trying:
rd! give me strength according to my day. I have been tried with wan-
ring thoughts; I could only read a few chapters in Jeremiah; we have
le time for our own improvement. I read the first epistle to Timothy.

Tuesday, 10. Rode to Andrew Purden's.[37] It was reported about that
re would be a horse race, and some opposition, but there was none.
any came to hear; I spoke long, and with liberty, on Heb. xii, 25. I
pe not in vain. Rode to William Virdenn's, where I preached some
onth's ago; the man was then quite an unfeeling person, but is now in
rnest for his soul's salvation.

Wednesday, 11. Rode to Richard Shaw's. I spoke to a simple and steady
ople on the righteousness of the law and righteousness of faith; a sub-
t with which they appeared to have but little acquaintance, therefore it
s necessary to inform their judgments: some were affected. I met the
ss: the people are faithful, in general; thank the Lord!

Thursday, 12. I renewed my covenant with God. O that every thought,
rd, and act were love!

xt year. (Garrettson: *The Experience and Travels of Freeborn Garrettson, Minister of
  Methodist Episcopal Church in North America.*)

[6] Asbury makes several references to Thomas White's home as "Choptank."
ewhere he means Greensboro, Caroline County, Maryland. (Lednum, *op. cit.*, 108,
; see *Journal* entry for July 7, 1796.)

[7] Andrew Purden lived near Canterbury, Kent County, Delaware.

Friday, 13. I rode to Wells's: there were many to hear for the time a
place. I spoke on Rev. xxii, 11–15, with a degree of liberty. Met the cla
the people were affectionate. I am kept from a wandering mind, in a h
exercise. I am afraid of the foot of pride. I hope the Lord will keep
faithful in all his ways, for I want only to please God. I preached
Sturgis's, to a small congregation.

Saturday, 14. I rested; have but little time for private exercises.

Sunday morning, 15. Read the law delivered by Moses, and our Lor
sermon on the mount; preached at nine o'clock at Boyer's; then went
the church at Dover; and preached in the woods at three o'clock on A
xvii, 30. I was plain and faithful; but the people will, and will not. C
own people do not keep so close to God as they ought; this injures
work.

Monday, 16. I went to Hilliard's, and the people attended very w
One is brought under deep distress, who some months back persecuted a
kept back his wife. I said at that time, perhaps he will be glad to co
himself; and so it is; thank the Lord for this. I preached from Psa
cxlv, 18–20. I had liberty and clear views in speaking; and believe
word went to the hearts of the hearers. I rode twenty miles to-day, a
if brother Cromwell does not come I must take the circuit.[38] I bless G
for health while many are sick around me. May I do the will of God, a
live and love! then, come life or death, all will be well.

Tuesday, 17. I spent part of the day with Mr. Magaw very comfortab
and find him a teachable man in his station. I met brother Alfrey, and hea
of the violent proceedings of some men at Lewis's, who were encourag
by persons who ought to know better; but what are Whigs, Tor
Presbyterians, Churchmen, or Methodists, if they have not the Spirit
Christ? All of one spirit. I rest contented, believing this will work f
good. God can and will vindicate his own cause.

Wednesday, 18. My spirits were flagged with a tedious ride to wid
Howard's; but found it was no time to give way to dejection. I preach
with difficulty, to a large congregation, on Isaiah lv, 6, 7.

Thursday, 19. Rode to Scotten's through heavy rain, preached to
crowded audience.

Friday, 20. Went to Forest Chapel, and spoke to a large congregatio
I returned to brother Shaw's, and wrote to brothers Philip Cox a
Daniel Ruff. I am grieved at the imprudence of some people; but w
should I be grieved?—the work is the Lord's. May I be faithful in
my ways, and attend to my own calling.

Sunday, 22. I went to a Presbyterian meeting, and heard a good sermo
on the epistle to the Church at Laodicea, truly applicable to the unfeeli
people, who are so full of politics that they seem to have turned
religion out of doors. It is time for the watchmen to cry aloud! I went

[38] Joseph Cromwell had been appointed to the Chester Circuit in April, 1779.

Draw-Bridge, and preached to about three hundred people. The work
the Lord goes on, and every denomination of Christians appear to be
red up. Well, if Christ is preached we will rejoice.

Monday, 23. I arose with a sense of God upon my heart. Preached on
l. i, 9–12, but not with much enlargement; in class, I found the people
ely; thus hath the Lord wrought for us according to his power.

Tuesday, 24. My soul is humbled. O, that I may feel Divine love every
ment, that my spirit may be holiness to the Lord! I preached from
alm vii, 11–13, at Andrew Purdin's, near Satan's synagogue, had many
hear; I did not spare them. Afterward I visited a distressed soul under
ep depression.

Wednesday, 25. I went to Richard Shaw's, and preached from Luke
i, 24–26. Had some opening, and the people appeared to hear, and
derstand what was said.

Thursday, 26. Rode to Wells's, and spoke close, but with little liberty,
a serious, but not very lively people, on Matt. xi, 4–6; brothers Joseph
yatt and Lewis Alfrey both spoke after me. This morning, I ended the
ading of my Bible through, in about four months. It is hard work for
e to find time for this; but all I read and write, I owe to early rising. If
were not to rise always by five, and sometimes at four o'clock, I should
ve no time only to eat my breakfast, pray in the family, and get ready
r my journey—as I must travel every day.

Friday, 27. I rode to Stockley's, and spoke pointedly on Hosea x, 12. I
et brother Wrenn in Dover, and we travelled together three days.

Sunday, 29. Preached at Boyer's, on Luke vii, 22, 23. Some awakenings;
t my spirits were dejected by false reports. O, what a shame to grieve
those things! What is our honour? Blessed are ye when men shall say
l manner of evil of you falsely for my sake, saith the Lord. O, how ought
o be humbled, that such trifles affect me! But I speculate too much, and
ason upon the dark side. I preached at Dover, at three o'clock, from
alm ix, 17. I spoke very plainly, and brother Wrenn spoke better than
er I heard him before.

Monday, 30. I rode to Hilliard's; there were about forty people, and a
tle melting among them; the members of society are slack. I rode to
wis Alfrey's the same afternoon. Brother Wrenn says, I should not ride
e circuit, and go where I am most wanted. I think it would be better
r me, and for the work of God.

Tuesday, 31. I preached at brother Alfrey's, on Luke xiii, 24–27; and
d but little liberty; but the people were melted, and stirred up. There is
evil here: I believe some were improperly taken into society who never
d any deep conviction; I am afraid of them. Some are fallen into sin,
hers have been on the verge. In the afternoon I preached at Mr. Wilde's,
Acts xiii, 26: "To you is the word of this salvation sent." The poor old
an is mourning after God, and was comforted a little. I had great sweet-

ness in speaking, and liberty of soul; but at times I am under some gloo
fears for the cause of God.

Wednesday, September 1, 1779. I went to the widow Howard's, and v
enlarged on Psalm vii, 11–13. I thought some felt the word; but O! h
great the work to bring sinners to God! It is the work of Omnipoten
Alas, how his poor dust labours and toils in vain, without him! I return
to Alfrey's, and employed my spare moments in taking notes from Ne
ton's third volume.

Thursday, 2. I was closely taken up in writing; but met the socie
they appeared to be humbled, and resolved to set out anew. I press
them to have prayer meetings, and they appointed one before they part

Friday, 3. I went to Poplar Neck, and preached on Isaiah lv, 6, 7; th
rode that night twenty miles to Dover, and was comforted in socie
meeting.

Saturday, 4. I changed my purpose, and instead of going to Williams
went to Thomas White's. Preached at night.

Sunday, 5. I rode to Williams's and preached at eleven o'clock, on Ma
xxi, 44; then rode to the Draw-Bridge, where about three hundred peo
were waiting. I preached on Mal. iv, 1, 2; and hope it reached some hear

Monday, 6. Preached at Caleb Furby's, on Rom. vi, 17, 18. I spo
strong words, and argumentative, on the subject of salvation from
sin, and answered some objections against the doctrine. I then met t
society, and gave a pointed exhortation, to stir them up. I have be
straitened in speaking, and sorely tempted; but the Lord will help me, a
has blest me to the people. I have had little time for anything but trav
ling: preaching is but half my work, and ought not to take up all my tin

Wednesday, 8. I preached at Richard Shaw's, to about two hundr
attentive people, from Rom. vi, 20–23. I hope the Lord's work goes o

Thursday, 9. I was unwell, and was relieved by Joshua Dudley, who to
the circuit. I have more time now for writing, and am kept humble,
think of the respect the people pay to such a poor creature. Lord, wh
am I, that thou hast brought me so far on my way? Though unwell,
completed my notes from Newton's third volume on the prophecies
cannot be idle.

Friday, 10. I have been employed in writing letters to the preache
Lord, help me to speak and write to thy glory, and the good of the peo
I have the charge of. I began reading Comber on Ordination.[39] Much po
was annexed to the clerical order, though plausible in its way. I belie
the Episcopal mode of Ordination to be more proper than that of Pre
byters; but I wish there were primitive qualifications in all who hand
sacred things.

Sunday, 12. I preached to the people, who came to church, at M

[39] Thomas Comber (1645–99), sometime dean of Durham, was the author of *Ordi
tion of Deacons, Priests, and Bishops.*

assett's door,[40] on Gal. ii, 19. In the afternoon, in the woods, to the
▲ost people I ever saw here, and had liberty; some living emotions ap-
eared amongst the people: we revive again! I had a very different feeling
◗ what I had the last time I was here. I hope we shall yet grow in Dover.
Monday, 13. I rode to Choptank, through heavy rain. I purpose for
'albot County, Maryland, to-morrow. I had pleasing views of a life
evoted to God, and felt determined to set out anew to do the will of the
,ord. I spent the afternoon in reading Mark's Gospel, making some
otes, and planning my future business.

Maryland

Tuesday, 14. I went to see brother Joseph Hartley, under his confine-
▲ent, who was in jail for preaching, and found him determined to marry.
▲e thought it was his duty before God. I could only advise a delay till he
▼as released from imprisonment. Persuaded him to give bail at court, if
ot released, as I thought he would have no trial. All that the opposers
▼anted was to prevent his preaching in the county. We thought his
▲prisonment was illegal, as he had taken the oath in the Delaware
▲tate.
Thursday, 16. We rode thirty miles yesterday. I am unwell and much
ejected, and lament the want of more grace. I rode to Reynear Williams's,
▲d met brother Pedicord, who copied some letters for me; we settled a
▶lan for our next quarterly meeting. I preached on *Friday*, at the widow
▶rady's,[41] and met a person with whom I laboured ten months ago to
onvince her of sin. Preaching is now at her mother's house, and a class
▶f twenty members. I preached on Rom. iii, 19–21; and brother Pedicord
xhorted.

Delaware

Saturday, 18. I returned to Choptank. Glory be to God this mortal
▲all put on immortality. Brother Pedicord informs me, that the Baptists
▶ppose stoutly, and also the devil, and a certain Woolf, his agent, near
,ewes. Brother Dudley being detained by his father being sick, brother
ohn Cooper is come in his place.

[40] Asbury first met Richard Bassett of Dover, Delaware, in 1778 at Judge Thomas
▼hite's. Bassett's first wife, Miss Ann Ennalls, was a member of an early Methodist
▲mily of Dorchester County, Maryland. From the time of his conversion through his
▲nure of such high offices as United States Senator and Governor of Delaware, he
efriended the Methodist itinerants at every opportunity. (*National Cyclopedia of
▶merican Biography*, XI, 530; Lednum, *op. cit.*, 272–78; Ware, *op. cit.*, 80, 234;
▲evens, *op. cit.*, I, 316–19.)
[41] The Widow Brady's home was in Jones Neck about five miles from Dover. (Hall-
▲an, *op. cit.*, 106.)

Sunday, 19. I went to a people whom I tried near two years ago i
vain. Now God is at work among them—several are under awakening
our people going to church, and Mr. Magaw's coming down, has remove
their prejudices. I had great liberty there, on Acts ii, 27–29. At Thoma
White's, on Gal. ii, 17–19, I had great breathings, and not a desire c
thought that tended to evil.

Monday, 20. I read thirteen chapters in Revelation, which was part c
what should have been read yesterday, but I had not time. I read als
about one hundred pages in Comber on the Consecrating Bishops; it
very well if properly attended to. Read fifty pages in Salmon's Grammar.
It is plain to me the devil will let us read always, if we will not pray; b
prayer is the sword of the preacher, the life of the Christian, the terror c
hell, and the devil's plague.

Tuesday, 21. I read a few chapters in the New Testament, and abo
seventy pages in Salmon's Grammar; wrote a letter to my dear friend M
Gough: spent the afternoon in visiting our friends.

Wednesday, 22. I am going up into Kent County, and then to Lewe
have hard trials, inward and outward. I spent this day in riding, and I m
brother Pedicord sick of a fever.

Thursday, 23. I called at the widow Beauchamp's, who was sick, bi
happy in the Lord. She said, "I was with my Saviour all night." She ha
been a constant church-woman; lately brought to seek justification b
faith, and is happy in God. I rode to Mispillion, to be near Reynea
Williams's, on my way to Lewes; was happy this day.

Friday, 24. Rode to Lewes. Am ashamed before God, under
sense of what he has done for me, and how unfaithful and unfruitful I ar
in everything. I rode thirty miles, and on my way called to hear M
Sydenham Thorne, an Episcopal minister. He took care to tell the peopl
they were not to be converted by thunder and lightning, like enthusiast
to know the time and place. In short, I could not tell what he would be at
but he was legal to all intents and purposes. I went to Abraham Harris's
the people were met, and brother Alfrey preached; afterward I delivere
a discourse on Acts xiii, 26, to an attentive congregation, and found m
mind at liberty.

Saturday, 25. Rode to Mr. Shankland's near Lewes, the son of
New-light.

Sunday, 26. Went to town, preached in the court house twice—first o
2 Cor. iv, 2, 3. Afternoon, on Psalm vii, 11–13. I was alarming, as th
people appeared to me to be careless. By the intercession of the friends,
preached at nine o'clock from Mark viii, 34, and following verses, t
about forty or fifty people.

Tuesday, 28. I preached to about fifty or sixty people, on Acts xxvi, 1£

---

[42] Thomas Salmon (1679–1767) was the author of *A New Geographical and Historic*
Grammar . . . and the Present State of the Kingdom of the World.

know not when I was more searching, though but little moving among the people. I was told that Mr. W. proclaimed a fast, to let the people know what the Methodists were, and told them we could not be sent and ordained of God—that we must be sent of the devil. I doubt not but souls will be brought to God here. I rode to Shockley's on *Wednesday*, and preached on Luke xiii, 24–26, to about fifty people; had great life. The work of God deepens here, though it is but low with some. I have rode about a hundred miles since this day week, and preached six times to not more than six hundred people.

Thursday, 30. Lord, keep me this day. I rose early, and preached at Gibson's to about sixty people, on Luke xii, 32. Some melting appeared amongst them. I spent the evening with Mr. Sydenham Thorne, an Episcopal minister.

Friday, October 1, 1779. I preached at the widow Brady's, to about fifty people, on 1 Pet. ii, 25. A great melting among the hearers. There is a good work: here three or four were weeping for pardoning love; they were greatly affected. The work declines at Williams's, but revives here. The Lord doth provoke them to jealousy for their slothfulness and divisions; but I hope they will revive again.

Sunday, 3. I preached on 2 Cor. ii, 11, with some vigour; about two hundred to hear. After this, I went to church. Mr. Neill preached a good sermon on these words, "I am determined not to know anything among you, save Jesus Christ and him crucified." I rode with haste to the Drawbridge, and spoke on 2 Pet. i, 20, 21, to about two hundred people. The Lord was with us of a truth.

Monday, 4. I preached at Caleb Furby's, on Heb. iv, 15, 16; afterward gave an exhortation to the society; and found great fervour among the people.

Tuesday, 5. I preached at Andrew Purdin's, on Acts xvii, 11; met the society; told the people the whole of our intention, and answered all the objections to the preachers and rules to the satisfaction of the serious; joined three in society, one a young lad, about thirteen, broken-hearted.

Wednesday, 6. I rode to Thomas White's. I met the people at Edward White's; they appeared to be stirred up, when I told them that they were some of the first-fruits of the Spirit in these parts, and that God was reviving his work a little distance off.

Thursday, 7. I prayed frequently; read the first epistle to the Corinthians. I am kept watchful, and have some holy breathings after God. I received a letter from brother Daniel Ruff: he says the work deepens in the Jerseys; it spreads in this (Delaware) State, also in Talbot County, in Maryland.

Friday, 8. Brother Thomas McClure came over. We settled a plan for the next half year, in Maryland, Delaware, Pennsylvania, and New Jersey. Our difficulties are great: we have not a sufficient number of proper preachers; some who are gifted cannot go into all the States, on accoun of the oaths; others are under bail, and cannot move far. I have not spen this day as I ought; perhaps not one in my whole life. I read eleven chap ters in the second of Corinthians, in course. Brother Hartley being baile from Talbot jail, after near three months' imprisonment, came to tak Kent in my absence: he preached on: "Persecuted, but not forsaken; cas down, but not destroyed."

Saturday, 9. I went to the Forks, and lodged at White Brown's.

Sunday, 10. The people had not proper notice at Twyford's. I preache on 1 Peter i, 8. In the afternoon I preached at Senior Turpin's, on Roman vi, 17, 18. About two hundred were at both places; some moving at the latte

Monday, 11. I rose at five o'clock, and returned to my study. I wan nothing but devotion to God, and to employ each moment for him. Thi day I preached at John Cannon's, near the chapel, to about three hundre people, on Acts xvii, 11. They did not understand much, and felt less. had a smart contest with a man upwards of seventy years of age, deaf t Scripture, sense, or reason, yet one that has been sorely afflicted; but age like the word, if it does not soften, hardens. I returned to White Brown's a few met me; I prayed and gave an exhortation. God was with us. Thes I call my children. I find my soul feels the good effects of prayer. O! wha can stand before faith and prayer?

Tuesday, 12. We are about to lay a plan to build a chapel at Brown's. I preached the funeral sermon of one Smith; it was thought he had a wor of grace on his heart before he died. There were about one hundred peo ple. I spoke loud and long, on Matt. xxiv, 44. I hope some felt, and wi remember it.

Wednesday, 13. I preached at Joseph Turpin's, to about one hundre people, on Luke xiii, 23–27. There was a move amongst the people. I me the class, and they were serious. I had a fever; went over to H. Keagey's returned at night, and made a plan for the house in the Fork. Next morn ing I set off at nine o'clock, called on the way to appoint preaching at new place. I met with an old man who had strange notions about th Methodists' rejecting the ordinances, and pulling down the Church whom I endeavoured to set right. I came to Joseph Moore's about on o'clock, and found myself better after my ride. I am kept, through grace and find daily growth therein, and am resolved to spend an hour in devo tion before I leave the room each morning. I am more than ever presse with the weight of my work and the worth of souls. Ah! what is preaching without living to God? It is a daily unction we want, that the word ma be like a hammer and fire from our mouths, to break hearts, and kindl life and fire.

Friday, 15. I spoke on 1 Pet. i, 7–4, to about thirty people. It was

---

[43] Brown's Chapel, named for White Brown, was erected in 1781. It housed the paren society of the present Bethel Church on the Seaford Circuit, Sussex County, Delawar

lessing to the people. I was a little unwell; did not, could not, employ my time as I wished. I live in hopes God will make me a blessing in his journey, after trials and disappointments. I read the epistles to the Philippians and Colossians, in the order of reading the Bible through.

Saturday, 16. I went to Joshua Moore's,[44] and met the society. There were about thirty people. I exhorted for near an hour, and spoke closely to the people, who are apt to jar about professions; they are too stiff on both sides.

Sunday, 17. I preached at George Moore's, to about two hundred people, on 2 Thess. i, 7–10. I was assisted to be very alarming, and hope not all in vain: in the afternoon I preached at Joshua Moore's, on Rom. vi, 20–23; some felt who were not at the morning sermon.

Monday, 18. I rose at five o'clock: Lord, help me under all my trials! I addressed the throne of grace fervently, but cannot be what I want to be, at all times, and in everything. Lord, think upon me for good! I was guided by my own experience, being much tempted, to speak on Heb. iv, 14–16, and found it was blessed to the serious part of my congregation. Here were about four hundred people. I found several had been greatly tempted, and ready to despair, as if there was no sacrifice for sin; but, blessed be God, we have a High Priest. My reading was only the first epistle to the Thessalonians. Days are short, and travelling every day, I do very little.

Tuesday, 19. I prayed often, read the second epistle to the Thessalonians, first and second epistles to Timothy, by half after nine o'clock in the morning. I am kept in peace and uprightness of heart, desire, and action. O, that every moment were devoted to God! that I could do more to his glory! I rode to Gitting Bradley's, and preached to about eighty people: was led out, in speaking on 1 John i, 7, 8, to a quiet, unfeeling people. I then drew a subscription for building a chapel here. My mind is in peace; praise God!

Wednesday, 20. I set out for Nanticoke, and found the family unwilling to part with me. Mr. Samuel Tingley preached at the church at Broad Creek. I had to meet the people at a new place; found about eighty or a hundred, rather wild, who looked with amazing wonder. I was exceedingly severe, from Isa. lv, 6, 7. Was invited to dine with Mrs. A——d, who seemed serious; I came to Joseph Turpin's, just at night, and spoke with a man under deep concern for his soul, and hope it will turn to good account in the end. I had a subscription bill, and plan, drawn for a preaching house in the Fork.[45]

---

[44] Joshua Moore, a leader in the Broad Creek Society, later moved to Georgia, where in 1805 and 1806 Asbury visited in his home.

[45] This preaching house was Moore's Chapel, built in 1780, now known as Mt. Pleasant. Samuel Tingley (1745–1800) was the rector of St. Peter's Parish in Sussex County, Delaware.

Thursday, 21. I preached at Turpin's, on 1 Cor. i, 20–25; but few peo ple, and they, too, unfeeling. I lodged at Henry Killen's.

Friday, 22. Preached at White Brown's, on Eph. ii, 19–22. I had some liberty, but it is a day of small things. We obtained some subscribers, and laid out an acre of ground for the purpose of erecting our preaching house I am kept by much prayer and grace. I had the curiosity to read Graham's Journey through England.[46] He gives a large account of the churches and noblemen's seats; but not so accurate on the face of the country, and distance of places.

Maryland—Delaware

Saturday, 23. I preached with some enlargement at Thomas Layton's on Heb. xii, 4, to about a hundred people: the work of God increases here.

Sunday, 24. Cloudy and rain. This day was appointed for Mrs. Jessop's funeral. There were about three hundred people; we had the use of the barn. I spoke with great opening, on Heb. ix, 27; was much assisted in showing to my hearers; first, What it is to die; second, The judgment with the certain consequences of both; third, The appointment for all men once to die; and controverted the argument against being saved from sin, drawn from death—that it is not a punishment to the righteous; that their constitutions being subject to decay, makes it necessary, and in imitation of Christ, to suffer as he did in death, without sin. I went home with Daniel Polk.

Monday, 25. I preached at William Laws's, on Luke vi, last three verses. There were about a hundred persons: the work goes on. I went to see John Laws, junior, sick, and perhaps near his end.

Tuesday, 26. Rode to the widow Maston's, and preached to about seventy people, on Rom. xi, 12. Brother Pedicord, and brother Micajah Debruler met with me; after more than a fortnight's trip. I am preparing for quarterly meeting, expecting it will be a great time of the Lord's power: souls are brought in every day. The death of Mr. Dickenson was something remarkable: full of the world, and judge of Caroline County court; he went to bed well, was taken in an hour after, and soon took his departure out of this to the unseen world. He was often heard to speak against the Methodists; he knows now the truth of these things we controvert.

Wednesday, 27. I was in close employment, bringing up my journal, and reading the Bible and Testament.

Thursday, 28. I was helping to make the arbour to preach under, and prayed frequently that God might be with us; was not so spiritual as I

---

[46] James Graham (1745–94), *Travels and Voyages in Scotland. England, and Ireland.*

ished. I read 2 Peter, and so to the end of my Bible. I rose at three
'clock, and spent an hour in prayer and retirement, and gave myself to
ading. I do not find the same life when at study, as when riding and
reaching every day; though I become tired of both too much.

Friday, 29. I visited the sick, and spent some time in retirement.

Saturday, 30. I preached a sacramental sermon from 1 Cor. xi, 28–30;
as directed to the awful consequence of an unworthy, and the blessings
f a proper, receiving it.

Sunday, 31. We all went to church, preachers and people, and received
ie sacrament. Messrs. Thorne, Neill, and Magaw were present. Mr.
[eill preached an affecting passion sermon; after the Lord's supper, Mr.
Iagaw preached an excellent sermon. At night I preached in the barn, on
He that saith he abideth in him, ought himself also so to walk, even as
e walked."

Monday, November 1, 1779. Our quarterly meeting began in Edward
Vhite's barn. The three clergymen attended with great friendship. I
reached on Isaiah lxvi, 6, 7, and had much liberty: there were about a
iousand or twelve hundred people, and the greater part were serious;
rother Richard Garrettson and brother Ruff exhorted.

Tuesday, 2. I preached again on 1 Thessalonians ii, 13, with more power
id application to the people: we held our love feast in the morning;
reaching at twelve o'clock; brothers Hartley and McClure exhorted.
'here were as many people, or rather more than yesterday; the barn and
eading-floor filled. We had a close conversation with the clergy, who
formed themselves of our rules, and were willing to give us all the
isistance they could by word and deed.

Wednesday, 3. We parted in much affection and great love. We ap-
pinted to meet at Mr. Thorne's, *Monday* three weeks. The Lord hath
one great things for us among the people: may he make and keep us
imble! I am unwell with so much exercise. The weather favoured us
iuch; after a little rain, it cleared away a fine, pure, healthy day, only
pol; all went well; there was great harmony among us, though men of
ifferent political principles; we suppressed these, and all was love. There
as an extraordinary deliverance this morning; brother Edward White's
oy, about six years old, fell into the well; was prevented by his sister
om falling head foremost, but no more; young as he was he held the
ucket: went down as far as the bucket would go, came up, let go the
ucket, took hold of the sides of the well, and saved himself; his father
ent down and brought him up: all these things demand notice and thanks-
.ving.

Thursday, 4. I rose early: prayed several times before I left the room,
id wrote to the stewards in Philadelphia. Most of my time to-day was
iken up in writing: I am kept in peace with God: I am watchful.

I here give a short and extraordinary account of the case of Achsah

Borden.[47] From her childhood she was attentive to reading her Bibl
and ofttimes had serious thoughts of eternity: one day, reading and med
tating, an uncommon light and comfort flowed into her heart. Her sou
cried out, "Sweet Jesus!" and was convinced Christ was her Saviour; he
friends observing for a season that she was very serious, feared a mela
choly; which to prevent, they gathered their friends and neighbour
with music and dancing, thinking to rouse her (as they said) from he
stupidity, or charm off her religious frenzy. Through various temptatio
she was prevailed upon to go into company, of course, into sin: she lo
her comfort, and afterward fell into deep distress: she had heard of th
Methodists, and was anxious to go to them that they might pray for he
Those with whom she was, paid no regard to her importunity, but locke
her up in a room, and ordered all the knives to be taken away. She kne
their meaning, but says she was under no temptation to destroy or la
violent hands upon herself. Soon after this her speech failed her, so tha
she only spoke half sentences, and would be stopped by inability; but b
grasping anything hard in her hand, she could speak with difficulty an
deliberation; but soon lost this power, and a dumb spirit took perfe
possession of her: she said, then it was impressed on her mind, "Th
effectual and fervent prayer of a righteous man availeth much." Sh
heard the Methodists were a people that prayed much, and still retaine
her desire to go amongst them, and by signs made it known to her friend
And after about one year's silence, her mother was prevailed upon to g
with her to New Mills, New Jersey, (about thirteen miles distant,) whe
there was a society and meeting house: they knew no Methodists, ne
could get any one to tell them where to find any, notwithstanding the
were now in the midst of them. Satan hindered: inquiry was made amon
the Baptists, who knew the Methodists, of whom we might have expecte
better things. They returned home, and after another year's waiting i
silence, by signs her mother was persuaded to come to New Mills agai
they fell in with the Baptists again; but turning from them, with muc
difficulty, and some hours' wandering, they found one to direct then
They went where a number were met for prayer; the brethren saw int
her case, believing it was a dumb spirit, and that God would cast him ou
Prayer was made part of three days: the third day at evening she crie
for mercy, soon spoke and praised God, from a sense of comfortin
pardoning love. During the two years of her silence, she would not wor
at all, nor do the smallest thing.

Friday, 5. Set apart for fasting and prayer: though tempted at times,
shall not be overcome: I had rather die than sin against God. I read abou
one hundred octavo pages, then applied to the Bible for the exercises o
the remaining part of the day: I began the reading of my Bible throug

[47] For accounts of Achsah Borden see Lednum, *op. cit.*, 234, 235; Atkinso
Memorials of Methodism in New Jersey, 130–33.

gain: read a few chapters in Genesis, visited the sick in the neighbour-
ood, but ate nothing till six o'clock at night; had various struggles, but
he grace of God is sufficient for me at all times: glory be to Jesus!

Saturday, 6. I set out for Boyer's, called at Joseph Purden's, who was
onvinced about two years ago by my preaching, but through fear and
ant of resolution was kept back: he said my preaching always came home
o him; now he has found peace.

Sunday, 7. I preached at Boyer's, on Luke vi, and last verse; then rode
o town, and heard a most excellent sermon, on "Follow peace with all
men, and holiness." The sermon was close, and much to the purpose. I
reached on 1 Corinthians i, 19–23, very close, and endeavoured to tear
way their props and false dependencies. I lodged at Mr. Magaw's.

Monday, 8. I rode to Hilliard's, where, with much comfort, I preached
o about forty people, and had the most liberty I ever felt here before. I
ead a part of the Confession of Faith; some good, and other very strong
hings in it. I thought the case of Robert Turner[48] worth notice: he came
om the Jerseys into this peninsula, and was useful in preaching. Lewis
lfrey was convinced by him, who had been an extravagant sinner, and
fterward became a useful preacher. The said Turner went home to his
amily, to settle his affairs, and intended to travel after a few weeks;
rother Ruff, from a great call, pressed him to go into the circuit before
he time he intended; Ruff said, "Suppose you had but a fortnight to live,
ould you not go?" Turner answered he would. By the time Ruff came
ound, about a fortnight, Turner died with the small-pox!

Tuesday, 9. I spent my time in reading a part of the Confession of Faith
nd Catechism, and transcribing a few sections; I read two chapters, and
reached on the Epistle to the Laodiceans; I was assisted in speaking,
nd inwardly mourned over the people. Though very severely tried at
mes, I have great feelings in prayer, and sweet consolation. I find the
ord revives my soul, and I am greatly assisted; I preached at Alfrey's to
bout thirty people. I have been greatly led out every time I have spoken
n this visit.

Wednesday, 10. I rose with a sense of the Divine presence, in wrestling
rayer; I find peace, though not without some darts from Satan: I read
ree chapters in the Bible; rode to the widow Howard's, and preached on
aiah liii, 1. I spoke as plain as I could, but I fear to little purpose; rode
o friend Heathers's,[49] and found more love to these people than formerly.

Thursday, 11. I preached to about forty people, at Hilliard's, thirty at

[48] Robert Turner, probably a local preacher from New Jersey, introduced Methodism
the northeastern part of Kent County, Delaware, in 1778 or 1779. (Lednum, *op. cit.*,
1, 222; Hallman, *op. cit.*, 234.)

[49] The Heather family lived between Dover, Delaware, and Sudlersville, Queen
nnes County, Maryland, near Holden's Chapel. This was the second chapel erected
 the Methodists in Queen Annes County. (Emory: *History of Queen Anne's County*,
8, 571; Lednum, *op. cit.*, 258; Hallman, *op. cit.*, 322, 326.)

Alfrey's, and forty at Howard's; I had liberty in speaking on the faithfu and wise servant, at the Forest chapel.

Friday, 12. I spoke on Galatians vi, 16–18, and was pointed, but ther was no great moving among the people: I dwelt upon the life and powe of religion: if they understood me, I fear they did not feel the word. I kep this day in fasting, till near four o'clock, then took a cup of milk an bread: I have read the Confession of Faith and the Assembly's Catechism they are calculated to convert the judgment, and make the people syst matical Christians.

Saturday, 13. I went to Wells's, and had about forty hearers. I spoke o Zechariah, eighth chapter and last verse: "We will go with you: for w have heard that God is with you." Brother Garrettson preached at Shaw at night. I received a letter from Mr. Jarratt, who is greatly alarmed, bu it is too late:[50] he should have begun his opposition before. Our zealou dissenting brethren are for turning all out of the society who will not sul mit to their administration. I find the spirit of separation grows amon them, and fear that it will generate malevolence, and evil speaking: afte all my labour, to unite the Protestant Episcopal ministry to us, they sa "We don't want your unconverted ministers; the people will not receiv them." I expect to turn out shortly among them, and fear a separatic will be unavoidable: I am determined, if we cannot save all, to save part; but for the divisions of Reuben there will be great heart searchings

Sunday, 14. I preached at the chapel,[51] to about four hundred seriou people, from John iv, 48: I spoke for near two hours; perhaps it is th last time. I preached at Shaw's in the afternoon, on Numbers x, 29, an following verses, to about three hundred people, and had much sweetnes surely there will be a work here. I have been pressed to go to Virginia time and circumstances must shortly determine whether I go to the nort or south.

Monday, 15. I rode twelve miles, to Stephen Black's, and preached c John xii, 48, to about sixty people. I had some opening, and met the clas I am kept in peace, though under reasoning about what is right and wrong but I am determined to be on the sure side.

Tuesday, 16. Rode to Callahan's,[52] and had about fifty people: spok on "The kingdom of God is not in word but in power." I then returne to Thomas White's.

[50] Devereaux Jarratt had reason to anticipate the policy of American Methodis concerning ordinances as hitherto officially declared at their conferences. From Asbury comment it appears that Jarratt was expressing alarm over the threatened cleavag (Sweet: *Men of Zeal*, 42; Jarratt, *op. cit.*)

[51] This was Thomas Chapel, originally called Forest Chapel and later White's Chap (Lednum, *op. cit.*, 234.)

[52] Edward Callahan's home was between Rising Sun and Magnolia, Kent Count Delaware. Henry Boehm conducted his funeral service in September, 1806. (Boehn *op. cit.*, 155.)

Wednesday, 17. I rode to Stradley's: had about sixty people to hear: met the society of about twenty-two members, all serious, and under good impressions. I was surprised to find them so clear in their ideas of religion, and was blest among them: returned to Thomas White's, met the people, gave a warm, searching exhortation. I am troubled about our separating brethren, in Virginia: I have read through the Book of Genesis; and again have read the Confession of Faith, the Assembly's Catechism, Directory of Church Government, and Form for the Public Worship: now I understand it better than I like it. I purposed to rise at four o'clock, as often as I can, and spend two hours in prayer and meditation; two hours in reading, and one in recreating and conversation; and in the evening, to take my room at eight, pray and meditate an hour, and go to bed at nine o'clock: all this I purpose to do, when not travelling; but to rise at four o'clock every morning.

Thursday, 18. Spent the day in reading and prayer, but was sorely tempted; wrote letters to William Lynch, William Watters, and the venerable Otterbein.

Friday, 19. I kept a day of fasting and humiliation.

Saturday, 20. Ended the reading of Salmon's Grammar, more than six hundred pages.

Sunday, 21. Preached on John v, 44, to the end of the chapter, and was clear and pointed: the people are stirred up, but there are disorders among them, occasioned by their unfaithfulness. Met the society, and afterward the Africans.

Monday, 22. Rose between four and five, spent an hour in prayer and meditation, read a few chapters in the Bible before it was day-light: I want to be all devoted to God; every moment given up to Christ. Rode to Maxfield's, and preached to about three hundred people; spoke on "Lord, are there few that be saved?" First, showed, What we are to be saved from. 2. How we are saved. 3. Why there are few. No open sinner can be in a state of salvation; no formalist, violent sectarian, having only opinions and modes of religion; no hypocrites or backsliders; no, nor those who are only seekers. I came back, was much tried, prayed to the Lord for peace, and opened my Bible on these words: "So the service was prepared, and the priests stood in their places, and the Levites in their courses, according to the king's commandment."

Tuesday, 23. Rode to Robert Layton's, and preached to about thirty people, from "Through much tribulation we must enter into the kingdom of God." Spoke as my own experience led me; then returned to Edward White's, and lectured on Moses meeting his father-in-law. (Exodus xviii.) There were not many people, but they were happy.

Wednesday, 24. Rode to the widow Jump's, and preached to about thirty souls, on "Why sayest thou, O Jacob, and speakest thou, O Israel," &c. There is a declension here; but I follow my own feelings. A great

sweetness has attended me this day, although I drank of the wormwood
and the gall in the morning. When I get out into the work, I am always
happy.

Thursday, 25. Rose at four o'clock, and had a sweet time in meditation
and prayer, from four to six; purpose to spend two hours in the morning,
and one at night, in these blessed exercises. Began this morning to read
books on the practice of physic: I want to help the bodies and souls of
men.

Friday, 26. Preached at William Laws's to about a hundred people;
spoke on Numbers x, 29. While meeting the class, some appeared greatly
affected: this evening I read in the Bible, and some books on physic: also
exhorted; for the people press upon us to hear the word.

Saturday, 27. Was kept in a calm after the devil had been tearing my
soul like a lion; but he hath left me for a season. I looked into Rutherford's Letters,[53] and they were blest to me: also looked into Doddridge's
Rise and Progress of Religion, and that was also blessed to me. My soul
is waiting on the Lord for full Christian perfection. I poured out my soul
to the Lord for this, and for my brethren in all parts of the world, that the
power of religion may continue with us, as a people. I tremble to think of
the cloud of the Divine presence departing from us; if this should be, I
hope not to live to see it; and with Mr. Wesley, desire that God may
rather scatter the people to the ends of the earth; I had rather they should
not be, than to be a dead society:—Amen, says poor William Spencer.

Sunday, 28. Preached at the widow Brady's before church, on Hebrews
x, 12, and following verses; had some liberty in speaking: afterward went
to church, received the sacrament, and returned to Brady's, and heard
Joseph Cromwell, an original indeed—no man's copy. Spent a day with
Mr. Thorne.

Tuesday, 30. I intended to go to Choptank, but Mr. Magaw was coming down to preach a funeral sermon, and desired me to stay. We spent
an evening at the widow Brady's together, and had some talk about
erecting a Kingswood school in America.

Wednesday, December 1, 1779. Rode twelve miles to Cardeen's,[54] and
preached to about one hundred serious people, and I hope there will be
good done: met Mr. Airey,[55] from Dorchester county, who was convinced

[53] Samuel Rutherford (1600-61), was a Scottish Presbyterian theologian and controversialist. His letters were published in 1664. Asbury sent this volume to Freeborn
Garrettson while he was a prisoner in the Cambridge, Maryland, jail. (Garrettson,
op. cit., 153.)

[54] The Cardeen home was south of Canterbury, Kent County, Delaware, an appointment later known as Laws' Meeting House. (Lednum, *op. cit.*, 257; Hallman, *op.
cit.*, 108, 237.)

[55] Henry Airey, in whose home southeast of Cambridge, Maryland, the first meeting
in Dorchester County was held, was converted under the influence of a relative, Mary
Ennals. Her sister was the first wife of Richard Bassett. In response to Airey's request

by reading the writings of old Mr. Perkins. Mr. Airey solicits preaching in that county. I have taken cold by some means, it has brought on an inflammation in my throat.

Thursday, 2. There fell a very heavy rain, that prevented my going to Johnny-cake Landing.[56]

Sunday, 26. Preached at Andrew Purden's to a large congregation: spoke with great power from "His name shall be called Jesus." Afterward preached at Jonathan Sipple's, on John ii, 8; there was some moving among the people.

Monday, 27. Visited the sick, Cranmer, a faithful soul, and Ruth Smith, wearing away fast with a consumption, but praising God, and continually preaching Christ.

Tuesday, 28. A stormy, rainy day: went to Lewis's, but none came. I must spend the whole night in prayer, after the example of my Lord; for temptation is to try me; perhaps for my good, as I have many things to lift me up. Brother Hartley is now married,[57] and begins to care for his wife. I have spent but little time to-day in reading or writing. There is a prospect of a work of religion in this State, if the preachers are faithful; but I fear none more than myself; yet, sure I am that I want to be the Lord's. The hard, cold weather is broke at last. People suffer much more in winter by cold, and in summer by heat, here than in England. I find the care of a wife begins to humble my young friend, and makes him very teachable: I have thought he always carried great sail; but he will have ballast now.

Wednesday, 29. Preached at D. Dehadway's, to about two hundred people, and spoke livingly from 2 Cor. vi, 17, 18. I was led out greatly. Preached at night at Joseph Purden's, from 1 Cor. xv, 58, and had much liberty. One of the devil's camps, a tavern, is broken up here; for most of their neighbours have forsaken them.

Thursday, 30. Rode to Stradley's, and preached on Luke iv, 17, 18. I had life, and there were more people than I expected. I came to Thomas White's, and went to see James Patterson, very ill; he appears to decline swiftly.

Friday, 31. I went to Cardeen's; a dreadful road, eight miles through the woods, and very cold. I spoke with great warmth on 1 John iii, 4, 5. Always, when most tried I have the greatest liberty.

For Methodist preaching in Dorchester, Asbury sent Freeborn Garrettson on February 20, 1780. Henry Airey and Caesar Rodney furnished $100,000 bond for Garrettson's release from the Cambridge jail. (Bangs, *op. cit.*, 108–13; Lednum, *op. cit.*, 261.)

[56] This was the present Frederica, Kent County, Delaware.

[57] After his marriage into one of the earliest Methodist families in Talbot County, Joseph Hartley resided in Miles River Neck near Easton, Maryland. (Lednum, *op. cit.*, 232, 233, 262.)

by reading the writings of old Mr. Perkins. Mr. Mair solicits preaching in that county. I have taken cold by some means; it has brought on an inflammation in my throat.

Thursday, 2. There fell a very heavy rain, that prevented my going to obtain—*cake I audited.*

Sunday, 26. Preached at Andrew Purden's to a large congregation: spoke with great power from "His name shall be called Jesus." Afterward preached at Jonathan Sipple's on Johns. 8.&here was some moving among the people.

Monday, 27. Visited the sick. C ranner, a faithful soul, and Ruth Smith, withering away fast with a consumption, but praising God, and continually preaching Christ.

Tuesday, 28. A stormy, rainy day; went to Lewis's that none othee, I must spend the whole night in prayer, after the example of my Lord: for temptation is to try me: perhaps for my good; as I have many things to lift me up. Brother Hartley is now married: and begins to care for his wife. I have spent but little time to-day in reading or writing. There is a prospect of a work of religion in this State, if the preachers are faithful: but I fear none more than myself yet, sure I am that I want to be the Lord's. The hard, cold weather is broke at last. People suffer upon more in winter by cold, and in summer by heat, here than in England. I find the care of a wife begins to humble my young friend, and make him very teachable: I have thought he always carried great sail: but he will have ballast now.

Wednesday, 29. Preached at D. Dehadway's, to about two hundred people, and spoke feelingly from 2 Cor. vii. 17. 18. I was led out greatly. Preached at night at Joseph Purden's, from 1 Cor. xv. 58, and had much liberty. One of the devil's camps is torn asunder up here; for most of their neighbours have forsaken them.

Thursday, 30. Rode to Stradley's, and preached on Luke iv. 17, 18, 19, and life; and there were more people than I expected. I came to Thomas White's, and went to see James Patterson, very ill; he appears to decline with.

Friday, 31. I went to Cordeon's; a dreadful road, eight miles through the wood, and very cold. I spoke with great warmth on 1 John iii. 1, 2, 3. Always, when most tried I have the greatest liberty.

For Methodist preaching in Dorchester, Maryland, see Freeborn Garretson on Cokesbury
0. 180. Henry Airey and Caesar Rodney furnished $10,000 bond for Garretson's
teased from the Continental jail (Bates op. cit. 108-11; Todman, op. cit. 264).

This was the present Frederica, Kent County, Delaware.

After his marriage into one of the earliest Methodist families in Talbot County, Joseph Hartley resided in Miles River Neck near Easton, Maryland (Colhoun, op. cit.
12, 213, 242.)

1780

CHAPTER NINE

Delaware

Saturday, January 1, 1780. I preached at Edward White's on Luke iii, 9, with great liberty; not in much order, but useful to the people. Went see James Peterkins; he is continually praying now death is before n. Lord, hear and answer his prayer! Now commences the new year; ese two years past have been trying years to me, and I doubt not but s will be so likewise; only, my God keep me through the water and e, and let me rather die than live to sin against thee!

Sunday, 2. Rode to Cardeen's, eight miles through the swamp, by ten :lock, and preached at eleven to about two hundred people, from, "To-y, if ye will hear his voice, harden not your hearts." I had the presence God, and spoke more than an hour. I believe good was done. We came ck safe through the snow and ice: preached at brother Edward White's little after two o'clock, on Deut. xxix, 10–13, upon renewing their venant: addressed the family at night. It was a dreary night of rain, nd, snow, and frost. I have been much tried and much blest. "It is ough much tribulation we must enter the kingdom."

Monday, 3. Exceeding cold weather: thank the Lord for a house and me, and all necessary things.

Tuesday, 4. Read a chapter in the Bible, read the Good Steward, a rmon upon the Reformation of Manners, and Mr. Wesley's Sermon on r. Whitefield's death:[1] was closely employed: prayed three times in the

For an account of the preparation and delivery of this sermon in Tottenham Court ad Chapel, London, and its repetition in the tabernacle at Greenwich, see Wesley's *rnal,* November 10, 23, 1770.

family, and attended private prayer my usual times. I long to be holy a
to make the best use of a short life. How much skill is required to b(
doctor! What diseases the human body is subject to! What regimen a
care are necessary! How many diseases hath the soul! What skill ough
preacher to have to know the causes and cures!—it will require all
time and study: the consequences of miscarriages are greater in the s(
than the body.

Wednesday, 5. Prayed and read closely till three o'clock in Mr. Wesle
fourth volume of Methodized Works.[2] I have my trials, and believe i
because I am not so extensively in the work as I hope to be shortly.

Thursday, 6. I did not travel; but read my Testament, and some
Young's poetry,[3] which is very sublime: was much taken up in praye
want to be employed in travelling and preaching, if the weather wo(
permit. Europeans cannot judge of the inclemency of our climate but
experience. I have hard struggles; but, glory be to God, his grace
sufficient.

Friday, 7. The ice on the ground, and the coldness of the weath
prevents my travelling. This was a day of fasting: I ate nothing till af
three o'clock, and then only a bowl of milk; amidst all my exercises, I f
as though I advanced in the Divine life; am thankful that I am so w
provided for, when, no doubt, thousands are suffering the want of fo(
firing, house room, and clothing. O! may I act worthy of these favou
At four o'clock began reading Mr. Fletcher's Checks.[4]

Saturday, 8. I spent in reading and prayer.

Sunday, 9. Preached on 2 Cor. xiii, 5: "Examine yourselves whether
be in the faith;" and was as pointed as I could be. Lord, make it a blessi
to souls!

Monday, 10. Spent part of the day in examining the list of Mr. Wesle
books; employed some time in prayer, but not so much as I had appoint(

Tuesday, 11. I read the Checks; went to view a spot of land for buildi
a preaching house[5] upon, formed a subscription paper, and obtain
subscribers for about £80.

Wednesday, 12. Was principally employed in assorting the books 1
sale.

[2] This was probably Wesley's *Christian Library*. Volumes II–XII were published
1751.

[3] This was probably *The Complaint, or Night Thoughts on Life, Death, and .
mortality*, 1742, by Edward Young (1683–1765). He was an English poet, playwrig
and clergyman.

[4] John Fletcher (1729–85) was a native of Switzerland. Although a clergyman of
Church of England, Fletcher became one of the most ardent and helpful associates
Mr. Wesley, who once designated him as his successor. Fletcher's *Checks on A
nomianism* is a work distinguished for scholarship and doctrinal disagreement with
bitterness.

[5] This house was familiarly called the White Brown Chapel, near the present Seafo
Sussex County, Delaware.

Thursday, 13. Finished reading the First Check: the style and spirit in ıich Mr. Fletcher writes, at once bespeak the scholar, the logician, and ⁄ine.

Friday, 14. A day of fasting, prayer, writing, and visiting the society: ıs kept in peace, but did not spend so much time in prayer as I wished do.

Saturday, 15. I am going into Sussex: my mind is serene, raised to God d heaven, and longing for the salvation of souls as much as ever. I de to Johnstown:[6] the roads are spread with sheets of ice; but my horse, ugh shod, went safe.

Sunday, 16. Read my selections, and part of the Revelation, and eached at Alexander Law's, to about a hundred and fifty people, an gumentative sermon, from John iv, 48. There were some opposers to- .y. I met the family, and spoke to the Africans.

Monday, 17. Spoke from 1 Timothy i, 15, with great enlargement, to out one hundred and fifty people; and *Tuesday* at Sharp's, on 1 John i, 9. I had much light and liberty while speaking. I lodged at Mr. Rawl- ɔn's, a candid, conversable Presbyterian elder.

Wednesday, 19. Preached on Mark viii, 34–36, at William Law's, to out one hundred and fifty people; met the society. I was led out upon e subject, and believe many felt it. The Presbyterians appeared to be ry attentive: truth will bear a strict scrutiny.

Thursday, 20. Preached at Spencer Hitchen's to about thirty people, on tus i, 15, 16. I was searching, and the weather very piercing: afterward nt to Mr. Daniel Polk's.

Friday, 21. Rode to White Brown's. This week past I have been in ıch haste, but have read a little every day, and finished the book of shua. O, for more holiness of heart! I cannot rise so early as I would, is so extremely cold these days and nights. I long to be more spiritual. am glad to hear that brother Joseph Cromwell's labours are blest in e Fork,[7] to the stirring up and awakening of several. Glory be to God! .ay I rejoice more heartily in the success of others, and yet be moved to ıulation, to live holier, to labour more, and preach with greater fervour!

Sunday, 23. About three hundred people flocked together upon short ɔtice, to whom I preached on Matt. i, 21: "Thou shalt call his name sus:" was very plain, but not methodical: met the society; the strangers ho stayed, fled when I had nearly done, for fear I should speak to them. the afternoon I had a long conference with a Nicolite,[8] who wanted to ıd out who were right—they or we; a man of no great argument, and I ar but little religion: this makes these people so troublesome to us.

---

[6] Johnstown is one mile east of Greenwood, Delaware.

[7] The Fork was a short term for North West Fork Hundred, Sussex County, in which hite Brown and other Methodist families lived.

[8] For a description of this sect see *Journal* entry for February 20, 1780.

Monday, 24. Preached a funeral sermon for Solomon Turpin, to ne
three hundred people, from Gen. 1, 24. Was much assisted, and spo
including the funeral service and exhortations in all, three hours: t
people stayed with great patience and seriousness, except a few w
young men. The work revives, and truth will spread.

Tuesday, 25. Preached to about thirty people at Joseph Turpin's.
Psalm xxvii, 10,—the "orphan's hope." I had not great enlargement, b
the few present, old and young, were in some degree affected. Satan h
tried me, but cannot prevail. I read but little: the weather is so sever
cannot keep from the fire; the rooms are cold and unfinished, and famili
are in the way. I kept my times for prayer; but not so long or so feeli
as I desire.

Wednesday, 26. Preached a funeral for one Sizer; though it was a co
day, I had about one hundred people: spoke from Psalm xc, 12. The hou
being uncomfortable, and the people cold, I had not the satisfaction
wished for, but hope there was some good done; cold as it was, I read t
burial service, and made some observations upon it that ought to impre
our minds. I returned to John Flowers's, spent some time in conversati
and prayer, and then came to R. Turpin's. There are three serious gir
left by their father in possession of a good plantation: they are youn
but if they are faithful, God will stand by them: Rebecca is a pattern
piety, and a stay to all the rest. I could not but advise them to keep hou
Lord, help me to improve! What is man! I am much troubled at times
must travel; I always find a blessing in it: God has given me health, t
best convenience, and some gifts; and I have some particular busine
that others cannot so well do. Lord, pardon my past slothfulness!

Thursday, 27. The weather was very cold, and the wind so exceeding
high, it was hardly safe to travel: as I had no appointment I stopt for o
day, and read my Bible in course, through Judges; read a part of Fothe
gill's Journal;[9] instructed Thomas Garrettson[10] a little in English.

Friday, 28. A fine day for travelling: yesterday was so cold, it w
hardly possible to travel without getting one's limbs frozen. I rose soo
after five o'clock, prayed four times before I left my room, and twice
the family. I then set out for Isaac Moore's below Broad Creek, met wi
some difficulty in the way from the ice, but came there safe. Was various
exercised with thoughts, and had hard fightings. After riding twenty-fi
miles I took a little food, this being a day of abstinence and prayer with m

Saturday, 29. Rose at five o'clock, prayed five times in private, once
the family, and transcribed into my collection a piece for the preache
from Baxter's Works. Read a few chapters in the Old and one in the Ne

<hr>

[9] John Fothergill (1712–80), member of a Quaker family, became an eminent Er
lish physician, author, and philanthropist.

[10] Thomas Garrettson, the uncle of Freeborn Garrettson, attended a service co
ducted by the latter at the Fork Chapel. (Garrettson, *op. cit.*, 173, 174.)

stament. My soul is more at rest from the tempter when I am busily
ıployed. Very cold weather yet; we are under great disadvantages in
ge families, people want much to talk; no glass in the windows; some
ıces not a room to sit in with any solitude. Went to visit a young woman,
ar her end, in a dropsy: she was in some doubt about her acceptance
th God, though a professor. I came in to her comfort—surely it is a
ious thing to die!

Sunday, 30. Preached on John, Second Epistle, 8th verse: had many to
ar, and I spoke with zeal.

Monday, 31. Rose at five o'clock, and prayed six times, and hope God
ıl be with and bless us, and make it a time of power; but O! I pass
rough the fire day after day. Lord let me rather die than live to dis-
·nour thee! I preached on Psalm cxiii, 1; had many to hear, but not
·at liberty in speaking. Joseph Cromwell came in and gave an exhorta-
·n: the people were very serious. In the evening we divided the circuit,[11]
·d settled the preachers' stations—John Cooper for Sussex and Somer-
·; Hartley and Stephen Black for Kent and part of Sussex.

Tuesday, February 1, 1780. At nine o'clock we had a love feast—a time
· great tenderness; after some time brother Cromwell spoke, his words
·nt through me, as they have every time I have heard him—he is the
·ly man I have heard in America with whose speaking I am never tired;
·lways admire his unaffected simplicity; he is a prodigy—a man that
·nnot write or read well, yet, according to what I have heard, he is much
·e the English John Brown, or the Irish John Smith, or Beveridge's
·epherd's Boy: I fear he will not stand or live long.[12] The power of God
·ends him more or less in every place, he hardly ever opens his mouth in
·in; some are generally cut to the heart, yet he himself is in the fire of
·nptation daily. Lord, keep him every moment. I preached on 1 Thess. i,
· and was much led out; there were about five hundred people. This
·eting will be attended with a great blessing—rich and poor approved
·e doctrine. I heard of the sudden death of my dear friend Jonathan
·pple. About eighteen months ago he was brought home to God, from
· open sinner, to be a happy, faithful man. He is soon taken away from
·e evil to come; he was loved, and is much lamented: in extreme pain,
·t full of patience, and rejoicing in God, he made a blessed end. All
·il, happy soul! Soon taken thy flight to rest! This is clear gains indeed—

[1] This was the Delaware Circuit. Asbury's division by counties was superseded at
· Baltimore Conference about three months distant by the creation of Sussex Circuit
· Delaware and Dorset, or Dorchester, Circuit on the eastern shore. Sussex County
· s in Delaware, and Somerset County was in Maryland. (Scharf: *History of Delaware*,
· 1159.)

[12] To Asbury the native ability and the reckless zeal of Cromwell were reminiscent of
·esley's eyewitness accounts of Brown and Smith, and the misfortunes of the former.
·'esley's *Journal*, April 24, 1747; September 28, 1749; June 13, 1759; and July 11,
·71; May 24, 1773.)

late brought in, soon taken away; my mind moves with mixed passions
joy and grief. Freeborn Garrettson spoke in his usual plainness, as
matter and manner, but it moved the people greatly.

Wednesday, 2. I preached a funeral sermon over a young woman
the name of Amelia Dodwell: I had hope in her death. I spoke on Eccle
ix, 10, with great fervour and clear views; brother Joseph Cromw
exhorted: I spoke at the grave; the people were serious. Strangers a
tended, that did not, would not, before quarterly meeting. These peop
were drawn, and friends refreshed; life begets life. I have been humbl
in spirit, but, blessed be God, all things go well in my own heart. Freebo
Garrettson had a desire to go to Dorchester; I consented to his goin
and the Lord go with him.

Thursday, 3. Rode to Mr. Freeny's, about ten miles, and preached
about one hundred people. I spoke upon "To-day, if ye will hear h
voice," &c. Brother Cromwell exhorted, and some were moved.

Friday, 4. Rode to Jonathan Boyer's, and preached to about eigh
people: the Baptists followed us about. Here we met with a woman
deep distress; we both spoke to her, and, I hope, sent her away comforte
I had today a providential escape: my horse started, turned round in t
woods, hardly escaped running me on the trees; which, if he had, wou
have overset me, and might have broken the carriage and my limbs, t
ground being so hard; but, thanks be to God, I received no hurt. I spol
at Boyer's from these words, "Will ye be also his disciples?"

Saturday, 5. Came to Morgan Williams's, and was received kindly f
the first time. I found one of my countrymen under deep distress, a bac
slider, and a man of sense; if restored it may be he will be a preacher. I
is afraid it is impossible he should be restored. I showed him the meanir
of Heb. 6th chap., that it must be one who denied the work of the Ho
Spirit, and opposed as the Jews did, and in enmity to crucify Christ, whi
he never did.

Sunday, 6. Spoke on Hosea xiii, 9. There were more people than t
house could hold, and they were very attentive. The people seem qui
ripe in the Fork for the Gospel. I rode to Choptank, near thirty miles.

Monday, 7. I went to see the old people, Mr. and Mrs. James Peterki
rejoicing in God, and willing to die. Made an addition to my book to t
preachers. I have done but little of account, but visiting the sick, ar
praying with them.

Tuesday, 8. I added to my book, and kept my times of prayer; I abridge
from Mr. Law. My mind was well taken up with God.

Wednesday, 9. Have peace, but long to be more employed in the publ
work. I hear the work spreads in Bolingbroke and Talbot.[13] So the Lor

[13] In this vicinity, in which Trappe, Maryland, is located, a Dr. Allen was the lead
in one of the earliest societies, from which Bolingbroke Chapel took its name. (Coke
Journal, 49; Lednum, *op. cit.*, 261, 262; Hallman, *op. cit.*, 337.)

ads us on through many hinderances. Perhaps there never was such a
ork carried on by such simple men, of such small abilities, and no
arning. The Lord shows his own power, and makes bare his own right
m! Brother Garrettson set off for Dorchester to preach the Gospel. We
mmitted the remains of Mrs. Peterkin to the dust at Thomas White's;
e died in full triumph of faith; many people were present, and we gave
hortations suited to the occasion.

Thursday, 10. I read a little in the morning, and visited the sick. Was
essed in talking with John White's family.[14] I must spend whole nights
prayer; I have been in peace, but want more love. Brother Hartley has
tained a discharge from Talbot jail, after much labour and pains; the
and jury returned the bill of indictment, *Ignoramus*. Thus God makes
ay for us in all trials. Prayed for an hour after I took my room; I took
y bed about ten o'clock. Had not prayed in the day so much as I should.
, my God, keep me in the spirit of prayer!

Saturday, 12. Visited my friends, and prayed from house to house; met
e class, and was much blessed. Spent some time in prayer; but Satan
th many devices.

Sunday, 13. I rode eight miles, and preached to about two hundred
ople, who seemed dead and unfeeling. Spoke on Romans v, 19, 20, and
boured hard to make them understand, but fear they did not. At three
clock preached on 1 Tim. iii, 5, with some life; we had but few people,
d most of them strangers.

Monday, 14. The work of God revives, but the people are not so faithful
they ought to be.

Tuesday, 15. A rainy morning: I had to go to Slaughter's; and on my
ay called at John Case's, prayed, and went on to the place of preaching.
here were about one hundred very attentive, poor, ignorant people.
oke on Acts xiii, 26, with great liberty. It was through great tribulation
went; I am tried as by fire. I called at Diall's, and spoke to him about
s soul; went to see old Mrs. Cox, a great professor of religion, but now
ing out of her senses on account of the loose behaviour of one of her
ildren; which makes me fear she was upon a self-righteous foundation.
e is now in a delirium, insensible of anything. Spoke rousingly to her,
t could not wake her at all. Went from thence to Mr. Peterkin's: he is
ck, but has no deep sense of religion.

Wednesday, 16. A bright, blessed morning, but I am in heaviness
rough manifold temptations; but trust the Lord will keep me. Have
ad in the intervals of these two days twelve of Mr. Wesley's Sermons;

[14] This was probably the family of John White, a brother of Dr. Edward White and
phew of Judge Thomas White. Freeborn Garrettson, who was with John White
en he was converted on his deathbed and conducted his funeral, says that he was
ce "a great persecutor." The widow and children became Methodists. (*The Arminian
agazine*, XVII, 228.)

and cannot read them without conviction and great instruction. God
with me: he is preparing me for great labours, and I hope yet to endure
the end; but must be more sanctified:

> "Lord, hasten the hour, thy kingdom bring in,
> And give me the power to live without sin."

Keep me holy and constant in thy work, always industrious, that Sata
may have no fair occasion to tempt. I lectured at Edward White's o
John xiv, 19–21, and had great liberty, love, and life; and the peop
likewise. After all my trials, God blesses me. Satan is a liar, and Christ
true, and will never leave nor forsake me.

Thursday, 17. I am going to preach a funeral sermon for Zach. Nichol
a schoolmaster, a reading Churchman, an Englishman, and wish I cou
say assuredly, a Christian. I found great liberty in preaching from Mat
xxiv, 44; read and explained the funeral service; there was a great meltir
among the people, and I hope not in vain.

Saturday, 19. I rode through bad roads to Morgan Williams's; and wa
in peace and prayer. Stepped into Johnson's, took dinner, and had son
close conversation with him; he is a mild, conversable man. I came i
late; the people were met; exhorted, and felt some life among the peopl

Sunday, 20. Was solemn in prayer. Spoke on James i, 22–24. I wa
assisted to be close, moving, and argumentative; but have in genera
hard labour. Here they are an unsettled people, and weak of understand
ing; preached in the afternoon at the widow Brady's, from James i, 8
"A double-minded man is unstable in all his ways." This text was presse
upon me to speak from, while at Williams's, and I could not get over i
In the afternoon I found there was a cause; the Nicolites had been work
ing upon several of our friends, and had shook them with their craf
These are a people who sprung from one Nicols, a visionary, but I hop
a good man: he held Quaker principles, but the Friends would not receiv
him. A certain James Harris is at present their leader; they clothe in whit
take everything from nature, and condemn all other societies that do no
conform to the outward: If a man were to speak like an archangel; if h
sung, prayed, and wore a black, or a coloured coat, he would not b
received by these people. They were almost asleep when the Methodis
came, but now are awake and working with simple, awakened peopl
They love, like some other denominations, to fish in troubled water. The
oppose family prayer as much as any sinners in the country; and hav
much to say against our speakers: profess what they will, there is nothin
in names.

Monday, 21. I am kept in peace. Preached twice yesterday, and met th
society. Joseph Hartley is sick. I see there is no way like prayer for th
life of my own soul. Some lazy, backsliding people among us are gone
after the Nicolites: let them go, for they were become as salt that had los

savour; we want no such people. I preached at the Draw-Bridge to about o hundred people; spoke on "Ye cannot serve God and mammon"— s clear and searching. Mr. ——, who has been a man much in pursuit the world, and who was condemned by our friends in his conduct, rose after I had done, and said, he was the man pointed at, and desired other hearing.

Tuesday, 22. Rode to Andrew Purden's, had about sixty people, and oke on Luke xi, 28: "Blessed are they that hear the word of God, and ep it"—met the class. John Beauchamp and Dr. Bowness, both pro- sed sanctification: I hope it is so. The society is much increased: but all not gold that shines.

Wednesday, 23. I rode to Richard Shaw's, it came up cold and snowed; d about fifty people; a solid society, tender, and in a measure faithful. ave been much in haste these two days, but had little time for prayer d private duties; but I take mornings and nights, and am resolved, that not in the day, I will have it at night and morning. I was tried in getting ; called at two of the friends' houses, and had prayer; and had my trials o. Spoke at Shaw's, on 1 John iii, 10; felt warm in spirit, although I suf- ed on the road with cold; have read but little, but am labouring for souls.

Thursday, 24. Rode ten miles out and ten miles in, to Joseph Wyatt's; out two hundred people: a very cold day; spoke on Titus ii, 11, to the d; was much led out, and kept in peace all day.

Friday, 25. A day of fasting and rest; sorely tempted: this made me nk, that had I gone to preach, or to town and met class, it would not ve been the case: so I must for the future be more employed, for this is will of God concerning me. This morning I read the Testament; and d a good time in general this week, but O! the workings of heart I our under! Have spent much time in prayer night and morning: I am ch led out at such times.

Saturday, 26. Rode to Boyer's, and met society; most of the hearers esent met in class. Spoke as searching as possible; and gave an exhorta- n: the people were much stirred up. At night I was greatly engaged in ayer.

Sunday, 27. Spoke from Luke xi, 24–27. There were many people, and ood time. I showed how the devil is cast out, and how he returns: then de to Dover, and came in just as church was ended. I preached with at labour on Acts xxiv, 25. Some had eaten and drank more than ough, and were fit to go to sleep; but the greater part were attentive. t O! what a continual burden have I to come and preach here! Went me with lawyer Richard Bassett,[15] a very conversant and affectionate

---

This was among the first of many visits to the three Bassett homes located in ver and Wilmington, Delaware, and in Bohemia Manor, Maryland. Mrs. Bassett s the former Ann Ennalls, sister of Henry Ennalls and niece of Judge Ennalls of rchester County, Maryland.

man, who, from his own acknowledgments, appears to be sick of s
His wife is under great distress; a gloom of dejection sits upon l
soul; she prayeth much, and the enemy takes an advantage of her l
state.

Monday, 28. I rode to Shaw's, spoke at three o'clock, on Acts xxv
28. I was blessed with a calm, sweet frame, and had great ease and freed
in my soul and subject; an attentive congregation. I feel a peculiar love
these people; and expect if Mr. Bassett ever comes to God, he is to prea
I have been kept in peace, and am ready to think sometimes God l
saved me from all sin, properly so called. Satan made one sudden strc
at me, but I looked to God. Last *Sunday morning* I was drawn out
prayer, and felt the effect in a particular manner in preaching at Boyer
the word went like fire; a little of it in the evening, but there is so mu
pride, and so much of unbelief in the Dover people, that a man needs t
faith and power of Stephen to bear up and speak to them.

Tuesday, 29. Rode to Scotten's, had about fifty people; they were d
appointed in expecting me the day before, and I was misinformed
spoke with liberty on 1 Tim. i, 5. The roads were bad beyond my c
pectation. I rode on horseback; returned to Shaw's, took dinner, heard
Freeborn Garrettson's being put in jail in Dorset. So Satan has stretch
his chain; but this shall work for good. Spent a night with Mr. Maga
had great satisfaction in conversing with him relative to his having
closer connexion with us.

Wednesday, *March* 1, 1780. Rode twelve miles to the Thomas chap
four or five miles the roads were so bad that I was obliged to get out of t
carriage and walk; I came late, and much fatigued. Spoke on Matt. v, l
"Let your light so shine before men;" spoke freely, and was blessed; t
work revives here, and over in Queen Annes County, a few miles dista
from this. Through bad roads with difficulty I rode to Fatad's mills—stay
that night—could not get to Choptank.

Thursday, 2. Heard of Mr. James Peterkin's death, he died last night
came to his house, and went to Thomas White's; find it is a fact th
brother Garrettson was put into jail last Sunday.[16]

Friday, 3. Rose between four and five o'clock, and prayed some tin
have begun reading Robertson's History of Scotland, in two vols.[17] We
to Stradley's, spoke on Rev. iii, 20, with liberty; met class, came back, a
spoke a few words to the people, who were met to put the remains
James Peterkin in the ground: at the repeated solicitations of Mrs. l
White, I attended those old people in life and death.

Saturday, 4. I wrote to Pedicord and Cromwell; and have appoint

---

[16] Freeborn Garrettson was lodged in the Dorchester County jail, Cambrid
February 27, 1780. (Garrettson, *op. cit.*, 152.)

[17] William Robertson (1721–93) was the author of *History of Scotland during*
Reigns of Queen Mary and of James VI until his Accession to the Crown of England.

shua Dudley for Dorset: he is qualified by law.[18] Rested and read
bertson's first volume. O! what treachery and policy attendeth courts!
d how does court policy, without design, give way to a reformation!
is has been the case in England and Scotland.

Sunday, 5. I went to church and heard Mr. Neill preach a good sermon
, "O! that they were wise." I preached at Edward White's, on Micah
6–8. The subject was too laboured for the congregation, yet searching,
d the people were solemn.

Monday, 6. I was kept close in reading the first volume of the History
Scotland, and was kept in quiet. In the morning I wrote to brother
rrettson to comfort him under his imprisonment.

Tuesday, 7. A rainy day, but went to my appointment: there were a
v people; I spoke on Eph. i, 8, 9, and had great liberty. I think a certain
rson here, that has been a high churchwoman, will yet be a Methodist.
lled at Vincent Dorothy's, took dinner, talked and prayed with the
nily. I am to preach at his house.

Wednesday, 8. I rose at five, and began reading in Mr. Wesley's Notes
the Acts of the Apostles. This day I visited the widow Cox, who has
arly lost her reason. She was pleased to see me, and showed some
derness and intervals of reason, though I had but little satisfaction
th her. Lectured on Jer. iii, 15–19, and was blest. Came back to Thomas
hite's.

Thursday, 9. I am under a gloomy heaviness through manifold tempta-
ns. Read Mr. Wesley's Notes on the Epistle to the Romans. Some of
sentiments I have adopted, and thought them my own; perhaps they
e not, for I may have taken them first from him. Prayed often, and shut
yself up. I find meditating on past unfaithfulness humiliating; but I
ust go on: pondering my ways so much dejects and weakens my faith.
rd, keep me; keep me, gracious Lord, and never let me go! I met class
night, though none but the Whites' families. It was made a blessing,
d made me examine my own heart.

Friday, 10. I rose between four and five o'clock, spent some time
private prayer and with the families; read Mr. Wesley's Notes on
Corinthians, and ended the reading of the second book of Kings, in my
ading in course the Bible through. To-morrow I am to go down into the
orth West Fork, where, I am told, the Lord revives his work. In the
ening was unwell, and went to bed early.

Saturday, 11. Rose under some exercise of soul, set off for the Fork
out eleven o'clock, stopped at brother Gozeley's, fed my horse, and
ard of the severity used to brother Garrettson in Cambridge jail, and
at they would not let the people come to speak with him. All this shall
ork for good, and we will rejoice that we are counted worthy to suffer
r righteousness' sake. Found it bad travelling; when I came into by-

This probably meant that Joshua Dudley had taken the Maryland oath of allegiance.

roads, my horse nearly overset; but with difficulty came to White Browr
and was blest in praying with and speaking to the family.

Sunday, 12. Rode to Solomon Turpin's; and fear something is the m
ter here. I cannot preach with freedom, and am not happy. Spoke
Ezek. xviii, 19, in light and liberty, and as searching as I well could.

Monday, 13. Received a letter from brother Garrettson: his enemies a
softened towards him. I think the Lord will deliver me yet from all ev
I heard Cromwell was put in jail, but did not credit it. I labour to
more spiritual, and to be holy in heart and life. I rode to John Cannor
and spoke on John i, 8, 9; had liberty. There were about a hundred pe
ple, and some little stir. One of the sons has a religious frenzy; he w
panic struck, and prayed some hours: he kneeled down in time of preac
ing; he may be sincere, and come to something. Rode to Morgan Williams
met brother Lowry, now rejoicing in God, his backslidings healed, a
his soul restored. Received another letter from brother Garrettson, whe
in he informs me the people want to get rid of him, and that they are n
so cruel to him as formerly, nor to the people who visit him.

Tuesday, 14. Rose in peace, spent near an hour in retirement, and w
blessed. Read some chapters in the Bible. My soul is kept in peace; glc
be to God! I wrote to Philip Rogers, and spent my time till noon
reading, writing, and prayer.

Wednesday, 15. Brother Garrettson expects to come out of jail by t
favour of the governor and council of Maryland in spite of his foes:
the Lord works for us. In Somerset they are using some of Bishop Wa
burton's Works[19] against Mr. Wesley and Mr. Whitefield. I was mu
blest in speaking at Spencer Hitchen's, on Titus iii, 2–8, to nearly tv
hundred serious people; their prejudices wear off: it is to be observe
bad as these people were, they never persecuted us, as they have done
some other places; it cannot be for our being falsely reported to be Tori
for in Somerset some of our greatest enemies are of that stamp.

Thursday, 16. I have peace; rose at five o'clock, read the Scriptur
ended the first Book of Chronicles. Last night I gave an exhortation;
young girl wept enough to break her heart. I hope she will seek the Lor
I am kept in faith, and feel my heart much melted and moved to po
opposers, and can pray for them as I do for myself.

Friday, 17. Rose at five o'clock, prayed, and read awhile in an c
author, who warmly attacks Popery in its capital errors, and in a stror
argumentative manner; but is full of Greek and Latin quotations. I ro
to Johnstown, and from thence to William Law's; met Freeborn Garre
son, who came out of jail by order of the governor and council of Mar
land, who had sent to the governor of Delaware to know if Freeborn Ga
rettson were not a fugitive, and had received satisfactory informatio

[19] William Warburton (1698–1779) was bishop of Gloucester. In 1762 he publish
his *Doctrine of Grace* directed against John Wesley's views.

other Garrettson preached on Matthew xxv, 10: "And they that were
dy went in with him to the marriage, and the door was shut." I spoke
ew words after him. 1. That the way some kept off convictions was,
neglect of prayer. 2. Some not uniform in prayer. 3. Others never
ended to give up all sin. 4. Others rest in present attainments, and
:e pride in what God hath done for them, and fall away: and closed
:h an application suited to the cases and consciences of the people.

Saturday, 18. Rose at four o'clock, and spent some time in prayer.
other Garrettson took my place and appointments: we drew some out-
es for our conference while together. I preached at John Lewis's, on
hn viii, 31–37, and had great liberty, and more people than I expected,
it rained.

Sunday, 19. Preached at Alexander Law's, and spoke searchingly; the
ople were attentive; some Presbyterians brought to think very seriously.
ode to William Law's, and spoke on 2 Thess. i, 7–13, had living liberty,
d I hope not in vain.

Monday, 20. Rose early, wrote an hour, and then rode twenty-four
les to Caleb Furby's to preach; was late, but came before Caleb Boyer
d done meeting the class. Spoke on John iii, 24, and felt quickenings.
ent home with Waitman Sipple;[20] he and Philip Barratt determined to
about the chapel, and to set it near the drawbridge.

Tuesday, 21. Rode to Purdin's, and had many people; spoke on Malachi
16–18. Had much power in speaking: then rode to Choptank, to the
eral of James Peterkin and Elizabeth his wife, at Thomas White's.

Wednesday, 22. Mr. Magaw preached the funeral sermon of James and
zabeth Peterkin, in Mr. White's barn: there were about four hundred
ople; I only stood as clerk. Joseph Cromwell gave an exhortation, pretty
ag and rough: Mr. Neill gave an exhortation. Mr. Magaw and myself
urned to the baptizing the children. I have been collecting all the
nutes of our conferences in America, to assist me in a brief history of
: Methodists; and an account of our principles.

Thursday, 23. Rose early: have some trials among my friends; but it is
well, God is with me. Company is not agreeable at all times; but the
ll of the Lord be done, if he calls me to it.

Good-Friday, 24. A cloudy day; it began raining when I was a few miles
my way; I could not turn back; about eleven o'clock it cleared away.
ame to the chapel, there were about forty people. Spoke on Isaiah liii,
, then rode to brother Richard Shaw's, and was much blest, as I always

---

' Waitman Sipple was the father-in-law of Philip Barratt (1730–84), for whom the
pel was named. The latter was converted in 1778 under the ministry of Freeborn
rrettson. The chapel was begun in May, 1780, dedicated in August, and opened for
vices that autumn. The deed of conveyance of land, August 17, 1780, from Philip
ratt, was made to Reynear Williams and eight other trustees. (Barratt: *Barratt's
ipel and Methodism*; Boehm, *op. cit.*, 50–52, 226, 227; Lednum, *op. cit.*, 265, 266;
ed Book W, I, 247, Dover Courthouse.)

am in this family. I have deep and sore trials: the remembrance of th
depresses my soul.

Saturday, 25. Have peace of soul, but am not enough given up to G
I purpose to be more devoted to God in prayer and meditation: rode
Boyer's, and met the society: the people appear to be more alive to G
than when I was here last; preached on 2 Tim. ii, 18, 19, and had mu
light and liberty.

Sunday, 26. Rode to church,[21] where we had a smooth, sensible d
course on 1 Peter i, 3. I attended the communion—communicants increa
daily, for people get awakened by us; when this is the case, they go to t
Lord's supper. In the afternoon I preached; many flocked to hear,
being Easter Sunday. Spoke plainer than ever on Acts xvii, 18; had e
largement of heart; the church minister was present.

Monday, 27. Called at the Rev. Mr. Magaw's; spent an hour, chang
books and sentiments, and came off to Mrs. Beauchamp's, then to Andr
Purdin's, there were near two hundred people; spoke on 1 Peter i, 7–1
was blest, and felt some things I spoke; nothing but hard trials cou
make me speak so.

Tuesday, 28. I rode to Stradley's, and spoke on 1 Peter iii, 18, w
great opening—entered deep into the nature of Christ's sufferings, a
some sublime truths of the Gospel.

Wednesday, 29. Spent what time I had to spare in transcribing fr
Robert Walker a part of one of his sermons to the preachers, and put
in my selections. I went to preach at Vincent Dorothy's, and spoke
Luke xxiv, 25, 26. Made a faithful discharge of truth to the people; th
were attentive. I have been very much exercised in mind; the time f
leaving this place draws nigh. Never was confinement in one State, De
ware, so trying to me. Lord, help me, I am weak! At night I went
Edward White's, and gave an exhortation; was greatly troubled in min

Thursday, 30. I am going to Sussex, on my way to the quarterly meeti
at the Fork. I fear there will be great commotions this summer; God or
knows what the end of these things will be; but "Blessed are those peo
that are found watching." I lost my way and wandered into the swam
and feared I must lie in the woods, but came to a friend's house, and th
pushed on and reached Mr. Daniel Polk's about seven o'clock. Read
wonderful book against Methodists, but it will do no great harm.

Friday, 31. Waked before three o'clock, though I did not go to bed t
after ten o'clock—was weather-bound, and read the second volume
Robertson's History of Scotland. The fate of unfortunate Mary Queen
Scots was affecting; and the admired Queen Elizabeth does not appear
advantage in the Scotch history. Prayed an hour this morning, and r
tired twice; used abstinence, though not so severe as I commonly use
Fridays.

[21] Christ Protestant Episcopal Church, Dover, Delaware.

Saturday, April 1. Rose about half-past three o'clock, and set out for oad Creek—was kept in peace all the way; when in temptation, I ay, and it flies. Came in about three o'clock; and found that the spirit lying and fury reigned! I received a satisfactory letter from William oore; he hopes a reconciliation will take place in Virginia, if healing easures are adopted.

Sunday, 2. Rose about six o'clock; I lay in a dark room, and was a tle unwell: I am kept near to God, but under some dejection; I believe was because the people of this house are not right toward God. Spoke -day on Acts xxviii, 22: "As for this sect, we know that everywhere it is oken against." Spoke long and freely, but the people were not greatly oved. Preached in the afternoon at George Moore's, on 1 Peter iv, 18: f the righteous are scarcely saved," &c.; and a blessing followed.

Monday, 3. Rose at five o'clock, spent some time in prayer, and my ading in course to the twenty-third Psalm. Preached at Thomas Jones's about sixty careless, ignorant people; had very little comfort; spoke om 2 Tim. ii, 19. Read in the afternoon the Appendix to the History of otland. I am in heaviness through the deadness of the people, and the s of the wicked about us—of which there appear to be enough; and it es seem now as if they could freely shed our blood: Lord, give me faith d patience! The present state of things is, *Report, say they, and we will ort it*; nothing can come amiss; all is fish that comes to the net: the cked will say anything; yes, all manner of evil against us.

Tuesday, 4. There came on rain, but I went to Gitting Bradley's; there re about forty people, though it rained rapidly. Spoke on Rev. iii, 20, d was much blessed; then returned to George Moore's.

Wednesday, 5. A snowy morning. Rode to Levin Bacon's: there were out thirty people; I was led out to speak close to them, and some felt to the heart.

Thursday, 6. Rode to Mr. Freeny's. I preached from 2 Chron. vii, 14, d was led, though with labour, to deliver my soul to them. Set off to seven miles, through a dreary road and deep swamps, to Calloway's; me in about seven o'clock, and found liberty as soon as I came. God has eople in these rude wastes: I expect to go, after preaching, to the sea- le.

Friday, 7. About three days ago I was moved to pray for good weather, en I saw what a condition we should be in: there is a change in the eather. I have peace this morning, and my heart is lifted up to God in ankfulness. An appearance of good weather: blessed be God! though, en the weather was so uncomfortable, I was tempted to murmur. Lord, rdon me in this also! Surely, what the Lord does is right, whether he es it against a single person or to a whole nation. Preached at Calloway's, 2 Peter iii, 18, and was blessed. There were about fifty souls—an at- tive, feeling people. After preaching, I rode thirty miles to the sea-side:

there met brother Garrettson, confident that God had, in a vision of tl night, sanctified him.

Saturday, 8. Went to the sea and bathed, though cold: and then ro< about nine miles from Evans's to Gray's. Our quarterly meeting began I preached on Rom. v, 6, 7, and had liberty. The Baptists show the enmity, and go from house to house persuading weak people to be dippe and not to hear the Methodists; and they bring their preachers in o absence.

Sunday, 9. I have peace: it has been very rainy; but clear this mornin We had a great day: preached on 1 John v, 19: "We know that we are God, and the whole world lieth in wickedness." Brother Garrettson e horted, there was some melting; John Cooper spoke to purpose; Josep Cromwell brought up the rear with great success. The people we serious.

Monday, 10. I have peace of soul; but too much talk like trifling; tl devil throws his firebrands, but grace is sufficient. I appointed broth Joseph Wyatt to keep the ground against the Baptists, and to supply o places here instead of the travelling preachers that are going to conferenc for John's people intend to come a fishing about, when we are gone. W had a love feast at eight o'clock; many spoke in a very feeling manne God was with us at eleven o'clock—I preached on 2 Cor. iv, 12. Broth Cromwell and brother Garrettson exhorted: the people were moved what was said, though simple, and the same things he frequently says; b he is a man of God, and their spiritual father.

Tuesday, 11. We rode fifty miles to Choptank.

Wednesday, 12. I was employed in writing a short history of the Metho ists; also in preparing my papers for conference. I am going from n home, Thomas White's.

Thursday, 13. I set off for Richard Shaw's, in Kent; and came in abo five o'clock, and kept a watch evening. I spoke on 1 Cor. xvi, 13, 1 Caleb Pedicord exhorted.

Friday, 14. A day of fasting. I was employed in preparing my pap for conference; Caleb Pedicord is my scribe. I am under some apprehe sions that trouble is near. Thomas M'Clure is confined sick in Philadelphi Henry Kennedy and William Adams are dead: so the Lord cuts off tl watchmen of Israel. But sure I am that it is better to die early, than t live, though late, to dishonour God.

Saturday, 15. I spent the afternoon with Mr. Magaw.

Sunday, 16. Rode twelve miles, and preached at the Thomas chape on Psalm cxxii, 6–8. Had some life among the people, but I fear they d not properly understand me. Preached at Richard Shaw's, my farewe

[22] Lednum locates the meeting "at the Sound," which is the present Sound Chap on the Roxana Charge, Sussex County. (Lednum, *op. cit.*, 279; Boehm, *op. cit.*, 12< Scharf: *History of Delaware*, II, 1949.)

rmon, on Acts xxi, 32. The people were solemn, but not deeply affected ith a sense of the worth of their souls.

Monday, 17. Our quarterly meeting began.[23] Our little chapel with gal-ries, held about seven hundred; but there were I judge near one thousand eople. I preached on Phil. i, 27: "Only let your conversation be as it ecometh the Gospel of Christ."

Tuesday, 18. After love feast, Mr. Magaw read prayers, and Mr. Neill reached a good sermon, on "Feed my sheep;" brother Garrettson and yself exhorted. The power of God was present in the love feast: many poke in our meeting with light, life, and liberty.

Wednesday, 19. I left Mr. Emory's, where we were very kindly enter-ined in the dreary forest; they live well; these people were brought off eir prejudices by Mr. Magaw's preaching in the chapel; they and their mily connexions promise fair. Brother Garrettson spoke on, "Ye now ve sorrow." But he could not move the people here as at the sea-side: ey are cooler, and he is not their spiritual father.

Thursday, 20. Set off for Baltimore,[24] and called at Mr. Magaw's; we rted in much affection. Called at Mr. Bassett's, and had a warm con-rsation with Warner Mifflin. We prayed, and Mrs. Bassett made a nfession of finding peace.

Maryland

We rode to Solomon Symmond's.

Friday, 21. We rode to Robert Thompson's, Maryland, Cecil County; ned, prayed, and spoke close to him, who had fainted in his mind, being ow left alone. We came to Susquehanna River a little before sunset, and ssed over in the night; rode six miles in the dark, and a bad road; but rovidence has preserved me hitherto. I had a very tender feeling for the eople I left behind; this makes me think I must return.

Saturday, 22. I could not pray for our friends we left behind without eeping. We rode to Mr. Gough's, Baltimore County; my friends ap-eared very joyful to see me; brother Glendenning[25] had his objections to ake, and pleaded some in favour of the Virginia brethren, who had made

[23] The participation in this meeting in Thomas Chapel of two clergymen of the tablished Church, Samuel Magaw and Hugh Neill, tended to reduce the local ejudice against the Methodists.

[24] Asbury was leaving the Peninsula. He was to attend the conference of the northern eachers set for April 24, 1780.

[25] Apparently Glendenning, who gradually grew more disputatious and erratic, on is occasion irritated Asbury. See the footnote by "W.S." below, which appears in e original *Journal*. (See *Journal* entries for November 6, 1780; December 26, 1790: e *Life of William Glendenning, Preacher of the Gospel*.)

a division.* We prayed after dinner, and God was with us: I had cause t talk more than I desired.

Sunday, 23. Lord give me wisdom that is profitable to direct. This is dumb Sabbath:[26] I have no freedom to preach; there are strange change what has taken place with our brethren seems parallel with the commotio of the southward; and the same spirit. I am kept in peace, through grac and am casting my care upon the Lord. If I cannot keep up old Methodis in any other place, I can in the peninsula: that must be my last retrea Spent some time in private, and prepared some conditions for a parti reconciliation, in hopes to bring on a real one in Virginia. Brother Fre born Garrettson preached in the afternoon, on these words, "Disallowe indeed of men, but chosen of God, and precious:" he was short and profi able; I prayed with my heart full. Met brother Samuel Selby, whom I hav not seen for near six years, one of my old friends from New York, drive about by the commotions of the present times: he with great joy fell upo my neck and wept. I am more moved than ever before, with leaving an meeting my friends; these are humbling times, and make the Christia love one another: I found the spirits of the preachers much melted an softened. I hope things will be made easy.

Monday, 24. We made a plan for the appointment of the preacher Received three epistles from the Jerseys, soliciting three or four preacher with good tidings of the work of God reviving in those parts. The pet tioners I shall hear with respect. I am kept in peace; praise the Lord, my soul! Rode to Baltimore, and my friends were much rejoiced to se me; but silence broke my heart. The act against non-jurors reduced me t silence, because the oath of fidelity required by the act of the State c Maryland, was preposterously rigid. I became a citizen of Delaware,[27] an was regularly returned. I was at this time under recommendation of th governor of Delaware as taxable.

Tuesday, 25. Our conference met in peace and love.[28] We settled all ou

---

* See what a poor unsettled creature this Glendenning ever was. This was long befor he went into his mighty trances, visions, &c., that he talks so much about. No wonde that a person of his selfish temper should behave as he has done to his brethren th Methodists.—W.S.

[26] Asbury applied the word "dumb" to any day on which he was prevented fro preaching.

[27] The name of Francis Asbury appears on the assessment list of Mispillion Hundre County of Kent, Delaware, in July, 1779. The governor of Delaware to whom Asbur refers was Caesar Rodney. (Original assessment list in Public Archives Commissio Hall of Records, Dover, Delaware; see *Journal* entry for February 5, 1781.)

[28] This conference met in the new Lovely Lane Chapel at Baltimore. The onl southern preachers were Philip Gatch and Reuben Ellis, who represented Virgini The meeting disapproved the action of the Virginians, regarded them as "no long Methodists," and asked them to suspend the ordinances for one year and meet in joint conference at Baltimore. (*General Minutes*, I, 11–12; Garrettson, *op. cit.*, 161 ff Watters, *op. cit.*, 79–80; Gatch, *op. cit.*, 73–4.)

orthern stations; then we began in much debate about the letter sent om Virginia. We first concluded to renounce them; then I offered onditions of union.

I. That they should ordain no more.

II. That they should come no farther than Hanover circuit.

III. We would have our delegates in their conference.

IV. That they should not presume to administer the ordinances where ere is a decent Episcopal minister.

V. To have a union conference.

These would not do, as we found upon long debate, and we came back o our determinations; although it was like death to think of parting. At st a thought struck my mind; to propose a suspension of the ordinances or one year, and so cancel all our grievances, and be one. It was agreed n both sides, and Philip Gatch and Reuben Ellis, who had been very iff, came into it, and thought it would do.

Wednesday, 26. Preached on Acts vi, 4, with liberty.

Thursday, 27. Read the advice to preachers. At twelve o'clock we had melting love feast; preachers and people wept like children. At night I reached on Acts ii, 48, with great liberty, to about six hundred people. oseph Cromwell and Freeborn Garrettson spoke. At the recommenda- on of the conference William Watters too; these three volunteered, and ere to be my spokesmen. Myself and brother Garrettson are going to the irginia Conference, to bring about peace and union. I am kept in peace, rough much business; little sleep, cold weather and damp. Lord, return, nd visit us!

Friday, 28. I have peace, and am going to brother William Lynch's is day. I had a melting sense of Divine love upon my heart after inner: this family professeth sanctification; whether this be so in the illest sense I know not; but this I know, that they are much more iritual than ever I knew them: so far it is well, and we go upon safe round.

Saturday, 29. Rode to Mr. Gough's; this is a good house to do business t.

Sunday, 30. I went to the Fork preaching house; an Episcopalian inister preaching just by. Spoke on Psalm lxxviii, 4–8. It was not made great blessing to the people: I was much tried to know if the subject was roper, and I think it was; I could not make choice of any other. Spoke t Mr. G——'s, on 1 Peter i, 5–10; had only the family to preach to. This not like Kent (in Delaware) for life and congregations. There were any of us, and much talking prevented my reading, writing, and raying.

Monday, May 1, 1780. I am going to Virginia; am kept, but not so much mployed for God as I ought to be. Preached at Baltimore on John v, 19. rainy night, but many came to hear.

Tuesday, 2. I rode to John Worthington's,[29] and spoke at night; God wa
present. I once had an opportunity of seeing Charles Scott,[30] apparent
full of the Holy Ghost; but what is he now! He died in a drunken revel.

Virginia

Wednesday, 3. I rode to Georgetown, from thence to William Adams
in Virginia; came in late and fatigued.

Thursday, 4. Prepared some papers for Virginia Conference. I go wit
a heavy heart; and fear the violence of a party of positive men: Lord, giv
me wisdom. I preached at the chapel in Fairfax;[31] and met Mr. Griffit
an Episcopal minister, who was friendly; and we spent the afternoo
together.

Friday, 5. Set out in company with brother Freeborn Garrettson,[32] rod
near forty miles, lodged at Garratt's tavern, where we were well ente
tained. Brother Garrettson talked to the landlord on the subject of re
ligion, and prayed with him at night and in the morning, though he woul
not consent to call his family together. We rode on to Mr. Arnold's,
about thirty miles, the roads good. Brother Garrettson will let no perso
escape a religious lecture that comes in his way. Sure he is faithful, bu
what am I? We found the plague was begun; the good man Arnold wa
warm for the ordinances. I spoke on "Strive to enter in at the strait gate.
There were about forty people, but dead enough.

[29] John Worthington and his wife Ann, a daughter of Nicholas Dorsey, resided i
the Jessup-Fort Meade Junction of Howard County. For nearly a decade the Worthin
ton home was open for preaching and quarterly meetings, but there is no evidence o
Asbury's being a guest there after June 8, 1783. (See *Journal* entry for that date.)

[30] Charles Scott, whose name appeared as "on file" in 1781, was appointed to th
Frederick Circuit that year. The tribute to Scott on October 30, 1780, Asbury later wa
obliged to retract. (See note under that date.)

[31] This was Adams' Chapel. (See note under June 16, 1777.)

[32] Sweet, *Men of Zeal*, 136, says, "Of all the native preachers, Freeborn Garrettso
undoubtedly stands at the head of the list in total influence exerted on the developmen
of American Methodism." He was born in Maryland in 1752. His parents belonged t
the Established Church. The first Methodist he met was Robert Strawbridge; an
through the influence of Strawbridge, Asbury, and Daniel Ruff he became a preache
It was Garrettson who was sent out to summon the preachers to the Christmas Co
ference, where he was ordained. In 1787 he was made presiding elder of the Baltimor
District and in the same year was appointed by Wesley to Canada. He married Cathe
ine Livingston, daughter of Judge Robert R. Livingston, and in later years they live
on the estate of Rhinebeck in New York. Both Garrettson and his wife inherited cor
siderable estates, and Garrettson declined to accept any salary during his entire mini
terial career of more than fifty years. (Bangs: *Life of Freeborn Garrettson*, 151.)

[33] This was George Arnold, who lived in Spottsylvania County and at whose hom
Asbury died in 1816. Asbury had traveled across Fairfax, Prince William, and Staffor
counties.

Sunday, 7. We rode eighteen miles to Brown's tavern.[34] I preached on a. lv, 6, 7. On entering into Virginia, I have prepared some papers for e conference, and expect trouble, but grace is almighty; hitherto hath the ord helped me.

Monday, 8. We rode to Granger's,[35] fifteen miles; stopped and fed our rses. These people are full of the ordinances; we talked and prayed ith them; then rode on to the Manakintown[36] ferry, much fatigued with e ride: went to friend Smith's, where all the preachers were met: I con-cted myself with cheerful freedom, but found there was a separation in art and practice. I spoke with my countryman, John Dickins, and found m opposed to our continuance in union with the Episcopal Church; rother Watters and Garrettson tried their men, and found them in-xible.

Tuesday, 9. The conference was called: brother Watters, Garrettson, d myself stood back, and being afterward joined by brother Dromgoole, e were desired to come in, and I was permitted to speak; I read Mr. 'esley's thoughts against a separation: showed my private letters of structions from Mr. Wesley; set before them the sentiments of the elaware and Baltimore conferences; read our epistles, and read my letter brother Gatch, and Dickins's letter in answer. After some time spent is way, it was proposed to me, if I would get the circuits supplied, they ould desist; but that I could not do. We went to preaching; I spoke on uth ii, 4, and spoke as though nothing had been the matter among the eachers or people; and we were greatly pleased and comforted; there as some moving among the people. In the afternoon we met; the preachers peared to me to be farther off; there had been, I thought, some talking it of doors. When we—Asbury, Garrettson, Watters, and Dromgoole—uld not come to a conclusion with them, we withdrew, and left them to

---

[34] Brown's tavern was in Caroline County.

[35] Bennett, *Memorials of Methodism in Virginia*, 127, says that Granger's and Thomas enshaw's were the same place. Here Asbury established the first Sunday school. adition places this event in 1786, though H. Bernard in the *American Journal of lucation* in the Library of Congress gives the date as 1783. Asbury visited the spot in e latter year, but there is no record of a visit to Crenshaw's in 1786. At least a dozen storians state that here was established the first Sunday school of the Raikes type in nerica. It was in the Crenshaw home. On June 14, 1791, Thomas Crenshaw and eight hers purchased a lot on Beaver Creek for a church in which Asbury and other persons ould preach, provided they adhered to the doctrines of Wesley. The Beaver Creek urch was one of three in the community, the others being St. Mark's and St. Peter's. e last named is still in existence and the direct descendant of the Crenshaw Sunday hool.

[36] Manakintown was in Powhatan County and was a French Huguenot settlement. lonel William Byrd in 1698 invited the Huguenots who had fled from France and ne to England to come to Virginia. They cleared the lands abandoned by the Manacan dians, the former foes of Powhatan. Manakintown was made famous in Methodist story by the conference held there this year and by the ordinances controversy. wathmey: *Twelve Virginia Counties*, 220–21.)

deliberate on the conditions I offered, which was, to suspend the measure
they had taken for one year. After an hour's conference, we were calle
to receive their answer, which was, they could not submit to the terms
union. I then prepared to leave the house, to go to a near neighbour
to lodge, under the heaviest cloud I ever felt in America: O! what I felt!—
nor I alone!—but the agents on both sides! they wept like children, b
kept their opinions.

Wednesday, 10. I returned to take leave of conference, and to go o
immediately to the North; but found they were brought to an agreeme
while I had been praying, as with a broken heart, in the house we went
lodge at; and brother Watters and Garrettson had been praying upstai
where the conference sat. We heard what they had to say; surely th
hand of God has been greatly seen in all this: there might have been twen
promising preachers, and three thousand people, seriously affected by th
separation; but the Lord would not suffer this; we then had preaching t
brother Watters on, "Come thou with us, and we will do thee good
afterward we had a love feast; preachers and people wept, prayed, ar
talked, so that the spirit of dissension was powerfully weakened, and
hoped it would never take place again.

Thursday, 11. I rode to Petersburg, thirty-five miles, through muc
fatigue and want of rest; found myself indisposed with the headache. Wi
difficulty I spoke at brother Harding's,[37] on, "We know that we are of God
but was so unwell I could scarcely speak at all. Though having prevail
with God and man, I yet halt on my thigh.

Friday, 12. I am a little better; rest this day to write to Mr. Wesley.
Petersburg, our friends who had a little religion before these times, ha
declined; I fear their hearts are worldly. Some who had religion befo
these times have lost it; and many who had none, have gained much; li
some who had no fortunes, have gained great ones; and many of those w
had great fortunes, are in a fair way to lose them, if these times hold lon

Saturday, 13. Went to Nathaniel Lee's, and preached to about fif
people, on Eph. v, 8, and had freedom; the congregation small, owing
a muster and cock-fighting not far off. I then rode to Wood Tucker's,
great friend to the old plan of Methodism; and was kept in peace.

Sunday, 14. Rode to George Booth's;[38] he is a curious genius for
mechanic. We had a great house, and about three hundred people; I spo
on 1 Cor. ii, 14, plain, warm and searching; but they seemed in gener
careless: I fear there is but little solid, pure religion here.

Monday, 15. Was much exercised; Lord! keep me every moment. A
this is rest day, I intend to employ my time in reading and writing princ
pally; but my spirit is restless various ways; and I think I ought always
be employed. I am for attending my twelve times of prayer, and resisti

[37] See note under June 29, 1775.
[38] Both Wood Tucker and George Booth lived in Dinwiddie County.

e devil steadfastly in the faith. I am much humbled before the Lord; a
essing I want, and will not cease crying to the Lord for it. I read Dr.
handler's Appeal to the Public; I think upon the whole he is right. Why
ight not the Protestant Episcopal Church have as much indulgence in
merica as any other society of people?

Tuesday, 16. Spent near an hour in private prayer, and twice in the
mily; then went to Nottoway church, where Mr. Jarratt gave an excellent
rmon on, "A man shall be a hiding-place." He was rather shackled with
s notes. We then had sacrament; afterward I returned to George
ooth's, spent the evening with Mr. Jarratt, and found him as friendly as
er. He labours, but the people give him little or nothing.

Wednesday, 17. Rode to the Widow Heath's;[39] about seventy people
ere waiting for me; it was twenty miles, my horse lame, and the road
ugh; the enemy tried me just before I came to the house, as he generally
es, if the distance is more than I expect; I spoke on Luke xiii, 23, and
as pointed, and had liberty; God moved upon the hearts of the people;
et the society, about fifteen pious people; most were blessed, and they
em all on stretch for holiness; spent my afternoon in reading and study.
here seems to be some call for me in every part of the work: I have
avelled at this time from north to south to keep peace and union: and O!
a rent and separation had taken place, what work, what hurt to thous-
ds of souls! It is now stopped, and if it had not, it might have been my
ult; it may have been my fault that it took place; but I felt a timidity
at I could not get over; preachers and people making the trial, they see
e consequences, and I hope will do so no more. They have suffered for
eir forwardness. May we all be more prudent!

Thursday, 18. When I came to Andrews's the people had no notice; I
as much tried on the way, my horse lame and the road rough; but I
ted up my heart to God. The family sent out and called in about sixty
ople, black and white. Spoke on Rev. xxii, 13–18. I had liberty, and felt
moving in my own soul. Two women were cut to the heart and were in
agony of soul for holiness: I prayed with them twice, while the people
ayed, and afterward spoke to them; they both, notwithstanding their
;ony, had a clear sense of the blessing they stood in need of, and believed
od had purified their hearts; I saw them both happily breathing a Divine
lm and heavenly sweetness. I see clearly that to press the people to holi-
·ss, is the proper method to take them from contending for ordinances,
· any less consequential things. I read and transcribed some of Potter's
hurch Government; and must prefer the Episcopal mode of Church
overnment to the Presbyterian. If the modern bishops were as the ancient
es, all would be right; and there wants nothing but the spirit of the thing.

Friday, 19. A very warm day. I rode over to Black Water to Bedding-

---

[39] Asbury was traveling through Sussex and Southampton counties to Nansemond,
d the places mentioned here were in those counties.

fields, and spoke with liberty to about one hundred people, on Acts xxv
19; when I came to treat on sanctification, I melted into tenderness, ar
the people also; met class, and had a blessed tenderness among the peopl
Kept a fast day till four o'clock, then ate no meat. It is a day of peace ar
purity, but I might have been more in prayer. I called to see Capt. Nichola
his wife is confined to her bed; but she was blessed: thank the Lord.

Saturday, 20. I rode to Bartlett's, ten miles, and preached to abo
thirty insensible people: afterward rode to Warren's, who was in distres
being of a melancholy cast, which is a family disorder. He is a man
understanding; and in time past followed the Quakers. He was in bed
perfect health: I raised him up, and after prayer he appeared better. Th
people are young, and have no deep sense of religion here; but they mu
have a trial.

Sunday, 21. I have a peace of mind, but fear we shall have few heare
today: it is not far from the rich and great upon James River. I read an
transcribed some of Potter's Church Government, till ten o'clock; wa
assisted in speaking to about two hundred people, who appeared ve
ignorant and unfeeling. After awhile, I gave them another sermon, no
very acceptable to me, and perhaps less so to them: however, I am clear–
they are warned. We then set out at four o'clock, rode sixteen miles ov
high hills, and deep valleys, in the dark; but came safe: went to bed
eleven o'clock, and was up at five o'clock. It is well if this will do lon
I am always on the wing, but it is for God.

Monday, 22. I laboured with brother Hill; I showed him the evil of
separation, which he seems to be afraid of. Our people's leaving th
Episcopal Church has occasioned the people of that Church to withdra
from our preaching. I preached on Rom. viii, 7–9, and had an opening
the people appeared pleased, and some wept, and I hope were profited.
advised our friends to attend the Episcopal Church, that prejudice migl
be removed; then their people will attend us: if I could stay, some wou
attend. We suffer much by young preachers and young people; yet the
would do their duty if they knew it; but those that knew a little of o
discipline, and have been first in the work, came into the notion
ordinances, and neglected the direction in the Minutes.

Tuesday, 23. I went to the great preaching house, in Nansemond: it ha
been a store house, now turned into a preaching house:[40] there we

---

[40] Nansemond Meeting House was an Established Church completed in 1752. It was
cross-shaped brick structure with a pipe organ and three galleries. It was torn down
1802. Other Anglican churches used by the Methodists were Somerton Chapel
Nansemond County; Holy Neck Chapel, about three miles northwest of Somert
which was later taken over by James O'Kelly, and used as a Methodist, then a R
publican Methodist, and later as a Christian church; Nottoway Chapel in the prese
Southampton County, and Cyprus Chapel in Nansemond County, one mile west
Dismal Swamp, which also was taken over by James O'Kelly and became a Christia
church. (See Mason: *Colonial Churches in Tidewater, Virginia*, 186.)

out three hundred people: I saw but one trifler among them; and he
ose and went out, when I came about the consciences of the sinners. I
oke on 1 Pet. iv, 18; had uncommon freedom; they appear to be an
ectionate, good people; they collected me money, but I took none; a
n offered me a silver dollar, but I could not take it, lest they should say
ame for money. There is a general prospect of a work; the minister,
. Burgess, is a very respectable man, and preaches, the people say, plain
od sermons. No doubt the introduction of the ordinances by us would
offensive where there is a clergyman so worthy. I had a meeting at
ht at Pinner's;[41] the society came. I exhorted them to holiness, and
ative duties, and spoke of Satan's temptations; there was a great melt-
. I read between preaching and the evening meeting, Bishop Burnett's
in and honest Account of the Earl of Rochester: it was a great thing to
such a man brought to God!—a check to infidels, a confirmation of
th. I was melted and filled with God. O, how the Lord blesses me among
se people! I have laboured to get our friends well affected to the
iscopal Church; what could I do better, when we had not the ordinances
ong us?

Wednesday, 24. I have peace, and power, and love to God. This was
pointed for a rest day, but one of my old friends gave out for preaching.
ile I have my health, and God is with me, I shall never say it is enough.
ere is a prospect of a good work in Nansemond, Virginia; near one
ndred people joined, in the neighbourhood. Rode to Philips's,[42] six
les, and preached to about one hundred people. After preaching, rode
to the widow Lane's, twenty-five miles; rode over Black Water,
ough Southampton,[43] and with hard riding (and some part bad roads)
ched there about nine o'clock; where I slept in peace, and arose early.
for faith to be saved from all sin! At twelve o'clock went to preach, and
d was with us of a truth, while I spoke upon 1 Pet. i, 7–12; afterward
t the society, and gave the people liberty to speak; many of them spoke,
d there were great meltings among them: one woman testified sanctifica-
n. I was blessed, and felt more spiritual; I can speak with a full heart
tears flow: the people are more moved by my easy speaking than ever
ore. Blessed be the Lord!

Sunday, 28. Yesterday I rode to William Graves's, spoke on Heb. iv,
-15, and had some life. There were about thirty people to hear: met the
ss, then rode to Robert Jones's, twenty-five miles.[44] Have peace this
rning, but not so tender as I would always wish to be. I read a pamphlet
tten by Mr. Jarratt, in answer to the Baptists, in a dialogue; and I think

Pinner's was in Nansemond County.
Philips's was in Nansemond County. (*Heads of Families, Virginia*, 73.)
The Blackwater River at this point is in Southampton, but the Widow Lane lived
ussex County.
William Graves and Robert Jones both lived in Sussex County.

it is well written, and ought to be published. I have had my mind tr
about approaching troubles; but I ought rather to mind my own busine
and trust all to God. Spoke at Robert Jones's, on Rev. xxi, 5–8. So
feared the soldiers would come to press our horses; but I had faith
believe they would not; and was led out much in speaking. Some w
young men kept talking, till I came to that part fitted for them, then th
listened. I met the class; they were stirred up, thirsting for full sanctifi
tion. I felt a tenderness for brother Hartley's sister,[45] who wept for
absence. Bless the Lord, who gives me to weep with them that weep! I
O! what must my dear parents feel for my absence! Ah! surely nothi
in this world should keep me from them, but the care of souls; and nothi
else could excuse me before God. I read my select Scriptures, the Law,
Sermon on the Mount, and the Revelation; and prayed often: God w
with me. Preached at Mabry's;[46] they have built a new house: there wa
woman sat by the desk, and cried, "Glory and praise! I drink of the wa
of life freely; I am at the fountain; my flesh praises God, I never hea
such singing in my life." I spoke with great power from 2 Thess. i, 6–9, a
then met society. This day has been a high day. Was led out to speak
saints and sinners; the people spoke in society; God was with us; so
expressed their joy in the union. I rode to Booth's; and am kept in pea
and love, and have great consolation in public and private.

Monday, 29. Read Mr. Wesley's second volume of Sermons; rode
Wood Tucker's; spoke on Heb. xii, 1–4. Then met society, or rather ga
them an exhortation; the people of the world were by, and God was w
us. I hope what was spoken was blessed to saint and sinner. I am kept
grace, though I have been in temptation.

Tuesday, 30. I arose at five o'clock, with peace of mind, and was e
ployed in writing letters to my friends in the Peninsula. Then rode
George Smith's, preached on 1 Peter iv, 17, to about sixty people: spe
some time in speaking; but had not as much liberty as at some other tim
Spoke to the class; the people spoke afterward of the goodness of Go
Afterward I rode to Boisseau's; some were gone home for fear of
horse-press. Captain Boisseau is dead, and the work dies with him. Befo
I had done prayer, there came up soldiers and horses; the people w
affrighted, but there was no need: the officers came in, and sat down; o
soon tired; the other could not stay it out. I spoke from 1 Peter v, 10, a
addressed myself according to my audience; the people were grea
alarmed; I was tempted to go back to the north, there is such a commoti
in the country; the troops are going to Camden, South Carolina. Bu

[45] Joseph Hartley was the preacher on the Dorchester, Maryland, circuit this ye
(See *Minutes*.)

[46] Joel Mabry lived in Brunswick County. This year, however, that part of Brunsw
County became Greensville County. Mabry's is sometimes listed in Brunswick a
sometimes in Greensville County.

1st go on, and not faint in the way. I have been very well off; but am 1owing trouble. What matters it, where I go, what comes upon me, if 1d is with me; or where I live or where I die, if holy and ready!

Wednesday, 31. I find some left the society here, at the time of the divi-1n; and between one thing and another, it is bad times here, and a 1rowful day with me.

Thursday, June 1, 1780. Rode to Mr. Jarratt's, and was kindly enter-1ned. Preached in the barn to about seventy people; but not so lively as 1en I was here four years ago; spoke on 1 John iii, 23, had much free 1nversation among the people; Mr. Jarratt is as kind as formerly.

Friday, 2. Went to White Oak;[47] and spoke on Titus iii, 2–5, and was 1ssed: then met the society and spoke to the people. Mr. Jarratt wept, 1d all the people, at the joy of union.

Saturday, 3. Rode to Gillum Booth's, had about sixty people, and I 1ke on Matt. vii, 21–23. Here Captain Benson[48] came twelve miles to 1 me; poor man, I wept over him, and exhorted him to seek the Lord; 1ich, if he does not, I fear he will never come back; but his family are 1ying for him: I felt an uncommon love for him, and a hope God will 1ss and keep him alive in the day of battle. (1810. Now General Benson 1iving in Talbot, Maryland.)

Sunday, 4. I rode twelve miles to Mrs. Merritt's meeting house: there 1re about three hundred people, white and black. Spoke on Rom. ii, 1; after sermon I spoke to the society, some of them are happy souls; 1 there is a slackness in meeting: the rules of the society have not been 1t up here. I spoke to some select friends about slave-keeping, but they 1ld not bear it: this I know, God will plead the cause of the oppressed, 1ugh it gives offence to say so here. O Lord, banish the infernal spirit 1 slavery from thy dear Zion.

Monday, 5. I have peace; though I am grieved at some things: it will be 1g, I fear, before the good Virginia brethren will be brought into close 1cipline; though there are many gracious people.

Tuesday, 6. Have peace of mind: preached at Walker's barn on Heb. 1. 2. Met some faithful people in society. Have been reading Knox's 1t volume of Sermons; they are sublime, though not deep: I approve the 1rit and principles of the man; he appears to be of the spirit of Mr. 1gaw; he gives some favourable hints of restoration; that natural evil 1uld purge out moral evil; but gave it not as his own opinion, but as 1t of others. In another place he says, "Perhaps the heathen world

1 This was White Oak Chapel where the revival broke out in Jarratt's work. It was 1inwiddie County.

1 Perry Benson (1751–1827), captain of Talbot County, Maryland, Militia in the 1olution, colonel of Maryland Militia in the Whiskey Rebellion of 1794, and cited 1810 as General Benson, was the ancestor of Charles C. Duke, retired Baltimore 1ker and prominent active Baltimore Conference layman. (Maryland Sons of the 1erican Revolution publication, *Patriotic Maryland*, 159.)

shall have an after-trial;" if in time, it is true. So it sometimes is, that i
man is a rigid Calvinist, and turns, he must go quite round; but gene
redemption and conditional salvation is the plan. I keep up prayer
public or private twelve times a day; and am exercised not a little. Lo
keep me through the approaching troubles of the continent! I preach
at Benjamin Johnson's; had many to hear, and some of the rich. Went
near the conscience as I could get; spoke on Luke xiii, 23–25, then n
society, and had a melting time: the people spoke their experiences, a
joyed in the union, and to see my face.

Wednesday, 7. Rode to Rose Creek; here my old friend William Wh
would not come to hear me. Spoke on Rom. xiii, 11–13; was much
sisted; all the friends were moved; but sinners are callous! God was w
us. Thus the Lord made us to rejoice; and although there has beer
falling off, I hope God will revive the people and his work in this pla
Rode home with friend Rivers; and think I am more given up than ev
I was in my life; I see the need of living near to God, to be able to prea
the travails of God's people, to get freedom and love to bear with sinne
and to deal faithfully. I am labouring for God, and my soul is pressi
after full salvation.

Thursday, 8. In my way I called to see friend Marks and family; he
worn down with family troubles: also called to see Mrs. Clayburn
Brunswick court house; she is under some despondency from weakness
body. Spoke at Mark Crowder's on 1 Peter i, 5–10. The word was bl
to believers. In society some spoke of the goodness of God. In the aft
noon, I rode through a steep, dangerous place, into the river; but thou
it was frightful, I came safe over to Wharton's. Edward Dromgoole i;
good preacher, but entangled with a family. We spoke of a plan for bui
ing houses in every circuit for preachers' wives, and the society to sup;
their familes with bread and meat; so the preachers should travel fro
place to place, as when single: for unless something of the kind be do
we shall have no preachers but young ones, in a few years; they w
marry and stop.

Friday, 9. Preached at Woolsey's barn, on Jude 20–22. James Mor
exhorted, and the people were moved very much. I rode to friend Ower
had the comfort to see my Portsmouth friends, and was pleased to fi
their faces Zionward.

Saturday, 10. Preached to about sixty people, was blest in speakir
rode on to my old friend, Samuel Yeargin's—as kind as ever, but a dissen
in heart. I spoke at the chapel with great power, on Isaiah iii, 10, 11. H
I was taken sick, a smart fever, I could get no farther; was very bad
Monday, Tuesday, and *Wednesday.* Providence dark; my spirits mu
dejected.

Wednesday, 14. Cannot read, write, think, pray, or speak much, I ha
such pain; but I trust in the Lord. It is no matter where I die, if in t

rd; I commend all to him: the more I suffer, the better it will be in the
d, if it is for souls I labour and suffer.

Thursday, 15. I am better in health; but have the toothache violently,
d am forced to use tobacco, that I had laid aside; but putting this in
v tooth, I found some relief. Lord, give me patience! I am never so holy
when travelling and preaching: I hope to set out again tomorrow.
rd, give me patience under all my suffering, and a happy issue out of
, in thine own time! Have read as far as Isaiah, in going through my
ole; have but little time. I see the need of returning to my twelve times
prayer; I have been hindered and interrupted by pains and fevers. Pain
rying; but I am kept from murmuring hitherto. Satan has tried me, and
ave had some dejection of spirit. Lord, keep me every moment!

North Carolina

Friday, 16. I crossed Roanoke (North Carolina),⁴⁹ felt a little better,
ough weak. We rode near thirty miles, was like to faint in the carriage;
t at brother Edward's⁵⁰ felt refreshed, and ease from pain; slept well;
ssed be God!

Saturday, 17. I am in peace, and much blest always when travelling.
ached at Jones's barn⁵¹ to about one hundred people; spoke on Heb.
11-15; was weak, but spoke long. A few felt and understood. The
awakened appeared unmoved; my discourse was not for them. I think
 immediate call is to the people of God: others seem in a hardened
te; they have heard much, obeyed little. Went to Mrs. Yancy's⁵² an

---

' Asbury entered Halifax County, North Carolina, near present Roanoke Rapids.
as his first tour through that state. His leading purpose was to heal the split caused
the action of the Virginians on the sacraments. Pilmoor had been in the state in
3 and preached the first Methodist sermon at Currituck Court House, being
ertained by Colonel Hallowell Williams, an active Methodist. There were Methodists
North Carolina much earlier, having come down from Virginia or converted by
orge Whitefield, who toured the state in 1739–40. No society was formed, however,
il Robert Williams extended his Petersburg Circuit across the state line to Bute
Halifax counties in 1773 or 1774. When Asbury arrived in 1780, there were four
uits in North Carolina, and Asbury covered three of them. He traveled for two
nths in twelve counties, and his movements can be traced only approximately and
1 great difficulty. (Grissom: *History of Methodism in North Carolina*, 29, 35;
odmason: *The Carolina Backcountry on the Eve of the Revolution*, 20.)
' Edwards probably lived in Northampton County near the Halifax line.
Jones's barn seems to have been in Halifax County, North Caroina. Jesse Lee
ached his first sermon "at a place called the Old Barn" on this circuit while assisting
n Dickins, who lived in the county. (Lee: *Life and Times of the Rev. Jesse Lee*, 64.)
re was a Jones Chapel in Sussex County, Virginia; and in a "barn near Brother
es' house" Methodist meetings were held. (Sweet: *Virginia Methodism*, 121, 122, 160.)
"Mrs. Yancy was one of the most self-denying, holy women that ever was; the
. John Dickins married a Miss Yancy." (Lednum, *op. cit.*, 173.)

afflicted, distressed woman, sunk into rigid mortification, thinking s
ought to fast excessively.

Sunday, 18. I rode fifteen miles to brother Bustion's,[53] and preached
about five hundred people; was much led out on Isaiah lv, 6, 7. The peo
were solemnly attentive: I was tempted to think I had done well; bu
opposed the devil and overcame him. Brother Dickins[54] spoke on char
very sensibly, but his voice is gone; he reasons too much; is a man
great piety, great skill in learning, drinks in Greek and Latin swiftly;
prays much, and walks close with God. He is a gloomy countryman
mine, and very diffident of himself. My health is recovered; thank
Lord. Thus he makes my strength sufficient for my day; glory
God!

Monday, 19. Rose about five o'clock, was a little disturbed in my r
with company. Brother Dickins drew the subscription for a Kingswc
school in America; this was what came out a college in the subscripti
printed by Dr. Coke.[55] Gabriel Long and brother Bustion were the fi
subscribers,[56] which I hope will be for the glory of God and good

---

[53] Mr. Bustion lived in Halifax County, not far from the home of John Dickins r
the present town of Halifax. Martha Bustion is listed in *Heads of Families, Cei
1790, N.C.*, as having three sons, three daughters, and sixteen slaves.

[54] John Dickins (1746–98), preacher on the Roanoke Circuit and one of Methodis
outstanding leaders, was born in London and educated at Eton. He came to Ame
in 1774 and entered the traveling ministry in Virginia in 1778. He had served the N
Carolina, Brunswick, and Roanoke circuits. In 1781 he located, presumably becaus
ill health, and lived in his own house near Halifax, North Carolina. He was readmi
in 1783 and appointed to New York; in his church there Thomas Coke preached
first sermon in America on the night of November 3, 1784; and it was to Dickins
Coke first communicated Wesley's plan for the consecration of Asbury and the organ
tion of the Methodists into a church. Dickins was a leading member of the Christ
Conference, where he was ordained a deacon and suggested the name of Metho
Episcopal Church for the new body. In 1786 while on the Bertie Circuit in North C;
lina he prepared the *Discipline* of 1786, the first in its present form. When the Metho
Book Concern was organized in 1789, he became book agent, and continued in
post until his death of yellow fever in 1798. (*Dictionary of American Biography*, V, 2
293; Sweet: *Virginia Methodism*, 101, 155; and various histories of Methodism;
Journal entries and notes for March 25, September 16, 1786.)

[55] The plan for the first Methodist school in America was prepared at John Dick
house on Fishing Creek near the Halifax and Edgecomb County line. Asbury had
cussed such a project on November 30, 1779. The phrase about "the subscription prir
by Dr. Coke" indicates a later entry, since Coke was not to appear on the scene
more than four years. It seems that the school was to be in North Carolina, though
funds were later used for Cokesbury College in Maryland. The North Carolina sch
was established some time before 1793 and was called Cokesbury. It was the first o
ference school in America. (See note under April 2, 1794. Cummings: *Early Schoo*
Methodism, 71, 72; Grissom: *Methodism in North Carolina*, 134, 135; Turner and B
gers: *History of Edgecomb County*, 468.)

[56] Messrs. Bustion and Long of North Carolina thus have the distinction of be
the first contributors to a Methodist school in America. The former lived in Hal
County, and the latter doubtless lived in Edgecomb, since Asbury rode twenty-

ousands. We set off in the rain, rode over Fishing Creek to Davis's, miles; I spoke on 1 Thess. i, 8, 9, had some light, but the people were ry little moved; rode twelve miles to Gabriel Long's, through the woods. ope John Dickins will ever after this be a friend to me and Methodism. y health is greatly restored; am blest among my friends.

Tuesday, 20. After an hour spent in prayer, private and in the family, I d a few chapters in the Bible; began reading Watt's first volume of rmons; was pleased and profited. Preached at noon to fifty people, on us ii, 11–14, had some liberty among the people; they were very little ected—but the faithful, for whom I principally spoke, were tender; n rode over to Joseph John Williams's, a rich man of this world, and I pe sincere. I am kept through mercy.

Wednesday, 21. I had to ride alone better than twelve miles to Mr. ike's; when I came there, found about thirty people, and they quite orant. After preaching I took dinner, and in talking found three or four them tenderly serious; gave them advice: the man and his wife have had nviction, and have sinned it away. They say it was the disputes of the ptists that turned them aside. I then rode home with a Mr. Green, a esbyterian; and was much blest in reading Watt's first volume of rmons.

Thursday, 22. I rode to Jenkins's[57] and spoke plainly to about eighty ople, and found the word was fitted to their cases; met class; it was a y of peace to me; the Lord was with me at this poor, but good man's use. I was kept by the power of God; my soul is breathing after the rd at all times. There is a hardness over the people here: they have had Gospel preached by Presbyterians, Baptists, and Methodists; the two mer appear to be too much in the spirit of the world; there is life ongst some of the Methodists, and they will grow because they preach wing doctrines. I heard of Mr. Hart,[58] from Charleston, passing north, one of the Countess of Huntingdon's[59] men turning Baptist. They ve soon turned about; but they may follow Mr. Whitefield in Calvinism.

Friday, 23. I have peace, the Lord is my portion; this was a day of ting; I rode fifteen miles, preached, prayed, and sung near two hours;

es from the chapel to his residence. (Turner and Bridgers, *op. cit.*, 468.) Jesse Lee d in the home of Gabriel Long before he became a traveling preacher. Lednum cribes Long as "a great Christian" and calls Bustion "another good man." (*Op. cit.*, ; Lee, *op. cit.*, 63, 64.)

Jenkins seems to have lived in Franklin County.

The Rev. Oliver Hart had resigned from the Particular Baptist Church (now First urch) in Charleston and was on his way to Hopewell, New Jersey, where he spent rest of his life. Pilmoor preached in his church in January, 1773.

The Countess of Huntingdon was the leader of the Calvinistic Methodists, to ch group George Whitefield also belonged. The person mentioned was probably of the preachers brought to Bethesda Orphanage by Whitefield, who perhaps ned to organize a Calvinistic Methodist group in America. (Lee and Luccock: strated History of Methodism, 134.)

ate a little about four o'clock, and preached at Nutbush Creek chape
(a little log-house, about twenty-five feet long and twenty wide,) to ab
one hundred and fifty people; here I found a broken society. Rode ho
with Dr. King; his wife was in society. I slept in peace, and rose ab
five o'clock: my heart is with God! Glory be to thee, O Lord! I had t
mean an opinion of Carolina; it is a much better country, and t
people live much better than I expected from the information gi
me.

Saturday, 24. Though the weather was extremely hot, I, yet weak
body, rode to Col. Edmund Taylor's;[61] and at the school house spoke
about seventy people, on 1 Peter iv, 18. Afterward was kindly entertain
at Col. Taylor's: they were for ordinances here, though not heated.

Sunday, 25. Rode six miles to the Tabernacle;[62] about four hund
people, rich and poor, attended; had very little liberty in speaking—t
people very insensible. I think these people must be awakened by ju
ments, for it appears the Gospel will not do it. I spoke near two hours
little purpose; held a love feast; all the friends were stirred up. Then r
eight miles, lodged over Nutbush Creek at brother Reeves's. I am kept
peace, but felt much ashamed for my unfaithfulness.

Monday, 26. Rose early; my legs are so inflamed I cannot tell what
do; but we must bear all things: I read Watts's first volume of Serm
last week, and transcribed a little of it. I preached at Turner's; he has l
the use of his limbs. I advised him to use the cold bath, or electric
either might help him. I had liberty in the word; the hearers were stir
up; many came to hear who do not, will not, attend the other preache
Now the end of this may be good; for if they get their hearts affect
they will come to hear others, and by constant travelling I may do go
I had in both meetings eighty or ninety people; the circuit preachers h
but about twenty. The Baptists appear to be very dead; their own peo
will not attend only on *Sabbath days*. The people are taken away, and tin
are so difficult that they appear to be under a judicial hardness, havi
heard so much and felt so little.

Tuesday, 27. Preached at William Price's, many came to hear. Lo
set home thy word to their hearts! Rode to Haw Tree,[63] many came

[60] Nutbush Creek Chapel was in Vance County about a mile north of Williamsb
and near the Roanoke River. It was built in 1757 by the Lewis family, and in 1772
moved to its present site in Williamsboro, where it is now St. John's Episcopal Chu
(S. T. Peace, Vance County, North Carolina, historian.)

[61] Colonel Taylor's family lived on Tar River, probably in Vance County, and "
a chief family in the beginning." (Lednum, *op. cit.,* 173.)

[62] The Tabernacle was in Vance County north of Colonel Taylor's according to
probable route being followed by Asbury.

[63] The 1808 map of North Carolina shows Haw Tree in upper Warren County. B
Haw Tree and Nutbush creeks flow into Roanoke River. Asbury was traveling in
northern counties near the Virginia line, and the persons mentioned lived there.

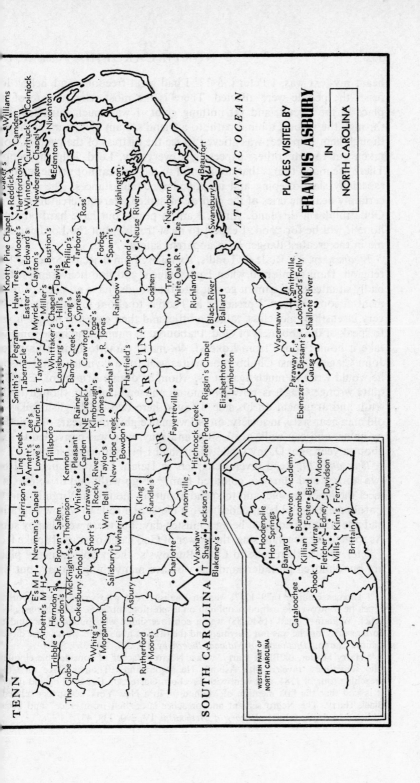

PLACES VISITED BY

FRANCIS ASBURY

IN

NORTH CAROLINA

ATLANTIC OCEAN

NORTH CAROLINA

SOUTH CAROLINA

TENN

WESTERN PART OF
NORTH CAROLINA

hear; my text was, 1 Peter i, 5–13. I had great freedom, and held a lo
feast, the people were affected. There is the most religion here of a
place in the circuit, and yet nothing great: I was much refreshed, ro
through the woods, a blind path, to a friend's. I am always upon the ru
though kept in peace; was grieved to see the distress of the people—so
taken out to war, others expecting it every day. Lord, help thy peopl
There are many things that are painful to me, but cannot yet be remove
especially slave-keeping and its attendant circumstances. The Lord w
certainly hear the cries of the oppressed, naked, starving creatures. O, 1
God! think on this land. Amen. I am in peace, but have hard labour
hope it will be for good: I expect to meet trouble, but the Lord can ke
me in the greatest danger as in apparent safety.

Wednesday, 28. Rode to Todd's, six miles: I am dejected to see so lit
religion. I am comforted when I pray much, and find deliverances. I a
badly situated: and cannot go out into the woods; have no place of reti
ment at some houses. I preached at Todd's, to about seventy people, b
very insensible; met class, talked a little, and then gave the people liber
to speak of the goodness of God. I laboured in public; and hope some w
take it home: spoke from Luke vi, 46, many came to hear. I have re
John Claget against Chubb:[64] he writes well for a layman; but I suspe
he would write as much against us, whom he deems Arminians. Chubb
quite wrong; Claget is no ways smooth and entertaining, though he h
truth and argument on his side. I found here two old English folks—
old man near sixty, in society; an old woman eighty-nine years old, Nodd
by name, and can walk, read, sing, and pray, who was converted to G
about a year ago. O, my God! when shall I be established in purity?

Thursday, 29. Read several chapters in Isaiah. I have thought if I h
two horses, and Harry (a coloured man)[65] to go with, and drive one, a
meet the black people, and to spend about six months in Virginia and t
Carolinas, it would be attended with a blessing. I rode to widow Pegram
had about sixty people, it being a muster-day; but these were happy sou
As soon as we began to sing, the power of God came over us; I spoke fro
1 Peter v, 6–8, then rode to Capt. Burrows's: the people in many plac
are but children in understanding; we have many things to say, but th

[64] Thomas Chubb (1679–1747) was an English Deist who wrote several works
which he controverted orthodox opinion on inspiration, miracles, and other articles
belief. William Clagett (1646–88) was a controversialist who published around t
dozen works, but he was not a layman and the titles of none of his works were direc
against Chubb. (*Dictionary of National Biography*, IV, 297, 298, 367, 368.)

[65] Harry Hosier, or Black Harry, was a Negro preacher of considerable eloque
who sometimes traveled with Asbury. He accompanied Thomas Coke on Cok
preaching tour in 1784, and went with Freeborn Garrettson to New England in 17
It is said that the first mention of Methodism in a New York newspaper related
Black Harry. The Negro servant and preacher later "fell from grace" and beca
addicted to drink. (Hurst: *History of Methodism*, IV, 290, 339, 437.)

ınot bear them now. I am much blessed in my own soul. I began to
m a plan for myself and all the preachers for next year, if we live. I am
l seeking full and final salvation. I preached at Burrows's; but fear
re is very little religion in this place: I was uncomfortable. The congre-
:ion about sixty people, but they were very dead; their minds and mouths
l of the world. I came off to the widow Ellis's,[66] and found the Lord was
re. There has been a heavy rain these two nights past; if it continues,
will destroy the full, ripe crops of wheat.

Friday, 30. Slept in peace last night; rose with a deep sense of God:
t with Henry Jones, a serious young man, and believe he is called to
: work of the ministry; I advised him to go with me.

Saturday, July 1, 1780. My soul pants after God more and more. O,
ıt I were filled with strong, constant, humble, suffering love! I preached
the widow Ellis's, on Heb. x, 21–24. I was fervent, had liberty, and
ɔke as searchingly as I could to saints and sinners. Here Edward
ʻomgoole[67] met me; and I appointed James Mallory[68] for Norfolk cir-
ıt, as there have been a few people kept together, notwithstanding the
sence of the preachers.

Sunday, 2. I rode to Lindsey's, a rough road; had about seventy people;
d spoke on 2 Cor. iv, 4–6. Now I have done in this circuit; the Lord has
:ssed me in body and soul. Tomorrow I am going to Tar River. Edward
ʻomgoole is hearty in good old Methodism; we have had great union;
ıope he will check the spirit of some of the divisive men. I wrote to
:uben Ellis;[69] read my select Scriptures. God is with us: it may be trials
: coming, but no matter; why should I fear?—the Lord liveth, and he is
y rock.

Monday, 3. Very rainy night, with thunder and lightning. I am grieved
see slavery, and the manner of keeping these poor people. I set out for
ır River: after riding about five miles I was told I could not cross Bear
vamp; but by the guidance of a Baptist friend, came through that and
ɔ very deep creeks.[70] Afterward I left my guide: we had travelled a few
ıles together, and talked in a friendly manner. Rode three miles farther,
d was stopped by what was called Bens Creek; the bridge was gone,

---

₆₆ The Ellis family was prominent in North Carolina Methodism. Reuben Ellis was
e of the first preachers. (Lednum, *op. cit.,* 173. Lednum identifies most of the persons
:h whom Asbury stayed on this trip.)
₃⁷ See note under January 30, 1774. Edward Dromgoole was living with his family
Brunswick County, Virginia. He had no regular appointment between 1778 and 1783.
₆⁸ James Mallory was a local preacher. The following year, in the conference held at
ıoptank, Delaware, he was admitted on trial and appointed to the Pittsylvania
rcuit; and he was admitted into full connection the year following and sent to the
uth Branch Circuit.
³⁹ Reuben Ellis had been on the Mecklenberg Circuit the previous year. (See *Minutes.*)
⁷⁰ The two creeks were probably Swift and Fishing creeks in Edgecomb County,
ɔrth Carolina. (Turner and Bridgers, *op. cit.,* 467.)

and a man said it was ten feet deep: I then made for Falcon's bridge,
little Fishing Creek; but the low ground was covered, and no bridge to
seen: lodged at Mr. John Falcon's, was known, and kindly entertain
I laboured to make Mrs. Falcon sensible of her danger, and hope not
vain; prayed evening and morning in the family.

Tuesday, 4. I rode by Miller's cross roads to Great Fishing Creek
rough way—but got safe along, and was comforted in mind; cross
Great Fishing Creek; stopped at Sandy Creek, where I found a kind (
man, brother Howell; lodged with him and spent my time peaceably.

Wednesday, 5. Set out to Green Hill's; but with difficulty I got alor
but this was not all, for in going the distance of four miles I rode eig
and was tried to purpose; on account of the waters, I have ridden abc
thirty miles out of my way; and am now twenty-six miles from the pla
of preaching tomorrow. Have been happy till today; but when lost
began to feel like fretting against persons and things. O, my God! pard
me in this. I was very kindly entertained, and blessed with fellowship
Green Hill's;[71] but never met with so many difficulties as I have met wi
in this circuit: I hope for the greater blessings; am kept by grace, and enj
health in this hot weather, though so far to the south; have peace of so
bless the Lord.

Thursday, 6. Rode twenty-six miles; exceeding hot, and my hor
suffered greatly. When I came to the place about seventy people were m
singing and praying. I spoke on Heb. iv, 13–16, had not much strength
soul or body. The people appeared inattentive and their minds full of t
present troubles.

Friday, 7. A day of fasting, till near three o'clock; I was weak, a
lodging on the floor was uncomfortable.

Saturday, 8. Rode to Cypress chapel;[72] had liberty in speaking
1 John i, 8, 9, to about one hundred people. Here James O'Kelly[73] m

[71] The Rev. Major Green Hill was a local preacher, prosperous farmer, and prom
ent political figure who lived in Franklin County, one mile from Louisburg. His ho
still stands, and after Hill's removal to Tennessee in 1799, it was occupied by
brother-in-law, Joel King, the son of Dr. John King. Here Asbury held the first co
ference after the organization of the Methodist Episcopal Church. (See note und
April 19, 1785.) Green Hill entertained four annual conferences in his home. (S
Journal entries and notes under April 19, 1785, and October 1, 1808. Davis, *op. c*
63, 279.)

[72] Cypress Chapel was in Franklin County on Cypress Creek, or in nearby Halif
County.

[73] James O'Kelly (1775–1826) was on the Tar River Circuit, one of the circu
through which Asbury was traveling. He was admitted to the conference in 1778 a
was one of those ordained elders at the Christmas Conference in 1784. Asbury had be
with him in the meeting at Manakintown, Virginia, in May, 1780. He traveled wid
in North Carolina and Virginia. He was a member of the short-lived Council, whi
was established in 1789. He became dissatisfied with Asbury's administration, and
the General Conference of 1792 he proposed a resolution providing that any preach
who was dissatisfied with an appointment given him by the bishop could appeal to t

; he spoke, and appeared to be a warm-hearted, good man; but he was
ubled with the people about these times. At Ross's I spoke on Rev.
ii, 10–19. I had an opening; and one Lindsay an exhorter, spoke; an
nest, zealous man: he has lost his little property by these times. I have
den near one hundred miles this week; and as severe, constant hot
ather as I ever knew.

Sunday, 9. Preached at Green Hill's to about four hundred souls, on
Thess. ii, 4. The subject was new, the people dead. I had not much
erty. James O'Kelly spoke on, "Have ye understood all these things?"
raised high, and was very affecting, but to little purpose. There are
ils here; the meeting not solemn; the women appeared to be full of
ess, the men full of news. These people are Gospel slighters. I fear some
avy stroke will come on them. James O'Kelly and myself enjoyed and
mforted each other: this dear man rose at midnight, and prayed very
voutly for me and himself. He cries, give me children or I die; but I
lieve no preaching or preacher will do much good at present. I was
ndemned for telling humorous anecdotes, and knew not whether it was
ilt or fear, lest my friends should think I go beyond the bounds of
udent liberty. It is dreadful, when a preacher is put to it to vindicate
mself.

Monday, 10. Through heat and for want of retirement, I suffer loss;
t bless God for health and faith. I made my journey to Roger Jones's.[74]
bout sixty people; God was with us; the people spoke of the goodness of
e Lord.

Tuesday, 11. Had a heavy night; rose up, and laid myself down on the
or upon my nightgown; slept in pain; rose at four o'clock; prayed in
ivate and in the family; then set off at six o'clock; had hilly roads; and
ter riding five or six hours, came to my appointment; had very little
eedom in speaking to about one hundred people: here I met with W.
rtridge. The Lord keeps me in health: I cast all my care upon him.

Wednesday, 12. I rode to Cooper's[75] upon Tar River, had about one
ndred and twenty people; I was under discouragement before I began,
t the Lord helped me. These people have heard Baptists and Presby-
rians, but I fear to little purpose. God assisted me to deliver my own

nference. When this resolution was defeated, O'Kelly withdrew and organized a
al denomination known as the Republican Methodist Church. Several preachers,
cluding William McKendree for a brief period, and numerous members followed
n, and the schism seriously affected the growth of the Methodist Episcopal Church
r several years. (Grissom, *op. cit.*, 175–86; Simpson: *Cyclopedia of Methodism*, 678–
; Hurst, *op. cit.*, V, 510, 513, 519–21, 886; Sweet: *Virginia Methodism*, 128–34.)

[74] Roger Jones lived near present Kittrell, North Carolina. From this meeting a
ciety was formed and a log chapel erected. This was later replaced by a building of
anks which was called Plank Chapel. It is still in existence under the same name and
the same form.

[75] Cooper probably lived in Granville County. Note the fact that Asbury seemed to go
ck and forth through the same areas.

soul. I rode to a friend's, and had great difficulty on the way; but I a
kept from murmuring: while labouring for other souls, my own is bless
—have felt nothing contrary to love for some days past.

Thursday, 13. Rode to the chapel: had an insensible people, full of t
spirit of the world. I laboured hard to preach on Luke xiii, 23–25. Th
rode to Captain Pope's;[76] I am distressed with the troubles of the tim
and hear there are great commotions. I went to the preaching house, a
poured out my soul to God for some time in the evening—my heart fou
rest, and felt power to trust God with my life and my all. O! why do
my cowardly flesh complain?

Friday, 14. God was with me; I was comforted with brother Pope,
lame, wise, and pious man; he has built a preaching house almost himse
Who can tell what a man may do under divine assistance? He makes
few cards, teaches a few children, and says he lives as well as ever he d
in his life. I was much comforted at the preaching house this morning
suffered much for want of a place of retirement; I cannot go into t
woods, there are so many ticks, chiegoes [chiggers], and such insects
this season upon the ground; retired at six o'clock to the chapel; it h
been a bethel to me: my day of fasting and humiliation has been blest
my soul.

Saturday, 15. After spending some time in the chapel alone, I set o
to Paschal's, about six o'clock; I came in before twelve, I spoke very clo
and plain on Acts xxvi, 18, to about thirty people, and had but little fai
for them. Rode on to B. Hartfield's,[77] about twenty miles, much fatigu
with the badness of the road.

Sunday, 16. I rose unwell, and somewhat dejected. Lord, keep me fro
the power of wicked men, devils, and sin. Sometimes I think, will th
Infinite Being we call God, who commands kingdoms, continents, a
worlds, take care of such a worm as I? Then I consider, he is INFINITE, a
cannot be hurried so as to forget any person. He can keep me as secure
as if there were none but myself in the world. Lord, give me faith to tru
in thee every moment, even in my greatest dangers! I spoke on 2 Thess.
6–9. I had great light; but the people seemed hardened. I fear judgment w
overtake them before they will be awakened; I never felt more engage
and hardly a person moved! I read my select Scriptures, and had my so
much taken up with God; the few people in society seemed tender
brother Hartfield's.

Monday, 17. I set out about five o'clock, and rode to Crawford's upo
Neuse River, about twenty miles, alone; was tried at times, but had son
sense of God; was not so free from my temptations, but kept from sinnin
or yielding in heart: there were many people. I spoke with liberty on

[76] Captain Pope lived in Wake County, and Pope's Chapel was located there.
[77] Paschal lived in lower Wake County, and B. Hartfield lived across the line
Harnett County.

:t. iv, 18. There was a melting among the people; but they are rich, and
e not cured of the love of money.

Tuesday, 18. Rode to Kimborough's, sixteen miles, crossed Neuse
iver. Many Baptists to hear; they were serious, and I spoke feelingly,
ıd aimed at their hearts, from Romans viii, 24–26. I met brother Poy-
ιress,[78] much cast down; the people are lifeless in religion; but, bless the
ord, I have had a good entrance, and a comfortable sense of the divine
:esence. After dinner, I was alone in the woods an hour, had sweet
eltings, came back and wrote these lines for future consolation.

Wednesday, 19. I rode to Abraham Hill's, and had great liberty in
ıeaking from Heb. iv, 10, &c., then brother Poythress spoke; and we
ıd a refreshing shower according to prayer: we afterward spent some
me in reading, out of what I had written and abridged, upon the art of
ıeaking and preaching. I find the spirit of separation on account of the
rdinances, is very high among preachers and people; but I hope it will
e checked.

Thursday, 20. Rode twelve miles to Tignal Jones's;[79] hilly, rocky roads;
bout eighty people to hear. While I was speaking General Hugine came
ı, and heard part of my sermon; he is a polite, well-behaved, conversable
entleman; we dined together. After dinner, I set out on my journey; we
ıme to a desperate creek called North-East, in Chatham county, where
ıe bridge was carried away by the freshet; we had to go through among
ocks, holes, and logs; I was affrighted; yea, it was wonderful that the
ırriage did not overset: brother Poythress said the horse was down twice,
ıd covered all but his head; however, the water kept up the carriage, and
·e came safe through all our difficulties, to brother Merritt's. Hitherto
ıe Lord hath helped—body, soul, horse, and carriage; there is a provi-
ence attending animate and inanimate creation. Here I met brother
·everly Allen[80]—a promising young man, but a little of a Dissenter.

[78] Francis Poythress was on the New Hope Circuit west of the Tar River Circuit, and
ne of the circuits through which Asbury was traveling.

[79] Tignal Jones lived in Wake County near present Apex, ten miles west of Raleigh,
Torth Carolina. There also were two Tignal Joneses in Virginia. (*Heads of Families,* 1790.)

[80] Beverly Allen was a brilliant preacher and one of the original elders ordained at
he Christmas Conference in 1784. He had preached on the New Hope Circuit with
ames O'Kelly in 1779, although his name does not appear in the *Minutes*. According
ɔ a letter from him to John Wesley he "was unable to travel at large" in 1780 and
spent most of the summer on New Hope and Bladen." He introduced Methodism in
alisbury, North Carolina, and formed a class there in 1783. He was the first preacher
ppointed to Georgia, in 1785, and in 1786 was among the first elders designated by
ppointment, being assigned to the Santee and Pee Dee circuits with three preachers
nder him. He later became an apostate and a criminal. (See notes under December 18,
785; January 11, 1786; and March 13, 1791. For his life and experiences see Smith:
Georgia Methodism, 27, 28; Bowen: *Wilkes County,* 118–19; Gilmer: *Early Settlers of
Jpper Georgia,* 105, 106; Grissom, *op. cit.,* 99; Strickland: *Autobiography of Peter
Cartwright,* 28; McIntosh: *History of Elbert County,* 71–73.)

Saturday, 22. We set out for Crump's, over rocks, hills, creeks, ar
pathless woods and low land; and myself in the carriage. The young ma
with me was heartless before we had travelled a mile; but when he sa
how I could bush it, and sometimes force my way through a thicket, an
make the young saplings bend before me, and twist and turn out of th
way, or path, for there was no proper road, he took courage; with grea
difficulty we came in about two o'clock, after travelling eight or nin
hours; the people looking almost as wild as the deer in the woods;
preached on Titus ii, 10–12.

Sunday, 23. We passed Haw River, wide, but shallow, bad going dow
and coming up; they took the carriage over by hand; then we had t
travel the pathless woods and rocks again: after much trouble, and fear
and dejection, we came to Taylor's preaching house,[81] where they wer
pressing horses, as we expected; but I came off safe, and spoke on
Peter i, 5–12. I had some liberty, but the people's minds were in confusion
poor souls, well they might, when there were such works carried on. Th
time to favour this people, I fear is past; and they seem hardened, and n
preaching affects them, at least not mine; they are exceedingly ignoran
withal. There are a few serious people, but much distressed one way o
another. I have travelled thirty miles, and could not avoid travelling or
Sunday, for I had not where to stay; rode to brother Beck's, and was mucl
fatigued: found brother Beck sick; he has a gracious wife.

Monday, 24. Cool, like the fall; I am kept in peace; rose with a sens
of God's presence; have only time to pray and write my journal; alway
upon the wing, as the rides are so long, and bad roads; it takes me man
hours, as in general I walk my horse. I crossed Rocky River about ter
miles from Haw River; it was rocky, sure enough; it is in Chatham county
North Carolina. I can see little else but cabins in these parts, built with
poles: and such a country as no man ever saw for a carriage. I narrowl
escaped being overset; was much affrighted, but Providence keeps me, and
I trust will. I crossed Deep River in a flat boat, and the poor ferryman
sinner swore because I had not a silver shilling to give him. I rode to
friend Hinton's,[82] borrowed a saddle, and rode near six miles to get there
as we were lost; when we came to the place there were about sixty people
I was at some loss whom to preach to, saints or sinners; but found sinner
as unfeeling as those who are out of the reach of mercy. I spoke on I

[81] Taylor's preaching house was probably in Chatham County, North Carolina.

[82] Dempsey and Sarah Hinton were among the earliest converts to Methodism ir
North Carolina. Their home was on Deep River in Randolph County, but they later
moved to the town of Washington on the Pamlico River in Beaufort, where they were
instrumental in establishing the Methodist Church. One of their sons, James Hinton
became a preacher and was admitted on trial in 1783 and appointed to Salisbury Cir
cuit. (Grissom, *op. cit.*, 150–51. See articles on Asbury's travels on Deep River and ir
neighboring counties by S. S. Robins in Chapel Hill *News Leader* June 20 and July 4
1955.)

ter v, 9–12. I was glad to get away, for some were drunk, and had their
ns in meeting. I expect to see some of these people again, and believe
ey will be humbled in time, but I fear not by the Gospel, which they have
ghted, but by judgments. We came back and found a serious family:
s blest in a family meeting; the Lord filled our hearts with his love. I
d a fever in the night; rose refreshed in the morning.

Tuesday, 25. Was engaged in private and family prayer for divine
otection; for I dwell as among briars, thorns, and scorpions: the people
e poor, and cruel one to another: some families are ready to starve for
nt of bread, while others have corn and rye distilled into poisonous
iskey; and a Baptist preacher has been guilty of the same; but it is no
nder that those who have no compassion for the non-elect souls of
ople should have none for their bodies. These people have had some
igion; but if any seeth his brother need, and shutteth up his bowels of
mpassion, so as neither to give nor sell, "how dwelleth the love of God
that man?" These are poor Christians. We left our worthy friend
nton's, a kind family, who parted with us in tears: I hope to see this
ace again (I have seen it many times) with a change for the better. We
rded Deep River, rode to White's, within ten miles of the camp,[83] into
settlement of people from Pennsylvania, some were Quakers. I preached
White's to about twenty people; was very unwell by a disorder in my
wels; then rode sixteen miles to R. Kennon's;[84] it was rainy, and we
de two miles in the dark through the woods, but came safe about ten
clock, fatigued, and under a temptation to stop; but reading Paul to
mothy, where he says, "I charge thee before God," &c., I resolved to
on; and though but little time and opportunity for retirement, not any
r reading or gaining knowledge, yet saving souls is better. But people
e so distracted with the times, they are afraid to leave their houses, or
le their horses. I acknowledge the providence and immediate hand of
od in my journey; though it be not of general benefit, I shall gain a
neral knowledge of the preachers and people, and strengthen our union.

Wednesday, 26. I preached at Harris's to about one hundred people
th some opening; it was well I did not give way and rest today.

Thursday, 27. Rose in some consolation, and read a few chapters in the
stament. I acknowledge the goodness of God in preserving my health,
e, and horse, from these people; they are very vile, and if there is any
schief done it is laid to the soldiers: people rob, steal, and murder one
other with impunity. Rode twelve miles to West's, about one hundred
ople; some faithful Baptists. I spoke with Thomas Brown, a preacher,
o, with twelve more, is separated from the separate Baptists on account
their slackness in discipline: I had fellowship with the man; we spent

[3] There were several camp grounds in the area. The parenthesis above must have
n inserted by another hand.
[4] White lived in Guilford County, and Kennon lived in Alamance.

some time together. I told him the danger of being alone; and advi*s*
them to meet in a class, one with another. My trials are great; rid*i*
twenty miles a day, or more; rocky roads, poor entertainment, uncomf*c*
able lodging; little rest night or day; but thanks be to God, he keeps *n*
the more I do and suffer, the greater the crown.

Friday, 28. Rode twelve miles to the chapel, and preached to *c*
hundred people, on 1 Peter iv, 18, with some life; but the people w*e*
unfeeling. I had an exceeding rough road, through woods, over roc*
through creeks, &c. I expect fewer trials every day, and frequently f*i*
more; I will therefore expect greater. I rode seven miles to Mr. Trice*
was kindly entertained; had the pleasure of seeing and conversing w*
brother Bailey, from Ireland,[85] a good and sensible man: I slept well, a*
am better. I praise God for health.

Saturday, 29. Rode to Roades's, and preached to about two hund*i*
people, on Titus iii, 2–8. I had some light: brother Bailey and Al*
spoke; I hope it will revive the work. I then went on to Alston's.

Sunday, 30. Preached at Neuse preaching house[86] to about four hund*i*
people—had not much liberty. These people have had an abundance
preaching from the Baptist and Methodists, till they are hardened. I *a*
kept in peace, power, and love to God, and from every moral evil. In *t*
evening a heavy rain came on. I lodged at Mr. Allen's. There are ma*
trials in my way, but the Lord hath brought me on—to him be all gl*e*
now and ever! I have lately passed through Cumberland, Chatham, Ora*n*
and Wake counties, in North Carolina: brother Bailey has agreed to g*
up all business and travel with me, and go to labour in the north. Beve*
Allen and Edward Bailey spoke at Neuse after me. I hope some good w*
done, and the work will revive. The people in these parts have been h*
with Calvinism; our first preachers moved their passions, and they has*
and improperly joined; and afterward they dropped off from society, a*
there was a great falling away. The ordinance places seem very barren

Monday, 31. A very rainy day. I rested at Mr. Allen's, read in the N*
Testament, and prayed in the family four times.

Tuesday, August 1, 1780. We were discouraged by the rivers, but
out late to Clenny's, crossed Eno[87] with difficulty—the water ran over *t*
foot-board of my carriage. After that, I rode a stony, hilly way ab*c*
twelve miles, came in by the time Edward Bailey had preached an alarm*
sermon on "Seek the Lord while he may be found." Then I preached fr*
Heb. ii, 1–3. Afterward Beverly Allen spoke, and prayed mightily. Thi*s*

[85] Edward Bailey was from Ireland and had been appointed to the Fairfax Circui*
the Virginia section of the conference the previous year. He fell ill and died while on *t*
journey with Asbury. (Larrabee: *Asbury and His Coadjutors*, I, 53, 54.)

[86] Neuse Meeting House was probably in the southeastern part of Durham Cou*
near the Wake County line. Asbury had turned eastward.

[87] Eno Creek was in Orange County; and Asbury crossed near Hillsboro, hav*
turned northward.

ettlement of Irish Pennsylvanians. Through all my troubles I am kept peace, faith, and love; we were blest in family prayer, speaking to them, i praying for them. I am this day to go towards Hillsboro with uctance—but at God's command I go, and from no other motive; I l no temper or desire but to do the will of God.

Wednesday, 2. Rode seven miles to Hillsboro, and preached in the use of Mr. Cortney, a tavern,[88] to about two hundred people, on osea x, 12: "It is time to seek the Lord." They were decent, and behaved ll; I was much animated, and spoke loud and long. Before I set off this orning, I felt dejected, but on the way it vanished. I felt faith to believe should have a peaceable, profitable meeting, and trust it was so: they ve had a warning. Edward Bailey and brother Allen gave exhortations. ame back to hold a watch night, without eating or drinking—though portuned to take refreshment; hitherto the Lord has helped me through ntinual fatigue and rough roads: little rest for man or horse, but souls e perishing—time is flying—and eternity comes nearer every hour.

Thursday, 3. We set off for Pittsylvania,[89] and travelled twenty-five les to John Lee's; came in about eight o'clock. God is at work, and I pe I shall be blessed here more than in the three circuits past. I felt a lemn, melting sense of God upon my heart in family prayer. I had a isible feeling for my northern friends, when I heard of the fighting in e Jerseys; I fear they will be distressed. I am kept in peace.

Friday, 4. I was never more devoted to God—it makes me think I am my duty. I was tempted and tried in Delaware to prepare me for, and ive me to, this work; and believe if I had not started I should have ffered great loss in my soul. I admire the hand of God in disposing of e, and wonder and own his providence.

Saturday, 5. Our quarterly meeting began at Henley's preaching use. I preached on Coloss. i, 27–29, then brother Bailey, Ivey, and orris[90] spoke, there was some reviving among the people. We lodged at hn Lee's—my mind was much drawn out; we retired to an old log shop, d prayed frequently, and found our hearts sweetly united together.

Sunday, 6. We had a great meeting, love feast at ten—very warm

[8] There was no Methodist society at Hillsboro, Orange County, at this time. The lsboro Methodist Church was organized about 1807.

[9] The Pittsylvania Circuit had been formed in 1776, embracing territory in Virginia d North Carolina. In 1780 the Yadkin Circuit in North Carolina was formed from a rt of the Pittsylvania. The Yadkin was west of the New Hope Circuit and extended to Blue Ridge and southward to the South Carolina line. Asbury was probably in swell County.

[0] Richard Ivey was on the Pittsylvania Circuit. In 1779 he served the Brunswick rcuit in Virginia with Thomas and James Morris. The Morrises do not appear in the pointments for 1780. Because the conference was split in two sections over the row Virginia about the sacraments, the appointments for all the preachers do not appear. 1779 there were forty-nine preachers, in 1780 there were forty-two, and in 1781 when breach had been healed there were fifty-four.

weather; a log house, covered with long shingles; the sun beating throu̟
At one o'clock preaching began, I spoke on Eph. iii, 16–18, to about ̍
hundred people; was blest, and the word went with power. Some w̍
moved, some hardened, yet I hope good was done and the work ͏
revive.

Monday, 7. Exceeding hot weather; I rose with a comfortable sense
the Divine presence on my heart; we prayed alone in the woods; I plead
in private; great labours are before me: the Lord keeps me. At te̍
preached in Lee's chapel, in Caswell county, to about sixty people,
Matt. vii, 21: "Not every one that saith, Lord, Lord, &c." I posses̍
clearness of ideas, liberty of speech, and the people serious: the preach̍
are under great difficulties here for want of places of study; most pla̍
but one room, or if a chamber, they cannot live there, it is so hot. I fou̍
the people much united to me, and appeared to think too highly of ͏
Lord, keep me from pride, and all high thoughts of myself; but da̍
travelling and other labours will humble me. There is a good work of G̍
here; but some of the Baptists rage because we have what they lost; ̍
while we keep close to God, and preach the power of religion, they c̍
do us no harm. (True!)[91]

Tuesday, 8. I rode to Baxter's, sixteen miles; about eighty people, ma̍
came that never attended at other times. My text was 1 John i, 8, 9. I h̍
great liberty, but was tried in getting there; we crossed the Line Cre̍
After preaching, rode six miles, but was an hour too late. About ei̍
o'clock, came to a cabin, an earthen floor, and damp bed. I was very we̍
and had a pain in my head; but the people were kind: I knew not how ͏
lie down. Edward Bailey lay down, and slept well.

Wednesday, 9. I rode sixteen miles to White's, came in about th̍
o'clock; no preaching appointed. I had time to write, and plan for anot̍
trip through Carolina. I have had little time or place for prayer till I ca̍
here: the roads are so bad, I have my carriage to refit almost every we̍
This is Caswell County; the poor people have been much put to it, t̍
year past, for bread; the present year they have exceeding fine grow̍
corn: Lord, remember the poor!

Virginia

Thursday, 10. I rode for the state of Virginia; we were lost, stopped ̍
Thomas Dickinson's, and took dinner; then rode on to Sylvester Adams̍
several creeks to cross, and bad roads to travel. Edward Bailey led ͏
horse down a steep hill, and the carriage overset, the horse struggled, ̍
kept his feet: one shaft broke which we strapped up; and rode on ne̍

[91] This interjection, True! was doubtless added by one of the early editors of ͏
Journal.

rty miles: we found the Rollinses there. Abraham is incurable: I have
iind to try Isaac again, having a hope that he is humbled: Lord, direct
what to do in this matter. I made proposals to him, but he rejected
m: I fear he is also incurable, being too lazy to ride a circuit.

Saturday, 12. I went down Dan River two miles, and preached to
ut eighty people on James iv, 8–11. Edward Bailey spoke very zealously
er me; it is very hot, myself weak and distressed; have no place for
irement but the woods, and the heat dispirits me: there is a great
ference between this and the northern part of the continent. I am kept
faith, and seek the glory of God.

Sunday, 13. I rode to Watson's preaching house,[92] a round, long build-
; after the plan of this part of the country. There were about five
ndred people; I spoke on the parable of the sower, a lengthy discourse.
ward Bailey preached much to the purpose about Christian discipline
d fellowship, from those words: "Where two or three are gathered to-
her, in my name," &c. There was a moving.

Monday, 14. I brought Isaac Rollins to some acknowledgment, and
pointed him to ride Pittsylvania, New Hope, and Tar River, till con-
ence. His greatest admirers saw his obstinacy, and would have disowned
n if he had not submitted; for they began to tire with his lounging about.
ope this will be a warning to him, and will make him take more care,
d submit to order. I preached at Colonel John Wilson's to about two
ndred people. I spoke on Heb. xii, 1–4.

Tuesday, 15. I rode thirty miles to Mr. Martin's, the roads and creeks
: rendered bad for travelling by the late freshets.

Wednesday, 16. I preached at Dowby's store to about three hundred
ople, some gay ones. I spoke on 1 John ii, 13–17, the people were at-
tive: Edward Bailey thundered away on "Is there not a cause?" I
ve been very unwell, and travelling down Dan River and among the
eks, am in danger of the fever and ague. We were obliged to swim the
rses over Birche's Creek,[93] and bring the carriage over the shattered
dge.

Thursday, 17. I stopped at friend Baker's, being very unwell. Brother
iley went to a chapel ten miles from this. I want to write, and to recover
ength, or I shall run myself down. I am kept in peace, humility and
tchfulness. I have been unwell for this week past; this has made it an
ditional burden to travel, and the sun is so violent, that it appears to
: I could not stand it, were it not for the top-carriage. I thought it would
well for me to have a person with me always, and I think Cromwell is
: man. If I should preach a systematical, dry sermon, he would pay the
ners off. I was kept in peace, my body some little recruited. I rested

² Watson lived at Chatham, Virginia, in Pittsylvania County.
³ Birche's Creek in Halifax County unites with other creeks and flows into Dan
ver.

comfortable, retired often to prayer, that God would go with me to t
next circuit. I suppose, upon a calculation, I have ridden better than
thousand miles since February last, when I was at quarterly meeting at t
seaside in Delaware.

Friday, 18. Felt unwell, something like an ague; this being an unhealt
spot amongst the rivers. I rode twelve miles to Boyd's church;[94] about si:
people; they had but little notice. I asked the people if they chose to ha
the service read; they did, and I read as far as the first lesson, not havi
time to read all: then spoke on 2 Chron. vii, 14, in great plainness; t
people did not feel. I prevailed on our preachers to use that church onc
fortnight.

Saturday, 19. I am unwell in body, but my mind is happy: this is
comfortable house to be at, (Mr. Griffin's,)[95] I shall have half a day's re
I preached on Acts xiii, 16, about eighty people, very wild and unfeelin
I rode to brother Parish's, ten miles, crossed Shoko Creek[96] at the Fi
trap, a very bad ford, occasioned by the late freshet that rose near fo
feet.

Sunday, 20. I could not read, write, think, or converse much.
twelve o'clock I preached to about five hundred souls; an unawaken
people, but the Lord assisted me greatly, from Luke iii, 23–25. So:
solemnity and quickening: brother Bailey exhorted. I cannot get clear
a cold, and a slow fever. I praise God for cooler weather, it is what I ha
prayed for, and God has sent it: for the heat is one cause of my bei
unwell.

Monday, 21. We rode to Carter's,[97] five miles: I was unwell, and Edwa
Bailey preached on "We preach not ourselves." We rode on, and cross
Dan and Stanton rivers at Sir Peyton's ferry; there is a short canal t
from one river to the other.[98] I rode through the woods to our frie
Crowder's, about ten miles from Carter's; came in about sunset.

Tuesday, 22. I am some little better in health; my spirit is refreshed
kind entertainment and a loving family, old Methodists of a right spi:
I hear the work revives in this circuit; bless the Lord! I shall have bet
entertainment, and better roads; but above all, better people: I thankfu
acknowledge the goodness of God in all my travels. May He, who alo
is able to keep my soul and body, be ever with me! I preached at D
Crowder's[99] to about three hundred people, on Titus iii, 2. Had libe:

[94] Boyd's Church in Halifax County seems to have been an Established Chur
(See *Heads of Families, Virginia*, 22–24, for the names of the people.)

[95] Mr. Griffin lived in Halifax County, Virginia. (See Virginia map, 1820.)

[96] Shoko Creek is in Pittsylvania County.

[97] Asbury returned to Halifax County to Carter's. (See Virginia map, 1820, for road

[98] Sir Peyton's ferry was near Clarksville. The old canal is now covered by the wat
of the Bugs Island Lake.

[99] Dr. Crowder's was in Mecklenburg County. Asbury went through the tip end
Mecklenburg going to Charlotte.

d life, though unwell. After preaching set out on the way, about
rteen miles, came in about eight o'clock: the people seemed not greatly
ased to see us. I slept some little, rose early for the quarterly meeting
Colonel Bedford's;[100] rode about ten miles to breakfast; met Henry
illis and Moses Parks,[101] rather stiff for ordinances. I spoke on Habak-
k iii, 2; spoke freely to them. I was a little grieved. Brother Parks preached
ermon on the "Grace of our Lord Jesus Christ," &c. He was much out
his harness; I thought they were but children, and that I ought to bear
th, and take care of them. I retired into the barn, prayed, and felt the
rd near. Next day, at nine o'clock, love feast: we had much prayer,
me singing and speaking; at last brother Parks prayed, and some of the
nest-hearted people broke out into a shout. At twelve o'clock I preached
der an arbour near the church, to about three hundred people, on
hn iii, 17, 18; was assisted at first, but was not close or clear in the
plication. Thomas Morris gave a good exhortation; Edward Bailey
oke very fervently. God blessed him; his greatest gift is exhortation. So
ended in peace. This day there came an account that the southern army
s defeated, and all taken to a man, except Gen. Gates, which cannot be
true. I am kept in resignation and faith, and praying that God may
ss my labours, and bring peace and union among the Methodists in
rginia. I received comforting letters from Mr. White and Mr. Gough:
these comfort me in the house of my pilgrimage. Mr. White informs me
Thomas Haskins, a young man that was convinced, who has a good
ucation, has been reading the law three years; now he must read and
each the gospel.

Friday, 25. I rode to Page Mann's, sixteen miles, was much assisted in
eaking on Heb. iv, 11–13, to about three hundred people, who appeared
rious and somewhat moved.

Saturday, 26. Rode to Robinson's, a smith, who braced up my carriage;
rode on to Little Falling River, and then to the New Store, where was
company stationed. The captain wanted our certificates; Bailey disputed
th him—I showed him mine. We rode on to Great Falling River:[102]
stopped at one Vincent Glass's; the man was kind, our entertainment
ain; I did not sleep well. We talked with our host, he had catched some
tions from the Baptists and Presbyterians; though he was going another
ay, he changed his purpose and came with us; we rode twelve miles,
er hills and creeks, and through woods. About eleven o'clock I spoke
Isaiah xxxv, 6, 7, to about five hundred people, wild enough: this is a

[100] Colonel Bedford's was in Charlotte County. (See *Journal* entry under February
–17, 1782.)

[101] Henry Willis and Moses Parks were the preachers on the Mecklenburg Circuit.
ee *Minutes*, 1780.)

[102] These rivers are in Campbell County, so it would seem that Asbury went to that
unty; however, he shortly returned to Charlotte County. (See Virginia map, 1820.)

running life. The devil roars, and men threaten; but God is with us.
laboured to come at the consciences of the people, but could not. I ke
my health to a wonder; but I want time for retirement; we had ne
thirty miles from Page Mann's to Staples's. I can hardly get time and pla
to note down anything. I spent some time at the quarterly meeting in t
barn, alone. O, how good did that feel!

Monday, 28. Rode sixteen miles to Fore's,[103] about one hundred peopl
some serious souls. Spoke to the society—about thirty members.

Tuesday, 29. Rode to friend Martin's;[104] came in about ten o'cloc
preached from 2 Corinthians iv, 1–4, to about five hundred hearers, son
Baptists, some Methodists, some old Churchmen, some independe
people, who have joined with one Mr. Roberts to be Independent Presb
terians. I see very little religion among the people in these parts; son
professors came to see what was going on.

Wednesday, 30. Rode thirty miles to Billups's barn;[105] about or
hundred and thirty people, rich and unfeeling: I could not get in till tw
o'clock, spoke freely from Heb. x, 12–16. I lodged at Col. Billups's.

Thursday, 31. Rode to Tucker's, spoke on 1 Peter iv, 18, had gre
light; met brother Parks, found him more teachable: we have hot weathe

Friday, September 1, 1780. A day of fasting. I was kindly entertaine
by the people, who refitted our clothing. Rode to Brown's, eightee
miles, came in about ten o'clock; spoke on 1 Peter v, 6–10, with some fre
dom, though very unwell by fasting and riding.

Saturday, 2. Rode fourteen miles to my old friend Johnson's, spoke fro
1 Peter iii, 17, 18, to about one hundred people; felt life; some of th
people were moved; then met society; some of them felt and spoke of th
goodness of God, and were put in mind of old times, and old preachin
Brother Johnson is a solid, true Methodist; he laments the falling awa
that I told him of. I am a true prophet of evil tidings, as it suits my cast
mind.

Sunday, 3. This day nine years past I sailed from Bristol, Old Englanc
Ah! what troubles have I passed through![106] What sickness! Wha
temptations! But I think, though I am grown more aged, I have a bette
constitution, and more gifts; and I think much more grace. I can bear di
appointments and contradiction with greater ease. Trials are before m
very great ones, but God hath helped me hitherto. I can with greate
confidence trust him! and, indeed, what have any of us to trust in fc
futurity, except the living God?

Monday, September 4, 1780. This being a day of rest, affords me a
opportunity of reading and writing. I enjoy a serene mind.

[103] Fore's was in Charlotte County.
[104] Martin's was in Charlotte County. (*Heads of Families*, 14.)
[105] Billups lived in Amelia County. (*Ibid.*, 12.)
[106] See Asbury's letter to John Wesley dated September 3, 1780.

Tuesday, 5. I rode to Easlin's preaching house;[107] where I spoke to
•out one hundred people. Some few warm hearts, I thought, among
any more cold. I spoke on Heb. xiii, 6; and had much liberty. At night
et the people at B. Clark's, and exhorted them closely to relative duties.
poor sinner who was drunk had prepared a bottle of spirits for the
sturbance of the congregation; his horse threw him, and the fall had
arly killed him. I had had a foreboding of mischief.

Wednesday, 6. At Morgan's, to about one hundred people, I spoke in
eat plainness of speech on 2 Cor. iv, 2, 3; preaching has not been ac-
mpanied with success here; the audience were, however, generally
tentive. I met with F. H., he is gone from the Methodists. I dealt very
ainly with him; he was, in his way, very affectionate to me; but what is
at to me?

Thursday, 7. At Malone's[108] spoke to about one hundred souls, on Matt.
iv, 12, 13. We had a love feast, some speaking. After meeting we had
me friendly contention with Andrew Yeargan and Watters[109] about the
dinances: so far as this was a loss of precious time, so far Satan pre-
iled, and I am sorry.

Friday, 8. My mind is calm; I have had close communion with God. My
•urs of retirement have been kept. When I can get a barn or a preaching
•use I am happy. Though I have talked much, I have kept my temper. I
el nothing but love; and no contradiction I meet with makes me angry.
ave a natural affection for my own countrymen; yet I can hear them
lled cruel people, and calmly listen to threatenings of slaughter against
em. Were a people spreading desolation with fire and sword in England,
as an inhabitant, whether the invaders were right or wrong, would
obably feel as the Americans now do, and use the same harsh expres-
ons: thus I reason, and cannot therefore condemn—but the grace of God
sufficient to set us all above the world, and all things here.

Saturday, 9. Rode to Edward Pegram's; about seventy people there. I
is under great dejection; and spoke with very little life on Heb. xiii, 6.

Sunday, 10. At Boisseau's chapel I spoke to about four hundred people
the parable of the sower; and although my fever came on before I
gan, I was greatly assisted. I spoke long, and was ready to weep over
em. After the meeting I rode seventeen miles, and came to Capt. Smith's.
ave travelled since *Friday* morning about sixty miles. I went to bed, and
d a strong fever on me all night, it was an intermittent. *Monday*, very
•ak, but happy! Received letters from Jesse Hollingsworth, from White,
d from Pedicord.

There is a great work of God in Delaware; but a drought, and very

07 This was probably Easter's meeting house. There is no record of Easlin, but fre-
ent reference is made to Easter's in Mecklenburg County.
08 Isham Malone lived in Mecklenburg County. (*Heads of Families*, 33.)
09 Lednum, *op. cit.*, 280, 283.

awful distresses in the land; I mourn with them, and I rejoice with them

Monday, 11. Though unwell, I spoke on Heb. iii, 12–14. I first stood u
and prayed, but was obliged, through illness, to commit my labours t
Edward Bailey, who spoke afterward: resuming my station, I preache
with liberty.

Tuesday, 12. I visited my friends. These kind people have made me
dress of Virginia cloth, which I much needed, as my dress approache
to raggedness. I saw L. Cole, a serious, good man, under a strong bias t
ordinances, because he opened his book on, "They shall not profit m
people:" with this he was affected. I saw brother Dromgoole, broth
M——s,[110] all loving, and showed me more respect than is due to me.

Wednesday, 13. A little better in health. Have read the first volume
Keysler's Travels through Switzerland. I am much unfitted for busine
by this tertian. Prayer, both in public and in private, has not been neglecte

Thursday, 14. Rode to Mr. Jarratt's, and was kindly received. I am ver
unwell.

Friday, 15. Preached with freedom at the barn, on Rom. xiii, 11.

Saturday, 16. Wrote to Mr. Wesley, at the desire of the Virginia Cor
ference; who had consented to suspend the administration of the ordi
ances for one year.* I want to be more devoted. I had liberty in speakin
God was with us. I am but feeble in body, and not so fervent in spirit a
I desire to be.

Sunday, 17. I had some close talk with Mr. Jarratt: he seems willing t
help what he can, and to come to the conference. My health is muc
restored. Rode to White's chapel—a miserable place it is; unfinished, an
one part lying open to the sun. A company of young men diverted them
selves under the trees, laughing and mocking while I discoursed wit
great plainness to about five hundred people on Heb. iv, 2, 3. I was dete
mined, if possible, they should hear. Rode on about twelve miles to Lew
Featherstone's,[111] a good man.

---

[110] Morris, Moore, Major, or Monroe. (Lednum, *op. cit.*, 280.)

[111] Lewis Featherstone apparently lived in Dinwiddie or Amelia County. There we
many Featherstones in Amelia County, but Lewis is not listed in *Heads of Famili*
in that county. However, Nelson Reed in his *Journal* refers to Lewis Featherstone
being in Amelia. White's Chapel was in Amelia.

* The answer to this letter was made through Dr. Coke, Richard Whatcoat, ar
Thomas Vasey, in 1784, who all came to America properly ordained. And here I w
take occasion to correct a mistake into which Dr. Whitehead has fallen in his Life
Mr. Wesley. It is in that work stated, that had Mr. Wesley obtained the consent of tl
American preachers and people, he might have sent ministers regularly ordained,
the society in that part of the world: the truth is, that the American Methodists, bo
ministers and people, wished to have such ministers among them, that they mig
partake, like other Christian societies, of the ordinances of the Church of God; ar
when ministers did thus come they received them generally and joyfully. I will furth
presume, that Mr. Wesley received few letters from America in which that subject wa
not pressed upon him. (This note is in the original *Journal*.)

Monday, 18. Peace! I preached on Psalm i, with some liberty, to a few
ithful souls.

Tuesday, 19. Rode to Green's, sixteen miles. What with opposers, the
ad times, and a worse devil, there has been a great falling away here. I
ooke on Gal. v, 16, 17, and was close and home, enforcing the power of
ligion to my hearers, among whom were some people warm for the *new
ay*.

Wednesday, 20. I came to Richard Walters's—sixteen miles. Spoke on
oloss. i, 26–28. Had light, and spoke long. Brother Bailey also spoke.
rother James Foster, a feeling, good soul, worn out in the Lord's work,
et me here; I felt much love and tenderness for him: he concluded by
rayer. My manner is, to pray in the morning for the prosperity of the
ork in every circuit: in the afternoon for all the travelling preachers, for
ur union, and the spirituality of each. I am greatly blessed in my soul by
ay and by night.

Thursday, 21. Travelled over rough roads sixteen miles, to Foster's.[112]
spoke on 2 Peter iii, 16, 17. I preached with some life. The people are
ind, and appear loving; but there is a great falling away; the devil has
ot been idle, and opposers have preached to them water, more than
oliness; and have thus brought confusion among the Methodists.

Friday, 22. I am weak, and not able to fast altogether, I eat sparingly.
ode twenty-seven miles, and came to a good house; yesterday it was
ery warm for the season. I feel the weight of the work, the greatness of
y charge, and resolve to be more given up to God than ever. From
rother Foster's conversation, I am led to hope our breaches will be
ealed.

Saturday, 23. I preached at Hayes's, to about five hundred people.
hey were gay and careless; I spoke with fervency, but they were unmoved.
Ve rode on to John Finney's, a serious man and a preacher.

Sunday, 24. I spoke long and in much plainness on the latter part of the
ighth chapter of Mark, to about seven hundred people; some of the gay
ort among them, and hope there was good done. I have enjoyed great
ellowship with brother Foster; he was once for the *new*, he is now for the
ood old way.

Monday, 25. Rode to Stoney Hill preaching house; spoke to about
fty serious, feeling people. Trials and blessings accompany me. After
inner retired to Benjamin Tucker's. I was much blessed in private, while
leading for wisdom to go before the people, and for a spirit of supplica-
on in my accustomed morning and evening prayers for all the preachers
nd circuits in America. I begin at the north and go to the south in order.
le that faithfully cares for others, others will care for him: above all, the
ord, who is not unrighteous to forget the work of faith and labour of
ove we show towards the saints, He will care for him.

[112] Foster lived in Amelia County. (*Heads of Families*, 12–13.)

Wednesday, 27. Rode to George Pegram's; preached to about eighteer great and small, on 2 Peter iii, 17, 18. I rode on to Mr. Yearbury's; l lives well; is kind and decent in behaviour: delivered a family lectur Rode ten miles to Petersburg. A heavy rain induced us to put off preachir until two o'clock: spoke on Rev. iii, 10; was led out—upon the who blessed; there were some old friends from the country present.

Thursday, 28. Rode twelve miles to Mr. Patrick's.[113] Some soldiers an officers came to hear the word. Rode on twelve miles to Baker's, and wa kindly received. Brother Davis went with me. I spoke on 1 John i, 8, { had some liberty. I sometimes feel gloomy: trying circumstances prevei me from making an exertion; yet if I would try to force myself on suc occasions it might be well.

Friday, 29. I have a sense of God upon my heart; although little res and much tempted. I was greatly led out in preaching at Baker's; bot parents and children wept in silent tears, while I spoke on Gen. xviii, 1 Rode that evening to the Manakintown, where a watch-night was held l brothers Finney, Bailey, and Foster. I spoke to our brethren upon a firr and lasting union; it was opposed, and with tears; tears and feelings wi not induce me to give up my charge. It began to be a doubt with me whethe I should leave Virginia until conference. I sent certain proposals by brothe Finney to the preachers at their quarterly meetings.

Sunday, October 1. I preached at the Manakintown to about fiv hundred people; I was led out and spoke plainly.

Monday, 2. Rode to Maxey's, twelve miles. Preached from Luke xii 23–25, and had some liberty.

Tuesday, 3. Rode twenty miles, crossed James River, and lodged a Tucker Woodson's. I spoke and prayed with an old Presbyterian, who once pleased with our preachers.

Wednesday, 4. We had not ridden far before it began to rain agair Edward Bailey was so unwell I feared for him, and stopped at a taverr it was Duke's, in Goochland, about twelve miles from our last stage. Her my companion was confined to his bed. I dried our clothes, and talke with the woman of the house, who had been under conviction by hearir our preachers in Carolina, but now unhappily in a way of life unfriendl to religion: we brought them to prayer,—forced prayer.

Thursday, 5. Set off without any breakfast. Passed onward to Lindsey tavern, inquiring the way to the Broken Back Church; we could not ge any positive directions until we came within eight miles of it, and foun it to be on this side of the fork of James River, about twenty miles distar from Duke's. We met about sixty people, after riding nearly as man miles. I spoke on Gen. xviii, 19; very little moving. O, how different wa it from the effect produced on Tuesday last, when discoursing on the sam

---

[113] This was Father Patrick, the old Methodist, in Chesterfield County. Asbur traveled from Amelia into Dinwiddie County to Petersburg.

xt! We crossed the North River in a canoe, and the carriage was brought
ver in the same way: were kindly received at Roger Thomson's;[114] and
ere it was the Broken Back Conference[115] was held, in which the subject
f the ordinances was brought into consideration. I have been much tried
i this journey by the lodging, people, and weather. O that I could bear all
iings! My companion is sick and much dispirited, and I myself am very
nwell. I expect some of this circuit is very inaccessible. O why should I
ike all this labour in vain, if it be yet in vain? my work and my reward
re with the Lord. Every morning and evening I pray for all the preachers
nd circuits; and as I am so led out to pray for them, I hope they will all
e united once more as they have been.

Friday, 6. We went forwards; the Fork Church seven miles distant.[116]

[114] Roger Thomson was the father-in-law of Philip Gatch, the second native American
Methodist itinerant. He was a native of Maryland.

[115] In 1779 there was the first split over the ordinances. The Virginia preachers no
onger professed adherence to the Established Church and took steps to become
idependent. It had been the rule (conference, 1773) that "all the people among whom
e labor [are] to be earnestly exhorted to attend the church and receive the ordinances
icre." At the conference held in 1777 in Harford County, Maryland, and in 1778 at
eesburg, Virginia, the question was asked, "What shall be done with respect to the
rdinances?" The answer was "Let the preachers and people pursue the old plan as
om the beginning." The crisis came at the Broken Back Church. The question was
sked, "Ques.: What are our reasons for taking up the administration of the ordinances
mong us? Ans.: Because our Episcopal Establishment is now dissolved, and, therefore,
. almost all our circuits the members are without the ordinances." Eighteen preachers
pproved. They were Isham Tatum, Charles Hopkins, Nelson Reed, Reuben Ellis,
hilip Gatch, Thomas Morris, James Morris, James Foster, John Major, Andrew
eargin, Henry Willis, Francis Poythress, John Sigman, Leroy Cole, Carter Cole,
imes O'Kelly, William Monroe (or Moore, Lednum, *op. cit.*, 280), Samuel Roe. Other
iestions were: "What form of ordination shall be observed to authorize any preacher
» administer? Ans. By that of a presbytery. Ques. Who are the presbytery? Ans. Philip
atch, Reuben Ellis, James Foster and in case of necessity, Leroy Cole. What power is
ested in the presbytery by this choice? First to administer the ordinances themselves;
cond, to authorize any other preacher or preachers, approved by them, by the form
f laying on of hands." Asbury disapproved and assembled the northern preachers at
altimore. They also asked questions: "Ques. 20: Does this whole Conference dis-
pprove the steps our brethren have taken in Virginia? Ans. Yes. Ques. 21: Do we
ok upon them no longer as Methodists in connection with Mr. Wesley and us until
iey come back? Ans. Yes. Ques. 22: Shall Brother Asbury, Garrettson and Watters
ttend the Virginia Conference and inform them of our proceedings in this and receive
ieir answer? Ans. Yes." In May, 1780, Asbury, Garrettson, and Watters went to
lanakintown in Powhatan County, Virginia, to the conference. There was no bitter-
ess but brotherly love and prayer. The committee from the north was about to leave
. failure and Asbury was praying alone in his room. Watters and Garrettson were also
raying when the conference suddenly decided to accept Asbury's proposition that the
rdinances be suspended for one year. They also agreed to submit the matter to Wesley
id to meet the next year in General Conference to settle the matter. Actually the
atter was not settled until the Christmas Conference in 1784 when elders were or-
ained, two for Nova Scotia and ten for the United States. (Bennett, *op. cit.*, ch. iv.)

[116] There were two Fork churches, this one in Fluvanna County and an old Estab-
shed Church in the western part of Hanover County. The Hanover church derived its

Brother Bailey was taken sick upon the road: I left him about two mile below the church, went on and preached on Rom. viii. Returning t brother Bailey, I found him very ill with a fever: he rode twelve miles i the carriage to brother Hopkins's, in Amherst. Riding on horsebac fatigued me.

Saturday, 7. Rode to Martin's; I spoke on Joshua's resolution, wit some pleasure, to about eighty people. Continued on seven miles int the mountains, to Mr. Haines's—the ways bad enough. Brother Baile travelling so far without eating anything, came in very sick.

Sunday, 8. Rode thirteen miles to the Sugar Loaf Mountains. Edwar Bailey, after riding a few miles, was taken with a second fit, and very il I left him in the carriage and proceeded on. About five hundred peopl had assembled, to whom I spoke on 2 Cor. iv, 2–4. Returning after preach ing to brother Bailey, I found him with all the symptoms of a sever bilious attack, and like a dead man in appearance; he passed the night i great distress—prayer was made for him; through mercy his fit went of I took brother Bailey to help me; his affliction has given me much troubl Greatly distressed for him as I have been, I am much consoled in bein able to leave him with Doctor Hopkins, who is a kind, skilful, sensibl man.

Monday, 9. Set out alone for Maupin's. After riding about twenty-fiv miles night overtook me at Wallace's mill; it was some time before I coul find my way, which I discovered to be under the trunk head race of th mill; here the top of the carriage being too high, set fast: I took the hors out, and with much trouble came clear without breakage of any kind. Th people of the house were Presbyterians; they gave me lodging. I praye night and morning with them.

Tuesday, 10. Rode over the mountains ten miles, came to the ne preaching house; spoke on 2 Cor. v, 17–19; was much blessed. Here I sa Robert Wagden, a soldier, and James Signal, Englishmen, captured wit Burgoyne. The first I saw in New York seven years ago; since then he fel and was restored at the barracks in Albemarle when a prisoner. I spe the night with them comfortably. Two soldiers in the neighbourhood hav occasioned scandal among the Baptists. Soldiers, I think, should be i society with one another, and exhort and preach among themselves.

Wednesday, 11. I rode to Fretwell's, twenty miles: was troubled i getting the carriage into the flat at the river-side. I spoke to about fort people on Acts xiii, 26. I rode to Mr. Grymes's, a comfortable house: arriving about eight o'clock, I was blessed and consoled for all my toil

Thursday, 12. I have peace and love, although unwell: I intend to spen

name from the location between two rivers, the North Anna and South Anna; ar many Methodists preached and worshiped there.

[117] Fretwell lived in Albemarle County, and Grymes's was in Orange Count (*Heads of Families*, 80, 98.)

is day in retirement. I preached at Mr. Grymes's at twelve o'clock to
out thirty people, white and black, on 2 Peter iii, 17, 18. I had great
berty and clear ideas. Though employed thus, I have had a little time for
tirement and writing. I am happy; but I see the great need of doing,
ing, and suffering, what I preach to others. I have travelled so much
at it seems like confinement to rest one day; I hope I shall travel as long
s I live; travelling is my health, life, and all, for soul and body. I am not
ell, but I am kept upright in heart; and am much concerned for a union
ith the preachers. I am alternately in hope and despair about it.

Friday, 13. Rode to Bohannon's, passing the Rapid Dan River. About
vo o'clock I arrived, after some difficulties, and found Henry Fry preach-
g to about eighty people.[118] I spoke after him on Luke xiii, 23–25: was
rvent; but the people thought I must speak like thunder to be a great
reacher. I shall not throw myself into an unnatural heat or overstrained
xertions. I rode home about ten miles with brother Fry; he is a serious
an. My carriage broke, and his overseer mended it very well; meantime
rested, and read at times the Valley of Lilies of à Kempis; it is much in
e style of his Pattern or Imitation. I wonder Mr. Wesley has never
bridged this work.

Sunday, 15. I rode to Roberts's, under the mountains, about ten miles.
poke to about five hundred people; I was zealous, but the people languid.
certain kind of preaching, of which these people have lately heard much,
aves the most stupid souls, to my mind, that I find anywhere. I have been
uch tempted; but I am stirred up to pray much; so I make a necessity
f a calamity: I remember all the preachers and societies twice a day. We
ad to ride back to Henry Fry's in the rain.

Monday, 16. I have peace. Rose at five o'clock, spent nearly an hour in
tirement; had all the circuits and preachers on my mind; I was led to
lead with God for a union: I have peace with, and love to all mankind.
rode twenty miles yesterday. Brother M'Clure[119] came in from the north,
n his way to see his parents in the west. I preached at Henry Fry's on
al. v, 16–18, had life in speaking. Spent some time with the family.

Tuesday, 17. Rode ten miles, preached at Stockdale's to about thirty
eople. Rode on fifteen miles; put in at Ragland's; a Baptist spoke to the
mily. Next morning rode eighteen miles to the Broken Back church;[120]
ot in a little after twelve o'clock. Preached on Zeph. i, 12. Here I received
e melancholy tidings of the death of my companion and friend, Edward
ailey: it was very distressing to me; riding together so long had created

[118] When Asbury crossed the Rapid Dan River, he entered Culpepper County. In
792 that part of Culpepper became Madison County, which accounts for Asbury's
ter reference to Fry's as being in Madison County.

[119] Thomas McClure is listed among the preachers in the *Minutes* of 1780, though his
ame is not included in the appointments.

[120] Stockdale's was probably in Orange County, and the Broken Back Church was
Fluvanna County.

a great sympathy between us. He died on Tuesday last, about five o'cloc
in full confidence; he spoke to the last, and bore a testimony to the goo
ness of God. He would sometimes get upon his knees in the bed, weak
he was, and pray. It troubles me to reflect that he was neglected so lon
yet it was unavoidable. The doctor supposed a mortification took place
his bowels, inflamed by the corrosive nature of the bile. It was a sorrowf
quarterly meeting to me: few people; they lifeless, and my dear frier
dead! I spoke to the preachers about a union.

Thursday, 19. I preached on John iii, 16, 17, to a very unfeeling peopl
friends parted in much love. On *Friday* I rode sixteen miles to Jol
Lasley's;[121] lectured on 2 Pet. i, 4–9, to some inanimate souls.

Saturday, 21. I set out as soon as it was light, and came about thr
o'clock to the widow Granger's, and Ground Squirrel Bridge; a distan
of forty miles. I travel very heavily now. I have lost my poor Bailey; s
suddenly called away! Lord, humble me, and make me more watchfu
He desired me to see into his temporal matters, for his poor sister, ar
wife, and children. I have reason to praise God that I have health und
such fatigue. I said I should have trouble, before I went into Fluvann
yet I little thought my friend would die there. If my affections were natu
ally tender, I should be bathed in tears, for I have great cause to weep
but the Lord hath ordered it: it may be that I suffer more than those wl
weep away distress. I was ready to say, "None shall ride with me hereafter
Satan works upon my gloomy mind greatly. I was comforted in meetir
John Beck and Caleb Boyer, Philip Bruce, Thomas Crenshaw;[122] a solen
meeting. We have lost three useful preachers within one year. The Lor
cuts Israel short.

Sunday, 22. I spoke long and freely on the parable of the sower to for
hundred people; but it appears as if sinners were Gospel-proof.

Monday, 23. I rode twelve miles to Friend Ellis's; spoke to about six
people, on 2 Cor. iv, 16–18. John Tunnell spoke after me. I wrote to tl
preachers jointly and severally about a union.

Tuesday, 24. Rode to Mr. Meredith's, thirty-five miles. We were er
tangled in the way; came in late, leaving the carriage in the woods. I w
unwell by long fasting, although among very kind people. We heard
rumour of the British landing up James River: I was afraid they wou
interrupt me in the circuit appointments.

Wednesday, 25. I am unwell, but happy in God; that is, I feel a solen
determination to labour more for God, because others desert the work.

---

[121] John Lasley lived in Louisa County, where was located Lasley's Meeting Hous
[122] (See note under May 8, 1780.) Bennett indicates that Crenshaw's and Grange
were the same place. Nelson Reed in his *Journal* says he was at Mrs. Crenshaw's c
this date, but mentions no other preacher than Asbury. John Kobler's *Journal* mak
frequent reference to visiting the widow Crenshaw. (See Kobler's *Journal*, Method
Historical Society, Baltimore Conference, Lovely Lane Museum.)

ached with great liberty at Tally's; there were some young preachers
sent; they shook whilst I showed the call to the ministry; how they
ght to evidence it, by having the same end in view our Lord had; "to
ach the Gospel to the poor; to bind up the broken-hearted, and to set
liberty them that are bound;" to imitate the prophetic and priestly
ce of Christ,—thus to set up Christ among the people, or to conclude
y had not the call. I met the society; some spoke, and the Lord blessed
At night the alarm was made for the seventh division of the militia.
e rumour was, that there were five thousand of the British troops;
t they had torn two counties to pieces, and had been within six miles
Williamsburg. As my appointments lay down that way, I put off to the
th across the river.

Thursday, 26. I set off; rode across Hanover to the court house, crossed
nunkey, a little below, and proceeded on to Collins's, thirty-seven
es.

Friday, 27. Rode on to Fredericksburg: my horse failed through fatigue,
t feed, and not enough of it. I stopped and fed by the way; mistaking
road, I met a serious man, and spoke to him about his soul; it may be,
losing my way was ordered by Providence. Came to Garratt's, at
fford court house: fell in with a Presbyterian, an acquaintance of Mr.
more; I spoke freely to him, and had prayer; two young men from
nchester joined us. Saturday morning, after paying eight continental
lars for my horse, and my supper and bed, I rode on to Dumfries, about
lve miles. Rode on four miles farther, fed my horse, and got a cup of
led milk for myself: here my paper-money failed, and I was obliged to
in silver. Rode on, carrying my corn, and fed upon the road. Missing
way to William Adams's, when on the south side of Colchester, I went
vn the state road within two miles of Alexandria, making my journey
r fifty miles; my horse was much fatigued, and myself in a fever with
d riding: I was blessed in the family I put up with. O, how sweet is
! But O, for eternal rest!

Sunday, 29. I am happy in the review of my labours; in the reflection
t my heart is in the work of God; and that it is not in vain. I rejoice in
prospect of returning home to Delaware.

Maryland

Monday, 30. Crossed Georgetown ferry; stopped at Baggerly's.[123] Rode
in great peace, and came to John Worthington's about five o'clock,

Henry Baggerly (1748–1831) was born on the western shore of Maryland and was
ng the first Methodist converts. He attended the first conference in Maryland. (See
of Henry Baggerly in Maryland, a manuscript fragment of an apparent auto-
raphy in the library of the Baltimore Conference Historical Society, Lovely Lane
ch, Baltimore, Maryland; memoir in *Advocate and Journal*, April 15, 1831, 132.)

after a ride of thirty miles. I was kindly entertained. I called at Mr. Thon
Dorsey's;[124] kind people. I breakfasted with them. I put forward to Ba
more: when within about two miles there came up an autumnal stor
there was fear of the trees falling, and that the wind would overset
carriage. I came in safe, stopped an hour, and proceeded on to N
Gough's, and arrived between eight and nine o'clock. There has been so
snow to-day, and the night is cold. I have spent my stock of money, th
guineas and two half johannas, given me by Mr. Gough and M
Chamier;[125] two guineas and a half, and a half-crown went in Virgir
Rode on about twelve miles to dinner, eight miles afterward to Sw
Creek, being kept in peace. Here I met that man of God and prisoner
Christ, Charles Scott; he is like a flame of fire; he has good sense, gc
utterance, and professes the sanctifying grace of God: a useful ma
dealing faithfully with the societies. I gave him some Virginia cloth to ma
him a suit of clothes. O, how sweetly were we united to each other!*

Thursday, November 2. I set out for Susquehanna ferry. I passed over
a calm, and gained Robert Thompson's about three o'clock. The old n
is stirred up.

Delaware

Friday, 3. Set off for my favourite Dover. (I believe Little Pipe Cr
now, 1813.) Mr. T. and B. are the offspring of very pious parents. I h
God has touched their hearts. I stopped awhile at Dr. Abraham Ridgel
to deliver a message to him from Colonel Thomas Dorsey of Elk Rid
in Maryland. While tarrying after dinner, Dr. Magaw came in. I w
home with the Doctor, and was kindly received. The Doctor's intenti
were not to go to the quarterly meeting; but having this opportunity, I w
and took him along. It was one o'clock before we arrived; about th
hundred people had been waiting for us. Mr. Magaw preached an excell

[124] Colonel Thomas Dorsey's mansion, "Troy Hill," is near the junction of Do
Road and Washington Boulevard. Colonel Dorsey commanded the Elk Ridge Batta
during the Revolutionary War. His second wife, Elizabeth Ridgely, was the daug
of Nicholas Ridgely of Dover, Delaware, and the niece of Dr. Abraham Ridgely. Y
after the death of the colonel, Asbury conducted services in the Dorsey home.

[125] Mrs. Achsah Chamier, the eldest sister of Captain Charles Ridgely, builde
Hampton. She married first Dr. Robert Holliday, whose estate lay south of Hamp
Her second husband was John Carnan; and their daughter, Prudence, married H
Dorsey Gough. Mrs. Carnan's third husband was Daniel Chamier (1720–78), merc
and high sheriff of Baltimore County. He was a Tory and went to New York C
where he died. Mrs. Chamier died in 1785 at Perry Hall, the home of her daug
Asbury conducted her funeral service. (*Maryland Historical Magazine*, XLV, 3
Journal entries for August 7–21, 1785.)

* He died an apostate—was in the habit of speaking maliciously of his for
friends; he became horribly wicked. (This note is in the original *Journal*.)

rmon on "Who shall ascend the hill of the Lord?" Brothers Hartley
d Glendenning exhorted. We all stayed at Mr. Barratt's; Mr. Magaw
ayed with much affection: we parted in great love.

Sunday, 5. We had between one and two thousand people; our house
rty-two by forty-eight,[126] was crowded above and below, and numbers
ll remained outside: our love feast lasted about two hours; some spoke
the sanctifying grace of God. I preached on John iii, 16–18; a heavy
use to preach in: brothers Pedicord and Cromwell exhorted.

Monday, 6. I preached to about four hundred people on 2 Chron. viii,
, and had liberty: I spoke of the necessity of getting and keeping the
wer of religion; William Glendenning exhorted afterward; then we
rted. I see the footsteps of Providence in my coming back. The people
gretted my absence, and the preachers would have been at variance one
th another. William Glendenning plead hard to come to Dover; but I
d not think him so fit as Thomas Chew. Brother Glendenning is a good
tle man, and though his utterance is less strongly marked with the Scotch
an formerly, it is not yet good. The British had almost thrown them-
ves in my way on my return through Virginia; I wished not to fall into
eir hands: they left it soon after I came away. Here there has been
od done in my absence; among believers we have been very solemn; and
e work of God has been deep among the brethren; not so in Virginia;
e preachers there do not know how to preach sanctification for want of
perience. I stationed the preachers thus: Thomas Chew, and the two
omwells, for Kent; for Dover, Pedicord and Law;[127] Samuel Roe[128]
d James White, for Sussex; William Glendenning, Stephen Black,
seph Wyatt, for Kent in Maryland; and Joseph Hartley and Joseph
erett, for Dorset.

Tuesday, 7. I was closely engaged in reading a volume of Mr. Wesley's
urnal of above three hundred pages; ended it on Wednesday morning.
elt dejection of spirits for want of public exercise: I have had so much
this, that within this six months, I have travelled, according to my com-
tation, two thousand six hundred and seventy-one miles; yet am uneasy
en still. I proposed meeting the children when I came again: I appointed
place for them to sit, and desired the parents to send a note with each,
ting me know the temper, and those vices to which the child might be
st subject. I long to spend a few minutes every hour in prayer. I see
eat need of living near to God—the people are so affectionate. Lord,
mble me!

26 This house was Barratt's Chapel.

27 James O. and Joseph Cromwell with Thomas Chew were appointed to Kent;
leb B. Pedicord and either Alexander or William Law were sent to Dover.

28 Samuel Roe (1756–91) was a Methodist itinerant from 1779 to 1784. (For his
eer in the Protestant Episcopal Church see Rightmyer's *The Episcopal Church in
laware*, 65, 66, 119–21.) Roe's name has been variously spelled; but it appears in its
rect form, Samuel Roe, on his tombstone in the Dover, Delaware, churchyard.

Wednesday, 8. Rode to Purden's, calling at Caleb Furby's and Dan
James's; at Purden's lectured on 1 Thess. iii, 6. Engaged the friends
subscribe seven hundred weight of pork towards the meeting house
Barratt's. I called at Laurence Combs's, and had preaching there, althou
the master of the house differs from us in some points. While we are bu
others are not entirely quiet; others, less in the habit of teaching by stat
speaking, can yet disseminate their books.

Thursday, 9. I came to my old lodgings at Thomas White's—met t
preachers. We spoke further about the work of God.

Friday, 10. This day I arranged my papers containing a brief account
the beginning and progress of our divisions: it was transcribed into a bo
by Caleb Pedicord.

Saturday, 11. I wrote to Mr. Gough, Mr. Lynch, and Mr. Skinn
To-day the quarterly meeting begins at Caroline. I am kept in faith a
love to God and all mankind. William Glendenning has handed me
book written by Jeremiah Burroughs, in the time of the commonweal
upon heart-divisions, and the evil of the times:[129] in this work I prom
myself good arguments against our separating brethren. The Lord do
greatly carry on his work; some little wild-fire; a few disorderly walke
Read a volume of Mr. Wesley's Journal.

Sunday, 12. I preached at Edward White's on 1 John iv, 14–18. I spo
on perfection strongly and clearly: some strangers attended. The wo
goes on here; but although I want rest it is no place for me to stay; the
is too much company. The quarterly meeting for Kent in Maryland w
large and powerful: there were twelve preachers present. I am kept
peace of soul; expecting my ministering brethren, that we may cons
about the work of God. Samuel Roe is going to Sussex[130]—one that h
happily escaped the separating spirit and party in Virginia, and the sna
laid for his feet;—and so also did poor William Spencer of late yea
Eternal thanks to God!

Monday, 13. I read Mr. Wesley's Journal. In the afternoon the preach
came to consult further about the stationing. They all agreed to my fi
appointment, except one brother; he was unwilling to go back to Ba
more, although we had no one so well qualified: on Monday evening a
Tuesday we met and conferred, when the judgment of the preachers p
vailed against Freeborn Garrettson. We were blest in prayer with ea
other. Our appointments were as follows: Kent in Maryland, Glend

[129] *Heart Divisions, the Evil of our Times*, by Jeremiah Burrough (1599–1646) a
The Cure of Church Divisions by *Richard Baxter* (1615–91). During the threate
division over ordinances Asbury arranged extracts from both books. They appeare
1785 as *The Causes, Evils, and Cures of Heart and Church Divisions, Extracted from
Works of Burrough and Baxter by Francis Asbury, One of the Bishops of the Metho
Episcopal Church*. The preface is a letter by Asbury. (See *Letters*.)

[130] Sussex Circuit in Delaware and Dorset Circuit on the eastern shore were form
in 1780 to provide for the expansion of the work of the Peninsula.

1g, Stephen Black, Joseph Wyatt; Kent in Delaware, Thomas Chew, seph and James Cromwell; Sussex, Samuel Roe, James Martin, James hite; Dorset, Pedicord.

Tuesday, 14. We parted in peace, united in heart and in judgment, and ounding in love. Glory be to God!

Wednesday, 15. I ended the reading of a volume of Mr. Wesley's urnal, giving an account of the rent made by Mr. Maxwell and Mr. ll. I read a part of what I had transcribed upon the art of preaching. At ;ht I met the society, and found them more and more spiritual— estioned closely—permitted some to speak: it was a solemn time. ursday morning we made our plans.

Thursday, 16. I examined Joseph Everett, as to his call and qualifica- ns, his circumstances, and his knowing and loving the Methodist ctrine: he gave full satisfaction; we, however, left the matter in suspense til Caleb Pedicord goes down, and we shall know from him what call re is in Dorset.

Friday, 17. A day of fasting. We all parted after much business. Samuel 1e went to Sussex; the two Cromwells for the circuit, (Kent, in Dela- re;) Pedicord to Dorset; myself to go through Kent and Sussex,—then the Jerseys, Philadelphia, and Chester. I wrote to Watters, Joshua 1dley, and Micaijah Debrular. *Friday*, set out for Murderkill,[131] stopping Combs's that night. I spoke freely to the man upon his mysticism, and the family about their souls.

Saturday, 18. Rode on to the chapel; Joseph Cromwell met the people :lass; I gave an exhortation, took down the names of the children, and)ke to some of them: I desired the preachers to meet the children when y came along;—an important but much-neglected duty—to the shame ministers be it spoken.

Sunday, 19. We met at the chapel; my text, Psalm lxxviii, 4–7; the)ple came in late; I was incommoded, but at last felt liberty; the serious ents were much affected: Joseph Cromwell exhorted. I met the society, l gave a close exhortation. Settled the rules of the house, and appointed vards.

Monday, 20. I went to Purdin's; spoke from 1 Samuel xii, 23–25. I had loud over me all the time I was speaking; was severely tried. I was nbled and solemn.

Tuesday, 21. Rode to young Lockwood's; spoke to about one hundred)ple from 1 Chron. xiv, 11. Was much blest. Joseph Cromwell spoke ch to purpose. I trust there will be a good work in this place. Rode to hard Shaw's. I was kept in much confidence in prayer—my soul was ch drawn out after these people. My text here from Phil. iv, 8. I had much liberty. I met the society, exhorting them, and pressing them to se communion with each other, and reminding them of their obligations

This was Murderkill Hundred, near Milford Hundred, Sussex County, Delaware.

to us; they appeared deeply sensible of it with cries and tears; brotl
Joseph Cromwell exhorted. My mind is kept very serene.

Thursday, 23. I am much given up to God. Joseph Cromwell part
from me to go into his circuit. Mr. Coleman[132] came up with me fr(
Virginia, either to take charge of Dover school, or to preach; he express
great satisfaction in the people of these parts. I went to see Mr. Lockwoc
I have been waiting some time for his coming to the Lord; he hath lo
stood it out, but I believe he is now deeply engaged, and so are almost
the adults of his family. I met a man who took occasion to abuse me
ringleader of sedition with many hard sayings:—he was in his cups
pitied, forgave, and prayed for him.

Friday, 24. I rode ten miles to Mr. Boyer's, and preached on Phil. iii,
Had liberty, and the people were affected: Mr. Coleman exhorted. I spc
to the society, addressing them with respect to the rules and their lo(
walk. Answered a very affectionate letter from John Finney, relative
the union in Virginia.

Saturday, 25. We rode to Mr. Magaw's, and had some talk with h
about his undertaking a plan for the education of youth, John Colem
being proposed as his assistant.

Sunday, 26. I rode to Shaw's, preached with liberty to about (
hundred people, from 1 Chron. xxviii, 9. In the afternoon again, at Dov
preached on Eph. iii, 11. Had some liberty, and spoke searchingly;
this people will, and they will not; they will in appearance be religious,
not in heart.

Monday, 27. I rode down to Jones's,[133] and preached from Prov
24–26. I had life, and some appearance of effect produced. In the aft
noon Mr. Magaw preached an excellent sermon on, "When Christ w
is our life shall appear, then shall we also appear with him in glory."

Tuesday, 28. I preached at Jos. Wyatt's on these words: "If any man
in Christ he is a new creature;" had not much liberty. I met the socie
many spake of the goodness of God. I went to lodge with Mr. Smith
strong Churchman. I am kept in faith.

Thursday, 30. I have peace of mind and the love of God. I preached
Liverson's, on Prov. xxviii, 13, 14; had Divine help. I found some sim;

[132] John Coleman (1758–1816) was a protégé of Devereaux Jarratt. After Colem
had withdrawn from the Methodist itinerancy (1781–85), his correspondence
published under the title *The Life of the Reverend Devereux Jarratt, Rector of I
Parish, Dinwiddie County, Virginia, written by Himself in a series of Letters addre.
to the Rev. John Coleman.* During his association with Asbury and Magaw an acade
was established at Dover, Delaware. Coleman married Pleasure Goodwin, niec(
Captain Charles Ridgely. (Ridgely: *Old Brick Churches of Maryland,* 99 ff.; Allen:
Garrison Church, 58–65; Lednum, *op. cit.,* 323.)

[133] This was a shortened form for St. Jones, near Dover, Delaware, where the Wi(
Brady and the Sipple families opened their homes for preaching. (Hallman, *op.
243; Lednum, *op. cit.,* 347.)

arted people here, but very ignorant of true religion. I met class, and
proved two disorderly walkers: I hope they will reform. I rode to Mr.
ook's,[134] who desired my company: I talked and prayed with him, and
oceeded on to the Cross Roads.[135] I here met many of my friends, among
out three hundred attentive people, to whom I spoke upon Matt. iii,
10. I hope good will be done here. I rode to Blackstown,[136] where I met
out one hundred and thirty people, and spoke on "Take heed to your-
ves:" some of them were greatly engaged. Lewis Alfrey has been made
blessing to these people; their number is increased, and they purpose
ilding a chapel.

Friday, December 1. I rode to Scotten's. Here they have been dis-
pointed in preaching, having had but two sermons this last quarter; the
nsequence was that they did not attend: they are not as steady as they
uld be. The day I rode to Richard Shaw's being damp, I caught cold.
ave suffered loss in my mind.

Saturday, 2. Rode to Fatad's, and although it snowed, there came to-
her about thirty people: preaching was a blessing to them.

Sunday, 3. Rode to the chapel:[137] the weather was so bad that not more
n thirty people attended; having a sore throat I spoke with difficulty.
ter meeting I went to Mr. Emory's.[138] *Monday,* I was bled. I rode to
njamin Blackiston's, but found myself unfit to speak. Leaving Mr.
leman I went on to Black's, fearing my throat would be worse: I was
icted. A useful letter from my trusty friend, Robert Furness,[139] came
me; I have also received one from Pedicord, giving an account of the
rk in Dorset.

Wednesday, 6. Rode twelve miles to Jarratt's, to preach the funeral of
ward Collins: for about eighteen months past he has attended our
aching; was convinced of sin, but had never joined us; in death was
st with the peace of God, departing in the faith. I spoke on these words,
Eccles. ix, 10: "Whatsoever thy hand findeth to do, do it with thy

---

[134] At this time Dr. Robert Cook lived in Greensboro, Caroline County, Maryland.
first wife was one of the three daughters of Judge Thomas White. Lednum says
t they lived a little below Smyrna, Delaware; but Asbury locates them in Dover.
dnum, *op. cit.,* 270; see *Journal* entries for May 25, 1801, and April 29, 1803.)

[135] This was the Duck Creek Cross Roads, the present Smyrna, Delaware.

[136] Blackiston's Corner or Crossroads is southwest of Clayton, Kent County, Dela-
e, and approximately three miles from the Maryland line. (Beers: *Atlas of the State*
Delaware, 5; Lednum, *op. cit.,* 317.)

[137] This was Blackiston Chapel.

[138] This probably was the home of the parents of John Emory, who later became a
op. In 1790 Spaniard's Neck Methodist Episcopal Church was erected in the
sent village of Burrsville. (Emory: *Queen Anne's County, Maryland,* 235, 447;
dnum, *op. cit.,* 328.)

[139] Robert Furness, keeper of an ordinary at New Castle, Delaware, "was a man of
ermined purpose and great force of character. At his home the first Methodist
tings were held." (Scharf: *History of Delaware,* II, 868.)

might." I was ill able to speak on account of my throat; but was bless
the people, among whom were some strangers, hearkened diligently
have been in greater heaviness lately, than for some months past. My s
is much humbled.

Thursday, 7. This is a day appointed for prayer and thanksgiving
the government: I intend to improve it for the Church and States. O wl
cause of thankfulness have we that there has not been a famine of bre
and water, and the word of God; that every place has not been delug
in blood! and what cause to praise God, that hundreds have been broug
to the Lord, year after year, in these times of trouble!

Friday, 8. Was under dejection. Read thirty chapters of Isaiah. Rode
Benjamin Dill's—had about forty people: was much led out to speak
the poor. Fasted, and intended to spend great part of the night in pray
but I felt weak through want of rest. I spent better than an hour in ferve
prayer and was much blest, having my soul divinely filled with love wl
I lay down. Rose about five o'clock in better health: passed some time
fervent prayer for the whole work—the preachers and people. Thon
Haskins[140] is a young man of learning, and has been studying the la
like William Spencer, he has given it up for grace and divinity. Glory
to God! I believe the Lord has called Thomas Haskins for a preacher;
was convinced in Dover some months ago.

Saturday, 9. I praise my God; I have great peace of soul.

Sunday, 10. I went to Mr. Thorne's church[141] and heard Mr. Thor
he preached a good sermon on the passion of our Lord, on, "Whom h
ing not seen, ye love;" the people seemed very solemn. I preached
Edward White's—was much assisted in speaking on, "Happy art thou,
Israel!" These people do grow in grace: four or five of them prof
sanctification—this I know, that they are very spiritual.

Monday, 11. I have faith, and am kept in life and the spirit of pray

---

[140] Thomas Haskins (1760–1816) was born near Preston, Caroline County, Ma
land. In 1780 while studying law in Dover, Delaware, he was converted under
preaching of Freeborn Garrettson. In his widowed mother's home the society
formed which in 1785 erected Frazier Flats Chapel, the second Methodist mee
place in Caroline County. It later united with the Preston church. Haskin's itinera
(1782–86) was followed by many years of service as a local preacher in Philadelp
During this period he became a business partner of Colonel Caleb North. They
in establishing the Charter Fund Society. (*Journal* of Thomas Haskins, Novem
1782; September 28, 1783; October 30, 1784; May 3, 1785. Library of Congr
Manuscript Division; Lednum, *op. cit.*, 265, 356, 357.)

[141] The Mispillion Church, Sydenham Thorne, incumbent, was westward some
tance from the site of the present Milford, Delaware. For refusing to observe fast d
and to cease praying for the royal family, he was not permitted to exercise his full p
fession during the Revolution. In 1787 he built a dam for a gristmill and sawmill a
ford on Tumbling Run, hence the name Milford. (Turner: *Some Records of Sus
County, Delaware*, 241; *Delaware, a Guide to the First State*, 208; Rightmyer, *op.*
66, 67.)

Tuesday, 12. I rode to Kent and performed the funeral rite over a child—
exhortation I endeavoured to enforce the necessity of a strict and pious
ducation; the people were much moved, and I felt some hope, that not-
ithstanding we have been greatly discouraged here in times past, this
vamp will bring forth some fruit of three years' labour.

Wednesday, 13. I visited S. White, she is near her end; possessing calm
1d solid peace, and sweetly resigned to the will of God. Preached at
aac Layton's: called to warn my brethren against the poisonous and
lse principles of opposing sectarists. I was doing only what it was my
ounden duty to do, and, indeed, acting on the defensive.

Saturday, 16. My soul is kept in constant peace and love to God.

Sunday, 17. Preached at Joseph Turpin's on "O that there were such a
eart in them," &c., Deut. v, 29; the congregation was larger, and there
as more of the power of God among them, than I have ever known at
is place.

Tuesday, 19. Rose at five—my soul stayed upon God. Preached at
lorgan Williams's on the prayer of Jabez, to a small, inattentive congrega-
on.

Wednesday, 20. I preached to a faithful people at Thomas Layton's, on
latt. iii, 9, 10. The Methodists, blessed be God! do grow as well as the
icked; their little stock increases; I am pleased with their temporal, and
joice in their spiritual prosperity.

Saturday, 23. I attended the funeral of E. T.; a man that had been
nvinced of sin many years ago, but had lost his convictions: about a
velvemonth past God made use of the Methodists to reach his heart
gain; he sought the Lord; joined our society, and at the last quarterly
eeting appeared to be a very happy man. He was poor—persecuted by
s wife, children, and family: he was so hardly treated that scarcely could
 live with them: he was sensible of his death, and died in peace.

Sunday, 24. I received a letter from Freeborn Garrettson, and another
om Thomas S. Chew, who promised me their filial obedience in the Gospel:
 the same day a letter from William Glendenning, who is well satisfied
ith his station, and mentions a letter from LeRoy Cole, who says, the
rring string is broken, and those who were friends at first are friends at
st, in Virginia. I rejoiced for the consolation, and many more will re-
ice with me.

Tuesday, 26. I preached to an unaffected people at J. Emory's, on Matt.
, 17. My soul is stayed upon God, and kept in peace. I rise early and
end my usual time in prayer, and remember my dear friends before God.

Thursday, 28. Wrote to Charles Twyford to take Samuel Roe's place,
hile he goes down to the eastern shore of Virginia; I believe God has a
ork for us to do there.

Friday, 29. I rode to Jonathan Boyer's, where there had been a work
eaking out; but so harassed are the people by opposers and their con-

trary principles, that I fear no lasting good will be done. "A double minded man is unstable in all his ways." From Boyer's I went to George Moore's,[142] and met with a people I had not seen for more than nin months: we mutually rejoiced to see each other. Blessed be God, my so is kept in peace.

Broad Creek, Saturday, 30. While I was preaching, I was seized with putrid sore throat; the attack was violent. *Sabbath day*, I took physic, an applied two blisters that drew kindly; afterward put one on the back my neck, and another behind the ear; had some blood taken from th arm, and some from the tongue; and it pleased kind Providence to reliev me sooner than I expected. I desire to give thanks to God for patience ar resignation.

[142] There were several Moore families in the Broad Creek Society. George Moore name appears in the *General Minutes* between the years 1780 and 1792. (Lednum, *c cit.*, 257.)

1781

1781

A hill woman rode without a saddle to guide Asbury

CHAPTER TEN

Delaware

January 1–4, 1781. Pain! Pain! Pain! 5th, found myself considerably mended, so that I sat up and did a little business.

Sunday, 7. The weather was rainy, so I stayed in the house: this is the second dumb Sabbath I have had; to this I could not submit were I not firm.

Wednesday, 10. I rose with a sense of God upon my heart. I preached many people at George Moore's, on the great salvation: my hearers appeared to be very stupid. The family where I lodged was a prayerless family; and if ministers (so called) can themselves visit without calling the household together for that purpose, it is not to be wondered at that there are so many without family prayer: lying in bed till sunrise, and drinking a dram after they are up, are, perhaps, the circumstances most prominently remembered of their clerical guests.

Thursday, 11. Preached in Quaker-Town:[1] from thence, being invited and pressed by Mr. Thomas Rodney,[2] I went to Lewes; found the court-house crowded, to whom I preached on 2 Cor. v, 13–15.

[1] Quakertown was between Westcott Corner and Lewes. In turn it later became Prettymanville and Westcott Corner.

[2] This was probably Thomas Rodney (1744–1811), brother of Governor Caesar Rodney. His career as a jurist included being a member and speaker of the Delaware Assembly, chief justice of Kent County, delegate to the Continental Congress, and United States judge for the territory of Mississippi. In 1775 he was a member of the Committee of Safety and was a colonel in the Revolutionary War. (*National Cyclopedia of American Biography*, I, 479.)

Lord's day, 14. Being rainy, we had only about one hundred and twen serious people at the place appointed. The people here are much mo gentle than they were a twelvemonth past. We have a society of mo than twenty members, some of whom have found the Lord; but I thin for ignorance of God and religion, the wilds and swamps of Delawa exceed most parts of America with which I have had any acquaintanc however, God is able of these stones to raise up children unto Abrahar

Monday, 15. Rose early; spent my usual time in retirement. Preache to about one hundred and fifty people at Stradley's; I find their prejudic abated, although the work on their hearts is not deep. My soul enjo peace; I was led out in prayer for the whole work of God, the circuits ar the preachers; this I do every morning as my first work. I have a sense God on my heart, and am sensible of the danger of falling; and what goc or harm may I do, as I am faithful or unfaithful!

I have been in heaviness, but I trust I am kept from sin. Indeed, I belie Satan is doing all he can to discredit the work of God that is carried c through our instrumentality, because he envies our success. It appears be high market day among every denomination of people; availing then selves of the work, they are labouring to detach those who would members from our society.

Thursday, 18. I called on the widow F., who had lately lost her husban He was a constant hearer of us, and as constantly resisted the doctri he heard, and could not bear the chapel so near him: he sickened and die in a short space; was delirious most of the time he was ill. What w remarkable, and awfully so, was, that his little son, of whom he w passionately fond, and on whom he frequently called, in his delirium, t go with him, went and hanged himself about the time his father die they went into eternity nearly together, and were laid out and buried the same time. This awful circumstance was the means of awakening stubborn son, who is now seeking the Lord. How wonderful are the way of God! He takes away a child to awaken a father, or removes a father t convince a child.

Friday, 19. I conversed with T. C., whom I visited under affliction abo a year ago: he then had an humble confidence of his acceptance with Go and a firm persuasion that God would save him from all sin. In the cours of his sickness he became somewhat delirious, and yielded to a suggestio that it was all delusion: he began to set in order his temporal affairs; b in about eight days there was a change in his disorder of body and mind his confidence in God returned; he professed that God had saved hi from all sin, and he appears to be always alive to God.

Sunday, 21. Mr. Magaw preached at Barratt's chapel, and was assiste by Mr. Thorne in the administration of the Lord's supper: it was a graciou time, and I hope it was not received in vain.

Monday, 22. On my way to Andrew Purdin's I came on a race groun

here the sons of Belial had been practising my horse; he ran away with
ᴍe when he came to the end of the paths, but stopped, and I received no
ᴅarm. I lifted my heart to God; and by the mercy of the Lord he stopped
ᴇar a point of woods, which, had he entered, I might probably have lost
ᴍy life: my heart was deeply humbled before the Lord, who preserved me
ᴏm such imminent danger.

Monday, 29. I learn that about six or seven years ago B. S. was deeply
ᴀwakened, and became a member of the Methodist society: some time
ᴀfter this he lost his convictions, and ran into sin. Last Christmas he was
ᴅtting up with a sick person, where were present two women who had
ᴀtely been awakened through the instrumentality of Lewis Alfrey: they
ᴅsked him what he thought of the Methodists; he, contrary to his better
ᴋnowledge, answered, "they are all hypocrites:" they asked him what he
ᴅought of Lewis Alfrey and Joshua Dudley,[3] he spake against them as
ᴡell as the rest. "How then, (rejoined they,) can they pray and exhort as
ᴅey do, if they are such men as you say;" he told them he could pray like
ᴅ minister himself, when he was in society. Next day he set off to go home,
ᴡhich he never reached: he was taken ill; was bereft of his senses, and so
ᴅe died.

Sunday, February 4. I preached, and had some of the Council and
ᴍembers of Assembly to hear me. I spoke plainly; intending my discourse
ᴅs a vindication of the doctrine of the Methodists.

Monday, 5. On my way to quarterly meeting, held at the Valley preach-
ᴅg-house,[4] I called on his Excellency, Governor Rodney,[5] to sign my
ᴄertificate, which he did with great readiness and politeness. At the
ᴍeeting we found some faithful souls, and the work revives among
ᴅem: they were greatly led out to speak in the love feast, six or seven
ᴅanding up as witnesses of a present salvation from all sin.

Pennsylvania

Saturday, 10. My soul enjoys peace, and I rejoice to hear that the work
ᴏf God is deepening and widening in the Jerseys. My old friends here in
ᴘhiladelphia appear loving to me; but they are not united as they ought
ᴅo be.

[3] Lednum, *op. cit.*, 266, 267, 317.
[4] The Valley Meeting House in Chester County, Pennsylvania, was first called Goshen.
ᴅee May 6, 1773.) It became Valley in 1774 and is now known as Grove. The society
ᴡas formed in 1769 or 1770, with George Hoffman (see August 9, 1783) and Daniel
ᴍeredith (see July 6, 1792) as the leaders. An account of its origins, written by Joseph
ᴍeredith, grandson of Daniel, is in the possession of Grove Church. (Reeves: *Method-
ᴅm in and Around Chester*; see *Journal* entries for October 7, 1781; August 25, 1782;
ᴅuly 3, 1787; July 7, 1792; August 22, 1800; June 2, 1804; August 7, 1805.)
[5] The Honorable Caesar Rodney was governor of Delaware.

Tuesday, 13. After casting in my mite, by saying and doing what
could in Philadelphia, I left my kind friends, and set off for New Jersey

New Jersey

Wednesday, 14. I met with and heard Benjamin Abbott[6]—his word
came with great power. Over in Chester, he informs me, twenty were
renewed in love, and eight on this side; the people fall to the ground
under him, and sink into a passive state, helpless, stiff, motionless. H
tried to attach himself to two other sects, but had such struggles within
that he was forced back—the Lord would not let him be anything but
a Methodist: such is his account. He is a man of uncommon zeal, and
(although his language has somewhat of incorrectness) of good utterance
Here, I find, remains the fruit of the labours of that (now) miserable man
Abraham Whitworth. How awful the thought, that God should own a
man and make him a blessing to many souls, and then lay him aside like
a broken instrument! Yet so it was, because of his sin. May others take
warning by his fall!

Thursday, 15. I have found the Lord with me in an extraordinary manner
ever since I left Delaware. Brother I——s tells me there is daily a grea
turning to God in new places, and that the work of sanctification goes on
in our old societies.

Tuesday, 20. Rode to Penny Hill: was much pleased with the simplicity
of our old German mother K. She says she lived in blindness fifty years
and was at length brought to God by the means of Methodism: she i
now rejoicing in the perfect love of God; her children are coming home
to the Lord; while she is preaching in her way to all she comes up with

Friday, March 2. My soul enjoys peace; and I have a little respite from
the haste I have been in for some time past; nevertheless I have read the
first and second volumes of Rollin's Ancient History (containing about
three hundred pages each) in about two weeks. We may justly admire the
policy and the temperance of the Persians; and it is very satisfactory to
find a more particular account corroborating the Scripture history of the
fulfilment of the prophecies concerning that great man Cyrus, called of
God.

Pennsylvania

Saturday, 3. Rode to Philadelphia, where I preached but twice: I me
the society, which was made a blessing to some; and I am persuaded
that my stay would be a means of the prosperity of the society here; bu
it is possible I may be more useful where I am going.

[6] See Abbott's autobiography, *The Experience and Gospel Labours of the Rev*
Benjamin Abbott. Also Atkinson, *op. cit.*, 107–13, 147–49, 157–60.

Tuesday, 6. Read the fourth volume of Rollin's Ancient History: it ontains the memorable life of Socrates, who was certainly a wise man; ut, as the worthy historian remarks, there were many blemishes in his iaracter.

Saturday, 10. Rode to French Creek,[7] and was kindly entertained by y much-respected friends Mrs. Rebecca Grace,[8] and her daughter Mrs. otts,[9] and her granddaughter Martha Potts, afterward Mrs. Haskins,[10] ho lived, and have since died in the Lord. O may the unfeigned ith which was in them be also in their children and their grand-ildren!

Sunday, 11. Preached to a small congregation. One of my hearers emed desirous I should form an independent church.

Wednesday, 14. Rode twelve miles into the forest to preach to the mnant of poor Demour's flock.[11] I. Demour, as well as S. Howe, died a artyr to labour and loud speaking; they were both disciples of good Mr. vans. He preached the last day of his life; afterwards, his people melted vay for want of preaching and discipline; we have been sent for, and vned and blessed among them. I have heard of a great work among e Germans towards Lancaster. Certain opposing sectarians hunt our reachers like partridges upon the mountains; they are trying to stop, but e going, I apprehend, the readiest way to establish us. God will stand y his people—blessed be his name. My soul is kept in peace.

Friday, 16. I preached at the Valley preaching house: and here I set my al to what Joseph Cromwell had done in expelling a member who had ng been troublesome to the society.

Monday, 19. A letter from Caleb B. Pedicord informs me that the work ʹ the Lord prospers in Dorset: glorious news this, at which my heart is eatly cheered.

[7] French Creek rises in lower Berks County, Pennsylvania, flows through the north-stern part of Chester County, and enters Schuylkill River near Phœnixville.

[8] See note under May 23, 1776.

[9] Mrs. Anna Potts was the daughter of Mrs. Grace and her first husband, Samuel utt, Jr. She married a partner of the Rutter family in the iron works.

[10] She was the wife of the Rev. Thomas Haskins. (See *Journal* entry under August 5, 08.) He settled later in Philadelphia as a wholesale grocer and was one of the editors Asbury's *Journal*.

[11] Forest Chapel in Berks County, Pennsylvania, was erected by the Rev. William mour, a Swedish minister. It is now St. Paul's Church, Geigertown; and the corner-ne date is 1773. The grave marker of Mr. Demour reads, "To the memory of Rev. illiam Demour who organized the first religious society at the Old Forest Church, w St. Paul's M.E. Church, about the year 1776. Died 1776." On March 17, 1780, e property on which Forest Chapel stood was sold by A. M. James and his wife, ary, to a group of nine trustees, Evan Evans, Samuel Haw, Valentine Carberry, raham Luris, John Davis, Joseph Haw, Henry Carberry, John Galloway, and Thomas itter. (Reeves: *Methodism in and Around West Chester*; Fulmer: *Historical Sketch of , Paul's Methodist Episcopal Church, Formerly Called Old Forest Church, Geigertown, nnsylvania, 1933.*)

Delaware

Dover, *Saturday*, 24. I was much led out in speaking of Peter's fa
at my favourite place. I am greatly comforted with the good news
Zion's prosperity. Upon a review of my travels I find that, from the fir
of last May to this present date, I have travelled nearly or quite fou
thousand miles.

Tuesday, 27. I resolve to spend an hour in enlarged prayer as soon as
rise in the morning; to retire again at eleven, at five, and at eight o'cloc
when in my power.

Wednesday, 28. My soul is comfortable. I daily find myself great
humbled.

Tuesday, April 10. I preached the funeral sermon of J. B., a *Freemason,*
a great sinner, and an enemy to the Methodists—persecuting his wife ar
children for coming to hear them. When sick he sent for the Methodis
to pray for him, and promised to come and hear them if spared.

Wednesday, 11. Since I have been here I am greatly kept from the fea
of men, and unholy desires to please them; I feel as free in speaking
masters as to their servants. I trust the Lord will humble and save tho
people.

Saturday, 14. Our quarterly meeting began at the Forest chapel—th
congregation was large: I spoke first, and was followed by brothe
Chew, Ruff, Cox, and Lambert; the people were quickened and appear
much alive to God. The next day, being Easter Sunday, our love fea
began at nine, and public preaching at eleven o'clock. After meeting v
rode about twenty miles to brother White's, where about twenty preache
met together to hold a conference.[12] Thence I attended Kent quarter
meeting, on the East shore of Maryland.

Maryland

Friday, 20. Crossed the Chesapeake Bay, and came to Mr. Gough
Saturday I rode to Baltimore, and preached on the *Sabbath day*.

Tuesday, 24. Our conference began in Baltimore, where several of th
preachers attended from Virginia and North Carolina. All but one agree
to return to the old plan, and give up the administration of the ordinance
our troubles now seem over from that quarter; and there appears to be
considerable change in the preachers from North to South: all was co
ducted in peace and love.

Monday, 30. I am relieved in mind relative to my visiting Virginia, ar
my soul is kept in peace, whilst I feel power to trust the Lord with my a

---

[12] This conference of the northern group appears in the *General Minutes*: "Held
Choptank, State of Delaware, April 16, 1781, and adjourned to Baltimore the 24th
said month."

Tuesday, May 1. Wrote to my father and Mr. Wesley.

Monday, 7. I employed this day in visiting my friends.

Tuesday, 8. I was preparing to set off to Virginia, but my horse failed.
hardly know how to proceed; Providence seems dark: I doubt if I can
de on horseback, and yet I am unwilling to give up my visit to the South.

Thursday, 10. I set off in the hope that the Lord will bless and keep me
r his own cause and glory.

Virginia

Saturday, 12. Reached Mr. Adams's[13] about eight o'clock at night: I
ways come to this house weary, but generally get my body and soul
freshed. I missed my watch, but found it again at the door where I had
ighted; my horse had trodden it and bruised the case, and not broken
e crystal, without otherwise injuring it.

Sunday, 13. Preached at the chapel; afterward Harry, a black man,
oke on the barren fig-tree. This circumstance was new, and the white
ople looked on with attention.

Thursday, 17. I had uncommon liberty in preaching in the court house
Leesburg. I see the need of a preacher's being well acquainted with his
ble, and yet not to think so; the word of God is one grand dispensatory
soul-diseases in every case of spiritual malady. I bless the Lord for
alth and peace: my soul was much drawn after God, and melted in
mily and private prayer.

Monday, 21. I preached in the afternoon at P. Hite's, and had
erty in urging purity of heart. Harry Hosier spoke to the Negroes, some
whom came a great distance to hear him: certain sectarians are greatly
spleased with him, because he tells them they may fall from grace,
d that they must be holy.

Tuesday, 22. We set off for Rectortown, being informed it was about
enty-two miles; we found it nearer thirty. I reached there, weary and
spirited, about half past two o'clock; I spoke for an hour with great
sistance, both loud and clear, to an apparently unconcerned people.

West Virginia

I have been kept back by the rain, the waters, &c., so as not to reach
hn Hite's[14] until Saturday evening.

[3] William Adams lived in Fairfax County, Virginia, where he was an outstanding
ethodist; and his home became a preaching place. He had four sons and two daughters,
of whom were useful members of the society. Two of the sons, William and Samuel,
:ame preachers, and the oldest daughter became the wife of the Rev. William Watters.
rmstrong: *History of Old Baltimore Conference,* 25.)

[4] John Hite, member of a prominent early family, lived about four miles from Charles
wn, West Virginia, where he built Hite's meeting house some time prior to 1788. Here

Sunday, 27. Had about two hundred people to hear. The society he
are not united in love; there is a consequent falling away among them.

Monday, 28. I found my heart deeply engaged with God on my way
J. Hite's; O what fellowship have I with God as I ride along! my soul
filled with love, and I witness that the Lord can keep me alive in the da
of famine.

Tuesday, 29. Felt solemn and much tempted. The Lord help his po
servant from day to day, from hour to hour, and from moment to momen
Alas, what a dearth of religion is here! My God, help us to go on und
these difficulties! Here brother Cooper (?)[15] was once taken up by T. H.,
man of property: he lived about one year afterward and languished o
his life; it may be he sinned the sin unto death; but there was hope in h
end. He spoke to all around him, exhorting them to repent. Whether I
was judicially visited I know not; but I do not recollect an instance
one preacher that has been thus treated, that something distressing ha
not followed his persecutors; it may not be for the preacher's holines
but rather the cause of God which the Eternal vindicates.

I have had great conflicts of mind for some time past. I believe Sata
has been hard at work, and has painted every possible danger he can
my imagination.

Thursday, 31. My soul enjoyed peace: I was blessed in reading tl
thirty-seventh Psalm; and was also comforted in reading a few pages
Bishop Hopkins, on the words "Count it all joy when ye fall into dive
temptations."

Saturday, June 2. Preached at Martinsburg:[16] afterward returned
Brother Bruce's;[17] he is a lily among the thorns.

Sunday, 3. Preached to about one hundred and fifty serious people, ai
was blest in meeting class.

Monday, 4. I preached to a few lifeless people at Stroud's.[18] I find m

Thomas Scott, preacher on the Berkeley Circuit in 1790–91, preached when Dr. Edwa
Tiffin, later governor of Ohio, was converted. (See Thomas Scott's manuscript in t
possession of the Rev. Lawrence Sherwood; Robert Ayer's *Journal* in the possessi
of the Historical Society of Western Pennsylvania at Pittsburgh; Whatcoat's *Jour*
for August 27, 1789; Finley: *Sketches of Western Methodism*, ch. xix.) Mrs. John H
was a sister of Mrs. Boydstone. (See *Journal* entry for July 18, 1782.)

[15] This was probably John Cooper, who had served the Fairfax Circuit in 17?
(Payton: *Our Fathers Have Told Us*, 20–21.) It may have been Philip Cox, who rode t
circuit in 1780. (Lednum, *op. cit.*, 248.)

[16] Martinsburg is the county seat of Berkeley County, West Virginia. It was charter
in 1778 and named for a nephew of Lord Fairfax.

[17] George Bruce probably lived at Brucetown on Opeguan Creek near the W
Virginia–Virginia line. Thomas Scott, a later circuit rider, referred to Bruce's mi
and said that one of Bruce's brothers kept a tavern at Monroe, Highland Coun
Ohio. (See the Scott manuscript; Ayer's manuscript *Journal*, 1788–89; Benne
Memorials of Methodism in Virginia, 139.)

[18] The widow Margaret Stroud lived near the mouth of Opeguan Creek, and I
house was a preaching place on the Berkeley Circuit. Captain James Stroud lived in t

If given to God in prayer, and am not peculiarly exercised; yet my irits feel depression.

Tuesday, 5. Had a rough ride over hills and dales to Guest's.[19] Here rother Pigman[20] met me, and gave an agreeable account of the work on e south branch of Potomac. I am kept in peace; and greatly pleased I n to get into the woods, where, although alone, I have blessed company, ad sometimes think, Who so happy as myself?

Wednesday, 6. We had twelve miles to Ross's, along a bushy, hilly ad.[21] A poor woman with a little horse, without a saddle, outwent us up nd down the hills, and when she came to the place appointed, the Lord et with and blessed her soul.

Thursday, 7. I set out for the south branch of Potomac[22]—a country of ountains and natural curiosities. Blessed be God for health and peace! he enemy strives against me; but I look to God from hour to hour. We und some difficulty in crossing Great Capon River;[23] three men very indly carried us over in a canoe, and afterward rode our horses over the ream, without fee or reward: about five o'clock we reached William annell's[24] [?]; I laid me down to rest on a chest, and using my clothes or covering, slept pretty well; here I found need of patience.

Friday, 8. Not being able to cross the South Branch, we had to bear way through the mountains, and to go up one of about two hundred me area near Martinsburg; and Asbury preached in his barn, according to Whatcoat, a August 25, 1789. (Whatcoat's *Journal* for August 19 and 25, 1789; see the Robert yres and Thomas Scott manuscripts.)

[19] Joseph Guest lived on Back Creek, Berkeley County, west of Gerrardstown, 'est Virginia. He erected a meeting house prior to 1788 near the present Glengary or anghai. Asbury was at Guest's again on July 17, 1782. (See Ayres manuscript.)

[20] Ignatius Pigman was on the Berkeley Circuit. He began traveling in 1780 and was ected deacon at the Christmas Conference in 1784 and ordained at Baltimore the llowing year. He located in 1788 and suffered a lapse of some kind. He went to New rleans as a flour speculator about 1812 and lost all his money. (See *Journal* entry for ptember 1, 1800; Lednum, *op. cit.*, 325; Stevens: *History of the Methodist Episcopal urch in the United States*, II, 89, 189.)

[21] The Ross family later moved to near Dayton, Ohio, where Asbury visited them irty years later. (See *Journal* entry for September 21, 1811.) Asbury had proceeded ong the old Redstone Road, later known as the Braddock Road because it was used / Braddock after his defeat. It had been laid out by Colonel George Washington. sbury used it on other occasions when he crossed the Alleghenies. (See *Journal* entries r July 12, 1782; July 1, 1784; and others.)

[22] Asbury traversed the fertile valley of the south branch of the Potomac River llowing Ignatius Pigman's good account of it two days before. He was so impressed ith it that at the next conference the name of the Berkeley Circuit was changed to uth Branch. (See *Minutes*, 1782.)

[23] Lost River rises in Hardy County, West Virginia, and disappears into the ground. hen it rises again, it is called Capon. There is a Little Capon which empties into the otomac about twenty-five miles above Great Capon. Asbury refers to both on July , 1782. (See also June 21, 1781.)

[24] This was probably William Rannell. (See Deed Book 2, p. 55, Hampshire Co., omney, West Virginia.)

yards' elevation; in some places the breaks in the slate served for step
in other parts of the ascent there were none: we at length reached tl
place appointed, and preached to about twenty, as I think, prayerle
people, on Isaiah lv, 6, 7. I hope some felt the word.

Sunday, 10. I preached at eleven o'clock to about two hundred peop
with a degree of freedom. I then rode to Richard Williams's.[25] On my wa
I had a view of a hanging rock[26] that appears like a castle wall, abov
three hundred feet high, and looks as if it had been built with square sla
stones; at first glance a traveller would be ready to fear it would fall c
him. I had about three hundred people; but there were so many wicke
whisky drinkers, who brought with them so much of the power of tl
devil, that I had but little satisfaction in preaching.

Monday, 11. I rose at five o'clock, with a determination to live near
to God. Here are a few believers groaning for full redemption, but mar
more are dying through controversy and for the want of urgent exhorta
tion to purity of heart: it is hard for those to preach this doctrine who hav
not experimentally attained it, or who are not striving with all their hear
to possess it. From Williams's I crossed the South Branch and went t
Patterson Creek.[27] I came to a Dutch settlement:[28] the people love preacl
ing, but do not understand class meeting, because they are not enoug
conversant with the English tongue; and we cannot all do as John Hagerty
and H. Weidner,[30] who speak both languages; could we get a Dutc
preacher or two to travel with us, I am persuaded we should have a goo
work among the Dutch. I love these people; they are kind in the
way.

[25] Richard Williams (1721–86) lived near present Romney, West Virginia. (S
Asbury's long account of him in *Journal* entry for July 31, 1784. See also Johnstoi
The South Branch of the Potomac.)

[26] Hanging Rock or Hanging Rocks, sometimes called Blue Rocks, are on tl
Wappatomaka (South Branch), about four miles north of Romney, West Virginia, c
route 28 between Romney and Springfield. The state of West Virginia has a mark
there. (Kercheval: *History of the Valley of Virginia*, 320.)

[27] Patterson Creek runs parallel with the South Branch. Asbury must have crosse
the latter near Romney, West Virginia, and proceeded to the former by way of tl
present Springfield.

[28] This Dutch settlement was Fort Ashby in Mineral County, West Virginia, bu
in 1755 under the direction of George Washington. Asbury stayed and preached in tl
home of John Jones. (See *Journal* entry for July 11, 1782. Also see Woodwortl
History of the Presbytery of Winchester.)

[29] See *Journal* entry and note under July 28, 1776.

[30] Henry Weidner was an associate of Philip William Otterbein. Before the foundii
of this church, Weidner was, as early as 1774, the leader of one of the Baltimore classe
On June 2, 1776, ministers, including Otterbein and Benedict Schwope, granted Weidn
a license to preach. By 1785 he was an elder in Otterbein's church in Baltimore. He w
a native of Switzerland and traveled and preached extensively in Maryland and Virgini
About 1790 he moved to Virginia. He died in 1811 near Baltimore. There was a clo
relation with the German preachers, and Asbury apparently considered Weidner
one of his own. (See Drury, *op. cit.*, 129, 137, 141, 155, 168, 250.)

We have many trials and threatenings; but God is with us. I have ately been reading Fletcher's Checks, and they have been greatly blessed me: however he may be now treated, and his works held in light estima-on, ages to come will bless God for his writings, as I have done for those f Baxter and other ancient divines.

I am now in a land of valleys and mountains, about ten or fifteen miles om the foot of the Alleghany—a mountain that, at this part of it, is two ays' journey across; thither some of our preachers are going to seek the utcasts of the people.[31] Blessed be God, I am kept in constant peace and ove, and am not so subject to dejection as in times past.

Sunday, 17. My soul enjoyed great peace in family and private prayer. here is much talk about some of our preachers being taken up; I have o fears from that quarter.

Monday, 18. I was led to wonder at myself when I considered the fatigue went through; travelling in the rain; sleeping without beds, &c., and in ae midst of all I am kept in health: this confirms me in the persuasion at I am about the work I am called to, and the Lord gives me strength ccording to my day. So let thy work spread, blessed Jesus, and let not ay servants labour in vain!

Wednesday, 20. We had hard work crossing the Fork Mountain,[32] being ometimes obliged to walk where it was too steep to ride. I was much lessed in speaking to about ninety Dutch folks, who appeared to feel ae word. Here is a spring remarkable for its depth,[33] and the quantity of ater it discharges sufficient for a mill within two hundred yards from the ource, which sometimes in freshets throws its mass of waters consider-bly above the ordinary level of the surface.

It does not appear that I do any great good; yet I am constantly happy nd measurably holy: I bless the Lord for this.

Thursday, 21. Last evening I rode a mile and a half to see some of the reatest natural curiosities my eyes ever beheld: they were two caves,[34] bout two hundred yards from each other; their entrances were, as in milar cases, narrow and descending, gradually widening towards the

---

[31] The preachers who were going across the mountains were evidently local preachers ich as Robert Wooster. (See *Journal* entry for July 2, 1784.) So far as is known, no inerants were sent into the transmontane region until 1782, when James Mallory, John aldwin, and James Haw pushed their South Branch circuit a little west of the summit. iee the Thomas Scott manuscript.)

[32] Fork Mountain divides Mill Creek and the South Fork of the South Branch of ae Potomac. Mill Creek joins the South Branch at Petersburg. The South Fork joins ae South Branch at Moorefield.

[33] This spring forms Spring Run, South Mill Creek, and has a flow of four thousand allons per minute. It is noted for the power generated because of its location. It was ormerly called Eyman's Spring and is now known as Spring Run or Spring 29. (West irginia Geological Survey, 1936, *Springs of West Virginia*.)

[34] There are several caves along this route. The cave here mentioned was probably eldon Cave, which seems to have been on Asbury's route.

interior, and opening into lofty chambers, supported, to appearance, t basaltic pillars. In one of these I sung,

"Still our of the deepest abyss."

The sound was wonderful. There were stalactites resembling the pipes an organ, which, when our old guide, father Ellsworth,[35] struck with stick, emitted a melodious sound, with variations according to their siz walls, like our old churches; resemblances to the towers adjoining the belfries; and the natural gallery, which we ascended with difficulty: all me was new, solemn, and awfully grand. There were parts which we d not explore; so deep, so damp, and near night. I came away filled wit wonder, with humble praise, and adoration.

In journeying through this mountainous district I have been great blessed, my soul enjoying constant peace. I find a few humble, happy sou in my course; and although present appearances are gloomy, I have n doubt but that there will be a glorious Gospel-day in this and every oth part of America.

There are but two men in the society at Lost River[36] able to bear arm they were both drafted to go into the army: I gave them what comfort could, and prayed for them.

Saturday, 30. I got alone into a barn to read and pray. The people he appear unengaged: the preaching of unconditional election, and its usua attendant, Antinomianism, seems to have hardened their hearts.

Sunday, July 1. More people attended preaching than I expected: I ha some liberty in speaking,[37] but no great fervour; neither seemed there muc effect produced. I retired to read and pray in the woods, the houses bein small, and the families large.

Friday, 13. For some days past my congregations have not been ver large, which is in part owing to the harvest-home. I fasted from yesterda noon until four o'clock to-day; though much tempted, I have been bles I have kept close to-day, and have read two hundred pages of Baxter Saints' Rest; surely this is a most valuable book—a book I should like t read once a quarter.

Monday, 16. We set out through the mountains for quarterly meetin It was a very warm day, and part of our company stopped after thirt miles' travelling; brother William Partridge[38] and myself kept on unt

[35] This was probably Thomas Elswick, Sr., who lived on Lost River, as did his so Thomas, Jr. The elder Elswick received land from his parents, John and Rachel El wick, on December 8, 1755. (Deed Book 4, p. 249, Hampshire County, West Virgini in Romney.)

[36] See note under June 7, 1781.

[57] Asbury probably preached at his "old friend S" mentioned in the entry for Ju 26, 1782, as having died. He lived on North River, a fork of Great Capon not far fro where Lost River sinks.

[38] William Partridge (1754–1817) was the preacher on the Berkeley Circuit. (See no under June 5, 1781.) He began preaching in 1775 and located in 1784. In 1814 he r

ght overtook us in the mountain, among rocks, and woods, and dangers
all sides surrounding us: we concluded it most safe to secure our
rses and quietly await the return of day; so we lay down and slept
ong the rocks,[39] although much annoyed by the gnats.

Virginia

Tuesday, 17. Next day I met several preachers, with whom I spent some
ne in conversation about the work of God. At twelve o'clock the people
Perrill's[40] met, and we all exhorted.

Friday, 20. I had some liberty on 2 Cor. vi, 2. I have been obliged to
ep on the floor every night since I slept in the mountains. Yesterday I
de twenty-seven miles, and to-day thirty.

Saturday, 21. I adore the goodness of God that I am kept in health;
d I may wonder at myself that it is thus, when I consider how rough the
·e is in this roughest of circuits.[41] I feel thankful to God for sending such
·nty for man and beast, and for the fine season to gather it, which, con-
lering how many men are called away to the armies, is a great mercy.

Tuesday, 24. I had some leisure for reading my Bible, which I have had
·le time for of late. I thank the Lord for peace, power, love, and a
vent spirit.

Monday, 30. Attended a quarterly meeting at Leesburg. I gave a brief
count of the Methodists, who and what they were, and repelled some
arges brought against them here. At twelve o'clock brother Ellis[42]
eached a solid good sermon on, "He that hath this hope in him purifieth
mself as he is pure."

Maryland

Tuesday, August 7. Our quarterly meeting began at Charles Penn's,[43]
ar Seneca. On *Wednesday*, many gave testimony to the goodness of God

tered the itinerancy, dying while on the Sparta circuit in Georgia. (Lednum, *op. cit.*,
3.)

[39] They probably slept near a gap on the West Virginia–Virginia border not far from
gh View, West Virginia. (See *Journal* entry for June 26, 1782.)

[40] Lednum says that Perrill lived in New Virginia. There was an early Perrill family
ing near Winchester, Virginia, which would be in the general direction of Asbury's
vels. On August 6, 1788, Robert Ayers preached at "John Parrel's" near Winchester.
s line of travel indicated a location about thirty-five miles from Guess's on Back
eek. (See the Ayres manuscript; Kercheval: *History of the Valley of Virginia*, 38.)

[41] This was the mountainous Berkeley Circuit.

[42] Reuben Ellis was on the Frederick Circuit in Virginia.

[43] Charles Penn was a member of the society and a trustee of the Goshen Meeting
ɔuse near Laytonsville, Montgomery County, Maryland. It was the second Methodist
ice of worship to be erected in that part of Maryland. Nelson Reed, who rode over

in the love feast. I preached a long sermon to many people assembled
a barn: the weather was very warm and trying to me; but if good is do
all is well. I hear the work of the Lord greatly revives and spreads
Dorset: there is some opposition, but God is with the young preache
who speak like old men. It appears as if the whole peninsula would
Christianized: go on, gracious Lord,

> "And let thy word o'er all prevail."

I am kept by the power of God, and filled with comfort under all my tria

Sunday, 12. Was a damp, unwholesome day. At Micah Dorsey's, E
ridge, I was seized with all the symptoms of an inflammatory sore thro
I bled, took medicine, and applied blisters; but the disease was too viol
to yield at once; very high fever followed, and I suffered more than I c
well express; I made use of poultice with better success; the gatheri
broke, and I found some relief. I praise God that his providence cast
lot among so kind a people; food, lodging, a physician, Dr. Pue,[44] a
whatever else was necessary, was not withheld. I am sensible I am not
humble as I should be; and it may be I am in danger of forming impro
estimates of my importance, among preachers and people: were t
disposition indulged, God might justly cut me off.

Monday, 20. I set out on my way in great weakness of body; bu
could not be satisfied to be at rest while able to travel: I stopped awh
at Dr. Pue's, and came in the evening to my old friend Thomas Cromwel

Sunday, 26. I had a warm ride of fifteen miles to G.'s, where I spo
with liberty to the poor, simple-hearted people. My body is weak, but
mind is kept in peace: I desire to trust to God with body and soul. It
now near four years since I was in these parts; in times past I labour
much here.

Preached at Fell's Point on Deut. xxxiii, 29, with a good degree of fr
dom; and in town at half past five o'clock: I trust the people felt, an
hope they will remember it. Spent *Wednesday* and *Thursday* in writing
still find my soul kept in peace, and I daily feel a deeper sense of God a
a greater concern for the prosperity of his work; yet I have no distressi
thought about it, being able to trust God with his own cause.

Friday, 31. I received a packet of letters from the Peninsula, by whicl
learn that the work of God still prospers there; that persecution, a
necessary consequence, rages with great violence; and that two or th
of the preachers are unable to preach through weakness of body.

Monday, September 3. I visited the Bush chapel. The people here o

from the Calvert Circuit, met there, besides Asbury, William Watters, Reuben E
and Jonathan Forrest. (Martz, *op. cit.,* 7; diary of Nelson Reed manuscript in Lo
Lane Church, Baltimore.)

[44] Dr. Michael Pue lived in the vicinity of Elkridge. His wife was Mary Dorsey
daughter of Caleb Dorsey. Fifteen years later Asbury met Pue's widow and paid h
tribute to her husband. (*Journal* entry for November 1, 1795.)

: us to follow another:[45] time was when the labours of their leader were
de a blessing to them; but pride is a *busy* sin. He is now no more: upon
whole, I am inclined to think the Lord took him away in judgment,
:ause he was in a way to do hurt to his cause; and that he saved him in
rcy, because from his death-bed conversation he appears to have had
pe in his end.

Wednesday, 5. I preached to about three hundred people at Deer Creek
h a good degree of freedom; and rejoiced to find that my old friends
itinued faithful.

Sunday, 9. After riding twenty miles, I preached at Jones's on the Manor,
about six hundred people, with great liberty; the audience were still
l attentive. Mr. Gough spoke after me.

Monday, 10. I learn that the Lord is reviving his work on the eastern
ore, more or less, in every circuit. The wicked persecute, and Satan
;es in Dorset; but God will carry on his own work and maintain his
n cause.

Tuesday, 11. My soul enjoys great nearness to God in private, and more
vour of spirit than I have known for some years; I also feel a greater
e for the circuit preachers, and for the work of God in general. I spent
rt of my time in marking Baxter's Cure for Church Divisions through.
ave little leisure for anything but prayer; seldom more than two hours
the day, and that space I wish to spend in retired meditation and prayer:
ing, preaching, class meeting, leaves but little for reading or writing,
d not always enough for prayer: something might be gained could I
re over a book on horseback, as Mr. Wesley does in England; but this
r roads forbid.

Saturday, 22. Spoke in a barn—a cold place, and cold people. Here I
t with T. Stephens, who heard me, and Mr. M., of Stroud, in England:
 wife was then a member with us: he has rambled until the Lord has
o found him out.

Pennsylvania

Tuesday, 25. Rode to York. I was met by Mr. Ranckle, who was once
Methodist, but now a German Presbyterian minister. Mr. Ranckle and
r. Wagner[46] appear as if they wished to be friendly; but they fear us,

⁵ Asbury refers to Robert Strawbridge, founder of Methodism in Maryland, who
l died at the home of Mr. Joseph Wheeler in the summer of 1781. For about five
rs Strawbridge had asserted his customary independence by taking charge of the
:ieties on Sam's Creek and at Bush Forest without recognizing any authority.

⁶ Daniel Wagner was pastor of the German Reformed Church in York, Pennsyl-
nia, from 1774 to 1786, and after serving in Berks County returned for a second
storate from 1793 to 1802. He entertained Freeborn Garrettson, who preached in
 church. Later the church was closed to Garrettson. In 1802 Wagner moved to
ederick, where Asbury visited him. (Prowell: *History of York County, Pennsylvania*,
589.)

lest we should get the good will of the people, and we should join them
our societies.

Sunday, 30. Under great weakness of body.

Wednesday, October 3. I began to amend. I am kindly and comfo
ably entertained by Mrs. Grace,[47] an old disciple; first awakened by N
Whitefield, afterward convinced by reading Mr. Wesley's sermon
Falling from Grace; and now a fast friend and member of our society

Sunday, 7. Preached at the Valley preaching house, on the "gre
salvation," to an attentive people, with some animation. From thence
rode to Benson's preaching house,[48] where there was a great gathering
people, like a quarterly meeting.

It is with difficulty I observe my morning and evening hour of reti
ment; I am, however, kept in constant peace.

Tuesday, 9. I preached at E. Jones's[49] to about a hundred people. He
I met with Isaac Rawlings,[50] mischievous and disappointed: having sep.
ated himself, he charges us with casting him off, and spares not his sec
abuse on conference and preachers: fallen, deceitful, self-deceiving man
leave thee to God and thy own conscience.

Friday, 12. Came to Philadelphia—found the people serious, lovin
and lively. The society here appears to be in a better state than they ha
been in since the British army was here.

Sunday, 14. I had some comfortable sensations in speaking on John :
14. Our congregations are large, and I hope for a revival of the wo
amongst us. I heard two good sermons at St. George's. I gave them a pla
discourse at night at St. George's, on 1 John i, 8, 9.

Tuesday, 16. I enjoy peace; but I soon grow tired of the city. There
a deepening of the work in some souls; but I feel the religion of othe
evaporates in talk.

Thursday, 18. I left the city of Philadelphia. In the evening I visited
German woman in distress for her soul. We spent an hour in prayer, a
God set her at liberty. Next day I returned to the city; and on *Sabbe
day*, the 21st, we had a love feast. I attended the Episcopal churcl
twice. Our own house was crowded. The work of God appears still
revive amongst us; and I trust the society increases in grace as well

[47] See note under May 23, 1776.

[48] Preaching began about 1774 in Uwchlan township, Chester County, Pennsylvan
and a society was formed near the Little Eagle. Here Benson's Chapel was erected
1781. It is no longer in existence.

[49] Jones lived at Hopewell Forge near the surviving Hopewell Church.

[50] Rawlings (also spelled Rollins) had been a preacher but located in 1782. He w
on the Chester Circuit with Pilmoor in 1773. (See *Minutes*.) He was thrown from a ho
and killed in 1783. (See *Journal* entry under August 5, 1783. Futhey and Cope: *Histo
of Chester County*, 280.)

[51] Asbury usually attended St. Paul's Church although he may have gone to Chr
Church on Second Street above Market.

numbers. Among too many of the citizens the spirit of politics has, in
.ole or in part, eaten out the spirit of religion. We have come to a con-
.sion to print the four volumes of Mr. Wesley's Sermons.

Delaware

Thursday, 25. Attended the quarterly meeting at Cloud's chapel.[52] I
.nd myself sweetly united to preachers and people. James Barton,[53] a
.blic speaker among *Friends*, bore his testimony that God was amongst

Saturday, 27. My intervals of time are employed in marking Baxter's
.ure for Church Divisions," for abridgment, which may some day see
.: light. My soul is drawn out to God to know whether I ought to go to
.rginia this winter, in order, if possible, to prevent the spreading of the
.: of division: I do not look for impulses or revelations—the voice of
.r brethren and concurrent circumstances will determine me in this
.atter. Harry[54] seems to be unwilling to go with me: I fear his speaking
. much to white people in the city has been, or will be, injurious; he has
.en flattered, and may be ruined.
Wilmington, Sunday, 28. I made an application to a discourse delivered
. another. At Newcastle many attended the word, while I enlarged on
.att. vii, 7.
Saturday, November 3. We had twelve preachers, and about one
.ousand people at quarterly meeting. This evening our quarterly meeting
.nference began. We scrutinized and dealt with fidelity one with the
.her. Nothing would satisfy the preachers but my consenting to go to
.rginia. There appear, at times, to be great movings among the people;
.it there seems to be a slackness of discipline among the preachers and
.em; this evil must be cured, or the work will be injured.
Monday, 12. For some days past I have been engaged in troublesome
.siness.
Saturday, 17. I am agitated in my mind: I want to be gone, for I am
.rsuaded my call for the present is to the south. I have often observed,
. others doubtless have, who have been similarly circumstanced, that the

[2] Cloud's Chapel, originally named for Robert Cloud who gave the ground for a
.; chapel, was changed to Bethel in 1799. It is now Chester-Bethel and is located in
.elaware just below the Pennsylvania state line on the state highway 261. Aaron Mat-
.1 was a trustee of the chapel in 1797. (Lednum, *op. cit.*, Intro., xv, xvi, and 58;
.*laware, a Guide to the First State*, 421.)
[53] See *Journal* entry for April 11, 1776.
[54] "Black Harry" Hosier, preacher and traveling companion of Asbury, Whatcoat,
.ke, and Freeborn Garrettson, later became a drunkard but was reclaimed. He died
. Philadelphia in 1810 and was buried in Kensington. (See William Colbert's *Journal*;
.ke's *Journal*, 46, 47, 49, 91, 118, 149; *Journal* entry and note for June 29, 1780;
.dnum, *op. cit.*, 281, 282, 410, 411; Boehm, *op. cit.*, 89–92.)

peace of mind which the preparations for a journey necessarily distu
returns to the traveller on his way.

Thursday, 22. I set out for Virginia: my horse gave me the slip, so tl
I got no farther than Dover by Sunday.

Saturday, December 1. I have attended my appointments on the w.
and am now as far as my old friend Mr. Robert Thompson's, in Bohen
Manor. My mind has been kept in peace ever since I left brother Thom
White's: I felt the pain of parting with him at Dover; he has the most r
affection for me of any man I ever met with. The Lord show kindness
him and his, for all their kindness shown to me!

Maryland

Sunday, 2. I preached at Robert Thompson's; and in the evening visit
his brother, Ephraim Thompson, who was very sick.

Monday, 3. Crossed the Susquehanna, and came to Josias Dallam's.

Thursday, 6. Came to Baltimore. Here I received letters from Virgin
by which I learn that affairs are not so bad in Virginia as I feared: a f
of the local preachers have made some stir, and the travelling preache
have withdrawn from them and their adherents. I have spent some tir
in Baltimore with satisfaction, and could freely stay longer; but there m
be danger in these trading towns, and my way south seems to be open.

Virginia

Monday, 17. Set out for Virginia.

Wednesday, 19. Preached in Leesburg. From thence I travelled a
preached through Hanover and Gloucester circuits. I find the spirit
party among some of the people: the local preachers tell them of t
ordinances, and they catch at them like fish at a bait; but when they a
informed that they will have to give up the travelling preachers, I appr
hend they will not be so fond of their new plan; and if I judge right, t
last struggle of a yielding party will be made at the approaching conferen
to be held at the Manakintown.

Saturday, 29. Rode to Stedman's, in Gloucester circuit. This man w
once famous for racing: he is now a servant of the Lord Jesus Christ. T
old man wept when I described the tenderness of a soul when first unit
to Christ: he was awakened by the instrumentality of Mr. Jarratt; and
am persuaded there have been more souls convinced by his ministry, tha
by that of any other man in Virginia.

1782

782 *Asbury and his companion slept on the rocks in the mountains*

CHAPTER ELEVEN

Virginia

..esday, January 1, 1782. Having preached several times in the neigh-
rhood of the Old Church,[1] to very unfeeling congregations, I rode to
..ley's ferry, in order to cross York River, but was disappointed, the
..t being on the opposite side. We returned to the widow Chapman's,
..g unwilling to stay at the tavern, and had a congregation of sixty or
..nty people: we then rode about five miles to a ferry, and passed over
..ediately. Arrived at the other side, we found the small-pox and camp-
..r raging, and heard of several poor creatures, white and black, that
..died on the road. Ah! we little know what belongs to war, with all its
..n of evils; churches converted into hospitals and barracks, houses
..ged or burnt,—which last has been the sad fate of the palace at
..iamsburg.

..met with five or six faithful souls on our fast day, and the Lord was
..ent with us. There is considerable distress amongst our societies,
..sed by some of the local preachers, who are not satisfied unless they
..inister the ordinances without order or ordination, and the whole
..iit appears to be more or less tinctured with their spirit.

..esday, 8. I rode to Mr. Jarratt's, and found him, as usual, quite
..dly.

..)ld Church was an Established Church where Asbury preached several times. The
..e now used by the Methodists is a half mile southeast of Shanghai and is the
..pper church of Stratton Major Parish. This old church was burned at least once
..was completely rebuilt in 1850. For a time it was used as a school taught by Robert
..bs. (Mason: *Colonial Churches in Tidewater Virginia,* 298.)

Wednesday, 9. I rested with Mr. Jarratt.

Thursday, 10. Brothers McKendree and Foster met me at White
chapel, where Adam Cloud, one of our young preachers, was bapt
by Mr. Jarratt. We spent the evening comfortably. I find the party-
among our societies grow weak, and I am persuaded this division
cause the sincere, among preachers and people, to cleave closer to
trine and discipline, and may be the means of purging our societie
those who are corrupt in their principles.

Saturday, 12. I preached at Captain Smith's: the matter was good,
I had not much liberty in speaking. I feel that talking about anything
the things of God is improper for me, and out of my line. I am not so
and flaming with the love of God as I was some time ago: I feel resol
through grace, to keep near to God at all times. O how many things
lawful in themselves that yet are not expedient, and damp the pure
of God in the soul! I have these words often in my mind, "The chil
which thou shalt have after thou hast lost the other, shall say again in t.
ears, The place is too strait for me; give place to me that I may dw

Tuesday, 15. Preached at Ellis's chapel to a simple, loving people.

Wednesday, 16. I preached at the widow King's. About eighteen mo
ago I preached in this neighbourhood, and then thought the people
with a witness, all except one poor old Englishman: now there are a
faithful souls.

Sunday, 20. I preached at the great preaching house in Nansemond
uncommon openings in my mind. About twenty months past I preac
here, and was then in hopes of a revival; but evil-speaking and other th
have prevented. How do unskilful surgeons often put their patient
pain without profit!

Tuesday, 22. I preached at brother Moss's; a place the circuit preac
had quitted, because there were no hearers: this good purpose my tr
ling answers—to get a few to hear me who will not come to hear otl

Wednesday, 23. At Lane's chapel I enlarged on 2 Cor. vii, 1, and fo
it was what the brethren wanted: they are a loving people, and may
with any of our north-country Methodists. My soul is refreshed; a
bless the Lord for what he has done for this society. My friend War
who was fond of our preaching, and rode thirty miles with me in my
visit here, is gone in *Quietism*, and would not come to hear: how cha
able a creature is man! This was a day of fasting and humiliation with
In describing the filthiness of the flesh, I treated on those sins that a
the flesh, and committed by the members of the body; the filthines
the spirit, those sins to which devils are subject—such as pride, envy,
will, bitterness, &c.: to cleanse ourselves from these, every mean of
denial and spiritual mortification is necessary; it must be sought by f
and expected as a present salvation.

² See *Journal* entry for May 20, 1780.

hursday, 24. God is with me, and has all my heart: I am not sensible
anything contrary to humble, thankful, constant love to God; pitying
e to poor sinners; and melting, sympathetic love for the dear ministers
1 people of God, wherever I meet them. I found great fellowship with
pious family of Davis, especially with Henry Davis, who, I trust, is
1 Israelite indeed, in whom there is no guile."

had about fifty hearers at ——, among whom were some high Cal-
ists: Mr. McKendree took my text to preach from, "The grace of God
t bringeth salvation, hath appeared unto all men."

riday, 25. I had a comfortable meeting with my old friends at R.
es's, and trust the word was felt among the people.

Saturday, 26. I had a large congregation at Richardson's, where the
rd has lately been at work. I met a class, and found many earnest seekers
salvation: the poor mourners came again at night, to whom I applied
zekiah's experience, at which all appeared deeply affected; they wept,
ked together, and seemed loath to leave the place.

Sunday, 27. I had a large, solemn congregation at Mabry's chapel. I
st the work revives in the souls of these people. I lodged with my old
nd, J. Mabry, who gave me the following account of the death of his
ighter, F. Mabry, who for some years past appeared to live the life of
h. In August last she was taken ill: when at the point of death, the
rd cut short his work in her soul, cleansing her heart; she testified what
d had done for her with great power, her language surprising all who
e present; she appeared to be kept alive one whole day almost miracu-
sly: her father said, he thought *the power of God was so strongly upon
, that she could not die.*

uesday, 29. I rode to Roses Creek; this is the coldest day I have yet
in Virginia. Mr. ——, who had lately lost his wife, desired me to
ach in his house, which I did to about fifty people. I spent the evening
h Freeborn Garrettson, and Enoch Matson, at T. Rivers's.

Wednesday, 30. I saw brother E. Dromgoole; he is very weak in body,
steady to old Methodism; I feel a great desire that he may travel again.

hursday, 31. I preached at Wolsey's barn, on "Where is the blessedness
spake of?" From thence rode to O. Myrick's.

riday, February 1. Brother S. Yeargan gave me an account of a light
former wife saw, whilst at prayer one day in a little thicket below the
ise; she said the light shone all around her, "above the brightness of
sun." This remarkable circumstance she had resolved not to com-
nicate even to her husband: on more mature reflection, however, she
ught it most proper to tell him; he observed to her, "Perhaps you will
soon,—are you willing?" "Yes," was her reply; but at the same time
ressed her fears of a long illness, "which," said she, "will burden the
ily:" within two weeks from this she died. She was my kind nurse the
time I was in Virginia; and she is the third woman of my former kind

friends, that I have heard of, who has died in the Lord during my absen
Blessed be the Lord for the great things he has done! After preaching t
few small congregations, on

Thursday, 7. I rode sixteen miles, and preached to a large assembl
of people at Isham Tatum's,[3] on the "great salvation." Though I am of
in haste, and straitened for want of time, I have gone through Mr. Wesle
third volume once, and am going through it again. I make it a rule
spend an hour, morning and evening, in meditation, and in prayer for
the circuits, societies, and preachers. I expect to see the work of C
revive in these parts, so soon as the spirit of disputation is cast
Blessed be God, I enjoy good health of body and peace of mind! I f
no preaching does good, but that which properly presses the use of
means, and urges holiness of heart; these points I am determined to k
close to in all my sermons.

Saturday, 9. We rode twenty-five miles up Meherrin,[4] and missing
way, did not reach the place until three o'clock: the people, meantime, I
waited for us, and I spoke to them on Luke xix, 10; I trust not in vain
this country I have to lodge half my nights in lofts, where light may
seen through a hundred places; and it may be, the cold wind at the sa
time blowing through as many: but through mercy I am kept from murm
ing, and bear it with thankfulness, expecting ere long to have be
entertainment—a heavenly and eternal rest.

Monday, 11. I rode to J. Martin's, Briery Creek,[5] and preached
nearly one hundred people from Acts xxvi, 18. After preaching I had so
conversation with Mr. McRoberts, who was formerly a clergyman of
Episcopal Church, but he is now set out on an Independent plan: altho
he has his peculiarities, I admire his candour as a Christian; his plan
fail, and his zeal may cool—if indeed that is not already observable.
McRoberts charged Mr. Wesley with inconsistency in some things,
disapproved of his sending what preachers he thought fit to any place
people. I observed, in reply, that Mr. Wesley did nothing without cons
ing the preachers; that he was no spiritual tyrant. Mr. McRoberts t
care to let me know that he did not believe that any one could finally
from grace: I felt great love to the man, and was pained that we had
agree to disagree.

Tuesday, 12. We rode to *solid* Robert Martin's, on Appomattox Ri
Brother Martin appears to be a man of piety—a professor of sanctificat
He informed me of the remarkable conversion of Captain Wood,
officer of the continental line: he was taken at the capture of Charlesto

---

[3] Lednum, *op. cit.*, 382.

[4] The Meherrin River comes down from Lunenburg County into Brunswick. As
was well up in Virginia.

[5] Briery Creek is in Prince Edward County at the upper end of the Meherrin Rive
flows into Briery River and on into Appomattox River. (See Virginia map, 1820.)

the British; obtaining a parole, he returned home to Prince Edward,—
e it was that he was convinced of sin. While labouring under deep
ress of soul he made frequent attempts to destroy himself, and would
'er no one to come near him but brother M.; at length the Lord set him
iberty; and he is now a serious man, and appears to be much devoted
God.

Wednesday, 13. I preached at S. Jones's, and was much led out on
n. xiii, 11. I enjoy peace from morning to night: was it only for what
el that I travelled and preached, my labours to myself would not be
, but I shall do good; God will not suffer the *word* he gives me to fall
he ground; it will be blessed to preachers and people. Bless the Lord,
ny soul, and all that is within me, forever and ever!

aturday and *Sunday*, 16, 17. Preached at Col. Bedford's, in Charlotte
nty: many appeared to be quickened and restored to the grace of God.

Monday, 18. Preached with pleasure and delight at Mr. Almond's on
"Almost Christian." While brother Ellis was exhorting, the congrega-
a was alarmed with the cry of fire, which had kindled in a house ading: willing hearts and ready hands sufficed to save the furniture and
ost every article of value from the destructive flames; but the house
t first took fire, and the dwelling-house, with a connecting piazza,
e consumed. We left this scene of awful solemnity and alarm, and rode
brother Crowder's for our dinners, which we needed, having ridden
nty-five miles since we took any refreshment.

uesday, 19. I preached to a mixed multitude, with great comfort, on
os. i, 27, 28, and hope the people will remember it. I praise the Lord
uninterrupted communion with him.

Wednesday, 20. I crossed the Dan and Staunton rivers, and came to
—s, poor and worthy people: the woman professes sanctification, and
man appears to be much given up to God. I had uncommon enlarge-
nt of spirit in speaking on Mark xi, 24.

Thursday, 21. I am filled with love from day to day. O bless the Lord
the constant communion I enjoy with him! Sanctification is the doc-
e which is most wanted to be preached among the people here, whom
more I know the more I love: Antinomians are labouring to spread
ir tenets among them; but they will give way, as holiness of heart and
is pointedly enforced and pressed home upon their consciences. This
ne best antidote to the poison.

unday, 24. I always find the Lord present when I go to the throne of
ce. O that the Lord may keep me from moment to moment! I received
tter from J. W., a faithful youth that bids fair to make a great man of
d, and a useful preacher of the Gospel. I began to fear I should have
one to travel with me, and pilot me in this strange land, when provi-
tially brother John Coleman[6] met me. I find my greatest trials to arise

[6] *Minutes*, 1782.

from "taking thought:" it is by this Satan trys to come in: it is
constitutional weakness to be gloomy and dejected; the work of God ⌐
life into me—and why despond? the land is before us, and nothing ⌐
hurt us but divisions among ourselves.

I preached the funeral sermon of Philip Adams, one of our preach⌐
He died last March. This duty I performed the more cheerfully believ⌐
that such would have been his choice had I been within reach at the t⌐
of his death. My subject was 1 Kings xiii, 30. P. A. was a man of gr⌐
and his gifts increased; he was steady, and closely attached to the doct⌐
and discipline of the Methodists: he died happy in the Lord, and I do⌐
not but that he has gone where the wicked cease from troubling, and ⌐
weary are at rest.

Sunday, March 3. I preached the funeral sermon of Mrs. Harrison,
wife of T. Harrison, on Dan River.[7] Although there was snow on ⌐
ground, many people attended; to whom I spoke on 1 Cor. xv, 57, ⌐
Mr. Harrison appears to be deeply distressed at the loss of his wife; I h⌐
it will terminate in a concern for his own soul. He offered me a large ⌐
ward for my services—money is not my object. I have great affection fo⌐
Kennon, one of the most sensible Calvinists in these parts: he ackn⌐
ledges he found his religion among the Methodists; his system he borro⌐
from Witsius. Fletcher has cured him of the disease of disputation; ⌐
reads him with delight even while he is prostrating the pillars aga⌐
which he leans.

Tuesday, 5. I enjoy great peace: my soul resteth in God from da⌐
day, and from moment to moment.

Saturday, 9. I have had hard work, but the Lord supports me, and d⌐
keeps me in his love; this bears up my spirit under all the usage and fati⌐
I undergo. Notice is taken here of a preacher's words and actions; ⌐
must therefore be cautious, and not lay a stumbling-block before ⌐
weak: it is my duty to labour for God and souls without a complai⌐
word.

North Carolina

Tuesday, 12. I have been much tried this day two various ways; I ⌐
myself greatly humbled. This morning I poured out my soul to God in ⌐
granary, and was refreshed in my spirit. When we came to New H⌐
Creek we could not ford it; so I crossed on a log. Hitherto the Lord ⌐
helped me. I would not live always; neither would, of choice, know w⌐
is before me.

Sunday, 17. I preached with great liberty to a solemn, attentive peo⌐
I met society, and the people spoke freely. I am willing to travel ⌐

[7] There is a Harrison Cross Roads near Dan River in Rockingham County, N⌐
Carolina. Harrisons and Kennons are also shown in Virginia. (*Heads of Families*⌐

ach as long as I live; and I hope I shall not live long after I am unable
ravel.

obtained the promise of brothers P. Bruce and O'Kelly to join heartily
ur connexion. I feel much led out in spirit for the preachers who are
meet in conference, that we may all be united together in love and
ce, and firm resolves to carry on the work which God hath called us to.
unday, 24. At Kimbrough I preached to a large congregation, but I
afraid the word preached will not profit them. I spoke warmly for
ut an hour; there came on a rain, and the people appeared to be more
id of their saddles being wet than their souls being lost.
Vednesday, 27. I preached to about one hundred people at the Taber-
le, on Deut. xxxiii, 29. I trust there is more of the life of God here now
a when I was here last.
hursday, 28. I have felt much this day from the coldness of the weather
ut no matter. Brother Henry Ogburn met me again: I am generally
t with the preachers; when one leaves me another meets me, and my
enjoys God as a satisfying portion.

Virginia

unday, *April* 7. I preached at Roanoak chapel on, "I have somewhat
inst thee, because thou hast left thy first love," &c.; it may be for the
time. I hasted on to preach a funeral sermon at brother John Seward's,[8]
1e interment of a young woman who had been a member of our society
ut five years; she died suddenly, and I trust rests from her labours.
riday, 12. I preached at the widow F——s, on "Work out your own
ation with fear and trembling." We rode to J. Keese's to be ready for
rterly meeting, to be held next day at White Oak chapel.
aturday, 13. We met Mr. Jarratt, but he had such a cold he refused to
ach. I spoke on "the children thou shalt have after thou hast lost thy
rs," &c. We had a love feast at four o'clock in the evening: it was
y a gracious season—many spoke freely and feelingly of the goodness
iod.
unday, 14. I preached at the chapel;[9] and we then went to church. I
l the lessons of Mr. Jarratt, who preached a great sermon on union
love, from the 123d Psalm: we received the sacrament, and afterward
t home with Mr. Jarratt, that we might accompany him to our con-
nce. I have been much tried, inwardly and outwardly. I have been
oly and solemnly engaged in public, in families, and more especially
rivate, for a blessing on the people, and for union and strength among
preachers at our approaching conference.

ohn Seward lived in Brunswick County, Virginia. (See marriage records of Bruns-
County.)
Vhite Oak Chapel, Dinwiddie County. (See *Journal* entry for June 2, 1780.)

Tuesday, 16. We set out; and on the next day (17th) reached Ell
at whose house we held a conference. The people flocked together
preaching: Mr. Jarratt gave us a profitable discourse on the 14th cha
of Hosea. In the evening the preachers met in conference: as there
been much distress felt by those of them of Virginia, relative to the
ministration of the ordinances, I proposed to such as were so dispo
to enter into a written agreement to cleave to the old plan in which we
been so greatly blessed, that we might have the greater confidenc
each other, and know on whom to depend: this instrument was sig
by the greater part of the preachers without hesitation. Next morni
preached on Phil. ii, 1–5. I had liberty, and it pleased God to set it ho
one of the preachers, James Haw, who had his difficulties, was deliv
from them all; and with the exception of one, all the signatures of
preachers present were obtained. We received seven into connexion,
four remained on trial. At noon, Mr. Jarratt spoke on the union of
attributes.

Friday, 19. We amicably settled our business and closed our confere
Mr. Jarratt preached on, "A man shall be as a hiding-place from
wind, and a covert from the tempest," &c. We had a love feast—the po
of God was manifested in a most extraordinary manner—preachers
people wept, believed, loved, and obeyed.

Saturday, 20. We rode upwards of thirty miles to Captain Smit
without eating or drinking.

Sunday, 21. Held quarterly meeting at Boisseau's[10] chapel: the glor
strangely departed here. I preached with liberty on, "They that sov
tears, shall reap in joy:" from thence I hasted to Mr. Jarratt's barn, wl
the people were waiting, to whom I enlarged on James iv, 7–10.
Jarratt seemed all life, and determined to spend himself in the worl
God, and visit what circuits he could.

I am persuaded the separation of some from our original plan ab
the ordinances will, upon the whole, have a tendency to unite the b
together, and to make preachers and people abide wherein they are cal
I feel abundant cause to praise God for what he has done.

Monday, 22. I rode thirty miles to brother Finney's, in Amelia, with
any refreshment. I have constant peace, and my soul enjoys more c
than heretofore; some pain, indeed, was felt in parting with my Virg
brethren, as though I had left something valuable behind me.

Thursday, 25. I rode forty-three miles in order to reach Fluvanna
cuit; and next day preached at the Broken Back Church.

Tuesday, 30. Rode to Doctor Hopkins's and preached with liberty f
Psalm cxlv, 17–19. I hope our meeting was not in vain. Lord, preach
word, by thy holy Spirit—let me not travel and spend my strength
naught—and thine shall be the glory!

[10] Boisseau's is the same as Boushell's. (Lednum, *op. cit.*, 140.)

Lord's day, May 5. I preached with freedom on the parable of the
ver, at brother H. Fry's, in Culpepper county[11]—he professeth sanctifi-
ion. I find many of the people and some of the local preachers quite
rm about the ordinances, on which subject there is much disputation:
ssed be God! in the midst of it all I have quiet and patience, and hope
rtly to get into a more peaceable clime—my face is to the north.
Friday, 10. I preached at Culpepper court house—the people were
ious and attentive. Here I heard the good news that Britain had ack-
wledged the Independence for which America has been contending—
y it be so! The Lord does what to him seemeth good.
Wednesday, 15. Our quarterly meeting began in Fairfax circuit. I
ached with but little consolation to my own soul: next day there was
ne move in the love feast—one sinner brought under conviction, and
backslider reclaimed.
Friday, 17. I set out with brother Garrettson, who has given up his
arating plan; the Lord has conquered him, and I hope that all who are
rthy will return.

Maryland

Monday, 20. A few of us began conference in Baltimore;[12] next day we
1 a full meeting: the preachers all signed the agreement proposed at the
ginia Conference, and there was a unanimous resolve to adhere to the
Methodist plan. We spent most of the day in examining the preachers.
had regular daily preaching: *Monday,* brother Reuben Ellis preached:
Tuesday, I spoke on 1 Tim. iv, 12.
Wednesday, 22. We had many things before us. Our printing plan was
pended for the present for want of funds.
Friday, 24. Was set apart for fasting and prayer: we had a love feast,
Lord was present; and all was well. The preachers in general were
isfied. I found myself burdened with labours and cares. We have now
y-nine travelling preachers; and eleven thousand seven hundred and
hty-five in society. Our young men are serious, and their gifts are
arged.
Saturday, 25. Rode to brother William Lynch's, to get quiet and rest
er so much haste, and bustle, and business. I want to be retired, to
swer my letters. I feel a great necessity of being more than ever given up
God: I hope he will yet do great things for us this year.
Saturday, June 1. I spent a considerable part of this week at Mr.

Asbury later says that Fry's was in Madison County, which was formed out of
pepper in 1792.
This conference decided unanimously to "choose Brother Asbury to act according
Mr. Wesley's original appointment, and preside over the American Conference and
whole work."

Gough's, in answering letters, in reading and retirement: I now return
Baltimore under a deep sense of the goodness of God.

Monday, 3. Set out for Calvert Circuit—preached on the way at W
River.[13] I spoke to about one hundred poor people, whom I exhorted
seek that they might *find*. After dinner I retired and sat down on a l
beside the water for nearly two hours, and had sweet communion wi
God. It is not the place, nor the posture of the body, that constitutes t
real worshipper; yet at proper times and convenient places, it is good
kneel before the Lord our Maker. We came to Herring Bay,[14] and then
went to a place formerly called Hell-Corner, and thus named because
the desperate wickedness of the people; yet even here hath God broug
many poor souls to the knowledge of himself.

Thursday, 6. Rose at four o'clock, and spent an hour in private. Ro
through the heat sixteen miles to Childs's barn[15]—where I spoke on 2 C
iv, 16; and where God has already wrought on the hearts of many, brin
ing them to the knowledge of the truth.

Friday, 7. We have a pleasant rain after great heat and drought; f
which we have cause to praise God.

Saturday, 8. There was an extraordinary hail near this place a few da
ago.

Sunday, 9. Rose in peace. My soul is solidly given up to God, althou
I am sorely tempted.

Friday, 14. I had many of the rich to hear, to whom I spoke on Jo
vii, 17. In the course of my preaching I was led to strike at Deism:
learned afterward that Doctor ——, a professed Deist, was present.
love these poor people, and I believe some of them love me: I hope t
time to favour them will yet come.

Virginia

Saturday, 22. I preached at Leesburg; and again on *Sunday* afternoo
I fear to little purpose. God be merciful to these people! I must now r
tire—my morning and evening hour is as my daily bread.

Wednesday, 26. Rode to S——'s under the Blue Ridge—neither t
place comfortable nor the people lively—I believe but few of the heare
understood me.

[13] West River is a branch of Chesapeake Bay in Anne Arundel County.

[14] On Herring Bay near the present Friendship, Anne Arundel County, lived sever
Methodist families, including those of David and William Weems.

[15] This was the home of Gabriel Childs, its site variously identified, but probab
near Mount Harmony in the northern part of Calvert County. When Nelson Re
was on the Calvert Circuit, he had "business with Mr. Childs about some ground for
preaching house." Coke states that when he and Childs left the latter's home for M
David Weems's, "we reached his house by dinner time." This seems to agree with t
distance of sixteen miles given by Asbury. (Coke, *op. cit.*, 229.)

I have read the lives of Mr. Gilpin and Mr. Latimer, and took good
ed of the life of Mr. Brainerd.[16] I admire their spirit, writing, and speak-
g; there is something in them all so Methodistical.
I find it difficult to get time, strength, and place for retirement; never-
eless, I do not neglect it.

West Virginia

From S——'s[17] we crossed the ridge to Hite's, where we rested and were
mforted.
We crossed the mountain at the Gap, near my bed where I slept last
mmer,[18] and riding up the North River made our journey near twenty
iles: when we came there, we found that the people had gone to bury
ir old friend S——;[19] so that we had seven miles farther to go: arriving,
: found them handing about their stink-pots of mulled whisky. We have,
it unfrequently, to lodge in the same room with the family, the houses
iving but the one room, so that necessity compels us to seek retirement
the woods; this, with the nightly *disagreeables* of bugs to annoy us,
ows the necessity of crying to the Lord for patience: in the midst of all,
hank God, I enjoy peace of mind. O how many thousands of poor souls
ive we to seek out in the wilds of America, who are but one remove from
e Indians in the comforts of civilized society, and considering that they
ive the Bible in their hands, comparatively worse in their morals than
e savages themselves: the want of religion among them arises, I appre-
nd, from the badness of their own hearts, and from their hearing cor-
.pt doctrines.
Saturday, July 6. We crossed the great mountain,[20] and being obliged
walk down its opposite side, I was much fatigued: arriving at the widow

16 Mr. Gilpin was doubtless the Rev. Bernard Gilpin (1517–83), called the "Apostle
the North," who underwent persecution because of his defiance of Queen Mary.
sbury probably read the biography by George Carleton which was published in
nglish in 1629 and reprinted in Wordsworth's *Ecclesiastical Biography*, Vol. III, 4th
. (*Dictionary of National Biography*, VII, 1257–59.) Hugh Latimer (1485?–1555) was
e bishop of Worcester who was burned at the stake with Ridley. David Brainerd was
e noted missionary to the American Indians whose biography by Jonathan Edwards
is abridged and published by John Wesley in 1768.
17 S must have lived in the western edge of Loudoun County, Virginia, in the Fairfax
rcuit.
18 See note under July 16, 1781.   19 See note under July 1, 1781.
20 Asbury's exact movements between June 26 and July 6 cannot be traced. After
iving Hite's, near Charles Town, in present West Virginia, he went briefly into Clark
id Frederick counties, Virginia, returning to Hampshire County, West Virginia. He
ems to have continued up the North River and then up Lost River, crossing back into
irginia (probably Rockingham County), then into present West Virginia near Sugar
rove. The spot is memoralized by the Francis Asbury Memorial Church at Sugar
rove, Pendleton County, West Virginia. The "great mountain" is now known as the
reat North Mountain or the Shenandoah Mountains. Its crest divides the two states.

Susannah George's,[21] I preached on, "My spirit shall not always strive wi man:" I had been sorely tried in body and mind—I now spoke with deligl

Sunday, 7. In recrossing the mountain, on my way to Mill Creek,[2] was obliged to walk up and down its sides, and was greatly tired. I d livered a short discourse, with pleasure, to about three hundred peopl afterward brother John Hagerty spoke to them: it rained before and aft preaching, but held up while we worshipped by the side of the stream, f want of a house. After preaching, we rode to the Branch,[23] making *Sabbath-day's* journey of nearly forty miles.

Monday, 8. I am sick and weary—ah! how few are there who would n choose strangling rather than life and the labours we undergo, and t hardships and privations we are compelled to submit to! Blessed be Go we have hope beyond the grave!

Thursday, 11. At Patterson Creek[24] I struck at the root of Antinomia ism, while speaking at John Jones's;[25] certain sectarians were not w pleased at this: once in Christ and always safe—this is a favourite mors to some.

Friday, 12. Rode to the north Branch, crossed the Nobbly Mountain at its foot we stopped, ate a little bread, drank fine water, prayed, a then went forward to Joseph Cresaps.[27]

Maryland

I was pretty plain on Isaiah lv, 6, 7. Here Colonel Barrett[28] met me, a conducted me two miles up the Alleghany: we were riding until near t

[21] Susannah George was the widow of Matthew George, who lived on the Sou Fork of the South Branch. (See Will Book, II, 45, 181, Romney, West Virginia.)
[22] The mountain was Fork Mountain. (See note under June 20, 1781.)
[23] The former Berkeley Circuit was named South Branch Circuit this year, from t South Branch of the Potomac. This was around the present Petersburg, West Virgini (Lawrence Sherwood, art. in *Delta*, Buckhannon, West Virginia, May 19, 1953; nc under June 5, 1781.)
[24] Patterson Creek was the present Fort Ashby. (See note under June 11, 1781.)
[25] John Jones lived at present Fort Ashby in Mineral County, West Virginia. (De Book, I, 59; II, 152; XVI, 59, Romney Court House. See note under June 11, 1781.
[26] Nobbly Mountain begins west of Petersburg, West Virginia. Asbury went fro present Fort Ashby to Short Gap, over Nobbly, and to the North Branch near Cresa town, Maryland.
[27] Joseph Cresap (1755–1827) was a member of a prominent family and lived present Cresaptown, Maryland. He was married four times. He was a Revolutiona officer, a farmer, member of the Maryland senate, and a Methodist preacher. H grandfather, Thomas Cresap, laid out a part of the Braddock Road; and his unc Michael's widow married the Rev. John Jeremiah Jacob. (See the *History of t Cresaps*; also notes under June 6, 1781; June 30, 1784; and July 21, 1785.)
[28] Colonel Barrett lived on the Braddock Road near Frostburg, Maryland. Asbu visited him in Kentucky on September 22, 1805, and in Ohio on September 5, 1811, a referred to his death on September 20, 1811. (See *Journal* entries for those dates.)

clock, the road was dreary, and the night was dark: I wanted rest and
und it. We had nearly two hundred people to hear in this newly-settled
untry—they were attentive; and I hope God will do something for them.
fter preaching on John vii, 17, we set out on our return: I was much
tigued, and it rained hard; my poor horse, too, was so weak from the
ant of proper food, that he fell down with me twice; this hurt my feelings
ceedingly—more than any circumstance I met with in all my journey.

West Virginia

Sunday, 14. Was rainy—however, it cleared away time enough to get
Richard Williams's, on the south Branch. Brother Hagerty preached
a excellent discourse on, "He would have all men to be saved, and come
the knowledge of the truth;" after which, I spoke about forty minutes
1 Prov. i, 23–25. I am not so pious as I want to be; I pray much, but I
) not watch and pray enough: in the course of the labours of the day I
irpose to do it more. Since *Thursday* we have ridden sixty miles along
credibly bad roads, and our fare was not excellent. O what pay would
duce a man to go through wet and dry, and fatigue and suffering, as we
)?—souls are our hire.
Tuesday, 16. We proceeded along to great and little Capon, over rough
d stony roads.
Wednesday, 17. We went on through devious roads and arrived at
uess's: here I set on a scheme to prevent my horse from falling lame,
at had yesterday lost a shoe; it was to bind round his foot a piece of the
ck of a bull's hide; my contrivance answered the purpose well.
Thursday, 18. I preached at Stephen Harland's,[29] under the spreading
ees, on David's charge to Solomon. Thence rode on to Boydstone's,[30]
here we stayed one day, which afforded us the first leisure time since
[onday morning, we have had to sit down and write. I am at times greatly
ncerned, that there are no visible movings and instantaneous conversions
nong the people.

[29] Stephen Harland's was a preaching point in the South Branch Circuit near
arrardstown, Berkeley County, West Virginia. Harland and his brother lived near
edges Chapel; and Stephen Harland often accompanied Thomas Scott, who was on
e circuit in 1790–91, and often exhorted for him. (See Ayre's manuscript for Berkeley
rcuit, 1788–89.)
[30] Thomas and Benjamin Boydstone, brothers, lived close together three or four
iles from Shepherdstown, West Virginia. It was a noted Methodist family. One of the
ughters married the Rev. William Talbot; the wife of one of the brothers was the
ster of Mrs. John Hite, William and Benjamin Talbot, and the wife of the Rev. John
ttleton on the death of her first husband. Benjamin Boydstone later became a preacher.
ee the Thomas Scott and Robert Ayres manuscripts; Smith, *op. cit.,* 167; *Journal*
tries and notes under May 22, 1781; May 25, 1784; August 15, 1786; August 17,
02.)

Saturday, 20. Preached at Shepherdstown,[31] to about two hundr
people: from thence, crossing the Potomac, came to Woods's.[32]

Maryland

Sunday, 21. I preached to a large congregation of poor sinners, wl
appeared hard and ignorant. We went forward to Fredericktown, whe
I arrived much fatigued and unwell; yet I preached in the court house
six o'clock, on Luke xix, 41, 42.

Saturday, 27. Being unwell, I declined going to Baltimore, and went
Perry Hall, where I found my dear friend Thomas White. On the Sabba
day we read prayers in the family, and I preached in the afternoon on
Chron. xxxii, 24, 25.

Monday, 29. Closely employed in answering letters from various part
I find it hard to keep the power of religion; yet I feel that my soul is staye
upon God. I want to be moving on; if I rest a few days I am tried: blesse
be God, who thus embitters inactive quiescence to me. I am impelle
forward by my desires of comfort for myself, and sincere wishes to l
useful to the Church, and to the world of sinners.

Thursday, August 1. Preached at the Fork preaching house[33] to abov
one hundred people.

Pennsylvania

Monday, 12. Rode to Little York,[34] and dined with Mr. Otterbein[35] an
Mr. Magner.[36] I had many hearers in the German school house. This is
day which I ought to remember with gratitude: I borrowed a young mar
and as I rode along with my hands in my pockets, she blundered and fe
in the scuffle I had thoughts of throwing myself off, but did not; aft
some time she recovered, and I praised the Lord who had preserved m
in such imminent danger.

[31] Shepherdstown, originally called Mecklenburg, has been called the oldest town
present West Virginia. It was named for its founder, Thomas Shepherd. Methodis
met strong opposition here in the early period, and Asbury said no society was forme
or meeting house secured for thirty years. (See *Journal* entries for June 1, 1786, ar
August 17, 1802; Thomas Scott's manuscript.)

[32] Woods probably lived in Washington County, Maryland.

[33] The Fork preaching house was in Harford County, Maryland. (See *Journal* ent
and note for June 9, 1776.)

[34] "Little York" is generally used to distinguish York, Pennsylvania, from New Yor

[35] Phillip William Otterbein was pastor of the German Reformed Church in Yoi
from 1765 to 1774 and of the Second Evangelical Reformed Church of Baltimore fro
1774 to 1813.

[36] This was probably Daniel Wagner.

Monday, 19. I see God will work among Menonists, Dunkers, Presby-
ians, Lutherans, Episcopalians, Dutch, English, no matter; the cause
longs to God.

Sunday, 25. Rode ten miles to Benson's preaching house, where there
re, I suppose, nearly four hundred hearers collected; after preaching
re, at ten o'clock, I rode six miles farther, and preached to about five
ndred people at the Valley preaching house.

Tuesday, 27. After preaching to a small congregation of unengaged
arers, we rode to Philadelphia. What a noisy, disagreeable place! O
r something of that simplicity which dwelt among the dwellers in tents!
it the souls of the people are precious.

Sunday, September 1. We had a solemn, melting season at the love feast
the morning, most of the society present; we afterward went to St.
ul's,[37] heard a sermon preached by Mr. Magaw,[38] and received the
crament.

Monday, 2. Met the leaders and stewards to look into the temporal
fairs of the society. After dinner we rode to Burlington, nineteen miles,
d preached on "My Spirit shall not always strive with man."

New Jersey

Tuesday, 3. Rode to Trenton; the town in a great bustle with the court,
d the French troops. My subject was the Syrophenician woman: the
ngregation was large and serious. Ah, poor Gospel-hardened Trenton!
it a few have been converted of late.

Thursday, 5. I spoke with plainness to a multitude of people at Egbert's;[39]
me, probably, came to see us taken up by the magistracy. At night a
unken man applied to have his wife's name blotted from the class
per; anon came two more to demand our passes: we were threatened
ith desperate work in the morning, an attack on the road; we saw
:ither harm nor them.

[37] St. Paul's Church, Third Street below Walnut, was the third Church of England
ngregation in Philadelphia, organized in 1760. Those that preceded it were Christ
urch in 1695 and St. Peter's in 1753. St. Paul's is now used as the office of the Epis-
pal City Mission and is to be preserved as a shrine. (Barratt: *Outline of the History
Old St. Paul's Church.*)

[38] The Rev. Samuel Magaw, D.D., was rector of St. Paul's in 1781–1804. He served
Dover, Delaware, where he and Asbury were fast friends. (See *Journal* entry for
ay 13, 1805.)

[39] Nicholas Egbert lived at Readington (sometimes written "Reading"), Hunterdon
unty, New Jersey. He moved to that place from Staten Island, New York, about
60. Asbury's services in his home were the beginning of the Grove Methodist
urch in the Barley Sheaf section of Readington township. Asher Atkinson, an early
nvert, gave the land for the first church. (Snell: *History of Hunterdon and Somerset
unties*, 499, 519.) Ezekiel Cooper (*Beams of Light on Early Methodism*, 53, 54) and
hers following his lead confused Readington with Reading, Pennsylvania.

In Germantown[40] there came a gentleman of the committee and
amined our passes; he treated us with great politeness, and told us wl
the law required: brother Tunnell's pass was pronounced valid; but m
was not, because I had not the signatures of the proper authorities in
counties through which I had travelled: I pleaded ignorance of
necessity of this. Here appeared to be the secret—the mob had been af
brother Everett with clubs, and, it was supposed, under the connivar
of their superiors; they found, however, that he was qualified according
law: the work of God prospers, and, it is possible, this is the real cause
offence to unfriendly ministers.

Saturday, 7. Rested from public labours, and spent some time in rea
ing and writing.

Sunday, 8. Preached to a very gay congregation, consisting of four
five hundred people: there appears to be a prospect of good among them

The priests of all denominations, Dutch and English, appear to
much alarmed at our success; some oppose openly, others more secret
the Episcopal ministers are the most quiet; and some of these are friend

Saturday, 14. I came to New Mills after preaching at Hunt's[42] a
Penny Hill. I passed through Monmouth and Upper and Lower Fre
hold.[43] Here lived that old saint of God, William Tennent,[44] who went
his reward a few years ago.

Pennsylvania

Monday, 16. After preaching at Mount Holly to a crowded congreg
tion, I rode, very unwell and under deep exercises of mind, to Philadelph

[40] This was Germantown in Hunterdon County, New Jersey, the present Lebanc
Asbury doubtless preached in the home of Mindurt Farley and probably in that
Tunis Melick also. It seems that Melick, Major Godfrey Rinehart, and Mrs. Hen
Miller became Methodists, "creating a great uproar in the [Dutch] church." In 18
the society built a chapel on James Street. This was evidently the beginning of
New Germantown Methodist Church and probably also the origin of the Fairmont
Fox Hill Church. (Snell, *op. cit.*, 481, 482; Mott: *The First Century of Hunterdon Coun*
14, 15; Lednum, *op. cit.*, 331; *Journal* entry for July 6, 1806.)

[41] This service seems to have been in Hunterdon County in the vicinity of New Germa
town, Tewksbury, and Fairmont.

[42] Asbury probably preached at Hunt's in what is now Clinton, New Jersey, whe
an industry known as Hunt's Mills was located. He passed from Hunterdon into Mo
mouth County on his way from Clinton to New Mills.

[43] Freehold was also called Monmouth. It was the county seat of Monmouth Coun
and the scene of the Battle of Monmouth. Upper Freehold was fifteen miles fro
Freehold, and Lower Freehold was a township of the county. Englishtown and Fre
hold were post towns and still extant.

[44] The Rev. William Tennent (1705–77) was the noted pastor of Old Scots Chure
or the Tennent church for over forty-three years. He died in the old parsonage on Mare
8, 1777. His church, now over two hundred years old and one of the most famous
the region, is still in existence about three miles from Freehold. (Wainright, *et. a*

twenty miles. I have preached seventeen times, and ridden above two undred miles in the last two weeks. I think God will do great things in e Jerseys: the prospect is pleasing, East and West.[45]

Saturday, 21. I received two letters from Virginia which gave me great nsolation; the divisions there are much abated; the work revives: the eachers are in health and well received.

Sunday, 22. After preaching on the Christian graces, I visited Mr. . W——, who opened himself to me on matters of religion with free-m. I went to St. Paul's; and to my great surprise, in comes my old end Barton.[46] He was brought up a Churchman, and was awakened thout human means: observing that ministers and members in that urch were dead and careless, and finding some living testimonies 1ong Friends, he was induced to join them, and thus adhered, for twenty ars, becoming a public speaker among them. He is now jealous for the rd's ordinances; he says he could never fully give them up, and must w come to the Methodists.

Monday, 23. I began begging for the society, that we might, if possible, lieve our preaching house from the incumbrance of ground-rent. I on got about £270 subscribed.[47]

Tuesday, 24. I think the Pennsylvanians are, in general, as ignorant of al religion as any people I have been amongst: when the power is lost here the forms were never cherished, the downright ignorance of the athen, who have only heard of Christ, is the necessary consequence.

Delaware

Saturday, 28. Preached in Thoroughfare Neck[48] (twenty miles) and then turned to Joseph Wyatt's, and preached with liberty; thence I hastened . to Dover, and at six o'clock delivered my third discourse, making a urney of forty miles: we know not what we can do until we try.

Sunday, October 6. I preached in White's new chapel for the first time:[49] is one of the neatest country chapels the Methodists have on the whole ntinent. My subject was Haggai ii, 9: "In this place will I give peace."

Tuesday, 22. I have had large congregations in several counties of the

story of Monmouth County, II, 453–56; *Historic Roadsides in New Jersey*, 70; Myers: ry of New Jersey, II, 250.)

⁵ The reference is to the designation of East and West Jersey. There were two circuits.
⁶ See note under April 11, 1776.
⁷ This was for St. George's Church in Philadelphia.
⁸ Methodism began in Thoroughfare Neck, between Smyrna Creek and Appo-ineamink Creek, New Castle County, in 1779. On this visit Asbury may have preached the newly erected Friendship Chapel, made of cedar logs from New Jersey. (Lednum, *cit.*, 258, 351; Hallman, *op. cit.*, 121, 251.)
⁹ This chapel was erected in 1780 on the farm of Judge White, Mispillion Hundred, nt County. Although Asbury had raised an initial subscription for the chapel, he s preaching in it for the first time.

States of Delaware and Maryland, and have been humbled before tł
Lord that so many people should come to hear such a poor worm as
am; if any good has been done by my poor labours, to God the Lord l
all the glory. I am this day in Dorset circuit, and have preached for tł
first time to about three hundred hearers.

Saturday, 26. Quarterly meeting at Thomas Airey's;[50] the first day ha
about five hundred people, (though rainy,) and I had life, and light, an
liberty in speaking to them.

Lord's day, 27. We met at seven o'clock; the people spoke with gre
life and simplicity: at noon it was supposed there were not less than twel
hundred people, to whom I spoke with Divine aid from the latter part
the eighth chapter of Mark's Gospel. Attended quarterly meeting
Barratt's chapel. I was greatly afflicted in mind; I could not accompli
my plan, to send preachers to the backwoods, where they are great
wanting. I have been counselled not to leave the peninsula; this advice
shall not follow.

Saturday, November 16. I have been employed in making large extrac
from Baxter and Burroughs on Church Divisions:[51] I think every minist
and Christian ought to read these works.

Monday, December 2. My soul is kept in constant peace, and shall mal
her boast in the Lord under all her trials.

Virginia

Sunday, 8. Preached to a wild, hardened people at the Old Church, i
King and Queen county. In the evening spoke at Stedman's. My spir
has been clothed in sackcloth since my coming into this state; my hop
begin to revive.

Wednesday, 11. I rode to Williamsburg—formerly the seat of goveri
ment, but now removed to Richmond; thus the worldly glory is departe
from it; as to Divine glory, it never had any. I preached in James Ci
court house. The place has suffered and is suffering: the palace, the ba
racks, and some good dwelling-houses burnt. The capitol is no gre
building, and is going to ruin; the exterior of the college not splendid, ar
but few students; the Bedlam-house is desolate, but whether because no
are insane, or all are equally mad, it might, perhaps, be difficult to te

Sunday, 22. We had a solemn time at the great preaching house i
Nansemond county.

Tuesday, 24. I rode through Suffolk. Alas! for these *Oliverian* times-
most of the houses here, except the church, are destroyed, or more
less injured.

[50] Probably Thomas H. Airey, a relative of Henry Airey, who according to the 17
census of Dorchester County also resided near Cambridge, Maryland. (Brumbaug
Maryland Records, II, 109.)

[51] See *Journal* entry and note for November 23, 1780.

1783

1783

Asbury preaching on the courthouse steps at Williamsburg

CHAPTER TWELVE

Virginia

New-Year's day, 1783. I have passed through Gates, Hertford, Bertie, ɪd Northampton counties, in North Carolina: I am now in Southampton ɔunty, in Virginia, and have this day preached in St. Paul's.

Monday, 6. After preaching at H. Cutherall's[1] we rode twenty miles to raves's, where I met with Mr. Jarratt: on *Tuesday* he preached for me R. Jones's; I exhorted; the meeting was lively.

Tuesday, 14. Woolsey's barn; cold day; cold house; cold people: there ʌs been preaching here for seven years past, yet the society declines.

Friday, 24. At brother Holmes's, in Mecklenburg county. My soul ɔurns for the deadness of the people in our old circuits. We have great lls to South Carolina and Georgia.

Monday, 27. I preached, and the people seemed attentive; at present ere is a good prospect of success.

Saturday, February 1. Our quarterly meeting began in Mecklenburg rcuit. I hope God will favour us, and revive his work here.

Sunday, 2. I was very unwell. Brother —— held a love feast: at noon was much led out on Mark viii, 4. I am quite dissipated with company, ɪd greatly desire retirement.

Tuesday, 4. I offended some at Col. Bedford's—they could not bear the ɔughts of a possibility of falling from grace.

Friday, 7. Being unable to reach the quarterly meeting at Henley's, I ɔnsented to preach at brother Crowder's; God is my hope and my help

[1] Lednum, *op. cit.*, 185.

at all times. My soul is kept in peace; and O that I could yet sink deepe
into God from day to day!

Sunday, 9. Rose with a sense of the Divine presence. I am great
blessed in reading the latter part of Jeremiah's Lamentations, and Ezekiel
prophecy. I discover how the prophets, who spoke in different ages an
places of the kingdom of God, accord in sentiment and language: so it
now with the preachers of the Gospel. I had great comfort in preachin
at noon; and so I always have after severe trials.

Monday, 10. Being disappointed in crossing Roanoak on *Saturday,* w
tried again this morning, and getting into Pittsylvania circuit, after ridin
about forty miles, reached brother Martin's; I felt weary, more than
have done for months past.

Thursday, 13. Rode twenty-five miles, but my horse failing, (bad far
and no fodder for him,) we did not get in until two o'clock; the peopl
however, had waited: I was much led out in speaking, although very unwe
from fasting, walking, and the exercise of my mind.

North Carolina

Monday, 17. We proceeded to the Yadkin circuit.[2] It is well we are o
this side the Dan River, the late rains might else have prevented our goin
on for a season. On our route we passed through Salem, a Moravia
town,[3] well built after the German manner: every one appeared to be i
business. We lodged at Mr. Thomson's, a settler on the Moravian land
which is a tract of sixteen miles square: neither was the cabin comfortabl
or our host pleasing.

Sunday, March 2. Came to Short's; and preached to a number of pec
ple, who appeared solemn, while I enforced "My Spirit shall not alway
strive with man." We rode on to L——'s, lodged in a cabin; but the be
was clean.

Monday, 3. Cold as it was, we rode from Guilford to Caswell count
a distance of twenty miles, and met with a considerable congregatio
among whom were a few warm-hearted people: I hope the Lord will wor

[2] The Yadkin Circuit was formed in 1780 and embraced all the counties in Nor
Carolina west of Guilford.

[3] The Moravians came to North Carolina in 1753, and most of them settled in wh
is now Forsythe County. Salem was selected as their central settlement. The first hou
in Salem was completed in 1769, and as early as 1794 a school for boys. In 1802 a gir
school was opened, which soon became known as Salem Female Academy. (Grissor
op. cit., 23.) Woodmason says that the twelve-thousand-acre tract of land on which t
Moravians settled was originally a grant to George Whitefield and sold by him
Count Zinzendorf, a German Moravian. (Hooker: *The Carolina Backcountry on th
Eve of the Revolution,* 64, 77.) No evidence has been found, however, to substantia
this claim.

re. Here was a cabin with one room, a barn, and stables. I have little me to write or place to read: the barn is my closet for prayer.

Friday, 7. I had a large congregation at Hillsboro,[4] and there was ore attention and solemnity observable than formerly. I visited three oung men who are to die shortly; they wept while I talked and prayed ith them. I walked to the church: it was once an elegant building, and ill makes a good appearance at a distance, but within it is in ruins.[5] he calamities and destructive waste of war have been severely felt in ese parts.

Tuesday, 11. Preached at Wims's to about thirty people—one or two ithful souls among them. The son of Mr. Wims has been cured of a nfirmed dropsy, by the recipe of Mr. P., of Brunswick, Virginia, who s thought proper to keep his remedy secret. Would it be a wonder if od should render it unsuccessful, or that some judicial dispensation ould light on those who will not make generally known a discovery so seful? O what a distressed people have they been in these parts during e late contest! to the fightings without were added all the horrors of a vil war within. Poor brother B——t was twice robbed, and escaped with s life.

Saturday, 15. Preached to some Calvinistic professors, and sinners. he people are very careless, and professors are unfaithful: what have I ffered on account of these things!

Rode twenty-eight miles to H——'s;[6] O how this family is changed for e worse! Black and white now wicked. We got our horses and took our ave about an hour by sun, and came to sister Kimbrough's, where we und the family at prayer. We were wonderfully directed along a road I d never but once before trod: here my soul is blessed, my burden is gone.

Saturday, 22. I preached to a poor, unfeeling people, at a place the rcuit preachers had left. We were fortunate enough to eat about eleven 'clock; we got nothing more until about that hour next day; we pushed n to get to M——'s, arrived there at eight o'clock at night, there was no dder, no supper, no prayer. Next morning we started at sunrise, and ith difficulty getting over the river, came to Winstead's about ten clock: here we breakfasted.

Sunday, 23. I have peace. I was close and fervent in speaking at the idow T——'s. Hard times—we can scarcely get food for man or beast.

Wednesday, 26. I spoke at Green Hill's, to a proud and prayerless eople, many of whom were backsliders.

Friday, 28. By getting my feet damp, I have taken cold, and have had a

---

[4] Asbury had turned eastward and had entered the New Hope Circuit.

[5] This must have been an Anglican church as the Methodists had no house in Hills-oro at this time. On August 2, 1780, Asbury preached at the home of Mr. Cortney, a vern keeper, in the town. (See note under that date.)

[6] This may have been Abraham Hill's. (See *Journal* entry for July 19, 1780.)

return of my old complaint; an inflammation in my mouth and throat
could not eat flesh, and have little else to eat.

Saturday, 29. My throat growing worse, I was bled in the arm a
tongue, which gave me some relief.

Monday, 31. Preached at T.'s and P.'s, with some fervency: the wo
revives. While I am enabled to praise God for health and peace, I lame
that I am too apt to catch the spirit of the people I am among: I want
be more habitually serious.

Saturday, April 5. I heard the news that peace was confirmed betwe
England and America.[7] I had various exercises of mind on the occasio
it may cause great changes to take place amongst us; some for the bett
and some for the worse. It may make against the work of God: our preac
ers will be far more likely to settle in the world; and our people, by ge
ting into trade, and acquiring wealth, may drink into its spirit. Believi
the report to be true, I took some notice of it while I treated on Acts
36, at brother Clayton's, near Halifax, where they were firing their ca
nons, and rejoicing in their way, on the occasion. This day I prevail
with brother Dickins to go to New York,[8] where I expect him to be f
more useful than in his present station.

Virginia

Thursday, 17. Quarterly meeting at White Oak chapel; next day (Goc
Friday) Mr. Jarratt preached and administered the sacrament. After I ha
preached on Peter iii, 18, J. Cromwell spake very pointedly at C.'s, a
apostate: he came with great assurance to the door, as if he had a min
to say or do something; but J. Cromwell called him "factor for the dev
full of all subtility"—and maintained his ground.

Monday, 21. Set out for Buckingham, to visit some who have bee
separated from us on account of ordinances, and my spirit was refreshe
among them. Preached at brother Baker's, to a kind and tender peopl
Brother Agee of this neighbourhood had a child of ten years of age, th
found the Lord in a gust of thunder and lightning, and straightwa
preached to all the family: at the same time, a poor backslider was cu

---

[7] This was doubtless a report of the provisional treaty of November 30, 1782. Th
final treaty was signed at Paris on September 3, 1783.

[8] See note under June 18, 1780. During the Revolutionary War, New York wa
occupied by the British and dropped from the list of appointments after 1777. This le
some historians to declare that the work ceased and Wesley Chapel was occupied by th
British army. (See Bangs, *op. cit.*, I, 119.) This was not the case. The work continue
throughout the war under the leadership of James Dempster, Daniel Ruff, Samu
Spragg, and John Mann, a local preacher. (*John Street Records*, I; Wakeley, *op. ci*
260–98; Seaman, *op. cit.*, 72 ff.) On Asbury's appointment John Dickins proceeded a
once to New York and took charge of the society.

the heart; he thought himself to be dying, and cried out against the
ctrine of not falling from grace as the means of his fall, and warned
ose about him of those destructive principles.

After long rides through Fluvanna and Orange circuits, I came to
tersburg on *Monday*, the *fifth of May*; and the next day to Ellis's
apel.

Wednesday, 7. Our conference began at this place. Some young labourers
re taken in to assist in spreading the Gospel, which greatly prospers in
e north. We all agreed in the spirit of African liberty, and strong testi-
onies were borne in its favour in our love feast; our affairs were con-
cted in love. From Petersburg I proceeded northward.

Thursday, 22. I enlarged on the fourteenth chapter of Hosea, at Adams's
urch; and fear the subject was nearly descriptive of the state of the
ople.

Maryland

On my way to Baltimore, I dined at Colonel Thomas Dorsey's. Here I
ve an exhortation: after reading the burial service over a child, I pro-
ded on to Baltimore.

Sunday, 25. Preached at town, and Point; and was assisted to be
rching.

Tuesday, 27. We began our conference[9] with what preachers were
sent. On *Wednesday*, we had a full assembly, which lasted until *Friday*.
had a love feast, and parted in peace.

Monday, June 2. Preached at Joshua Cromwell's, on my way to Cal-
t; thence rode on through dust and heat to Worthington's;[10] I found
old friends tender; here was a young woman in deep distress of mind,
casioned by the flight of a whip-poor-will close to her, which strangely
her to fear her end was nigh.

Rode to Mrs. Heneliss's—a few poor people and Negroes, and the
nister, Mr. Gates,[11] from Annapolis, attended: I was as close as I could
ll be. Mr. Gates and myself had some talk on religion; he is a polite
n.

went alone to the silent woods, and my soul was much melted in
ayer; entreating the Lord to go with me and preserve me through all
weary journeys.

This was the first meeting of a conference following the official announcement of
cessation of hostilities by Washington on April 19. (Lee: *Short History of the
thodists*, 84, 85.)

John Worthington and his wife Ann, a daughter of Nicholas Dorsey, resided in
Jessup-Fort Meade Junction of Howard County. For nearly a decade the Worthing-
home was open for preaching and quarterly meetings, but there is no evidence of
ury's being a guest there after June 8, 1783. (See *Journal* entry for that date.)

Thomas Gates, D.D., was rector of St. Ann's Church in Annapolis.

I had the pleasure of receiving a letter (with a sermon) from M
Ogden,[12] a man of piety, who, I trust, will be of great service to t
Methodist societies, and the cause of God in general.

Friday, 6. I rode to Gabriel Childs's; was close and pointed. Po
Childs was very kind. I admire the piety, prudence, and good sense of t
Misses Childs: since they have experienced religion, none of the gro
will employ them; their patrons, alarmed at the deep and graci
impressions apparent on the young minds of some of the scholars, wit
draw their children at once.

Sunday, 8. I have been well exercised, although I am not so weary a
expected: I have preached three times, and the weather is very warm
believe the more we do, the more we shall be enabled to do for God a
for our souls.

I visited sister R——y, sick of the putrid fever: I prayed with her, a
trusted God with my safety from infection. I went to John Worthington
but I beheld such cruelty to a Negro that I could not feel free to stay
called for my horse, delivered my own soul, and departed.

Sunday, 15. Rode to Bennett's chapel;[13] a pretty octagon house, bu
of logs: there was an insensible, but attentive people: I hope the time
favour them will come.

I had a comfortable time at John Willson's; they were kind beyo
measure. I visited the old gentleman, hoping he had done with disputatio
the subject of slavery being introduced, he acknowledged the wrong do
the blacks by taking them from their own country, but defended the rig
of holding them: our talk had well-nigh occasioned too much warmth.

West Virginia

Wednesday, 18. After preaching at Shepherdstown, I rode to Boydsto
and rested one day.

[12] Uzal Ogden (1744–1822) was elected the first bishop of New Jersey, his native sta
However, consent for his consecration was withheld by the General Assembly. This I
been attributed by some to his tendency to associate too much with evangelical religic
bodies. He encouraged the early Methodist leaders, as his letters to Asbury and Ran
indicate. (*The Methodist Magazine*, V, 424; VI, 28; *Dictionary of American Biograp.*
XIII, 643, 644.)

[13] Lednum (*op. cit.*, 377) may be in error in placing Bennett's and Willson's in t
Calvert Circuit. Asbury might have arrived in Montgomery County and preached in Su
Loaf Chapel, which he called Bennett's Chapel because it was near Bennett's Cro
or one of its trustees was John Bennett. In that case he was the guest of John Willse
son of Jonathan Willson, "the old gentleman." (Scharf: *History of Western Maryla*
I, 729; Martz, *op. cit.*, 7.) Or Asbury may have meant by Bennett's Chapel the me
ing house which later became the Tabernacle; it was "close to the big patuxent"
Anne Arundel County. (See Hartman: *History of of Methodism in Maryland, 17.*
1912, microfilm in Library of Congress; Records of Anne Arundel County, April
1783, liber NH No. 1, folio 323.)

Virginia

Saturday, 21. Preached to a few people in Winchester. For several days
st I have had to ride the whole day, and to preach without eating, until
e or six o'clock in the evening, except a little biscuit; this is hard work
man and horse: this, however, is not the worst—religion is greatly
nting in these parts. The inhabitants are much divided; made up, as
y are, of different nations, and speaking different languages, they agree
scarcely anything, except it be to sin against God.

West Virginia

July, 13. Preached at John Hite's at ten, at W. Hendrick's[14] at twelve,
d at Willis'[15] at four o'clock: all these were funeral discourses. Rachel
by[16] was a professor of religion: she dreamed that within three weeks
e should die of the smallpox; she thought she heard something strike on
top of the house like the nailing up of a coffin; she took it as a warning,
nt to prayer, was exceedingly happy, sickened, and died triumphantly.
Friday, 25. The weather has been uncommonly warm; I felt weak, yet
oke closely to a few people; thence I rode to Paup's, where I fell sick,
d became unfit for service. I went alone into the fields and poured out
soul to God.

Pennsylvania

Saturday and *Sunday*, 26, 27. Our quarterly meeting was held at
orley's,[17] near Little York: many spoke in our love feast with great
iplicity, and my spirit was refreshed among them.

[a] The Hendricks family lived about four miles from Shepherdstown and six miles
m John Hite's in present Jefferson County, West Virginia. The home was a Methodist
aching place. (See note under May 22, 1781; Scott and Ayres manuscripts.)
[b] In 1788, entry for August 15, Robert Ayres mentions the Widow Willis. Asbury
haps preached the funeral of her husband. The home was five miles from Boydstones
d five miles from Mrs. Margaret Strode on Opeguan Creek. (See entries and notes
der June 4, 1781, and July 18, 1782.)
[c] A family named Selbey lived in this area, but the identification is doubtful.
[d] James Worley, an Episcopalian, lived one mile west of York. On January 24, 1781,
hired man returning from Baltimore was caught in a snowstorm and compelled to
y at a tavern twelve miles from York. Worley learned of it and took a fresh team
orses to help him. While at the tavern that evening he heard Freeborn Garrettson
ach. As a result he became a Methodist, and a close friendship with Garrettson
eloped. The next day Mrs. Worley heard Garrettson preach in Daniel Wagner's
rman Reformed Church in York and was also converted to Methodism. Their home
ame the stopping place and often the preaching place of both Garrettson and Asbury.
e *Experience and Travels of Mr. Freeborn Garrettson*, 175–76; Prowell, *op. cit.*,
–11.)

Thursday, 31. Preached at Martin Boehm's[18] to many people.

Saturday, August 2. Indisposed and dejected. This is a barren land
religion, yet fruitful for everything else.

Monday, 4. Rose early to pour out my soul to God. I want to live
him, and for him; to be holy in heart, in life, and in conversation: thi
my mark, my prize, my all—to be, in my measure, like God.

Tuesday, 5. I preached on "It is a fearful thing to fall into the hands
the living God."

Having lately heard of the death of Isaac Rollins, and having had
intimate acquaintance with him for some years, I will here notice some
the circumstances of his life. He was born and brought up in Patap
Neck; and when grown up was uncommonly wicked. The Methodi
about this time, coming into those parts, he professed conviction a
conversion through their instrumentality: some time after this he beg
to speak in public; roughly, but I believed in sincerity. I took notice
him, and appointed him to travel on the eastern shore; there he did so
good and some harm: I then sent him to Pennsylvania; it was the sa
thing there. Eight years ago he was sent to Virginia: the first year he
much good; refusing, however, to take his appointment from conferen
he stayed about Brunswick, causing disaffection among the peop
whence sprung disorder: thence we removed him to Pittsylvania, where
was also useful; here he would not long remain, but went off to Jan
City. After a considerable time we received him again, although contra
to the advice of some who knew him better. About two years past he w
appointed to Pennsylvania: this appears to have placed him where
wished to be, and he presently set about making a party, enjoining secr
upon his followers; after one quarter he left us, and set up for hims
and he and his few adherents took from us the Forest chapel. He beg
now to be forsaken; and being too lazy to ride a circuit, took to baptiz
and begging, by way of subscription. There were many reports abo
him, which decency forbids to mention; which, nevertheless, were pro
ably true. From these scandalous imputations on his character, he felt
seems, the necessity of defending himself; and being at the Yellow Sprin
he was for some hours employed in having his defence written: he did
times drink freely, but whether he was in liquor while there, I know ne
so it was, that setting off on a mettlesome horse, he had not ridden ma
yards before he was thrown to the ground, and died on the spot. I h
said, "I think he cannot stay long," because he did pervert the right wa
of the Lord. To the Lord I leave him, desiring that his sad example m
be a warning to me and all preachers of the Gospel.

Saturday, 9. Our quarterly meeting begun in Philadelphia circuit, a
was well attended; our love feast was spiritual, and many spoke feeling

[18] Martin Boehm lived in Conestoga Township, Lancaster County, Pennsylvan
(See numerous references to Boehm and his son, Henry, throughout the *Journal*.)

he goodness of God. From the quarterly meeting I went to Hoffman's,[19] the Valley, where they are building us a new stone chapel: I spoke to m on 2 Chron. xv, 17.

Vednesday, 13. Preached at Fisher's[20] on my way, and in the evening ched the city of Philadelphia in lowness of spirits.

Saturday, 16. Visited the sick, and was a little refreshed. I have constant ce with God, and my heart is dead to every unlawful pursuit. The city ll in motion—stores full of goods, great trade going on; all things sper but religion.

Sunday, 17. Was a melting time to me and many others at our love-st. Brother Jacob Baker[21] (?) felt the power of God as soon as he came: had been engaged some days before; and so had I. O that all in the se had been so predisposed, surely it would have been a great time of Lord's power! I preached on 2 Thess. i, 6–8, striking a side-blow at Universalist system; I made one of our sisters sick for a day.

Friday, 22. I have ridden about one hundred miles since I left Phila-phia, and preached nine times: the weather is very warm, and the poor h complains; yet I bless God for health to drag along while so many seriously afflicted. My dear old friend, Mrs. Maddox, aged one dred and two last May, went into eternity about a month ago.

New York

Monday, 25. Set out for New York: arrived there, I found brother kins preaching.[22]

Vednesday, 27. I was close and searching; a few felt it—a little of the d old spirit yet prevails among these people. We had preaching

George Hoffman lived a mile south of the Valley preaching house and was the member of a regularly organized circuit in Chester County. (See *Journal* entries February 5, 1781; August 2, 1784.)

Asbury stopped at the Fisher home near Radnor. William C. Fisher, then a boy, ght Asbury's horse to him.

Jacob Baker was a wholesale dry-goods merchant who joined the Methodists in . He lived at 62 Front Street in Philadelphia and was a trustee of St. George's rch and president of the board of the Chartered Fund. (Lednum, *op. cit.*, 44. There possibility that the man was James Barton, mentioned on April 11, 1776, and where.)

See notes under July 5, 1780, and April 5, 1783. Asbury had not been in New York e November 28, 1774. John Dickins and his family occupied the small house on the Street property, which for the first time became the parsonage of a married cher. The house was carefully refurnished for him. The British still occupied the although evacuation had been ordered. By mutual consent there was a delay of ly four months during which numerous loyalists removed. Among these were Mann, Charles White, Philip Marchinton, and others from the John Street Society, went to Nova Scotia and established a society there. The trustees had a meeting eptember 16, 1783, for that purpose. (*John Street Records*, I; Seaman, *op. cit.*, 76 ff.)

generally morning and evening, and I trust the seed sown will not
be lost.

Sunday, 31. In the evening I thought it necessary to put them on
examination whether they were Christians or not. I spoke on 2 Cor. x
15.[23] I was very much led out; a power went forth, and I hope some r
good was done.

Monday, September 1. Left the city, and spent some time at I
Woglom's[24] (?) in reading the additional works of Mr. Fletcher.

Wednesday, 3. My soul is serene. I find it expedient to spend an h
in prayer for myself alone; and an hour each morning and evening for
the preachers and people.

New Jersey

Thursday, 11. At Mount Holly[25] I had more people than I expected.
Friday, I rode a long, barren way to the Forks of Egg Harbour.[26]

Sunday, 14. I injured myself by speaking too long and too loud. I r
seven miles, got wet, had poor lodgings, with plenty of mosquitoes; r
day, poorly as I was, I had to ride seventeen miles, and spoke while I I
a high fever on me. I laid me down on a plank—hard lodging this fo
sick man.

Tuesday, 16. Rode fifteen miles; could hardly preach: my subj
yesterday and to-day were, Paul to Titus ii, 2–12, and 1 Peter iv, 18.

Sunday, 21. I had a wild chase—first, to New Englandtown; but tl
minister had warned the people against hearing us:[27] thence to Cohanse
here Mr. Vantull had appointed to preach at the same hour, although
appointment had been given out some time before; arriving, howe
before him, I preached in the court house—and cleared out; those w
remained met with hard blows.

[23] There is no such verse. The text may have been 2 Cor. 13, 5.

[24] Asbury probably stayed with Abraham Woglom on the south shore of St
Island or with Mr. Ward on the east shore.

[25] Mount Holly is in Burlington County, New Jersey.

[26] Asbury was now in Atlantic County, where Egg Harbor City is located. As
doubtless preached in the old Presbyterian church, known as Clark's Mill Mee
House, in Port Republic. The Methodist church now there probably stems from Asbu
visit. The mileage indicates that the bishop also preached at Blackman's Meeting Ho
built by Presbyterians at Cedar Bridge where Zion's Methodist Church in Barga
town now stands. Methodism in both Bargainstown and Tuckahoe stems from Asbu
visit. (Heston's *Annals*, I, 180–85.)

[27] See Asbury's letter to Wesley dated September 20, 1783.

[28] New Englandtown was a village of Fairfield township, Cumberland, sout
Bridgetown. Cohansey was the present Bridgetown. There was a "free church
May's Landing in which Asbury may have preached in this ten-day preaching mis
in South Jersey. (Gordon: *Gazeteer of New Jersey*, 108, 197; *Story of the First Meth*
Church, Bridgeton, 4; Wilson: *The Jersey Shore*, I, 188.)

Monday, 22. In the evening at Salem;[29] a number of Friends attended,
1 were serious. Here a few of our scattered people have attempted to
ld a house of worship, but found themselves too weak to accomplish
they applied to some of the people, called Quakers, for assistance, who
scribed liberally; the matter was talked over, as I am informed, at
ir quarterly meeting; when it was objected, "that we spoke for hire;"
vas answered, "No—it was only for a passing support,"—so there was
sent given that *Friends* who were free to do it, might give.

Delaware

*assed through Philadelphia, and came on *Saturday*, the twenty-
enth, to Dover, where I preached at nine o'clock on the *Sabbath day*,
1 at Barratt's chapel at three o'clock.

Thursday, October 2. I preached at Queen Anne's chapel,[30] where a
siderable number attended, and where many profess religion.

Friday, 3. Preached at Anderson's,[31] in Kent county, to a large com-
1y, and was much assisted. Of late I have been greatly subject to
ection and gloominess of mind, which I have been ready to attribute
excessive exercise, and the drinking of tea and coffee: I mean to quit
use of these for a season, and see what effect this will produce.

Saturday, 11. I found some faithful people at brother Joseph Hartley's,
Talbot. Here I met with brother Garrettson, and heard him speak
h pleasure: we spent the evening together at Mr. Benson's[32] in reading,
iversation, and prayer.

Sunday, 12. We had about five hundred people at the Bay side.[33] I find
prejudices of the people in Talbot County grow weaker: and there is

Salem, New Jersey, was settled by the first English emigrants to West Jersey.
iiel Ruff introduced Methodism in 1774; and the first society was formed in the
se of John Murphy, a Presbyterian. Benjamin Abbott was converted and baptized
. Henry Ffirth and John McClaskey, who later became a preacher, were early con-
s; and Ffirth was one of the builders of the church here mentioned by Asbury.
ott formed a society at Quinton's Bridge, three miles from Salem, in the home of
jamin Weatherby in 1781 or 1782. (Atkinson, *op. cit.*, ch. xi.)

This was Dudley's Meeting House near Sudlersville. Because it so far surpassed
r local Methodist places of worship, some gave it the more dignified title, Queen
ie's Chapel. (Lednum, *op. cit.*, 379; Emory, *op. cit.*, 568–71.)

James Moat Anderson, M.D. (1752–1820), was educated at the University of
nburgh. He achieved a reputation enjoyed by few other people in the neighborhood
Chestertown, Maryland. He was conscientious and eminently pious, and in early
th he united with the Methodist Episcopal Church and wore the white lawned stock
broad-brimmed hat so characteristic of the leaders of that sect. (Cordell: *Medical
als of Maryland, 1799–1899*, 302: *The Methodist Magazine*, XI, 135.)

Brigadier-General Perry Benson, of the Maryland Line of the Continental Army,
d at St. Michaels, Maryland.

This was Bayside Chapel, near the present Wittman in Talbot County, Maryland.

some revival of religion among them. I preached on Heb. iii, 12–14. O
that was formerly full of pride and contempt for religion, ran to the b
while I was speaking, and lay there till after sermon. She went home si
I trust of a wounded conscience. I crossed the ferry to Cambridge.

Wednesday, 15. Met brothers Joseph Wyatt and Leroy Cole, at Jo
McKeel's, and our spirits were refreshed together. I am happy, thou
often something unwell. I have great liberty in preaching and in prayer
feel nothing contrary to love to God and all mankind. Bless the Lord,
my soul!

Thursday, 23. I enjoy much peace with God, although I am left to ser
alone. But God is with me. O healthful sickness, blessed pain, if the Lo
supports! I am now beside the Chesapeake Bay, here Calvert and Dors
lie opposite to each other; eight years ago, when going down the ba
little thought I of the great things God was about to do for both shor

Saturday, 25. Our quarterly meeting began at Kane's barn. Our lo
feast was large, powerful, and lively; we had very sensible tokens of t
goodness of God. Here is a blessed work of God among a people who we
once brutish and wicked.

Tuesday, 28. I had to hasten away to John Phoebus's, sixteen miles,
perform the funeral rites of William Wright,[34] a native of Ireland. I
began to preach about three years ago: last conference he was receiv
as a travelling preacher, and appointed to Annamessex circuit, where
laboured very faithfully. From the best accounts we are warranted
believing that he died happy in God. We had a solemn time at our mee
ing, and I hope the impressions made will be lasting. I want to feel a
live the holiness I preach to others; and this I might do, were I mo
diligent in watchfulness and prayer:—God will always help those who
all they can to help themselves.

Sunday, November 2. There were few at Captain Downing's when
began to speak, but before I had done preaching we had a considerab
company; thence we returned to Melvin's,[35] where I enforced Luke xi, 1
to a few people. The word was made a blessing to the woman of the hous
who went with us weeping to quarterly meeting. Our love feast was
life and power, although there were not so many and clear testimonies
in Dorset.

Riding leisurely to brother Farley's, I missed my road, and stopped
a poor man's house; so poor that the furniture within was not, perhap
worth twenty shillings; the woman listened to me with great attenti
while I spoke to her about her soul: after praying with her and h

---

[34] This was William Wright, the first American Methodist itinerant to die. The fa
that at the time no obituaries were printed in the conference *Minutes* accounts for t
meager information concerning him. (Hedges: *Crowned Victors*, 1.)

[35] This preaching place was established prior to 1780 by Charles Twyford. Melv
Chapel stood east of the Pocomoke River. (Hallman, *op. cit.*, 355.)

ildren, I pursued my journey. I bless God I have seen so much of rough
d smooth, that neither makes any impression on me; I know how to be
ased and how to abound.

I spoke at Mr. Bassett's, in Dover, to many people; thence rode on
the Crossroads.[36] Here a design had been formed to prevent my
eaching; and Mr. Bishop came, as I was told, to advise me to forbid
sistance; had he and another honestly discouraged those who had got
gether to interrupt preaching on a former occasion, resistance and for-
arance would have been equally unnecessary. I rode on through the rain
d darkness to Mr. Thompson's [Cecil County, Maryland].

Sunday, 23. Preached on Romans ii, 8–10, with some openings.

Tuesday, 25. I visited some families, and my soul was grieved at the
ckslidings of some of my old friends. O may the Lord reach their
arts!

Made a short stay in Baltimore, and preached at Elk Ridge on my way
Virginia. When we reached the Potomac, brother Phoebus[37] was un-
ling to cross; so we stayed at the public house without fire, candle, or
pper; and the host drunk. Next morning we crossed the river, and were
dly received at brother Bushby's.

Virginia

Friday, 28. Preached to a large congregation in the court house at
exandria. On my way to Fredericksburg I fell in with some gentlemen,
d conversed with them on the subject of religion; they sought refuge in
d's foreknowledge, and thence drew their proofs that their Creator
uld not eternally damn them.

Sunday, 30. Came to Collins's, in Caroline county, in time to escape the
n; but the people had no notice of my coming. I enjoy peace of soul.
ek nothing but God; and I feel uncommon tenderness for the people.

Thursday, December 4. I preached to about thirty people at old father
dman's, in King and Queen county, Gloucester circuit: myself and
people were blessed in waiting on God.

Sunday, 7. I went to Williamsburg, and found the people waiting: the
of the court house being lost, or mislaid, I stood without, and was
isted on Acts xvii, 30, 31. I feel some faith that God will call out a
ple in this place.

Thursday, 11. Went down to James River in hopes of getting an early

Georgetown Crossroads is the present Galena, Maryland. Asbury had been across
line in Delaware for the brief visit to Bassett's.

William Phoebus (1754–1831), a native of Somerset County, was admitted on trial
appointed to the Frederick Circuit. This eccentric but respected Methodist was
quarian, author, physician, and scholarly preacher. (Wakeley, *op. cit.,* 326–34;
ens, *op. cit.,* II, 114, 115; *Minutes,* 1832.)

passage across, but was detained till twelve o'clock. I spoke and pray
at Mrs. Ellis's: since I last prayed in her house, one of her children, a s
has died of a consumption; he would not allow himself to speak of worl
affairs on the Sabbath day; we have good cause to believe he died in
Lord; and doubtless there are hundreds whom we know not of, that t
go to God and rest from their labours.

After being detained by a storm on Craney Island, on

Thursday, December 18, set out, through a dripping rain, for Po
mouth; and reached there about one o'clock.

North Carolina

Saturday, 20. I spent the evening at Colonel Williams's,[38] in Curritu
county, North Carolina, in company with brothers Ivy, Baldwin, a
Morris.[39] The work revives; many are brought to God; and I am comfort

Sunday, 21. I suppose we had five hundred people at Coinjock chape
Monday at White's, and *Tuesday* at Winfield court house,[41] I presume
had six or seven hundred people, inattentive and wild enough: I had li
faith, and less liberty. From this neighbourhood I went to Nixonto
where numbers also attended; but I spoke with little comfort to mys
Spirituous liquor is, and will be, a curse to this people.

Wednesday, 24. Set out in the rain to Hertford[43] town; I spoke i
tavern; the people seemed wild and wicked altogether. I journeyed
through the damp weather, and reached Pettigrew's about six o'clock.

Here I received a letter from Mr. Wesley, in which he directs me to
as general assistant; and to receive no preachers from Europe that are
recommended by him, nor any in America, who will not submit to
and to the minutes of the conference.

[38] Colonel Halowell Williams was a prominent Methodist and a member of Cong
held at Halifax in 1776. He was the first man who entertained a Methodist preac
in North Carolina. Pilmoor visited him in 1772, and Coke was in his home in 1
(Grissom, *op. cit.,* 34–36, 148.)

[39] Richard Ivy was on the Nansemond Circuit, John Baldwin was at Norfolk,
Edward Morris was on the Bertie Circuit. (*Minutes,* 1783.)

[40] Coinjock Chapel was an Anglican church in Currituck County which was regul
used by the Methodists. Pilmoor preached there in 1772, and Coke preached ther
1785. Coke referred to it as a "pretty chapel" and remarked that "we do regular d
in it." The Methodists have never established permanent work at Coinjock, howe
(Grissom, *op. cit.,* 35.)

[41] Winfield Courthouse was two miles south of Elizabeth City in Pasquotank Cou
North Carolina. It was located there from about 1758 until the 1780's. The buil
said to have been the courthouse is now a residence.

[42] Nixonton was on Little River in Pasquotank County.

[43] Hertford was in Perquimans County.

preached in Edenton, to a gay, inattentive people: I was much pleased
h Mr. Pettigrew;[44] I heard him preach, and received the Lord's supper
is hands. Thence I crossed the Chowan river, and preached, journeying
ough Bertie, Hertford, and Northampton counties, to considerable
gregations.

Charles Pettigrew was the Anglican pastor at Edenton in Chowan County. He
rtained the circuit riders, and his chapel on his plantation was a regular Methodist
ching place and a point on the Columbia Circuit until 1839. Asbury doubtless
ched in his church, though the courthouse was sometimes used. The Methodist
ety was formed in 1808 by Enoch Jones. (Records of Edenton Methodist Church;
s Alma Browning.)

1784

1784

Coke and Asbury meet at Barratt's Chapel, with Whatcoat and Vasey

CHAPTER THIRTEEN

North Carolina

riday, January 2, 1784. Rode to Doctor P——'s. After preaching here,
w Henry Metcalf,[1] who travels through this circuit, a man of a sorrow-
spirit, and under constant heaviness.

Monday, 5. A few met me at Northampton court house; after preach-
we rode on through the rain, to brother Anthony Moore's, where I
warm, dry, and comfortable.

have read two volumes of Sermons written by Mr. Knox, of the West
ies. I am much pleased with his defence of revealed religion; and,
.ed, through the whole work there is something sublime and spiritual;
atholic too, and free from peculiar doctrines: I esteem him as one of
best writers amongst the Presbyterians I have yet met with.

Virginia

unday, 11. I had five hearers, beside the family; we then rode through
and snow to brother John Seward's.

Monday, 12. On my way to Isham Malone's my horse fell on the ice,
caught my leg under him: I had some bread in my great-coat side-
ket that was under me in my fall, which made it worse, and I hurt my

_____

lenry Metcalf was admitted to the conference in 1783, appointed to the Pasquo-
Circuit, and died in 1784. (*Minutes.*)

knee too: I had presence of mind, and prayed as I fell. The snow bei
deep saved me much from damage. I lament the love of the wor
covetousness, and other evils that lie heavy on the Church of God.

Tuesday, 13. I preached.

Thursday, 15. After preaching at Easter's, I rode to Tignall Jones's: I
wife has waded through deep waters. I have spent some time in Meckle
burg circuit; but such has been the weather that I have had but few heare
We tried to cross Staunton River at Owen's ferry, but could not for the i
we then had a long cold ride to Coles's ferry, and here we got over. V
lodged where we had nothing to eat or drink but a little toast and wat
I went shaking to bed as if I had an ague on me.

North Carolina

After riding some miles to Halifax court house, about ten o'clock
the morning I had some coffee for my breakfast.

Saturday, 31. Preached at a church, and held a love feast. My t
which has been inflamed for some time past, is now very troublesor
Sister Martin's kindness has been a plaster for all my sores.

Thursday, February 5. Rode to Guilford quarterly meeting;[2] then
twenty-five miles, to Short's; and thence to Madeira's; here my toe
came so bad, I was obliged to halt. I applied different poultices to ta
out the inflammation.

Wednesday, 11. I feel much better, and hope shortly to be able to
on the Lord's work again; this is my life, my all. During my confinem
I have been reading the sacred text.

Lord's day, 15. Lord, my soul thirsteth for holiness in myself and oth
I found my heart led out in prayer for those I cannot preach to. The Lo
is my witness, that if my whole body, yea, every hair of my head, co
labour and suffer, they should freely be given up for God and so
During my heavy affliction I could scarcely have met with a greater o
appointment than my being unable to go to the Yadkin,[3] but it might i
be to any great purpose; and Providence has hindered. By the help o
stick, I can now visit the barn and stable. The more I pray, Satan tem
the more—but this is according to custom. I hope to live the life of lo
and holiness below, triumphing over all my foes.

[2] Guilford Circuit was carved out of the New Hope Circuit in 1783. Its bounda
are uncertain; but it covered most of the area between Raleigh and Greensboro,
cluding Guilford County. The place of the quarterly meeting attended by Asbur
not known but was probably not as far west as Guilford Courthouse. (See Griss
op. cit., 97.)

[3] The Yadkin Circuit, which Asbury did not visit on this journey, covered the wl
of North Carolina west of Guilford County. It was formed in 1780 and first serve
Andrew Yeargin. (See *Minutes*; Grissom, *op. cit.*, map.)

Wednesday, 18. Being sent for, I went to Mr. Bostwick's (?), on Dan ver.[4] I have been engaged in reading Baxter's Saints' Rest;[5] and my ul was often drawn to God in secret prayer.

Sunday, 22. Preached at the funeral of Absalom Bostwick's daughter.

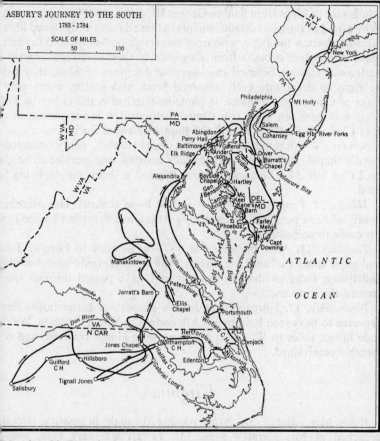

ASBURY'S JOURNEY TO THE SOUTH
1783 - 1784

SCALE OF MILES
0   50   100

Monday, 23. Preached twice: began to fear I should stop again—my foot elled, and my toe inflamed.

Tuesday, 24. Rode forty miles—next day preached to fifteen people.

Thursday, 26. Rode to Hillsboro. The snow was deep—the street ty—my horse sick—the people drinking and swearing. I endeavoured preach on "A man's gaining the whole world," &c.

This was probably in Rockingham County.
Richard Baxter (1615–91), one of the greatest of English theologians, wrote his ous *The Saints' Everlasting Rest* in 1650. John Wesley printed extracts from Baxter's *horisms of Justification* in 1745 and his *A Call to the Unconverted* in 1782.

Friday, 27. Brothers Allen and J. Cromwell[6] were with me: we to sweet counsel together, and refreshed each other's bowels in the Lord

Thursday, March 4. Preached at Browder's, and then hasted to the wid Kimbrough's. Here I was wonderfully entertained with a late publicati by Silas Mercer, a Baptist preacher, in which he has anathematized whole race of kings from Saul to George III. His is republicanism run m Why afraid of religious establishments in these days of enlightened liber Silas has beaten the Pope, who only on certain occasions, and for cert reasons, absolves subjects from allegiance to their sovereigns; and if nations of Europe believed the sweeping doctrines of Silas, they wo be right to decapitate every crowned head, and destroy every existi form of Church government. If plunging-baptism is the only true ord ance, and there can be no true Church without it, it is not quite clear t ever Christ had a Church until the Baptists *plunged* for it.

Sunday, 7. Although the day was unfavourable, many attended Pope's chapel, where I was wonderfully assisted, and enabled to be cl on 2 Cor. xiii, 5—a favourite subject. We had a short, simple, living l feast.

Monday, 8. I enlarged on Isa. lv, 6, 7, at Pope's chapel. This neighbo hood has been poisoned by preaching Antinomianism; but I hope it w yet come to something.

Thursday, 11. After preaching at S——'s, we rode to Long's.[7] I h had great times in Tar River circuit;[8] the congregations have been la and living, more so than in any circuit I have passed through sinc crossed the Potomac.

Wednesday, 17. I preached at Jones's chapel[9]—a better house tha expected to have seen built by the Methodists in North Carolina. We t rode fifteen miles to W——'s, where we were kindly received, and co fortably entertained.

Virginia

Wednesday, March 31. After passing through Brunswick circuit preached at Mr. Jarratt's barn. Mr. Jarratt was very kind, and people very attentive.

Sunday, April 4. Preached at Finney's old place, where I suppose th might be some that had hardly heard preaching since I was here

[6] Beverly Allen was on the Salisbury Circuit and James O. Cromwell on the Pitt vania Circuit.

[7] Long lived in Edgecomb County near the Halifax County line.

[8] Tar River Circuit lay east of the New Hope and stretched from near Raleigh thro the valleys of the Tar, Neuse, and Pamlico Rivers. (Grissom, *op. cit.*, map.)

[9] Jones lived in the western part of Halifax County. Jesse Lee preached his sermon in Jones's barn.

ır: thence I rode through Powhatan, Cumberland, and Buckingham
ınties, where there is poor encouragement for religion. O my Lord,
se for thine own glory, visit the people in mercy, and make known thy
wer in the salvation of poor sinners!

We crossed James river in a canoe; our horses by wading and swimming
t over. I found some people of feeling at T. Key's, to whom I preached
John iii, 19; thence we rode the river seventeen miles along a very
le, uneasy path, to preach to fifteen people. After getting a little cold
con, we rode on to Crenshaw's, where we fared better.

Sunday, 11. Preached at Granger's[10] church to perhaps five hundred
ople. From the church we rode on to Dr. Hopkins's. I could not see;
ling the hills and dales, we pushed on about thirty miles. We got in,
d and fatigued, about eleven o'clock. A drunken man we fell in with
ıducted us four or five miles. The labour of the day has been performed
'h little refreshment for either man or horse. Since yesterday week at
on, I have ridden one hundred and fifty-four miles in this rough country.
riving, through the woods, at Martin Key's,[11] I found a happy change
ce I was here last year—bless the Lord! I will take it as an answer to
ıyer. Now, the whole family are called together for worship—the
n is seeking, the woman has found the Lord, and the children are
ious.

Saturday, 17. Quarterly meeting at brother Fry's: a living power went
ough the people in our love feast. It was supposed the congregation
ısisted of nearly, or quite, seven hundred people. I hope the word was
led to some hearts. I do not love, live, or labour as I desire. O, my soul!
up thyself to take hold of the Lord by diligence and faith every
·ment.

Sunday, 25. I preached at the Manakintown on the Epistle to the
urch at Smyrna.

Monday, 26. Rode on to Walthall's, and thence to Petersburg, where we
ınd a house full at six o'clock. On Tuesday we reached Mabry's chapel
quarterly meeting, just as preaching was over.

Thursday, 29. Rode to Ellis' chapel, in Sussex county, where we held
· conference the two ensuing days. Brother O'Kelley gave us a good
mon: "I keep under my body, and bring it into subjection," &c. Mr.
ratt gave us a good discourse on 1 Tim. i, 4. Our business was con-
:ted with uncommon love and unity.

'rom this conference I proceeded on and crossed James River on my
y to the north, and was led to cry to God to go with us and meet us
re.

Asbury had been at Granger's, Hanover County, before and mentions Thomas
ınshaw. Bennett says that Granger's and Crenshaw's were the same place. Coke
ıched at Granger's in 1785. (See Lednum, *op. cit.*, 419.)
Martin Key lived in Amherst County.

Maryland

Thursday, May 20. Reached Baltimore about seven o'clock. I ha
ridden about fifty miles to-day. In crossing the Potomac, when abc
midway, we turned back to meet the stage, and I found Dr. Lusby
learned by letter that my father and mother are yet alive.

Tuesday, 25. Our conference began, all in peace. William Glendenni
had been devising a plan to lay me aside, or at least to abridge
powers.[12] Mr. Wesley's letter settled the point, and all was happy. T
conference rose on *Friday* morning.

I find the spirit and conversation of those I am among steal upon n
My soul is in travail to be holy in all manner of conversation and godline

It is amazing to behold how the ice, coming down the Potomac,
swept the banks, cutting through large trees, removing rocks of incredi
size, and smoothing the river banks, as though many hundreds of n
had been employed for that purpose.

I was solemn and blessed at Sharpsburg. A poor Irish woman, who h
treated the Methodists ill, was convicted, and sent for me to pray with h
God grant that the impressions made may be lasting!

Virginia—West Virginia

From Sharpsburg I hastened on to Shepherdstown, where the Lord
home his word. Came to sister Boydstone's, one of the kindest wom
in Virginia. Here all things were comfortable. I was sleepy, weary, a
feeble, but my body and soul were refreshed; thanks be to God for ev
friend! I covenanted with God to be more in prayer; my soul is humb
before the Lord.

Thursday, June 17. Lord, strengthen my resolution to be thine in he
more and more. Make, and keep me always watching unto prayer!

I preached at Martinsburg to a hundred people or more, and was
out while I enlarged on, "What is the Almighty that we should serve hin
&c. Thence to Stroud's at seven o'clock, and spoke with great plainne
the people stared upon us. Next morning we had all the workmen
prayer. The mother and two daughters appeared tender, and wept wh
we took our leave of them. Who knows what God may do for them?

Sunday, 20. I attempted to preach at Newtown.[13] I raged and threaten
the people, and was afraid it was spleen. I found, however, that N

[12] Wesley's letter of October 3, 1783, settled the devices of Mr. Glendenning. Wes
said: "I do not wish our American brethren to receive any (English preachers) w
make any difficulty on receiving Francis Asbury as the general assistant." The sessi
at Ellis's preaching house and at Baltimore in 1784 reiterated those sentiments with
latent implication that it applied to such troublemakers as Mr. Glendenning. (Bar
op. cit., I, 148, 149; *Minutes;* Ware, *op. cit.,* 83, 84.)

[13] Newtown was the present Stephens City in Virginia.

terbein,[14] a worthy German minister, had done the same a little time
'ore.

Friday, 25. We had hard work in crossing a mountain six miles over,
d it was still worse the next day in crossing the greater mountain.[15] I
ind it very warm work, though stripped. We struggled along neverthe-
s, and met with about four hundred people at Strader's,[16] to whom I
oke on 2 Cor. xiii, 5,—I hope not in vain. While I was at prayer, a
ge limb fell from a sycamore tree in the midst of the people, yet not one
-eived the least injury; some thought it was a trick of the devil; and so
leed it might have been. Perhaps he wanted to kill another, who spoke
er me with great power.[17]

Sunday, 27. At Hyder[18] I was much tried in spirit, yet I was enabled to
:ak pure, living truth, on Titus iii, 2–5, at three o'clock. I was assisted
speak feeling words to some souls at Isaac Van Meter's[19] though in pain
d weariness. Thence I hasted to preach at six o'clock at Conrad
offman's,[20] a third time this day, where I enlarged on Job xxi. 15. About
a o'clock at night I came to brother Samuel Dew's,[21] very weary, and
lged there. I hope this day's labour will be useful to my own soul and
: souls of others.

Monday, 28. Preached twice[22]—speaker and hearers too dull. Alas!

[4] The Rev. Philip William Otterbein was one of the founders of the United Brethren
urch. He assisted Coke in the ordination of Asbury at the Christmas Conference in
!4.

[5] These mountains were apparently the Great North and South Branch Mountains
Hardy County, West Virginia, on the Virginia border.

[6] Christopher, John, and Michael Strader lived in Hampshire County, Virginia,
.v either Grant or Hardy County, West Virginia. (Maxwell: *History of Randolph
unty, W. Va.*, 474.)

[7] This was perhaps Hezekiah Bonham, who accompanied Asbury on this tour. He
s a local preacher and a member of the first class established by Strawbridge in
iryland. (See *Minutes*, 1785; Payton, *op. cit.*, 22-23, 99; Armstrong: *History of the
l Baltimore Conference*, 7, 17.)

[3] This preaching place seems to have been the home of Adam Hyder (or Heider)
ir Morefield, West Virginia. (See *Journal* entry for August 10, 1790.) Robert Ayres
nuscript journal for February 23–March 23, 1788, lists the preaching place on the
eghany Circuit, and Hyder's seems to be the only point at which Asbury could have
ached and reached Dew's that night.

[9] Isaac Van Meter (1757–1837) lived at Old Fields, Hardy County, West Virginia.
 and his wife, Elizabeth, gave the land for an early Methodist meetinghouse in the
a. (Deed Book, XII, 340, Moorefield, West Virginia; Halterman: *History of Method-
: in the South Branch Valley*; Kercheval: *History of the Valley of Virginia*, 50, 55;
dnum, *op. cit.*, 314; *Journal* entry for August 10, 1790.)

[0] Conrad Hoffman lived near Old Fields, West Virginia.

[1] Samuel Dew at this time lived a few miles south of present Romney, West Virginia.
 later moved to Potts Creek in present Monroe County where he built Dew's Chapel.
e *Journal* entry for July 10, 1790, and May 28, 1793. Also Whatcoat's *Journal* for
ly 10–11, 1790.)

[2] Asbury probably preached at Samuel Dew's and Richard Williams'. (See note
der June 10, 1781, and entry for July 30, 1784.)

Tuesday, 29. Although my body is weak, my soul is filled with love God. He is my portion.

Maryland—Pennsylvania

Wednesday, 30. I had freedom of spirit and utterance, at Joseph Cresap to a large congregation; and although still weak in body, I preach again at Barratt's in the evening.

Thursday, *July* 1. We began to ascend the Alleghany, directing c course towards Redstone.[23] We passed the Little Meadows, keeping t route of Braddock's road[24] for about twenty-two miles, along a rou pathway: arriving at a small house, and halting for the night, we ha *literally*, to lie as *thick as three in a bed*. My soul has peace. For three da I had a fever; the excessive labour I have undergone may have nourish it. When I rose yesterday morning I was very unwell. After riding abo seven miles, I was taken with a trembling and profuse perspiration. I something, and felt better, and my fever is now abated. My soul has be blessed in an uncommon degree; and thou, my soul, bless the Lord; a O that he may be pleased to make me a blessing to the people in this pa of the world!

Friday, 2. I was amongst a dull, kind people: I spoke closely, and pe haps laboured much in vain; here are some of Wooster's disciples this man set up prayer meetings, and preached for twenty-five pounds p annum; he left his people because they would not increase his salary.

West Virginia—Pennsylvania

Sunday, 4. At Cheat River we had a mixed congregation of sinne Presbyterians, Baptists, and it may be, of saints: I had liberty, and ga

[23] Richard Owings, first American-born Methodist preacher and raised up Strawbridge, crossed the mountains in the fall of 1783 and laid out the plan of the fi western circuit. Many of the first settlers west of the mountains were Maryland from the region evangelized by Strawbridge. There is evidence that there were Methodi west of the mountains as early as 1772, and apparently their appeal to Owings led the laying out of the original Redstone Circuit. John Cooper and Samuel Breeze we assigned to the Redstone Circuit in the spring of 1784. This is Asbury's first crossi of the mountains to the great central valley of America, made within two months of assignment of circuit riders to the new field. (*Journal* of Thomas Scott; Smeltz *Methodism on the Headwaters of the Ohio*, 46 ff.)

[24] The road cut by the three hundred axmen who moved in advance of the army General Edward Braddock in the disastrous campaign of 1755 to attack Fort Duques at "the forks of the Ohio." It became one of the two main roads across the mountai and approximates Route 40 today. (See note under June 6, 1781.) Asbury along he was crossing the borders of these states.

[25] There is evidence that Robert Wooster, a Methodist local preacher, lived alo the Braddock Road from about 1778 to 1790. He did some preaching and possib

to them as the Lord gave it to me—plain enough. After me brother
nham spoke with life and power. I think God will bring a people to
nself in this place. Blessed be the name of the Lord for a plentiful rain
er a long drought!

Three thick—on the floor—such is our lodging—but no matter: God is
th us:—

> "Labour is rest, and pain is sweet,
> Whilst thou, my God! art here."

Wednesday, 7. We had nearly seven hundred people at Beeson Town:[26]
y were, in general, serious and attentive.

Thursday, 8. I preached at Dennis',[27] to a wild people, on Acts xiii, 26.
ce last Friday we have ridden one hundred and sixty or more miles,
 rough roads, through a rough country, and with rough fare: I trust
 r labour will not all be lost.

West Virginia

Tuesday, 13. I preached to many people at Old Town, where they
ound in intemperance.

Wednesday, 14. I preached at Bath—I was shut up.

Maryland

Sunday, 18. I preached in the new market-house at Fredericktown;
ny attended both from town and country.

Wednesday, 21. We had many to hear at Winchester (Westminster); they
peared to be orderly and solemn, and I hope it will appear that some
re convicted.

Sunday, 25. I preached at Reisterstown on, "Take heed that the light
ich is in you be not darkness."

Pennsylvania

Tuesday, 27. We had about thirty people, and a poor time at Rock
apel.[28] We came to Squire William McClellan's(?); a kind, inquiring
n, who received and entertained us hospitably.

anized some societies before the Redstone Circuit was formed, but was not under
ointment. (Smeltzer, *op. cit.*, 40–41.)

[6] This is Uniontown, Pennsylvania, laid out as a town in 1776 by Henry Beeson.
[7] Dennis', a little southwest of Washington, Pennsylvania, indicating that Asbury
 that far west on his first crossing of the mountains.
[3] Rock Chapel was the first Methodist Church built in Adams County. The corner-
ne was laid in 1773 and the building completed in 1776. Prior to that services were
d in the home and orchard of Peter Group. (Cathcart: *Historical Address at Anni-
sary of Old Rock Chapel, 1887*, 7; Warner and Beer: *History of Cumberland and
ams Counties*, 293–94.)

Saturday, 31. I praise God for health of body, peace of mind, and
desire to be holiness to the Lord: I am led into a deep and sweet uni
with God.

My mind was solemn at the love feast, and the people appeared to
stirred up: I was very searching on Luke xviii, 11, and there was so
move. Thence I hasted to Daniel Worley's,[29] where I found about o
hundred and fifty people waiting for me. I want to be very spiritu
seeing that it is by continual prayer alone this state is to be attained
will endeavour to watch thereunto with all perseverance.

Richard Williams, on the north branch[30] of the Potomac, was tak
prisoner by the Indians. It may be satisfactory to many to record in t
journal his own account of the wonderful deliverances he experience
and the extraordinary combinations of providences by which he w
restored to his family.

A few days before Braddock's defeat, nineteen Indians beset the hou
killed his father, his mother, and one of his brother's sons: Williams a
his child they secured as prisoners, and took them away to Fort Pi
(now Pittsburg,) tying his hands to a tree every night to prevent his escap
the child he fed with wild cherries or sawice berries; but it was taken fro
him at the fort. On the day of Braddock's defeat, he was taken across t
Ohio River, and guarded to Detroit, where he found the garrison reduc
to the extremity of eating horseflesh. After staying some time at Detro
he made his escape, taking with him a Frenchman's gun and ammunitio
and pushed homeward, first by curve lines, and then in a more straig
direction.

The Indians pursued and headed him, which obliged him to alter
course: wading through a deep stream, the water went over his head, a
wet his powder. For three days he travelled on, until, being pressed
hunger, he stopped to dry his wet powder, but on examination he fou
it all dissolved away: his next shift was to dig sarsaparilla for sustenan
He went on, and by good fortune found a fish which a bird had droppe
and eat that. Continuing on, he came to a large river, where he saw tv
canoe loads of Indians pass; from these he hid himself: the Indians bei
out of sight, he made a raft of two logs, and by this contrivance gain
the opposite shore. After this, he was three days without eating or drir
ing, and reduced to extreme suffering: he saw an Indian, and escaped hi
and came to a stream of water of which he drank, and soon after a plv
tree, some of the fruit of which he took along with him. The day followi
he fared something better, having found part of a fawn, which he roaste
picking the bones and the marrow, and carefully preserving the meat
future need. After the venison was all eaten, on each succeeding day,
three days, he found a squirrel. He afterward caught and eat a pole-ca

[29] Daniel Worley lived in York County, Pennsylvania. (Armstrong, *op. cit.*, 50–51.
[30] This should be the South Branch. (See note under June 10, 1781.)

another time he saw a hawk fly up, and going to the spot he found a
ld turkey. Travelling on, he came to the Ohio and waded it: near this
ace an Indian threw a tomahawk at him; he tried to escape, by climbing
● a wild-cherry tree, but found himself too weak, and he fell into the
ınds of two Frenchmen and five Indians, and thus found himself once
ore in the power of his enemies. With these he feigned derangement;
ey, however, took him along with them to Fort Pitt. On the way he
·ed, and they threatened to kill him; he told them he was willing to die.
rriving at the fort, an Indian charged him with being a prisoner from
etroit: he was forthwith put under a guard, and a council held in the
·ench language to determine what was to be done with him. The sentence
′ the general was, that he should be shot: to this some objected, saying
at his *spirit* would haunt them if he was killed there, and advised his
·ing taken to the island and buried in the sand. He was told that he
ould eat no more meat there, that the crickets should eat him. He be-
ιved himself as though he understood nothing they said, yet he knew the
·neral purport of their conversation, although they spoke in French. He
ιates, that one morning before day, while in the fort, he fell into a
ance: he beheld spirits for his conductors, and lightning also: the guards
·ing both asleep, he climbed up the high wall, and clambering over the
●ike palisades, got out safe. Having still to pass the sentinels, and not
ιowing where they were placed, he was discovered just as the cock crew
·r day; the sentinels mistook him for a comrade, and let him pass. At
ιis time he felt a conviction that his wife prayed for him, and this was
●mmunicated in an unusual manner: and she, during his absence, had
·eat comfort, and an assurance that she should see her husband again.
·scaping thus he made the best of his way without interruption until the
·ening, when he heard a gun fire some distance behind him; presently
ιother—these were his pursuers, who had found his track in the woods:
· strove to run, but he was too weak. Another gun yet nigher to him went
ſ: he made what way his strength would allow, and when he came to
·aces where he left no track, he made *zigzag* courses to deceive them, and
·ve him time to get ahead; but there were so many of them, they would
·ill discover his track again. Thus he struggled on until seven guns were
·ed, the last of which he supposes to have been within two or three
ιndred yards from him; now his heart began to fail, and he thought he
·as gone, yet he resolved to labour onward as long as he had life. At the
·ring of the last gun, his pursuers crossed his track and got ahead of him;
·king advantage of this circumstance, he turned out of the path, letting
ιe Indians who were behind tread in the footsteps of those before. Follow-
ιg the direction now taken, he had not gone far until he came to a path
·hich led to a settlement of the whites; this he did not long keep, but
·oing round the head of the ravine, laid himself down, concluding that, if
·s track was again discovered, he would be favoured by the darkness.

The Indians did get his track twice, but never overtook him. He went o
in the dark as well as he could, sometimes feeling the bushes with h
hands: among the rocks he often fell down from weakness; having gaine
smoother ground, he stopped and lay down until day.

His enemies, it seems, had not given up the pursuit. He had not lor
left his hard lodgings when he heard the report of two guns; but comir
to a hill where no mark of a footstep could be traced, he steered his cours
for Bedford, and came on a trading path in which he kept. Five days I
lived on acorns; afterward he found some wild cherries; but lo! while I
was eating, up comes an Indian. The Indian asked him where he wa
going; he said, "To the Delaware:" the Indian then took him by the han
and gave a *whoop*, when presently others joined him. By these he was ke
a prisoner for some time: he appeared bold; was active in cooking, an
by his cleverness got the favour of the captain, who praised him, and sai
he could do everything like an Indian. He had more than he needed t
eat: the captain, however, was very careful to secure him every night, t
making him lie down in one corner; here he drew a cord over some hoo
poles and tied deer's hoofs to the end, so that if Williams pulled open th
poles they would rattle and the deer's hoofs would strike the captain
face. With these Indians Williams stayed a long time: they went to wa
and left him to provide deer for the squaws. At last he found an oppo
tunity of escaping, which he improved, and arrived safe at his own hom
He is now a faithful man—his wife a pious woman; and they have preac
ing at the house.

Our quarterly meeting in Philadelphia circuit began the 21st of *Jul*
I addressed the congregation on the Epistle to the Church of Sardis. W
had a gracious time on *Sunday* the 1st of *August*. At four o'clock I preache
again, in the Valley church, on Isaiah lxvi, 1: "Heaven is my throne, an
the earth my footstool."

Monday, August 2. After preaching at brother Hoffman's, on Luke x
13, I went to the city and preached to many people, on 1 Peter ii
15.

Friday, 6. I was blessed in preaching on "Blessed are they that mour
for they shall be comforted." I was weak and faint from the extrem
warmth of the weather.

Sunday, 15. I was very weak, and had to lie down on the floor; howeve
although faint, I was enabled to speak to nearly a thousand people i
Philadelphia.

New Jersey

Monday, 16. Went to Burlington.
Tuesday, 17. Went to Trenton: although unwell and greatly oppresse
by heat, I preached at both these places.

Tuesday, 24. I rode to Mr. Ogden's.[31] Next day I spoke, but with little
eedom, to an attentive yet unfeeling audience, in Sussex court house.
y host, who appears to be a man of liberal sentiments, entertained me
ndly.

I preached at New Market Plains[32] to about one hundred hearers. I
oke freely in vindication of Methodism: it was strange; for I knew not,
til afterward, that there were present those who come at no other time.

New York

Friday, 27. We had a trying journey to New York; the weather being
cessively warm. I found my old friends John Chave and William Lupton
Newark, who appeared pleased to see me.[33] We took the stage, and
ached New York about eight o'clock. At New York we found the people
ve to God: there are about one hundred in society,[34] and, with those in
iladelphia, to my mind, appear more like Methodists than I have ever
t seen them. My first discourse was for the benefit of poor stragglers,
ho have not yet returned to the fold: the subject chosen was Rev. iii, 1–4.
Sunday, 29. In the evening I preached for the benefit of poor sinners,
 Job xxi, 15.
Monday, 30. My soul is alive to God: I visited, prayed, read, wrote,
et the classes, and in the evening preached. I have found great consola-
n and fellowship in the classes.
Monday, September 6. I took leave of my dear friends in New York:
ey showed their love in deed and in truth, liberally supplying me with
at was necessary. On *Tuesday* brother Hagerty met me, and we re-
iced together.

New Jersey

Sunday, 12. Preached at Penny Hill, and afterward at New Mills. I
ve been kept in peace, but find my adversary is not dead; neither am I

[1] The Rev. Uzal Ogden was Anglican rector at Newton in Sussex County, and had
out forty appointments in that and neighboring counties. He was author of several
rks, including one on *Revealed Religion*, and a friend of the Methodist preachers.
 carried on a friendly correspondence with Asbury. Later he moved to Newark,
ere Asbury again saw him. (See his letters in Atkinson, *op. cit.*, 288–92.)
[2] New Market was a village in Hunterdon County, New Jersey. Asbury's preaching
ce was probably the locality called Woodsville, one mile south, where a class was
med which became the New Market Methodist Church. (Snell, *op. cit.*, 356, 364.)
[3] The misunderstanding between Asbury and the two New York laymen had been
led during the 1774 residence of Asbury.
[4] The preceding conference had reported only sixty members, the total having been
uced by the migration of the loyalists. (See note under August 25, 1783.) An in-
ase had been made under the ministry of John Dickins.

out of the body, or what I may be, or must be, before I see the kingdom
God. O my soul, keep near to God, and always watch and pray!

Monday, 13. I was weak and feverish—sorely tempted, and much com
forted. I walked over to John Budds's, a son of affliction: we spoke of t
dealings of God with our own souls—not in vain: we prayed, and part
in love. Two things seem to dim my prospects of heaven, in point of qua
fication,—First, I do not speak enough for God; and, Secondly, I am n
totally devoted to him. Lord, help me to come up to my duty!

Sunday, 19. I spoke at Peter Cressy's;[35] and at Godfrey's in the evenin
I cannot sufficiently praise God for health, while others are sick in alm
every house. I have felt great nearness to God for a few days past.

Tuesday, 21. I was tried when I missed my way, but I was blessed
speaking to the people. It is a great time of sickness with the ague a
fever.

Thursday, 23. I found a dearth at Haddonfield.[36] A poor sot came in a
muttered awhile: after meeting he acknowledged he was a sinner, a
seemed sorry for his conduct, drunk as he was.

Saturday, 25. I was weary and faint as I journeyed towards Philadelph
After preaching twice in the day, I was refreshed by a glass of wine and
piece of bread.

Delaware

Saturday, October 2. I preached in our new chapel at Dover,[37] in t
state of Delaware, on faith, hope, charity. At Barratt's I believe I w
alarming, on Isaiah iii, 10, 11. I was moved in the evening towards t
boys to school at Coleman's.[38] I spoke till they wept aloud. O my Go
their parents fear thee—bring them home, with them, to thyself.

Maryland

Thursday, 7. I rode in the afternoon to Queen Annes County, visit
and prayed with Brother Reuben Ellis in affliction, and was persuad
God would spare him. Poor F. is overtaken by the adversary; and R.
gone astray. Alas, how are the mighty fallen!

Friday, 8. Came to Angiers. Here they had the flux; but I did not f

---

[35] See Lednum, *op. cit.*, 294, 395.

[36] Asbury preached at Joseph Thorne's in Haddonfield on June 3, 1772.

[37] This was Wesley Chapel on South State Street, organized in 1779, the year in whi
Asbury first preached in Dover.

[38] Francis Asbury and Samuel Magaw had planned a school for boys and had plac
John Coleman, a Virginian and friend of Devereaux Jarratt, in charge. (Rightmyer, c
cit., 162; Powell: *History of Education in Delaware*, 55.)

e to leave the house, until I had delivered my message: my testimony as low, but serious and weighty.

Wednesday, 13. At Hooper's,[39] the congregation was large indeed. I as greatly at liberty; and I hope the seed was not all lost. Here I met th brother Garrettson—all love and peace.

Thursday, 14. I rode twenty miles to visit Kent Island[40] for the first ne. Here we had an unusual collection of people, and surely all was not vain. We had a good time at Robert Newcomb's:[41] the word of God as greatly triumphed over the prejudices of rich and poor. We went on Cambridge. Here George, a poor Negro in our society, we found under ntence of death for theft committed before he became a Methodist; he peared to be much given up to God: he was reprieved under the gallows: merchant, who cursed the Negro for praying, died in horror. I pity the or slaves. O that God would look down in mercy, and take their cause hand!

Wednesday, 20. I was distressed by the levity of some spirits. We had long ride to Taylor's Island;[42] we had a profitable season there: and xt day going twenty-four miles to Levin Todd's, I found a warm people deed. I injured myself by speaking too loud.

Saturday, 23. Rode thirty miles to Mr. Thomas Airey's, preaching by e way. We had a great time—multitudes attended: Dorset is now in ace, and the furies are still.

Sunday, 24. This day has been so much taken up, that I had no time to are. My mind is with the Lord, and every day is a Sabbath with me. ere B. T., who was a great Churchman, after hearing Freeborn Garrettson second time, was seized with conviction on his way home, and fell down the road, and spent great part of the night crying to God for mercy. It as suggested to him that his house was on fire; his answer was, "It is tter for me to lose my house than my soul."

Virginia

Sunday, 31. We rose early, and rode twenty miles to Downing's. I ctured at Burton's[43] in the evening.

[39] Asbury probably visited the society organized in 1780, now known as Hooper's emorial. Hooper's Island is in Dorchester County about opposite the mouth of the tuxent River.

[40] Kent Island, largest island in Chesapeake Bay, is a part of Queen Annes County. eeborn Garrettson found a society there on his first visit in 1778. (Emory, *op. cit.*, Hallman, *op. cit.*, 326.)

[41] Robert Newcomb lived north of Royal Oak in Talbot County, Maryland.

[42] Methodism was introduced on Taylor's Island in Dorchester County at an early date.

[43] Several historians have placed this in the northern neck of Virginia; however, it is the Eastern Shore, and the Burton Oak Grove Church grew out of this preaching ace.

Monday, November 1. After riding twenty miles to Col. Paramore's, preached with liberty. The family is kind; the father, mother, son, an niece have tender impressions. The people hereabout are gay, blind spiritual matters, well-featured, and hospitable, and good livers.

Tuesday, 2. After preaching at Garrettson chapel,[44] I rode to Co Burton's, and was kindly received.

Friday, 5. I came back to Col. Burton's. Since I went from this hous I have ridden about one hundred miles, spent five hours in delivering fi

THOMAS COKE

public discourses, and ten hours in family and public prayer, and rea two hundred pages in Young's Works. I have enjoyed great peace, an hope to see a great and glorious work.

The Presbyterians came down here about thirty years ago; many we moved, and some advances were made towards a reformation. A hous was built for public worship. About six years past the Baptists visite these parts, and there was some stir among the people. I think the Methoc ists are most likely to have permanent success, because the inhabitants ar

[44] This was one of the earliest preaching places on the eastern shore of Virginia ar is now called Garrison's Church.

nerally Episcopalians. We preached some time before any regular circuit
s formed, or any people had joined us; now brother Willis is stationed
re, and there are one hundred in society.

The land here is low and level, and is refreshed with fine breezes from
e sea; there is an abundance in the productions of the earth and
the waters; the people are generous, social, and polished in their
anners.

Saturday, 6. Came to Downing's, and had a large congregation for the
ne and place. I see a difficulty in saying anything of any denomination
 people—it is so much like evil speaking to mention their faults behind
eir backs: I will avoid it, and endeavour to prevent others doing it in my
esence.

Maryland

Sunday, 7. I rode twelve miles to Snow Hill.[45] Here the judge himself
)ened the court house, and a large congregation of people of different
nominations attended: the subject was the certainty, universality, and
stice of God's proceeding at the day of judgment.

Sunday, 14. I came to Barratt's chapel: here, to my great joy, I met these
ar men of God, Dr. Coke, and Richard Whatcoat,[46] we were greatly
mforted together. The Doctor preached on "Christ our wisdom,
ghteousness, sanctification, and redemption." Having had no oppor-
nity of conversing with them before public worship, I was greatly
rprised to see brother Whatcoat assist by taking the cup in the ad-
inistration of the sacrament.[47] I was shocked when first informed of the
tention of these my brethren in coming to this country: it may be of
od. My answer then was, if the preachers unanimously choose me, I shall
)t act in the capacity I have hitherto done by Mr. Wesley's appointment.
he design of organizing the Methodists into an Independent Episcopal

[45] Asbury came up the Peninsula from Accomack County, Virginia, to Snow Hill, in
orcester County, Maryland. His activities during the ensuing week are partly covered
Thomas Haskins, then on the Somerset Circuit. He heard Asbury at the Line Chapel
:ated on the Maryland-Delaware border, southeast of Laurel, on Monday, November
and traveled with him through Thursday. (Ms. *Journal* of Thomas Haskins, Library
Congress.)

[46] Thomas Coke and Richard Whatcoat had arrived in Delaware and preached at
e present Smyrna on Friday, November 12. They then traveled southward to Barratt's
aapel while Asbury was approaching from below. The occasion was the midyear
arterly meeting at which pastoral exchanges were to be made. This was the first
eeting of Coke and Asbury. A bronze star on the floor of Barratt's Chapel indicates
e historic spot. (Coke, *op. cit.*, 35, 44, 45; Cooper: *The Substance of a Funeral Dis-
urse—on the Death of Francis Asbury*, 104, 105.)

[47] Apparently Asbury was unaware that on September 2 Richard Whatcoat had
:eived ordination from John Wesley, assisted by Coke and Thomas Creighton, both
esbyters in the Church of England.

Church was opened to the preachers present,[48] and it was agreed to c
a general conference, to meet at Baltimore the ensuing Christmas;
also that brother Garrettson go off to Virginia to give notice thereof
our brethren in the south.[49]

Delaware

I was very desirous the Doctor should go upon the track I had just be
over, which he accordingly did. I came to Dover, and preached on Eph.
6; was close, and, I hope, profitable.

Maryland

Tuesday, 16. Rode to Bohemia Manor where I met with Thom
Vasey,[50] who came over with the Doctor and Richard Whatcoat. My so
is deeply engaged with God to know his will in this new business.

Wednesday, 17. Rode to quarterly meeting at Deer Creek; thence,
Mr. Gough's, to Baltimore. I preached in the evening to a solemn peop
on, "O wicked man, thou shalt surely die:" about the ending of t
sermon the floor of the house gave way, but no injury followed.

Tuesday, 23. We rode twenty miles to Frederick quarterly meetir
where brother Vasey preached on, "The Lord is my Shepherd; I shall n
want." Our love feast was attended with the power and presence of Gc
Leaving Frederick, I went to Calvert quarterly meeting. Brother Poythre
and myself had much talk about the new plan. At our quarterly meeti
we had a good time; the love feast was in great life and power. I admi
the work of God among the coloured people in these parts.

Friday, 26. I observed this day as a day of fasting and prayer, that
might know the will of God in the matter that is shortly to come befc
our conference; the preachers and people seem to be much pleased wi

[48] The plan was first presented at the home of Mrs. Philip Barratt, whose husba
had recently died. There Asbury, Coke, and eleven other preachers had Sunday dinr
The house, still used as a dwelling, is about one-half mile behind Barratt's Chap
(Barratt, *op. cit.*, 49; Hallman, *op. cit.*, 15.)

[49] Garrettson said, "I set out for Virginia and Carolina. . . . My dear Master enabl
me to ride about twelve hundred miles in about six weeks." Coke's description
Garrettson's mission was ". . . like an arrow from North to South." (Bangs: *Life
the Rev. Freeborn Garrettson*, 146; Coke: *Journal*, 46.)

[50] Thomas Vasey (1742?–1826) was one of Wesley's three commissioners who land
in New York on November 3, 1784, with Coke and Whatcoat. After two years as
American itinerant he was reordained by Bishop William White and returned to E
land, where he accepted a curacy. After a brief period he re-entered the Wesleyan fell
ship and was stationed until shortly before his death in London. (Stevens, *op. cit.*,
156, 157.)

e projected plan;[51] I myself am led to think it is of the Lord. I am not
:kled with the honour to be gained—I see danger in the way. My soul
iits upon God. O that he may lead us in the way we should go! Part of
y time is, and must necessarily be, taken up with preparing for the
nference.

Tuesday, 30. I preached with enlargement to rich and poor, on, "That
: may have boldness in the day of judgment." The Lord has done great
ings for these people. The Rev. Mason Locke Weems and myself had an
teresting conversation on the subject of the Episcopal mode of Church
vernment. I spent the evening with David Weems,[52] and spoke to the
ack people.

Saturday, December 4. Rode to Baltimore, and preached on Mark xiv,
, 30, with freedom. I spent some time in town, and was greatly grieved
the barrenness of the people; they appear to be swallowed up with the
res of the world.

Sunday, 12. At the Point my heart was made to feel for the people,
iile I enlarged on, "Blessed are the pure in heart," &c. I was close and
rvent in town at four o'clock. A young man pushed the door open
iile we were meeting the society; he was carried before a justice of the
ace, and committed to jail, but he was bailed out.

Tuesday, 14. I met Dr. Coke at Abingdon, Mr. Richard Dallam kindly
king him there in his coach;[53] he preached on, "He that hath the Son
th life." We talked of our concerns in great love.

Wednesday, 15. My soul was much blest at the communion, where I
lieve all were more or less engaged with God. I feel it necessary daily
give up my own will. The Dr. preached a great sermon on, "He that
veth father or mother more than me," &c.

Saturday, 18. Spent the day at Perry Hall, partly in preparing for
nference.[54] My intervals of time I passed in reading the third volume of

[51] This plan was that set forth in John Wesley's letter of September 10, 1784, to Coke,
sbury, and "Our Brethren in America," and also the subsequent action taken by the
eachers on November 14 to call a conference at Baltimore to consider the organiza-
n of an "Independent Methodist Church." (Townsend, Workman, and Eayrs: *A
w History of Methodism*, II, 85.)

[52] David Weems, a brother, lived in St. James Parish, Herring Bay, the southern part
Anne Arundel County. The Weems family led in the erection of a chapel near the
e of the present Methodist church in Friendship, Maryland. (*Calendar of the Ezekiel
oper Collection of Early American Methodist Manuscripts* in Garrett Biblical Insti-
te, 6, 7; *Journal* entry and note for December 16, 1789.)

[53] It is probable that Asbury and Coke met to inspect Abingdon as a site for Cokesbury
ollege. Richard Dallam was a heavy contributor and an original trustee of the institu-
n. Coke says, "Mr. Asbury met me on this side of the Bay (Chesapeake); between us
: have got about one thousand pounds sterling subscribed for the College." (Coke,
. *cit.*, 51.)

[54] By prearrangement Asbury and Coke met at the home of Harry Dorsey Gough,
out twelve miles from Baltimore, to draw up the agenda for the approaching con-
rence. Among others who arrived were Whatcoat, Vasey, and William Black.

the British Arminian Magazine. Continued at Perry Hall until *Friday,* t
twenty-fourth. We then rode to Baltimore, where we met a few preachers
it was agreed to form ourselves into an Episcopal Church, and to ha
superintendents, elders, and deacons. When the conference was seate
Dr. Coke and myself were unanimously elected to the superintendency
the Church, and my ordination followed, after being previously ordain
deacon and elder, as by the following certificate may be seen.

Know all men by these presents, That I, Thomas Coke, Doctor of Ci
Law; late of Jesus College, in the University of Oxford, Presbyter of t
Church of England, and Superintendent of the Methodist Episco;
Church in America; under the protection of Almighty God, and with
single eye to his glory; by the imposition of my hands, and prayer, (bei
assisted by two ordained elders,) did on the twenty-fifth day of this mon
December, set apart Francis Asbury for the office of a deacon in t
aforesaid Methodist Episcopal Church. And also on the twenty-sixth d
of the said month, did by the imposition of my hands, and prayer, (bei
assisted by the said elders,) set apart the said Francis Asbury for the offi
of elder in the said Methodist Episcopal Church. And on this twent
seventh day of the said month, being the day of the date hereof, have,
the imposition of my hands, and prayer, (being assisted by the said elder
set apart the said Francis Asbury for the office of a superintendent in t
said Methodist Episcopal Church, a man whom I judge to be well qua
fied for that great work. And I do hereby recommend him to all whom
may concern, as a fit person to preside over the flock of Christ. In tes
mony whereof I have hereunto set my hand and seal this twenty-seven
day of December, in the year of our Lord 1784.   THOMAS COKE.

Twelve elders were elected,[55] and solemnly set apart to serve o

[55] On Friday morning, December 24, the party assembled at Perry Hall traveled
Baltimore, and the first session of the Christmas Conference began at ten o'clock
Lovely Lane Meeting House. Coke presided as Wesley's representative and presen
the plan. John Dickins offered a resolution, the unanimous adoption of which crea
the Methodist Episcopal Church in the United States. Asbury was unanimously elec
superintendent, as was Coke. On Christmas Day, the second day of the conferen
Asbury was ordained deacon by Coke, assisted by Whatcoat and Vasey; the followi
day he was ordained elder; and on Monday, December 27, he was consecrated super
tendent. William Philip Otterbein, a German minister and Asbury's friend, assis
in the consecration service. Nearly sixty preachers were present at this conference, c
of a total of eighty or more. Time and distance prevented the others from attendi
(Tipple, *op. cit.,* 140–55.)

[56] Bishop Asbury wrote of "determining all things by a majority of votes," but he d
not elucidate the procedure by which the "twelve elders" were presented. Because
minutes of this conference are extant, some doubt exists concerning those who receiv
ordination and of those who comprised the sixty preachers in attendance. (Ridgawa
"Personnel of the Christmas Conference," in *Proceedings of the Centennial Methoc
Conference,* 119–36.) Those ordained for Nova Scotia were Freeborn Garrettson a
James O. Cromwell. Jeremiah Lambert was ordained for Antigua, in the West Indi
but died before reaching the field.

CONSECRATION OF FRANCIS ASBURY, 1784

Those officiating are Thomas Coke, Philip William Otterbein, Richard
Whatcoat, and Thomas Vasey

societies in the United States, one for Antigua, and two for Nova Scot
We spent the whole week in conference, debating freely, and determini
all things by a majority of votes. The Doctor preached every day at noo
and some one of the other preachers morning and evening. We were
great haste, and did much business in a little time.

1785

Home of Green Hill, in North Carolina, site of the first Conference

CHAPTER FOURTEEN

Maryland

Monday, January 3, 1785. The conference is risen, and I have now a [littl]e time for rest. In the evening I preached on Ephes. iii, 8, being the [firs]t sermon after my ordination: my mind was unsettled, and I was but [weak] in my own testimony.

Virginia

[T]uesday, 4. I was engaged preparing for my journey southward. Rode [fort]y miles through frost and snow to Fairfax, Virginia, and got in about [t]en o'clock.

[T]hursday, 6. We had an exceeding cold ride to Prince William—little [less] than forty miles, and were nearly two hours after night in getting to [bro]ther Hale's.

[F]riday, 7. A calm day. I had brother Hickson for my companion. We [pas]sed Fauquier court house; came to the north branch of Rappahannock, [whi]ch we found about waist high, and frozen from side to side; we pushed [the] ice out of the track which a wagon, well for us, had made, and got [ove]r safe. Pursuing our journey, we came to a little *ordinary* kept by one [Wh]itehead: here were some wagonners at cards in the front room; this [did] not prevent our having prayers in the one adjoining: we slept in peace, [and] had only nine shillings and six-pence to pay in the morning.

[S]aturday, 8. Rode to brother Fry's to dinner, where I met with brother [El]lis, who had stopped there on his way to the conference.

Sunday, 9. We read prayers, preached, ordained brother Willis deac and baptized some children. I feel nothing but love. I am sometir afraid of being led to think something more of myself in my new stat than formerly.

Tuesday, 11. In the morning I discovered that my horse was very lar after some time he grew better. The adversary tries to get me into a fret spirit—our journey was attended with some difficulties; but I do murmur. I had dreaded the ice in James River, but we crossed with greatest ease. We directed our course to Staunton River; and here waited some time at Hunt's landing. Mr. Hunt was so kind as to insist our staying with him; and we were tired enough to want rest. I lectu in his family night and morning.

Saturday, 15. Preached and administered the sacrament at Royst church; then rode to brother Phelps's, where I was pointed, on R xvii, 14.

Sunday, 16. Although there was only a probability of my coming, a people met at Doby's store, where I preached with some life, on Jc iii, 19–21.

Tuesday, 18. Brother Willis was ordained elder at Carter's church: Lord was with us in this, the sacrament, and the love feast; and all in life.

North Carolina

Thursday, 20. My horse was lame. I rode with patience to A. Arnet and was blest: we rejoiced in the Lord together.

Friday, 21. After preaching at Thompson's,[2] and baptizing so children, we set out for Short's.[3] Travelling onward we came to a cre it was so dark by this time that we could not find the ford; we rode b a mile, and engaged a young man who undertook to be our guide, but himself was scarcely able to keep the way. We rode with great pain Waggoner's chapel, and after pushing on through deep streams, I only nine hearers; this was owing to the carelessness of the person w should have published the notice of our coming.

Sunday, 23. I had about one hundred hearers; to whom I spoke Josh. xxiv, 15. We lodged with F. C., who was very kind, although could afford but one bed for three. The horses fared well. Next morn we set off, and came to Old Town instead of Salem:[4] by the evening,

---

[1] Arnet must have lived in Rockingham County, North Carolina. Asbury a stayed there on March 1, 1786.

[2] Thompson lived in Forsythe County.   [3] Short lived in Rowan County.

[4] Salem was a Moravian community in Forsythe County, founded in 1766. It one of the communities of the "Wachovia Tract," an area of 100,000 acres secure Bishop Spangenburg in 1753. George Washington visited the community in 179

ched brother Hill's, on the Yadkin circuit. Thus far the Lord has led
on; and I still hope to get along according to appointment.

Friday, 28. My horse being unfit to travel, I borrowed another, and
nt on seventeen miles to Fisher's River, where I met with a few poor
ople. Thence we rode through the barren mountains, and crossed the
quent rivers in our course, and came to W——'s: 29*th*, next day I
ached at Heady's, and rode on to Herndon's[5] in Wilkes county: here
were kindly entertained, although there were few people to preach to.
thing could have better pleased our old Church folks[6] than the late
p we have taken in administering the ordinances; to the *catholic* Pres-
terians it also gives satisfaction; but the Baptists are discontented.

Thursday, February 3. Rode twenty miles to Witherspoon's: here was a
ge assemblage of people; some to pay and receive taxes; some to drink;
d some to hear me preach: I gave them a rough talk on Rev. ii, 5–8.
om this place we rode to Allen's. The people here are famous for talking
out religion: and here and there is a horse thief.

Sunday, 6. Yesterday some were prevented from offering their children
God in baptism, by a zealous Baptist: to-day brother Willis spoke on
right of infants to baptism; our opposer soon took his leave.

Monday, 7. I preached at Elsberry's, and rode thirty-one miles to Mor-
n Bryan's. The weather has been cold and uncomfortable. I have ridden
the horse I borrowed, nearly three hundred miles in about nine days.

Tuesday, 8. I observed this as a day of abstinence. I preached and
ministered the sacrament; held a love feast—our friends were greatly
mforted. Here I plunged four adults,[7] at their own request, they being
rsuaded that this was the most proper mode of baptizing.

Thursday, 10. Rode to Salisbury,[8] where, as it was court time, I had

s later united with Winston, which was chartered in 1851 to become Winston-Salem.
vers: *Forsyth County*, 14–18.) Old Town is a community a few miles north of
nston-Salem.

Colonel Joseph Herndon lived in "a hospitable mansion on the headwaters of the
edee," or Yadkin, River in Wilkes County, North Carolina. (Shipp: *Methodism in
uth Carolina*, 152.) Jesse Lee, who had not attended the Christmas Conference, came
m Salisbury and joined Asbury here. The party now consisted of Asbury, Henry
llis, Woolman Hickson, and Lee. Asbury was wearing "black gown, cassock, and
nd," and Lee objected to this dress as unbecoming to Methodist simplicity. Asbury
d it aside and seldom wore it again. Strickland says he wore gown and bands when
dedicated Cokesbury College, but Smith denies this. (Lee: *Life and Times of Jesse
*, 149; Strickland: *The Pioneer Bishop*, 163; Smith: *Francis Asbury*, 89, 94.)

The "old Church folks" were the former Anglicans.

"In one of his letters Asbury declared that owing to the encroachments of the
ptists in Virginia, baptism by immersion was practiced, but abandoned at the end
the year." (Tipple: *Heart of Asbury's Journal*, 234.)

Methodism was introduced in Salisbury in 1783 by Beverly Allen, and a circuit
s formed with thirty members. An account of the first sermon preached in a school-
use there was written by a convert and is preserved in Lednum. (*Op. cit.*, 372–76;
issom, *op. cit.*, 245–47.)

but few hearers; and some of these made their escape when I began
insist on the necessity of holiness—a subject this which the Antinomi:
do not like to hear pressed too closely.

Tuesday, 15. I gave up my horse, and borrowed one of Mr. Randa
I fear my horse will lose his eyes. I visited B——; one who has depar·
from God; he appeared to be sensible of, and lamented it; yet, he sa
he had not power to pray and seek.

South Carolina

Thursday, 17. We set off for Charleston, South Carolina. When at ·
Cheraw Hills,[10] we thought of going to ——'s, but he was not at hor
A family which had moved from Virginia sent after me with an invitati
to come and dine;[11] I accepted their kindness, and arriving, found t·
they had been Methodists: after spending some time in the church
prayer,[12] we prepared to pursue our journey, but being pressed to s·
until the morrow, we remained with them. Came to the Long Bluff co·
house[13]—found few people: thence journeying on, we arrived at Jo·
Kimbro's,[14] and were kindly entertained.

[9] John Randall lived in the present Stanley County, North Carolina, a few m·
north of Norwood. Jesse Lee, traveling the Salisbury Circuit, preached in his hom·
1784. "The man of the house was always deaf and dumb," said Lee, but "he is estee·
as a pious man." The community became a regular preaching place and Asbury stop·
there on numerous occasions (February 15, 1785; April 3, 1789; December 20, 17·
November 16, 1798; February 23, 1800; December 8, 1804.) Services were first c·
ducted in the Randall house and then in a brush arbor. A church was erected bef·
1800. Randall Church is now the oldest in Stanley County. (Grissom, *op. cit.*, 2·

[10] The Cheraw District was one of the seven judicial districts into which So·
Carolina was divided in 1768 and included the present Marlboro, Chesterfield, D·
lington, and parts of Florence and Lee Counties. Its name was derived from the Che·
Indians. The town of Cheraw, or Cheraw Hill, was on the west side of the Great ·
Dee River. The name was for a brief period changed to Chatham in honor of the E·
of Chatham, but anti-British feeling engendered during the Revolution caused the
name of Cheraw to be retained when the town was incorporated in 1820–21. (
Gregg: *History of the Old Cheraws*; Bulletin of the First Methodist Church, Cher·
S.C., 1953.)

[11] Their host at Cheraw was a merchant who had in his employ a young man fr·
Massachusetts who described the low state of religion in his native state. This so ·
pressed Jesse Lee that he resolved to go to New England. (Lee: *Life and Times of*
Rev. Jesse Lee, 150.) Lee became the virtual founder of Methodism in New Engla·
preaching first under "the old elm" on Boston Common on July 11, 1790.

[12] St. David's Episcopal Church was built in 1770–73 and is still in use. There ·
a hiatus of thirty-four years, 1785–1819, when it was dormant because of anti-Brit·
feeling. (Bulletin of Saint David's Church, 1953.)

[13] Long Bluff Court House was on the west side of the Great Pee Dee River and ·
the first business center in the colony, founded around 1735 or 1740. It was ten·
twelve miles south of Cheraw, about where Society Hill in Darlington County r·
stands. A lot had been purchased at Cheraw, but the location was changed in 1·

Tuesday, 22. I heard of that impostor, T—y—t,[15] who was fleecing the
ople of one hundred guineas per annum: were he a good man, I doubt
they would supply him thus. The greatest consolation I had was
ilst alone in the woods. I was comfortable in brother Jesse Lee's
mpany.

Wednesday, 23. We crossed Lynch's Creek, Black Mingo, and Black
ver, and arrived at Georgetown,[16] where we met with a kind reception.
elt my mind solemn, and devoted to God, but was in great doubt of
ccess. If God has not called us by his providence into these parts, I
sire and pray that we may have no countenance from the people;
hough we have ridden four or five hundred miles, and spent our
oney.

Thursday, 24. I preached in Georgetown on 1 Cor. ii, 14, to a serious
ople. A Mr. William Wayne, a nephew of the celebrated General [Mad
thony] Wayne, introduced himself to us,[17] with whom we took break-
t; on parting, he showed us the way to the ferry, and paid our ferriage.
ound the Lord had brought him through deep exercises of soul. We
velled on through a barren country, in all respects, towards Charleston.[18]
e came that evening to Scott's, where the people seemed to be merry;
y soon became mute: we talked and prayed with them: in the morning,
en we took our leave of them, they would receive nothing. We met
ther Willis; he had gone along before us, and had made an acquaint-
ce with Mr. Edgar Wells, a respectable merchant of the city, to whom he
d carried letters of introduction, from Mr. Wayne, of Georgetown: I
ged on, dejected in spirit, and came to Mr. Edgar Wells's. We obtained

en a committee from the lower part of the district made an appeal to the General
embly for a more nearly central site. (Williamson: "Historical Sketch" in *Bulletin
he University of South Carolina*, No. 196, February 1, 1927.)

John Kimbrough went from Wake County, North Carolina, and settled in the
tral part of Darlington District south of Cheraw in 1756. (Gregg: *History of the
Cheraws*, 90–91.)

Miss Cora Page Godfrey suggests that this may have been Governor Tryon who
s regarded as a tyrant.

Asbury went southward through Darlington, the present Florence, Williamsburg,
Georgetown Counties to Georgetown on the coast. Lynch's Creek formed the
ndary between Darlington and Williamsburg Counties (Florence County had not
n been formed). Black Mingo Creek rises in the upper part of Williamsburg County
flows southeast into Black River near the northern border of Georgetown County.
ck Mingo community was about four miles above the junction of the two streams
ten miles north of Andrews. It was an important rural travel and trading center
ch was later called Willtown. Black River flows through central Williamsburg
nty to the sea near Georgetown.

Asbury's party first lodged at another house in Georgetown. As they were leaving
the meeting, their host excused himself to attend a ball, whereupon Jesse Lee
yed that another home might be opened to them. The prayer was answered by the
roach of Wayne. (Lee: *Life and Times of the Rev. Jesse Lee*, 151.)

The party doubtless crossed Santee River at Myzack's Ferry near Honey Hill and
r the Cooper to Charleston.

the use of an old meeting house belonging to the General Baptists,[19] which they had ceased to preach: brother Willis preached at noon brother Jesse Lee morning and evening. I first went to the Episco Church,[20] and then to the Independent meeting-house:[21] at this last heard a good discourse.

Monday, 28. The Calvinists, who are the only people in Charleston w. appear to have any sense of religion, seem to be alarmed. Yesterd morning [*Sunday*], and again at noon, the congregations were small; night we were crowded. There is a great dearth of religion here; some s: never more so than at this time.

The people were a little moved while brother Lee preached to them *Sabbath* evening. My first sermon was on *Wednesday,* the second *March,* on 2 Cor. v, 20. I had but little enlargement. I preached again t next day on Eccles. xi, 9; the people were solemn and attentive. I find the are here who oppose us—I leave the Lord to look to his own cause told my hearers that I expected to stay in the city but seven days; tha should preach every night, if they would favour me with their compar and that I should speak on subjects of primary importance to their sou and explain the essential doctrines taught and held by the Methodists.

Friday, March 4. I gave them a discourse on the nature of convicti for sin, from John xvi, 8; many serious people attended, and some appear to feel.

Saturday, 5. I spoke on the nature and necessity of repentance. T —— ministers, who had before this held meeting at the same hour w us, and had represented our principles in an unfavourable light, a striven to prepossess the people's minds against our doctrines—ev these ministers came to hear. This afternoon Mr. Wells began to f conviction; my soul praised the Lord for this fruit of our labours—tl answer to our prayers.

---

[19] Chreitzberg (*Early Methodism in the Carolinas,* 41–43) says this was the old S man's Bethel in which Joseph Pilmoor twelve years earlier preached the first Metho sermon in Charleston, but this is refuted by the old Baptist records. The Calvini or Particular Baptists organized first. Then the Arminian or General Baptists came Both used the same house until the former tried to oust the latter. The colonial cou gave equal rights to each group, and the Particular body bought the Seaman's Miss where Pilmoor preached. After the Revolution the General Baptists dwindled, a Asbury and his party used the original house which they abandoned. The Particu congregation later reclaimed the property, which was on the site of the present F Baptist Church. Asbury, Lee, and Willis used it during this visit to Charleston. 1 Methodists were later ejected, the seats were thrown into the streets, and the do and windows barred. Mrs. Stoll, grandmother of Bishop William W. Wightman, tl opened her home for Methodist worship until the services were moved to an unfinisl house on Wentworth Street. (Betts: *History of South Carolina Methodism,* 481–82.)

[20] St. Phillip's Church.

[21] Circular Congregational Church, called the "White Meeting House." (Shi, *History of Meothdism in South Carolina,* 164.)

Sunday, 6. I had but few hearers this morning; these few appeared to ve feeling hearts: in the evening I preached to a large, wild company, Acts xvii, 30, 31. My soul is in deep travail for Mr. Wells—I hope God ll set him at liberty. The sore throat and scarlet fever prevail in this y, yet are the inhabitants vain and wicked to a proverb. I bless God for alth.

Wednesday, 9. I had a good time on Matt. vii, 7. In the evening the ·uds about Mr. Wells began to disperse; in the morning he could re-·ce in the Lord. How great is the work of God—once a sinner, yesterday seeker, and now His adopted child! Now we know that God hath ›ught us here, and have a hope that there will be a glorious work among ‹ people—at least among the Africans.

Thursday, 10. This day I delivered my last discourse on 1 Pet. iii, 15. oved and pitied the people, and left some under gracious impressions. ‹ took our leave: and had the satisfaction of observing that Mrs. Wells peared to be very sensibly affected.[22]

We had rough crossing, in going over the Bay to Hadrell's Point.[23] I ptized two children at Mr. Scott's,[24] for which I was offered a great re-·rd—but it was by persons who did not know that neither my own ·lings nor the constitution of our Church permitted me to receive any mpensation for such services.

We reached Georgetown time enough to give notice for preaching in ‹ evening.

Sunday, 13. The people generally attended and were serious. We found ·s. Wayne under deep distress of soul.

From Georgetown[25] we came by Kingstree[26] and got to Mr. Durant's,[27]

---

[2] Asbury left Henry Willis as preacher in Charleston, taking him from Holston :cuit to which he had been appointed at the 1784 conference. He formed a society l was the first pastor, though John Tunnell appears in the minutes. The explanation hat Willis served only a few weeks between conferences. At the conference at Green l's soon to follow Willis was given oversight of the Yadkin and Holston circuits, l Tunnell was assigned to Charleston. (Betts: *History of South Carolina Methodism*,)

[3] Asbury crossed the harbor eastward to Hadrell's Point, now Mount Pleasant, and owed the old King's Highway to Georgetown.

[4] Perhaps the Scotts with whom Asbury stayed on the night of February 25.

[5] Woolman Hickson was doubtless left in Georgetown since he was appointed to · circuit the following April. It became the Pee Dee Circuit a year later.

[3] This was doubtless Kingston instead of Kingstree, since a visit to the latter would ·e involved a wide detour without apparent reason. Chreitzberg (*op. cit.*, 42) noted l queried the contradiction, and Betts agrees in thus correcting the *Journal*. Asbury lt via the Yuahannah Ferry to Kingston, the present Conway in Horry County.

[7] Durant lived forty-five miles northeast of Georgetown and six or seven miles ·ond Kingston (now Conway) where Durant's Church now stands. Several Durant lilies are indicated on old maps of the region. (Henry Mougon's map, 1773, published Robt. Sayer and J. Bennett, London; Series of County Maps by Robert Mills, 1825.) ·re were meetinghouses in Horry County and the lower neck of Marion County

who, I had heard, was a Methodist: we found him, in sentiment, one
Mr. Hervey's[28] disciples, but not in the enjoyment of religion: I deliver
my own soul before I took my leave of him.

North Carolina

Hearing of brother Daniel at Town Creek,[29] I resolved to make a pu
for his house; it was forty miles distant, and I did not start until ni
o'clock. I dined at Lockwood's Folly,[30] and got in about seven o'cloc
O, how happy was I to be received, and my dear friends to receive m
I have been out for six weeks, and ridden near five hundred miles amo
strangers to me, to God, and to the power of religion. How could I li
in the world if there were no Christians in it!

Saturday, 19. After preaching at Town Creek, I rode in the evening
Wilmington;[31] night came on before we reached there, and from the ba
ness of the causeway, I ran some risk; we went to ——, but he was n
prepared to receive us; afterward to ——, where we had merry, singi
drunken raftsmen; to their merriment I soon put a stop. I felt the pow
of the devil here.

Sunday, 20. The bell went round to give notice, and I preached to
large congregation. When I had done, behold, F. Hill came into the roc
powdered off, with a number of fine ladies and gentlemen. As I could n
get my horse and bags, I heard him out: I verily believe his sermon was I
own, it was so much like his conversation. I came away well satisfied th
I had delivered my own soul.

near Bradley's Ferry where Asbury probably crossed the Great Pee Dee. (*Geographi*
Statistical and Historical Map of South Carolina, 1823, by J. Wilson, reduced by
Drayton.)

[28] James Hervey was one of the original Oxford Methodists who broke with
Wesleys and became a Calvinist.

[29] Town Creek is in North Carolina about ten miles south of Wilmington, near
South Carolina line.

[30] Lockwood's Folly was the present Supply, North Carolina, thirty-seven mi
below Wilmington on Lockwood's Folly River. The settlement was established by a
named for a Mr. Lockwood from Barbados, who was driven away by the Indians.
New Voyage to Georgia, in Georgia Historical Society Publication, Vol. II, quoted
the *Wilmington Messenger*, August 22, 1897, 16.)

[31] The Methodists had difficulty in establishing a permanent society in Wilmingt
North Carolina. A class was formed on the Cape Fear River near Wilmington befo
the Revolutionary War by Philip Bruce and James O'Kelly, but it did not endure.
1784 Beverly Allen and James Hinton were sent to form a circuit, but their sm
classes were not permanent. They reported only eighty members in the whole Ca
Fear area, and in 1786 Wilmington was merged with the Bladen Circuit. The first cl
of white people was formed in Wilmington in 1797, and it was said that "the blac
were much more attentive to religion than the whites." (Lee: *History of the Methodis*
209; Grissom, *op. cit.*, 219, 224.)

Monday, 21. On my way I stopped at A——'s and baptized some chil-
:n: the poor mother held out a piece of gold to me. This is the pay of
priests here for such service: Lord, keep me from the love of honour,
ney, and ease.

Wednesday, 23. I had a few hearers at the Lake Waccamaw chapel.
ere has been much injury done here to the cause of religion by some who
omised much in this way, and performed little. I lodged near the Wacca-
w Lake, which is seven miles in circumference, fed by several streams
ning through the adjacent marshes, and surrounded nearly on all
es by a sandy beach: this is a desert country; has few inhabitants, and
ver still who have any deep sense of religion.

Tuesday, 29. Rode to Elizabethtown, crossing the north-east branch of
pe Fear River. I called at S——'s and offered baptism to his sick wife,
ich she declined accepting; after I came away she was distressed at her
usal, and sent her son four miles after me; myself and my horse were
th weary, but I returned and had a solemn time.

Wednesday, *April* 6. I preached at Swansboro[32] in sight of the sea.
re are a wicked people indeed; nevertheless, a few have joined society.

Monday, 11. Preached in the court house at Kinston. I was entertained
y kindly by Governor Caswell.[33]

Tuesday, 19. Preached at the Cypress chapel, and had many people to
ar. I met Doctor Coke at Green Hill's that evening: here we held our
nference in great peace.[34]

Monday, 25. I rode to Doctor Peets: this man has given up family and
vate prayer, and yet is in distress about his soul.

Asbury had followed a roundabout route from Wilmington, turning back west-
d to Lake Waccamaw in Columbus County, northward to Elizabethtown in Bladen
unty, and then eastward on a long ride to Swansboro.

Richard Caswell (1729–89) was governor of North Carolina in 1776–80 and served
cond term in 1785–87. (*Dictionary of American Biography*, III, 571.) The capitol of
state was at New Bern. Caswell lived at Kinston and is buried there.

This conference which Asbury mentions so briefly was the first conference of the
ly formed Methodist Episcopal Church and the fourteenth in America. It repre-
ted the Carolinas and Virginia, in which there were 31 circuits and 9,063 members.
was held in the home of the Rev. Major Green Hill, one mile from Louisburg, North
olina. Hill was a man of prominence, a large holder of slaves, a member of each
vincial Congress, treasurer of the state, and a major and chaplain in the Provincial
ny. The house in which about twenty preachers were entertained at this conference
till standing and occupied. Hill later moved to Tennessee, and in his home near
hville, called "Liberty Hill," Bishop McKendree held the first Tennessee conference
808. At the 1785 conference Coke spoke harshly of slavery and was rebuked by
se Lee, whereupon Coke objected to the passage of Lee's character, although he
ented and apologized. The few ordained elders were placed over groups of circuits
his conference and thus originated the office of presiding elder, although the term
not used until 1789. Here also Beverly Allen was ordained deacon and elder,
bably the first Methodist ordinations in North Carolina. (Lee: *Life and Times of
Rev. Jesse Lee*, 159; Smith: *History of Georgia Methodism*, 27–28; Shipp: *History
Methodism in South Carolina*, 157.)

Tuesday, 26. I preached at Bridge Creek chapel.[35] I was very ill, and w
tempted to think the Lord was about to lay me aside, or take me aw
and detain Doctor Coke in America.

Virginia

Saturday, 30. I am much better in health—my sickness was mad(
blessing to me. Rode to W. Mason's, where we are to meet in conferen
I found the minds of the people greatly agitated with our rules agai
slavery, and a proposed petition to the general assembly for the emar
pation of the blacks. Colonel Bedford and Doctor Coke disputed on t
subject,[36] and the Colonel used some threats: next day, brother O'K(
let fly at them, and they were made angry enough; we, however, came
with whole bones, and our business in conference was finished in pea

Thursday, *May* 5. At Robert Jones's, I found a blessing in my labou
Spent the evening with William Graves; I am weak in body, but I hav
constant sense of the presence of God. Rode to Lane's chapel, wher
found a serious, loving people.

Sunday, 8. Rode to Ellis's chapel—read prayers and preached. It a
pears to be low times here. I was happy with brothers Nichols and Spr
ley in the evening.

Monday, 9. Set off for James City, came to James River, and missi
the house where the ferrymen stay, I was detained some time befor
found them.

Tuesday, 10. Had a large congregation at Chickahominy church.[3]
administered the sacrament to a number of communicants, and we ha
very gracious season.

Thursday, 12. Rode to Yorktown, lately the seat of war. Here L(
Cornwallis surrendered to the combined armies of America and Fran
The inhabitants are dissolute and careless. I preached to a few seri(
women at one o'clock; and, at the desire of the ladies, again at four o'clo(
I came to Mrs. Rowe's: the son was once on our side;[38] he has left
and now we have the mother. I lodged in the poor-house.

[35] Bridge Creek Chapel in the old colonial precinct of Bertie was an Anglican ch:
and a regular preaching place for the Methodists. (*Historical Papers of Trinity I
torical Association*, 9–13, 57.)

[36] This is one of several occasions on which Coke aroused animosity by his opposi
to slavery. He urged the conference, which met at Mason's May 1–4, to send a peti
to the Virginia Assembly for the emancipation of the slaves, and this was done.

[37] Chickahominy Church was the upper church in James City Parish. It stood a
country crossroads two miles south of Toano and has long since disappeared, hav
been burned some time after the Civil War. Asbury refers several times to preach
there. (Mason, *op. cit.*, 22.)

[38] Samuel Rowe entered the itinerancy in 1779. He desisted from traveling in 1
and became a preacher in the Protestant Episcopal Church. (Lednum, *op. cit.*, 244–

Saturday, 14. I directed my course for Urbanna. I was apprehensive of
ɡust, while crossing the Rappahannock; but I reached the other side in
ɛty, lodging with Colonel Gordon and Captain Owings. I waited on
lonel Carter, a Baptist; a man of a most excellent spirit: we had much
ɛ conversation on the subjects of religion, Churches, and slavery.

Maryland

We crossed the Potomac at Hoe's ferry, and found the people vulgarly
ɛked, drinking and swearing: we paid a dollar for our ferriage, and
ɛ them. Perhaps the providence of God led me this way, that I might see
ɑ learn to pity the state of the people in the northern Neck of Virginia;
ɑ those also of Charles and St. Mary's counties in Maryland—I have
ɛn sensibly affected with their situation.

Thursday, 19. Preached at Gabriel Childs's, and at David Weems's; at
ich last place they are building a chapel. I hasted on to Annapolis; but
ɾough neglect, the people had no notice of my coming. Brother William
ɪl was here a few weeks past, when one S——, a barber, came to mock;
ɑ, it is said, stood up to preach, and said his sins were forgiven: he
s soon seized with sickness, and made a sudden exit; here we will
ve him.

Sunday, 22. Notwithstanding it rained, many attended, of both rich
ɑ poor: but in the afternoon, the wind, or the rain, kept the gentry
ay; many of the common people heard gladly.

Virginia

From Annapolis, we rode to Alexandria, to meet Dr. Coke; he did not
ne, however, until the next day.

Thursday, 26. We waited on GENERAL WASHINGTON, who received us
y politely, and gave us his opinion against slavery.[39]

Maryland

Friday, 27. We returned to Annapolis. The Doctor preached at six
lock, to a crowded congregation: thence, passing through Baltimore,
came to Mr. Gough's.

ᵍ At this famous meeting Washington informed Coke and Asbury that he shared
ir sentiments on emancipation but that he did not think it proper to sign the petition;
vever, he stated that he would signify his sentiments by letter if the Assembly con-
ɛred the subject. The General invited the two preachers to spend the night with him,
they could not accept because of an engagement at Annapolis the following day.
ɔke: *Journal*, 73; see letter to George Washington, April 24, 1786.)

Monday, 30. We went to Abingdon, to settle our college business and took a bond for the conveyance of the ground: we then returned, a fixed our plan for the approaching conference.

Wednesday, June 1. Our conference began.[41] I was unwell during session, a blister running, applied for a pain in my breast. On *Thursd* the Doctor took his leave of America for this visit. We parted w heavy hearts. On *Friday* we rested from our labours, and had a l feast.

Saturday, 4. I spent three hours profitably, in reading the print minutes of the conference.

I left Baltimore at three o'clock to take a little breath after such press of business.

Sunday, 5. I rode to Abingdon, to preach the foundation sermon Cokesbury College: I stood on the ground where the building is to erected, warm as it was, and spoke from Psalm lxxviii, 4–8. I had libe in speaking, and faith to believe the work would go on.

Monday, 6. From Abingdon I returned to Perry Hall, and there co tinued until *Friday*.

Saturday, 11. Preached in Baltimore, on "Ye know not what manner spirit ye are of." In the town I spoke three times, and at the Point on

Friday, 17. Preached at the Garrison church to a dull, backslid people.

Friday, 24. I crossed the mountains to Sharpsburg, and preached some honest Germans.

West Virginia

Came on to Shepherdstown.

Tuesday, 28. Rode to the Springs called Bath; now under great impro ment. I preached in the play-house, and lodged under the same roof w the actors. Some folks, who would not hear me in their own neighbo hood, made now a part of my audience, both night and morning. Leav Bath I came to brother Dew's (on the South branch of the Potom very unwell.

Sunday, July 3. The day was rainy: nevertheless I preached, administe the sacrament, and baptized some children.

[40] On January 5 Coke "gave orders that the materials should be procured for erection of the College." An item of business was the purchase of four acres of gro from Josias Dallam for sixty pounds sterling. (Coke: *Journal*, 53, 74; Lee: *A S History of the Methodists*, 112–18; Bangs, *op. cit.*, I, 229–40.)

[41] This conference, held in Baltimore, was one of three this year. It was presided by Coke, who after the second day sailed for England, whereupon the burden fell u the ailing Asbury. At this conference St. Mary's Circuit in southern Maryland created. (Coke: *Journal*, 76.)

Saturday, 9. Rode to Peter Dewit's,[42] where I had many to hear, and ne to have their children baptized.[43]

Sunday, 10. My congregation was large. Hard labour has almost over-ne me. I rode to Simpkin's,[44] where I found some life among the peo-. A long, dreary ride, brought us to Morgantown.[45] I preached and bap-ed, and was much spent.

Pennsylvania

Thursday, 14. I was taken with an inflammation in my throat: I preached Col. Charles Martin's:[46] afterward I went on, in the night, and very well, to Seaton's.[47]

Friday, 15. I had a high fever; I however bore up to ride eight miles, 1 preached and baptized.

Saturday, 16. Rode to Litten's,[48] but could not preach.

Tuesday, 19. Came to Besontown;[49] gave an exhortation, and rode on ——.

West Virginia

Thursday, 21. Went to Mr. John Jeremiah Jacob's,[50] Old Town; he and wife appear to be much engaged.

Peter Dewit was a prominent man who lived in present Mineral (then Hampshire) nty, West Virginia, about seventeen miles from Colonel Barrett. (See note under *rnal* entry for July 12, 1782.) He later moved to Clarke County, Kentucky. (Ayres iuscript, February–March, 1788; *Glade Star*, Oakland, Maryland, March 31, 1945.)

Between July 3 and 9, for which there is no record, Asbury made his second crossing he mountains to the headwaters of the Ohio. This is the record of the first Methodist tisms west of the mountains by Asbury.

Judge, or Squire, John Simpkins was a noted innkeeper on the Braddock Road. inn was on what was called the Bear Camp on Mill Run, thirty-two miles from ontown. (*Glade Star*, March 31, 1942; March 31, 1946; September 30, 1947; March 1950; June 30, 1950.)

Morgantown, in present Monongalia County, West Virginia, had no Methodist tinghouse as late as 1794, although there was one five years later. (See the Ayres iuscript; Smeltzer, *op. cit.*, 70; Smith: *Recollections of an Old Itinerant*; *Journal* ·y for July 24, 1790.)

Colonel Charles Martin lived just south of the Pennsylvania-West Virginia line a little west of the Monongahela River. He erected in 1788 the sixth chapel in this on west of the mountains. It is in West Virginia, half a mile south of the state ndary and a mile or more west of the river. (Smeltzer, *op. cit.*, 68, 69.)

Seaton lived across the line in Pennsylvania, in which state Asbury spent the next ral days. He probably spent the nights of July 19, 20, at John Simpkins (see note er *Journal* entry for July 10, 1785) and continued down the Braddock Road through tern Maryland and back into present West Virginia on July 21.

Samuel Litten lived about two miles southeast of Bentleyville, Pennsylvania.

Besontown was the present Uniontown, Pennsylvania.

John Jeremiah Jacob (1757–1839) was a merchant, Revolutionary officer, and il preacher who lived across the river from Old Town, Maryland, in present West

Sunday, 24. As an appointment was made for me to-day, I read pray
and preached with some pain, and to little purpose.

Monday, Tuesday, Wednesday. Very unwell, with a relapse of an
flammatory complaint in the throat; or some time I could get no reli
honey, a remedy so excellent in such cases, was not to be had: meanti
I ate with pain, and was called to the exercise of patience.

Thursday, 28. Being in a good degree recovered, I felt thankful.
spirit is grieved at so much vanity as is seen here at Bath, by the ma
poor careless sinners around me. The living is expensive, four dollars
week. Capt. —— is here, raised almost from the grave: I feel tende
for him; I hope God will convert his soul.

Sunday, 31. Mr. Keith gave us a sermon; very legal and to little purpo
In the afternoon I gave them my last discourse on Rom. i, 16.

Maryland

Monday, August 1. Rode thirty miles: I was almost spent; I ate a lit
and was glad to get to bed.

Tuesday, 2. I felt better: the weather is very warm.

Wednesday, 3. I rode fifty miles: I felt weary, but better in health.

Thursday, 4. Reached Baltimore. Our friends here have bought a l
and are building a new chapel thereon, seventy by forty-six feet: it is w
fixed for entrances and light.[51]

Sunday, 7. From preaching so frequently in the evenings, and con
quent exposure to night air, I have suffered a relapse, and the inflammati
of my throat has returned: to this was added a bilious lax; so that I w
laid up at Mr. Gough's until Saturday, the 20th inst. During my st
Mrs. Chamier has departed this life, and is gone, I trust, to Abraha
bosom. It has been a school of affliction to me; but I am thankful that
my sufferings, I had a skilful physician, and constant attendance from

Virginia. In early life he lived with and conducted stores for Captain Michael Cre
(see notes under *Journal* entries for July 12, 1782; June 28, 1784), and in 1781 he marr
Cresap's widow. Asbury stayed often in his home, held a conference there in 1793,
ordained him on August 25, 1813. In 1826 Jacob wrote *A Biographical Sketch of the*
of the Late Captain Michael Cresap, and a letter to Asbury in 1803 was printed
Letters to Bishop Asbury and Whatcoat, which was published early in the ninetee
century. (See *Journal* entries and notes for July 12, 1782; June 28, 1784; July
1784; July 11, 1786; June 25, 1808; August 25, 1813; Stevens, *op. cit.*, II, 136, 1
Cresap: *The History of the Cresaps; Heads of Families, 1784*.)

[51] This was the first Light Street Chapel, which stood on the northwest corner
Light Street and Wine Alley, Baltimore. It was built to accommodate the congregati
that had become too large for Lovely Lane Meeting House. (Roberts: *Centen*
Album of Methodism, 76; *The Methodist Quarterly Review*, July, 1856, 445.)

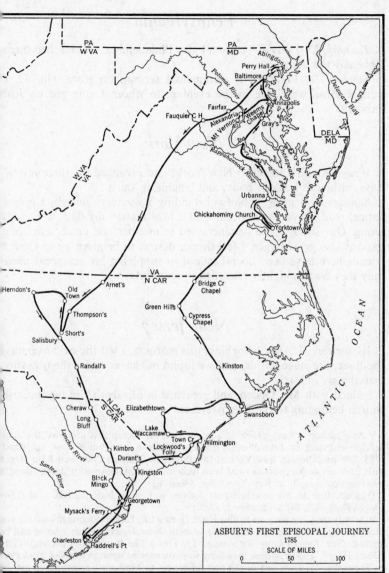

ASBURY'S FIRST EPISCOPAL JOURNEY
1785
SCALE OF MILES
0   50   100

nd nurses, and I was in a house where prayer was wont to be made. I
ve been taught the necessity of walking more holily and humbly with
od; to pray more fervently, and to preach more faithfully.

Sunday, 21. I was just able to perform the funeral rites of Mrs. Chamier. I
preached to about one thousand people, and had a very serious time.

Pennsylvania

Tuesday, 23. I set off, very weak, for Philadelphia, and reached there
Thursday the 25th.

Sunday, 28. Preached a sacramental sermon on Rom. viii, 32. C
congregation was large in the evening, to whom I enlarged on Josh
xxiv, 19.

New York

Wednesday, 31. Reached New York; and preached the three followi
days, although weak in body, and languid in spirit.

Sunday, September 4. Notwithstanding I was very unwell, I preach
thrice, read prayers twice, and held a love feast:[52] my flesh went heav
along. Our society here has increased in number and grace; our cong
gations also grow larger. I feel deeper desires to be given up to God. N
friends here have been liberal indeed in supplying my temporal needs
may they be abundantly rewarded in spirituals!

New Jersey

Wednesday, 7. After preaching, this morning, I left the city: overstayi
the hour, the stage left us, and we found ourselves under the necessity
walking six miles.[54]

I dined with Mr. Ogden, and preached in Elizabeth,[55] in the unfinish
church belonging to the Presbyterians.[56]

[52] As a bishop Asbury probably administered the sacraments and used the Sund
Service sent over by John Wesley. See the *Discipline and Prayer Book* published
1785. The preachers in New York at this time were Thomas Chew and John Hager
with Ezekiel Cooper, who had just been received on trial, assigned to Long Island a
assisting occasionally at New York. (See *Minutes.*)

[53] In addition to his entertainment Asbury was given four pounds. (*John Str*
Church Records, I, for September 5, 1785.)

[54] Asbury took the ferry to Paulus Hook (Jersey City) and evidently missed the sta
necessitating the walk of six miles to Elizabeth, New Jersey. Asbury's horse had be
injured. (See *Journal* entry for August 15, 1786.) The bishop was accompanied
"Black Harry" Hosier, whose preaching was commented upon in the *New York Pack*
on September 11, 1786, one of the first references to Methodist preaching in any N
York newspaper. The John Street society had paid two pounds for Harry's tra
expenses. (*John Street Church Records*, I, for these dates; Seaman, *op. cit.*, 92 ff.; a
note under *Journal* entry for June 29, 1780.)

[55] Methodism was introduced in Elizabeth, New Jersey, this year. It was on the Ne
ark Circuit on which John Haggerty was stationed. One of the leaders was Elias Cra
who was converted by Uzal Ogden. He was a descendant of Stephen Crane, a found
of Elizabeth, and a relative of a signer of the Declaration of Independence. In 1791

Friday, 9. Heard Mr. Woodhull[57] preach a funeral discourse on "Lord, ou hast made my days as a handbreadth." In my judgment he spoke ell.

Saturday, 10. I had liberty in preaching to the people at Monmouth,[58] i Josh. xxiv, 17, and felt much for the souls present.

Saturday, 17. Quarterly meeting at Morris's River:[59] our house was not ite covered, and it was falling weather; the people, nevertheless, ayed to hear me preach; afterward brother Abbott and brother Simon icas[60] spoke to them.

Sunday, 18. We had a great time; the people spoke freely of the deal-gs of God with their souls.

Wednesday, 21. Rode to brother Fisler's. I received my wagon for forty-ur pounds. Will it not bring me into trouble in travelling, and in getting orses?

Saturday, 24. Preached at Salem and at Stow Creek,[61] with some conso-tion: many attended, although it rained, and we had a comfortable ne at sacrament. I plunged H. T. and S. M. in Salem Creek: this unusual iptismal ceremony might, perhaps, have made our congregation larger an it would otherwise have been. Lord, help me to keep on, under all my oubles of body and mind! From Salem we proceeded on thirty miles rough a great storm; we were glad to stop at Gloucester, where we had

oved to Uniontown, Pennsylvania, where he became a class leader and local preacher d where he entertained Asbury, Coke, and Whatcoat. In 1813 he moved to Leesburg, ere he opened his house for preaching and became instrumental in building a church use. He died on June 4, 1830. (Atkinson, *op. cit.*, 318, 319.)

[56] The First Presbyterian Church on Broad Street in Elizabeth was founded in 1664. rned during the Revolution in 1780, it was at this time being rebuilt. (*Historic adsides in New Jersey*, 104.)

[57] The Rev. Mr. Woodhull was the successor of William Tennent, Jr., at the First esbyterian or Old Tennent Church. (See note under *Journal* entry for September , 1782.)

[58] Monmouth or Freehold was three miles from the Tennent church. Asbury prob-ly preached in the courthouse. However, a society must have been formed there out 1780. In that year Job Throckmorton was converted there by the Rev. Richard irrettson. (Atkinson, *op. cit.*, 345.)

[59] The church on Morris, or Maurice, River was doubtless at Mauricetown in imberland County, although Atkinson (*op. cit.*, 344) thought it was at Port Eliza-th. Here lived the Fisler family from which came the Rev. Benjamin Fisler. Asbury turned here a year later. (Gordon, *op. cit.*, 175; Lednum, *op. cit.*, 295; Atkinson, *cit.*, 344.)

[60] Benjamin Abbott was one of the most noted preachers of New Jersey. Lucas had en a captain in the Revolution, after which he became a local preacher. According tradition he was converted by the Rev. John Brainerd and for more than twenty ars preached in the old Brainerd Free Church. (Heston: *South Jersey, a History*, II, 2; Lednum, *op. cit.*, 295–96.)

[61] Stow Creek flows through Salem and Cumberland Counties to Delaware Bay. township bears the same name. There does not seem to have been a church there. ordon, *op. cit.*, 244.)

a room to ourselves, enjoying our Christian privileges, and were comfo
able.

Pennsylvania

Next morning we came on to Cooper's ferry,[62] and although the wi
blew violently in the morning, when we came to the ferry all was cal
We breakfasted in Philadelphia early enough for church.

Monday, 26. Set out for the south; and arrived at Chester. Next d
preached at Matson's;[63] arriving at Wilmington, I preached there
James i, 27.

Delaware

Friday, 30. At Blackiston's chapel. I felt the necessity of watching agai
the spirit of politics, and of being more in the spirit of prayer: the peopl
minds are agitated with the approaching election of delegates to t
assembly.

October 1. Came to Dover. I had the court house full of people, bu
was not in possession of liberty of mind or strength of body to preac
The election is not yet over.

Monday, 3. We had a gracious season at the sacrament at Purdin
That evening I rode to brother White's, and was closely occupied wi
temporals.

Maryland

Saturday, 8. We had an open time, and the souls of the people we
stirred up at Angiers; the Lord was also with us at Worton chapel in
afternoon.

Sunday, 9. I preached at Kent Old Chapel, on, "Ye have said it is va
to serve God:"—in the afternoon and at night in Chestertown. I alwa
have an enlargement in preaching in this very wicked place: the peoj
to-day were very serious and attentive.

[62] Cooper's ferry was between Camden, New Jersey, and Philadelphia, across
Delaware River.

[63] Aaron Matson lived at West Branch near Rockdale, Delaware County, Pe
sylvania. His father, Morris Matson, had opened the house to preaching a few ye
after Captain Webb preached in the Marcus Hook area. Mount Chapel was b
there in 1797. It is now Mount Hope. Hallman (*Garden of Methodism*, 116) says t
Matson lived north of Wilmington, New Castle County, Delaware, and that
present Mount Pleasant Church was formerly called Matson's Chapel.

Monday, 10. Came to Brown's Chapel; there was a spirit of life among the people, and my own soul felt comfortably. Some of our principal members here are men who have not been successful; had they prospered in their pursuits, perhaps they never would have sought the Lord: being now in possession of religion, there is the less of danger in prosperity; I therefore counselled them to go to the western country, where the means of rearing a family, and advancing in the world, were more within the reach of the inhabitants.

October 24. Set off from brother White's, for Dorset circuit. I preached at brother William Frazier's[64] in the evening. After visiting the societies in this quarter, I came on *Saturday* to Caroline quarterly meeting, at the widow Haskins's; here we had a gracious season.

Rode to Dover quarterly meeting. Our brethren preached and exhorted, and I administered the sacrament.

Wednesday, November 2. I preached on Caleb's following the Lord fully. I left Dover, and felt some pain in parting with my friends.

Saturday, 5. I crossed the Chesapeake, and found some difficulty in getting my wagon over: I missed my appointment at the college, and came late to Mr. Gough's.

Sunday, 6. Came away early, and arriving in Baltimore, preached at noon, on Heb. xi, 2–8; and at night, on Caleb's fully following the Lord. I found the means of conveyance by my carriage, or Jersey wagon, would not do.

Tuesday, 8. I preached at Annapolis to a multitude of people, part of whom were serious.

Wednesday, 9. I was under considerable exercise of mind about my carriage; I at length resolved to decline travelling in it, and buying a second-hand sulky, left it to be sold. I now travelled light and easy, and came to Childs's church.[65]

Being disappointed in crossing at Holland's Point,[66] I shaped my course for Alexandria. I preached on the Sabbath evening on my way, to an attentive congregation, and reached town on *Monday*, 14.

---

[64] Captain William Frazier, a wealthy and influential convert to Methodism, lived near Preston, Caroline County, Maryland. From his family Frazier's Chapel, second Methodist meetinghouse in Caroline County, took its name. In the churchyard of Bethesda Methodist Church is a memorial to Captain Frazier, which in 1953 was one of the four historical markers in Caroline County. (Lednum, *op. cit.*, 265; Hallman, *op. cit.*, 112, 282, 288; *Federalsburg, an Historical Souvenir.*)

[65] This is the first mention of a church named for the family of Gabriel D. Childs. In 1781 Nelson Reed, when on the Calvert Circuit, discussed the prospects of erecting a church. (Manuscript *Journal* of Nelson Reed, June 11, 1781.)

[66] Holland's Point on the east side of the Patuxent River opposite Benedict in Charles County derived its name from the custom of travelers wishing to cross "hollering" for the ferryman. William Colbert while on the Calvert Circuit refers to the "Hollowing Point Meeting House." This was replaced by Asbury Church at Barstow, one-half mile from the original site. (See *Journal* of William Colbert, March 14, 1790.)

Virginia

Tuesday, 15. I dined with Dr. Samuel Smith and Mr. M'Kendree, a General Roberdeau's.[67] Our conversation turned upon slavery; th difficulties attending emancipation, and the resentment some of the mem bers of the Virginia legislature expressed against those who favoured general abolition. I preached in the court house. I took cold by comin out into the open air whilst in a profuse perspiration; and this I seldo fail to do, if I preach to a large congregation in a close, warm place. I the afternoon I set out, and spent the evening with brother Foster,[68] a Mr. V——'s: it rained, and the house was like a sieve—they could n even keep the beds from the wet.

Thursday, 17. The morning was very damp, and I imprudently set o an hour before day; I thus increased the cold I had caught in Alexandri and brought on a regular attack of my old complaint—an inflammatic in the throat. The day was very cold, and we suffered much: we stoppe at a very indifferent house, where there were no beds fit for use, and n candles: we had to wait about two hours for some boiled milk. My fev and inflammation increasing, I rode on thirty-three miles, to Collins's, i Caroline county, where I became indisposed indeed.

Saturday, 19. I could not think it safe to stop here; I went on, passin by Hanover court house, Hanover and Newcastle towns,[69] anxious to g into a good lodging and amongst kind people. I called at one tolerab house; plain people they were, but ill as I was I could not stay her Journeying on, I came to a petty *ordinary*, where the host recommende me to a widow Chamberlayne, who, he thought, would receive me an use me well: it was growing late, and it was cold; and it was still fi miles to her house; on, however, I went; the Lord opened the heart this widow, and she kindly received me under her roof: I found her to be motherly woman, and to have some skill in my complaint. I was doubtf whether it were best to bleed or blister; my throat inflamed and ulcerate In this situation I continued with little amendment, until on *Wednesd* morning the 23d, one ulcer broke; and on *Thursday* the other. I was no

[67] General Roberdeau introduced Asbury and Coke to General Washington. (S Lednum, *op. cit.*, 419.)

[68] This evidently was Thomas Foster, presiding elder of the district which includ Redstone, Allegheny, Berkeley, Fairfax, St. Mary's, Lancaster, and Calvert. T districts were not named in the *Minutes* at that time. (See *Minutes*, 1785.)

[69] These two towns were flourishing ports on the Pamunkey River. The former w known first as Page's Warehouse, being about fifteen miles from the present bridge the Tappahannock Highway, and New Castle Town was a short distance below Both are now abandoned. As late as 1830 New Castle was an important shipping poi for tobacco. In the debates which preceded the removal of the Virginia capitol fro Williamsburg to Richmond, Hanover Town came within a few votes of being made t capitol of the state. (Gwathmey, *op. cit.*, 86–88.)

a fair way for recovery; but having taken cold by frequent bathing my
et, a violent pain and swelling settled in the joint of my great toe, to
hich I applied a bath and poultice of bitter herbs. My spirits have not
iled. I find myself humbled before the Lord; and hope that this affliction
ill be for his glory and my good.

Friday, 25. This day I rode to James City.

Sunday, 27. I went to Chickahominy church, where conditional notice
ad been given for brother Reed: I preached on Acts vi, 31, and spent the
ening at Mr. Welden's. My foot continuing in such a state as to prevent
y going to my appointments, I was led to reflect on this dark providence.
nwilling to be idle, I wrote to the preachers to do what they could in
llecting money to carry on the building of our college. For some time
ast, I had not been quite satisfied with the order and arrangement of our
rm of discipline; and persuaded that it might be improved without
fficulty, we accordingly set about it, and during my confinement in
mes City completed the work, arranging the subject-matter thereof
der their proper heads, divisions, and sections.

December 4, 5. I felt somewhat better, and had a great desire to go on
y way. We set out and came to the James River; after long waiting we
t over, but with difficulty—the high wind meeting the tide, made so
ugh a sea that the water came with great violence into the boat, as we
eat out of the creek's mouth to get into the river: thus exposed, I took
ld, which brought on a slight inflammation, and next day increased, and
oduced a fever.

North Carolina

Saturday, 17. Having proceeded on, I arrived at brother Reddrick's, in
ates's county, North Carolina, where I spoke a little.

Sunday, 18. I had more hearers at Winton[70] than I expected; they were
tentive to what I said on Joshua xxiv, 19.

At Wicocon the glory is departed. A few Baptist women stood at a
stance and wept, whilst I administered the sacrament: they dared not
me to the table, lest they should be discovered by their own people.

On *Thursday* last we made an attempt to cross the Roanoke at Cashie[71]
t could not get a flat; we then made for Oliver's ferry, and having no
owledge of the way, I waded through Rock West twice, and wet my
oks. The river was rising rapidly, and we had still six miles to Long
rry: I was very unwell, and my spirits greatly sunk. After getting over,
r difficulties did not cease; we had to wade several deep and dangerous

---

[70] Winton is across Chowan River in Hertford County, North Carolina.
[71] The Cashie River flows into the Roanoke. The present crossing is at Windsor in
rtie County, North Carolina.

swamps: we, at length, by kind Providence, were brought safely to brothe Currell's, where we met brother Morris.[72] The two following days we wen on in the same manner, both horses and riders sometimes in danger a they worried through the swampy wilds.

A solitary day this!—plenty of water, if nothing else. We employed black man to ride our horses, and we took to a canoe; being remounted and journeying on, we came to a stream that was impassable—we foun ourselves under the necessity of going round by Martinsburg, and thu got into the road, and now pushed forward with spirit, until we came t Swift's Creek;[73] here the causeway was overflown, and the logs most o them afloat; my horse fell, but I was preserved by his securing a fore-foc hold on the timber after falling: thus we toiled over our swampy route and crazy bridges, till seven o'clock; and about that time arrived at Neus Ferry, having ridden about forty tedious miles.

Came to Newbern.[74] Found brothers Allen and Baldwin[75] in th church; I preached at three o'clock, on, "The world by wisdom knew nc God." The assembly was in session, and some of the members wer friendly.[76]

Wednesday, 21. Sailed down to Beaufort, and preached in the church: the people are kind, but have very little religion. On the same evening pushed down to the Straits,[78] and the next day preached at the Strait chapel; thence I returned to town, and preached again; after which w sailed back to Colonel Bell's,[79] whence we first started.

[72] Edward Morris was one of the preachers on the Roanoke Circuit which extende into this section of North Carolina. (See *Minutes.*)

[73] Asbury probably reached Swift's Creek in Pitt County. Since entering Nort Carolina he had proceeded through the present Gates, Hertford, Bertie, and Edgecom counties. This whole section was a "swampy route" traversed by the Roanoke, Ta Neuse, and Pamlico rivers, Swift and Fishing creeks, and other streams.

[74] New Bern in Craven County was laid out by Baron Christoph von Graffenrie shortly after 1710 and named for the capitol of his native Switzerland. Here was estal lished in 1762 the first school authorized by legislative enactment in North Carolin Pilmoor preached in New Bern at Christmas in 1772 and stayed with William Woc there. Methodism flourished in the town during the early period, and Asbury frequent visited it. (*Account of the Founding of New Bern*; Grissom, *op. cit.,* 7, 37, 169, 320

[75] John Baldwin was serving the Wilmington Circuit. Beverly Allen had been on th circuit the previous year and had remained in North Carolina in 1785 even though l had been appointed to Georgia. (See *Minutes*; Betts: *South Carolina Methodism,* 55

[76] New Bern at this time was the capitol of North Carolina.

[77] The church at Beaufort was an Anglican church which was used by preachers various denominations and also for school purposes. (Grissom, *op. cit.,* 149.)

[78] The Straits was a mainland community fourteen miles by land from Beaufor bordering the straits of Core Sound. The Straits Chapel was Tabernacle Church, a Anglican meetinghouse.

[79] Colonel and Mrs. Bell and Mrs. Bell's sister were the first Methodists in t New Bern area, and Bell's Chapel was one of the first meetinghouses for Methodis Colonel Bell's two sons, Caleb and Jacob, became Methodist preachers. (Grisson *op. cit.,* 150.)

Saturday and *Sunday*, 24, 25. We held quarterly meeting at Swansboro; any people—little religion.

We came to Ford's ferry on Drowning creek.[80] The waters had risen, nd extended far outwards from the banks of the stream; here we were rought to a full stop: providentially, we found a man there who was aiting for his brother to fetch him over; the brother came, and we all rossed over together; not, however, without danger—bushes would rike the horses, and their capering about had well-nigh overset the boat.

[80] Drowning Creek rises in Moore County and flows through Scotland and Robeson unties. East of Robeson it is known as Lumber River. Asbury probably crossed in obeson County.

1786

Asbury at Beesontown in Pennsylvania, on his first western trip

CHAPTER FIFTEEN

South Carolina

January 4, 1786. I rode my sore-backed horse about thirty miles to ␣nham's, in Britton's Neck.[1] Dunham is in despair: this, perhaps, is ␣nstitutional—or it may be owing to his circumstances; the awakening ␣ God's Spirit, or the combination of all these may have produced this ␣ect. I borrowed brother A——'s horse, and we went on. We crossed ␣reat Pedee, and Lynch's creek, and wet my books: coming to Black ␣ingo, we lodged at a tavern, and were well used.[2] Sleeping upstairs, I ␣s afraid the shingles, if not the roof of the house, would be taken away ␣th the wind.

Saturday, 7. I preached at Georgetown twice to about eighty people ␣ch time; this is a poor place for religion. Here I was met by brother ␣enry Willis.[3]

[1] Asbury entered the state in upper Marion (now Dillon) County, crossing the Little ␣e Dee River. Britton's Neck is in lower Marion County. Britton's Neck Methodist ␣urch is no longer active, having merged with Central Church on the Centenary ␣arge. There were then or soon thereafter four meetinghouses along the route, one ␣ which was near the junction of Great Pee Dee and Lynch's Creek. (See Map, 1823.)

[2] This was doubtless at Port's (Porter's) Ferry where Asbury frequently stayed. It ␣s five miles west of Britton's Neck. The Bishop crossed the Great Pee Dee here and ␣ssed Lynch's Creek at Wrag's Ferry into Williamson County. He followed Black ␣ingo Creek and Black River to the Black Mingo settlement along the route of his ␣evious trip in 1785. This became his favorite route through the region.

[3] Henry Willis was the "presiding elder" of the district which included the Yadkin ␣d Holston circuits covering northern and western North Carolina and all the Holston ␣untry of Tennessee and Virginia.

Tuesday, 10. Rode to Wappetaw. It was no small comfort to me to a very good frame prepared for the erection of a meeting house for us, that very road[4] along which, last year, we had gone pensive and distress without a friend to entertain us.

Wednesday, 11. Preached at Sinclair Capers's[5]—we had a good ti and many hearers, considering that neither place or weather was favo able: my soul enjoyed great peace, and I was much engaged with God t my labours might not be in vain. From Capers's I came to Cain Hoy water. I was grieved at Beverly Allen's[6] conduct; hurt to the cause of G may follow.

Friday, 13. I came to Charleston: being unwell, brother Willis suppl my place.

Sunday, 15. We had a solemn time in the day, and a full house a good time in the evening. My heart was much taken up with God. C congregations are large, and our people are encouraged to undertake building of a meeting house this year. Charleston has suffered much—fire about 1700—again in November, 1740—and lastly, the damage s tained by the late war: the city is now in a flourishing condition.

Friday, 20. I left the city, and found the road so bad that I was thank I had left my carriage, and had a saddle and a good pair of boots.[7] were water bound at Wassamaw, where I found a few who had be awakened by the instrumentality of our preachers. I was comforted reading Mr. Zublee's account of the death of some pious Germans; a also Mrs. Fletcher's[8] account of her husband's death.

[4] This was the coast road to Wappetaw Swamp just below Awendaw. He had cros the Santee at Myzack's Ferry.

[5] Leaving Georgetown, Asbury proceeded along his 1785 route until he was wit twenty-five miles of Charleston. Then he turned southwest over the Wappetaw Swa Bridge to Cainhoy, which was inland from Caper's Island and Caper's Inlet on coast. Between the bridge and Cainhoy lived Captain George Sinclair Capers, uncle of William Capers who was to become famous as the founder and superintend of the Plantation Missions and a bishop. Bishop Caper's mother, née Mary Singleta and her parents are buried at Cainhoy. Bishop Capers says that his father, Willi Capers, was converted this year under the preaching of Asbury's companion He Willis. (*Life of William Capers, D.D.*, autobiography completed by Wightman, 12, 41.)

[6] Beverly Allen, soon to become an apostate and a criminal, had not gone to appointment in Georgia but worked around Cainhoy, South Carolina, and Ans North Carolina. Asbury apparently did not trust him in spite of his standing and confided to Bishop Coke.

[7] Leaving Charleston, Asbury followed a new route. He went northward along old State Road to Wassamaw Swamp in the present Berkeley County.

[8] John Fletcher of Madeley died August 14, 1785, in his fifty-sixth year. He wa saintly man, second in the Methodist command, and chosen by Wesley as his success He wrote two famous works, *Appeal to Matter of Fact and Common Sense*, on hum depravity, and *Checks to Antinomianism*, against Calvinism. He married Mary Bos quet, who became a preacher and took his place in the parish of Madeley after death.

Monday, 23. The Wassamaw being still impassable, we directed our
irse up the low lands through the wild woods,[9] until we came to Mr.
inter's, an able planter, who would have us to dine with him and stay
night. His wife's mother being ill and desiring the sacrament, we went
her apartment, and there had a melting, solemn time: in this worthy
nily we had prayer night and morning.

Tuesday, 24. We made an early start. We stopped at a tavern for break-
t; the landlord had seen and heard me preach three years before in
rginia, and would receive no pay. That evening we came to Mrs. B.'s.
rode fifty miles to the Congaree: we lodged where there were a set of
mblers: I neither ate bread nor drank water with them. We left these
cklegs early next morning, and after riding nine miles, came to a fire,
ere, stopping and broiling our bacon, we had a *high* breakfast. At
aver's ferry we crossed the Saluda.[10] Here once lived that strange, de-
iged mortal, who proclaimed himself to be God: report says, that he
led three men for refusing their assent to his godship: he gave out his
e to be the Virgin Mary, and his son Jesus Christ; and when hanged at
arleston, promised to rise the third day.

Friday, 27. I had near four hundred hearers at Parrott's log church,
ir Broad River.[11] We have ridden about two hundred miles in the last
ht days.

Sunday, 29. Having, by appointment, to preach on Sandy River, we set
in the rain which had been falling all the night before: the first little
eam we attempted to cross had well-nigh swept brother M'Daniel
ay. We rode on to Little Sandy, but found it too much swollen for us to
d; going up the stream, we crossed over on a log, our horses swimming
er; having gained the opposite bank, we continued on about twenty
les, and had a trying time: I was happy, although brother Willis was
aid we should be obliged to sleep in the woods.

Monday, 30. We rode to friend Terry's;[12] but here we met with our old
ficulties, and were compelled to go up higher. Coming to Great Sandy,
crossed the river at Walker's mill; and here we were in danger of losing

Detouring around Wassamaw Swamp, Asbury proceeded along the route of the
sent Holly Hill and Cameron, and a little west of the present St. Matthews.
The Saluda and Broad rivers unite at Columbia to form the Congaree. The
ongarees" and the tavern were in the upper part of the present Calhoun County.
iury proceeded along the lower or western bank of the Congaree via Granby, south
he present Columbia, and crossed the Saluda at Weaver's Ferry, later called Hart's
ry, at a point which is now the eastern shore of Lake Murray above Columbia.
Asbury followed the road up the west side of Broad River through Newberry
inty. Parrott's Log Meeting House has not been certainly identified, but it was
bably in Newberry County near the present town of Blair in Fairfield County, and
evidently due to the work of the Rev. James Foster from Virginia.
Asbury crossed the Broad River near its junction with the Enoree near Blair and
ered Fairfield County. Terry's was on the border of Fairfield and Chester counties
appears as "Tan Yard" on the old maps.

both our horses; the water came with such rapidity from the dam t
it swept them down the stream under a log: we at length came to fat
Seally's:[13] here we stayed to refit, and had everything comfortable
preached on *Wednesday*, after which I had one hundred and fifty mile
ride to White's, Mulberry Fields, near the mouth of John's River.

North Carolina

Thursday, February 2.[14] We made a push for the Highlands, and go
far as brother Smith's. On *Friday* we aimed to get to the Horse Ford;
missing our way, we made but twenty-five miles, reaching Herman's, v
treated us kindly, and would receive nothing—this was well for us, for
had but little to give.

Saturday, 4. Was a very rainy day; however, we pushed on, and r
this day about fifty miles. We crossed the north branch of the Catav
River, and arriving late at the south branch, we providentially met wit
man who was acquainted with the ford and piloted us safe over; it v
dark, and the river mild: through a heavy day's journey we came, wet a
weary, to Mr. Moore's.

Sunday, 5. I preached at brother Connelly's, where there is a la
society, and a revival of religion.

Monday, 6. We rode to W. White's, and appointed preaching for
next day; here I had about one hundred hearers.

Wednesday, 8. We rode forty computed, and, perhaps, in truth, f
miles, to quarterly meeting at Gordon's, at the Mulberry Fields, on
Yadkin River: here we met with brothers Ivey, Bingham, and Willia
son.[15] *Thursday*, the sacrament was a time of refreshing.

Saturday, 11. I rode through rain and hail to B——'s, and preached
a few serious people on Psalm cxxviii, and we were blessed together.
what happiness do they lose who never visit the poor in their cottages

Sunday, 12. At Joseph Herndon's[16] it was a chilly day, but there v
some life among the people.

Monday, 13. There were many to hear at K——'s.

[13] Father Seally lived a little west of the present town of Chester (Chesterv
probably on Seally's Creek. From this point the bishop proceeded through Y
County into North Carolina.

[14] Asbury entered North Carolina into present Cleveland County and procee
northward.

[15] The quarterly conference was for the Yadkin Circuit. Richard Ivey was the e
over the Caswell, Salisbury, and Halifax circuits; and Henry Bingham and Thoi
Williamson were on the Yadkin Circuit. (*Minutes*, 1785.) Asbury was in Caldwell
Wilkes counties.

[16] Colonel Joseph Herndon lived in eastern Wilkes County, North Carolina. (
note under *Journal* entry for January 28, 1785.)

√ly rides are little short of twenty miles a day in this mountainous
√ntry, besides my public labours: my soul has peace, but this body is
√vy and afflicted with pain.

Tuesday, 14. We rode through the snow to Heady's, where, to my
prise, I found that the poor people had built a good house of logs; and
satisfied with this, they must needs collect a little money for me, if
√ould receive it.

Sunday, 19. Preached at Morgan Bryan's. Next day I set off in the rain,
l travelled with it: we swam Grant's creek, and reached Salisbury in
evening, wet and weary. I thought we should scarcely have preachers
the time appointed, but the bad weather did not stop their coming. We
√nt three days in conference, and went through our business with
√isfaction.[17] Having sent our horses into the country, we could not get
√m when they were wanted; I therefore borrowed brother Tunnell's[18]
√se, and went on to my appointments.

Wednesday, March 1. I found many waiting at Newman's church,
√ckingham county, to whom I enlarged on, "Christ our wisdom,
√hteousness, sanctification, and redemption." Provisions here are
√rce: some of our friends from the Delaware are suffering. I arrived in
√ night at A. Arnett's: my being in a poor cottage did not prevent my
√ng happy, for God was with me.

Thursday, 2. I preached on, "This do in remembrance of me;" and it
√s a solemn, good time.

Saturday, 4. At the widow Dick's the preachers fell in with each other:
√re were Foster, Ellis, L., and Hull;[19] the latter is a smooth-tongued
√tty speaker, a youth that promises fair for future usefulness.

Tuesday, 7. At Stanfield's I had many hearers, and more liberty in
√aking than I have had for some time past. It is hard to get and preserve
√ spirit of preaching: it seems as if God, at times and places, withholds

[17] The conference at Salisbury was one of three held in 1786, the others being at
√e's Chapel in Virginia the following April and at Baltimore in May. Twenty-four
√achers attended the Salisbury conference, seven of them being entertained by Mr.
√ Mrs. Fishburn. The latter had joined the society under Beverly Allen in 1783.
√dnum, *op. cit.*, 374; Grissom, *op. cit.*, 126. See note under *Journal* entry for Feb-
√ry 10, 1785.)

[18] John Tunnell (1755–90) was one of the preachers ordained at the Christmas Con-
√ence and had been stationed at Charleston, South Carolina, but later became one
√the pioneers of Methodism in the Holston country, where he died at Sweet Springs,
√ginia, in July, 1790. Asbury preached his funeral. (See *Journal* entry for July 10,
√0; Price: *Holston Methodism*, I, 176–83.)

[19] James Foster was elder in Georgia, Reuben Ellis an elder in North Carolina, and
√pe Hull was on the Pee Dee Circuit. The *L* might have been Jesse Lee, who had strong
√rth Carolina connections but who was at this time on the Caroline Circuit in Mary-
√d. He was on that circuit until March of this year and was at the conference in
√ginia on April 10. It would have been possible for him to attend the North Carolina
√sion in the interim. (Lee: *Life and Times of the Rev. Jesse Lee*, 182.)

his Spirit from his servants; or else the power of Satan is so strong as
depress the life and liberty of the speaker.

Friday, 10. I rode once more to Hillsboro, where I met with a c
reception: I am now satisfied never to visit that place again until they ha
a society formed, constant preaching, and a desire to see me. O, wha
county this is! We can but just get food for our horses. I am griev
indeed, for the sufferings, the sins, and the follies of the people.

Tuesday, 21. Came to Whitaker's chapel, near Fishing Creek,[20] wher
spoke, with but little consolation to myself, to about seventy souls. I f
my body unwell; but my soul is stayed in cheerful dependence upon G

Wednesday, 22. Rode to D.'s chapel, where I was met by about fi
hearers: spirituous liquors have greatly injured the people here.

Friday, 24. At Conniconnara chapel. I had nearly gone through
subject, when a man began to talk; his brother carried him away, af
fruitless endeavours to silence him. Brother Dickins spoke, and I ca
away in great pain to brother Clayton's.

Saturday, 25. I took some Hiera Picra,[21] and felt better. Read our Fo
of Discipline, in manuscript, which brother Dickins has been prepari
for the press.[22]

Sunday, 26. We had a large congregation, and a solemn time at broth
Clayton's. After meeting returned to brother Dickins's. He and his w
cleave to God; but there is a great declension elsewhere.

Tuesday, 28. I called on sister Bruce, at whose house I preached wh
she lived near Portsmouth, Virginia. I found her at the point of dea
her soul filled with the peace and love of God.

Virginia

I came on to Roanoak chapel, where I was led to be sharp while
treated on the form of godliness without the power.

I found the Lord was working among the people at Young's,
Mecklenburg, and felt myself to be in a warmer clime. We had a gracio
time at quarterly meeting, especially at the sacrament: the words of o

[20] Whitaker's Chapel on Fishing Creek in Halifax County, North Carolina, w
notable and was perhaps the meetinghouse of John Dickins when he lived in t
county. Nearby lived Mr. Long and Mr. Bustian who made the first gifts to the scho
which Dickins had planned. (See *Journal* entries for June 19, 1780.)

[21] Hiera Picra was "a cathartic powder made of aloes and canella bark." (*Webste
New International Dictionary*.)

[22] This was the first *Discipline* in its present form. Dickins after two years at Wes
Chapel in New York had returned to North Carolina to serve the Bertie Circuit. T
circuit was formed from a part of the Roanoke Circuit in 1783 and contained some
the points served previously by Dickins. At the Salisbury Conference he was ag
sent to New York, later to become the first Book Agent. (See note under *Journal* ent
for June 18, 1780; *Minutes*; Moore: *Pioneers of Methodism in North Carolina a
Virginia*, 106–17; Grissom, *op. cit.*, 60–61, 103.)

ellent sister Jones, both in speaking and in prayer, were sweetly and
verfully felt. The second day was great, both in preaching and love
st: my soul was melted; I have not witnessed such a meeting in the South.
aturday, April 1. Rode through the rain twenty-four miles to the
low Bedford's, where but a few, besides the society, came. I met the
rried men and women apart, and there were tenderness and tears,
atly felt, and copiously shed, among them.

riday, 7. I preached at Merritt's chapel, with but little life. I rode down
Mason's that night, much weakened through abstinence. A deep de-
:ion seized my spirits, so that I could hardly bear up. On the *Sabbath*
' I preached at Moss's, to a large congregation. We went forwards to-
rds Lane's church: here our conference was held—some spirits were
d before it ended. Here ten young men offered themselves on probation.
'hursday, 13. Rode through the rain to N. Lee's.
'riday, 14. Arrived in Petersburg, and had but a dull time.
Sunday, 16. Being Easter-day, I preached at the Manakintown on
loss. iii, 1–4, with some freedom.
Monday, 17. I directed my course northward, and on *Thursday* the
ntieth reached Alexandria.
Sunday, 23. Hail, glorious Lord! After deep exercises of body and mind,
el a solemn sense of God on my heart. I preached by day in the court
ise, on 1 Pet. iii, 10; and in the evening at the Presbyterian church, on
ke xix, 41, 42. Alexandria must grow: and if religion prospers among
m, it will be blessed. I drew a plan, and set on foot a subscription for a
eting house.

Maryland

Wednesday, 26. Arrived in Baltimore, and was occupied until the
lowing *Saturday* in collecting money for the books, and inspecting the
counts of the Book Concern.[23]
Sunday, 30. I preached three times, and made a collection to defray the
enses of sending missionaries to the western settlements;[24] I spoke
ce on the same subject through the course of the week.
Monday, May 8. Our conference began at Abingdon,[25] where love, can-
ur, and precision, marked our deliberations.

[23] This is Asbury's first reference to the Book Concern. Although its management
h before and after its official organization in 1789 caused Asbury much work and
rry, he left his estate to the Concern. (See *Journal* entry for June 6, 1813.)
[24] These missionaries were doubtless James Haw and Benjamin Ogden, first preachers
ointed to Kentucky, and Thomas Humphreys and John Majors, volunteers for
rgia. (Lee: *A Short History of the Methodists*, 121, 123, 360, 361; Barclay, *op. cit.*,
26, 197.)
[25] The session of the preceding conference decided that the conference for 1786
uld be held on May 8 in Baltimore. Apparently the change to Abingdon was made
romote interest in Cokesbury College. (*General Minutes*, 1785 and 1786.)

Saturday, 13. We find that the college is now only fit for covering, a we are already in debt nearly £900, and money is scarce. Came to Ba more to spend another tedious week.

Friday, 19. My soul is stayed upon the Lord; and all within me lo for God—even the living God.

Sunday, 21. I preached in the new meeting house in Light street, "I had rather be a door-keeper in the house of the Lord, than to dv in the tents of wickedness." And in the evening I spoke on 1 Kings 6–9; it was a very solemn time, a warning to our young people.

Tuesday, 23. We had a watch night, brother Whatcoat preached; it v a moving season.

Wednesday, 31. Came to Antietam settlement,[26] and spoke in a Du church: a travelling ministry would be more productive of good am these people; their preachers and people are too fond of *settling*, and h ing things established on the *regular plan*.

West Virginia

Thursday, June 1. I reached Shepherdstown with difficulty, and in pa I was blest, and delivered my own soul. The people here are displea with me because I do not send them brother Thomas Vasey.[27] Rid through so much wet and damp weather has caused the inflammation my foot, and I am afraid of being stopped: this is a great trial to r Lord, give me a perfect resignation! We have had rain for eighteen d successively, and I have ridden about two hundred miles in eight or n days; a most trying time indeed.

Virginia

Saturday, 3. We rode twenty-eight miles along very bad roads Milburn's.[28] Brother Watters preached.

Sunday, 4. The Lutheran minister began a few minutes before I

[26] The settlement was on Antietam Creek, Washington County, Maryland, near present Sharpsburg. The population was mostly German, and through Otter doors were opened for Methodist preaching. The Beeler family led in promo Methodism in that region. (Scharf, *op. cit.*, II, 1207, 1209, 1210.)

[27] Thomas Vasey (1742–1826) was ordained as presbyter, or elder, by John We in 1784 and sent to America with Coke and Whatcoat. He was elder in Pennsylva and New Jersey, and then accepted reordination by Bishop White of the Angl Church and returned to England. In 1789 he re-entered the Methodist itinera (Stevens, *op. cit.*, II, 155–57; see *Journal* entry for September 1, 1787.)

[28] John Milburn lived about four miles from Winchester, Virginia, where he I Milburn Chapel. He was a traveling preacher from 1787 to 1799. (Scott and A manuscripts; Whatcoat's *Journal*, August 22, 1789.)

:o Winchester. I rode leisurely through the town, and preached under me spreading trees on a hill,[29] on Joshua xxiv, 19, to many white and ick people. It was a solemn, weighty time; all was seriousness and ention. I then went once more to Newtown;[30] here I preached on 2 Tim. , 16, 17. I had but little freedom in speaking. I called on Mr. Otterbein: : had some free conversation on the necessity of forming a church nong the Dutch, holding conferences, the order of its government, &c.

West Virginia

[31]Rode to Col. Seymour's,[32] as welcome as snow in harvest. My soul is pt in peace; but my poor body is much fatigued, and I am lame withal. ame over a rough road to Johnson's,[33] and preached to a most insensible ople.

Monday, 12. Rode thirty-one miles; spoke at Dewitt's to about fifty ople; rather hard this, after riding so far: I shall go elsewhere, and do ore good, I hope.

Maryland

Tuesday, 13. I had an open time at Col. Barratt's. My lameness dis-urages me. Praise the Lord! there is a little religion on the Maryland le of the Potomac, and this is some comfort, without which this Alleg-ny would make me gloomy indeed. Sick or lame, I must try for Red-one to-morrow. My mind has been deeply impressed with the necessity getting our people to set apart the five o'clock hour wholly for prayer; establish prayer meetings, and to speak evil of no man.

Thursday, 15. We rode about twenty-two miles, and were kindly enter-ined for five shillings and sixpence.[34]

West Virginia

Saturday, 17. We had a heavy ride to Morgantown. I was to have been ere at four o'clock, but missing my way, I made it six.

[29] There was no Methodist meetinghouse in Winchester, Virginia, until 1793. (See Scott manuscript.)

[30] Newtown was the present Stephens City, Frederick County, Virginia.

[31] This entry is undated in the *Journal*, but June 11 seems likely.

[32] Colonel Felix Seymour (1728–98), a Revolutionary officer who came from Ireland 1740, lived near Petersburg; and his home was a preaching place. The community Seymoursville in Grant County, West Virginia, is named for the family. (See the res manuscript, March 12, 1788.)

[33] This family is unidentified, though it may have been Abraham Johnson. The ott manuscript says he lived on Patterson Creek in present Grant County, West rginia.

[34] The place of entertainment was at John Simpkins' inn. (See note for *Journal* entry der July 10, 1785.)

Sunday, 18. We had a great day. When I had done preaching broth
Enoch Matson[35] exhorted with life and power, and the power of God w
felt among the people. I suppose there were nearly six hundred hear
present.

Pennsylvania

Tuesday, 20. Being court time at Beesontown[36] our congregation w
large; perhaps not less than six hundred people. My foot continues swell
and uneasy; but I desire to praise the Lord under every affliction.

Thursday, 22. Crossed the Monongahela at Redstone at Old Fort
where they are building a town. I am now among some of my old frien
that moved from Maryland to this country.

Friday, 23. I was much blessed, and had many to hear at S. Litton
We are now going to the frontiers, and may take a peep into the Indi
land.[38] This is a fruitful district, and I hope it will prosper in religic
I have lately been sorely assaulted by Satan, and much blessed of t
Lord.

Saturday, 24. The people were very still, and very lifeless at Lackey':
I felt the power of death, and my spirits were low. This is death—wh
religion and every comfortable accommodation are wanting. Lo
sanctify all these for my humiliation!

Sunday, 25. We had a wild company at Dennis's, to whom I was l
to be pointed, on Isaiah lv, 6, 7. After preaching we ate a little bread a
butter, and rode fifteen miles to Doddridge's Fort.[40] We arrived just

[35] Enoch Matson was elder over the Redstone and Allegheny circuits. (See *Minute*

[36] Beesontown was the present Uniontown, Pennsylvania.

[37] Brownsville, Pennsylvania, at the point where Redstone Creek flows into
Monongahela River, was often called "Redstone Old Fort" because of prehisto
earthworks nearby. (Buck, *op. cit.,* 98.)

[38] The limits of white occupation were defined as the line of the Allegheny and O
rivers, according to the terms of the Treaty of Fort Stanwix of 1768 with Iroqu
Confederacy. Across the rivers was Indian land. Asbury does not make record of hav
crossed the river, but the manuscript *Journal* of John Smith, one of the circuit rid
on the Redstone Circuit this year, shows that he did make the crossing and set foot
the soil of Ohio.

[39] Thomas Lackey (1745–1816) emigrated from New Jersey and settled on the he
waters of North Ten Mile Creek, just south of Washington, Pennsylvania, in 1772. Th
is good evidence pointing to his home as a preaching place by Eli Shickle, one of Stra
bridge's local preachers, as early as 1772, though no official society was organi:
there until the laying out of the Redstone Circuit in 1784. This society at Lackey'
the direct predecessor of the First Methodist Church in Washington, Pennsylvar
(Smeltzer, *op. cit.,* 38–40.)

[40] John Doddridge (1745–91) settled in Independence Township near the Penn
vania–Virginia line in 1773 and built a fort that same year. The fall after this visit
Asbury, Doddridge built a Methodist chapel near the fort, it being the fourth Metho
chapel in the region west of the mountains. Joseph Doddridge, son of John, ser

nset, and I was comforted in the company of brother Smith,[41] and others
my old friends from Maryland.

West Virginia

Monday, 26. Preached in Coxe's Fort[42] on the Ohio river,[43] on "Trust
the Lord, and do good, so shalt thou dwell in the land." Psalm xxxvii,
3. We found it necessary to return, they said twelve, but I thought
een miles. We were lost in the woods, and it rained all the way. We,
wever, came in about eight o'clock, and about ten laid ourselves down
rest in peace.

Pennsylvania

Tuesday, 27. I had a large congregation, and Divine aid. We hasted
ay to a little town called Washington—wicked enough at all times, but
ecially now at court time. We had uncomfortable lodgings. Riding
rd all day, and loss of sleep at night, never fail laying me under affliction.
Thursday, 29. I had enlargement in speaking to three or four hundred
ople, at Roberts's chapel,[44] on Luke iv, 18.

a Methodist itinerant from 1788 to 1791. He then entered the Episcopal ministry.
also qualified as a physician and served as missionary in the Upper Ohio Valley.
eph Doddridge was the author of *Notes on the Settlements and Indian Wars of the
stern Parts of Virginia and Pennsylvania, from 1763 to 1783, inclusive.* (Smeltzer, *op.
, 67–68; Payton: *Our Fathers Have Told Us*, 75–76; Mulkearn and Pugh: *A Traveler's
ide to Historic Western Pennsylvania*, 339–40.)

 John Smith (1758–1812) was appointed to Redstone Circuit this year. He was a
ive of Kent County, Maryland. (*Minutes*, 1813; Stevens: *History of Methodist
scopal Church*, II, 147.)

 Coxe's Fort was a Methodist preaching place on the original Redstone Circuit,
 miles north of Wellsburg, Brooke County, West Virginia. (Smeltzer, *op. cit.*, 49.)

 Asbury and John Smith went into the present state of Ohio on this day, being the
t Methodist preachers within that state of whom there is record. The opinion has
n that George Callahan was the first preacher in what was to be the state of Ohio
that his visit took place in September of 1787. (See article *Introduction of Methodism
Ohio* in "Ohio Archaeological and Historical Society Publications," 165 ff.) Proof
Asbury's "peep into the Indian land" (*Journal* entry for June 23, 1786) is found in
manuscript *Journal* of John Smith: "June 26, 1786: Crost the great Ohio into the
ian Contry in company with Mr. Asbury, Henry, and several others. This river
s into the Missesippy bordering upon south Amarica inhabited by the spanyards. . . ."
ith's reference to "south Amarica" means the section that later became the Louisiana
chase. It is not known whether Asbury or others preached in Ohio in 1786, but there
 possibility that there was preaching at the blockhouse at Carpenter's station or at
e other fortification.

 Robert's Chapel was the first Methodist meeting house west of the mountains,
ted in 1784 or 1785. It was 4·5 miles south of Brownsville, Pennsylvania, on the
n of Roger Roberts. It has continuity in the West Bend Methodist Church of the
sburg Conference. (Smeltzer, *op. cit.*, 66–67.)

Friday, 30. Occasion was given to-day for expressions of wonder by clerical character, that any one should be able to preach who had i acquired learning. What Jesuitical stupidity was here manifested! V came to the widow Murphy's.[45] The family are kind, and the motl professes religion.

July 1 and 2. I spoke in the new church at Beesontown.[46] We hac feeling, gracious season. The sacrament was, I trust, attended with blessing.

Maryland

Monday, 3. We came in haste to Simpkins and thence to Barratt' We rode through gloomy mountains, and over rough roads for two hoi in the dark, where both man and horse were in danger; but the Lc was our preserver, and no accident happened to us.

Tuesday, 4. I came to Barratt's, where God spoke to the hearts o few souls, who were not a little moved. Here I was almost ready to dr for want of sleep.

I found an appointment had been made for me at Friend's Cove.[4] hesitated to go, but being unwilling to disappoint the people, I set o and must needs stray two miles out of my way to see a curious sprii which ebbs and flows, but not regularly. What with rocks and logs in c route, the way was so rough, it was a mercy that ourselves and our hor escaped unhurt. I came to the Cove, and preached on Luke xi, 13. I ha been greatly tempted to impatience and discontent. The roads are ba my horse's hind feet without shoes; and but little to eat. To this I may a that the lodgings are unclean and uncomfortable. I rode across t

---

[45] Mrs. Ann Murphy (1731–1814) was an early leader of Methodism in Unionto Pennsylvania, having moved from Ellicott's Mill in Maryland in 1780 and settled v of Uniontown. Her home was a regular stopping place for the Methodist itinera On Saturday, May 26, 1787, during the quarterly meeting on the Redstone Circ Robert Ayres made the following entry in his *Journal*: "After Meeting we walked to Sister Murphy's and tarried and fifteen or twenty of us slept in one spliced long be

[46] This was the first Methodist meetinghouse in Uniontown, Pennsylvania, predecessor of the present Asbury Methodist Church. It must have been built in spring of 1786 since both Asbury and Ayres refer to it as "new" that spring. 1 makes it the second oldest Methodist building in the region, being preceded only Roberts Chapel. (Smeltzer, *op. cit.*, 67.)

[47] (See note under *Journal* entry for July 12, 1782.) Colonel Barratt resided on Braddock Road, eight miles northwest of Cumberland. (Manuscript diary of Rol Ayres, Historical Society of Western Pennsylvania, Pittsburgh.) Later Asbury fo "Colonel Barratt of Alleghany and his wife" at Mount Gerizim, three miles southeas Cynthia, Kentucky. (*Journal* entry for October 22, 1805.) In 1811 Asbury met Colc Barratt's third son, probably Abner, at Urbana, Ohio. (*Journal* entry for Septem 20, 1811; Henry Howe: *Historical Collections of Ohio*, II, 372.)

[48] Friend's Cove was a preaching place on the Bath Circuit.

untain to Spurgin's,[49] where I met with a number of serious souls. I not repent coming fifteen miles. I preached on, "That we may have ldness in the day of judgment."

. rode twenty-two miles to Foster's,[50] along a blind path, and came in out nine o'clock, and was thankful. I have, in six days, ridden about e hundred and fifty miles, on as bad roads as any I have seen on the ntinent.

Sunday, 9. I rested from riding. Preached on, "Who hath warned 1 to flee from the wrath to come?" I had sweet communion with God the woods. My soul hath rest in the Lord.

Monday, 10. Came to Old Town, and preached on 1 Tim. i, 15; and ninistered the sacrament.

Tuesday, 11. I rested to look over some papers and prepare some rchments. Spent nearly a third of the day in prayer, that the Lord would with me to the Springs. O what hath God wrought for brother John emiah Jacob and his wife since I lodged with them four years ago! I ieve from that day the Lord heard our prayers for them.

There has been a remarkable storm of hail at and about the warm ings, by which great damage has been sustained. Some of the hail, it s said, measured seven inches in circumference.

West Virginia

Thursday, 13. I came to Bath; the water made me sick. I took some ls, and drank chicken-broth, and mended. I am ill in body, and dis-ited. I am subject to a headache, which prevents my reading or writing ich, and have no friends here; but I desire to trust the Lord with all my icerns. Having no appointments for three weeks to come, I have con-ded to stay here awhile; and I am the more inclined so to do, as I am orehensive my stomach wants all the healing efficacy of the waters to tore it to its proper tone.

Sunday, 16. I had some Divine assistance in speaking to the people der the trees, on "Lovers of pleasure more than lovers of God." In the ernoon I enlarged on, "Having the form of godliness, but denying the wer thereof."

Monday, Tuesday, and *Wednesday*. Quite weak, and considerably ected by the water.

Thursday, 20. I am better. Employed in reading Mr. Harvey, and Brooks's ictice of Physic. More than ordinary in prayer, and spoke in public ry other night.

S. Spurgin's house was a preaching place on the Bath Circuit.
John Foster lived about eleven miles from Old Town and six miles from Cumber-l, Maryland. He was ordained deacon by Asbury in 1787. (See the Ayres manuscript August and September, 1787.)

Sunday, 30. I spoke plainly and closely in the playhouse, on "(
wicked man, thou shalt surely die." The people were serious. I cann
get the people to attend preaching except on the Sabbath. This evil
to be remedied only, I presume, by our getting a preaching house, a
preaching therein by candle-light.

Saturday, August 5. I began to pack up, in hopes of moving on Monda

Sunday, 6. I had a serious, little congregation in the country.[51] Return
to town, and preached at four o'clock.

A pleasing thought passed through my mind: it was this, that I w
saved from the remains of sin. As yet, I have felt no returns thereof. I w
solemnly impressed with the account of the death of poor Styor,[52]
German, who dropped down suddenly, and died. He was a man of piet
and had a gift to preach; had a noble spirit, and sound judgment. I ha
spent twenty-three days at this place of wickedness (Bath). We are tryi
what can be done towards building a house for worship:[53] we collect
something on the Sabbath for that purpose, and it appears the business
entered upon with spirit. My horse was running in the pasture last wee
and hurt himself, so that I find him utterly incapable of travelling, a
that I am compelled to linger here another week. This, as it is, I am willi
to do, for the sake of the people, the cause of God, and my health; and
am disposed to consider it a providential call, although I should not
main, were my horse able to carry me away. I sent brother Caleb Boye
to my appointments, and directed him when and where to appoint f
me. My hopes revive here, and I trust my labour is not all in vain.

Tuesday, 15. I preached for the last time during this visit, but t
people showed but little affection for the word.

Capon River being full, I crossed in a canoe, and found my horse b
ter. The cut was a deep one, but we applied a piece of bacon to the woun
bound some leather round it, and on Thursday I took my departure fro
this unhappy place.

Came to my old friend, Benjamin Boydstone's. I had the happiness
seeing that tender woman, his wife, who careth for the preachers as f
her own soul; full oft hath she refreshed my spirit: her words, looks, a
gestures, appear to be heavenly. Here I could make no stay, lest I shou
miss my appointments in Philadelphia; and if so, be too late for those ma
in the Jerseys and New York.

[51] The preaching place was probably the home of Archibald Wiggins about fo
miles from Bath. He later moved to Mason County, Kentucky, and settled on Licki
Creek. (Whatcoat's *Journal* for August 7, 1789; Ayres and Scott manuscripts.)

[52] This man was probably a lay preacher of the Otterbein group.

[53] The Methodist meetinghouse which Asbury wanted at Bath (see *Journal* entry
July 13, 1786) was started this year but was not completed for more than a year. (S
Journal entries for July 16 and August 10, 1787.)

[54] Caleb Boyer was elder over the Philadelphia and Little York circuits. (See Lednu
op. cit., 413; and *Minutes*.)

Maryland—New Jersey

Sunday morning. Rode twenty miles to Pipe Creek chapel,[55] and preached a large congregation.

Monday, 21. Reached Mr. Gough's, where I spent two days. The weather s very warm; but for one hundred miles and upwards I have had it ficiently agreeable.

Came to Abingdon. Our college is still without a cover, and our nagers, as I expected, almost out of breath. I made but little stay, but sted on to Philadelphia, and arrived there on the twenty-sixth, Saturday.

Monday, 28. I came to Trenton; and thence proceeded on to Brunswick. vas accidentally, or rather providentially, favoured with a ride in a riage; else I know not how I should have proceeded on my journey.

New York

i reached New York on the thirty-first of August, having travelled three ndred and fifty miles since I left Bath, in Virginia. I was taken ill, and s confined about eight days, during which time I was variously tried d exercised in mind. I spent some time in looking over my journals, ich I have kept for fifteen years back.[56] Some things I corrected, and ne I expunged. Perhaps, if they are not published before, they will be er my death, to let my friends and the world see how I have employed ' time in America. I feel the worth of souls, and the weight of the storal charge, and that the conscientious discharge of its important ties requires something more than human learning, unwieldy salaries, clerical titles of D.D., or even *bishop*. The eyes of all—both preachers d people, will be opened in time.

Saturday, *September* 16. It was a very solemn season at the ordination brother Dickins to the eldership.[57] I gave the charge from 1 Tim. iii, 14. In the afternoon I preached to the people from these words, ray for us;" and in the evening from "The world by wisdom knew not

---

Pipe Creek Chapel was occasionally used in referring to Stone Chapel, erected in 3 on the site of Poulson Chapel, successor to Strawbridge's Log Meeting House. It till in use.

The *Journal* so faithfully kept by Asbury was carefully edited several times by ious persons. John Dickins and his wife, Eliza, were the first to whom Asbury sub- ted his manuscripts for revision. (See the Introduction to this volume.)

John Dickins had been sent to the Bertie Circuit in North Carolina in 1785 and rned to New York in 1786. He was ordained deacon at the Christmas Conference 1784 and elected an elder at one of the Conferences in 1786, though he was not ained when elected, probably because he was not present. This solemn service of ination of a prominent man may have been on Sunday, September 17, rather than Saturday as indicated.

God: it pleased God, by the foolishness of preaching, to save them t̶
believe." I met the society, and opened my mind to them on vari
subjects.

Tuesday, 19. I rose with a sense of God upon my soul.

I have been a little grieved with letters from ——:[58] but it is in vain
look for more than *man* in the best of men. My witness is on high; an̶
shall have respect to my Great Shepherd in all things. After preaching
"The grace of our Lord Jesus Christ, and the love of God," &c., a̶
settling some temporal matters relative to the support of the statio̶
preachers,[59] I left the city and came to Elizabethtown. At seven o'clo̶
preached, and had much liberty.

New Jersey

Friday, 22. We dined at Amboy, and reached Monmouth at night.

Saturday, 23. I preached with life and love at Leonard's.[60] The peo̶
here appear very lifeless. I have lately been much tried and much bless̶

Tuesday, 26. I had many to hear at Potter's church,[61] but the peo̶
were insensible and unfeeling.

Wednesday, 27. I met with brothers Phoebus [?] and Budd.[62] We sai̶
over the bay to the sea, for the benefit of the air.

Thursday, 28. Since this day week we have ridden about one hund̶

---

[58] The undesignated correspondent may have been Thomas Vasey. (See *Jou*
entries for June 27, July 14, and September 1, 1787.)

[59] These preachers were John Tunnell, elder; John Dickins, New York; Tho̶
Ware, Long Island; and Robert Cloud, Newark. Full support for the year was pai̶
Tunnell and Dickins, and a small payment was made to Cloud. Asbury received se̶
teen pounds for personal requirements and cost of his illness. (See *John Street Ch̶
Records*, I.)

[60] The present community of Leonards is on the site of former farms of the Leon̶
family, a mile from Atlantic Highlands in Monmouth County, New Jersey. Cap̶
William Leonard and his son William entertained the preachers. (Lewis: *Histor̶
Monmouth County*, II, 149, 150; *New Jersey, a Guide to its Present and Past*, 675.)

[61] The Potter Church was at Good Luck, now Lanoka Harbor, in Ocean Cou̶
New Jersey. Here John Murray, founder of Universalism in this country, first preac̶
in America. Thomas Potter built the church in 1766 because his wife objecte̶
preaching in the home. He left it to Murray on his death, and the Methodists bo̶
it in 1809. It was rebuilt in 1841 and now stands in its cemetery at Murray's Grove ̶
a brick church of later construction. (Heston, *op. cit.*, I, 249; *New Jersey, a Gui̶
its Present and Past*, 557, 558.)

[62] William Phoebus was assigned to New Jersey in 1785; his name does not ap̶
in 1786, and he may have remained there. William Budd was a local preacher f
New Mills who accompanied Pedicord and the other itinerants frequently and ̶
may be the person referred to, although there were several Budds. They sailed ̶
Great Bay through Little Egg Inlet. Asbury had come via Wareton and Tuckert̶

d fifty miles over dead sands, and among a dead people, and a long
ace between meals.[63]

Friday, 29. I preached in a close, hot place, and administered the
crament. I was almost ready to faint. I feel fatigued and much dispirited.
e lodged at Freedom Lucas's, near Batstow, an honest-hearted man.[64]
e shall see whether he will continue to be the same simple-hearted
iristian he now is, when he gets possession of the estate which, it is
id, has fallen to him in England.

Sunday, October 1. We had a very large congregation; to whom I en-
rced, "Look unto me, all ye ends of the earth, and be saved.'

Cape-May.—We stopped at the Cape.[65] I find there is a great dearth of
igion in these parts; and my spirit is clothed in sackcloth before the
>rd.

Tuesday, 3. At Peter Cressy's[66] we had a few cold hearers—the glory is
angely departed.

Thursday, 5. There are a few pious souls at Gough's;[67] but here also
ere is an evident declension. My soul is under deep exercise on account
the deadness of the people, and my own want of fervour and holiness
heart.

Friday, 6. At Morris River church,[68] I was warm and close on, "Lord,
ᵉ there few that be saved?" The people were attentive to the word.

Sunday, 8. At New England Town we had a small house and large
ngregation. I had liberty in preaching on, "By grace are ye saved through
th." Thence I proceeded to M——'s, where I had poor times. Next day
elt quite unwell for want of rest, so annoyed were we the night before.

Thursday, 12. I was shut up in speaking on 1 Cor. i, 30. At Murphy's[69]
ᵉ had many dull, prayerless people. We came to the widow Ayres's;[70]

³ Asbury had now gone inland to Batstow, the present Pleasant Mills. Here was the
Brainerd Free Church, which later became a Methodist meetinghouse where Simon
cas preached and died. (For the complicated road system of southern New Jersey
Heston, *op. cit.*, I, 249, 274–86, 287–99; *Historic Roadsides in New Jersey*.)

⁴ Freedom and Simon Lucas were brothers. (See note under *Journal* entry for
>tember 17, 1785.) A later descendant was the Rev. Arthur Lucas of the Newark
nference, who died in 1944. Simon was known as "Daddy" or "Father" Lucas. He
s the original "Father Lawrence" of Charles J. Patterson's novel *Kate Aylesford*.

⁵ This was Cape May.

⁶ Peter Cressy lived in Cape May County and was a magistrate. (Lednum, *op. cit.*,
■.)

⁷ The Gough, or Goff, family lived near the Cape May-Cumberland County line.
ijamin Abbott had a fine meeting there around 1783. (Lednum, *op. cit.*, 294.)

⁸ See note under *Journal* entry for September 17, 1785.

⁹ John Murphy lived at the Friendship Church on Salem Circuit. (Atkinson, *op.*
, 234.)

⁰ Mrs. Susannah Ayres (Ayars) was one of the first Methodists in Pittsgrove, ten or
:lve miles from Shiloh. She was probably related to the family of Robert Ayres, a
/enth-Day Baptist, who in 1705 founded Shiloh, first called Cohansey Corners.
ien a log church was moved, it stuck on some rocks, whereupon Ayres announced

the mother and daughters are serious, and the son thoughtful. T
weather is oppressively warm, and I feel weary and faint. I was much sh
up at Bethel,[71] on 1 Peter iii, 18. Three times have I been here, and alwa
straitened in spirit.

Saturday, 14. Came to Sandstown:[72] the weather very warm, and t
people dull: I administered the sacrament, and rode away to Coope:
ferry,[73] where we left our horses and crossed to the city, (Philadelphi;
here I found brother Whatcoat, with whom I took sweet counsel.

Pennsylvania

Sunday, 15. I had some energy in speaking, and at sacrament. In t
afternoon it was a feeling time, on "The Lord will give grace and glory

New Jersey

Monday, 16. Rode to Mount Holly, where I preached on "Come,
blessed of my Father," &c.; and then at New Mills, on "Suffering affl
tion with the people of God."

At Burlington I enlarged on, "Neither is there salvation in any othe
&c.: these are not a zealous people for religion.

Pennsylvania

Wednesday, 18. We returned to the city of Philadelphia. Next day
preached, and was close and pointed.

Friday, 20. I was led to treat on the sufferings of God's people;
entirely distinct from those they endure in common with other men, a
certainly unavoidable by all who are really alive to God. I found

that "the Ark of the Lord rested at Shiloh." He had two thousand acres of land wh
he sold to people of his own faith. (*Historic Roadsides in New Jersey*, 38.)

[71] Bethel is the present-day Hurffville. The church was instituted as early as 17
and ten years later a Methodist society was also started at nearby Paulsboro. Bet
gave its name to one of the circuits in 1790. (Heston: *South Jersey: A History*, I, 4
Journal entry for September 29, 1790.)

[72] Sandstown was the present Mount Royal, New Jersey. Its former designations w
Sandstown and also Berkely, a village in Greenwich Township, Gloucester County,
Mantua Creek, four miles southwest from Woodbury. It is not to be confused with
present Sandtown in Burlington County. Atkinson (*op. cit.*, 366) says, "There m
have been a society there, or else it does not seem probable he would have hel
sacramental service." (Gordon's *Gazetteer of New Jersey*, 1834, 233; Heston, *op. c
I, 397.)

[73] Cooper's ferry was at Camden.

:essary to change some official men; and to take proper steps in pre-
ring to defray our church debt, which is now £500. I gave them a
mon on "By this shall all men know that ye are my disciples, if ye
e one another."

Sunday, 22. In the afternoon I left the city, and preached in the evening
Chester.

Delaware

Monday, 23. I rode forty-five miles to Dickerson's,[74] in the Delaware
ite. Preached at Little Creek,[75] and then rode five miles to Dover, and
:ached in the court house. I bless God for peace of mind, and com-
 union with him.

Sunday, 29. I had many to hear at Dover, and had power and liberty in
eaking on Gal. i, 5: we also had a good sacramental time. In the after-
on I spoke on the latter part of my text—how and what it is to suffer
:ording to the will of God. Thence to Thomas White's, where I was
»sely employed.

Maryland

Sunday, November 5. I preached at Cambridge, on "We preach Christ
icified," &c.; little light, and less heat. I was blessed in my own soul,
d had liberty in preaching at M'Keel's[76] in the afternoon, where there
some revival among the people.

Thursday, 9. I rode to Mr. Bartholomew Ennals's;[77] the notice was
ort, and the congregation small; the word, nevertheless, reached some
arts. I crossed at Vienna, a dead and dark place for religion.

Friday, 10. We had more than I expected of hearers at Quantico chapel.
ence I went to Wicomico River, and lodged at Captain Conaway's,[78]

[4] Joseph Dickerson, who in July, 1789, donated land on which a chapel named
  him was erected near Dexter's Corner, New Castle County. It was the successor
White's Chapel located between Townsend and Pine Tree. (Scharf, *History of Dela-*
·e, II, 1021.)

[5] Methodist preaching began in 1778 in Little Creek Hundred, Kent County,
laware. That year Gum Swamp Chapel was built and occupied its original site until
'5 when the improved structure was moved to Little Creek Landing about a mile
tant. (*Ibid.*, II, 1121.)

[6] John McKeel, or McKell, lived near Cambridge, Dorchester County, Maryland.
illman, *op. cit.*, 116; *Journal* of Thomas Haskins, November 26, 1782.)

[7] Bartholomew Ennalls played an early and conspicuous part in planting Methodism
Dorchester County, Maryland. He was among those who joined in the persecution
Freeborn Garrettson at Cambridge. (Boehm, *op. cit.*, 58; see *Journal* entry for April
1802.)

[8] Captain Conaway resided in Wicomico County near the river of that name.
:hard Whatcoat rode with the captain from Thomas Garrettson's near Vienna to
antico. (Sweet: *Religion on the American Frontier*, IV, 84; Hallman, *op. cit.*, 108.)

where we met with a kind reception. I feel the need of being more tha
ever given up to God. I preached in Curtis's chapel:[79] our love feast w
lively: several holy women spoke of the perfect love of God.

Sunday, 12. According to the custom of the place, I preached to a
commodate them; my subject was Joshua xiv, 8.

Monday, 13. I had about fifty hearers at Miles's chapel,[80] where
preached a funeral sermon on Ezek. xxxvi, 25.

Tuesday, 14. I crossed Pocomoke River, and had some enlargement
preaching at Melvin's chapel.

Virginia

Thursday, 16. Rode to Paramore's. The winter comes on apace. I a
at times beset with temptation; but sin is as hateful to me as ever.

Friday, 17. The weather was cold and rainy, so that there were but fe
people at the widow Burton's; among these there were some who enjoye
and others panting after, the perfect love of God.

Sunday, 19. I rode about twenty miles through the rain to Garretts
chapel, where about fifty whites, and as many blacks met me, to whom
preached with liberty.

Maryland

Monday, 20. I rode about forty-five miles; and on *Tuesday* preached
Snow Hill[81] to about one hundred people. Here I visited some prison
under sentence of death; they were sunk down with fear and horror.

Delaware

Friday, 24. My soul has peace under sore temptation. I want to li
from moment to moment under a sense of God.

Saturday, 25. We had a cold, long ride to the sound.[82] On *Sunday*
had an open house, and the weather was very cold; but my preaching w
not all in vain: I spoke from these words, "I will give them a heart of flesl

[79] Curtis Chapel, erected about 1784, stood three miles east of Westover, Somer
County. It was long a preaching place on the two-hundred-mile Annamessex Circu
Coke visited the chapel in 1784, and Whatcoat visited there November 5 and 7, 17
(Boehm, *op. cit.*, 68, 69; Sweet, *op. cit.*, IV, 83.)

[80] Miles Chapel was erected in 1784 by members of a society organized two ye
earlier. In 1813 when a new church was built, it was given the name St. Peters an
located two miles northeast of Crisfield, Somerset County. (Hallman, *op. cit.*, 117, 35

[81] Snow Hill is in Worcester County, Maryland.

[82] Old Sound Chapel was built in 1784 by the society which Freeborn Garrettso
organized in 1779 near the present village of Roxana, Sussex County, Delawa
(Garrettson, *op. cit.*, 107, 110; Scharf: *History of Delaware*, II, 1343.)

Monday, 27. I rode thirty miles to Lewes very unwell. I preached at ankland's,[83] and the people were serious, but I was compelled to cease m speaking by a violent pain in my head, accompanied by a fever.

Tuesday, 28. I preached in the court house at Lewes and I trust the rd went with some weight; the congregation was large.

Maryland

I attended a quarterly meeting at William Frazier's, where I rested m travelling two days: the first day I spoke on "Fight the good fight faith;" and on the second, "Look unto me, all ye ends of the earth, d be saved." My soul was blessed, although our meeting was cold; and r dwelling-house crowded with a dozen preachers, besides others.

Sunday, December 3. Preached at Tuckahoe chapel,[84] on "These shall away into everlasting punishment, but the righteous into life eternal." poke again at widow Lyder's[85] at four o'clock.

Monday, 4. I rode to the bay-side through snow and hail, and met out one hundred people:[86] this we owe to the revival of religion among :m. Our return thence was through heavy roads. I stopped in my way Henry Banning's,[87] whose wife felt conviction under my preaching ree years ago.

[3] Asbury first visited the Shankland home near Lewes, Delaware, September 25, 79. Listed among the persons taxable in Lewes and Rehoboth Hundred in 1785 re Robert, David, and Rhoads Shankland. The last named sold a lot on May 7, 38, on which Ebenezer Church, near Lewes, was built. (Scharf, *op. cit.*, II, 1220; llman, *op. cit.*, 120, 268; Turner, *Some Records of Sussex County, Delaware*, 46, 340, 341.)

[4] Tuckahoe, or Ebenezer, Chapel was the first Methodist place of worship in Caro- e County, Maryland. Its origin dates from a day in 1776 when Freeborn Garrettson, aching from horseback to the militia, won the converts who became the nucleus the society. Historically it is associated with Squire Henry Downs who was con- ted while Thomas Chew, whom he had sentenced for preaching, was serving his l sentence in the former's home. It was at a camp meeting at Hillsboro that Jesse e was stricken and his body was first interred near Ebenezer Chapel. (*Extracts of Journal of Thomas Coke*, 49, 54; Hallman, *op. cit.*, 122, 286.)

[5] Mrs. Lyder was a resident of Dorchester County, Maryland. (Hallman, *op. cit.*, .) Robert Ayres in his plan of the Dorchester Circuit, 1785, lists as a preaching place "Widow Tyler." Inasmuch as the "Widow Lyder" is unmentioned by Ayres, it ms probable that "Tyler" is the correct name. (Manuscript *Journal* of Robert Ayres.)

[6] The Bayside Society organized in 1777 frequently met in the home of a Mr. nnall. About 1782 the society erected the first Methodist meetinghouse in Talbot unty. The records indicate its successor was built on land called "Miles End," one le from Wittman. When in 1906 the congregation moved to Wittman, its church k the name of the village. Wittman Church is now on the Bayside Circuit.

[7] Henry Banning lived in Hopkins Neck, Miles River, Talbot County, Maryland. s name appears in the census of Mills Hundred, 1776. (Brumbaugh, *op. cit.*, 227; llman, *op. cit.*, 104.)

Tuesday, 5. I had a few people at Bolinbroke,[88] and spent the even**i**
with Colonel Burkhead, who wants to know the Lord; he opened **l**
mind to me with great freedom and tenderness. Brother James Whit**e**
says that five hundred souls have joined society in this circuit (Talb**ot**
this year; that half that number profess to have found the Lord; and m**o**
than one hundred to have obtained sanctification: good news this, if tr**ue**

Delaware

At Barratt's chapel there was some move during the course of **the**
quarterly meeting, especially at the love feast. I rode in the evening **to**
Dover, and preached on "So is every one that layeth up treasure **for**
himself, and is not rich towards God."

Maryland

Friday, 15. We had a heavy ride to Queen Anne's chapel. I did **not**
arrive there until near two o'clock. My soul melted for backsliders. I w**as**
much led out on Hos. xiv, 14; and hope it will never be forgotten. **We**
dined, and then rode to Newtown by sunset.

Sunday, 17. A day of rest to my soul. I preached and administered **the**
sacrament in Newtown.[90] They have a comfortable house for wors**hip**
here, especially in the winter. Came to Worton chapel,[91] and had so**me**
life in speaking to a few people.

[88] Bolinbroke Chapel stood on the road between Trappe and the Cambridge Fer**ry,**
Talbot County. When this chapel was built is unknown, but Bishop Thomas C**oke**
preached and administered the Sacrament there on December 6, 1784. (Coke, *op. c*
49; Hallman, *op. cit.*, 106, 337.)

[89] James White, a native of Maryland, was a traveling preacher from 1781 to **his**
death in 1789. He was serving the Talbot Circuit at the time of Asbury's visit. (*Minut*

[90] Although the name of the county seat of Kent County was officially changed fr**om**
New Town to Chestertown in 1780, use of the former persisted. Strawbridge preac**hed**
the first Methodist sermon in Kent County two or three years before Asbury visited**.**
In 1773 a society was organized in Chestertown, although Kent Meeting House ab**out**
five miles south became the focal point for Eastern Shore Methodism. In 1776 Thom**as**
Rankin used the courthouse as a preaching place. In 1780 a lot was purchased **in**
Chestertown, and soon thereafter the erection of a church was begun. (Phoebus, **op.**
cit., 24, 25; Lee: *Life and Times of the Rev. Jesse Lee*, 186; Rankin: manuscript *Journ**al***
160; *Methodist Magazine*, XI, 135–41; *Journal* entries for December, 1772; April **29,**
1802; April 20, 1803.)

[91] Near Worton, several miles northwest of Chestertown, Maryland, a log struct**ure**
was erected about 1780 by the congregation that formerly had met in the home of He**nry**
Randall. Apparently because of its proximity to Worton, it took the name of Wor**ton**
Chapel, although that village was without a Methodist church until 1901. (Hallm**an,**
op. cit., 318, 319; Rankin manuscript *Journal* for numerous references.)

We waited at the widow Frisby's[92] for a boat to cross the Chesapeake
y; but none was to be had. We rode round the head of Elk River, and
ossed the Susquehanna: we came in, after riding that evening in the
in and snow, with the wind in our faces, about twenty miles.

Thursday, 21. Reached the college; and on *Friday* went to Baltimore,
ere I was in great haste to settle the business of the Book Concern,[93]
d of the college.

Saturday, 23. We called a meeting of the trustees, formed our constitu-
n, and elected new members. I preached twice on the Sabbath, and
dained Woolman Hickson[94] and Joseph Cromwell to the eldership. I
et the trustees and adjusted the accounts. We find we have expended
wards of £2,000; we agreed to finish two rooms, and to send for Mr.
eath for our president.[95] On *Tuesday* I left town, and came to Annapolis
out seven o'clock. Finding my appointments were not made, I deter-
ined to direct my course towards Alexandria. The Lord has been power-
lly at work at Annapolis since I was here last autumn; twenty or thirty
ites and some blacks have been added to the society.

Virginia

I reached Alexandria, and on *Saturday* preached in the court house, on,
f we suffer, we shall also reign with him."

[92] Mrs. Frisby lived in or near Rock Hall, Kent County, Maryland, which was then
e terminus of the post road from the North. Here ferry service was long in opera-
n across Chesapeake Bay. (*Maryland, a Guide to the Old Line State,* 384; Phoebus,
ams of Light, 24.)
[93] While John Dickins was stationed in New York City from 1783 to 1789, with the
ception of one year, it is believed that he was following Asbury's instructions to
ntract for the printing of certain books. Toward the close of 1786 the bishop was
ger not only to settle the current accounts but to launch a more extensive program
ich appeared in the *Discipline* the next year. Jesse Lee wrote, "From that time we
gan to print more of our books in the United States . . . principally in New York."
iscipline, 1787; Lee: *Short History of the Methodists,* 129.)
[94] At this time Woolman Hickson, who became a traveling preacher in 1782, was
ving the Baltimore Circuit. (Lednum, *op. cit.,* 342–44; Wakeley, *op. cit.,* 313–15;
kinson: *Memorials of Methodism in New Jersey,* 305–13; Warriner: *Old Sands Street
ethodist Church of Brooklyn, N.Y.,* 5–7, 59–61.)
[95] Levi Heath received Anglican orders at the hands of the Bishop of Hereford,
gland, in 1783. After serving as principal of Cokesbury College, he became the rector
parishes in Maryland, New Jersey, western Pennsylvania, and Virginia. He died in
05 or 1806 while in charge of Norbone Parish, Berkley County, Virginia. (Rightmyer:
e Anglican Church in Delaware, 121.)

1787

Asbury arriving for the opening of Cokesbury College in Maryland

CHAPTER SIXTEEN

Virginia

January 1, 1787. Preached at brother Moss's[1] on 2 Chronicles xv, 12, 13, ◄ the people's entering into covenant with God.

Tuesday, 2. We rode near fifty miles on our way to Westmoreland; next ◄y, by hard riding, we came to Pope's, in Westmoreland; but I have not ◄en more weary many times in my life.

Saturday and *Sunday*. Attended the quarterly meeting in the Northern ◄eck: there were many simple and loving testimonies delivered in the ◄ve feast.

Thursday, 11. Rode through the snow to Fairfield.[2] Here a Captain R. ◄d turned the people out of the barn in which worship was held, and ◄reatened to take brother Paup to jail if he did not show his authority for ◄eaching; after all this vapouring of the valiant Captain, when the affair ◄s brought before the court, Captain R—— found it convenient to ask ◄rdon of our brother, although he sat upon the bench in his own cause:— ◄ the matter ended. The Lord is at work in the Neck: more than one ◄ndred have been added to the society since conference, who are a simple, ◄ving, tender people.

◄We had a good time on *Friday*, the 12th; I spoke on Acts xxvi, 18. I ◄ink God has spoken by me to S——s, a wild man—but the Lord can ◄me him. O Lord, speak for thyself!

◄ John Moss lived in Fairfax County, Virginia. (*Heads of Families*, 17.)
◄ Fairfield was in Northumberland County, near Heathsville. Asbury was passing ◄wn the Northern Neck of Virginia. (Butts: *From Saddle to City by Buggy, Boat, and* ◄ilway, 52.)

Sunday, 14. We had a crowd at the Presbyterian meeting house Lancaster, to whom I delivered a very rough discourse: it was a close ar searching time, and we had many communicants, both white and coloure

Tuesday, 16. Preached at the church on the love of Christ. I find hard to the flesh to ride fifteen or twenty miles every day, and perfor the duties of my station; especially when indisposed and suffering ther from the bodily pain incident thereto. Lord, give me patience! I feel u common affection for the people here.

Wednesday, 17. I had a crowd of careless sinners at Mrs. Agatha Ball who is a famous heroine for Christ. A lady came by craft and took h from her own house, and with tears, threats, and entreaties, urged her desist from receiving the preachers, and Methodist preaching; but all vain. She had felt the sting of death some years before, and was a mo disconsolate soul; having now found the way, she would not depa therefrom.

Thursday, 18. Rode ten miles to the ferry; but being unable to cros I returned to Mrs. Ball's: next morning I came away before day, a reached Shackelford's.

Saturday, 20. Preached at Douglas's[3]—very low in body and spirit.

Sunday and *Monday*, 21, 22. Cold times in religion in this circu (Gloucester), compared with the great times we have had in Lancaster.

Tuesday, 23. Came off early, and preached in Yorktown to some we behaved women. Dined with Mr. Mitchell, and went on to dear broth Weldon's,[4] whose heart and hands were open.

Wednesday, 24. According to appointment, I attended at Williamsbur I had about five from the country, and about fifteen hearers from the tow besides a few blacks and children. I spoke with freedom on, "They ma light of it." I returned through the rain, but hope to receive no harm.

> "He guards our souls, he keeps our breath,
>   Where thickest dangers come;
>   Go, and return; secure from death,
>   Till God commands thee home."

Friday, 26. We waited four hours in the rain before we could cross t ferry at old Jamestown; it was two hours after night when we came brother Mooring's.[5]

Tuesday, 30. We held a quarterly meeting at Craney Island; the weath prevented many from attending. I was blessed in the company of t preachers.

[3] Douglas lived in Gloucester County. Asbury had passed through Lancaster, sto ping at Ball's, and at Shackelford's, King and Queen County.

[4] Weldon lived in James City County.

[5] Mooring lived in Surry County. Out of this family came Christopher S. Moori the Methodist preacher. (*Heads of Families*, 43.)

Wednesday, 31. I enlarged on, "What shall the end be of them who obey ɔt the Gospel of God?" I observed to them that the Gospel had once ɛen taken away from them; and that they ought to lay it seriously to ɛart, lest it should be the case again. We had some quickening in the ɪcrament and at the love feast. Thence I went through Portsmouth, and ɾeached on, "Ye are now returned to the Shepherd and Bishop of your ɔuls."

Saturday, *February* 3. Visited my old friend Fullford:[6] he is feeble in ɔdy, and not much at ease in his worldly possessions, yet happy in God.

Brother Poythress[7] frightened me with the idea of the Great Swamp, the ɪst end of the Dismal; but I could not consent to ride sixty miles round; ɔ we ventured through, and neither we nor our horses received any injury. ɾaise the Lord! Our passing unharmed through such dangers and un-ɛalthy weather, feelingly assures me that I am kept by the immediate ɪterposition of His providence. I preached in the new chapel. I hope not ɪ vain. I am now surrounded with waters and hideous swamps, near the ɛad of the Pasquotank River.

North Carolina

Thursday, 8. Came on, wet and unwell, to Proby's.

Went on to Nixonton,[8] where I had many to hear, and was blessed in ɪy own soul, and, I think, spoke to the cases of some of my audience.

Friday, 9. I had a long ride of nearly fifty miles to Gates county. We ɔpped at one Newby's, one of the Society of Friends, who entertained s kindly. We reached sister Gipson's,[9] cold and weary The poor flesh ɔmplains, but my soul enjoys peace and sweetness.

Sunday, 11. We had a large congregation and an open time at Knotty ine chapel. Here we have a little revival.

Tuesday, 13. I had about sixty people at Wicocon: I spoke as I felt, on ʔr xiii, 11. I mourned over the people and left them.

I came to Hardy's, where I spoke with some light on Matt xxii, 5. I ɪhappily ran a splinter into my leg, which has alarmed me.

[6] Fullford lived in Norfolk County. (*Ibid.*, 95.)

[7] Francis Poythress was presiding elder on the district, which included Brunswick, ɪssex, and Amelia counties.

[8] Nixonton was on Little River in Pasquotank County, North Carolina. Asbury had ɪtered the state through Camden County and proceeded southward along the general ɔurse pursued by him in 1784.

[9] In a letter to Asbury written from Knotty Pine Chapel in Gates County, North ɪarolina, on March 17, 1799, Mrs. I. (or J.) Baker, wife of a preacher, mentioned Ann ɪipson among those who had died in the community. "Ann Gipson, converted from ɪe height of pride and vanity to a humble lover of God and man; full of good works." Ⅎoore: *Pioneers of Methodism in North Carolina and Virginia*, 35; also *Letters.*)

I found we had to go twelve miles by water, and send the horses anoth
way. O what a world of swamps, and rivers, and islands, we live in her
I met brother B—— and A——; two devoted young men; the former
native of Maryland, the latter of Virginia. At the desire of several of t
brethren I preached at Washington,[10] where many collected in the cou
house, whom I addressed on my favourite text, 1 Tim. i, 15. Three mil
on the water, and riding three more on roads under the water (such
the inundated state of the country), made our jaunt unpleasant.

Thursday, 22. We set off for Newbern. Stopped at Kemp's Ferry, ke
by Curtis, where we were kindly entertained *gratis*. I feel heaviness throug
labour and temptation, yet I am given up to God.

Friday, 23. I arrived at Newbern. I felt the power of death as I journeye
along. We rode round the town, and could get no certain informatio
about preaching, brother Cole[11] being absent. We were at last taken in
Mr. Lathrop's. The place and people were in such a state, that I judge
by my own feelings, it would be as well to leave them just as I found the
—and so I did.

Tuesday, 27. It was rather a dry time at the love feast and sacramer
There was some life and melting while I enforced, "Look unto me, a
be ye saved, all ye ends of the earth." We then rode to H——'s on Isla
Creek. I went alone into the woods, and had sweet converse with Go
At night we were poorly provided against the weather; the house w
unfinished; and, to make matters worse, a horse kicked the door ope
and I took a cold, and had the toothache, with a high fever.

Thursday, *March* 1. I had more hearers, and they were more attenti
than I expected: I trust it was a profitable time. Rode to brother Johnsor
—without the labour of slaves he manages to have abundance for man ar
beast.

Tuesday, 6. My horse is stiff, and almost foundered, and there is
appearance of a swelling on his head. I have always had hard struggl
to get to Charleston. Lord, give me patience, and bear me up!

Wednesday, 7. Crossed the main fork of Black River, and came throug
a wild country to Colonel R——'s: the colonel's wife is a tender, devote
woman.

Thursday and *Friday*, 8, 9. Directed our course to the south: cross

[10] There were Methodists in Washington, Beaufort County, as early as 1784. It w
taken into the Pamlico Circuit in 1789. The first meetinghouse was built in 1789, large
by Ralph Potts, an Englishman who is regarded as the father of Methodism in Washin
ton. It was on the east side of Market Street near the courthouse. Asbury visited t
community in 1801 and 1802. (Grissom, *op. cit.*, 150, 152.)

[11] Lee Roy Cole (1749–1830) was the elder over the circuits which included Newber
He was licensed to preach by George Shadford and went to North Carolina in 17
He was ordained at the Christmas Conference. For some reason he was suspended
1785 but was readmitted the following year. (See note under December 20, 178
Grissom, *op. cit.*, 61–63.)

ape Fear, and reached Drowning Creek. Rested a day at W——'s, a
nd people, but without religion.

South Carolina

Sunday, 11. Preached at Robinson's new court house.[12] Rode in the
ening to M——'s. Crossed Little Pedee; stopped at Smith's,[13] ate a
orsel, and came on to Buck Swamp.[14]

Thursday, 15. Preached at the new church at Sweet's[15]: here I heard
at Doctor Coke was in Charleston. Proceeded thence to the widow
ort's, where I had much ado to prevail on brother Hull to stay.[16]

We rode nearly fifty miles to get to Georgetown. Here the scene was
eatly changed—almost the whole town came together to hear the word of
e Lord.

We arrived at Charleston, and met Dr. Coke. Here we have already a
acious house prepared for us,[17] and the congregations are crowded and
olemn.

Sunday, 25. I enlarged on, "I had rather be a doorkeeper in the house

[12] The new courthouse was the present Lumberton in Robeson County, North
arolina.

[13] The Rev. Moses Smith, a local preacher, lived near the present Mullins, South
arolina. Macedonia Church at Mullins is the successor of the society formed by him.

[14] Asbury entered South Carolina on this trip through the present Dillon (then
arion) County and crossed the Little Pee Dee River east of the present town of Dillon.
e map of 1823 shows three bridges over the river in the general area of the present
illon–Marion County line. Buck Swamp was in the upper part of Marion County
mediately west of the Little Pee Dee, extending from near the community called
oringville to the river near its junction with the present Lumber River, then known as
rowning Creek. He went southward by way of the present Dillon, Latta, Marion, and
entenary to Britton's Neck. (See note under January 4, 1786.)

[15] Sweet's church was fifteen miles south of Marion. It became Bare Pond Church
d is now Soule's Chapel, located on the original site.

[16] Asbury crossed the Great Pee Dee River at Port's (Porter's) Ferry. The "Widow
ort" may have been the widow of the man who established the ferry. He then followed
s previous route over Lynch's Creek, Black Mingo, and Black River to Georgetown.
ee notes under February 23, 1785; January 4, 1786.) Hope Hull, later to be the father
Methodism in Georgia, was then on the Pee Dee Circuit with Jeremiah Mastin.

[17] From Georgetown he went along the route of his first tour in 1785 to Charleston.
e "spacious house," just completed, was the Cumberland Street Church, then known
the "blue meeting house" to distinguish it from the "white meeting house" or
rcular Congregational Church. This first Methodist meetinghouse in Charleston was
plain wooden structure sixty by forty feet in size, with galleries for Negroes, and cost
e thousand pounds in addition to the three hundred pounds paid for the lot on
umberland Street. The Cumberland Street Church was only a block from St. Phillip's
piscopal Church and a block from the Independent or Circular Congregational
urch. (Shipp: *Methodism in South Carolina*, 164, 169; Betts: *History of South Carolina
ethodism*, 60.)

of God, than to dwell in the tents of wickedness"; at night again on Isaia
xlv, 22. We held our conference[18] in this city.

Tuesday, 27. We exchanged sentiments on matters freely.

Wednesday, 28. The Doctor treated on the qualifications and duties «
a deacon.

Thursday, 29. Our conference ended.[19]

Friday, 30. I left the city, and rode thirty miles, although my horse ha
been injured by over-feeding. Next day I rode forty miles through the rai
and begged a lodging with Doctor W.

Sunday, April 1. We came to Santee Ferry, and there was such a
overflowing of water in our route that we had to swim upon our hors«
several times: my horse performed so well that I was not wet much high«
than my knees: that day we rode thirty miles, and the next day fifty mile
and came to Moore's.[20] Here we met with brother R. Swift, who had bee
near death, but then was recovering: we advised him to go with us for h
life. The people here begin to feel, and yield to the power of truth.

Wednesday, 4. At Camden I preached on, "They made light of it'
thence we rode on to quarterly meeting, where I met with a multitude «
people who were desperately wicked—but God hath wrought amor
them: we had little rest by day or night.

Friday, 6. Rode forty miles to preaching at Jackson's; and then t
brother Pace's.[21]

North Carolina

Saturday and *Sunday*, 7, 8. Attended Anson quarterly meeting, i
North Carolina: the Doctor preached on, The love of Christ, and I o«
"The grace of God that bringeth salvation"; sacrament followed.

From *Saturday* to *Saturday*. I have ridden about three hundred mile

[18] See letter to Richard Whatcoat, March 25, 1787.

[19] This four-day conference was the first ever held in South Carolina. Jesse L«
(*History of the Methodists*, 128) says that in this year Asbury prepared a new form «
the minutes which stated that one of the duties of the conference was the "electing ar
ordaining of Bishops, Elders and Deacons." "This was the first time that our Superi«
tendents ever gave themselves the title of Bishops in the minutes. They changed t«
title themselves without the consent of the conference." At the next conference a majo«
ity of the preachers agreed to let the word remain, and in the minutes of 1788 Asbu«
and Coke were called bishops.

[20] Captain Moore lived near Wedgefield. Asbury followed the route taken in 178
going seventy miles northwest on the old State Road which approximates the prese«
U.S. Highway 176. A little east of Orangeburg he turned more directly north, crosse
the Santee River at the ferry near the present Lone Star at the northern end of La«
Marion, and proceeded along the east bank of the Wateree River to Camden.

[21] From Camden the bishop went along a route now traversed by U.S. Highway 6(
through the present Kershaw and a little north of Pageland crossed into Anson Count
North Carolina.

d have preached only about half the time. O may the Lord seal and
ter his own word, that all this toil of man and beast be not in
in!

Tuesday, 10. The Doctor and myself preached to a few simple people at
.'s, I hope not in vain. At our next meeting we had many hearers. We
ve scarcely time to eat or sleep.

Thursday, 12. I preached at Salisbury. Afterward rode to Huggins's,
ere we had many hearers, and a melting among the people.

Good Friday, 13. I was much led out at Caton's. Thence to M'Knight's
apel,[22] where we found a living people.

Saturday, 14. We hasted to C——y church, where we had many people:
er riding twenty-two miles, we had another meeting about six o'clock;
d about midnight got to bed.

Sunday, 15. Rose about six o'clock, and went to Newman's church,[23]
ere the Doctor and myself both preached: the people were rather wild,
d we were unwell. I came to Arnat's about eight o'clock, having ridden
rty miles: the Doctor went by Dick's ferry, and did not get in until near
dnight.

Virginia

Monday, 16. Rode to Jeremiah White's,[24] and on *Tuesday*, about fifty
les to Page Mann's, in Charlotte county, Virginia.

Wednesday, 18. Rode to Rough Creek.[25] On *Thursday*, the 19th, our
nference began at William White's.[26] We had much preaching, morning,
on, and night, and some souls were converted to God.

Saturday, 21. I gave them a discourse on Jer. iii, 15: "And I will give
u pastors according to my heart."

Sunday, 22. Doctor (Coke) spoke on the qualifications of a deacon;
d I gave them a charge. Some said there were three thousand people
hear: it was a solemn, weighty time.

[2] McKnight's Chapel, named for George McKnight, was in Yadkin, now Forsyth
unty, North Carolina, near Clemmonsville, now Clemmons. Conferences were held
e in 1789, 1790, and 1791. McKnight's home was one of the earliest preaching places
the Methodists. An inscription on his tombstone in the cemetery of Sharon Church
r Lewisville reads: "The memory of George McKnight Senu [Senior] born July 8,
5. Departed this life March 22, 1847. He livd 81 years 8 mont and 14 days. In
th he joind the Methad [Methodist] then maryed got sotfkt [sophisticated]
nd the Morafens [Moravians] then moved to Stoks had preaching in his oan house."
rissom, *op. cit.*, 95, 126 ff. Inscription furnished by G. R. Stafford of Lewisville.)
[3] Newman's Church was in Rockingham County, North Carolina.
[4] Jeremiah White lived in Pittsylvania County, Virginia. (*Heads of Families*, 42.)
[5] See letter to an unnamed person, April, 1787.
[6] William White lived in Charlotte County, Virginia, and there was a Rough Creek
urch in the same county.

Monday, 23. We called at Hampden and Sydney college,[27] in Prin
Edward: the outside has an unwieldy, uncommon appearance, for
seminary of learning; what the inside is, I know not. The president, M
I. Smith, is a discreet man, who conducts himself well. About half p:
eleven o'clock we reached John Finney's, in Amelia, having ridden abo
sixty miles. I want to live more constantly in the spirit of prayer.

Wednesday, 25. Preached at I. Anderson's,[28] and then rode to Manch(
ter,[29] where I preached again. The Doctor preached in Richmond.

Thursday, 26. Went onwards to the north. We have made it a point
pray in the families where we lodge, whether public or private; and gen(
ally where we stop for refreshment.

Saturday, 28. At night the Doctor preached in Alexandria; and ag:
on the *Sabbath* morning, to many hearers.

Maryland

We were kindly entertained on *Sunday* night at Shadrach Turner's
near Bladensburg, Maryland, and on *Monday* reached Baltimore abo
noon.

We had some warm and close debates[31] in conference; but all end
in love and peace. After much fatigue and trouble, our conference end
on *Monday,* the seventh of May. We went forward to Perry Hall. Then
we went to Cokesbury; drew a deed for the conveyance of the proper
of the college, and settled our temporal matters there.

[27] Hampden Sydney College is one of the oldest Presbyterian colleges in America

[28] Probably Anderson's in Chesterfield County. (See *Journal* entry for April 16, 18C

[29] Manchester, now South Richmond, first appeared as an appointment in 1793 un(
the name "Richmond and Manchester." In the same year the appointment dropped (
of the *Minutes,* and the churches in Richmond and Manchester were evidently put o:
circuit. However, out of this movement grew Manchester Methodism and Cent
Church, the mother church.

[30] Bishop Asbury had held the Frederick Circuit quarterly meeting at the home
Shadrach Turner near Bladensburg, Maryland, ten years previoulsy. Even earlier it h
been a Methodist preaching place. (*Journal of Thomas Rankin,* June 30, 1775; May
and August 14, 1776.)

[31] The "warm and close debates" were occasioned by Bishop Coke, acting un(
instruction from Wesley, changing the conference from Abingdon, Maryland, July
as set by the previous conference, to Baltimore, May 1, and by Wesley's further instr:
tion that Richard Whatcoat and Freeborn Garrettson be appointed superintende:
with Asbury. The protest against absentee superintendency resulted in Dr. Coke sign:
a certificate to the conference never "to exercise any government whatever in s:
Methodist Church during my absence from the United States." The conference refus
to elect Whatcoat and struck the name of Wesley from the list of superintendents, la
restoring it. (See *Minutes of the General Conference,* 1787; Ware, *op. cit.,* 129; L(
A Short History of the Methodists, 124, 125; Lee: *Life and Times of the Rev. Jesse L*
188–97.)

Wednesday, May 9. Many attended at Elkton, and we were received by e Rudolph family[32] with great respect.

Pennsylvania—New Jersey

Thursday, 10. We attended at Wilmington (Delaware) at noon; and at hester at night.

Friday, 11. We reached Philadelphia, where the Doctor[33] preached that d the following evening. We spent the *Sabbath* in the city, and on *onday* came to Trenton, where we found a lifeless people.

Tuesday, 15. The Doctor preached with life in the Episcopal church at izabethtown (New Jersey), and we had a good time.

New York

Wednesday, 16. Arrived in New York and rested. On *Friday, Saturday, unday,* and *Monday,* the Doctor preached[34] with great energy and accept-ce.

Tuesday, 22. After long silence,[35] I preached on, "For Zion's sake I will t hold my peace, and for Jerusalem's sake I will not rest."

Rode twenty miles on Long Island, to Hempstead Harbour,[36] and reached with some liberty in the evening. I am now out of the city, and ve time to reflect: my soul turns to its rest, and to its labour for souls, in hich I can live more by rule.

---

[32] This family lived in the residence built by Tobias Rudolph in 1768. It stood three ors east of the courthouse in Elkton, Cecil County, Maryland. The Rudolphs were piscopalians and hospitable to Methodist itinerants. (Johnson, *History of Cecil County, aryland,* 447.)

[33] Asbury was accompanied by Thomas Coke and "Black Harry" Hosier and perhaps ' other preachers who were appointed to their posts by the Baltimore Conference. e *John Street Records* show that the church paid a part of "Black Harry's" travel pense.

[34] Coke had come to New York to sail for England. No ship was available, and he turned to Philadelphia on the following Tuesday and sailed for Dublin on the twenty-venth. According to the *Records,* the congregation at John Street gave him more an nineteen pounds for his expenses. (Coke, *Journal, ad. loc.*; Seaman, *op. cit.,* –97.)

[35] Asbury's "long silence" indicates that Coke must have done all the preaching dur-g his stay in New York.

[36] The trip to Hempstead Harbor, the present Roslyn, was probably made on Wednes-y, May 23. Peter Moriarty had been appointed to the Long Island Circuit, where homas Ware during the previous year had developed the work started by Ezekiel ooper in 1785.

Thursday, 24. I rose very sick—felt solemn and devoted to God
preached in a paper mill[37] on, "If any man will do his will he shall know
the doctrine, whether it be of God."

I preached at Mosquito Cove,[38] where many attended notwithstandi
the rain: there was a power went with the word.

Saturday, 26. Rode to ——: our friends had procured the Pr
byterian church[39] for me. I felt a spirit of life on these words, "
ready to give an answer to every man that asketh you a reason of the ho
that is in you." I called to see my old friend and assistant, James Gla
brook,[40] who was the first preacher I travelled with upon a regular appoi
ment in England. He is now a Presbyterian minister; much changed in
outward man, but I believe his sentiments are much the same as whe
first knew him. The Lord be with and bless him!

Sunday, 27. I came to Harper's, where we have a little new house, a
about thirty members:[41] I hope, and expect, in a few years, to see a circ
of six weeks formed here, and four or five hundred members in socie
The people on this island, who hear the Gospel, are generally poor, a
these are the kind I want, and expect to get. I have had great assistance a
freedom in speaking.

Monday, 28. Came to New York. Preached at night on, "They that
after the flesh do mind the things of the flesh, and they that are after t
Spirit, the things of the Spirit." I found it necessary to stop brot

[37] The paper mill, where Asbury had probably preached also on the previous d
was a large building frequently used for meetings. It was near a small lake in wha
now Roslyn Park. The original foundations still exist. The American Legion build
now occupies the spot and has a replica of the old mill wheel.

[38] This paragraph should probably be dated Friday the twenty-fifth. Mosquito Co
the present Glen Cove, was about four miles from Hempstead Harbor or Roslyn.
was the birthplace of Nicholas Snethen, who later traveled with the bishop and
known as "Asbury's Silver Trumpet." (Seaman, *op. cit.*, 149; Warriner: *Old Sands Str
Church*, 493.)

[39] Asbury's preaching place was probably Hempstead, where the Presbyterians ha
good church.

[40] Asbury had been appointed to assist Glassbrook on the Bedfordshire Circuit wh
Asbury was admitted on trial at the English Conference of 1767. Glassbrook was
ceived by the New York Presbytery in 1786, but there is no record of a pastorate u
1788 and 1789, when the Minutes of the Philadelphia Presbytery mention him
connection with congregations at Pettigrew and Fairfield. He may have been the Mr.
mentioned by Asbury on July 4, 1794.

[41] This church was at Newtown, where Captain Thomas Webb began preaching
1768 at the home of James Harper (1742–1819), and the class was related to the N
York society. Joseph Harper, son of James, had four sons who were outstand
Methodists and founders of the publishing house of Harper Brothers. The chapel v
at the intersection of Dry Harbor and Juniper Swamp roads. In 1836 a larger chu
was erected on land secured from Joseph Harbor. It is now the Middle Village Meth
ist Church, second oldest in the New York area. (Records of Middle Village Method
Church and 185th anniversary brochure.)

ckson from going to Nova Scotia: brother Cromwell is married, and
xpect brother Jessop will go alone.[42]

Tuesday, 29. I delivered a close and awful discourse on, "They shall
me from the east, and from the west, and from the north, and from the
uth, and sit down with Abraham, and Isaac, and Jacob," &c. 1. A
riptural view of the kingdom of heaven. 2. The subjects or citizens
reof. 3. Sit down with Abraham, famous for faith; Isaac, for justice,
th, meditation, and walking with God; and Jacob, mighty in prayer.
vas in prayer until near midnight. O Lord, make me all life and love,
tience and resignation under the troubles of the Church, and disap-
intment of its ministers.

Sunday, June 3. I had a gracious time on 2 Cor. iv, 1–4. Ordained
ekiel Cooper[43] a deacon. In the afternoon my soul had peace whilst I
larged on Matt. xviii, 15, to the end.

Tuesday, 5. Preached on, "No man having put his hand to the plough
d looking back, is fit for the kingdom of heaven." I felt freedom and
wer in speaking.

Wednesday, 6. Met leaders and trustees and after some explanation,
tled matters relative to singing in public worship. I preached at the
or-house[44] on "Whosoever shall call on the name of the Lord shall be
ved." My soul has peace. I keep myself busy in visiting the families of the
ciety, or the sick, or meeting class, if some other business does not call
.

Sunday, 10. I had some life in preaching on Luke iv, 18, and in the

[2] Freeborn Garretson and James Cromwell had been sent to Nova Scotia by the
ristmas Conference in 1784, and they had laid the foundations of the work there.
Coke's request they returned to the United States in this year, and Coke and Asbury
Wesley's suggestion asked Garrettson to accept ordination as superintendent over
the work in British North America and the West Indies. The plan was not carried
t, however, largely because Garrettson did not want to sever his connection with the
thodist Episcopal Church, and soon the Nova Scotia work was wholly British. (For
iscussion of this affair see Candler: *Life of Thomas Coke* and Barclay, *op. cit.*, I,
5–75.) Woolman Hickson's health was impaired, and Cromwell's married state made
going inadvisable. William Jessop went alone, but he fell ill and returned after a few
nths. Hickson formed the first class in Brooklyn; he died the following year and was
ried in John Street Church.

[3] Ezekiel Cooper (1763–1847), one of the most notable of the early Methodist
ders, was born in Maryland and converted by Freeborn Garrettson. He was ap-
inted to a circuit at the Christmas Conference in 1784. He preached in New York
1 New Jersey with distinction and became Book Editor and Publishing Agent in
90 on the death of John Dickins. He was a member of seven General Conferences
04–32) and at his death was the only survivor of the Christmas Conference. His
luminous correspondence is at Garrett Biblical Institute. (See Sprague's *Annals*, VII,
3 ff.; Stevens, *op. cit.*, III, 180 ff.; Seaman, *op. cit.*, 87–90, 122, 128–33; *Dictionary of
erican Biography*, IV, 397, 398. Phoebus' noted *Beams of Light on Early Methodism
America* is based on Cooper's documents.)

[4] The New York Poor House was located deep in The Commons, apparently near
northeast corner of the present City Hall Park.

afternoon on "I thank thee, O Father, Lord of heaven and earth, becau
thou hast hid these things from the wise and prudent," &c.

Monday, 11. I left the city in great union with the Lord and with t
Church. My soul is variously exercised: I want the country air, and to li
more in the spirit and solitude of prayer. Came to East Chester a
preached in the shell of the new church[45] on "To-day if ye will hear l
voice, harden not your hearts"; the power of God was felt. I came to t
widow Bartow's,[46] where I lay sick fifteen years ago, and was treat
with the greatest tenderness. May the Lord reward them all a hundr
fold, and convert their souls!

Tuesday, 12. I found it the same at New Rochelle town as in time pa
will it always be so? If there is no change I shall trouble them no moi
In the afternoon I rode to C——'s, where I laboured many years ago, a
there is some fruit remaining to this day.

Wednesday, 13. We had a long and warm ride to North Castle.[47] He
a multitude were gathered together, to whom I spoke in an orchard
"Him hath God exalted with his right hand to be a Prince and Saviour,
give repentance unto Israel, and remission of sins." I was quite unwe
faint yet pursuing.

Rode to R——'s, of the society of Friends,[48] who received us wi
great love.

At Hall's[49] a multitude came to hear, whom I exhorted to "seek t
Lord while he might be found."

I was happy in being alone. I poured out my soul to God for the who
work, and the dear people and preachers of my charge. My body is we
—my soul enjoys peace. I have power over all sin, and possess a spirit
prayer and watchfulness: I feel myself dead to all below, and desire to li
only for God and souls.

[45] The new church was probably in New Rochelle, which was less than a mile fro
East Chester. The church at East Chester was not erected until 1797. (*Journal* entry
September 27, 1797; De Vinne: "History of Methodism on New Rochelle Circui
Methodist Magazine and Quarterly Review, XIV, 203, April, 1832.)

[46] This was the widow of Theodosius Bartow. She cared for Asbury in a serious illn
during his first winter in America. (See *Journal* entry for January 23, 1772.)

[47] There are two townships in Westchester County with similar names, New Cas
and North Castle. Asbury had not previously visited North Castle, which had be
covered by Thomas Ware the preceding year. The village and township was seven mi
or more north of White Plains and was the scene of the capture of Major John And
the British spy connected with Benedict Arnold's treasonable plot to deliver West Poi
(See *Journal* entry for June 16; Lossing: *Pictorial Field Book of the Revolution*, I, 698
A short time previously a chapel, outgrowth of the New Rochelle Society, had be
built near the center of North Castle Township at School Street and Cox Avenue in
present village of Armonk, and it was here that Asbury preached.

[48] The Quaker center was the Chappaqua Monthly Meeting of New Castle townsh

[49] James Hall lived between present Chappaqua and Mount Kisco and was active
the class organized by Ware at Bedford in the area in 1786. (See *Journal* entry for M
27, 1805; Scharf, *op. cit.*, II, 627.)

Friday, 15. I preached to a listening multitude at Peekskill;[50] and was rming and close on, "By grace ye are saved through faith. I thought re were no people here of spiritual understanding; but I was informed, my comfort, that a number of simple-hearted people had formed emselves into a society for prayer: perhaps these will be some of the t-fruits in this place.

Saturday, 16. Rode over the mountains, and was gratified with the ht of a remarkable recess for the Americans during the last war: the mes of Andre and Arnold, with which misfortune and treachery are so happily and intimately blended, will give celebrity to West Point, had it en less deserving of notice than its wonderful appearance really makes It is commanded by mountains rising behind, and appears to be pregnable: there are block houses on the east; and on the west, stores, rracks, and fortifications. From West Point we crossed a high moun-n,[51] and came to Newburg.[52]

Sunday, 17. In the love feast, sacrament, and public exercises, we were ployed nearly seven hours : there was some life in the love feast, but congregation appeared very little moved under preaching.

Monday, 18. I presume I had nearly seven hundred hearers at Allen's,[53] whom I spoke with some power on Luke xi, 13. I baptized several adults, d some children; and came to Wyatt's,[54] and baptized others. Thence Mr. Ellison's[55], whose wife (a Dutch lady) entertained us *like a queen*.

[50] Peekskill was named for an early Dutch explorer, Jans Peek, who anchored near re while exploring the area. Whitefield preached in the mansion of a merchant, niel Birdsall, there in July, 1770. Asbury preached either in the Birdsall home or in t of Jonathan Ferris, who was a leader in the class which Garrettson formed in 1788. harf, *op. cit.*, 391, 394.)

[51] This mountain was Storm King. Asbury crossed the Hudson at King's Ferry from plank's Point to Stony Point. (Patterson: *Peekskill in the American Revolution*, 6.)

[52] In 1786 Ezekiel Cooper and John McClaskey preached in this section. The latter ached in the home of Elnathan Foster on the site of the present Calvary Presbyterian urch at Newburgh and formed a class there. Asbury probably preached at Foster's this occasion. (Ruttenber: *History of Newburgh*, 324, 325.)

[53] This "Allen" was probably the widow Allison who lived in the outskirts of New-gh and whose home was noted as a Methodist preaching place. (*Historical Records Newburgh*.)

[54] Samuel Wyatt lived in New Marlboroughtown, the present Marlboro, between wburgh and Middlehope. The place was also called Keytown. Cooper and Mc-skey had formed a class in his home. (Ruttenber, *op. cit.*)

[55] This was John Ellison, who lived at New Windsor, the present Vail's Gate, about r miles southeast of Newburgh. He inherited a large estate from his father and lived a stone mansion which is now preserved by the state of New York as a historic site. was the Methodist leader in the vicinity, and in 1790 he built a structure of which the ond story was a chapel. The present church at Vail's Gate was built on a lot provided Ellison in 1806 and is the oldest in continuous use on the west bank of the Hudson. wife was the former Catherine Johnson (Jansen) of a leading family in Kingston, w York. Their marriage license was dated September 7, 1760. (Records of town of gston.)

I visited Colonel P——, supposed to be at the point of death: after close examination, I administered the sacrament to him.

Wednesday, 20. I came to Warwick,[56] where I suppose not less than thousand people were collected: I was very low both in body and spirit but felt stirred up at the sight of such a congregation, and was moved and quickened while I enlarged on Gal. i, 4. I baptized some and administered the sacrament to many communicants.

New Jersey

Thursday, 21. A multitude attended at Benjamin's,[57] in a barn. Here G has wrought a great work for a poor, blind, ignorant people.

Friday, 22. I preached at the stone church,[58] after riding upwards thirty miles: we then rode until ten o'clock in the night through a hea rain. I was much tried in body and mind: I had nothing to eat but a lit bread and milk, and that made me sick.

Saturday, 23. We had a good time at Sweezy's.[59] After administering sacrament, we had another long ride after night.

Sunday, 24. I preached in the woods[60] to nearly a thousand people was much oppressed by a cold, and felt very heavy in body and so Like Jonah, I went and sat down alone. I had some gracious feelings in sacrament—others also felt the quickening power of God. I baptized

[56] Methodism was introduced in Warwick, New York, in 1786, the first service be held in the home of Colonel David McCamley. (Ruttenber and Clark: *History of Ora County, New York*, 591.)

[57] Nathan Benjamin developed the society at or near Hamburg in Vernon Townsh Sussex County, New Jersey, in 1786 or 1787, under the ministry of Ezekiel Coop He was a Revolutionary soldier and late in life was a trustee in the church at Vern (Phoebus, *op. cit.*, 46, 68; Snell: *History of Sussex and Warren Counties, New Jers* 70, 356; Ruttenber and Clark, *op. cit.*, 134, 135.) Atkinson in *Memorials of New Jer Methodism* erroneously identifies Asbury's preaching place as Banghart's, but Bangh lived in Oxford Township of present Warren County around fifty miles away.

[58] The stone church was in Johnsonburg, which was early designated as "Log Ja because it was the county seat of Sussex County. It is now in Warren County. The ste building is now known as the Van Ness house. (See *Journal* entries for June 27, 17 and April 25, 1807; Snell, *op. cit.*, 692; *New Jersey Guide*, 455; Gordon's *Gazetteer*, 1

[59] Joseph Sweezy lived near Hope in present Warren County, New Jersey, eight m from the Delaware River. There were several other members of the family in the a Methodism was established there in 1785 by Adam Cloud and Matthew Greentree, preachers on the circuit. A log meetinghouse was erected two miles northeast of H in 1810. (Atkinson, *op. cit.*, 381; Phoebus, *op. cit.*, 68; Shampanore: *History and Di tory of Warren County*, 24; Honeyman: *Northwestern New Jersey*, II, 706, 707; Sr *op. cit.*, 665, 666.)

[60] This was probably at Flanders, near the present Budd Lake. It was one of Ezek Cooper's preaching places. (Phoebus, *op. cit.*, 68; Pitney, *History of Morris Cour* 193.)

PLACES VISITED BY

Francis Asbury

IN

NEW JERSEY

Benjamin's
Pepper Cotton
Nicholas
Warwick, N. Y.
Nyack, N. Y.

Newton

Union Chapel
Albertson
Cummins
Hackettstown
Freeman's
Lockwood
Shearman
Rockaway

Mt. Bethel
Budd's
Lawrence
Morristown
Second River
Newark
Bull's Ferry

Asbury
New Vernon
New Providence
Elizabeth

Hunt's Fy
W. Wallace
Germantown
Bridgetown
Ward's Ferry

Kingwood
Brunswick
Drake's
G. Totten
J. Totten

Jas. Throckmorton
John Rule
Leonard's
Throckmortons

Pennington
Mt. Pleasant
Shewsbury
Monmouth (Freehold)
P. White's.

Trenton
Princeton
Milford
Barcalows

Crosswicks
Shark River

D. Longstreet
Burlington
Mt. Zion
Squan River

Penny Hill
Haddenfield
Mt. Holly
A. Coates
Polhemus Chapel

Gloucester Point
Lumberton
New Mills

Woodbury
Gloucester
Chews
Lanoka Harbor

Perkintown
Bates
Taper's
Waretown

New Kirk's
Squire Robert
Forks

Union Chapel
Newkirk's
Pittsgrove
Price
Peacocks

Penn's Neck
Salem
Murphy's
Little Egg Harbor
Tuckerton

Deerfield
Champlons

Bridgeton
Blackwood

May's Landing
Greenwich
New England
Absecon

Town
Port Elizabeth
Tuckahoe
Great Egg Harbor

Peter Cressey's
Gough's

Cape May

number of infants and adults, by sprinkling and by immersion. I felt r
body quite weary *in*, but my spirit not *of*, the work of God.

Tuesday, 26. Preached at William Wallace's[61] to a dull, contracted peop
Since last *Monday* two weeks, I have ridden about three hundred and fi
miles.

Wednesday, 27. We had a warm ride through a fertile, pleasant count
to Trenton.

Pennsylvania

On *Thursday*, the 28th, to Philadelphia. Here I found Thomas Vase
had scattered firebrands, and thrown dirt to bespatter us.

Friday and *Saturday* 29, 30. Taken up in writing letters, packing
books and begging for the college.

Sunday, July 1. Preached three times in the city of Philadelphia—
Monday, 2, to a few simple-hearted souls at Radnor.[63]

Tuesday, 3. We had a flat time at the Valley.[64]

Wednesday, 4. We had a few feeling souls at Uwchland;[65] afterwa
went to Coventry Forge.[66]

Saturday, 7. I had some energy in preaching to a few people at Morga
town.[67]

Sunday, 8. Preached at Evans's, Uwchland;[68] a poor people for religic
I hope, nevertheless, that God will visit them.

Monday, 9. Preached at John Miller's,[69] who has a pious wife.

[61] William Wallace kept an inn, which is still standing, in Somerville, Some
County, New Jersey. It is a noted landmark which was occupied by Washington in 1
and 1779. This was a Dutch Reformed community not hospitable to Methodis
(Snell, *op. cit.*, 145, 646, 656, 678; *New Jersey, Guide to Present and Past*, 551.)

[62] Thomas Vasey had left the Methodists and been ordained by Anglican Bish
White. (See *Journal* entry for June 1, 1786. Also July 15 and September 1, 1787.)

[63] The Radnor church, which is still active, is on the old Lancaster or Conest
Road in Delaware County, Pennsylvania. The society was formed in 1780 or 1781
the Rev. George Main. The first meetinghouse was built in 1783 on land deeded
Evan James, in whose mansion services were previously conducted.

[64] See note under February 5, 1781.

[65] Uwchland was a township in Chester County, site of Benson's meetinghouse. (
note under October 7, 1781.)

[66] Coventry, in Chester County, Pennsylvania, was the home of Mrs. Grace. (
note under May 23, 1776; also July 6, 1792; July 24, 1799; April 10, 1812.)

[67] Morganstown, Berks County, Pennsylvania, was settled by a Welchman, Thon
Morgan, in 1730.

[68] Thomas Evans lived in Uwchland Township near the Friends meetinghouse.
Hollingsworth's transcription of the *Journal* Uwchland was called Richland.

[69] John Miller lived at Strasburg, Lancaster County, Pennsylvania. A Metho
class met in his house, and William Colbert preached in his barn. (See Colbert's ma
script *Journal*.)

Maryland

Friday, 13. We rode to Hagerstown; and found it a journey of about
ty miles: we and our horses were weary enough. I was sorry to hear
at the people came twice to hear me last year, and the lameness of my
rse caused me to disappoint them.
Saturday, 14. At five o'clock in the evening the court house was opened;
few of the great and many of the poor attended, to whom I spoke with
ivine assistance. I preached again on *Sunday* at eleven o'clock.
I find Thomas Vasey has misrepresented us as having cast off Mr.
esley, making this a plea for his re-ordination.[70]

West Virginia

Monday, 16. Set out for the Springs.[71] In the first place we missed our
iy; then my baggage-horse ran back two miles: I was tried not a little.
how sad the reflection, that matters trifling as these should make a
rson so uneasy. We reached the Springs about seven o'clock. I preached
e two following days with some satisfaction. By advancing nine pounds,
r nails and planks, I engaged brother Eaton to have our chapel covered
first of August.

Maryland

Friday, 20. We had a heavy ride to Oldtown: we met with a kind recep-
n; and had a reviving season in the family.
Saturday, 21. Was a day of rest to my soul and body. Preached on
ant. iv, 16.
Sunday, 22. We had sacrament, attended with some power, in the
ening.
Tuesday, 24. There were to have been great doings at Cumberland, but

[70] Vasey's dissatisfaction arose from his belief that faith had not been kept with the
mmitment made by the Christmas Conference which reads: "During the life of the
v. Mr. Wesley, we acknowledge ourselves his sons in the gospel, ready in matters of
irch government to obey his commands." Wesley's name had been omitted from the
neral Minutes, and the conference had acted unfavorably on Wesley's appointment
Whatcoat and Garrettson as general superintendents. Vasey was critical of Asbury,
whose consecration he had assisted, for not protesting against changing the name of
office from superintendent to bishop, a move opposed by Wesley. (Lee: *A Short
story of the Methodists*, 126; Bangs, *op. cit.*, I, 258, 259.)
[71] The Springs were at Bath, the present Berkeley, West Virginia.

Mr. Bower,[72] a minister, failed coming. I had a good time in N
Bell's mill,[73] on, "Thou art fairer than the sons of men."

We had feeling and weeping at Barratt's; my subject, "I sleep, but *
heart waketh," &c., eight or nine verses. I feel a sweetness of spirit, a
much of the love of Christ. Came to Cresap's.

Friday, 27. Ordained brother Phœbus deacon,[74] and had a serious tim

West Virginia

Sunday, 29. At Jones's,[75] all death! death! death! My mind was devot
to God. I administered the sacrament, but could find no openings. Ro
to Oldtown, Maryland. Six years ago I preached in this place, when th
was scarcely a soul that knew anything of God; now there are sixty
membership, many of whom are happy in the knowledge of the truth. \
held a love feast and had a quickening time.

Tuesday, 31. Rode to the Springs (Bath), much tried in spirit. I ga
myself to reading and prayer.

Wednesday, August 1. Preached at Bath.

Sunday, 5. Preached on 1 Pet. iii, 9, to a large congregation, with t
little liberty.

Monday, 6. I began my lectures on the Prophecies by Bishop Newt
and had more hearers than I expected. The weather is very warm; ma
are sickly; and continued changes of comers and goers; all this leaves t
little opportunity for prayer. I forbear reading on account of my ey
lest I should not be able to read in public.

Tuesday and *Wednesday*, 7, 8. Had very few to hear, so I gave them u
everything that is good is in low estimation at this place. I will retu
to my own studies: if the people are determined to go to hell, I am cl
of their blood. My soul is clothed in sackcloth and covered with asl
before the Lord.

Thursday, 9. I enjoy some peace.

Friday, 10. I feel calm within, and the want of more life, and m
love to God, and more patience with sinners. I read my Testament.
what a weariness would life be without God, and love, and labour! T

---

[72] This may have been the Rev. George Bower who was the incumbent of the pai
of the Protestant Episcopal Church which embraced much of western Maryla
(Scharf: *History of Western Maryland*, II, 1078, 1084; Rightmeyer: *Maryland's Es*
lished Church, 164.)

[73] Bell's Mill, probably on Evitts Creek near Cumberland, was operated by Tho
Bell. (See manuscript *Journal*, George Wells, October 9, 1790, Lovely Lane Muse
Baltimore.)

[74] William Phoebus (1754–1831) was on the Redstone Circuit at this time.

[75] Jones was the present Fort Ashby, Mineral County, West Virginia.

st two weeks of my time at Bath have been spent in carrying on the
ilding of the new chapel, reading Newton on the Prophecies, visiting,
thing, &c. My soul has been under great trials, at times, but hitherto
e Lord has helped.

Tuesday, 21. O, how sweet will labour, and Christian society, and the
litary woods be to me!

Thursday, 23. I have been under great exercises, but was divinely
sisted in preaching on, "The eyes of the Lord are over the righteous,"
c.

Sunday, 26. I preached on, "How beautiful upon the mountains are the
et of him that bringeth good tidings," &c. It was a solemn time—my
ul was stayed upon God. We had a melting sacrament and love feast,
d many spoke. The devil is angry, and so are his children: brother
hatcoat spoke at the steps, and it was with difficulty the people kept
emselves within decent bounds of respect.

Friday, 31. I gave them my farewell address at Bath, and had many
arers.

Saturday, September 1. I set out in the rain, and came to the widow
roud's, where I met with Thomas Vasey who made some acknowledg-
ents for what he had said in the heat of his zeal at Philadelphia and at
th.

Sunday, 2. I attended at a place where every one has liberty to preach;
t it so happened that no one had an appointment there but myself. The
ethodists would do well to withdraw from this as a preaching place
their circuit. I had a large congregation at Shepherdstown, to whom I
oke, on Luke iv, 18. I have had some trials and great consolations; and,
times, it is a Paradise regained with me since I left Bath and the wicked
ere.

Maryland

Friday, 7. I had a cold time at Reistertown, on, "Woe to them that are at
se in Zion." Thence I rode to the new church,[76] where I had much more
e. Came to Baltimore. The weather is extremely warm.

Sunday, 9. Preached in the morning—my text, "Thou art fairer than
e sons of men:" in the afternoon at Mr. Otterbein's church: and at
ght on, "They shall come from the east, and from the west, and from
e north, and from the south," &c. Large crowds attended: I was strait-
ed in speaking. The following was a week of haste and business.
ednesday, I went to Perry Hall; thence to Cokesbury—fixed the price of

---

[6] This chapel, only two years old, occupied the site of the one in which Robert Straw-
dge preached. Stones from it were used in the erection of the present Old Stone Chapel
Pikesville, Maryland. The cornerstone reads 1786 for the first building, 1862 for the
ond.

board, and the time for opening the college. On *Friday*, I returned
Baltimore. In the midst of business my mind is calm.

Sunday, 16. Preached at Baltimore and Fell's Point. On *Monday*, t
people waited nearly two hours at Daniel Evans's before I arrived, owi
to my horse being out of the way: I found he had stuck a nail into I
foot, so that I had to leave him. Under these discouraging circumstanc
I was much exercised: nevertheless, I had liberty in speaking, and the
was a melting time among the people. Thence I hastened to Hunt's chap
where I enlarged on, "I know you, that you have not the love of God
you."

I rode by John Colgate's gate—an old stand of mine. It is now, in tv
senses, fallen into decay. The want of religion oftentimes causes the wa
of economy. Ah! how do the persons and fashions of this world pass awa

Tuesday, 18. I found the work of God in a reviving state at G——'s.

Wednesday, 19. I had a liberal opening at John Wilson's, on "Whos
ever shall call on the name of the Lord shall be saved." Thence I hasten
to the Fork church, and preached on Cant. iii, 1–6. I lamented the gaye
of the children of Methodists; but yet they do not appear to be so full
enmity against God and his people as other children.

I hastened to Cokesbury, it being the examination: some gentlemen a
some triflers were present. *Friday*, I preached at Josias Dallam's.

Saturday, 22. I preached at Havre de Grace, on Acts ii, 23.

Sunday, 23. I had a large congregation at Elkton, and some pow
attended the word. In the evening spoke at Isaac Tussey's.

Monday, 24. I had a large, solemn congregation at Wilmington. I fee
persuasion that God will revive his work at this place.

Pennsylvania

Tuesday, 25. I attended at Chester; and next day came to Philadelph
I had liberty in speaking on Cant. v, 6–10. On *Thursday* and *Friday*
had not freedom as I wished. I was seized with a violent headache, exce
ing anything, as I thought, I had ever felt.

Saturday, 29. I felt a little better. My mind was stayed upon God.

Sunday, 30. We had a good sacramental occasion. In the afterno
brother Willis[77] preached; and at night I had some enlargement
Ephes. iv, 17–19.

Wednesday, October 3. I met the people, and explained the nature a
design of the college.[78]

Thursday, 4. I preached on the primitive design of the Church.

[77] The Rev. Henry Willis was the elder at New York. He was the first man to
ordained by Asbury. (See *Journal* entry for January 18, 1785.)

[78] The college was Cokesbury College in Maryland.

Friday, 5. We had an uncommon love feast—a gracious season—much
eaking. On *Saturday* I met a class.

Sunday, 7. There was life in the administration of the sacrament. I felt
mbled before the Most High. I trust the Lord will revive his work, and
ake his power known.

Monday, 8. I came to Chester, and preached on, "My grace is sufficient
r thee."

Tuesday, 9. I had unusual freedom in speaking at Aaron Matson's.
ence I pushed on through the rain, and was sorely tempted to complain.

Delaware

Wednesday, 10. I was at Wilmington; and next day came late to Joseph
ckerson's.

I visited Duck Creek Cross Roads,[79] where we have a comfortable
use, which cost about two hundred pounds.

Saturday, 13. Came to Dover very unwell, and brother Ira Ellis[80]
eached in my stead.

Sunday, 14. I read prayers, and preached on 2 Tim. iii, 10; and solemnly
apart Jacob Brush[81] and Ira Ellis, for the office of deacon: I trust it was
rofitable time. I spent two days at Thomas White's.

Tuesday, 16. I preached the funeral sermon of Joshua Barwick—a
thful steady man, who had followed the Lord about ten years; my text
s, "These all died in the faith."

Thursday, 18. I had Divine aid in preaching at Milford's:[82] the house
s open, and the day was cold.

Friday, 19. Came in the evening to Shanklands. Here I found the people
disorder and violence about the election; some had gone so far as to
e up fire-arms.

> This was the present Smyrna.
> Ira Ellis, a brother of Reuben Ellis, was then on the Kent Circuit. (For "A Sketch
he Labours and Travels of Ira Ellis," 1781–95, by himself, followed by a certificate
ecommendation by Asbury and Whatcoat with a tribute from the former, see *Journal*
ry for February 17, 1805; Sweet: *Religion on the American Frontier*, IV, 710, 711.)
Jacob Brush was born near Merrick, Long Island, in 1762 and died of yellow fever
New York City on September 24, 1795. He was interred at the Forsyth Street Church.
the time of Asbury's visit he was on the Dover Circuit. (*General Minutes*, I, 66;
man: *Annals of New York Methodism*, 114, 136; Hallman, *op. cit.*, 60; Wakeley,
cit., 367–70.)
More than a decade before Milford, Delaware (Sussex County), was laid out in
7, John Cooper preached in the nearby home of Renyear William. The old Method-
Cemetery, North and Third Streets, was the site of the unfinished chapel to which
ury refers. Asbury, who preached in the community in 1778, records about eighteen
ts to Milford. (Scharf, *op. cit.*, II, 1198; Hallman, *op. cit.*, 117; Lednum, *op. cit.*,
, 255; Colbert's *Journal, Milford Circuit*, II, 65–115.) Milford Circuit first appears
1789. (Hynson: *Historical Etchings of Milford and Vicinity*, 47–49.)

Sunday morning, 21. Before sacrament I preached on Psalm ii, 24, 25
and then in Lewes, on, "God sent not his Son into the world to conde▮
the world," &c.

Tuesday and *Wednesday,* 23, 24. I had a good time at quarterly meeti▮
at the Sound church: thence, through a barren, sandy country, we came
Evans's church,[84] where we had a good and gracious time, more so tha▮
have felt for some time. From Evans's we rode to the beach, and gratifi
our curiosity with the sight of the raging, roaring sea.

Wednesday, 24. I spoke closely upon the discipline of the Church: ▮
subject, "All Scripture is given by inspiration of God, and is profital
for doctrine," &c. After meeting, we had a very long ride to brot▮
Bowen's.[85]

Virginia

Friday, 26. After preaching at Parnell's, on, "I will give them a heart
know me," &c., I rode in the evening to Downing's.[86]

Saturday, 27. Reached Paramore's[87] at night.

Sunday, 28. We had a gracious time indeed.

Monday, 29. There were life and power among the people in the sac
ment and love feast. I was greatly comforted to find the Lord had grea
blessed the labours of brother Sparks,[88] and that a revival had taken pl▮
all round the circuit. In the evening I rode to Burton's, in Virginia. ▮
former inhabitants have gone to the dust.

It seemed as if I was let into heaven, while I enlarged on, "Behold w▮
manner of love the Father hath bestowed upon us, that we should
called the sons of God.' We have twenty miles, and sometimes mo▮

[83] Psalm 2 has only twelve verses. There is no indication as to what passage this ▮

[84] The site of this chapel has not been definitely identified. It is probable that Asb▮
meant the Old Line Chapel of which Jacob Evans was a trustee. It was on his rout▮
Accomack County, Virginia.

[85] The singular experience of how an early circuit rider, inquiring the way to Accom▮
County, Virginia, was misdirected into the Cypress Swamp only to emerge at the h▮
of Jephthah Bowen is often told. The visit of the stranger led to the conversion of
Bowen family, the introduction of Methodism into that region, and the erection
Bowen Chapel, the first in Worcester County. (Boehm, *op. cit.,* 66, 67; *Journal e*▮
for July 12, 1796.)

[86] William Downing, Richard Drummond, and Jonathan Garrettson of Accom▮
County, and John Johnson of Northampton County, each donated land for the build
of a chapel, thereby perpetuating their names in the Methodist annals of the East
Shore. (Clark: *Eastern Shore of Maryland and Virginia,* 175.)

[87] Paramore's, Burton's, and Downing's were the earliest preaching places on
Eastern Shore of Virginia. In 1787 a survey of William Paramore's plantation sho▮
911 acres. "He took his religion seriously and set free his ten slaves." (Whitel▮
Virginia's Eastern Shore, 869.)

[88] *Minutes,* Northampton Circuit, 1787.

a day to travel; but we have fine roads, kind friends, and good entertainment.

Thursday, November 1. The people coming in still after I began, caused me to lengthen out my discourse. Came afterward to Captain Burton's, and spoke with life and consolation.

Maryland

Friday, 2. Was a day of sore exercise of soul, and barren preaching. I visited Mr. R., and administered the sacrament to him. Rested that evening with Mr. Thomas Curtis.

Saturday, 3. Quarterly meeting. I was close on keeping the feast, and on discipline—some felt the word.

Sunday, 4. Preached on, "Thou shalt arise and favour Zion." I believe God will make his power known; and I trust brother Joseph Everett will be made a blessing, as well by strictness of discipline, as by faithful preaching.

Monday, 5. I had a few living people at John Phœbus's.[89] My soul is given up to God; but I have felt Satan near. Lord, help, or I perish!

Sunday, 11. I had some light in preaching at the Fork chapel.[90] Spent the evening with brother Ennall.[91]

Monday, 12. I preached at Hopper's.[92] Thence I rode to Johnson's chapel,[93] and spoke on 2 Tim. 1: 8–12. I had some enlargement.

[89] Probably John Phoebus of Quantico Neck, Somerset County, to whose home Asbury hastened on October 28, 1783, to conduct the funeral of William Wright. He was a brother of the Rev. William Phoebus, M.D. Annemessex Chapel, which became Phoebus Chapel, is now the Oriole Church. (Colbert's *Journal*, IV, 27, 34, 42; Boehm, *op. cit.*, 70.)

[90] The Fork's Chapel was located in Dorchester County.

[91] Henry Ennalls lived near the Choptank River about twelve miles from Cambridge. His sisters were instrumental in establishing Methodism in Dorchester County. Ennalls was a trustee of Cokesbury College, led in the erection of Ennall's Chapel, and by his hospitality and generosity became one of the most influential Methodists of the Eastern Shore. (Boehm, *op. cit.*, 57–64; Phoebus, *op. cit.*, 116; Stevens, *op. cit.*, II, 254.)

[92] In September, 1783, Philip Cox, then on the Annamessex Circuit, wrote Thomas Haskins that "Colonel Hopper and several great men have been brought in since Christmas." (See original letter in the Harper Memorial Library, University of Chicago.) Earlier, while a resident of Caroline County, the colonel had served six years as sheriff and three years in the Assembly. Following his arrival in Queen Annes County he opened his house for preaching, and the society became the nucleus of the present Epworth Church, Centerville. A daughter married the Rev. Hugh Neill. (Hallman, *op. cit.*, 325; Emory: *History of Queen Annes County*, 175, 231, 367.)

[93] Johnson's Chapel, the site of which cannot be identified, was probably somewhere in Queen Annes County. (Hallman, *op. cit.*, 114; Ware, *op. cit.*, 108.)

After riding thirty miles and preaching twice, we held a watch night at Todd's.[94]

Sunday, 18. We went to church at Cambridge, and heard a sermon. Afterward I spoke to a large congregation at Tucker's, on Rom. x, 1–4. Upon the whole, it has been a laborious, trying time of late.

Tuesday, 20. We rode through excessive rain thirty miles. Our quarterly meeting at Frazier's chapel was large and lively. I had very few to hear at Doctor Allen's,[95] the fiery edge is greatly worn off there.

Thursday, 22. We had a feeling time at Bolingbroke; but it is not here as in months past. O how soon does the power or religion decline! I came to Easton, Talbot county, where we had a watch night, and the gentry had a ball.

Friday, 23. We had a gracious season at the Bayside, where many attended.

Saturday, 24. My soul is dejected. O that it were perfectly resigned to the will of God!

Sunday, 25. I stopped at Keet's,[96] on my way to Kent Island. Although under a great depression of spirits, I was uncommonly led out whilst I enlarged on, "Woe to them that are at ease in Zion," to a large assembly of people.

Monday, 26. My mind is still depressed. I called on poor Colonel H. who bears his imprisonment for debt with great fortitude. I had a good time at Boardley's,[97] notwithstanding two drunken men came in and made some disturbance.

Friday, 30. Cold, straitened for time at Tuckahoe; something better at Choptank. I here heard of the conduct of Adam Cloud;[98] he is gone from

[94] This was the home of Levin Todd, located in Mispillion Hundred, Kent County, Delaware. The successor to this society, organized about 1777, is Todd Chapel, west of Farmington on the Farmington Circuit. (Scharf, *op. cit.*, II, 1177; Lednum, *op. cit.*, 202, 261; Hallman, *op. cit.*, 121, 245.)

[95] This was Moses D. Allen, M.D. After meeting him on December 6, 1784, at Boling broke, near Trappe, Talbot County, Thomas Coke wrote: "Dr. Allen is a physician of great eminence in these parts, and a most precious man of excellent sense, and of the greatest simplicity." (See Coke's *Journal*, 49.) He was one of the original trustees of Cokesbury College. (Armstrong: *Old Baltimore Conference*, 89; Hallman, *op. cit.*, 104.)

[96] The presence of several Keets families in both Talbot and Queen Annes counties makes identification of this preaching place uncertain. However, since Asbury visited it while en route from Bayside Chapel (Wittman) to Kent Island, it must have been in Talbot County rather than the home of Thomas Keets, a trustee of Wye Chapel, Queen Annes County. (Hallman, *op. cit.*, 115, 329.)

[97] John W. Boardley, or Bordley, lived southwest of Wye Mills, a village located in both Queen Annes and Talbot counties. The last of the three services conducted by Asbury at Boardleys was in a barn. (See *Journal* entry for October 13, 1792.) In 1818 John W. Boardley was a committeeman from Corsica, Queen Annes County, to obtain subscriptions for a parsonage for Queen Anne's Circuit. (Emory, *op. cit.*, 236.)

[98] Adam Cloud, brother of Robert, and a member of a pioneer Methodist family of New Castle County, Delaware, became a traveling preacher in 1781. Although in the

at last. There were many people at Barratt's chapel during quarterly
:eting, but I had little life in speaking.

Monday, December, 3. We had a melting time at Queen Anne's chapel.
:nforced, "Because iniquity shall abound, the love of many shall wax
ld."

Tuesday, 4. At Chestertown, I had but little life on Isa. liii, 1–5. At
ght the Lord was with us indeed, while I enforced, "Let your modera-
>n be known to all men."

Wednesday, 5. After preaching at Worton chapel, we set out to cross
e Chesapeake Bay, and were on the water until ten o'clock at night.

Thursday, 6. We opened our college, and admitted twenty-five students.
>reached on, "Trust in the Lord, and do good." On the *Sabbath* I spoke
ı, "O man of God, there is death in the pot;" and on *Monday,* "They are
e seed of the blessed of the Lord, and their offspring with them." From
>kesbury I came to Baltimore, where I was closely employed and much
haste about temporal concerns.

Saturday, 15. I had a cold ride to Annapolis; and but few to hear me on
ınday morning. Brother Hagerty[99] attempted to travel with me, but was
•on glad to resign. My soul has been kept in peace, and for three weeks
ıst I have enjoyed a most devoted frame of mind.

Thursday, 20. We must now direct our course for Lancaster, Virginia,
rough a barren route of sixty miles. This is the only uncultivated part of
[aryland; and God will surely visit these people, and bless them in his
vn time, if they hear his voice. We crossed Patuxent River at sunrise:
·other James Riggin having undertaken to be our guide, led us ten miles
ıt of our way.

Virginia

Bearing near to Port Tobacco, we came to the ferry, crossed about
ınset, and put up at Mrs. Hooe's,[100] where we paid eight shillings for
ır oats, and six for our fodder—all this exclusive of charge for lodging,
 she said.

Friday, 21. Reached Pope's some time in the night. On *Saturday* I read

---

inutes of 1788 his name appears under those who "desist from traveling," he actually
ıs expelled for improper conduct. (*Minutes of the Annual Conferences,* 1773–1828,
»; Lee, *op. cit.,* 136; Lednum, *op. cit.,* xv, 57, 58; Adkinson: *Methodism in New Jersey,*
·0, 351; Bangs, *op. cit.,* I, 275; letter of Jesse Lee to Ezekiel Cooper, April 16, 1807;
[anuscript 37, Ezekiel Cooper Collection, Garrett Biblical Institute, Evanston,
linois.)

[99] John Hagerty was one of the traveling elders of the circuits through which Asbury
ıas en route to Virginia.

[100] This was Hooe's (Hoe's) Ferry, which crossed the Potomac River from Cedar
oint, Maryland, to Colonel Richard Hooe's in Virginia. (Wilstach: *Tidewater
irginia,* 295, 296.)

the apostolical canons, published by Johnson—curious enough. He is
violent Churchman, and appears to have little charity for the Presbyteriar
upon whom he is unmercifully severe. I have been sorely tempted, and
sword's point with the enemy.

Sunday, 23. I had very little life in preaching to a few dead souls
Pope's.[101] On *Monday*, at Hutt's, it was nearly the same both in preachii
and sacrament. In the evening, at brother Cannon's,[102] the Lord powerfu
broke into my soul, and the cloud disappeared. That night while sleepir
I dreamed I was praying for sanctification, and God very sensibly fill
me with love, and I waked shouting glory, glory to God! My soul was ;
in a flame. I had never felt so much of God in my life; and so I continue
This was on Christmas day—a great day to me.

I rode to the Widow Woolard's,[103] and preached on, "For this purpo
was the Son of God manifested, that he might destroy the works of t
devil." During the last five days, we have ridden one hundred and for
miles. We crossed Wicomoco, and came to G's. Death prevails here. N
spirit was clothed in sackcloth.

Saturday and *Sunday*, 29, 30. Held quarterly meeting at Lancast
meeting house. There was a large gathering, and some life on the first da
On Sunday there was much snow, and only about three hundred peop
attended. I ordained E. Ellis a deacon.

[101] Pope lived in Westmoreland County.
[102] Hutt and Cannon also resided in Westmoreland County. (Butts, *op. cit.*, 93.)
[103] The Widow Woolard lived in Westmoreland County. (See Asbury's letter to Ezek
Cooper dated December 24, 1788, and written from Woolard's.)

1788

1788

Asbury reaching the home of General Russell at Saltville, Virginia

CHAPTER SEVENTEEN

Virginia

Tuesday, January 1, 1788. Preached at the Widow Agatha Ball's, on alm xc, 12.

Thursday, 3. Crossed the Rappahannock, and came to G.'s, but did not el free to stay. I went on to Blake's.[1] Came to brother Billups's,[2] in ingston parish, Gloucester county.[3] Here we were at home, and happy our religious exercises. During the last one hundred miles of our journey have preached very little for the want of appointments. We left brother llups's, and, riding after forty miles, and preaching by the way, we came Cappahosie Ferry; but being unable to cross we rode on ten miles to e widow Rowe's.

Tuesday, 8. There being a storm of rain and a thaw, we set out to cross e river at York: we succeeded, but with some difficulty: I had had some stressing apprehensions of this. I preached at B——'s, on "How beauti- l upon the mountains are the feet," &c. We came to James River: the e was in the way, yet we pushed through safely to the opposite shore, d arrived at Mooring's just as the quarterly meeting ended; nevertheless,

[1] There were several Blakes living in Middlesex County. (*Heads of Families,* 56.)

[2] Thomas Scott, the Methodist preacher who served Gloucester Circuit in 1789-90, ys, "A seacaptain named Billups resided at New Point Comfort where a large and eply pious society had been formed. . . . Captain Billups possessed a handsome estate, ed great hospitality, was a member of our church, a zealous local preacher, greatly loved by the people, and very influential." (Scott's *Journal.*)

[3] In 1791 Kingston Parish was cut off from Gloucester County to form the present athews County. (Mason: *Colonial Churches of Tidewater Virginia.*)

we too had a meeting, and the cry of glory! was heard in great life: G*
is among these people. Brother Cox[4] thinks that not less than fourte*
hundred, white and black, have been converted in Sussex circuit the pa*
year; and brother Easter thinks there are still more in Brunswick circu*
I preached at Pinner's[5] in Nansemond circuit; thence to Cowling's, a*
preached on Isa. liii, 1–4. We came on to Sleepy Hole Ferry,[6] being unab*
to get our horses over, we walked five miles to Turner's.[7]

Sunday, 13. I had some liberty on Isa. lii, 6–8.

Monday, 14. We continued our meeting nearly four hours, but h*
little satisfaction by reason of the extreme cold. There is a growth
religion here since last year.

We came to Portsmouth, but too late, the ice hindered: however,
preached at three o'clock. Next day it rained, and few attended; so th*
upon the whole, we had but a low time there. I preached at N. Wilson*
Here I had an interview with James Morris[8] he wants to go into the O*
Church. I had a great and good time at brother Williams's on Isa. xxx*
3–5, the power and love of God were manifested and felt.

North Carolina

Sunday, 20. I preached at Col. Jarvis's; and on *Monday* at Saunders'*
dull times at both these places.

Tuesday, 22. At Coinjock[9] there is a death here. —— has been expe*
menting on extremes; wise doctrine—hard discipline. I doubt whether
will end well.

I have ridden about eighty miles, and preached four times to abo*
eight hundred people, most of whom were dead and ignorant; yet I ho*
God will arise.

Currituck—a pleasant place: I rode along the shore and enjoyed t*
view of its banks of evergreen.

I preached at Camden court house with freedom, but the people a*

[4] Philip Cox was on the Brunswick Circuit in 1786 and the Sussex Circuit in 178*
Edward Dromgoole says 1,800 were added to Brunswick Circuit in 1787, the reviv*
being greater than that of 1786. (Dromgoole's Papers, University of North Caroli*
Library.)

[5] *Heads of Families*, 92.

[6] Sleepy Hole Ferry was on the Nansemond River, three miles east of Driver. Bened*
Arnold, returning from his Richmond raid, crossed the river there on January 16, 178*
and Cornwallis, going to Portsmouth, crossed there in July, 1781. There is a historic*
marker at Driver.

[7] This was Pasco Turner, who lived in Nansemond County. (*Heads of Families*, 7*

[8] James Morris later entered the Episcopal ministry. (See *Journal* entry for March *
1799.)

[9] Asbury traveled through Currituck and nearby counties in December, 1784. (S*
notes on that journey.)

ared insensible: after meeting, we rode, hungry and cold, to brother
——'s.[10]

Thursday, 24. We had a violent storm; so we kept within doors; and
an and beast were well provided for.

Friday, 25. Was an uncommonly cold and windy day; I neverthe-
ss attempted to preach at Richardson's chapel. In the evening visited
'. P.

Saturday, 26, and *Sunday*, 27. We had cold weather, and a cold people
the quarterly meeting at Flatty Creek chapel.[11] On *Sabbath* evening I
eached at Nixonton.[12]

Monday, 28. Rode to Gates's; and next day preached at Knotty Pine
apel:[13] there were but few people, and it was a barren meeting.

Wednesday, 30. Preached on "The grace of God that bringeth salvation
th appeared unto all men."[14] Alas for the rich! they are so soon offended.
ode to Winton,[15] is a little town on Chowan River; here I had a dry meeting
th a few people in the court house. I housed for the night with W——.
seldom mount my horse for a ride of less distance than twenty miles on
dinary occasions; and frequently have forty or fifty in moving from
e circuit to the other: in travelling thus I suffer much from hunger and
ld.

I preached at W——'s, with some liberty. Our brother Chastaine
amped to purpose.

Saturday, February 2. At Wicocon[16] I enlarged on Peter's fall.

Sunday, 3. I preached on Heb. vi, 11, 12. I rode that evening to friend
eeman's, whom I had not visited for five years past: I found him still an
nest Baptist, and we were kindly entertained.

Rode to Ross's in Martin's county. The rise of the waters of the
oanoke River had inundated the lowlands more than a mile from

[10] Brother C. must have been one of the Chamberlains who lived in the north end of
mden county near the present South Mills. (J. F. Pugh, Camden.)
[11] Flatty Creek is in Pasquotank County on Pasquotank River. The chapel is no longer
existence there. (J. F. Pugh, Camden.)
[12] Nixonton is in Pasquotank County on Little River.
[13] Knotty Pine Chapel was six miles north of Gatesville on the Sommertown Road in
ates County. It was an Anglican chapel and was connected with the Edenton Parish
ssibly from 1701 to 1740. Nearby was the colonial home of Colonel William Baker
ich Asbury sometimes visited. (See *Journal* entry for April 1, 1801.) On March 17,
99, Mrs. I. Baker, a minister's wife, wrote from Knotty Pine Chapel to Asbury and
ve him a list of persons who had died there. (Moore: *Pioneers of Methodism in North
rolina and Virginia*, 35.)
[14] Asbury seems to have preached in a room at the south end of the Old Tavern at
rtford in Perquimans County, North Carolina. (*Historical Papers of the Trinity
llege Historical Association*, Secs. 9–13, p. 56.)
[15] Winton is the county seat of Hertford County.
[16] Wicocon was not a community but a stream in Bertie County, North Carolina,
ich gave its name to an area. (*Colonial Records, North Carolina*, II, 330; IV, 332.)

the banks, and made the ferry altogether a wonderful sight. We came to our lodging about nine o'clock, and found a plain, kind-hearted host.

I preached a funeral sermon; my text, "The sting of death is sin." I spoke on the nature of the law; of sin—its guilt, power, nature, and punishment; and the victory through Christ. Does it not appear that those who live in sin, which is a breach of the law, wish to abolish the law, seeing they must know the necessary consequence of its violation? And if this *postulation* is just, what saves them from theft, murder, rape? Self preservation. Alas, poor world! is this all thy virtue?

Wednesday, 6. Rode twenty miles and had the ice to break in two swamps. Preached at Lloyd's, near Washington.

Saturday, 9. I had a very unfeeling people at Mr. O.'s, to whom I preached with some freedom on Luke iv, 18. Death! death! death! in the lowlands.

Sunday, 10. I had many to hear at S.'s; but it was an uncomfortable time: thence I rode to Cox's on Neuse River, where we had an open time and there is a prospect of good. We then had to move towards Trent.[1] Our rides are still long—from fifteen to twenty miles a day.

Wednesday, 13. We had many dead souls at the quarterly meeting a Lee's.

Thursday, 14. My heart melted for the people: they do not, will not pray and if they so continue, must be undone.

Friday, 15. Came to poor J.'s, where I spoke dreadful things to a lifeles people on Isa. liii.

Saturday, 16. We rode to T——'s, an old stand in Duplin county where I was met by a few souls. We had naught to eat, nor where to lodg short of Colonel C——'s; we pushed for that shelter, and reached ther about nine o'clock at night; a poor place for religion it is, but we me with good entertainment.

Sunday, 17. I had about five hundred hearers at Samson court house to whom I enlarged on Peter's denial of his Master. 1. He was self confi dent. 2. Followed afar off. 3. Mixed with the wicked. 4. Denied hi discipleship, and then his Lord.

Tuesday, 19. At Fayetteville I was unable to preach. *Wednesday* w pushed on for the south state, but being unacquainted with the way we fell ten miles too low: after riding as many in the night, w ended our blunders and our fatigue for that day at S.'s, who used u kindly.

Thursday, 21. We rode twenty miles in the rain through the woods an sands, and had but a poor time at Col. M.'s: thence we descended to th

---

[17] Asbury went to the Trent River area around the present town of Trenton in Jone County. The Trenton Circuit, mainly in Jones and Lenoir counties, was formed fror part of the New River Circuit in 1792. (Grissom, *op. cit.*, 165.)

een Ponds,[18] fifteen miles, where we were very comfortable at Cross-
ıd's.[19]

South Carolina

Saturday, 23. I attended the quarterly meeting at the Beauty Spot:[20]
e weather was cold, but I had great assistance on Isa. xxxv, 1–6.
Sunday, 24. I preached on Zech. xi, 12: we had a gracious, moving time.
Monday, 25. We crossed Peedee at the Long Bluff, and rode nearly fifty
iles to brother Gardner's.[21]
I preached at Black Creek[22] on Psalm cxlv: I was much fatigued, and
d a high fever; but my soul had peace, and was stayed upon God.
Wednesday, 27. After preaching at D.'s, I had to ride ten miles out of
y way to cross Lynch's Creek. We moved forwards to our worthy
.end Rembert's,[23] who entertained us kindly, and supplied us with
ɔrses to ride to our appointments at Lenoir's and Moore's,[24] where we
ıd few hearers and dead times. After our meetings at these places we
turned to Rembert's, at whose house our quarterly meeting began, on
ıturday the first of *March*, which was not without some life; in our love
ast there appeared to be more feeling than speaking.
Monday, March 3. We rode through the snow to Bradford's,[25] and next
ıy had no small difficulty in crossing the swamps in order to get to
ıntee Ferry: we made it a ride of about fifty miles to Hart's[26] and did
ɔt get in until about nine o'clock at night.
Wednesday, 5. I passed Dorchester, where there are the remains of
hat appears to have once been a considerable town: there are the ruins

[18] Green Ponds was in Richmond County, North Carolina, near the South Carolina
ιe. On this trip through North Carolina Asbury had passed through Currituck,
ımden, Pasquotank, Perquimans, Gates, Hertford, Bertie, Martin, Beaufort, Pitt,
nes, Lenoir, Duplin, Samson, Cumberland, Hoke, Scotland, and Richmond counties.
[19] The Crosslands probably lived at the extreme upper border of Marlboro, South
ırolina, near the present town of Gibson, North Carolina. The family is prominent in
e county.
[20] Beauty Spot was three miles north of the present Bennettsville in Marlboro County.
ıe Methodist society was active there for a hundred and fifty years.
[21] Long Bluff was near Society Hill in Darlington County. Gardner lived on Black
reek a little west of Darlington.
[22] Black Creek flows through Darlington County to the Pee Dee River.
[23] James Publius Rembert was a large planter of French descent who lived south of
ynch's Creek in Sumter County. At Rembert Hall he often entertained Asbury. The
embert Church is still in existence. Boehm says "there was a church called Rembert's
hapel and James Rembert was the honored patriarch." (*Reminiscences*, 216.)
[24] Lenoir's was about twenty miles north of Wedgefield on the east side of the Wateree.
Ioore lived near Wedgefield.
[25] Bradford's was near Sumter, South Carolina. Asbury rode southward through the
resent Clarendon, Orangeburg, and Dorchester counties.
[26] Hart lived five miles north of Holly Hill.

of an elegant church, and the vestiges of several well-built houses.[27] W
saw a number of good dwellings and large plantations on the road leadi
down Ashley River.[28] In the evening we reached the city of Charlesto
having ridden about fifty miles.

Sunday, 9. Brother Ellis[29] preached in the morning. In the evening
felt some liberty in enlarging on Rom. x, 1–3. On *Monday* my soul a
body enjoyed some ease and rest.

Friday, 14. Our conference began, and we had a very free, open tim
On *Saturday* night I preached on "I have set watchmen upon thy walls
&c. On the *Sabbath*, on "The Lord turned and looked on Peter," &c. It w
a gracious season, both in the congregation, and in the love feast. Wh
another was speaking in the morning to a very crowded house, and ma
outside, a man made a riot at the door; an alarm at once took plac
the ladies leaped out at the windows of the church, and a dreadful co
fusion ensued. Again whilst I was speaking at night, a stone was throv
against the north side of the church; then another on the south; a thi
came through the pulpit window, and struck near me inside the pulp
I however continued to speak on; my subject, "How beautiful upon t
mountains," &c.

Upon the whole, I have had more liberty to speak in Charleston th
visit than I ever had before, and am of opinion that God will work her
but our friends are afraid of the cross.

Monday, 17. Preached in the morning and took my leave of the ci
When I reached Mr. Givhan's[30] the congregation had been dispers
about ten minutes.

I preached at Rumph's,[31] at L.'s,[32] and at Cattle Creek church,[33] in t
Edisto circuit. The people are insensible, and, I fear, are more in love wi
some of Christ's messengers than with Christ. I now changed my cours
and went through Orangeburg, by the Congarees, to Saluda, and then
up to Broad River quarterly meeting. We rode till one o'clock on *Frida*

[27] The deserted village of Dorchester, four miles below Summerville, had been found
by an Independent (Puritan) congregation from Massachusetts, but it had moved
Midway, Georgia, in 1754. Its pastor, the Rev. James Osgood, became a dear friend
the Rev. James Andrew, who named his son, Bishop James Osgood Andrew, for hi
(Betts, *op. cit.*, 49.)

[28] Along this road are located the world-famous Magnolia and Middleton garden

[29] Reuben Ellis was the elder of the district which included the Santee and Pee D
circuits and the Yadkin and Salisbury circuits in North Carolina.

[30] Givhans lived on Edisto River in Dorchester County. A Givhans community a
a Givhans Ferry State Park are near Summerville, South Carolina.

[31] General Jacob Rumph lived in Orangeburg County, five miles north of Orangebu
He was a Revolutionary officer and had two sons, Jacob and Christian, both of who
became preachers. Jacob was born on January 9, 1777, and joined the conference
1808. He died at Charleston on September 11, 1812.

[32] This may have been a Mr. Lindsay, who lived near Branchville.

[33] The Cattle Creek Church is now a church and campground between the towns
Bowman and Rowesville.

21st of March.[34] I believe we have travelled about two hundred miles
five days: dear brother Isaac Smith accompanied me. I was so unwell
at I had but little satisfaction at the quarterly meeting. My service was
rdensome; but the people were lively.

Wednesday, 26. We rode from Finch's to Odell's new church,[35] where
had a good time, whilst I enlarged on Titus ii, 14, and administered the
rd's Supper. Thence to Smith's,[36] thirty miles. After preaching we had a
ght meeting, that prevented our getting to bed until about twelve o'clock.
e had a comfortable cabin, and were very well entertained.

Thursday, 27. I had but little freedom on, "The foundation of God
ndeth sure." Brothers Mason and Major[37] spoke after me. I went alone
o the woods, and found my soul profitably solitary in sweet medita-
n and prayer.

Friday, 28. Rode about thirty miles to Brook's.[38] My soul was tired, but
was also comforted in the Lord. I was much led out on Eph. vi, 18, and
were employed till nearly twelve o'clock at night.

Sunday, 30. I had some liberty in preaching, but the people began to move
out when they were pointedly dealt with. Brothers Mason and Major
oke after me. I found it good to be alone by the solitary stream and
ent woods, to study the welfare of Zion, and to pray for her prosperity.

Monday, 31. We rode within a mile of Savannah river. The land in
neral, during our route, is very fine. We were benighted, and moping in
e woods made our journey a long one of about fifty miles.

Georgia

Tuesday, April 1. We crossed the Savannah at the Forks,[39] and came
ere I much wanted to be—in Georgia. Nevertheless, I fear I shall have
t little freedom here.

Wednesday, 2. I rested; and compiled two sections which I shall
commend to be put into our form of discipline, in order to remove from
ciety, by regular steps, either preachers or people that are disorderly.

Saturday, 5. I was led out in preaching at the quarterly meeting, on
ch. xii, 10.

Sunday, 6. There was a moving of the souls of the people; and I felt
uch life on Isa. xlv, 22.

[4] Asbury proceeded through Orangeburg and Lexington counties and crossed the
uda to the Finch home in Newberry County, probably at Weaver's Ferry.
[5] O'Dell's Church was near the present Whitmire, South Carolina, just across the line
Laurens County.
[6] Smith probably lived near the present town of Ninety Six in Greenwood County.
[7] John Mason was on the Board River Circuit and John Major was on the Burke Circuit.
[8] W. Brooks lived five miles south of Ninety Six.
[9] The Forks was the junction of the Broad and Savannah rivers where the old town
Petersburg, now submerged, was located.

PLACES VISITED BY

FRANCIS ASBURY

IN

GEORGIA

TENNESSEE NORTH CAROLINA

SOUTH CAROLINA

Redwine • Oliver's
Carroll's • Rembert
Thompson's • Cherokee Ford
Freeman's • Tait's • Martin's Ferry
Coke's Chapel • Petersburg
Washington • X Roads
Wakefield • Grant
Apalachia • Little River • Scott's
Greensboro • Stewart's
Liberty Chapel • White Oak • Haynes
Heath's • Augusta
Butler's • Rehoboth
Sparta • Hardwick's • Cox's • Jarvis
Harris • Waynesboro
Milledgeville • Louisville • Buckhead
Williams Swamp • Galphin's • Lovell's
Blackburn Chapel
Hudson's Ferry • Black Swamp
Goshen
Tiebout's • Ebenezer
Savannah
Bethsada

ALABAMA

G E O R G I A

FLORIDA

I have been told, that during the last rupture the Indians butchered
arly one hundred people.

Wednesday, 9. Our conference began at the Forks of Broad River,
here six members and four probationers attended.[40] Brother Major was
ck, and could not meet us. Soon after, he made his exit to his eternal rest.

Thursday and *Friday*, 10, 11. I felt free, and preached with light and
erty each day. Many that had no religion in Virginia, have found it
ter their removal into Georgia and South Carolina. Here at least the
ed sprung up, wherever else it may have been sown. Our little con-
rence was about sixty-one pounds deficient in their quarterage, nearly
1e-third of which was made up to them.

South Carolina

Sunday, 13. I called at a Presbyterian meeting house,[41] and heard Mr.

[40] The community of Petersburg was in the forks of the Broad and Savannah rivers,
d it has been said that Asbury went a few miles westward because of an epidemic in
e town; the site is now covered by the waters of the Clark-Hill Reservoir. This first
nference in Georgia is said to have met in the home of Colonel Charles Tate (Tait),
e of Asbury's friends who lived in Wilkes (now Elbert) County, five miles south of
e present Elberton on the Elberton–Washington highway. A house now stands there
iich is said to contain materials from the original Tate building. This site was de-
gnated by the North Georgia Conference in 1934, and a granite marker was erected
ere. Unanimity of opinion does not exist among authorities, however. The Georgia
storian George C. Smith in his *Life and Labors of Francis Asbury* (108) and *History of
orgia Methodism* (35), says that it met at or near the home of James Marks, a
ethodist whom Asbury had known in Virginia, but on page 40 of the latter work he
ys that the second conference was held in Grant's Church but "before the church was
ilt the conference met at their house." Elbert Augustine Banks in his *Genealogical
cord of the Banks Family* (254) says that the first conference in Georgia met in the
me of Ralph Banks in the present Elbert County, a house which still stands fifteen
les north of Elberton near the village of Neuberg and Cold Water church house. On
e other hand Bishop Hurst in his *History of Methodism* (IV, 461) and Bishop Mc-
eire in his *History of Methodism* (363) say that the place of meeting was the home of
neral David Meriwether in the present Elbert County, and the same view is taken by
e writer of the history of the First Methodist Church at Athens, Georgia. The historian
Wilkes County, Miss Eliza Bowen (1828–98), in her *The Story of Wilkes County
20) says that Meriwether joined the church in 1788, in which case it may be doubted
at the conference would have been held in the home of a nonmember when Methodists
ed in the same neighborhood. Smith, however, says he became a Methodist in 1787.
iss Bowen says that he lived in the forks, but this was not the case, although Frank
d Thomas Meriwether lived in or near other forks considerably to the north of David,
ile both John and James Marks also lived in forks and were related to the Meri-
thers by marriage. (Gilmer: *Sketches of Some of the first Settlers of Upper Georgia*,
-84, 115–16. See especially Governor Gilmer's map showing the location of the homes
early settlers.) McIntosh in his *History of Elbert County* (69) says that the first
signated place of meeting was Thompson's Meeting House several miles away, but
bury and his party stopped at Tate's (Tait's) because of the unpleasant weather.

[41] This was the Long Cane Presbyterian Church, located two miles north of the present
beville, South Carolina.

Hall, the minister preach a good sermon on Isa. lv. After the meeting w
rode to brother Moore's,[42] twenty miles on the Saluda.

Monday, 14. Was almost entirely occupied with writing letters to tl
north.

Tuesday, 15. I had many people at the widow Bowman's.[43] While he
we had a most awful storm. I was afraid the house would come dow
We rode in the night to M. Moore's.[44] I was seized with illness on the wa
which continued during the night. Next day, however, I was able to pu
sue my journey.

Friday, 18. We rode along crooked paths to Kasey's,[45] where we r
ceived the afflicting account of the death of dear brother Major, wl
departed this life last Saturday. He was a witness of holiness, and died i
peace and love.

Saturday, 19. I preached at Wilson's, with some liberty, on 1 Peter iii,

Sunday, 20. I spoke with little enlargement. Our friends here on Tyg
River are much alive to God, and have built a good chapel. We rode t
Buffington's in the evening, on Fair-forest Creek,[46] and were kindly ente
tained.

North Carolina

Tuesday, 22. Rode to Rutherford court house; and the next day
Burke court house: it being court time, we went on, and reached broth
White's, on John's River,[47] about ten o'clock at night. Here I found bo
the saddles broke; both horses foundered; and both their backs sore—
we stopped a few days.

I preached on Rev. xxii, 5-8; and had liberty in speaking to the peopl
our souls were blessed in a near access to the Lord. Our preachers in tl
Yadkin circuit have been sick; they have had hard travelling the pa
winter; and the work has consequently suffered. I have read D.'s Stuc
of Divinity—the catalogue of books at the end I thought of more valu
than all the rest of the work.

Sunday, 27. I preached at the Globe, on the main branches of John
River, where there are a few who fear God. There was some stir, and
hope some good done.

Monday, 28. After getting our horses shod, we made a move f

---

[42] Moore lived near Ware Shoals.
[43] Mrs. Bowman probably lived near Enoree.
[44] M. Moore lived twelve miles south of Spartanburg.
[45] Kasey probably lived near Reidville.
[46] Buffington probably lived near Woodford. Fairforest Creek was in Spartanbu
County.
[47] John's River is in Burke County, North Carolina, between Morganton and Leno

Iolston,[48] and entered upon the mountains; the first of which I called
:eel, the second stone, and the third iron mountain: they are rough, and
ifficult to climb. We were spoken to on our way by most awful thunder
nd lightning, accompanied by heavy rain. We crept for shelter into a
ttle dirty house, where the filth might have been taken from the floor
ith a spade. We felt the want of fire, but could get little wood to make it,
nd what we gathered was wet. At the head of Watauga we fed, and
:ached Ward's that night. Coming to the river next day, we hired a
oung man to swim over for the canoe, in which we crossed, while our
orses swam to the other shore. The waters being up we were compelled
) travel an old road over the mountains. Night came on—I was ready to
unt with a violent headache—the mountain was steep on both sides. I
rayed to the Lord for help. Presently a profuse sweat broke out upon
ue, and my fever entirely subsided.

Tennessee

About nine o'clock we came to Andrew Greer's.[49] After taking a little
:st here, we set out next morning for brother Edward Cox's[50] on Holston

[48] Stephen Holstein (Holston) settled in what is now Smyth County, Virginia, before
748 and gave his name to the Holston river and valley of Southwest Virginia and East
:nnessee. (State Historical Marker K-30, Smyth County, 8·5 miles east of Marion.)
sbury crossed the mountains from Morganton, North Carolina, through the gap just
ist of Roan Mountain near the present town of Elk Park. His route approximated
resent Highways 181, 19, and 11E, through Bluff City, Elizabethton, and Bristol. The
rst Methodist society in the region was probably in Pulaski County, Virginia, at
age's meetinghouse, a log church and a campground said to have been the earliest
. the area. Holston Circuit appeared as an appointment in 1783 with Jeremiah
ambert as preacher. It included all the settlements on the Watauga, Nollichucky,
nd Holston rivers in the present Greene, Washington, Carter, Johnson, Sullivan and
awkins counties in Tennessee, and Washington, Smyth, Russell, and perhaps Scott
id Lee counties in Virginia, with one or two appointments on the headwaters of New
iver, in Grayson County, Virginia, or Ashe County, North Carolina; some of these
)unties had not then been formed. The circuit had sixty members. (Price: *Holston
1ethodism*, I, 77, 94; Lundy: *Holston Horizons*, 12). When Asbury entered, the circuits
ere the Holston and Nollichucky and the conference this year appointed preachers to
e Holston, French Broad, New River, and Greenbrier circuits.
[49] Andrew Greer, a prosperous Indian trader, lived across the river from the present
lizabethton above the mouth of the Doe. He was probably on the Wautauga as early
. 1770. Asbury stayed with him on other occasions. (Williams: *Early Travels*, 291;
awn of History, 271.)
[50] Edward Cox was perhaps the earliest Methodist in this region. He was born in
altimore County, Maryland, in 1750, of Methodist parents, and was converted by
sbury in 1773. He went to the Holston country soon thereafter and settled on the
orth bank of the Holston River in the present Sullivan County, Tennessee, near
ristol. In 1775 he returned to the east and married Sallie Meredith and took her to
ast Tennessee. On the way they had prayer in their tent about one mile northeast of
luff City which was "probably the first prayer by a Methodist family in Tennessee."

River. I had trouble enough. Our route lay through the woods, and m
pack-horse would neither follow, lead, nor drive, so fond was he (
stopping to feed on the green herbage. I tried the lead, and he pulle
back. I tied his head up to prevent his grazing, and he ran back. The weathe
was excessively warm. I was much fatigued, and my temper not a litt
tried. I fed at I. Smith's,[51] and prayed with the family. Arriving at the rive
I was at a loss what to do; but providentially a man came along wh
conducted me across. This has been an awful journey to me, and this
tiresome day, and now, after riding seventy-five miles, I have thirty-fiv
miles more to General Russell's. I rest one day to revive man and beast.

Virginia

Friday, May 2. Rode to Washington,[52] where I met brother Tunnell
on the way to Mr. Cox's. We have to put up in houses where we have n
opportunity for retirement.

Saturday, 3.   We came to General Russell's; a most kind family i
deed and truth.[54]

After returning from service in the Revolutionary War, Cox opened his house fe
religious services which he conducted himself, even to the extent of administering th
sacraments, it is said, and took the names of those who desired to be Methodists when
preacher arrived. Asbury visited his home on other occasions. He died in 1852 at th
age of 102. The old Cox log house is still standing on an eighty-five-acre tract about or
mile northeast of Bluff City, Tennessee. (Price: *Holston Methodism,* I, 77–85; Lundy
Holston Horizons, 12–13.)

[51] Isaac Smith was a humble settler who frequently fed travelers. (Williams: *Earl*
Travels, 291.) It could have been Jonas Smith, who owned eight hundred acres of lan
south of Walker's Mountain on little Holston and in the section where Asbury wa
(Summers: *Annals,* 1247.)

[52] The present Abingdon, Virginia, seat of Washington County.

[53] John Tunnell (1755–90) was the presiding elder on the Holston District. He wa
born in Fredericksburg, Virginia, and had two brothers, William, who was a Bapti
preacher, and Stephen, both of whom went to Tennessee. John was converted in 177
under William Watters, and the next year he began to travel as a minister. His firs
appointment was to the Brunswick Circuit. (See *Journal* entries for May 31, 1790, an
July 10, 1790, for references to his illness and death.)

[54] General William Russell was an officer in the Colonial and Revolutionary armie
for whom Russell County was named. He married Mrs. Elisabeth Henry Campbel
widow of General William Campbell of King's Mountain fame and a sister of Patric
Henry, in 1783, and five years later settled at the "Salt Lick" or Saltville in Smyt
County, Virginia, where he engaged in the production of salt. The names of Genera
and "Madam" Russell are famous in Holston Methodist history, and the Saltvill
Methodist Church is today called the Madam Russell Memorial. In 1812 the widowe
Mrs. Russell moved to a large log house near Chilhowee Depot on the present Norfol
and Western Railway in Smyth County. Price says that Madam Russell is probabl
more eminent in the Methodist pioneer history than any other woman. (Price: *Holsto*
Methodism, I, 130–34.)

Sunday, 4. Preached on Phil. ii, 5–9. I found it good to get alone in prayer.

Tuesday, 6. I had many to hear at Easley's[55] on Holston. I was much wearied with riding a strange horse, having left mine to rest. It is some grief that I cannot be so much in prayer on the road as I would be. We had a good time, and a large congregation at Keywood's.[56]

Tennessee

The people are in disorder about the old and new State: two or three men, it is said, have been killed.[57]

At Nelson's[58] I had a less audience than was expected; the people having been called away on an expedition against the new State men. My subject was Heb. vi, 11, 12. Rode to Owens's,[59] and met our brethren from Kentucky, where I preached on Psalm cxlv, 17–19, with some fervour.[60]

[55] Stephen Easley, one of the early Tennessee Methodists, settled in Sullivan County soon after the Revolution. His home was on a promontory above Horse Creek valley near the present Kingsport. (Williams: *Early Travels*, 294.) Asbury had retraced his path from Saltville to Bristol and followed the Wilderness Road (now Route 11W) to Easley's. He returned to Virginia and then went back to Tennessee.

[56] Stephen Keywood lived between Saltville and Glade Spring, about fifteen miles east of Abingdon, Virginia. There is a marker there with the inscription: "Site of the Keywood House in which the first Methodist Conference west of the Blue Ridge was held by Bishop Asbury May 13–15, 1788." (Price: *Holston Methodism*, I, 113–15; Lundy: *Holston Horizons*, 13–14.) It has been claimed that the first conference west of the Alleghanies was at Uniontown, Pennsylvania, but this meeting was on July 22, 1788.

[57] The disorder was the little civil war between Governor Sevier of the State of Franklin and Colonel Tipton, who represented the State of North Carolina. In the rivalry between the two states Tipton refused to comply with laws of the new state and Sevier threatened military force against him, but the expedition failed. The Rev. Thomas Ware on the Nollichucky Circuit was seized by Sevier's men, who threatened to hang him, but he escaped on his horse while the men were disputing his fate. (Price: *Holston Methodism*, I, 111.) The Holston country was in the Watauga Association from 1769 to 1777, North Carolina from 1777 to 1784, the State of Franklin from 1784 to 1788, North Carolina from 1788 to 1790, the Territory of the United States south of the Ohio from 1790 to 1796, and Tennessee since 1796.

[58] William Nelson lived near Jonesborough in the New Territory or State of Franklin, later Tennessee, the present Johnson City. In Nelson's Chapel the third Holston Conference was held in 1793. Just west of Johnson City there is now a marker on the spot with the following inscription: "Ancient home for Methodists and Methodist preaching. First sermon by Methodist Bishop in Tennessee preached here, May, 1788, by Asbury. Site of Annual Conferences 1793–1796–1797." (Price: *Holston Methodism*, 188, 189; Lundy: *Holston Horizons*, 14–15.)

[59] John Owens' was a preaching place south of the Clinch River nearly opposite Fort Blackmore. It was on a road which approximated the present Highway 17. An old church there now bears the name of Owen's Chapel. Asbury stopped at the Owens house on later occasions.

[60] The date set for the conference was May 13, and Asbury reached the region ten days early and spent the intervening time in preaching at various places. The preachers

Virginia

Came to Half-Acres (Huffakers) and Keywoods, where we held conference three days, and I preached each day.[61] The weather was cold; the room
without fire, and otherwise uncomfortable. We nevertheless made out to
keep our seats, until we had finished the essential parts of our business.

Thursday, 15. We came to General Russell's,[62]—and on *Friday* to Isaac
Smith's, on the south fork of Holstein (Holston) River.

Sunday, 18. Rode to a chapel near New River, where I preached on
"How beautiful upon the mountains are the feet," &c. After eating a

from Kentucky arrived on an uncertain date, and Asbury met them and proceeded to
the conference. There are no definite dates in the *Journal* between May 6 and May 15,
but there was probably some misunderstanding as to dates. Asbury must have known
the date that had been set, and it has been assumed that he and the Holston preachers
would hardly have gone ten days in advance. Price thinks Asbury changed the date of
the conference from the thirteenth to the sixth, but at the salt works he learned that the
Kentucky preachers were not aware of the change and filled in the time while waiting
for them. On the other hand Thomas Ware, who was present, stated that Asbury
reached the conference site a "week after the time appointed to commence it" because
he was detained by the presence of hostile Indians, though the *Journal* made no mention
of such danger. Ware says the Holston preachers themselves filled in the time by
evangelizing. On this theory the date of the conference had been changed by Asbury to
a period a few days at least before his arrival in early May. (For a discussion of these
themes regarding the date see Price: *Holston Methodism*, I, 118–25.)

[61] There is some confusion in Asbury's account of this conference. The name is
Halfacre or Huffaker. Michael Halfacre, an emigrant from Germany, lived in a large
log house three miles southwest of Saltville, Virginia, one-half mile south of the later
Mahanaim Church erected on a lot given by Halfacre. Keywoods, where the conference
was actually held, was the residence of Stephen Keywood. The two locations were not
the same, and Price supposes the error of linking them together was due to the fact that
the Halfacres and Keywoods were the leading Methodists in the community. Probably
some of the preachers lodged at Halfacres. The second conference in the Holston
country was held at Halfacres in 1792. Price was informed the Keywood house had
but one chimney, and the conference met in an upstairs room. (Summer's *Annals*;
Price: *Holston Methodism*, I, 113–15; Lundy: *Holston Horizons*, 13–14.)

[62] Mrs. (Madam) Russell was deeply convicted by a sermon preached by John
Tunnell at the conference on Sunday, May 11. She said to Thomas Ware, "I though
I was a Christian; but, sir, I am the veriest sinner upon the earth. I want you and Mr
Mastin to come with Mr. Tunnell to my house and pray for us, and tell us what we
must do to be saved." The preachers went and spent much of the afternoon in prayer
When they retired briefly to a nearby grove, General Russell read to his wife from
Fletcher's *Appeal*. Ware's account continues: "At length we heard the word 'Glory!'
often repeated, accompanied with clapping of hands. We hastened to the house, and
found Mrs. Russell praising the Lord, and the General walking the floor and weeping
bitterly, uttering at the same time the plaintive appeal to the Saviour of sinners: 'O
Lord, thou dost bless my dear wife while thy poor servant was reading to her. Hast
thou not also a blessing for me?'" The General was also converted. The incident made
a deep impression on the people and led to many other conversions at the conference
(Price: *Holston Methodism*, I, 126–27.)

orsel, we hasted on our way to Gideon Farris's.[63] A twenty miles' ride
rough the mountains brought us to our lodgings for the night at Francis
incannon's, near the Flower Gap.[64]

North Carolina

Monday, 19. We rode about fifty miles to S——'s: the weather was
arm in the extreme; we had rain, thunder, and lightning—and were
eary enough.

Tuesday, 20. After riding nearly thirty miles we came to M'Knight's
apel in North Carolina. Here I preached on Peter's denial of Christ.
hence we went to Hill's. After meeting, we proceeded to the neat and
ell-improved town of Salem; making a journey, besides the labours of
e day, of nearly forty miles.

I came to the quarterly meeting at C——'s, where I spoke feelingly and
ointedly; and the word appeared to have effect.

Thursday, 22. Preached at P——'s chapel: we then rode to C——'s,
bout seven miles from Guilford court house, where we had a good time.

Friday, 23. Was a damp, rainy day, and I was unwell with a slow fever
nd pain in my head: however I rode to Smith's chapel and preached;
nd thence to brother Harrison's on Dan River, and preached. In the
ace of one week we have ridden, through rough, mountainous tracts of
untry, about three hundred miles. Brothers Poythress, Tunnell, and
yself have had serious views of things, and mature counsels together.

Sunday, 25. Preached, and had a love feast and sacrament. I then rode
the widow Dick's: many were waiting here, and the power of God was
lt by some, whilst I enlarged on Isaiah lv, 1–3.

Monday, 26. We had a good time at Martin's. Leaving this, on our way
Stamfield, we were obliged to swim our horses across Dan River, and
sing our road, made it late before we arrived.

Riding thirty miles brought us to Hammon's: here we had a serious,
eling time, while I spoke on Isaiah lxi.

Thursday, 29. Reached Edmund Taylor's[65] about two o'clock, and gave
short discourse on "Happy is he that hath the God of Jacob for his
elp." Thence to Pope's, to Green Hill's, to Long's, and to Jones's chapel:

---

[63] See Summers: *Annals of Southwest Virginia,* 1214.

[64] En route to North Carolina Asbury seems to have followed a southeastern course
ong the south fork of the Holston, where Isaac Smith lived, from Aspenville to Flower
ap, now called Low's Gap, in Grayson County, Virginia. The "chapel near New
iver" was probably on Bridle Creek. He probably ate his "morsel" with Enoch
sborne, who lived on Bridle Creek and in whose home Asbury stayed on later occa-
ns. (See Nuckol: *Pioneers of Grayson County,* 171.)

[65] Edmund Taylor lived in Granville County, North Carolina.

on our way to the latter place we got out of our route when within a mil
of the chapel, and did not reach it till two o'clock.[66]

Sunday, June 1. At Clayton's there are a hundred blacks joined i
society; and they appear to have real religion among them—her
Ethiopia doth stretch out her hand unto the Lord. I suppose there wer
not less than a thousand souls at preaching.

Monday, 2. Preached at Moore's in Northampton—once a poor, dea
people, but now revived, and increased from eleven to sixty members.

We had much of the power of God at Clark's: sixty members, amon
whom are some children, are the subjects of this work. I feel life amon
these people—preaching and praying is not labour here: their noise
heed not; I can bear it well when I know that God and Christ dwells i
the hearts of the people.

Virginia

Thence I passed through Southampton,[67] where I also beheld the powe
of God manifested in several lively meetings.

Rode to and rested with Phillip Davis. On *Saturday* I had a feelin
living time on Psalm lxxxv, 9, 10.

Sunday, 8. We had a gracious season: it was a memorable day, and m
soul was much blessed. After meeting, we hastened to Petersburg, whe
I preached on 2 Cor. v, 20. Our elders and deacons met for conference
all things were brought on in love. The town folks were remarkably kin
and attentive; the people of God in much love. The awful circumstance
B. C——'s losing his religion, and lately attempting to pull out R. Swift
eyes, may yet be sanctified to some, and explained by his conduct hereafte

Friday, 13. I preached a pastoral sermon, under a large arbour near th
borders of the town, on 1 Tim. iv, 13–16, with considerable consolatio
Ordained Henry Ogburn and John Baldwin, deacons; and Edward Morr
and Ira Ellis, elders.

Sunday, 15. I preached at the Manakintown; then rode to Maxey's.

Monday, 16. Rode about fifty miles to brother Agee's in Buckingha
county; and thence to Bedford circuit; in our route we were compelled
ford the James River, not without danger: we were hospitably entertaine

Wednesday, 18. At night, I had some opening whilst I enforced "Wh
soever shall call upon the name of the Lord shall be saved."

---

[66] Asbury traveled through Granville, Franklin, and Halifax counties.

[67] This was probably Southampton Court House, later Jerusalem, and now Cou
land, Virginia. Asbury passed through Southampton, Sussex, and Prince Geor
counties to Petersburg.

[68] Maxey's was in Powhatan County. Out of this family came Bennet Maxey,
preacher, who was admitted on trial in 1787.

Heavy rains, bad roads, straying, bewildered in the woods—through
these I worried to Murphy's:[69] great was the cross under which I
•oke on "The grace of God that bringeth salvation," &c. I had a high
ver, and was otherwise distressed in body, and ill at ease in mind: I was
raid the medicine I had made use of would be injurious to me in conse-
1ence of my getting wet.

Saturday, 28. I had considerable liberty, though unwell, at Ayres's[70]
•w chapel.

Sunday, 29. After preaching I went to V——'s, and after trying, had to
ence him. O, my God, what awful subjects come before me!

West Virginia

Monday, 30. Crossed the high mountains, and came to Hogg's[71] in
reen Brier.

Tuesday, July 1. I enlarged on Gal. iii, 22. We then rode to Alexander
'Pherson's, a serious family on Sinking Creek, where I preached with
me freedom. After crossing some considerable mountains, and preach-
g occasionally, on *Friday* we arrived at the Sweet Springs: here I
eached and the people were very attentive.

Saturday and *Sunday,* 5, 6. I had large congregations at Rehoboth.[72]
•reached with some satisfaction.

Monday, 7. Our troubles began; it being the day we set out for Clarks-
1rg. Thirty miles brought us to Watt's,[73] on the Great Levels.[74]

Tuesday, 8. Reached John M'Neil's, on the Little Levels,[75] where almost
e whole settlement came together, with whom I found freedom on Matt.

---

[39] John Murphy lived in Bedford County. (Sweet, *op. cit.,* 106.)

[70] John Ayers also lived in Bedford County. (*Ibid.*)

[71] See *Journal* entry for May 17, 1792.

[72] Rehoboth Church is two miles east of Union, Monroe (formerly Greenbrier)
•unty, West Virginia. It was built in 1785 on land given by Edward Keenan and is
w the oldest Methodist meetinghouse west of the Alleghanies, maintained as a shrine
the West Virginia Methodist Historical Society. (See McGann, "Old Rehoboth," in
ristian Advocate, July 1, 1954, 8; *Journal* entries for May 24, 1793; May 25, 1796;
ril 9 ff., 1797.) The area surrounding Rehoboth Church was known as the "Sinks of
eenbrier." On this occasion Asbury ordained John Smith as deacon, this being the
t ordination west of the Alleghanies. It has previously been believed that the first
lination was that of Michael Leard at Uniontown, Pennsylvania, but Smith's manu-
ipt *Journal* at Garrett Biblical Institute shows that his ordination preceded Leard's
several weeks. (See also "A New Distinction for Old Rehoboth," by Lawrence Sher-
•od in the *West Virginia Christian Education Bulletin,* February, 1954; Lawrence
erwood in *West Virginia State Magazine,* August, 1954.)

[73] Lednum, *op. cit.,* 187.

[74] Great Levels was an area around present Lewisburg, West Virginia.

[75] Little Levels was an area round present Hillsboro, West Virginia. (See *Journal* of
Rev. John Smith for data on McNeil.)

xi, 28–30. Our brother Phœbus had to answer questions propounded 1 him until evening.

Wednesday, 9. We rode to the Clover Lick,[76] to a very remote and e: posed house. Here we found good lodgings for the place. The former tena» had made a small estate by keeping cattle, horses, &c., on the *range*, whic is fertile and extensive.

Thursday, 10. We had to cross the Alleghany mountain again, at a ba passage. Our course lay over mountains and through valleys, and the mu and mire was such as might scarcely be expected in December. We came 1 an old, forsaken habitation in Tyger's Valley. Here our horses graze about, while we boiled our meat. Midnight brought us up at Benjam Jones's, after riding forty, or perhaps fifty miles. The old man, our hos was kind enough to wake us up at four o'clock in the morning. W journeyed on through devious lonely wilds, where no food might be foun except what grew in the woods, or was carried with us. We met with tw women[77] who were going to see their friends, and to attend the quarter meeting at Clarksburg.[78] Near midnight we stopped at William Anglin' who hissed his dogs at us; but the women were determined to get 1 quarterly meeting, so we went in. Our supper was tea. Brothers (Willial Phoebus and (Valentine) Cook[79] took to the woods; old —— gave up h bed to the women. I lay on the floor on a few deer skins with the fleas. That night our poor horses got no corn; and next morning they had to swi across Monongahela. After a twenty miles' ride we came to Clarksbur and man and beast were so outdone that it took us ten hours to accor plish it. I lodged with Col. Jackson.[81] Our meeting was held in a long, clo

[76] This community is northeast of Marlinton, Pocahontas County. Jacob Warwi had moved here from southeastern Virginia, erecting a small fort and bringing seve» slaves. He had vast numbers of horses and cattle running at large through the fores (Hardesty: *Historical and Geographical Encyclopedia*, 366; John Smith's *Journal*.)

[77] These two women were sisters, Miss Margaret Hadden and Mrs. Edward (Ma Hadden) Jackson. Mrs. Jackson was the grandmother of General Stonewall Jacksc (Arnold: *Early Life and Letters of General Thomas J. Jackson*; Barnhart: *History Bridgeport*.)

[78] In 1787 the original Redstone Circuit reported 756 members, so Bishop Asbu divided it into three circuits: Redstone, Ohio, and Clarksburg, placed Joseph Cromw over it as presiding elder, and named seven circuit riders to the region. In this tour 1788 Asbury was present for the quarterly meetings on each of the three circuits a: then held his first district conference in western Pennsylvania. (Smeltzer, *op. cit.*, 59–6 *Early Conferences in the Redstone Region*.)

[79] William Phoebus was on the Rockingham Circuit, and Valentine Cook was on 1 Calvert Circuit. (See *Minutes*, 1788.)

[80] The party spent the night at or near the present site of Philippi, West Virgin» (*Delta*, Buckannon, West Virginia, May 19, 1953.)

[81] Colonel George Jackson (1756–1831) was a brother of "Stonewall" Jacksor grandfather. He was a soldier in the Revolution, a prominent lawyer in Clarksburg member of the General Assembly of Virginia, and a member of the Fourth, Sixth, a: Seventh Congresses. He later moved to Zanesville, Ohio, where he spent the remaind of his life. (Third Biennial Report of the Department of Archives and History of W«

₁om belonging to the Baptists. Our use of the house it seems gave offence. ₁ere attended about seven hundred people, to whom I preached with ₁eedom; and I believe the Lord's power reached the hearts of some. ₁fter administering the sacrament, I was well satisfied to take my leave. 'e rode thirty miles to Father Haymond's,[82] after three o'clock, Sunday 'ternoon, and made it nearly eleven before we came in. About midnight ₁e went to rest, and rose at five o'clock next morning. My mind has been ₁verely tried under the great fatigue endured both by myself and my ₁rse. O, how glad should I be of a plain, clean plank to lie on, as ₁eferable to most of the beds; and where the beds are in a bad ₁ate, the floors are worse. The gnats are almost as troublesome here, ₁ the mosquitoes in the lowlands of the seaboard. This country will ₁quire much work to make it tolerable. The people are, many of them, of ₁e boldest cast of adventurers, and with some the decencies of civilized ₁ciety are scarcely regarded, two instances of which I myself witnessed. ₁he great landholders who are industrious will soon show the effects of ₁e aristocracy of wealth, by lording it over their poorer neighbours, and ₁ securing to themselves all the offices of profit or honour. On the one ₁nd savage warfare teaches them to be cruel; and on the other, the ₁eaching of Antinomians poisons them with error in doctrine: good ₁oralists they are not, and good Christians they cannot be, unless they ₁e better taught.

Tuesday, 15. I had a lifeless, disorderly people to hear me at Morgan-₁wn, to whom I preached on "I will hear what God the Lord will speak." ₁is matter of grief to behold the excesses, particularly in drinking, which ₁ound here. I preached at a new chapel near Colonel Martin's,[83] and felt ₁uch life, love, and power. Rode to the widow Robinson's,[84] and re-₁eshed with a morsel to eat; thence to M. Harden's, where, though we ₁d an earth floor, we had good beds and table entertainment.

Friday, 18. Rode forty miles to quarterly meeting at Doddridge's,[85] ₁here we had a melting season.

Sunday, 20. From twelve o'clock to-day we rode forty miles—my soul ₁n sweet peace.

₁rginia. 1911; Withers: *Chronicles of Border Warfare*, 121, 313, 342, 378; *Bulletin of ₁ West Virginia Sons of the Revolution for 1925*, 76.)

[82] Calder Haymond, son of John Haymond, an English architect and builder, lived ₁ar the present Fairmont, West Virginia. His son, Thomas, was a Methodist circuit ₁ler. (Smith: *Recollections and Reflections of an Old Itinerant*, 12; Maxwell: *History ₁ Randolph County, West Virginia*, 399–400.)

[83] This was the fifth Methodist chapel west of the mountains, built by Colonel ₁arles Martin just south of the Pennsylvania line in 1788. It continues as the Fort ₁artin Church of the West Virginia Conference. (Smeltzer, *op. cit.*, 68–69.)

[84] Robert Ayres records in his *Journal* on November 4, 1786, that he "tarried at ye ₁dow Robinsons" at about this same location on the Redstone Circuit.

[85] This records the Bishop's presence this year at the summer quarterly meeting of ₁ Ohio Circuit, near the Pennsylvania line and not far from the Ohio River.

Pennsylvania

Tuesday, 22. Our conference began at Union Town.[86] We felt gre
peace whilst together; and our counsels were marked by love and pr
dence. We had seven members of conference and five probationers.
preached on 1 Peter v:7; and brother Whatcoat gave us an excellent d
course on "O! man of God, flee these things."

Friday, 25. We concluded our conference.

Saturday and *Sunday*, 26, 27. Attended quarterly meeting.[87]

Monday, 28. Came over the mountains along very bad roads. Broth
Whatcoat[88] and myself were both sick. We stopped at Simpkins's, and we
comfortably entertained.

Tuesday, 29. Reached Barratt's, where we had a little rest and peace.

West Virginia

We had left our horses at Oldtown, Maryland, on the other side of t
river, but I thought it best to have them brought over, and so it was; f
that night there were two stolen. On *Monday* we rested; on *Tuesday* ro
down to Capon; and on *Wednesday* visited Bath. I took lodgings
brother Thomas Williams's, was well fixed, and found the waters to
of service to me.

Sunday, August 10. Preached at Bath. I received heavy tidings fro
the college—both our teachers have left; one for incompetency, a
the other to pursue riches and honours: had they cost us nothing, t
mistake we made in employing them might be the less regretted. I ha
read one volume of Church History, by Mosheim, containing an accou
of the state of ecclesiastical matters in Germany, and the differe
Churches.

Sunday, 17. I attempted to preach at Bath, on "the lame and the blind
the discourse was very *lame*; and it may be, I left my hearers as I fou
them—*blind*.

I am now closely engaged in reading, writing,[89] and prayer—my sc

[86] Bishop Asbury expanded the number of his district conferences from three in 17
to eight in 1788. Two of these conferences were held west of the mountains, the first
the Holston on May 11, and the second at Uniontown, Pennsylvania, July 22–25. T
Journal of Robert Ayres states that the preachers Asbury called to meet him at Unic
town were those on the six circuits on both sides of the mountains that divide the hea
waters of the Ohio and Potomac. (Smeltzer, *op. cit.*, 60–63.)

[87] This was the quarterly meeting of the Redstone Circuit. At it Asbury ordair
Michael Leard a deacon, his second ordination west of the mountains.

[88] Richard Whatcoat was presiding elder this year over Alleghany, Bath, and Berke
circuits, just east of the mountains, so he and his preachers were included in the Unic
town conference.

[89] See letter to Jasper Winscom, August 18, 1788.

joys much of God. We have great rains, and are obliged to keep close
ouse; but we have a little of almost everything to improve the mind—
e languages, divinity, grammar, history, and belles-lettres; my great
sire is to improve in the best things.

Sunday, 24. Preached at Bath, on Isaiah lxiii, 1, with little liberty and
or attendance. But we have some stir among the poor people in the
untry.

Friday, 29. We left Bath, and on the *Saturday* and *Sunday* following
tended a quarterly meeting. I felt enlargement on Peter's case, and also
the love feast.

Monday, September 1. I enlarged with some freedom on the case of
e man who brought the child to our Lord.

Wednesday, 3. Rode from John Hite's[90] to the Blue Ridge: the weather
as warm, and so were the hearts of the people.

Virginia

Thursday, 4. I preached at Leesburg, and was very warm, on, "Thou
lt arise and favour Zion"; and the people appeared to be somewhat
rred up. To-day I received a letter from brother Tunnell, informing of
e spreading of the work of God in West New River, and several parts
North Carolina. Glory be to God, for his great and glorious power!

Maryland

Wednesday, 10. Our conference began in Baltimore.[91] I chose not to
each while my mind was clogged by business with so many persons
d on so many subjects.

Sunday, 14. I felt considerably moved at our own church in the morn-
g, and in the Dutch church in the afternoon: the Spirit of the Lord
me among the people, and sinners cried aloud for mercy: perhaps not
ss than twenty souls found the Lord from that time until the *Tuesday*
llowing.

Monday, Tuesday and *Wednesday* were spent at Cokesbury in exam-
ing and arranging the temporal concerns of the college.

---

90 John Hite lived near Charlestown, West Virginia.

91 Revision of the *Discipline*, anxiety over Cokesbury College, and fatigue caused by
e of the longest and most strenuous journeys of his career caused Asbury to complain
at his "mind was clogged." He was facing his sixth conference of the year held in as
any states, and preachers were in short supply to meet the unparalleled expansion of
ethodism. (Lee: *A Short History of the Methodists*, 135, 139; Strickland, *op. cit.*, 184,
5.)

Pennsylvania

Sunday, 21. I preached with some satisfaction, morning and evening, Philadelphia. On *Monday*, our conference began and held until *Friday*, *Saturday*, 27. We left the city.

New Jersey

Sunday, 28. Preached with some assistance in Elizabethtown.

New York

Monday, 29. Rode to New York. Next day (*Tuesday*, 30) our conferer began,[92] and continued until *Saturday*, the 4th of *October*.

New Jersey

Sunday and *Monday*, *October* 5, 6. My soul was uncommonly led c in prayer and preaching—I found it a very gracious season. My retu brought me through Elizabethtown, Amboy, Hightstown,[93] Crosswicks and Burlington.

Delaware

Sunday, 12. I was much depressed in spirit whilst in Philadelphia left there on *Wednesday*, and preached at Chester, where I had so

[92] In his listing of the conferences held in 1788 Jesse Lee (*op. cit.*, 134,135) omit this New York Conference and Bangs, following Lee, also ignored it. This error I been perpetuated even in the records of the present New York Conference. Steve (*op. cit.*, II, 275) referred to it, however, and it is proved by the records of John Str Church. At this conference Thomas Morrell was ordained, and his original certifica signed by Asbury, is at John Street Church, dated October 2, 1788. (Seaman, *op. c* 101; Wakeley, *op. cit.*, 328.)

[93] Hightstown, New Jersey, in Mercer County, was then a post town in Middle County. Methodist preaching was started in 1785. The services were held in Ad Shaw's tavern. The location was regarded as undesirable, and the meetings were la transferred to the home of Joseph Hutchinson at Milford, two and a half miles aw where a chapel was subsequently built. A church was established at Hightstown al the Milford Chapel was abandoned about 1835. (Atkinson: *Memorials of New Jer Methodism*, 364–65, 412–15, 423–33; Gordon: *Gazetteer of New Jersey*, 157; Phoeb *Beams of Light on Early Methodism*, 64, 71.)

[94] There was no Methodist meetinghouse at Crosswicks, in Burlington County, a Asbury preached at the home of a Mr. Smith. (Phoebus, *op. cit.*, 64, 70; Heston: *So Jersey, a History*, II, 674; Gordon: *Gazetteer*, 124, 125.)

ergy; and had openings at Wilmington and Duck Creek,[95] where I also
ministered the word of life.

Monday, 20. Our meeting in Dover was attended with some power.
: Milford we had liberty and love. At Johnstown I was very unwell, and
as under the necessity of going to bed, but our friends were alive: God
with them of a truth. Preached at Shankland's. My soul enjoys great
ace and love. On *Sunday* I was under bodily affliction, but I went to the
urt house[96] and spoke a few words on, "Ye will not come to me that ye
ight have life." We have a house now building, and I hope something
ll be done here.

Maryland

Monday was remarkably warm weather, and I was ready to faint whilst
ode to the Sound. We reached Powell's[97] about three o'clock.

Wednesday, 29. I was very alarming—seldom, if ever, have I felt more
oved. We came away, and rode twenty-five miles, having nothing to eat
om eight o'clock in the morning till six at night. My body was weak, but
y soul was kept in peace. Knowing the obligations I am under to pay
oney to several persons to whom the college is indebted, my mind is
uch exercised, and I feel very heavily the weight of such responsibility.
ie Lord opened the heart of ——; and I thankfully received the kindness
from God and man.

Preached at Jepthah Bowen's, and I trust the Lord was present; as also
the Lord's supper.

We then hasted to the widow Paramore's, about nineteen miles: the
ople were moved whilst I exhorted them to come boldly to the throne of
ace.

On *Friday* I met with an engaged people at Parnell's, and they appeared
der whilst I enlarged on, "My grace is sufficient for thee."

Virginia

After meeting we rode to Burton's, nineteen miles.

Saturday, November 1. Attended a quarterly meeting at Garrettson
apel. O how changed! A preacher absent nearly nine weeks from his

---

⁵ Duck Creek was the present Smyrna.

⁶ The Sussex County Courthouse, erected between 1740 and 1750, stood on the north-
t corner of the Episcopal Church yard of that time in Lewes, Delaware. In 1791 a
nsfer of the county seat to the present Georgetown was authorized. (Scharf, *op. cit.*,
1204–6; Garrettson, *op. cit.*, 127–29.)

⁷ The Powell house was near Berlin, Worcester County, Maryland. The family may
e been members of Perdeaux Chapel in Sinepuxent Neck. Stevenson Church, Berlin,
he descendant of the original society. (Hallman, *op. cit.*, 356.)

circuit, failing to give proper notice of the quarterly meeting. Oth
persuasions are less supine; and their minister boldly preaches agai
the freedom of the slaves. Our brother Joseph Everett[98] with no le
zeal and boldness, cries aloud for liberty—emancipation.

Sunday, 2. Brother Whatcoat preached, and I exhorted a little. My so
and body are deeply impressed. We rode fifteen miles that evening, a
held meeting again.

Monday, 3. Myself and the people were comforted at Seymour's
we had a meeting in the evening.

Wednesday, 5. I preached at the school house, on Peter's denial
Christ: it was a time of refreshing—there were few present that did n
feel the word. Spoke again in the evening at Seymour's to a very u
feeling people.

Friday. 7. Preached at the court house, to many people, with liber
We have had heavy riding; dust, heat, and fevers. Our meeting at Dow
ing's almost overcame us with heat and fatigue.

Maryland

At Annamessex quarterly meeting[100] I was at liberty on Rev. iii,
Again I preached on, "Fear not, little flock," &c.: most of our memb
in these parts have freed their slaves.

Wednesday, 12. We had a precious season at the Line chapel[101] on R
iii, 18: "I counsel thee to buy of me gold tried in the fire," &c. Af
meeting I rode to Broad Creek. We have travelled little less than t
hundred miles a week.

Thursday, 13. At quarterly meeting I preached on, "Thy teachers sh
not be removed into a corner."

Friday, 14. My subject was, "Is my hand shortened at all that I can
redeem, or have I no power to deliver?"—there was some moving on
souls of the people. Rode twelve miles to Lewis's[102] and preached at ni
on "Search the scriptures."

---

[98] Joseph Everett was the preacher in charge on the Caroline Circuit, Maryla
(See *Minutes.*)

[99] See *Journal* entry for April 4, 1806.

[100] Annamessex Circuit first appears in 1783. This quarterly meeting was held
Annamessex Chapel, once called Phoebus, near Crisfield, Somerset County. (Lee,
cit., 82; Hallman, *op. cit.*, 104, 330.)

[101] Line Chapel, organized in 1779, was erected on a site called Pleasant Grove.
proximity to the Delaware–Maryland boundary accounts for its name. It now sta
on the Delaware side in Gumboro Hundred. (Scharf, *op. cit.*, II, 1345.)

[102] John Lewis probably lived in Nanticoke Hundred, Sussex County. Asbury, Co
bury, and St. Johnstown are congregations in Nanticoke Hundred that had their ori
under the ministry of Asbury. (Scharf, *op. cit.*, II, 1297, 1298.)

Delaware

After preaching at North West Fork, I rode twenty-five miles to
arterly meeting at Henry Ennall's chapel: here we had a good time.
reached at Johnson's, Levin Todd's, and at the chapel. I feel myself
ak, but the Lord is present.

Maryland

riday, 21. I felt some power in speaking on Matt. xi, 5, 6, at Mr. Keel's.
came on to Hooper's,[103] where we had a time of refreshing.

Saturday and *Sunday*, 22, 23. Attended quarterly meeting at William
azier's: there was some quickening among the people each day.
We crossed Choptank River to Bolingbroke—death! death! The
ond day of our meeting a great power went through the congregation,
1 a noble shout was heard among the people.

was much led out at the Bay-side chapel. At Doctor Moses D. Allen's
as greatly comforted, after a wet ride of thirty miles.

preached at Queenstown to a few people, who appear to be far gone
orgetfulness of God.

went to Kent Island, and found about two hundred and fifty people,
ong whom were some of the rich and great: we had a good meeting.
hen returned to Queenstown, and gave the citizens another *rally*;
re were more to hear than before.

Saturday, 29. I felt some power in preaching at John Boardley's. We
1 a little move among the people at Choptank. My soul is kept in peace.
imes past I have felt some disagreeable impressions on my mind about
college being burnt; now I have heard of an attempt to do it; but I
st the Lord will encamp about the house. We had a very good meeting
Dover, although the weather was very cold. We had meeting again that
ht in town—I hope not in vain. Next day I rode to Dudley's church,
een Annes; and thence to Chestertown, and preached on, "Let us have
ce whereby we may serve God acceptably, with reverence and godly fear."

aturday, *December* 6. I had some freedom in preaching at Stillpond
rch,[104] on, "Simon, Satan hath desired to have you, that he might sift
as wheat," &c.

unday, 7. I preached at the widow Woodland's;[105] was not in a good

---

This was Colonel William Hooper.

Still Pond, Kent County, was a preaching place as early as 1773. Benjamin Abbott
tions meeting the class at Howard's in that vicinity. (Ffirth: *The Experience and
el Labours of the Rev. Benjamin Abbott*, 121, 122; Colbert's *Journal*, II, 71; Hall-
, op. cit., 318.)

For a description of a class meeting at Woodlands in Kent County, see Jesse Lee's
nal, quoted by Minton Thrift in *Memoir of Jesse Lee*, 187.

frame of body or mind. At Georgetown I felt still worse; and to crown a
I had a long dispute with Mr. B——[106] about ordination and experiment
religion.

Monday, 8. Rode to Cecil court house, and had, I trust, a profitab
time. We crossed Elk River to brother Ford's,[107] and had a gracious mee
ing at his house.

Tuesday, 9. We had a damp ride to Cokesbury, and found it was ev
as it had been reported to us: an attempt had been made to burn t
college by putting fire into one of the closets; but some of the studer
made a timely discovery, and it was extinguished. I stayed two days a
expended more than £100, and felt my spirit tried. I put the young men
board in the college. We have some promising youths among them f
learning, but they want religion.

I came to Baltimore, and found some tokens of the Divine presence,
the quarterly meeting, on 2 Chron. xiv:11, "Thou canst save by many,
by those that have no might."

Monday, 15. Came to Cromwell's and preached with some satisfactic
Thence I hasted to Annapolis, where the Lord was present while I c
clared "The Lord's hand is not shortened."

Tuesday, 16. Rode to Weem's chapel, and preached with fervour c
"O Zion, that bringest good tidings," &c. Thence to Calvert quarte
meeting: the weather was very cold, but there was some spiritual he
among the people.

Virginia

Friday, 19. Rode thirty miles to Hoe's ferry; and thence to Pope
about thirty miles more: the weather is still excessively cold.

Sunday, 21. I preached to a few tender souls at Pope's, on Isaiah xx
17: "Yet a very little while and Lebanon shall be a fruitful field."

Tuesday, 23. Had a few lively people at Woolard's. I read, write,[108] pra
and ride; and hope to see much of the power of God on this journey.

Christmas day. I preached in the open house at Fairfield's, on Isa
ix, 6. I felt warm in speaking; but there was an offensive smell of r
among the people.

[106] This may have been the Rev. John Bowie, a controversial figure whose r
nounced Toryism had caused him to be banished from the Western Shore of Maryla
About 1780 he appeared on the Eastern Shore, where he taught school and became
incumbent of several parishes. (Rightmyer, *op. cit.*, 164, 165.)

[107] John Ford lived on Turkey Point between Elk River and North East River th
miles southwest of Rock Point. He was a trustee of the new church at North Eas
well as of Harts Meeting House. (Whatcoat's *Journal* in Sweet, *op. cit.*, IV, 80; Jc
ston: *History of Cecil County, Maryland*, 449.)

[108] Woolard lived in Westmoreland County. (See letter to Ezekiel Cooper, Decem
24, 1788.)

Saturday, 27. At the Presbyterian church in Lancaster, there was a
ine stir in the congregation. Envy and disputation have been injurious
the work of God in these parts. O may the Lord yet help us and revive
work! I found our opposing the doctrine of final perseverance had
en offence: a house of our own will alone fix us properly.

1789

1789

Asbury, Coke, Morrell, and Dickins visiting Washington

CHAPTER EIGHTEEN

Virginia

January 1, 1789. After waiting about two hours the wind suddenly
lmed, and I crossed Rappahannock and came to Cheesecake.[1]

We had a comfortable meeting at Richard (or Robert) Matthews's,[2] in
ingston,[3] thence to Billup's;[4] and afterward to Douglas's,[5] where, al-
ough I had an unfeeling audience, I had satisfaction in my own soul.

We came to James City; where God has wrought a glorious work; as
so in New Kent county in the same circuit: a number of young people
ive been made the subjects of this grace.

Thursday, 8. I had a most agreeable passage, for the season, across
imes River. Arrived at Mooring's about three o'clock, and found a
vely people. Christians here appear to stand faithful, but sinners are not
:ought in.

Friday, 9. Was a good day at Ellis's: my soul felt peace, and I was happy
) find our old friends standing fast.

Saturday, 10. We had a happy meeting at Lane's chapel. I went to the
idow Lane's: I felt uneasy; but I found it needful for me to be there.

[1] Cheesecake was a large tract of land across the Piankatank River from the
:esent Urbanna, Virginia, which had been inhabited by the Kiskiacs or Chiskiacs
dians, who were known locally as the "Cheesecake" Indians.

[2] Gwathmey: *Twelve Virginia Counties*, 16.

[3] Kingston Parish, Gloucester. (See *Journal* entry for January 3, 1788.)

[4] See *Journal* entry for January 3, 1788.

[5] See *Journal* entry for April 17, 1800.

Sunday, 11. Preached on, "Kiss the Son," &c., and afterward rode f
teen miles to Moss's. They are a dear people at Lane's chapel: slavery
greatly on the decline among them.

Tuesday, 13. An appointment had been made at Mabry's chapel, b
the sleet and rain hindered the people from attending; so I preached
brother Thweat's[6] to about six preachers, and as many members.

North Carolina

Wednesday, 14. I had about three hundred hearers at the Low Grou
chapel: our brethren shouted whilst I enlarged on Isaiah lxiii, 1. I ha
felt very solemn for two or three days past, as though God would spe
through me to the souls of the people.

Thursday, 15. Rode to Moore's; had a dead, dull people, except tho
few who came from a distance. Crossed Roanoak, and arriving at t
place of preaching a little after night, I spoke on, "Comfort ye, comfo
ye my people," &c.

Saturday and *Sunday*, 17, 18. Preached at Whitaker's chapel,[7] whe
we had a profitable time; I found God had been working, and that ma
souls had been awakened.

We came to J——'s: in this neighbourhood the Christians are sing
larly devoted, but sinners yet stand it out. The Lord has begun to wo
on Sandy Creek, in Franklin county, where twenty souls have been late
brought to God. Came to Bemnet Hills, hungry and unwell. My so
enjoys much of God.

We had a shaking time at Hill's; a sweet love feast and sacramen
Thence I went to Pope's chapel: I came to G——'s.

Saturday, 24. Rode to Kimbrough's,[8] twenty miles, where there we
many people, and but little engagedness among them. After attending
few appointments on *Tuesday* 27, I crossed Haw River, and rode twen
miles to brother Kennon's, in Chatham county: I had not been in th
county for eight years; we had a meeting at night, but I was strange
shut up.

[6] Thweats are listed in both Greensville and Brunswick counties. Greensville w
formed from Brunswick in 1780. (*Heads of Families*; Knorr: *Marriages of Brunswi
County, Virginia*, 1750–1810.)

[7] Whitaker's Chapel is near Enfield, North Carolina, in Halifax County. R. Whitak
lived twenty miles from Pollock's Ferry on Roanoke River. (See *Journal* entry f
March 16, 1801.) Grissom notes also a Whitaker's Church on Dutchman's Creek
present Davie County, then Rowan County. (*Op. cit.*, 214, 267.)

[8] John Kimbrough had lived in Wake County, North Carolina, but went to Sou
Carolina in 1756. (See note under February 17, 1785.) Some of his descendants probab
remained in North Carolina. Either the *Journal* account is not strictly chronological
Asbury took a zigzag course in Chatham and Wake counties.

Thursday, 29. Rode to W.'s, wet and water-bound: we found the poor
ntinomian drunk; however, as the rain was great, we made out to stay.
Friday, 30. Rode through the rain to Bowdon's. Deep River was very
gh; and we had an awful time crossing it.
Saturday, 31. Came to Fair Creek, which was nearly swimming high.
hen to Little River, but we could not cross; we stopped at M'D.'s, and
e our own morsel; afterward we rode down the river, and were thankful
be housed.
Monday, February 2. I attended an appointment made for another
reacher at Mask's, where there were a few serious souls.
Tuesday, 3. I stopped on my way at Dr. King's,[9] and took dinner, and
ad my horse shod. By some means my appointments have not been
ublished.

South Carolina

Came to the Green Ponds,[10] where there was an appointment for me;
felt a little comforted. I have ridden about one hundred and forty miles
the last seven days, through a very disagreeable part of the country to
avel when the waters are high: I have had various exercises, and have
affered hunger, fatigue, and fever, and have not had a comfortable bed
r a week past.
Wednesday, 4. I was much moved at the Beauty Spot,[11] on, "Ye did run
ell," &c. I found it had been the case here; but ah! the use of strong liquor.
We rode to Rogers's[12] a long stretch across a deep swamp: we came in
te, and I preached with little liberty. I lodged at ——, a poor, kind man.
Sunday, 8. Notwithstanding the rain, we had many to hear at Flower's.[13]
was in due season that I was led out here on Peter's denial of his Master;
r there has been a great falling away, particularly by drunkenness: this
as not told me till after preaching.
Monday, 9. Rode to Rewell's meeting house:[14] my soul was in peace

[9] Dr. John King lived in Franklin County, North Carolina, near Louisburg, but "in
'89 or 1790" he moved to Wake County near Raleigh. (Grissom, *op. cit.*, 59.) If he
ved in Franklin County at this time, Asbury doubled back on his trail from Chatham
ounty. (See notes under May 29, 1772, and June 23, 1780.)
[10] Asbury again entered Marlboro County, South Carolina, from Green Ponds in
ichmond County, North Carolina, along his previous route in February of this year.
[11] From Beauty Spot near Bennettsville, which he had previously visited, he proceeded
uthward along the route of the present Blenheim and Brownsville in Marlboro
ounty and Latta in Dillon County, approximating Highways 38 and 917.
[12] Rogers lived on Reedy Creek, seven miles southeast of Clio.
[13] Flower's meetinghouse was on the land of General Williams, one mile north of
arion. It was later moved southwest of Marion and called Bethel, and about 1833 it
as brought into Marion and became the present First Methodist Church.
[14] Rewell's meetinghouse was Rowell's in Marion County, nine miles south of
arion, which became Centenary Methodist Church.

and uncommonly led out in preaching. Thence to Port's,[15] Long Ferr three miles across Pee Dee: the inundation of the river, occasioned by tl rains, has made a mere sea. My mind has been variously tried and strong exercised by dejection. Lord, give me faith and patience!

Tuesday, 10. Came, after a ride of forty miles, to Georgetown, ar lectured on Isa. xl, 1–9.

Friday, 13. Rode forty-five miles to Wappetaw[16]; and next day arriv in Charleston in sweet peace of soul.

Sunday, 15. Preached in the morning with some light; in the afterno on Matt. xi, 28–30. I preached again on *Tuesday* and on *Wednesday*. M heart was drawn out greatly for these people.

Friday, 20. I spoke very pointedly on Rev. iii, 20–22, but the peop are of small spiritual understanding. Lord, stir them up! I was close employed in making my plan, and arranging the papers for conferenc I made out a register of all the preachers on the continent who bear tl name of Methodists.

Saturday, 21. I was very ill with a fever and colic; and it being rainy kept within doors.

Sunday, 22. Very rainy, but I had about a hundred blacks, and near fifty whites to hear me. I preached also in the afternoon, and at night.

Tuesday, 24. I set out for Edisto circuit, journeying up the south si of Ashley River. Here live the rich and great who have houses in the ci and country, and go backward and forward in their splendid chariots the land, however, with the exception of the rice fields, is barren, tl weather is cold: but my soul has peace—full and flowing peace. After ridi thirty-six miles, I was kindly entertained by Mr. Givhan,[18] but there w still something wanting.

Wednesday, 25. They were out of bread at P——'s, and we found o own stores of use. We had to send one of our weary horses eight miles fetch the flour from the mill.

Thursday, 26. Rode to Bruten's, and enjoyed uncommon happiness God. Some time in the night Dr. Coke came in: he had landed in Charle ton about three hours after I left the city: next day he and myself bo spoke at Ridgell's.[19]

[15] Crossing the Pee Dee at Port's (Porter's) Ferry as previously, Asbury followed l old route over Great Pee Dee, Lynch's River, and Black Mingo to Georgetown.

[16] He proceeded to Charleston via Wappetaw Swamp and bridge and the Cape home at Cainhoy.

[17] He passed Magnolia and Middleton plantations, then the homes of wealthy Car linians and now world-famous gardens.

[18] (See note under March 17, 1788.) Givhan lived six miles west of Ridgeville.

[19] Bishop Coke was delayed by the uncertainties of ocean travel, having come fro England. He overtook his colleague on the evening of the third day at Mr. Bruten's a traveled with Asbury to Georgia. (Shipp: *Methodism in South Carolina*, 199; see Ship 200, 201, for a description of the journey to Georgia and its hazards.) Bruten liv near Bamberg. Ridgell probably lived near Canadys.

Sunday, March 1. We spent the day at Chester's:[20] we had very few
arers, occasioned, in part, by a black man's preaching not far distant.
Monday, 2. I was violently exercised. The Doctor and myself both
ached at Puckett's. Thence we set out with a design to reach Tread-
y's, but were greatly deceived, and went up the road that leads to
nety-Six;[21] at last we thought we had gone far enough, and stopped at
house twenty-one miles from the place whence we started, and still
ther from the place we aimed at.

Georgia

Came to Doctor Fuller's,[22] at Beach Island, and next day arrived in
igusta, Georgia. Riding late two nights past has much disordered me;
ving taken a cold, attended with a fever and a pain in the head.
Thursday, 5. I obtained a little rest at brother Haynes's.[23]
Friday, 6. Although it rained, we had a few people at Brownsborough.
·xt day there was some life at Scott's.[24] Here they have built us a large
apel.
Sunday, 8. Our conference began at Grant's.[25] Here we have a house for

) The Chester family lived halfway between Edgefield and Augusta.
⁴ Instead of crossing the Edisto at Givhan's Ferry and following the more direct
·r road south of the river to Augusta, Georgia, he proceeded into present Orangeburg
unty and got on the old Ninety Six road by mistake. Discovering his error in upper
·en County, he turned westward to Beech Island, seven miles below Augusta on the
·t side of the Savannah River. Thence he went into Georgia for a fortnight.
² Fuller lived on the South Carolina side of the Savannah River six miles below
gusta.
³ Thomas Haynes left Virginia partly to escape the Methodist evangelists who had
verted his wife. He settled on Uchee Creek in what is now Columbia County in
orgia, where he was converted. He had a church nearby, and such Methodists as
·ury, Coke and Lorenzo Dow were entertained in his home. (Smith: *Georgia
·thodism,* 38, 39.)
⁴ Scott's meetinghouse was built by Joseph Scott in the Gatrell neighborhood on
·le River or near the Augusta road in the southeastern part of present Wilkes
unty. (Bowen: *Wilkes County,* 122.) Pierce's Chapel in the same neighborhood is an
growth of Scott's.
⁵ Daniel Grant and his son Thomas had been Presbyterians in Hanover County,
ginia. They became Methodists after moving to Georgia in 1784. They were pros-
·ous merchants at Grant's Store near Washington in present Wilkes County, where
y built the first Methodist church in Georgia five miles east of Washington. A
·man who lived in the Grant house in 1820 thought there was a Piny Grove Methodist
·rch between the house and Washington. (*Ibid.,* 120, 121.) The preachers were enter-
·ed in the home, and conference met in the chapel. Thomas Grant had been a revolu-
·ary soldier and became an outstanding Methodist in Georgia. At his home he had a
·ophet's chamber" with clothing of various sizes for the cold and wet preachers who
·ved. After new counties were opened east of the Ocmulgee, he established a store in
·ndolph, now Jasper, County, and later moved to Monticello. When he died in 1828,

public worship; and one also at Meriwether's.[26] On *Thursday* we a
pointed a committee to procure five hundred acres of land for the esta
lishment of a school in the State of Georgia. Conference being ended, v
directed our hasty steps back to Charleston, calling at the several plac
we attended on our journey hither.

South Carolina

Sunday, 15. We reached the city, having ridden two hundred miles
about five days and two hours.[27] Here I received a *bitter pill*[28] from o
of my greatest friends. Praise the Lord for my trials also—may they all
sanctified!

Tuesday, *Wednesday*, and *Thursday*, 17, 18, 19, were spent in confe
ence; it was a time of peace and love. My mind was much hurried wi
book, and other temporal concerns. We had an unkind attack publish
against us relative to our slave rules; it was answered to purpose. I h
not much doubt who the author of this unworthy work was.

Saturday, 21, was spent in preparing to move on Monday next.

Sunday, 22. Doctor Coke preached an ordination sermon in the for
noon; and in the afternoon I felt lively in soul whilst I enlarged on Eze
xxxiii, 5.

Monday, 23. We left the city, and rode upwards of forty miles.

he left a bequest to the South Carolina and Georgia conferences from which the lat
received fifteen hundred dollars and some land. His funeral was preached by I
Lovick Pierce. (Smith: *Asbury*, 116, 117; *Georgia Methodism*, 38–44; *Georgia Peop
140, 141.) There is a granite marker on the site of Grant's meetinghouse, a few mi
from Washington. Two miles away is Mount Zion Church, successor to Grant's Chap
which contains parts of the pulpit and altar from the first Methodist meetinghouse
Georgia.

[26] See note for April 9, 1788. General David Meriwether came from Virginia w
George Mathews, who became governor of Georgia. Meriwether was a wealthy m
who became prominent in political affairs. He was related by marriage to the two o
standing Methodists of Georgia, Hope Hull and John Andrews. The church built
him was in the southern part of present Elbert County, west of Broad River and pr
ably near Long Creek. The conference in 1789 decided to buy five hundred acres
land for a school to be named in honour of Wesley and Whitefield. (Smith: *Asbu
116–17; *Georgia Methodism*, 38–44; *Georgia People*, 140–41; Bowen: *Wilkes Coun
120–22.)

[27] Asbury returned to Charleston on the Edisto River road via Givhans.

[28] This bitter pill was a letter from John Wesley which criticized Asbury and Cc
bitterly for calling themselves bishops and other reasons. Wesley wrote: "I study to
little; you study to be great. I creep: you strut along. I found a school; you a colle
nay, and call it after your own names! . . . How can you, how dare you suffer yours
to be called Bishop? I shudder, I start at the very thought! Men may call me a knave
a fool, a rascal, a scoundrel, and I am content; but they shall never by my consent c
me Bishop!" (*The Letters of the Rev. John Wesley, A.M.*, Standard Edition, ed. Jo
Telford, VIII, 91; also *Letters of Francis Asbury*.)

Tuesday, 24. Crossed the Santee, and came to brother Bowman's.[29]
Wednesday, 25. Preached at Gibson's; then rode to Ramsay's, near
atesburg, sixteen miles.[30]
Thursday, 26. I was hurried away to preach a funeral sermon. I have
Iden about one hundred and fifty miles, and preached three times
Ice I left Charleston, last Monday morning. I am at times tempted to
;htness; yet, blessed be God, my soul has sweet communion with
m.
Saturday, 28. At Bradford's chapel[31] I preached on Heb. xi, 16, 17. At
Embert's, on Isaiah xl, 1. My soul was blest among the people.
Sunday, 29. I was led out in preaching and prayer; the people were
Elted; and the work of God progresses. I trust the Lord will get himself
Eat glory here.
Monday, 30. We rode about fifty miles to Colonel Marshall's.[32] the
Eather was very warm, and we were hungry and weary.

North Carolina

Wednesday, April 1. The people came together at Jackson's[33] at twelve
Clock. I did not reach there until three. I enlarged a little on Zech. xiii,
,[34] and was somewhat severe. I rode to Savannah Creek, and met with
 Antinomian people. Reached Threadgill's; having been out twelve
Durs, and ridden nearly forty miles, without food for man or beast.
Friday, 3. Preached by the way, and came to Randall's,[35] twenty miles.
E have ridden three hundred miles in about nine days, and our horses'
Icks are bruised with their loads. I want more faith, patience, and
Signation to the will of God in all things. I wish to send an extra
Eacher to the Waxsaws, to preach to the Catabaw Indians: they have
Ettled amongst the whites on a tract of country twelve miles square.
Sunday, 5. We had a move whilst I was speaking on Isa. xxxiii, 14, 15.
Ime souls were brought to experience peace with God. Here Doctor
Ike came up with us. We expect to continue together for some time.
E had a long ride to Jones's. I preached there, and continued on to
'Knight's, on the Yadkin.
Friday, 10. We opened our conference, and were blessed with peace and

[29] Bowman lived in Clarendon County, near Summerton.
[30] Gibson and Ramsay lived in Sumter County, near Statesburg.
[31] Bradford's was four miles northwest of Sumter, South Carolina. See note under
Arch 3, 1788.
[32] Colonel Marshall lived on Lynch's River near Chesterfield County but on the
Ershaw side.
[33] Jackson lived just across the line in Anson County, North Carolina.
[34] Zech. 13 has only nine verses. There is no clue as to the correct passage.
[35] See note under February 15, 1785.

union. Our brethren from the westward met us, and we had weigh
matters for consideration before us.[36]

We left M'Knight's, having about two hundred miles to ride in fo
days.

Virginia

We had a tedious ride to Almond's, and a blessed season of grace. S
out from Almond's, and reached Good's.[37]

Saturday, 18. We rode thirty-six miles to Petersburg. On *Sunday* t
Doctor preached. I had nothing to say in public. We met the preachers
Saturday and *Sunday* evenings, and brought our work forward. I h
disagreeable feelings while here. There is a spiritual death among t
people. I spoke a little on *Monday* and on *Wednesday*.

Thursday, 23. We came to Manchester. My exertions, want of rest, a
distress of mind, brought on a violent headache. Instead of preaching
found myself under the necessity of going to bed. Doctor Coke had go
over the river to Richmond, and preached there.

Friday, 24. We rode about fifty miles; and next day reached Frederick
burg, but found no door open. We met with one soul in distress.

Sunday, 26. Having no appointment to preach, we pushed on and ro
forty-five miles, and lodged in Prince William county.

Monday, 27. Arrived at Leesburg, and opened the conference. We fou
a little rest comfortable to man, and advantageous to beast.

Maryland

Thursday, 30. We crossed Potomac into Maryland. My soul cleaves
God; but I am again afflicted in my head. Reaching brother Nicholson
in Montgomery, we were kindly entertained.[38]

[36] This conference at McKnight's Chapel in the present Forsyth County, No
Carolina, was an important meeting. It included the Holston preachers. Thomas W
says that Asbury passed through his New River Circuit and that he accompanied t
bishop to the conference by way of the Flower Gap (*Life and Travels*, 160), but sir
Asbury came from South Carolina this is an obvious error; Asbury came throu
Holston in 1788. Among the "weighty matters" transacted was the launching of
American *Arminian Magazine*, which the newly appointed (1789) Book Steward, Jo
Dickins, published at Philadelphia. The preface of the first edition was signed by Asbu
and Coke at "North Carolina, April 10th, 1789." (Ware: *Sketches of the Life a
Travels of Rev. Thomas Ware*, 160; Price: *Holston Methodism*, I, 143, 144; Grisso
op. cit., 140, 141. See note under April 13, 1787; preface to *The Arminian Magazi*
April 10, 1789.)

[37] Almond lived in Charlotte County, Virginia. (*Heads of Families*, 15.) Good liv
in Prince Edward County. (Sweet, *op. cit.*, 185.)

[38] Asbury probably entered Maryland over White's or Conrad's Ferry. The Nichols
home was somewhere between the Potomac River and Laytonsville. John Nicholson
enrolled in the 1790 Federal Census of Montgomery County.

Friday, May 1. I felt life in speaking.

Saturday, 2. We attended quarterly meeting. Not being permitted to
e the chapel, we went into a tobacco house. Many attended; and the
ung converts shouted aloud.

Sunday, 3. Was a great day to saints and sinners. God has wrought
onderfully in brother Pigman's neighbourhood.[39] Fifty or sixty souls
ve been suddenly and powerfully converted to God.

Came to Baltimore, and had very lively meetings. Multitudes came to
ar, and great cries were heard among the people, who continued to-
ther until three o'clock in the morning. Many souls professed to be
nvicted, converted, sanctified.

On reaching Cokesbury, we found that here also God was working
nong the students. One, however, we expelled. We revised our laws,
d settled our temporal concerns.

Tuesday, 12. We were detained at Susquehannah Ferry, so that we were
mpelled to ride in the night to reach Chestertown.

We had a blessed work of God on our way. Loud shouting was heard
almost every meeting. At sacrament especially, the Lord's power and
esence were great indeed. At Duck Creek we had a good season.

Saturday, 16. Doctor Coke preached in Wilmington, Delaware.

Pennsylvania

Sunday, 17. The Doctor preached at Chester; and in Philadelphia in the
ening.

Wednesday, 20. In the evening the Lord's power came down among the
ople in the city; and I hope to hear he is doing great things.

New Jersey

Thursday, 21. Rode to Burlington, in Jersey. In crossing the Delaware
e encountered an uncommon storm, but were providentially brought
fely over. We were comfortable in our meeting; but we had a painful
terview and explanation with L. H. H. O, my soul, keep near to God!

Friday, 22. We rode to Trenton; and on *Saturday,* 23, opened our con-
rence in great peace. We laboured for a manifestation of the Lord's
wer, and it was not altogether in vain.

[39] The Pigman family lived near Laytonsville, Montgomery County. Joshua and
seph were among the trustees to whom the land on which the Goshen Meeting House
s conveyed. The deed bears the date February 2, 1791. Ignatius Pigman, a brother,
s an eloquent itinerant from 1781 to 1788. (Lednum, *op. cit.,* 325; Martz: *History of
e Clarksburg Methodist Church,* 7; *Journal* entries for August 31, 1790, and September
1800.)

Sunday, 24. We had abundance of preaching.

Monday, 25. We rode through a heavy rain to Elizabethtown, and ne
day reached New York. I was under great travail of soul for a revival
religion.

New York

Thursday, 28. Our conference began. All things were conducted
peace and order.[40] Our work opens in New York State.[41] New Englai
stretcheth out the hand[42] to our ministry, and I trust thousands will short
feel its influence. My soul shall praise the Lord. In the midst of haste
find peace within.[43]

Sunday, 31. We had a gracious season to preachers and people, whi
I opened and applied Isaiah xxv, 6–8: "And in this mountain shall t
Lord of Hosts make unto all people a feast of fat things; a feast of win
on the lees; of fat things full of marrow; of wines on the lees well refined

Friday, June 5. Doctor Coke left us and went on board the Union f
Liverpool. My soul retires into solitude, and to God. This evening
was enabled to speak alarmingly, and felt my heart much engaged f
about thirty minutes on Isaiah xxix, 17–19. The power of God, and
baptizing flame came among the people.

[40] The conference met at John Street Church. Asbury was accompanied by Whatco
and the church records show payment for feeding the latter's horse. A notable eve
transpired here. On April 30 George Washington had been inaugurated at Wall a
Nassau Streets as the first President of the United States. The conference adopted
congratulatory address, and John Dickins and Thomas Morrell made an appointme
with Washington to receive it. On June 1 Asbury and Coke presented the address,
which Washington replied. (See the document in the *Letters* under the proper dat
This event caused a stir in the city and the *New York Packet* noted it in its colum
declaring that the "affectionate and respectful address" indicated that the "who
Society are warmly attached to the Constitution and government of the United States
The Methodists were the first church group so to address Washington. Coke, as a
Englishman, was criticized for signing the paper, but Asbury's devotion througho
the Revolution identified him as an American. (Seaman, *op. cit.,* 104, 462 ff.; Mo
"Asbury Knew Washington" in *Christian Advocate,* February 10, 1955; see letters
Thomas Morrell, May 20, 1789; to George Washington, May 29, 1789; and to t
Friends of Cokesbury College, May 29, 1789.)

[41] The previous conference had appointed Garrettson to work north of Westchest
to Lake Champlain. He formed new circuits and added around seven hundred membe
(*Minutes*; Bangs: *Life of Garrettson,* 171 ff.)

[42] Jesse Lee was appointed to New England and became the founder of Methodis
there.

[43] The notable conference also decided to build another church in New York a
appointed Thomas Morrell to the task, which he so successfully accomplished th
Asbury preached in it on October 3, 1790. (See *Journal* entry for that date. See al
Asbury's letters to Morrell of June, 1789; October 3, 1789; and December 10, 179
The conference also established a "Book Room" in Philadelphia and named Jo
Dickins as "Book Steward." (See the analysis of the work of this conference in *7
Methodist Quarterly Review,* April, 1857.)

I have lately read Whiston's Translation of the Apostolical Institutions, ɔ called). Also Cave's Lives of the Apostles and Fathers.

Sunday, 7. Was a good day. I felt inwardly quickened towards the close my morning's discourse, and the people were moved. In the afternoon any were divinely drawn, and my own soul was humbled and filled with e love of God. Several souls have been stirred up this conference. I trust e Lord will claim the people of New York for his own.

Tuesday, 9. We left the city of New York, and came to Kingsbridge.[44] fter refreshing ourselves and our horses, we pushed on to East Chester. ie appointment for us was to have been made at Deveau's. There came gether about two hundred people, among whom there was a consider-•le move.

Wednesday, 10. My horse was lamed (by fetters, I suppose) so that I ιd to walk part of the way to New Rochelle. Proper notice of my coming ɔt having been given, I had but one hundred and fifty hearers. We have good house here,[45] a large society; and several of the old members, whom formed into a society some years past, are still alive to God.

Thursday, 11. My horse continues lame;—the journey is long, and the ιy unfavourable—yet I must go.

I came on to Crom Pond,[46] and expected to have preached at Oakley's ιurch;[47] but my appointment was made at Badeau's,[48] where I had but w. Returned to Fowler's.[49] We had a comfortable time at Oakley's ιurch at seven o'clock.

Friday, 12. We rode four miles and stopped at Kirkham's[50] for some freshment, then hasted on to Peekskill Hollow, where I found a poor, mple-hearted people, to whom I enforced, "Repent, and be converted, ιat your sins may be blotted out"; there was a power attended the ɔrd.

[44] Asbury followed the usual Post Road route accompanied by Whatcoat and ιrrettson and probably by Peter Moriarty and Lemuel Smith, appointed to the New ɔchelle Circuit, and Samuel Talbot and Benjamin Abbott, appointed to Duchess ɔunty.

[45] This church was first mentioned in the *Journal* on June 10, 1787. The society was ganized on June 23, 1773. (See *Journal* entry and note for that date.)

[46] This was a small community on the edge of Cortland and Yorktown townships, estchester County, named after a group of small lakes in the vicinity known in pre-evolutionary days as the Crom Ponds.

[47] A small church had recently been completed on the property of either Timothy or hn Oakley. Thomas Ware had first preached in this vicinity in 1786; others had llowed in succession on the circuit. The present Shrub Oak Methodist Church is the ιeal descendant of the group at Oakley's. (Scharf, *op. cit.*, II, 454–56.)

[48] Jacob Badeau, in whose father's house Thomas Ware had preached the first ethodist sermon in Yorktown Township. Jacob joined with the Oakleys and others incorporating the church in April, 1792. (*Ibid.*)

[49] Solomon Fowler was one of the trustees of the Oakley church.

[50] Thomas Kirkham was also a trustee of the church. He lived on the road to Peek-ill, and his home was one of the earliest preaching places.

Saturday, 13. We rode about twenty miles to brother Jackson's where brother Cook[52] lay sick: we had heard that he was dead. I labour under violent temptation; vast consolation followed. Glory! Glory God! He bears me up, body and soul. In our way we stepped into a hou exhorted and prayed with the mother and daughter, who appeared than ful for our services.

Sunday, 14. Preached at Jackson's, in Dutchess county, to a considerat number of quiet hearers; I hope not in vain. Brother Cook is low in bod but his soul is solidly happy in God, who will be glorified in his life death. The people here are a still kind of folks; but God can work in storm or a calm.

Monday, 15. We rode about twenty miles to Dover:[53] the settlers in tł neighbourhood are mostly Low Dutch. It is a day of small things with ʋ yet I trust there are a few feeling souls. We had very alarming meetings noon and at night. Thence to Oblongs,[54] where I found a dull peopł I exerted myself sick as I was; and had I been well, I should have made ɪ little noise. After meeting we rode to ——, where an Antinomian carr drunk as he was, to tell his experience: he gabbled strangely until I stopp his mouth; he then left us. Rode to Livingston's,[55] and preached o "Seek ye first the kingdom of God," &c.; the people appeared like rocł O that the hammer and fire of God's word and love might come doʋ among them!

[51] Garrettson had established Lagrange in Dutchess County as a central point in ſ circuit, and Jackson's home was the preaching place.

[52] Cornelius Cook was born in England, converted and called to preach in Ameriɛ He was quite young and frail in health, suffering from a chronic kidney ailment. Co was received on trial in 1787 and appointed to East Jersey, during which time he assisɪ in New York, following close after Ware in Westchester County. He was received full connection in 1788 and appointed to Dutchess County, and in 1789 was ordair deacon and assigned to Schenectady, but he died before he could leave Dutchɛ County. Garrettson saw him a week after this visit of Asbury and thought him dyir but he rallied and lived until mid-August. (Bangs, *op. cit.*, 177.)

[53] Dover was a village north of Lagrangeville in the same valley east of Hudsɛ Highlands.

[54] The exact location of Oblongs is indefinite. It was also mentioned by Garrettsɛ as a place for occasional preaching.

[55] This was most probably one of the several homes of persons in the noted Livingstɛ family, whose original manor holdings covered a wide sweep along the Hudson aɪ back into the country in the general vicinity of Rhinebeck. Robert R. Livingston, fiɪ chancellor of the state of New York, was the head of the family at this time. He waɛ member of the committee which framed the Declaration of Independence and h administered the oath of office to Washington at his inauguration in New York, Apɪ 30, 1789. When Garrettson preached first at Rhinebeck in 1788, he was entertained bɣ Mr. Tillotson, whose wife was a sister of Chancellor Livingston. Another sister, Cathɛ ine, was to become Mrs. Garrettson in 1793. There were also others of the family liviɪ in adjacent properties, and one of these appears to have been Asbury's host on tł occasion.

Friday, 19. I preached in a barn on the North River:[56] my hearers were chiefly Low Dutch. Our congregations are small; *the craft is in danger*; we are therefore not to wonder if we meet with opposition. To begin at the right end of the work is to go first to the *poor*; these *will*, the rich *may possibly*, hear the truth: there are among us who have blundered here. I feel as if I wanted to get across the river; I am pressed in spirit, and pity our preachers who labour here;[57] it seems as if I should die amongst this people with exertions and grief.

Sunday, 21. Preached at Latin Town[58] to a poor, dull people; some, however, appeared to be moved. At Allison's[59] I was more enlarged, and many wept, and felt the word. We have had a trying, warm day to ride in, and preach twice.

Monday, 22. Rain and business prevented most of the people from attending at Newburg, except a few women. I felt moved while I spoke on Isaiah lxiii. I hope the Lord will water the word sown.

Thursday, 25. I was sick. Brother Whatcoat gave them a sermon at Warwick,[60] on the "wages of sin"; and I gave them a finishing exhortation: have no desire to see them again until there is some change.

New Jersey

Friday, 26. The power of God came down among the people at Benjamin's,[61] and there was a great melting. After meeting we rode through the heat fifteen miles to Pepper Cotton.[62]

Saturday, 27. Rode to the stone church, and found stony hearts. The Methodists ought to preach only in their own houses; I have done with

[56] This place is unidentified, but it was probably a short distance below Rhinebeck.

[57] See letter to Thomas Morrell, June 19, 1789.

[58] This community was fifteen miles north of Newburgh and four miles inland from the Hudson River. First Methodist preaching there was in 1786, by either Ezekiel Cooper or John McClaskey. Two classes were speedily formed, one in the village itself and the other, called Jacob Dayton's class, for the section eastward to Milton on the Hudson River. Dayton later became a trustee of the Milton Methodist Church when it was incorporated.

[59] This was probably the Widow Allison, who lived at Pochuck just north of Newburgh. (See *Journal* entry for June 18, 1787.)

[60] The preaching place in Warwick was either the residence of Colonel David McCamey or the inn.

[61] Nathan Benjamin lived in Sussex County, New Jersey. (See note under June 21, 1787).

[62] Pepper Cotton is a corruption of Papakating, a valley in Frankford Township, Sussex County, New Jersey. Asbury doubtless preached in the frame church built about 1787 to replace a log union meetinghouse built earlier. It is now the Frankford Plains Methodist Church near Branchville, oldest in the county, which is the fourth on the site and the third to be occupied exclusively by the Methodists. (Phoebus, *op. cit.*, 7; Snell: *History of Sussex County*, 356, 390-97; Lantz, "History of the Frankford Plains Churches," in *The Sussex Independent*, August 30, 1912; *Historical Sketch, Frankford Plains Methodist Episcopal Church*; Honeyman: *Northwestern New Jersey*, I, 524; Atkinson, *op. cit.*, 421; Gordon: *Gazetteer*, 143.)

the houses of other people: brother Whatcoat bore the cross, and preached for me here. When I see the stupidity of the people, and the contentiousness of their spirit, I pity and grieve over them. I have hard labour in travelling amongst the rocks and hills.

Sunday, 28. My body is weak; my spirits are low; and I am burdened under the spiritual death of the people: yet, O my soul, praise the Lord I spoke a few words with freedom at Sweezey's,[63] to insensible people we then drove through the heat to Axford's,[64] where I found life and liberty amongst my hearers.

Monday, 29. We had a heavy ride to Cummins's,[65] where brother Whatcoat preached, while some of the audience slept. Thence we came to M'Cullock's.[66] I had no small trial with Adam Cloud,[67] who was once a preacher amongst us and disowned. He had, in some instances, fallen short of his quarterage during his ministry, and now insisted on my paying him his deficiencies: I did not conceive that in justice or conscience this was required of me; nevertheless, to get rid of him, I gave him £14.

Pennsylvania

Wednesday, July 1. I had a good time at Newman's, near Hunt's ferry.[6] We crossed the ferry on *Thursday*, about six o'clock, got some refreshment at Hinkletown,[69] whence we proceeded to Clymer's,[70] where we had a good meeting.

[63] See note under June 23, 1787.

[64] John Axford lived at Buttzville in present Warren County, New Jersey. Of Quaker ancestry, he opened his house to Asbury and became a devoted Methodist. (Snell, *op. cit.*, 592–93, 608, 610, 615; New Jersey Archives, Abstracts of Wills, VIII, 19.)

[65] Philip Cummins lived at Pequest, the present Vienna, New Jersey. The church there was called the Pequest Methodist Church. Methodist preaching was in the old stone house of Philip Cummins until a church was built in 1810. The house is still standing. (Snell, *op. cit.*, 740; Honeyman, *op. cit.*, II, 707–16. See *Journal* entries for April 23, 1807; May 11, 1811.)

[66] Colonel William McCulloch (1759–1840), a Revolutionary soldier, lived in the village of Hall's Mills, which he was instrumental in changing to Asbury, the present town in Warren County, New Jersey. Here he was also instrumental in building the Asbury Methodist Church, the cornerstone of which was laid by Asbury on August 9, 1796. (See *Journal* entry for that date.) The town and church were the first to bear Asbury's name. In 1811 McCulloch built a hotel at nearby Mansfield, which he renamed Washington. He was buried at Asbury. (Snell, *op. cit.*, 160, 569, 577, 705–8; Honeyman, *op. cit.*, III, 676; Gordon, *op. cit.*, 95, 233–34; Phoebus, *op. cit.*, 68.)

[67] Adam Cloud appeared in the *Minutes* as a traveling preacher in 1781. He "desisted from travelling" in 1788.

[68] Hunt's Ferry was between Riegelsville, New Jersey, and Riegelsville, Pennsylvania, or in that locality.

[69] Hinkletown is in Plumstead Township, Bucks County, Pennsylvania. The transcriber spelled it Inkletown.

[70] The Clymer family lived near Kitnersville, Pennsylvania. (See Davis: *History of Bucks County.*)

Friday, 3. Came to Philadelphia; here I found enough to do. My soul longs for more religion in this city; I am distressed for these people: twenty years have we been labouring in Pennsylvania, and there are not one thousand in society: how many of these are truly converted God knows.

Sunday, 5. We had a dead time. O that the Almighty would bless and stir up this people!

Rode to Radnor[71] where there were a few feeling souls.

Tuesday, 7. It being harvest-home, and short notice, we had few hearers. I love God supremely, and feel myself greatly weaned from earth: I have a glorious victory; sweetly resting and suffering in Christ. Yesterday I felt so unwell that I could scarcely sit on my horse. My soul was so filled with God, that it appeared as if all sense of pain was suspended by the power of faith. I was so led out in speaking at the Valley church[72] that all my sufferings were forgotten. I spoke very loud a part of the time; we had a gracious season.

Wednesday, 8. After riding thirty miles, I preached at Rodfong's[73] at night, with satisfaction, and souls were brought to God.

Friday, 10. I called on Mr. Hendel,[74] a Dutch Presbyterian minister; he and his wife were both very kind: I believe they are children of God. I had an interview with Mr. Muhlenberg,[75] a Lutheran minister, and teacher of languages: he is a childlike, simple-hearted man, and has a considerable knowledge of the arts and sciences. We came to York; but I felt no desire to preach. I proceeded on to Carlisle; in the morning I was permitted to preach in the church; but in the evening, this privilege was denied me: it was said, the reason was, because I did not read prayers, which I had forborne to do because of my eyes; I apprehend the true cause might be found in the pointed manner in which I spoke on "Blessed is he whosoever shall not be offended in me." I went to the court house and called them to repentance, from, "Look unto me, and be ye saved, all ye ends of the earth"; to the great offence of all who set themselves up for judges, and who declared it was no preaching.

Wednesday, 15. Came to Juniata River; we were well nigh being lost in

---

[71] See *Journal* entry for July 1, 1787.

[72] See *Journal* entry for February 5, 1781.

[73] This was probably near Strasburg.

[74] John William Hendel (1740–98) was born in Bad Duerkheim in the Palatinate and educated at the University of Heidelberg. He offered his services for Pennsylvania before the deputies of the Holland Synod at The Hague in June, 1764, and was ordained and sent to Pennsylvania, arriving in Philadelphia in December, 1764. He immediately began his ministry as pastor of the German Reformed Church in Lancaster. He was elected vice-principal of Franklin College when it was opened in 1787. In 1794 he became pastor of the Reformed Church in Philadelphia, where he prepared a new hymnbook and a German Reformed liturgy.

[75] The Rev. G. H. E. Muhlenberg was pastor of the Lutheran Church of the Holy Trinity at Lancaster, Pennsylvania, 1780–1815.

the woods, but kind Providence brought us safe in company with brother Whatcoat[76] to I. C——'s, and we lodged there.

Thursday, 16. Came to G——'s, nine miles from Bedford.[77] and being informed that the people thereabouts were willing to hear, we yielded to the persuasion of some who desired us to stay and preach.

Friday, 17. We rode on to Wells's, a place visited by our preachers: here we had a good night's rest.

Saturday, 18. We passed Greensburg, stopping at Hanover Davis's, a man who has trouble and conviction: his three sons were killed by the Indians, his wife and two children taken prisoners, and detained from him eighteen months.

Sunday, 19. Came to Rowlett's and dined; thence we set out and reached Pittsburg,[78] twenty-five miles; I preached in the evening to a serious audience. This is a day of very small things: what can we hope? yet, what can we fear? I felt great love to the people; and hope God will arise to help and bless them.

Monday, 20. I preached on Isa. lv, 6, 7; had some zeal, and the people were very attentive; but alas! they are far from God, and too near the savages in situation and manners. We were not agreeably stationed at ——, who was continually drunk, and our only alternative was a tavern.

Tuesday, 21. I spoke on "The Son of Man is come to seek and to save that which was lost:" we were crowded, and I felt more courage. The night before, the rude soldiers were talking and dancing about the door; but now they were quiet and mute; this, I judged, might be owing to the interference of the officers, or magistracy.

Wednesday, 22. We left Pittsburg, and came by the Allegheny River to Wilson's, who was formerly an elder in the Presbyterian Church. Brothers Green, Willis, and Conaway[79] were my companions on the road.

Thursday, 23. We had a number of poor attentive people at M'G——'s: the weather was excessively warm, and we were in a close log house, without so much as a window to give us air.

[76] Phoebus: *Memoirs of the Rev. Richard Whatcoat*, 25.

[77] This was Asbury's first westward tour along the route of Forbes Road. This road was cut through the wilderness by the army of General John Forbes in his successful attack upon Fort Duquesne in 1758. It is now the Lincoln Highway, or Route 30. It, and Braddock's Road which was cut in 1755, were the two main routes by which the pioneers reached the land west of the mountains.

[78] This was Asbury's first visit to Pittsburgh, then a frontier village of about four hundred population. The Pittsburgh Circuit, embracing the land between the Youghiogheny and the Kiskiminetas Rivers, had been set apart as a new circuit at the Uniontown conference in 1788, but it did not include a preaching point in Pittsburgh until 1796. (Smeltzer, *op. cit.*, 94–103.)

[79] This year Asbury had placed the eight circuits in Pennsylvania in one district, with two presiding elders, Lemuel Green and Henry Willis. Green and Willis accompanied the Bishop to Pittsburgh over the Forbes Road and on the return over Braddock's Road. Charles Conaway was one of the two preachers on the Pittsburgh Circuit this year.

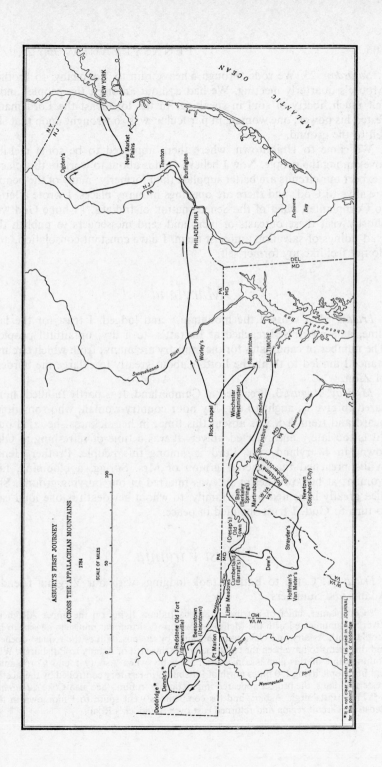

ASBURY'S FIRST JOURNEY
ACROSS THE APPALACHIAN MOUNTAINS
1784

SCALE OF MILES

0   50   100

*It is not clear whether "D" as used in the JOURNAL for this point) refers to Dennis or Doddridge

Saturday, 25. We rode through a heavy rain to Yohogany, to brother Moore's quarterly meeting. We had a shout amongst the people, and I felt much liberty of soul in speaking. In the love feast the Lord manifested his power; one woman, in particular, was so wrought upon that she fell to the ground.

We came to Uniontown, where there appeared to be some melting love among the people. Now I believe God is about to work in this place: I expect our circuits are better supplied than formerly; many of the people are alive to God; and there are openings in many places. I wrote a letter to Cornplanter, chief of the Seneca nation of Indians.[80] I hope God will shortly visit these outcasts of men, and send messengers to publish the glad tidings of salvation amongst them. I have constant consolation, and do not feel like my former self.

Maryland

Friday, 31. I crossed the mountain,[81] and lodged, I trust for the last time, at Simpkin's. Preached at Barratt's, to a dry, unfaithful people. The number of candidates for the ministry are many; from which circumstance I am led to think the Lord is about greatly to enlarge the borders of Zion.

Monday, August 3. Preached at Cumberland. It is partly fulfilled; none cared to give us aught to eat. My poor country-woman, who sometimes heard and trembled, was absent this time; in her sickness she cried out, "it is too late," and rejected prayer. It was a time of refreshing at Oldtown, in Maryland; the Lord is among this people. Brother Henry Willis preached the funeral sermon of Mrs. Sprigg, a blooming, fair woman; at her own desire she was interred in our burying ground. She died greatly lamented by her family, to whom her death is one loud call to turn to God. I trust she died in peace.

West Virginia

Friday, 7. Came to Bath. I took lodgings with our Virginia friends, Adams and Summers.

[80] Cornplanter, chief of a tribe of Seneca Indians living on the upper Allegheny River, communicated with the Methodist bishops desiring that ministers be sent to his people. Both Asbury and Coke were intrigued by the possibilities the request opened, and this seems to have been the chief reason for this visit of Asbury to Pittsburgh. Why nothing came of this plan is conjectural. Probably when Asbury found Cornplanter and his people living 150 miles north of Pittsburgh in territory controlled by the hostile western Indians, the project appeared impracticable to him. (See also Coke's *Journal*.)

[81] From Pittsburgh, Asbury and his companions went south to Uniontown in the Redstone Circuit region and returned east over Braddock's Road.

Saturday, 8. My soul has communion with God, even here. When I behold the conduct of the people who attend the Springs, particularly the gentry, I am led to thank God that I was not born to riches; I rather bless God, that I am not in hell, and that I cannot partake of pleasure with sinners. I have read much, and spoken but little since I came here. The water has been powerful in its operation. I have been in great pain, and my studies are interrupted.

August, 19. I left Bath; which was much sooner than I expected.

God was powerfully present at Hendrick's, where there were twelve or fifteen hundred people: many professed to be converted to God—Glory be to his name! My body enjoys better health; and blessed be God! my soul is wholly kept above sin: yet I blame myself for not being more watchful unto prayer; and I sometimes use unnecessary words. We made a tour through Berkley circuit, where I had some freedom, and where we found not a little living affection in the congregations.

Sunday, 23. We had alarming words at Winchester,[82] from Ezek. xxxiii, 11. I feel the worth of souls, and their disobedience gives me sorrow of heart. O Jehovah! work for thine own glory.

Saturday, 29. Our quarterly meeting began in the woods near Shepherdstown: we had about seven hundred people: I felt energy and life in preaching, and power attended the word. Brother Willis spoke, and the Lord wrought powerfully.

Sunday, 30. Was a high day—one thousand or fifteen hundred people attended; sinners began to mock, and many cried aloud; and so it went. I was wonderfully led out on Psalm cxlv, 8–12; and spoke, first and last, nearly three hours. O, how the wicked contradicted and opposed!

Maryland

Wednesday, September 2. I came to brother Philips's,[83] in Maryland, and had a quickening time. God has preached to the whole family by the death of his daughter, and the fire spreads throughout the whole neighbourhood.

We needs must go through Samaria. I called at Fredericktown, and had a number of wild, unfeeling hearers. Thence to Liberty, where the Almighty is working among the people. I preached in the day, and again at night—I hope not in vain.

---

[82] Winchester was in the present state of Virginia.

[83] Samuel Phillips, who lived four miles from Middletown, Frederick County, Maryland, opened his house for preaching at an early date. He probably was of the family of Methodists of that name who resided in the neighborhood of Woodsboro, Frederick County. (Scharf, *op. cit.*, I, 615, 616; Sweet, *Religion on the American Frontier*, IV, 111; *Journal* entry for August 16, 1802; Robert Ayres, Manuscript *Journal* for June 3, 1786.)

Friday, 4. I rode to Seneca. O what hath God wrought for these people Many precious souls have been brought to the knowledge of salvation.

Monday, 7. Preached at Rowle's: here fifty or sixty souls profess to have been brought to God in a few weeks. We had a shout, and a soul converted to God. I preached in the evening at Baltimore, on "Lord, increase our faith."

Tuesday, 8. Preached in town and at the Point. The last quarterly meeting was a wonder-working time: fifty or sixty souls, then and there, appeared to be brought to God; people were daily praying from house to house; some crying for mercy, others rejoicing in God, and not a few, day after day, joining in society for the benefit of religious fellowship. Praise the Lord, O my soul! I spent some time in visiting from house to house, and begging for the college. The married men and the single men, the married women and the single women, I met apart, and was comforted. Many of the children of the Methodists are the happy subjects of this glorious revival. We have more members in Baltimore[84] (town and Point) than in any city or town on the continent besides.

Sunday, 13. I preached three times; baptized and administered the sacrament twice; and ordained Archibald Foster and William Losee deacons. I trust it was a profitable time to many. I took cold, and was much hurt by labour, so that I could hardly move my body.

Monday, 14. Came to Daniel Evans's, one of our oldest members, and his house one of our oldest stands; to this day he has continued to be steadfast. The Lord has now made bare his arm, and brought in forty or fifty young people, among whom are some of his own children, for whom so many prayers have been offered up to God: the fire of the Lord spreads from house to house, and from heart to heart.

Tuesday, 15. I had but few hearers at Hunt's chapel, but the Lord was present, and I am persuaded there was not an unfeeling soul in the house. I spent the evening with one of the great: the Lord and his own conscience will witness that I did not flatter him. O that his soul were converted to God!

Friday, 18. At Gough's we had a solemn time; the power of the Lord has been displayed here to great purpose.

Sunday, 20. Was an alarming time at the Forks church—a number of serious people—no trifling here now: how many dead souls restored from a backsliding state! and their children converted too!

[84] In 1789 Baltimore had three principal sections. They were served by these Methodist churches: Baltimore Town, west of Jones Falls, near the waterfront, by Light Street Church, successor to Lovely Lane Meeting House; Fells Point by Strawberry Alley Chapel; and Old Town, east of Jones Falls, probably by a meeting place later known as Exeter Street Church. Because of the recording of members on circuits rather than in congregations, the number of Methodists in Baltimore in 1789 is unknown. However, that year the Baltimore Circuit reported a total membership of 937. (*General Minutes,* I, 35.)

Monday, 21. Rode in the evening to Cokesbury. I found I. Steward had gone to his final rest: he was a pious lad who kept too close to his studies. He praised God to the last, even when he was delirious: it made the students very solemn for a season.

Sunday, 27. Preached at Gunpowder chapel in the forenoon and at Abingdon at three o'clock.

Monday, 28. After a long absence I preached at Bush Forest chapel: this was one of the first houses that was built for the Methodists in the state of Maryland; and one of the first societies was formed here. They had been dead for many years; of late the Lord has visited this neighbourhood, and I suppose, from report, fifty souls have been converted to God.

I preached at Havre de Grace with Divine illumination and authority. Thence I went to ——; I was hardly welcome—perhaps I wrong him; I shall know when I call again. Called at Isaac and Solomon Hersey's, and found the Lord had not departed from these houses; I hope their children will all come to God.

Delaware – Pennsylvania

Wednesday, 30. At Wilmington I was warm in spirit. Thence I rode to Philadelphia; where I gave a short discourse on another man's appointment; my subject—Jacob's wrestling with God. On *Friday* night I spoke on "Who may abide the day of his coming?"

Sunday, *October* 4. We were not without the presence of the Lord at our love feast and sacrament this day. Brother Willis[85] spoke feelingly in the afternoon.

Monday, 5. We had a meeting of the principal members, in order to consult about the incorporation of our church.

New Jersey

Tuesday, 6. After twenty years' preaching, they have built a very beautiful meeting house at Burlington,[86] but it is low times there in religion. At

---

[85] See *Journal* entry for September 30, 1787.

[86] The first Methodist class meeting at Burlington was on December 14, 1770. The courthouse was used for preaching until it was torn down after the Revolutionary War and the court moved to Mount Holly. The people were then compelled to meet in the home of George Smith, a faithful member. About 1787 Major Joseph Bloomfield, later governor of New Jersey, inquired of James Sterling as to why there was no house of worship. Sterling replied, "We are too poor, we have no ground to build it on, and nothing to build it with." The Major generously gave a lot of ground, and Sterling and Smith secured the necessary money and materials. The church, 29 by 35 feet and two stories high, was considered quite commodious in that day. It was located on Library Street. It is recorded that no layman did more for New Jersey Methodism in the early

New Mills,[87] both preachers and people appeared to feel, and the watch night was attended with some breathings after God.

Thursday, 8. We had a poor, dry meeting, at Mount Holly: some were alarmed with fear, lest we should make a noise as we had done in Philadelphia; some dear country friends felt the Lord powerfully, and carried home the flame.

Friday, 9. I felt inward strength at Bethel, on Isa. lxiii, 12. The power was present, but there is not as much religion amongst them as formerly.

Saturday, 10. My ride to Bethel was thirty miles, and thirty miles more brought me to Deerfield;[88] I spoke very alarmingly, and to little purpose at the Methodistico-Presbyterian Church.

Sunday, 11. At the Glass-House[89] I felt myself, and the Lord made others feel—to purpose, I hope. Thence to Salem, at three o'clock: it was levelling work, storm and thunder, whilst I opened and applied Isaiah xxx, 20, 21.

Monday, 12. I returned to Philadelphia, where there were five criminals hanged; one of them professed conversion.

Tuesday, 13. Was the day of election for representatives; preaching in the evening was to little purpose, on, "Arm of the Lord, awake." "O Lord of life! when shall it be?"

Delaware

I preached at Wilmington, on the dedication of our new chapel:[90] thus far are we come after more than twenty years' labour in this place.

Thursday, 15. I preached at Dickinson's. Here we have a good house

days than did James Sterling. He was a prosperous merchant and often accompanied the preachers, rendering valuable assistance in establishing Methodism at other points. His daughter, Mrs. Rebecca Sterling Cowperthwaite, was the founder of the church school. (Pamphlet on 150th Anniversary of Broad Street Methodist Church, 1933; Heston, *op. cit.*, II, 646; Schermerhorn: *History of Burlington*, 195.)

[87] New Mills was the present Pemberton.

[88] Deerfield was the present Deerfield Street. Asbury preached in the Deerfield Stone Church, then used jointly by Presbyterians and Methodists. It was erected in 177- and is still in use by the Presbyterians. (Gordon's *Gazeteer of New Jersey*, 128; New Jersey Guide—Federal Writers Project, 655; New Jersey Annual Conference *Minutes*, 1954.)

[89] This was undoubtedly the famous glassmaking center which had been established by Casper Wistar in 1739 and which resulted in the establishment of a manufactory and village known as Wistarburg. Wistarburgh was located on Alloways Creek in Salem County. The New Jersey Guide states that "Caspar Wistar's glass factory was founded at Allowaystown," so that may be considered today the successor of the former Wistarburgh, and the Alloways Methodist Church the immediate descendant of Asbury's preaching. (Gordon's *Gazeteer of New Jersey*, 93; New Jersey Guide; Cunningham: *New Jersey: A History of Her Industries*, 17–23; Map of New Jersey, 1822.)

[90] Methodism in Wilmington, Delaware, introduced in 1767 by Captain Webb's open-air meetings, had advanced through temporary quarters in Joseph Gilpin's store house on King Street Wharf and the schoolroom of John Thelwell until 1789 when

ᴜilt; and a blessed foundation of living stones fixed on the chief corner-ᴊone. After preaching at Severson's and Duck Creek Cross Roads,[91] we ᴊame on *Saturday* to Dover quarterly meeting; here the congregation was ᴊrge and serious.

Sunday, 18. Preached on, "The Lord whom ye seek shall suddenly come ᴊ his temple." Ordained William Jessop and Jacob Brush elders. We ᴊave had encouraging intelligence of an opening in New England: we ᴊall send Jacob Brush to assist Jesse Lee, who has been some time visiting ᴊose parts.

Reached Judge White's in the evening, and rested there on *Monday.*

Tuesday, 20. Rode to Milford; where we had a great move and noble ᴊouting. I felt myself very unwell. We had a very comfortable love feast ᴊext morning. I was taken with a sore throat, and brother Whatcoat sup-ᴊied my lack of service. I was laid up four days; a violent headache and ᴊver attended the inflammation in my throat, with little or no perspira-ᴊon. I made use of flaxseed tea, and a very great expectoration followed.

Wednesday, 28. I came to Lowry's,[92] at the head of Nanticoke. I still ᴊel much pain, with a fever and hoarseness. I must take blame to myself ᴊr riding sometimes in the night and cold evenings without an upper coat: ᴊam growing old; and I live much in southern climes. I lodged at brother ᴊitchen's[93] who was ill with a bilious and nervous complaint.

Thursday, 29. Came to Wicomico, and was kindly entertained.

Virginia

Friday, 30. We rode in the rain—it was almost enough to kill healthy ᴊen. After steeping our feet in warm water, we came to brother Down-

ᴊected its first chapel. It was thirty-five feet square and stood near the southeast corner ᴊᵗ Walnut and Third streets on a lot conveyed to the trustees May 12, 1789. The ᴊᴊrnerstone was laid by Richard Whatcoat, who as late as June, 1793, in Baltimore ᴊnade up 50 dollars for the Wilmington Church." It was named for Bishop Asbury, ᴊho preached in Wilmington in 1772. (Lednum, *op. cit.*, 56–59; Scharf, *op. cit.*, I, 717, ᴊ8.)

[91] On May 13, 1783, James Severson conveyed to seven trustees the site upon which ᴊ1784 a chapel was erected one and one half miles from Rothwells Landing in Duck ᴊreek Hundred. It was dedicated on December 27, 1784. This 25 × 28 foot structure, ᴊeceded by one built of logs, is believed to have been the first frame meetinghouse ᴊiilt by Methodists in Kent County, Delaware. In Asbury's *Journal,* November 30, ᴊ'80, the name "Liverson" erroneously appears. Because of changing conditions the ᴊ urch fell into disuse about 1921 and was removed in 1940. (Scharf: *History of Dela-* ᴊᴊre, II, 1097, 1103; Hallman, *op. cit.*, 120, 257.)

[92] James Lowry lived at Lowry's Mills, Northwest Fork Hundred. For a day by day ᴊccount of Asbury's illness during the week before his arrival at Lowry's, see Sweet, ᴊeligion on the American Frontier, IV, 82, 83.

[93] Asbury first preached in the home of Spencer Hitchens January 20, 1780. He lived ᴊ Northwest Fork Hundred, Sussex County. (Scharf: *History of Delaware,* II, 1279; ᴊallman, *op. cit.*, 113.)

ing's. Next day we rode twenty-eight miles to Colonel Paramore's. My rest being interrupted, I rose early, and rode through the cold to the love feast,[94] where we had great shouting.

Although very weak in body, I rode thirty miles; a dish of tea, and a biscuit and a half, was all my food till six o'clock in the evening.[95]

Monday, November 2. I rode forty miles to Magotty Bay,[96] and preached to a few people. The Antinomians please them and gain them—alas! for us. O, that the Lord would send an earthquake of his power among them!

Tuesday, 3. We had an open time at brother Johannes Johnson's.[97] The school for the charity boys[98] much occupies my mind. Our annual expenditure will amount to two hundred pounds, and the aid we get is but trifling. The poverty of the people, and the general scarcity of money, is the great source of our difficulties. The support of our preachers, who have families, absorbs our collections, so that neither do our elders nor the charity school get much. We have the poor, but they have no money; and the worldly, wicked rich we do not choose to ask.

I have ridden about one hundred miles from Sunday morning till Tuesday night; at the same time very unwell with a cold and influenza, which spreads in almost every family.

Wednesday, 4. We had many people at Accomack (Accomac) court house, and power attended the word whilst brothers Joseph Everett and Richard Whatcoat spoke.

Thursday and *Friday, 5, 6.* We held quarterly meeting at William Downings. The first day the Lord was powerfully present, and the people were greatly agitated. On the second day at the love feast and sacrament there was a shout, and I believe two hundred souls praised God at one time. My soul was happy among them.

Maryland

Saturday, 7. At Annamessex quarterly meeting[99] the Lord was amongst the people on the first day. On *Sunday*, at the love feast, the young were greatly filled, and the power of the Most High spread throughout. I appeared as if they would have continued till night if they had not been

[94] (See Whatcoat's *Journal* for November 1.) Whatcoat says that they were at Garretson's Chapel where Joseph Everett administered the sacrament to three hundred people and Asbury ordained Christopher Spry and Conner Simpkins.

[95] See letter from Wesley, October 31, 1789.

[96] Magotty or Magothy Bay at the southern tip of Eastern Shore of Virginia, north of Smith's Island.

[97] Whatcoat's *Journal*, Sweet, *op. cit.*, 83.

[98] The reference is to Cokesbury College. (See *Journal* entry for December 16, 1791.)

[99] Whatcoat stated that the quarterly meeting was in Curtis Chapel near the Pocomoke River, Somerset County, and that on Friday, Asbury rode fifteen miles from Downings in Accomac County, Virginia, to Littleton Longs.

n some measure forced to stop that we might have public worship. I tood near the window, and spoke on Isaiah lxiv, 1–5. There was a stir, nd several sinners went away. There were very uncommon circumstances f a supernatural kind said to be observed at this meeting. The *saints of he world* are dreadfully displeased at their work; which, after all, is the est evidence that it is of God.

The preachers urged me to preach at Princess Anne. I did so, and many oor, afflicted people came out. I trust some will be able to say of Christ, He is altogether lovely!"

I felt uncommon power in preaching at Thomas Garrettson's.[100] Surely he Lord will work.

At the quarterly meeting I did not speak the first day. The second, I reached on Rom. x, 14, 15. There was a little stir; yet this is said to be the ullest, or one of the dullest places in the peninsula.

Thursday, 12, was a warm day, and we had a heavy ride to the Line hapel.[101] There were but few hearers, owing to the great affliction that revails. The influenza, and other complaints, carry off many people; nd it is an awful time.

Friday, 13. Came to Broad Creek chapel, where some of the wicked had roken the windows. There had been a stir at the quarterly meeting, and testimony borne against their revellings, and it was judged, that on this ccount the injury was committed on the house. My throat was sore, and ny testimony feeble on 2 Cor. vi. 1. I rode to the head of Nanticoke, here brother Whatcoat preached a warm sermon.

Saturday, 14. Preached at Brown's chapel: the general affliction hin- ered many from attending; but we were happy together, and it was a trengthening, confirming time to many tried souls.

Sunday, 15. The people were shouting the praise of God when I came. After the noise and fervour had subsided, I preached on the men of Nineveh's repenting at the preaching of Jonah; and the word sunk into ome hearts.

Monday, 16. We had a noble shout, and the people rejoiced in the Lord.[102]

Friday, 20. Being the day of our quarterly meeting fast, we strove to eep it as well as our feeble bodies would admit.

Saturday and *Sunday*, 21, 22. There was a shaking among the people: ome were alarmed; some professed to be justified, and others sanctified;

[100] Thomas Garrettson lived in or near Quantico. (Colbert's *Journal*, III, 123, July 5, 1800.)

[101] When soon after January, 1785, a church was erected on an acre lot through which assed the Delaware-Maryland boundary, the church, also called Vincent's Chapel, ecame known as Line Church. It is now on the Whitesville Charge. A new church uilt in 1874 was located in Gumboro Hundred, Delaware. (Scharf: *History of Dela- are* II, 1345; Hallman, *op. cit.*, 272.)

[102] See letter to Ezekiel Cooper, November 16, 1789.

whilst the wicked brought with them much of the power of Satan. I received some relief for my poor orphans. For some days past I have been kept in an humble, living, holy, conquering frame.

Monday, 23. Although the north-west wind blew very strong, we crossed Choptank River, and came to Bolingbroke. Here we had loud shouts and living testimonies from many of our oldest members, whilst some of our gay young Methodists were mute. Being a day of public thanksgiving, I rode to Wye,[103] where there is a good new chapel. The rain hindered, so that we had but few hearers. Came through the rain to Tuckahoe.

Friday, 27. There was a good move at Choptank Bridge. I ordained five persons to the office of deacons.

Saturday, 28. Preached with some freedom at Dover.

Sunday, 29. I preached at Duck Creek. Stopped, and gave them a discourse at Middletown;[104] and spent the evening with a worthy, kind friend. A number of dear old brethren accompanied me to Cokesbury, where we had an examination of the boys, and stationed eleven on charity. Thence we hastened on to Baltimore.

Thursday, December 3. Our council[105] was seated, consisting of the following persons, viz.: Richard Ivey, from Georgia; Reuben Ellis, South Carolina; Edward Morris, North Carolina; Philip Bruce, North district of Virginia; James O'Kelly, South district of Virginia; Lemuel Green, Ohio; Nelson Reed, Western Shore of Maryland; Joseph Everett, Eastern Shore; John Dickins, Pennsylvania; James O. Cromwell, New Jersey; and Freeborn Garrettson, New York. All our business was done in love and unanimity. The concerns of the college were well attended to, as also the printing business.[106] We formed some resolutions relative to economy and union, and others concerning the funds for the relief of our suffering preachers on the frontiers. We rose on the eve of Wednesday following. During our sitting we had preaching every night; some few souls were stirred up, and others converted. The *prudence* of some had stilled the noisy ardour of our young people; and it was difficult to re kindle the fire. I collected about twenty-eight pounds for the poor suffer ing preachers in the West. We spent one day in speaking our own experi ences, and giving an account of the progress and state of the work o

[103] Wye Chapel stands on ground deeded by William Hindman to the Methodists i Wye Mills, Queen Annes County, September 15, 1795, for five shillings. The claim tha the first sermon was preached in the new chapel by Ezekiel Cooper on December 13 1789, was made without knowledge that Asbury had preceded him by about thre weeks. (Phoebus, *op. cit.*, 110, 111; Hallman, *op. cit.*, 329.)

[104] Asbury often traveled the old Kings Road which passed through Middletowr New Castle County. The present Bethesda Church is the offspring of the earliest societ in that community. (Scharf: *History of Delaware*, II, 998.)

[105] See letter of November 16, 1789.

[106] See preface to the second volume of *The Arminian Magazine*, Philadelphia December 8, 1789, and also the preface to the *Discipline*, 1790.

God in our several districts; a spirit of union pervades the whole body, producing blessed effects and fruits.

Thursday, 10. This and the two following days were spent in writing, and other necessary business. I also preached at town and Point.

Sunday, 13. I delivered some alarming truths at our meeting house with some life. I preached at the German church in the afternoon; and in the evening I spoke on, "The men of Nineveh shall rise up in judgment against the men of this generation, and condemn it," &c.

Monday, 14. To my comfort I found one of Thomas Cromwell's children under deep distress. When I formerly frequented the house she was a child.

Came on to Annapolis, and found the work rather dead.

Tuesday, 15. I preached with more liberty than the evening before.

Wednesday, 16. Set out for Herring Bay. It rained, and our ride was heavy. I lodged with William Weems,[107] once a great zealot for the Old Church.

Thursday, 17. We rode to Gabriel Childs's—it was an awfully stormy, rainy day, and we had no meeting. The Lord has made bare his arm since my last visit here, and souls have been converted and sanctified.

Friday, 18. Rode to Gray's. Here also the Lord hath wrought powerfully amongst the children.

Virginia

Saturday, 19. Rode through Charles county, Maryland, to Hooe's ferry. Death! death! We had prayer at our lodgings. Mr. Hooe treated us very kindly.

Sabbath morning, 20. I read part of the thirty-third chapter of Ezekiel's prophecy, and gave an exhortation. We then rode twenty-five miles through the snow to Pope's, where I spoke with some liberty. We found ourselves not at home, so we went to our friend Richard Sanford's.[108] My spirit has been wounded not a little. I know not which to pity most— the slaves or their masters. Thence we went on to the widow Hutt's. I am ill, and have little to do, which makes me worse.

On Christmas eve I made a visit to counsellor Carter;[109] a very social

[107] Captain William Weems was born near Herring Creek, Anne Arundel County. Among his nineteen brothers and sisters were David, who became an ardent Methodist, and Mason Locke Weems. The latter, who was known as "Parson Weems" whose account of truthful young George Washington, his hatchet and the cherry tree, is still remembered, had just been installed rector of All Hallows Parish when Asbury met him at the home of David Weems. (Kellock: *Parson Weems of the Cherry Tree*, 38–51; *Journal* entry for November 30, 1784.)

[108] See Whatcoat's *Journal*; Sweet: *Religion on the American Frontier*, IV, 87.

[109] See Whatcoat's *Journal* for December 24. He says the party rode to "Nomeny Hall" and spent the afternoon with Colonel Robert Carter, Mr. Dawson, a Baptist

gentleman, a Baptist. After preaching we had fifteen miles to ride to sister Woolard's; and twenty miles the next morning to Lancaster quarterly meeting.[110]

Sunday, 27. Feeling myself unwell, brother Whatcoat preached; and our public and society meeting occupied six hours and a half. Notwithstanding the rain, we had many to hear, both white and black. I was very sensible that the work of grace was deepened in the souls of the people: several spoke of the pure love of God.[111]

Monday, 28. I felt much enlarged in spirit. It seemed to me as if the Lord was only beginning to work; but the Antinomians oppose. Nevertheless, I have growing hopes that the glory of Zion will shortly appear.[112]

Tuesday, 29. After waiting at the ferry about four hours, we made an attempt to cross in an old boat, with tattered sails, which gave way near the middle of the river: through mercy we got safe over. Thence directing our course to Turks Ferry,[113] a poor old Negro made out to get us across in a little flat: about eight o'clock we arrived safely at sister Davis's,[114] where we found three of the preachers waiting for us, preaching having been appointed for the morrow. We had the presence of God with us in the meeting,[115] and at the sacrament.

Thursday, 31. We had a few attentive people at brother Bellamy's.[116] O Gloucester! Gloucester! when will it be famous for religion? Finding my appointments not made, we crossed York River, and came once more to my dear old friend Weldon's. I was much indisposed.

preacher, and Dr. Hearington, with religious services in the evening. Asbury was in Westmoreland County.

[110] Whatcoat says this quarterly meeting was held in a former Presbyterian church and that they slept at the home of John Diggs. (Sweet, *op. cit.*, 88.)

[111] The preachers dined this day with Captain Diggs and spent the evening with Colonel Gordon.

[112] Whatcoat says that on this day Asbury preached at Mary Tapscott's, that he and Brother Bruce exhorted to a full house, and they all then rode to Widow Ball's. (Sweet *op. cit.*, 88.)

[113] Turk's ferry was over Piankatank River. Cheesecake was on Gloucester County side.

[114] (Sweet, *op. cit.*, 88.) Scott says in his *Journal* that he stayed at Sister Davis's. Asbury stayed there November 17, 1795.

[115] This was in Cheesecake. The church was the forerunner of Salem Church. (Sweet *op. cit.*, 88.)

[116] Dr. Walter Reed, who contributed so greatly to the eradication of yellow fever, was born in Bellamy's parsonage in Gloucester County, September 13, 1851, the son of the Rev. Lemuel S. Reed and Mary Catherine Boyd Reed. William Bellamy became an itinerant in 1792 and located in 1796. A thriving church is there today named Bellamy's.

1790

1790

Asbury traveling with an armed party to the Kentucky Conference

CHAPTER NINETEEN

Virginia

January 1, 1790. No appointment for preaching. We are bound to the south, and shall proceed on as fast as we can.

Saturday, 2. We were refreshed in the evening. Next day (*Sabbath*) I preached at Chickahominy[1] church once more: sinners, Pharisees, backsliders, hypocrites, and believers, were faithfully warned; and of all these characters there were, doubtless, a goodly number in the large congregation which attended. Brother Philip Bruce went to Brown's, and brother Whatcoat and myself to Weldon's; at both these places the Lord was powerfully present in our meetings.

Monday, 4. We crossed James River,[2] with a fresh wind ahead, and only two poor blacks, where four ferrymen are necessary. Two brigs under sail came down full upon us, and we had hard work to get out of their way. These large ferries are dangerous and expensive: our ferriages alone have cost us £3 since we left Annapolis.

Tuesday, 5. Rested, and next day preached at brother Mooring's. I felt some power among the people; but the glory is measurably departed; the imprudent haste of the young people to marry unbelievers, and divisions excited by other causes, have done much injury.

[1] Chickahominy Church was an Established Church two miles south of the present Toano, Virginia. It was the successor of the Wilmington Lower Church which had been on the same site, and was built about 1750. (Mason: *Colonial Churches of Tidewater, Virginia.*)

[2] Whatcoat says they crossed at Swan Point ferry and narrowly escaped being run down by two brigs. (Sweet, *op. cit.*, 89.) They went through Surry and Sussex Counties.

Thursday, 7. Was an ameliorating time at Ellis's church. The next da
at Lane's, I had many people, although it rained; I felt comfortable i
speaking to them.

Saturday, 9. Was a cold time in a cold house at brother Moss's. I fe
unwell, and much dejected at the situation of the people, whom I foun
divided about the merits of a certain character, once a preacher among th
Methodists, but now disowned, and striving to make a party; this mar
and the disputes for and against slavery, have been hurtful.

Sunday, 10. Came to Jones's church, and was much lifted up in spiri
Monday, 11. I had many to hear at Mabry's.

Tuesday, 12. From Mabry's we came to Brunswick quarterly meetin;
where there was a considerable quickening, and manifestation of th
Lord's power. We had a good meeting at Roanoke chapel;[3] I rejoiced tha
the society had increased to more than a hundred souls.

I received a letter from the presiding elder of this district, Jame
O'Kelly;[4] he makes heavy complaints of my power, and bids me stop fo
one year, or he must use his influence against me. Power! power! there i
not a vote given in a conference in which the presiding elder has no
greatly the advantage of me; all the influence I am to gain over a compan
of young men in a district must be done in three weeks; the greater par
of them, perhaps, are seen by me only at conference, whilst the presidin
elder has had them with him all the year, and has the greatest opportunit
of gaining influence; this advantage may be abused; let the bishops loo
to it: but who has the power to lay an embargo on me, and to make c
none effect the decision of all the conferences of the union?

North Carolina

Friday, 15. Crossed Roanoke, and was met by several preachers at siste
Pegram's, where the Lord was with us.[5]

[3] Roanoke Chapel was on the Greensville Circuit and was formerly an Establishe
Church in St. Andrews Parish, Brunswick. Whatcoat says they had services at Woo
sey's and Drumgoole's and slept at William Owen's in Mecklenburg County on th
way to Roanoke Chapel. (*Ibid.*)

[4] See letter to O'Kelly, January 12, 1790, and excerpts from Deveraux Jarratt t
John Coleman.

[5] Whatcoat, who accompanied Asbury, says they reached the Roanoke on January 1
and slept at Stephen Shels in Warren County, North Carolina. Asbury preached, an
the exhorter was Philip Bruce, a North Carolinian who was presiding elder of the nort
district in Virginia. Bruce was of Huguenot descent and a zealous patriot who wa
present "as a sort of chaplain" at the battle of King's Mountain near his birthplac
On the fifteenth they rode to "Widow Pegram's," where Bruce exhorted and the sacra
ment was administered. They slept that night at John Falcon's in Warren County
Whatcoat's spelling is very uncertain. (*Journal of Bishop Richard Whatcoat*, printed b
Sweet in *Religion on the American Frontier, The Methodists*, 90.)

Saturday, 16. I had a long ride to Roger Jones's:[6] we had a good season at the sacrament; several spoke powerfully of the justifying and sanctifying grace of God. A hundred souls have been brought to God: thus the barren wilderness begins to smile. I found it a time to speak from Isaiah li, 1.

We had to ride sixteen miles; and here, O what my spirit felt! It is a day of very small and feeble things, and but little union among the people. I found it needful to enforce that prayer: "O Lord, revive thy work!" One poor black fell to the ground and praised God.

Tuesday, 19. I had some freedom in preaching at Bruce's; but I fear there is too much vanity and Antinomian leaven amongst them to permit much good to be done.

Rode to Thomas Tomlinson's; but here they made no appointment. At Merritt's chapel, on New Hope Creek, Chatham county, I enforced, "How shall I give thee up, Ephraim?"—there was some feeling among them; but they are not a united people.[7]

Thursday, 21. I rode to the widow Sarah Snipe's,[8] twenty miles, and preached on Isaiah xlv, 22; then crossed Haw River, and came to M——'s, about two hours in the night, where I found a congregation waiting, to whom I spoke on, "I am not ashamed of the Gospel of Christ," &c.; the people were tender.

Friday, 22. Came to William Rainey's,[9] in Orange county, to a quarterly meeting, where seven of our preachers met together: the first day the people were dull; the second, our congregation was large; my subject was, "We will give ourselves to prayer and the ministry of the word." I ordained Thomas Anderson[10] to the office of an elder. We rode through a heavy rain sixteen miles to our friend Gerald Burr's;[11] here they have built us a complete house of the heart of oak. Proceeded twelve miles to Rocky River, and preached at William M'Master's chapel;[12] afterward we had a

[6] *Ibid.*

[7] On the seventeenth the party rode to Pope's Chapel, where Asbury preached. Whatcoat and Bruce rode with James Lester. On the eighteenth they proceeded to Bruce's, where Asbury preached, and on the nineteenth they went on to the home of Thomas Tomlinson on the Neuse River in Wake County. On the following day Reuben Ellis, a North Carolinian and notable figure in early Methodism, then presiding elder of the South Carolina district, was with the party. They went on to the home of William O'Kelly, presiding elder of the North Carolina district. Merritt's Chapel or New Hope Chapel was in Chatham County. The New Hope Circuit was formed in 1778 and appeared in the *Minutes* in 1779. It included parts of Orange, Chatham, Cumberland, and Wake counties, and took its name from a creek that flowed into Haw River in Chatham County. (*Ibid.*, 91; Grissom, *op. cit.*, 64, 67.)

[8] Whatcoat, *op. cit.*, 91.

[9] *Ibid.*

[10] Thomas Anderson was serving the New Hope Circuit. (See *Minutes.*)

[11] Gerald Burr (or Burrough) lived in Chatham County. (Whatcoat, *op. cit.*, 91.)

[12] The chapel named for William McMasters was in the same county. (*Ibid.*)

night meeting and upon the whole I believe we were speaking about fou hours, besides nearly two spent in prayer. We came to our frien Key's,[13] and were kindly entertained. Thence we went to Mr. Willian Bell's,[14] on Deep River, and were received in the kindest manner; before left the house, I felt persuaded that that family would come to experienc the power of religion.

Tuesday, 26. We had to make our way through a dreary path, and rod about fifty miles; we were favoured by only getting a sprinkling of rain which became very heavy after we were housed at Thomas Chiels's,[*] about eleven o'clock. Rode to Doctor Miles King's,[16] twenty-five miles and performed the funeral rites of Captain Clark,[17] who was sick when was here last year. I then prayed for him, and felt as if his sickness wa unto death: now, I preached his funeral sermon; my text was, "It i appointed unto men once to die," &c. I felt some enlargement in speaking and a few people appeared to be moved.

I have read an account of the wonderful revolution in France; may th good of Protestantism and the glory of God be advanced by it!

Since we crossed Roanoke River, we have passed through Warren Granville, Wake, Chatham, Orange, Randolph, and Richmond counties in North Carolina.

After passing Hedge Cock creek, I preached at Night's chapel, on "My grace is sufficient for thee:" there was some quickening, and I wa blest. It is no small exercise to ride twenty miles, or more, as we frequentl

[13] James H. Keys lived at Hillsboro in Orange County. He later moved to Murfrees boro, Rutherford County, Tennessee, where Asbury stayed with him on February 12 1807. From both places he carried on correspondence with Edward Dromgoole, whose papers are in the library of the University of North Carolina and have been publishe in part by Sweet. Dromgoole (1751–1835) was from Sligo, Ireland, a Roman Catholic who publicly recanted after hearing the Methodists. He came to America in 1770 an settled near Baltimore, and became a preacher under the influence of Robert Straw bridge. He was a conspicuous figure in the Christmas Conference. In 1777 he marrie Rebecca Walton of Brunswick County, Virginia. He located in 1786; Asbury remarke that "Edward Dromgoole is a good preacher, but entangled with a family." He was unti his death a local preacher in Brunswick County, where he entertained Asbury and othe Methodist leaders on numerous occasions. The church at his home came to be know as Dromgoole's Chapel, later united with Olive Branch. (Sweet, *op. cit.,* 159.)

[14] William Bell lived on Deep River in Randolph County above Randleman. He wa the stepfather of John and William McGee, leaders of the great Kentucky revival an founders of the camp meeting movement. (Whatcoat, *op. cit.,* 91.) His wife was th Revolutionary heroine Martha Bell, who won local renown by capturing a desperad called Steve Lewis. This exploit is described by Caruthers in *The Old North State in 1776* (Sidney Swaim Robins, "Bishop Asbury on Deep River," in *Chapel Hill News Leader* July 4, 1955.)

[15] *Ibid.,* 92.

[16] Miles King lived in Montgomery County. The party reached his home on th twenty-eighth. (*Ibid.*)

[17] The man whose funeral was preached by Asbury was designated as Crark, perhap Clark, in Whatcoat's untrustworthy spelling. (*Ibid.*)

o, before twelve o'clock; taking all kinds of food, and lodging, and veather too, as it comes, whether it be good or bad.

I saw the hand of the Lord in preserving my life and limbs when my orse made an uncommon start and sprung some yards with me; it was ith difficulty I kept the saddle.[18]

South Carolina

We had a severe day's ride; and called at the Beauty Spot:[19] the beauty ere has somewhat faded; the society is disjointed, and in a poor state. Ve made it a fifty miles' ride, or thereabouts, to Pryor's.[20]

Sunday, 31. There were some signs of remaining life seen under preach-ng, and a little spirit and feeling in the love feast. I felt great enlargement n, "How shall I give thee up, Ephraim?" &c. I found it heavy work.

Monday, February 1. Brother Whatcoat preached at the Grove;[21] ohn Ellis and myself spoke after him, and there were gracious signs of enderness among the people. An elderly Baptist preacher attended, whose eart the Lord touched, and he acknowledged the power of the Most High o be present. We lodged at old friend Jones's,[22] having ridden twenty-ive miles; we were weary and hungry, having breakfasted on tea at eight 'clock, and taken nothing more till six o'clock at night. Lord, help me o bear all things without murmuring or disputing!

At Flower's[23] there was a living stir: one soul found peace; and I had reedom in preaching.

After riding fifteen miles to Sweet's meeting house,[24] on a cold day, we ad about a dozen people: of these few, some were drunk, and began to augh and trifle round the house. After three exhortations and prayers, we ame to Port's ferry, and had to cross in the night, and wade the low laces.

[18] According to Whatcoat they entered South Carolina on the twenty-ninth and were ntertained by Jacob Abit, or Abbott. (*Ibid.*)

[19] On this sixth trip through South Carolina, Asbury followed the same route taken 1 1789 as far as Augusta, Georgia, though he passed through the western section of he state over a new route after leaving Georgia. (See the notes for February 4–March 2, 789.)

[20] Pryor's has not been identified. It is also mentioned by Whatcoat. It may have een Bryan's on Catfish Creek, near Latta, South Carolina. John Ellis of the Anson Circuit and Thomas Humphries of the Little Pee Dee accompanied Asbury and Vhatcoat as exhorters, and they sometimes preached. (Whatcoat's *Journal, op. cit.*, 92.)

[21] The Grove has not been identified. There are Pine Grove and Oak Grove churches n Marlboro County.

[22] Frederick Jones lived in Prince George's parish, in which the present Marion County was included. He "was born in 1709 and his wife is 77." (Whatcoat, *op. cit.*, 2.)

[23] Flowers was one mile north of Marion on General William Evans' place.

[24] Sweet's meetinghouse was fifteen miles south of Marion. It became Bare Pond Church and is now Soule's Chapel. (See note under March 11, 1787.)

Came to sister ——, and had a comfortable table spread before us which, to us, who had ridden thirty miles through heavy rain, without eating or drinking, was almost necessary. I think our kind hostess has several of the marks St. Paul gives of a widow *indeed.*[25]

I have lately read Thomson's Seasons, containing upwards of two hundred pages. I find a little wheat and a great deal of chaff: I have read great authors, so called, and wondered where they found their finery of words and phrases; much of this might be pilfered from the "Seasons," without injury to the real merit of the work; and doubtless it has been plucked by literary robbers; and my wonder may cease.

My own soul has peace; but I feel a death amongst the people. I hope the Lord will come and visit them in power; if they do not turn to God, expect they will be cut off, and that soon.

Saturday, 6. Rode to Georgetown;[26] and on the Sabbath, brother Whatcoat preached on, "In all places where I record my name, I will come in to thee, and I will bless thee."[27]

Monday, 8. I gave them a close and serious address on rightly dividing the word of truth.

Tuesday, 9. Came to Wappetaw,[28] and preached on 1 John iv, 16, 17.

Wednesday, 10. Came to Charleston.[29] Here I received good news from Baltimore and New York: about two hundred souls have been brought to God within a few weeks. I have been closely occupied in writing to Europe and to different parts of this continent. We feel a little quickening here: brother Whatcoat preaches every night.

Saturday, 13. The preachers are coming into the conference. I have felt fresh springs of desire in my soul for a revival of religion. O may the work be general! It is a happy thing to be united as is our society. The happy

[25] Whatcoat says Asbury preached and Ellis preached and exhorted on the second presumably at the Frederick Jones home; they rode to Valentine Rowell's church on Catfish, nine miles below Marion, on the third, where there were about eleven people; "we were very wet but rode to the Widow Port's in safety, though one of the horses getting his hind feet over the side of the boat made it dangerous for the others. On the fourth Asbury preached at Britain's Neck. Whatcoat says they "returned, perhaps to the Widow Port's. He says that "William Balson died soon after we left the house," and Asbury preached his funeral on the fifth. On the fifth also Asbury administered the sacrament and exhorted the black people on Great Pee Dee. (Whatcoat *op. cit.,* 93.) Sister —— across Port's Ferry may have been Mrs. Kimbrough.

[26] Asbury presumably went to Georgetown by the usual route of Port's Ferry, Lynch's River, and Black Mingo. The party spent the night at William Wayne's. (*Ibid.*)

[27] On this Sunday, Asbury preached in the afternoon, and Whatcoat preached in the evening, after which they drank tea at the home of Miss Judy Raggs. (*Ibid.*)

[28] Wappetaw was near the Capers' home at Cainhoy. They visited George S. Capers there. (*Ibid.*)

[29] They slept at John Huse's. During the period spent in Charleston they also took meals with Mrs. Patton, Brothers Cook and Seaver, Captain Doral, Brother Welsh, Mrs. Wright, Mr. McGowin, and Jonathan Crook "on the warf (Amen Street or Rag Alley)" according to Whatcoat's peculiar spelling. (*Ibid.,* 93, 94.)

ews of the revival of the work of God flies from one part of the continent
o the other, and all partake of the joy.

Sunday, 14. I preached twice.[30] Next day (Monday) our conference
egan. Our business was conducted in great peace and love. The business
f the council came before us[31]; and it was determined that the concerns
f the college, and the printing, should be left with the council to act
ecisively upon; but that no new canons should be made, nor the old
ltered, without the consent of the conference; and that whatever was
one on this head, should come in the shape of advice only. We had some
uickening seasons, and living meetings. Several young people come under
wakenings.

Wednesday, 17. I preached on, "If thou take forth the precious from
he vile, thou shalt be as my mouth." It was a searching season: several
poke and prayed; and we had noise enough. The evening before an ex-
ract of sundry letters from New York and Baltimore was read in the
ongregation, at which saints and sinners were affected. But we have not
sufficient breastwork. Our friends are too mute and fearful, and many
f the *outdoors* people are violent and wicked. I have had a busy, trying
ime for about nine days past; and I have hopes that some hundreds
n the city will be converted by this time next year. Our conference
esolved on establishing Sunday schools for poor children, white and
lack.[32]

Friday, 19. We rode to Edisto. At Gueham's[33] I preached on the "Great
alvation." There appeared to be attention, and some were affected.

Saturday, 20. Was a dry time at Linder's.[34] Brother Whatcoat preached.
was very unwell with a headache.

[30] See letter to parents, February 14, 1790.

[31] The newly organized controversial and short-lived council was discussed at this
onference, and it was agreed that the powers of the body should be supervisory only.
Betts, *op. cit.*, 63.)

[32] The following action was taken: "Q.: What can be done in order to instruct poor
hildren, white and black to read? A.: Let us labor, as the heart and soul of one man to
stablish Sunday Schools in or near the places of worship. Let persons be appointed by
ie Bishops, elders, deacons and preachers to teach (gratis) all that will attend and have
capacity to learn, from 6 o'clock in the morning until 10; and from 2 o'clock in the
fternoon till 6; where it does not interfere with public worship. The Council shall
ompile a proper school book to teach them learning and piety." (Betts, *op. cit.*, 63.)
esse Lee says that Sunday schools were now established in several places, most of
iose attending being black children. The parents were backward about sending them,
nd only a few attended regularly, and the teachers soon became discouraged and gave
p the work. (Lee: *History of the Methodists*, 161.)

[33] This was probably Givhans, since the party went that way to Augusta. Whatcoat
ays they rode through Dorchester to Philip *Gibham's*, where Asbury preached to a
w people. (Whatcoat, *op. cit.*, 94.) They probably proceeded through Orangeburg
'ounty and the present towns of Springfield and Williston to Beech Island.

[34] This was Jacob Linder, according to Whatcoat. (*Ibid.*) He probably lived near
;reen Pond Church on the Edisto.

Sunday, 21. We had a better season at Cattle Creek,[35] on Mal. iii,
May God arise to help these people, and revive and work mightily for an
amongst them!

Monday, 22. We had a heavy ride to Burton's.[36] It was still more s
when we came to preaching. Poor souls! the Antinomian leaven bring
forth death here. Some appeared hardened; others, nevertheless, appeare
a little melted. May God help these people! I was unwell—could eat bu
little. I was not at home. I felt as if God had departed from this house
and was miserable until I left it.

Tuesday, 23. We rode to Rigdall's.[37] Here we found people of anothe
spirit. We had a large congregation—but very blind, deaf, and dumb. (
Lord! can these dry bones live? I spoke very close, but to litttle purpose
May the Lord help, and stand by the poor preachers who labour on thi
side Edisto!

Wednesday, 24. At Chester's, and next day at David Pucket's[38] ther
was a small stir. Some here have been awakened; but they lean to Calvir
ism, and the love of strong drink carries almost all away. My spirit wa
bowed down amongst them. I spoke a little, and so did brother Whatcoa
We appointed a night meeting. There came only two men, and they wer
drunk.

Friday, 26. There came about a dozen people to hear us at Treadwell's,
to whom brother Whatcoat preached on the "works of the flesh," and th
"fruits of the Spirit."

After riding thirty miles through heavy sands, we came to Docto
Fuller's.[40] I am strongly inclined to think I am done with this road an
people. They pass for Christians—a prophet of strong drink might su
them. I was clear in not receiving anything without paying for it.

Saturday, 27. Rode to Campbelltown, and stopped at brother Willia
Guyin's.[41] Since Friday, the 19th, we have ridden about one hundred an
sixty miles.

I have been under various trials and exercises, and have some dejecte
hours. This also shall tend to my humiliation, and work for my good.

Sunday, 28. I preached on 1 Tim. i, 15. I had a very still and unfeelin

[35] Cattle Creek Church was in Orangeburg County. Whatcoat refers to it as Kett
Creek Church, remarking that Satan's bulwarks were very strong there and that the
slept at Brother Berry's. (*Ibid.*)

[36] George Burton. (*Ibid.*)

[37] Whatcoat said they rode to Jones' Church and rested at John Rigdall's in Orang
burg County. (*Ibid.*)

[38] It was tax gathering day, and Asbury preached to three people, two of whom wer
drunk. (*Ibid.*)

[39] There were thirteen people at Treadwell's, Tredwys according to Whatcoat
spelling. (*Ibid.*) He lived just west of Cedar Creek in Aiken County.

[40] Fuller lived at Blueberry Hill. (*Ibid.*)

[41] William Guyin (Whatcoat's spelling) lived at Campbelltown, the present Nort
Augusta. His name was probably Guyton.

congregation. The inhabitants of this little town (Campbelltown) seem to be sober and industrious; but even here I found some drunkards.

Georgia

Monday, March 1. We crossed at Augusta, in Georgia, and rode to Sandy Creek church. I had some enlargement on Luke iv, 18, 19. Thence we proceeded to Briar Creek.[42]

Tuesday, 2. I preached in an old church, near Waynesborough; at Thomas Wyche's,[43] in the evening; and next day at Golphin's, Old Town.[44] The house was open, and the day cold.

Thursday, 4. I preached with liberty in a new church, near Fenn's bridge.[45] We have been exercised in public night and day; frequently we have not more than six hours' sleep; our horses are weary, and the houses are so crowded, that at night our rest is much disturbed. Jesus is not always in our dwellings; and where he is not, a pole cabin is not very agreeable. Provisions for man and horse we have plenty of. Our journeys are about thirty miles, day by day; but under all these trails I enjoy peace and patience, and have much of the love of God.

Sunday, 7. We had a crowded congregation at Harvey's.[46] Brother Whatcoat attempted to preach, but soon concluded. We lodged with brother Scott, above the forks of Ogeeche.[47] My mind has been much tried under so much bodily fatigue.

I went to view four hundred acres of land, and found it not suitably situated for a seminary of learning.[48] Came to Star's; a cold place, and cold congregation there.

[42] The Sandy Creek Church was the first in Richmond County. Its exact location is not known. The church at Briar Creek was on a bluff near the great Briar Creek Swamp, and was probably the first in Burke County. It was later turned over to the Negroes. (Smith: *Georgia Methodism,* 41.) Whatcoat says they rode to old Sandy Run Church on March 2.

[43] See Whatcoat's *Journal.*

[44] The old church near Waynesboro was St. George's Episcopal Church, the first in Burke County. It was abandoned after the Revolution and later came into the possession of the Methodists. It still stands six miles south of Waynesboro. "Golphin's" was the post of the Indian trader George Galphin, near Louisville. (Smith: *Georgia Methodism,* 41.)

[45] Fenn's Bridge was on the Ogeechee River in Jefferson County. (Smith: *Georgia Methodism,* 41.)

[46] See Whatcoat's *Journal.*

[47] The Mr. Harvey lived in Warren County. Bishop Richard Whatcoat traveled with Asbury on this southern tour. (Phoebus: *Memoirs of the Rev. Richard Whatcoat,* 26.) Joseph Scott lived on Little River.

[48] The bishop was looking for land on which to locate the Wesley and Whitefield School which had been projected at the previous conference. No suitable location was found, and the school was never built. In August, 1790, the Academy of Commissioners of Wilkes County appointed Florence Sullivan and James Williams as a com-

Wednesday, 10. Our conference began at Grant's. We had preachin, every day, and there were some quickenings amongst the people. Ou business was conducted in peace and unanimity. The deficiencies of th preachers, who receive a salary of sixty-four dollars per annum from thi conference, amounted to seventy-four pounds for the last year.

Thursday, 11. We had a rainy day, yet a full house, and a living lov feast. Some souls were converted, and others professed sanctification. had some opening in speaking from Ezek. ii, 7. We have a prospec of obtaining a hundred acres of land for every one hundred pounds w can raise and pay, for the support of Wesley and Whitefield school. O *Monday* we rode out to view three hundred acres of land offered for th above purpose. My soul has been much tried since conference began. must strive to keep from rising too high, or sinking too low.

Tuesday, 16. We set out on our journey, and came to the new chapel a Bibb's Cross Roads.⁴⁹ I preached with some life and liberty, and ordaine brother Bennet Maxey⁵⁰ to the office of deacon. I spent the evening a brother Isaac Herbert's, where lie interred the remains of dear brothe Major. I was told that a poor sinner was struck with conviction at hi grave, and thought he heard the voice of God calling him to repentance I was also told of a woman who sent for brother Andrew⁵¹ to preach he funeral sermon while living. She was blest under the word, and died i peace.

South Carolina

Wednesday, 17. We were kindly entertained at Patrick Calhoun's;⁵

mittee to "write to Bishop Asbury." The contents of the communication are not known but the commissioners probably urged the bishop to establish the school. (Smith *Georgia Methodism,* 41; *Asbury,* 125; Bowen: *Wilkes County,* 121.)

⁴⁹ The exact location of the chapel at Bibb's Cross Road is not definitely known but it was in Wilkes County. There were cross roads at Sandtown Danburg, and Delhi and one of these may have been known as Bibb's. (Bowen: *Wilkes County,* 122.) The Bibb family came from Virginia. Dr. William Wyatt Bibb located near the old town o Petersburg in the forks of the Savannah and Broad Rivers, later moving to Wilke County, "a mile or two from Broad River, and a few miles from the residence of Col Taliaferro." He was a member of the House of Representatives in 1806, a Senator and later was governor of Alabama. His brother Thomas was also governor of Alabama (Gilmer: *First Settlers of Upper Georgia,* 85–87.)

⁵⁰ Bennet Maxey, who was ordained deacon, had served the Burke Circuit with Hope Hull and was appointed to the Richmond Circuit with John Holliday.

⁵¹ John Andrew, father of Bishop James O. Andrew, was on the Cherokee Circui with Philip Matthews and was appointed to the Burke Circuit with Wheeler Grissom John Andrew was the first native Georgian admitted as traveling preacher. (Smith *Asbury,* 125; *Georgia Methodism,* 41.)

⁵² Patrick Calhoun was the father of Hon. John C. Calhoun, who was eight years old when Asbury and Whatcoat were there. He lived ten miles south of Abbeville court- house near the present Wilmington and on Long Cone Creek and worshiped at the Lower Cane Creek Presbyterian Church. (Whatcoat, *op. cit.,* 96.) After his two weeks

and next day, after riding twenty-two miles to Porter's,[53] we had an evening meeting, and were happy with a few living souls. The Presbyerians are very kind, giving us freely whatever is needful for man and horse. I have great consolations, and severe trials.

Friday, 19. We had some stir, especially amongst the young people, at he widow Bowman's, on Reedy River.[54]

Saturday, 20. Rode to Moore's;[55] and finding brother Ellis was to be at C——'s,[56] we hasted to see him, and rode twenty miles, crossing Enoree River, near the *slaughter ground*, where a battle was fought in the last war.

Sunday, 21. Preached to a quiet people, and had a small stir. We had a meeting in the evening at Brother Smith's.

Monday, 22. I feel myself unwell with a sick and nervous headache, which returns once a month, and sometimes oftener. We have travelled about six hundred miles in about three weeks, besides the time taken up in conference. Thou, Lord, wilt have mercy, and save both man and beast! I expect Providence brought us this way, to pity and to help the people. Dear brother and sister Smith[57] are unspeakably kind.

North Carolina

Friday, 26. Rode about twenty-two miles. Stopped at Col. William Graham's,[58] dripping wet with rain. He received us, poor strangers, with great kindness, and treated us hospitably. We had awful thunder, wind, and rain. I was still unwell with a complaint that terminated the life of my grandfather Asbury, whose name I bear; perhaps it will also be my end. We were weather-bound until *Monday* morning, the 29th of March. For several days I have been very sick and serious. I have been enabled to look

in Georgia, Asbury was returning northward, probably via Abbeville and Laurens counties to Musgrove Mill, crossing the Broad and Savannah rivers at the old town of Petersburg.

[53] Hugh Porter. (*Ibid.*, 97.) According to Whatcoat they visited John Hambleton at Abbeville courthouse, who fed their horses free. They also went by Gabriel Smathers'.

[54] The Widow Bowman on Reedy River lived in Laurens County, probably near Cross Hill.

[55] Whatcoat, *op. cit.*, 97.

[56] Whatcoat says that Sister Foster piloted them to Kersey's. (*Ibid.*) He may have meant Casey's. They crossed the Enoree at the historic Musgrove's Mill, which was only a few miles from Cross Keys.

[57] Whatcoat says that he and Asbury reached Broad River near Smith's Ferry on March 24. They crossed the river in a canoe, swimming their horses. Whatcoat preached that night at Josiah Smith's, where they remained through the twenty-fifth. (*Ibid.*) Smith lived on Broad River just below Cherokee Falls.

[58] Josiah Smith rode with them sixteen or eighteen miles. In a storm they reached Colonel William Graham's on Little Broad River and remained there until the twenty-ninth, when they rode to George Moore's. (*Ibid.*) He was a Revolutionary soldier and a leading citizen of Rutherford County. (Griffin: *Essays on North Carolina History.*)

into eternity with some pleasure. I could give up the church, the college and schools; nevertheless, there was one drawback—What will my enemies and mistaken friends say? Why, that he hath offended the Lord and he hath taken him away. In the afternoon I felt somewhat better Brother Whatcoat preached a most excellent sermon on, "The kingdom of God is not in word but in power"—not in sentiments or forms, but in the convincing, converting, regenerating, sanctifying power of God. I am making close application to my Bible. Reading the Prophets at my leisure whilst on my journey, I met with a pious Baptist. Glory to God for what religion there is still to be found amongst all sects and denominations of people!

Wednesday, 31. Rode to Gilbert Town, and preached at Holland's[59] with some freedom, but was very unwell in the afternoon.

Thursday, *April* 1. Rode about fifty miles through Rutherford and Burke counties: it is a day of small things here.

Crossed Catawba River at Greenlee's ford, and came to our good friend White's,[60] on John's River, about eight o'clock at night. When I set off in the morning it seemed as if I should faint by the way, I was so ill with a mixed internal complaint to which I am subject. We arrived in the very nick of time, Friday being a very rainy day, and there being no necessity that day to ride. I feel happy in the prospect of death and rest; yet I am willing to labour and to suffer the Lord's leisure.

Saturday, 3. Quarterly meeting began. Brother Whatcoat and myself both preached, and there was a reviving among both white and black; and I trust some souls were blessed.

Sunday, 4. Was a serious day; none were admitted to our private meetings but members: many spoke, and most felt the power of God. We then hasted to the Globe chapel, where the people met, but had not patience to wait: we had a rough road, and John's River to cross twenty times. I was desired to preach sister Eliza Biggerstaff's[61] funeral. She was formerly a Presbyterian; then a Methodist; and last of all a Christian; and there is good hope that she died in the Lord. I was resolved to fulfil her desire, and preached on 1 Cor. xv, 56, 57, to about eight souls.

Monday, 5. We made an early move. After worming the stream for a while, we took through the Laurel Hill, and had to scale the mountains, which in some places were rising like the roof of a house. We came to the head of Watauga River; a most neglected place. Here the people have had their corn destroyed by frost, and many of them have moved away It was thus we found it in Tyger's Valley. We passed by W——'s, a poor

[59] This was Major James Holland, a member of Congress, merchant, and lawyer. (Griffin: *Essays on North Carolina History*.)

[60] The travelers held a quarterly conference at the home of William White, at which Thomas Anderson, presiding elder of the eastern district in South Carolina, exhorted Here they remained until April 4. (Whatcoat's *Journal*.)

[61] *Ibid.*

odging, and slept at the Beaver Dam in a cabin without a cover, except vhat a few boards supplied: we had very heavy thunder and lightning, nd most hideous yelling of wolves around; with rain, which is frequent 1 the mountains.[62]

Tennessee

Tuesday, 6. We were compelled to ride through the rain, and crossed he Stone Mountain: those who wish to know how rough it is may tread 1 our path. What made it worse to me was, that while I was looking to ee what was become of our guide, I was carried off with full force against tree that hung across the road some distance from the ground, and 1y head received a very great jar, which, however, was lessened by my aving on a hat that was strong in the crown. We came on to the dismal lace called Roan's Creek, which was pretty full. Here we took a good reakfast on our tea, bacon, and bread. Reaching Watauga, we had to wim our horses, and ourselves to cross in a canoe; up the Iron Mountain e ascended, where we had many a seat to rest, and many a weary step o climb. At length we came to Andrew Greer's,[63] and halted for the night.

Wednesday, 7. We reached William Nelson's chapel[64] about one o'clock, fter riding about eighteen miles.[65] Now it is that we must prepare for anger, in going through the wilderness.[66] I received a faithful letter from rother Poythress in Kentucky, encouraging me to come. This letter I hink well deserving of publication. I found the poor preachers indiffer- ntly clad, with emancipated bodies, and subject to hard fare; yet I hope hey are rich in faith.

Friday, 9.[67] After receiving great kindness from dear sister Nelson, we ame on to brother Bell's, who wrought for us, *gratis*, what we wanted in hoeing our horses.[68] Thence we went on to brother Gott's, and to brother —'s; and thence, groping through the woods, to brother Easley's; epending on the fidelity of the Kentucky people, hastening them, and eing unwilling they should wait a moment for me. We crossed Holston

[62] "We were saluted with a tremendous storm of lightning thunder and rain which lmost put out our fire. Oh, that we may reign with Christ in His glory." (Whatcoat: *ournal*.)

[63] See note under April 28, 1788.

[64] See note under May 6, 1788. At Nelson's Chapel, Asbury preached and Thomas nderson, presiding elder in eastern North Carolina, who accompanied the party, xhorted. (Whatcoat, *op. cit*.)

[65] It was only eight miles from Greer's to Nelson's. (Martin.)

[66] They were to travel the old Wilderness Road. The pioneers were pouring over that rail, and the Indians were angrily resisting them.

[67] The party spent the night of April 8 at Stephen Easley's near the present Kingsport. See note under May 2, 1788; Whatcoat, *op. cit*.; Price, *op. cit*., I, 147.)

[68] Asbury usually mentioned the blacksmith who shod his horses.

at Smith's ferry,[69] and rode thirty miles to Amis's,[70] where we were wel
entertained for our money. Coming along, I complained that the peopl
would take no pay for their food or services; that complaint has ceased
Very unwell as I was we pushed down Holston to the last house; here w
had no hope of company from the eastern or western side. We turned ou
our horses to graze, and they strayed off; so here we are anchored indeed.[7]

The unsettled state of my stomach and bowels makes labour and life *
burden. We are now in a house in which a man was killed by the savages
and O, poor creatures! they are but one remove from savages themselves
I consider myself in danger; but my God will keep me whilst thousand
pray for me.

Sunday, 11. My soul is humbled before God, waiting to see the solutio
of this dark providence. The man of the house is gone after some horse
supposed to be stolen by Indians. I have been near fainting; but my sou
is revived again, and my bodily strength somewhat renewed. If thes
difficulties, which appear to impede my path, are designed to prevent m
going to Kentucky, I hope to know shortly. I spent the *Sabbath* at Rober
Bean's.[72] In the evening a company of eleven came to go forward. Ou
horses were not to be found without a great sum.

Monday morning, 12. We loaded brother Thomas Anderson's littl
horse with my great bags, and two pair smaller; four saddles, witl
blankets and provender. We then set out and walked ten miles, and ou
horses were brought to us, and those who brought them were pleased t
take what we pleased to give. Brother Jeremiah Abel[73] sought the Lor
by fasting and prayer, and had a strong impression that it was the will o
God that I should not go with that company.

Tuesday, 13. We came back to Amis's—a poor sinner. He was highly
offended that we prayed so loud in his house. He is a distiller of whisky
and boasts of gaining £300 per annum by the brewing of his poison. W
talked very plainly; and I told him that it was of necessity, and not o

---

[69] Smith's Ferry was on the North Fork of the Holston River, near Moccasin Ga
in Virginia, but near the Tennessee line.

[70] Thomas Amis kept a tavern three miles west of Rogersville. His stone house is stil
standing. (Martin.) Whatcoat says that they "arrived at Captain Eamie's near sunset
a place well prepared for travellers."

[71] On April 10 the party rode to Robert Bean's Station at the forks of the Cumberlan
and Kentucky roads in what Whatcoat called "Hukin (Hawkins) County near Clincl
Mountain in Grassy Valley." (See Whatcoat's *Journal*.) His father, William Bean, wa
the first white settler in Tennessee. He established Bean's Station on a section of th
Wilderness Road near Tate Springs; its site is now beneath Cherokee Lake. (Williams
Dawn of Tennessee Valley History, 337, 338; Kincaid: *The Wilderness Road*, numerou
references.)

[72] Robert Bean was the son of the noted pioneer and founder of Bean's Station i
Granger County.

[73] Jeremiah Abel was preacher on the West New River Circuit with Joseph Dod
dridge. (See *Minutes*.)

choice, we were there; that I feared the face of no man. He said, he did not desire me to trouble myself about his soul. Perhaps the greatest offence was given by my speaking against distilling and slave holding.

Having now been upon expenses from *Friday* until this day, for four horses and three men, I judged it high time to move.

Virginia

Thursday, 15. We rode fifty miles; and next day preached at Owens's.[74]

Saturday, 17. We rode on with great violence, which made me feel very serious.[75]

Sunday, 18. Brother Whatcoat preached at General Russell's,[76] on the birth, character, and office of John the Baptist.

Monday, 19. I resolved on taking a *proper* dose of Tartar emetic; this has wrought me well, and I hope for better health.

From *December* 14, 1789, to *April* 20, 1790, we compute to have travelled two thousand five hundred and seventy-eight miles. Hitherto hath the Lord helped. Glory! glory to our God!

We had a good prayer meeting at General Russell's. This family is lavish in attentions and kindness: I was nursed as an only child by the good man and woman of the house, and indeed by all the family. God Almighty bless them and reward them!

Thursday, 22. We had a lively prayer meeting at Keywood's.[77] Come, Lord, like thunder, and break in upon these dear young people!

Friday, 23. We had a very lively prayer meeting and exhortation.[78] We trust the Lord will do something for these people before we leave the rich Holston Valley: I feel for their state; they are settled, and dwindling. I have been happy in my own soul, and have gained bodily strength. Two weeks are now spent, one in waiting on the Kentucky business, and one, illness has prevented my improving, except that it has furnished time to publish my appointments on Clinch and Nolachucky.

Saturday, 24. Many attended a prayer meeting at John M'Henry's,[79] but there was little life.

[74] (See note under May 6, 1788.) Whatcoat says that they reached James Carr's at Beaver Creek, Washington County, Virginia, about ten o'clock in the evening on April 15, having traveled fifty miles, and that they walked to John Owens' on the sixteenth. They probably returned to Carr's, since Whatcoat says he preached and Asbury exhorted there on the evening of the sixteenth.

[75] According to Whatcoat they rode by Washington Court House to Michael Halfacre's on April 17. (See note under May 8, 1788.)

[76] See notes under May 3 and May 6, 1788.

[77] See note under May 6, 1788.

[78] This prayer meeting was at Michael Halfacre's according to Whatcoat.

[79] John McHenry lived near Saltville. He was the father of Barnabas McHenry (1767–1833), a preacher of some prominence during the period. During this year he was serving the Kentucky Circuit. (Finley: *Sketches of Western Methodism*, 143–45.)

Sunday, 25. Preached at General Russell's[80] on Ezekiel xxxiii, 11. I saw, I felt, I knew that some of my congregation were touched.

Monday, 26. We rode through the Poor Valley,[81] calling on F——, who had been sick and frightened with convictions and the fear of death; we prayed, fed our horses, and rode on to Clinch River.[82]

Tuesday, 27. We had a house well crowded,[83] but there was but little stir among them. I felt for these dear souls, and judged that Providence was about to open a way for a circuit to be formed here in Russell county,[84] for one preacher.

Wednesday, 28. I preached at brother Beckel's,[85] a frontier house, and a *station*. In time past, a person was killed here by the Indians. The people showed their zeal in purchasing two magazines and several hymn books. Some say, nothing but whisky will bring money; but I proved the contrary, and I give them credit. We have had cold weather, and severe frosts for two nights past.

We had a dreary ride down to the Ford of Clinch, through a solitary plain: many attended at Looney's.

We rode down to Joseph Blackmore's station:[86] here the people have been *forted* on the north side of Clinch. Poor Blackmore has had a son and daughter killed by the Indians. They are of opinion here, that the Cherokees were the authors of this mischief: I also received an account of two families having been killed, and of one female that was taken prisoner, and afterward retaken by the neighbours and brought back.

Friday, 30. Crossed Clinch about two miles below the fort. In passing

[80] Whatcoat was impressed by the "perfection" of the salt works operated by General Russell, remarking that "it must be a great privilege to these back parts as they can buy it at nine shillings a bushel in produce." (Whatcoat's *Journal*.)

[81] Poor Valley is between Clinch Mountain and Walker's Mountain in parts of Washington, Russell, and Smyth counties. It is part of the valley of the North Fork of the Holston. The south side of the river is called Rich Valley.

[82] They rode to Richard Price's on Clinch River, where both Asbury and Whatcoat preached. (Whatcoat's *Journal*.)

[83] Whatcoat says this was at Richard Price's. He settled at Elk Garden in Russell County, Virginia, in 1770, and was the grandfather of the Rev. R. N. Price, historian of Holston Methodism.

[84] Russell County was named for General Russell. Russell Circuit was one of the first circuits named for a county. (Martin.)

[85] This frontier house and station or tavern was at Castlewoods, the first home of General Russell. It was kept by Captain Charles Beckel, Bickley, or Beckley. He took his religion seriously, setting free his slaves in 1795. (Whatcoat's *Journal*. See Asbury's entry under September 24, 1801; also Summers: *History of Southwest Virginia*, 367, 368.)

[86] This place still bears the name of Fort Blackmore. It is on Clinch River a short distance above Clinchport. Whatcoat says they called at James "Ausbands" (Osborne's?) on April 29. Here Asbury preached and Whatcoat performed a wedding ceremony for John Alley and Mary Porter, after which they rode to Joseph Blackmore's. "Lord pity the people in these backwoods," he wrote. "Though they live in jeopardy every day yet the greatest part of them seem to have no more religion than savage tribes." (*Journal*; *Annals of Southwest Virginia*, 984.)

long I saw the precipice from which Blackmore's unhappy son leaped into the river after receiving the stroke of a tomahawk in his head; I suppose, by the measure of my eye, it must be between fifty and sixty feet descent; his companion was shot dead upon the spot; this happened on the 6th of *April*, 1789.

We came a dreary road over rocks, ridges, hills, stones, and streams, along a blind, tortuous path, to Moccasin Gap and Creek;[87] thence to Smith's ferry across the north branch of Holston. Here I found some lies had been told on me; feeling myself innocent, I was not moved.

Tennessee

Saturday, May 1. Rested. Next day (*Sabbath*) I preached to a hardened people.

Monday, 3. I preached at brother Payne's, and had some encouragement among our Maryland people. Sabbath night, I dreamed the guard from Kentucky came for me; and mentioned it to brother Whatcoat. In the morning I retired to a small stream, for meditation and prayer, and whilst there saw two men come over the hills: I felt a presumption that they were Kentucky men, and so they proved to be; they were Peter Massie and John Clark, who were coming for me, with the intelligence that they had left eight men below: after reading the letters and asking counsel of God, I consented to go with them.[88]

Tuesday, 4. We prepared ourselves and horses for our journey, and the next day came once more to Amis's.

Thursday, 6. Came to Joseph Crabbe's, at the lower end of the Grassy Valley, and were occupied in collecting our company.

Virginia

Friday, 7. We formed the whole of our company at the Valley station;[89] besides brother Whatcoat and myself, we were sixteen men, having

[87] They were among the rugged hills above the Natural Tunnell in Scott County, Virginia. Whatcoat says that Stephen Easley and Thomas Rubey met them at Moccasin Gap and conducted them to Easley's. (See note under May 6, 1788.) Asbury was traveling the famous Wilderness Road. Near these places was the Block House, a well-known inn.

[88] Whatcoat mentions Asbury's dream and its fulfilment in the coming of "two sedate men" in his *Journal*. Eight other men, including Hope Hull and John Sewell, accompanied Massie and Clark to escort Asbury's party through the dangerous wilderness to Kentucky. Peter Massie was the first Kentuckian to become an itinerant preacher and the first to die. He died on December 18, 1791, in the house of a Mr. Hodges four miles west of Nashville, Tennessee, while traveling the Limestone Circuit. (Arnold: *History of Methodism in Kentucky*, 47, 53; Redford: *Methodism in Kentucky*, I, 68.)

[89] Valley Station was five miles from Wallen's Ridge and two miles from Powell River in Lee County, Virginia. (Pusey: *The Wilderness Road to Kentucky*, 26–27.)

thirteen guns only. We moved on very swiftly, considering the roughness of the way, travelling, by my computation, thirty-five miles to-day.[90]

Kentucky

Next day we reached Rich Land Creek,[91] and encamped on the road about nine o'clock at night, having made, by computation, forty-five miles.

Sunday, 9. We travelled about fifty miles; and next day forty-five miles, and reached Madison court house,[92] passing the branches of Rock Castle River: on our journey we saw the rock whence the river derives its name;[93] it is amazing and curious, with appearances the most artificial I have ever seen—it is not unlike an old church or castle in Europe. We stopped at McGuire's,[94] whose wife, now a tender, gracious soul, was taken prisoner by the Indians during the last war, and carried to Detroit.

Tuesday, 11. Crossed Kentucky River. I was strangely outdone for want of sleep, having been greatly deprived of it in my journey through the wilderness; which is like being at sea, in some respects, and in others worse. Our way is over mountains, steep hills, deep rivers, and muddy creeks; a thick growth of reeds for miles together; and no inhabitants but wild beasts and savage men. Sometimes, before I am aware, my ideas would be leading me to be looking out ahead for a fence; and I would, without reflection, try to recollect the houses we should have lodged at in the wilderness. I slept about an hour the first night, and about two the last; we ate no regular meal; our bread grew short, and I was much spent.

I saw the graves of the slain—twenty-four in one camp.[95] I learn that

[90] Escorted by his armed guard, Asbury now started his first trip to Kentucky, accompanied by Richard Whatcoat, Hope Hull, and John Sewell. An old powder horn with large lettering, "Francis Asbury, May 1, 1790," was discovered at Medina, Ohio, in a collection made by a Kentucky physician. It is presumed to have been carried by Asbury on this trip, indicating that the Bishop was also armed. The route was tedious. The party traveled the old Wilderness Trail to Cumberland Gap and then over a narrow Indian trail.

[91] Richland Creek is in Knox County. The party camped near the present town of Barbourville. Whatcoat says that they reached New Station near Cumberland Gap and spent the night at Joseph Lewis' on May 7, and rode to the Rich Valley on the eighth. (*Journal*, in Sweet, *op. cit.*, 100, 101.)

[92] Madison courthouse is the present Richmond, county seat of Madison County, Kentucky. On the ninth they rode to "near the Hazel Patch" and on the 10th to "Wm. Maguyer near Mattason Courthouse." (*Ibid.*, 101.)

[93] Rock Castle is in Laurel County, Kentucky, about four miles south of Livingston.

[94] Sweet, *op. cit.*, 101.

[95] Evidently the graves of the victims of what is known as "McNitt's Defeat," which occurred the night of October 3, 1786. Twenty-four persons were killed and scalped, and five women carried away. The leaders of the party were members of the McNitt, Ford, and Barnes families from Botetourt and Rockbridge counties in Virginia. The victims were buried at the camp site, and the graves are still preserved in the Levi Jackson State Park, near London, Kentucky. This camp site and the graves were fre-

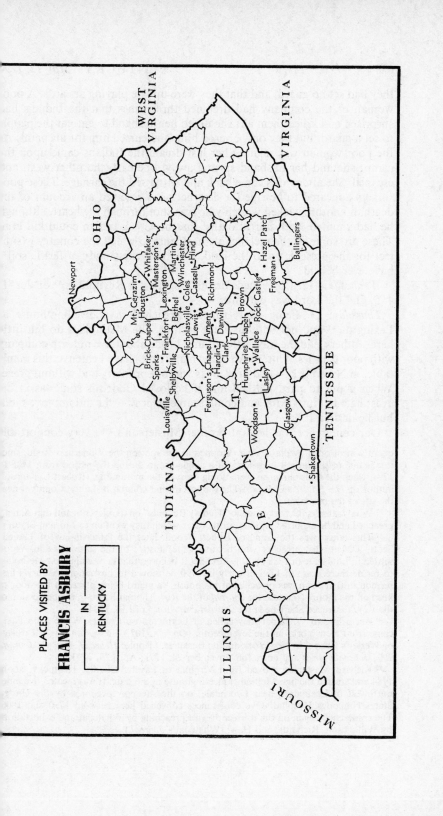

PLACES VISITED BY

FRANCIS ASBURY

IN

KENTUCKY

they had set no guard, and that they were up late playing at cards. A poo
woman of the company had dreamed three times that the Indians ha
surprised and killed them all; she urged her husband to entreat the peopl
to set a guard, but they only abused him, and cursed him for his pains. A
the poor woman was relating her last dream the Indians came upon th
camp; she and her husband sprung away, one east, the other west, an
escaped. She afterwards came back and witnessed the carnage. These poo
sinners appeared to be ripe for destruction. I received an account of th
death of another wicked wretch who was shot through the heart, althoug
he had vaunted, with horrid oaths, that no Creek Indian could kill him
These are some of the melancholy accidents to which the country is sub
ject for the present; as to the land, it is the richest body of fertile soil
have ever beheld.

Wednesday, 12. I preached for the first time at Reynolds's,[96] on Jer. 1
4, 5, and the Lord was with me.

Thursday, 13. Being court time, I preached in a dwelling house a
Lexington,[97] and not without some feeling. The Methodists do but littl
here—others lead the way. After dinner I rode about five miles in compan
with poor Charles White.[98] Ah! how many times have I eaten at this man'
table, in New York!—and now, he is without property and without grace
When about to part, I asked him if he loved God: his soul was in hi
eyes; he burst into tears, and could scarcely speak—"he did not love God
but he desired it."

Our conference was held at brother Masterson's,[99] a very comfortabl

quently mentioned by diarists who stopped at the spot on the Wilderness Road, sinc
it was one of the largest massacres of a single group during the period from 1785 t
1794, when the Chickamaugas were doing most of the marauding. (Robert L. Kincaid
author of *The Wilderness Road*.) The Camp Ground Church in Laurel County is nea
the site of the massacre.

[96] Whatcoat says the party rode to "Henery Renolds" on the eleventh and that Asbur
preached and he exhorted on the twelfth, after which they went on to Morgan Bryan's

[97] This house was the home of Robert Wood, later the father-in-law of Thoma
Scott, a Methodist preacher who became Chief Justice of the state of Ohio. Woo
settled in Louisville in 1788 or 1789, and Scott believed that he was the first Methodis
to reside there. Late in 1789 or early in 1790 he moved to Lexington. Asbury's firs
sermon in that town was preached at his house, "a guard being placed at the door t
keep off the mob." (Manuscript *Journal* of the Rev. Thomas Scott, in the possession o
the Rev. Lawrence Sherwood; see *Journal* entry for April 14, 1794.)

[98] According to Whatcoat they called at Lexington on Charles White, who latel
came from New York, on the seventeenth. (*Op. cit.*, 102.) He was an original truste
of Wesley's Chapel in New York and its treasurer. (Tipple: *Heart of Asbury's Journa*
299; *Journal* entries and notes for November 24, 1771; April 29, 1793.)

[99] Richard Masterson moved from Virginia to Fayette County, Kentucky, abou
1784 and erected the first Methodist meetinghouse in the state. It was located five mile
northwest of Lexington, near Greendale, on the site now occupied by the Unite
States Narcotics Hospital. Five conferences convened here between 1790 and 180
The conference began on the thirteenth with preaching by Whatcoat and exhortation
by Williamson, Richards, and Haw. (Whatcoat's *Journal*.)

house, and kind people. We went through our business in great love and harmony. I ordained Wilson Lee, Thomas Williamson, and Barnabas M'Henry, elders.[100] We had preaching noon and night, and souls were converted, and the fallen restored. My soul has been blessed among these people, and I am exceedingly pleased with them. I would not, for the worth of all the place, have been prevented in this visit, having no doubt but that it will be for the good of the present rising generation. It is true, such exertions of mind and body are trying; but I am supported under it: if souls are saved, it is enough. Brother Poythress[101] is much alive to God. We fixed a plan for a school, and called it *Bethel*; and obtained a subscription of upwards of three hundred pounds, in land and money, towards its establishment.[102]

Monday, 17. Rode to Coleman's chapel,[103] about ten miles from Lexington, and preached to an unengaged people. We thence rode to John Lewis's,[104] on the bend of Kentucky River. Lewis is an old acquaintance, from Leesburg, Virginia; I was pleased to find that heaven and religion were not lost sight of in this family. Brother Lewis offered me one hundred acres of land for *Bethel*, on a good spot for building materials.

[100] Wilson Lee (1761–1804) was a native of Delaware. He was admitted on trial in 1784, and prior to migrating to Kentucky he served circuits in Virginia, Pennsylvania, and Maryland, on one of which he was an assistant to Whatcoat. Thomas Williamson was admitted in 1785 and had traveled the Yadkin and Salisbury circuits in North Carolina. Barnabas McHenry (1767–1833) of North Carolina was admitted in 1787 and went to Kentucky the following year. Whatcoat says that Lee and McHenry were ordained deacons on the fifteenth, and the three were made elders on the sixteenth. He also says that James Haw and Joshua Hartley desisted from traveling. Haw was one of the pioneer preachers in Kentucky. He was received into full connection in 1782 and served in Virginia until going to the newly created Kentucky Circuit in 1786. According to the *Minutes* he was appointed to the Cumberland Circuit at this conference, but he is listed in the O'Kelley defection and joined the Republican Methodists, later becoming a Cumberland Presbyterian. Hartley was admitted on trial in 1785 and served in North Carolina and Virginia before going to Kentucky in 1789. (Whatcoat's *Journal*.)

[101] Francis Poythress (1732–1810) of Virginia was one of Deveraux Jarratt's converts and a noted early preacher. He began preaching in 1775 and served the Carolina circuit with Edward Dromgoole in 1776. He was presiding elder in Virginia, North Carolina, Kentucky, and Tennessee. He went to Kentucky in 1787 and was the first presiding elder there. He was one of the founders of Bethel Academy and was to Kentucky what Jesse Lee was to New England, virtual founder of Methodism. He suffered mental derangement after 1800. (See note under October 15, 1810.)

[102] At the conference in North Carolina in 1789 Coke said he had letters from friends in Kentucky asking that a college be established. Bethel, near Lexington, became the first Methodist school in the state. (For its history see note under October 4, 1800.)

[103] Coleman's Chapel was at or near the home of Benjamin Coleman and was probably erected by him. (Whatcoat, *op. cit.*, 102.)

[104] This was Captain John Lewis. Lewis' Chapel was nearby, and the conference met there in 1794. (*Ibid.*; Arnold: *Methodism in Kentucky*, I, 181.) The Lewis farm was in Jesamine County on Highway 29 between Wilmore and High Bridge.

We rode through mire and rain twenty-one miles to Francis Clark's,[105] near Danville, where we had a numerous congregation.

Saturday, 22. We had a noble shout at Brown's,[106] and four souls professed to be converted to God. Reached the Crab Orchard, and lodged under a tree,[107] very feverish and unwell; a poor beginning this.

Monday, 24. We set out on our return through the wilderness with a large and helpless company; we had about fifty people, twenty of whom were armed, and five of whom might have stood fire. To preserve order and harmony, we had articles drawn up for, and signed by, our company, and I arranged the people for travelling according to the regulations agreed upon. Some disaffected gentlemen, who would neither sign nor come under discipline, had yet the impudence to murmur when left behind. The first night we lodged some miles behind the Hazel patch.[108] The next day we discovered signs of Indians, and some thought they heard voices; we therefore thought it best to travel on, and did not encamp until three o'clock, halting on the east side of Cumberland River. We had gnats enough. We had an alarm, but it turned out to be a false alarm. A young gentleman, a Mr. Alexander, behaved exceedingly well; but his tender frame was not adequate to the fatigue to be endured, and he had well-nigh fainted on the road to Cumberland Gap. Brother Peter Massie was captain; and finding I had gained authority among the people, I acted somewhat in the capacity of an adjutant and quartermaster among them. At the foot of the mountain the company separated; the greater part went on with me to Powell's River; here we slept on the earth, and next day made the Grassy Valley. Several of the company, who were not Methodists, expressed their high approbation of our conduct, and most affectionately invited us to their houses. The journeys of each day were as follows: *Monday* forty-five miles; *Tuesday* fifty miles; *Wednesday* sixty miles.

[105] Francis Clark's home was in Lincoln County, now Boyle County, about six miles west of Danville. He and John Durham had moved to Kentucky from Virginia in 1783. Clark, a local preacher, organized the first Methodist society in Kentucky in John Durham's home. A historical marker on Highway 150 between Danville and Perryville marks the location of the Durham home. Clark probably preached the first Methodist sermon in Ohio at Fort Washington, the present Cincinatti, in 1793. Asbury reached Clark's on the eighteenth and preached and administered the sacrament the following day. (Whatcoat, *op. cit.*, 102.)

[106] This was Absolom Brown. On the previous day Asbury and his party had been at the home of Willis Green "on Salt Water River." He was a Virginian who went to Kentucky at an early date and served in the Kentucky legislature and as a trustee of Bethel Academy and Transylvania Seminary. He lived in Lincoln County. (*Ibid.*, 102, 103; Arnold, *op. cit.*, I, 27.)

[107] Whatcoat says they rode to an undisclosed place on the twenty-third, where he and Asbury preached to six or seven hundred people. They then went on to Crab Orchard. Crab Orchard was in Lincoln County.

[108] Hazel Patch was about eight miles north of the present town of London, Kentucky.

Thursday, 27. By riding late we reached Capt. Amis's where I had a bed to rest on.

Virginia

Friday, *Saturday*, and *Sunday*, 28, 29, 30. I spent at General Russell's[109] whose wife is converted since I left the house last; I thought then that she was not far from the kingdom of God.

I found myself dispirited in public preaching. I afterward ordained I. Ragan[110] and B. Vanpelt,[111] local preachers, to the office of deacons.

Monday, 31. Rode to New River,[112] forty-five or fifty miles; here I saw John Tunnell, very low; a mere shadow; but very humble and patient under his affliction.[113]

North Carolina

Tuesday, June 1. I rode about forty-five miles to Armstrong's, and next day about four o'clock reached M'Knights on the Yadkin River, in North Carolina;[114] here the conference had been waiting for me nearly two weeks: we rejoiced together, and my brethren received me as one brought from the jaws of death. Our business was much matured, the critical concern of the council understood, and the plan, with its amendments, adopted.

Saturday and *Sunday*, 5, 6. Were days of the Lord's presence and power —several were converted. We had an ordination each day. We have admitted into full connection some steady men, with dispositions and talents for the work.[115]

[109] There is a chronological divergence in the accounts of Asbury and Whatcoat. The latter in his *Journal* for these dates says they lost their way on the twenty-eighth of May and slept in a little cabin "under the widow's roof." On the twenty-ninth they rode about fifty miles to Michael Halfacre's and did not reach General Russell's until the thirtieth.

[110] "Ragan" was probably James Riggin, a local preacher, who visited Asbury at the home of Mitchell Porter in Sevier County, Tennessee, on October 18, 1808.

[111] Benjamin Van Pelt, was a brother of Peter Van Pelt, who welcomed Asbury to Staten Island in 1771. Benjamin went to Tennessee in 1780 and built one of the first meetinghouses in that section. It was on Lick Creek in Greene County.

[112] According to Whatcoat they stayed at Michael Lee's on New River and passed through Flower Gap to North Carolina.

[113] John Tunnell, one of the noted pioneer preachers, was dying with tuberculosis. Asbury soon returned to preach his funeral.

[114] Asbury and Whatcoat rode up Cripple Creek to Armstrong's near the Flower Gap. George McKnight lived a mile and a half west of Clemmonsville, the present Clemmons, in Yadkin, now Forsyth County, near the Yadkin River. McKnight's Chapel was an important preaching place where several conferences were held. On the fourth Whatcoat rode to Adam Peathree's to have the horses shod. (Whatcoat, *op. cit.*, 103.)

[115] At this conference Asbury preached and ordained seven elders. The exhorters were Thomas Anderson, presiding elder in South Carolina, and Isaac Lowe, who was serving the Guilford Circuit. On leaving McKnight's the party rode to John Hill's. *Ibid.*, 104.)

Monday, 7. Rode through Salem Town; the Moravian brethren hav* the blessing of the nether springs, and houses, orchards, mills, stores mechanics' shops, &c. I rode about three hundred miles to Kentucky i* six days; and on my return about five hundred miles in nine days. O wha* exertions for man and horse![116]

Virginia

Wednesday, 9. Came forty-five miles to John Cannon's,[117] and next da* thirty miles to sister Jones's.[118]

Friday, 11. Rode to brother Isaac Johnson's,[119] and next day late i* the evening reached Petersburg.[120]

Sunday, 13. I preached on Psalm lxxxv, 6. I was weak and unwell wit* excessive labour and want of rest.

Monday, 14. Our conference began; all was peace until the council wa* mentioned. The young men appeared to be entirely under the influenc* of the elders, and turned it out of doors. I was weary, and felt but littl* freedom to speak on the subject. This business is to be explained to ever* preacher; and then it must be carried through the conferences twenty* four times, that is, through all the conferences for two years. We had som* little quickenings, but no great move among the people at our publi* preaching. Mr. Jarratt preached for us; friends at first are friends agai* at last.[121] There were four elders and seventeen deacons ordained; te* young men who offered to travel, besides those who remained on tria* We have good news from a far country—Jersey flames with religion; som* hundreds are converted. The work of God does revive here, although no* in the same degree as it did two years ago. In the midst of all my labou* and trouble I enjoy peace within.

Saturday, 19. Ended my week of business. I am crowded with letters—

[116] Whatcoat says that they rode to Isaac Lowe's home in Rockingham County o* June 7. On the following day they refreshed themselves at Nathan Williamson's an* lodged with James Rice in Caswell County. On the ninth they called at Gabriel Lee* and lodged with John Cannon in Granville County. The next day they were at Colon* Smith's, crossed the Roanoke at Taylor's Ferry, and lodged with Tignal Jones in Mecl* lenburg County, Virginia. Thus Whatcoat's chronology varies somewhat from that c* Asbury.

[117] John Cannon lived in Granville County, North Carolina.

[118] Sister Jones lived in Mecklenburg County, Virginia. (Whatcoat's *Journal*, Swee* *op. cit.*, 104.)

[119] See Whatcoat's *Journal*, Sweet, *op. cit.*

[120] Whatcoat says they stayed at Gressett Davis's. (See *ibid.*, 104.)

[121] Relations between the old friends were not as good as this statement indicate* Jarratt seems never to have entirely forgiven Coke and Asbury for forming th* Methodist Church. (See the *Letters* of Asbury for January 12, 1790, and January 1* 1796.)

have much reading and writing, and the temporal concerns of the college, and the printing to attend to.

Sunday, 20. I spoke melting words on Hosea xi, 8; many felt; one found peace with God. In the afternoon, I believe the power of God was felt in the hearts of some of my congregation. I did not wonder that there was not a greater work of religion in this place, when I learned that they were sometimes three or four weeks without preaching; thus Satan tries to keep preachers and people asunder—yet some cry out, "We have no faith for Petersburg!" My dear old friend and fellow-traveller, Whatcoat, is smitten with boils, so that he cannot go on. Stopped at brother Garrettson's.[122]

Monday, 21. We had the Divine presence in our worship at sister Stringer's.[123] I am often blessed at the houses of the fatherless and widows. Now, I say to my body, return to thy labour; to my soul return to thy rest, and pure delight in reading, meditation, and prayer, and solitude. The shady groves are witness to my retired and sweetest hours: to sit and melt, and bow alone before the Lord, whilst the melody of the birds warbles from tree to tree—how delightful!

Tuesday, 22. The Lord was with us at Finney's church; and God's dear children praised his name, whilst sinners felt and looked serious.

Wednesday, 23. I preached at Paine's, an ancient, and almost wornout place. At Ryall's, the next day, I was quite unwell; and what made the matter worse, was, that I imprudently walked out, and sat upon the ground, and took fresh cold. From Ryall's I proceeded to the old court house,[124] where I spoke with great pain—from head to foot was pain, all perspiration appeared to be quite stopped. I lodged at Thomas Jones's—whole family snatched as brands from the burning.

Saturday, 26. I was so unwell that I could not preach at Pride's church.

Sunday, 27. Rode to brother Strong's, where, as there were many who had come expecting to hear me, I made a feeble attempt in the woods, on Thess. i, 5–9; my head was greatly afflicted.

Monday morning, 28. I took a strong decoction of rue and wormwood. My fever breaks, and I feel a little better. I found perfect patience in great misery of body. Lord, make me perfect through suffering.

Monday, 28. I had a few Christians and a few sinners at the widow Lackland's; and there was a small reviving among the people. The leaven of Antinomianism prevails here, and the Methodists talk much about persons and opinions, when they should be looking to God.

Tuesday, 29. I am very weak and low in body. Lord, sanctify affliction, and make it a means of health to my soul! Brother Whatcoat preached on,

---

[122] This was Richard, the brother of Freeborn Garrettson. (See Whatcoat's *Journal*.)
[123] Whatcoat's *Journal*, Sweet, *op. cit.*, 105, says that Baptist delegates attended the conference to ask the Methodists to join in a petition for an act to sell the glebes and church. "But our preachers chose to be Neuters."
[124] This was Amelia Court House. Asbury was in Amelia from Finney's to Strong's.

"He that believeth shall not make haste." I have felt grieved in mind that there is a link broken out of twelve that should form a chain of union. I hope God will sanctify some providence to the explanation of this matter, and heal the whole.

Wednesday, 30. Brother Whatcoat gave us a weighty discourse on the prophetic, priestly, and kingly offices of Christ. In great weakness, I enlarged on 1 Peter iii, 15, and showed that it is not enough to sanctify the Lord God in his name, word, Sabbath, ordinances, ministers, people, and worship; but that the heart must be filled with a holy, constant fear of, confidence in, and love to, God. But how common is it for different denominations to ask each other of their distinguishing peculiarities; and how very rare it is for them to talk closely of the dealings of God with their own souls!

As we rode on, there was a great appearance of immediate rain; I prayed that it might pass, fearing its effects in my very weak state; I was mercifully preserved, a few drops fell on me only, and I found, as I proceeded, that it had rained very heavily ahead.

We had a few unfeeling souls at Swiney's:[125] one man appeared to be hardened to an extraordinary degree; I thought I felt his spirit as soon as I came.

Thursday, July 1. I preached in a school house, near brother Robert Moseley's,[126] with some enlargement, but, I fear, to little purpose: one woman appeared to be under conviction.

Friday, 2. I had a painful ride of twenty-five, or thirty miles, to brother Caloway's.[127]

Saturday, 3. My mind was afflicted, and my body weak. I was led to speak on, "Be ye also ready,"—and some felt the word.

Sunday, 4. I was set at liberty, and there was a little shaking and breathing after God, while I opened and explained, "And there is none calleth upon thy name, that stirreth up himself to take hold of thee." Afterward rode to brother John Murphy's.[128] I felt very weak, but patiently happy in God.

Monday, 5. We had some move at Ayer's church; brother Whatcoat was much led out in exhortation and prayer. I spent the afternoon in reading and spiritual exercises.

Tuesday, 6. We rode to Liberty,[129] the county town of Bedford. We set out towards Botetourt, and reached brother Mitchell's about ten o'clock the next day, and found some zeal amongst the people. Next

---

[125] Swiney lived in Prince George County. (Whatcoat's *Journal*, Sweet, *op. cit.*)

[126] *Ibid.*

[127] Caloway lived in Bedford County. (*Ibid.*)

[128] Whatcoat says they rode to Joseph Wilson's and then to John Murphy's.

[129] Liberty was the county seat of Bedford County after its separation from Campbell County. The present county seat is Bedford (old Liberty).

day at Edward Mitchell's,[130] on Craig's Creek, one soul found the Lord.

Friday, 9. We had a tedious, tiresome journey over hills and mountains to Potts' Creek. After a melting season at brother Joseph Carpenter's,[131] we came to brother James Wright's,[132] where we were informed of the death of dear brother John Tunnell.

Saturday, 10. Brother Tunnell's corpse was brought to Dew's chapel.[133] I preached his funeral: my text, "For me to live is Christ, and to die is gain." We were much blessed, and the power of God was eminently present. It is fourteen years since brother Tunnell first knew the Lord; and he has spoken about thirteen years, and travelled through eight of the thirteen States: few men, as public ministers, were better known or more beloved. He was a simple-hearted, artless, childlike man: for his opportunities, he was a man of good learning; had a large fund of Scripture knowledge, was a good historian, a sensible, improving preacher, a most affectionate friend, and a great saint; he had been wasting and declining in strength and health for eight years past, and for the last twelve months sinking into consumption. I am humbled. O, let my soul be admonished to be more devoted to God!

West Virginia

Sunday, 11. The morning was rainy. About noon I set out for the Sweet Springs,[134] and preached on 1 Cor. i, 23–29. A few of the gentry were kind enough to come and hear—and some were enraptured with the sermon; or—it was very like the subject. The three following days I rested, and was very unwell. I had no place to preach, but under the trees, and preaching here seems unseasonable with the people except on Sundays.

Thursday, 15. Rode to Rehoboth,[135] where brother Whatcoat preached, and brother Jeremiah Abel and myself spoke after him, and the people appeared somewhat affected.

[130] Whatcoat says they rode from Liberty with Henry Ogburn across the Peaks of Otter and down Jennings Creek to James River and arrived at James Mitchell's. (Sumners: *Annals of Southwest Virginia*, 444.) Edward Mitchell was a local preacher, and he and his brother, Samuel, manumitted their slaves.

[131] See Whatcoat's *Journal*.

[132] *Ibid.*

[133] Dew's Chapel was in Botetourt County, Virginia. Sherwood says Samuel Dew had lived in Hampshire County, West Virginia, and Asbury visited him there in 1784 and 1785. He moved to what was later Monroe County, but the boundary was changed several times. He lived on Potts Creek, which is in both Virginia and present West Virginia.

[134] The party was now in present West Virginia.

[135] Whatcoat says the party rode to Edward Keenan's and gave the sacrament at Rehoboth Chapel in Greenbriar (now Monroe) County. This chapel stood on land given by Keenan, who was originally a Roman Catholic. (Bennett: *Memorials of Methodism in Virginia*, 306–8.)

Friday, 16. We had twenty miles to Green Brier court house:—her some sat as critics and judges. We had to ride thirty-one miles withou food for man or horse, and to call at three houses before we could ge water fit to drink—all this may serve to try our faith or patience.

Saturday, 17. Some very pointed things were delivered relative t parents and children, from Gen. xviii, 19. After being in public exercise from ten till two o'clock, we rode in the afternoon twenty miles to th little levels of Green Brier. On my way I premeditated the sending of preacher to a newly-settled place in the Kenhaway county.[136]

Sunday, 18. We had a warm sermon at M'Neil's, at which many wer highly offended; but I trust their false peace is broken. There are man bears in this part of the country; not long since, a child in this neighbour hood was killed by one.

Monday, 19. Rode to Thomas Drinnon's, whose wife was killed, and hi son taken prisoner by the Indians.

Tuesday, 20. I believe I never before travelled such a path as I thi day rode over the mountains to reach Mr. Charles Nelson's, in Tyge Valley.

Wednesday, 21. I preached at Wilson's.[137] Here many careless people d not hear a sermon more than once in one or two years; this one of ther told me; and that he and his wife had not been to preaching since I wa here on my last visit. I endeavoured to apply, "My people are destroye for lack of knowledge."

Thursday, 22. My horse lost a shoe on a bad road, and next day on th mountains dropped two more; so I rode my old baggage horse along most dreary, grown-up path, to brother James Coburn's.

Saturday, 24. Attended quarterly meeting at Morgantown—I spoke o superstition, idolatry, unconditional election, and reprobation, Antinc mianism, Universalism, and Deism.

Sunday, 25. Preached on Matt. xxv, 31, to the end; brother Whatcoa also gave us a sermon; and a Presbyterian minister two: so here we had in abundance.[138]

[136] Kanawha County was organized in 1789. The newly settled place was Charlesto the present capital of West Virginia. In 1790 Asbury did appoint Jacob Lurton ar Thomas Boyd to Kanawha, but the difficulties were too great and the work was n accomplished. Methodism waited until 1804 to enter the Great Kanawha Valley, ar then it came from the Ohio River rather than from the Greenbrier region.

[137] John Wilson (1756–1827) lived at Beverly, West Virginia. At the age of eighteen l had been severely wounded in an Indian fight at Wheeling. He held several publ offices, including county clerk, justice of the peace, sheriff, and was a major in tl Virginia Militia in 1787. He and his brother Benjamin were the delegates from Randolp County to the Virginia Convention of 1788 which ratified the Constitution of tl United States. (Maxwell, *op. cit.*, 488–94.)

[138] (See Whatcoat's *Journal* for this date.) He says they slept at William Lenham's, saddler at Morgantown, and that the Presbyterian minister was a Mr. Marshal. The dined at the home of John Stealey, a tanner. (See letter "To a Quaker," July, 1790

Pennsylvania

Monday, 26. Preached at Thomas Batting's;[139] and the next day at John Hudson's.[140] Our conference began at Uniontown[141] on *Wednesday* the twenty-eighth of July:—it was conducted in peace and love. On *Thursday* I preached.

Saturday, 31. I spoke on education, from Prov. xxii, 6. I was led to enlarge on the obligations of parents to their children; and the nature of that religious education which would be most likely to fit them for this, and which alone could qualify them for the next world.

Sunday, August 1. I ordained Charles Conway, Isaac Love, and George Callahan, elders, and four deacons.[142] Here there is a revival among preachers and people; some of the societies are much engaged with God and after we have had a few more conferences in Uniontown, I hope we shall drive Satan out, and have a glorious work.

Maryland

Tuesday, 3. Rode to Colonel Barratt's, and next day came to Cresap's, where I rested the following day, and was employed in reading, mediation, and prayer. I had very solemn thoughts of God and his work. want a closer walk with God; and to be more alone, and in prayer.

Friday, 6. We had Divine breathings at the chapel.

West Virginia

Saturday, 7. We held a quarterly meeting at the widow Coulson's. There was much rain; we had many people, and but little room. These circumstances rendered the meeting in some respects uncomfortable; yet, I trust, it was profitable. Many souls felt the Divine power, among whom were some poor backsliders.

Tuesday, 10. I had an attentive, well-behaved congregation at Squire Vanmeter's. O that they may feel the truth and effects of godliness on earth, and in heaven!

At Doctor Naves's, formerly Hyder's, I applied, "O Ephraim, how shall give thee up?" I felt a vast weight upon my spirits for these people.

[139] Whatcoat's *Journal*, Sweet, *op. cit.*, 108.

[140] *Ibid.* Smeltzer cites Whatcoat also, but calls this man "Hutson."

[141] This was Asbury's second district conference held in the Redstone region of western Pennsylvania. (Smeltzer, *op. cit.*, 63.)

[142] Whatcoat's *Journal* gives the full names of the elders and also the deacons, by their last name only, listing five instead of four, as follows: (Joseph) Doddridge, (Tasley) Matthews, (Anthony) Banning, (?) Cochran, and (Joseph) Cheuvront. The first names are inserted from the *General Minutes*. (*Ibid.*)

Wednesday, 11. We had about forty miles to ride to Green's,[143] and Brock's Gap, over a severe mountain to cross. The weather was extremely warm. I viewed and pitied the case of the people on the south fork of the south branch of the Potomac: they are Germans, and have no preaching in their own language, and English preaching is taken from them—none careth for them. I am of opinion, that if a preacher would come and continue amongst them for one year, riding up and down the river, preaching from house to house, it would answer a very good purpose.

Virginia

Came to brother Baker's, a pious German, well settled on a branch of Shenandoah River. I had an attentive congregation of his countrymen.

Saturday and *Sunday*, 14, 15. I preached at Rockingham,[144] where there is the beginning of a good work. We have a church built on a hill, that cannot be hid. People came as far as thirty miles to preaching; and some found the Lord during my stay. We have some very respectable friends here.

Tuesday, 17. We had a crowd of people at Bethel, who appeared very insensible. Rode on to Miller's Town, properly Woodstock. Here I was permitted to preach in the Episcopal church. Many attended, and behaved well, and I had light and liberty in speaking.

Wednesday, 18. We had twenty-two miles to Newtown.[145] Here they have built a spacious chapel. Our horses are stiff, and lame, and sore, and the weather is oppressively warm. We have many sick, hungry, weary rides through the heat, and over hills, rocks, and mountains.

Saturday and *Sunday*, 21, 22. We held our quarterly meeting at Newtown. Many felt the power of God—particularly at the love feast. Some were of opinion that twenty were converted.

Tuesday, 24. We had a melting time while I opened these words, "Neither is there salvation in any other," &c. I feel a persuasion that these people will come home to God. One was deeply distressed under preaching. I rode about an hour after night, in order to reach brother Donaldson's, by which I found I had taken cold.

Wednesday, 25. Our conference began at Leesburg; and we continued together until the Sabbath following: and had a happy time of peace and union.

[143] (Whatcoat's *Journal*, Sweet, *op. cit.*, 111.) Brock's Gap is on the Virginia–West Virginia border.

[144] Rockingham was the present Harrisonburg, Virginia. The church there was a log house erected in 1789 on an acre conveyed for the use of Bishop Asbury, his successors and their appointees, who were to preach no other doctrine than those "contained in Mr. John Wesley's notes upon the New Testament and four volumes of sermons." (Wayland: *History of Harrisonburg*, 16.)

[145] Newtown was the present Stephens City.

To conciliate the minds of our brethren in the south district of Virginia, who are restless about the council, I wrote their leader a letter, informing him, "that I would take my seat in council as another member"; and, n that point, at least, waive the claims of episcopacy; yea, I would lie down and be trodden upon, rather than knowingly injure one soul.[146]

Maryland

Monday, 30. Preached at the Sugar Loaf mountain with great freedom, n: "For Zion's sake I will not hold my peace," and found the work of God had been greatly furthered. Here I preached sixteen years ago.

Tuesday, 31. I had a blessed season at Pigman's church, where the Lord ath wrought wonders.

Wednesday, *September* 1. There was an appearance of good at John Holland's;[147] and the work goes on there.

Thursday, 2. At the widow Hood's, I put them in mind of my first labours mongst them from house to house, and some sinners felt and shook. Next day at Rowe's there was a shaking.

Friday, 3. At night I preached in Baltimore: "O Ephraim! how shall I give thee up?"

Monday, 6. Our conference began;[148] was conducted in great peace and nion, and ended on *Wednesday*, 8.

Thursday, 9. I rode to Cokesbury.

Friday, 10. In the morning philosophical lectures were delivered; and n the afternoon the boys delivered their orations, some parts of which ere exceptionable, and duly noticed.

Saturday, 11. We made some regulations relative to the order and overnment to be observed in the college.[149]

[146] Asbury refers here to James O'Kelly, who was leading the fight in the South district of Virginia against the Council. (See letter to "The Virginia preachers," utumn, 1790.)

[147] John Holland, whose home was an early preaching place, lived near Seneca, Montgomery County. (*Journal* of Thomas Rankin, October 29, 1774; *Journal* of William olbert for January 15, 1794: "It was in this house that it pleased the Lord to find a ay to my heart.")

[148] The conference convened in Light Street Chapel during an unusual revival which ad progressed for months in Baltimore and the Baltimore Circuit. (*A Brief Account of the Work in Baltimore*, by Ezekiel Cooper, Maryland, December 1, 1790, quoted by hoebus, *op. cit.*, 85-101.)

[149] This may have pertained to the four items concerning the college in the *Minutes* of the council for December 1, 1789, or to a revision of the original thirty-two rules rescribed for forty-six students enrolled. Failure to obtain and keep suitable faculty embers stood next to a shortage of funds as a continual worry to Asbury. (*Journal* atry for December 9, 1788; Bangs, *op. cit.*, I, 236-42; Lee, *op. cit.*, 151-58.) In his count of his visit the preceding May, Coke praised the members of the faculty, but

Sunday, 12. I preached in the college hall, on Matt. xxv, 31, to forty-six scholars. Brothers Dickins and C—— spoke after me.

Delaware

Monday, 13. Set out, and next day reached Duck Creek Cross Roads where we held our conference for the Eastern shore of Maryland and Delaware.[150] One or two of our brethren felt the Virginia fire about the question of the council, but all things came into order, and the council obtained. While in session I preached twice; first, on Jos. iii, 5, and the second time, on Psalm cxxxvii, 6. We had a solemn, uniting, melting season, and great power attended our last meeting.

Saturday, 18. At noon I set out for Philadelphia; but my saddle horse being lame, I was compelled to ride my old horse, which is only fit to carry my baggage.

Sunday, 19. Dined with brother John Bond, and came on to Wilmington. Whilst preaching we had Satan inside and outside of the house,[151] and through the windows. I believe good was done, at which he was not well pleased.

A daughter of my old friend, Stedham,[152] had not forgotten me. She invited me, with much affection, to her house. She remembered the living and dying monitions of her father, and was mindful of his friends.

Pennsylvania

Monday, 20. I reached the city of Philadelphia. Our brethren have built a new chapel, thirty feet square, at the south end of the city.[153] I feel myself fatigued and unwell, occasioned by riding a rough-going horse.

spoke of "expelling a young lad of fifteen years of age" for "trifling, irreligious conduct, and open ridicule among the students, of experimental religion." (Coke, *op. cit.*, 134.)

[150] This was the third conference held in Delaware, the first in Smyrna, and also was the first in the state over which Asbury had presided as a bishop. The council against which Ezekiel Cooper anticipated "dreadful work among the preachers in opposition" was approved with only two dissenting votes. (Phoebus, *op. cit.*, 119.)

[151] Wilmington was notorious for its rudeness toward early Methodist preachers (Ware, *op. cit.*, 185, 186; *The Centennial Services of Asbury Methodist Episcopal Church, Wilmington, Delaware*, October 13–20, 1889, 124, 125, 144–46.)

[152] This was a daughter of Jacob Stedham, whom Asbury on his first visit to the vicinity of Wilmington, Delaware (April 9, 1772), described as a "friend to the Methodists." (In the "Persons Taxable" in Brandywine Hundred he is listed as "Stidham." See Scharf: *History of Delaware*, II, 902.)

[153] This new chapel was Ebenezer Church, erected on Second near Queen street in Philadelphia. Preaching had previously been in the shop of Robert Fitzgerald in Southwark. After Ebenezer was used for twenty-eight years, a new building was erected between Third and Fourth streets on Christian Street. The congregation later

Tuesday, 21. This day was spent in reading, writing, and visiting.

Wednesday, 22. The conference began in poor Pennsylvania district: all was peace and love. Our printing is in a good state.[154] Our society in the city of Philadelphia are generally poor: perhaps it is well; when men become rich, they sometimes forget that they are Methodists. I am weak, and have been busy, and am not animated by the hope of doing good here. I have therefore been silent the whole week. "I must needs go through Samaria."

Friday, 24. There was some feeling, and profitable speaking. We also had a love feast. Next day, *Saturday*, I was closely employed in writing.

Sunday, 26. Many felt and wept, whilst I enlarged on "The Lord is in his holy temple." At the new chapel, called Ebenezer, in the afternoon, my subject was 1 Sam. vii, 12. I first explained the text; then showed the Methodist doctrine and discipline, and the work God had wrought by them in this country.

New Jersey

Monday, 27. Rode to Burlington, the place appointed for our next conference. Here I preached on, "Searching Jerusalem with candles," and it was a searching season. On *Tuesday* night we had a shout—then came the bulls of Basham and broke our windows. It was well my head escaped the violence of these wicked sinners. I hope the strong power of Satan will feel a shake this conference. The session has been in great peace; harmony prevailed, and the council has been unanimously adopted.

Wednesday, 29. We have a love feast; and a genuine, sweet melting ran through the house. S. Strattan stood up and declared he had followed the work of God for six months, and that he believed six hundred souls had professed conversion in that time. There is a most genuine work in several places; viz. in Flanders, Trenton, Burlington, Salem, and Bethel circuits— glory to our wonder-working God! All hail, eternal Father, coequal Son, and everlasting Spirit, in time and forever! Amen, and Amen!!!

I delivered a discourse on Psalm cxxii, 6. On *Friday* I rode through Cross Weeks, and Allentown, and Cranbury, lodging at Doctor Jacques's.[155]

moved to 52nd and Parrish streets in West Philadelphia, and still later the property was sold and the assets and name given to a new church in Manoa in Delaware County. (Lednum, *op. cit.*; also *Journal* entries for September 26, 1790; July 8, 1792; October 11, 1795; and others.)

[154] The Methodist Publishing House had been established at Philadephia with John Dickins as Book Steward and pastor of St. George's Church in 1789.

[155] Cross Weeks is the present Crosswicks. Allentown was a post town of Upper Freehold on the road from Bordentown to Freehold. Cranberry was settled in 1682 and was partly in South Brunswick Township and partly in South Amboy Township. David Brainerd, a young follower of George Whitefield, often preached to the Indians

Saturday, October 2. As we could not reach New York, I stopped and
gave them a discourse at Elizabethtown. We afterward had a safe, although a long passage, by water to New York;[156] and found all in peace

New York

Sunday, 3. I preached at the old church;[157] and in the afternoon at the
new, on Matt. xxv, 31–46. The new church is commodious, elegant, yet
plain.[158]

Monday, 4. We began our conference,[159] and sat with close application
to business until Thursday morning: all was peace, order, and unanimity.
On Thursday evening I returned to Elizabethtown.

Friday, 8. Rode twenty-five miles to Trenton, and preached at night.
Next day I rode through a heavy rain to Philadelphia.

Pennsylvania

Sunday morning, 10, was rainy. I however preached at St. George's
church, and again in the evening. Henry Willis is come hither to settle
himself in life, and will probably go into trade. The Church has thereby
lost, in part, a faithful servant.

Thursday, 14. I left the city; dined at Chester; and here I saw one whose
soul was made dear to me by long acquaintance, now feeble in body, and
deeply affected in mind.[160]

there. Ezekiel Cooper, who followed the same general itinerary in 1786, says he lodged
at Samuel Jaques in Cranberry, and that it is probably the same person Asbury
mentions. (Phoebus, *op. cit.*, 28, 44, 71.)

[156] Elizabethtown lay on the shore of New Jersey across the narrow Arthur Kill
from the northwest corner of Staten Island. The distance from Elizabethtown to
Whitehall at the southern tip of Manhatten Island was approximately fourteen miles

[157] This was John Street Church, built on the original property purchased by the
society in March, 1768.

[158] This new church, the second in New York, was the Forsyth Street Church, referred to by Asbury in numerous *Journal* entries as the Bowery Church or the new
church. Thomas Morrell had been appointed in 1789 to raise the funds and build the
church. (See letters dated May 20, June 19, October 3, and one undated, 1789;
Journal entry for May 28, 1789.) It stood on Forsyth near Division streets on seven lots
purchased from George Workheart on August 17, 1789, for 350 pounds. The site was
on the former estate of James Delancey, which had been forfeited to the state because
of his loyalist activities. The church was of blue stucco over rough stone, 50 × 70 feet in
size, and cost around $2,500 exclusive of the lots. It was held by the same board of
trustees as the John Street property, a custom which prevailed until 1835. (Seaman, *op
cit.*, 104–14.)

[159] *John Street Records,* I, shows that the church entered wholeheartedly into meeting
the costs of the conference. One entry indicates that the church paid the costs of
"keeping the preachers' horses" for £26/6/8.

[160] The person referred to was Mrs. Mary Withey. (See note under July 6, 1773.)

Delaware

Reached New Castle, in Delaware, and once more preached there, and had a few serious hearers.

Friday, 15. I did not reach Dickinson's in time; however, I spoke a little. I found sister Dickinson[161] wrapped in clay, whom I left sick about three weeks ago: she has been an attentive, devoted woman, has washed the saints' feet, and kindly served the dear servants of God; and I trust her soul is now in peace. I spoke a little at Duck Creek Cross Roads, where nearly thirty members have been added to the society since last conference.

Sunday, 17. We had a gracious love feast, and a very powerful meeting; many bore a living testimony; there was great life and shouting among the people of God. In the evening I rode to brother White's.

Monday, 18. At Thomas White's my soul has been made to feel very solemn: a view of the remarkable work of God; the death of some, and the deep spirituality of others; the sending out young men for the ministry; and the providing for the fatherless and widows; these are all weighty matters, and greatly occupied my mind. In the midst of all my soul panteth after God.

Wednesday, 20. We rode twenty miles to Milford quarterly meeting. They have ceiled the chapel, and put the galleries in order; and what is still better, there were many living souls among them.

Thursday, 21. At the love feast many spoke of the dealings of God with their souls. I once more visited B. Williams, and felt my soul powerfully drawn out towards the children. The people are alive; but I fear they are not as much engaged as they were this time last year.

Friday, 22. Came once more to sister Sharkley's;[162] now my dear old friend is gone, perhaps the Gospel must go out of the house: I trust the dear woman is gone to heaven. I then visited the fatherless and the widow (sister Abbitt:) I felt sweet peace, and a solemn sense of the presence of God.

Saturday, 23. Came to Lewiston. There being no preaching appointed, we rode to the light-house:[163] I could but praise God that the house was kept by people who praise and love him; no drinking or swearing here. Brother Hargus is a Christian and a preacher; and God has owned his labours. An Irish vessel had been cast away with three hundred souls on

[161] This was probably the wife of Joseph Dickenson, who in 1789 donated the site for the chapel that bore his name. (Hallman, *op. cit.*, 109, 249.)

[162] This is probably a misspelling of Shockley. Elias Shockley was one of the Trustees to whom a lot for the Milford Church was deeded on December 3, 1787. (Scharf, *op. cit.*, II, 1198.)

[163] The keeper of historic Henlopen Lighthouse on Cape Henlopen was then J. R. Hargus.

board, all of whom perished but about forty: I asked him concerning it, and I learned that they were within sight of land; and that if they had timely thrown themselves into the sea, they were nigh enough the land to have been washed ashore, so that many more would have probably been saved. So much for a drunken captain, who threw these precious lives away. Brother Hargus told me that he did not go near the wreck until after his return from Lewistown, with a guard; that it was reported some of the crew were as ready to plunder the goods on board as others: stricter laws are now made; and the people on this shore are greatly reformed; for which they may thank the Methodists. We have a chapel built at Lewistown; and we had an agreeable Sabbath day. The people, however, have their prejudices. Mr. Wilson,[164] a minister of thirty or forty years' standing, has gone (since I was here last) to give an account of his stewardship, as we must all shortly do.

Tuesday, 26. I preached at the Sound chapel. Brother Joseph Everett then spoke of the sin of unbelief as the chief sin that keeps people from the blessings of the Gospel. We administered the sacrament, and in the afternoon rode to Buckingham.[165] I rejoiced in the account brother William Powell gave me of the state of religion at the Sound: he said that the Lord had owned and blest their prayer meetings; that he thought one hundred souls had been affected and shaken, and perhaps eighteen or twenty converted in the space of eighteen or twenty months; that brother Arthur Williams, a local deacon, was in the spirit of the work—formerly he pleased all with his smooth speaking, but that now they cry out against him.

Wednesday, 27. I felt glad in my soul, notwithstanding brother Jesse Lee is on forbidden ground;[166] and, in spite of prejudice and Antinomianism, that souls are awakened by his ministry. I feel myself under some temptation; but I fight and conquer in the strength of Christ.

Thursday, 28. I finished reading the second volume of the Arminian Magazine.[167] Notwithstanding its defects, I am persuaded it is one of the best and cheapest books in America: the life of Mr. John Fletcher, the tracts, letters, and sermons are good; the poetry might be better.

---

[164] The only resident minister with such a record of long service was the Rev. Matthew Wilson who was installed as pastor of the Lewes Presbyterian Church in 1756 and served until his death in 1791, which may have been erroneously ascribed to 1791 rather than the date Asbury here gives.

[165] Buckingham, the present Berlin in Worcester County. The Mother of Methodism in this vicinity was Perdeaux Chapel, located in Sinepuxent Neck, Worcester County.

[166] New England, a new field to which Lee had been appointed in 1789, had been generally inhospitable to Methodism. (Lee, *op. cit.*, 142, 163–67.)

[167] The second and final issue of *The Arminian Magazine*, published in Philadelphia, 1790 (John Dickins, Editor), is not to be confused with the London publication of the same name, begun in 1778. To the Arminian publication Asbury contributed a letter "in behalf of the Council."

Virginia

Saturday, 30. I feel the weakness and infirmities of flesh and blood, having ridden seventy miles the two last days. At the quarterly meeting, at Garrettson's, I was unwell, but felt Divine assistance in my preaching.

Sunday, 31. We had a powerful love feast; and I believe it would have been more so had God's dear children had time to speak. We had a vast crowd of people. Brother Thomas Foster preached first, and I after him: I had a solemn sense of God, and sinners were serious.

Monday, November 1. Preached at Accomack court house, on Rom. i, 16. We had a weighty season. A poor man, who had lately professed religion, appeared to be somewhat distracted: he has been a vile sinner but I hope he will recover his right mind: the family is subject to derangement. There are some unreasonable things among the people here; but we are afraid of gathering out the tares, lest we should root up the wheat also. We must continue to observe the order of God and our own discipline; attend to preaching, prayer, class meeting, and love feast: and then, if they will shout, why let them shout.

Wednesday, 3. I preached on education, from "Come, ye children, hearken to me; I will teach you the fear of the Lord." The word was felt by the parents.

Maryland

After preaching I rode to Littleton Long's.[168] This neighbourhood is supplied with preaching by the Episcopalians, Presbyterians, Baptists and Methodists. All is well, if the people are saved.

Thursday, 4. We had but few hearers, and an uncomfortable time, at our quarterly meeting in the Annamessex chapel. Next day we had a full house, and I preached on education; my text, "Train up a child in the way he should go, and when he is old he will not depart from it." After meeting we rode eighteen miles without our dinner, which, with the disagreeable weather, made me sick. Rode twenty-five miles to Broad Creek quarterly meeting, and preached on Matt. x, 37, 38; and the next day on Hosea vi, 4—it was a searching time. We came off, and found the wind blowing fiercely; but when we had entered the boat, we had a sudden calm: if this were not an answer to prayer, it was as I prayed. I reproved myself for a sudden and violent laugh at the relation of a man's having

---

[168] William Colbert says, "I rode from Salisbury to Littleton Long's in Worcester County on the south side of Pocomoke River and the first house in Northampton Circuit." (Colbert's *Journal*, II, 32, 41.)

given an old Negro woman her liberty *because she had too much religion for him.*

Monday, 8. We held a quarterly meeting in Dorset, in a new, unfinished house.[169]

Tuesday, 9. We had a gracious love feast; and I addressed parents very seriously, on Deut. vi, 6–7. I lodged with brother Henry Ennalls, who, with his wife, has been powerfully brought to God; his slaves were freed immediately. His sister, Nancy Bassett,[170] has gone to rest: the other two have followed the example of a dear brother; God has heard their prayers.[171]

Wednesday, 10. I came to Frazier's chapel: my spirits were very low; and I felt that there was death amongst the people.

Thursday, 11. Our love feast was living and powerful. I have seen a wonder of grace in Capt. B——: this has been the wish of my heart, the desire of my soul, and the answer to prayer; for which I am thankful to God.

Friday, 12. I preached at Bolingbroke to a full house, on Ephraim's mixing himself among the people.

Saturday, 13. We had a gracious season at the love feast. In the evening I came to Allen's.[172] The next day, being rainy, we had about one hundred hearers at Tuckahoe Chapel; whereas, we expected that, had it been a clear day, we should have five or six hundred. I preached in the evening at Choptank Bridge to a few people.

Monday, 15. I see the wonders of grace; and have had severe conflicts: my soul is more and more established in God; but so many persons and things occupy my time, that I have not as much leisure and opportunity for prayer and communion with God, and for drinking into the Holy Spirit of life and love as I could wish. We had a seasonable time at brother Thomas White's: I was very pointed on 2 Peter ii, 9. Perhaps I have spoken my last admonition to some who were present.

Thursday, 18. Rode to Dover, Delaware; and next day we had quarterly meeting at Dudley's chapel.

Saturday, 20. At Duck Creek Cross Roads a spirit of prayer prevails amongst the people, and God is with them.

Sunday, 21. At Cecil quarterly meeting, held at Dickinson's, we had

---

[169] Dorchester County, formed in 1668, was named for Earl Dorset, a family friend of the Calverts. In Asbury's day the name Dorset was in common use. (Mathews: *The Counties of Maryland*, 421.) This "new, unfinished house," if a place of worship, may have been Ennall's or Airey's Chapel.

[170] This was the wife of Richard Bassett.

[171] The other two sisters (besides Mrs. Richard Bassett) were Catherine, who married William Bruff, and Mary, who became the wife of George Ward, a local preacher of Snow Hill, Maryland. (Boehm, *op. cit.*, 69; Hallman, *op. cit.*, 299 ff.; Bangs: *Life of Garrettson*, 253; Stevens, *op. cit.*, iv, 177.)

[172] This was Dr. Moses D. Allen. (See note under November 20, 1787.)

many people, and some life. On *Monday* I rode to Dr. Clayton's;[173] and next day to Cokesbury, where I continued until *Monday* the 29th. We then examined the students relatively to learning and religion, paid debts, and put matters in better order. We have forty-five boys. The charitable subscriptions to the establishment amount to £300 per annum.

December 1. The council was seated in Philip Rogers's chamber in Baltimore.[174] After some explanation, we all agreed that we had a right to manage the temporal concerns of the Church and college decisively; and to recommend to the conferences, for ratification, whatever we judged might be advantageous to the spiritual well-being of the whole body. For the sake of union, we declined sending out any recommendatory propositions: we had great peace and union in all our labours. What we have done, the minutes will show.

Sunday, 5. I preached a funeral discourse on the death of Mrs. Murray,[175] on I Cor. xv, 29–31: it was, I hope, not altogether in vain. In the afternoon I preached in Mr. Otterbein's church. I have kept no journal during the sitting of the council: I enjoy peace of soul, but such a variety of persons and subjects agitates my poor mind. Lord, keep me in perfect peace!

Thursday, 9. The council rose after advising a loan of £1,000, payable in two years, for Cokesbury; and giving directions for proper books to be printed.

Friday, 10. I left Baltimore, and reached my old friend, Shadrach Turner's: the girls, who were babes when I first visited this house, are now grown up, and, I trust, possess religion.

---

[173] Joshua Clayton (1744–98), a resident of Upper Bohemia Manor, was a surgeon and aide to General Washington in the Revolutionary War. He was the first governor of Delaware and had served two years in the Senate of the United States when he fell victim to the yellow fever epidemic in Philadelphia. He married Mrs. Rachel McCleary, an adopted daughter of Governor Richard Bassett. Their son, Thomas, also was a senator from Delaware. Another son, Dr. James Lawson Clayton, married Elizabeth Nutter Polk, a granddaughter of Judge Thomas White. Dr. and Mrs. Joshua Clayton were buried in Bethel Church. (Scharf, *op. cit.*, I, 479; *Biographical Directory of the American Congress*, 1774–1927, 821; *National Cyclopaedia of American Biography*, XI, 530, Delaware Historical Society Papers, Numbers 31–40.)

[174] The council was instituted by order of the annual conferences of 1789. It was to be comprised of the bishops and presiding elders, not to be fewer than nine in number. It was authorized to survey almost every function and phase of Methodism and submit its recommendations to the conferences. The first meeting convened on December 3, 1789. The provision that no measure would be binding until unanimously approved by the council and by the several conferences rendered the experiment unacceptable. (*Journal* entry for December 3–10, 1789; Lee, *op. cit.*, 149–59; Buckley: *Constitutional and Parliamentary History of the Methodist Episcopal Church*, 61; Tigert: *A Constitutional History of American Episcopal Methodism*, 250 ff.)

[175] Mary, aged forty-four, wife of Edward Murray, a Baltimore merchant, died November 24, 1790, and was buried in St. Paul's Churchyard. A religious service, days after the interment, was not unusual in those times.

Virginia

Saturday, 11. We rode through heavy rain to Alexandria, in Virginia.

Sunday, 12. I preached morning and evening; but the streets being muddy, and but few friends attending from the country, we had a thin congregation.

Monday, 13. We set out for Stafford. The weather being uncomfortable, and the roads deep, we turned in at twenty miles, to Mr. Dawning's, who treated us kindly.

Tuesday, 14. We hasted to Mrs. Waller's,[176] where we found a few people, to whom I spoke on Rom. ii, 7–9. Finding Tommy (a son of Mrs. Waller's) had genius, I gave him a pass to Cokesbury: it may be that he may serve himself, his family, and his country. O that he may serve his God!

Wednesday, 15. Came to King George; and, cold as it was, I found nearly one hundred people had assembled at the widow Bombry's.

Saturday, 18. Attended the quarterly meeting at brother Edwards's: the weather was extremely cold, and we had but few hearers.

Sunday, 19. After preaching at the quarterly meeting, I visited Counsellor Carter; and spent the evening in much peace and love: he has the manners of a gentleman, the attainments of a scholar, and the experience of a Christian.

Monday, 20. The weather softening, I made haste to get across the Rappahannock, and reached brother Ball's, about twenty-five miles: I found myself much chilled by my ride. My soul has been kept in great peace; and almost in constant prayer: I wish to feel so placid as not to have any acid in my temper, nor a frown or wrinkle on my brow; to bear all things, do all things, suffer all things, from the ignorance or weakness of the children of God, or the wickedness of the sons and daughters of Satan. I think my soul momently pants after more of God.[177]

Thursday, 23. I preached at brother Collin's; and was very pointed: I hope it will have the good effect of preventing the sin and vanity that too often prevail at Christmas.

Friday, 24. Came to the widow Clayton's; where there has been a work of God: I preached with liberty, from, "Put ye on the Lord Jesus Christ and make no provision for the flesh to fulfil the lusts thereof." I cautioned the people against the sins of the times.

Christmas day. I had thirty miles to Hanover. William Glendenning[178]

[176] Thomas Scott says the Widow Waller's was one of the preaching stations. Mrs Waller was the mother of John Waller of Kentucky, one of the delegates sent from that state to the legislature of Virginia to obtain the consent of the latter for Kentucky to form a constitution and state government. (Scott's *Journal.*)

[177] See letter to friends at Taunton, England, 1790.

[178] William Glendenning had been one of the early preachers but had become a recalcitrant who later made severe attacks on Asbury and the episcopacy.

began before I came; when he had done, I went into the tavern keeper's porch; but I afterward judged it best to withdraw, and speak in another place. I stood in the door of a public house, and with about half of my congregation out of doors, preached on, "Behold, I bring you good tidings of great joy:" the people behaved exceedingly well; and the town was very still.

Sunday, 26. I had a large congregation at Newcastle,[179] to whom I spoke on, "Thou shalt call his name Jesus; for he shall save his people from their sins." William Glendenning spoke after me: I am clear he is not right in his head or heart, and am therefore resolved he shall speak no more at my appointments.

Monday, 27. Preached at Colonel Clayton's.[180] The people hereabouts are wealthy, and few attend preaching; nevertheless, I was favoured with their company, and had great liberty and sweetness in speaking to them: I feel as if God would yet work among them. It was in this neighbourhood I was laid up four years ago.

Tuesday, 28. I had many people at the widow A——'s; but they did not appear to be in a good frame to receive instruction: their Christmas company; sinful, worldly joy; full feeding; together with the severity of the weather—all appeared to make against a profitable meeting.

Wednesday, 29. Preached in James City[181]—crowded with company. I was informed of some painful circumstances relative to our dissatisfied brethren: I leave these things to God, who will bring all things to light. Contrary to my expectations, I found there was an appointment made for me to preach in Williamsburg, being the day I had intended to cross the river.

Thursday, 30. I preached in the city of Williamsburg, according to appointment: I felt much liberty; and had some hope that Providence was about to open the way for a work in this place.

Friday, 31. I came on to the (Jamestown) ferry, chilled with the cold. We had to ride seven miles; the wind was high about the time we embarked; presently a snow storm came on; and although wind and tide were in our favour, we had rough work in crossing. Our horses were smooth, the bottom of the boat icy; so that it was with difficulty they could keep their feet; however, kind Providence brought us safe to Cobham, whence we hasted along to brother Mooring's, and found brother Paup speaking, and the people shouting. I preached on Ephes. v, 17–19. I

[179] "In the early years there were two flourishing ports in Hanover on the Pamunkey River. One was Hanover Town, once known as Page's Warehouse, and Newcastle, the former some fifteen miles above the present bridge on the Tappahannock Highway, and the latter a short distance below it. Both are now abandoned. As late as 1830 Newcastle was an important shipping point for tobacco." (Gwathmey: *Twelve Virginia Counties*, 86.)

[180] Colonel Clayton lived in Hanover County.

[181] On this route Asbury usually preached at Chickahominy Church.

afterward had an interview with brother Paup,[182] and a more full account of matters relative to our disaffected brethren. Thence I rode on to brother William Blunt's;[183] but there were none to preach to.

[182] In 1790 John Paup was pastor on the Sussex Circuit.
[183] William Blunt's was a regular preaching place in Isle of Wight County.

1791

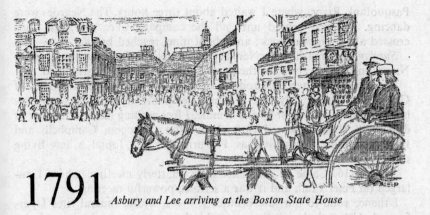

1791 *Asbury and Lee arriving at the Boston State House*

CHAPTER TWENTY

Virginia

Sunday, January 2, 1791. Notwithstanding the snow was deep, we rode to brother Cowling's. Few people attended; but we had a comfortable meeting, especially at the sacrament.

Monday, 3. We rode hard to get to Craney Island, and came within three miles by two o'clock; the people being dispersed, we came back to brother Joliff's.[1]

Tuesday, 4. I had a few to hear, to whom I spoke on Rom. xiii, 11. I engaged R. I——, as a French teacher for Cokesbury.

Wednesday, 5. We had a blessed time at Norfolk, whilst I applied Zech. xii, 10. Many praised the Lord aloud. I was closely employed until the moment I left town. I find the Lord has wrought in Norfolk, Portsmouth, and the country round about.

North Carolina

Thursday, 6. I did not reach chapel until three o'clock. Next day I reached Colonel Williams's, Currituck, North Carolina.[2] Here we had a quickening time. I possess peace of mind; and feel no murmuring nor discontent. My horse is very lame, and the roads in this country are very deep.

Saturday, 8. After preaching at B——'s, I hasted to S——'s ferry, on

[1] The church at Joliff's is still extant, though not the same building.
[2] See note under December 20, 1784.

Pasquotank River, where I waited about three hours. The Negroes were dancing. I stayed behind until all the company were over, and then crossed about eight o'clock; and about nine, reached brother P——'s.

Sunday, 9. Preached at New-begun church in the morning, and at Nixonton in the evening, in the court house, which was nearly filled.

Tuesday, 11. Yesterday I rode to brother B——'s, within five miles of Gates court house.[3] My fare is sometimes poor, my rides are long, my horse is lame; yet, whilst Christ is mine, I feel nothing like murmuring or discontent. I have passed through Winton, Wicocon, Campbell, and Hardy counties,[4] preaching as I journeyed, and found a few living souls.

Sunday, 16. Came to Gardener's, to quarterly meeting, where I enlarged on Peter's fall, and it was a serious, powerful meeting.

I thence rode to our late brother F——'s, whose funeral rites I performed. Although the weather was cold, the congregation was large. I was importuned to visit the town; but found there were but few who really wished me to go. I however, went, and preached to them at candlelight, and many of them laughed at the foolish old prophet. Perhaps, when I next come to see them, they will be more serious. Thence we hastened to brother Jones's, whose wife lately departed this life in the full triumph of faith—and his son is engaged in horse-racing. This brought to my mind young P——; who, after the death of his pious father, turned away the preachers, and sinned with a high hand; but the Lord followed him; and after he had spent a good deal of the substance left him by his father, he was made a happy subject of the grace of God. I will not give up all hope for young Jones.

Saturday 22 Crossed Neuse River, at Smith's ferry, and came to the dwelling the late Gen. Hardy Bryan[5]—a man I had often heard of, and wished to see; but death, swift and sudden, reached the house before me. His son H—— died the 18th of last November; his daughter Mary, December 28th; and himself the 10th instant: each of them feared the Lord, and were happy souls. I felt strangely unwilling to believe the General was dead, until I could no longer doubt it: at the grave-yard I had

[3] The present Gatesville in Gates County, North Carolina.

[4] No such counties have ever existed in North Carolina. Asbury or Hollingsworth must have meant communities instead of counties. Winton then and now is the county seat of Hertford County. Wicocon (spelled variously) is a river near Winton which gave its name to a geographic area. Hardy and Campbell may have been communities. (William G. Tarlton, Researcher, North Carolina Department of Archives and History, Raleigh.)

[5] General Bryan was a barrister who lived in the bounds of the New River Circuit which took its name from a stream in Onslow County, though it embraced several counties. He had recently been converted from deism through the instrumentality of his wife and the ministry of Thomas Ware, who was elder of the circuits in the area the previous year. He died shortly thereafter. (Grissom, *op. cit.*, 165; Ware: *Life and Travels of Rev. Thomas Ware*, 164–67.)

Sunday, 6. Notwithstanding the heavy rain, we had many to hear at brother Stafford's;[20] where I enforced, "Let this mind be in you which was also in Christ Jesus."

Georgia

Monday, 7. I preached at Hudson's ferry with some freedom; but the people appeared wild and stupid. I was alarmed at hearing a man talking large and loud, thinking he was drunk, and would come in and disturb the congregation; but he was, as I afterwards learned, an Antinomian. I came, in a heavy storm, to brother H——'s.[21] This day I passed Savannah Swamp, parts of which are not unlike the Santee and Kentucky lands.

Tuesday, 8. We had nearly four hundred people at R——'s; and I trust the Lord, in some good degree, breathed upon the souls present. We then rode sixteen miles, and had a comfortable evening exercise at brother R——'s.

Wednesday, 9. Preached at an old church.[22] I was much fatigued, and felt unwell. At the invitation of Mr. C——, I came to Waynesborough. I lodged with Mr. Henry, a Jew. We read Hebrew part of the night, and I should have been pleased to have spent the night thus occupied with so good a scholar.

Thursday, 10. I preached at C——'s church. My body was wearied with labour and want of sleep.

Sunday, 13. Came to Georgetown at Ogechee Shoals, and found Satan was there. I levelled away on the parable of the sower. I came to brother H——'s. Heard heavy tidings.[23] My soul is calm. Let the Lord look to his

[20] Stafford lived near Black Swamp Church in the lower corner of Hampton County.

[21] Asbury seems to have entered Georgia over Hudson's Ferry and proceeded through Screven and Burke counties. "Brother H——" probably lived in Screven.

[22] The old church near Waynesboro in Burke County may have been the one he used on his previous visit. (See note under March 2, 1790.) Asbury was accompanied by Bishop Thomas Coke, who now made his first visit to Georgia. (Smith: *Asbury*, 129; *Georgia Methodism*, 45.)

[23] The "heavy tidings" was the news of the defection of the popular preacher Beverly Allen, who was on the Edisto Circuit in South Carolina and who was expelled the following year for a "flagrant crime." He then went to Georgia, where he and his brother, Billy, operated a store on the road between Fishdam Ford on Broad River and Cherokee Ford on the Savannah in Elbert County. In 1795, while he was buying goods in Augusta, a warrant was secured against him by a creditor from whom he purchased his original stock. Allen armed himself and barricaded himself in his hotel room, and when the U.S. Marshall, Major Forsyth, forced the door, he was shot dead by Allen. The former preacher was then arrested for murder, but he escaped and fled to his home in Georgia. There the sheriff, William Barnett, arrested him by setting fire to the house in which he was hidden and lodged him in jail. Sympathy was with Allen, however, not only because of his great popularity as a preacher, but also because the political contests of the period had involved the federal courts in unpopularity. Learning that a mob would attempt to rescue his prisoner, the sheriff tried to take Allen

own house. I hasted to Scott's. Doctor Coke came in time enough to preach; and then we opened a conference.[24]

We sat very closely to our work; and had some matters of moment to attend to in the course of our deliberations. I have ridden about two hundred and fifty miles in Georgia, and find the work, in general, very dead. The peace with the Creek Indians, the settlement of new lands, good trade, buying slaves, &c., to take up the attention of the people.

Sunday, 20. There was a shaking amongst the people whilst I spoke on Rom. x, 21.

South Carolina

After meeting, I came away, and rode twenty miles to brother Herbert's[25] that evening.

Whilst Doctor Coke stayed behind to preach at Ninety-six Town, I came on and made an appointment and preached at Finche's;[26] and some, I know, felt the word.

Wednesday, 23. We crossed the Ennoree, Tyger, and Broad Rivers.

Saturday, 26. We had white and red Indians at Catawba;[27] the Doctor and myself both preached. I had some conversation with the chiefs of the Indians about keeping up the school we have been endeavouring to estab-

to Washington in Wilkes County, but he was intercepted and forced to return. The following night the Elbert County jail was attacked by two hundred men, and Allen was released. It developed that the powder had been taken from the guns of fifteen guards, and the one other was prevented from firing while the prisoner escaped. Allen went to Logan County, Kentucky, which was known as "Rogue's Harbor" because of the large number of criminals there. Here he practiced medicine and became a Universalist. The famous Peter Cartwright boarded in Allen's house when he was a boy attending school in Russellville and was with him when he died. When Cartwright asked him "if he was willing to die and meet his final Judge with his Universalist sentiments," Allen replied that "he could make the mercy of God cover every case but his own." (*Autobiography of Peter Cartwright*, 28; Smith: *Georgia Methodism*, 27, 28; Bowen: *Wilkes County*, 118–19; Gilmer: *Early Settlers of Upper Georgia*, 105–6. Cartwright's eyewitness account that Allen died warning his hearers "not to come to that place of torment to which he felt himself eternally doomed" does not support the statement of McIntosh, *History of Elbert County*, 71–73, that Allen became a preacher in Kentucky and lived to the age of ninety years.)

[24] For the location of Scott's meetinghouse where the conference was held, see the note for March 6, 1789. There was a decrease of two hundred members in Georgia, though the Savannah River Circuit increased. Hardy Herbert from North Carolina was placed on the Washington Circuit with John Andrew. He was sent to Virginia the following year. (Smith: *Georgia Methodism*, 45.)

[25] Herbert's store was east of Chappell about where Silver Street, South Carolina is now located.

[26] Finch lived just south of the Enoree River and five miles west of the Broad in upper Newberry County where the Bethel School was soon to be located.

[27] They crossed the Broad at Smith's Ferry ten miles above Sockhart into York County and met the Indians beyond Fort Mill.

lish amongst them. I asked for one of their children; but the father would not give consent, nor would the child come. My body is weak; but my mind has heaven and peace within. We closely employed our intervals of leisure, in preparing different tracts for the press.

North Carolina

Lord's day, 27. We found the people insensible at the Waxsaws church: some few seemed alarmed whilst Isa. xxxiii, 14 was opened and enforced.

Wednesday, 30. We came to Salisbury: I felt unwell, and no freedom to speak. Doctor Coke gave them a sermon, and we then rode five miles to B——'s. Next day we reached Jones's; and the day after (*first of April*) M'Knight's, where we opened conference in great peace. Many of the preachers related their experience, and it was a blessed season of grace.

Monday, 4. We rose, after sitting each night (Sabbath excepted) until twelve o'clock. Several of our brethren expressed something like the perfect love of God, but they had doubts about their having retained it.

Tuesday, 5. We rested awhile at Salem on our way, and came in the evening to brother W——'s, and had a meeting there. I believe trouble is at hand: but I trust God with his cause, and Christ with his Church. My soul drinks into holiness.

Friday, 8. I observed as a day of abstinence and prayer, reading and meditation. O for more of heaven! Poor Minters's case has given occasion for sinners and for the world to laugh, and talk, and write.

Saturday, 9. We had a large congregation at Arnett's; I felt life in speaking, although weak and weary in body. We rode seven miles to the banks of Dan River, but knew not where to cross. At length we came to the Fishery, crossed in a canoe, and walked two miles, in the night, to T. Harrison's: thus ended the labours of the day.

Virginia

Sunday, 10. Doctor Coke and myself both preached at Watson's church; and there was some little effect produced. I spent the evening with George Adams, a true son of his worthy father, Silvanus Adams, for kindness to the preachers. I am constantly weak and feverish in body; but my soul is uncommonly happy and calm. We moved from G. Adams's to the widow Dick's; and thence, next day to brother Marten's.

Wednesday, 13. Came to Difficult church,[28] where we were honoured with the company of some of the *great*: Doctor Coke preached a noble

[28] Difficult Church was evidently on Difficult Creek. (See map of Halifax County, Virginia.) Watson's was in present Chatham County.

sermon on the Divinity of Christ; and I urged, "It is time to seek the Lord."
Afterward we preached in Charlotte and Mecklenburg; and on *Sunday*
following came to quarterly meeting at sister Walker's, in Brunswick.
Doctor Coke went to the barn;[29] and I preached in the house: the rain
rendered our meeting uncomfortable.

Monday, 18. Near Dinwiddie court house I waited, it being the day of
the election, until our brethren returned from the court house, and then
preached in the new church on 2 Cor. vi, 17, 18.

Tuesday, 19. We rode to Petersburg.[30] We agreed to take different
lodgings during the sitting of the conference—the Doctor at brother
Davis's, and myself at brother Harding's.

Wednesday, 20. I preached on "Our light afflictions which are but for a
moment," &c.; and there was some warmth amongst the preachers and
the people. The business of our conference was brought on in peace; and
there was a blessing attended our speaking on our experiences, and in
prayer. The affair of the council was suspended until a general conference.

Friday, 22. Late in the evening our conference rose.

Saturday, 23. I preached at E. West's, to a large congregation: and had
a little spring of power.

Sunday, 24. Came to Colonel Clayton's;[31] who was very ill. We had a
large collection of people, and a good meeting: we were to have held our
conference[32] at the colonel's, but his illness prevented. We sat at his son,
B. Clayton's; and were amply provided for: the son is not a member; but
he was very kind.

Monday, 25. Doctor Coke and brother I. Ellis preached; and there was
some power attended the word. I found the Doctor had much changed his
sentiments since his last visit to this continent; and that these impressions
still continued. I hope to be enabled to give up all I dare for peace' sake;
and to please all men for their good to edification.

We hastened our business; and on *Tuesday, twenty-sixth*, came to New
Castle: here I preached on "How often would I have gathered thy children
together as a hen gathereth her brood under her wings, and ye would
not:" I have no doubt but the people felt the word. We came on to Hanover Town; where the Doctor preached in the afternoon.

Wednesday, 27. We rode thirty miles to the widow Collins's, Caroline
county, much wearied in body, but greatly comforted in God.

Thursday, 28. At eleven o'clock, at Pope's chapel,[33] the Doctor preached
on, "Pray without ceasing." Myself, on, "By grace are ye saved, through

[29] This was the preaching place called Old Barn in Brunswick County, Virginia.
(See Early's *Journal*, Randolph-Macon College.)

[30] See letter to Ezekiel Cooper, April 19, 1791.

[31] Colonel Clayton lived in Hanover County.

[32] See letter from Coke to Bishop White, April 24, 1791.

[33] Pope's Chapel was in Caroline County.

'aith": I was long and very close. We hasted to Port Royal,[34] where a number of fine people were waiting, to whom the Doctor preached on 'Ye are dead, and your life is hid with Christ in God:" they expressed a desire for me to preach also; but it being late, I declined it.

Friday, 29. The solemn news reached our ears that the public papers had announced the death of that dear man of God, John Wesley. He died in his own house in London, in the eighty-eighth year of his age, after preaching the Gospel sixty-four years. When we consider his plain and nervous writings; his uncommon talent for sermonizing and journalizing; that he had such a steady flow of animal spirits; so much of the spirit of government in him; his knowledge as an observer; his attainments as a scholar; his experience as a Christian; I conclude, his equal is not to be found among all the sons he hath brought up, nor his superior among all the sons of Adam he may have left behind. Brother Coke was sunk in spirit, and wished to hasten home immediately. For myself, notwithstanding my long absence from Mr. Wesley, and a few unpleasant expressions in some of the letters the dear old man has written to me occasioned by the misrepresentation of others), I feel the stroke most sensibly; and, I expect, I shall never read his works without reflecting on the loss which the Church of God and the world has sustained by his death. Dr. Coke, accompanied by brother Cox, and Dr. Glendenning,[35] set out for Baltimore in order to get the most speedy passage to England; leaving me to fill the appointments. I had a large congregation at sister Bombry's. In the afternoon I rode to sister Waller's, making a journey of forty miles for this day. Next day I overtook Dr. Coke and his company at Colchester. Brother Coxes's horse being sick, I put my old horse in his place to carry them to Alexandria; where we arrived about three o'clock, after riding forty miles by our reckoning. At Alexandria[36] Dr. Coke had certain information of Mr. Wesley's death. On *Sabbath day* he reached Baltimore, and preached on the occasion of Mr. Wesley's death; and mentioned some things which gave offence.

Maryland

Thursday, May 5. This day, and the two following days we held conference in Baltimore;[37] and great love and sweetness prevailed throughout

---

[34] Port Royal, established in 1744, was one of the principal shipping points on the Rappahannock River in colonial times. Near here John Wilkes Booth, Lincoln's assassin, was killed while resisting arrest.

[35] See *Minutes* and *Letters*, especially the Bishop White correspondence.

[36] See letter to Daniel Fidler, May 1, 1791.

[37] Three sermons were delivered daily. Bishop Asbury, John Dickins, Jonathan Forrest, and Ezekiel Cooper are mentioned. On Friday the Bishop examined the candidates. Monday, about thirty preachers were seated for breakfast at one table in the

the sitting. I preached to a large congregation on the *Sabbath*, and we had a gracious time.

Monday, 9. Came to Cokesbury. I found there was a vast demand for money for the establishment, there having been an expenditure of £700 in five months.

Tuesday, 10. Crossed Susquehannah and came to Cecil; and next day reached Duck Creek. Our conference began,[38] and was conducted in much peace and harmony amongst preachers and people. Our meetings in public were attended with great power.

Sunday, 15. Two elders and three deacons were ordained. After the ordination, I rode to Middletown, Delaware, and preached to a large congregation.

Monday, 16. I rode to New Castle, and had the last interview with Dr. Coke. Surely the time to favour New Castle is swiftly coming.

Pennsylvania

In the evening I came to Chester; and next day (the 17th) arrived in Philadelphia, and opened conference. We had a tender, melting account of the dealings of God with many souls; and settled our business in much peace. Mr. Hammett came from Charleston with a wonderful list of petitioners desiring his return: to this, as far as I had to say, I submitted, but I see and hear many things that might wound my spirit, if it were not that the Lord bears me up above all.

Wednesday, 18. I preached on, "The Lord liveth; and blessed be my rock, and let the God of my salvation be exalted."

Friday, 20. We had a fast day; and in the afternoon a feast of love. It was a time to be remembered: some precious souls were converted.

Saturday, 21. I left Philadelphia for New Jersey. On the road I felt much of the spirit of prayer.

New Jersey

Sunday, 22. I preached in Trenton, on Joel ii, 17. Several preachers exhorted, and the Lord made sinners tremble. Eighteen years ago often slipped away from Philadelphia to Burlington one week, and to

home of Philip Rogers. In a large adjoining room the business of the conference was concluded. (*Journal* of William Colbert, I, 36, 37; Phoebus, *op. cit.*, 130; see Coke's letter to James O'Kelly, May 4, 1791.)

[38] The conference met in the chapel built in 1786 in Smyrna, then known as Duck Creek Cross Roads. Ezekiel Cooper noted that the "Governor of the State (Richard Bassett, Delaware) who has opened his house on the circuit as a place for preaching was present during the Conference Session." Nearby Queen Anne was one of the twelve new circuits created. (Phoebus, *op. cit.*, 130, 131; Hallman, *op. cit.*, 244.)

Trenton another, to keep a few souls alive: I had then no conferences to take up my time and occupy my thoughts; and now—what hath God wrought!

We attended to the business of the conference with a good spirit. In the course of our sitting we had some pleasing and some painful circumstances to excite our feelings.

Tuesday, 24. I set out for New York. At Princeton[39] I preached, and I trust a few felt the word. Passing through Kingston,[40] I proceeded on to Mr. Samuel Jaques's, near Brunswick, making thirty-two miles. My soul is in peace; my body weak and weary.

Wednesday, 25. Rode to Elizabethtown. After dinner, I went by water to New York; and found all in peace.

New York

Thursday, 26. Our conference came together in great peace and love. Our ordinary business was enlivened by the relation of experiences, and by profitable observations on the work of God.

Nothing would satisfy the conference and the society but my consenting to preach on the occasion of Mr. Wesley's death, which I did on *Sunday*, *May* 29: my text was 2 Tim. iii, 10, 11.[41] I took the same subject at the old church in the morning; and in the afternoon at the new church, varying, but retaining the substance.[42]

Monday, 30. Our conference rose; and after love feast, the preachers dispersed. We had had about thirty preachers at this conference, and not a frown, a sign of sour temper, or an unkind word was seen or heard amongst us:—but I am sick, and quite outdone with constant labour. Mr. Hammett's preaching was not well received; it was supposed to be aimed at our zealous men and passionate meetings: at the new church his preaching was still more exceptionable to those judicious persons who heard him. I expect some things will be retailed to my disadvantage. Be it so—I trust the Lord.

[39] Princeton was settled about 1681 and was first called Stony Brook. In 1724 the name was changed to Prince's Town and then shortened to Princeton. Hageman *History of Princeton*, II, 195) says the first Methodist sermon in Princeton was given by Ezekiel Cooper in 1802, but Asbury's entry above disproves this statement. Attempts to organize a society were not successful until 1841. (Gordon's *Gazetteer of New Jersey*, 834, 221; Phoebus, *op. cit.*, 63.)

[40] Kingston was a prominent stopping place on the stage road from Philadelphia to New York. It is in Middlesex County and was founded about 1700. Most of the stage passengers commonly dined at the inn of Mr. P. Withington, now Kingston House. Gordon, *op. cit.*, 165.)

[41] Ezekiel Cooper was to use this text many years later when called upon to preach a similar sermon after Asbury's death.

[42] See letter to Nelson Reed, May 29, 1791.

Wednesday, June 1. I preached at New Rochelle church:[43] the weather was unfavourable: but we had a living meeting.

Thursday, 2. We had a decent, lifeless congregation, at the court house on the Plains.[44] In the afternoon I preached at Northcastle,[45] on Phil. ii, 12. My clay is heavy, and my spirits low.

Friday, 3. I very sensibly feel the cold I had taken on my way to New Rochelle by riding in the rain; however, I rode to Bedford,[46] and preached in the town house to about two hundred serious and deeply-attentive hearers. Rode on to brother H——'s,[47] and was much indisposed.

Connecticut

Saturday, 4. I rode over rocks and hills, and came to Wilton; and preached to a serious, feeling, well-behaved people at Squire Rockwell's.[48] In the evening I went on to Redding.[49] Surely God will work powerfully amongst these people, and save thousands of them. We have travelled about twenty-four miles this day over very rough roads: the weather is cold for the season; my horse is very small, and my carriage is inconvenient in such rocky, uneven, jolting ways. This country is very hilly and open— not unlike that about the Peak of Derbyshire. I feel faith to believe that this visit to New England will be blessed to my own soul, and the souls of others. We are now in Connecticut; and never out of sight of a house; and sometimes we have a view of many churches and steeples, built very neatly of wood; either for use, ornament, piety, policy, or interest—or it may be some of all these. I do feel as if there had been religion in this country once; and I apprehend there is a little in form and theory left. There may have been a praying ministry and people here; but I fear they are now spiritually dead; and am persuaded that family and private prayer is very

[43] Asbury had formed the society in New Rochelle in 1773–74, and though badly shaken, this group had persisted across the Revolution. Jesse Lee accompanied Asbury from New York at this time.

[44] White Plains was a thriving community north of Scarsdale Township. At the close of the war business was promptly resumed, a new courthouse was built, and by act of state legislature the community was incorporated in its own right. Asbury preached in the new courthouse on this occasion. (Scharf, *op. cit.*, I, 714 ff.; Lossing, *op. cit.*, II, 616 ff.

[45] Northcastle was about ten miles north of White Plains.

[46] Bedford Village is about eight miles northeast of Armonk on present Highway 22

[47] Turning eastward to Connecticut, Asbury crossed Poundridge Township in Westchester County and stopped at a small community known as Dantown. Thomas Ware brought Methodism to this community in 1786, and the H—— mentioned was doubtless of this society. (Scharf, *op. cit.*, II, 572.)

[48] This was probably John Rockwell, who entertained Jesse Lee on January 1, 1790

[49] Jesse Lee preached in a schoolhouse in Redding on June 24, 1789, and on December 28 he organized the first class with two persons, Aaron Sanford and Mrs. William Hawley. The society leased the Town Hall in 1803, and the first church was erected in 1811.

little practised: could these people be brought to constant, fervent prayer, the Lord would come down and work wonderfully among them. I find my mind fixed on God, and the work of God.

Lord's day, 5. About ten o'clock we assembled in a barn at Redding, where we had, perhaps, three hundred serious, attentive people to hear: my subject was Eph. ii, 8, 9. I felt freedom, and the truth came clearly to my mind. Rode in the evening twelve miles over rocks and uneven roads to Newtown: I found multitudes of people in a Presbyterian meeting house,[50] many of whom appeared wild in their behaviour—the young laughing and playing in the galleries; and the aged below seemed to be heavy and lifeless. I was sick and weary; nevertheless, I attempted to preach on Acts v, 31, 32, and endeavoured to enlarge on—1. The humiliation of Christ; 2. His exaltation in his resurrection, ascension, glory, Head of the Church, a Prince to give repentance and pardon to rebels. I felt the power of Satan, and soon ended my feeble testimony. Brother Jesse Lee preached at six o'clock. I felt much weakened and wearied. My impressions relative to the people in these parts are unfavourable.

Monday, 6. Came to Stepney, and found a few people waiting for us at brother O——'s, to whom I gave an exhortation, and we had an awakening and melting time. Came on to Chestnut Hill, about twenty miles from Newtown; the people here had not had proper notice of our coming; a few, however, being informed of it, let others know, so that by the time I had exhorted and prayed many joined them: I exhorted again about forty minutes in as pointed a manner as I well could. After meeting we called at E. H——'s, and obtained refreshment for man and beast; after conversing and praying with the family, we set out and reached J. H——'s, in the evening, where we had a small family meeting, at which I spoke on Hosea x, 12: "Break up your fallow-ground; for it is time, to seek the Lord, till he come and rain righteousness upon you." To-day I have felt weary and heavy, and yesterday I was agitated in mind, and sorely buffeted by the enemy—but I have peace with God.

Tuesday, 7. Body and mind more tranquil and serene. Time was when I should have thought the prospects here were very great—the people attend in great multitudes. I find it necessary to guard against painful anxiety on the one hand, as well as against lukewarmness on the other. I judge that the spirits of men must be stirred up to expect more than in former times, and pray, preach, and converse accordingly. We came to Stratford[51]—good news—they have voted that the town house shall be

[50] The minister of the Presbyterian Church in which the "First Ecclesiastical Society of Newtown" met was the Rev. Zephaniah Smith.

[51] Jesse Lee preached in Stratford on July 4, 1789, and was entertained in the home of Solomon Curtis on Main Street opposite the library. The first class was formed on May 9, 1790. Meetings were held in the homes of Captain John Peck and Elnathan Wheeler. A church was built on Main Street opposite the town hall in 1810 and was destroyed by fire in 1865.

shut: well—where shall we preach? Some of the selectmen—one at least, granted access. I felt unwilling to go, as it is always my way not to push myself into any public house:—we had close work on Isaiah lv, 6, 7; some smiled, some laughed, some swore, some talked, some prayed, some wept: had it been a house of our own, I should not have been surprised had the windows been broken. I refused to preach there any more; and it was well I did—two of the esquires were quite displeased at our admittance. We met the class, and found some gracious souls; the Methodists have a society consisting of twenty members, some of them converted; but they have no house of worship—they may now make a benefit of a calamity—being denied the use of other houses, they will the more earnestly labour to get one of their own: the Presbyterians and the Episcopalians have each one, and both are elegant buildings.

Wednesday, 8. We rested at Stratford; and had meeting in brother Peck's house:[52] finding that most of those who attended were serious people, I spoke on our blessed Lord's words, Matt. xi, 28–30; it was a time of comfort to the few seekers and believers present.

Thursday, 9. Came to New Haven, and found my appointment to preach had been published in the newspapers. Everything was quiet; we called on the sheriff—he was absent: we then put up our horses at the Ball tavern, near the college yard. I was weary and unwell. I had the honour of the president Stiles, Dr. Wales, and the Rev. Mr. Edwards,[53] to hear me, and several of the collegians, with a few scattering citizens. I talked away to them very fast, telling them some little stories, whilst the sun shone full in my face. The judges looked very grave while I endeavoured to show—1. What we must be saved from; 2. What has been esteemed by the men of the world as the wisdom of preaching; 3. What is meant by the foolishness of preaching. When I had done, no man spoke to me. I thought to-day of dear Mr. Whitefield's words to Mr. Boardman and Mr. Pilmoor at their first coming over to America:—"Ah!" said he, "if ye were Calvinists, ye would take the country before ye." We visited the college chapel at the hour of prayer: I wished to go through the whole, to inspect the interior arrangements, but no one invited me. The divines were grave, and the students were attentive; they used me like a fellow-Christian, in coming to hear me preach, and like a stranger in other respects: should Cokesbury or Baltimore ever furnish the opportunity, I, in my

---

[52] Captain John Peck's home "seems to have been on the south side of Stratford Avenue just west of Keating Brothers salesroom." (*History of Stratford*, 567.) He was one of the four original members of the first class formed in Stratford.

[53] Ezra Stiles was president of Yale and professor of ecclesiastical history. The record of this day also appears in his diary. "I attended a Methodist lecture at the State House by Bishop Asbury [*sic*] of Maryland. The Methodists [are] now about 70 Th. in America." (Osterweis: *Three Centuries of New Haven*.) Samuel Wales was professor of divinity at Yale. Jonathan Edwards, the younger, son of the great Jonathan Edwards, was the minister of the White Haven Church in New Haven.

turn, will requite their behaviour, by treating them as friends, brethren, and gentlemen. The difficulty I met with in New Haven for lodging, and for a place to hold meeting, made me feel and know the worth of Methodists more than ever. My body is fatigued and listless—my spirit tried and tempted: infirmities cleave to me.[54]

From New Haven, through a poor country, we passed on to Northbury,[55] where there is a large Independent church. In Wallingford the meeting house of the Separatists[56] supplied a place for our preachers; we have also used a neat Episcopal church—small indeed, compared to others.

I am reminded of England in travelling here; this country more resembles my own than any I have yet seen on this side of the Atlantic. I preached at five o'clock, in the meeting house of the Separatists—a large room, and small company. My subject was I Cor. vi, 20. I alarmed the town by the excessive noise I made, and thereby enlarged my congregation. I felt more assisted than I expected.

Saturday, 11. At Wallingford Farms.[57] Here has been some stir about religion; but the people say *new divinity* has put out the fire—Methodists, Baptists, Separatists, &c. I felt somewhat warmed while I opened and applied "Strait is the gate, and narrow is the way that leadeth into life." Some were tender, and some appeared a little alarmed. I then came to Middlefields, and lodged at the house of a niece of David Brainerd.[58] Here we enjoy the quiet use of a meeting house.

Lord's day, 12. Very unwell, but had to preach three times. I began at ten o'clock, on "Blessed is he whosoever shall not be offended in me." I had the attention of the people much more than I expected. In the afternoon I enlarged, under very great weakness, on "How shall I give thee up, Ephraim?"

Came in haste to Middletown, where the committee favoured me with the meeting house belonging to *the standing order*.[59] I felt exceedingly low in body, while I spoke to a very large, serious, and attentive congregation, and I had liberty in preaching on 1 John iii, 23. After meeting we rode a mile out of town to get lodging. It was the poorer classes of people that this preaching on love and charity was anciently blest.

[54] See excerpt from Asbury's letter to unnamed person and Coke's letter to Asbury, Summer, 1791; September 23, 1791.

[55] Asbury doubtless meant North Haven since there is no record of a Northbury in the state. North Haven is immediately south of Wallingford and directly on the route Asbury was traveling.

[56] The Separatists were the Congregationalists.

[57] A map of 1861 shows North Farms about three miles northeast of Wallingford and East Farms about two miles directly east. Asbury's reference was probably to North Farms since he was traveling northeastward from Wallingford toward Middletown.

[58] See note under June 13, 1791.

[59] *"The standing order"* referred to the Congregational Church.

Monday, 13. Rode to Haddam, where David Brainerd was born.[60] We came through dreadful rocky ways to Captain Lee's: a Congregational minister had just finished his sermon as we came in. As we did not wish to force ourselves on any one, we went forward to Lyme and found a free, open-hearted Baptist minister, who rose from his bed, and received us kindly. By this time we were weary and sleepy. I trust the Lord had a dwelling in this man's heart and house—his wife is a kind, loving soul; their children obliging, and ready to serve us cheerfully.

Tuesday, 14. We came over rocks, and through heat and dust, to New London. My mind has felt but little temptation to impatience until yesterday and this day; but, through grace, I do not yield thereto. It is both unreasonable and unchristian to murmur—it betters nothing: to deny ourselves, and to take up our cross daily, is our duty—let us not flee from it.

New London stands upon the River Thames—almost newly built since the war. This town suffered in the general burning carried on by Arnold in this quarter. The new meeting house stands on an eminence; the Episcopal church is a pleasant, well-formed building. The New Light Baptists were very kind, and some of them appeared like Methodists. My church was the court house—my subject 2 Peter iii, 15: I was not happy in speaking. Brother Lee gave them a sermon at half-past eight o'clock. I understood there was a work of religion in this place last year; little of it now remains. I came on to Stonington, properly so called, a distance of ten miles, over a most dreadful road for a carriage: I would almost as soon undertake to drive over the Alleghany mountain. From Stonington I came to Westerly, crossing the line-bridge between Connecticut and Rhode Island. I dropped a few words to the woman of the house where we dined, and saw very clearly that she felt them. I had some life in speaking to about one hundred people at Mr. Stanton's,[61] in Charlestown, on Rev. iii, 20. One said, I had fitted the people well: another said, that I had the signs of the times.

Rhode Island

Thursday, 16. Came to Newport—the roads were comparatively good— the ferry three miles wide; which, however, we safely crossed in a spacious open boat, excellent in its kind. In Newport are two Presbyterian meeting

[60] David Brainerd was the famous missionary to the Indians in western Massachusetts. John Wesley in 1768 published an extract from his life which was really an autobiography prepared for publication by Jonathan Edwards. Brainerd was betrothed to Jerusha Edwards, daughter of Jonathan Edwards, but died of tuberculosis in 1747 at Northampton. Jerusha Edwards, seventeen years of age, died four months later of the same disease which she contracted while nursing Brainerd.

[61] This was probably Mr. Stanton who kept the coffeehouse in Charlestown, Washington County, Rhode Island. (Thrift: *Memoir of Rev. Jesse Lee*, 124.)

houses—one, New Divinity, so called; three others, regular Baptists, New Lights, and Sabbatarians[62]; one Friends' meeting, and one Episcopal church. We stayed two nights at our kind friend's, brother Green, a New Light Baptist. I lectured the second night from Isaiah lxiv, 1–7; there was some life amongst the people, although it was late, and the congregation like our Lord's disciples before his passion. There is also a Jews' synagogue,[63] and a Moravian chapel. I expect before many years the Methodists will also have a house for worship here. I feel the state of this people —they are settled upon their lees, and want emptying from vessel to vessel. My soul enjoys peace.

Saturday, 18. We go hence to Providence, attended by our kind friend for guide. Blessed be the Lord for a refreshing rain last night. On this journey I feel much humbled; I am unknown, and have small congregations, to which I may add, a jar in sentiment—but I do not dispute. My soul is brought into close communion. I should not have felt for these people and for the preachers as I now do, had I not visited them: perhaps I may do something for them in a future day. We came to Bristol,[64] and should have gone farther, but Captain Gladding[65] saw us, and took us to his house. At the request of a few persons I preached in the court house to about a hundred people, and enforced "The Son of man is come to seek and to save that which was lost," and found a degree of liberty. Some time ago there was the beginning of a work here, but the few souls who began are now discouraged from meeting together: I fear religion is extinguished by confining it too much to church and Sunday service, and reading of sermons. I feel that I am not among my own people: although I believe there are some who fear God; and I find reason to hope that souls have gone to glory from this town.

Sunday, 19. Came to Providence.[66] I attended the ministry of Mr.

[62] The "New Divinity" Presbyterian Church stood for a somewhat modified Calvinism in theology and advocated participation in political matters as against "old school" Presbyterianism. After the Whitefield tours in the colonies a dispute arose which divide them into "Old Lights" or "Regulars," who registered distrust of revivalism, and "New Lights" or "Separates," who stood for a reborn membership. The Sabbatarian Church was a Seventh-Day Adventist Church. (David: *Methodism in Newport*, 921.)

[63] The synagogue at Newport, still in use, is the oldest in America, having been dedicated in 1763.

[64] Jesse Lee preached in the state house at Bristol on July 2, 1790, and the first class was formed the following spring. Permission was granted for the erection of a Methodist church on the southwest corner of the common in 1803. Thomas Coke visited the town in 1804 and preached in St. Michael's Episcopal Church.

[65] Captain Daniel Gladding, a sea captain, was converted in Philadelphia in 1791. His name headed the list of sixteen nembers of the first class in Bristol.

[66] Freeborn Garrettson preached the first Methodist sermon in Providence in April, 1787. On July 4, 1790, Jesse Lee preached several times in a private house and the courthouse. Ten miles from the town he met Freeborn Garrettson and "Black Harry" Hosier returning from Nova Scotia, and both of these preached for several days in

Maxcy, a Baptist, in the forenoon; and Mr. Snow,[67] a New Light, in the afternoon. In the evening I preached with some life, on Isai. lxi, 1–3. There are Presbyterians, Episcopalians, Independents or Congregationalists, here: but the Baptists appear to be the leading people. I found a few gracious souls, and some seeking. It has been a season of deep exercise with me while here: I have had some weighty sensations; I think the Lord will revive his work in Providence.

Monday, 20. I visited some serious families that truly love and fear God. The afternoon I spent very agreeably with the old prophet Mr. Snow, aged about seventy years: he was awakened by the instrumentality of Gilbert Tennent[68] whose memory I revere. He told me much about Mr. Whitefield, and old times, and of the ministers of old times—of himself, his awakening, and conversion to God—of his riding thirty miles to Newport, in exceeding cold weather, to bring Mr. Tennent to Providence.

Having obtained more knowledge of the people, my subject was Gal. vi, 14, plain and pointed: my audience was serious and attentive. I endeavoured to show,

1. What is it for a man to glory in a thing.
2. What men glory in, which is not the cross of Christ.
3. What it is to glory in the cross of Christ.
4. How a person may know when he glories in the cross of Christ—namely, by the world's being crucified to him, and he unto the world.

The people here appear to be prudent, active, frugal—cultivating a spirit of good family economy; and they are kind to strangers. They have had frequent revivals of religion: I had faith to believe the Lord would shortly visit them again, and that even we shall have something to do in this town.

Massachusetts

We rested a day at Easton, and appointed meeting at five o'clock. I had good freedom on Acts xvii, 27, and the people felt the word. We have

Providence. On one occasion Hosier's congregation numbered more than one thousand persons. In 1794 Providence was one of the four circuits in New England, and the following year it was connected with the Greenwich Circuit. On November 24, 1798, Joshua Hall organized a class of five persons which had grown to thirty by 1803. The first meetinghouse was dedicated on June 8, 1816. It was on the corner of Aborn and Washington streets.

[67] The Rev. Jonathan Maxcy was the pastor of the First Baptist Church and a former tutor in Brown University. The Rev. Joseph Snow was a "Whitefield Congregationalist."

[68] Gilbert Tennent (1703–64) was a Presbyterian clergyman, as were his three brothers, William, John, and Charles. Their father, William Tennent (1673–1746), was the founder of the famous "Log College." The Tennents were evangelistic in spirit and friends of Whitefield. Gilbert Tennent and Samuel Davies visited Whitefield and John Wesley in England seeking funds for the college. There are three letters from Davies to John Wesley in Wesley's *Journal*, written while Davies was pastor in Hanover, Virginia.

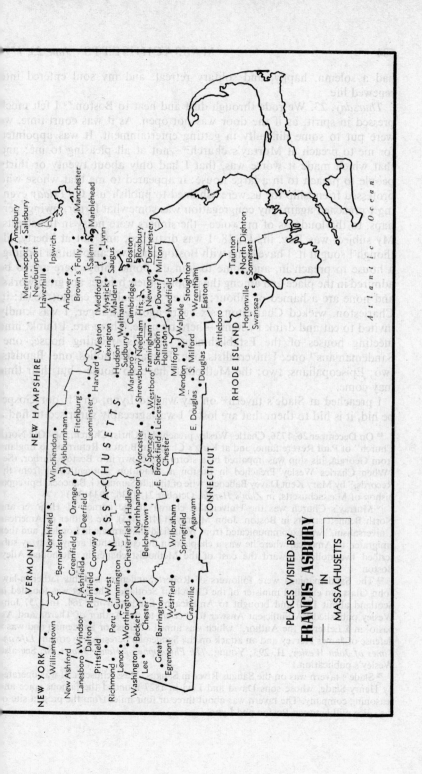

PLACES VISITED BY FRANCIS ASBURY IN MASSACHUSETTS

had a solemn, happy, and solitary retreat, and my soul entered into renewed life.

Thursday, 23. We rode through dust and heat to Boston.[69] I felt much pressed in spirit, as if the door was not open. As it was court time, we were put to some difficulty in getting entertainment. It was appointed for me to preach at Murray's church[70]—not at all pleasing to me; and that which made it worse was, that I had only about twenty or thirty people to preach to in a large house: it appeared to me that whose who professed friendship for us were ashamed to publish us. On *Friday* evening I preached again: my congregation was somewhat larger, owing, perhaps, to the loudness of my voice—the sinners were noisy in the streets. My subject was Rev. iii, 17, 18. I was disturbed, and not at liberty, although I sought it. I have done with Boston until we can obtain a lodging, a house to preach in, and some to join us. Some things here are to be admired in the place and among the people—their bridges are great works and none are ashamed of labour; of their hospitality I cannot boast: in Charleston, wicked Charleston, six years ago, a stranger, I was kindly invited to eat and drink by many—here by none. There are, I think, nine meeting houses of the Establishment; Friends' meeting house, one; Sandemanians[71] one; Universalists, one; Roman Catholics, one; Baptists, two; Episcopalians, two; the Methodists have no house—but their time may come.

I preached at Slade's tavern[72] on my way to Lynn, on "If our Gospel be hid, it is hid to them that are lost." I was agreeably surprised to find a

---

[69] On December 26, 1736, Charles Wesley preached in Christ Church, the "Old North Church" of Paul Revere fame, and at King's Chapel in Boston. Returning to England from Georgia, his ship was impaired by a storm and blown into Boston Harbor. (See "When Charles Wesley Preached in Boston, a Tradition Authenticated from the Records," by Mary Kent Davey Babcock, wife of the late Samuel G. Babcock, Episcopal bishop of Massachusetts, in *Zion's Herald*, October 21, 1936, 1034–36.)

[70] Murray's Church was the Universalist church at the corner of Hanover and North Bennett streets in Boston. John Murray (1741–1815), the "father of American Universalism," was excommunicated from Whitefield's tabernacle in London, and then emigrated to America, where he was a chaplain in the continental army. Murray subscribed five dollars toward the cost of the Methodist chapel in Methodist Alley, Boston.

[71] The Sandemanians were followers of Robert Sandeman and his father-in-law John Glass, an expelled minister of the Church of Scotland. The sect was founded in Scotland about 1730 and brought to America by Sandeman in 1764. In 1757 John Wesley published "A Sufficient Answer to 'Letters to the Author of Theron and Aspasio' in a Letter to the Author," which was aimed at Glass or Sandeman and was a defense of James Hervey and an attack on the Sandeman heresies. (Tyerman: *Life and Times of John Wesley*, II, 293; Young: *The Philosophy of Henry James, Sr.* See also Wesley's publication.)

[72] Slade's tavern was on the Saugus River in Saugus, Massachusetts. It was operated by Henry Slade, whose sons David and Levi in 1827 founded the famous spice and seasoning company. The tavern was about three or four miles from the present site of the spice mill between Boston and Lynn.

house raised for the Methodists.[73] As a town, I think Lynn the perfection of beauty; it is seated on a plain, under a range of craggy hills, and open to the sea: there is a promising society—an exceedingly well-behaved congregation—these things, doubtless, made all pleasing to me. My first subject was Rom. viii, 33, in the afternoon Acts iv, 12: here we shall make a firm stand, and from this central point, from Lynn, shall the light of Methodism and of truth radiate through the State. Our brother Benjamin Johnson[74] is simple-hearted, and hearty in the cause: we owe our entertainment and house for worship chiefly to him.

Tuesday, 28. Rode to Marblehead. When I entered this town, my heart was more melted towards its inhabitants, than to any in those parts, with the exception of Lynn. After consultation, and some altercation among themselves, the committee invited me to preach in Mr. Story's meeting house,[75] which I did accordingly at four o'clock, on Acts xxvi, 17, 18. I was led to speak alarmingly, whilst I pointed out the Gospel as descriptive of their misery and need of mercy: brother Lee preached in the evening to a great number of people in and about Mr. Martin's house.[76] Next morning, weak as I was, I could not forbear speaking to them on "Seek ye first the kingdom of God."

Wednesday, 29. Rode to Salem. Here are five meeting houses, two of them on the New Divinity plan—that is, regeneration the first work—no prayer, repentance, or faith, until this is accomplished; the other three belong to the Establishment, one Episcopalian, and one Friends' meeting house. I found no access to any. I lectured in the court house, on Rom. v, 5–9. I looked upon the greater part of my congregation as judges; and I talked until they, becoming weary, began to leave me. I have done with

---

[73] This was the first Methodist church in Lynn. Jesse Lee preached the first sermon in the town on December 14, 1790, and on February 20, 1792, organized here the first society in New England. Lynn claims the first society, the first church, the first conference, the first native New England preacher, the first Sunday school, the first missionary society, and the first regularly appointed missionary. In the steeple of the present church is the bell made by Paul Revere. Bishops Joshua Soule, Elijah Hedding, W. F. Mallalieu, and George R. Grose all served the church. (Clark: *Discourse on the Formation and Progress of the First Methodist Episcopal Church in Lynn*, 31, 32.)

[74] Benjamin Johnson invited Jesse Lee to Lynn in 1790, and the first sermon was preached in his home on Market and Essex streets.

[75] On May 1, 1771, the Rev. Isaac Story was ordained as assistant to the Rev. Simon Bradstreet, pastor of the Second Congregational Church. Bradstreet died on October 5, 1771, and Story assumed full pastoral charge of the church and continued in that position until February 4, 1802. (Roads: *The History and Traditions of Marblehead*, 379.)

[76] Ebenezer Martin had been south and brought home favorable reports of the Methodists. Upon the coming of Jesse Lee, Martin opened his home to the preachers and to services. The house was situated on Darling Street, next to the pump, and was used as a tavern during the Revolution. The preaching was held in a large unfinished upper room which had been used as a billiard room when the house was a tavern. The original membership of the first class consisted of seven females. (Candlin: *History of the Methodist Episcopal Church in Marblehead, Mass.*)

Salem until we can get a better stand. I had the curiosity to visit the calvary of the witches[77]—that is, those who were destroyed on the charge of
witchcraft. I saw the graves of many innocent, good people, who were put
to death, suffering persecution from those who had suffered persecution—
such, and so strangely contradictory, is man. I have felt weakness of body,
and deep exercise of mind, and, at times, good liberty in speaking. I am
now convinced that the Methodists, as a body, have the most religion,
and am more and more confirmed in my choice.

We rode to Manchester. Mr. Foster[78] received us with great kindness.
The selectmen granted us the privilege of the meeting house. I lectured on
Malachi iii, 13, at five o'clock. Here are some feeling and understanding
souls. This place has been visited for many years, and a society kept up,
although the ministers did not favour the stir. Of this work, father Lee's
ministry, an aged man of that country and town has been the principal
means; for a long time he has faithfully stood his ground, praying with,
and exhorting the people. We were invited to lodge at a place where provision is made for the entertainment of ministers, and in the morning
money was offered. I declined accepting their invitation, and refused their
money.

Friday, July 1. Came to L——'s to dinner. After praying with them, and
speaking to each in the family, I left them to God. Thence I proceeded to
T——'s, and preached at Browne's Folly,[79] to many people; my subject,
Luke ii, 10.

Saturday, 2. I returned home to brother Benjamin Johnson's, in
Lynn.

Sunday, 3. My first subject was, "The great salvation." In the afternoon
I spoke on Titus ii, 11, 12, and had liberty. In the evening my subject was
Matt. xi, 28–30. The congregation was attentive, and my mind enjoyed
sweet peace; although, outwardly, we were uncomfortable, the meeting
house being open, and the weather very cool for the season. I feel as if
God would work in these States, and give us a great harvest. My intervals
of leisure have been spent in close application to my Bible, and reading
Baxter's Call to the Unconverted.

Monday, 4. I took the benefit of the sea air, and began visiting.

Tuesday, 5. My soul is in great peace and love. Here it is a day of small
things: the people have been neglected, but now the Lord has opened their
eyes. O what skill, and patience, and wisdom are needful to deal with

[77] The "calvary of the witches" was Gallows Hill, where a number of witches were
executed during the witchcraft hysteria in 1692.

[78] This was probably Israel Forster, who studied at Phillips Academy in Andover,
was selectman for many years, and had great influence in the town. (Lawson: *History
of the Town of Manchester,* 336–37.)

[79] Browne's Folly was a building erected by William Browne about 1740 in Danvers,
Massachusetts, at the summit of Folly Hill between Danvers and Danversport. (*History
of Essex County,* I, 424.)

souls! I was happy in meeting the women in class. I found but few believers, but I do believe that God will bring them all into full liberty.

Wednesday, 6. Found my mind stayed upon God. In the evening I had a large, attentive congregation.

Thursday, 7. I was engaged closely in reading. I visited and conversed freely with two families. I am informed that Lynn and Lynnfield afford upwards of two thousand two hundred souls (1791). This day brother Jesse Lee put a paper into my hand, proposing the election of not less than two, nor more than four preachers from each conference, to form a general conference in Baltimore, in December, 1792, to be continued annually.

Saturday, 9. I preached a sacramental sermon on, "Let a man examine himself, and so let him eat of that bread and drink of that cup."

Sunday, 10. Preached on the great supper, Luke xiv, a very solemn, baptizing, and sacramental season. The people chose to receive the elements sitting, as is the practice amongst Presbyterians. In the afternoon I enforced, "What shall the end be of them that obey not the gospel of God?" At night I spoke on, "These shall go away into everlasting punishment." The Lord was among the people, and I hope and trust some real good was done.

Monday, 11. I labour under deep exercises of soul. The sea-bath I found to strengthen me. In the evening I met the men's class in Lynn, and was led to hope that a glorious work of God will be wrought here. Several people are under awakenings at this time. My staying so long among them may be of the Lord.

Tuesday, 12. We had a blessed rain after nearly a month's drought.

Wednesday, 13. We came through Waltham, Sudbury, and Marlborough. At this last place there is a grand meeting house, and one not less elegant in its kind for the minister. Thence we proceeded on through Northborough and Shrewsbury, to Worcester,[80] through rain, and with pain and weariness. Mr. Chandler[81] received us with kindness more than common, and courtesy anxious to please, calling his family together with softness of address, and in all things else being agreeable; perhaps more so than any man I have met with in America. This reception shall comfort us a little in our toil. From Worcester we journeyed on, passing through

[80] On October 15, 1740, George Whitefield on his way to visit Jonathan Edwards at Northampton stopped in Worcester and "preached a powerful sermon on the Common." Fifty years later Freeborn Garrettson was denied the privilege of preaching in the courthouse. "A meeting was early established at what is now 1055 Main Street in the house of a liberal Baptist brother by the name of Bryant; after a while the services were transferred to the school house that stood on the hill in the Square, about where the drinking fountain is now located." (See *Year Book of the Webster Square Methodist Episcopal Church, Worcester, Mass.*)

[81] Samuel Chandler lived on Sumner Street in Worcester.

Leicester, Spenser, Brookfields, and another town.[82] We dined at a place where "the people are united, and do not wish to divide the parish"— their fathers, the Puritans, divided the kingdom and the Church too, and when they could not obtain liberty of conscience in England, they sought it here among wild men and beasts. At Grave's tavern[83] I saw a man from Vermont, who said the number of their inhabitants was ninety thousand. He invited me to send preachers among them.

Friday, 15. My mind has been dejected; Satan has assaulted me. I could not be fixed in prayer as I desired. We have made it one hundred and eight miles from Lynn to Springfield. I want to be with the Methodists again. O how unworthy of such fellowship! yet am I seated among the princes of thy people! At six o'clock I delivered a discourse in Mr. C——'s house, on "It is time to seek the Lord till he come and rain righteousness upon you." The people were a little moved; and one sister under deep conviction. This place is a haunt of soldiery; the armoury being kept here. There appears to be little religion among the inhabitants.

Connecticut

Sunday, 17. Passed through Suffield to Turkey Hills,[84] where I had a large and very criticising congregation, to whom I preached my first discourse on John vii, 17. My second subject was Heb. vi, 1. There were some feeling hearts present; the Lord will work here. On Monday I had a crowd at Proquonac, in a school house, to whom I preached on 2 Cor. iv, 1, 2. Some were frightened, some melted, and some were offended. We came to Windsor. Mr. Strong[85] received us kindly, but did not fail to let us know how lightly he thought of *us* and of our principles. Here my feelings were very gloomy, and I secretly wished myself out of the way. I went to the school house and found it crowded with people: the Lord lifted me up whilst I opened and applied Gal. iii, 22. I think I was given to see and feel the true state of these people; some of them were melted, and praised God for the gospel.

Tuesday, 19. I came to the city of Hartford. At Mr. Strong's[86] meeting house I was attended by three ministers. I was clear not to keep back any

[82] The other town was probably Warren, between Brookfield and Palmer.

[83] Major Aaron Graves kept a tavern at Palmer, where he at one time entertained Washington and Lafayette. He was an officer in the Revolution and a leading citizen who held several public offices. (Graves: *Genealogy of the Graves Family in America*, I, 52.)

[84] Turkey Hills was a section four miles from Suffield near East Granby, Connecticut, not far from Old Newgate Prison.

[85] This was Timothy Strong, with whom Jesse Lee talked on April 3, 1790, respecting his theological views.

[86] This was the Rev. Nathan Strong, minister of the First Congregational Church at Hartford. (See note under July 14, 1794.)

part of the truth, whilst I enforced Luke vii, 23. The people were mostly serious and attentive.

I had an interview with Dorcas Brown, who was converted forty years ago, and in the history of whose experience there were some remarkable manifestations of the power of God, and of the interposition of his providence in answer to prayer in times of persecution and violence. Her son's case was also remarkable. He had been captured by the Indians, and was returned *killed*. In contradiction to this account, and the general belief, she pronounced that she should again see him in the flesh. Contrary to the expectation of all but herself, he did return after an absence of three years and eight months.

Wednesday, 20. At East Hartford I felt more than usually assisted on Luke xix, 10. I had an attentive, feeling congregation. On *Thursday* we had a gracious shower at the quarterly meeting at West Farmington, where I delivered a pointed discourse on Acts xvi, 31, 32, which was blessed to some souls.

Friday, 22. The Episcopal church was open at Litchfield,[87] where I preached, with very little faith, on the love of Christ. I think Morse's account of his countrymen is near the truth. Never have I seen any people who would talk so long, so correctly, and so seriously about trifles.

Saturday, 23. By a rocky, mountainous way, we came to Cornwall in the midst of the harvest home. We had about one hundred and fifty hearers. I had openings of mind whilst I spoke on 1 Pet. iii, 15.

Sunday, 24. Came to Canaan, after preaching at a new meeting house. Here naught would satisfy but my going to the acient Presbyterian church. I reluctantly complied, and made a feeble attempt on Luke xi, 13. I offended, and was offended: the people seemed uneasy, and wished to be gone. This is the first, and I expect will be the last time I shall speak in that house, if not in that place. Twenty-five years ago the people in this place had religion; at present, it is to be feared, there is little or none. How it is I know not; but at such places I feel dreadfully,—as if such people were the worst of all under the sun, and at the greatest distance from God.

Wednesday, 27. Although under considerable affliction of body and mind, I rode over rough ways, to New Britain, where, in general, the people appeared unfeeling; nevertheless, I found a few among them who felt the need of Christ. I was led to exhort them, and to pray with them. I am persuaded some are not far from the kingdom of God.

Thursday, 28. I felt some freedom at T——'s, while speaking on 2 Tim. iii, 16. The length of the ride, and the languor of my bodily powers, had not enfeebled my mind. We found some gracious souls in the society.

[87] Litchfield was the birthplace of Henry Ward Beecher, June 24, 1813. Freeborn Garrettson came to Litchfield with "Black Harry" Hosier June 23, 1790, and preached in St. Michael's Episcopal Church one mile west of the town and also in the "old church on the Green." The Litchfield Circuit was organized the same year .

New York

Friday, 29. Came to Albany.[88] My mind felt impressed with the value of the souls in this place. By the curves I have made in my course from Hartford to this place, I suppose I have not travelled less than one hundred and fifty miles: perpetual motion is no small trial to my body and mind; but I must cast my care upon the Lord. I am led to think the eastern church will find this saying hold true in the Methodists; namely, "I will provoke you to jealousy by a people that were no people; and by a foolish nation will I anger you:" they have trodden upon the Quakers, the Episcopalians, the Baptists—see now if the Methodists do not work their way: the people will not pay large money for religion if they can get it cheaper.

I preached to about three hundred people in a barn at Coeyman's Patent,[89] the new stone church not being ready. Our society is promising in this place.

Tuesday, August 2. Came to Hudson.[90] I felt disagreeable sensations— a chill, hoarseness, headache, and fever.

Wednesday, 3. The day was unusually warm, and I was sick and felt like Jonah; I was ready to faint in my carriage; at last, through mercy, I arrived safe at kind sister Livingston's.[91] I went to bed, took some chicken broth, and after a comfortable sleep felt revived. No more rest—I took the road again, and arrived at Rhinebeck by noon. My soul is in peace—I

---

[88] A small society was organized in 1789 in Albany by Freeborn Garrettson, who preached in the assembly chamber there. Albany appeared as the name of a circuit in the *Minutes* of 1790. In June, 1791, Garrettson dedicated the first Methodist church building in Albany, on the corner of Pearl and Orange Streets, the building being 32 × 44 feet. It was in this church, scarcely six weeks old, that Asbury preached on the present occasion.

[89] In 1789 Garrettson sent John Crawford to Coeyman's Patent, a small farming community about twelve miles south of Albany, to begin his work. At the end of his first year Crawford reported ten members in society, and he had organized a circuit of some size back into the hills. Growth was steady and interest mounted rapidly. A commodious stone church was begun in the late spring of 1791 but was not completed when Asbury passed through at this time. When he returned in 1792, he mentioned the church with pleasure. Although the church has long since disappeared, there is a marker on Route 9W indicating the site. While at Coeyman's this time, Asbury became ill and was cared for at the home of James Waldron, an early leader of the group and later a trustee for many years. (See *Journal* entry for August 20, 1792.)

[90] Hudson is on the east bank of the Hudson River, about fifteen miles below Coeyman's Patent. Garrettson made this town a focal point early in his progress up the Hudson valley. Early services were held in a building on Cherry Lane, but a church building was erected in 1790 at North Third and Diamond streets, where Asbury preached on this occasion. (Records of First Methodist Church, Hudson.)

[91] This was apparently the same member of the Livingston family, living not far north of Rhinebeck, referred to in the *Journal* entry of June 15–18, 1789.

want more prayer, patience, life, and love—I walk daily, hourly, and sometimes minutely, with God.

Saturday, 6. I had a few serious people at the Mountain meeting house.[92] I lodged at C——'s, who was formerly a Shaking Quaker.

Sunday, 7. We received the sacrament; and then went to a small grove, where we had a green carpet of nature's spreading underneath, and an umbrella of variegated leaves above us. I preached on Zech. xii, 10, to about a thousand or twelve hundred people, as it was judged: I felt solemn and recollected, and was assisted in speaking: I had some faith to believe it would be the beginning of days, and of a revival of religion.

Connecticut

Preached at Salisbury, on Acts v, 31, 32. My mind is in peace.

I came to Sharon time enough to preach at three o'clock: the women crowded the house, whilst the men stood at the door, with patient attention, in the rain, which indeed many seemed scarcely to perceive; I spoke with life and freedom on Ephes. ii, 8–10. Here are some praying souls. I read, much to my comfort, Corbit's Memoirs of the Secrets of his Heart, brought to public view after his death.

New York

Friday, 12. I preached at B——'s,[93] on Luke xix, 10, to a number of simple-hearted people. Rode to brother Richard Jackson's to attend quarterly meeting; I felt weak and unwell, yet happy in God. My soul enters into deeper union with God, and into a sweet resignation and confidence in him for his work and Church. I judge that my journey to Lynn, and my rides through the country thereabouts, have made a distance of little less than five hundred miles; and thence to Albany, nearly the same; and from Albany to New York not much less; with, occasionally, very rough roads for a carriage: well, it is all for God, and Christ, and souls: I neither covet nor receive any man's silver or gold—food, raiment, and a little rest, is all I want.

Saturday and *Sunday*, 13, 14. We began our meeting in a barn at Jackson's: I had freedom whilst enlarging on Joshua xxiv, 15: there was

[92] This was near the present Pine Plains, New York, twelve miles east of Rhinebeck and halfway to Salisbury, Connecticut. It was probably the chapel erected by John Rowe.

[93] This unidentified person probably lived near Amenia, New York, five miles from Sharon, Connecticut, a place that was to see rapid Methodist development in the near future.

a large collection of people from far to our sacrament and love feast; among these there was life, but the people about this place are dead— dead! there is a curse somewhere. I doubt if one soul has been converted to God since I was here two years ago.

Monday, 15. I feel great power to trust God with his Church and work; and am resolved on more frequent access to the throne of grace, not continuing so long as heretofore: I feel greater sweetness in so doing, and it tends more to an hourly and momently walk with God.

Tuesday, 16. This is a day of rest from public labour. I have uncommon trials, and great liberty of spirit: my addresses to a throne of grace are frequent to-day.

Wednesday, 17. Felt a good degree of liberty at Jacob Badeau's, on Col. i, 28: "Christ formed in you the hope of glory"—perfect in Christ Jesus. Ours is not the perfection of God, of Christ, of angels; such perfection must be ours as excludes evil tempers from the heart, and yet supposes us liable to ignorance and error, while in tenements of clay. As I came along to P——'s[94] I was ready to complain of the roughness of the roads, but I was suddenly stopped, when I beheld a poor Irishwoman with a heavy child on her shoulders, and without covering for head or feet; she said she was from Canada, and thus far had begged her way:— pity for her at once stilled all murmur of complaint for myself.

On *Thursday* we had a gracious season at Stoney Street,[95] amongst sinners, seekers, and believers, while I applied Gal. vi, 10.

Saturday, 20. Quarterly meeting at North Castle: it began well; I was happy in mind, although unwell, whilst I spoke to many who attended, on 1 Sam. vii, 3.

Sunday, 21. Our congregation became unwieldy and restless; my subject, Luke xxiii, 3, was new, to me at least: although my mind enjoyed some degree of peace, my frame was agitated, and my spirits hurried. I received the olive-branch from Virginia. All is peace—it was obtained by a kind letter from me to O'Kelly.[96]

Saturday, 27. Quarterly meeting in Newtown: I felt freedom of mind whilst treating on Deut. v, 26.

Sunday, 28. We had a good sacramental time, and a melting love feast. There are four houses of worship[97] in this place, but I fear the Church of Christ is very small. I have lately been led into great depths of God, and sight of my danger and constant need of prayer.

[94] This was possibly Jean Poilleau, of French Huguenot descent and a distant relative of Mr. Bonnet of New Rochelle.

[95] Stoney Street was the chapel previously referred to as "Oakley's." Garrettson used both designations on occasion.

[96] See letter, September 21, 1791.

[97] These four churches were the Protestant Episcopal, Dutch Reformed, Presbyterian, and Methodist. The present Middle Village Methodist Church is the lineal descendant of the original class in Newtown.

Monday, 29. Came to New York: the weather is warm, and here is an awful season of affliction.[98]

I preached at the new church, on Heb. v, 12; we had an acceptable time, and some gracious movings.

Wednesday, 31. We had a serious, heart-affecting time;[99] many were ready to break out in praises to God. I respect the kindness of the dear people here, and leave New York in faith that the Lord will return to visit them.[100]

Thursday, September 1. I visited my old friends on Staten Island:[101] many whom I have preached to and prayed for still keep at a distance.

Friday, 2. I preached in our new chapel[102] to a large congregation on, "Ye that have escaped the sword, go away, stand not still; remember the Lord afar off, and let Jerusalem come into your mind." Jer. li, 50. It was a gracious season: after preaching the society met, and several declared the Lord's dealings with their souls.

New Jersey

Monday, 5. I rode through much rain to Monmouth, New Jersey, where I preached to a considerable congregation,[103] on, "The just shall live by faith; but if any man draw back, my soul shall have no pleasure in him." There is some stir among the people: at Long Branch,[104] within eighteen months, as I am informed, nearly fifty souls have professed conversion.

[98] An epidemic of yellow fever was in process. This and kindred maladies were frequent serious scourges in cities along the Atlantic seaboard. (Seaman, *op. cit.*, 118.)

[99] This service was probably at John Street Church.

[100] On this occasion the people of John Street provided Asbury with a new suit of clothes, outer coat, boots, and hat, costing over twenty-two pounds, and also gave him two pounds in cash. (*John Street Church Records*, I.)

[101] See note under November 7, 1771.

[102] This was the chapel on Woodrow Road near Rossville, the first Methodist meeting-house on Staten Island, which had been erected in 1787. A meeting was held May 5, 1787, at the home of Abraham Cole to consider the matter of erecting a suitable place for public worship. The trustees elected at this meeting were Abraham Cole, Benjamin Drake, John Hillier, Gilbert Totten, John Slaght, Joseph Wood, Joseph Totten, Elias Price, Israel Disosway. (Hubbell: *History of Staten Island Methodist Churches*, 19–35; Hampton: *Francis Asbury on Staten Island*, 8–9, 12.)

[103] Monmouth was the present Freehold. Asbury probably preached at Job Throckmorton's, William Grandin's, or Leonards's. (Atkinson, *op. cit.*, 345–46; Phoebus, *op. cit.*, 63–64.)

[104] Long Branch has been famous as a beach resort since 1788. The First Methodist Church there is the direct descendant of Asbury's visitations. Ezekiel Cooper mentions the Drummond and King families as active Methodist supporters. (Phoebus, *op. cit.*, 71, 221; Gordon, *op. cit.*, 170.)

Tuesday, 6. I found the Lord had not left himself without witnesses at Kettle Creek.[105]

Wednesday, 7. At Potter's church[106] I learn some were offended: blessed be God! my soul was kept in great peace.

Friday, 9. At Little Egg Harbour[107] I endeavoured to speak very point-edly on Acts xiii, 46: my spirit was much moved, and I think, as a preacher and a visitor, I am thus far free from the blood of saints and sinners.

Saturday, 10. Rode a dreary, mosquito path, in great weakness, to Batsto works.[108]

Sunday, 11. Preached on Luke xix, 10. I advised the people to build a house for the benefit of those men so busily employed day and night, Sabbaths not excepted, in the manufacture of iron—rude and rough, and strangely ignorant of God.

Thursday, 15. Having exerted myself more than my strength would well bear last evening, I feel faint, *yet pursuing*. I gave an exhortation to a house full of people. The evening was spent with S. Hewes:[109] gracious souls, mother and children.

Friday, 16. Preached at C——'s:[110] here are some under awakenings;

[105] Kettle Creek is a stream of two branches, north and south, which flow east and by their union form an arm of Barnegat Bay. The town no longer exists, but the arm of water still bears the name. (Gordon, *op. cit.*, 164–65.)

[106] Potter's Church, also known as "Good Luck," is the present Lanoka Harbor in Ocean County. (Phoebus, *op. cit.*, 63–64.)

[107] Little Egg Harbor bay and inlet, and Great Bay, form a sheet of salt water separated from the sea by Brigantine, Tucker's, and Long beaches. Tuckerton was the principal sailing and mercantile center of Little Egg Harbor. Ezekiel Cooper mentions preaching places in the locality as Esquire Tucker's, Hankins', and Egg Harbor, probably Bargaintown which is below Little Egg Harbor. (Gordon, *op. cit.*, 254; Phoebus, *op. cit.*, 64.)

[108] The Batsto Works were extensive bog iron works in Burlington County on the Mullica River. The Batsto, Atsion, and other furnaces of the area operated for nearly one hundred years, having been established as an industry in 1766 by Charles Read at Batsto. Colonel William Richards, operator of the works at Batsto, opened his home to Bishop Asbury. A rude church was later built by Elijah Clark near the site of the present Methodist church and was known as Clark's log meeting house. It was used by various denominations, but preference was given the Methodists. (Lednum, *op. cit.*, 297; Heston: *Absegami*, I, 187, 188; II, 248–50; Gordon, *op. cit.*, 97; *Letters*, 406.)

[109] Samuel Hewes, Sr., had died in 1784, and his son, Samuel, Jr., inherited part of the estate. The Hewes place was near May's Landing on Great Egg Harbor River. Asbury had turned southward from Batsto, going to May's Landing so as to take the road leading toward Bethel and Gloucester Point where he could cross the Delaware to Philadelphia, thus avoiding travel through the desolate pine barrens. (Lednum, *op. cit.*, 294–95; New Jersey Archives, Abstracts of Wills, VI, 192.)

[110] This was probably Champion's, who lived at Buena Vista, once a stage-coach station. James Crowell and Benjamin Abbott preached at Buena Vista as early as 1781, and a society was formed by Aquila Dorms and Ambrose Pancoast in 1794. A church, known as Friendship Church, was built in 1808 near Landisville less than a mile from Buena Vista. (Heston, *op. cit.*, I, 186–87; Atkinson, *op. cit.*, 233–34; Wilson:

and the prospect is pleasing. Many attended the word on the Lord's day: several of our sisters and of our brethren on this day (and on *Monday* at Bethel) after sacrament, testified to the goodness of God.

Pennsylvania

Tuesday, 20. Rode to Philadelphia.[111] Here, as usual, I was closely employed in writing; I had several meetings, and some awful seasons that will be remembered in eternity. This city abounds with inhabitants—it is the London of America.

Wednesday, 28. We rode to Strasburg[112] thirty miles, where I preached at night in a respectable tavern,[113] on Acts iii, 19. I was very plain, and had some energy in preaching although unwell in body. I have faith to believe we shall have a house of worship, and that the Lord will have a people in this place.

Thence to Martin Boehm's:[114] hitherto the Lord hath been our helper in spite of sin and Satan. We had a good time whilst I spoke on Zechariah xii, 10: after sacrament several bore their testimony for the Lord. My soul is much humbled, and brought into close communion with God; yea, I rejoiced greatly to find so much religion among the people. We went hence to brother Musselman's,[115] where, for two days, we had a gracious season: I preached on Acts ii, 37, 38. I had openings, and was made to feel after the souls of the people. How will Satan take advantage to raise prejudice in the minds of many! At first the cry was, "They are enemies to the country!" that tale worn out, it is said, "They will pull down the churches—they hold erroneous doctrines!" aye; we will labour to raise a true spiritual Church; and if, in doing this, we injure wolves in sheep's clothing, let unfaithful ministers look to it: we shall deliver our own souls.

Delaware

Came to Wilmington. Alas for poor Wilmington! when will this people open their eyes? We rode in haste thirty miles to Dickerson's, but the

---

The Jersey Shore, I, 122. See preface to the *Minutes*, September 16, 1791; Hall: *History of Atlantic County*, 457–58.)

[111] See letter to Thomas Morrell, September 17, 1791.

[112] The Methodist class at Strasburg met in the home of John Miller. The first Methodist meetinghouse was erected in 1807 on Decatur Street. (See *Journal* entries for July 3, 1792; July 21, 1799; August 16, 1812.)

[113] Amos Slaymaker operated a tavern at Salesburyville, fourteen miles east of Lancaster. (Ellis and Evans: *History of Lancaster County*, 312.)

[114] See note under July 31, 1783.

[115] David Musselman lived seven miles from Lancaster. His home was a Methodist preaching place. (See Boehm, *op. cit.*, 115; also *Journal* entry for August 12, 1805.)

people had met three hours before our arrival, and brother Everett[116] had preached to them. I preached at the Cross Roads, but the minds of the people were so occupied by the approaching election,[117] that I fear there was little room for things of more importance. Finding there were no more appointments published for me, I rode, through the dust, thirty-two miles to Judge Thomas White's. O Lord, help me to watch and pray! I am afraid of losing the sweetness I feel: for months past I have felt as if in the possession of perfect love; not a moment's desire of anything but God. I have an awful view of the reformed Churches, and am determined to speak to the very hearts of the people. After attending a quarterly meeting at Barratt's chapel, I came to W——'s; we had a large congregation: after public service, we had a meeting for the local preachers, leaders, and stewards. Next morning we had a love feast for the coloured brethren at sun-rise; and at nine o'clock for the whites. We find new members are added every year ; many living experiences, and miracles of grace in this society.

Friday, October 14. Came to brother L———'s.[118] Hail, happy souls! three out of four in this family love God.

Virginia

Saturday, 15. Came to Downing's chapel; had a blessed love feast; most of those who spoke professed sanctification. My soul was filled with God. I did what I could to put those in band who had witnessed perfect love in love feast. There is a great work of God in the lower counties of Virginia; but the Antinomian doctrines, so liberally set forth by some, greatly hinder. We have rough weather.

Thursday, 20. The storm continued; it was thought no one could go out; we, nevertheless, ventured through heavy rains and came to Paramore's; at night we reached Downing's, making a journey of nearly forty

---

[116] Joseph Everett (1732–1809) was then the presiding elder of the eleven circuits on the Peninsula, other than Wilmington. Few of Asbury's helpers were more dependable, laborious, and effective than was Everett who left the home of Dr. Edward White, his spiritual monitor, as an itinerant in 1780 and died there nearly thirty years later. He served twice as a presiding elder on the Peninsula, a total of ten years. (See *The Arminian Magazine* (Philadelphia), 1789; *Minutes* of the Annual Conferences 1773–1828, I, 179, 180.)

[117] Although political parties in the modern sense then were nonexistent, there was feverish rivalry between the Federalists led by Alexander Hamilton and the Anti-Federalists by Thomas Jefferson.

[118] Robert Layton lived near Federalsburg, then Marshy Hope, Caroline County, Maryland. In this home Asbury had preached as early as September 26, 1778. (Hallman, *op. cit.*, 115.) Some students have identified him as Littleton Long, who lived in the southern section of Worcester County, Maryland.

miles; we were wet and uncomfortable; but the Lord preserves our goings out and our comings in.

Maryland

Friday, 21. Preached at brother Littleton Long's on Heb. viii, 10–12. I think the Lord will work in this neighbourhood, and take away the covering and the veil that are spread upon the minds of the people. Temptations have oppressed my soul, and disease afflicted my body; it is the Lord's power alone that can help me; I fear I am not so constant in prayer as I should be. I made an effort to establish a female school, under sister G——, and sister B——; and endeavoured to impress the necessity and expediency of band meeting, on men and women, both married and single.

Tuesday, 25. At M——'s, there was a living stir among some who came to the quarterly meeting from a distance. My soul is bowed down for this neighbourhood.

Wednesday, November 2. We crossed Choptank River and came to Talbot quarterly meeting. My subject on the first day was, "O! let the wickedness of the wicked come to an end." We had a close love feast, and some living souls.

Sunday and *Monday,* 6, 7. Attended quarterly meeting at Greensburg,[119] commonly called Choptank Bridge: we had a strict and living love feast, and powerful testimonies.

Wednesday, 16. Came to Havre de Grace, and thence hurried to Cokesbury, where I found all in peace.[120]

Thursday, 17. Came to the old meeting house at Bush, and preached on "Enoch walked with God:" the meeting house at Bush is the second house built for the Methodists in the State: it is a poor building, remaining unfinished to this day, and likely so to continue.

Friday, 18. We had a powerful, melting time, at Deer Creek: my subject was Jeremiah xiv, 8–10.

Sunday, 27. I preached at Baltimore a searching discourse on Zeph. i, 12. In the afternoon I preached at the Point, to some unfeeling souls; and in the evening performed the funeral solemnity of my dear old friend sister Triplett, on Acts xvi, 13–15. I was uncommonly drawn out this day, and truly laboured in body and spirit.

Monday, December 5. I went from house to house through the snow and cold, begging money for the support of the poor orphans at Cokesbury.

Rode to Annapolis and preached at night.

Wednesday, December 7. A day to be remembered. We stopped once in forty-three miles: when we reached Oxon Hill Ferry, opposite to Alexandria, I was nearly frozen, being hardly able to walk or talk.

[119] This is the present Greensboro in Caroline County, Maryland.
[120] See letter to Jacob Hall, November 12, 1791.

Virginia

We crossed the Potomac in an open boat, on whose icy bottom the horses with difficulty kept their feet; and still worse it would have been, had I not thoughtfully called for some straw to strew beneath them; we had five of them on board, and the waves were high.

Friday, 9. Rode forty miles to Mrs. Waller's:[121] I suffered not a little with cold: I thank God my life is spared.

Sunday, 11. I could not find the way to the hearts of an unfeeling people at the widow Bombry's; thence we went in haste to Port Royal; the inhabitants, seeing us, ran together, to whom I spoke on Acts ii, 27: the people were respectful and attentive.

Monday, 12. Rode through a storm of snow to brother Adams's. My mind enjoys peace; and although by constant travelling I am kept from the privilege of being so frequently in private prayer, yet I am preserved from anger and murmuring; my soul is wholly given up to God.

I am now about entering upon the business of the conferences for the present year; all is peace. Notwithstanding I have been so highly favoured, my sufferings may be lessened by an earlier move to the south; I will therefore remember to be on the south side of the Potomac by the middle of November, if circumstances allow.

Wednesday, 14. Came to brother Dickenson's, Caroline county, and waited for the preachers composing the conference in the central district of Virginia.

In the evening the brethren came together; we opened conference, and went through a great part of our minute work; all was peace and love. We had searching work in speaking experiences and in examining the young men who offered as candidates for the ministry.

Friday, 16. After fasting and prayer our conference rose. My subject at the new chapel was 1 Chron. xxix, 15–17. *Saturday* I rode to Hanover Town.

Sunday, 18. I preached at Hanover on 2 Cor. ii, 17. I rode in the evening to brother Clayton's. My mind was in peace. I journeyed on through Richmond, Manchester, and Petersburg, accompanied by brothers Ellis and Kobler;[122] on *Friday* 23d, arriving at Lane's chapel,[123] where our conference began and ended in great peace.[124]

Sunday, 25. I preached on John iv, 14, and had a comfortable season; many spoke of the dealings of God with their souls: the examination

---

[121] See *Journal* entry for December 14, 1790.

[122] Ira Ellis was the elder over some of the Virginia circuits, and John Kobler was on the Bedford Circuit with Bennet Maxey. (See *Minutes,* 1791.)

[123] Lane's Chapel in Sussex County was one of the earliest preaching places.

[124] See letters to William Glendenning, December 23, 1791, and to Edward Dromgoole, December 24, 1791.

among the preachers relative to character and experience, was very close; all was meekness and love.

Tuesday, 27. We had a long, cold ride to our kind brother Blunt's.

Wednesday, 28. I preached on 1 Peter iv, 1–4.

Thursday, 29. I rode twenty-five miles, through very cold weather, without taking any refreshment, to sister Pinner's, on our way we had a meeting at brother Cowling's,[125] where many attended, to whom I spoke with freedom on 2 Tim. ii, 19–21: here some wicked young men behaved quite out of character.

[125] Mrs. Pinner and Cowling lived near Suffolk.

1792

1792
Asbury has breakfast with Lieutenant Governor Van Cortlandt

CHAPTER TWENTY-ONE

Virginia

Sunday, January 1, 1792. On this beginning of the new year, I preached and had liberty on Isai. lxv, 1, 2. In the evening I once more cried to the people of Norfolk, "Repent, and be converted:" my audience was attentive and tender. My body was greatly fatigued, my soul much comforted in the Lord. Religion revives here, the seed which has been sowing for twenty years begins to spring up: Norfolk flourishes; Portsmouth declines, and is already low.

Thursday, 5. Rode to William Blount's: there were but few people. On our way thither brother Morrell[1] would stop to feed: I believe the Lord sent me to speak a word to a broken-hearted, forsaken, distressed woman. My soul enjoys peace; but excessive labour, and bodily suffering from the cold, prevent that deep communion with God I wish for: I do little except reading a few chapters in my Hebrew Bible.

[1] The Rev. Major Thomas Morrell (1747–1838) was a notable figure in early Methodism. He was an officer under Washington in the Revolution and was incapacitated by a leg wound received at the Battle of Brandywine. Converted by John Hagerty in 1786, he became an itinerant preacher in 1787 and served in New Jersey and New York until his retirement in 1804. In 1789 he with John Dickins arranged an appointment with President George Washington for the presentation of an address by Asbury and Coke. In that year he was commissioned to raise funds and build the Forsyth Street Church in New York, and in 1791 he accompanied Asbury to Charleston to deal particularly with the Hammett controversy. Morrell's portrait, ordination papers, and swords are at John Street Church. (Sprague: *Annals of the American Pulpit*, VII, 145 ff.; Wakeley, *op. cit.*; Seaman, *op. cit.*, 105, 119, 125.)

North Carolina

Sunday, 8. I preached at the widow Hardy's to a large congregation: I felt freedom in speaking, and the souls of the people appeared tender. The prospect of our journey ahead seemed gloomy; however, we came down in the snow, and got on board a leaky *flat*, which we were obliged to bale as we went; the ferry was five miles wide, our horses restless, the river (Roanoke) rough, and the weather very cold; but the Lord brought us safe to shore,[2] twelve miles from our destined place: we were strangers to the road, and had not an hour's sun; nevertheless, kind Providence brought us through the dark and cold to brother Ward's about eight o'clock: here I sold my carriage and took horse again.

Thursday, 19. I rode with no small difficulty to Green Hill's, about two hundred miles, the roads being covered with snow and ice.[3] Our conference began and ended in great peace and harmony: we had thirty-one preachers stationed at the different houses in the neighbourhood. I find we have had a good work in the eastern district of North Carolina in the past year. For some time back I have travelled with much difficulty, having few hearers, much weakness of body, and uncomfortable weather.

Monday, 23. Our conference rose. I rode twenty miles through severe cold to Brother B——'s.

Tuesday, 24. Brother Morrell, my fellow traveller, was unwell: we had our horses *roughed*, which detained us an hour or two after the appointed time. I reached brother T——'s, and said a little from Philip. ii. 14–16; but the people could not hear, their souls and their bodies were cold. Finding it was twenty-two miles to my next appointment, I set off without refreshment, intending to reach brother D——'s near Hillsboro;[4] on the way, however, hearing of brother S——, a local preacher, we called on him, and he gave us freely of such things as he had.

Thursday, 26. I was led out with freedom on the last two verses of Heb. xii, at M——'s. I find outward difficulties in my progress; the roads are covered with ice and snow, and the severity of the weather prevents my having an opportunity, when I wish, of spending time in private exercises; but, blessed be God! I am resigned, and am kept from sin, and my soul is stayed upon God.

Friday, 27. After riding thirty miles through ice and snow to Rainey's, I found many people waiting for me, and I began, without any refresh-

[2] Asbury seems to have entered North Carolina on this trip from Nansemond County, near Whaleyville, Virginia. Contrary to his usual custom, he did not cross Roanoke River until he was near its mouth in Tyrrell County, North Carolina.

[3] During the eleven days that elapsed between entries in the *Journal*, Asbury must have traveled through some of the counties mentioned on January 27. Green Hill lived one mile north of Louisburg. (See entry under April 19, 1785.)

[4] Hillsboro is in Orange County, about fifty miles west of Green Hills.

ment, to speak on, "This is the victory that overcometh the world, even our faith." 1. I endeavoured to point out the object of this faith; 2. Its subjects; 3. Its nature; and 4. Its victory. In our route through North Carolina we passed through Bertie, Gates, Tyrrel, Tarborough, Franklin, Wake, Chatham, Orange, Guilford, and Randolph counties.[5] We have travelled nearly eight hundred miles since the 7th of *December* last past. Seldom have I been tempted to a murmuring thought; it is now the 29th of *January*: I want nothing but more mental and private prayer.

Tuesday, 31. Yesterday and to-day we have ridden about sixty miles, a great deal of the way through heavy hail and rain. I gave an exhortation at C——'s on *seeking the kingdom of God*. Here we had all things richly to supply our wants; and what was still better, we found the Lord had souls in this family.

February 1. I preached to a considerable congregation at M'D——'s[6] on Acts xiii, 38.

Saturday and *Sunday*, 4, 5. I attended a quarterly meeting.

South Carolina

Monday, 6. At Fowler's (Flowers) church.[7] For some time past I have enjoyed much of God, though suffering under indisposition of body, and frequently in a crowd: I feel nothing but peace in my soul, and find power to trust Jehovah with his own cause.

Tuesday, 7. We reached sister Port's.[8] I find there is a great commotion among the people, excited by the conduct of William Hammett, who has divided the society in Charleston, and taken to himself some chaff and some wheat. This is not all—they say our house will go too.

Wednesday, 8. We set off after six o'clock in the morning; our horses being over-fed we did not push them, so that we did not reach Georgetown until near six in the evening. After my trials and hard riding my cordial is to preach at night. Except Georgetown and Charleston, there are few places where I have not a good congregation when weather permits. I can praise God—my soul is happy in Him; by his grace I am kept from sin, and I still hope this dark cloud that lowers over us will yet break with blessings on our heads.

[5] The counties through which Asbury traveled covered a large part of northern North Carolina. His itinerary involved much wandering through that section of the state. Tarboro is not a county but a town in Edgecomb County.

[6] M'D—— was probably M'Donalds, North Carolina, between Rowland and Fairmont in Robeson County, from where Asbury passed into Dillon County, South Carolina.

[7] Flowers Church was one mile north of Marion, South Carolina.

[8] Asbury was following his former route via Port's Ferry, Lynch's River, and Black Mingo to Georgetown.

Thursday, 9. We rested; and next day came to Wappetaw, and found that brother Sinclair Capers had moved. We then went to his brother's, whose wife was buried that day.[9] We were fatigued and cold, and rejoiced to find that we were not compelled to take up our lodgings under a pine tree.

Saturday, 11. Arrived in Charleston.[10] I received a full and true account of Mr. Hammett's proceedings. Brothers Ellis and Parks[11] have done all things well. Mr. Hammett has three grand objections to us:—1. The American preachers and people insulted him. 2. His name was not printed in our *Minutes*. 3. The *nota bene* cautioning *minute* was directed against him. He has gone to the New Market, to preach, and has drawn about twenty white members after him. We are considered by him as seceders from Methodism!—because we do not wear gowns and powder; and because we did not pay sufficient respect to Mr. Wesley![12]

Sabbath, 12. My subject was Isa. liii, 11. Brother H. preached in the afternoon.

Tuesday, 14. Our conference began. I preached at night on Luke xxiv, 17, and endeavoured to show the low estate of the interest of Christ at that time. In our conference we were unusually close in examination of characters, doctrines, and experience: we had great peace and some power amongst us, and received the good news of eighty souls being converted in Philadelphia, and of a revival in Connecticut.

[9] The brother was Captain William Capers, whose wife, Mary Singletary Capers, was buried that day at Cainhoy. Their two-year-old son became Bishop William Capers.

[10] See letters to Thomas Haskins and Nelson Reed, January 1, 1792.

[11] Reuben Ellis was presiding elder and James Parks was pastor at Charleston.

[12] William Hammett, a missionary in the West Indies who was brought to Charleston by Coke in 1791, was an attractive personality and a correspondent of Wesley's. Although a member of the British connection he complained because his name was not printed in the American *Minutes*, and he insisted that he be given the Charleston appointment and James Parks removed. He secured a petition to that end and followed Coke and Asbury to Philadelphia and New York to present it. He declared that the two bishops were tyrants, Coke was a murderer, and the American church was in schism because the preachers did not wear robes and powder nor have sufficient respect for Wesley. These charges he communicated in letters to Great Britain, and the British Conference replied in a letter to Asbury in which Hammett was repudiated and ejected from the connection. The first schism in American Methodism ensued. Hammett formed the Primitive Methodist Church and secured a considerable following. He erected Trinity Church at Hasell Street and Maiden Lane in Charleston; St. James Chapel, later Spring Street Church and now St. James Church, also in Charleston; and other churches in Georgetown, Savannah, Georgia, and Wilmington, North Carolina. He also secured three parsonages and a cemetery. After Hammett's death in 1803 there was litigation with the Episcopal Church over Trinity Church, but all the Primitive churches and other property were soon ceded to the Methodist Episcopal Church and the schism was healed. (Betts: *History of South Carolina Methodism*, 65–67; Shipp: *Methodism in South Carolina*, 210–12; Chreitzberg: *Early Methodism in the Carolinas*, 57–58, 71; Candler, *op. cit.*, 145–50.)

I preached a sermon to the preachers, on "Endure hardness as a good soldier of Jesus Christ."

Saturday, 18. I received an abusive, anonymous letter (I believe from Mr. Smith)[13] on several subjects.[14] My spirits were low; I came from my knees to receive the letter, and having read it, I returned whence I came; I judged it prudent and expedient, and I think I was urged thereto by conscience, to tell the people of some things relating to myself. I related to them the manner of my coming to America; how I continued during the war; the arrival of Dr. Coke, and the forming of the American Methodists into a Church; and finally, why I did not commit the charge of the society in Charleston, to Mr. Hammett, who was unknown, a foreigner, and did not acknowledge the authority of, nor join in connection with, the American conference.

Sunday, 19. I preached on "Who is on the Lord's side?" Mr. Matthews[15] sent in his resignation. For certain reasons we were led to pass over his character, but we were wrong; it might have been better to subject it to scrutiny, although none grieved at his going from us.

Monday, 20. *I came out of the fire*. Rode to Parker's ferry.[16]

Tuesday, 21. Came to Mr. Lambright's, and next day had a heavy ride to Maixer's, and missed my congregation after all, and so I did at Hudson's, in Georgia;[17] however, I spoke a few words to a few people, and it was felt.

Georgia

Friday, 24. We had fifty miles to ride, but had the advantage of good roads. Stopped at Finch's, and then came on to brother M——'s; he and his father have kindly entertained us as the servants of the Lord.

Saturday, 25. I had an attentive and feeling people at Providence, where I saw C——, and learned that poor Henry, the Jew mentioned *March 9*, 1791, was dead, and died wretched in body and mind, a few months after my departure. Let preachers or people catch me in Waynesborough until things are altered and bettered. Since last *Monday* I have ridden one hundred and eighty miles, and was obliged to ride on, though late, to prevent man and beast being on the road on the Sabbath day. My mind was powerfully struck with a sense of the great duty of preaching in all

[13] Tipple: *Heart of Asbury's Journal*, 331.

[14] Asbury wrote on this date to Freeborn Garrettson in New York, though the letter has no relation to the one described here. (See letter to Garrettson, February 18, 1792.)

[15] (Shipp, *op. cit.*, 213.) Philip Matthews had been pastor at Georgetown.

[16] He crossed the Ashley and Edisto at Parker's Ferry near Jacksonboro, then proceeded across present Colleton and Hampton counties to Hudson's Ferry and into Georgia.

[17] Lambright lived at Coosawhatchie Court House. Maixer is unidentified unless he was Maner at Black Swamp Church. Asbury crossed the Savannah at Hudson's Ferry.

companies; of always speaking boldly and freely for God as if in the pulpit.

Sabbath morning, 26. I made frequent visits to the throne of grace, and feel my soul comforted in God's word, "Instead of thy fathers, thou shalt have sons, whom thou shalt make princes in all the land:" I feel solemn; the burden of the work lies on me; the preachers have left and are leaving the field.

Monday, 27. We rode thirty miles to White Oak meeting house[18]—a painful journey; the weather was cold, and the house open; the people, however, were attentive. It is not pleasing to the flesh to take only a little tea at seven o'clock in the morning, and then go until six at night before we have a table spread; and ah! how few Christian houses! I had my trials in the evening.

Tuesday, 28. We rode through the snow to Little River,[19] and a few people met us at Scott's: I preached on 2 Tim. iv, 2–4. Without staying to eat, we rode on to Washington,[20] making thirty miles this day also. We collected our conference, and had great searching and sifting, and were under the necessity of suspending one; we were very close in examining characters and principles: each preacher spoke his experience, and made his observations relative to the work of God since last conference. Brother Hull accompanies me, and H. Herbert repairs to Alexandria in Virginia. I hope in future there will be harmony among the brethren: if souls are converted to God it answers no valuable purpose thereafter to disciple them to ourselves. I preached on the marriage supper, and took occasion to

[18] White Oak Meeting House was in Columbia County. (Smith: *Georgia Methodism*, 46.)

[19] Little River is along the southern boundary of the present Wilkes County. On this stream was located the home and meetinghouse of Joseph Scott. Pierce's Chapel, successor to Scott's meetinghouse, and Mount Zion, successor to Grant's meeting-house, the first in Georgia, are both on the present Little River Charge in the North Georgia Conference.

[20] Washington was laid out in 1780 and was the first town to be named for George Washington; a county in Virginia was called Washington in 1776, and Washington, North Carolina, was so named in 1782. Washington, Georgia, was Heard's Fort during the Revolution. Its name was changed to Georgetown for a brief period. Here or nearby Hope Hull conducted the first Methodist school in the state, and he published at Washington in 1803 the first Methodist hymnbook in Georgia, *Hymns and Spiritual Songs*. Not much is known about the school, but it was probably established by the Rev. John Springer, a Presbyterian, about 1790. Hull became his assistant, and he later turned it over to Hull, who moved it to a site donated by General David Meriwether, Hull's brother-in-law, near Coke's Chapel and named it Succoth Academy. The conference did not meet in the town, and there was no Methodist church there for forty years after this date. Asbury did not preach there until 1794. It seems that he rode through the town and collected some Methodists and proceeded to Coke's Chapel, where the conference was held. This chapel was three miles from Washington and probably on the Fishing Creek Road. (Bowen: *Wilkes County*, 49, 122; Smith: *Asbury*, 116–17; *Georgia People*, 140–41; Pierce: *Lest Faith Forget*, 24 n.)

show how some are kept from, and others lose, the grace of God, by the unlawful use of lawful things.

Saturday, March 3. Rode to Fishing Creek, and had an uncomfortable time on the Sabbath at Bibb's Cross Roads.²¹

South Carolina

Monday, 5. I left Georgia, and lodged near Whitehall in South Carolina.²²

Tuesday, 6. Rode fifty miles to brother Finch's;²³ here the brethren gave me a meeting on *Wednesday*; the congregation was small, and the people unengaged; rode that evening to O'Dell's, and the next day to Watter's.

North Carolina

Sunday, 11. Preached at Smith's²⁴ on Romans v, 1–3; and kept the holy, solemn Sabbath as a day of rest for man and beast.

Monday, 12. Rode forty miles to Major Moor's, cold and weary. I have read two volumes of Gordon's American Revolution, containing about one thousand pages. We came to the widow M——'s: here we heard that fifty poor wandering sinners had been brought back to God in this wild place, and we rejoiced at the glad tidings.

Friday, 16. I was very much chilled in riding twenty-five miles over the mountains to Wiltshire's: at three o'clock I preached on Heb. iii, 12–14. I was very unwell and in much pain. There was a poor man in the house who was wild enough to swim the river on a mare with another man behind him—what a mercy that he was not drowned!

Saturday, 17. I felt death in some measure at this place. Brother Hull preached and I exhorted.

Sunday, 18. We had a close love feast, and a few testimonies of the power and love of Christ: there was some little melting also amongst the people; but it is hard to civilize, methodize, and spiritualize; sin, Satan, flesh, and hell are against us.

²¹ For the location of Bibb's Cross Roads see the note under March 16, 1790.

²² Asbury again crossed the Broad and Savannah rivers at the now submerged town of Petersburg in the "forks" and went to Ninety Six in South Carolina. White Hall was probably in the lower part of Saluda County.

²³ Finch lived in upper Newberry County. Asbury proceeded from there through the present Whitmire to O'Dell's in the edge of Laurens County. Then he crossed the Enoree to Watter's, who probably lived near Union.

²⁴ He crossed the Broad into North Carolina at Smith's Ferry, having traveled through Newberry, Laurens, Union and Cherokee counties after leaving Ninety Six. Entering Rutherford County, North Carolina, he proceeded northward through the state.

We have rested two days besides Sabbaths, and ridden two hundred and fifty miles in about two weeks: our entertainment is generally mean.

Monday, 19. Our horses' backs being bruised, we had our difficulties in getting to Rehoboth.

We were well-nigh cast away in going to the widow W——'s. It was very dark, and we were bewildered in the woods. My saddle turned, and I slipped from my horse, but received no harm. I had to walk nearly half a mile through mud and water to reach the house.

Tuesday, 20. I came to Gordon's, on the Yadkin. It is seven years since I was here—dead! dead! The world—the devil—Antinomianism in doctrine and practice. I was led out in preaching on Deut. xxxiii, 29.

Virginia

Wednesday, 21. We started for Holston.[25] After riding about fifteen miles, we stopped to feed, and a woman directed us along the new way over the Elk Spur. We found ourselves in a wilderness. The weather was very cold, and the night coming on, we were at a loss what to do. Whilst we were wishfully looking about us, to our great satisfaction we discovered a house. It was clean and comfortable, and we were well entertained.

Thursday, 22. We made an early start for friend Enoch Osborne's,[26] on New River, fifteen miles distant. Here we were generously entertained. After talking and praying together, we were guided across the river, for which I was thankful. Arriving at Fox Creek, we crossed it eleven times, and tarried that night with C——, a *nominal* member of the Society of Friends, who used us very well.

Friday, 23. Rode twelve miles to Smith's.[27] After dinner, exhortation, and prayer, we came down the south fork, and crossed the middle fork of Holston river.

Saturday, 24. Came to the Salt Works,[28] and on *Sunday* preached on, "Happy is the people whose God is the Lord."

Monday, 26. I had enlargement in preaching to an attentive congregation at Abingdon court house.[29]

Tuesday, 27. Preached at Owens'[30] on, "This people have I formed for myself."

[25] The party crossed from the Yadkin in North Carolina to the Holston country by the way of Flower Gap, now Low's Gap, near Galax, Virginia.

[26] Enoch Osborne lived near Bridal Creek in Grayson County, Virginia. (Nuckols: *Pioneer Settlers of Grayson County*, 171.)

[27] See *Journal* entry for May 16, 1788.

[28] The Salt Works refers to the home of General Russell at Saltville.

[29] Abingdon is the county seat of Washington County.

[30] From Abingdon the party went to the Owens' home by way of Moccasin Gap.

Tennessee

Thursday, 29. We had many people to hear at Charles Baker's,[31] to whom I preached with some life. We took half a day to have the smith's work done in fitting our horses for the journey through the wilderness.

Rode twenty-four miles to Mr. Young's, on the main Holston, and the next day, eighteen miles to Hawkins court house,[32] and thence to Crabb's.[33] We have confused accounts of Indians. Our guard rested on the Sabbath day within four miles of the wilderness.

Saturday, 31. I heard a company had arrived from Kentucky at Crabb's. This man's son and a Mr. Henderson have been killed by the Indians since I was here last.

Sunday, April 1. I preached to all the people I could collect.

Kentucky

Monday, 2. We entered the wilderness and reached Robinson's station.[34] Two of the company were on foot, carrying their packs; and women there are with their children. These encumbrances make us move slowly and heavily.

Tuesday, 3. We reached Richland Creek, and were preserved from harm. About two o'clock it began to rain, and continued most of the day. After crossing the Laurel River, which we were compelled to swim, we came to Rock Castle station, where we found such a set of sinners as made it next to hell itself. Our corn here cost us a dollar per bushel.[35]

Wednesday, 4. This morning we again swam the river, and also the West Fork thereof. My little horse was ready to fail in the course of the day. I was steeped in the water up to the waist. About seven o'clock, with hard pushing, we reached the Crab Orchard. How much I have suffered in this journey is only known to God and myself. What added much to its disagreeableness, is the extreme filthiness of the houses. I was seized with a severe flux, which followed me eight days: for some of the time I kept up, but at last found myself under the necessity of taking to my bed.

Tuesday, 10. I endured as severe pain as, perhaps, I ever felt. I made

[31] From Owens' they went by way of Big Moccasin Gap to the home of Charles Baker on the Holson River.

[32] Hawkins courthouse was the present Rogersville in Hawkins County.

[33] Crabb was a trader who lived below Bean's Station. Asbury was there on May 7, 1790.

[34] Robinson's Station was on the Wilderness Road north of Cumberland Gap in Kentucky.

[35] Asbury's party went through Cumberland Gap, Knox, Laurel, and Rock Castle counties in Kentucky along the general route followed in May, 1790. (See the notes for that trip.)

use of small portions of rhubarb; and also obtained some good claret, of which I drank a bottle in three days, and was almost well, so that on Sunday following I preached a sermon an hour long. In the course of my affliction I have felt myself very low. I have had serious views of eternity, and was free from the fear of death. I stopped and lodged, during my illness with Mr. Willis Green, who showed me all possible attention and kindness.

I wrote and sent to Mr. Rice, a Presbyterian minister, a commendation of his speech, delivered in a convention in Kentucky, on the natural rights of mankind.[36] I gave him an exhortation to call on the Methodists on his way to Philadelphia, and, if convenient, to preach in our houses.

Wednesday, 11. I wrote an address on behalf of Bethel school. The weather was wet, and stopped us until Friday.

Friday, 20. Rode to Clarke's station;[37] and on Saturday preached on David's charge to Solomon.

Sunday, 22. I preached a long, and perhaps a terrible sermon, some may think, on "Knowing therefore the terror of the Lord, we persuade men."

Monday, 23. I rode to Bethel.[38] I found it necessary to change the plan of the house, to make it more comfortable to the scholars in cold weather. I am too much in company, and hear so much about Indians, convention, treaty, killing, and scalping, that my attention is drawn more to these things than I would wish. I found it good to get alone in the woods and converse with God.

Wednesday, 25. Was a rainy, damp day. However, we rode to meet the conference,[39] where I was closely employed with the travelling and local preachers; with the leaders and stewards. I met the married men and women apart, and we had great consolation in the Lord. Vast crowds of people attended public worship. The spirit of matrimony is very prevalent here. In one circuit both preachers are settled. The land is good, the country new, and indeed all possible facilities to the comfortable maintenance of a family are offered to an industrious prudent pair.

Monday, 30. Came to L——'s. An alarm was spreading of a depredation committed by the Indians, on the east and west frontiers of the settlement. In the former, report says one man was killed. In the latter, many men, with women and children. Everything is in motion. There having been

[36] The Rev. David Rice from Virginia established the first Presbyterian church in Kentucky ten years earlier. He wrote a letter to the convention protesting against the introduction of slavery into Kentucky. This was the occasion of Asbury's letter of commendation to Rice.

[37] See note under May 17, 1790.

[38] Bethel Academy was not completed. (See notes under May 13, 1790, and October 4, 1800.)

[39] The conference met at Masterson's. (See note under May 13, 1790.) On Highway 68, five miles from Greensburg in Green County, Kentucky, is Mount Lebanon Church, which local tradition says was founded by Asbury in 1792. The date appears over the door, and there is a marble memorial to Asbury there. It does not appear, however, that Asbury was there in 1792.

so many about me at conference, my rest was much broken. I hoped now to repair it, and get refreshed before I set out to return through the wilderness; but the continual arrival of people until midnight, the barking of dogs, and other annoyances, prevented. Next night we reached the Crab Orchard, where thirty or forty people were compelled to crowd into one mean house. We could get no more rest here than we did in the wilderness. We came the old way by Scaggs Creek, and Rock Castle, supposing it to be safer, as it was a road less frequented, and therefore less liable to be waylaid by the savages. My body by this time is well tried. I had a violent fever and pain in the head, such as I had not lately felt. I stretched myself on the cold ground, and borrowing clothes to keep me warm, by the mercy of God I slept four or five hours. Next morning we set off early, and passed beyond Richland Creek. Here we were in danger, if anywhere. I could have slept, but was afraid. Seeing the drowsiness of the company, I walked the encampment, and watched the sentries the whole night. Early next morning we made our way to Robinson's station. We had the best company I ever met with—thirty-six good travellers, and a few warriors; but we had a pack-horse, some old men, and two tired horses—these were not the best part.

Tennessee

Saturday, May 5. Through infinite mercy we came safe to Crabb's. Rest, poor house of clay, from such exertions! Return, O my soul, to thy rest!

Monday, 7. I came to Young's: a comfortable, quiet house, within six miles of Ratcliffe's, whose wife and children were murdered by the Indians. Here I slept comfortably.

Tuesday, 8. We came to brother Baker's, where we rested two days and had our horses shod.

Virginia

Friday, 11. Rode to Michael Halfacre's, about fifty miles, and came in about eleven o'clock.

Saturday, Sunday, and *Monday,* 12, 13, 14. We were engaged in the business of conference at Holston.[40] I had a meeting with the men; a lively one with the women, most of whose hearts the Lord touched.

Tuesday, 15. We came to Russell's old place,[41] at Seven Mile Ford, and

[40] The conference met at Halfacre's, or Huffacres. (See notes under May 6, 1788.)

[41] General Russell lived in the old home of his wife, the former Mrs. William Campbell, at Aspenville, until they moved to Saltville in February, 1788. Cook lived in the present West Virginia.

next day set out for Greenbrier, and reached Cook's. My spirits were too lively and disposed to gayety, which indulged, perhaps too far, made me feel mean before the Lord.

Thursday, 17. Rode to Hogg's, and next day to McPherson's; forty miles each day. The roads were better than I expected.

Saturday, 19. Rode twenty miles. My weary body feels the want of rest; but my heart rejoiced to meet with the brethren who were waiting for me. I am more than ever convinced of the need and propriety of annual conferences, and of greater changes among the preachers. I am sensible the western parts have suffered by my absence. I lament this, and deplore my loss of strict communion with God, occasioned by the necessity I am under of constant riding, change of place, company, and sometimes disagreeable company, loss of sleep, and the difficulties of clambering over rocks and mountains, and journeying at the rate of seven or eight hundred miles per month, and sometimes forty or fifty miles a day. These have been a part of my labours, and make no small share of my hindrances.

I crossed the Kanawha at Paris's ferry.[42] Here I conversed with a man who informed me a brother preacher had called there, and, as he said, was peevish. The dear man was just at death's door, and though his exercises and bodily infirmities may have pressed him sore, and excited expressions of discontent, he was, nevertheless, a meek and holy servant of God. My informant also mentioned another, who *had been* a member, and who would swear horribly and drink to excess. It is proper I notice, that I did not receive these accounts from a professor of religion. I thought within myself—See how we are watched! Ah! we little think oftentimes how narrowly our conduct, our tempers, are observed by the world; and poor sinners still less imagine how strictly we watch them, and how well this habit of observation, and the intimate knowledge we gain of our own hearts, makes us competent judges of their cases, and enables us so justly and so powerfully to condemn their wickedness.

Sunday, 20. I preached at Rehoboth,[43] on Isa. lv, 12; there was no great move: brothers Hope Hull[44] and Philip Cox[45] both spoke after me.

"Weary world, when will it end?"

My mind and body feel dull and heavy, but still my soul drinks deeper into God. We rode about one hundred and sixty miles from the Rich Valley to Greenbrier conference; talking too much, and praying too little, caused me to feel barrenness of soul. We had a hope that not less than ten souls were converted during the conference: at preaching I myself, having a violent headache, retired; the Lord was with them at the sacrament;

[42] Paris' Ferry was at Pearisburg, in Giles County, Virginia.
[43] Rehoboth Church, one of the oldest in that region, is near Union, West Virginia. It is still kept in its early simplicity. Asbury preached there on July 15, 1790.
[44] See *Journal* entry for May 25, 1792.
[45] Bennett, *op. cit.,* 306.

after which, the doors being opened, many came in and the meeting continued until nearly sunset.

We had a most solemn ordination on *Thursday* morning. Afterward we rode through Greenbrier by the town, on to brother Watts's,[46] a distance of thirty-six miles. My headache still continuing, brother Hope Hull preached, and I retired to rest.

Friday, 25. We rode twenty-six miles to the Little Levels. O what a solitary country this is! We have now one hundred and twenty miles before us, fifty of which is a wilderness: there is a guard at two houses on our route; but I do not fear: nature is spent with labour; I would not live always; hail! happy death: nothing but holiness, perfect love, and then glory for me!

Saturday, 26. My body is much wearied; my bowels being much disordered, the water, the milk, and the bread, are like physic to me. We now thought it necessary to be moving; it was dreary work as we rode along the dreary path to Drinnon's;[47] one of my companions, as well as myself, was unwell. From Drinnon's we had still forty miles to go, over hills and mountains: this I think, equalled, if not exceeded, any road I had ever travelled: we at length reached Tygers Valley. We stopped at Capt. Shannon's,[48] where there were several families crowded together, for fear of the Indians. The upper end of the valley has been depopulated, one family has been destroyed since I was last here. The Captain's wife was decent, kind, and sensible. Thence we went on to Wilson's,[49] where I got some fowl soup; thence a few miles to Maxwell's, where the woman of the house was kind and attentive; but a still, a mill, a store, cause much company and some not of the most agreeable kind.

Tuesday, 29. We hasted to Osman's in the Cove, where we met with a most kind and affectionate reception. But O the flies for the horses, and the gnats for the men! And no food, nor even good water to be had. I slept well, although forced, ever and anon, to stir a little.

Wednesday, 30. We had a dreary path, over desperate hills, for fifty miles; no food for man or beast, which caused both begin to fail very sensibly: my bowels continued to be disordered, and had I not procured a little wine, I suppose I should have failed altogether.

Pennsylvania

Thursday, 31. Both men and horses travelled sore and wearily to Uniontown. O how good are clean houses, plentiful tables, and populous villages, when compared with the rough world we came through! Here I turned out our poor horses to pasture and to rest, after riding them for nearly three hundred miles in eight days.

[46] Lednum, *op. cit.*, 187.   [48] See *Journal* entry for April 6, 1797.
[47] See *Journal* entry for July 19, 1790.   [49] See *Journal* entry for July 21, 1790.

Friday, June 1. Wrote letters to send over the mountains.

Saturday, 2. I began to feel lame, and had a severe touch of the rheumatism, accompanied with a high fever, which occasioned great pain to me while sitting in conference.[50] I found it necessary to remove, by exchange, six of the preachers from this to the eastern district.

Sunday, 10. Having been too unwell to attend preaching through the week, I now ventured in public: a great crowd of people attended, and there was some melting and moving among them. I feel the death of this district; I see what is wanting here—discipline, and the preaching a present and full salvation, and the enforcement of the doctrine of sanctification. I have been variously tried, and was constrained to be cheerful.

We have founded a seminary of learning called Union School;[51] brother Charles Conaway is manager, who also has charge of the district: this establishment is designed for instruction in grammar, languages, and the sciences.

I have had some awful thoughts lest my lameness should grow upon me, and render me useless. I sometimes have fears that I am too slack in speaking in public, at conferences; I also feel the want of time and places to pursue my practice of solitary prayer, being frequently obliged to ride all the day and late at night, that I may in time reach the appointed places to preach.

Tuesday, 12. We ascended Laurel hill, and after forty miles' riding reached M——'s, quite weary. Came to I. C——'s, and found the Lord was still in this house: I preached, and felt a melting heart, and there was some move in the congregation. I find myself recruited in body and mind; and I feel as if God would work once more amongst this people.

I was informed that Mr. Hammett had sent abroad circular letters, and had been railing against the presiding eldership, &c. I am not surprised that he should find fault with the office—its duties he was a man not likely to fulfill; yet had it not been for the power attached to it, how greatly

---

[50] This was Asbury's third district conference held at Uniontown, Pennsylvania, being one of a series of four such conferences which he held in succession in the West in the spring of 1792. He held his second conference in Kentucky on April 26–29, his second on the Holston on May 13–15, and his first conference at Rehoboth on the Greenbrier on May 23–25.

[51] In June, 1793, while en route to his appointment on the Ohio Circuit, Thomas Scott paused in Uniontown and made the following entry in his *Journal*: "The next morning we visited the Methodist Academy at Uniontown, situated on a beautiful eminence overlooking the town, on the northeastern bank of Redstone Creek. The building was of brick, two stories high, and just finished for the reception of students. A young gentleman who had been educated at Cokesbury College had just arrived to take charge of the Seminary. The erection of that Academy was approved by Bishop Asbury, and carried to its completion through the indefatigable efforts of the Reverend Charles Conaway." This school was the predecessor of Madison College, which was organized in Uniontown in 1826, with the Rev. Henry B. Bascom (later bishop) as the president. It has a direct continuity in Allegheny College at Meadville, Pennsylvania. (Smeltzer, *op. cit.*, 162 ff.)

might Mr. Hammett have confused the society in Charleston, and perplexed the preachers in the district! The Lord will see to his own house.

Maryland

I preached at Fort Cumberland, in our new house to many people.[52] Dined with Mr. D——, at whose house I was entertained the first time I visited this town: O that each of the family may be everlastingly saved! It is now three years since I came down this road. Swift-winged time, O how it flies! My body is in better health, and my soul in great peace; I feel no wrong temper. O that my whole heart might be running out in holiness after God!

Lord's day, 17. We had a solemn meeting, whilst I enlarged on, "Blessed are they that hear the word of God and keep it." It was a good season.

West Virginia

Monday, 18. Rode to Bath. Here I had the opportunity of writing to all the connected preachers in the district.

Friday, 22. In the evening I preached with some assistance on Luke xix, 10.

Saturday, 23. I attended quarterly meeting at the widow Flint's. Here I had the first sight of Mr. Hammett's and brother Thos. Morrell's attacks on each other—or rather Mr. Hammett's against the Methodists, and brother Morrell's reply. Had brother Morrell known more, he would have replied better. Mr. Hammett's[53] quotation of a clause in my confidential letter to brother Shadford, is not altogether just. He has also misquoted the *caution*, leaving out the word "District," which, when retained, shows it to have been *American*, and to have been directed against *American* apostates and impostors.

Sabbath day, 24. We had a living love feast, although the house was crowded, and warm, almost past sufferance.

Tuesday, 26. I had a sweet opening at the quarterly meeting, on Ephes. ii, 12. I met the preachers, leaders, and stewards, and they resolved to

---

[52] This frame building, 32 × 40 feet in dimension, preceded by one of logs on Quality Hill, now Smallwood Street, housed the parent congregation of the present Center Street Church. The earlier structure is believed to have been the first Methodist Church erected in western Maryland. A deed in the record office reads, "Conveyed in 1799 by Thomas Beall to John J. Jacob and Joseph Cresap." (Scharf: *History of Western Maryland*, II, 1411; Hartman: *History of Methodism in Maryland, 1770–1912*, manuscript copy, Baltimore Conference Historical Society, Baltimore.)

[53] William Hammett, the South Carolina schismatic, had gone as far north as New York in 1791 and had written a pamphlet against the Methodists. Both Thomas Morrell and Bishop Coke had published replies. (Lee: *History of the Methodists*, 206–8.)

enter more fully into the spirit of discipline. Next day I preached on, "My Spirit shall not always strive with man."

Rode twenty-two miles to Shepherdstown,[54] weary and warm; the people were waiting, and I began on "An adulterous and sinful generation." This is a poor place for religion.

Pennsylvania

Friday, 29. I rode nearly fifty miles through excessive heat, and felt somewhat like Jonah.

Saturday, 30. I was taken up with writing letters, having received accounts from Cokesbury. The college seems to be the weighty concern for the present.

Sunday, July 1. I had heavy work; no freedom at Daniel Worley's,[55] nothing will do here but discipline. I felt my spirit much humbled before the Lord, and a willingness to suffer.

Tuesday, 3. Rode to Abraham Keaggy;[56] it was the harvest home. I feel it my duty to press the people of God to go on to holiness of heart and life. As the next morning was rainy, we stayed until the afternoon, and then rode to see our old brother Martin Boehm.[57] We had a tender, feeling season on 1 John i, 8, on *Salvation from all sin.* At Strasburg, in the afternoon, we had a solemn meeting; a young woman, who was married a few minutes before worship began, was powerfully struck under the word, and wept greatly. O may she mourn until her second marriage takes place in her soul!

Friday, 6. We had a long ride to Morgantown:[58] we came in at eleven o'clock, being much fatigued. I discoursed on the likeness between Moses and Christ, in the academical church.[59] This building is well designed for a school and a church. I directed Esquire Morgan to one of our local preachers as a teacher.

We set out for Coventry Forge,[60] but we missed our way, and came to brother Meredith's, in the valley.[61] I prayed heartily for, and spoke plainly to, the young people. O that the Lord would follow them powerfully!

[54] Shepherdstown, West Virginia, is about twenty miles from Berkley Springs, which was known in Asbury's day as Bath.

[55] Daniel Worley lived in Conewage Township, York County, near Strinestown. (Prowell, *op. cit.,* I, 958.)

[56] Abraham Keaggy (or Keaggey) lived at Strasburg, Pennsylvania. The transcriber spelled the name "Kageell."

[57] See note under July 31, 1783.   [58] See note under July 7, 1787.

[59] There was an academy in Morgantown conducted by Jacob Morgan.

[60] See note under May 23, 1776.

[61] Daniel Meredith lived near Goshen, Chester County, Pennsylvania, and was a class leader for fifty years. (Reeves: *Methodism in and Around West Chester,* 21–22; see note under February 5, 1781.)

Saturday, 7. This day my soul enjoyed the presence of God. I dined at Radnor,[62] and went into Philadelphia.

Sunday, 8. I preached at Ebenezer church[63] on James iv, 8; at St. George's church on Mark viii, 38. I had large accounts from the eastward, and am requested to send them more preachers. After twenty years' standing of the house in our hands, the galleries are put up in our old *new* church.

Monday and *Tuesday*, 9, 10. Employed in reading and writing. I wish to be alone. O how sweet is solitude!

Wednesday, 11. I sought and obtained peace between two brethren who had, unhappily, been at variance.

New Jersey

Thursday, 12. Rode through great heat and dust to Burlington, New Jersey. Here I had many of my old, and some new hearers: but some are much wiser than they were twenty years ago. We had a cold time of it, whilst I spoke on Heb. iv, 7.

Friday, 13. After preaching at ——'s, we rode on to brother Hancock's.[64] He is resolved that after he and his wife are served, the remainder of his whole estate shall go to the Church; his plantation to be rented, and the annual income to be applied as the conference held for Pennsylvania and the Jerseys shall please to direct.

New York

Sunday, 15. Preached at our church on Staten Island.[65] I was very close on the law and the Gospel—a few felt; but it was a dry time. Lord, help us!

Monday, 16. We hasted to Van Duzer's[66] ferry; but found ourselves detained by the absence of both boats, so that we did not so soon as we expected reach New York. I did not find that life and harmony here that have been in times past.[67] I have just now obtained and am reading Mr. Wesley's Life, the work of Dr. Coke and Mr. Moore, containing five

---

[62] See note under July 1, 1787.   [63] See September 20, 1790.

[64] This was probably Hewlet Hancock. Asbury appears to have stopped here regularly in going to and from Burlington. (See *Journal* entries for October 1, 1794; October 4, 1797; October 2, 1798; July 28, 1802; and August 8, 1804.)

[65] This was the Woodrow Church near the village of Rossville. (See note under September 2, 1791.)

[66] Van Duzer's ferry was on the East Shore of Staten Island, where Asbury took the boat to Whitehall in New York.

[67] Probably the loss in spiritual power and unity at New York developed from the Tory proclivities of James Mann of Nova Scotia, who had been appointed to New York in 1791 for the only assignment ever given him in the United States.

hundred and forty-two pages. It is in general well compiled; but the history of American Methodism is inaccurate in some of its details, and in some which are interesting. For some days past I have been occupied in reading, and in meeting the several women's classes, and found the Lord was amongst them.

As very probably all of my life which I shall be able to write will be found in my journal, it will not be improper to relate something of my earlier years, and to give a brief account of my first labours in the ministry.

I was born in Old England, near the foot of Hampstead Bridge, in the parish of Handsworth, about four miles from Birmingham, in Staffordshire, and according to the best of my after-knowledge on the 20th or 21st day of August, in the year of our Lord 1745.

My father's name was Joseph, and my mother's, Elizabeth Asbury: they were people in common life; were remarkable for honesty and industry, and had all things needful to enjoy; had my father been as saving as laborious, he might have been wealthy. As it was, it was his province to be employed as a farmer and gardener by the two richest families in the parish. My parents had but two children—a daughter, called Sarah, and myself. My lovely sister died in infancy; she was a favourite, and my dear mother being very affectionate, sunk into deep distress at the loss of a darling child, from which she was not relieved for many years. It was under this dispensation that God was pleased to open the eyes of her mind, she living in a very dark, dark, dark day and place. She now began to read almost constantly when leisure presented the opportunity. When a child, I thought it strange my mother should stand by a large window poring over a book for hours together. From my childhood I may say, I have neither

> "—dared an oath, nor hazarded a lie."

The love of truth is not natural, but the habit of telling it I acquired very early; and so well was I taught, that my conscience would never permit me to swear profanely. I learned from my parents a certain form of words for prayer, and I well remember my mother strongly urged my father to family reading and prayer; the singing of psalms was much practised by them both. My foible was the ordinary foible of children—fondness for play; but I abhorred mischief and wickedness, although my mates were amongst the vilest of the vile for lying, swearing, fighting, and whatever else boys of their age and evil habits were likely to be guilty of: from such society I very often returned home uneasy and melancholy; and although driven away by my better principles, still I would return, hoping to find happiness where I never found it. Sometimes I was much ridiculed, and called *Methodist Parson,* because my mother invited any people who had the appearance of religion to her house.

I was sent to school early, and began to read the Bible between six and

seven years of age, and greatly delighted in the historical part of it. My
schoolmaster was a great churl, and used to beat me cruelly; this drove me
to prayer, and it appeared to me, that God was near to me. My father
having but the one son, greatly desired to keep me at school, he cared not
how long: but in this design he was disappointed; for my master, by his
severity, had filled me with such horrible dread, that with me anything
was preferable to going to school. I lived some time in one of the wealthiest
and most ungodly families we had in the parish: here I became vain, but
not openly wicked. Some months after this I returned home; and made
my choice, when about thirteen years and a half old to learn a branch of
business at which I wrought about six years and a half: during this time I
enjoyed great liberty, and in the family was treated more like a son or an
equal than an apprentice.

Soon after I entered on that business, God sent a pious man, not a
Methodist, into our neighbourhood, and my mother invited him to our
house; by his conversation and prayers, I was awakened before I was
fourteen years of age. It was now easy and pleasing to leave my company, and I began to pray morning and evening, being drawn by the cords
of love, as with the bands of a man. I soon left our blind priest, and went
to West Bromwich church: here I heard Ryland, Stillingfleet, Talbot,
Bagnall, Mansfield, Hawes, and Venn—great names, and esteemed
Gospel ministers. I became very serious; reading a great deal—Whitefield
and Cennick's Sermons, and every good book I could meet with. It was
not long before I began to inquire of my mother who, where, what were
the Methodists: she gave me a favourable account, and directed me to a
person that could take me to Wednesbury to hear them. I soon found this
was not the Church—but it was better. The people were so devout—men
and women kneeling down—saying *Amen.* Now, behold! they were singing
hymns—sweet sound! Why, strange to tell! the preacher had no prayer-
book, and yet he prayed wonderfully! What was yet more extraordinary,
the man took his text, and had no sermon-book: thought I, this is wonderful indeed! It is certainly a strange way, but the best way. He talked about
confidence, assurance, &c.—of which all my flights and hopes fell short.
I had no deep convictions, nor had I committed any deep known sins.
At one sermon, some time after, my companion was powerfully wrought
on: I was exceedingly grieved that I could not weep like him; yet I knew
myself to be in a state of unbelief. On a certain time when we were praying
in my father's barn, I believed the Lord pardoned my sins and justified my
soul; but my companions reasoned me out of this belief, saying, "Mr.
Mather said a believer was as happy as if he was in heaven." I thought I
was not as happy as I would be there, and gave up my confidence, and
that for months; yet I was happy, free from guilt and fear, and had power
over sin, and felt great inward joy. After this, we met for reading and
prayer, and had large and good meetings, and were much persecuted,

until the persons at whose houses we held them were afraid, and they were discontinued. I then held meetings frequently at my father's house, exhorting the people there, as also at Sutton Coldfield, and several souls professed to find peace through my labours. I met class awhile at Bromwich Heath, and met in band at Wednesdury. I had preached some months before I publicly appeared in the Methodist meeting houses; when my labours became more public and extensive, some were amazed, not knowing how I had exercised elsewhere. Behold me now a local preacher!—the humble and willing servant of any and of every preacher that called on me by night or by day; being ready, with hasty steps, to go far and wide to do good, visiting Derbyshire, Staffordshire, Warwickshire, Worcestershire, and indeed almost every place within my reach, for the sake of precious souls; preaching, generally, three, four, and five times a week, and at the same time pursuing my calling. I think, when I was between twenty-one and twenty-two years of age I gave myself up to God and his work, after acting as a local preacher near the space of five years. It is now the 19th of July, 1792: I have been labouring for God and souls about thirty years, or upwards.

Some time after I had obtained a clear witness of my acceptance with God, the Lord showed me, in the heat of youth and youthful blood, the evil of my heart: for a short time I enjoyed, as I thought, the pure and perfect love of God; but this happy frame did not long continue, although, at seasons, I was greatly blessed. Whilst I was a travelling preacher in England, I was much tempted, finding myself exceedingly ignorant of almost everything a minister of the Gospel ought to know. How I came to America, and the events which have happened since, my journal will show.

Saturday, 21. Yesterday I preached in New York, on, "Who is on the Lord's side?" I had some life in speaking, but there was little move in the congregation. O Lord, hasten a revival of thy work! This city has been agitated about the choice of Governor:[68] it would be better for them all to be on the Lord's side. The standard is set up—who declares for the Lord? The wicked; the carnal professors; carnal ministers, and apostates, are the Lord's enemies.

Sunday, 22. Was a melting time with many hearts in the old church: my subject, 1 John i, 6, 7. In the afternoon, although very unwell, I laboured hard in the new church, but the people were exceedingly insensible. There was a little shaking under brother Hope Hull[69] in the old church in the evening.

[68] George Clinton and Pierre Van Cortlandt were the candidates for governor and lieutenant governor on the Anti-Federalist ticket, while the Federalist aspirants were John Jay and Stephen Van Renssalaer in an acrimonious campaign. Asbury was doubtless interested because of his friendship for the Livingston and Van Cortlandt families.
[69] Hope Hull (1763–1818) was born in Worcester County, Maryland, and was received on trial in 1785 to Salisbury, North Carolina. He spent the next several years at appointments in North Carolina, Georgia, Virginia. In 1792 he was appointed to

Monday, 23. We set out for Lynn, and made our way through Bedford, riding fifty miles the first day: I prayed in four houses,[70] and felt much given up on the way.

Connecticut

Tuesday, 24. Rain to-day: after which, we came to Redding; and although it was late, and the evening damp, I was unwilling to omit the opportunity of speaking to the people. Brother Hope Hull, my fellow-traveller, went to bed very ill. God has wrought in this town: the spirit of prayer is amongst the people; and several souls have been brought to God.

Wednesday, 25. We came to Newtown and fed—thence to Waterbury: brother Hull is still very ill. Here we were entertained kindly, and at small charges; the people submitted, and were attentive to prayer. Thence we continued on to Southerington: we dined at a public house, where we had cheap, good, plain usage: our host told us, "It was the misfortune of the Methodists to fall in with some of the most ignorant, poor, and disreputable people in the State." My answer was: the poor have the Gospel preached to them—that it had been aforetime asked, "Have any of the rulers believed on him?"

Came to the city of Hartford, and thence went on to East Hartford. I was alarming on Rev. xxi, 8: brother Hull is still very sick; and for my poor self, I am tempted to fretfulness; but by grace I was kept in peace, and blessed in speaking. The next day we came through the extreme heat to Stafford, and attended a quarterly meeting, where we had a crowd of people in a new, open house: I was very unwell, and much tempted, but I had good liberty in preaching; my subject was Colos. ii, 6: on *Sunday* I was very pointed on Rom. i, 18.

There has been a work in Tolland circuit: I suppose one hundred and fifty souls have been converted, and twice the number under awakenings in different societies around: I felt very solemn among them. Brothers Smith and Raynor[71] have been owned of the Lord in these parts.

Massachusetts

We came through Ashford, Pomfret, Menden, and Douglass: we lodged at a tavern, where the people were very obliging, and attentive to

Hartford, Connecticut, hence his traveling with Asbury to that place. Hull located in 1795, marrying soon thereafter, and in 1802 he moved to Athens, Georgia, and became a founding trustee of the University of Georgia.

[70] The four churches where Asbury prayed were at New Rochelle, White Plains, North Castle, and Bedford.

[71] Lemuel Smith was on the Providence Circuit, and Menzies Rainor was on the Lynn Circuit. (See note under July 23, 1793.)

prayer: thence we rode to Medfield's to dinner; thence through Dover, Newton, Cambridge, Malden, to Lynn; which we reached about midnight, having travelled sixty-five miles—my soul, meanwhile, continually filled with the goodness of God.

Thursday, August 2. Our conference met, consisting of eight preachers, much united, beside myself. In Lynn, we have the outside of a house completed; and what is best of all, several souls profess to be converted to God. I preached on 1 John iv, 1–6, and had some life, but was too formal. There was preaching every night through the sitting of the conference.

Saturday, 4. I preached an ordination sermon to a very solemn congregation, on 2 Cor. iii, 5.

Sabbath morning, 5. I preached on 1 Cor. vi, 19, 20. In the afternoon brother Allen[72] preached; and I afterward gave them a farewell exhortation, and there were some affectionate feelings excited amongst the people. Many were moved, and felt a great desire to speak in the love feast, but they had not courage. O that we had more apostolical preaching.

Monday, 6. We took leave of town, making a hasty flight. We dined at Cambridge. The rain drove us for shelter under the hospitable roof of Mr. How[73]; the kind family here accepted of family worship.

Tuesday, 7. We came through Brookfield and Shrewsbury to Worcester; after resting, we briskly pursued our way to Brookfield.[74] We found that we had stopped at the wrong house: some wicked labouring young men were intoxicated, singing psalms and song tunes for their amusement; one man railed on, and cursed us because he was not told all he wanted to know.

Wednesday, 8. We came to Belcher Town, and were kindly entertained at W——'s: thence we pushed on to Hadley, crossed Connecticut River, and stopped at Northampton. Ah! where is the blessedness of which we formerly heard in this place? I inquired of our host, but received little satisfactory information. I proposed prayer, but found it was not well received. I went to bed weary and unwell; and about half-past six o'clock next morning set out again over the rocks and uneven roads, across the mountain, having passed through Worthington, Chesterfield, and Partridgefield (Partridge).[75] I wondered to see the people settled here so thickly, among the rocks, where the soil can only be cultivated by the iron hand of active, laborious industry: I should prefer any part of the Alleghany where it is not too rocky, because the land is better. We made it nearly forty miles to Pittsfield; and our journey was more disagreeable from the falling of a heavy shower. We have now ridden about one

---

[72] The Rev. John Allen was pastor at Needham. (*Minutes.*)

[73] Paige: *History of Cambridge, Mass., 1863–1878.*

[74] Shrewsbury is east of Worcester and Brookfield is west. Asbury must have passed through Worcester going from one to the other.

[75] In 1806 the name of Patridge or Partridgefield was changed to Peru.

hundred and seventy miles from Lynn in four days. My mind has been variously exercised, and my body much fatigued: if I have been kept from sin, to the Lord's name be all the glory! Pittsfield is a pleasant plain, extending from mountain to mountain; the population may consist of two thousand souls. There is a grand meeting house and steeple, both as white and glistening as *Solomon's temple*. The minister, as I learn, is on the New Divinity plan. I heard the experience of one of the first settlers in the town, who was clearly brought out of bondage; but by resting in unfailing perseverance, he again grew cold: of late he has been stirred up and restored by the instrumentality of the Methodists. I was pleased to enjoy the privilege of retiring alone to the cooling sylvan shades in frequent converse with my best Friend.

Saturday, 11. We held our meeting in a noble house, built for Baptists, Separatists, or somebody, and is now occupied by the Methodists. There was a large and attentive congregation, and some melting amongst the people, with whom the Lord is at work.

Sunday, 12. I was so unwell, that I concluded not to go to meeting, but was at last persuaded along. I felt enlargement in preaching, and the people were tender and attentive. It has been said, "The Eastern people are not to be moved": it is true, they are too much accustomed to hear systematical preaching to be moved by a systematical sermon, even from a Methodist; but they have their feelings, and touch but the right string, and they will be moved. I became weary of staying three days in one house; Mr. Stevens[76] was very kind, his wife was under heavy heart-awakenings.

New York

We set out and came to Lebanon[77] in the State of New York. The medical waters here are warm and very soft; pure and light, with no small quantity of fixed air. I found a poor bath house. Here the devil's tents are set up, and as is common at these his encampments, his children are doing his drudgery. I baptized F——'s child: he and his wife came out from amongst the Shakers, where they had lived in celibacy many years. At the request of the people, notwithstanding my barrenness at brother Williams's,[78] I delivered a discourse on 1 Peter iii, 15; my audience ap-

[76] Captain Joel Stevens was a prosperous man of Pittsfield. He lived at the base of the Taconic Mountains near the road to Lebanon, New York. (See *Some Early Chronicles of the M.E. Church in Pittsfield, Mass.*)

[77] Present Route 20 passes through this community, now called Lebanon Springs, about eight miles west of Pittsfield, Massachusetts.

[78] This was probably Nathan Williams, one of the first trustees at Coeyman's Patent. If this is correct, Asbury had crossed the Hudson River at or near Coeyman's. Although he does not mention this center until his return from Albany, it was necessary for him to go through Coeyman's in order to reach Bethlehem.

peared to be strangers to our way. Mr. K——a, a Presbyterian minister, bore his testimony in favour of the word delivered, and recommended it to his people. We then came to Bethlehem[79] and the next day I preached at the house of a Baptist to about three hundred people: it was a searching, moving time. I also baptized and administered the Lord's supper; I then went a small distance to lodge, but I felt not myself at home, the worship of God not being in the house. I now began to bring up my reading in the New Testament.

Wednesday, 15. Came to Albany, and had a joyful, happy conference, twenty-one preachers being present. We constituted two deacons and four elders. Each preacher was called upon to speak of his exercises and observations since our last annual session: we examined our doctrines, and whether our faith was still firm in those which were believed and taught amongst us. We appointed Jonathan Newman[80] as a missionary to the whites and Indians on the frontiers. We also sent another to Cataraqui.[81] Before we rose, we propounded a few questions of theology namely,

1. How are we to deal with sinners?
2. How should we treat with mourners?
3. Which way should we address hypocrites?
4. How can we deal with backsliders?
5. What is best for believers?

We had preaching in the market-houses in Albany; and notwithstanding our hurry and crowd we were happy, and had living testimonies from preachers and people. I trust two hundred have been converted in the district since last conference.

Monday, 20. I came to Coeyman's Patent, and had a degree of light in preaching in the new church on Ephes. i, 18, 19. After preaching we hasted to Hudson, thirty-two miles. On our way we called on a friend whose wretched wife had made an attempt to poison him and two others by strewing bane on the meat they ate:[82] the dose wrought so powerfully

---

[79] Bethlehem was about five miles north of Coeyman's and an important preaching place on the Coeymans Circuit, established during John Crawford's early work in 1790.

[80] Jonathan Newman was received into full connection in 1791 and appointed to Otsego, New York. In 1793 he became an elder, appointed to Herkimer; in 1794 his appointment was Saratoga; and in 1795 he located. (Barclay, *op. cit.*, I, 200 ff.)

[81] Cataraqui was the old Indian name for the locality of the present Kingston, Ontario, on the Canadian side of the head of St. Lawrence River. This is the first notation of any point in Canada to appear in the *Journal*. In 1789 Garrettson had sent William Losee "to range at large in Canada," and his success was definite. At this conference he appealed for aid, and Darius Dunham volunteered and was appointed to Cataraqui. Dunham had been educated as a physician. He entered the Methodist ministry on trial in 1788, coming into full connection in 1790. He became elder in charge of the Upper Canada District in 1794, continuing in that capacity until 1800, when he located. (Barclay, *op. cit.*, I, 177; Bangs, *op. cit.*, II, 122 n.)

[82] Garrettson reported this incident in his *Journal*, indicating that he himself had narrowly escaped the insane woman's mania against Methodists when as a guest in the

that they threw it up; and so she, Satan, and hell, were all disappointed. I lodged with brother Waldron:[83] he and his wife were kind, dear souls to me, when sick here last year—now I am well: praise the Lord, O my soul!

I had to ride thirty-five miles to Rhinebeck; the weather was extremely warm and dry. We hasted along, and arriving a little before five o'clock, found the people waiting. I preached in a school house, which, by enlargement, makes a good church, so called.

I had reason to fear, from former and later information, that brother Hallock was not as useful nor as acceptable here as I could wish: from a sense of duty I mentioned this to him with great tenderness. At first, it proved some trial to him; but when brother Garrettson and brother Moriarty confirmed what I had said, and I assured him that a desire to promote the cause of God was the only motive that led me to mention this to him, he resumed his former cheerfulness, and we parted in peace.[84]

It was appointed for me to preach at a place forty-five miles distant[85]; but the weather being extremely warm, and our horses weary, we did not get in until eight o'clock, in consequence of which many people were disappointed.

Thursday, 23. I breakfasted at Governor Van Cortlandt's.[86] I feel as if the Lord had been striving here.

Saturday, 25. Came to the quarterly meeting at New Rochelle. The Lord gave light and liberty in speaking. We had a meeting with the local preachers, stewards, and leaders who were present. Mr. Hammett's rejoinder has made its appearance. N. Manners has also come to town, to spread his doctrine and distribute his books: were he a gracious man, I

house just a day before Asbury's visit there, he had declined certain food and drink she had set before him. (See "The Onward Way," Brochure of 150th Anniversary of New York Annual Conference, 1949, 44–45.)

[83] James Waldron was an early leader on Coeymans Circuit and first trustee for the stone church.

[84] At the 1791 conference Peter Moriarty and "—— Hallock" were appointed to Dutchess Circuit, with Freeborn Garrettson as elder in charge. Hallock was then admitted on trial. The nature of his problem is not indicated, but it was serious enough for the work to require episcopal admonition, with Garrettson and Moriarty concurring. Hallock's name disappears from the *Minutes* at this point.

[85] This was at the town of Croton below Peekskill on the east shore of the Hudson River.

[86] Pierre Van Cortlandt (1720–1814), frequently referred to as "Governor," was lieutenant governor of New York from 1777 to 1795. A member of a rich and prominent family, he lived at the Manor House near Croton, where he entertained Washington and his generals. Whitefield had preached at the Manor House. The house was open to the Methodist preachers and Van Cortlandt gave the land for the first meetinghouse at Croton and provided a tract for a camp meeting. He and his wife were active in the society but were not members. Asbury enjoyed warm friendship with them for many years. (See *Journal* references under September 20, 1795; June 26, 1799; August 13, 1800; May 15, 1815; Scharf, *op. cit.*, II, 423–36. See Asbury's letters to Van Cortlandt's two sons.)

cannot think he would write as he does against Mr. Wesley and Mr. Fletcher. Perhaps he will find it rather easier to write and print books, than to sell and pay the cost of publishing them.

Sunday, 26. I preached to a vast congregation, with liberty, on 1 Cor. iii, 15, 16. Many hearts were touched, and we had a blessed season at love feast and sacrament.

Monday, 27. Came to New York, and opened conference,[87] twenty-eight preachers being present. We spent most of the afternoon in prayer; and nearly all the preachers gave an account of what each one had seen and felt since last conference. The young gave us their experience, and there were several who professed sanctification. Awful Hammett haunted us one day, requesting us to give him an honourable discharge from the connexion; but we shall publish him expelled—he is the Wheatley of America.

Friday, 31. We had a solemn love feast, the lower floor of the house being nearly filled: several of the brethren professed perfect love; others had lost the witness.

My mind has been so bent to the business of the conference, that I have slept but little this week. Connecticut is supplied much to my mind, several very promising young men having been admitted to this conference. The societies are in harmony, but not as lively as they ought to be. I went to hear Dr. Livingston,[88] but was greatly disappointed: he had such a rumbling voice that I could understand but little in that great house. How elegant the building! How small the appearance of religion! Lord, have mercy upon the Reformed Churches! O ye dry bones, hear the word of the Lord! I was much obliged to my friend for renewing my clothing and giving me a little pocket money; this is better than £500 per annum. I told some of our preachers, who were very poor, how happy they were; and that probably, had they more, their wants would proportionately increase. My soul is humble, and by grace is kept holy: I do the best I can, and leave the event to the Lord; if others do wrong, they must answer for themselves now, and at the day of judgment.

Sunday, September 2. I preached a preparatory sermon on 1 Cor. v, 7, 8, previously to the administration of the sacrament. It was observed what a fitness of similarity there was between the passover and the supper

---

[87] This conference was held at John Street Church. The *General Minutes* of 1791 indicate that the New York session of conference was appointed for July 19. There is no clue to the reason for deferring it to this date.

[88] John H. Livingston, D.D. (1745–1825), was chief minister of the Reformed Dutch Church in New York. He was admitted to that ministry in 1770 and continued until 1810, when he accepted a professorship in the Theological Seminary at New Brunswick, New Jersey. Asbury heard him on this occasion either in the Middle Dutch Church at Nassau and Cedar streets or in the North Dutch Church on William Street at Fulton, a short block around the corner from John Street Church. (Greenleaf: *A History of the Church in the City of New York*, 12–19.)

of the Lord. The simplicity and purity of the latter—*bread*, instead of the flesh of an animal, and *wine* instead of the blood of the creature; *wine*, the blood of Christ, and *grace* the life of our souls. It was shown who were proper communicants—true penitents and real believers. Not with the leaven of malice and wickedness—acid, bitter, and puffing up, but the unleavened bread of sincerity and truth—uprightness of heart, and sound experience.

I now leave New York for one whole year, under the hope and prophecy that this will be a year of the Lord's power with them.

New Jersey

We had severe crossing the North River;[89] it was as much as ever the horses could do to keep their feet. We came to Newark, and thence to Elizabethtown, in Jersey. I now began to unbend my mind, and became very heavy. I went upstairs, sat in my chair, rested my head, and slept solidly; but a kind friend would have me waked, which made me sick.

Tuesday, 4. I pursued my journey through Woodbridge, and came to Brunswick. The weather was very warm; the roads dusty, and our journeys long. We reached Milford town in the evening.

Pennsylvania

Wednesday, 5.—Passed through Crosswicks and Burlington, and came to Philadelphia: I found I was too late, the preachers having waited a day for me to come and open the conference.

Thursday, 6. We had great peace in our conference. The preachers gave a feeling account of the work of God. We had more preachers than we needed this time; both they and the people were lively: most of our brethren in the ministry can now stand the greatest exertions.

Sabbath morning, 9. We had a melting love feast; the mouths of many were opened to declare the loving kindness of the Lord. I preached, but did not like their ill-contrived house. At Ebenezer I had an attentive congregation, to whom I spoke on Philip. i, 18. At night the *mobility* came in like the roaring of the sea: boys were around the doors, and the streets were in an uproar. They had been alarmed by a shout the night before, which, probaby, was one cause of the congregation being so large. Brother Armstrong[90] went to prayer; a person cried out; brother Clem-

[89] This crossing was probably made at Powles Hook, known as Paulus Hook today, and the present Jersey City. Henry Boehm describes this route from Newark to New York via Powles Hook in 1809, and it became a favorite route for Asbury hereafter. (Boehm, *op. cit.*, 234.)

[90] John Armstrong was a member of Ebenezer Church in 1805 according to William Colbert's *Journal*.

ents[91] joined in prayer; the wicked were collected to oppose. I felt the powers of darkness were very strong. After ending my discourse, brother Mosely[92] rose up and mentioned the shocking conduct he had observed among them; fighting, swearing, threatening, &c. But where are the watchmen? asleep. Where are the magistrates? dozing at home. This is a wicked, horribly wicked city; and if the people do not reform, I think they will be let loose upon one another, or else God will send pestilence amongst them, and slay them by hundreds and thousands: the spirit of prayer has departed, and the spiritual watchmen have ceased to cry aloud among all sects and denominations; for their unfaithfulness they will be smitten in anger: for sleepy *silence* in the house of God, which ought to resound with the voice of praise and frequent prayer, the Lord will visit their streets with the *silence of desolation.*

Delaware

Monday, 10. I left Philadelphia, dined at Chester, and preached at Wilmington in the evening. The next day I rode to Duck Creek Cross Roads, State of Delaware, to hold conference. We were full of business, and had life and liberty. I met the leaders and local brethren in the ministry, and we had a powerful time. I requested them to give an account of their past and present experience; the state of their respective families; and the classes they had the charge of, together with the prospects of religion where they lived: they understood me, and spoke much to the purpose. We parted with a good love feast, from which the gay and the worldly, at least, were excluded, if we did not keep out sinners, Pharisees, and hypocrites.

Saturday, 15. Rode to Camden. To Dr. Barrett,[93] a true son of a worthy father, we are chiefly indebted for a neat, economical meeting house. I had so many friends I knew not where to go. My attendance on conferences and quarterly meetings has lately been so constant, I found it expedient to make a sudden change and come home. In my way I stopped at a friend's house: the woman had been early a member; the man, not of us; I pressed family prayer upon her from Divine authority; I saw her tears and heard her promises. Came home to Thomas White's. I resolved on the establishment of a prayer meeting for the women before I go hence.

[91] David Clements was a member of Ebenezer Church.

[92] Richard and George Mosely were members of Ebenezer Church.

[93] This was Dr. Elijah Barratt (1770–1809), son of Philip Barratt of Barratts Chapel. Barratt, a physician in Camden, earlier called Piccadilly and Mifflins Cross Roads, apparently provided only a temporary meeting place as the records show that the chapel was not erected until 1796. At this time Barratt was one of the five trustees to whom the lot w s deeded. (Barratt, *op. cit.,* 23, 38, 54; Scharf: *History of Delaware,* I, 473, 483, and II, 1133.)

I have felt my soul greatly quickened of late to bear and suffer all things, and to feel nothing but love: if we are tried by Christian people, it is chiefly for want of grace or knowledge in them, or us, or both; they are objects of pity, not of anger.

This day is spent in reading, writing, meditation, and prayer. To be retired and solitary is desirable after the presence of crowds, and the labours, various and unceasing, to which I am called: when our Lord was pursued by the people, he, as a man, would hide himself. I thought, if my brethren would not spare me, I must spare myself.

I have been reading Doctor Langdon on the Revelation,[94] and find little new or very spiritual; he is like the Newtons and all the historical interpreters—one thing is wanting. And might not an interpreter show the present time foretold by these signs, which plainly point to the *why* and *wherefore* it is, that some are Christian bishops and Christian dissertators on prophecy? A bishopric with one, or two, or three thousand sterling a year as an appendage, might determine the most hesitating in their choice: I see no reason why a heathen philosopher, who had enough of this world's wisdom to see the advantages of wealth and honours, should not say, "Give me a bishopric and I will be a Christian." In the Eastern states also there are very *good and sufficient* reasons for the faith of the favoured ministry. Ease, honour, interest: what follows? idolatry, superstition, death.

Tuesday, 18. Continued at Judge White's, and spoke a few words to a few people.

Wednesday, 19. We came to Milford, and had a solemn time on Genesis vi, 3. Here I held a conference with the local preachers, and was pleased at the accounts they gave of their prospects of religion in their neighbourhoods.

Thursday, 20. We had a moving feast of charity, and a close, searching time in public; my subject, 2 Tim. iii, 20, 21.[95]

Friday, 21. I came to Broad Creek with a heavy heart. We had a blessed time in the love feast; many souls had longings for sanctification, and some boldly professed it. I felt as if it would be long before I should again visit this house. A poor man attempted to come near me; being encouraged by my speaking to him, he approached, and told me, with a full heart, that about that time, five years past, the Lord spoke through me to his conviction, at Moore's chapel.

Tuesday, 25. Attended quarterly meeting at Myle's chapel, where I met with a few serious people: the second day we had a few Church folks—something wild.

---

[94] Samuel Langdon (1723–97), twelfth president of Harvard University, became a Congregational minister and published several theological works.

[95] This chapter has only seventeen verses. It is possible that the passage was II Tim. 3:10–11, which text Asbury often used.

Virginia

Thursday, 27. Crossed Pocomoke to Long's (in Maryland): at Downing's at night. Brother Everett was sick. I had a large congregation at Garrettson chapel; and was much blessed on Rom. viii, 29, 30. I had a comfortable conference with the leaders, stewards, local preachers, and exhorters; and we had a living love feast.

Sunday, 30. We had a crowded congregation and some melting amongst the people while I enlarged on, "Almost thou persuadest me to be a Christian." 1. I endeavoured to point out the genuine marks of a Christian: 2. Remove the objection against these marks; and 3. Persuade by applying to the hopes and fears of my hearers.

Maryland

Monday, October 1. I had a kind of chill and headache, and was very unwell; yet I rode about forty miles to Littleton Long's. I went quick to bed.

I attended the quarterly meeting in Dorset on the last day. We had few people. Thence to Henry Ennall's, where young sister Kane[96] was struck with conviction at family prayer. She followed us to quarterly meeting, at Easton, under deep distress; and returning, found peace where she found conviction three days before. We had great plainness, and were much stirred up in the conference with our local brethren. The congregation was large the second day, and the people were more quiet than common—perhaps because we were so.

Thence we rode to Choptank, now Greensboro, and preached on Ephes. ii, 17; and some power went through the house. I had a good conference with the local brethren; making close inquiries relative to themselves, their families, and the societies to which they respectively belong.

I stopped a day at Judge White's, and read in haste the most essential parts of "Jefferson's Notes."[97] I have thought, it may be I am safer to be occasionally among the people of the world, than wholly confined to the indulgent people of God. He who sometimes suffers from a famine will the better know how to relish a feast.

Saturday, 13. We had many gracious souls at John Boardley's barn. I was greatly weakened by preaching; but I hope souls were spiritually strengthened. We had a gracious season in conference with the local brethren, men who felt for the cause of God. Two professed to find the

---

[96] This was probably a member of the Kane family in whose barn Asbury held a quarterly meeting. (See *Journal* entry for October 25, 1783.)

[97] "Notes on the State of Virginia," first American publication, Philadelphia, 1788, contained the passage which aroused charges of infidelity against the author, Thomas Jefferson. (Winsor: *Narrative and Critical History of America*, VII, 307.)

Lord; and it was said two were awakened the first evening of the quarterly meeting.

Sunday, 14. We had a great love feast, the women led the way. I preached on, "Thou knowest not the time of thy visitation." A larger or more attentive congregation has not, perhaps, been seen in these parts. I feel more than ever the necessity of preaching sanctification.

Monday, 15. Rode to Chestertown. Here I was warmly importuned to preach; and submitting to the desire of my friends, I enlarged on 1 John ii, 18, and was very pointed and alarming, at which some were offended.

Saturday, 20. Rode to Back Creek. Being detained at the ferry, I did not get in until after night, which made me unwell.

Monday, 22. Rode to Cokesbury. All is not well here.

Saturday, 27. I came to Baltimore. Here I only stopped to feed myself and horses, and then proceeded on to Thomas Cromwell's,[98] and had a little rest and peace.

Sunday, 28. Contrary to my wish, I was constrained to ride to Annapolis, which I reached about eleven o'clock, and gave them a sermon on 1 Peter iii, 18, with some help and liberty.

Monday, 29. We opened our district conference in great peace and love; and so it ended.

Tuesday, 30. Came to Baltimore in a storm of rain. Whilst we were sitting in the room at Mr. Philip Rogers's, in came Dr. Coke,[99] of whose arrival we had not heard, and whom we embraced with great love.

I felt awful at the General Conference,[100] which began *November* 1, 1792. At my desire they appointed a moderator, and preparatory committee, to keep order and bring forward the business with regularity. We had heavy debates on the first, second, and third sections of our form of

[98] This was Thomas Cromwell to whom Asbury referred on August 20, 1781, when recuperating from a week's illness near Elkridge. He may have been a kinsman of the early itinerants James O. and Joseph and of Joshua Cromwell of Annapolis.

[99] This meeting between Asbury and Coke was not on Tuesday, October 30, as the *Journal* indicates. On that day Coke disembarked at New Castle, Delaware, on his fifth voyage to America. That night he lodged at Elkton, and "about nine o'clock, Wednesday night, October 31, I arrived at the house of my friend Mr. Philip Rogers of Baltimore." (Coke, *op. cit.*, 185, 186.)

[100] This General Conference, authorized by the annual conferences of that year, replaced the council which had failed. The *Journal* of this conference remains unpublished owing to the disappearance of the original. Asbury was the guest of Philip Rogers during the conference, which met in the Light Street Church. He preached once, but if he spoke on controversial issues, there is no record of it. The first great major debate in Methodist deliberative assemblies was on the "Right of Appeal," the historic name given the resolution offered by James O'Kelly. (For accounts by those present see Whatcoat's manuscript *Journal*, November 1–15, 1792; Thrift: *Memoir of the Rev. Jesse Lee*, 182, 183; Lee, *op. cit.*, 176–93; William Colbert, *Journal*, typed manuscript, I, 84, 85; Phoebus, *op. cit.*, 152, 153; Coke, *op. cit.*, 186, 187; Lee: *Life and Times of Jesse Lee*, which contains excerpts from Jesse Lee's *Journal* and from O'Kelly's *Apology*, 268–87.)

discipline. My power to station the preachers without an appeal was much debated, but finally carried by a very large majority.[101] Perhaps a new bishop, new conference, and new laws would have better pleased some. I have been much grieved for others, and distressed with the burden I bear, and must hereafter bear. O, my soul, enter into rest! Ah, who am I, that the burden of the work should lie on my heart, hands, and head?

Thursday, 8. Having taken cold, and had my rest broken, I went to bed to bring on a free perspiration; and from this I received relief, my soul breathed unto God; and I was exceedingly happy in his love. Some individuals among the preachers having their jealousies about my influence in the conference, I gave the matter wholly up to them, and to Dr. Coke, who presided. Meantime I sent them the following letter:—[102]

MY DEAR BRETHREN:—Let my absence give you no pain—Dr. Coke presides. I am happily excused from assisting to make laws by which myself am to be governed: I have only to obey and execute. I am happy in the consideration that I never stationed a preacher through enmity, or as a punishment. I have acted for the glory of God, the good of the people, and to promote the usefulness of the preachers. Are you sure that, if you please yourselves, the people will be as fully satisfied? They often say, "Let us have such a preacher;" and sometimes, "we will not have such a preacher—we will sooner pay him to stay at home." Perhaps I must say, "his appeal forced him upon you." I am one—ye are many. I am as willing to serve you as ever. I want not to sit in any man's way. I scorn to solicit votes. I am a very trembling, poor creature to hear praise or dispraise. Speak your minds freely; but remember, you are only making laws for the present time. It may be, that as in some other things, so in this, a future day may give you further light. I am yours, &c.

FRANCIS ASBURY.

I am not fond of altercations—we cannot please everybody—and sometimes not ourselves. I am resigned.

Mr. James O'Kelly,[103] being disappointed in not getting an appeal from any station made by me, withdrew from the connexion, and went off. For himself, the conference well knew he could not complain of the regulation. He had been located to the south district of Virginia for about ten succeeding years; and upon his plan, might have located himself, and any preacher, or set of preachers, to the district, whether the people wished to have them or not.

[101] See letter to William Glendenning, November, 1792.

[102] Of all Asbury's letters this ranks among the wisest and most disarming.

[103] In a letter to Thomas Morrell at the close of the General Conference, November 15, 1792, Bishop Asbury sets forth his view of the motives which prompted the conduct of James O'Kelly. O'Kelly, who received ordination at the Christmas Conference, led a large defection in American Methodism and became the founder of the Republican Methodist Church. (See letter.)

The general conference went through the Discipline, Articles of Faith, Forms of Baptism, Matrimony, and the Burial of the Dead; as also the Offices of Ordination. The conference ended in peace, after voting another general conference to be held four years hence. By desire of my brethren, I preached once on 1 Peter iii, 8. My mind was kept in peace, and my soul enjoyed rest in the Stronghold.

Thursday, 15. I was comforted at the women's class meeting. I appointed three prayer meetings for them, sisters Keener, Owings, and Fonderen,[104] to be the leaders of them. If this is regularly attended to, I think good will follow.

Friday, 16. I left Baltimore, and, contrary to my first intention, called on the widow Rachel Hulings, whose daughter was awakened the last time I was here, and still continues to be happy in the Lord. I met the sisters here, and urged prayer meeting. Perhaps it was for this I unexpectedly came here.

Virginia

Saturday, 17. Brother Ira Ellis and myself came on to Georgetown, and thence to Alexandria, making a ride of forty miles. Here the preachers were waiting for the district conference.

Sunday, 18. I preached in our small, neatly finished house.

Monday, 19. We had a close sitting in conference, and completed our work in one day.

Tuesday, 20. We set out southwardly. The day was very stormy, and we had a gale in crossing the river at Colchester,[105] and came to our newly-made friend Ward's, near Dumfries.[106]

Wednesday, 21. Six of us set out, and rode fifty-three miles to D. Dickinson's, in Caroline county—so much for an American *episcopos*. Travelling in such haste, I could not be as much in mental prayer as I desired; although I enjoyed many moments of sweet converse with God.

The mischief has begun. Brother O'Kelly called here and vented his sorrows, and told what the General Conference had done. I was closely employed in reading "The Cure of Divisions," and my Hebrew Bible.

Sunday, 25. Came to Manchester, and preached in the afternoon, and felt life amongst the people and the preachers who were met for the district conference. I met the preachers in band, and found their fears were greatly removed: union and love prevailed, and all things went on well.

[104] At this time Mrs. Christian Keener, Mrs. Richard Owings, and Mrs. Adam Fonderen were active in Baltimore Methodism. The last named was a class leader. (See original manuscript of Richard Whatcoat, January 30, 1792; August 22, 1793, Library of Congress.)

[105] Colchester was on Occuquan Creek, a tributary of the Potomac River.

[106] Dumfries was in Prince William County.

W. M'Kendree and Rice Haggard[107] sent me their resignation in writing. We agreed to let our displeased brethren still preach among us; and as Mr. O'Kelly is almost worn out, the conference acceded to my proposal of giving him his forty pounds per annum,* as when he travelled in the connexion, provided he was peaceable, and forbore to excite divisions among the brethren. The General Conference and the district conferences have kept us a long time from our work; but after all Satan's spite, I think our *sifting* and *shaking* will be for good. I expect a glorious revival will take place in America, and thousands be brought to God.

Thursday, 29. Came to Petersburg. Myself, and several others preached during our stay.

Saturday, December 1. I had a few attentive hearers at brother Bonner's of whom I inquired, "Where is the blessedness ye spake of."

Sunday, 2. Rode fifteen miles to Graves' chapels where we had a full house, and I felt life and love in speaking to the young people. I lodged with brother Graves and was very much moved to lay a plan for a district school.

Monday, 3. Preached at River's chapel: cold house and languid people. Came to brother Cox's in the evening. I am not conscious of inward or outward sin, yet I do not feel that inward life I wish. I have lately read our "Cure of Church Divisions," and much of the word of God.

Tuesday, 4. Preached at Mabry's chapel;[108] and the next day at J. Mason's, where we had a full house and a comfortable time.

Thursday, 6. Rode through the rain to Edward Drumgoole's: here I found a few friends, and formed a constitution for a district school, which, with a little alteration, will form a general rule for any part of the continent.

Saturday 8. I once more visited Owen Myrick, whose wife is gone, and from all we can learn departed in a good old age, in triumph to glory the dear old man is much dispirited. We spent the evening together very solemnly, remembering the occurrences of nineteen years ago, now gone as yesterday—

> "Short as the watch that ends the night
> Before the rising sun."

The cause of his slaves was not forgotten.

*For a part of that year he received it; but refused, and left us to form a new and pure Church.

[107] James O'Kelly "was President of the Quarterly Conference when McKendree was recommended to the Annual Conference and was regarded with peculiar veneration by his young friend." (Bennett, *op. cit.*, 314, 323–26.) Though McKendree came back to the church, Rice Haggard went off with O'Kelly and formed the Christian Church. Haggard later went to Kentucky and was active there. (MacClenny: *The Life of Rev. James O'Kelly*, 125.)

[108] Mabry's Chapel was in Greensville County. Originally Mabry's had been in Brunswick, but at this date Greensville had been taken from Brunswick.

Sunday, 9. I came once more to Roanoak chapel, and gave them a discourse on Eph. ii, 13. Reuben and Ira Ellis gave an exhortation: I met the society. We then rode six miles, and got to our quarters about sunset.

North Carolina

Monday, 10. We crossed Roanoak at Black's ferry, and directed our course for Lewisburg. We passed Warrington, and missed our way. We remembered the name of William Myrick, and inquiring after him, found he lived nearly on our way; we accordingly called on him, and were gladly received, and kindly entertained. Memory is good in distress: had we not housed here, we should have had our difficulties in getting to sister L——'s.

Tuesday, 11. Rode to Green Hill's, near Louisburg. Here I met the preachers in conference, and we were closely employed until *Saturday* morning. We had about forty preachers from the two districts in North Carolina. Our labours finished, we rode to Neuse River.

Sunday, 16. Preached at Merritt's.

Monday, 17. Rode fifteen miles to S——'s: preached on *Christ*, the believer's *wisdom, righteousness, sanctification,* and *redemption.* We had a difficult road in going to Haw River, but a kind Providence brought us along very well, although the weather was exceedingly cold: we crossed the stream by fording, about half-past eight o'clock, and about ten arrived at R——'s, very cold and in much pain. I know not why, but so it is, that I cannot feel that I hold such sweet communion with God in cold weather as in warm; it may be that—

> "Nature being oppress'd,
> Commands the mind to suffer with the body."

The great love and union which prevailed at the late conference makes me hope many souls will be converted in the ensuing year: an account was brought in of the conversion of about three hundred souls last week within its limits—chiefly in the Lowland circuits. Glory be to God! I feel that he is with us; and I have good evidence that fifteen or eighteen hundred souls have professed to have been converted in the United States within the last twelve months. At Rainey's, a congregation of willing, patient souls was called hastily together, to whom I preached on 2 Peter i, 4. I was led out on the corruption that is in the world, arising from three grand sources,—the lust of the flesh; the lust of the eye; and the pride of life.

Wednesday, 19. I was detained until about ten o'clock, and then rode on to S——'s, and dined: we then hastened on to Deep River, and lodged at Mr. B——'s. Lord, show kindness to those who have succoured me!

Thursday, 20. I took a route along a new path below the Narrows of

Pee Dee; and after riding forty-five or fifty miles, came in, cold and hungry, about seven o'clock, and found a congregation waiting: I was fatigued, and could say but little to them.

Friday, 21. I rode thirty miles to Rocky River; had few to hear.

Saturday, 22. The people were attentive and behaved well at Anson court house. In the evening we had a weary ride to brother Jackson's.

South Carolina

Sunday, 23. We attended from ten till one o'clock in a house built of *poles*—here were light and ventilators plenty. We rode this evening twenty miles to Mr. Blakeney's[109]: the rain caught us in the woods, and we were steeped. Arriving, we found a good house, table, and bed, which was some relief to weather-beaten pilgrims.

Christmas Eve. We rode in the rain twenty-five miles to our kind brother Horton's,[110] and found many people had gathered.

Christmas day. Although the weather was cold and damp, and unhealthy, with signs of snow, we rode forty-five miles to dear brother Rembert's[111]—kind and good, rich and liberal, who has done more for the poor Methodists than any man in South Carolina. The Lord grant that he, with his whole household, may find mercy in that day.

Wednesday, 26. Preached at quarterly meeting on 1 Peter iv, 13. I was pleased to hear the young men exhort and sing after sacrament. I felt uncommonly melted—tears involuntarily burst from my eyes. God was there.

Thursday, 27. I had a long, cold ride of forty-five miles to brother Bowman's,[112] near Santee. I was overtaken on my way by rain mingled with hail which ended in snow, covering the ground six or eight inches deep. The unfinished state of the houses, lying on the floor, thin clothing, and inclement weather keep me in a state of indisposition.

Friday, 28. We had to cross Santee, and ride thirty-five miles to dear sister Browning's.[113] The weather still very cold.

Saturday, 29. Rode thirty-three miles to Charleston, and found our little flock in peace, and a small revival amongst them.

Mr. Hammett has raised a grand house, and has written an appeal to the British conference. He represents Dr. Coke as a sacrilegious tyrant and murderer. I have no doubt but the Doctor will be able to make good his

---

[109] Blakeney lived in the western part of Chesterfield County in South Carolina. The Jackson with whom he had spent the previous night lived in the same section.

[110] Horton lived at Hanging Rock near the present Kershaw in Lancaster County.

[111] James Rembert. (See note under March 27, 1788.)

[112] Bowman lived near Summerton in Clarendon County.

[113] Mrs. Browning lived near Ridgeville in Dorchester County. Asbury crossed the river at Vance's ferry.

cause. As to Hammett, time will show the man and the people who have made lies their refuge.[114]

Sunday, 30. Brother Isaac Smith[115] preached in the forenoon. In the afternoon I said a little on Isaiah ix, 6, 7. The blacks were hardly restrained from crying out aloud. O that God would bless the wild and wicked inhabitants of this city! I am happy to find that our principal friends have increased in religion. Accounts from Philadelphia are pleasing—souls are converted to God. There is also a move in New York, and their numbers are daily increasing. On reviewing the labours of the last six weeks, I find we have rested about fourteen days at conferences, and ridden at least seven hundred miles.

[114] For the schism of William Hammett see note under February 11, 1792.
[115] Isaac Smith was on the Santee Circuit. (See *Minutes*.)

1793

1793 *Asbury at the ruins of Whitefield's Orphan House in Savannah*

CHAPTER TWENTY-TWO

South Carolina

January 3, 1793. From *Wednesday, December* 26, to this day, *Sunday* excepted, we sat in conference in this city.

Friday, 4. I was unwell, yet I set out and reached Mr. Givhan's, on Edisto River. A few people met me here in the evening; but I was unwell, and weary, and sleepy, and very unfit for public exercise.

Saturday, 5. Rode fifty miles to Rumph's,[1] and rested on the Sabbath. I had a meeting with eight or ten souls. The people in these parts are much given up to sin; they have a little charity for the Baptists, but none at all for the Methodists.

Monday, 7. We rode thirty-seven miles to Treadwell's;[2] where, had we not begged and promised to pay well for it, I know not if we should have been taken in.

Georgia

Tuesday, 8. We passed Augusta, and rode thirty-seven miles to Haynes's, where we were treated kindly. Thence, next day, to Washington, forty-four miles. I was taken ill at brother Meriwether's.[3]

[1] This Mr. Rumph lived on the South Edisto near Blockville in Barnwell County. General Jacob Rumph lived in Orangeburg County near Orangeburg. (See note under March 17, 1788.)

[2] Treadwell lived in Aiken County.

[3] Crossing the Savannah River at Augusta, Asbury rode to Thomas Haynes' in the present Columbia County.

Thursday, 10. Met our dear brethren in conference.⁴ We had great peace and union: the Carolina preachers came up to change with those in Georgia: all things happened well. Bless the Lord, O my soul! We now agreed to unite the Georgia and South Carolina conferences⁵—to meet in the fork of Seleuda and Broad Rivers, on the first of January, 1794. Our sitting ended in exceeding great love.

Sabbath, 13. We had sacrament, love feast, and ordination. I felt very serious, and was very pointed on Acts xx, 26, 27. I have now had an opportunity of speaking in Washington: most of the people attended to hear *this man that rambles through the United States*. In due time I shall, with permission, visit Georgia.

Monday, 14. I preached in the new house at Grant's,⁶ on, "He that overcometh shall inherit all things, and I will be his God, and he shall be my son."

1. The Christian soldier has to overcome the world, sin, and the devil, with his temptations.

2. He fights under the banner of Christ, who is the Captain of his salvation.

3. His armour is described by St. Paul, Ephes. vi.

4. His inheritance—Christian tempers, and the things promised to the seven Churches; and finally, glory—"Will be his God"—giving him wisdom, truth, love—"He shall be my son"—a son partakes of the nature and property of the father, and doeth his will; so it is with those who are the children of God.

Our dear Georgia brethren seem to think some of us shall visit them no more: they appear to be much humbled, and will not give up the travelling preachers. I am now bound for Savannah; where I may see the former walks of a dear Wesley and Whitefield, with whom I hope to meet in the new Jerusalem.

⁴ The conference probably met in the courthouse at Washington. (Bowen: *Wilkes County*, 122–23.) Here again confusion is encountered in conflicting statements by Smith. In his *Francis Asbury* (148) he says the conference met at Grants, but in his *Georgia Methodism* (48) and his *Methodism in Georgia and Florida* (59) he says it met at Washington. In the last two works he uses the word "again" although it had not met at Washington before, as Smith himself says in the preceding page in each case. (See note under February 28, 1792.)

⁵ The conferences in Georgia and South Carolina were merged and so continued for nearly forty years. The conferences during these periods were really regional meetings of one conference. They appeared in the *Minutes* as districts in 1801 and as independent conferences in 1802. At the time of the merger there were 5 charges, 10 preachers, and 1,894 members. When the first conference was held in the state in 1788, there were 2 charges, 7 preachers, and 1,100 members.

⁶ The fact that Asbury here mentions his sermon at Grant's Chapel three days after the adjournment of the conference indicates that the conference was held elsewhere. (See note under January 10, 1793.)

Wednesday, 16. We had to swim Long Creek. We had few to hear at Haynes's;[7] but they felt the word, and we had a good time.

When the weather is open and the sun shines, the days are generally warm in this country; but the nights are cold, and the houses open.

Saturday, 19. Was taken up in reading Ostervald's Christian Theology; it is simple, plain, and interesting.

Sunday, 20. I preached at Bethel on 1 Peter ii, 24, 25. I had a full congregation, and great freedom in speaking: the house was a miserable one.

Wednesday, 23. I came to Buckhead: a few people had gathered, to whom I gave an exhortaton. Reached J——'s; making it thirty-three miles without refreshment, being out from seven to seven o'clock again.

Friday, 25. I rode fifteen miles to my very loving friend brother D——'s: here my mind was exercised with what I heard and felt. Mr. Matthews wrote brother D—— he had been taught *my iniquity*, to which Mr. Hammet (his brother) gave his sanction. And why was I thus charged? Because I did not establish Mr. Wesley's absolute authority over the American connexion:—for myself, this I had submitted to; but the American's were too jealous to bind themselves to yield to him in all things relative to Church government. Mr. Wesley was a man they had never seen—was three thousand miles off—how might submission, in such a case, be expected? Brother Coke and myself gave offence to the connexion by enforcing Mr. Wesley's will in some matters; for which I do not blame Mr. Wesley: like other great men, he had his elbow friends; and like other people I had my enemies.

Tuesday, 29. We reach Savannah. Next day I rode twelve miles along a fine, sandy road to view the ruins of Mr. Whitefield's Orphan House:[8] we found the place, and having seen the copperplate, which I recognized, I felt very awful; the wings are yet standing, though much injured, and the school house still more. It is reported that Mr. Whitefield observed, whilst eating his last dinner in the house, "This house was built for God; and cursed be the man that puts it to any other use." The land for the support of the school is of little value, except two rice plantations, which we passed in our route.

I returned to Savannah, and preached on Luke xix, 10, to a serious people, with whom I had liberty.

Friday, February 1. I came to Ebenezer, and had a pleasing interview with Mr. Bergman; he cannot speak much English. The Lord has certainly

---

[7] Asbury returned to the home of Thomas Haynes and continued through Buckland in Burke County and southward to Savannah.

[8] The Orphan House was founded by George Whitefield in 1749, and its successor is still in operation. There were two churches in Savannah, Lutheran and Presbyterian. It was a difficult field for the Methodists. In 1790 Hope Hull was appointed to the town but was driven away by a mob, as were other preachers later. Jesse Lee was able to form a class with four members in 1807, and the first church was built in 1812. (Smith: *Georgia Methodism*, 48; Simpson: *Cyclopedia of Methodism*, 784.)

something in design for this man, more than to be buried in this place. We rode through rice plantations for nearly two miles, and were entangled in the swamp. O, how dreadful to be here in the dark!

Saturday, 2. I am not enough in prayer. I have said more than was for the glory of God concerning those who have left the American connexion, and who have reviled Mr. Wesley, Mr. Fletcher, Doctor Coke, and poor *me*. O that I could trust the Lord more than I do, and leave his cause wholly in his own hands.

This being *Saturday*, we rest to read and write, having ridden, since *Monday* morning, about one hundred and twenty-four miles.

I reflect upon the present ruin of the Orphan House; and taking a view of the money expended, the persons employed, the preachers sent over, I was led to inquire, where are they? and how has it sped? The earth, the army, the Baptists, the Church, the Independents, have swallowed them all up at this *windmill end of the continent*. A wretched country this! —but there are souls, precious souls, worth worlds.

I was offered the use of the court house to preach in, but the night being cold and windy, prevented: I preached at Mr. M——'s.[9] We want a house here, which I expect we shall obtain. I suppose there are five hundred houses of all sorts; and if I guess well, about two thousand inhabitants. There is one Lutheran Church, with, perhaps, fifty or sixty members. Goshen church is about forty by twenty-five, well-finished: Mr. Bergman and the congregation have given it to us, on condition that we supply them with preaching on Sabbath days—once in two, or even three weeks.[10]

I lodged at our kind W——'s. Crossed the Savannah at the Sister Ferry; and came on to Blackswamp, and in the dark got pretty well scratched by the trees.

South Carolina

Sunday, 3. Preached at Blackswamp church[11] on 2 Cor. iii, 9: the subject was pointed; and the people were attentive.

Monday, 4. I preached at Purysburg[12] to a full house: some of the women appeared to feel the word. We had a heavy ride: I was faint, and low-spirited at the view which I could not fail to take of the state of

[9] Mr. M—— was probably Mr. Miller, a Presbyterian.

[10] The Goshen church, offered to the Methodists by Mr. Bergman, Lutheran pastor at Ebenezer, was in Effingham County north of Savannah. (Smith: *Georgia Methodism*, 48.)

[11] Black Swamp Church was in lower Hampton County, near Garnett, South Carolina. The church still stands and is maintained though inactive.

[12] Purysburg was a Swiss Protestant settlement established in 1726 just west of Hardeeville in Jasper County on the Savannah. It endured until around 1726. When Joseph Pilmoor preached there, the settlers desired him to remain as their pastor.

professors and sinners. I had about fifty hearers, and was invited to a friend's house, but thought it best to pursue my journey. We came to Salt Ketchers [Salkehatchie] bridge, where we stopped to pay our fare—but O, the scent of rum, and men filled with it! How shocking! Who could enter such a house! I hoped for quiet private entertainment at Red Hill![13] but the gentleman refused to receive us for love, money, or hospitality's sake. I then sent brother R. to know if we could get in at the next Negro quarter: into the house we might be permitted to enter, but we could get no corn for our horses, and no bed for ourselves: overseers dare not, and their employers will not, receive strangers: they are too proud to sell, and too covetous to give. At length we providentially reached a Mr. C——'s, a schoolmaster and minister: we bought some corn for our horses, and had tea, and bread and cheese for ourselves. I saw some beautiful boys at this house: had these children the opportunity of a northern education, what choice young men they might make! I was happy in the house, and pleased with two poor blacks, who were much moved under prayer. Next morning I set out about six o'clock, and passing the Fish-pond we came on slowly to Parker's ferry. I found my appointment to meet brother Jackson was not properly made; and as it was out of my way, I made a sudden turn to Givhan's, on Edisto River. After dinner I met with —— who offered to be our guide; but when I began to show him his folly and the dangerous state of his soul, he soon left us, and we had to beat our way through the swamps as well as we could: he said he had killed a Negro worth sixty pounds, and a valuable horse with racing. Pushing on we found our way to the ferry, and crossed about eight o'clock.

I laid me down at nine, and rose again at seven o'clock in the morning and set out: travelling through heavy rains, deep swamps in dark nights, makes both man and beast feel the effect of yesterday's journey of forty-five miles. My mind has been severely agitated this tour; I have ridden about six hundred and fifty miles in one month, lacking one day.

Friday, 8. I have got through Mr. Wesley's Journal as far as 1782. Finding the subscription set on foot at the conference to purchase a burying-ground and build a house, was likely to succeed, we began to think about looking out for a lot.[14] I also see a prospect of stationing two preachers here.

Sunday, 10. I preached with some life on Ezek. xxxvi, 25, 26: but alas! the people are so dissipated, and so ignorant of Gospel truth, that it is difficult to preach to them; but I cannot spare, though they keep their course to hell. At night I spoke on Isaiah vi, 8–10. Our congregation consists of five hundred souls and upwards; three hundred being black.

I have seen Mr. Johnson, the last president of the Orphan House in Georgia, who confirmed what I had written respecting it.

[13] Red Hill was in Collenton County.
[14] This was the beginning of Bethel Church in Charleston.

Charleston is a growing, busy, dreadfully dissipated place. The printed list of vessels in the harbour sets forth, fifty-three ships, fifty-five brigs, twenty-five sloops, twenty-five schooners, seven scows, and two barques, besides pilot-boats and coasters.

Monday, 11. Met the women's class, white and black, and had a powerful meeting. They agreed to hold a prayer meeting, once a week, amongst themselves.

Tuesday, 12. I make it my work to visit every afternoon. I happily met with Mr. Wesley's Journal, bringing the date down to two years before his death. I could not but specially notice that his latter days were more abundant in labours; and that he preached in places formerly unnoticed. He made this observation (so fixed on my mind), that it is rare—a mere miracle, for a Methodist to increase in wealth and not decrease in grace. I have now read the third volume of Gordon's History; Burnham's Select Martyrology; and Memoirs of Dying Saints. We have two hundred and seventeen travelling preachers; and about fifty thousand members in the United States. Glory to God in the highest!

Saturday, 16. I met the stewards and leaders: it was agreed that every other meeting should be purely spiritual—speaking experience and opening their hearts to each other.

Sunday, 17. I preached on Romans iii, 11–21. In the evening was very low, but was very plain on Luke xvi, 31. The building of a new house, and stationing another preacher in this city, and the state of this and the Georgia districts, with things relative to individuals in this society, do not work to my mind; I felt as if the charm was near breaking—some wish union; others will come back. The union must first take place with Dr. Coke, then with the British conference, and then with the American: I ask; who made us twain, and strove to scatter fire-brands, arrows, and death, through the whole continent?

Wednesday, 20. I had an interview with Dr. A., who came from the north for his health; seeing him so low, and fearing he would die if he stayed here, I hastily invited him to ride out in the country with me.

Thursday, 21. We left the city on small horses, with heavy baggage. We came to the Cypress Swamp in the night, following a poor Negro, who waded through as a guide, and not expecting to find it as bad as it was: at length we came to sister Browning's,[15] and were kindly received; I found no appointments were made for me, owing to brother —— being sick.

Friday, 22. We set out for Santee, but missed our way, and took the road to Fourholds Bridge, being six miles out of our course. We again directed our course to Santee; and after coming within sight of Mangoe's

[15] Mrs. Browning lived near Ridgeville. Asbury left Charleston along the route of present Highway 78.

ferry,[16] I took a wrong road, and went three miles up the river. We came to Mr. H.'s, where we were comfortable, and had whatever we wanted.

Saturday, 23. We had our difficulties in getting across the river—the overseer had moved the flat to the middle ground, and would not suffer any one to have it; I entreated him in behalf of the sick, but in vain. Had we waited a few minutes longer, our dear brother B. would have been there to conduct us. I have lately had cross winds; the roads, myself, Satan and my sick companion, Dr. A——, have all been matter of trial to me.

Sunday, 24. I preached the funeral of our brother B——, on Isaiah lvii, 1. The congregation was large and attentive, but appeared stupid and unfeeling.

Monday, 25. Came to brother B[radford's?], the weather as sultry as in the month of July in the north. We rode thirty miles.

Thursday, 28. The weather was exceedingly cold, so that we declined going to the chapel, but had a comfortable meeting at brother Rembert's, on Ephes. vi, 10–20.

Saturday, March 2. We crossed the water at English's[17] ferry, and came to father Marshall's, an Englishman, from Epworth; who was formerly converted, but living under Antinomian dotages, he lost the blessing. I trust the Lord hath again restored him by means of our labours. Here we have a chapel and society.

Sunday, 3. This day was rainy, yet nearly four hundred souls came together; but I could not fix the attention of the people, nor get them to understand.

Monday, 4. Came to H——'s, and thence through Columbia, the capital of South Carolina. Brother Reuben Ellis, who is nearly risen from the dead, accompanied me from M——'s: having left one sick man, I now take up another. We came to a house five miles from Columbia; we got a little bread, drank our own tea, had our horses fed, and paid two dollars next morning—so the matter ended.

Tuesday, 5. We had our difficulties in crossing the river, which was rising; and in beating up Cedar Creek fifteen miles, much of it through the woods: in the evening, we came greatly wearied to R——'s, and were kindly entertained; it may be that Providence sent us here for some good —the man and his wife feel the want of religion.

Wednesday, 6. We came to Little River Bridge;[18] crossed at S——'s ferry,[19] and at length came, thoroughly wearied, to brother Finch's.[20] I

[16] Managoe's Ferry was just below the junction of the Congaree and Wateree rivers, which form the Santee. The "Fourholds Bridge" was at Four Holes Swamp in Dorchester County.

[17] He crossed the Wateree at English Ferry below Camden.

[18] Little River Bridge was in upper Richland County.

[19] This ferry was across Broad River. Its later name was Ruff's Ferry.

[20] Mr. Finch lived in Newberry County. The district school mentionedbe low was Mount Bethel School.

expect we have been forced to ride twenty or thirty miles out of our way among strangers on account of high waters; my mind has been variously tried: I have been employed in improving myself in the Hebrew tones and points; this being my horseback study.

Thursday, 7. Preached at Finch's. I consulted the minds of our brethren about building a house for conference, preaching, and a district school; but I have no grounds to believe that our well-laid plan will be executed —our preachers are unskilful, and our friends have little money.

Friday, 8. The rains continued, and the waters kept up; crossed Enoree —high, and rising powerfully. Tyger River being impassable, we rode to Cokesbridge, and had a hungry time: came to brother Wright's, near Union court house.[21]

I next day preached to a few people at the open meeting house with some spiritual opening and sweetness. We were closely employed in writing subscriptions for the district school, and copies of the constitutions. Great rains still continue.

Thursday, 14. I preached at Flat Rock, in an open house, to an unfeeling people. Thence we came to Pacolet:[22] the waters were up; but for our money we got across in a flat that had drifted and was taken up.

Friday, 15. Came to father Smith's,[23] a German; first a Baptist, then a Methodist, but last, and best of all, a Christian.

North Carolina

Saturday and *Sunday*, 16, 17. Attended quarterly meeting in Union circuit. There were no elders present. I preached on Eph. vi, 10–18, and felt a great death among the people. *Sunday*, we administered the sacrament and held love feast. I desired Daniel Asbury to preach, and brother William Gassaway to exhort, whilst I retired to write to Isaac Smith,[24] desiring him to take the presidentship of Union, Catawba, Little Pee Dee, Great Pee Dee, Anson, and Santee circuits.

[21] Cokesbridge was later Henderson's. Wright lived near Union, and the courthouse was at the county seat of Union County.

[22] He crossed Pacolet River near the Cherokee County line on his way to Smith's Ferry across Broad River to North Carolina.

[23] Smith lived at Smith's Ford over the Broad into York County.

[24] For the identity of these preachers see Shipp: *Methodism in South Carolina*, 215. For biographical data see Betts, *History of South Carolina Methodism*, 85, 171, 172. A full day's ride must have taken Asbury eastward to Union County, North Carolina, for his quarterly conference. Union Circuit had just been formed. From there he went to Burke County, North Carolina, near Morganton. Union Circuit was called Lincoln when formed by Daniel Asbury in 1790. It became Union in 1793 and changed to Lincoln again in 1805. It embraced the whole area along the state line, including Lincoln, Burke, parts of Mecklenburg, Cabarrus, and Union counties in North Carolina, and parts of York and Spartanburg counties in South Carolina. (Grissom, *op. cit.*, 273.)

The people hereabouts have been poorly handled by those who, whilst they made a great profession of religion, maintained Antinomian principles and practice. I have been unwell, occasioned by the change of seasons, houses, and tables. Came to brother M——'s on *Sunday* evening, to get a day of rest. I feel the want of religion in families, congregations, and societies. I have travelled about three hundred miles the last three weeks; and have escaped the excessive rains, but have had to wrestle with floods.

Monday, 18. I spent in writing sundry letters to the north; and in my favourite study.

Tuesday, 19. I had a full house at L——'s. I felt very unfit for public exercises, both in body and mind. I have little desire to come here again:— we can hardly get entertainment. We want brethren and children here. A woman invited us to her house; but when I understood the distance, I determined to haste along, and made it about thirty miles to F——'s, in the cover of the mountain; where we rested in peace, after getting a little Indian bread, fried bacon, and drinking some of our tea. Our lodging was on a bed set upon forks, and clap-boards laid across, in an earthen-floor cabin. But worse than all the rest, these people decline in religion. I feel awful for them on this account. Next morning, about sunrise, we took the path up the mountain.

I sent Daniel Asbury to Dr. Busnell's, to inquire if there was any expectation of my coming to Burke to preach; for, being indisposed, I intended to turn aside to Johns River. Daniel Asbury returned; and the Doctor's nephew pursued, and brought us to town, where I gave them a plain, pointed sermon on, "The Son of man is come to seek and save that which was lost": every one, young and old, lawyers, doctors, and clerks, were obliging, attentive, and serious. Doctor Busnell is a man I have heard of these twenty years, but knew him not until now. He descended from the Bohemians. His son Joseph was happily brought home to God by means of the Methodists; he lived to God, and died in Winchester about twelve months ago. The Doctor's usage to me was that of a gentleman and Christian. The transition with respect to entertainment was very great; here we had a table, bed, room, and whatever we wanted; but all this could not give me rest, having a return of my rheumatic and nervous complaints.

Friday, 22. Rode up to Johns River: I am heavy; cannot attend study nor mental prayer, and company is irksome. O that my soul were always flaming with perfect love! In the evening eight of us met together, and conversed on the work of God: all was love. Brother P. gave us an animating sermon on, "By whom shall Jacob arise? for he is small."

Sunday, 24. I preached on 1 Cor. xiv, 3; there was a noise, and a shaking each day: some were awakened, one professed to be converted, and several to be quickened: the meeting lasted from nine, A.M., to four o'clock, P.M. "While he was yet speaking there came also another." I heard there was a conference appointed at Reese's chapel, in Charlotte county, Virginia, to form what they call a free constitution, and a pure Church; and to reject me and my creatures.[25] I know not whose hand is in this; I hope they will call themselves by another name. Only let them settle in congregations and tax the people, and I know how it will work. If we (the itinerant connexion) would give the government into the hands of a local ministry, as some would have it, and tax the people to pay preachers for Sabbath work—this would please such men: but this we dare not do. Whenever the people are unwilling to receive us and think they can do better, we will quietly withdraw from them; and if those who wish the change can serve them better than we have done, well. Perhaps some of them may think with Hammett, in Georgia, that I am the greatest villain on the continent; I bid such adieu, and appeal to the bar of God. I have no time to contend, having better work to do: if we lose some children, God will give us more. Ah! this is the mercy, the justice of some who, under God, owe their all to me, and my *tyrants*, so called. The Lord judge between them and me! There appears to be a general quickening in the Yadkin circuit, and about eight souls have professed conversion there in the last three months.

Monday, 25. I rested and prepared to cross the *Harmon harim*—the multitude of mountains.

Tuesday, 26. We wrought up the meanders of Johns River to the Globe,[26] and met a few people at Mr. Moor's, a Baptist, a very kind head of a respectable family.

Wednesday, 27. We began our journey over the great ridge of mountains: we had not gone far before we saw and felt the snow; the sharpness of the air gave me a deep cold, not unlike an influenza. We came to the head of Watauga River. Stopped at Mr. S——'s, and had some enlargement on, "The promise is to you and to your children," &c. My soul felt for these neglected people. It may be, by my coming this way, Providence will so order it, that I shall send them a preacher. We hasted on to Cove's Creek, invited ourselves to stay at C——'s, where we made our own tea, obtained some butter and milk, and some most excellent Irish potatoes: we were presented with a little flax for our beds, on which we spread our coats and blankets, and three of us slept before a large fire.

Thursday, 28. We made an early start, and came to the Beaver Dam; three years ago we slept here in a cabin without a cover. We made a breakfast at Mr. W——'s; and then attempted the iron or stone mountain, which is steep like the roof of a house. I found it difficult and trying to my lungs to walk up it. Descending the mountain, we had to jump down the

---

[25] The reference here is to the O'Kellyites who were organizing the Republican Methodist Church in Virginia. (See letter of November 23, 1793.)

[26] John's River is in the northern area of Burke County, North Carolina, between Morganton and Lenoir. Globe is in Caldwell County, North Carolina. There was a chapel at Globe. (See *Journal* entries for April 27, 1788, and April 4, 1790.)

steep stairs, from two to three and four feet. At the foot of this mountain our guide left us to a man on foot; he soon declined, and we made the best of our way to Julius Dugger's[27] ford, on Roans Creek. We came down the river, where there are plenty of large, round, rolling stones, and the stream was rapid. My horse began to grow dull: an intermittent fever and a deep cold disordered me much. I was under obligations to Henry Hill, my new aid, who was ready to do anything for me in his power. Perhaps Providence moved him to offer to travel with me, and his father to recommend him. Twenty years ago a rude, open loft did not affect me—now it seldom fails to injure me.

Tennessee

Friday, 29. We took our journey deliberately. We passed Doe River at the fork,[28] and came through the Gap; a most gloomy scene—not unlike the Shades of Death in the Alleghany mountain.[29] Mr. L——, a kind Presbyterian, fed our horses gratis.[30] I must give the Presbyterians the preference for respect to ministers. We prayed, and came on to a kind people;[31] but to our sorrow we find it low times for religion on Holston and Watauga Rivers. In Green circuit there is some increase. My way opens; and I think I shall go to Kentucky. I laid my hands on what is called "The Principles of Politeness," imitated from Chesterfield: it contains some judicious remarks, and shows the author to have been a man of sense and education, but of no religion. He recommends some things contrary thereto.

Tuesday, April 2. Our conference began at Nelson's, near Jonesboro in the new territory.[32] We have only four or five families of Methodists here. We had sweet peace in our conference.

Wednesday, 3. I gave an exhortation after brothers Henry Hill and Barnabus M'Henry[33] had preached, and there was a melting among the people.

[27] Ramsay's *Annals*, 142.

[28] This was at the outskirts of the present Elizabethton, Tennessee. (Williams: *Early Travels*, 299.)

[29] The "Shades of Death" refers to a section along the state highway from Elizabethton to Bristol. (*Ibid.*)

[30] Asbury was in the neighborhood of the New Bethel Presbyterian Church, one of the oldest in that region. (*Ibid.*)

[31] Asbury probably stopped at the home of William Cobb, which is still standing. Here was the first seat of a government of the Southwest Territory under Governor William Blount in 1790. (*Ibid.*)

[32] This was the first Methodist conference held within the limits of Tennessee. (*Ibid.*)

[33] Barnabus McHenry was the elder over several circuits in Virginia. He was appointed at this conference to the Salt River Circuit.

Thursday, 4. I had a happy time at my old friend Cash's;[34] I am pained for his children, who are yet unconverted.

Friday, 5. Rode to Nolachucky, and attended a meeting at Squire Ernest's,[35] where I had about two hundred hearers. We have formed a society in this place of thirty-one members, most of them new. There are appearances of danger on the road to Kentucky; but the Lord is with us. We have formed a company of nine men, (five of whom are preachers,) who are well armed and mounted.

Saturday, 6. Rode to Greenville, and crossed the grand island ford of Nolachucky: the lowlands are very rich, the uplands barren. Stopped and fed at Green court house; here was brought a corpse to the grave in a covered carriage drawn by four horses. Solemn sight! Be instructed, O my soul! A whisky toper gave me a cheer of success as one of John Wesley's congregation! I came on alone through heavy rains, over bad hills and poor ridges, to brother Benjamin Van Pelt's,[36] on Lick Creek; he is brother to Peter, my old, first friend on Staten Island: I was weary, damp, and hungry; but had a comfortable habitation, and kind, loving people, who heard, refreshed, and fed me. We had a large congregation at brother Van Pelt's chapel,[37] where I had liberty in speaking. I left the young men to entertain the people awhile longer, and returned and read Mr. Wesley's Sermon on Riches.

If reports be true, there is danger in journeying through the wilderness; but I do not fear—we go armed. If God suffer Satan to drive the Indians on us; if it be his will, he will teach our hands to war, and our fingers to fight and conquer.

Monday, 8. Our guard appeared, fixed, and armed, for the wilderness. We came down to E——'s, and were well entertained. Thence we proceeded on to the main branch of Holston which, being swelled, we crossed in a flat; thence to R——'s, where I found the reports relative to the Indians were true—they had killed the post and one or two more, and taken some prisoners. I had not much thought or fear about them.

Tuesday, 9. We came off: there were only eight in our company, and eight in the other; two women and three children. We had two poor sinners, that set themselves to work wickedness: they would not let us go foremost: so we took it patiently, and followed up to the Cumberland station. I went to Robinson's station, where the soldiers behaved civilly. We gave them two exhortations, and had prayer with them. They honoured

[34] Mr. Cash lived in Washington County, Tennessee. (*Ibid.*)

[35] This meeting was held at the home of Henry or Felix Ernest in Green County. Both were ardent Methodists and had descendants who are members of Ebenezer Church today. (*Ibid.*)

[36] Benjamin Van Pelt, brother of Peter Van Pelt, who first welcomed Asbury on Staten Island, moved westward in 1780.

[37] The chapel erected by Benjamin Van Pelt near Mosheim was one of the earliest Methodist meetinghouses in Tennessee. (*Ibid.*)

me with the swinging hammock (a bear skin), which was as great a favour to me as the governor's bed; here I slept well.

Kentucky

Wednesday, 10. We hasted on our way, meeting with our troubles at the foot of Cumberland mountain; we then went foremost, and travelled at a great rate, the roads being uncommonly good.[38] We fed on the banks of Cumberland River, and kept up the head of Rich Lands. We then pushed through Little and Big Laurel to the Hazel Patch,[39] Hood's station. Here there was high life below stairs, talking, laughing, &c. We had a troop of poor, very poor sinners; I gave dreadful offence by a prayer I made. After resting here from three to six, we urged our way along the new road to Rock Castle. Fed at the deserted station, and hasted to Willis Green's; but, missing our way, did not get in until eight o'clock: a supper at that time was good, and a bed was better, having not slept in one for three nights, and having ridden one hundred miles in two days. I felt so well in the morning I was ready to set out for Salt River. I went to Danville, and set myself down in Mr. Rice's church[40]; thence to Francis Clark's,[41] where I was not expected, but was quite welcome. I left my aid and pack-horse at G——'s, to rest.

Saturday, 13. We rode thirty-three miles down to a quarterly meeting at Humphries chapel.[42] Here my presence surprised the brethren. The state of the work here appears to be low. I had some light, life, and liberty in preaching, and some felt the word. We closed our meeting after several had joined in prayer. Lord, remember the labours of this day! Let not thy faithful word fall to the ground! From the quarterly meeting we came to Col. Hardin's.[43] He has been gone some time, as a commissioner, to treat with the Indians; if he is dead, here is a widow and six children left. I cannot yet give him up for lost. We had a large congregation at W——'s,

[38] Asbury's party was traveling on the famous Wilderness Road. (Kincaid: *Wilderness Road*, 201.)

[39] The Hazel Patch was a clump of hazel bushes at the important junction of two prongs of the Wilderness Road, eight miles north of present London, Kentucky. (Kincaid, *op. cit.*, 113; see map.)

[40] The Rev. David Rice was a pioneer Presbyterian minister in Kentucky.

[41] The Rev. Francis Clark, a local preacher from Virginia, settled near Danville, where he organized the first Methodist society in Kentucky in 1783. (Redford, *op. cit.*, I, 149; Arnold: *Methodism in Kentucky*, 22–25.)

[42] Humphries Chapel was in Casey County, Kentucky, about thirty miles south of Danville. (*U.S. Geological Survey of Kentucky*, 1938.)

[43] Colonel John Hardin went from Virginia to Kentucky and in 1786 settled near Sandusky Station, a few miles from Springfield. He was a prominent citizen and Methodist and the father-in-law of the Rev. Barnabus McHenry. He was killed in 1792 by the Indians. (Redford, *op. cit.*, I, 117–19, 317–18; Roosevelt: *Winning of the West*, V, 176, 177.)

where I was led out on Psa. xxxiv, 17–20. I cannot stand quarterly meetings every day; none need desire to be an American bishop upon our plan,
for the ease, honour, or interest that attends the office: from my present
views and feelings, I am led to wish the conference would elect another
bishop, which might afford me some help.

Tuesday, 16. Rode thirty miles without food for man or horse. I was
uncomfortable when I came into the neighbourhood of W——'s: there is
a falling away among the people. Lord, help me to bear up in the evil day!
Let me not disquiet myself, and kill man and horse in vain.

Thursday, 18. I rode sixteen miles to Francis Clark's station to attend
the quarterly meeting. My winter's clothing, the heat of the weather, and,
my great exertions in travelling, cause me to be heavy with sleep; yet
blessed be God, I live continually in his presence, and Christ is all in all
to my soul!

Friday, 19. I preached a short, pointed sermon; and the preachers and
members were moved.

Sunday, 21. We had sacrament and love feast; and some spoke much
to the purpose: my subject was Heb. vi. 4–8. The congregation was very
large. I endeavoured to show, 1st. How far people may advance in the
grace of God; 2d. By what degrees they may apostatize; 3d. The impossibility of a recovery when they arrive at a certain degree of wickedness:—
(1.) Because they sin against God, Christ, and the Eternal Spirit, and lose
all they ever felt or knew;—(2.) Every means is lost upon them; to sin
against the remedy, is to be undone without it. The difference between
those who are recoverable and those who are not: such are not who deny
the work to be of God, persecute, and say the devil was the author of it;
the others acknowledge the work that it was of God, and have some
regard for his people. Lastly: that the only security pointed out by the
apostles against apostasy, is to go on to perfection.

Tuesday, 23. I was at Bethel—the place intended for a school.[44]

Sunday, 28. We had sacrament and love feast, and some living testimonies.

Monday, 29. Rode through the rain to Lexington. I stopped at Charles
White's[45] once more. O that God may help him safe to glory! Came to
brother Morgan's. I felt awful and solemn, and some dejection of mind.
Ah! want of religion is too visible in most houses.

Tuesday, 30, *Wednesday*, *May* 1, *Thursday*, 2. We spent in conference;
and in openly speaking our minds to each other. We ended under the
melting, praying, praising power of God. We appointed trustees for the
school; and made sundry regulations relative thereto: we read the Form
of Discipline through, section by section, in conference.

Friday, 3. I preached on Habakkuk iii, 2. I first pointed out the distin-

[44] Bethel Academy was located in Jessamine County on land donated by John Lewis.
See note under May 17, 1790.)   [45] See note under May 13, 1790.

guishing marks of a work of God; 2d. The subjects; 3d, The instruments; 4th, The means. If ever I delivered my own soul, I think I have done it this day. Some people were moved in an extraordinary manner, shouting and jumping at a strange rate.

Saturday, 4. Came to Bethel to meet the trustees.

Sunday 5. We had an awful time whilst I opened and applied "Knowing therefore the terror of the Lord, we persuade men." It was a feeling, melting time, among old and young; and I am persuaded good was certainly done this day. I feel a good deal tried in spirit, yet, blessed be God, I still have peace within; God is all to me: I want more faith to trust him with my life, and all I have and am.

Tuesday, 7. We rode down to the Crab Orchard, where we found company enough, some of whom were very wild: we had a company of our own, and refused to go with them. Some of them gave us very abusive language; and one man went upon a hill above us, and fired a pistol towards our company. We resolved to travel in our order, and bound ourselves by honour and conscience to support and defend each other, and to see every man through the wilderness. But we could not depend upon wicked and unprincipled men, who would leave and neglect us, and even curse us to our faces. Nor were we at liberty to mix with swearers, liars, drunkards; and, for aught we know, this may not be the worst with some. We were about fourteen or fifteen in company; and had twelve guns and pistols. We rode on near the defeated camp,[46] and rested till three o'clock under great suspicion of Indians: we pushed forward; and by riding forty-five miles on *Wednesday*, and about the same distance on *Thursday*, we came safe to Robinson's station, about eight o'clock.

Friday, 10. We rode leisurely from the edge of the wilderness, crossed Holston and about one o'clock came to brother E——'s, it being about sixteen miles.

Tennessee

Saturday, 11. We came to brother Van Pelt's, with whom we rested on the Sabbath. I have travelled between five and six hundred miles in the last four weeks, and have rested from riding fifteen days at conferences, and other places. I have been much distressed with this night work—no regular meals, nor sleep; and it is difficult to keep up prayer in such rude companies as we have been exposed to; I have also been severely afflicted through the whole journey.

Monday, 13. Was a day of great trial; we rode about forty-six miles; stopped at ——, where, through carelessness, I nearly had been burnt up.

Tuesday, 14. At eleven o'clock we came to Baker's.[47] The subject was,

[46] This refers to McNitt's defeat. (See note under May 11, 1790.)
[47] Charles Baker lived near Blountville, Tennessee.

"Let this mind be in you which was also in Christ Jesus." Sisters W——, and H——, making some clothing, and repairing my burnt raiment next day, we could not move until eight o'clock. We then set out without a guide, missed our road, and came in about two o'clock: we found the people patiently waiting, to whom I preached on "Ye will not come to me that ye might have life."

Virginia

Thursday, 16. Came to Abingdon—felt very heavy; I however preached in the court house to a very genteel people on the words of Joshua, "Ye cannot serve God," &c.

Saturday, 18. Came to sister Russell's[48]; I am very solemn. I feel the want of the dear man who, I trust, is now in Abraham's bosom, and hope ere long to see him there. He was a general officer in the continental army, where he underwent great fatigue: he was powerfully brought to God, and for a few years past was a living flame, and a blessing to his neighbourhood. He went in the dead of winter on a visit to his friends; was seized with influenza, and ended his life from home: O that the Gospel may continue in this house! I preached on Heb. xii, 1–4, and there followed several exhortatons. We then administered the sacrament, and there was weeping and shouting among the people: our exercises lasted about five hours. I have little rest by night or by day. Lord, help thy poor dust! I feel unexpected storms—within from various quarters; perhaps it is designed for my humiliation. It is a sin in thought that I am afraid of: none but Jesus can support us, by his merit, his Spirit, his righteousness, his intercession; that is, Christ in all, for all, through all, and in every mean, and word, and work.

West Virginia

Monday, 20. Rode to Cook's, and was well steeped in rain; here I wrote a plan for a district school.

[48] Madam Russell, Patrick Henry's sister, was one of the great early Methodists in Virginia. Having been at first the wife of General William Campbell and after his death the wife of General William Russell, she was the best-known woman in southwestern Virginia and was devoted to the Methodist cause. A short note is extant in Miss Nelly Preston's, her descendant's, possession written to Colonel William Preston, her son-in-law, instructing him to pay for an addition to her house with salt from the salt works which belonged to Mrs. Russell and her family. The tradition is that she was adding to her house because of need for a better place for Asbury and the preaching services he held in her home. She had also a pulpit made, and tradition is also well established that she had a beaver hat made for Asbury and kept his old one, which she wore the remainder of her life. She manumitted her slaves, as did Colonel Preston, after joining the Methodists.

Wednesday, 22. We rode forty-five miles to Elias Harmon's,[49] where we had many people. About five o'clock, on our way over the hills, we felt the rain without, and hunger within: next day we crossed Walker's Mountain, and in the evening met brother M—— at Munday's.

Friday, 24. Came to Rehoboth, in the sinks of Green Briar; where we held our conference. I was greatly comforted at the sight of brothers B. J. and Ellis Cox. We had peace in our conference, and were happy in our cabin. I learn that mischief is begun in the lower parts of Virginia; J. O'Kelly, and some of the local preachers, are the promoters and encouragers of divisions among the brethren.

Tuesday, 28. We passed the Sweet Springs,[50] and crossed a rough mountain to brother Dew's on Potts Creek. I wrote many letters to the south district of Virginia, to confirm the souls of the people, and guard them against the division that is attempted among them.

Virginia

Came to Edward Mitchell's.[51] Crossed James River, near the mouth of Craigs Creek;[52] but was prevented by the rain from pursuing our journey. We spent the evening comfortably at sister Pryer's.

Friday, 31. Rode forty-five miles to Moore's furnace; and lodged with kind brother R.

Saturday, June 1. We came to Staunton, a very unpleasing place to me. There are an Episcopal church, a court house, good taverns, and stores here. We went to Mr. ——'s, expecting to find a friend; after making the trial, we thought it best to return and take lodging in a tavern. Thence we proceeded on to Rocktown,[53] a beautiful place; here I felt myself stiff, and weary, and troubled with rheumatic pains: sweet sleep was quite welcome. My congregation was small, the people not having proper notice of my coming. Satan has been sowing discord here, and has hindered the work of God; but I hope the approaching quarterly meeting will be a blessing to them, and that we shall not toil in vain. The loss of sleep, and other circumstances, made me very heavy, and brought on a sick headache, which I had not felt for some time. I spent the evening with Doctor Dulany. Rose, and took the rain next morning as usual, having had rain

[49] Elias Harmon lived in Giles County, Virginia, near New River. He emancipated a number of slaves in 1827–28. (Harmon's *Annals of Tazewell County*, 455.)

[50] Sweet Springs was in present West Virginia.

[51] Edward Mitchell lived in Bottetourt County and was one of the original Methodists in this section. He and his brother, Samuel, both became local preachers. Later the two brothers moved to the West, Edward to Illinois and Samuel to Ohio. (Bennett, *op. cit.*, 336.) Both Edward and Samuel freed their slaves after becoming Methodists.

[52] Craig's Creek enters into the James River near the present Eagle Rock.

[53] Rocktown was the present Harrisonburg. This was the second of ten visits made to the community by Asbury.

for eight or ten days successively. On my way I was met by an old German, who shook me by the hand, and said he wished he might be worthy to wash my feet. Yea, thought I, if you knew what a poor sinful creature I am, you would hardly look at one so unworthy; but Jesus lives—O precious Christ, thou art mine and I am thine!

Came to Newtown:[54] the roads exceedingly miry, and our horses very tired: we are glad to get a little rest at brother Phelps's. My soul has been much tried by Satan, and I am pained for the work of God. In my six months' travel I find that six acceptable preachers are preparing to settle themselves in the world, and leave the itinerancy.

Thursday, 6. We came to Winchester; where they have built an excellent house, and we have better times than I expected: here nothing would do but I must preach, notwithstanding the lanes and streets of the town were so filled with mire, owing to the late rains.

West Virginia

Friday, 7. We rode to Bath, that seat of sin: here we continued to rest ourselves: my public work was a sermon on the Sabbath. A number of our society from various parts being here, I have an opportunity of receiving and answering many letters. I am afraid I shall spend nine or ten days here to little purpose; I employ myself in reading Thomas à Kempis and the Bible: I also have an opportunity of going alone into the silent grove, and of viewing the continent, and examining my own heart. I hope for some relief from my rheumatic complaint which has so oppressed me for six months past. The people here are so gay and idle, that I doubt there being much good done among them. The troubles of the east and west meet me as I pass.

Maryland

Sunday, 16. A number of us crossed the ferry at the mouth of Great Capon; and made our way through great heat to Oldtown, thirty-two miles: we were obliged to ride moderately, or the excessive warmth of the weather might have killed our horses. We had no small consolation in uniting the brethren from three districts in conference;[55] whose names only were before known to each other. I gave them one sermon on, "Pray for the peace of Jerusalem; they shall prosper that love thee." Our conference sat three days successively, very closely employed.

[54] Newtown was the present Stephens City.

[55] The preachers were from districts over which Charles Conaway, Nelson Reed, and Barnabas McHenry were the elders. The region included parts of Maryland, Virginia, Pennsylvania, and Ohio. (See *General Minutes,* 1793.)

Thursday, 20. I had some little time to read, write, and pray. My congregation was careless and unfeeling. I enforced David's charge to Solomon. Methinks it ought to be with those who have to do with souls, as with a tender feeling physician that attends a patient: does the fever rage, or the delirium continue? his countenance is sad; and when labour and medicine fail, and the symptoms continue or grow worse, he is then forced, as a skilful physician, to pronounce his patient incurable—whilst a quack flatters and sees no danger: such is the difference between a true minister of Christ and a false teacher, when applied to the souls of men.

Pennsylvania

Friday, 21. We rode thirty-five miles to Fidler's,[56] and thirty-five more the next day to Fort Littleton. Our roads are rough; I am sick; our fare is coarse; but it is enough—I am to die. I have been under violent temptations—Lord, keep me every moment! Our horses were out of the way, so that we could not pursue our journey. I was desirous to be doing good somewhere; and was led to speak to a woman unknown to me, and urged her to pray three times a day: she appeared tender; and with tears promised to do so—perhaps this labour may not be lost. I have had the happiness to hear that my labour of this kind at the widow H[ollopeter's?] when there last, was successful, and that a woman was wrought upon to give herself to God, and found peace. We collected the little persecuted society, to whom I preached on, "All that will live godly in Christ Jesus shall suffer persecution": they were poor, but very kind. Thence we proceeded on to Juniata; crossed to Mifflin Town, and came to Henry Moore's.[57]

Thursday, 27. Was to me a day of trial. We set out late towards Northumberland: night coming on, we stopped at Penn's Creek. Next morning we went to Northumberland to breakfast. It has a little chapel (that serves as a school house) belonging to the Methodists. We have a few kind, respectable friends, whose circumstances are comfortable. I gave them a sermon on John xiv, 6; and in the afternoon paid Sunbury a visit. The people here are almost all Dutch. I was enabled to speak alarming words on Acts iv, 12.

July 2. After preaching on "the grace of God appearing to all men,"[58]

[56] This was the home of the parents of Daniel Fidler, located between Oldtown and Fort Littleton, Pennsylvania. (See Asbury's letter to Daniel Fidler, June 22, 1793.)

[57] Henry Moore's home near Mifflintown was a frequent stopping place of early Methodist itinerants. William Colbert stayed there and preached at "Henry Moore's Meeting House." (Manuscript *Journal* of William Colbert, entry for July 2, 1792.)

[58] Asbury was accompanied by James Campbell, William Colbert, and Henry Hill. The last named was his official traveling companion. (*Journal* entry for March 28, 1793; Palmer: *Heroism and Romance, Early Methodism in Northeastern Pennsylvania*, 87.)

we wrought up the hills and narrows to Wyoming.[59] We stopped at a poor house; nevertheless, they were rich enough to sell us a half bushel of oats, and had sense enough to make us pay well for them. We reached Mr. Parish's[60] about eleven o'clock. I found riding in the night caused a return of my rheumatic complaint through my breast and shoulders. But all is well, the Lord is with us.

Thursday, 4. Being the anniversary of the American independence, there was a great noise among the sinners: a few of us went down to Shawnee:[61] called a few people from their work, and found it good for us to be there.

[62]On the 5th, after very sultry weather, there came a whirlwind, and a very great storm; in which there fell hail of such a size that three stones filled a pint measure: this went through Hudson, some distance from us.

Sunday, 7. The Lord has spoken in awful peals of thunder. O, what havoc was made here fifteen years ago! most of the inhabitants were either cut off, or driven away.[63] The people might have clothed themselves in sackcloth and ashes the third, if in white and glory the fourth of July. The inhabitants here are very wicked; but I feel as if the Lord would return. I hope brothers Frisby, Richard Inman, and Parish will be owned of the Lord. The man at whose house I was to preach,[64] made a frolic the day before; it was said he sent a mile across the river for one of his neighbours, taking him from his work, and telling him he was about to bleed to death: this falsity was invented, I suppose, to incline the man to come: the people would not come to his house. I had to walk a mile through burning heat

---

[59] Wyoming, meaning plain or valley, was an area about four by twenty miles along the Susquehannah River within which are Kingston and Wilkes-Barre, Pennsylvania; it is not to be confused with Wyoming Borough, organized in 1885. It was set up as a Methodist circuit in 1791 and included Newberg and New York. (*Minutes*, I, 42 ff.) In 1793 it was a district with four circuits extending from Northumberland, Pennsylvania, to Seneca Lake, New York. Valentine Cook was the elder. (Palmer: *op. cit.*, I, 100 ff. See letter to Thomas Morrell, July 3, 1793.)

[60] Captain Ebenezer Parish lived on Ross Hill, two miles south of Kingston, Pennsylvania, and was the leader of the class that had been formed in his cabin. The house stood just east of the present Edwardsville high school. From here Methodism spread through the whole area and into central and western New York. Prominent in this work was the converted blacksmith circuit rider Anning Owen. Parish was the first class leader in Wyoming. (Palmer, *op. cit.*, 61 ff., 109.)

[61] Shawnee was the present Plymouth.

[62] In the original edition of the *Journal* this entry followed that for Monday, July 8. In order to preserve the acting sequence of events, it has been inserted here. A tornado was rather unusual as far east as the Hudson River Valley. In passing through Hudson the following week, Asbury does not mention the occurrence.

[63] This reference was to the Wyoming "Massacre" in early July, 1778.

[64] This man was Captain Satterthwaite. (Palmer, *op. cit.*, 88; manuscript *Journal* of William Colbert.)

to preach;[65] I was severely exercised in mind, hardly knowing where to go to get a quiet, clean place to lie down.

Monday, 8. I took "The Wilderness," through the mountains, up Lackawanna on the Twelve-miles Swamp;[66] this place is famous for dirt and lofty hemlock. We lodged in the middle of the swamp at Stanton's;[67] and made out better than we expected. Next morning we set out in the rain, without breakfast: when we came to the ferry,[68] a man took us to his house, and gave us some bread, butter, and some buckwheat, and then charged us four shillings and twopence, although we found our own tea and sugar,—the place we should have called at was a little farther on the way.

Wednesday, 10. We came to Broadhead's,[69] and were totally unknown;

[65] Colbert says the "people met at Rosencrantz's but the captain was so affronted that he would not attend." Rosencrantz presumably lived on the west side of the Susquehanna in the Kingston area or possibly at Forty Fort. There is, however, a possibility that he lived on the east side of the river north of Wilkes-Barre, since Asbury does not mention crossing the river as he walked a mile through the heat. Asbury preached and William Colbert, Henry Hill, and Anning Owen exhorted on Sunday at the meetinghouse in Hanover just below Wilkes-Barre. In the afternoon both Asbury and Hill preached at the courthouse in Wilkes-Barre. Asbury had preached there on Saturday also and had gone home with Richard Inman. (Colbert's *Journal*; Palmer, *op. cit.*, 87, 88.)

[66] The swamp was east of Hamlin, Wayne County, Pennsylvania. The party had separated, Asbury and Hill going toward New Jersey and the conference at Albany and Colbert returning to the Northumberland Circuit. (Palmer, *op. cit.*, 6, 88–89.)

[67] William Stanton was the son of Jacob Stanton who had built a home at what was called Little Meadows. This small tract of tillable land had been redeemed from the swamp by several beaver dams and for long years had been an Indian camping site. In 1770 Seth Strong had built a house and fort there, and a few people had joined him. Soon after the Wyoming massacre in 1778, they were all killed by Indians except Jacob Stanton, who escaped. He and his son, William, returned the next year and buried the remains, and in 1781 they came again with equipment and built the simple establishment Asbury found so comfortable. The spot, still known as Little Meadows, lies a short distance off Route 590, about four miles east of Hamlin, Pennsylvania. (Matthews: *History of Wayne, Pike and Monroe Counties, Pennsylvania*, 746–48, 771, 857, 901, 945; old maps and records of Wayne and Pike counties at Wayne County Historical Society, Honesdale, Pennsylvania.)

[68] Asbury crossed the Delaware River at Carpenter's Point, seven miles north of Milford, Pennsylvania. The present bridge of Route 6, connecting Port Jervis, New York, and Matamoras, Pennsylvania, stands exactly where Carpenter's ferries plied. (*Ibid.*, 901.)

[69] Four families named Broadhead lived in the vicinity of Marbletown. The most likely one to have been host to Asbury was Daniel Broadhead, then a trustee of the town of Marbletown. Although not a Methodist, he was known as a religious man, hospitable to travelers on the trail. The heads of the other Broadhead families were Samuel, Charles, and Lewis. (Records of Marbletown.) Some students believe the Broadhead mentioned here lived on Brodhead Creek in present Monroe County, Pennsylvania, which Henry Boehm identifies as one of his preaching places. However, the Brodhead location in Pennsylvania would have been over sixty miles out of the way for Asbury on this trip, and surely someone there would have known him.

I was sick, and stopped for breakfast—they suspected we were preachers; one asked brother Hill[70] who I was: being informed, the mother, son, and daughter came running with tears to speak with me.

New York

I stopped and gave them a sermon at Marbletown.[71] I found the work of God going on among the Low Dutch:—these, of all the people in America, we have done the least with.

Saturday, 13. We rode to Coeyman's Patent; we had a good quarterly meeting; many newly-converted souls testified of the goodness of God, and of the power of his grace. From thence to Albany with reluctance; and lectured, being Sabbath evening: I felt the wickedness of the people: but we had a melting season among the preachers in our conference. Great changes will be made among the preachers from this conference: some will be sent to New Jersey; others to Rhode Island and Massachusetts. The people of Albany roll in wealth: they have no heart to invite any of the servants of God to their houses; unless a great change should take place, we shall have no more conferences here. I am tired down with fatigue and labour, under great weakness of body. Yet I must haste to Lynn—it may be, to meet trouble. But my days will be short.

> "My suff'ring time will soon be o'er;
> Then shall I sigh and weep no more:
> My ransom'd soul shall soar away,
> To sing God's praise in endless day."

We hope two hundred souls have been awakened, and as many converted, in Albany district the past year. Our friends are happy here, not being distressed with divisions in the Church, nor by war with the Indians, as they are to the southward. According to our reckoning, we make it about four hundred and forty-seven miles from Old Town to Albany—to come the mountainous road through the woods; and to come by Baltimore, Philadelphia, and New York, it is six hundred miles.

Saturday, 20. The congregation being small, and the preachers sleepy, made it a task for me to preach at Rowe's chapel.[72]

[70] John Hill had been serving at Tioga and met Asbury at Wyoming, traveling with him to conference at Albany.

[71] Marbletown is a small hamlet on the road from Port Jervis to Kingston, New York, and was in 1793 one of the towns on a circuit of Dutch churches. The town was named from the eight-mile ledge of limestone from which much of the stone for the old houses was quarried. (Snell: *History of Sussex County, New Jersey*, 368; *New York Guide*, 404.)

[72] This chapel was also known as Rose Chapel and was erected by John Rowe at Milan, southeast of Hudson. Henry Boehm stopped here with Asbury on July 6, 1810, and found that the "old man still lives, and has consecrated his money to God by building a church and parsonage." (Boehm, *op. cit.*, 295–96.)

Sunday, 21. There was a breath of life in the love feast. I was enabled to be close in preaching on Matt. xviii, 3: "Except ye be converted, and become as little children, ye cannot enter into the kingdom of heaven." In my introduction I showed that the being converted here mentioned is the same word which in other places is translated, "born again"; answering to the new creation and resurrection. In this discourse I took occasion to show the miserable state of the unconverted, both present and future, and the exercises that converted souls do, and must pass through;—that they must be made as little children, wholly dependent on God; possessing meekness of spirit, and freed from the guilt, power, and nature of sin. My mind enjoyed peace; but I was grieved at seeing a number of young, unfeeling sinners, assembled at a tavern on the Lord's day.

Connecticut

Monday, 22. We rode fifteen miles to Sharon, two miles from Litchfield:[73] there is a little move among the people of this place.

Tuesday, 23. Came to H——'s.[74] I rested in a very solitary shade, and was comforted in my own mind. Perhaps the old man is right who says, not many of this generation will enter into the promised land, but their children. Came to East Hartford, and find it still a day of small things. Falling under deep dejection, (such as I had not known for months), I concluded to preach this evening for my own consolation on, "Thou that teachest another, teachest thou not thyself?" We passed through and spent a night at Windham—a pleasant town. Thence through Canterbury and Plainfield; where our preachers from Connecticut have visited—but it is a dry land—little rain in a double sense. Thence I came upon the State of Rhode Island; stopped in Coventry, and found that the two preachers stationed here have been running over almost the whole State, and had formed but few societies.[75] When I came to Providence, I. Martin told me, that under the present difficulties they had agreed not to forward the preachers of the Methodists among them, nor to befriend them; I asked for a tavern, and was directed to General Thayer's,[76] where I was used well:

[73] Sharon is about two miles from the New York border, and Litchfield is about twenty miles from Sharon.

[74] Possibly Samuel Hitchcock, who lived in the south part of Sharon. (Sedgewick: *History of Sharon*.)

[75] These two preachers were probably Lemuel Smith and Menzies Rainor. The latter became an Episcopalian and then a Universalist. The eccentric Lorenzo Dow was born in South Coventry and converted in the Methodist church there in November, 1792. He left his circuit and went "ranging." (See McTyeire: *History of Methodism*, 434.)

[76] General Simeon Thayer, a Revolutionary officer who served under Arnold in his march to Quebec, operated the Montgomery Hotel. It was named after General Montgomery and was built in 1781 on a triangular lot at the head of Constitution Hill. (*Narragansett Historical Register*, V, 145–46.)

some were displeased at our praying; and acted much like Sodomites. O, the enmity and wickedness that is in the human heart! In the morning I was visited by Mr. Wilson; I gave him my mind freely, and left him: the secret of the matter was, that many in that congregation would have been kind to us, but meeting with Mr. Wilson,[77] coming from Ireland (once a travelling preacher), he settled with them: their convenience suited his interest. But the people can hear us in the school house; and if any are awakened, they will join the Church over the bridge.

Massachusetts

We had heavy work for man and horse to reach Easton—our money grew short.

Sunday, 28. Reading the Scripture in the congregation appeared to be a new thing among the people. I gave them a lecture under the apple trees, on Isaiah xxxv, 3-6; and trust my labour was not lost.

Monday, 29. We rode upwards of thirty miles, through great heat to Lynn. On our way we fed our horses, and bought a cake and some cheese for ourselves; surely we are a spectacle to men and angels! The last nine days we have ridden upwards of two hundred miles, and all things taken together, I think it worse than the wilderness: the country abounds with rocks, hills, and stones; and the heat is intense—such as is seldom known in these parts.

Tuesday, 30. Preached in Lynn, on 2 Chron. xv, 2, the prophecy of Azariah by the Spirit.

I. We are to seek Jehovah in the means; by the direction of the word and Spirit; through Christ, by repentance and faith.

II. The Lord will be with his people, as a Father and God; in his wisdom, love, truth, and mercy; at all times and places; in every strait and difficulty.

III. We should be with God as his children, to fear, trust in, worship, and serve him.

IV. The breach of the covenant by idolatry, departing from the love, fear, and confidence they have in him.

V. That the Lord will withdraw from such souls.

---

[77] James Wilson was born in Limerick, Ireland, in 1760. John Wesley sent him to the Limerick Circuit, and he became a probationer in the Irish Conference. Marrying against the rule, he was returned to the local ranks. He entered into business and later came to America. For a while he was in Providence, then went to Baltimore, where he worked with the Rev. William Hammett. He never entered the Conference. He returned North in 1793 and became the colleague of the Rev. Joseph Snow of Broad Street Congregational Church, Providence. Wilson became severely critical of Methodism and published a book entitled *Apostolic Church Government, and Massachusetts the Government and System of the M.E. Church Investigated.*

August. We have only about three hundred members in this district, yet we have a call for seven or eight preachers; although our members are few, our hearers are many.

Sunday, 4. We had preaching at six, twelve, two, and seven o'clock, and administered the Lord's supper also. I have now finished my work at Lynn. Circumstances have occurred which have made this conference more painful than any one conference beside.[78]

Monday, 5. We rode to Cambridge. On our way we called on Mr. Adams,[79] and found him and his wife under deep exercise of mind. We then came to Waltham where many attended. Things appear strange here; but several souls are under awakenings, and there is hope the Lord will work. The harvest is great; the living, faithful labourers are few.

We hasted to Weston;[80] and found a congregation at the Baptist meeting house. From Weston we came two miles to Needham:[81] here the majority of the people prefer the Methodist preachers, and want to pay them by a tax on the people; but brothers Smith and Hill[82] absolutely refused this plan,—for which I commended them. I gave them a sermon, and found some feeling souls.

Wednesday, 7. We passed several little towns, and came to Milford, about nineteen miles from Needham: here they have a good priest's house, and meeting house; all appear to be in peace and fulness of bread. About three hundred were soon collected, to whom I preached on, "The love of Christ constraineth us," &c. The man at whose house we lodged was very kind, and told me his father held society meeting in the house where we preached, and, except conditional perseverance, preached our

[78] The painful circumstances at the Lynn Conference related to Jesse Lee's reluctance to take his appointment to the province of Maine and Lynn because he did not want to leave Lynn. But he had given dissatisfaction there by interdicting fugue tunes in the music, and some persons had threatened to return to the Congregational society. He finally consented to go to Maine, however. (Phoebus: *Beams of Light on Early Methodism*, 169, 170; Mudge: *History of the New England Conference*, 47.)

[79] This was probably Lieutenant-Governor Samuel Adams who lived in a large old-fashioned house on Purchase (now Winter) Street, Boston. After the death of Governor John Hancock on October 8, 1793, he became governor of Massachusetts. In the Adams household "grace preceded every meal and morning and evening prayers were read from the old Bible." (Wells: *Life of Samuel Adams*, III, 336.)

[80] The Weston society was formed in the home of Abraham Bemis in 1792, and his name was the first on the roll. It is said that over four hundred preachers and nine bishops were entertained by him in his mansion in the extreme northwestern section of Waltham near the Weston line. (*Story of Methodism in Waltham*, 5, 6, 16.)

[81] Jesse Lee preached the first sermon in Needham and founded the Needham Circuit on October 6, 1791. This circuit spread from Worcester to Boston and had twenty-one societies at various times. The first Needham church was in a section known as "The Hundreds" and "Pine Plain," now Wellesley, Massachusetts. The lot was given by "Father" William Bogle. (*Story of Methodism in Waltham*, 16; Clarke: *History of Needham*, 259; see also *Origin of Old Needham M.E. Church.*)

[82] Lemuel Smith was preacher at Litchfield, and John Hill was at Needham. (See *Minutes.*)

doctrines. We rode through Mendon, Douglas, Thompson, Woodstock, up to Pomfret: missing our way, and being very unwell, as I have been for some time with an inflammation in my throat, we concluded to turn in at a tavern, and spend the night in pain: pain begets invention. I now began to think, What shall I do? I am my own physician. I sent for two blisters; applied both to my ears; and then began to march to Ashford. I turned in at Mr. Woodward's, and met brothers Taylor and Smith[83] and was dragged out to baptize a household, whilst I had a fever; the weather was excessively warm, like Carolina: I had an awful night.

Connecticut

Saturday, 10. Came to brother Howard's:[84] here I grew worse: this night I had some discharges, and was somewhat relieved. For a few days I have felt some pain in my left foot: it now inflamed more and more until I could scarcely put it to the floor; I applied a poultice, and spent the Sabbath in private; and was closely engaged in reading the Scriptures.

Monday, 12. Our conference sat at Tolland. Lame as I was, I went through the business; and notwithstanding I was tired out with labour, heat, and pain, and company, I must also preach; so I submitted; and endeavoured to apply 2 Tim. ii, 24–26. Being unable to ride on horseback, I drove on in a carriage through the rain, over the rocks, in the dark, and came to Doctor Steel's[85] at Ellington.

Yesterday the pain seized my right foot. I am now not able to move from my horse to a house; an attack of this kind generally terminates in about eight days.

Thursday, 15. Came in brother Steele's carriage to Hartford. From what we can gather, we are encouraged to hope that upwards of three hundred souls have been awakened, and more than two hundred converted to God the last year: if this work goes on, Satan will be labouring by all means, and by every instrument. From Hartford I came to Middletown. I slept at Ebeneezer Frothingham's,[86] who was the first separate minister on the west of Connecticut River; a man who had laboured, and written much:

[83] Joshua Taylor was on the Middletown Circuit, and Lemuel Smith was on the Litchfield Circuit. They were probably on their way to the conference at Tolland.

[84] Joseph and Henry Howard leased for 199 years a lot on their estate for the erection of the Methodist chapel at Tolland.

[85] Dr. Steel was probably the Rev. Elephalet Steele (1770–1817), a Congregationalist who was once minister at East Hartford. In Shay's Rebellion he suffered persecution for his attitude favorable to the government.

[86] The Rev. Ebeneezer Frothingham of Cambridge was the first minister of the Strict Church in Middletown. It grew to sufficient strength for two churches, the second being in Westfield. At the time of the formation of the second church, Frothingham was dismissed from the Middletown church and "found guilty by jury for false and railing speeches against Rev. James Loskwood." (See Roberts: *Historic Towns in the Connecticut Valley*.)

had his learning been equal to his piety and good sense, the *standing order* would have trembled under his hand. Who would think his Church would vote him out, when old and gray-headed, because he could not subscribe to the new divinity? He is now, as he saith, like a broken vessel; upwards of fourscore years of age: his wife and children favour us.

I came to New Haven; thence to Derby; and had a return of the inflammation in my throat. Came to West Haven—very unwell. I had heavy work to get to Reading, being lame in both feet: I laid myself down on the road-side, and felt like Jonah or Elijah. I took to my bed at Reading.

New York

Monday, 19. Rode ten miles on horseback, and thirteen in a carriage, to Bedford, and rested a day at dear widow Banks's,[87] where I was at home. O, how sweet is one day's rest!

Wednesday, 21. When I came near the White Plains, my horse started, and threw me into a mill-race knee deep in water, my hands and side in the dirt; my shoulder was hurt by the fall. I stopped at a house, shifted my clothes, and prayed with the people. If any of these people are awakened by my stopping there, all will be well. This day I made out to ride thirty-three miles.

Thursday, 22. Came to New York. The weather is extremely warm. Great afflictions prevail here—fluxes, fevers, influenzas. It is very sickly also in Philadelphia.[88] I have found by secret search, that I have not preached sanctification as I should have done: if I am restored, this shall be my theme more pointedly than ever, God being my helper. I have been sick upwards of four months; during which time I have attended to my business, and ridden, I suppose, not less than three thousand miles. I kept close house in New York until *Sunday,* 25; then I attempted to preach on Romans xiii, 10–12. The weather being warm, and dry, I caught an influenza which held me four days[89]—and this in addition to my fevers, and lameness. The effects of this weather were sensibly felt by every member of the conference, some of whom were so indisposed that they could not attend. We made a collection of forty pounds for the relief of the preachers on the frontiers of New York and Connecticut.

We have awful accounts from Philadelphia; which made me feel too much like a man, and too little like a Christian.

Monday, September 2. I rested.

[87] The Banks house was close to Byram Pond and Bridge, two miles south of Bedford Village on the road to White Plains. This home of Methodist people was to become Asbury's frequent stopping place on subsequent journeys. (See *Journal* entries for September 5, 1796; September 13, 1797; July 2, 1798; June 30, 1800.)

[88] The port cities along the Atlantic coast were frequent victims of scourges brought, apparently, by shipping from the West Indies.

[89] See letter to parents, September 1, 1793.

New Jersey

Tuesday, 3. Dined at Elizabethtown on my way to Philadelphia.

Wednesday, 4. I reached Trenton, and received a letter from brother M—k—y, requesting me to come to Burlington, and that it was doubtful whether it were prudent to go to Philadelphia on account of the contagion that then prevailed in that city; I did not reach Burlington so soon as was expected, and the preachers went on to Philadelphia. I preached in Burlington, and the people were very solemn.

Pennsylvania

Friday, 6. We rode to the city. Ah! how the ways mourn! how low-spirited are the people whilst making their escape! I found it awful indeed. I judge the people die from fifty to one hundred in a day: some of our friends are dying, others flying.[90]

Sunday, 8. I preached on Isa. lviii, 1: "Cry aloud, spare not, lift up thy voice like a trumpet, and show my people their transgressions, and the house of Jacob their sins." The people of this city are alarmed; and well they may be. I went down to Ebenezer (a church in the lower part of the city), but my strength was gone: however, I endeavoured to open and apply Micah vi, 9. The streets are now depopulated, and the city wears a gloomy aspect. All night long my ears and heart were wounded with the cry of fire! O! how awful! And what made it still more serious, two young men were killed by the fall of a wall: one of them was a valuable member of our society. Poor Philadelphia! the lofty city, He layeth it low! I am very unwell; my system is quite weak; I feel the want of pure air. We appointed *Tuesday*, 10th, to be observed as a day of humiliation: I preached on 1 Kings viii, 37–40; and had a large and very serious, weeping congregation. The preachers left the city on *Monday*; I continued in order to have the minutes of conference printed.

Delaware

Wednesday, 11. We left the city—solemn as death! The people of Darby[91] and Chester are sickly: and they are greatly alarmed at Wilmington. I found a quiet retreat at friend Bond's,[92] near New Castle.

[90] There was an epidemic of yellow fever in Philadelphia. Nearly four thousand deaths occurred in September and October. (Hardie: *The Philadelphia Directory*, 1794, 218 ff.)

[91] There was no Methodist society at Darby. A class was organized in 1807, and a stone church was erected on the site of the present Mount Zion Cemetery.

[92] This was probably the same John Bond twice visited by Bishop Coke, whose place of residence he describes thus: "proceeded to visit Mr. and Mrs. Bond, formerly of our Society in Lambeth Marsh, London, but now (1792) residing on a large plantation within half a mile of New Castle (Delaware)." (Coke, *op. cit.*, 180, 185.)

Came to the quarterly meeting at the Cross Roads, where there were crowds of people: I gave them a sermon on, "Yea, in the way of thy judgments have we waited for thee." I showed, 1. That God sent pestilence, famine, locusts, blasting, mildew, and caterpillars; and that only the Church and people of God know, and believe his judgments. 2. That God's people waited for him in the way of his judgments; and, 3. That they improved and profited by them. About one o'clock we set out and rode thirty-two miles to Thomas White's; and spent one day at my former home.

Sunday, 15. We rode twenty miles to Milford, and had a comfortable love feast; I preached to many on 2 Chron. vii, 13–15. I preached a laboured sermon at Quantees[93] quarterly meeting: the second day brother G. preached, on, "There remaineth therefore a rest to the people of God." My finishing stroke was to show them the way to ruin—so we parted.

Virginia

Thursday, 19. We rode to Accomac: and had a comfortable quarterly meeting at Downing's. I met the located official members, and we had sweet fellowship together.

Sunday, 22. After a gracious love feast and preaching on Jer. xvii, 9, 10, I returned, weak in body, and under dejection of mind, to Churn's chapel,[94] a ride of twenty miles: this is one of the most awful places I ever visited, according to my feelings: I had only courage to exhort for a few minutes. Brother Smith,[95] one of our elders, gave it as his opinion that two hundred people had died in the bounds of Somerset circuit the last summer.

I searched the continent for the Travels of Sin and True Godliness; now they are printed and bound together, and sell well: our Americans are not fools; no books sell like those on plain, practical subjects; as the Saint's Rest, Baxter's Call, Alleine's Alarm, and Thomas à Kempis.

Maryland

I came to Bartholomew Ennall's to quarterly meeting: we had a solemn time, though our congregation was small.

Friday, 27. We came to Easton, twenty-five miles; here the people pretended to be afraid of my communicating the infection of the yellow fever, although I had been out of Philadelphia from the 9th to the 26th instant.

[93] This was the present Quantico, Maryland.
[94] Westcott Churn's was the last place at which William Colbert preached before he was transferred to the Milford Circuit in 1795. Some students think this may have been Curtis Chapel in nearby Maryland. (See William Colbert's *Journal*, II, 62.)
[95] This was probably John Smith. (See *Minutes*, 1793.)

I gave them a long discourse, and then rode to Hillsboro; and thence to Judge White's. Sickness prevails in every house; but there are not so many deaths as might be expected from general afflictions.

Monday, 30. I preached at quarterly meeting, on, "The Lord is good, a strong hold in the day of trouble, and he knoweth them that trust in him." 1. Originally, independently, communicatively good. 2. He knoweth, loveth, approveth, and delivereth those that put their trust in him.

Tuesday, October 1. I came early to Churchhill; and felt myself solemnly engaged with God. In the evening I was enabled to give a close, alarming exhortation on the present alarming and awful times.[96]

Wednesday, 2. I endeavoured to enforce, at Worton's, "Let us search and try our ways, and turn again to the Lord." The wind being contrary, we rode twenty miles to brother Stephen Black's, through dust and drought. Brother Black conveyed me to North East on *Thursday*; and *Friday*, 4, after disputing the passage at the ferry with Mr. R——, I rode to Cokesbury. I had left Philadelphia, and knew not that a pass was necessary until I came to the ferry. Mr. Barney, who was a health-officer, behaved like a gentleman, and gave me a true and honourable certificate. I found matters in a poor state at college—£500 in debt, and our employees nearly £700 in arrears.

Thursday, 10. Came to Baltimore; passed the guard against the plague in Philadelphia, set for prudence, one hundred miles off. O! the plague of sin! Would to God we were more guarded against its baleful influence! I was sick, weary, and feeble; yet, preaching being appointed for me in town, I sounded the alarm on Jer. xiii, 16: "Give glory to God before he cause darkness," &c.

Friday, 11. I hasted to Annapolis.

Saturday, 12. Attended a quarterly meeting at Bignall's,[97] in a large tobacco-house, where I enlarged on the weighty words of our Lord: "Because iniquity shall abound, the love of many shall wax cold."

Monday, 14. I opened and applied the charge given by David to Solomon, at Gassaway Rawling's, well adapted to the children of the Methodists.

Tuesday, 15. I had a large congregation of serious women at Capt. William Weems's. To these I preached on John xiv, 16. 1. Christ is the way to God by precept, example, and power. 2. The truth; the true Messiah, revealing the truths of God, the standard and judge of all. 3.

[96] "Citizen" Genet's fiery appeal to American voters to join France in her war against Great Britain and the yellow-fever scourge then raging in Philadelphia were causing anxiety throughout the land. The latter Asbury interpreted as a possible visitation of their sins upon Philadelphians because of God's wrath. (See letter to William Watters, October 29, 1793.)

[97] This was Thomas Bignall, resident of Anne Arundel County, whose name in the census of 1800 is spelled "Bicknell." (Lednum, *op. cit.*, 189.)

The life, by his merit and Spirit, leading to the knowledge of God in his perfections and glory.

Wednesday, 16. I enlarged on "Without me ye can do nothing," and applied it to sinners, Pharisees, hypocrites, backsliders, believers, and sanctified souls.

Saturday, 19. I attended a quarterly meeting at Hardestie's; where I exhorted the people to "Forget the things that are behind, and to reach towards the things that are before"—i.e. establishment in grace, walking with God, resignation to his will, meekness, humility, perfect love, a glorious resurrection, and eternal glory. "Leave the things that are behind" —see Heb. vi, 1, and v, 12. "Leave these"; so as not to rest in conviction, repentance, faith, justification, nor in Church ordinances, as being the whole of religion, or any part thereof, any farther than as they lead us to Christ. We had some life in the love feast, and in public service; but there is a dearth here. The circuit has suffered for want of a preacher.

Sabbath, 20. I came to Baltimore, and preached on Amos iii, 6–8.

Monday, 21. Our conference began.[98] I was well pleased with the stations, and the faithful talk most of our brethren gave us of their experience and exercises. I preached a charity sermon, on, "Hath God cast away his people?" We collected £27, which was augmented to £43, and applied it to the supplying the wants of the distressed preachers.

Sunday, 27. I preached, and ordained elders and deacons, at the Point, and at night, in town, spoke on Jeremiah ix, 12–14.

Monday, 28. I left Baltimore in a cool, stormy day. We dined with Capt. White,[99] on the north branch of the Patuxent, and had only time to warm, eat, drink, and pray. We hasted on to Shadrach Turner's. We stopped on the way at the house of some old, forgotten English people: I talked plainly to the poor old woman, and commended the family to God in prayer.

Virginia

I rode to my old friend Adams's;[100] and spent the evening in Christian conversation, writing, and prayer.

Tuesday, 29. Five of us came to Stafford court house. The next day we dined and prayed at Falmouth's,[101] and in the evening reached Collins's, an old stand in Caroline county.

[98] This conference met at Baltimore with sessions at Cokesbury College. Although Asbury had been indisposed during four months, this was one of the most laborious years of his life. It was at this session that the Prince George's Circuit in Maryland was created.

[99] Captain Charles White, who during the Revolutionary War commanded a company of militia, lived about ten miles southwest of Elkridge in the present Howard County.

[100] William Adams lived in Fairfax County, Virginia.

[101] Falmouth lived across the Rappahannock River from Fredericksburg.

Friday, November 1. We breakfasted at Ellis's tavern, and next day rode to Richmond and Manchester, and came to Baugh's, and preached to a congregation mostly women. Thence we proceeded to J. Anderson's. I was so hoarse it was with difficulty I spoke to the people. In six days we have ridden two hundred and twenty miles.

Sunday, 3. We had to ride ten miles to quarterly meeting at Tucker's chapel.[102] I did not expect to be heard; but, to my great surprise, I had not spoken long before my voice was clear. We had a melting time under brother John Easter; was much blessed with the local brethren. Brothers Wynn[103] and A—— were recommended to the office of deacons, and ordained. Brother W—— with two others, are appointed to wait on me at the ensuing conference; what for, will then be better known.

Tuesday, 5. I rode to brother Baugh's, and the next day preached at Charity Chapel.[104] It was a day appointed by the bishop and committee of the Episcopal Church to be observed as a day of fasting. I feel my mind greatly eased relative to those who have lately separated from us and set out as reformers. Let the Lord look to his own Church.

Thursday, 7. We had a serious congregation at Cumberland quarterly meeting: some appeared to be much engaged.

My *Sabbath day's* journey was from sister Ligon's[105] to a new chapel in Prince Edward,[106] twenty miles, where, after preaching on Matt. xxiv, 12–14, I was led to say a few things for myself: as to my coming to and staying in America—of the exercise of that power which was given by the first and confirmed by the last general conference. Many of the people thought me not that monster I had been represented. I thought this the more necessary here, as great pains had been taken to misrepresent and injure me in this congregation and neighbourhood. So it is; when I am absent some will say what they please of me. After sacrament we came, weary and hungry, to brother Ryall's, by whom we were kindly entertained. My soul is stayed on the Lord, although Satan will push at me by means of the world, the flesh, and false brethren.

Tuesday, 12. I preached at brother Tilman's, on Nottaway River. The people here have been unsettled by the divisions which a few persons have endeavoured to make in our societies.

Thursday, 14. Rode from brother N——'s to Salem, and, after preaching to brother Merritt's, in Brunswick, making it about thirty miles, without eating or drinking.

Friday, 15. I had a few serious souls at Roses Creek.[107] Here I received

---

[102] This was evidently Wood Tucker in Dinwiddie County, now Petersburg.

[103] John Wynn was on Hanover Circuit. He died in 1794 at the age of twenty-eight. (*Minutes.*)

[104] Charity Chapel was in Powhatan County.

[105] This was probably Elizabeth Ligon. (*Heads of Families*, 59.)

[106] See letter to Jacob Hall, November 10, 1793.

[107] This was one of the chapels in Brunswick County.

the happy tidings from John Dickins, that he, with his family, had been preserved during the late contagion in the city of Philadelphia.

Sunday, 17. At Merritt's chapel; the weather was rainy and uncomfortable, and brother Ellis very unwell. The next day I rode from brother F——'s, about twenty miles, to preach a funeral discourse on the death of our dear brother Cox. The Lord's power was present. Brother Philip Bruce[108] preached at Jones's chapel on "Sowing to the flesh." I was happy in God at brother Paup's, in the evening. The next day I stayed at the chapel until it appeared as if I was well nigh chilled through, and to cure me had to ride twelve miles to brother Moss's[109]; thence twenty miles to brother Bonner's, where I met several of the brethren in great peace and love. Came to J. Smith's,[110] and had a good season on Eph. iv, 22–25. The seeds of discord have been sown here, but they have not taken deep root. Several of the preachers came in, and we spent the evening, and were happy together.

Sunday, 24. Hasted to Petersburg.[111] Came in a little before noon, and preached on Isa. lxvi, 4, 5.

Monday, 25, and the following days, were spent in conference. The preachers were united, and the Lord was with us of a truth. There were fifty-five preachers present. I had some difficulties respecting the stations; but there was a willingness among the brethren to go where they were appointed, and all was well.

Our disaffected brethren have had a meeting at the Piney Grove, in Amelia circuit, and appointed three men to attend this conference. One of these delegates appears to be satisfied, and has received ordination amongst us since he was delegated by them; the other two appeared, and we gave them a long talk. My mind has been closely employed in the business of the conference, so that I have slept only about sixteen hours in four nights.

Friday, 29. Rode nineteen miles, and preached at Mrs. Cox's barn.[112] The next day we reached brother Mooring's in Surry.

Sunday, December 1. My mind was in a state of heaviness. I endeavoured to preach on 2 Cor. xiii, 5. It is heavy times here; but the work is the Lord's, and I wish to leave it all to him. In discoursing on the above text I pursued nearly the following method—

I. Such as profess to have experienced religion should examine whether they have not let some fundamental doctrines slip.

II. Examine into the nature and effects of faith—it is the substance of

---

[108] Philip Bruce was presiding elder on the Northern Virginia District.
[109] Moss lived in Sussex County.
[110] Evidently Bonner and Smith lived in Prince George County, since Asbury traveled more than twenty miles from Sussex Court House toward Petersburg.
[111] See letter to Ezekiel Cooper, November 23, 1793.
[112] Mrs. Cox lived in Prince George County.

things hoped for, in a penitent state; and the evidence of things not seen, in a justified state.

III. They should know themselves, whether they are seekers, believers, or backsliders.

IV. They should prove themselves, to themselves, to their ministers, the world, and the church of God.

V. That if they have heart-religion, Christ is in them—the meek, loving pure mind of Christ.

Monday, 2. Came to Ellis's chapel, in Sussex.

Tuesday, 3. Preached at Lane's chapel: it was low times and cold weather. Thence to my old friend Moss's, near Sussex court house. I have lately read Blair's Sermons,[113] where I find some very beautiful things: they contain good moral philosophy; and his Sermon on Gentleness is worthy the taste of Queen Charlotte; and if money were anything towards paying for knowledge, I should think that sermon worth two hundred pounds sterling—which some say the Queen gave him.

Thursday, 5. After riding several miles out of my way, I came to dear brother and sister Parham's—two Israelites indeed. I was unwell, yet spent the evening comfortably. Next day I had a long ride to Pelham's,[114] in Greensville; where I enlarged to a small, serious congregation, on 2 Cor. xii, 15—the grand subjects of the faithful minister's care.

Saturday, 7. Rode through the rain to Woolsey's barn—now Drumgoole's chapel.

Next day we had but twenty miles to ride for our Sabbath day's journey. Came to Roanoke Chapel and enlarged on Eph. iii, 7, 8: in which I showed, 1st, How a minister of Christ is made; 2d. To whom he is to preach; 3d. What he is to preach—namely, the unsearchable riches of Christ; 4th. The humble opinion the ministers of Christ entertain of themselves.

North Carolina

Monday, 9. Crossed Roanoak in a flat, with seven horses; but we were mercifully preserved. Came to Warrenton. I had a violent pain in my head, and, my horse's back being injured, I stopped at Myrick's, having ridden only twenty miles.

Tuesday, 10. Came to Louisburg, and held our conference at Green

---

[113] Hugh Blair (1718–1800) was a Scottish clergyman whose sermons were published through the aid of Dr. Johnson. He was widely read. Wesley called him an "elegant but not a deep writer" and wrongly thought he was the translator of Ossian's poems. (Wesley's *Journal*, VI, 234, 507.)

[114] Pelhams intermarried with the Drumgooles, and some of both families moved to Ohio because they were against slavery. (See Drumgoole's papers, University of North Carolina library.)

Hills, about a mile from town. Great peace and unity prevailed amongst us. The preachers cheerfully signed an instrument, expressing their determination to submit to, and abide by, what the General Conference has done.

Friday, 13. Our conference rose: it was agreed that the next conference should be held in Petersburg; there the preachers from North Carolina, Greenbrier, the Center and South Districts of Virginia, may all meet, and change properly, and unite together for their own and the people's good.

Saturday, 14. Rode to father P. B——'s. O that the last days of ancient Methodists may be the best! I have a cold and pains; but there is ease in peace, and love, and communion with God.

Sunday, 15. We had as many people at father B——'s as we could find room for: I delivered some alarming words from Isaiah lxv, 2.

Monday, 16. Rode up the Neuse; fed at Tomkins's, and hasted to the widow Carson's (about forty miles).

Tuesday, 17. After riding about twenty-six miles to R——'s, I gave them a short discourse on, "The foundation of God standeth sure": after eating, we had to ride sixteen or eighteen miles in the evening home with brother M'Gee.[115] In the morning we crossed Deep River, in a flat, not without danger; thence down Caraway Creek to Randolph town; thence to Uwharrie at Fuller's Ford. Here we were assisted by some young men with a canoe. Thank the Lord, both men and horses were preserved! The young men *sometimes prayed* and *sometimes swore.* After riding three miles, came to Wood's, but Russel's was the place of preaching, where I found some who had heard me in Virginia many years past; I laboured to speak, although my throat was very sore: the hearts of the people appeared to be cold, as well as their bodies.

Friday, 20. I had to ride thirty miles by two o'clock; but was so poorly I declined preaching. *Saturday* and *Sunday* I spent at John Randle's: I gave place to brothers George M'Kenney[116] and Jonathan Bird.[117] On Sunday evening, I gave the family a discourse at Wyatt Randall's.[118]

Monday, 23. Crossed Rocky River: this is a bold stream; it rises in Mecklenburg (County), North Carolina, and, after running eighty or ninety miles, empties itself into Pee Dee, a little below Montgomery.

[115] See *Journal* note and entry for January 22, 1790.
[116] George McKenney was on the Caswell Circuit.
[117] Jonathan Bird was on the Anson Circuit.
[118] John and Wyatt Randall lived in Stanley County, and Asbury frequently stopped there. He was there first on February 15, 1785, when he borrowed a horse. Randall's Church is still active a little west of the Yadkin at Tillery Lake and north of Norwood. The property of three and one-half acres was deeded by John Snugg in 1813 to Henry Ledbetter, John Christian, George Allen, John Randall, and Wyatt Randall as church trustees. Ledbetter was an itinerant preacher from 1787 to 1795. (Correspondence, Jeffrey F. Stanback, Mount Gilead, N.C., 1953.)

South Carolina

Came to Blakeney's,[119] on the waters of Lynch's Creek: here I preached to about forty people; it being Christmas day.

Thursday, 26. We crossed various branches which empty into Pee Dee about ten miles below Port's Ferry: we passed the hanging rock to J. Horton's.[120]

Friday, 27. We set out at sunrise: the weather was cold and frosty: we made it twenty-two miles to Camden. After dinner we crossed the river, and came to Marshall's.[121]

Saturday, 28. We set out very early, and came through pine and oak barrens, twenty-five miles: about one o'clock I was willing to sit down and rest. I have lately felt all the grace I had put to trial: through mercy I am kept from sin, and long to be perfect in faith and patience, love and suffering: I am sometimes tempted to wish to die; but I fear it is wrong: I rather choose to wait the Lord's time.

Sunday, 29. With some difficulty I attended at the meeting house near Marshall's.

Monday, 30. We rode forty-five miles to brother Cook's,[122] on Broad River; and the next day to brother Finch's: here we are to have about thirty preachers from South Carolina and Georgia.[123] We were straitened for room, having only twelve feet square to confer, sleep, and for the accommodation of those who were sick. Brother Philip Bruce was attacked with the dysentery.

[119] The Blakeney home was near Pageland. On November 27, 1798, Asbury stopped at Blakeney's on Thompson's Creek. There is no evidence that two Blakeney families lived in South Carolina, but Thompson's Creek rises in western Chesterfield County in six or seven miles of Lynch's Creek. The distances indicate that the Blakeney's mentioned were the same and lived near enough to both streams for both to be mentioned.

[120] For Asbury's route on this and the previous days see notes under December 21–25, 1792.

[121] Leaving Camden he turned to the west and crossed the Wateree to Marshall's in upper Richland County, sixteen miles east of Columbia, South Carolina.

[122] Cook lived on the Broad River above Columbia. Asbury probably crossed at Ashford's Ferry from Fairfield County to Newberry County.

[123] This conference at the Finch residence in Newberry County was the eighth in South Carolina and the first which also included Georgia. It was notable in its personnel. Two future bishops, William McKendree and Enoch George, were present, the former coming with Asbury, as were Tobias Gibson, founder of Methodism in Mississippi, Hope Hull, Reuben Ellis, and other pioneer leaders. Bethel Academy, the first Methodist school in South Carolina, was under construction but was not opened until next year. The Presbyterian Church was offered for worship. James Jenkins was ordained deacon, Asbury remarking, "You feel the hands of a bishop very heavy, but the devil's hands will be heavier still." Coleman Carlisle was expelled unjustly; a young man whom he had reproved hid a pistol in his saddlebags and had the preacher arrested for stealing it. The young man confessed as he was dying two years later, and Carlisle was restored to conference membership. He died a member of the Tennessee Conference in 1838. (Betts, *op. cit.*, 70; Chreitzberg: *Early Methodism in the Carolinas*, 60, 61.)

Dat